Germany

Steve Fallon
Anthony Haywood
Andrea Schulte-Peevers
Nick Selby

Germany

1st edition

Published by
Lonely Planet Publications
Head Office: PO Box 617, Hawthorn, Vic 3122, Australia
Branches: 150 Linden St, Oakland, CA 94607, USA
10a Spring Place, London NW5 3BH, UK
71 bis rue du Cardinal Lemoine, 75005 Paris, France

Printed by
Colorcraft Ltd, Hong Kong

Photographs by
Anthony Haywood
Marie Oamek
David Peevers
Nick Selby
Jonathan Smith
Stuttgart-Marketing GmbH

Front cover: Flag on a half-timbered house in Bacharach, Rhine Valley (David Peevers)

First Published
March 1998

National Library of Australia Cataloguing in Publication Data

Germany.

1st ed.
Includes index.
ISBN 0 86442 487 6

1. Germany - Guidebooks. I. Fallon, Steve.

914.304879

Steve Fallon

Steve wrote the Berlin and Brandenburg chapters, contributed to the Facts for the Visitor chapter and was coordinating author of the book.

Born in Boston, Massachusetts, Steve can't remember a time when he was not obsessed with travel, other cultures and languages. As a teenager he worked an assortment of jobs to finance trips to Europe and South America, and he graduated from Georgetown University in 1975 with a Bachelor of Science in modern languages. The following year he taught English at the University of Silesia near Katowice, Poland. After he had worked for several years for a Gannett newspaper and obtained a master's degree in journalism, his fascination with the 'new' Asia took him to Hong Kong, where he lived and worked for 13 years for a variety of publications and was editor of *Business Traveller* magazine. In 1987, he put journalism on hold to open Wanderlust Books, Asia's only travel bookshop. Steve lived in Budapest for 2½ years from where he wrote *Hungary* and *Slovenia* before moving to London in 1994. He has written or contributed to a number of other Lonely Planet titles.

Anthony Haywood

Anthony wrote the Facts about the Country and Harz Mountains chapters as well as the Göttingen section in Lower Saxony and contributed to the Facts for the Visitor chapter.

Born in the port town of Fremantle, Australia, in 1959, Anthony first pulled anchor at 18 to spend two years travelling through Europe and the USA. He studied literature and then Russian language at university, and has variously turned Holeproof socks the right way round on the night shift, baked and cracked soil samples for an oil multinational in London, taught English, translated everything he could get his hands on, and worked as a technical writer and trainer. Pleasantly diverted on a Russian jaunt in 1991, he now lives with his wife Sylvia in Germany, where he works as a writer and translator.

Andrea Schulte-Peevers

Andrea wrote the chapters of North Rhine-Westphalia, Schleswig-Holstein, Rhineland-Palatinate, Hamburg, Saarland, Bremen and Thuringia, and co-authored those of Mecklenburg-Western Pomerania (Western Pomerania), Lower Saxony (west of Hanover), Baden-Württemberg (Black Forest) and Facts for the Visitor.

Andrea is a Los Angeles-based writer and editor who owes her love for languages and travel to her mother who showed her around Europe and North Africa when she was just a toddler. Having finished school in Germany, Andrea left for London and stints as an au pair, market researcher and foreign language correspondent. In the late 1980s, she swapped the gloomy skies of England for the perpetual sunshine of Los Angeles where she enrolled at UCLA. Armed with a degree in English literature, she then embarked on a career in travel journalism which has taken her to all continents but Antarctica. With husband David Peevers, Andrea wrote Lonely Planet's first guide to *Berlin*.

Nick Selby

Nick clocked major miles in writing all the Bavaria, Saxony, Saxony-Anhalt and Hesse chapters, as well as a good whack of the Lower Saxony, Baden-Württemberg and Mecklenburg-Pomerania chapters and contributed to the Facts for the Visitor chapter. Not to mention the Trabant joke.

A native New Yorker, Nick gave up a career as a TV sound engineer in 1990 to work in Poland for Warsaw's Radio Zet and then for a multinational advertising agency (which fired him). In 1991 he moved to Russia and wrote *The Visitor's Guide to the New St Petersburg*, before travelling through Europe, Asia and America. In 1994, he started to work with LP. Since then he's worked on guides to *Russia, Ukraine & Belarus*, *St Petersburg*, *Florida* and *Miami*. Nick lives at Europe's southernmost point, Tarifa, in Spain with his wife, Corinna.

From the Authors

Steve Fallon My share of *Germany* is dedicated to *mein Lieber* Michael Rothschild – so close to and yet so far from Deutschland. In Berlin I'd like to thank Bernd Buhmann of Berlin Tourismus Marketing and Andreas Becker, Peter Löllmann and staff at the Circus Hostel for their help and hospitality. In Brandenburg, *Danke schön* to Herr Bracht of Tourismusverband Land Brandenburg and Tom Sehrer of City Rad in Potsdam.

A special mention also goes to authors Andrea Schulte-Peevers and David Peevers for performing with grace under pressure that would have given Ernest Hemingway a ride for his money, and to editor Suzi 'Suzip' Petkovski for her encouragement, professionalism and good humour. Much appreciated.

Anthony Haywood Thanks especially to Frau Spier in Thale and Frau Garn and Frau Hoppe in Quedlinburg. Thanks also to Allo and Christa, Sylvia, Christine and Falk, Gunnar, Horst and Burghard.

Andrea Schulte-Peevers My portion of this book would not have possible to complete without the indefatigable support and love from my mother, Ingrid Schulte, to whom I am endlessly grateful. The same is true of my husband, David Peevers, who assisted throughout the entire research process. Without his patience, tolerance and commitment – compounded by his resourcefulness and wonderful sense of humour – this project would not nearly have been as much fun over the 30,000km of German roads we drove together. Profound thanks also to my colleagues, Steve Fallon and Nick Selby, whose guidance and encouragement were much appreciated during days of crisis and frustration.

Much gratitude goes to James Carberry, Helga Stehli and Heinz Dallmann of LTU airlines for accommodating our many special needs and requests during some times of real emergency; to our friend, Uwe Petry, and to Rainer Schlageter for assisting with official German press accreditation; to Gunter Winkler of the German National Tourist Office, Frankfurt, for his continued support and assistance; to Dr Wolfgang Riecke of Mercedes Benz for solving part of the transportation problem; and to Irvin Matsukiyo for taking care of numerous details during our absence from Los Angeles.

The staff at countless tourist offices provided invaluable help, with special kudos going to Wolfgang Thieme, Hella Ackermann and Karin Mass (Rhineland-Palatinate); Maria Antoinette Ritter and Dr Peter Rohrsen (Cologne); Bernd Goebel (Black Forest); Horst David (Mecklenburg-Western Pomerania); Kerstin Dietrich (Thuringia); Barbara Kotte (Schleswig-Holstein); Ralf Ostendorf (Lower Saxony-North Sea) and Reiner Büchtmann (Hamburg).

Klaus and Andrea Bürkle of Traben-Trarbach get special mention for their charming hospitality, as do Olaf and Thomas Drubba of Drubba Hotels & Tourism in the Black Forest.

Finally, a big round of thanks to LP's own Suzi Petkovski, especially for her encouragement and meticulous attention to detail, and to Rob van Driesum for his continued confidence and support.

Nick Selby Huge heartfelt thanks to Gunter Winkler and Tanja Pintschovius at the German National Tourist Office, and to Corinna Selby. Also, thank you Knut Dinter at Deutsches Jugendherbergswerk and to the tourist offices and hostels throughout Germany that gave me so much assis- tance. Thanks also to Clem Lindenmayer and David Peevers and Andrea Schulte-Peevers for the *Western Europe on a shoestring* work in my territories!

And, in Germany, thank you Oliver Bengl, Barbara Klöver, Rainer Flotow, Ryan Ver Berkmoes, Sara Marley, Katherine & Michl Kolter, James Stoker, Karen Sparshuh, Marie Oamek, Sabina Jörs, Anja Bolata, Hakan Evcin, Patrick Phelps, Alan Wissenburg and Marlies Arnold.

In Tarifa, thanks to Christina & Axel

Guddas, Melanie & Antony, Butch, Olivia, Spijkerman and Arrancha Sanchez.

And, of course, thanks to Bernard Goldstein and Angela Wilson and Irwin Stein.

From the Publisher

This spanking 1st edition of Germany was coordinated by Rachel Black (mapping and design) and Suzi Petkovski (editing).

Vielen dank to the countless conscripts who helped bring the monster to life. On the mapping front, Jacqui Saunders, Trudi Canavan and Mark Griffiths drew endless Altstadts and Neustadts and sorted the Hauptbahnhofs from your run-of-the-mill Bahnhofs. Illustrations were lovingly drawn by Rachel Black and Jacqui Saunders.

On the editing front, heaps of nasty jobs were performed, with nary a complaint, by (deep breath): Craig 'Macca' MacKenzie, Katie Cody, Sarah Mathers, Tom Smallman, Rebecca Turner, Anne Mulvaney, Wendy Owen, Martin 'training wheels' Hughes, Paul Harding, Justin Flynn and Russell Kerr.

Final checks were conducted with unnerving thoroughness by Jane Fitzpatrick and Tamsin Wilson. The cover was designed by Simon Bracken.

Our thanks also to the Berlin transport office (BVG), the German national tourist office in Sydney and the Goethe Institute in Melbourne.

To our authors, thanks for your professionalism and good humor in answering a string of (often inane) queries.

Finally, to the travellers who've waited patiently for a Germany guide (about bloody time, eh?), we did our best to do justice to Germany and we look forward to all your comments.

Warning & Request

Things change – prices go up, schedules change, good places go bad and bad places go bankrupt. Nothing stays the same. So, if you find things better or worse, recently opened or long since closed, please tell us and help make the next edition even more accurate and useful.

We value all of the feedback we receive from travellers. Julie Young coordinates a team who read and acknowledge every letter, postcard and email, and ensure that every morsel of information finds its way to the appropriate authors, editors and publishers.

Everyone who writes to us will find their name in the next edition of the appropriate guide and will also receive a free subscription to our quarterly newsletter, *Planet Talk*. The very best contributions will be rewarded with a free Lonely Planet guide.

Excerpts from your correspondence may appear in new editions of this guide; in our newsletter, *Planet Talk*; or in updates on our Web site – so please let us know if you don't want your letter published or your name acknowledged.

Contents

HAMBURG 781

SCHLESWIG-HOLSTEIN 807

GLOSSARY 837

ALTERNATIVE PLACE NAMES 841

INDEX 842

Boxed Text

Map Legend

BOUNDARIES

	International Boundary
	Provincial Boundary
	Disputed Boundary

ROUTES

A25	Freeway, with Route Number
	Major Road
	Minor Road
	Minor Road - Unsealed
	City Road
	City Street
	City Lane
	Train Route, with Station
U	U-Bahn Route, with Station
	Cable Car or Chairlift
	Ferry Route
	Walking Track

AREA FEATURES

	Building
	Cemetery
	Desert
	Market
	Park, Gardens
	Pedestrian Mall
	Reef
	Urban Area

HYDROGRAPHIC FEATURES

	Canal
	Coastline
	Creek, River
	Lake, Intermittent Lake
	Rapids, Waterfalls
	Salt Lake
	Swamp

SYMBOLS

CAPITAL	National Capital
CAPITAL	Provincial Capital
CITY	City
Town	Town
Village	Village
	Place to Stay
	Camping Ground
	Caravan Park
	Hut or Chalet
	Place to Eat
	Pub or Bar
	Airport
	Ancient or City Wall
	Archaeological Site
	Beach
	Castle or Fort
	Cave
	Church
	Cliff or Escarpment
	Dive Site
	Embassy
	Hospital
	Lookout
	Mosque
	Mountain or Hill
	National Park
	One Way Street
	Parking
	Pass
	Petrol Station
	Police Station
	Post Office
	Shopping Centre
	Swimming Pool
	Synagogue
	Telephone
	Tourist Information
	Transport
	Zoo

Note: not all symbols displayed above appear in this book

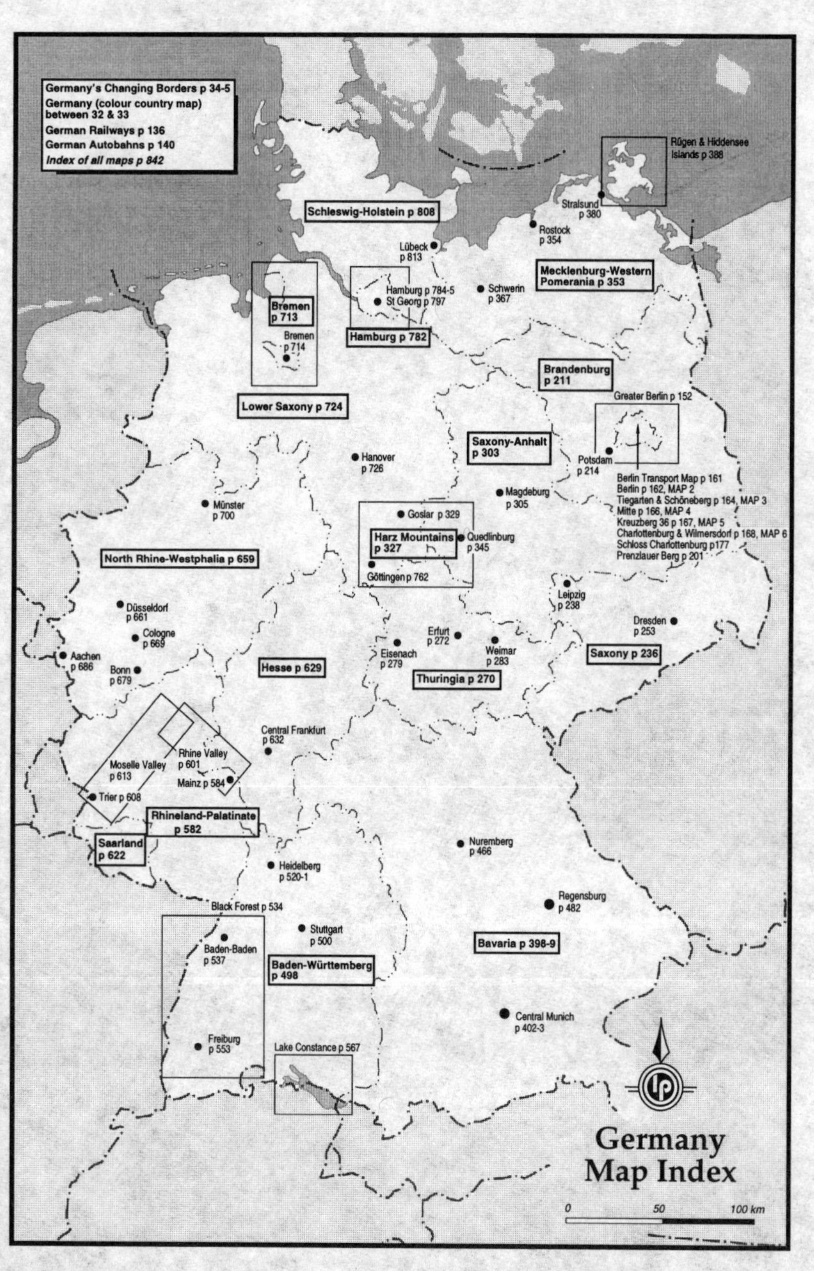

Germany's Changing Borders p 34-5
Germany (colour country map) between 32 & 33
German Railways p 136
German Autobahns p 140
Index of all maps p 842
Rügen & Hiddensee Islands p 388
Stralsund p 380
Rostock p 354
Schleswig-Holstein p 808
Lübeck p 813
Mecklenburg-Western Pomerania p 353
Schwerin p 367
Hamburg p 784-5
St Georg p 797
Hamburg p 782
Bremen p 713
Bremen p 714
Brandenburg p 211
Greater Berlin p 152
Lower Saxony p 724
Saxony-Anhalt p 303
Potsdam p 214
Hanover p 726
Berlin Transport Map p 161
Berlin p 162, MAP 2
Tiegarten & Schöneberg p 164, MAP 3
Mitte p 166, MAP 4
Kreuzberg 36 p 167, MAP 5
Charlottenburg & Wilmersdorf p 168, MAP 6
Schloss Charlottenburg p177
Prenzlauer Berg p 201
Magdeburg p 305
Münster p 700
Goslar p 329
Harz Mountains p 327
Quedlinburg p 345
North Rhine-Westphalia p 659
Göttingen p 762
Leipzig p 238
Düsseldorf p 661
Cologne p 669
Dresden p 253
Erfurt p 272
Aachen p 686
Eisenach p 279
Weimar p 283
Saxony p 236
Bonn p 679
Hesse p 629
Thuringia p 270
Central Frankfurt p 632
Rhine Valley p 601
Moselle Valley p 613
Mainz p 584
Trier p 608
Rhineland-Palatinate p 582
Saarland p 622
Nuremberg p 466
Heidelberg p 520-1
Regensburg p 482
Black Forest p 534
Stuttgart p 500
Baden-Baden p 537
Bavaria p 398-9
Baden-Württemberg p 498
Central Munich p 402-3
Freiburg p 553
Lake Constance p 567
Germany Map Index
0 50 100 km

Introduction

Germany (Deutschland), situated in the heart of Europe, has had a greater impact on the continent's history than any other country. From Charlemagne and the Holy Roman Empire to Otto von Bismarck's Reich, two world wars and the fall of the Berlin Wall, no other country has moulded Europe the way Germany has – for better or for worse. It is the home of Bach and Wagner, of Goethe and Schiller, of Einstein and Marx, of the fairy tales of our childhood. Until the late 19th century the English-speaking world looked not to Italy and France for its cultural cues but to Germany, and German was the most popular foreign language learned in schools.

But there's another Germany: a Germany of war, land-grabbing *Lebensraum* and genocide committed in the name of Reich and Führer. The human race owes it to the victims and survivors of the Holocaust to never forget their pain, and to remain vigilant so that never again will such a civilised and cultured nation sink to such depths.

Germany's reunification in 1990 was the beginning of yet another chapter. Though it's now one country, the cultural, social and economic differences of the formerly separate Germanys will take many years to disappear altogether. Nevertheless, the integration of the two is proceeding well, and first-time visitors to Germany may not notice big differences between them at all.

Much of Germany's history and culture is easily explored by visitors today. There is a huge variety of museums, architecture from most periods and a heavy emphasis on cultural activity. Infrastructure is extremely well organised, there is plenty of accommodation and the beer, food and wine are all excellent.

But Germany is not just a mecca for history buffs and culture vultures. It is also a land of staggering physical beauty, from the Bavarian Alps and the majestic, castle-lined Rhine River to windswept North Sea islands, the enchanting Black Forest, 'museum'

towns of half-timbered houses and Gothic cathedrals.

Outdoor activity is part of the German way of life and the opportunities for cycling, skiing, hiking and mountaineering, horse riding or just relaxing in a thermal spa are endless.

Gute Reise!

Facts about the Country

HISTORY

The origins of German history can be found in the Teutonic tribes that once inhabited northern Europe. But a 'German' history only dates from about the 9th century, when the Frankish Reich was first divided up and regions east of the Rhine began to develop a cultural identity. Compared with Britain and France, Germany was slow to shake off the yoke of regional dynastic rule and become a centralised state. The subsequent development of its principalities into the Federal Republic of Germany is a history of feudalism, unification and fascism, occupation, division and reunification.

Today, Germany is the main player in pushing for a united Europe, and the German nation is finding a new voice as a mediator between established capitalist countries to the west and former communist countries to the east.

Early History

The first inhabitants of Germany were Celts, who were gradually displaced by Germanic tribes from the north. The exact origins of the tribes are uncertain, but Bronze Age populations are believed to have inhabited a region extending south from Sweden and Denmark to the North German plains and Harz Mountains. By about 100 AD, six broad settlement groups had formed, scattered roughly between what is today Denmark in the north, Kaliningrad in the north-east, the Danube in the south-east and the Rhine region in the west.

Romans

Early clashes between Germanic tribes and conquering Romans occurred in the 1st century BC. The Romans suffered defeats, but their opponents found it difficult to hold onto land gains and were usually pushed back east across the Rhine. In 71 BC regions west of the Rhine were taken by Atovius, a powerful tribal military leader hailing from the north, before reoccupation under Julius Caesar in 58 BC led to alliances that temporarily kept the peace. After the defeat of Roman legions at the hands of Arminius in the Teutoburger Wald in 9 AD, the Romans abandoned plans to extend control to the Elbe River. They consolidated southern fortifications in about 90 AD and began Romanising conquered populations. Arminius was a talented tribal leader who had enjoyed Roman citizenship and fought with the legions before staging his own revolt.

Trade contacts ensured that something of the Romans rubbed off on the tribes. Many signs of the occupation can be found today, especially in Trier, one of the most important administrative centres in the Western Empire. Others were Cologne, Mainz, Koblenz, Augsburg and Regensburg.

A lot of what we know about the early Germans comes from the Roman scholar, Tacitus, and his work *Germania*, published in 98 AD. According to Tacitus, who often idealised the tribes, they cultivated crops, produced most of their goods within the household, traded in slaves with the Romans, and lived on a diet largely consisting of milk, cheese and meat. He was probably the first scholar to draw attention to their proclivity for beer and a bet.

The arrival of Hun horsemen from central Asia in the 4th century marked the beginning of the Great Migration throughout Europe, causing the displacement of Germanic tribes in the 5th century, who then overran southern Europe. The Hun threat ended with the death of Attila in 453.

In 486, with the collapse of the Western Empire, the tables turned and the Romans began seeking protection among resettled Germanic tribes. By that time there had already developed a Germanic population that benefited from Roman administrative, financial and political structures. The later use of the title *Kaiser* (from 'Caesar') was a direct legacy of Roman times.

The Frankish Reich

Based in lands on the west bank of the Rhine, the Frankish Reich was the most important European political entity in the early Middle Ages. In its heyday it included present-day France, Germany, the Low Countries and half the Italian peninsula. One reason for its success was a policy by Clovis (482-511), its first Merovingian king, and his successors of uniting diverse population groups. His conversion to Christianity marked the start of campaigns to convert pagan tribes and create unified foundations. Missionaries, such as the English St Boniface, were sent across the Rhine. When fighting broke out among the aristocratic clans in the 7th century, the Merovingians were replaced by the Carolingians.

The Carolingians exerted power over duchies east of the Rhine by establishing hierarchical Church structures. The granting of newly cleared and reclaimed land (and the pacification of the tribes) became dependent on a hotchpotch of religious, economic and political factors – a fateful combination that would later play a crucial role in Germany's development. Charlemagne (768-814), the Reich's most important king, conquered Lombardy, won territory in Bavaria, successfully waged a 30-year war against the Saxons in the north, and was crowned Kaiser by the pope in 800. Charlemagne took up residence in Aachen, emphasising Germany's significance to the crown. By subduing the Lombards, Charlemagne affirmed the Franks' role in protecting the newly created papal state in Italy, granted to the popes by his father.

Attacks by Danes, Saracens and Magyars in the 9th century resulted in a decentralisation of military, political and economic power, and eventually four main tribal duchies formed in the eastern portion of Charlemagne's empire: Bavaria, Franconia, Swabia and Saxony.

On Charlemagne's death, a bunfight ensued between his sons, resulting in the Treaty of Verdun and a gradual carve-up of the Reich. Louis the German, who ruled Bavaria, was the first to seriously promote the German language and culture. When Louis the Child, a grandson of Charlemagne, died in 911 without leaving an heir, the East Frankish (ie German) dukes elected a king from their own ranks, creating a first 'German' monarch.

Holy Roman Empire

A cultural identity had been forged under Louis the German. This was reinforced by the election of Konrad I (911-18) as king by the dukes, which was accompanied by a concentration of political and economic power in the hands of German princes and the low nobility.

Konrad proved to be a hapless ruler. When he died and the crown passed to Heinrich I (919-36), a leading figure from Saxony's gentry, Saxon power began to grow. So, too, grew a reliance on the support of clerics, who sometimes assumed the characteristics of nobility. This coincided with Saxon military campaigns in 925 to establish hegemony over French-speaking Lorraine.

Heinrich's son, Otto I (936-73), continued Charlemagne's policy of integrating Church figures into civil administration, and reasserted the Reich's power over Italy as far south as Rome. He also consolidated *Markgrafschaften* (marches) on the eastern border, administrative buffer regions that gradually turned into duchies.

In 962 Otto answered a call for help from the pope, renewing Charlemagne's promise of protection to the papacy. The pope, who traditionally crowned Kaisers, cordially obliged by promising his own loyalty, reinforcing an interdependence of pope and Kaiser that complicated future struggles for power. The Holy Roman Empire survived, under various names, from the 8th century until 1806.

Otto III (983-1002), grandson of Otto I, was three years old when elected to the throne, and for 11 years the Reich was successively ruled by two women, Theophano, his mother, and Adelheid, his grandmother. Otto then tried to make Rome the capital of the Holy Roman Empire and resurrect its former classical glory. He failed, and most of the gains under Otto I were forfeited. In 1024 power fell to the Salians, an established Franconian noble house. Konrad II (1024-39) and his reformist successor, Heinrich III (1039-56), relied on a power base of *Ministeriales*. These were bonded crown servants who received fiefdoms for their services, but could not bequeath them. Under Salian rule, vassal fiefdoms would be created in the west of Poland and Hungary, as well as in Bohemia and Moravia, and Burgundy would be added to the Reich.

Early Papal Reforms

The lack of clear distinctions between clerical and secular positions of power meant that papal reforms, begun around 1050, greatly affected Germany. Rulers had often sold Church positions, a practice opposed by reformers. This led to a power struggle, the Investiture Conflict, between Heinrich IV (1056-1106) and the pope over the main issues of simony (selling religious office) and the right to appoint bishops.

In 1076 Heinrich was excommunicated – for the first of two times – but absolved a short time later in a sensational act of penance, when he stood barefoot in the snow for three days in front of the castle at Canossa, in northern Italy, begging the pope's forgiveness. This divided his enemies, resulting in a 20-year civil war to control bishoprics and, of course, their wealth. The Salian downfall was merely delayed when Heinrich V (1106-25) took power, for he would fail to deliver the dynasty an heir.

The Treaty of Worms (1122) regulated the appointment of bishops, who became independent of the Reich. This hailed the end of the Ottonian system, whereby the Church had provided a direct power base for the monarchy.

Hohenstaufen Rule

Despite land gains, Salian rule had weakened the crown. Kings had always had to submit to some form of election in Germany, but a relative usually held the best cards. By 1125, however, this principle had been abandoned, and rather than dust down an obscure nephew of Heinrich V's, the *Kurfürsten* (prince electors) chose one of their own number in Lothar III (1125-37), a Saxon noble who had scaled the dynastic ladder by marriage. Another good marriage, this time between his daughter and a member of the powerful Welf family, allied Bavarian and Saxon rulers against the rival Swabian family of the Hohenstaufens. When Lothar died, however, the electors opted for Konrad III (1138-52), thus beginning a period of Hohenstaufen rule.

Under Friedrich I Barbarossa (1152-89), attempts were made to consolidate imperial power on the old linchpins of Germany, Italy and Burgundy, and to create an efficient feudalist state. Friedrich's move on Burgundy was achieved by another clever dynastic marriage. He also honoured the old custom of leading an Italian campaign, being crowned Kaiser by the pope, then falling out with His Holiness. In Friedrich's case, the reaffirmation of rule in Lombardy made Pope Alexander III nervous about territorial control in Italy. An agreement was finally reached (the Treaty of Venice, 1177), whereby both pope and Kaiser temporarily abandoned demands for respective subservience.

In the meantime, Henry the Lion, a Welf whose interests lay in Saxony and part of Bavaria, had been extending influence eastwards in campaigns to Germanise and convert the Slavs. When he went into exile after a dispute with Friedrich I, Saxon interests were carved up and handed over to the Reich. Bavaria ended up in the hands of another powerful family, the Wittelsbachs. Friedrich died in 1189 on the 3rd crusade, at the threshold to the Holy Land.

With Heinrich VI (1190-97), the Reich under the Hohenstaufens reached its peak. It married into Sicily (causing another papal nerve attack), but Heinrich's sudden death caught the Reich unawares, bringing a fight for the crown between Welfs and Hohenstaufens. This led to the election of a king and (a pope-backed) anti-king in Phillip von Schwaben and Otto IV, Henry the Lion's son.

The papacy, jittery at Hohenstaufen gains, assumed the role of holy umpire, exploiting the conflict to reassert power.

One effect of a system of electing monarchs was to make central power dependent on the fickle will of prince electors, who placed their own dynastic interests before those of the Reich. Authority had all but fallen to local rulers by 1250, and dynastic conflict took on a new quality as rival dynasties, especially the Welfs and Hohenstaufens, contested bishoprics and newly-formed principalities.

Friedrich II (1212-50), a papal nominee replacement for the murdered Phillip von Schwaben, left government administration to the princes, accelerating fragmentation. The princes built castles, established local mints and customs tolls, and enjoyed judicial autonomy.

Friedrich tried to resurrect Hohenstaufen policies in Italy, however, and was nullified by Pope Innocent IV, leading to the Great Interregnum, or 'Terrible Time' (1254-73), when the Reich was over-endowed with kings and central authority collapsed. Richard of Cornwall, an obscurely-related English nominee, managed four visits to his realm, making sure he never strayed far from the Rhine, while his anti-king, Alfons X from Spain, did not manage to pay his subjects even a flying visit.

Settlement in the East

Chaos and dynastic rivalry in the German Reich did not, however, inhibit expansion eastward, which had always been the prerogative of individual princes. By the mid-12th century a large number of German peasants and city dwellers had settled east of the Oder River in Silesia and Moravia. Settlement really got underway in the early 13th century, however, with the Teutonic Knights. Originally part of a charity organisation formed in the Holy Land to care for fallen crusaders, the knights took on a military character and, with the crusades behind them, returned to Europe. After answering a call from the king of Poland to fight the Prussians, they pushed eastwards, establishing fortresses under their grand master, Hermann of Salza, which later grew into towns, such as Königsberg (present-day Kaliningrad). Granted protection rights over their conquests, the knights subsequently built a unified state that, at its peak, stretched from the Oder to Estonia.

By the mid-14th century, plague and trouble with Poland and the gentry had brought decline, and by 1525 a reduced area controlled by the knights became the Duchy of Prussia, a vassal state of Poland until the rise of Brandenburg-Prussia around the 17th century.

Cities & the Hanseatic League

From about the mid-11th century, population growth, land pressure and greater mobility had accelerated the growth of cities. Some were imperial (once controlled by the Reich and subsequently granted autonomy by crown charter), others were free cities (those that had shaken off clerical rulers). Imperial cities still had certain military and financial obligations to the Reich. Both had their own administration and generally more liberal laws than the countryside, which was often under the decree of regional feudal lords. Any peasant who managed to flee to a city and stay there for one year and one day could become a resident. This gave rise to the expression *Stadtluft macht frei* ('city air liberates').

Leagues were established to protect common interests, the most important of which was the Hanseatic League, whose origins lay in guilds and associations formed by out-of-town merchants. By 1358 these had formally come together to create the Hanseatic League, dominated by Lübeck, which controlled a large slice of European shipping trade. At its zenith, the League had over 150 member cities. It acquired a say in the choice of Danish kings after the Danes inspired Hanseatic wrath by sinking a flotilla of the League's ships off Gotland in 1361. The resulting Treaty of Stralsund turned the League into northern Europe's most powerful economic and political entity.

As well as Lübeck, the League included such cities as Rīga and Danzig (now Gdańsk) on the Baltic Sea, Hamburg and Bremen on the North Sea, and inland cities such as Cologne, Dortmund and Hildesheim. By the 15th century, however, competition from Dutch and English shipping companies, internal disputes and a shift in the centre of world trade from the North and Baltic seas to the Atlantic had caused decline. Today, Hamburg, Bremen and Lübeck are still known as Hanse cities, and Hamburg and Bremen remain separate German states in their own right.

Plague

The 'Terrible Time' brought untold misery, but the plague, which wiped out about 25% of Europe's population in the mid-14th century, was worse. It hit Germany from 1348 to 1350 and produced panic lynchings, pogroms towards Jews, labour shortages and a rush to the cities, where tensions rose between old and new city dwellers. Large tracts of marginal farmland were abandoned. The bright side of the plague, however, was that anyone who survived it enjoyed slightly better conditions by being able to demand more for labour.

Guilds

The higher price of labour corresponded to an increase in the power of craft guilds (precursors to trade unions), which, during the 13th and 14th centuries, developed into important institutions that posed a challenge to merchant dominance. Leadership of a guild was usually in the hands of old masters, who regularly met to discuss work issues. Guilds operated a closed-shop system, and often came in conflict with city authorities. They formed alliances with powerful families, and sometimes held their own church services. Those excluded from the guilds, such as journeymen or day labourers, usually endured serious hardship in the cities.

The Habsburgs

All this was still to come, however, when the Habsburg dynasty, in the person of Rudolf (1273-91), took the throne thus ending the Terrible Time. The dynasty would dominate much of European affairs into the 20th century.

Under the Habsburgs, the focus of the Reich was shifted to the south-east and Austria, the family's traditional stamping ground. By Rudolf's time, the power to elect kings had fallen to seven Kurfürsten – three secular and four clerical – who shaped the politics of the Reich. Rudolf gave Austria to his son, made a hash of Switzerland, which struggled for independence, and built on his influence in Italy. In the 15 years after his death the crown changed hands four times to other powerful dynasties, who continued to promote their own interests at the expense of the Reich's. Rudolf had merely been a flicker of light in what was still a pretty bad time, and something had to change.

The first change came in 1338 with the Declaration of Rense, which dispensed with the pope's confirmation of elected kings. Election to king now automatically bestowed the title of Kaiser, thereby ending centuries of built-in conflict. The second change was introduced under Karl IV (1347-78) with the signing of the Golden Bull (1356), Germany's most important early constitutional document. This laid down electoral procedures in writing and codified the relationship between the Kaiser and the princes, giving the princes formal sovereignty in a range of matters, including customs levies and the status of Jews. But the very weakness of the Reich meant it was a princes' solution, for it prevented the establishment of a powerful central authority, setting the tone up to the 19th century.

The reign of Karl IV (a Luxemburg) saw the establishment of Prague University (he was king of Bohemia as well). It was followed in the next half century by other universities in Heidelberg, Cologne, Erfurt, and in Leipzig in 1409 when anti-German feelings in Prague caused the German professors to pack their bags and found their own university. The Reich (as opposed to local rulers) soon asserted itself in European affairs after the Great Schism (1378-1417) brought forth two popes (one French, the other Italian), weakening Church power and further reducing the Church's influence in German affairs.

By the time of Maximilian I (1493-1519), the Reich was Habsburgian again, and would stay that way until its collapse in 1806. Maximilian was an impressive ruler who had command of seven tongues and was often referred to as 'the last knight', which said as much about his predilection for medieval tournaments as the fact that the days of knights were numbered. Under pressure from the princes, he reformed the Reich's finances and administration to prevent its total collapse, and established a *Reichsregiment* (a decision-making body made up of the Kaiser and the princes) and a court to settle disputes. He himself 'married' Burgundy and Holland, and when his son married the heir to the Spanish throne, he acquired Naples and Sicily as well, winning back some of the territory lost in the years after the Hohenstaufen reign.

Martin Luther: the central figure of the Reformation.

Reformation

The Great Schism was a low point for the Church. By squandering Church money on self-aggrandisement, competing popes created a rift between themselves and the common folk. This brought a rise in the practice of selling 'indulgences', whereby the wealthy could buy freedom from punishment for sin. Jan Hus, a cleric at Prague University, had raised a storm about this around 1400, inflaming Czech nationalist sentiments, ending with the departure of the German professors. The Church solved that problem by burning him at the stake in 1415.

On 31 October 1517, plagued by the questions of faith and salvation, Martin Luther, a theology professor at Wittenberg University, made public his '95 Theses' in which he questioned the selling of indulgences. Though in Latin and intended only for theologians, the theses quickly spread by word of mouth across Germany and found popular support.

The following year Luther was given a hearing by anxious Church authorities in Augsburg. Having refused to repudiate the theses, he broke from the Catholic (ie 'Universal') Church and expanded on his beliefs in reformist writings in 1520. In the same year the pope threatened Luther with excommunication. Luther burnt the letter. Increasingly under pressure, he was invited to a *Reichstag* (one of the many meetings to discuss issues of the day) by Karl V (1519-56), nephew of Karl IV, where he again refused to repudiate his theses. He was banned by the Reich, only to be hidden in Wartburg (south of Eisenach in Thuringia), where he translated the New Testament into German.

Spurred on by Luther's teachings, townsfolk in Wittenberg began destroying their church. Luther returned to restore order, with the outcome that Latin mass was replaced by the Protestant service, which relied heavily on German hymns.

Meanwhile, similarly inspired by Luther and growing weary of their feral nobility, peasants elsewhere began to demand better conditions from lords and the free election of priests. Insurrections occurred. Luther, to the dismay of many, sided with the lords, who repressed the violence. The *Bauernkriege*

(Peasants' War) of 1524-25 ensued, immediately following a failed uprising by the knights, who wanted to save the last of their power by carving up principalities.

Karl V was too distracted by dynastic crises to fully recognise the impetus of the Reformation. After initially trying to force the Lutherans back into the Catholic Church, he succumbed to the princes' demands in the Peace of Augsburg (1555). Each ruler had the right to decide the religion of his principality, and the Catholic and Lutheran Churches now enjoyed equal status. With the exception of small diasporas, the more secular northern principalities adopted Luther's teachings, whereas the clerical lords in the south, south-west and Austria adhered to the Catholic Church. This compromise is reflected in the religious make-up of Germany today. When Rudolf II took the throne in 1576, a Counter-Reformation gained momentum.

Thirty Years' War

The religious issue would not die. What began as a conflict between newly-formed Protestant and Catholic leagues degenerated into one of Europe's most bloody dynastic wars. The Thirty Years' War (actually several wars) began in 1618 in Bohemia. In 1625 it was picked up by an alliance of Protestant Danes and Saxons, who felt threatened by attempts to re-Catholicise the north. Sweden jumped in from 1630, joined in 1635 by France, which saw a chance to weaken the Habsburgs by taking the Protestant side.

By the time calmness was restored with the Peace of Westphalia (1648), the Reich was ravaged. It consisted of over 300 states and about 1000 smaller territories. Switzerland and the Netherlands gained independence, France won chunks of Alsace and Lorraine, and Sweden took the mouths of the Elbe, Oder and Weser rivers. The Reich had turned into a nominal, impotent state, its population depleted by the war. Whole regions lay empty, and the nobility began to exact more in taxes and labour from their dependent peasants. The cities lost old trade contacts and fell into poverty.

Absolutism & Enlightenment

Much can happen in a century, but in Germany it took that long to recover from the war. From the middle of the 17th century, the Reich's fortunes were in the hands of a rabble of autocratic princes who competed to assert authority. Some developed the nasty habit of selling their subjects as cannon fodder for foreign wars, notably to the British in America's War of Independence. They built grand baroque residences such as those in Würzburg, Karlsruhe, Mannheim and Ludwigsburg. Although the Enlightenment was slow to gain momentum in Germany, when it did it produced composers like Bach and Händel, and a wave of *Hochkultur*. All this, of course, excluded the masses, who remained largely illiterate and at the mercy of absolutist rulers. In 1714 the English crown fell into the hands of the House of Hanover, beginning a union between Hanover and Britain that only ended with the death of William IV in 1837.

Areas formerly controlled by the Teutonic Knights had been united under Brandenburg-Prussia and, largely through the efforts of kings Friedrich Wilhelm I (the Soldier King), and his son Friedrich II (Frederick the Great), the Hohenzollerns rose to challenge the power of the Habsburgs. This marked the rise of Brandenburg-Prussia.

Brandenburg-Prussia annexed Silesia after the Seven Years' War (1756-63) with Austria, and subsequently sliced up Poland in a series of partitions. When peace returned in 1763, both Prussia and the Habsburgs set about revamping their administrations and armies.

The Habsburgs, meantime, had extended imperial power across south-east Europe to Hungary and the Balkans, having repelled an army of 200,000 Turks near Vienna in 1683. This created the foundation for an Austro-Hungarian empire. Nevertheless, with Austria distracted by the Turks, France had gradually helped itself to the rest of Alsace, including Strasbourg and the Palatinate in the 1680s.

Towards the end of the 18th century, the Age of Enlightenment was in full swing and the scales had tipped in favour of a centralised state. Rulers were quick to recognise the expediency of the Enlightenment for the survival of their own government. At the same time, a self-made class of public servants, academics, theologians and merchants questioned the right of the nobility to rule and stressed individual achievement.

A newly established imperial deputation secularised and reconstituted German territory between 1801 and 1803, much of this at the behest of Napoleon, who would do more for German unity than any German had ever done. In 1806 the Rhine Confederation was formed, which supported Napoleon's ambitions by eradicating about 100 principalities. Sensing the end of the Holy Roman Empire, Kaiser Franz II (1792-1806) packed his bags for Austria, renamed himself Franz I of Austria, and finally abdicated altogether in 1806. This marked the end of the Holy Roman Empire. Thus, it was not a frightened pope or an ambitious prince who had sounded the death knell to this anachronism, but a Frenchman.

Its fragmentation meant that Germany was no serious match for Napoleon. In 1806 Brandenburg-Prussia fell to the French armies, which occupied Berlin. But Napoleon abandoned plans to completely abolish this new power. The humiliation of defeat prompted Brandenburg-Prussia to reform, bringing it closer to civil statehood. Restrictive guild regulations were lifted and agricultural reforms abolished bonded labour, providing the basis for industrialisation. Jews won social equality.

In 1813, with French troops driven back by the Russians, Leipzig was the scene of one of Napoleon's most significant defeats. At the Congress of Vienna (1815), held to hammer out a post-Napoleon Europe, Germany was reorganised into a confederation of 35 states, an unsatisfactory solution that only minimally improved on the now-defunct Holy Roman Empire. Under the auspices of the charismatic Austrian diplomat, Klemens von Metternich, an ineffective Reichstag was established in Frankfurt. It poorly represented the most populous states, however, and failed to address Austro-Prussian rivalry.

Industrial Age

The first half of the 19th century was a crucial period in the development of Germany and Europe as a whole. The decay of feudal structures, an accumulation of wealth in new hands, and industrial innovation changed the economic and social ground rules, feeding into nationalist calls for a centralised state.

In 1837 construction of the first substantial railway line in Germany was begun between Dresden and Leipzig. This was expanded on in later years to become an efficient transportation system, coinciding with new customs unions that abolished feudal tariffs. Also significant was the growth of an industrial, urban proletariat. Workers' movements were banned, which is why the Trier-born Karl Marx and his collaborator, Friedrich Engels, would publish their enormously influential works in exile.

With the scrapping of monarchical birthright in France in 1830, calls by liberals for reform in Germany grew louder. Fearing revolution, many states belatedly introduced the constitutions promised to the people at the Congress of Vienna. The 'Young Germany' movement of satirists formed and lampooned the powerful of the day. In Prussia, Friedrich Wilhelm IV had taken the throne and disappointed everyone who wanted substantial change.

The French revolution of 1848 soon found its own counterpart in Germany. Metternich was dispensed with. Berlin erupted in riots. The response by German leaders was to quell demands for more radical reforms by setting up a provisional parliament in the Paulskirche in Frankfurt. However, delays in agreeing on a constitution slowly sapped its prestige. One reason for this tardiness was the so-called *Grossdeutsch-Kleindeutsch* question (greater or lesser Germany) – mainly whether or not Austria would belong to a reconstituted Germany.

Austria wrote its own constitution, broke away and then relapsed into monarchism.

Friedrich Wilhelm IV drafted his own constitution in 1850 (it remained in force until 1918), but failed in his attempt to form a North German Confederation.

Although revolution fizzled, it did turn Prussia into a constitutional state, albeit with limited franchise. The confederation was revived in Frankfurt under Austrian presidency, and the clock turned back on reforms in the German parliament, the *Bundestag*. One member of the Bundestag was Otto von Bismarck.

Unification

When a new era of reform began in Prussia in the 1850s, Otto von Bismarck went into 'cold storage on the Neva' in Russia, returning to become Prussian prime minister only after a constitutional crisis had changed the political atmosphere. Bismarck's grand ambition was to create a unified Germany, preferably with Prussia at the helm. An old-guard militarist, he successfully waged war against Denmark (with Austria his ally) over Schleswig-Holstein in 1864, and in 1866 he unified northern Germany after the Seven Weeks' War against Austria itself, creating his own North German Confederation the following year.

With northern Germany under his belt, Bismarck turned his attention to the south. Through skilful diplomacy, he isolated France and manoeuvred it into declaring war on Prussia in 1870. The pretence he used was a dispute with France over nominating a successor to the Spanish throne. Prussia backed down on the nomination issue, renouncing all future claims to the Spanish throne, but some tricky editing of a telegram to this effect (the *Emser Depesche)* by Bismarck offended the French. Bismarck then surprised Napoleon III by winning the backing of most south German states. War with France resulted in Bismarck's annexation of Alsace-Lorraine.

By 1871, having won over the south German princes, he had created a unified Germany with Berlin as its capital. The Reich extended roughly from Memel (Klaipeda in present-day Lithuania) to the present-day Dutch border, and included Alsace-Lorraine in the south-west and Silesia in the south-east. It was a masterful achievement, and western Europe's largest state. On 18 January 1871 the king of Prussia was crowned Kaiser of the Reich at Versailles (an ultimate humiliation of the French), with Bismarck its 'Iron Chancellor'.

Otto von Bismarck: the 'Iron Chancellor' who united Germany in 1871.

The new Reich was a bicameral, constitutional monarchy dominated by Prussia. Suffrage was limited to men, and real policy decisions were often made outside the elected Reichstag. The national colours were black, white and red, those of the old North German Confederation. Bismarck's power was based on merchants and *Junker*, a noble class of landowners (without knighthood) that had formed in the Middle Ages.

He quickly embarked on a campaign, his *Kulturkampf*, to curb Catholic power. With the Catholic Zentrum (Centre) party the second-largest in the Reichstag, Bismarck feared a possible alliance of party interests with France and Austria. Laws designed to nip the Catholic Church in the bud only increased support for Zentrum, however, and the policy was eventually abandoned.

The achievements of the Bismarck era were largely based on a dubious 'honest Otto' policy, whereby he acted as a broker between European powers, encouraging colonial vanities to divert attention from his own deeds. He built up a web of alliances to cover his back against Russia, Austria-Hungary, France, Italy and Britain, and even enjoyed good press in Britain. Germany began to catch up to Britain industrially, and the number of Germans emigrating tailed off substantially from the peak levels of the 1840s and 1850s. Bismarck belatedly graced the Reich of Kaiser Wilhelm I with a few African jewels after 1880, acquiring colonies in central, south-west and east Africa as well as numerous South Sea paradises, such as Tonga, where a weary Prussian prince might one day lay down his steel helmet and crack coconuts.

The mid-19th century saw the rise of democratic socialist parties, including predecessors of the present-day German Social Democratic Party (SPD). This was founded in 1875 as the Socialist Workers' Party, and got its present name in 1890. One leading social democrat, August Bebel, antagonised Bismarck with repeated calls for universal suffrage and economic equality. The chancellor's chief opponent, he was sentenced to two years' prison in 1872 for high treason and offence to the monarchy. In 1886, after a crackdown on socialists, he was convicted of belonging to a 'secret society'.

By the late 19th century, Germany was a wealthy, unified country. Bismarck had painted himself in liberal colours to buy inches and stop socialist demands for miles, providing health and accident benefits and invalid pensions. But the reform issue was to be his downfall, and when Wilhelm II became Kaiser in 1888 (Friedrich, son of Wilhelm I, was sickly and ruled for only 99 days), divisions arose between the Kaiser, who wanted to extend the social security system, and Bismarck, who enacted his stricter anti-socialist laws.

Europe badly missed Bismarck's diplomacy after the Kaiser's scalpel finally excised him from the political scene in March 1890. The period up to the outbreak of war in 1914, called the 'new direction', was an aimless one under the personal rule of Wilhelm II, who brought his weak chancellors to heel. Although industrially advanced (especially in chemical and electrical industries) and having produced some of the best social-revolutionary minds, Germany paddled towards the new century with incompetent leaders at its helm.

Bismarck's diplomacy slowly unravelled. Wilhelm II had already given up Zanzibar for the return of Helgoland from Britain in 1890, frightening Russia, which fled into amorous French arms and a treaty in 1894. England came out of isolation and signed up with Japan against Russian hegemony in East Asia, later with France, and then with Russia itself in 1907. Austria-Hungary teetered on the brink of collapse and dreamed of pan-Germanism. Meanwhile, the decline of the Ottoman empire had thrown the Balkans into disarray and local wars.

The Great War

No war can be great, but technological advances and the hardening of Europe into large colonial power blocs made WWI probably the worst since the Thirty Years' War. It began with the assassination of the heir to the Austrian throne, Archduke Franz-Ferdinand, in 1914 in Sarajevo, which triggered off war between Serbia and Austria-Hungary. Russia mobilised, ready to jump in on the side of Serbia, its ally. With the Russian rejection of a German ultimatum to demobilise, Germany declared war on Russia, followed two days later by a war declaration on France, based on the Schlieffen Plan. This dictated that, in the event of a two-front war (ie against Russia in the east and France in the west), Germany would attack France where it was most vulnerable, via Belgium, then fight the Russians afterwards. By doing so, however, this drew Britain, Belgium's ally, into the war. The lights of Europe, as the British foreign minister noted, had gone out. It escalated into a European and Middle East war. The major allies Britain, France, Italy and Russia fought against Germany, Austria-Hungary and Turkey.

The horror of the Great War was to change the psychological landscape of Europe forever. It began well enough for Germany, but when in 1915 one of its submarines sank the British passenger liner, the *Lusitania*, killing 120 US citizens, the Americans began to reconsider non-interventionism. Fearful of arousing American hostility, Germany abandoned its submarine attacks. By 1917, however, these had been unwisely renewed, and America entered the war.

In the meantime, hunger had produced widespread pessimism in Germany. In Russia, communist revolution had deposed the tsarist government. Russia won peace with Germany in March 1918 through the humiliating treaty of Brest-Litovsk, which saw Russia renounce vast territories. With an allied counter-offensive and Germany's collapse on the western front following many bloody battles, Germany was prepared to negotiate a ceasefire and the acceptance of US president Woodrow Wilson's 14-point peace plan.

Peace & Abdication

To facilitate negotiations, Prince Max von Baden, a liberal, took over leadership of the government and the constitution was changed to make the chancellor responsible to parliament. This gave Germany its first truly parliamentary party system. Though a good idea on paper, it in fact successfully shifted any blame for peace negotiations onto the parties, creating a potent link between the stigma of defeat and democracy. This, a revolution from above that excused the military of defeat, would heavily burden Germany's first democractic experience, the Weimar Republic.

What began as a sailors' mutiny in Kiel in September 1918 escalated into a workers' revolt, then turned into revolution on 9 November 1918 in Berlin. Kaiser Wilhelm II was forced to abdicate, ending monarchical rule once and for all. Two days later, on 11 November 1918, the armistice was signed.

Weimar Republic

Peace meant the end of war, but it did not create stability at home. The period after the armistice hailed a struggle between socialist and democratic socialist parties, including the radical Spartacus League. Founded by Rosa Luxemburg and Karl Liebknecht, the Spartacus League sought to establish a republic based on Marx's theories of proletarian revolution. In practice, this meant transferring power to a soldiers' and workers' council (a council was established, but only briefly). Opposed by moderate socialists, in 1919 the Spartacus League came together with other groups to form the German Communist Party (KPD). Following the bloody quashing of an uprising in Berlin, both Luxemburg and Liebknecht were arrested and murdered by *Freikorps* soldiers (war volunteers) and their bodies dumped in Berlin's Landwehrkanal. In the meantime, a new democratic republic had been proclaimed.

Germany paid dearly for the war. The Treaty of Versailles forced it to relinquish its colonies, to cede Alsace-Lorraine and territory in western Poland, and to pay high reparations. Article 231 of the treaty made Germany responsible for all losses incurred by its enemies. The treaty was passed by a newly elected national assembly in 1919.

The federalist constitution of the new republic was adopted in July 1919 in the city of Weimar, where the constituent assembly had sought refuge from the chaos of Berlin. It gave women the vote and established basic human rights, but it was also unwieldy and gave too much power to the president, who could rule by decree in times of emergency – a clause that would be abused by Paul von Hindenburg, Germany's second president.

A broad coalition government was formed by left and centre parties, led by president Friedrich Ebert of the SPD, the largest party until 1932. Too many forces in Germany rejected the republic, however, and it satisfied neither communists nor monarchists.

More trouble occurred in 1920 when a right-wing military circle staged the 'Kapp Putsch', occupying the government quarter of Berlin. Called on by the government to act (it had fled to Dresden), workers and trade unions went on strike, and the Putsch collapsed.

By August 1923, economic difficulties had alienated the middle classes, whose savings were ravaged by hyper-inflation. A new currency, the *Rentenmark*, was introduced but for many it was already too late.

In 1923 another attempt was made to topple the republic with the Munich Putsch, led by a young Austrian by the name of Adolf Hitler. Born in 1889 in Braunau am Inn, Austria, Hitler quit school after the death of his father in 1903 and dedicated himself to painting and a self-conceived mystical philosophy based on anti-Semitism, knights and Germanic folklore. In 1913 he moved to Munich and enlisted as a volunteer in the German army during WWI, rising to the rank of corporal and returning to civilian life after a gas attack left him temporarily blind.

A bad watercolour painter who had been twice rejected by the Vienna Institute of Art as talentless, Hitler exploited anti-Berlin ('red Berlin') sentiments and a Bavarian state of emergency. He tried to persuade the Bavarian government to march on the capital, imitating Mussolini's march on Rome a year earlier. He and other members of his National Socialist German Workers' Party set off through the Munich streets and were promptly arrested. The party was banned and Hitler wound up in jail, where he wrote his turgid, nationalist and anti-Semitic work, *Mein Kampf*. After his early release in 1925, he set about rebuilding the party, having sworn to authorities that he would thereafter only pursue legal means of change.

Reparations had bitten deeply into the German economy, breeding widespread dissatisfaction. The French, increasingly distrustful of Germany meeting its demands, had occupied the Ruhr region in 1923, leading to passive resistance by workers, the creation of a French-backed Ruhr separatist movement, and a German backdown to save the already ailing economy. Although the French ultimately let the separatist issue slide, the conflict spelled out a need to solve the reparation problem.

This was done by the Dawes Plan, which provided for cheap loans. (Payments would later again be readjusted under the Young Plan in 1930.) The Locarno Pact (1925), largely the work of Gustav Stresemann as foreign minister, saw Germany accept its western borders with France and Belgium, which incited the wrath of nationalists but eased Franco-German tensions.

The most ambitious project in international relations, however, was the establishment of the League of Nations, originally part of Wilson's 14-point plan and the Treaty of Versailles. It was an early, commendable attempt to create international order (Germany joined in 1926, the USSR in 1934), but its power was undermined by the fact that, ironically, the USA never joined.

After 1923 the economic situation began to stabilise and the Weimar years brought forth a cultural explosion. *Die wilden Zwanziger* ('the wild twenties') saw film and radio gain importance and *Kabarett* (cabaret) capture the public imagination. Germany witnessed the literary flowering of the likes of Thomas Mann and Bertolt Brecht and the creative outpourings of the Bauhaus and dada art movements.

Following the death of Ebert in 1925, Field Marshal Paul von Hindenburg became president. The election of the 78-year-old Hindenburg, a monarchist, would prove disastrous to the Republic.

Karl Marx was 111 years old and had long met his maker when the stock market crashed on Black Friday, 25 October 1929. The ensuing depression undermined an already fragile German democracy and bred support for extremist parties. Hindenburg, who had his own views on the crisis, used Article 48, the emergency powers, to circumvent parliament and appoint the Catholic Centre Party's Heinrich Brüning as chancellor. Brüning deflated the economy, forced down wages and destroyed whatever savings – and faith – the middle classes might have built up after the last economic debacle. It earned him the epitaph 'the hunger chancellor'.

The Hitler Era

In 1930 Hitler's NSDAP made astounding gains, winning 18% of the vote. Hitler set his sights on the presidency in 1932, running against Hindenburg; he received 37% of the second round vote. In the same year, Brüning was replaced by Franz von Papen as chancellor. Papen was a hard-core monarchist associated with the *Deutscher Herrenklub*, a right-wing club for industrialists and gentry in Berlin. He called two Reichstag elections, hoping to build a parliamentary base, but Hindenburg soon replaced him with Kurt von Schleicher, a military old boy.

Schleicher's attempt to pump-prime the economy with public money – a policy begun by Papen – failed when it alienated industrialists and landowners. Finally in January 1933, won over by the right and advised by both Papen and Schleicher to nominate Hitler, Hindenburg continued his tradition of ignoring parliament, dismissed Schleicher and appointed Hitler as chancellor, with a coalition cabinet consisting of National Socialists and Papen's Nationalists. The National Socialists (Nazis) were by far the largest single party but still short of a majority.

The Nationalists, conservatives, old aristocrats and powerful industrialists who controlled Hindenburg thought they could do the same with Hitler, but they were gravely mistaken. Hitler consolidated power by creating new ministries, which he filled with his own henchmen. In March 1933, without a clear majority, he called Germany's last halfway free pre-war elections. With the help of his intimidating party militia, the *Sturmabteilung* or SA, and the dubious Reichstag fire, which gave him an excuse to use emergency laws to arrest communist and liberal opponents, he won 43% of the vote – still not a majority.

The turning point was reached with the Enabling Law, which gave him the power to decree laws and change the constitution without consulting parliament. A state of emergency remained in place until 1945.

By June 1933 the SPD had been banned and other parties disbanded. Hitler's NSDAP governed alone. So began the Third Reich.

In the early 1930s laws limited the independence of the states and banned unions, whose members were reorganised into the *Deutsche Arbeitsfront*, a crony association designed to eliminate worker opposition (the workers had voted against Hitler in 1933). SA and SS *(Schutzstaffel)* troops stepped up their terror campaigns. Meanwhile, Joseph Goebbels, head of the well-oiled Ministry for Propaganda, had begun to crack down on intellectuals and artists. This resulted in the burning of 'un-German' books on 10 May 1933 by students in Berlin and university towns across the country. Many intellectuals and artists packed their bags for America and elsewhere. The respected author, Ricarda Huch, boldly resigned her post as head of the Prussian Academy of the Arts in protest at the expulsion of Jews. Membership of the *Hitlerjugend* (Hitler Youth) became compulsory for young women and men aged between 10 and 18, and all other youth organisations were disbanded except those of the Catholic Church.

Hitler, aware of the problems caused by unhappy popes in German history, signed an agreement that protected the Catholic Church (it was, after all, keen to sign up against 'godless Bolshevism') but excluded it from party political activities. In these early days, Hitler also enjoyed the support of the Protestant Church.

Röhm Putsch

Originally formed to guard public meetings, by 1934 the SA had become a powerful force that pushed to accelerate change. With rumours of revolt circulating, on 30 June 1934 elite SS troops (originally Hitler's bodyguards) rounded up and executed high-ranking SA officers. This gave the SS unchallenged power, but Hermann Göring and his lieutenants also exploited the occasion to settle old (sometimes homophobic) scores with Hitler's opponents. In the same year the death of Hindenburg allowed Hitler to merge the positions of president and chancellor.

The Plight of Jews

Although anti-Semitism in itself was not unique to German society, its level of institutionalisation and brutality was. A boycott of Jewish businesses and medical and legal practices was organised by Goebbels in April 1933. A few days later Jews were expelled from the public service, followed by an Aryanisation of the economy, prohibiting non-Aryans from engaging in many professions, trades and industries. With the Nuremberg Laws of 1935, non-Aryans (ie mostly Jews, but also Gypsies and other groups) were deprived of German citizenship and forbidden from marrying or having sexual relations with Aryans. The death penalty was usually passed on Germans and 'non-Germans' who broke race laws. Those sentenced to death were made to pay for their own trial and execution costs.

On the night of 9 November 1938 the horror escalated with the *Reichspogromnacht* (often called 'the night of broken glass'). In retaliation for the assassination of a German consular official by a Polish Jew in Paris, synagogues and Jewish cemeteries, property and businesses across Germany were desecrated, burnt or demolished. About 90 Jews died in the course of the pogrom and another 30,000 were arrested and incarcerated. Businesses were expropriated and transferred to non-Jews through forced sale at below-market prices.

The Road to War

Economic success was one reason for Hitler's phenomenal popularity among the middle and lower-middle classes. He achieved this by pumping large sums into employment programmes, such as *Autobahn* construction, and by encouraging employers to adopt military principles ('the employer is the *Führer*, the employee takes the orders').

Hitler reintroduced conscription and built up the airforce. His first major lick of the Versailles wounds came in March 1936 with the occupation of the Rhineland, which had been demilitarised under the treaty. He would later describe the 48 hours during which he awaited international reaction as the most exciting of his life. Mild protest was registered. A non-aggression pact with Poland, a friendship agreement with Mussolini, and a naval agreement with Britain already tucked under his belt, in 1936 Hitler introduced a four-year plan to rearm Germany and develop heavy industry. The SS established its own industries, initially relying on a compulsory 'volunteer workforce' made up of all women and men aged 18 to 25 (women worked on the fields or in farmhouses). The Volkswagen factory was opened in Wolfsburg in 1938.

In the same year Hitler's troops marched into Austria, greeted by enthusiastic crowds. This created the greater Germany that had been deliberated on back in the 19th century. The annexation boosted Hitler's popularity at home. Meanwhile, foreign powers, hopelessly unprepared both militarily and psychologically for another war, pursued an increasingly untenable policy of appeasement.

With the Munich Agreement of September 1938, signed by Hitler, Mussolini, Britain's Neville Chamberlain and France's Édouard Deladier, the largely ethnic German Sudetenland of Czechoslovakia was relinquished to Hitler. The British and French compromise, intended to buy time and save the remainder of Czechoslovakia, left the Czechs defenceless. Chamberlain returned home and declared there would be 'peace in our time', but began to rearm. By March 1939, Moravia and Bohemia had fallen into German hands.

When Hitler signed a non-aggression pact with Stalin's USSR in August 1939, the Tokyo-Berlin-Rome axis was expanded to include Moscow, clearing the way for an invasion of Poland. A secret Soviet-German protocol divided up Eastern Europe into spheres of interest, thus ensuring Soviet neutrality.

In late August an SS-staged attack on a German radio station in Gleiwitz (Gliwice) gave Hitler the excuse he needed to march into Poland. Three days later, on 3 September 1939, France and Britain declared war on Germany.

World War II: Early Victories

Although it resisted strongly, Poland was no match for Hitler's army, and the persecution and murder of intellectuals left it without effective leadership; Jews were driven into ghettos and forced to wear the yellow Star of David. Meanwhile, ethnic Germans were resettled (about 900,000 up to 1944) in the west of Poland from areas occupied by the USSR under the terms of the secret protocol. The thumbscrews of the SS under Heinrich Himmler were tightened a notch. It ran concentration camps, the Gestapo (secret police), and provided elite fighting troops. War brought food shortages at home and greater political oppression.

Belgium and the Netherlands fell quickly, as did France, where a collaborationist government was installed under Marshal Pétain. Hitler signed the French armistice in the same railway carriage used for the signing of the humiliating 1918 armistice. By summer 1940, the British had evacuated mainland Europe at Dunkirk but withstood the Battle of Britain and the bombing of major cities, including Coventry, which was almost completely destroyed.

In June 1941 Hitler attacked the USSR in Operation Barbarossa, opening up a new front. Delays in staging the operation – caused by problems in the Mediterranean – would be his downfall. Although Barbarossa was initially successful, lines became overstretched. Hitler's troops, bogged down and ill-prepared for the bitter winter of 1941-42, were forced into retreat. With the defeat of the German 6th army at Stalingrad (Volgograd) the following winter, morale flagged both at home and on the fronts.

In 1941 the USA signed the Lend-Lease Agreement with Britain to finance badly needed military equipment. In December of the same year the Japanese attacked the American fleet at Pearl Harbour, prompting the USA to formally enter the war.

The Final Solution

The treatment of Jews deteriorated after the outbreak of war. Himmler's SS troops systematically terrorised or executed local populations in occupied areas, and war with the USSR was portrayed as a fight against 'sub-human' Jews and Bolsheviks. The Nazis, abandoning vague plans to resettle European Jewry on the African island of Madagascar, began deportation to the east.

At Hitler's behest, Göring commissioned his functionaries to find an *Endlösung* (final solution) to the Jewish question. A conference held in January 1942 on the shores of Berlin's Wannsee resulted in a protocol clothed in bureaucratic jargon that laid the basis for the murder of millions of Jews. The Holocaust would be an efficient, systematic, bureaucratic and meticulously documented genocidal act carried out by about 100,000 Germans, but with the tacit agreement of a far greater number.

Concentration Camps

Concentration camps, although not a Nazi invention, reached a new level of efficiency under Nazism. Among the main groups incarcerated were Jews, Gypsies, political opponents, priests (especially Jesuits), homosexuals, resistance fighters and habitual criminals. The network of camps was expanded throughout the war, reaching a total of 22 (mostly in Eastern Europe) and another 165 work camps, with many (Auschwitz-Birkenau, for example) providing a labour force for large industrial concerns such as IG Farbenindustrie AG, producer of Zyklon B, a cyanide gas. Initially tested on Soviet prisoners, the gas was later used in the gas chambers to murder over three million Jews. About seven million people were sent to concentration camps. Only 500,000 survived to be liberated by Soviet and Allied soldiers.

Resistance

Resistance to Hitler from socialist, social democratic and workers' groups had been effectively quashed during the 1930s, with members either sent to camps or forced to go underground or abroad. Following the outbreak of war with the USSR in 1941, the Gestapo successfully smashed the Rote Kapelle, a Soviet spy ring that had penetrated Nazi ministries. The efficiency of the SS meant that, with notable exceptions, resistance tended to be small-scale or individual.

In 1942 a group of Munich students formed the Weisse Rose (White Rose) group, led by siblings Sophie and Hans Scholl. Exploiting the pessimism after Stalingrad, they distributed anti-Nazi leaflets. The following year the Scholls and four other members were arrested and sentenced to death.

When the war seemed lost, a plan was hatched by Claus Graf Schenk von Stauffenberg and other high-ranking army officers to assassinate Hitler and seize power from the SS on 20 July 1944. The attempt failed, and when sensitive documents fell into Nazi hands, over 200 women and men from the underground were immediately arrested and executed. Over 7000 people would be arrested as a result of the plot, several thousand of whom were executed.

Total War

With the Normandy invasion of June 1944, the Allies returned to the European mainland, supported by systematic air raids on German cities. The brunt of the bombings was carried by the civilian population. Over a year earlier, Goebbels had delivered his speech on total war to a gathering of the high and mighty in Berlin, rejecting Allied demands for unconditional surrender. Children and the elderly were called to join the newly formed *Volkssturm* (People's Army). An end, however, was in sight.

The Soviet advance from the east continued, often with brutal retributions. Rape and a particularly nasty strain of venereal disease, the so-called 'Russian syphilis', worsened the lot of women. The British bombed Dresden on 13 February 1945, killing 35,000 people, many of them refugees.

Hitler, broken and paranoid, ordered the destruction of all German industry and infrastructure, a decree that was largely ignored. He committed suicide, along with his wife Eva Braun (they married the previous day) and Goebbels, on 30 April 1945, with Soviet troops just outside Berlin. The capital fell two days later.

On 7 May 1945, after a delay that allowed refugees to reach Allied areas, Germany capitulated and peace was signed at the US headquarters in Rheims. It was signed again, at Stalin's request, the next day at Soviet headquarters in Berlin.

Surrender & Occupation

With the declaration of unconditional surrender on 8 May 1945, Germany lay in ruins. In line with agreements reached at the Yalta Conference (1944), it was divided into four zones of occupation. Similarly, Berlin was carved up into 12 administrative areas under British, French and US control and another eight under Soviet control. At the Potsdam Conference in July and August 1945, regions east of the Oder and Neisse rivers were transferred to Poland as compensation for earlier territorial losses to the Soviet Union.

Soviet demands for high reparations, a bone of contention between the Allies and Soviets that soon led to a breakdown in cooperation, were ultimately met from its own zone of occupation. In practice, this meant factory production was requisitioned, and able-bodied men and POWs were marched away and put to work in forced-labour camps on Soviet reconstruction.

Resettlement & Persecution

The westward advance of the Red Army had caused the displacement of millions of ethnic Germans in the east. At Potsdam a 'humane expulsion' of remaining ethnic German populations in Poland, Czechoslovakia and Hungary was provided for. This was accompanied, however, by retribution by the local populace. About 6.5 million ethnic Germans migrated or were expelled in a matter of months. The *Aussiedler* (foreign German settlers) and their descendants formed their own support groups to help locate missing family members, but these soon developed right-wing overtones. Many of these groups, often a source of friction with eastern neighbours today, remain an arch-conservative force in present-day German politics.

Political & Economic Developments

In the Soviet zone, the German Communist Party (KPD) and the Social Democratic

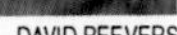

DAVID PEEVERS

DAVID PEEVERS

DAVID PEEVERS

MARIE OAMEK

DAVID PEEVERS

DAVID PEEVERS

Landscapes and half-timbered facades

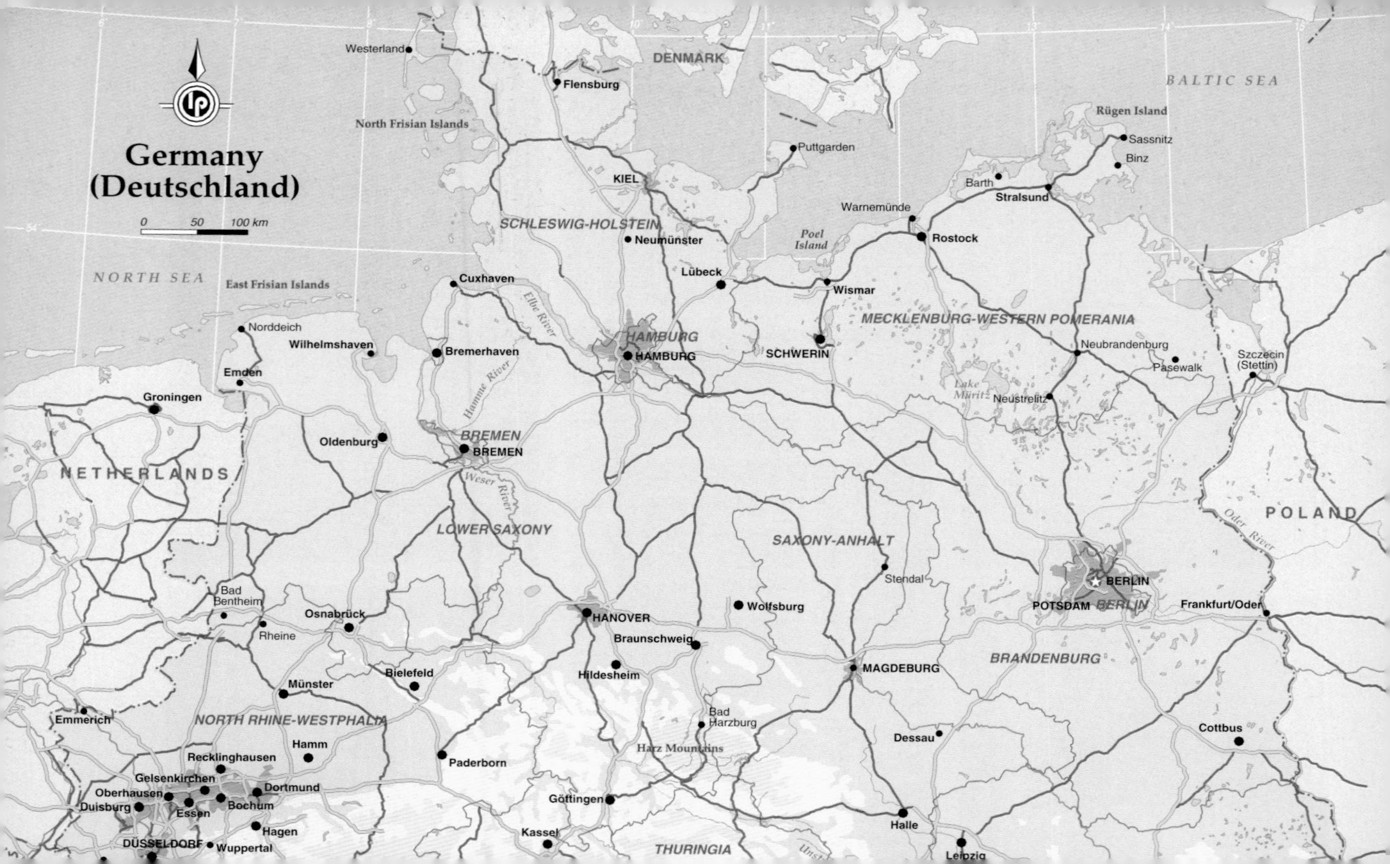
Germany
(Deutschland)
0
50
100 km
NORTH SEA
BALTIC SEA
DENMARK
NETHERLANDS
POLAND
North Frisian Islands
East Frisian Islands
Rügen Island
Poel Island
SCHLESWIG-HOLSTEIN
MECKLENBURG-WESTERN POMERANIA
HAMBURG
BREMEN
LOWER SAXONY
SAXONY-ANHALT
BRANDENBURG
BERLIN
NORTH RHINE-WESTPHALIA
THURINGIA
Elbe River
Hamme River
Weser River
Oder River
Lake Müritz
Harz Mountains
Westerland
Flensburg
KIEL
Neumünster
Puttgarden
Lübeck
Cuxhaven
Norddeich
Wilhelmshaven
Bremerhaven
Emden
Groningen
Oldenburg
BREMEN
HAMBURG
SCHWERIN
Wismar
Warnemünde
Rostock
Barth
Stralsund
Sassnitz
Binz
Neubrandenburg
Pasewalk
Szczecin
(Stettin)
Neustrelitz
BERLIN
POTSDAM
Frankfurt/Oder
Stendal
Wolfsburg
HANOVER
Braunschweig
Hildesheim
MAGDEBURG
Bad Bentheim
Rheine
Osnabrück
Bielefeld
Münster
Emmerich
Bad Harzburg
Dessau
Cottbus
Hamm
Recklinghausen
Paderborn
Gelsenkirchen
Dortmund
Oberhausen
Duisburg
Essen
Bochum
Hagen
DÜSSELDORF
Wuppertal
Göttingen
Kassel
Halle
Leipzig

ELEVATION
3000m
1500m
1000m
500m
200m
0
Cologne
Aachen
Bonn
Siegen
HESSE
Giessen
Fulda
Eisenach
ERFURT
Jena
Gera
Chemnitz
Zwickau
Thuringian Forest
Suhl
Ilm
Saale
River
BELGIUM
Koblenz
Rhine
RHINELAND-PALATINATE
Moselle
River
Plauen
Hof
Coburg
PRAGUE
CZECH
REPUBLIC
Frankfurt/Main
WIESBADEN
MAINZ
Schweinfurt
Bayreuth
Aschaffenburg
Darmstadt
Würzburg
Bamberg
LUXEMBOURG
Trier
Pilsen
SAARLAND
Saar River
Erlangen
Mannheim
Kaiserslautern
Heidelberg
Nuremberg
SAARBRÜCKEN
Rothenburg
Schwandorf
Heilbronn
BAVARIA
Karlsruhe
Regensburg
Pforzheim
Danube
River
STUTTGART
Ingolstadt
Baden-Baden
Nördlingen
Strasbourg
Black Forest
BADEN-WÜRTTEMBERG
Passau
Offenburg
Landshut
Freudenstadt
FRANCE
Ulm
Augsburg
MUNICH
AUSTRIA
Freiburg
Memmingen
Salzburg
Singen
Kempten
Berchtesgaden
Basel
Konstanz
Lake
Constance
Lindau
Garmisch-
Partenkirchen
Kufstein
Bavarian Alps
Zürich
SWITZERLAND
Oberstdorf
Zugspitze
(2963m)
Mittenwald
LIECHTENSTEIN
Innsbruck

ALL PHOTOS: DAVID PEEVERS

Faces of Germany

Party (SPD) were forcibly united into the Socialist Unity Party (SED) and given preferred status. Meanwhile, having removed a ban on political parties, the Allies set up regional and state administrative bodies – institutional forerunners of West German federalism. The SPD was joined by the Christian Democratic Union (CDU) and its Bavarian offshoot, the Christian Social Union (CSU).

Free elections were held in the Allied zones in 1946-47, the first since 1933, resulting in the formation of elected state parliaments.

The Marshall Plan

War had devastated the German economy. Inflation strained the currency and critical food shortages meant many city dwellers went hungry. About 50-70% of all houses in Cologne, Hamburg, Dortmund and Kiel had been destroyed in air raids, a problem aggravated by the need to house German refugees from Eastern Europe.

The Allies, keenly aware of the role an unhealthy German economy had played in the Nazi rise to power, founded economic councils, took control of some of Germany's non-military industries and, in 1948, implemented the Marshall Plan, an economic aid package. The plan provided for the delivery of goods, food parcels, credit and raw materials. Money paid for aid was deposited in European bank accounts, creating a pool of funds to inflate the economy. The Marshall Plan provided the basis for West Germany's *Wirtschaftswunder* (economic miracle). One side-effect of this, however, was to widen the rift between Soviet and Allied zones.

Blockade

Currency reform in Allied zones in June 1948 prompted the USSR to issue its own and, angry at the lack of consultation, begin an economic blockade of West Berlin that would last almost a year and see over 200,000 flights supply the city.

In this climate of frosty East-West relations, the Allies went ahead with the establishment of government institutions. In September 1948, representatives of West German states met in Bonn to discuss a draft constitution for a Federal Republic of Germany (FRG, or BRD by its German initials), which was subsequently approved by the Allies. Elections were held in 1949 and Konrad Adenauer, 73, a former mayor of Cologne during the Weimar years, became West Germany's first chancellor. Bonn was chosen as the provisional capital.

Reaction in the East

With the foundation of a West German state, the idea of creating a unified Germany faded. Tension in Korea led to greater East-West polarisation, and Tito's independent policy course in Yugoslavia complicated the situation and created a Soviet need to consolidate power in East Germany. At the same time, the idea of an independent, uniquely German socialism was abandoned in favour of Stalinism.

East Germany adopted its own constitution for a German Democratic Republic (GDR, or DDR by its German initials) in 1949. The constitution was based largely on the Weimar model and, on paper at least, guaranteed press and religious freedom and the right to strike. Berlin became the East German capital. A bicameral system was set up (one chamber was later abolished), Wilhelm Pieck was voted the country's first president and Otto Grotewohl became its premier and cabinet head.

Although East Germany was nominally a parliamentary democracy, the dominance of the SED was such that party boss, Walter Ulbricht, was the country's real leader. The early years saw a party takeover of economic, judicial, and security functions, including the establishment of the Ministry for State Security, or Stasi, which set about neutralising opposition to the SED. In keeping with centralist policies, the states of Mecklenburg-Western Pomerania, Saxony, Saxony-Anhalt and Thuringia were reorganised into 14 regional administrations, thus removing a source of possible opposition.

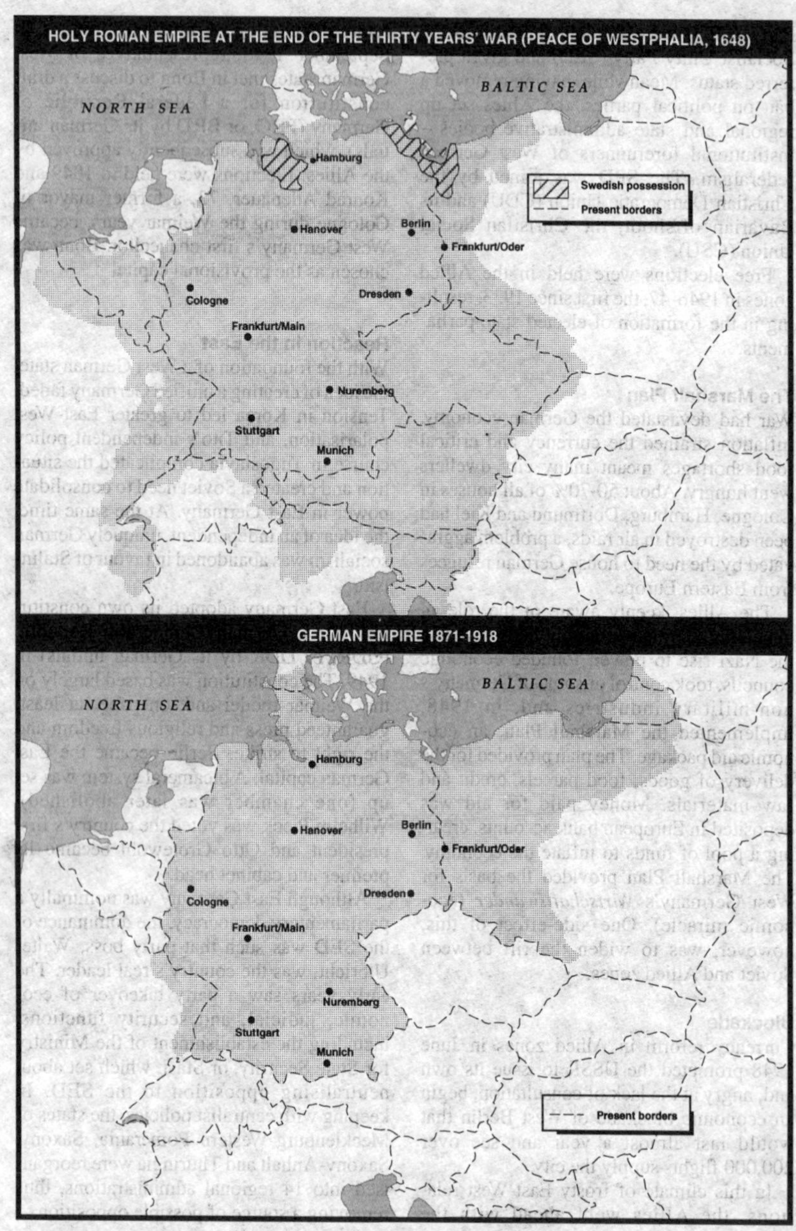
HOLY ROMAN EMPIRE AT THE END OF THE THIRTY YEARS' WAR (PEACE OF WESTPHALIA, 1648)
BALTIC SEA
NORTH SEA
Hamburg
Swedish possession
Present borders
Hanover
Berlin
Frankfurt/Oder
Cologne
Dresden
Frankfurt/Main
Nuremberg
Stuttgart
Munich
GERMAN EMPIRE 1871-1918
BALTIC SEA
NORTH SEA
Hamburg
Hanover
Berlin
Frankfurt/Oder
Cologne
Dresden
Frankfurt/Main
Nuremberg
Stuttgart
Munich
Present borders

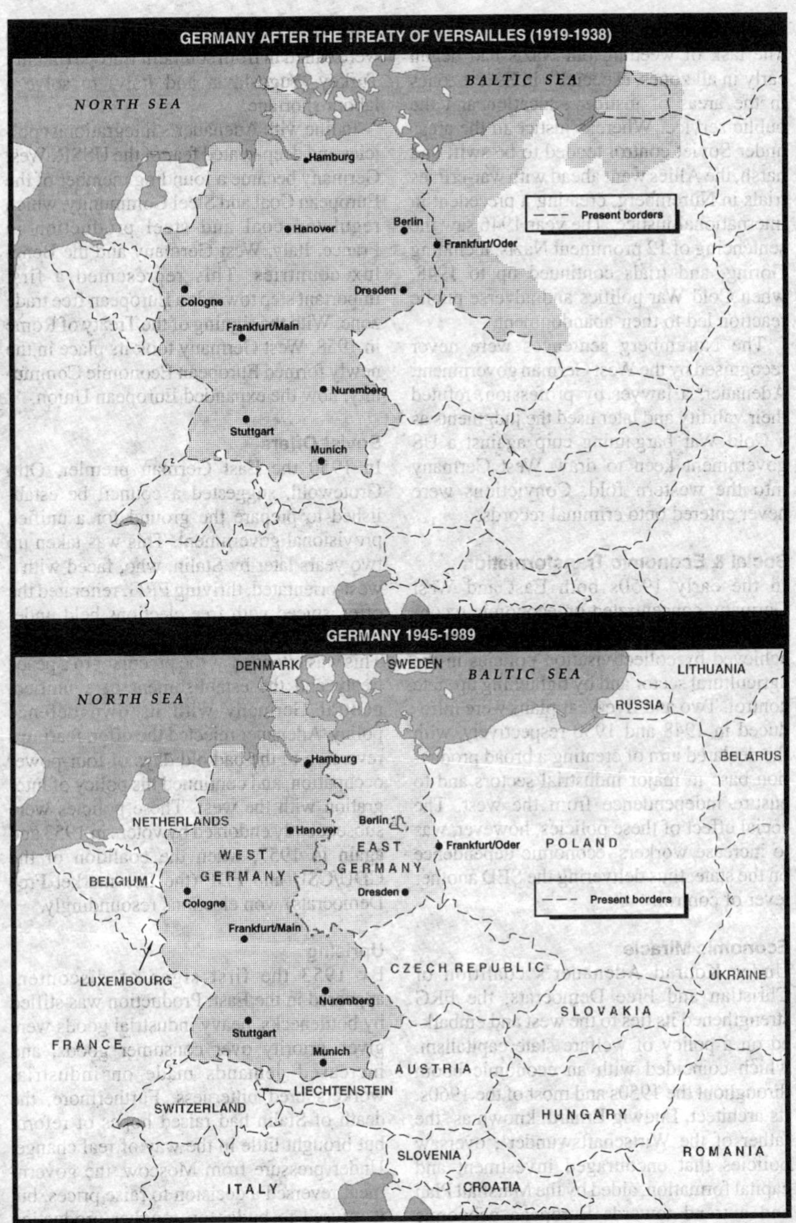
GERMANY AFTER THE TREATY OF VERSAILLES (1919-1938)
BALTIC SEA
NORTH SEA
Hamburg
Present borders
Berlin
Hanover
Frankfurt/Oder
Dresden
Cologne
Frankfurt/Main
Nuremberg
Stuttgart
Munich
GERMANY 1945-1989
DENMARK
SWEDEN
BALTIC SEA
LITHUANIA
NORTH SEA
RUSSIA
Hamburg
BELARUS
NETHERLANDS
Berlin
Hanover
WEST
GERMANY
EAST
GERMANY
Frankfurt/Oder
POLAND
BELGIUM
Dresden
Cologne
Present borders
Frankfurt/Main
CZECH REPUBLIC
UKRAINE
LUXEMBOURG
Nuremberg
SLOVAKIA
Stuttgart
FRANCE
Munich
AUSTRIA
LIECHTENSTEIN
SWITZERLAND
HUNGARY
SLOVENIA
ROMANIA
ITALY
CROATIA

De-Nazification

The task of weeding out Nazis had begun early in all zones, especially in Soviet zones in the areas of justice, education and the public service. Whereas justice in the areas under Soviet control tended to be swift and harsh, the Allies went ahead with war-crimes trials in Nuremberg, creating a precedent in international justice. The year 1946 saw the sentencing of 12 prominent Nazis, including Göring, and trials continued up to 1948, when Cold War politics and adverse public reaction led to their abandonment.

The Nuremberg sentences were never recognised by the West German government. Adenauer, a lawyer by profession, refuted their validity and later used the judgments as a Cold War bargaining chip against a US government keen to draw West Germany into the western fold. Convictions were never entered onto criminal records.

Social & Economic Transformation

In the early 1950s both East and West Germany concentrated on economic reconstruction. In East Germany, this was largely achieved by collectivisation policies in the agricultural sector and by tightening up state control. Two and five-year plans were introduced in 1948 and 1950 respectively, with the declared aim of creating a broad production base in major industrial sectors and to ensure independence from the west. The social effect of these policies, however, was to increase workers' economic dependence on the state, thus delivering the SED another lever of control.

Economic Miracle

Under Konrad Adenauer's coalition of Christian and Free Democrats, the FRG strengthened its ties to the west and embarked on a policy of welfare state capitalism, which coincided with an economic boom throughout the 1950s and most of the 1960s. Its architect, Ludwig Erhard, known as 'the father of the Wirtschaftswunder', oversaw policies that encouraged investment and capital formation, aided by the Marshall Plan and a trend towards European economic integration. *Gastarbeiter* (guest workers) were called in from southern Europe (mainly Turkey, Yugoslavia and Italy) to solve a labour shortage.

In line with Adenauer's integrationist policies and deep-seated fear of the USSR, West Germany became a founding member of the European Coal and Steel Community, which regulated coal and steel production in France, Italy, West Germany and the Benelux countries. This represented a first important step towards a European free trade zone. With the signing of the Treaty of Rome in 1958, West Germany took its place in the newly formed European Economic Community, now the expanded European Union.

Soviet Offers

In 1950 the East German premier, Otto Grotewohl, suggested a council be established to prepare the ground for a unified provisional government. This was taken up two years later by Stalin, who, faced with a west-orientated, thriving FRG, reiterated the offer, spiced with free elections held under the observation of the occupying powers. This was intended as the precursor to a peace treaty and the establishment of a unified, neutral Germany with its own defence policy. Adenauer rejected the offer, fearing a reversion to the bad old days of four-power occupation, and continued his policy of integration with the west. These policies were subsequently endorsed by voters in 1953 and again in 1957, when the coalition of the CDU/CSU and FDP (the free-market Free Democrats) won elections resoundingly.

Uprising

By 1953 the first signs of discontent appeared in the East. Production was stifled by bottlenecks, heavy industrial goods were given priority over consumer goods, and increased demands made on industrial workers bred bitterness. Furthermore, the death of Stalin had raised hopes of reform but brought little in the way of real change. Under pressure from Moscow, the government reversed a decision to raise prices, but it refused to budge on tougher production norms proposed for factories and the building industry. Strikes and calls for reform turned to unrest in the urban and industrial centres, culminating in demonstrations and riots on 17 June 1953 that involved about 10% of the country's workers. The government proved incapable of containing the situation. Soviet troops stationed on East German soil quashed the uprising, with scores of deaths and the arrest of about 1200 people.

Defence Alliances

In May 1955 the FRG joined the North Atlantic Treaty Organisation (NATO), thus completing its military integration into the west. The constitution was changed to allow German-based armed forces, followed a year later by the introduction of conscription. East Germany responded by joining the Warsaw Pact defence alliance and the trade organisation in the Eastern bloc, Comecon.

As early as 1957 there were calls to arm West Germany with nuclear weapons, a policy supported strongly by both the USA and leading West German political figures, including Adenauer. Despite public protests, a parliamentary resolution to this effect was passed one year later, though never acted upon. In the same year, a proposal by Poland (Rapacki Plan) to ban all nuclear weapons on German, Polish and Czechoslovakian soil failed miserably. The reason for its lack of success – the fact that Warsaw Pact troops clearly outnumbered NATO's – would subsequently dominate talks on disarmament right into the 1970s.

The Wall

The flow of refugees seeking better fortunes in the West increased. In 1953 about 330,000 East Germans fled to the West, most of them young, well-educated and employed, thus placing strain on an already troubled economy. The exodus reached such a level that it threatened East Germany's Comecon commitments. On the night of 12 August 1961, with the approval of Warsaw Pact countries, the wall was erected between East and West Berlin, thus creating one of the Cold War's most potent symbols. At the same time, the entire FRG/GDR border was fenced off and mined.

Building walls to keep people out may be one thing, but building one to keep your own citizens in amounted to an admission of failure by the SED. In a period of economic stabilisation in the 1960s, the East German government tried to make the system more flexible and attractive. Their New Economic Policy was extremely successful: the standard of living rose to the highest in the Eastern bloc and East Germany became its second largest industrial power (behind the USSR). Party head Walter Ulbricht, who had been slow to pick up on changes in Moscow under Khrushchev, was considered too inflexible. In 1971 he was replaced by Erich Honecker, opening the way for rapprochement with the West and greater international acceptance.

Ministry for State Security (Stasi)

Based on the Soviet KGB, the Stasi was founded in 1950. The 'shield and sword' of the SED, it soon developed into a state within the state that, by 1989, had a spy network of about 90,000 full-time employees and 180,000 *inoffizielle Mitarbeiter* (unofficial co-workers). The Stasi accumulated about six million files in its lifetime, and in January 1990 its Berlin headquarters was stormed by angry protesters demanding to see them. With the fall of the SED, the Stasi was disbanded and a public office, the Gauck Behörde, established to assess records, which continue to provide a source of controversy today.

Developments in the West

By the end of 1956 Warsaw Pact troops had crushed Hungarian reformists, the last German internee was released by the USSR, and the German Communist Party (KPD) had been banned in West Germany for its rather rash call for the violent overthrow of the 'Adenauer regime'. Undeterred, Adenauer pushed ahead with his 'love your friends, don't recognise your enemies' policy by signing a friendship treaty with

France in 1963 and maintaining the Hallstein Doctrine, which rejected recognition of East Germany. His 'I'm OK, you're OK' meeting with Charles de Gaulle was to be his last triumph. Later that year the aged Adenauer was replaced by Ludwig Erhard, who still rested on his laurels as the 'father of the Wirtschaftswunder' but now faced a troubled economy. In 1966 the three major parties (CDU/CSU and SPD) formed a broad coalition, a period of government during which there was no effective opposition.

The absence of parliamentary opposition in the late 1960s served to fuel radical demands by the student movement. Students sought reform of West Germany's antiquated university system and teaching programmes (many of Germany's textbooks either ignored Nazism or took a soft line), an open discussion of the Hitler years, and a more flexible policy towards the Eastern bloc. New emergency acts passed to protect the FRG's political system evoked public outrage. In 1969, the Social Democratic Party, having dispensed with revolutionary elements of its platform, formed a government (with the FDP) under Willy Brandt.

Whereas Adenauer had spent the Hitler years quietly tending his garden in Cologne, Brandt (a pen-name – his real name was Herbert Ernst Karl Frahm) had worked as a journalist in exile in Scandinavia, where he was stripped of German citizenship for anti-Nazi writings, and later served as mayor of Berlin from 1957-66. Brandt took the broom to the Hallstein Doctrine and instigated an *Ostpolitik* of co-existence to normalise East-West relations.

In December 1972 the two Germanys signed the Basic Treaty. This guaranteed sovereignty in international and domestic affairs, but fudged formal recognition, which was precluded by the West German constitution. Nevertheless, it normalised German-German relations and paved the way for both countries to join the United Nations.

Brandt signed separate treaties with Poland, recognising the Oder-Neisse border, and with Czechoslovakia. In Poland he kneeled after laying a wreath to pay his respects to Jews killed in the Warsaw ghetto uprising, provoking outrage among hard-liners at home and approving nods abroad. On top of this came the Four-Power Agreement, which eased conditions in Berlin. Somewhat of a legend in his own time, Willy Brandt was to drag more retrograde elements of German society kicking and screaming into a new era.

He was replaced by Helmut Schmidt in 1974 after a scandal (one of Brandt's close advisers turned out to be a Stasi spy). A period of government followed that, opposed by Schmidt, saw anti-nuclear and green issues move onto the agenda, ultimately leading to the election of Green Party representatives to the Bonn parliament in 1979.

The 1970s had also brought a rise in terrorism in West Germany, with the abduction and assassination of prominent business and political figures by the notorious Red Army Faction. By 1976, however, its leading members, Ulrike Meinhof and Andreas Baader, had committed suicide (both in prison) and remaining members found themselves either in prison, in hiding, or taking refuge across the border in East Germany, where political change would one day expose them to West German attempts to bring them to justice.

In 1982 the SPD lost power to a conservative coalition government under Helmut Kohl, who set about grooming relations in both East and West, while dismantling parts of the welfare state at home. Kohl would fulfil Erich Honecker's dream by receiving him with full state honours on a visit to Bonn in 1987. It might have been Erich's kiss of death.

Reunification

The Honecker era saw changes to the East German constitution. Ominously, hopeful reunification clauses were struck out in 1974 and replaced by one declaring East Germany's irrevocable alliance to the USSR. Nevertheless, the Basic Treaty of 1972 had created some semblance of order in the East German household. Honecker fell in line with Soviet policies, rode out world recession and an oil crisis in the early 1970s, and oversaw a period of housing construction, pension rises and help for working mothers.

In the mid-1980s, however, prices for consumer goods rose sharply and, with East Germany struggling to keep pace with technological innovations elsewhere in the world, stagnation set in. Reforms in Poland and Hungary, and especially Mikhail Gorbachev's new course in the USSR, put pressure on an increasingly recalcitrant SED leadership to introduce reforms.

The end began in May 1989, when Hungary announced it would suspend its Travel Agreement, which had once prevented East Germans from entering the West via Hungary. It began to dismantle installations along its Austrian border, suddenly making it possible for East Germans to cross safely, which they did in numbers. The SED responded to the exodus by tightening up travel restrictions. East German discontent peaked, with heavy-handed police actions against demonstrators and the falsification of regional election results. Adding insult to injury, the party prepared to celebrate East Germany's 40th anniversary.

Replying to a question about reforms in the USSR, party ideologist Kurt Hager was quoted as saying you didn't need to wallpaper your flat just to keep up with your neighbours. However, it was Gorbachev's decision not to intervene in German affairs that ultimately brought change.

In the meantime, the churches had become a focal point of opposition, and more and more East Germans filled West German consulates and embassies in East Berlin, Warsaw, Prague and Budapest, seeking to emigrate. The turning point was reached on 10 September 1989, when Hungary's foreign minister, Gyula Horn, officially opened the Hungarian border to Austria, allowing refugees to cross legally to the West. Two weeks later the SED arranged transport to the West for several thousand of those who had taken refuge in diplomatic buildings. This triggered another wave of refugees seeking asylum.

In Leipzig the number of demonstrators attending traditional Monday church services swelled throughout October to more than 250,000. A wave of opposition groups, notably *Neues Forum* (New Forum), formed and led calls for human rights and an end to the SED political monopoly, supported by church figures. This brought about a leadership crisis in the SED and the replacement of Honecker by Egon Krenz. About 500,000 demonstrators turned up on Berlin's Alexanderplatz on 4 November and whistled as Markus Wolf, the Stasi head, tried to lodge a defence of Stasi activities. By this time, East Germany was losing its citizens at a rate of about 10,000 per day.

Five days later, on 9 November, the floodgates opened when the Politburo of the GDR approved direct travel to the West. Tens of thousands passed through border points in Berlin, watched by perplexed guards. Amid scenes of wild partying, the Wall had fallen.

Under pressure from opposition groups, so-called 'round table talks' were established between government representatives and opposition groups to hammer out a course. In March 1990 free elections were held in East Germany, the first since 1949, in which an alliance, headed by Lothar de Maizière of the CDU, won convincingly. The SPD, which took an equivocal view of reunification, was punished by voters accordingly. The old SED administrative regions were abolished and the *Länder* (states) revived. Currency and economic union came into force in July 1990.

In September 1990 the two Germanys, the USSR and Allied powers signed the Two-Plus-Four Treaty, ending postwar occupation zones. One month later East Germany recognised the West German constitution (with a few changes) and formally ceased to exist. On this basis, Germany's first unified post-WWII elections were held in December 1990, resulting in a victory for the CDU/CSU and Liberal coalition.

Recent Trends

Since reunification, Germany has been preoccupied with the task of economic, social

The Rise & Fall of Erich Honecker

A miner's son, Erich Honecker was born in Neunkirchen, Saarland, on 25 August 1912. He worked as a roof tiler, joined the central committee of the communist youth organisation in the 1920s, and led the group's underground activities in southern Germany after Hitler took power. He was imprisoned for 10 years from 1935, and on release became president of the youth organisation Freie deutsche Jugend (Free German Youth).

One of the SED's promising talents, in 1958 he was appointed Politburo member and secretary of the central committee, handling state security matters. A diligent if unspectacular functionary, by 1976 he rose to party general secretary and head of East Germany.

Honecker continued the established policy of limiting relations with West Germany, and made himself unpopular in the west by raising the minimum sum of money West Germans had to exchange when visiting the GDR. Like West German chancellor Helmut Schmidt, he tried to prevent international tensions from flowing over into friction between the two German states.

Honecker's period of leadership was one of lethargy and disillusionment in East Germany. He stepped down as leader of the SED in October 1989 and was stripped of all party and political functions shortly afterwards. In December of the same year he was investigated for treason, corruption and abuse of public office, and put under house arrest. He was tossed in jail in 1990, released shortly afterwards due to bad health and transferred to a Soviet military hospital.

With an arrest order hanging over him, Honecker fled to the USSR in March 1991. By November he had sought refuge in the Chilean embassy. When the Russians applied pressure on Chile, he was returned to Germany and placed on trial for manslaughter (for his role in giving the order to shoot fleeing East Germans), but Honecker's ill health led to the case being abandoned.

In 1993 Honecker went to Chile, and died of liver cancer the following year. ■

and political integration. On the economic front, the *Treuhand* (literally 'trust'; see Economy) was established to privatise industry, while in foreign policy, Germany strove to placate worried neighbours. It signed friendship treaties with Poland (renewing recognition of the Oder-Neisse border), the ex-USSR and the Czech Republic. All Soviet troops were withdrawn from German soil by August 1994, and shortly afterwards the Allied powers withdrew from Berlin. Relations with the Czech Republic have remained politically strained, however, with the 1997 joint declaration on the Sudeten German resettlement (or persecution) fudging issues of guilt and compensation. The greatest obstacle to good political relations remains the Sudeten German lobby, which continues to press for compensation.

Attempts were made to bring former East German functionaries to justice, notably Erich Honecker. This contradictory policy – bearing in mind that West Germany did not formally recognise the Nuremberg convictions – has only been partly successful. Former Defence Minister Heinz Kessler and his deputy, Fritz Streletz, lost appeals against convictions and were imprisoned for their role in issuing the order to shoot fleeing East Germans. Scores of other cases, however, have degenerated into farce or have been abandoned.

Having regained its status as 'the land in the middle', Germany now finds itself torn between an inward-looking reunification process and outward-looking European integration.

GEOGRAPHY

Germany covers 356,866 sq km and shares borders with Poland and the Czech Republic in the east, Austria and Switzerland in the south, France, Belgium, the Netherlands and Luxembourg in the west, and Denmark in the north. The landscape tends to be flat in the north and north-east, gradually building up in height further to the south. Its highest mountain, the Zugspitze, rises to 2962m and is near the Austrian border.

Most of Germany's rivers run to the north or north-west, following the lie of the land,

and drain into the North or Baltic seas. The Danube, an exception, flows eastward. Of all its natural features, the Rhine River is Germany's most potent national symbol. It begins in the Swiss Alps and winds 1320km to the Netherlands' North Sea coast. The Rhine has long been an important natural border between Germany and France. The middle Rhine between Bingen and Bonn is the most beautiful stretch.

The North Sea coast is mostly flat, partly consisting of drained land and dykes. Islands extend from East Friesland near the Netherlands up to Schleswig-Holstein. The shallow North Sea along this coast is known as the Wattenmeer, and is subject to extreme tides that make it possible to walk to some of the islands across the tidal flats at low tide. Storm tides sometimes submerge a group of smaller islands, known as the Halligen, leaving only dyked houses visible above the sea.

In Schleswig-Holstein, the Baltic Sea coast is slightly hillier and has numerous bays and fjords. These give way to sandy inlets, spits and occasional cliffs in eastern Germany. Rügen, Germany's largest Baltic Sea island, is famous for its chalk cliffs. In cold winters the Baltic Sea freezes, as does the North Sea in the Wattenmeer.

The north of Germany is characterised by the Northern Lowlands, a broad expanse of low-lying land that sweeps across about one third of the country. This is part of a larger European plain extending from the Netherlands to the Urals. Some parts consist of marshland and heath, such as around the lower Elbe, and others of glacial lakes, mainly in Mecklenburg-Western Pomerania. The Spreewald, a favourite holiday area south-east of Berlin, is a picturesque wetland with narrow, navigable waterways.

The Central Uplands region is a complicated patchwork of mountain ranges, rifts and valleys. In German it is called the *Mittelgebirge*, which refers to the region itself and a type of medium-altitude mountain range, mostly less than 500m. The Central Uplands roughly includes the area between the Black Forest, the Sauerland (near Cologne), the Elbsandsteingebirge (south-west of Dresden), and the Bavarian Forest, which runs along the Czech border. The Danube marks its southern boundary. Although physically a Mittelgebirge, the Harz Mountains lie north of the main body of ranges.

The Central Uplands are especially picturesque in the west around the Rhine massifs and the Moselle River, where the slopes of warm valleys provide Germany's best winegrowing conditions and some good hiking. The Black Forest, Elbsandsteingebirge, the Harz Mountains and the Bavarian Forest are other beautiful areas. The Eifel Upland north of the Moselle River is volcanic and famous for its *Maare* or crater lakes.

The Alpine Foothills, a wedge between the Danube and the Alps, are typified by moorland in eastern regions near the Danube, low rolling hills and subalpine plateaus. Some of Germany's most beautiful villages can be found here. Also here are several large glacial lakes such as the Chiemsee and Ammersee, and hundreds of smaller ones.

The German portion of the Alps lies entirely within Bavaria and runs from Lake Constance (Bodensee), Germany's largest lake, to Berchtesgaden in the east. Though lower than their brethren to their south, many peaks are well above 2000m, rising spectacularly from the Alpine Foothills.

CLIMATE

Germany has a much milder climate than its eastern neighbours, but a collision of Atlantic westerly winds and continental air masses from the north-east can sometimes cause changeability. Conditions also fluctuate greatly from year to year, which makes it difficult for the visitor to know exactly what to expect.

In a harsh winter, temperatures plunge well below zero and can remain there for several weeks, with much of the country blanketed by snow. The next year might be mild and damp, however; in that case you can count on daytime temperatures of about 0°C. The temperature is approximately between 14°C and 20°C in July, and -4°C and 3°C in January, depending on the region.

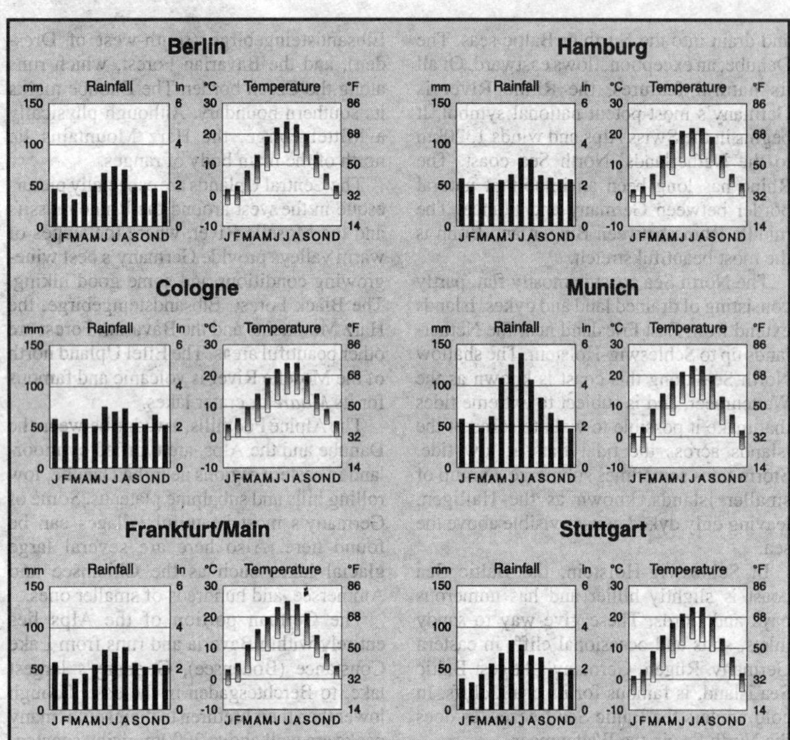

Annual rainfall distribution is fairly even, although regional summer droughts sometimes occur. November can often be drizzly, with overcast conditions adding to the climatic misery of the locals. Most of Germany gets between 600mm and 800mm annually, but the north-east averages less. Areas in the Alpine Foothills, the Alps, the western Harz Mountains and the Black Forest receive over 1200mm. The western slopes of mountain ranges are generally wetter than eastern slopes, and afternoon thunderstorms are fairly common in summer.

Spring is especially beautiful but it can be slow to arrive. In a good year, however, jackets can be stripped off in early April, and summer temperatures reach the high 20s or low 30s. An indian summer might set in around October and the winter remain crisp and dry. Cross your fingers, though: all too often spring can be a cold washout, run into a cool, wet summer with temperatures that only occasionally rise above 20°C in some regions, and turn into dark, equally wet November weather that lingers until the following spring.

Generally, areas in the east and south-east are subject to a more continental climate and greater temperature extremes, with colder, drier winters. It is not uncommon for bays, lakes and rivers to freeze over in winter. When the Alster in Hamburg freezes, half the city heads for the ice to eat, drink and be merry.

The western third of Germany is milder. The wind can make the lowlands a couple of degrees cooler, and the breezy North Sea coast is often cooler again. Germans say the North Sea coast has a *Reizklima*, a healthy, bracing climate. Windmills dot the landscape in Schleswig-Holstein and East Friesland. Bathers rent *Strandkörbe*, large wicker shelters, as protection from the wind.

The warmer latitude enjoyed by the south is generally offset in winter by its higher altitude. The south-west corner, around Freiburg, has a reputation for receiving more sunshine than any other part of Germany, and the valleys of the Central Uplands often enjoy summer daytime temperatures a little higher than elsewhere.

Germans have a few indigenous expressions for their weather patterns. A brief cool period that occurs regularly in May is called *die drei Eisheiligen* (the three ice saints). *Schafskälte* (loosely a 'sheep's cold spell') corresponds with shearing time in June. *Altweibersommer* (literally 'old maid's summer') is an indian summer, and frequently warmer weather between Christmas and New Year is called *Weihnachtstauwetter* (Christmas thaw weather).

One interesting phenomenon is the *Föhn*, an autumn wind that occurs in the German Alps and Alpine Foothills. It is caused by the rapid descent and warming of cool air as it passes over the Alps. The Föhn can bring clear skies and temperatures of over 20°C in autumn while the rest of Germany is being rained on. If it doesn't give you a headache (locals blame it for all sorts of ailments), it may be worth seeking out during a wet spell. Winds can intensify unexpectedly, however, so you need to be careful if boating on one of the lakes during *Föhnig* weather.

ECOLOGY & ENVIRONMENT

Germany's population density and long history of settlement have placed enormous pressure on the environment, with few areas escaping human impact. Industrialisation, urban encroachment and an extensive road system have dramatically reduced the amount of natural open space, especially in urban conglomerations such as the Ruhr region.

Furthermore, many watercourses have been altered to facilitate internal shipping, and levels of air and water pollution remain relatively high. This is complicated by the fact that some of the pollution comes from neighbouring countries, and that only coordinated Europe-wide agreements can bring about significant improvement.

Nevertheless, the situation has improved a lot in the past few years, with a shift away from the use of brown coal in power stations and the introduction of more efficient emission filtering systems. A vehicle tax system strongly encourages the use of advanced catalysers, but the car is worshipped as a symbol of freedom in Germany and a speed limit has yet to be introduced on Autobahns. Smog alerts are commonplace during the summer months, a situation that is unlikely to change until Germans wean themselves off their cars.

Germans have become fiercely protective of their natural surroundings, and environmental science is one area where they excel. Households and businesses participate enthusiastically in waste-recycling programmes. In 1994 a newly created article of the German constitution made it the duty of government to protect the nation's natural resources. Germans zealously wash and sort their rubbish into yellow recycling bags, and receive a rubbish rebate for maintaining a compost heap. A refund system applies to a wide range of bottles and jars, especially for foodstuffs bought in health-food shops, and nonrefundable glass is disposed of according to colour (green, clear and brown) in special containers placed throughout towns and cities.

Greenpeace is extremely active in Germany. In 1995 it successfully opposed controversial plans by Shell to sink the Brent Spar oil platform in the North Sea. It is also involved in attempts to prevent the storage of reprocessed nuclear waste in an underground facility near the north German town of Gorleben. The issue has resulted in demonstrations, clashes and the sabotage of railway links, with a massive police presence required to protect trains transporting the waste.

The Bergwald Projekt group is an interesting option for anyone wishing to become actively involved in environmental field work. Based in Switzerland, the group organises land-care programmes to improve and safeguard forests in Germany, Austria and Switzerland. For more information, see Volunteer Work in the Facts for the Visitor chapter.

Environment in Eastern Germany

The Unification Treaty of 1990 aims at ironing out differences in environmental conditions by the year 2000. Some of the problems faced have been contaminated industrial land, poor sewage facilities, uncontrolled rubbish dumping, high levels of water, soil and air pollution around Leipzig, Bitterfeld, Halle and Merseberg, a dependence on brown coal for power plants, and the heavy-handed use of pesticides and manures on farmland. Particularly insidious were uranium slag heaps in parts of Saxony and Thuringia.

Sewerage connection and repair programmes, industrial closures and the conversion of power stations to oil and natural gas have all greatly improved the situation. Many of the subsidised employment programmes in eastern Germany relate to environmental improvement, financed with enormous sums from both Germany and the EU.

Despite the environmental destruction, large areas of East Germany have survived intact. Areas along the Oder River and some estuaries on the Baltic coast are a haven for species, mainly birds, now rare or extinct elsewhere in Germany.

Forest Destruction

Deforestation reached a peak in the late 18th century, when early industries such as glassmaking created a high demand for wood. Cleared areas were then replanted with fast-growing conifers, turning what were once mixed deciduous forests into a monoculture. The lower Harz Mountains, which originally consisted of beech and oak, are one such example. This practice has been abandoned and attempts are being made to re-create original forest conditions using species mixtures.

The problems associated with acid rain first emerged in the 1970s, when an alarming rate of disease was noticed among spruce. This soon spread to beech and oak, especially at higher altitudes in the Mittelgebirge. About 73% of all forest stands in eastern Germany are presently affected to some degree, compared with a national figure of about 60%. The rate among mature trees in the Erzgebirge, the Bavarian Alps, and the Rhön and Harz mountains is as high as 90%! Damage initially occurs in the crown, which means it is often barely noticeable.

Acid rain, which develops when emissions (especially sodium dioxide and nitric oxide) alter the pH level of water, inhibits growth by rinsing nutrients out of tree foliage or by directly damaging the fine root system. This causes trees to shed their leaves. They also become susceptible to disease or extreme weather conditions. Attempts to reduce soil acidity by applying lime have helped in some areas, but the only real solution is to reduce air pollution levels.

Rivers & Seas

Environmental disasters in the 1970s and 1980s have led to increased awareness of pollution in Germany's rivers and seas. In 1988 about 18,000 seals were washed up dead along the Atlantic coast, 8300 alone in the Wattenmeer in Germany. Scientists established that pollutants, mainly heavy metals, had weakened the seals' immune system, making them susceptible to viruses. High nitrogen and phosphate levels have also produced algae blooms in the Baltic Sea. Better sewage disposal systems in eastern Germany are helping to reduce the problem, but both seas are still recognised as being in a sorry state. The Wattenmeer in particular is showing signs of stress, which poses a threat to the feeding and breeding grounds of migratory birds.

The Rhine River has seen its fair share of accidents – a chemical spill in 1986 temporarily turned it green. A couple of years later,

Germany's environment minister, Klaus Töpfer, donned a wetsuit and swam a few laps to reassure the populace, but aquatic ministers aside, the situation for marine life remains critical.

FLORA & FAUNA

Flora

Despite environmental pressures, German forests remain beautiful places to relax and get away from the crowd – especially in summer, when most Germans prefer to soak up light in various states of undress in open parks and meadows. Most cities and towns have their own forest *(Stadtwald)*, which can be easily reached by public transport or on foot. The prettiest ones are planted with varieties of beech, oak, birch, chestnut (mostly with non-edible fruit), lime, maple or ash.

Many forest regions of Germany consist of mixed deciduous forest at lower altitudes, changing to coniferous species as you ascend, so with a little planning it's possible to find the type of forest you want. River valleys are usually the best place to find deciduous forest.

Waldfrüchte (berries) are particularly colourful and, for the most part, extremely poisonous in Germany, so it might be wise to avoid the taste test unless you know exactly what you are about to eat. The same applies to mushrooms, which are essential for the development of healthy root systems in trees, especially in deciduous forests. It is always a good idea to limit your pick. *Pfifferlinge*, or chanterelle mushrooms, are just one of the seasonal culinary delights.

Alpine regions have a wide range of wildflowers – orchids, cyclamen, gentians, pulsatilla, alpine roses, edelweiss and buttercups, just to mention a few. Meadow species are particularly colourful in spring and summer, and great care is taken these days not to cut pastures until plants have seeded. Visitors can help by keeping to paths, especially in alpine areas or coastal dunes where ecosystems are especially fragile.

One popular attraction is the heather blossom on the Lüneburg Heath north of Hanover in late August. It draws visitors each year from all over Germany, and a couple of towns in the region compete to elect their own *Heideköniginnen*, or Heather Queens, who lead parades through the streets.

Fauna

Germany remains host to a wide variety of animals, although many have found their way onto the endangered species list. Gone are the days, however, when declining numbers only caused concern if there was too little game for the hunter to bag. That said, the most common large mammals you are likely to see in forests will be game species like deer and wild boar, or those that have adapted well to human activities, such as squirrels and foxes.

Raccoons were introduced from America and are common, if difficult to observe due to their nocturnal lifestyle. The alpine marmot can be found in the Alps up to the treeline. They live in colonies and let out a shrill warning when disturbed. Wild goats were almost wiped out by hunters in the 19th century, and those now found in the Alps (above the tree line) were reintroduced from northern Italy. Chamois are widespread in the Alps and Alpine Foothills, and small introduced populations also exist in the Black Forest, the Swabian Alps and Elbsandsteingebirge (south of Dresden).

Beavers were endangered as early as the Middle Ages, faced extinction in the 19th century and are now becoming more common. Originally found throughout Germany, these days populations cluster around the Oder and Elbe rivers in eastern Germany. Attempts are currently being made to reintroduce them into other wetland areas.

The hare is on the list of endangered species but can be observed frequently in fields in less populated regions. Collectivised farming methods virtually wiped them out in East Germany. The snow hare, whose fur is white in winter, is fairly common in the Alps. Visitors may also come across martens, badgers, hamsters and otters.

Lynx died out in Germany in the 19th century. Reintroduced populations were then illegally hunted to extinction in the 1980s. Since the removal of fences along the Czech border, about 25 to 30 brave souls have tried their luck again in the national park of the Bavarian Forest, which unfortunately means that your chances of seeing one in the wild are virtually zero. Others have been sighted in upland regions of eastern Germany. The wild cat, another indigenous feline, has returned to forest regions after being almost hunted to extinction in the 1930s. The Harz Mountains has the largest population. They often breed with domestic cats, making it hard to distinguish between the two.

Wolves regularly cross the Oder River from Poland into eastern Germany. Elk, which also torment guards with their border activities, are occasionally sighted in mixed forests and on moors in eastern Germany.

It is common to see seals on the North Sea and Baltic Sea coasts, especially on sandbanks in northern Germany's Wattenmeer. The Wattenmeer is also excellent for observing migratory birdlife. Sandpipers, marsh geese, eider and shelduck abound approximately from March to May and August to October, when many different species make a stopover to feed on the region's rich marine life.

Sea eagles, almost extinct in West Germany, survive now as small populations in eastern Germany. If you are very lucky, you might see a golden eagle in the Alps. More common are falcons, jays, white storks and cranes, especially in eastern Germany. Forests everywhere in Germany provide a habitat for a wide variety of songbirds as well as woodpeckers.

National Parks

Germany has 12 national parks. The following is an overview of what you can expect to find. For information on facilities and accommodation refer to the relevant section in the regional chapter.

Bavarian Forest National Park Near the Czech border, the Bayerischer Wald National Park covers an area of 131 sq km and consists of mountain forest (mostly beech, fir and spruce) with upland moors. Parts of the forest have been severely damaged by acid rain. Nevertheless, it has some fine walking tracks.

Berchtesgaden National Park This park covers 210 sq km and is near the Austrian border, rising in altitude from about 60 to 2700m. The landscape is a contrast of lakes, limestone and dolomite cliffs, meadows, mixed forests and subalpine spruce stands. Arguably Germany's most beautiful park, this, of course, is where you can best view alpine plants and wildlife.

Saxon Switzerland The main attraction of the Sächsische Schweiz, a 93-sq-km national park south of Dresden, is its spectacular sandstone and basalt rock formations, especially in the Bastei region on the Elbe. Its proximity to Dresden means the park can get a bit crowded in summer, but things quieten down on the walking tracks further away from the river. Kurort Rathen and Königstein are the two main centres.

National Parks in the Wattenmeer The three national parks of the Wattenmeer, in Schleswig-Holstein, Lower Saxony and around the mouth of the Elbe River near Hamburg, have a combined area of 5367 sq km. The largest of the parks is in Schleswig-Holstein. The tidal flats are rich in sea life and host an extraordinary variety of birds. The islands are also very attractive, especially the sand dunes and beaches on Amrum and Sylt. The best time to observe birds is in spring and autumn. Summer, late spring and early autumn are the best times to walk the Wattenmeer, but it is highly advisable to have a guide.

Boddenlandschaft Covering an area of 805 sq km, this park takes in the Baltic Sea coast from Rostock to Stralsund, several islands and peninsulas, as well as Rügen's west coast. Its main feature is the coastal landscape, with dunes, pine forests, meadows and heath.

Jasmund On the island of Rügen and covering only 30 sq km, this small national park protects the chalk cliffs along the Jasmund Peninsula. Forest, creeks and moors can be found inland. It can get extremely crowded in midsummer.

Unteres Odertal An example of European cooperation, this 329-sq-km German-Polish park (105 sq km in Poland) is a unique wetland with an enormous range of flora and fauna, especially water fowl. Meadows, marshland and deciduous forest make up a large proportion of it. Many of Germany's rarer species are found here, including migratory species.

Müritz The designated national park area covers about 318 sq km. This includes the Mecklenburg Lakes between the eastern shore of Lake Müritz and Neustrelitz. The park consists largely of moorland, with about 60 lakes, some comprising important breeding grounds for sea eagles and cranes.

Harz & Hochharz Located near the former East German border, these parks are largely made up of spruce forest, with occasional meadows, moorland and deciduous forests. There are also caves and several spectacular rock formations in the area. The western portion (Harz) covers an area of 158 sq km and is more developed than its neighbour, the Hochharz (about 58 sq km), to the east. Weekends can turn the more popular walking tracks (especially those leading to Brocken, northern Germany's highest peak) into crowded ant trails.

GOVERNMENT & POLITICS

Germany is a constitutional democracy with a president and a bicameral system based on the Bundestag (lower house) and the Bundesrat (upper house). The lower house is a popularly elected people's chamber, the upper house made up of delegates who represent the 16 states.

With reunification, eastern Germany's original (pre-1952) states of Brandenburg, Mecklenburg-Western Pomerania, Saxony, Saxony-Anhalt and Thuringia were re-established. Berlin, now the capital, became a separate city-state. These are often referred to as *neue Bundesländer* (new states). The *alte Bundesländer* (old states) are Hamburg, Schleswig-Holstein, Lower Saxony, North Rhine-Westphalia, Bremen, Hesse, Saarland, Rhineland-Palatinate, Bavaria and Baden-Württemberg.

The president is elected by an unwieldy body consisting of parliamentary representatives, state parliament delegates and respected public figures. The term is five years, and presidents can only be re-elected once. The position is largely ceremonial, with a few built-in safety mechanisms for troubled times. Presidential powers to dismiss a government, as existed in the Weimar constitution, were abolished to prevent a repeat of the chaotic circumstances that culminated in Hitler becoming chancellor in 1933. Roman Herzog is the current office holder. His predecessor, Richard von Weizsäcker, served two terms, earned much respect for his leadership and acuity during the reunification phase, and is proving a hard act to follow.

The whole Bundestag elects the chancellor (currently Helmut Kohl) and initiates most legislation, often relying on closed door parliamentary commissions which consult experts to hammer out compromises. A simple majority is required for ordinary laws, a two-third majority in both houses for constitutional changes. The term of parliament is four years and the chancellor can only be unseated by a so-called 'constructive vote of no confidence', which means a new chancellor must already have been assured a majority before the old one can be dispensed with. The only time such a motion has been successful was when Helmut Kohl replaced Helmut Schmidt in 1982.

About half the Bundestag is made up of direct candidates, those elected from constituencies, and the other half of listed candidates, who are party delegates and do not have electorates. The idea behind this is to prevent parochial issues from dominating the political agenda. A party has to gain 5%

of the national vote in order to be represented in the Bundestag. This has often prevented small radical parties and splinter groups from gaining a seat in parliament. Bundesrat members are appointees of the state parliaments.

The next tier of government is the state parliament or Landtag. Each Landtag has its own prime minister – a lord mayor in city-states – and cabinet. States also have their own constitution. A federal law overrides state law on any single issue. In practice, cooperation means there is a high degree of uniformity between state and federal laws. Below state level are several tiers of local government, including city administrations.

Women have had the vote in Germany since 1918 and make up 26% of the Bundestag. The federal election turnout among Germans is consistently high, usually around 80%.

In 1996 the current CDU chancellor, Helmut Kohl, broke Konrad Adenauer's record of 14 years in office. The following year he announced his intention to contest the 1998 Bundestag elections. Kohl's leadership has come under pressure several times from within his own party, but a process of weeding out possible threats has left it short of real talent. His coalition of Christian Democrats and Liberals (CDU/CSU and FDP) controls the agenda of German politics today, despite an opposition SPD majority in the upper house. Gregor Gysi, the leader of the Democratic Socialists (PDS, formerly the SED), summed up the situation by saying: 'The only strength of the Kohl government is the current weakness of the opposition.' His comment is directed at the Napoleonesque Oscar Lafontaine, who currently heads the SPD opposition, and the failure of the SPD to formulate clear policies. In the last election, held in 1994, Gysi's party failed to achieve the 5% minimum required for federal representation, but received about 20% of the vote in eastern Germany. The Greens, after some ups and downs in the early 1990s, have recovered lost ground under their current head, Joschka Fischer. In coalition with Bündnis 90, which grew out of the protest movement in East Germany, the Greens are presently the third largest party in the Bundestag. The Liberals, who had lost support in recent years, are now showing signs of recovery.

Economic problems dominate public debate today, particularly cuts in the welfare state, but issues such as racism and racist attacks, deployment of the German army abroad, political-asylum laws and environmental protection remain firmly on the political agenda. In eastern Germany, disenchantment (especially among the youth), unemployment, factory closures, and the struggle to find a role in a reunited Germany very much dominate discussion.

ECONOMY

Germany is the world's third largest economic power (behind the USA and Japan), a committed member of the EU, and a member of the powerful G7 group of industrial nations since 1974.

Although Germany was already a leading industrial power in the late 19th century, its real economic success was achieved in the postwar years with the Wirtschaftswunder in West Germany. In the 10 years from 1951-61, the economy averaged an annual growth rate of about 8%. This was helped to a large extent by the multiple effects of the Marshall Plan (see History), a labour supply swelled by returned soldiers, refugees and foreign workers, and a system known as the social market economy.

Although the Sozialmarktwirtschaft is taking somewhat of a hammering today, it still ensures a broad safety net of benefits for employees and unemployed that is anchored in the constitution. This is coupled with a free market guaranteeing private ownership and competition.

Of particular importance to German economic success has been the centralised wage-bargaining system and the creation of 'super unions', industry-based unions that often act in economic partnership with employer groups to fix wage levels and conditions. It means that all employees of one industrial sector, regardless of their specific job, belong to a single union. Until recently, this system has helped keep industrial disputes to a minimum.

Employees are represented on works committees, and often have a say in decisions made by management – the *Mitbestimmungsrecht* (right of co-determination). Much of the social security system is run by private insurance institutions.

The mainstay of the German economy is the manufacturing sector, which employs about 30% of the total workforce. It mainly consists of medium-sized companies of less than 100 employees and excels in automotive, chemical, electronics and machine-building industries. Its industrial giants like Siemens, Hoechst, BASF and Daimler-Benz produce worldwide. Siemens employs about 200,000 people in Germany alone, although a trend towards offshore production is shrinking that number yearly.

Other important industrial sectors are environmental technology, which has cornered 20% of the world market, and food processing, clothing and steel. Almost a million Germans work in fields directly or indirectly related to environmental protection (as many as are employed in the automotive industry), many of these in waste management.

The economy is heavily focused on exports, and approximately one third of workers are employed in export industries. About half of Germany's trade is with other EU countries, and another 15% with countries in Asia or the Pacific region. Its major trading partners are France, Great Britain, Italy, the Netherlands and the USA.

The German economy has come under strong pressure recently from foreign competition, and many of its companies have moved production abroad, especially to Eastern Europe, where wages and social security overheads are lower (Germany's are the highest in the world). Political figures have tried to reverse the trend by appealing to business leaders' loyalty, but the decisions are financial, not sentimental, and it is unlikely a change will occur in the near future.

Germany is eager to join the European Monetary Union due to be introduced in 1999. Like other EU countries, however, it is struggling to meet the Maastricht criteria, and many Germans, mindful of the extreme hyperinflation of the Weimar period, are loath to abandon the solid D-Mark. In early 1997 the unemployment rate reached a post-WWII record of almost 12% in western Germany (19.9% in eastern Germany), underscoring the country's troubled economic times. The economy was expected to grow by about 2.5% in 1997 – a modest 1% in eastern Germany.

Costs of Unification

East Germany's postwar recovery was even more remarkable given the wartime destruction, looting by the USSR, loss of skilled labour, and isolation from Western markets. By 1989, however, stagnation had set in. A secret paper prepared for the government revealed that its deficits could not be reversed without a 20-25% cut in living standards. Such a cut, however, would have made the country ungovernable. It became ungovernable anyway.

About 80% of the East German workforce was engaged in state industries prior to reunification, mostly in the manufacturing sector, an old West German stronghold. After initial optimism, the problems became clear: its industries were overstaffed, massively subsidised, and too heavily focused on Eastern European markets, which dried up with the collapse of the Comecon trading bloc. Its capital stock was badly run down, and productivity lagged behind West German levels.

The introduction of a 1:1 exchange rate for the *Ostmark* (East German Mark) has been seen as a big setback for economic development. Overnight, this gave East Germans the means to buy Western consumer goods, but robbed East Germany of its greatest advantage – low wage costs. Nevertheless, wage levels in eastern Germany are currently about 70% of those in western Germany, and as one union official pointed out, a tub of yoghurt costs the same regardless of where you buy it – the question was whether you would let eastern Germans go hungry.

In March 1990 the *Treuhandanstalt* (Trust Agency) was set up to privatise East German assets. Its brief ranged from selling off the large industrial combines through to flogging Erich Honecker's holiday home and the SED party organ *Neues Deutschland* (New Germany). But West German companies were reluctant to invest, and sales proceeded more slowly than was envisaged. Many East German companies were returned to former owners, others scaled down, broken up, or bought out in management takeovers. About 14,500 companies were privatised in all, creating losses for the government and adding to Germany's not inconsiderable debts.

Top 10 German Towns

Germany has 19 cities with over 300,000 inhabitants. The greatest proportion of the population (40.7 million, or about one half) lives in small cities of between 2000 and 100,000 inhabitants. About 26 million (nearly one third) lives in the 84 cities with over 100,000 inhabitants.

The 10 biggest cities in Germany (and their populations) are:

1. Berlin	3,500,000
2. Hamburg	1,706,000
3. Munich	1,250,000
4. Cologne	964,000
5. Frankfurt/Main	652,000
6. Essen	617,000
7. Dortmund	601,000
8. Stuttgart	589,000
9. Düsseldorf	573,000
10. Bremen	549,000

POPULATION & PEOPLE

Germany has a population of approximately 81 million, 16 million of whom live in eastern Germany. This makes it one of Europe's most densely populated countries (third behind the Netherlands and Belgium). It is highly decentralised, with only one third of all citizens living in cities of over 100,000. Most Germans live in villages and small towns, and even Germany's largest cities tend to be modest by world standards. Berlin, its largest, has a population of about 3.5 million, Hamburg 1.7 million and Munich 1.3 million. Its decentralisation is a direct legacy of a history of political fragmentation. Nevertheless, Berlin has enjoyed a boom since again becoming the capital, and its population is expected to hit 5.5 million by the year 2000.

The most densely populated areas are Greater Berlin, the Ruhr industrial region, the area around Frankfurt am Main, Wiesbaden and Mainz, and another taking in Mannheim and Ludwigshafen. The east is much less densely populated, with about 20% of the total German population living on about 33% of the land area. In fact, the population of eastern Germany today has fallen to the 1906 level. The most sparsely populated state is Mecklenburg-Western Pomerania.

Modern Germany has become an *Einwanderungsland* (country of immigrants), and today it is almost as culturally diverse as New World countries or former colonial powers such as France and Britain. Historically, it has always had many immigrants, whether French Huguenots escaping religious persecution (about 30% of Berlin's population in 1700 consisted of Huguenots), Polish mineworkers who settled in the Ruhr region in the 19th century, postwar Gastarbeiter, or asylum seekers in the 1990s.

There is one legal peculiarity, however. It is called *Ius sanguinis* (law of the blood), which, in practice, means that blood is more important than birthplace or residence. It dates back to 1913 and produces an absurd situation whereby generations of 'foreigners' born in Germany are not automatically entitled to citizenship. Those most affected by this are the former Gastarbeiter and their descendants. So, for instance, children of Turkish families who were born and raised in Germany and have never lived elsewhere are deemed foreigners. Meanwhile, descendants of ethnic Germans in Eastern Europe have been given favour, although they may have little connection with Germany society and culture (see the section on Spätaussiedler).

Nevertheless, the laws lag behind the people on this score, and the majority of Germans are open-minded towards foreigners (less so towards asylum seekers). About half of all foreigners have lived in Germany for 10 years or more. Anyone wishing to become a German citizen (it usually takes 10 to 12 years, less for schoolchildren) must renounce their original citizenship, which means a lot of people decide not to apply.

Germany has an aging population and a low birthrate, making immigration necessary if the present standard of living is to be maintained. About 200,000 immigrants per year would be required to hold the population (and keep pension funds afloat) at 74 million in 2040.

Ethnic Minorities

The Sorbs, a Slavonic minority, live in the south-east in Saxony and Brandenburg. They developed their own written language around the time of the Reformation and enjoyed a nationalist revival in the 19th century. Hitler tried to eradicate the Sorbs, and in GDR times the SED attempted to politically integrate them into its power monopoly by offering generous cultural support. They have their own Institute for Sorb Studies at Leipzig University, as well as schools, press and 'national' literature. There is also a Danish minority based around Flensburg with its own schools and cultural life.

Gastarbeiter

Rather than develop an immigration programme to solve a labour shortage in the 1950s, Germany signed treaties with a range of mostly Mediterranean countries to import foreign workers. The first treaty was signed with Italy in 1955, followed by others with Greece, former Yugoslavia, Portugal, Spain, Morocco, Tunisia and Turkey. About 1.6 million Gastarbeiter ('guest workers') worked in Germany throughout the 1960s, rising to a peak of 2.3 million in 1973, when the oil crisis and economic recession ended the programme. Instead of returning home, as was envisaged, many stayed on. They were joined by families, or established families of their own, and today form an important component of German society.

The Turkish ethnic community is the largest (about 2 million), followed by Italian (563,000) and Greek (351,000) communities. A smaller Gastarbeiter community of Vietnamese lived in East Germany before reunification – about 200,000 workers in all arrived from 'fraternal socialist countries', most living in housing ghettos for foreigners. Despite attempts by the German government to repatriate them, stalling tactics by Vietnam have posed difficulties, and many live a marginalised existence selling cigarettes on the streets.

Spätaussiedler

Though German by legal definition (ie having German blood), *Spätaussiedler* (literally 'German settlers from abroad') form another important ethnic group. Since 1987 about two million immigrants with distant German connections have settled in Germany, most hailing from Eastern Europe, and Kazakstan. These days the government is applying strict language tests, while pumping aid into German villages in Kazakstan to encourage people to stay.

Asylum Seekers

One indirect effect of the Nazi years was the creation of liberal asylum laws for the politically persecuted. In 1992 almost 80% of all asylum seekers accepted by EU countries were living in Germany. This amounted to about 438,000 people, mainly due to war in former Yugoslavia. Most were housed in hostels and in temporary container block settlements on vacant land or on moored ships. Some were put up in cheap hotels. In 1993 the German constitution was changed to tighten up regulations. The current number of asylum seekers is about 100,000 per year, of whom about 7% are allowed to stay.

EDUCATION

Germany has a highly educated population and one of the world's most thorough education systems, providing the country with a skilled workforce and a strong research industry. Education is compulsory for 12 years and financed by the state. There is a large number of private and religious schools; the overwhelming majority of students, however, attend government schools. Reunification and the fact that education is a state government responsibility mean there are quite a few regional differences.

The first port of call for many is kindergarten (indeed, a German word). Children then attend a *Grundschule* (basic school), usually at age six. In most states, this lasts for four years. They then spend two years in an orientation phase, after which they are divided into streams and allocated a school type. Here is where the whole system becomes more complicated.

Excluding schools for the disabled, there are five different types of school. The first three are the *Hauptschule* (main school), *Realschule* (practical school) and a combined *Hauptschule-Realschule*. Students who have been to one of these schools then enter the workforce and/or attend a *Berufsschule* (vocational college) after the ninth or 10th year. In addition to vocational college, there are several types of specialist colleges – some trades orientated, others focusing on a specific field of business or industry. All of these colleges are integrated into the school system, and attendance in one form or another is compulsory until the full 12 years have been completed.

The equivalent of English O-levels is called the *Mittlere Reife*, which students receive after successfully completing the 10th year.

Gesamtschule (comprehensive school) combines all types of schools. The *Gymnasium* (senior secondary school) is usually where students do the *Abitur* – the university entrance qualification. Most students do the exam when they are 19 years old. It is extremely rigorous, sometimes lasting six hours in one subject. All students, regardless of their school type, have to take at least one foreign language.

Germany has some of Europe's most respected universities, with Heidelberg, its first, founded in 1386. This followed the foundation of Prague University in 1348 – at that time part of the German Reich. Based on the ideas of Wilhelm von Humboldt, who founded the University of Berlin, universities were originally devoted to pure learning, but this has changed recently. There are about 290 universities or equivalent institutions in Germany, mostly under the wing of the individual states and funded in part by the federal government.

The high demand for a university place these days means that it is almost impossible for students to pick and choose the town in which they want to study, and most places are allocated by a central board. Often students then swap places among themselves.

Students study for a *Diplom* (diploma) or *Staatsexam* (state examination), *Magister* (master of arts), or *Doctortitel* (doctorate). The minimum study period is nine semesters, about 4½ years, but the usual length of stay at a German university is seven years. Together with the late entry age and military service for men, this means a lot of students are 28 before they leave the education system. Women comprise 46% of uni students.

Parents are legally obliged to support their children's education, and those who cannot afford it receive income-tested assistance.

The third pillar of the education system is vocational training. Germans are very proud of their 'dual training system', which combines on-the-job training with formal classes. Formal qualifications are highly regarded in Germany, untrained experience less so.

Influenced by the USSR, East Germany dispensed with the streamed-school system and most of its students attended the *Einheitsschule*, something like West Germany's Gesamtschule. There were also schools offering courses in specialised areas such as music, sport, languages and certain sciences. Officially, the tenet of this system was to create a 'harmoniously developed socialist personality'. Despite this wild claim, the system did function, and the strong involvement of parents in school matters ensured that there was much more to it than the official line suggests. However, the number of students able to study at university was much lower than in West Germany. With reunification, English replaced Russian as the first foreign language (making some teachers redundant), Marxist-Leninist programmes were axed and many universities had trouble gaining formal recognition. The proportion of women attending university in East Germany was generally 5% higher than in West Germany.

ARTS

Music

Early Forms The Church was the focal point of much early German music. The *Lied* (song) describes a variety of popular styles sung as marching tunes or to celebrate victory or work. These later divided into *Volkslieder* (folk songs) and *Kunstlieder* (artistic songs). Among the latter were religious songs, such as the *Marienlied*, which had a mixture of German and Latin lyrics.

From 1100-1300, the *Hof* (court) was the focus of music. *Minnesang*, as the new style was called, had Moorish origins and was imported from southern France. These love ballads praised the woman of the court, and were often performed by knights. The most famous minstrel was Walther von der Vogelweide (about 1170-1230), whose work has been re-recorded by modern artists.

Meistergesang Around the 15th century the troubadour tradition was adopted by a class of burghers who earned a living from music and were often tradesmen on the side. They established schools and guilds, and created strict musical forms. Their model was the tradesmen's guild, with *Altmeister* and *Jungmeister* (old and young masters). To become a *Meistersinger*, a performer had to pass a test and bring something new to melody and lyric. One famous Meistersinger, Hans Sachs (1494-1576), was the subject of a Richard Wagner opera, *Die Meistersinger von Nürnberg*, in the 19th century.

Renaissance The Lied remained an important secular form in the 15th and 16th centuries, with Ludwig Senfl (1486-1546) one of the most important composers.

The most significant development took place in the Church when Martin Luther (1483-1546) created the tradition of Protestant hymns. He collaborated with Johann Walther (1496-1570) to publish a first book of hymns sung in German. He also translated Latin hymns and, an amateur musician himself, wrote a dozen of his own, some set to the melodies of Volkslieder.

Baroque Dietrich Buxtehude (1637-1707) was one famous organist who influenced Johann Sebastian Bach (1685-1750). The latter is said to have walked several hundred kilometres to Lübeck to hear Buxtehude play. Bach and Georg Friedrich Händel (1685-1759) are synonymous with the baroque period.

Händel's music was greatly influenced by his Italian travels. He wrote operas, instrumental works and oratorios such as his *Messiah*. From 1714 he lived and worked almost exclusively in London. Halle and Göttingen both celebrate his works with annual festivals.

Bach's legacy includes his *Brandenburg Concerts*, passions, cantata and oratorios.

Johann Sebastian Bach: synonymous with baroque music.

Wiener Klassik The late 18th century saw a shift to Vienna, although none of the three great names associated with the movement came from there. Both Joseph Haydn (1732-1809) and Wolfgang Amadeus Mozart (1756-91) were Austrian (but not Viennese), and therefore not really German in today's sense. Nevertheless, their influence on German music is immeasurable. Ludwig van Beethoven (1770-1827), the third great name, was born in Bonn and went to Vienna, where he was taught by Haydn and Salieri. His work reflects the Enlightenment, and he intended to dedicate his third symphony, *Eroica*, to Napoleon until he saw a betrayal of democratic ideals in Napoleon accepting the imperial crown. Beethoven's compositions became more abstract with the onset of deafness. By 1819 he had lost all hearing. Four years later, inspired by a Schiller ode, he composed his monumental ninth symphony, which included a choral finale.

One of Europe's best orchestras was at the Residenz in Mannheim. Bach's son, CPE Bach (1714-88), became a significant composer in his own right. Christoph Willibald Gluck (1714-87) was an early composer who began with Italian opera styles and moved on to a simpler, classical style.

Romantic Romantic composers of the 19th century continued the tradition of musical independence (ie living from their work) established in Beethoven's time. This fitted in well with the ideology of the free, if sometimes hungry, artist. Felix Mendelssohn-Bartholdy (1809-47) from Hamburg gave his first concert recital when nine years old and at 17 composed his first overture, based on Shakespeare's *A Midsummer Night's Dream*. He later dug up works by JS Bach and gave the latter the fame he enjoys today.

Carl Maria von Weber (1786-1826) set the Romantic tone early with idealisations of Germanic myths. But the most influential composer of the 19th century was Richard Wagner (1813-83), who balanced all the components of operatic form to produce the *Gesamtkunstwerk* (complete work of art). He was strongly influenced by Weber, Beethoven and Mozart. He once described his *Die Meistersinger von Nürnberg* as his most perfect work. *Der Fliegende Holländer* (The Flying Dutchman) is another of Wagner's famous operas popular today. His choice of mythological themes also made him popular with Nazis – Friedrich Nietzsche, another Nazi favourite, fell out with him metaphysically and condemned his works. Wagner's

The National Anthem

Germans have had an ambiguous relationship with their national anthem. Although a lot of young West Germans were familiar with the words, those who sang it before reunification were generally dismissed as either fools or hard-core nationalists. These days Germans feel less inhibited about singing along.

Based on an obscure Croatian folk song, the music for the German national anthem was composed by Joseph Haydn in 1797 and set to words penned by Hoffmann von Fallersleben in 1841 (including the original words 'God preserve Franz the Kaiser' – an Austrian, in fact). It didn't become the formal anthem until 1922. During the Nazi period it was usually sung in conjunction with *Die Fahne hoch* (Raise the Flag), an uninspiring ditty composed in 1927.

The national anthem was retained after 1945 largely due to the efforts of Konrad Adenauer – minus the first two verses, which either listed a set of borders that now lie in neighbouring countries or sounded like a drinking song. A 1990 court decision ruled that only the third verse was protected as a national symbol.

The East German national anthem, *Auferstanden aus Ruinen* (Resurrected from Ruins) joined the long list of unsung communist golden oldies once the socialist fatherland was abolished. Proclaimed in 1949, its pro-unification lyrics fell out of favour among party honchos after the construction of the Berlin Wall in 1961, when only the tune was permissible. In November 1989, it was sung in protest by demonstrators. This received the blessing of the Ministry of Culture a couple of weeks later, and the anthem was played accordingly on radio and television before being finally abolished in 1990. ■

innovations in opera made him controversial even in his own time, and no post-Wagner composer could ignore him.

Johannes Brahms' (1833-97) fine symphonies, chamber and piano works and Lieder were important landmarks. Robert Schumann (1810-56) began his career as a pianist, turning to composition after suffering paralysis of the fingers. In 1840 he married Clara Wieck (1819-96), a gifted pianist in her own right who had begun concert tours at 13. In 1843 Schumann opened a music school at Leipzig in collaboration with Mendelssohn-Bartholdy.

The Hungarian-born Franz Liszt (1811-86) was at the centre of a group of composers in Weimar from 1844 to 1860. Wagner married his daughter. Richard Strauss (1864-1949) worked in the late-Romantic tradition of Wagner, only to delve into a style reminiscent of Mozart at the end of his career.

20th Century Arnold Schönberg (1874-1951) was born in Vienna and died in Los Angeles. Between that, however, he lived in Berlin (in the 1920s) and exerted an enormous influence on Germany's classical music. He is arguably the inventor of a new tonal relationship.

Hanns Eisler (1898-1962) was a pupil of Schönberg's who went into exile in 1933 and returned to teach in East Berlin in 1950. Eisler wrote classical music, pop songs, film music, scores for Bertolt Brecht and, his most notorious work, the East German national anthem. Paul Dessau (1894-1979) also collaborated with Brecht and composed in a broad range of styles. Paul Hindemith (1895-1963) emerged as a talented composer before WWII. Banned by the Nazis, he emigrated to the USA in 1938 and only returned for tours and brief visits after the war. His early works had baroque leanings; his late orchestral compositions, mostly completed in America, confirm his status as one of Germany's best modern composers.

The German classical tradition continues to thrive: the Dresden Opera and Leipzig Orchestra are known worldwide, and musical performances are hosted almost daily in every major theatre in the country.

The Studio for Electronic Music in Cologne is a centre for cutting-edge developments in music. German also has a strong jazz tradition, which had a flavour of protest in the 1950s. One of the world's best exponents of free jazz is the trumpeter, Albert Mangelsdorff. Passport, headed by Klaus Doldinger, is one of the most interesting German bands playing jazz-rock fusion.

Contemporary Many Germans shun their indigenous rock musicians, and the music community is presently divided on whether local talent would be best supported by introducing radio quotas.

German rock began to roll in 1969, when Amon Düul released its first album – a psychedelic work with long instrumental breaks. Can, a Cologne-based experimental group, earned a name with their *Monster Movie* album. Better known internationally is Tangerine Dream, which gained recognition with its 1974 *Phaedra* album, and went on to record with Virgin.

Old hands will remember Kraftwerk's *Autobahn* album, which hit the turntables worldwide in the early 1970s. This band, one of the first to recognise the potential of computer-assisted music, is hailed as the 'mother of techno'.

Rolf Kaiser was an important producer in the 1970s who did much to promote German music, but British and American bands usually thrived at the expense of local talent. The advent of punk initially left the industry gaping at its guitars. A local movement – *neue deutsche Welle* (German new wave) – soon took shape with German lyrics.

Nena's extremely tame *99 Luftballons* (released in Britain as *99 Red Balloons)* was a No 1 in the UK; in the USA, where the original German version was released, it was No 2. Spliff, Ideal and Palais Schaumberg were other bands that built up strong reputations.

Nina Hagen, born in East Berlin, was the foster child of the writer Wolf Biermann. After Biermann was stripped of East German citizenship, she followed him to West Germany and soon became a symbol of German punk. She worked with the British all-girl group The Slits and, as The Nina Hagen Band, struck gold with her first album. Her laconic Berlin style blended well enough with English-American punk for the *New Musical Express* to describe her as an epileptic Edith Piaf and a cross between Johnny Rotten, Maria Callas and Bette Midler.

Neue deutsche Welle grew weary and lost momentum around the early 1980s, with few new bands to emerge. Nevertheless, Udo Lindenberg, who was involved in early bands, went solo with political engagement, and anarchists still have a soft spot beneath their leather for the old rocker. Generally, however, rock became more conservative, a lot of it indistinguishable from *Schlager* (see the following section).

Herbert Grönermeyer ('the German Springsteen') achieved success in 1984 with his *Bochum* album, which stayed in the charts for 79 weeks. His single *Männer* was another big hit. Grönermeyer's strained vocal style is not everyone's cup of tea, but his lyrics often have a nice irony. BAP is a renowned Cologne-based band which sings in the local *kölsch* dialect, which means most Germans can't understand them either. Cologne has a lively rock scene, and BAP is worth seeing if rock archaeology is your interest.

Marius Müller-Westernhagen is a friend of Boris Becker, which makes him doubly famous. His *Freiheit* single became the unofficial reunification anthem after the Berlin Wall fell (sung by the audience, cigarette lighter held aloft, fingers getting sizzled).

Fury in the Slaughterhouse and Poems for Laila are a couple of other important bands. Die Toten Hosen (literally 'the dead trousers', but based on an expression to say nothing much is going on) continue to serve up their orthodox punk, much of it in English. Die Ärzte have threatened to fade away several times but always come back. Their lyrics range from the bland to the inspired, as in a single released in the early 1990s about neo-Nazis ('Your violence is just a cry for love – asshole!'). The Scorpions have made a name abroad with their own brand of heavy metal, choosing to groom an international image at the expense of their German roots.

The rap group, Die Fantastischen Vier, won a big following with its *Die da* single in 1992. The all-girl Lassie Singers have enjoyed limited success recently with their slow, if somewhat flat, mesmerising style.

Techno fans might like to return to the womb of creation by dropping in on the Love Parade, held in Berlin each summer. It has turned into Germany's most important rock event, and about 750,000 fans thronged to the capital in 1996, many arriving in special 'love trains'.

Schlager & Chanson Schlager is what Germans call your traditional nondescript pop song. Some have a country & western or folk flavour, others are influenced by French and Italian pop. You can hear it all over Germany, but especially in mountain-top restaurants, and as *Meyers*, one highbrow music encyclopaedia, points out: 'All attempts to raise the standard of Schlager have failed so far – even the last resort of parodying it. What was intended as a parody ended up a Schlager success.'

Before the term was coined in 1881, the style was known as 'street' or 'alley' music. One of the first songs was penned in 1821. Since then we've had such greats as *We're Drinking Away Granny's Little House*, *I Only Kissed You on the Shoulder* and *Love Came Overnight Like a Miracle*. All, as you can imagine, riveting stuff.

Those in the know try to distinguish between Schlager and the more respectable *Chanson* or Lied. The Lied can be traced back to medieval times (see Early Forms at the start of the Music section) and is an integral part of *Kabarett* (German cabaret). One of Germany's more fascinating Schlager singers is Heino, something like a tranquillised albino 'Ken' doll who sports dark glasses and is fast achieving the status of a national treasure.

Cabaret Originally imported as cabaret from Paris' Montmartre district in the late-19th century, Kabarett, the German form, has a strong political flavour and relies heavily on satire and the Lied.

In Berlin in 1922 there were over 38 venues to help Germans forget about the troubled Weimar Republic. A few of these, such as Schall und Rauch (Noise and Smoke), were political snakepits.

Many well known creative figures of the era worked in Kabarett – Bertolt Brecht, Erich Kästner and Kurt Tucholsky, just to mention a few. Tucholsky wrote lyrics for one famous performer, Gussy Holl (nicknamed 'the silver-blonde elegant witch'). Annemarie Hase, Trude Hesterberg and Rosa Valletti were three other Kabarett stars of the 1920s.

It is said that when Brecht read his *Legende vom toten Soldaten* (Legend of the Dead Soldier) before a full house, its anti-militarism was so provocative that brawling broke out among the divided public.

Hesterberg, who was Jewish, tormented Nazis in the audience by hanging swastikas and Star of David symbols on the curtain during one of her numbers, *Die Dressur* (The Taming).

In 1933 the stakes were raised by Hitler's power takeover. Almost all political Kabarett was closed down, with performers and writers forced into exile. Others died in concentration camps.

Nevertheless, the tradition is still alive and kicking in Germany today. If you think your German is up to the humour, you might like to keep an eye on theatre listings in major cities.

Dieter Hildebrandt is one old hand on the scene who now crops up on television with his mostly political sketches.

Jutta Wübbe's stage persona, Marlene Jaschke, is an awkward, drab, middle-aged woman who stumbles through life.

Sybille Schrödter is another name to watch out for. Rüdiger Hoffmann bases his humour on that of a pedestrian country lad, with a strong Westphalian element. It is innocent, dry and very funny.

Literature

Early Literature The earliest form of German literature was an oral tradition among the tribes. It was usually polytheistic and based on an epic deed. During Charlemagne's reign (circa 800) educated clerical figures diligently recorded what remained of the oral tradition, giving us the *Hildebrandslied*, a father-son epic with shades of the Oedipus myth. Christian and Teutonic traditions were sometimes combined, as in *Ludwigslied*, which celebrated victory over the Normans, or *Heliand*, a story about Christ in which Jesus is recast as a tribal leader.

Clerical dominance continued under the Ottonian dynasty. Hrotsita von Gandersheim (circa 960) was a nun who wrote religious moral dramas. In the 12th century, however, *Hofliteratur* (literature of the royal court) brought a shift away from the Church. It was French-inspired, epic and performed by the author, who was often a knight. The *Nibelungenlied*, an anonymous work, draws heavily on Germanic mythology.

Wolfram von Eschenbach's (circa 1170) epic, *Parzival*, took the themes of mortal beings, God and compassion, and was later turned into a libretto by Richard Wagner. Less conventional is Gottfried von Strassburg's (circa 1200) *Tristan and Isolde*. It tells the tale of a rarified illicit love that clashes with social custom, belief and the heroes' duty. Minnesang, a musical cousin of Hofliteratur, was directed at the women of the court. Walther von der Vogelweide (circa 1170-1220), the best lyricist, went beyond love themes to produce works with a political and philosophical edge.

Meister Eckhard (1260-1327), Heinrich Seuse (1295-1365) and Johannes Tauler (1300-61) were three writers whose works have strong mystical tones, an important element of the 13th and 14th centuries.

Martin Luther (1483-1546) revolutionised literary language in the 16th century with his translation of the Bible into common German. As he once wrote: '...look at their gobs to find out how they speak, then translate so they understand and see you're speaking to them in German.' Luther's translation was printed using a revolutionary technique invented by Johannes Gutenberg (1397-1468). Reusable lead printing blocks replaced wooden blocks, providing the technological basis for mass circulation.

Baroque Much of baroque literature reflects the Thirty Years' War and conflict surrounding the Reformation. The 17th century saw a conscious attempt to groom the German language. Language societies were established to formalise grammar and oversee usage, and with this came a dose of literary absolutism.

Martin Opitz (1597-1639) created the basis for a new German poetry with his influential and theoretical work *Buch der deutschen Poeterey* (Book of German Poetry). Andreas Gryphius (1616-54) was a poet and playwright who played on baroque ideas of earthly transience and the grandiose meaninglessness of life. In his *Katharina von Georgien* (Katharine of Georgia) the heroine dies a Christian martyr rather than marry the Shah of Persia. His sonnet *Tränen des Vaterlandes* (Tears of the Fatherland) thematised the horrors of the Thirty Years' War.

HJC von Grimmelshausen's (1622-76) classic *Simplicissimus* (Adventures of a Simpleton) is a picaresque tale about a peasant youth who, having become caught up in the war, returns home as a hermit. It is an important predecessor of the German novel and its influence can be found today in the work of Günter Grass.

Enlightenment Led by the French philosopher, Descartes, and his German counterpart, GW Leibniz (1646-1716), the Enlightenment dispensed with superstition and baroque folly and turned to human reason.

Johann Christian Gottsched (1700-66) left his native Königsberg allegedly because Friedrich Wilhelm I liked his size and wanted to conscript him. He went to Leipzig and became Professor of Philology and Poetry, where he remodelled German theatre along French lines. His theoretical work *Versuch einer critischen Dichtkunst* (Essay on Critical Poetics) was a milestone of the era.

Also significant was Christoff Wieland (1733-1813), whose *Geschichte des Agathon* (Agathon) is considered Germany's first *Bildungsroman* (a novel showing the development of the hero). At the centre of the novel is an ambitious attempt to find a harmony of emotion and reason.

Gotthold Ephraim Lessing (1729-81) wrote critical works, fables and tragedies, throwing his hat into the ring with Gottsched, whose French inclinations he rejected in favour of Shakespearian dramatic forms. He dug up the old Greek idea whereby tragedy employed empathy and fear to evoke the audience's passion (Bertolt Brecht later threw his hat into the same ring). Lessing's *Miss Sara Samson*, *Emilia Galotti* and *Nathan der Weise* (Nathan the Wise) are his best known dramatic works. One recurring theme in his plays is of the daughter who is 'created' by the father but later becomes his sacrifice.

Sturm und Drang (1767-85) Literally 'Storm and Stress', this marks the beginning of a golden age dominated by the two heavyweights, Johann Wolfgang von Goethe (1749-1832) and Friedrich von Schiller (1759-1805).

Goethe, who, unlike his Sturm und Drang contemporaries, came from the upper class and lived to a ripe old age, earned fame with his early work *Götz von Berlichingen*, following up with the movement's first novel, *Die Leiden des jungen Werthers* (The Sorrows of Young Werther). During this period Schiller wrote his *Die Räuber* (The Robbers) and *Kabale und Liebe* (Cabal and Love). The importance of Goethe and Schiller is immeasurable, and their arrival signalled the start of a modern national literature.

Neoclassicism Storm and Stress was merely a short stopover in a greater literary flight plan. Neoclassicists looked to ancient Greece and Rome for inspiration and ideals, tightened up formal aspects and cultivated

Johann Wolfgang von Goethe: the heavy-weight of German *Hochkultur.*

the idea of the 'beautiful soul'. This artistic ideal, which aimed at human improvement, often meant authors hailed their own, alleged, genius.

Goethe's *Italienische Reise* (Italian Journey) was a new turn in his development. The years 1794-1805 saw a fruitful collaboration with Schiller in Weimar and Jena, during which *Wilhelm Meisters Lehrjahre* (Wilhelm Meister's Apprenticeship) was published, a Bildungsroman. Goethe's finest work, however, is often seen to be his two-part *Faust*, which he worked on for most of his life. Based on a pact with the devil, *Faust* thematises the human struggle for ultimate power and knowledge. Among Schiller's important works are his Wallenstein trilogy, and *Maria Stuart*, *Die Jungfrau von Orleans* (The Maid from Orleans) and *Wilhelm Tell.*

Romanticism Early Romanticism began as a complement to neoclassicism. It kept and developed the Greek and Roman elements but took the individual deep into fancy and imagination. Friedrich Hölderlin (1770-1843) was one important figure who, like Goethe, spanned several periods. Germany's best Romantic poet, he strove for perfect balance and rhythm in his work – much of which was in classical meter or free verse. His career was cut short, however, by the onset of madness in his 30s.

John-Paul (1763-1825) wrote novels which often had a whimsical, sentimental edge. Novalis (1772-1801) created the symbol of Romantic yearning, the blue flower, in one of his early novels. His best work, the poems *Hymnen an die Nacht* (Hymns to the Night), deals with death and grief.

ETA Hoffmann (1776-1822) is best known for his bizarre tales. His *Mademoiselle de Scudérie* is considered the forerunner of the mystery genre. Annette von Droste-Hülshoff (1797-1848) was a Catholic socialist whose *Die Judenbuche* (The Beech Tree of the Jews), like most of her work, has a tranquil mood and is set in a village.

The brothers Jacob (1785-1863) and Wilhelm (1786-1859) Grimm are famous worldwide for their collections of fairy tales and myths. As scholars, however, they created a basis for the serious study of German language and literature. In the field of philosophy, the idealist Wilhelm Friedrich Hegel (1770-1831) explored ideas of being and spirit.

Heinrich Heine & Junges Deutschland
The Junges Deutschland (Young Germany) movement grew up around the 1830s as a reaction to non-political Romanticism. Literature was subject to harsh censorship at the time, causing many writers to resort to satire. Heine's (1797-1856) *Deutschland: Ein Wintermärchen* (Germany: A Winter's Tale) is a politically scathing work based on a trip from Aachen to Hamburg. His early *Buch der Lieder* (Book of Songs) is ranked as one of Germany's best collection of love poems. Heine's work was banned in 1835 – and it had nothing to do with the love poems. In Georg Büchner's (1813-37) *Woyzeck*, one of the best plays of the era, a simple hero gets caught up in hostile social forces. Büchner lent his characters a complex psychology, and employed plot structures that anticipated Theatre of the Absurd.

Realism The realist movement, which broke in Germany around 1840, saw the novel become the dominant form. Many novels took on a regional flavour. Theodor Storm

(1817-88) wrote poetry, short stories and novels set in his native Schleswig-Holstein, often creating a raw North Sea atmosphere. Wilhelm Raabe (1831-1910) is hailed for his social descriptions. His *Else von der Tanne* is about a woman killed by fellow villagers made distrustful by war. Better known is Wilhelm Busch (1832-1908), whose illustrated *Max und Moritz* delights adults and children today. Busch's skill was in the simplicity of his tales and cartoons, which are full of wit and irony.

With the crossover to naturalism, things became grimier and more descriptive. Arno Holz's (1863-1929) *Buch der Zeit* (Book of the Times) was a landmark in big-city poetry. Gerhart Hauptmann's (1862-1946) *Bahnwärter Thiel* (Thiel the Crossing Keeper) is a bleak novella with madness, murder, sexual dependence and a railway theme – just the thing for a long train journey.

20th Century The 20th century kicked off in fine style with the poetry of Rainer Maria Rilke (1875-1926), who, like Franz Kafka, was born in Prague. Rilke is one of Germany's best lyric poets. His *Das Stunden-Buch* (The Book of Hours) is a search for spiritual well-being in an industrial age. Rilke travelled twice to Russia, and later to Paris, where he became Auguste Rodin's private secretary.

Thomas Mann (1875-1955) has a place of honour approaching Goethe. Born in Lübeck, he moved to Munich around 1900 and later travelled to Italy. His greatest novels focus on the society of his day. In *Buddenbrooks* he described declining bourgeois values. *Der Zauberberg* (The Magic Mountain) linked personal and social illness around the time of the Great War, and in *Doktor Faustus* the central character makes a pact with the devil, exchanging health and love for creative fulfilment. Its tone, however, is set by the menace of Nazism. A good Mann starter is his magnificently crafted *Tod in Venedig* (Death in Venice).

Hermann Hesse (1864-1947), like Mann, was a Nobel Prize winner. His *Steppenwolf* took the theme of the outsider. A 'new Romantic', he was profoundly influenced by a journey to India in 1911, and imbued his work with spirituality.

Ricarda Huch (1864-1947) was described by Thomas Mann as 'Germany's first lady'. She stands out in her own right as a courageous opponent of Nazism, having resigned in protest from the Prussian Academy of the Arts. Her work includes poetry, novels and biographies, including one on the Russian anarchist, Mikhail Bakunin.

Heinrich Mann (1871-1950) took a stronger political stance than his younger brother, Thomas. His *Professor Unrat* was the raw material for the film *Der blaue Engel*, with Marlene Dietrich (see the boxed text on Dietrich later in this chapter). Alfred Döblin's (1878-1957) *Berlin Alexanderplatz*, another important novel of the era, provides a dose of big city lights and the underworld during the Weimar Republic.

The Prague-born Franz Kafka (1883-1924) only fleetingly graced Germany, but his influence on its literature is enormous. Guilt and the human condition underscore most of his works. In *Die Verwandlung* (Metamorphosis), the hero inexplicably wakes up one morning as a dung beetle. The hero of *Der Prozess* (The Trial) is condemned by an imaginary court on charges he never learns.

Erich Maria Remarque (1898-1970) achieved worldwide success with his anti-war novel from 1929, *Im Westen nichts neues* (All Quiet on the Western Front), one of the most widely read of all German books. It was banned in 1933 and Remarque emigrated to America in 1939.

Bertolt Brecht The 'epic theatre' of Brecht (1898-1956) was loosely Marxist, rejecting Lessing's Greek leanings for political, didactic forms. His *Leben des Galilei* (Life of Galileo) and *Die Dreigroschenoper* (The Threepenny Opera) are two of his most popular dramatic works, which generally overshadow his fine poetry.

Brecht went into exile during the Nazi years, surfaced in Hollywood as a scriptwriter, was called in to explain himself during the McCarthy communist witch hunts, and ended up in East Berlin after the war – where he could count on a sympathetic audience. Empathy, Brecht claimed, numbed the faculties of the theatre audience: his epic theatre relied on alienation techniques designed to allow the audience to reason.

Kurt Tucholsky (1890-1935) and Erich Kästner (1899-1974), two political satirists, are also recommended for anyone interested in the period between the wars.

Post-1945 The postwar period saw the return of many writers-in-exile and the emergence of Heinrich Böll (1917-85) and Günter Grass (1927-) as key figures in West Germany. Both were members of the political Gruppe 47 circle of writers, which focused on postwar social questions and the German psyche. In Böll's *Ansichten eines Clowns* (The Clown), the central character, a washed-up pantomime artist, takes a sceptical look at family, society, Church and state. Grass' tour-de-force, *Die Blechtrummel* (The Tin Drum), humorously traces recent German history through the eyes of Oskar, a child who refuses to grow up. This first novel turned Grass into a household name, and he has followed up with an impressive body of novels, plays and poetry.

Christa Wolf (1929-) grew up in East Germany and is one of its best, if controversial, writers. *Der geteilte Himmel* (Divided Heaven) has an industrial backdrop and tells the story of a woman's love for a man who fled to the West. Sarah Kirsch (1935-), who emigrated from East Germany, has earned a reputation as a highly respected poet. Stefan Heym (1913-) was one writer who, like Brecht, went into exile and returned after the war to settle in East Germany. He has been politically active with the PDS (the former East German SED) and his *Auf Sand gebaut* (Built on Sand), a collection of stories, looks at the situation of East Germans around 1990.

Heiner Müller (1929-95) had the honour of being unpalatable in both Germanys. It is said that Müller worked for the Stasi, but that his messages were so ambiguous as to be worthless. His acerbic wit produced gems such as 'five Germans are more stupid than one'. His *Der Lohndrücker* (The Man who Kept Down Wages) is a good place to start.

Since the late 1980s, Patrick Süskind has been one of Germany's more popular young writers. Süskind's *Das Parfum* (Perfume) is the extraordinary tale of a psychotic 18th-century perfume-maker with an obsessive genius.

Architecture

Visitors to Germany are often surprised by the number of fine buildings that survived the ravages of wartime bombing. Many damaged buildings were restored, others so painstakingly reconstructed from rubble as to defy the believability of films and pictures of ruins. Whether you like baroque palaces, half-timbered houses, wooden or onion-dome churches, or anything Romanesque, you will find more than enough of interest.

Carolingian The grand buildings around the 9th century were loosely based on styles and techniques used in Italy. The finest remaining example is the Pfalzkapelle of Charlemagne's palace in Aachen, which dates from about 800. It was probably inspired by San Vitale in Ravenna, and its classical columns were brought from Italy.

Romanesque The main influences of the Romanesque era (c.1000) were Carolingian, Christian (Roman) and Byzantine. Bishop Bernward, Otto III's tutor, returned from Rome wanting to turn Hildesheim into the cultural centre of the empire. The Michaelskirche in Hildesheim and the elegant Stiftskirche in Gernrode are fine examples of the style, which aimed for a proportional interior and integrated columns. The cathedrals of Worms, Speyer, Mainz and Bamberg are considered Germany's most significant examples of Romanesque.

Gothic The Gothic movement, which began in northern France around 1150, was slow to reach Germany. The Magdeburger Dom (begun in 1209), one of Germany's first

Gothic cathedrals, was based on a French design but kept many Romanesque elements. Gothic interiors usually had ribbed vaults, pointed arches and flying buttresses – allowing height and larger windows. The Elizabethkirche in Marburg an der Lahn and Liebfraukirche in Trier (both about 1240) are good examples.

Germany's most famous Gothic building is the massive Dom in Cologne (a World Heritage building), which was begun in 1248 and not completed until 1880. The Ulm Münster is a good example of how high Gothic can go in Germany (161m, in this case). Freiburg's Münster and the Marienkirche in Lübeck are others. Late Gothic (from about the 15th century) tended to have more elaborately patterned vaults, and hall churches (where the nave is the same height as the aisles) became more common. Munich's Frauenkirche and Michaelkirche are good examples of late Gothic. The *Rathaus* (town hall) buildings in Bremen and Lübeck are both secular Gothic styles.

Renaissance The Renaissance had a slow birth in Germany, gaining importance only around the mid-16th century and overlapping with late Gothic. Its main centre was in southern Germany and around the trade routes of the Rhine, where there was much contact with Italy. Herms (usually stone heads of Hermes) placed on structural features, leafwork and sculptured human figures used as columns and pillars became popular. The Ottheinrichsbau (1556), the part of Heidelberg Castle built by Count Ottheinrich, is an example of German Renaissance architecture matching Italian standards. The Haus zum Ritter, also in Heidelberg, is another.

The 16th century brought colour and decorative façades to half-timbered houses, many of which have elaborately carved surfaces.

Weser Renaissance is a northern German secular style found in regions near the Weser River. Typical is a balanced multiple-wing castle with winding staircases ascending a tower. The finest example is the picturesque castle and grounds in Celle. Early styles often incorporated Gothic decoration on facades.

Baroque Loosely describing a period in German architecture from the early 17th century to the mid-18th century, baroque is linked to the period of absolutism following the Thirty Years' War, when feudal rulers asserted their importance through grand residences. Many took their inspiration from the palace of Versailles. Structures tended to dominate their surroundings, with grand portals, wide staircases, and wings that created enclosed courtyards. Ornate and excessive, baroque buildings also incorporated sculpture and painting into their design, and during this period many Italian architects such as Barelli and Zuccalli worked in Germany. Barelli created Schloss Nymphenburg in Munich.

Karlsruhe was founded in the baroque period, with the castle its focal point. Dresden's Zwinger, the Residenz in Würzburg and portions of Dom St Stephan in Passau are also fine examples.

The Protestant north was Dutch-influenced and more geometric; in the Catholic south, however, baroque tended to be freer and more ornamental. Schloss Sanssouci, in Potsdam, was begun during the late baroque, or rococo, period.

Neoclassicism In the late 18th century, baroque folly and exuberance were replaced by the strict geometry of neoclassicism, typified by Berlin's Brandenburger Tor, which was based on a Greek design. Friedrich Wilhelm II tried to turn Berlin into a European centre of culture by linking Prussian nationalism with the greatness of ancient Greece. Columns, pediments and domes were the dominant architectural forms. A leading architect of the style was Karl Friedrich Schinkel. His Altes Museum, Neue Wache and Schauspielhaus, all in Berlin, are pure forms of neoclassicism.

In Munich, meanwhile, Leo von Klenze, another leading figure, chiselled his way through virtually every ancient civilisation, with eclectic creations such as the Glyptothek and Propyläen on Munich's Königsplatz.

Revivalism The late 19th century brought a wave of derivative architecture based on old styles. This lent impetus to the completion of the Dom in Cologne after original plans were discovered in 1814 and 1816. Georg von Nauberisser's Munich Rathaus (Marienplatz) is secular neo-Gothic.

A German peculiarity was the so-called 'rainbow style', which blended Byzantine and Roman features. The Heilandskirche in Potsdam typifies the style. Georg Adolph Demmler's Schloss in Schwerin is an example of Renaissance revivalism.

One prominent example of neo-baroque, often called 'Wilhelmian style', is Paul Wallots' Reichstag building (begun 1884) in Berlin. It was damaged in the fire of 1933, repaired without the original cupola, and, when renovations are completed, will again house the German parliament.

Neuschwanstein, Ludwig II's grandiose, fairy-tale concoction, was built in a neo-Romanesque style.

Art Nouveau The use of steel in the late 19th century allowed greater spans and large glass surfaces (exemplified by your average German Hauptbahnhof), which was taken up by the Art Nouveau movement in the early 20th century. German impetus for the movement came from a group called Der Deutsche Werkbund, founded in 1907. It consisted of architects, designers, tradespeople and industrialists, and was aimed at raising the quality of German industrial products. One of the many Art Nouveau factories built at this time is the AEG Turbinenhalle in Berlin. Alfred Messel's Wertheim department store in Berlin is another good example of Art Nouveau.

Between 1910 and 1925, an expressionist style arose that employed more fantasy, typified by the stalactite interior of the Grosses Schauspielhaus in Berlin or Erich Mendelsohn's Einsteinturm (1920) in Potsdam.

Bauhaus The Bauhaus movement took the industrial forms of Art Nouveau and drove them to functional limits. It began in 1919 with the founding by Walter Gropius of the Staatliches Bauhaus, a modern art and design institute in Weimar. The institute was later moved to Dessau and then to Berlin, before being closed by the Nazis in 1933. Gropius' aim, which he set out in his *Bauhaus Manifest*, was to bring together architects, painters, furniture designers and sculptors to create a unity of the arts. Detractors claim that it was often functional and impersonal, relying too heavily, for their liking, on cubist and constructivist forms. The institute's building in Dessau is typical of the style, but you can find the influence of Bauhaus everywhere in modern design. Wassily Kandinsky and Paul Klee, both painters, taught at the institute before going into exile.

Post-1945 Nazi architecture, like Nazism itself, revelled in pomposity. Hitler's architect and political crony, Albert Speer, received the order to create works that would befit the Thousand Year Reich. Unfortunately for Speer, classicism had two 'neo' prefixes by the time he got his hands on it, which perhaps explains why Nazi monumentality often seemed absurd. Werner March's lavishly embellished Olympisches Stadion and grounds in Berlin is one of the better examples to survive.

After Hitler, it took German architects a few years to plug back into the world scene. Postwar reconstruction demanded cheap buildings that could be erected quickly. Hubert Petschnigg's Thyssenhaus in Düsseldorf is considered one of the best works of the 1960s. The interior of Hans Scharoun's Philharmonie (1963) in Berlin hints at a terraced vineyard. Günther Behnisch and Frei Otto's Olympisches Stadion, built for the 1972 Munich games, is tent-like and one of Germany's best postwar constructions. Otto had achieved fame a few years earlier with his German pavilion at the 1967 Montreal World Expo.

The 361.5m-high Fernsehturm in the former East Berlin, built in 1969, is to the memory of GDR architecture what Donna Summer is to disco. A tradition of monumentalism continued in the East (Berlin's Frankfurterallee is a sugar-cake version) until political disappointment among East Germans made monumentality untenable in the 1960s. East Germany also inadvertently created one of the world's most potent architectural symbols in the Berlin Wall.

More recently, Richard Meier has integrated an old villa into a design with ramps, blocks and ship motifs for his Museum für Kunsthandwerk (1984) in Frankfurt am Main.

There is currently much activity in Berlin, with what is referred to as the 'project of the century' at Potsdamer Platz. This, and other ambitious post-reunification projects, will create a new skyline for the capital.

Film

Silent Film Germany's first public film screening was in Berlin in 1895. Early films were shown in booths at annual town fairs or in refurbished shops. In 1917 Ufa (Universum Film AG) was established by the government to raise production standards and improve the image of Germany abroad.

Silent films in Germany often took up morbid, pathological themes and used images and clever cutting to create character psychology. The influence of Sigmund Freud is clear in Stellan Rye's 1913 classic *Der Student von Prag* (The Student from Prague), which tells the story of a student who sells his mirror image to a stranger and ends up fleeing his own self. *Das Kabinett des Dr Caligari* (The Cabinet of Dr Caligari, 1919) by Robert Wiene, about a hypnotist who brings his patients to commit murder, has expressionist influences and deals with tyranny. Another *Gruselfilm* (horror or Gothic film) is FW Murnau's *Nosferatu* (1921), a seminal Dracula work in which the plague is brought to a north German town. It hints at collective fear in the early days of the Weimar Republic.

The 1920s was a period of intense creativity, with quality films such as GW Pabst's *Die freudlose Gasse* (The Joyless Street, 1925) and Joe May's *Asphalt* (1929). Pabst, who worked in New York theatre before WWI, dominated the film scene in the 1920s and 1930s, using montage intelligently to elucidate character and create visual sequence. In the *Die freudlose Gasse*, he takes two women – one a society lady, the other a prostitute – to illustrate a perceived loss of values.

Fritz Lang's *Metropolis* (1926) stands out as an ambitious cinema classic. It depicts the revolt of a proletarian class that lives underground. Walther Ruttmann's *Berlin – Die Sinfonie einer Grossstadt* (Berlin – Symphony of a Big City, 1927), set over a 24-hour period, provides excellent early documentation of Berlin.

Sound Films of the 1930s In 1927 Ufa passed from the Deutsche Bank into the hands of the Hugenberg group, which was sympathetic to right-wing movements. The new film era resulted in the Marlene Dietrich classic *Der blaue Engel* (The Blue Angel, 1930), directed by Joseph von Sternberg and loosely based on Heinrich Mann's novella *Professor Unrat*. It tells the story of a pedantic professor who is hopelessly infatuated with a sexy Kabarett singer, played by Dietrich. It destroyed our learned man in the end, and created the vamp image Marlene enjoyed all her life.

Pabst's *Dreigroschenoper* (Threepenny Opera, 1931) was based on the play by Brecht (music by Kurt Weil) and set in the gangster milieu around Mackie Messer (Mack the Knife). Apparently Brecht was unhappy with changes, and tried to prevent its screening. A year earlier, Pabst had made *Westfront – 1918* (The Western Front – 1918), a pacifist film that depersonalised characters to depict them caught up in the machinery of war.

Leontine Sagan's *Mädchen in Uniform* (Girls in Uniform, 1931) is set in a girls' boarding school, where pupils are taught obedience and prepared for a future as good mothers and soldiers' wives. *Das Testament des Dr Mabuse* (The Testament of Dr Mabuse, 1932) was Fritz Lang's first talkie.

Marlene Dietrich

Marlene Dietrich, whose real name was Marie Magdalena von Losch, was born in Berlin into a good middle-class family on 27 December 1901. After attending acting school, she worked in the fledgling German silent film industry in the 1920s, stereotyped as a hard living, libertine *flapper*. In the 1927 film *Wenn ein Weib den Weg verliert* (When a Girl Loses the Way) she played a well-mannered young woman who falls into the clutches of a gigolo. She soon carved a niche in the film fantasies of lower middle-class men as the dangerously seductive *femme fatale*, best typified by her 1930 talkie *Der blaue Engel* (The Blue Angel), which also made her a Hollywood star.

Dietrich landed the role only through the insistence of Josef von Sternberg, the film's director, who had watched her perform in a theatre review. Nevertheless, he still had to convince Heinrich Mann. Mann had written the novel and wanted to give the part to his lover, Trude Hesterberg, a cabaret artist. Meanwhile, the film's scriptwriter was doing his best to get his own lover into the role. Dietrich won the part and Mann lost his lover.

Working closely with Sternberg, Dietrich built on her image of erotic opulence – dominant, severe, always with a touch of self-irony. When she put on men's suits for *Marocco* in 1930, she lent her 'sexuality is power' attitude bisexual tones, winning a new audience overnight.

Marlene stayed in Hollywood after the Nazi rise to power, though Hitler, no less immune to her charms, reportedly promised perks and the red carpet treatment if she moved back to Germany. She responded with an empty offer to return if she could bring Sternberg, a Jew and no Nazi favourite.

When Allied GIs rolled into Paris in 1944, Marlene was there, too. Asked once whether there was any truth to the rumour that she had slept with General Eisenhower, she reportedly replied, 'How could I have? He was never at the front'.

After the war, Dietrich made only occasional appearances in films, choosing instead to cut records and perform live. Discrete, uncompromising and, contrary to the film image, always the well-bred woman from Berlin, Dietrich retreated from the public eye as age and illness slowly caught up with her.

She died in 1992, aged 90. The Deutsche Bahn named one of its ICE trains after her – *Der blaue Engel* to Berlin. ■

It is about a psychiatric patient who devises plans to take over the world. If that somehow rings a bell, it is worth remembering that the Nazis prevented the German premiere, forcing Lang to shift it to Austria.

Nazi Period Hitler's power takeover ruptured German cultural life, and film was no exception. Financial trouble at Ufa between 1933 and 1937 allowed the Nazis to anonymously buy out Hugenberg and step up control over the industry (the Nazi government owned 99.25% of the shares). All films now had to get the nod of approval from Goebbels' *Reichskulturkammer* (chamber of culture). Censorship laws and bans drove over 500 actors and directors into exile. Many were murdered. Others, a large number of whom were Jewish, went to Hollywood and played parts as stereotypical German Nazis. Some directors and actors were successful, but the majority struck a language barrier and sank into oblivion.

László Loewenstein, an ethnic-German Hungarian better known as Peter Lorre, had already played a pathological child-killer in Fritz Lang's 1931 film *M* before cropping up as the edgy, hunted Ugarte in *Casablanca*. Lorre later returned to Germany to act and direct.

Carl Froelich's *Traumulus* squeezed past the censors in 1935. It is a period film, set in the provinces, about an idealistic school director who loses touch with reality. Emil Jannings, an Austrian, played the leading role in a masterful performance.

Post-1945 Films shot directly after the war are known as *Trummerfilme* (literally 'rubble films') and usually deal with Nazism or war. DEFA (Der Deutsche Film AG), a new East German film corporation, was established in the Soviet zone (the USSR was its chief shareholder), producing Germany's first postwar film, *Die Mörder sind unter uns* (The Murderers Are Among Us), in 1946 by Wolfgang Staudte. Set in 1945 at Christmas, it tells the story of a guilt-ridden army doctor who encounters a commanding officer responsible for the execution of women and children in Russia. He threatens the officer with a pistol as the latter is celebrating with his wife and children.

Bernhard Wicki's *Die Brücke* (The Bridge, 1959) is an exceptional and highly recommended film about a group of young boys who faithfully try to defend an insignificant bridge against advancing Americans in the last days of the war.

Strassenbekanntschaft (Street Acquaintance, 1948), a Soviet-zone educational film about the dangers of venereal disease, is an interesting document for its conservative portrayal of women's roles in peacetime. The East German *Sterne* (Stars, 1958) is about a love that develops between a prisoner and a guard in a concentration camp in Bulgaria. Konrad Wolf earned a name as East Germany's best director, and the film won an award at Cannes.

1960s to the 1990s The new decade brought the Oberhausener Gruppe, a group of directors who rejected old cinema norms with the declaration 'Papa's cinema is dead' in its 1962 manifesto. A highlight was Vesely's *Das Brot der frühen Jahre* (The Bread of Early Years, 1962), an adaptation of a Heinrich Böll work about an electrical mechanic who surrenders his humdrum existence after encountering an old friend and falling in love. Vesely's film paved the way for a new wave of directors.

Volker Schlöndorff emerged as a key figure in a movement known as Der junge deutsche Film, a German form of the French new wave. His *Der Junge Törless* (Törless) from 1965 is set in a boys' boarding school and deals with hierarchy and power, culminating in the maltreatment of a Jewish boy. *Abschied von Gestern* (Goodbye to Yesterday, 1966) by Alexandra Kluge, and Edgar Reitz's *Mahlzeiten* (Meals, 1967), are two other fine films.

Der geteilte Himmel (Divided Heaven) is a 1964 adaptation by Konrad Wolf of a novel by the East German writer Christa Wolf. *Nackt unter Wölfen* (Naked Among Wolves, 1963), directed by Frank Beyer, has a concentration-camp plot. When a child is smuggled into Buchenwald it presents moral dilemmas for other inmates by endangering a resistance movement.

Werner Herzog, Rainer Werner Fassbinder, Margarethe von Trotta, Wim Wenders and Doris Dorrie all emerged to join Schlöndorff as significant directors in the 1970s and 1980s. Terrorism became a popular theme. Schlöndorff's 1975 film *Die verlorene Ehre der Katharina Blum* (The Lost Honour of Katharina Blum) was an adaptation of a Böll story on the subject. Margarethe von Trotta worked with Schlöndorff on the film and later dealt with the theme again in *Das zweite Erwachen der Christa Klages* (The Second Awakening of Christa Klages, 1978) and *Die Bleierne Zeit* (Leaden Time, 1981).

Werner Herzog's *Kaspar Hauser – Jeder für sich und Gott gegen alle* (Kaspar Hauser – Every Man for Himself and God Against All, 1974) is based on the true story of a foundling in 1829 who, having grown up isolated from civilisation, is misused as an object of research. As was the case for so many German films from the 1970s, Herzog portrayed society as a threat to self-identity. His *Fitzcarraldo* (1982), which took four years to complete and received mixed reviews from critics, is about a dreamer who defies social norms and self-limits to drag a boat inland across Peru.

Rainer Werner Fassbinder's films are more eclectic, at times more grotesque, in their exploration of society, sexuality and the human psyche. They have won nine awards in Germany alone, and his trilogy *Die Ehe der Maria Braun* (The Marriage of Maria Braun, 1979), *Lola* (1981) and *Die Sehnsucht der Veronika Voss* (The Longing of Veronica Voss, 1982) is highly acclaimed.

Wim Wenders won a Golden Palm at Cannes for *Paris, Texas* (1984). He pushed the *Erzählkino* (literally 'narrative cinema') style to its limit, as, for example, in *Der Himmel über Berlin* (The Sky Over Berlin, 1987), starring Peter Falk, based on two angels who move through divided Berlin.

With the collapse of the Wall, the GDR's Babelsberg film lot was sold to a French corporation. Headed by Schlöndorff, it has been upgraded to a tourist attraction – he refers to it as 'sacred ground' – while continuing to produce films and provide production services and studios.

The 1990s have brought a shift to relationship themes, with some good films emerging from Munich. Sönke Wortmann's 1992 *kleine Haie* (a pun on 'little sharks' and the title of a book of elocution exercises for actors) is a gentle comedy about male friendship. Katja von Garnier's *Abgeschminkt* (released as Making Up) from the same year is about love, life and work crises from a woman's point of view. Its lack of box office success in America, however, has caused consternation about the saleability of German humour. In *Keiner liebt mich* (Nobody Loves Me, 1994), Doris Dorrie created an offbeat film with black humour about the single woman in the 1990s.

Detlev Buck's 1993 *Wir können auch anders* (titled No More Mr Nice Guy in English) is arguably the best film to emerge since reunification. It is a comic road movie about two innocent brothers from the backwoods of Schleswig-Holstein who set off for the wilds of eastern Germany to claim an inheritance.

Film buffs should drop into the Deutsches Filmmuseum on the 'Museum Bank' in Frankfurt. It has a book and video library, and screenings of German and international films.

Painting & Sculpture

Early Works The two dominant art forms during the Carolingian period (around 800) were frescos and manuscript illumination. Few frescos have survived, but one example can be found in the crypt of St Maximin in Trier, which was excavated in the 1930s. Reichenau, an island in Lake Constance, was an early centre of Christian culture and manuscript illumination. Other schools sprang up in Trier, Cologne, Fulda and Hildesheim. The Stiftskirche St Georg on Reichenau has frescos from the late 10th century depicting miracles. These are among Germany's most important early works. Stained glass, such as in the cathedral at Augsburg (about 1100), was common during the Salian dynasty. The cycle in Augsburg cathedral is the earliest in Central Europe and depicts Jonas, Daniel, Hosea, Moses and David. Augsburg's stone *Bischofsthron* (Bishop's Throne), which is set on two lions, dates from the same period. The ceiling painting of the Michaelskirche in Hildesheim, dating from around 1200, depicts biblical scenes.

Gothic Building techniques enabling large windows meant that stained glass played an important role between the 12th and 15th centuries. However, the price paid by Gothic art was the loss of space for frescos. Good examples of glass painting can be found in Cologne in St Kunibert and in the choir of the Dom. An excellent early Gothic work is in the cathedral in Limburg an der Lahn. Manuscript illumination gained a density of colour with solemn shades of gold, dark green and purple. Iconography became common on church panels.

The Cologne school dropped the usual gold background and began painting rudimentary landscapes. The best example of an early realistic landscape depiction is *Die Meerfahrt der Heiligen* (Sea Voyage of Mary Magdalena), probably painted by Lukas Moser in 1432. It's in the Pfarrkirche in

Tiefenbronn near Pforzheim. The background depicting ships is remarkably evocative and realistic, creating a great sense of movement. Another famous work is Meister Bertram's religious panel *Erschaffung der Tiere* (Creation of the Animals, circa 1340), with its fine depiction of animals. Originally in the Petrikirche in Hamburg, it is now in the Kunsthalle.

Renaissance This era saw human elements gain importance in painting: religious figures were often depicted surrounded by mortals. In Germany, the Renaissance is synonymous with one great figure, Albrecht Dürer (1471-1528), who was born in Nuremberg. His influence was so great that the period is often referred to as the *Dürerzeit* (Age of Dürer). Dürer began as an apprentice goldsmith and travelled widely throughout Germany before spending time in Venice and Bologna. He was the first German to grapple seriously with the theory and practice of Italian Renaissance art. Closely tied to a Gothic tradition in early years, his woodcuts often had apocalyptic elements. His drawings of nature and animals were exact in their detail, and he left a surviving legacy of about 70 paintings, 350 woodcuts and 900 drawings. Some of his work is displayed in the Alte Pinakothek in Munich.

Dürer had an important influence on Lucas Cranach the Elder (1472-1553) and Hans Holbein (1497-1543). Cranach's landscape paintings contain many Gothic elements, as in his *Apollo und Diana in waldiger Landschaft* (Apollo and Diana in a Forest Landscape, 1530), in Berlin's Dahlem Museum. It depicts both figures naked in primal forest, Diana seated upon an acquiescent stag. Cranach formed the centre of a south German school of Mannerism, a movement that idealised beauty and dropped some of the Renaissance naturalist elements. Portraits often depicted stylised figures detached from their environment.

Of the Renaissance sculptors, Tilman Riemschneider (1460-1531) was the best known. He fell foul of authorities by supporting the peasants in the Bauernkriege of 1525, lost his job as mayor and was tossed in jail and tortured. His greatest skill was in giving his stone sculpture qualities resembling wood. His woodcuts show a strong play of light and shadow, as indeed did his life.

Baroque & Rococo The period around the 17th and 18th centuries brought an elaborate integration of painting, sculpture and architecture to form a *Gesamtkunstwerk* (total artwork). Sculpture was integrated into architectural design and gardens. Andreas Schlüter (1660-1714) was both a sculptor and architect whose *Reiterdenkmal des Grossen Kurfürsten* (Horseman's Monument of the Great Prince Elector), one of his most famous works, now stands before Berlin's Schloss Charlottenburg. He was called to St Petersburg by Peter the Great in 1713.

The fresco re-emerged as an important form, employed in the palaces to create the illusion of extended space. But baroque German painters were thin on the ground, with the two most important figures, Adam Elsheimer (1578-1610) and Johann Liss (1597-1630), both working in Italy. Many of Germany's palace frescos of the time were done by Italians. Johann Baptist Zimmermann (1680-1758) was an important southern German fresco painter who worked in pastels typical of the rococo style. In northern Germany Friedrich I employed the Frenchman Antoine Pesne (1683-1757) to satisfy his taste for the French rococo style.

Neoclassicism From about the mid-18th century neoclassicism brought a formal shift to line and body, with an emphasis on Roman or Greek mythology. The human figure also came back into fashion. In Germany the movement was influenced by the theorist Johann Winckelmann (1717-68), who, before being murdered in Italy, published works on classical painting and sculpture, including a history of classical art. His influence extended to Anton Mengs (1728-79), who became a painter of the royal court in Dresden. Johann Heinrich Tischbein (1751-1829) painted still lifes, animals and Goethe.

He belonged to Goethe's circle of friends during the latter's Italian journey, and his *Goethe in der Campagna* (1787) shows Germany's most famous writer reclined in a suitably classical landscape surrounded by an assortment of antique objects. The painting is now housed in the Frankfurt am Main Städel Art Institute.

Johann Gottfried Schadow (1764-1850) was the most important sculptor of the time. His most prominent work is the four-horse chariot with Victoria on Berlin's Brandenburg Gate. Napoleon liked it so much he took it with him in 1806. Returned in 1816, it was damaged during WWII and restored in 1956. After several decades of looking east, Victoria now faces west, her original position.

Romanticism The 19th century saw a shift back to more conventional religious themes. Great emphasis was placed on inner spirituality. Caspar Friedrich's (1774-1840) paintings had a religious symbolic element, such as his *Das Kreuz im Gebirge* (Cross in the Mountains). It depicts Christ's crucifixion among fir trees on a hilltop, light filtering supernaturally through a mackerel sky. Otto Runge (1777-1810) belonged to the Dresden school and also imbued his paintings with mysticism. He was a founder of the German Romantic movement and wrote several theoretical works. His work is well represented in Hamburg's Kunsthalle. Raphael's influence can be seen in a group of artists known as *Nazarener* (Nazareths), a derogatory term for intensely religious painters such as Johann Overbeck (1789-1869) and Franz Pforr (1788-1812), both of whom had studied in Vienna.

Realism & Naturalism Romanticism stagnated by the mid-19th century. The industrial age saw painters set up their easels outdoors and strive to re-create detail, whether natural or urban. Cologne-born Wilhelm Leibl (1844-1900) studied in Munich and specialised in painting Bavarian folk. His style gradually became more impressionistic. Some of his work can be seen in Hamburg's Kunsthalle.

Hans Thoma (1838-1924) belonged to Leibl's circle and produced still lifes, portraits and lithographs. Adolph Menzel (1815-1905), who is now ranked alongside Leibl as one of the best realist painters, was largely self-taught and went unnoticed until he began doing works based on the life of Friedrich I. His 1852 *Das Flötenkonzert* (The Flute Concert), now at Berlin's Dahlem Museum, accurately re-creates costume and a room interior with a realist brush.

Impressionism A truly impressionist school of painting emerged in Germany in the 1880s and 1890s, with Max Liebermann (1847-1935) and Fritz von Uhde (1848-1911). Liebermann's work was often dismissed as 'ugly' and 'socialist', and the movement itself was long considered un-German, which perhaps reflects the lingering social influence of Romanticism. Liebermann began by painting gloomy naturalist works of the proletariat before adopting brighter impressionistic tones. Lovis Corith's (1858-1925) late work *Die Kindheit des Zeus* (Childhood of Zeus, 1905) is a richly coloured frolic in nature with intoxicated, grotesque elements, now housed in the Bremen Kunsthalle with others of its ilk.

Expressionism In the same year that Corith painted *Die Kindheit*, a group calling itself Die Brücke (The Bridge) emerged from the Dresden art scene. The movement worked with bright, dynamic surfaces, striving for a direct and true representation of creative force. They admired the work of Paul Gauguin and often employed primitivist and cubist elements. Its founding members were Ernst Kirchner (1880-1936), Erich Heckel (1883-1971) and Karl Schmidt-Rottluf (1884-1976). Members often lived in artists' communes, turning their studios into exhibition space.

Emil Nolde (1867-1956), arguably Germany's best expressionist painter, was an artistic lone wolf who only fleetingly belonged to Die Brücke. Nolde was forbidden from working by the Nazis in 1941.

A second group of expressionists known

as Der Blaue Reiter (Blue Rider) was based in Munich around the key figures of Wassily Kandinsky (1866-1944), Gabrielle Münter (1877-1962), Paul Klee (1879-1940) and Franz Marc (1880-1916). Like Die Brücke, the movement tried to find a purer, freer spirit through colour and movement. Kandinsky's 1909 *Eisenbahn bei Murnau* (Railway at Murnau) shows a train passing through an evocatively colourful landscape. It is in Munich's Städtische Gallerie im Lenbachhaus, where many of the movement's works are housed. The Russian-born Kandinsky wrote much about expressionist theory, saying the creation of form was the creation of life. Oskar Kokoschka (1886-1980) was an Austrian (also briefly a British citizen) who exerted great influence on the expressionist scene both as an artist and as a professor in Dresden.

Neue Sachlichkeit 'New Objectivity' describes a loose movement in the early 20th century that reached its zenith with Bauhaus. Architecture formed the basis of Bauhaus, but ideas spilled over into painting with the publication of the movement's ninth book by Kandinsky, who had moved on from expressionism.

Kandinsky's work *Punkt und Linie zu Fläche: Beitrag zur Analyse der Malerischen Elemente* (Point and Line to Surface: Contribution to the Analysis of Elements of Painting) was a landmark in Bauhaus art theory. As well as Kandinsky and Klee, the movement included the sculptor Gerhard Marcks (1889-1981).

Otto Dix's (1891-1969) work crossed from expressionism into dadaism, a movement mocking bourgeois that developed briefly in Germany around 1916, whereas Max Ernst (1891-1976), a painter, sculptor and graphic artist, moved in later years from dadaism to grotesque surrealism.

George Grosz (1893-1959), co-founder of German dadaism and, later, the Rote Gruppe (Red Group), took the pencil and brush to society in the 1920s with witty, skilful caricatures. He escaped execution by the skin of his teeth after a military court sentenced him to death in 1918, and went on to be received by Lenin on a 1922 trip to Russia. None of this made him the favourite artist of Hitler, who stripped him of German citizenship and classified him as *entartet* (degenerate). Many of Grosz's works in private hands were confiscated or destroyed. He went into exile in New York, returning only in 1957.

John Heartfield (1891-1968) was another member of the futurist-dadaist club who kicked around Berlin in the 1920s and 1930s. He worked closely with Grosz on satirical magazines. His *Die Saat des Todes* (The Seed of Death, 1937) depicts a skeleton in a wasteland sprinkled with swastikas. Käthe Kollwitz (1867-1945) was a 'Renaissance woman' active in virtually all fields of visual art. She worked her way through naturalist and expressionist movements to arrive at agitprop and socialist realism. Some of her works are housed in Berlin's Käthe Kollwitz Museum.

With war approaching, art became increasingly bleak, often taking the themes of silence and death. Many artists suffered the fate of being classified 'degenerate' like Grosz or were forced to resign their positions and go into exile. Others were murdered or went into 'internal exile'.

Nazi Art Hitler was no great fan of 20th-century painting unless he had done it himself. Very few people today place much value on Nazi art. It lay stacked in a basement for 50 years before being rolled out for an exhibition in 1996, attracting the scorn of the art world.

Post-1945 After the war, respected figures such as Nolde, Schmidt-Rottluf and Kandinsky returned to pull Germany's destroyed cultural scene back onto its feet. Willi Baumeister and Ernst Nay are considered two of Germany's best postwar abstract expressionists. Nay tried to capture rhythm in his work, often using erotic motifs and mythology.

The Düsseldorf-based Gruppe Zero (Group Zero) plugged into the Bauhaus legacy. Otto Piene and Heinz Mack were two key members who used light and space cleverly in endeavours to create a harmonious whole. Mack's sculpture is predominantly of metal, whereas Piene has used projection techniques to create his so-called 'light ballets'. More recently, Anselm Kiefer has gone for size in his 32-tonne work *Zweistromland* (Mesopotamia), which consists of 200 lead books arranged on shelves.

The Neue Wilde (New Wild Ones) movement of the late 1970s and early 1980s brought together new-wave music and the visual arts, with Cologne, Berlin and Hamburg its main centres.

In the GDR, the Leipzig Kunsthochschule was one important centre of socialist realism. Wolfgang Matheuer emerged as a respected painter and sculptor who relied on mythological personae (Icarus, Sisyphus) and has produced a large body of work that includes self-portraits and landscapes.

Germany is paradise for any museum lover. Some of the best museums to visit for a good overview of German painting and sculpture are Hamburg's Kunsthalle, the Alte and Neue Pinakothek in Munich, Dresden's New Masters Gallery, the Dahlem Museum in Berlin, the Städel Art Institute in Frankfurt am Main, and Stuttgart's Staatsgallerie. Schwerin's Staatliches Museum has an excellent collection of Dutch 17th-century masters.

PHILOSOPHY & SCIENCE

Germany, with its rigorous education system based on the ideas of the philologist and statesman Wilhelm von Humboldt (1767-1835), has made enormous contributions to the disciplines of philosophy and the natural sciences. The importance of Germans in the social sciences and physics in particular is inestimable. Up to 1939, 10 out of 45 Nobel Prizes in physics had gone to Germans.

Immanuel Kant (1724-1804), who was born in Königsberg (now Kaliningrad in Russia), provided Germany with a philosophy for the Enlightenment in his *Critique of Pure Reason* (1781) in which he claimed that natural laws were merely human constructs to explain our surroundings. As a founder of German idealism, he paved the way for Georg Wilhelm Friedrich Hegel (1770-1831).

In *The Phenomenology of the Spirit* (1807), Hegel developed a theory of dialectics, or opposites. For Hegel, the world consisted of polarities that were resolved and threw up new opposites, culminating in an idealised pure consciousness. His influence extended to Arthur Schopenhauer (1788-1860), an idealist with pessimist predilections, who was associated with Goethe and Schiller in Weimar.

If Schopenhauer drove German idealism to its subjective limits, the Trier-born Karl Marx (1818-83) injected it with a historical basis and reinterpreted Hegel's pure consciousness as proletarian revolution. Marx's *Das Kapital*, written in the reading room of London's British Museum, is arguably the most influential work of the past two centuries.

As an economist, Marx occupies a place alongside his British predecessor, David Ricardo (1772-1823). As a social theorist, his brilliance was in describing the change from feudalism to modern capitalism. As a revolutionary, he laid the groundwork for 20th-century political developments.

Friedrich Nietzsche (1844-1900) shared Schopenhauer's idealism but saw subjectivity as a positive condition. Much of his work focuses on power and the human will. His ideas on an Übermensch (superman), however, were distorted by Hitler, and used to justify racial abuses.

Max Weber (1864-1920), who was born in Erfurt, is considered the founder of modern sociology.

The ideas of Martin Heidegger (1889-1976), who was influenced by Dane Søren Kierkegaard, formed the basis of existentialism.

Germany's achievements in the natural sciences are no less impressive. Geographer and naturalist Alexander von Humboldt (1769-1859), the younger brother of Wilhelm, stands out as an important figure for his study of flora and species geography, physical geography and meteorology. His

Karl Marx: economist and revolutionary social theorist.

data from expeditions to Cuba, and Central and South America contributed greatly to the knowledge of our environment.

Physics, however, is the field in which Germany has particularly excelled and three distinguished Germans stand out in the pantheon of Nobel Prize laureates. Albert Einstein (1879-1955) was born in Ulm and emigrated to Switzerland at 15 years of age, where he worked in the patents office in Bern. His theories on the atomic structure of matter were followed by his theory of relativity. In 1933 Einstein moved to the US and became an American citizen in 1940. Max Planck (1858-1947) is considered the founder of quantum physics. Werner Heisenberg (1901-76) achieved recognition with his research into hydrogen.

The German tradition of excellence in the social and natural sciences continues to this day, supported by a network of elite Max Planck Institutes and the financial backing of private research by large German international corporations.

SOCIETY & CONDUCT

Though politically united, Germany is still marked by 40 years of Cold War division. For better or worse, it still isn't possible to talk of a single German society. Optimistic predictions of integration within five years have now given way to vague hopes of social unification within a generation or two.

The difficulties of reunification come on top of old ones relating to Germany's Nazi past, which, after 50 years, still dominates attitudes both at home and abroad. A 1996 survey among British schoolchildren conducted for the Goethe Institute revealed that, for 68% of those asked, Adolf Hitler was still the most well known German. Next came Jürgen Klinsmann, Boris Becker and Steffi Graf. About 16% mentioned Ludwig van Beethoven. This comes as no surprise to many Germans, who feel that their country's postwar role as a model for peace continues to be under-emphasised.

In Germany itself, the Nazi experience eliminated certain words from the language (so-called 'Nazi words'), interrupted a rich cultural tradition and lent a few seemingly innocuous ideas a sinister quality. The very idea of a Tidy Town competition, for example, runs the risk of sounding like an ethnic purge in German. As for a Neighbourhood Watch campaign ... forget it.

National Identity

German society predates the German nation. Compared with other European countries, Germany achieved nationhood very late. This, and the fact that nationhood was closely associated with periods of confusion, war or authoritarianism, still lends the very idea of a German nation negative connotations. Germans cannot celebrate their country as innocently as, say, Americans or French can theirs – the stigma is too great.

Günther Grass, Germany's most famous modern writer, is quoted as saying his people didn't deserve a country of their own after Auschwitz. One consequence of Hitler's nationalist programme was that, until recently, most 'good' Germans rejected national sentiment as part of their rejection of Nazism, preferring to dress themselves in the colours of Europe. Waving a flag or singing the national anthem in the FRG after 1945 was generally avoided. Meanwhile, good East Germans were taking their government's advice and busily turning 'swords into ploughshares'. The mood has changed since reunification, however, and now you can even hear the German football team struggling through the approved third verse of *Das Deutschland Lied* – which doesn't stop reporters asking them *why* they sing.

Just how far Germany has come (or not come) in creating a confident, post-WWII national identity was spelled out by the hysterical reaction in 1996 to Daniel Goldhagen's *Hitler's Willing Executioners*, when the entire political spectrum sprang nervously to its country's defence. Many historians falsely believed Goldhagen wanted to cast doubt on the German national character by resurrecting the so-called 'collective guilt thesis', which attributes responsibility for the Holocaust to all Germans. It was probably the post-reunification debate Germany needed to have, and now, the dust having settled, is seen as a new station in the search for a balanced national self-image.

Volkhard Knigge, who is responsible for the upkeep of the Buchenwald concentration camp memorial outside Weimar, probably best summed up the situation in an interview with *Der Spiegel* magazine: 'When you talk about Goethe, you can't hold your tongue on Buchenwald.'

Wall in the Head

In East Germany, national identity was thrown into one bag with class struggle and socialism. Although this potpourri had taken on a bitter flavour by the 1980s, a lot of East Germans did develop a sense of nation. Stripped of socialist clothing, many still cling nakedly to a now defunct national identity. Some feel done out of a country, and most eastern Germans will tell you that it was not all a nightmare. Their identity may be expressed in *Ostalgie* (a pun on 'east' and 'nostalgia') or a predilection for Rotkäppchen sparkling wine ('Little Red Riding Hood', as if she were always a paid-up party member) and other eastern products.

Paradoxically, however, East Germans were more predisposed to reunification than West Germans, using it to express discontent with the SED. But isolation bred unrealistic expectations: the grass was always greener on the other side of the wall.

Daniela Dahn, an ex-GDR journalist who wrote what has come to be seen as a survival handbook for eastern Germans, believes one of the biggest culture shocks occurred in the workplace. Eastern Germans, she says, were unused to the level of competition between employees in western Germany. Many East Germans identified with their workplace and co-workers, even if that meant less work was done. 'It was ineffective,' she explained in an interview with the *Frankfürter Rundschau*, 'but effectiveness knows no human measure'. Dahn has become something of a high priestess of *Ost-Trotz* (eastern pride).

Eastern Germans identify strongly with their town or region, especially in those parts affected most by industrial closures. This combination of looking inward at their region and outward at a forbidden West seems to have left traces of a 'broad-minded provinciality'. Overseas travellers often emerge from a visit to the 'wild east' surprised by its friendliness, and it is probably worth bearing in mind that eastern Germans reveal things to foreigners that they wouldn't reveal to western Germans. The tip, in this regard, is to ask questions.

Oddly, 89% of all eastern Germans believe conditions have deteriorated since reunification. Much of this can be attributed to Ostalgie. While valuing freedom of movement and choice, a cleaner environment and better leisure facilities, many miss the security they believe they once had. Only 20% feel they now have more influence on the state than under single-party rule.

Changes for Women in the GDR

Almost 90% of all women in the GDR were employed or in training programmes. By June 1992, 63% of women in eastern Germany were unemployed. Reunification also brought the closure of childcare centres, an end to free contraception, and cuts in health programmes. It pushed some women back into more traditional roles.

SED ideology did draw women into the economic life of the state, based on the official line that an independent income was good for family and the economy. It didn't harm the party much either. But, in practice, it amounted to a double burden, with women taking sole responsibility for the family. This in turn lowered work status. Women's overall earnings were 25 to 30% less than those of men, and two incomes were essential for a reasonable standard of living. For women, the *Wende* (change) meant a loss of, albeit limited, economic power.

Abortion

Abortion within three months of conception was legal in the GDR. Due to strong opposition from women's groups to the adoption of less liberal West German abortion laws, the issue was fudged in the Unification Treaty. Abortion, according to old West German law, was illegal, but certain preconditions made it unpunishable. One of these, a 'social indication', meant termination within 12 weeks was often possible after counselling. Each state enforced this law as it saw fit, resulting in abortion tourism, whereby women sought abortions in states with a pro-choice approach.

In 1992, a *Fristenlösung* (based on a time limit, as with the old GDR law) was passed by the SPD, FDP and CDU in the Bundestag. Parts of this law were subsequently declared unconstitutional, however, by the *Bundesverfassungsgericht*, the German High Court, which prescribed detailed changes.

The issue remained unresolved until 1995, when a compromise was reached, keeping a couple of the indications and, in practice, allowing abortion on demand. Abortion is now illegal (except when medical or criminal indications exist, which make it legal) but unpunishable if carried out within 12 weeks of conception and after compulsory counselling. The Catholic Church is still debating whether it should play a role in abortion counselling.

Right-Wing Violence

A disturbing social phenomenon to emerge in the 1990s has been attacks on foreigners. This is often attributed to youth unemployment and readjustment problems in eastern Germany. Nevertheless, the problem is not confined to eastern Germany, and government leaders in both regions have been blamed for failing to unequivocably condemn attacks when they increased in the early 1990s. Police have also been criticised for focusing too heavily on the substantial *Autonom* (left-wing anarchist) scene and too little on the skinhead problem.

Right-wing extremists had been an active but insignificant group at Monday demonstrations in Leipzig in 1989. In 1991 the level of right-wing violence increased fivefold. In the same year, encouraged by many locals, who obstructed the police, skinheads attacked a refugee hostel in Hoyerswerda, south of Cottbus. Instead of clamping down on the skinheads, authorities carted off the refugees, relocating them in a nearby town. This further encouraged extreme right-wing elements. Rostock erupted a year later with similar scenes. Other attacks followed: a house in Solingen (in the Ruhr region) occupied by Turks was burnt to the ground, killing five people; arsonists set fire to the Lübeck synagogue; a group of Africans was brutally beaten up in Magdeburg. Sensitive to matters concerning foreigners, Germans demonstrated in large numbers against the violence and established solidarity groups to protect hostels.

Dos & Don'ts

There are arguably more stereotypes of Germany and Germans than of any other European nation. Many of these images are media-generated, leftovers from wartime or Cold War propaganda. Then there are comic clichés about the cool, efficient Prussian, or of Bavarians in *Lederhosen* (leather trousers) descending from the hills twice a year to dance and slap together hands or various other body parts. Mention of such images usually induces bewilderment and frustrated groans among young Germans at home.

Nevertheless, tradition does remain dear to the German heart. Hunters still wear green, master chimney sweeps get around in pitch-black suits and top hats, some Bavarian women don the *Dirndl* (skirt and blouse), while Bavarian menfolk occasionally sport Lederhosen, a *Loden* (short jacket) and felt hat. However, most young Germans these days graduate from nappies to jeans and Nikes, completely side-stepping the leather phase. You are also likely to find people relaxed, personable and interested in enjoying life. English-speaking travellers readily identify with Germans and find it easy to strike up a conversation with them.

It *is* OK to mention the war, if done with tact and relevance. After all, a lot of people you will meet have grown up demanding explanations. What causes offence, however, is a 'victor' mentality, which is perceived as righteous and gloating, or the idea that fascist ideas are intrinsically German.

You might find yourself tripping up occasionally (you'll notice the blank stare) on German historical or cultural taboos. What may be an innocuously 'liberal' view at home can sometimes go down in Germany as political dynamite. No discussion of euthanasia can ignore abuses under the Nazi regime. Similarly, abortion has almost always been illegal (see the earlier section in this chapter), but under the Nazi regime criminals and non-Aryans – notably Jews and Gypsies – were encouraged and often forced to have abortions as a means of population control.

Push firmly but politely in dealings with German bureaucracy. Shouting will invariably bring down the shutters. In fact, Germans often lower their voice, not raise it, in mildly heated moments. Insist on talking to the boss. Ask for it in writing *(eine schriftliche Begründung)*. German work hierarchies are still rock solid, and obstinacy crops up occasionally as a form of passing the buck. In that case, unfortunately, the boss will quite possibly be a higher and more unpleasant manifestation of your lowly buck-passer.

Give your name at the start of any phone call. This is especially important when booking a room by telephone. Germans consider it impolite or simply get annoyed when no name is given. If you don't want to (when dealing with bureaucracy, for instance), make one up.

Germans usually face each other squarely in conversation, and a lot of eye contact is used to signal interest and attention. If John Wayne had been German, he would have intently analysed the pupils of his interlocutor during those big moments, not gazed meaningfully at the horizon. Depending on your momentary state of mind, this stance can seem overbearing and unnerving or refreshingly direct. Shaking hands is common both among men and women, as is a hug or a kiss on the cheek among young people.

Much importance is still attached to academic titles (Herr or Frau Doktor), and addressing someone by the surname is a must unless you are on informal *du* terms. If you have a title yourself, you might like to move mountains with it (it's legally part of your name and you can insist on its use). If Herr Professor Doktor Vollschnauze nods or bows his head slightly when he shakes your hand, he's signalling respect for you as an equal, not that he feels humbled by your presence (always good to know). In that case, a subtle nod in response is the usual grace. If he insists on being addressed with both 'Dr' titles, you might like to think seriously about the kind of people you attract.

Great importance is also placed on the formal 'Sie' form, which is used more often than most non-Germans expect. It is worth trying to get it right, as correct use will make things a lot easier.

In the workplace, only employees who are also good friends say 'du'. It is quite common to use 'Sie' even after 20 years of close contact. This, of course, can turn your average German Christmas office party into a minefield once the drink and 'du' start flowing. One psychologist, interviewed on TV about inadvertently becoming 'familiar under the influence', suggested that fellow workers innocently revert to 'Sie' and

Jews in Germany

The first Jews arrived in what is now Germany with the conquering Romans, settling in important Roman cities on or near the Rhine such as Cologne, Trier, Mainz, Speyer and Worms. As non-Christians, Jews had a separate political status. Highly valued for their trade connections, Jews were formally invited to settle in Speyer in 1084, granted trading privileges and the right to build a wall around their quarter. A charter of rights granted to the Jews of Worms in 1090 by Henry IV allowed local Jews to be judged according to their own set of laws. With 2000 Jews, Mainz had one of the largest communities.

The First Crusade (1095-99) resulted in a wave of pogroms in 1096, usually against the will of local rulers and townspeople. Many Jews resisted before committing suicide once their predicament had become hopeless. This, the *Kiddush ha-shem* (martyr's death), established a precedent of martyrdom that became a tenet of European Judaism in the Middle Ages. But the attacks also set the tone for persecution by mobs during troubled times. Jews fared better in the Second Crusade (1147-49), taking refuge in castles until the danger had passed.

In the 13th century Jews were declared crown property by Frederick II, an act that afforded protection but exposed them to royal whim. The Church also prescribed distinctive clothing for Jews, which later meant that in some towns Jews had to wear badges.

Things deteriorated with the arrival of the plague in the mid-14th century, when Jews were accused of having poisoned Christians' drinking wells. Persecution, including trials and burnings, was now sanctioned by the state. Political fragmentation meant Jews were financially exploited by both the Kaiser and local rulers, and libellous notions circulated throughout the Christian population. One of these, the 'blood libel', accused Jews of using the blood of Christians in rituals. The even more bizarre 'host-desecration libel' accused Jews of desecrating or torturing Christ himself by, among other dastardly deeds, sticking pins into communion wafers, which then wept tears or bled.

Moneylending continued to be the main source of income for Jews in the 15th century, but many moved back into local trade, including the wine trade in southern Germany. Expulsions remained commonplace, with large numbers emigrating to Poland, where Yiddish, essentially medieval German with large borrowings from Hebrew and Slavic languages, developed. The Reformation marked another low point, with Martin Luther calling at various times for the confiscation of Jewish religious texts, expulsion, serfdom and the destruction of Jewish homes. Deeper fragmentation after the Thirty Years' War again exposed Jews to the whims of competing territorial and central authorities, but by the 17th century they were valued once more for their economic contacts. Jews expelled from Portugal founded the Hamburg Bank and were important traders in wine, tobacco and textiles. Those invited to Saxony promoted trade with Switzerland, Holland, Italy and Britain. Nevertheless, their lives remained strictly regulated.

Napoleon granted Germany's Jews equal rights, but reforms were repealed by the 1815 Congress of Vienna, and anti-Jewish feelings in the early 19th century coincided with German nationalism and a more vigorous Christianity. Pressure was applied on Jews to assimilate. Famous assimilated Jews, such as Heinrich Heine, often exerted a liberal influence on society.

With unification in 1871, Jews enjoyed almost equal status in Germany, but they were still barred from government and could not become army officers. In the late 19th century Germany became a world centre in the study of Jewish culture and history. There was a shift to large cities such as Leipzig, Cologne, Breslau (now Wrocław in Poland), Hamburg, Frankfurt, and to the capital, Berlin, where one third of all German Jews lived.

The advent of the Weimar Republic in 1919 meant emancipation for the 500,000-strong Jewish community, and many assumed a direct political role in democratic and socialist parties (Hugo Preuss, who was Jewish, drafted Germany's first democratic constitution). But economic disasters in the 1920s soon brought a backlash. Despite the fact that over 100,000 of their numbers had served Germany in the armed forces during WWI, Jews became scapegoats for Germany's defeat, the humiliating peace and ensuing economic woes.

Large numbers of unassimilated Jews from Eastern Europe immigrated to Germany in the 1920s. Meanwhile, German Jews continued to assimilate, and about half of all marriages by Jews in the 1920s were mixed. Germany also became an important centre for Hebrew literature after Russian writers and academics fled the revolution of 1917.

After Hitler came to power, the fate of German Jewry was sealed by new race laws. Increasing persecution led many to emigrate, and by 1939 only 214,000 Jews remained in Germany, less than half the 1933 figure. By 1943 Germany had been declared *Judenrein*, or clean of Jews. This ignored the hundreds of thousands of Eastern European Jews incarcerated on 'German' soil. In all, around six million Jews died in Europe as a direct result of Nazism and its unspeakable barbarity.

Germany's Jewish community numbers around 60,000 today, a figure boosted by the influx of Jews from the former Soviet Union. ■

pretend they were too drunk to remember. This might be worth a try in other predicaments too. Germans often celebrate the change to the familiar. Young people and eastern Germans are much more relaxed about 'Sie' and 'du' (in bars, where a lot of young people gather, 'du' is often used), but don't even consider saying 'du' to a shop assistant unless you want to incite bad service.

On the whole, Germans are not prudish. Nude bathing and mixed saunas are commonplace (many women, however, prefer single-sex saunas). Nude bathing areas are marked FKK, or form spontaneously in certain areas on beaches or the shores of lakes.

RELIGION

The constitution guarantees religious freedom in Germany. The two main religions are Catholicism and Protestantism, each of which has about the same number of adherents. This situation dates back to the Peace of Augsburg (1555), when, as a result of the Peasants' War (see the earlier History section), the Catholic and Protestant churches were granted equal status. Each ruler was free to choose the denomination of his principality, which left the south predominantly Catholic and the north Protestant. Nevertheless, several Catholic diasporas continue to exist in the north, and there are both Catholic and Protestant Sorbs – the Slavonic minority in eastern Germany. A large influx of Huguenots (French Protestants) occurred in the late 17th century, making up a substantial chunk of Berlin's population (about 30%) by 1700. There are also about 1.7 million Muslims, 40,000 Jews and many smaller denominations.

About 500,000 Jews lived in Germany in 1933, before the community was devastated by emigration and the Holocaust. Some surviving Jews chose to remain, and the Jewish community has grown recently due to immigration from the former Soviet Union. The largest groups are in Berlin, Frankfurt am Main and Munich.

Germans who belong to a recognised denomination have to pay a Church tax. Many leave the Church for financial reasons. A survey conducted in 1996 for *Der Spiegel* magazine produced the interesting statistic that only 51% of all Germans believed in God. In eastern Germany, the figure was 20%.

In the former GDR, Protestants overwhelmingly outnumbered Catholics. Church membership was officially frowned upon by the party, and no party member could belong to the Church. Religious lessons were conducted solely outside the school system. Church and state existed side by side with formal agreements regulating Church activities. For example, a 1957 agreement allowed Protestant pastors to visit military barracks, but the state paid for this, and also organised and controlled all visits. The Protestant Church played a major role in the overthrow of the SED by providing a forum for anti-government protesters.

On the whole, the Church in former East Germany took a distrustful view of the armed forces and supported conscientious objectors. This contrasted with a more conservative approach to the issue of pacifism in West Germany. This fact, and the much closer relationship between Church and state in unified Germany, means many eastern Germans view the current role of the Church with scepticism. In 1991 about 40% of eastern Germans claimed to have had no religious upbringing. About 20% stated they had no confession.

LANGUAGE

German belongs to the Indo-European language group and is spoken by over 100 million people in countries throughout the world, including Austria and part of Switzerland. There are also ethnic-German communities in neighbouring Eastern European countries such as Poland and the Czech Republic, although expulsion after 1945 reduced their number dramatically.

High German used today comes from a regional Saxon dialect. It developed into an official bureaucratic language and was used by Luther in his translation of the Bible, gradually spreading throughout Germany. The impetus Luther gave to the written language through his translations was followed by the establishment of language societies in the 17th century, and later by the 19th-century work of Jacob Grimm, the founder of modern German philology. With his brother, Karl Wilhelm Grimm, he also began work on the first German dictionary.

Regional dialects still thrive throughout Germany, especially in Cologne, rural Bavaria, Swabia and parts of Saxony. The Sorb minority in eastern Germany has its own language. In northern Germany it is common to hear Plattdeutsch and Frisian spoken. Both are distant relatives of English, and the fact that many German words survive in the English vocabulary today makes things a lot easier for native English speakers.

That's the good news. The bad news is that, unlike English, German has retained clear formal distinctions in gender and case. Though not as difficult as Russian, for instance, which has more cases, German does have its tricky moments. Germans are used to hearing foreigners – and a few notable indigenous sports personalities – make a hash of their grammar, and any attempt to speak the language is always well received.

All German school children learn a foreign language, usually English, which means most can speak it to a certain degree. You might encounter greater communication problems in eastern Germany, however, where Russian was the main foreign language taught in schools before the *Wende* (change).

Pronunciation

English speakers sometimes hold onto their vowels too long when speaking in German, which causes comprehension problems. Nevertheless, there are long vowels, like *pope*, and short ones, like *pop*. One other common mistake is a tendency to pronounce all vowels as if they have umlauts (ä, ö and ü). It is worth practising the difference, as they often change the tense and meaning of a word. Otherwise German pronunciation is fairly straight forward. There are no silent letters, and many foreign words (eg *Band*, for 'rock band') are pronounced roughly the same as in English.

Vowels

a short, like the 'u' in 'cut', or long, as in 'father'.
au as in 'vow'.
ä short, as in 'act', or long, as in 'hair'.
äu as in 'boy'.
e short, as in 'bet', or long, as in 'day'.
ei like the 'ai' in 'aisle'.
eu as in 'boy'.
i short, as in 'in', or long, as in 'see'.
ie as in 'see'.
o short, as in 'pot', or long, as in 'note'.
ö like the 'er' in 'fern'.
u like the 'u' in 'pull'.
ü similar to the 'u' in 'pull' but with stretched lips.

Consonants

Most consonants and their combinations are roughly similar to English ones, with a few exceptions. At the end of a word, consonants **b**, **d** and **g** sound a little more like 'p', 't' and 'k' respectively. No consonants are silent.

ch throaty as in 'ch' of Scottish 'loch'
j 'y' as in 'yet'
ng always as one sound, like in 'strong'
qu as 'kv'
r trilled or guttural
s sharp as in 'see' or almost a vocalised 'z' as in 'zoo'
ß sharp 's', sometimes written as 'ss' or 'sz'; written as 'ss' in this book
sch as in 'shore'
st usually pronounced 'sht'
sp usually pronounced 'shp'
v more like an English 'f'
w like an English 'v'
z 'ts', like in 'tsar'

Articles, Gender, Case & Plural

These four elements of the language can be a nightmare for English speakers. German has three genders (masculine *der*, feminine *die* and neutral *das*). They decline according to the case (nominative, accusative, dative and genitive). The basic plural form is *die*. German nouns always begin with a capital.

Verbs

Many German verbs have a prefix that is often detached from the stem and placed at the end of the sentence. For example, *fahren* means to go (by mechanical means). *Abfahren* means to depart. A simple sentence with the prefixed verb *abfahren* becomes: *Um wieviel Uhr fährt der Zug ab?* (What time does the train leave?).

The following words and phrases should help you through the more common or difficult situations. Travellers interested in finding out more might like to pick up a copy of Lonely Planet's *German phrasebook*, a comprehensive guide for getting around in German.

Language Problems

I (don't) understand.	*Ich verstehe (nicht).*
Do you speak English?	*Sprechen Sie Englisch?* (formal) *Sprichst du Englisch?* (informal)
Does anyone here speak English?	*Spricht hier jemand Englisch?*
How do you say that in German?	*Wie sagt man das auf Deutsch?*
What does ... mean?	*Was bedeutet ...?*
Please write it down.	*Bitte schreiben Sie es auf.*
Can you show me (on the map)?	*Könnten Sie mir (auf der Karte) zeigen?*

Paperwork

first name	*Vorname*
surname	*Familienname*
nationality	*Staatsangehörigkeit*
date of birth	*Geburtsdatum*
place of birth	*Geburtsort*
sex (gender)	*Geschlecht*
passport	*Reisepass*
identification	*Ausweis*
visa	*Visum*

Greetings & Civilities

Hello.	*Hallo./Grüss Gott.* (in Bavaria and Austria)
Good morning/ Good day/Good evening.	*Guten Morgen/ Guten Tag/Guten Abend.*
Goodbye.	*Auf Wiedersehen.*
Bye.	*Tschüss.*
Yes.	*Ja.*
No.	*Nein.*
Where?	*Wo?*
Why?	*Warum?*
How?	*Wie?*
Maybe.	*Vielleicht.*
Please.	*Bitte.*
Thankyou (very much).	*Danke (schön).*
You're welcome.	*Bitte* or *Bitte sehr.*
Excuse me.	*Entschuldigung.*
I'm sorry/Forgive me.	*Entschuldigen Sie, bitte/Verzeihen Sie mir, bitte.*
I'm sorry (to express sympathy).	*Das tut mir leid.*

Small Talk

What's your name?	*Wie heissen Sie (heisst Du)?*
My name is ...	*Ich heisse ...*
How are you?	*Wie geht es Ihnen?* (formal) *Wie geht's dir?* (informal)
I'm fine, thanks.	*Es geht mir gut, danke.*
Where are you from?	*Woher Kommen Sie (kommst du)?*
I'm from ...	*Ich komme aus ...*
Have you already eaten?	*Haben Sie (Hast du) schon gegessen?*
How old are you?	*Wie alt sind Sie (bist du)?*
I'm ... years old.	*Ich bin ... Jahre alt.*
Are you married?	*Sind Sie (Bist du) verheiratet?*
I'm (not) married.	*Ich bin (nicht) verheiratet.*

How many children do you have?	*Wieviele Kinder haben Sie (hast du)?*

Getting Around

I want to go to ...	*Ich möchte nach ... fahren.*
What time does the ... leave/arrive?	*Um wieviel Uhr fährt ... ab/ kommt ... an?*
the boat	*das Boot*
the bus	*der Bus*
the train	*der Zug*
the tram/trolleybus	*die Strassenbahn*
What time does the plane leave/ arrive?	*Um wieviel Uhr fliegt /kommt das Flugzeug ab/an?*
Where is the ...?	*Wo ist ...?*
bus stop	*die Bushaltestelle*
metro station	*die U-Bahnstation*
the train station	*der Bahnhof*
main railway station	*der Hauptbahnhof*
airport	*der Flughafen*
tram/trolleybus stop	*die Strassenbahn-haltestelle*
the next	*der/die/das nächste*
the last	*der/die/das letzte*
Where can I buy a ticket?	*Wo kann ich eine Fahrkarte kaufen?*
1st class	*erste Klasse*
2nd class	*zweite Klasse*
platform number	*Gleisnummer*
ticket office	*Fahrkartenschalter*
timetable	*Fahrplan*
one-way ticket	*einfache Fahrkarte*
return ticket	*Rückfahrkarte*
left-luggage locker	*Gepäckschliessfach*
I'd like to hire ...	*Ich möchte ... mieten*
a bicycle/motorcycle	*ein Fahrrad/ Motorrad*
a car	*ein Auto*

Directions

Where is ...?	*Wo ist ...?*
How can I get to ...?	*Wie erreicht man ...?*
Is it far from here?	*Ist es weit von hier?*
street	*die Strasse*
suburb	*der Vorort*
town	*die Stadt*
north	*Nord*
south	*Süd*
east	*Ost*
west	*West*
behind	*hinter*
in front of	*vor*
opposite	*gegenüber*
straight ahead	*geradeaus*
(turn) left	*(nach) links*
(turn) right	*(nach) rechts*
at the traffic lights	*an der Ampel*
at the next corner	*an der nächsten Ecke*

Around Town

I'm looking for ...	*Ich suche ...*
a bank	*eine Bank/Sparkasse*
the church	*die Kirche*
the city centre	*das Stadtzentrum*
the ... embassy	*die ... Botschaft*
my hotel	*mein Hotel*
the market	*den Markt*
the museum	*das Museum*
the post office	*das Postamt*
a public toilet	*eine öffentliche Toilette*
a hospital	*ein Krankenhaus*
the police	*die Polizei*
the tourist office	*das Fremden-verkehrsbüro*
I want to change some money/ travellers' cheques.	*Ich möchte Geld/ Reiseschecks wechseln.*
What time does ... open/close?	*Um wieviel Uhr macht ... auf/zu?*
I'd like to make a phone call.	*Ich möchte telefonieren.*
bridge	*die Brücke*
beach	*der Strand*
castle/palace	*die Burg/das Schloss*
cathedral	*der Dom*
monastry/convent	*das Kloster*
town square/market	*der Marktplatz*
tower	*der Turm*
gate	*das Tor*
mountain	*der Berg*

forest *der Wald*
island *die Insel*
river *der Fluss*
sea *das Meer/die See*
lake *der See*
coast *die Küste*
valley *das Tal*

Useful Signs

Camping Ground *Campingplatz*
Entrance *Eingang/Einfahrt*
Exit *Ausgang/Ausfahrt*
Push *drücken*
Pull *ziehen*
Arrival *Ankunft*
Departure *Abfahrt*
Full *voll/besetzt*
Vacant *frei*
Occupied *besetzt/belegt*
Closed for the Day *Ruhetag*
Open *auf/offen/geöffnet*
Closed *zu/geschlossen*
Service Counter *Theke*
Till *Kasse*
Youth Hostel *Jugendherberge*
Rooms to Let *Fremdenzimmer/ Zimmer frei*
No Smoking *Rauchen Verboten*
Police *Polizei*
Telephone *Telefon*
Toilets *WC/Toiletten*
Ladies *Damen*
Gents *Herren*
Customs *Zoll*
Guesthouse *Pension*
Railway Station *Bahnhof*
Main Railway Station *Hauptbahnhof (Hbf)*
Emergency Exit *Notausgang*

Accommodation

I'm looking for ... *Ich suche...*
a hotel *ein Hotel*
a guesthouse *eine Pension*
a youth hostel *eine Jugendherberge*
a camping ground *einen Campingplatz*

Where is a cheap hotel? *Wo findet man ein preiswertes Hotel?*

Could you give me the address, please? *Bitte könnten Sie (könntest du) mir die Addresse geben?*

Do you have a room available? *Haben Sie ein Zimmer frei?*
How much is it per night/person? *Wieviel kostet es pro Nacht/Person?*
May I see it? *Darf ich es sehen?*
Where is the bathroom? *Wo ist das Badezimmer?*
It is very noisy/dirty/expensive. *Es ist sehr laut/dreckig/teuer.*
I'd like to book (a) ... *Ich möchte ... reservieren.*

bed *ein Bett*
cheap room *ein preiswertes Zimmer*
single room *ein Einzelzimmer*
double room *ein Doppelzimmer*
room with two beds *ein Zimmer mit zwei Betten*
room with shower and toilet *ein Zimmer mit Dusche und WC*
dormitory bed *ein Bett im Schlafsaal*
for one night *für eine Nacht*
for two nights *für zwei Nächte*

I am/We are leaving today. *Heute verlasse ich/verlassen wir das Zimmer.*

Food & Drink

breakfast *Frühstuck*
lunch *Mittagessen*
dinner *Abendessen*
menu *Speisekarte*
restaurant *Gaststätte/Restaurant*
pub/bar *Kneipe*
supermarket *Supermarkt*
snack bar *Imbiss*

I'm a vegetarian. *Ich bin Vegetarier(in).*

I'd like something to drink, please. *Ich möchte etwas zu trinken, bitte.*
It tasted very good. *Es hat mir sehr geschmeckt.*

I'd like to pay/have the bill, please?	*Ich möchte bezahlen/ die Rechnung, bitte.*
Please keep the change.	*Das stimmt so.* (literally: that's OK as is)

Shopping

I'd like to buy ...	*Ich möchte ... kaufen*
How much does that cost?	*Wieviel kostet das?*
I don't like it.	*Es gefällt mir nicht.*
Can I see it?	*Könnte ich es anschauen?*
I'm just looking.	*Ich schaue nur.*
It's too expensive for me.	*Es ist mir zu teuer.*
Can I pay with a credit card?	*Kann ich mit einer Kreditkarte bezahlen?*
department store	*Kaufhaus*
bookshop	*Buchladen*
chemist/pharmacy (for medicine)	*Apotheke*
chemist/pharmacy (for toiletries etc)	*Drogerie*
laundry	*Wäscherei*
more	*mehr*
less	*weniger*
smaller	*kleiner*
bigger	*grösser*

Times & Dates

What time is it?	*Wie spät ist es?*
It is (10) o'clock	*es ist (zehn) Uhr*
in the morning	*morgens/vormittags*
in the afternoon	*nachmittags*
in the evening	*abends*
at night	*nachts*
It is half past nine.	*Es ist halb zehn.*
When?	*wann?*
today	*heute*
yesterday	*gestern*
Monday	*Montag*
Tuesday	*Dienstag*
Wednesday	*Mittwoch*
Thursday	*Donnerstag*
Friday	*Freitag*
Saturday	*Samstag/Sonnabend*
Sunday	*Sonntag*
January	*Januar*
February	*Februar*
March	*März*
April	*April*
May	*Mai*
June	*Juni*
July	*Juli*
August	*August*
September	*September*
October	*Oktober*
November	*November*
December	*Dezember*

1	*eins*
2	*zwei /zwo*
3	*drei*
4	*vier*
5	*fünf*
6	sechs
7	*sieben*
8	*acht*
9	*neun*
10	*zehn*
11	*elf*
12	*zwölf*
13	*dreizehn*
14	*vierzehn*
15	*fünfzehn*
16	*sechzehn*
17	*siebzehn*
18	*achtzehn*
19	*neunzehn*
20	*zwanzig*
21	*einundzwanzig*
22	*zweiundzwanzig*
30	*dreissig*
40	*vierzig*
50	*fünfzig*
60	*sechzig*
70	*siebzig*
80	*achtzig*
90	*neunzig*
100	*einhundert*
1000	*eintausend*
10,000	*zehntausend*
100,000	*hunderttausend*

one million *eine Million*

Health

I am ill.	*Ich bin krank.*
I feel nauseous.	*Mir ist übel.*
It hurts here.	*Es tut hier weh.*
I need a doctor.	*Ich brauche einen Arzt.*
Where is a hospital?	*Wo ist ein Krankenhaus?*
I'm diabetic/epileptic/asthmatic.	*Ich bin Diabetiker/ Epileptiker/ Asthmatiker.*
I'm allergic to antibiotics/penicillin.	*Ich bin allergisch auf Antibiotika/ Penizillin.*
I'm pregnant.	*Ich bin schwanger.*

antiseptic	*Antiseptikum*
aspirin	*Aspirin*
condoms	*Kondome*
the pill	*die Pille*
contraceptive	*Verhütungsmittel*
diarrhoea	*Durchfall*
medicine	*Medikament*
sunblock cream	*Sonnencreme*
tampons	*Tampons*

Emergencies

Help!	*Hilfe!*
Call a doctor!	*Rufen Sie einen Arzt!*
Call the police!	*Rufen Sie die Polizei!*
Leave me in peace.	*Lassen Sie mich in Ruhe.* (formal)
Get lost!	*Hau ab!* (impolite and informal)
I don't know where I am.	*Ich weiss nicht, wo ich bin.*
Thief!	*Dieb!*
I've been raped/ robbed!	*Ich bin vergewaltigt/ bestohlen worden!*

Facts for the Visitor

PLANNING

When to Go

Any time can be the best time to visit Germany, depending on what you want to do. However, the climate can vary quite a bit according to the location, season and even the year, so it's best to be prepared for all types of weather at all times. The most reliable weather lasts from May to October, coinciding, of course, with the standard tourist season (except for skiing). The shoulder seasons can bring fewer tourists and surprisingly pleasant weather. In April and May, for instance, flowers and fruit trees are in bloom, and the weather can be surprisingly mild. Indian summers that stretch well into the autumn are not uncommon.

Eastern Germany lies in a transition zone between the temperate Atlantic climate of Western Europe and the harsher Continental climate of Eastern Europe, and the two air masses meet here. The mean annual temperature in Berlin is 11°C, the average range of temperatures varying from -1°C in January to 18°C in July. The average annual precipitation for all of Germany is 690mm and there is no special rainy season. The camping season generally runs from May to September though some sites open as early as Easter and close in late October or even November.

If you're keen on winter sports, ski resorts, slopes and cross-country trails in the Alps, Harz Mountains and Black Forest begin operating in (usually late) November and move into full swing after the New Year, closing down again when the snows begin to melt in March.

The Climate section and the Climate Charts in the preceding Facts about the Country chapter explain what to expect and when to expect it.

What Kind of Trip?

Go Solo? Travelling alone is not a problem in Germany; the country is well developed and generally safe. Hostels and camping grounds are good places to meet fellow travellers so even if you're travelling alone, you need never be lonely.

The Getting Around chapter has information on organised tours. See also Tourist Offices later this chapter for a list of German tourist offices abroad.

Move or Stay? 'If this is Tuesday, it must be Munich.' Though often ridiculed, the mad dash that 'does' an entire country the size of Germany in a couple of weeks can have its merits. If you've never visited Germany before, you won't know which areas you'll like, and a quick 'scouting tour' will give an overview of the options. A rail pass that offers unlimited travel within a set period can be the best way to do this.

If you know where you want to go, have found a place you like or have specific interests like hiking or folk culture, the best advice is to stay put for a while, discover some of the lesser known sights, make a few local friends and settle in. It's also cheaper in the long run.

Maps

Locally produced maps of Germany are among the best in the world. Most tourist offices distribute free (but very basic) city maps. Two auto associations, Allgemeiner Deutscher Automobil Club (ADAC) and Automobilclub von Deutschland (AvD), produce excellent road maps. More detailed maps can be obtained at most bookshops. Among the best city maps are made by Falkplan, with a patented folding system, though some people prefer the one-sheet maps published by Hallwag or RV Verlag's EuroCity maps. If you are going to stay for a considerable length of time in any one city, you might invest in a street atlas such as the *Städte Atlas* series published by RV Verlag and available in bookshops and tourist offices everywhere in Germany.

What to Bring

Take along as little as possible; if you forget to bring it, you can buy it in Germany.

In general, standard dress in Germany is very casual, but fairly conservative outside the largest cities. Jeans are generally accepted throughout the country though denim and trainers (sneakers) are banned at certain upmarket discos. Men needn't bother bringing a necktie; it will seldom – if ever – be used except maybe at certain casinos. Layers of clothing are best, as weather can change drastically from region to region and from day to night.

If you plan to stay at hostels, pack or buy a towel and a plastic soap container when you arrive. Bedclothes are almost always provided, though you might want to take along your own sheet bag. You'll sleep easier with a padlock on one of the storage lockers usually provided at hostels.

Other items you might need include a torch (flashlight), an adapter plug for electrical appliances (such as a cup or coil immersion heater to make your own tea or instant coffee), a universal bath/sink plug (a plastic film canister sometimes works), sunglasses, a few clothes pegs and premoistened towelettes or a large cotton handkerchief that you can soak in fountains and use to cool off while touring cities and towns in the warmer months.

SUGGESTED ITINERARIES

Depending on the length of your stay, you may want to see and do the following things:

One week
: Berlin/Potsdam, Munich and an alpine resort like Berchtesgaden

Two weeks
: As for one week, plus Trier, Cologne, Heidelberg, the Rhine Valley, Freiburg and the southern Black Forest

One month
: As for two weeks, plus Aachen, Hamburg, Lübeck, one or two of the North Frisian Islands, Rügen Island, Weimar and Dresden

Two months
: As for one month, plus the Romantic Road, Harz Mountains, Münster, Ahr Valley, Mainz, Worms, Speyer, German Wine Road, Bamberg, Moselle Valley, Erfurt and the Thuringian Forest

HIGHLIGHTS

Castles

With castles of all periods and styles, Germany is a great place to indulge in fairy-tale fantasies. If you're into castles, make sure to visit Heidelberg, Neuschwanstein, Burg Rheinfels on the Rhine River, Burg Eltz on the Moselle, medieval Wartburg Castle in Eisenach, Renaissance Wittenberg Castle, baroque Schloss Moritzburg near Dresden and romantic Wernigerode Castle.

Museums & Galleries

Germany is a museum-lover's dream. Munich has the huge Deutsches Museum, and Frankfurt's Museumsufer (Museum Embankment) has enough museums for any addict. The Dahlem Museum complex in Berlin and the New Masters Gallery in Dresden are among the chief art museums.

Theme Roads

Germany has several scenic theme routes. Car is generally the best way to explore them. Check with the route's tourist office (if there is one) or the regional tourist office for maps and highlights of the route. Theme roads covered in this book include the Romantic Road in Bavaria, the Fairy-Tale Road from Hanau to Bremen, the German Wine Road in the Rhineland-Palatinate, the Black Forest Road and the Vineyard Road in Saxony-Anhalt.

Historic Towns

Time stands still in many parts of Germany, and some of the best towns in which to relive the 'days of yore' include Rothenburg ob der Tauber, Goslar and Regensburg. Meissen and Quedlinburg have a fairy-tale atmosphere, Weimar holds a special place in German culture, and Bamberg and Lübeck are two of Europe's true gems. The old district *(Altstadt)* remains the heart and the highlight of many large cities.

TOURIST OFFICES

Tourism in Germany runs like the train system – very efficiently. Small and large tourist offices are incredibly helpful and well informed. Don't hesitate to make use of their services.

Local Tourist Offices

Germany's national tourist office (Deutsche Zentrale für Tourismus, DZT) has its headquarters at Beethovenstrasse 69, 60325 Frankfurt/Main (☎ 069-974 64 0; fax 069-751 90 3; email www.germany-tourism.de). For local information, the office to head for in cities and towns throughout Germany is the *Verkehrsamt* (tourist office) or, in spa or resort towns, the *Kurverwaltung* (resort administration). These are listed in the Information section of each town.

Tourist Offices Abroad

DZT branch and representative offices abroad include:

Australia
: c/o German-Australian Chamber of Industry & Commerce, PO Box A980, Sydney South, NSW 2000 (☎ 02-9267 8148; fax 02-9267 9035)

Austria
: Schubertring 12, 1010 Vienna (☎ 0222-513 2792; fax 0222-513 2791)

Canada
: 175 Bloor St East, North Tower, Suite 604, Toronto, Ont M4W 3R8 (☎ 416-968 1570; fax 416-968 1986)

France
: 9 Blvd de la Madeleine, 75001 Paris (☎ 01 40 20 01 88; fax 01 40 20 17 00)

Japan
: 7-5-56 Akasaka, Minato-ku, Tokyo 107 (☎ 03-3586 5046; fax 03-3586 5079)

Netherlands
: Hoogoorddreef 76, 1101 BG Amsterdam (☎ 020-697 8066; fax 020-691 2972)

Russia
: c/o Lufthansa German Airlines, Hotel Olympic Penta, Olimpinski Prospekt 18/1, 129 119 Moscow (☎ 095-975 3001; fax 095-975 2383)

South Africa
: c/o Lufthansa German Airlines, 22 Girton Rd, Parktown, Johannesburg 2000 (☎ 011-643 1615; fax 011-484 2750)

Switzerland
: Talstrasse 62, 8001 Zürich (☎ 01-221 1387; 01-212 0175)

UK
: Nightingale House, 65 Curzon St, London W1Y 7PE (☎ 0171-495 0081; fax 0171-495 6129)

USA
: Chanin Building, 122 East 42nd St, 52nd Floor, New York, NY 10168-0072 (☎ 212-661 7200; fax 212-661 7174)
: 401 North Michigan Ave, Suite 2525, Chicago, IL 60611 (☎ 312-644 0723; fax 312-644 0724)
: 11766 Wilshire Blvd, Suite 750, Los Angeles, CA 90025 (☎ 310-575 9799; fax 310-575 1565)

There are also offices in Brussels, Budapest, Chicago, Copenhagen, Helsinki, Hong Kong, Madrid, Mexico City, Milan, Oslo, Prague, São Paulo, Stockholm and Tel Aviv.

VISAS & DOCUMENTS

Passport

Your most important travel document is your passport, which should remain valid until well after your trip. If it's just about to expire, renew it before you go. This may not be easy to do overseas, and some countries insist your passport remain valid for a specified minimum period (usually three months) after your visit.

Applying for or renewing a passport can be an involved process taking from a few days to several months, so don't leave it till the last minute. Bureaucracy usually grinds faster if you do everything in person rather than relying on the mail or agents. First check what is required: passport photos, birth certificate, population register extract, signed statements, exact payment in cash etc.

Australian citizens can apply at post offices, or the passport office in their state capital; Canadians can apply at regional passport offices; New Zealanders can apply at any district office of the Department of Internal Affairs; and US citizens must apply in person (but may usually renew by mail) at a US Passport Agency office or some courthouses and post offices.

Visas

Citizens of Australia, Canada, Israel, Japan, New Zealand, Singapore and the US require only a valid passport (no visa) to enter Germany for stays of up to three months. Citizens of the European Union (EU) and those from certain other European countries including Switzerland and Poland can enter on an official identity card.

Photocopies

The hassles brought on by losing your passport can be considerably reduced if you have a record of its number and issue date, or even better, photocopies of the relevant data pages. A photocopy of your birth certificate can also be useful.

Also add the serial numbers of your travellers' cheques (cross them off as you cash them) and photocopies of your credit cards, airline ticket and other travel documents. Keep all this emergency material separate from your passport, cheques and cash, and leave extra copies with someone you can rely on back home. Add some emergency money, US$50 in cash, say, to this separate stash. If you do lose your passport, notify the police immediately to get a statement, and contact your nearest consulate.

Travel Insurance

You should seriously consider taking out travel insurance. This not only covers you for medical expenses and luggage theft or loss but also for cancellation or delays in your travel arrangements. (You could fall seriously ill two days before departure, for example.) Cover depends on your insurance and type of airline ticket, so ask both your insurer and your ticket-issuing agency to explain where you stand. Ticket loss is also covered by travel insurance.

Paying for your airline ticket with a credit card often provides limited travel accident insurance, and you may be able to reclaim the payment if the operator doesn't deliver. In the UK, for instance, institutions issuing credit cards are required by law to reimburse consumers if a company goes into liquidation and the amount in contention is more than £100. Ask your credit card company what it's prepared to cover.

Driving Licence

If you don't hold a European driving licence and plan to drive in Germany, obtain an International Driving Permit from your local automobile association before you leave – you'll need a passport photo and a valid licence. They are usually inexpensive and valid for one year only. An IDP helps Germans make sense of your unfamiliar local licence (make sure you take that with you, too) and can make life much simpler, especially when hiring cars and motorcycles.

Camping Card International

Your local automobile association can also issue the Camping Card International, which is basically a camping ground ID. Cards are also available from your local camping federation, and sometimes on the spot at camping grounds. They incorporate third-party insurance for damage you may cause, and some camping grounds offer a small discount if you sign in with one.

Hostel Card

You must be a member of a Hostelling International-affiliated organisation in order to stay at hostels run by the Deutsches Jugendherbergswerk (DJH), but it's usually possible to buy a membership when checking in; see Hostels in the Accommodation section for more details. Independent hostels, usually called 'non-DJH hostels' in this guide, don't require a card, but you may be charged less if you have one.

Student & Youth Cards

The most useful of these is the International Student Identity Card (ISIC), a plastic ID-style card with your photograph, which provides discounts on many forms of transport (including airlines and local public transport), cheap or free admission to museums and sights, and cheap meals in some student restaurants.

There is a worldwide industry in fake student cards, and many places now stipulate a maximum age for student discounts or, more simply, they've substituted a 'youth discount' for a 'student discount'. If you're aged under 26 but not a student, you can apply for a GO25 card issued by the Federation of International Youth Travel Organisations (FIYTO) or the Euro<26 card, which go under different names in various countries. Both give much the same discounts and benefits as an ISIC.

All these cards are issued by student unions, hostelling organisations or youth-oriented travel agencies. They do not automatically entitle you to discounts, and some companies and institutions refuse to recognise them altogether, but you won't find out until you flash the card.

Seniors' Cards

Museums and other sights, public swimming pools, spas and some forms of transport such as Deutsche Bahn (DB) may offer discounts to retired people/old-age pensioners/those over 60 (slightly younger for women). Make sure you bring proof of age; that helpful Herr in Hamburg or that friendly Fräulein in Frankfurt – polite to a fault – is not going to believe you're a day over 39.

For a small fee, European nationals aged over 60 can get a Rail Europe Senior Card as an add-on to their national rail senior pass. It entitles the holder to reduced European fares; savings vary according to the route.

EMBASSIES

German Embassies Abroad

German embassies around the world include the following:

Australia
: 119 Empire Circuit, Yarralumla, ACT 2600 (☎ 02-6270 1911)

Austria
: Metternichgasse 3, Vienna 3 (☎ 0222-711 54)

Canada
: 1 Waverley St, Ottawa, Ont K2P 0T8 (☎ 613-232 1101)

France
: 13-15 Ave Franklin Roosevelt, 75008 Paris (☎ 01 53 83 45 00)

Japan
: 5-10, 4-chome, Minami-Azabu, Minato-ki, Tokyo 106 (☎ 03-3473 0151)

Netherlands
: Groot Hertoginnelaan 18-20, 2517 EG The Hague (☎ 070-342 0600)

Russia
: Ul Mosfilmovskaya 56, 119285 Moscow (☎ 095-956 1080)

New Zealand
: 90-92 Hobson St, Wellington (☎ 04-473 6063)

South Africa
: 180 Blackwood St, Arcadia, Pretoria 0083 (☎ 012-344 3854)

Switzerland
: Willadingweg 83, 3006 Bern (☎ 031-359 4111)

UK
: 23 Belgrave Square, London SW1X 8PZ (☎ 0171-824 1300)

USA
: 4645 Reservoir Rd NW, Washington, DC 20007-1998 (☎ 202-298 8140)

Foreign Embassies in Germany

The transferral of the German capital from Bonn to Berlin will begin in earnest from 1998, but until the German Foreign Ministry moves to Berlin the main diplomatic missions will stay in Bonn. The following list includes embassies in or near Bonn, where the telephone area code is ☎ 0228; for embassy branches and consulates in the new capital, see the Berlin chapter.

Albania
: Dürenstrasse 35-37, 53173 Bonn (☎ 351 04 5)

Australia
: Godesberger Allee 105-107, 53175 Bonn (☎ 810 30)

Austria
: Johanniterstrasse 2, 53113 Bonn (☎ 530 06 0)

Bulgaria
: Auf der Hostert 6, 53173 Bonn (☎ 363 06 15)

Canada
: Friedrich-Wilhelm-Strasse 18, 53113 Bonn (☎ 968 0)

China
: Kurfürstenallee 12, 53117 Bonn (☎ 955 97 0)

Croatia
: Rolandstrasse 45, 53179 Bonn (☎ 953 42 0)

Czech Republic
: Ferdinandstrasse 27, 53127 Bonn (☎ 919 70)

France
: An der Marienkapelle 3, 53179 Bonn (☎ 362 03 13 6)

Hungary
: Turmstrasse 30, 53175 Bonn (☎ 371 11 2)

Ireland
: Godesberger Allee 119, 53175 Bonn (☎ 959 29 0)

Israel
: Simrockallee 2, 53173 Bonn (☎ 934 65 00)

Italy
: Karl-Finkelburg-Strasse 51, 53173 Bonn (☎ 822 0)

Japan
Godesberger Allee 102-104, 53175 Bonn (☎ 819 10)
Netherlands
Strässchensweg 10, 53113 Bonn (☎ 530 50)
New Zealand
Bundeskanzlerplatz 2-10, 53113 Bonn (☎ 228 07 0)
Poland
Lindenallee 7, 50968 Cologne (☎ 0221-937 30 0)
Romania
Legionsweg 14, 53117 Bonn (☎ 683 80)
Russia
Waldstrasse 42, 53117 Bonn (☎ 312 07 4)
Slovakia
August-Bier-Strasse 31, 53129 Bonn (☎ 914 55 0)
Slovenia
Siegfriedstrasse 28, 53179 Bonn (☎ 858 03 1)
South Africa
Auf der Hostert 3, 53173 Bonn (☎ 820 10)
Switzerland
Gotenstrasse 156, 53175 Bonn (☎ 810 08 0)
UK
Friedrich-Ebert-Allee 77, 53113 Bonn (☎ 916 70)
Ukraine
Rheinhöhenweg 101, 53424 Remagen (☎ 02228-941 81 2)
USA
Deichmanns Aue 29, 53179 Bonn (☎ 339 1)
Yugoslavia
Schlossallee 5, 53179 Bonn (☎ 344 05 1)

CUSTOMS

Articles that you take to Germany for your personal use may be imported free of duty and tax with some conditions. The usual allowances apply to *duty-free goods* purchased at the airport or on ferries: tobacco (200 cigarettes, 50 cigars, or 250g of loose tobacco), alcohol (one litre of strong liquor or two litres of less than 22% alcohol by volume; two litres of wine), coffee (500g or 200g of extracts), perfume (50g of perfume and 0.25 litres of toilet water) and other products to a value of DM350. Do not confuse these with *duty-paid* items (including alcohol and tobacco) bought at normal shops and supermarkets in another EU country and brought into Germany, where certain goods might be more expensive. Then the allowances are more than generous: 800 cigarettes, 200 cigars, or 1kg of loose tobacco; 10 litres of spirits (more than 22% alcohol by volume), 20 litres of fortified wine or aperitif, 90 litres of wine or 110 litres of beer; petrol reserves of up to 10 litres.

Tobacco products and alcohol may only be brought in by people aged 17 and over; the importation of duty-free coffee, interestingly, is barred to those under 15. There are no currency import restrictions.

MONEY

Costs

The secret to budget travel in Germany is cheap accommodation. Germany has a highly developed network of camping grounds and hostels, some of them quite luxurious, and they're great places to meet people.

Other money-saving strategies include preparing your own meals and avoiding alcohol, using a student card (see the previous Student & Youth Cards section) and buying any of the various rail and public transport passes (see the Getting Around chapter).

Including transport but not private motorised transport, your daily expenses could work out to around US$30 to US$40 a day if you're operating on a rock-bottom budget. This means camping or staying in hostels, eating economically and using a transport pass.

Travelling on a moderate budget, you should be able to manage on US$60 to US$80 a day. This would allow you to stay at cheap hotels, guesthouses or B&Bs. You could afford meals in economical restaurants and even a few beers! Prices have almost reached Western European levels in the cities and towns of eastern Germany, but food and accommodation are generally quite affordable.

Cash

Nothing beats cash for convenience ... or risk. If you lose it, it's gone forever and very few travel insurers will come to your rescue. Those that will, limit the amount to about US$300.

It's still a good idea, though, to bring some local currency in cash, if only to tide you over until you get to an exchange facility or find an automatic teller machine (ATM). The equivalent of, say, US$50 should usually be enough. Remember that banks will always accept paper money but very rarely coins in foreign currencies.

Travellers' Cheques

The main idea of carrying travellers' cheques rather than cash is the protection they offer from theft though their popularity is falling as more travellers – including those on tight budgets – deposit their money in their bank at home and withdraw it as they go along through ATMs.

Travellers' cheques are widely used and accepted in Germany, especially if issued in Deutschmarks. If that's the case, you'll usually get the full amount, though bank branches at borders often charge a small commission, and post offices charge a flat DM6 for each cheque cashed. A commission of up to DM10 (ask first!) is charged every time you change foreign currency into Deutschmarks.

The most widely accepted travellers' cheques are American Express, Thomas Cook and Barclays; all of them have efficient replacement policies. American Express charges no commission on its own cheques, but the exchange rates aren't great if the cheques have to be converted into Deutschmarks.

Credit Cards & ATMs

If you're not familiar with the options, ask your bank to explain the workings and relative merits of credit, credit/debit, debit, charge and cash cards.

Credit cards are not always accepted outside major cities in Germany, but are handy for emergencies. Hotels and restaurants often accept MasterCard, Visa and American Express. German banks prefer Eurocard, which is linked with Access and MasterCard, and in small towns you may have difficulty drawing cash with cards other than those three. Typically, an over-the-counter cash advance against a credit card at major banks costs a flat DM10 per withdrawal, so it's better if you have ATM linkage (check fees and availability of services with your bank before you leave home).

International Transfers

Money sent by telegraphic transfer should reach you within a week; by mail, allow at least two weeks.

Having money sent to Germany is fairly straightforward. American Express' MoneyGram service is a good bet, and transfers to large commercial banks are also easy, although you may have to open an account. For emergencies, Thomas Cook and Western Union offer ready and fast international cash transfers through agent banks such as Postbank or Reisebank, but commissions can be costly. Count on about US$40 for amounts up to US$300 and US$70 for amounts over US$500 but under US$1000.

Guaranteed Cheques

Guaranteed personal cheques are another way of carrying money or obtaining cash. The most popular of these is the Eurocheque. To get Eurocheques, you need a European bank account and a cheque-cashing card; depending on the bank, it takes at least two weeks to apply for the cheques. In Germany Eurocheques are widely accepted (up to DM400 per cheque). Most banks charge a commission of DM4 to DM6 for cash payments on Eurocheques.

Currency

The German Mark, or Deutschmark (DM), usually just called the Mark or D-Mark (pronounced 'day-mark'), consists of 100 Pfennig. Coins include one, two, five, 10 and 50 Pfennigs, as well as DM1, DM2 and DM5. There are banknotes of DM5, DM10, DM20, DM50, DM100, DM200, DM500 and DM1000. Beware of confusing the old DM5 and new DM20 banknotes, which are the same colour and have similar designs, although the DM20 note is larger. Watch out for counterfeit banknotes made on colour photocopy machines!

Currency Exchange
Exchange rates at the time of writing were as follows:

Australia	A$1	=	DM1.24
Austria	AS1	=	DM0.14
Canada	C$1	=	DM1.23
Denmark	Dkr1	=	DM0.26
France	1FF	=	DM0.30
Japan	¥100	=	DM1.41
Netherlands	f1	=	DM0.89
New Zealand	NZ$1	=	DM1.08
South Africa	R1	=	DM0.36
Switzerland	Sfr	=	DM1.23
UK	UK£1	=	DM2.89
USA	US$1	=	DM1.72

Changing Money
The easiest places to change cash in Germany are banks or foreign-exchange counters at airports and train stations, particularly those of the Reisebank.

Post offices often have money-changing facilities as well, and rates for cash – but not for travellers' cheques – tend to be better than at banks. Post offices charge DM2 for cash transactions if the exchanged amount is under DM200 and no fee if it's higher.

Main banks in larger cities have machines outside that exchange more than a dozen different foreign currencies, but they don't give very good rates.

Tipping & Bargaining
Tipping is not widespread in Germany. In restaurants, service *(Bedienung)* is usually included, but it is normal to round up the bill if you're satisfied with the service. Do this as you pay, rather than leaving money on the table. Taxi drivers, too, expect a small tip. A tip of 10% is considered generous and is gratefully received.

Bargaining rarely occurs in Germany, but when paying cash for purchases of more than, say, DM100, you could try asking for *Skonto*, which is a discount of 3%. This doesn't apply to hotel and restaurant bills, however.

Taxes & Refunds
Most German goods and services include a value-added tax (VAT) called *Mehrwertsteuer* (or MwSt) of around 15%. Non-EU residents leaving the EU can have this tax refunded for goods (not services) bought, which is definitely worth it for large purchases.

Check that the shop where you're buying has the necessary Tax-Free Shopping Cheque forms. The shop will issue you a cheque for the amount of VAT to be refunded, which you can have stamped and cash in when leaving the country. The Tax-Free Shopping Cheque, together with the invoices/receipts, must be stamped by German customs as you're leaving the country. You're not allowed to use the items purchased until you're outside the country.

Bus drivers and train conductors aren't likely to want to wait at the border while you're getting your paperwork stamped, so if you're travelling this way, ask the shop (or the tourist office) for the nearest customs authority where you can do this beforehand. If you're flying out, have the paperwork stamped at the airport *before* you check in for your flight (with the exception of Frankfurt airport, where you check in first and then proceed to customs with your luggage). Note that you will have to show the goods. Refunds are made directly at VAT Cash Refund desks at airports, land borders, train stations and ferry terminals. Otherwise, the stamped forms, together with the bills, must be returned to the shop where the goods were bought. The shop will mail the refund, minus costs, to your home address.

Some 17,000 shops, including Germany's biggest department stores, are affiliated with the Tax-Free Shopping Cheque service; they can be identified by a special label on their window reading 'Tax-Free for Tourists'. You can obtain printed information at affiliated shops, some tourist offices, major hotels, airports and harbours.

POST & COMMUNICATIONS
Main post offices in larger cities are usually open from 8 am to 6 pm on weekdays and till

noon on Saturdays. Occasionally there will be a late counter offering limited services to 8 pm, and to 2 pm on Saturday. In major cities, the main post office may also open for an hour on Sunday morning, usually from 11 am to noon. Branch offices in the suburbs or those in small towns and villages close at lunchtime and after 5 or 5.30 pm. You'll often find main post offices located at or near the main train station.

Stamps are available at post offices, though there will often be stamp machines outside the main entrance. Letters sent within Germany usually take only one day for delivery, those addressed to destinations within Europe or to North America four to six days and to Australasia five to seven days. Most post offices also exchange currency and travellers' cheques and are a good place to fall back on when the banks are closed (see the earlier Money section).

Postal Rates

Within Germany and the EU, normal-sized postcards cost DM1, a 20g letter is DM1.10 and a 50g letter is DM2.20. Postcards to North America and Australasia cost DM2.20, a 20g airmail letter is DM3 and a 50g airmail letter is DM4. If the postcard or letter is oversized, there is a significant surcharge, sometimes up to triple the base rate. A parcel up to 2kg within Germany costs DM6.90. Surface-mail parcels up to 2kg within Europe are DM12 and to destinations elsewhere DM15. Airmail parcels up to 2kg cost DM20 within Europe; otherwise it's DM46.

Sending & Receiving Mail

Mail can be sent poste restante to the main post office in most cities. German post offices will hold mail for only two weeks, so plan your drops carefully. Ask those sending you mail to clearly mark the letter or package *Hauptpostlagernd* and to write your name clearly, followed by the address of the post office. Bring your passport or other photo ID when picking up mail. There is no fee for this service.

You can also have mail sent to American Express offices in large cities if you have an American Express card or travellers' cheques. Make sure to include the words 'Client's Mail' somewhere on the envelope. American Express holds mail for 30 days but won't accept registered mail or parcels.

Telephone

Making phone calls in Germany is simple, but rates are extraordinarily high thanks to the monopoly still enjoyed by Deutsche Telecom. You can make phone calls anywhere in the world from pay phones marked 'International'. Many public telephones also receive calls, which can save you money if you have to make a collect call. Somewhere on the phone or in the box/booth will be the notation '*Standort*' (location) plus the number. Tell whoever you're trying to reach to call you back by dialling their international access code plus 49, the area code and that number, and they'll save substantially over paying for reverse charges.

Most public phones in Germany accept only phonecards nowadays, which saves you carrying around a pocketful of change. To avoid frustration, though, it's a good idea to carry both a card and a few coins to cover contingencies. Cards are sold at post offices and occasionally at tourist offices, news kiosks and public transport offices.

Phone cards are available for DM12 and for DM50. When using coins or the DM12 card, call units cost DM0.20; with the DM50 card it's DM0.19 per unit. If you call from a private phone, units cost only DM0.12. If you can, refrain from calling from your hotel room, since you'll often be charged DM0.60 or even DM0.80 per unit. If you're calling home, or someone is willing to call you back, you could just place a short call to give that person the number of the hotel where you can be reached. Also note that, as elsewhere, calls made *to* cellular phones cost a lot more than those to a regular number, though how much more depends on the service used by the cellular-phone owner.

For directory assistance within Germany, dial ☎ 11833. Charges for the call are DM0.96 for the first 30 seconds, then

DM0.12 every 3.8 seconds. For numbers abroad, you must dial ☎ 11834 and will be charged the DM0.96 base price plus an immediate DM0.12 for every 3.8 seconds. If a number starts with 0130, it's toll-free, but these numbers are still rare in Germany.

Telephone Rates Deutsche Telecom has devised an incredibly confusing rate plan divided into zones and time periods. How long you can talk per phone unit depends on where and when you are calling.

For example, a three-minute call from Berlin to Munich made at 3 pm on a weekday costs DM1.80; the same call after 9 pm costs DM0.96. If you're in Cologne and calling Düsseldorf, you pay DM0.72 at 3 pm and DM0.36 after 9 pm for three minutes.

International calls are also subject to zones and time periods. Reduced rates are available after 6 pm and before 8 am to EU countries and between 3 am and 2 pm to the USA and Canada. Calls to Australia and New Zealand cost the same all day.

The length of time you can talk per unit is:

Country	*Standard Rates*	*Reduced Rates*
Australia/NZ	3 seconds	3 seconds
EU countries	7 seconds	9 seconds
USA/Canada	5 seconds	5.46 seconds

In other words, a three-minute call at standard rates to the USA will cost you DM4.32, to the UK DM3 and to Australia DM7.20.

To ring abroad from Germany, dial 00 followed by the country and local area codes and number.

The country code for Germany is 49.

A reverse-charge call (or *R-Gespräch*) from Germany is only possible to a limited number of countries. For calls through the German operator, dial ☎ 0010.

To reach the operator direct in the USA and Canada dial ☎ 0130 followed by ☎ 0010 (AT&T); ☎ 0012 (MCI), ☎ 0013 (Sprint) or ☎ 0014 (Canada).

To Australia, dial ☎ 0130-800 66 1 for the Optus operator and ☎ 0130-800 06 1 for Telstra.

Fax, Telegraph & Email

Most of the main post offices have handy public fax-phones that operate with a phonecard. The regular cost of the call, plus a DM2 service charge, will be deducted from your card if the connection succeeds. Occasionally you will also find public fax-phones in train stations.

Telegrams can be sent through the post office, from many hotels, or by calling ☎ 01131.

Maintaining your Internet connectivity while you are in Germany can be done with a little planning and forethought. Access is becoming easier all the time.

You have a few options. You can take your laptop PC and modem and dial your home country service provider, or take out a local account in the region where you will be spending the most time (there are kits to help you cope with local telephone plugs). For more information, have a look at Lonely Planet's site at www.lonelyplanet.com.

Internet cafés, where you can buy online time and have a coffee, have sprung up all over Germany. Before leaving home, contact your service provider to see if they can offer any specific advice about Germany. See also the Online Services section later in this chapter for useful Germany sites.

BOOKS

Lonely Planet

Lonely Planet's *Central Europe* and *Western Europe* both include a big Germany chapter for those on a grand 'shoestring' tour, in which case the *Central Europe Phrasebook* might also come in handy. Lonely Planet also publishes a *German Phrasebook*.

Guidebooks

Those able to read German will find a seemingly endless choice of guidebooks, many of which focus on just one region. Cultural guidebooks are very popular, and any German speaker with a special interest in architecture and the arts should pick up a copy of *Knaurs Kunstführer*. The German-language *Varta* guide has quite a lot of useful addresses of restaurants and hotels, mostly comprehensible to non-German speakers.

The Michelin *Red Guide* is good for quality hotels and restaurants if you are on a gastronomic tour of Germany.

The DCC *Campingführer, Europa '97* is one of the best annual camping guides on the market, with special entries on environmentally friendly camping grounds and those set in particularly attractive surroundings.

Travel

The Continental Journals, 1798-1820 by Dorothy Wordsworth, sister of William Wordsworth, is a fascinating account of a Continental jaunt. The author keeps track of the party's movements, recording its everyday trials and tribulations from Hamburg to the Black Forest. The book's strength is its descriptions of daily life and towns in the early 19th century; its weakness is a mania in early parts to record prices for *everything*.

A Tramp Abroad by Mark Twain includes chapters on Germany during one of the author's two visits in the 1880s. In his postscript 'The Awful German Language', he wittily vents his spleen on the language. During the visit, a companion was prompted to say, 'Speak in German, Mark – some of these people may understand English', which is more or less the tone of the whole book.

Twilight in Italy and Other Essays by DH Lawrence has a couple of mildly interesting early chapters in which Lawrence wrestles hopelessly with English and German national characteristics before rather preciously describing a near-arrest, all inspired by a 1912 stopover while Lawrence was on his way to Italy.

The Temple by Stephen Spender is an autobiographical novel by one of Britain's most celebrated 20th-century poets. It was reworked from a 1929 draft based on time the author spent in Germany during the Weimar Republic. *European Witness*, by the same author, picks up the threads in 1945, when Spender travelled the Rhine region and the British zone of occupation.

From the same school of writing, *Mr Norris Changes Trains* and *Goodbye to Berlin* by Christopher Isherwood should provide enough for those interested in literary or semi-autobiographical accounts of life in Berlin during the Weimar Republic.

In a German Pension by Katherine Mansfield is a collection of short stories by this New Zealand-born author, whose great skill in extracting meaning out of vignettes makes it a worthwhile read.

History & Politics

The Origins of Modern Germany by Geoffrey Barraclough is an excellent introduction to the complex history of this country. *A History of Modern Germany* by Hajo Holborn is a three-volume work that begins with the 15th century and traces developments up to the division in 1945. *The German Empire 1871-1918* by Hans-Ulrich Wehler is a translation of an authoritative German work on the period from Bismarck to the Weimar Republic. Another highly readable translation is *The History of Germany since 1789* by Golo Mann. *Germany 1866-1945* by Gordon Craig is also worthwhile as a general overview.

The Course of German History by AJP Taylor outlines developments since 1815. *Bismarck, the Man and the Statesman* by the same author is a revealing study of the Iron Chancellor placed in historical context. *The Wars of Frederick the Great* by Dennis Showalter focuses on 18th-century Prussia.

Of the books dealing with Martin Luther, *Here I Stand* by Roland Bainton is one of the best. *Young Man Luther* by Eric Erikson focuses on Luther's early development from a psychoanalytical perspective.

The German People and the Reformation by Ronnie Hsia examines the Reformation through the lives of ordinary Germans. Those interested in basing a trip around the life of Luther and his work should try to get hold of *Luther* by Wolfgang Hoffmann, a travel guide translated from German that deals with towns and localities associated with the reformer. It is published by Schmidt-Buch-Verlag.

The Great War, 1914-18 by Marc Ferro is

considered one of the best books on WWI. *The Struggle for Europe* by Chester Wilmot is an interesting account of WWI by a British journalist who was in the thick of things. *German Liberalism and the Dissolution of the Weimar Party System* by Larry E Jones is recommended for those interested in the politics of the 1920s.

Worthwhile books on Hitler include *Hitler: The Führer and the People* by JP Stern, which analyses the reasons why Germans fell for the charms of a maniac, and the classic *Hitler: A Study in Tyranny* by Allan Bullock. *Hitler and Stalin: Parallel Lives* is a related work by this highly respected historian.

The Rise and Fall of the Third Reich by William L Shirer is a very readable history of the Nazi years. *Mothers in the Fatherland: Women, the Family and Nazi Politics* by Claudia Koonz examines women's social conditions between 1933 and 1945. *Inside the Third Reich* by Albert Speer is a memoir by the Nazi henchman who wound up in Berlin's Spandau prison.

The Origins of the Second World War by AJP Taylor is another good work by the well known British historian. *The Longest Day* by Cornelius Ryan is an account of the D-Day landings. *The Desert Fox* by Desmond Young is arguably the best biography of WWII Field Marshal Erwin Rommel.

Jews & the Holocaust *Hitler's Willing Executioners* by Daniel Goldhagen is the best place to start for a detailed analysis of who was responsible for the Holocaust. It raised a storm in Germany in 1996, but both the book and Goldhagen himself emerged favourably from the subsequent historical debate. *The Holocaust* by Martin Gilbert is one of the best general histories on the subject. *The Course of Modern Jewish History* by Howard M Sachar provides an overview of European Jewry from the mid-19th century up to the establishment of the state of Israel. Other works are *A Mosaic of Victims: Non-Jews Persecuted by the Nazis* by Michael Berenbaum and *Justice at Nuremberg* by Robert Conot. *A Train of Powder* by Rebecca West is one of the most informative books on the Nuremberg trials.

Society & Recent History *The Divided Nation* by Mary Fulbrook traces German history from 1918 to reunification. This has also been published as *The Fontana History of Germany 1918-1990*. *Anatomy of a Dictatorship* by the same author focuses on East Germany from 1949 to its collapse in 1989. *The GDR, Moscow's German Ally* by David Childs is another recommendation. Two books dealing with the occupation zones are *The Russians in Germany* by Norman M Naimark, which focuses on the period from 1945 to 1949, and *The American Occupation of Germany: Politics and the Military 1945-49* by John Gimbel. *The Adenauer Era* by Richard Hiscocks examines the period under Germany's postwar political architect. *Hitler's Children* by Jillian Becker is an accessible account of the Red Army faction, telling the story of the Baader-Meinhof group of terrorists.

The Germans by Gordon A Craig is one of the most intelligent books available on German life and an excellent introduction to the country's politics, religion, the Jews, women, academic life and literature, dealt with from a historical perspective. It ends with a chapter on the German language, playing on Mark Twain's ironic contribution. *After the Wall* by Marc Fisher is a less detailed but no less interesting book on German society, with great emphasis on life after the *Wende* (change of 1989). Fisher was bureau chief for the *Washington Post* in Bonn and gives us some perceptive social insights. It is both a professional and personal account.

Germany and the Germans by John Ardagh is similar in tone to Craig's book, and has been revised since reunification; it is highly recommended for anyone interested in finding out how the country and its people tick. *The Rush to German Unity* by Konrad H Jarausch is more academic, mostly focusing on the 1989-90 period and the issue of reunification.

There are several worthwhile books on the

practicalities of life in Germany for those intending to spend a long time in the country. Two very similar works are *Coping with Germany* and *Long Stays in Germany*, both by JAS Abecasis-Phillips. The latter is probably more useful for business travellers, but both include some good tips on avoiding pitfalls.

The *Xenophobe's Guide to the Germans* by Stefan Zeidenitz and Ben Barkow is the irreverent work of two German Anglophiles. The wit might wear thin at times, but beneath this and the book's unashamed stereotyping are some worthwhile tips on Germans and codes of conduct in Germany. Be warned, though – not all Germans will appreciate the humour.

Special Interest

Art *Artists and Revolution: dada and the Bauhaus, 1917-25* by Allan C Greenberg is an informative look at the Bauhaus movement and art in the Weimar Republic. *The Berlin Wall Book* by Hermann Waldenburg is a photographic collection of graffiti on this symbol of the Cold War.

The Nazification of Art: Art, Design, Music, Architecture and Film in the Third Reich by Brandon Taylor is worth dipping into for an overview of the period.

New German Cinema: A History by Thomas Elsaesser covers the area of German films from 1950 to 1980.

Art as History: Episodes in the Culture and Politics of Nineteenth Century Germany by Peter Paret is for more serious art buffs as is *The Classical Centre: Goethe and Weimar, 1775-1832* by TJ Reed.

The Brecht Memoir by Eric Bentley is a reasonable biography of Bertolt Brecht. *Brecht: A Choice of Evils* by Martin Esslin is highly recommended for anyone interested in Brecht and Germany's cultural scene in the 1920s. *Bertolt Brecht: Chaos According to Plan* by John Fuegi focuses on Brecht's methods.

Gastronomy *German Menu Guide and Translator* by Bernard Rivkin will be useful if you intend to tour the culinary scene in a big way. *The Wine Atlas of Germany* by Hugh Johnson and Stuart Pigott is highly recommended for wine buffs. Crammed with maps and information on all German wine regions, it is probably the best book on the subject.

ONLINE SERVICES

There's a bewildering amount of information on all aspects of Germany (culture, institutions etc) on the Internet. Most towns have their own web site. Look via the usual search engines. Most of the sites listed here also provide useful cross links.

Please note that web site addresses, though correct at press time, are particularly prone to change.

www.germany-info.org
: Run by the German Information Center in New York and the German Embassy in Washington, this site is packed with useful general information and links to just about everything, be it language or exchange programmes, German media, the postal-code directory, political foundations, business, law and, of course, travel. In English.

www.webfoot.com/travel/guides/germany/germany.html
: Great site with info about the country, language, cities and even such practical matters as rail passes. In English.

www.germany-tourism.de
: Information on travel in Germany from the German national tourist office. In English.

www.traxxx.de
: One of Germany's largest publishers, Burda, maintains this site. Lots of tips on travel, leisure, events etc. In German.

www.dwelle.de/english
: English news from Deutsche Welle. In English.

www.dino-online.de/seiten/go01t.htm
: German and international phone numbers online. In German.

www.dino-online.de/seiten/go01a.htm
: German addresses online. In German.

www.web.de & www.yahoo.de & www.dino-online.de
: All three are German-language search engines.

www.goethe.de
: Site of the nonprofit Goethe Institute language and cultural centres, with info on German-language courses in Germany and around the world. In English.

NEWSPAPERS & MAGAZINES

German

The most widely read newspapers in Germany, which generally cost DM1 or DM2, are *Die Welt*; the sensationalist *Bild* (actual headline: 'Sex Waves From Space!'); the fine, centrist and respected *Süddeutsche Zeitung* of Munich and the green-leaning *Die Tageszeitung*. The sometimes shockingly politically incorrect *Frankfurter Allgemeine Zeitung* is the voice of Frankfurt.

Germany's most popular magazines are *Der Spiegel*, *Die Zeit* and *Stern*, all of which offer hard-hitting investigative journalism, a certain degree of government criticism, and other deep thoughts between covers often featuring scantily clad models.

English

You'll almost always find English-language newspapers and magazines in the newsstands at major city railway stations, and at a surprising number of ones in smaller towns as well. They are mainly – in fact almost exclusively – from the UK and USA, though in very big cities you'll find papers from all over the world.

The *International Herald Tribune*, edited in Paris with wire stories from the *New York Times* and *Washington Post*, is the most commonly available English-language daily paper; it sells for DM3.50.

The biggies on offer from the UK include *The Independent*, the *Financial Times* and Fleet Street tabloids like the *Daily Mirror* and *The Sun*. From the USA, *USA Today* has made huge inroads, and you'll also sometimes find, for some reason, copies of the conservative *Washington Times*. Copies of the Sunday edition of the *New York Times* are on sale in Frankfurt, Munich and Berlin, but at DM35, they're not exactly moving like hotcakes.

The European and *The Economist* are available in most major cities, as are the international editions of *Time* and *Newsweek*. *Spotlight* is a monthly English-language magazine for Germans who want to learn English, with good feature articles and travel pieces.

MainCity, an excellent English-language monthly magazine (edited by LP author Ryan Ver Berkmoes) and a subsidiary of the *Frankfurter Allgemeine Zeitung*, covers the Main-Rhine region.

RADIO

German

German radio is much like that of many other estern countries; pop, rock, adult contemporary and oldies dominate, with classical and opera offerings at the lower end of the dial. The inevitable Morning Zoo format is in great vogue here, so during commuting time you'll hear several jovial German DJs giggling, honking horns and making fart noises.

English

The BBC World Service (on varying AM and FM wavelengths depending on which part of the country you happen to be in) and National Public Radio (NPR; available via cable channel 22) have radio programmes in English. NPR is also available on AM radio in and around Frankfurt and Berlin. It features the excellent international news programme *Morning Edition* daily from noon to 3 pm.

The American Armed Forces Radio & Television Service (AAFRTS) is available in parts of southern Germany on the AM dial; it offers news broadcasts read by US service people, public-service spots and the American blabbermouth Rush Limbaugh.

TELEVISION

Free to Air

Germany has two national channels: ARD (Erstes Deutsches Fehrnsehen) and ZDF (Zweites Deutsches Fehrnsehen). In addition, there are the 'Dritten Programme', regional stations like the Cologne-based WDR (Westdeutscher Rundfunk) and the Munich-based BR (Bayrischer Rundfunk).

Regional television stations closely echo the political sentiments of the regions they serve. On Bayern 3 you'll be seeing highly conservative programming, on Berlin's Nord3 and on WDR you'll see the most radically left-wing programming available.

WDR produces *Monitor* with Klaus Bednartz, a programme and host so left-wing it's allegedly been censured by the government.

German soap operas are big, with *Lindenstrasse* still about as popular as *Eastenders* was in the UK in the late 1980s.

Reality and chat shows are the latest big movement; a hugely entertaining way to burn off jet-lag is to tune in to *Strassenfeger* (Street Sweeper), a late-night show that puts you in a car racing through the streets of cities around the country. Crime shows aspire to the level of *Tatort* (Scene of the Crime), a well produced programme that follows inspectors investigating crimes in different cities.

Chat shows explore sexual issues in fascinating detail and with surprising forthrightness while maintaining a sober, intellectual approach – a discussion with a panel of men and women discussing the pros and cons of circumcision is a good example of this. But sensationalism has the predominant role, and sometimes 'news' shows border on pornography, especially shows like *Explosiv*, which takes on subjects it claims are at the heart of national debate: penis size, men who have relationships with young girls etc.

Every third German advertisement, it seems, features a naked or partially naked woman, regardless of the product.

Cable

Cable TV is becoming more and more common in Germany, and in addition to the broadcast channels also offers DSF and EuroSport (sport channels), Pro7 and Kabel1 (predominantly American films dubbed into German), news and weather options, and English and other language programming.

English Language There are three main English-language channels on German cable television, and where you are determines what you'll receive. In the former West Germany this is broken up on the lines of the Allied forces division of Germany: in formerly American-controlled territory you'll receive CNN, 24-hour news and information, and NBC SuperChannel, which features business news programming all day, American news magazines and the alleged humour of Jay Leno and Conan O'Brien at night. It also broadcasts NBC Nightly News with Tom Brokaw at 12.30 and 6.30 am.

In 'British' territory you'll receive BBC World, with news and limited entertainment programming and, rarely, SKY News. SKY also rebroadcasts American ABC News with Peter Jennings in the evenings.

VIDEO SYSTEMS

German video and television operates on the PAL (Phase Alternative Line) system that is predominant through much of the world, including the UK and almost all of Europe. It is not compatible with American and Japanese NTSC or French SECAM standards; pre-recorded video tapes bought in countries using those standards won't play in Germany and vice versa. Dual standard VCRs, which play back NTSC and PAL (but only record in PAL) are available in better electronics and duty-free shops; expect to pay somewhere around DM500 for a decent one.

PHOTOGRAPHY & VIDEO

Germany is a photographer's dream, with the Alps in the south, the stark North Sea and Baltic Sea coasts in the north, and countless castles and picturesque old towns.

Film & Equipment

German photographic equipment is among the best in the world and all makes and types are readily available. Print film is widely available at supermarkets and chemists throughout the country. Colour print film has a greater latitude than colour slide film; this means that print film can handle a wider range of light and shadow than slide film. However, slide film, particularly the slower speeds (under 100 ASA), has much better resolution than print film. Like B&W film, the availability of slide film outside major cities is rare or at inflated prices when found.

We found that for sharpness, vivid colour and ease of commercial developing, the best widely available slide film was Fuji Velvia. Unlike Kodachrome, whose developing is easy to screw up and must usually be sent out by developers, Velvia is developed using the standard E-6 process, and it's virtually idiot-proof. And while Kodachrome is certainly fine film when used and developed correctly, there are just more user-friendly types around.

For a roll of 36-exposure standard print film (Kodak Gold or Agfa) expect to pay around DM7. Higher-end film like Fuji Velvia and especially Provia is more difficult to find and generally costs from DM11 to DM13.

You'll pay around DM8 for a standard VHS tape and DM12 for a 60-minute Video 8 tape.

It's worth carrying a spare battery for your camera to avoid disappointment when your camera dies in the middle of that Rhine River cruise. If you're buying a new camera for your trip do so several weeks before you leave and practice using it.

Chemists and supermarkets are good places to get your film processed cheaply. Developing will cost about DM6 for standard developing (two to four days), and about DM24 for one-hour service. If it's dropped off by noon, you can usually pick it up the next day. A roll of 100 ASA 35mm colour film with 24 exposures will cost about DM14 to get processed.

Many 24-hour processing outlets also handle slides. The Porst chain offers specials on developing, as do other chains like Photo Dose.

Photography

When the sun is high in the sky, photographs tend to emphasise shadows and wash out highlights. It's best to take photos during the early morning or the late afternoon when light is softer. This is especially true of landscape photography. Always protect camera lenses with a haze or ultraviolet (UV) filter. At higher altitudes, a UV film may not adequately prevent washed-out photos; a polarised filter can correct this problem and, incidentally, dramatically emphasise cloud formations in mountain and plains landscapes.

Film can be damaged by excessive heat. Don't leave your camera and film in the car on a hot day, and avoid placing your camera on the dash while you are driving.

Frame-filling expanses of snow come out a bit grey unless you deliberately *overexpose* about a half to one stop. Deep cold can play tricks with exposure, so 'bracket' your best pictures with additional shots about one stop under and overexposed.

Video

American-bought video recorders can record with German-bought tapes and then play back with no problems. The size of the tapes are the same, only the method of recording and playback differs between PAL and NTSC standards.

Airport Security

In general, airport X-ray technology doesn't jeopardise lower-speed film (under 1600 ASA), but it's best to carry film and cameras with you and ask the security people to inspect them manually.

TIME

Throughout Germany clocks are set to Central European Time (GMT/UTC plus one hour), the same time zone as Madrid and Warsaw. Daylight-saving time comes into effect at 2 am on the last Sunday in March, when clocks are turned one hour forward. At the end of October they're turned back an hour. Without taking daylight-saving times into account, when it's noon in Berlin, it's: 11 am in London, 6 am in New York, 3 am in San Francisco, 8 pm in Tokyo and 9 pm in Sydney.

In Germany, official times (eg shops, trains, films etc) are usually indicated by the 24-hour clock, eg 6.30 pm is 18.30.

ELECTRICITY

The electric current in Germany is 220V, 50 Hz AC. Plugs are the European type with two round pins. Do not attempt to plug an American appliance into a German outlet without a transformer.

WEIGHTS & MEASURES

Germany uses the metric system – there's a conversion table at the back of this book. Like other Continental Europeans, Germans indicate decimals with commas and thousands with points. Cheese and other food items are often sold by the *Pfund* (pound), which means 500 grams.

LAUNDRY

You'll find a coin-operated laundrette *(Münzwäscherei)* in most cities. Expect to pay about DM5 to DM6 for a basic wash (including soap powder) plus DM1 per 10 minutes for drying; you won't get back much change from DM10 in exchange for a clean, dry load.

The dryers in German laundrettes are cooler than those in the USA or Australia, which means a sopping wet load can take up to an hour to dry. To save time and money, use the extractor. It's the bomb-shaped aluminium device that costs DM0.50. Spread your clothes inside it (making sure to balance the load), close it up and start it. It takes about five minutes to spin vigorously, removing much of the excess water from the clothes and cutting drying time by at least half.

Some camping grounds and a few hostels have washers/dryers for guests' use. If you're staying in a private room, your host might take care of your washing for a fee. Most major hotels provide laundering services for fairly steep fees.

TOILETS

Finding a public lavatory when you need one is not usually a problem in Germany, but you may have to pay anything from DM0.20 to DM1.50 for the convenience. All train stations have toilets, and at some main stations you can even shower for between DM2 and DM10. The standard of hygiene is usually very high, although occasionally toilets can be surprisingly grotty – even in places where you'd least expect it, such as Nuremberg train station or an otherwise pleasant pub. Public toilets also exist in larger parks, pedestrian malls and inner-city shopping areas, where ultra-modern self-cleaning pay toilet pods (with wide automatic doorways that allow easy wheelchair access) are increasingly being installed. Some public toilets are notorious gay hang-outs, such as the large one in Berlin below Alexanderplatz near the World Time Clock.

HEALTH

Germany is a clean and healthy nation, with no particular health concerns, but by all means don't get lulled into a false sense of security. One of the authors picked up a particularly virulent and stubborn case of crabs at a Berlin hostel without – he insists – coming into contact with anything more stimulating than a hostel towel (the hostel has been warned).

No vaccinations are required to visit Germany, except if you're coming from an infected area – a jab against yellow fever is the most likely requirement. If you're going to Germany with stopovers in Asia, Africa or Latin America, check with your travel agent or with the German embassy or consulate nearest you. Tap water is safe to drink everywhere in Germany.

Most major hotels have doctors available. In an emergency, look in the telephone book under *Ärztlicher Notdienst* (emergency medical service). First aid and emergency health care is free for EU citizens with an E111 form; any other form of treatment can be very expensive, so make sure you have travel insurance (see that heading in the previous Visas & Documents section).

WOMEN TRAVELLERS

Women should not encounter particular difficulties while travelling in Germany. The Lübeck-based organisation Frauen gegen Gewalt (☎ 0451-704 64 0), Marlesgrube 9, can offer advice if you are a victim of harassment or violence. Frauenhaus München (☎ 089-354 83 11, 24-hour service ☎ 089-354 83 0) in Munich also offers advice, and Frauennotruf (☎ 089-763 73 7) at Güllstrasse 3 in Munich can counsel victims of assault.

The women's movement is very active in Germany. Most larger cities have women-only cafés, ride and accommodation-sharing services, or cultural organisations just for women such as the Frauenkulturhaus (☎ 089-470 52 12), at Richard-Strauss-Strasse 21 in Munich, or the Frankfurt Frauenkulturhaus (☎ 069-701 01 7) at Industriehof 7-9.

There are also courses tailored specifically for women; see the Courses section.

GAY & LESBIAN TRAVELLERS

Germans are generally fairly tolerant of homosexuality, but gays, who call themselves *Schwule* (formerly a pejorative term equivalent to 'queer' but now a moniker worn with pride and dignity), and lesbians (or *Lesben*) still don't enjoy quite the same social acceptance as in certain other northern European countries. Most progressive are the largest cities, especially Berlin, Cologne and Frankfurt, where the sight of homosexual couples holding hands is not uncommon (kissing in public is rather less common). Larger cities have many gay and lesbian bars as well as other meeting places for homosexuals, such as Berlin's Mann-O-Meter (☎ 030-216 80 08), Motzstrasse 5, Schöneberg, or the Lesben- und Schwulen Zentrum, Mehringdamm 61, Kreuzberg, or in Frankfurt, the Lesbisch-Schwules Kulturhaus (☎ 069-297 72 96) at Klingerstrasse 6.

DISABLED TRAVELLERS

Germany caters well to the needs of disabled travellers, with access ramps for wheelchairs and/or lifts where necessary in public buildings, including toilets (see that heading above), train stations, museums, theatres and cinemas. All InterCity Express (ICE), InterCity/EuroCity (IC/EC), and InterRegio (IR) trains, suburban (S-Bahn) and underground (U-Bahn) trains and ferry services have easy wheelchair access, but stepped entrances to trams and buses remain obstacles.

SENIOR TRAVELLERS

Senior citizens are entitled to discounts in Germany on things like public transport, museum admission fees etc, provided they show proof of their age. In some cases they might need a special pass. See Seniors' Cards in the Visas & Documents section for more information.

TRAVEL WITH CHILDREN

Successful travel with young children requires planning and effort. Don't try to overdo things; even for adults, packing too much into the time available can cause problems. And make sure the activities include the kids as well – balance that day at the Museumsufer in Frankfurt with a visit to the city's wonderful zoo or even the two visitors' terraces at Frankfurt airport, much beloved by children. Include the kids in the trip planning; if they've helped to work out where you are going, they will be much more interested when they get there. Lonely Planet's *Travel with Children* by Maureen Wheeler is a good source of information.

Most car-rental firms in Germany have children's safety seats for hire at a nominal cost, but it is essential that you book them in advance. The same goes for highchairs and cots (cribs); they're standard in most restaurants and hotels, but numbers are limited. The choice of baby food, infant formulas, soy and cow's milk, disposable nappies (diapers) and the like is great in German supermarkets, but the opening hours may be restricted. Run out of nappies on Saturday afternoon and you're facing a very long and messy weekend.

DANGERS & ANNOYANCES

Theft and other crimes against travellers are relatively rare. In the event of problems, the police are helpful and efficient.

Be careful in crowded train stations, where pickpockets are often active. Don't allow anyone to help you put your luggage into a coin locker. Once they've closed the locker, they might switch keys and later come back to pick up your things. Begging for small change is becoming prevalent in crowded city centres.

Africans, Asians and southern Europeans may encounter racial prejudice, especially in eastern Germany where they have been singled out as convenient scapegoats for economic hardship, though the animosity is directed against immigrants, not tourists. People in eastern Germany are becoming used to foreigners, though a few may still feel a bit awkward in your presence. See Dangers & Annoyances in the individual cities and towns for more specific warnings.

In the event of a real emergency, the following are the most important telephone numbers:

Police ☎ 110
Fire/Ambulance ☎ 112
Medical Emergencies/Ambulance ☎ 115

LEGAL MATTERS

The police in Germany are well trained, fairly 'enlightened' and usually treat tourists with respect. Most members of the police force can speak some English, but you may encounter communication problems in remote villages or in eastern Germany.

German law states that you must be able to prove your identity if asked by a police officer, which means you should always carry your passport or a national identity card. A driving licence with a photograph will usually suffice. Carrying a passport, however, may save you a lot of trouble.

Reporting theft to the police in Germany is usually a simple, if occasionally time-consuming, matter. The first thing you will have to do, however, is show your passport or identity card.

If driving in Germany you should carry your driving licence and obey road rules carefully (see Road Rules under Car & Motorcycle in the Getting Around chapter). Penalties for drinking and driving are stiff. The highest permissible blood-alcohol level is 0.08% nationwide. If you are caught exceeding this limit, your licence will be confiscated immediately and a court then decides within three days whether or not you get it back. The same applies if you are involved in an accident with a blood-alcohol level exceeding 0.03%, regardless of whether or not the accident was your fault.

You would have to be extremely unfortunate to lose your driving licence for riding a bicycle while over the limit, but this is theoretically possible. It is probably not a good idea, anyway. More likely are offences such as riding through a pedestrian zone or on a footpath, or crossing an intersection against the red bicycle signal. The 'Greens', one of the more affectionate terms for the police in Germany (based on the colour of their uniforms), take a dim view of cyclists' misdemeanours, and you will receive an on-the-spot fine if caught. It is also illegal to use a bicycle path on the left-hand side of a road (ie against the flow of traffic); the keep-right law applies for cyclists even when the road and bicycle path are separated. Cyclists are not required to wear helmets. As a pedestrian, you will be expected to keep off bike paths.

Penalties for the possession of drugs are generally harsh. Travellers coming from Amsterdam should be aware that German authorities are less liberal in this regard than their Dutch cousins. Despite the abolition of border formalities, customs officers still check passengers on trains. Though treated as a minor offence, the possession of even small quantities of cannabis for personal consumption remains illegal and, if you are caught, entails a court appearance.

German political demonstrations can quickly take on a violent character, especially when the *Autonomen*, a left-wing anarchist group, is involved. It is not uncommon for police to seal off side streets and entire blocks and ask passers-by to prove their identity. If you want to participate in a political demonstration, it is probably a good idea to avoid the hard core of anarchists at the front, some of whom will be masked or possibly armed. You should be aware that you will probably be photographed or filmed by the police.

Every now and again cases of abuse of a public servant crop up, as do rarer cases of highly sensitive citizens going to court over the supposedly derogatory use of the familiar *du* (you) form of address used among friends, relatives and with animals. It is expected that the police address members of the public with the formal *Sie*.

BUSINESS HOURS

Shop trading hours in Germany have recently been extended to 7 am until 8 pm on weekdays, until 4 pm on Saturday, and for a maximum of three hours on Sunday. Larger stores – particularly supermarkets – are expected to take full advantage of this though most smaller shops, with the exception of bakeries, remain shut on the 'Lord's Day'.

Banking hours are generally from 8.30 am to 1 pm and from 2.30 to 4 pm Monday to Friday (many stay open till 5.30 pm on Thursday). Travel agencies and other offices are usually open weekdays from 9 am to 6 pm and on Saturday till noon. Government offices, on the other hand, close for the weekend as early as 1 pm on Friday. Museums are almost universally closed on Monday in Germany; opening hours vary greatly, although many art museums are open late one evening per week.

Restaurants tend to open from 10 am to midnight, with varying closing days. Many of the cheap restaurants are closed on Saturday afternoon and all day Sunday. All shops and banks are closed on public holidays.

PUBLIC HOLIDAYS & SPECIAL EVENTS

National public holidays include: New Year's Day, Good Friday & Easter Monday, May/Labour Day, Ascension Day (40 days after Easter), Whit/Pentecost Monday (May or June), Corpus Christi (10 days after Pentecost), Unification Day (3 October), and Christmas and Boxing/St Stephen's Day. In addition, Epiphany (6 January) is a state holiday in Baden-Württemberg and 20 November is designated Prayer & Repentance Day in Saxony.

There are many festivals, fairs and cultural events throughout the year in Germany. Highlights include the following:

January
: The Carnival *(Fasching)* season before Lent begins with many colourful events in large cities, notably in Cologne, Munich, Düsseldorf and Mainz. The partying peaks on Shrove Tuesday, the day before Ash Wednesday.

February
: International Toy Fair in Nuremberg; International Film Festival in Berlin

March
: Frankfurt Music Fair; Frankfurt Jazz Fair; Thuringian Bach Festival; many spring fairs throughout Germany; Sommergewinn Festival in Eisenach

April
: Stuttgart Jazz Festival; Munich Ballet Days; Mannheim May Fair; Walpurgis Festivals (May Day's Eve in the Harz Mountains)

May
: International Mime Festival in Stuttgart; Red Wine Festival in Rüdesheim; Brahms Festival in Lübeck; Dresden International Dixieland Jazz Festival; Dresden Music Festival (late May/early June)

June
: Moselle Wine Week in Cochem; Händel Festival in Halle; sailing regatta in Kiel; Munich Film Festival; International Theatre Festival in Freiburg

July
: Folk festivals throughout Germany; Munich Opera Festival; Richard Wagner Festival in Bayreuth; German-American Folk Festival in Berlin; Kulmbach Beer Festival; International Music Seminar in Weimar; Love Parade in Berlin; Rheingau Music Festival in Wiesbaden (July/August)

August
: Heidelberg Castle Festival; wine festivals throughout the Rhineland area

September & October
: Munich's Oktoberfest, the world's biggest beer festival; Canstatt Folk Festival in Stuttgart; Berlin Festival of Music & Drama; Frankfurt Book Fair; Bremen Freimarkt; Gewandhaus Festival in Leipzig; Berlin Jazzfest

November
: St Martin's Festival throughout Rhineland and Bavaria

December
: Many Christmas fairs throughout Germany, most famously in Munich, Nuremberg, Berlin, Lübeck, Münster, Stuttgart and Heidelberg

ACTIVITIES

The Germans are outdoors people, which means there are plenty of facilities for visitors in search of active pursuits.

Cycling

Cycling is popular both in cities and the countryside, with over 170 long-distance cycling tracks totalling some 35,000km.

Many routes are marked, and eastern Germany has much to offer cyclists in the way of lightly travelled back roads and a well developed hostel network, especially in the flat, less populated north. Offshore islands, especially the North Frisian group, are tailor-made for pedal-pushers. The eastern Harz is also excellent. If you want to do some rural cycling in one region, pick up a local topographic map and look for the *Forstwege* (forestry tracks), which are often part of the network of hiking tracks. With a compass and a good map, you can completely avoid traffic.

Bicycles can be hired in most towns; see the Getting Around sections of the individual cities and towns. For details on Deutsche Bahn's Fahrrad am Bahnhof (Bike at the Station) network and more tips, see Bicycle in the Getting Around chapter. Always have a good lock for your bike.

Skiing

The German Alps have the most extensive downhill and cross-country skiing in the country, and Garmisch-Partenkirchen is the most popular alpine resort. Those who want to avoid the glitz, glamour and high prices there may want to try the Black Forest or the Harz Mountains, both excellent for cross-country skiing and ski hikes. The compact upper Harz (Hochharz), with its national parks and well developed tourist facilities, is a good region for anyone wishing to undertake a ski hike of several days or more. Full clothing and safety precautions should be taken for ski hikes and a good topographic map is indispensable for anything more than a local loop.

The skiing season generally runs from late November/early December to March. In the shoulder season, discounted ski package weeks are advertised by Weisse Woche (White Week) signs in tourist offices, hotels and ski resorts. Daily ski-lift passes start at around DM30.

All winter resorts have equipment-rental facilities. The lowest daily rate for downhill gear is about DM20; less if you rent gear for longer periods.

Hiking & Mountaineering

Trails crisscross the German countryside, with more than 100,000km of marked trails throughout the country. Popular areas for hiking are the Black Forest, the Harz Mountains, the Bavarian Forest, the so-called Saxon Switzerland area and the Thuringian Forest. The German Alps offer the most inspiring scenery, however, and are the centre of mountaineering in Germany, with some 50 mountain huts available to climbers and walkers.

The Verband Deutscher Gebirgs- und Wandervereine (Federation of German Mountain and Hiking Clubs; ☎ 0681-390 46 50), at Reichsstrasse 4, 66111 Saarbrücken, and the Deutscher Alpenverein (German Alpine Club; ☎ 089-14 00 30) at Von-Kahr-Strasse 2-4, 80997 Munich, are the best sources of information on walking and mountaineering in Germany.

Hikers should always seek information on weather conditions and make sure their footwear, clothing and provisions are adequate for the hike. Always carry water and high-energy food. Although conditions are less extreme in the Central Uplands, you should still be prepared for sudden changes, especially outside the summer months. Weather conditions are particularly changeable in the Alps. It is always advisable to let someone know where you intend to hike.

Thermal Spas & Saunas

Germans love to sweat it out in the sauna, and most public baths *(Stadtbäder)* have sauna facilities, usually with fixed hours for men and women as well as mixed sessions. Prices start from around DM12. Booking in for a regimen of sauna, bath, massage and exercise in a spa resort *(Kurort)* is also popular. Treatments vary according to the qualities of the region. The local spa centre *(Kurzentrum)* or spa administration *(Kurverwaltung)* will have price lists for services. Expect to pay upwards of DM25 for a full massage. Sauna/massage combinations are popular. Services can usually be booked at short notice, and most spa towns have regular activity programmes such as short guided hikes or a programme of music and theatre.

Horse Riding

Anyone with a passion for horse riding will have no trouble finding well equipped *Reiterhöfe* (riding stables) in Germany. Most towns have one, and many riding centres also rent out rooms or holiday flats. Options range from individual lessons for beginners through to dressage, jumping and riding excursions *(Ausritt)*, often in the forest. Prices vary considerably, but adults can expect to pay DM15 to DM35 per hour for excursions. The best place to pick up addresses is from local tourist offices.

Sightseeing Flights & Ballooning

For a real experience, consider the special Lufthansa flights available from some 40 airports around Germany. Flights in these slow, angular 1930s Junker planes, though expensive, give breathtaking views of German towns in a 30-minute circuit. One way to cut the DM275 cost per person is to head to eastern Germany, where flights are only 20 minutes long and cost DM190. Hour-long flights are also available from Lübeck and Munich. All flights must be booked in advance using a booking card. To obtain a timetable/booking card, write or fax Deutsche Lufthansa Stiftung (fax 040-507 06 1), Postfach 630300, 22313 Hamburg. State your preferred flight date, and Lufthansa will inform you of seat availability. A German-language information service is in Hamburg on ☎ 040-507 01 71 7.

Serious balloonists should head straight for the Lüneburger Heide north of Hanover, where they can expect to pay DM400 for a 1½-hour excursion. The central organisation for ballooning is the Deutscher Freiballons-Verband (☎ 0201-208 44), Huyssenallee 87, 45128 Essen.

Steam Trains

Railway enthusiasts will be excited by the wide range of special excursions on old stream trains organised by DB. For more information, ask for the free booklet *Nostalgiezüge* at any large train station in Germany. The eastern Harz has a spectacular network of narrow-gauge lines, popular with enthusiasts and general visitors alike. A permanent steam-train service runs to the Brocken (1142m) and regular steam services operate on other lines. There are also lots of special excursions on trains drawn by historic steam locomotives. For information on timetables and excursions, write, call or fax Harzer Schmalspurbahnen (☎ 03943-558 14 3; fax 03943-558 14 8) at Friedrichstrasse 151, 38855 Wernigerode. Information on services and prices can also be found on the Internet at www.hsb-wr.de.

COURSES

You need pretty good German-language skills for most courses, but you may get by with English on more practical courses such as pottery, sculpture or skiing. If in doubt, contact the course leader; most speak a little English and, where practicable, may be prepared to help you out with rudimentary translations.

The best sources of information are the local or regional tourist offices, particularly in popular resort areas like the Black Forest or German Alps. Newspapers are another good place to look, especially national dailies, or weekly magazines such as *Die Zeit*. The DZT (see the previous Tourist Offices section) can point you in the right direction, but the sheer number and variety means courses are mostly publicised at the regional level.

Courses conducted over several days often include accommodation packages. If that involves sharing, you can usually pay a supplement for a single room. Some institutes may even offer child-care facilities for seminar participants.

Women who can speak German reasonably well might like to enrol in programmes run by the Frauen Gesundheitszentrum. The central contact address is Dachverband der Selbstverwalteten Frauengesundheitszentren (☎ 0551-48 45 30), Goethe Allee 9, 37073 Göttingen. Courses, which are held throughout Germany, range from group information-exchange sessions to formal courses on women's health and health issues.

Foreigners who want to study at a German university do not have to pay more than the standard guild fees and administration fees paid by Germans. However, you will have to take a language-proficiency test, known as the DHS. The only exemptions are if you can show Goethe Institute certificates or have qualified for university entrance at a German school. Information can be obtained from the Deutscher Akademischer Austauschdiest (☎ 0228-88 20; fax 0228-882 44 4), Kennedyallee 50, 53175 Bonn (Postfach 20 04 04, 53134 Bonn if inquiring by post) or contact your nearest German embassy or consulate.

Universities also offer a wide range of summer courses, a few of which are held in English or aimed at foreigners wishing to improve their German. Most courses include accommodation in student hostels. The Deutscher Akademischer Austauschdienst publishes a multilingual *Sommerkurse in Deutschland* booklet with useful course descriptions, locations and prices.

Language

A *Sprachaustausch* (language exchange), whereby you help someone out with English or another language in exchange for German lessons, is an informal way to learn the language and make German friends. University language faculties are the best places to start looking.

Formal language courses are extremely well organised, divided into *Grundstufe* (basic), *Mittelstufe* (intermediate) and *Oberstufe* (advanced) levels, with several degrees of difficulty at each. The Goethe Institute has centres in Berlin, Bonn, Boppard, Bremen, Dresden, Düsseldorf, Frankfurt am Main, Freiburg im Breisgau, Göttingen, Iserlohn, Mannheim, Munich, Murnau, Prien, Rothenburg ob der Tauber, Schwäbisch Hall and Staufen, as well as summer schools in Konstanz and Rosenheim. Intensive eight-week courses start at DM2710 excluding accommodation and meals. The institute also runs three-week summer programmes for children and youths aged 10 to 20 years from DM3050. Course information can be obtained from German embassies or consulates abroad and from branches of the Goethe Institute or its central registration office (☎ 089-15 92 10; fax 089-159 21 450; email: esb@goethe.de), Helene-Weber-Allee 1, 80637 Munich. You can also find information on the Internet at www.goethe.de.

Volkshochschule (VHS; adult education centre) courses are good value and open to everyone. Most reasonably sized towns have their own VHS, which might offer anything from Japanese origami to language courses. The length of courses varies from several hours to several months. Language courses, which usually last three or four months and include an examination and certificate, cost around DM30 per teaching hour. One popular option is to combine au pair work with an evening German course.

Wine

The focus here is on the southern wine-growing regions, especially around the Moselle, Ruwer and Saar rivers. Those doing a grand wine tour will find more than enough to tickle both nose and palate, as well as regional food specialities such as *Sauerbraten* (a marinated, braised beef) around the middle Rhine, game and mushroom dishes from the Nahe region, and Chancellor Helmut Kohl's favourite dish, *Saumagen* (a pork haggis), in Rhineland-Palatinate.

Numerous wine courses are conducted by the Deutsches Weininstitut (German Wine Institute; ☎ 06131-282 90; fax 06131-282 95 0), Gutenbergplatz 3-5, 55116 Mainz (Postfach 1660, 55006 Mainz by post). Your choice of courses will be much greater if you can speak German, but a couple of seminars are held each year in English for tourists during the main tasting season (Easter to October). A typical English-language seminar lasts six days and costs DM2100 per person (single supplement DM250), including tastings, bus and Rhine steamer transportation through the major regions, and all meals, accommodation and lectures. You'll be busy from 8.30 am to about 10 pm.

Those going it alone should pick up the wine institute's pamphlets, called *Vintners to Visit*, which are packed with information in six languages on the wine regions, vineyard practicalities, eating and accommodation facilities. Some vineyards have restaurants that are open all year, others have wine pubs known as a *Besenwirtschaft* or *Strausswirtschaft*, 'broom' or 'wreath' wine pubs identified by a birch broom or wreath above the doorway. The latter, smaller outlets open for a few months each year, often sell traditional snacks to accompany their wine.

WORK

Finding work in Germany is much tougher than it used to be. Gone are the days of the 'economic miracle' when workers could pick and choose jobs in a climate of full employment. Today you have to be well qualified and able to back up your skills with an impressive array of certificates. Germans place great importance on formal qualifications, and the country has a highly trained workforce. On the whole, local qualifications are more highly valued than those gained abroad.

All non-EU citizens who wish to work in Germany require both a work permit *(Arbeitserlaubnis)* and a residency permit *(Aufenthaltserlaubnis)*. Special conditions exist for citizens of so-called 'recognised third countries', including the USA, Canada, Australia, New Zealand, Japan, Israel and Switzerland. Citizens of these countries who have a firm job offer may apply for the necessary permits, providing the job cannot be filled by a German or EU citizen.

You can begin your job search either before leaving home or on arrival in Germany. Once you receive a firm offer, the local employment office *(Arbeitsamt)* checks that the position cannot otherwise be filled, then issues a specific work permit for that position. You will also need to apply for the residency permit from the *Ausländerbehörde* (foreigners' office). EU citizens don't need a work permit, and basically enjoy the same rights as Germans. However, they do need an EU residency permit *(EU-Aufenthaltserlaubnis)* from the local authority.

The same conditions apply for seasonal work such as fruit picking, but Germany has agreements (mostly with its neighbours to the east) allowing citizens of some countries to engage in seasonal jobs for a maximum of three months.

The best places to look for work are local Arbeitsamt offices, which have an electronic data bank (SIS) on vacant positions throughout the country. National newspapers are also a good option, especially the *Frankfurter Allgemeine Zeitung* and *Süddeutsche Zeitung*. It is also possible to find work teaching English at language schools in the large cities, but you will still need work and residency permits, and you should make sure you have valid health-insurance cover at all times. Hospital costs in Germany are astronomical, so it might spare you a lifetime of debt. Many schools will ask you to work on a semi-freelance basis, which means you are entirely responsible for your own social-security payments and health insurance. These secondary costs are high – health insurance for around DM250 per month is quite usual.

You won't get rich teaching English privately to adults or school children, but it might help keep your head above water or prolong a trip. The hourly rate varies dramatically – from a low of DM20 per hour to DM70 for qualified professionals in large cities. Local papers are the best way to advertise, but other good places to start are notice boards at universities and in photocopy shops or even in local supermarkets.

In these days of record postwar unemployment, authorities are cracking down on illegal workers, especially on building sites, where raids are fairly common. You are unlikely to make friends among your German colleagues either, who will see you as a threat to their wage and work conditions.

Busking is always an option in large cities and university towns, but you might find stiff competition from the homeless, and it is often equated with begging.

Work as an au pair is easy to find. *The Au*

Pair and Nanny's Guide to Working Abroad (Vacation Work) by Susan Griffith & Sharon Legg will help. *Work Your Way Around the World*, also by Susan Griffith and published by Vacation Work, is another suggestion. There are numerous approved au pair agencies in Germany and it is hoped that lists will soon be available from German embassies abroad. For more information in Germany itself, enquire at the local Arbeitsamt or *Landesarbeitsämter*, the state head offices of the Arbeitsamt.

Volunteer Work

Voluntary environmental field work is a good way to meet people and do something for the environment as well. The Switzerland-based Bergwald Project, supported by Greenpeace and the WWF Switzerland, is active in reforestation programmes in Germany, Switzerland and Austria, working in conjunction with local foresters. Accommodation is usually in forest huts or tents food is provided, and you pay your own travel costs. Projects usually last one week, and are run almost weekly from spring to autumn. They are very popular, so register several months in advance. The address for information and registration is Bergwald Project (☎ 081-252 41 45; fax 081-252 41 47), Rigastrasse 14, 7000 Chur, Switzerland.

ACCOMMODATION

Accommodation in Germany is generally well organised, though since reunification eastern Germany has been a little short on budget beds; private rooms are one option in these emergencies.

The best quality and value in eastern Germany is in newly renovated hotels, where owners have made an effort to upgrade the standard of rooms and service. Double rooms in such hotels can be especially good value.

Accommodation usually includes breakfast, but not all breakfasts include a boiled egg. If you ask politely, most owners will be happy to cook one for you. In the better hotels you will find elaborate buffet breakfasts. Sometimes breakfast is brought to your room; most times you will have to sit in what are mostly smoky and poorly ventilated breakfast or dining rooms.

A nightly *Kurtax* (resort tax) is charged in recognised resorts and spas. This may be a nominal DM0.50 or a hefty DM5, and is generally not included in the quoted price. If a resort tax is charged, you should receive a resort card *(Kurkarte)*, which usually entitles you to discounts on anything from museum entry to a glass of mineral water from a spa fountain.

Reservations

The DZT associate called ADZ Room Reservation Service (☎ 069-74 07 67; fax 069-75 10 56), Corneliusstrasse 34, 60325 Frankfurt/Main, is a national booking agency. Reservations can also be made through tourist offices – some will require written confirmation – or by calling hotels directly. If making a reservation by telephone, remember to give your name at the start. Always tell the owner what time they can expect you and stick to it or ring again. Many well meaning visitors have lost rooms by turning up late.

Camping

With over 2000 organised sites, camping makes an excellent budget alternative. If camping is to be your main form of accommodation, however, you will probably need your own transport, since sites tend to be far from city centres.

Most camping grounds are open from May to September, but several hundred stay open throughout the year. The range of facilities varies greatly, from the primitive to the over-equipped and serviced. Some camping grounds, especially in eastern Germany, rent out small bungalows. For camping on private property, permission from the landowner is required. Nightly costs in camping grounds vary according to the standard, but DM10 is common for sites. Many then charge around DM7 per person and DM3 for cars. The best overall source of information is the Deutscher Camping Club (☎ 089-380

14 20; fax 089-334 7 37), Mandlstrasse 28, 80802 Munich.

Rental Accommodation

Renting an apartment for a few days or more is a popular form of holiday accommodation in Germany. Tourist offices have lists of *Ferienwohnungen* or *Ferien-Appartements* (holiday flats or apartments). Most have cooking facilities (which means breakfast isn't included) and can be rented both in cities and the country for a minimum period, usually three days. Some guesthouses and hotels also have a couple of apartments, and occasionally owners are willing to rent holiday flats for one night in cities. This can be truly budget accommodation for groups of two to four people. Another place to look for holiday flats is in newspaper classifieds.

Mitwohnzentralen, accommodation finding services, are a good bet for long-term accommodation in cities. These match up visitors to apartments, houses or vacant rooms in shared houses. Rates vary widely, but are invariably lower than in hotels and decrease dramatically with the length of stay. The Verband der Mitwohnzentralen (☎ 089-194 45; fax 089-271 20 19), Georgenstrasse 45, 80799 Munich, is an umbrella association of over 40 such services throughout Germany that can help with long-term needs in major cities.

Private Rooms If you are after a private (or even a hotel) room, head straight for the tourist office and use the room-finding service *(Zimmervermittlung)*. The cost of this service varies from DM3 to DM5, or it may be 'free', in which case the tourist office often takes a commission from the owner. The latter means that in some cases you can rent rooms slightly cheaper by dealing directly with owners. Tourist office staff will usually go out of their way to find something in your price range, although telephone bookings are not always accepted.

Many owners will often enquire about the length of your stay before giving room prices. Generally, the longer you stay, the cheaper the daily room price; if you intend to stay for more than one night, it is always a good idea to say so at the start. In some resort towns, owners are reluctant to let rooms for just one night. It is generally a little more difficult to find singles than doubles, and for use of a double room as a single room *(Einzelbelegung)* you might end up paying 75% of the double-room rate.

In eastern Germany the quality and price of accommodation is less predictable. Tourist offices have often weeded out the absolute hovels, but occasionally you stumble upon unlisted rooms let at exorbitant prices by owners with unrealistic expectations. This can be Dickensian and highly amusing at first when, for example, the owner throws open the door to a crumbling dump and proudly announces, 'The Quedlinburg Room', but the amusement soon wears off.

In the absence of a tourist office, look for signs saying '*Zimmer frei*' (rooms available) or '*Fremdenzimmer*' (tourist rooms) in house or shop windows in many towns.

Farm Stays

Tourist offices can help with rooms or holiday flats on farms. This may be a basic room on a fully fledged farm where 'Junior', waving from the tractor, makes hay while the sun shines, or one holiday flat among many, nominally on a farm, where tourists are the main crop. Bavaria is a popular place for farm stays, but you will find them throughout most of Germany. In parts of eastern Germany and Lower Saxony these are sometimes called *Heu* (hay) hotels. Germany also has lots of riding stables *(Reiterhöfe)*, where horsey types can find accommodation, mostly holiday flats. In the wine-growing regions, it is possible to stay at wine estates. Facilities range from the rustic and simple through to modern hotels where visitors arrive by the coach load.

Hostels

The Deutsches Jugendherbergswerk (DJH; ☎ 05231-740 10; fax 05231-740 14 9, or write to Hauptverband, Postfach 1455, 32704 Detmold) coordinates all affiliated

Hostelling International (HI) hostels in Germany.

With more than 600 hostels throughout the country, Germany's hostel network is arguably the best and most extensive in the world – which is to be expected of the country that pioneered the concept. Almost all hostels in Germany are open all year. Guests must be members of a Hostelling International-affiliated organisation, but it's possible to join the DJH for an annual fee of DM19/32 juniors/ seniors when checking in.

The charge for a dorm bed in a DJH hostel varies from about DM18 to DM30. Camping at a hostel (where permitted) is usually half that price. If you don't have a hostel-approved sheet bag, it usually costs from DM5 to DM7 to hire one (some hostels insist you hire one anyway). Breakfast is always included in the price. Lunch or an evening meal costs between DM5 and DM9.

Theoretically, visitors aged under 27 get preference, but in practice prior booking or arrival time determines who gets the room – not age. In Bavaria, though, the strict maximum age for anyone except group leaders or parents accompanying a child is 26. Check-in hours vary, but you must usually be out by 9 am. You don't need to do chores at the hostels and there are few rules. Most have a night curfew (as early as 10 pm but often midnight) and some are regularly filled with rambunctious German school groups. The DJH's *Jugendgästehäuser* (youth guest-houses) offer some better facilities, freer hours and sometimes good single rooms from DM35.

Germany also has plenty of independent (non-DJH) hostels, especially in large cities. Usually slightly more expensive than member youth hostels, they tend not to have curfews.

Pensions & Guesthouses

Pensions offer the basics of hotel comfort without charging hotel prices. Many of these are private homes somewhat out of the centre of town with several rooms to rent. The worst-case scenario in this category is a wood-panelled attic room that has a permanent smell of scorched chicken or pork, a plump owner whose culinary inspiration was taken from the Teutonic tribes, and a tacky ensemble of furniture procured at the height of the *Wirtschaftswunder* of the 1950s. A single at one of these places should only cost about DM30. Most pensions and guest-houses, though, are perfectly reasonable, if not superior to many hotels, and charge around DM40 to DM60 for a single.

Hotels

Budget hotel rooms can be a bit hard to come by in Germany during summer, although there is usually not much seasonal variation in price. The cheapest hotels only have rooms with shared toilets and showers in the corridor. Prices here don't differ much from those of private rooms. It's increasingly rare to find single rooms with facilities for less than DM45, and most are in the DM50 to DM70 bracket. Doubles work out substantially cheaper – you will find good quality ones in many cities for DM120 or less. Prices are higher in larger centres such as Berlin, Frankfurt, Hamburg and Munich.

Expensive hotels in Germany provide few advantages for their up-market prices. The best time to splurge on them is on weekends or during a lull in trade-fair and conference activity, when you can sometimes take advantage of a package deal or special discounts. Top-end hotels really only come into their own when they have sauna and gym facilities. Otherwise, you would be better off sticking to quality medium-priced hotels. The sky is the limit for big-city splurges in Germany; of course, luxury comes at a cheaper price in rural areas. Spa towns are a good place to go the whole hog as you can also splash out on massages.

FOOD

Germans are hearty eaters. But while this is truly meat-and-potatoes country, vegetarian and health-conscious restaurants are beginning to sprout up. Restaurants always display their menus outside with prices, but watch for daily specials listed on black-boards. Beware of early closing hours, and of the dreaded *Ruhetag* (rest day) at some establishments.

At home Germans might eat their heaviest meal at lunchtime and then have lighter evening fare *(Abendbrot* or *Abendessen*, consisting of cheeses and bread). That's not to say that dinner in the evening isn't important; especially in business, it's a full meal, and going out to dinner in large cities on Friday and Saturday night can get crowded, so it's best to book ahead.

Paying & Tipping

Everywhere but in Stehcafés (stand-up cafés) and at snack bars, bills are paid directly at the table and waiters carry a large leather change purse. They'll present you with a written bill and state the amount. Tipping is not necessary – serving staff are well paid in Germany and a service charge is almost always included – but, if you're happy with the service, you might round up the bill as you're paying to the nearest Deutschmark. To add a tip, tell the server the total amount you're paying, not the amount of the gratuity (eg to give a DM1 tip on a DM59 bill, tell the waiter '*Sechzig Mark, bitte.*'

Meals

Breakfast A good German breakfast *(Frühstück)* usually includes bread rolls, butter, jam, cheese, several sliced meats, a boiled egg and coffee or tea. Most hotels and hostels and even some camp sites include a buffet breakfast as part of the cost of a night's stay, or indicate what part of the hotel bill is for the breakfast. Buffets, in hotels and restaurants that have them, offer all of the above with the addition, in the better ones, of yoghurt, quark, and fresh or canned (or both) fruit salads.

If your hotel doesn't serve breakfast or you arrive in the morning, your best bets are bakeries with Stehcafés, designer restaurants that feature breakfast buffets, and, if all else fails, McDonald's.

Lunch Lunch *(Mittagessen)* is traditionally the main meal of the day. Getting a main meal in the evening is never a problem, but you may find that the dish or menu of the day only applies to lunch.

In larger cities, many restaurants offer lunch specials, usually a main course, salad or soup or an appetiser and sometimes a drink as well, for a fixed price. These are especially prevalent in Chinese restaurants throughout the country and in many restaurants in business centres like Frankfurt. In many places, these are offered by top-end restaurants trying to increase their lunchtime turnover, and have the same menu as at dinnertime at a third or half off.

Dinner There are no surprises here. Restaurants serve dinner (Adendessen) from about 4 pm to about 11 pm. Restaurant prices are highest at dinnertime.

Eating Out

Restaurants German restaurants can be formal places, with uniformed waiters, full menus, tablecloths and better service. And higher prices. Many town halls have an atmospheric restaurant, or *Ratskeller*, in the basement, serving traditional German dishes, but in our research we found that with few exceptions, these are usually the most expensive in town, and generally the ones with the worst food. If you're fine with paying for atmosphere, great, but if you like your food, check carefully.

Gaststätte A *Gaststätte* is somewhat less formal than a restaurant, though they'll have a large menu, daily specials and perhaps a beer garden attached out front or back.

Wine & Beer Cellars A *Weinkeller* or *Bierkeller* is, literally, a cellar serving wine or beer. But many small bistros call themselves this as well, and generally they're nice places to have a glass of either wine or beer and a light meal.

Cafés & Bars Much of German social life revolves around these institutions, which are often hard to separate as both coffee and alcohol are usually served. They're great places to meet local people without spending too much money – you can sit for hours mulling over your cup of coffee or beer. Note that almost every café is shrouded in cigarette smoke.

A wonderful German invention is the quick-and-cheap Stehcafé, a stand-up café where you indulge that sinful European habit of coffee and cakes – without spending too much time and money doing so.

Street Stalls & Fast Food Chains You can get a quick feed at any stand-up food stall *(Schnellimbiss* or simply *Imbiss)* throughout the country. There are almost always Imbisse in railway stations and, in the east, around the centre of town. The food is usually quite reasonable and filling, ranging from doner kebabs to traditional German sausages with beer.

Doner kebab, a sandwich made from slices of roasted beef or lamb on pitta bread with onions, tomato, tahini and spices, is a popular fast food throughout Germany. It usually costs between DM5 and DM6.

Almost all places that do doner will accommodate vegetarians by making a vegetarian version, and almost all sell salads as well, from DM3.50 to DM7. Salads and some sandwiches are covered with tzatziki, a Greek-style garlic, cucumber and yoghurt sauce (the Turkish version is called *cacik*).

Other street offerings include small square slices of pizza (DM3 to DM5), sausage (DM1 to DM3), simple sandwiches (a ham sandwich in Germany is likely to contain bread and ham, *maybe* butter but usually nothing else; from DM2 to DM5) and, in the north, herring and other pickled fish.

Nordsee, a fast-food chain with branches throughout the country, serves inexpensive and sometimes even creative seafood, along with beer and wine. Some are stehcafés, some are sit-down restaurants and some are kiosks.

Imbiss stalls and some vans sell excellent roasted chicken (DM4.50 per half).

American-style fast-food restaurants are taking over Germany at a jaunty clip. Offerings include McDonald's, Burger King and Pizza Hut, but for some reason no Taco Bell. The price of burgers at the first two establishments is far higher than in the USA, and the quality is generally not as good. Additionally, you have to pay for ketchup and mayonnaise (up to DM0.50 per serving). Burger King and McDonald's have meat-free vegie burgers at all their German outlets.

Bakeries Bakeries are some of Germany's best features, offering a mind-boggling array of breads, rolls, sweets and snacks, usually very cheaply and always freshly prepared. Some are also Stehcafés, serving coffee, chocolate and cappuccino in addition to their bakery goods.

Chain Bakeries Pfisterbrot is a chain of environmentally friendly bakeries that use brick ovens. Their breads are reduced in price after a certain time in the afternoon.

Müller is perhaps the most ubiquitous national chain; many of its bakeries also have stand-up cafés attached. Each supermarket chain has its own bakery chain attached as well.

Bread & Bread Rolls German bread is arguably the best in the world; there are almost 100 varieties of it, coming in everything from light and crusty French-style baguettes to corkboard-like *Vollkornbrot* that's heavy enough to kill someone with. *Bauernlaib* is a dark, sour brown bread, and *Sonnenblumenbrot* is another sour brown bread covered on the outside with sunflower seeds.

Bread rolls *(Semmeln* in southern Germany, *Brötchen* in the north) also come in dozens of varieties, including those covered in melted cheese *(Käsesemmel)*, nuts and grains (several types), made from whole grain *(Vollkornsemmel)*, covered in sesame seeds *(Sesamsemmel)* or rye rolls covered in caraway seeds *(Kümmelsemmel)*. All are made fresh daily or more often. Müller does freshly baked pretzels every hour or so. Brez'n, the scrummo traditional pretzels covered in rock salt, are available at bakeries throughout the country.

Biscuits & Cakes If you have a sweet tooth, welcome to heaven. Every German bakery offers dozens of types of cakes and biscuits/cookies, pre-sliced and chopped into snack-size pieces that sell for between DM0.50 and DM2. Quark and cream-filled treats topped with fruit and laced with chocolate abound.

Self-Catering

It's very easy and relatively cheap to put together a picnic. Head for the local market or supermarket and stock up on breads, sandwich meats, cheeses, wine and beer. Chains such as PennyMarkt, Aldi and Norma are good places to start, though they may lack a wide range.

City and town markets are a great source of some of the best, freshest and either cheapest or dearest ingredients. In much of the country they're held daily or several times a week, usually in the centre of the city, almost always at the Markt or Marktplatz.

German Cuisine

Sausages Sausage *(Wurst)*, in its hundreds of incarnations, is by far the most popular dish in Germany. It's traditionally served with either sweet *(süss)* or spicy *(scharff)* mustard *(Senf)*, with either sauerkraut or potato salad, and a piece of bread or a *Semmel*.

Regional favourites (found throughout the country but mainly in certain areas) include:

Bratwurst – spiced sausage, found throughout Germany
Weisswurst – veal sausage, found mainly in southern Germany
Bregenwurst – yes, brain sausage, found mainly in Lower Saxony and western Saxony-Anhalt
Blutwurst – blood sausage
Frankfurter – hot-dog type sausage

Side Dishes Main courses in Germany are almost invariably accompanied by a small salad and either *Sauerkraut* (shredded cabbage marinated in white wine vinegar and cooked slowly with apple), *Blaukraut* or *Rotkohl* (much the same but made with red cabbage), or any number of potato dishes, mainly the ubiquitous *Kartoffelsalat* (boiled potatoes mixed with vinegar, chives, spices and sometimes sausage or cucumber).

Potatoes, which feature prominently in German meals, are prepared in countless ways – indeed, there are restaurants throughout the country called Kartoffelhaus (or some variation on the word Kartoffel), which base their entire menu around what most of the world considers to be a side dish.

Potatoes can also come either fried *(Bratkartoffeln)*, mashed *(Kartoffelpüree)*, grated and then fried (the Swiss *Rösti*, known in the USA as hash browns), or as chips/French fries *(Pommes frites)*. A Thuringian speciality is *Klösse*, a ball of mashed and raw potato which is then cooked to produce something like a dumpling. This is similar to the Bavarian *Kartoffelknödel*. In Baden-Württemberg, potatoes are often replaced with *Spätzle*, essentially wide, flat noodles.

Other Specialities See the introductions and Places to Eat sections of each chapter for suggestions on local specialities. Some of the more renowned specialities include:

Schnitzel – Pork, veal or chicken breast pounded flat, coated in egg, dipped in breadcrumbs and pan-fried; is a standard German menu item. Unless otherwise stated, it's pork.
Eisbein – pickled pork knuckles, popular in Berlin
Rippenspeer – spare ribs
Rotwurst – black pudding
Rostbrätl – grilled meat
Sauerbraten – marinated and roasted beef served with a sour cream sauce
Rosthänchen – roast chicken
Putenbrust – turkey breast

Vegetarian Vegetarians are looking for *Vegetarisches Gerichte* on the menu. Note that Germans sometimes won't consider vegetables that are cooked with meat to contain meat and sometimes will offer chicken as an alternative to meat – this whole vegie thing is new here. Vegans have a serious problem, as most salads come with cheese and/or a mayonnaise-based salad dressing. Some 'vegetarian' pizzas contain eggs *(Eier)*. Always ask, and say (for men) '*Ich bin ein*

Vegetarier' or (for women) '*Ich bin ein Vegetarierin*'.

Desserts Germans are keen on rich desserts *(Nachspeise* or *Nachtisch)*. A popular choice is the *Schwarzwälder Kirschtorte* (Black Forest cherry cake), which is one worthwhile tourist trap. Desserts and pastries are often enjoyed during another German tradition, *Kaffee und Kuchen* – the 4 pm coffee break.

Fruit Except, perhaps, for bananas, Germans are modest fruit eaters. However, groceries and markets generally have a broad, if expensive, selection of fruits, which are often air-freighted from as far away as California, South Africa and New Zealand.

The most expensive way to buy fruit is at specialised neighbourhood fruit shops, which have the very finest of everything, and also stock excellent wines and sometimes high-end pasta and other delicacies. Prices are usually twice that of the supermarkets.

Menu Items

A German menu *(Speisekarte)* and daily specials (on the *Tageskarte)* are usually broken up by category; meat, fish, vegetable. Menu vocabulary includes:

Fleisch – Meat
Rindfleisch – Beef
Schweinefleisch – Pork
Lammfleisch – Lamb
Kalbfleisch – Veal
Hackfleisch – Chopped or minced meat
Hähnchen or *Huhn* – Chicken
Schinken – Ham

Fisch – Fish
Forelle – Trout
Dorsch – Cod
Karpfen – Carp
Lachs – Salmon

Wild – Game
Wildschwein – Wild boar
Hirsch – Male deer
Reh – Venison
Kaninchen – Rabbit
Truthahn – Turkey

Geräuchert – Smoked
Gebacken – Baked
Frittiert – Deep-fried
Paniert – Breaded
Gegrillt – Grilled
Gebraten – Pan-fried
Gefüllt – Stuffed
Gekocht – Boiled

DRINKS

Buying drinks can get very expensive in Germany. Be very careful at restaurants and, if you like lots of liquids, make a point of buying your drinks (alcoholic or not) in supermarkets or, even better, in drink shops that specialise in beer and soft drinks.

Almost all bottles in Germany are subject to a deposit *(Pfand)* which varies according to the manufacturer. You get your deposit back when you bring the bottle back to a shop – not necessarily the one that you bought it from.

Nonalcoholic Drinks

Soft drinks are available throughout the country and each region produces its own brand of mineral water. It comes with bubbles *(mit Kohlensäure)* or without *(ohne Kohlensäure)* and lots of variations in between (slightly fizzy, for example, is *wenig Kohlensäure)*. Bottled water costs from DM0.69 to DM1 per 75cl bottle in drink shops, DM1.25 to DM2 in supermarkets and as much as possible in petrol stations and other convenience shops.

Soft drinks, all known as *Limonade*, come in cans *(Dosen)* as everywhere in the world, and in bottles from 33cl to two litres. The only real shock here is *MezzoMix,* a brand name for a type of drink known as *Spezi,* which is cola mixed with sparkling lemonade. *MezzoMix* is the best, made by the Coca-Cola company; all the rest are generic brands. Nonalcoholic beer *(alkoholfreies Bier)* is very good and has become quite popular. Löwenbräu makes a tasty nonalcoholic beer that is frequently served on tap.

Beer

Beer, the national beverage, is one cultural phenomenon that must be adequately explored. The beer is excellent and usually relatively cheap. Each region and brewery has its own distinctive taste and body.

Beer drinking in Germany has its own vocabulary. *Vollbier* is 4% alcohol by volume, *Export* is 5% and *Bockbier* is 6%. *Helles Bier* is light, while *dunkles Bier* is dark. Export is similar to, but much better than, typical international brews, while *Pils* is more bitter. *Alt* is darker and more full-bodied. A speciality is *Weizenbier*, which is made with wheat instead of barley malt and served in a tall, half-litre glass with a slice of lemon.

Eastern Germany's best beers hail from Saxony, especially *Radeberger Pils* from near Dresden and *Wernesgrüner* from the Erzgebirge on the Czech border. *Rostocker Pils* is quite good as well. *Berliner Weisse*, or 'Berlin White', is a foaming, low-alcohol wheat beer sometimes mixed with red or green fruit syrup. The breweries of Cologne produce their own speciality called *Kölsch*, and in Bamberg *Schlenkerla Rauchbier* is smoked to a dark-red colour.

Wine

German wines are exported around the world, and for good reason. They're typically white, light and 'reflect a unique interplay of fruit and acidity' – which is wine-speak for 'relatively sweet'. As with beer, the cheaper wines are almost as cheap as bottled water or soft drink, and quite good. The most popular German wines are the whites, which are generally lower in alcohol (between 8% and 11%) than other European wines.

There's a big difference between cheap *Tafelwein* (table wine) which can be had for as little as DM2.99 per 75cl bottle; *Deutsche Tafelwein* (German table wine), which is still cheap but made entirely from German grapes; and *Qualitätswein*, quality wine, at the top of the heap.

Of the quality wines, Riesling, Müller-Thurgau and Silvaner are the three most celebrated German varietals abroad, but in the country you'll see plenty of other varieties, including Scheurebe, a crossing of Silvaner and Riesling, and Weissburgunder. Each varietal is available in different levels of sweetness and acidity (see Wine Varieties).

Germans usually ask for a *Schoppen* of whatever – a solid wine glass holding 20 or 25cl. A *Weinschorle* or *Spritzer* is white wine mixed with fizzy mineral water. Wine is drunk as an apéritif or with meals.

Regions There are 13 wine-growing regions in Germany. The Rhine and Moselle valleys are the best known, but Franconian labels are also popular, and the vineyard areas of the Saale-Unstrut region in southern Saxony-Anhalt are coming back from a long sleep.

Wine Varieties With typical German breeziness, there are several distinctions in the Qualitätswein category. QbA (*Qualitätswein eines bestimmten Anbaugebietes)* denotes specific regional wines that are put through official tastings.

Qualitätswein mit Prädikat (QmP) are totally natural wines that are broken down into six sub-categories based on the ripeness of the grapes at harvest:

Kabinett – light and relatively low in alcohol
Spätlese – wine from grapes harvested a week after ripening
Auslese – another late harvest, these tend to be sweeter
Beerenauslese – made from individually picked over-ripe grapes
Trockenbeerenauslese – a concentrated sweet wine made from dried and individually picked grapes that are practically raisins
Eiswein – made from grapes that have frozen on the vine.

All levels of German wine up to Beerenauslese can be produced in dry styles, known as *trocken* (dry) or *halbtrocken* (semi-dry). More than 50% of German wine production is now in these drier styles.

If you want to know a whole lot more, a great source is the Deutsches Weininstitut (☎ 06131-282 90; fax 06131-282 95 0), Gutenbergplatz 3-5, 55116 Mainz (Postfach 1660, 55006 Mainz by post) or in the USA, the German Wine Information Bureau

(☎ 212-213 7028), 79 Madison Avenue, New York, NY 10016. Both have publications including the very helpful *Balance of Flavours – German Wine and Food Pairing Guide*.

Other Wines *Sekt* is German sparkling wine. The *Ebbelwei* (or *Ebbelwoi*) of Hesse is a strong apple wine with an earthy flavour, and *Glühwein*, a hot mulled wine drink, is served throughout the country around Christmas. Sweet and easily drinkable, it will sneak up on you, so take it slowly.

Wine Tastings & Tours Tourist offices in all wine-producing regions can give you loads of information on local wine tastings, winery routes and organised tours prepared by them or the local wine-production organisation. The German Wine Information Bureau also distributes free pamphlets called *Vintners to Visit*. For a more organised approach to learning about wines, see the previous Courses section.

Schnapps

Schnaps is the German word for booze – spirits or hard liquor – and it's drunk more as an apéritif or digestive than as a method of getting blotto (though the latter is by no means unheard of). Most German schnapps is made from apples *(Apfelschnaps)*, pears *(Williamsbirne)*, plums *(Pflaumenschnaps*, or, in Bavaria, *Zwetschgengeist)*, or wheat *(Kornschnaps)*. But there are others made from different fruits as well, like *Himbeergeist*, from raspberries. Schnapps is best served at room temperature, tipped back in shots.

Austrians make a superb dark rum called *Stroh Rum* that's available in extremely limited quantities in southern Bavaria. A highly potent firewater, it's absolutely exquisite when tipped into a cup of hot tea on a cold winter day. It's not officially for sale in Bavaria, but some family-owned pubs will sometimes offer it. *Der Gute Pott* is a readily available brand of dark rum.

German digestive liquors have been coming into vogue over the last few years, especially in the USA, where college fraternity parties centre around a tap of *Jägermeister*, a sickly sweet herbal concoction. Each region produces its own type of digestive; each is said to be incredibly healing – and at 45 to 60% alcohol, it had bloody well better be.

ENTERTAINMENT

The German heritage is associated with high culture, and the standard of theatre performances, concerts and operas is among the highest in Europe. Berlin is unrivalled when it comes to concerts and theatre, Dresden is famed for its opera, and Hamburg is now synonymous with the musical *Cats*.

Tickets to all cultural performances – classical music, dance, theatre, cabaret, pretty much anything except films – are almost always available through the local tourist office and at the box office of the venue itself. Except for travelling shows, there's usually no need to reserve far in advance. Student discounts usually apply to all performances.

Cinemas

Films are widely attended in Germany, but foreign films are usually dubbed into German. English-language subtitled options (usually identifiable by the letter-code 'OV', 'OmU' or 'OF') are mostly limited to large cities like Berlin, Munich, Hanover, Hamburg and Frankfurt.

Alternative cinemas – usually called *Kommunales Kino* – are wonderful places to see movies from around the world in their original language, sometimes with German subtitles, but usually not dubbed.

Discos & Clubs

Germany is infamous as the home of techno music, Kraftwerk's *(I Am the Operator of my Pocket Calculator)* neat invention, and discos are hugely popular in larger towns and cities. In many smaller towns, the blaring thud, thud, thud is overpowered by more traditional German meeting places such as cafés and pubs.

Germans are very good at freeing up unorthodox spaces for discos – old city airports, bomb shelters, bank vaults, and, in Ferropolis, a lignite strip coal mine. As in many other places in the world, old places become boring and new places become flash very quickly. Check the Entertainment section in the individual cities and towns for listings guides, which are the best source of what's hot at the moment.

Discos in business hotels are usually filled with suits in complicated eyewear and pastel ties bopping the night away and doing thumbs-up-sign waves on the dance floor.

Generally, admission to discos is between DM5 and DM10. In some cities, like Leipzig and Berlin, there aren't any mandatory closing times, but in most places discos close between 1 and 3 am.

Opera & Classical Music

Most cities in Germany have active musical calendars, featuring either their own or visiting philharmonics and opera companies, and there are many opportunities to hear classical and choral works in churches – particularly in the hometowns of some of the country's most famous sons.

Ballet and opera are usually held in the same venues as classical music performances, though in larger cities like Munich, Frankfurt, Berlin, Leipzig and Dresden they have their own venue.

Theatre

Traditional German theatre is a treat even if you're not following the language, as productions are usually lavish and the acting, well, let's just say it can get very over the top. A treat in larger cities is *Kabarett* (cabaret), usually highly political in nature and sometimes screamingly funny. Also in larger cities, road shows of West End and Broadway musicals – *Rocky Horror Picture Show*, *Evita*, *Cats* etc – pass through regularly.

Rock

Local bands are best heard in bars, beer halls, beer gardens and small arenas. There are frequent big-name rock concerts throughout the country, and there's an energy to German local bands that's absolutely unique. Venues are unpredictable and in many instances as creative as those used for discos – the Olympic Stadium in Munich, a huge tent in Berlin's Tiergarten, the Volkswagen employee car park in Wolfsburg etc. Check each city's Entertainment section for a listing of what's-on magazines.

Jazz

Jazz is big in Germany and most larger cities have dedicated jazz clubs. Check the Entertainment sections of each chapter for more information. Some city tourist offices publish jazz calendars (usually free), showing upcoming performances.

Folk & Traditional Music

Much of the folk and traditional music you're likely to encounter during a trip to Germany is found at Irish pubs, where it's traditionally *Irish*. Most people think of oompah band music as typically German, but it's typically Bavarian; you'll find it at beer gardens throughout the state. In fact, German folk music is played mostly in drinking venues throughout the country, though sometimes there are special performances at theatres and small concert halls.

Pubs & Bars

Pubs and bars are less common in Germany than are beer gardens and cafés, where most casual drinking is done. Beer gardens are outdoor areas, usually in parks or outside castles, where you sit at long wooden tables drinking huge glasses of beer and eating. In many Bavarian beer gardens, you're permitted to bring your own food, but not in other states. Beer garden food is usually things like roast chicken, Wurst and other quick snacks, along with huge pretzels. You'll be required to pay a deposit on the glass.

In all German cities and towns there are *Kneipe* (pubs), which range from absolute dives packed with drunks slugging down rotgut to stylish affairs with good food and drink. You'll usually be able to tell rather quickly which one you're in. There are also standard American-style stand-up bars in most larger cities. While beers are relatively inexpensive, mixed cocktails are outrageously priced – sometimes as high as DM15 or DM20.

SPECTATOR SPORT

Germans are mad about sport, and on the whole they play it well. At the heart of German sporting success are the *Sportvereine*, small, well organised sports associations that are as much social clubs as sports clubs. The idea of the Sportverein dates back to the 19th century, when many were founded to remedy 'unhealthy' industrialisation. Today, around 26 million people, or about one in three Germans, belongs to some sort of sports club.

The GDR usually outshone its larger neighbour West Germany in the Olympic Games, and the rigorous East German system of early talent identification and special training centres paid dividends in national prestige.

Doping, informally sanctioned by some sports clubs, tarnished the image of GDR sport and when East Germany won 12 out of 13 Olympic gold medals in women's swimming events in Montreal in 1976, even good GDR citizens began to harbour doubts. After reunification, many top competitors received suspensions. But even without the doping, a strong sporting tradition had taken hold, and a new generation of eastern Germans, especially swimmers, excels in international competition.

Football

Football *(Fussball)*, or soccer, is by far the most popular sport, and one of Germany's most important football figures was Sepp Herberger; the centenary of his birth was celebrated in 1997. Herberger's great achievement was to coach the West German side to victory against Hungary in the 1954 World Cup in Switzerland, a triumph referred to as 'the miracle of Bern'. The victory, which restored pride to a defeated Germany, was greeted in West Germany by spontaneous public celebrations – no simple matter after WWII. It was West Germany's first real mass celebration as a country, and its significance became embodied in the popular phrase '*Wir sind wieder wer*' ('We're someone again').

West Germany had to wait 20 years to repeat the triumph, this time with a new generation of players under the leadership of Franz Beckenbauer, one of the most technically proficient players the world has seen. Also important for national prestige was the success of the unified German side (this time coached by Franz 'the Kaiser' Beckenbauer) in the 1990 World Cup in Italy.

East Germany was less successful than its larger neighbour, although it seemed to be set for a rosy future when it picked up the European Championship for juniors in 1986. One member of this team, Matthias Sammer, went on to become the first eastern German to play in the unified German team. He has won both the German Footballer of the Year award and the German Championship twice with his team, Borussia Dortmund.

Among other renowned players, Jürgen Klinsmann, who comes from Stuttgart, won accolades in Britain with Tottenham Hotspur, one of his stopovers after Monte Carlo and Italy. As national captain, he led Germany to victory in the 1996 European Championship. At home, he was captain of Bayern-München, the bickering Bavarians often referred to as 'the millionaires' club' because of the high salaries. The club's infighting is one highly entertaining aspect of German football, but not for Klinsmann, who quit the club in 1997 and moved back to Italy.

Some of the best matches are the derbies, such as those between Bayern-München and TSV 1860 Munich, usually held at Munich's Olympic Stadium, or Schalke 04 (from Gelsenkirchen) and Borussia Dortmund. Other first-division teams to watch out for are VfB Stuttgart, VfL Bochum, Bayer Leverkusen, Hamburger SV, Karlsruher SC, Borussia-Mönchengladbach and 1FC Köln. Clubs from eastern Germany have gradually dropped out of the first division, and in 1997 only Hansa Rostock remained.

National League Championship *(Bundesliga)* games are usually played from

Friday to Sunday. The DFB Cup, based on a knockout system and often more exciting, is usually played during the week, as are European Cup play-offs. The season runs from mid-August to June, with a winter break from Christmas to mid-February. Tickets, which can be bought at the grounds or in advance from designated ticket offices locally, cost DM10 to DM20 for *Stehplätze* (standing room places) and around DM30 for cheap seats.

Tennis

Tennis was a minor sport in Germany until a somewhat awkward carrot-top by the name of Boris Becker won Wimbledon in 1985 at 17 years of age and became the youngest player, first unseeded player and first German ever to do so. He won again in 1986 and 1989, and has also picked up the US Open in 1989, and the Australian Open in 1991 and 1996. Becker, who has assumed guru-like qualities over the years – 'Mankind is a creature without foundation'– has consistently failed to win a major tournament on clay, but remains one of tennis' most enthralling champions. Dramatic by nature, he often drives Germans to despair for two sets before releasing the primal Becker scream and turning the tables in the third. Now in the twilight of his career, Becker is gradually assuming a training role with German juniors.

Michael Stich, despite his extraordinary skill, was condemned to the role of the eternal No 2 of German tennis. Not even a win over Becker in the 1991 Wimbledon final could make him Germany's No 1 in the public's eyes. His best year was 1993, when he was ranked second in the world and won the Davis Cup for Germany. Having suffered a string of injuries and failing to win another major title despite final finishes at the French and US Opens, Stich announced his retirement in 1997, aged 28.

Steffi Graf is the most consistently brilliant of all German tennis players. She has ranked number one for longer than any other player in history, man or woman. Graf also holds a special place in history as the only player to achieve the Golden Slam – all four Grand Slam titles and the Olympic gold medal, in 1988.

Less dramatic on court than Becker – German tennis fans had always hoped for a Boris-Steffi marriage – Graf's ability to roll over opponents exposed her to unfair accusations of having made tennis dull.

The same cannot be said of Steffi's off-court activities. Her father, Peter Graf, was imprisoned for tax evasion in 1997, and Graf narrowly escaped charges herself. Perfectionism has taken its toll on Graf physically and psychologically. This merely reinforces her public image as a modern-day symbol of sacrifice, of *Fleiss und Arbeit* (diligence and work).

Thanks largely to the success of Becker and Graf, Germany has become the biggest tennis market in the world, hosting plenty of top tennis tournaments. The men's outdoor season gets under way in Munich in late April, followed by the German Open in Hamburg in early May. The World Team Cup is held in mid-May in Düsseldorf. A grass tournament is then played in Halle in mid-June in preparation for Wimbledon. Then it's back on clay in Stuttgart in mid-July, and indoors for the Grand Slam Cup in Munich in late September. The men's professional tour culminates with the ATP World Championship in early November in Hanover.

Women's tournaments are held in Hanover in mid-February, Hamburg in late April, Berlin in mid-May, Leipzig in late September/early October, and Stuttgart in early October.

The address of the Deutscher Tennis Bund (☎ 040-411 78 0; fax 040-411 78 22 2) is Postfach 13 02 71, 20102 Hamburg.

Athletics

Germany has lots of quality athletics meetings. Locations vary from year to year. The most important indoor event is the Leichtathletik-Hallenmeisterschaft, held in February each year, which is the German qualification for international indoor events that usually follow in May.

Other good events are held annually in

February and March in Chemnitz, Karlsruhe, Stuttgart and nearby Sindelfingen.

The outdoor season runs roughly from May to early September. Its highpoint, the Deutsche-Leichtathletik-Meisterschaften, is reached each year at the end of June, when top athletes compete to represent Germany in the next international championship.

There are also numerous commercial gatherings, usually 'parade events' after the completion of important international championships (usually by late August), two of which (both Grand Prix events) are the Internationales Stadion-Fest in Berlin's Olympic Stadium and ASV Sportfest in Cologne.

For more information on track & field events, contact the Deutscher Leichtathletik-Verband (☎ 06151-770 80; fax 06151-770 81 1), Postfach 11 04 63, 64219 Darmstadt.

Other Spectator Sport

For information on swimming events, contact the Deutscher Schwimm-Verband (☎ 0561-940 83 0; fax 0561-940 83 15) at Korbacher Strasse 93, 34132 Kassel.

Exciting alpine and ski-jumping events are held annually in southern Germany. The top ski-jumping events are held in Oberstdorf in late December and in Garmisch-Partenkirchen on 1 January. The dates and locations of alpine events vary; tourist offices in ski areas are the best sources of information.

Information on equestrian events can be obtained from the Deutsche Reiterliche Vereinigung (☎ 02581-636 20; fax 02581-621 44) Postfach 110265, 48204 Warendorf.

Fans of Michael Schumacher might like to watch the FIA Formula 1 World Championship, normally held in the last week of July at the Hockenheim-Ring near Heidelberg. A motorcycle grand prix is usually held in late May or early June.

A calendar of events is published each year by Hockenheim-Ring (☎ 06205-950 0; fax 06205-950 29 9). The address of the Deutscher Motorsport Verband (☎ 069-695 00 20; fax 069-695 00 22 0) is Otto-Fleck-Schneise 12, 60528 Frankfurt/Main.

THINGS TO BUY

Products made in Germany are high quality but rarely cheap.

Munich is a good place to buy Bavarian traditional dress, which is Germany's most interesting. Much of it is aimed at the children's market, but you will also find a large range of adult wear. It is hard to find a quality adult leather jacket or *Dirndl* (women's dress) for less than DM400. Bavaria is also the place to buy hunting gear, especially if you have a penchant for traditional hunting hats.

Germany excels in optical goods such as binoculars and lenses, and its Leica and Zeiss brands have an excellent reputation worldwide. Beer steins are best bought from breweries or beer halls.

In the Harz Mountains there's a roaring trade in puppets, marionettes, carved wooden figures and embroidered cloth, much of this on the theme of witches. A good wooden marionette witch costs around DM200.

Anyone seeking quality toys should visit Nuremberg, where a tradition of toy manufacture dates back to the 16th century. The city was famous for its wooden dolls with movable limbs, and later for toys made out of tin. It remains a centre for toys, traditional as well as modern plastic, many of which can be found at its Christmas market.

Glassware is another Harz speciality. The Bavarian Forest is famous for its crystal glassware, and Meissen should be a port of call for anyone interested in modern or antique porcelain. The symbol of Meissen porcelain is the crossed swords, and a much imitated local form is the so-called *Einschnitt*, which has distinctive curved rims and rich decorative patterns. Quality antique porcelain designed by Graf Marcolini in the late 18th century has a small star beneath the crossed swords.

Germany produces some fine regional white wines which, due to the cool climate, have a distinctive refreshing acidity. The most famous vineyards are along the Rhine and Moselle rivers, but throughout most of southern Germany you will find places selling vintages from the cellar door (see Wines in the earlier Drinks section).

Other typical shopping items include colourful heraldic emblems, cuckoo clocks from the Black Forest, ships in bottles from coastal towns in northern Germany and the black Prince Heinrich caps, which were *de rigueur* for Chancellor Helmut Schmidt in the 1970s. Therapeutic footwear, such as the sandals and shoes made by Birkenstock and orthopaedic inlays by Scholl, is a niche market where Germany excels. Birkenstock sandals can be picked up at shoe stores from around DM80.

Art reproductions, books and posters are sold in some museums and speciality shops. Also of high quality are illustrated calendars and coffee-table books.

The annual Christmas markets (*Christkindlesmarkt* in Nuremberg, *Weihnachtsmärkte* elsewhere) are good places to pick up presents. Wax candles and ceramic goods are always well represented. Wooden toys and wooden boards (used by Germans for the *Abendbrot* evening meal or breakfast) are other options. The latter come in a variety of shapes and are often sold with names or motifs engraved.

If you are proficient in the language, German paperbacks are cheap, and mini-editions of classics, such as the Reclam series, won't take up much space in your bag. Collectors of antiquarian books will find a large selection in *Antiquariat* bookshops in major centres or university towns. English-language books, except for those used in schools, tend to be overpriced; if you need to stock up on reading material, go to larger second-hand bookshops or shop around before you buy.

Being one of Europe's largest ports, Hamburg has a wide range of goods imported from all over the world – from international wines and teas to carpets and Asian antiques. It is difficult to find real bargains at flea markets, where 1970s junk dominates. But collectors of kitsch will be in their element; records and cassettes can usually be picked up for a couple of Deutschmarks and second-hand souvenirs for much less.

Window shoppers will enjoy Germany's many *Passagen* (arcades), and Berlin's Kaufhaus des Westens (KaDeWe) and Wertheim department stores are well worth a visit for their sheer range of goods.

Getting There & Away

If you live outside of Europe, flying is pretty much the only way to get to Germany. Even if you're already in Europe, a flight may still be the fastest and cheapest option, especially from faraway places like Greece, Spain or southern Italy.

Otherwise, train travel is the most efficient and comfortable option, though buses are a viable, and usually cheaper, alternative from some capital cities. Keep in mind that seats fill up quickly and prices often increase considerably during the summer school holidays.

No matter which way you're travelling to Germany, be sure to take out travel insurance. Depending on the scope of your coverage, this will protect you against sudden medical or legal expenses, luggage theft or loss, personal liability and cancellation or delays in your travel schedule. Before you take out any insurance, be certain that you understand all the ramifications and what to do in case you need to file a claim. Also check your medical policy at home, which may already provide coverage worldwide, in which case you only need to protect yourself against other problems. Buy travel insurance as early as possible. If you buy it the week before you leave you may find, for example, that you are not covered for delays to your trip caused by strikes or industrial action. Some policies also cover ticket loss, so make sure to keep a photocopy of your ticket in a separate place. It's also a good idea to make a copy of your policy, in case the original is lost.

WARNING

This chapter is particularly vulnerable to change – prices for international travel are volatile, routes are introduced or cancelled, schedules change, special deals come and go, and rules and visa requirements are amended. Airlines seem to take a perverse pleasure in making price structures and regulations as complicated as possible. You should check directly with the airline or travel agent to make sure you understand how a fare (and ticket you may buy) works. In addition, the travel industry is highly competitive, with many specials and bonuses. The upshot of this is that you should get opinions, quotes and advice from as many airlines and travel agents as possible before you part with your hard-earned cash. The details given in this chapter should be regarded as pointers; they are not a substitute for careful, up-to-date research. ■

AIR

Airports & Airlines

The main gateways are Frankfurt/Main, Munich and Düsseldorf. Most of the cheaper tickets will get you as far as Frankfurt – the busiest airport in Europe after London's Heathrow – from where you can catch connecting flights to other German cities.

Lufthansa is Germany's premier airline, with services within Germany, Europe and overseas. Its subsidiary Condor does charter flights mainly to holiday destinations in southern Europe.

LTU is an independent charter airline with flights to cities around the world. Eurowings is a regional airline that does primarily short hops from major European cities to regional and international airports in Germany. It's also a feeder airline for KLM, Northwest Airlines and Air France.

One major domestic competitor for Lufthansa is Deutsche BA, a subsidiary of British Airways.

Buying Tickets

If you're flying to Germany from outside Europe, the plane ticket will probably be the single most expensive item in your budget, and buying it can be an intimidating business. There is likely to be a multitude of airlines and travel agents hoping to separate you from your money, and it is always worth putting aside a few hours to research the current state of the market. Start early: some of the cheapest tickets have to be bought months in advance, and some popular flights sell out early. Ask other travellers for recommendations, look at the ads in newspapers and magazines (including those catering specifically for the German community in your country), consult reference books and watch for special offers. Then phone several agents for bargains. Find out the fare, the route, how long the ticket is valid and any restrictions on the ticket.

Cheap tickets are available in two distinct categories: official and unofficial. Official ones have a variety of names including advance purchase tickets, advance purchase excursion (Apex) fares, super-Apex and simply budget fares. Unofficial discount tickets are released by the airlines through selected travel agents, and it is worth shopping around to find them. If you call the airlines directly, they may not quote you the cheapest fares available, except perhaps if there's an airfare war on between competing airlines. In most cases, return tickets work out cheaper than two one-way tickets.

If you are flying to Germany from the UK, USA or South-East Asia, you may find that the cheapest flights are being advertised by obscure agencies whose names haven't yet reached the telephone directory. Many such firms are honest and solvent, but there are a few rogues who will take your money and disappear, to reopen elsewhere a month or two later under a new name. If you feel suspicious about a firm, don't give them all the money at once – leave a deposit of 20% or so and pay the balance when you get the ticket. If they insist on cash in advance, go somewhere else or be prepared to take a big risk. And once you have the ticket, ring the airline to confirm that you are actually booked onto the flight.

You may decide to pay more than the rock-bottom fare in favour of the safety of a better-known travel agent. Firms such as STA Travel and Council Travel with offices worldwide, Travel CUTS in Canada and Flight Centre in Australia are not going to disappear overnight, leaving you clutching a receipt for a nonexistent ticket.

Once you have your ticket, make a photocopy or at least write down its number, the flight number and other relevant details, and keep the information somewhere separate. If the ticket is lost or stolen, this will help you get a replacement.

Round-the-world (RTW) tickets are often real bargains, and can work out to be no more expensive – or even cheaper – than an ordinary return ticket. Official airline RTW tickets are usually put together by a combination of two or more airlines and permit you to fly anywhere you want on their route systems so long as you do not backtrack. Other restrictions are that you (usually) must book the first sector in advance (cancellation penalties then apply). There may be restrictions on how many stops (or miles/km) you are permitted. Usually the tickets are valid for 90 days up to a year from the date of the first outbound flight. Prices start at about UK£1000/US$1500/A$1800, depending on the season and length of validity. An alternative type of RTW ticket is one put together by a travel agent using a combination of discounted tickets. These can be much cheaper than the official ones but usually carry a lot of restrictions.

Travellers with Special Needs

If you have special needs of any sort – you're vegetarian or require a special diet, you're travelling in a wheelchair, taking the baby, terrified of flying, whatever – let the airline know as soon as possible so that they can make the necessary arrangements. Remind them when you reconfirm your booking (at least 72 hours before departure) and again when you check in at the airport. It may also be worth ringing around the airlines before you make your booking to find out how they can handle your particular needs.

Airports and airlines can be surprisingly helpful, but they do need advance warning. Most international airports will provide escorts from check-in desk to plane where needed, and there should be ramps, lifts, accessible toilets and reachable phones. Aircraft toilets, on the other hand, are likely to present a problem; travellers should discuss

Air Travel Glossary

Apex Tickets Apex ('advance purchase excursion') fares are usually between 30 and 40% cheaper than full economy ones, but there are restrictions. You must purchase the ticket at least 21 days (sometimes more) in advance, be away for a minimum period (normally 14 days) and return within a maximum period (90 or 180 days). Stopovers are not allowed, and if you have to change your travel dates or routing, there will be extra charges. These tickets are not fully refundable; if you cancel your trip, the refund is often considerably less than what you paid for the ticket. Take out travel insurance to cover yourself in case you have to call off your trip unexpectedly (eg due to illness).

Baggage Allowance This will be written on your ticket; you are usually allowed one item weighing 20kg to go in the hold, plus one item of hand luggage. Many airlines flying transatlantic routes allow for two pieces of luggage with relatively generous limits on their dimensions and weight.

Bucket Shops At certain times of the year and/or on certain routes, many airlines fly with empty seats. This isn't profitable (or good PR) and it's often more cost-effective for them to fly full, even if that means having to sell a certain number of drastically discounted tickets. They do this by off-loading them onto bucket shops (or consolidators), travel agents who specialise in such discounted fares. The agents, in turn, sell them to the public at reduced prices. These tickets are often the cheapest you'll find, but you usually can't purchase them directly from the airlines, restrictions abound and long-haul journeys can be extremely time-consuming, with several stops along the way. Availability varies widely, so you'll not only have to be flexible in your travel plans, you'll also have to be quick off the mark as soon as an advertisement appears in the press.

Bucket-shop agents advertise in newspapers and magazines, and there's a lot of competition – especially in places like Amsterdam, London and Hong Kong. It's always a good idea to telephone first to ascertain availability before rushing to some out-of-the-way shop. Naturally, they advertise the cheapest available tickets, but by the time you get there, these may be sold out (or were nonexistent in the first place), and you may be looking at something more expensive.

Bumping Having a confirmed seat doesn't mean you're going to get on the plane (see Overbooking).

Cancellation Penalties If you have to cancel or change an Apex or other discounted ticket, there may be heavy penalties involved; travel insurance can sometimes be taken out against these penalties. Some airlines now impose penalties on regular tickets as well, particularly against 'no show' passengers.

Check In Airlines ask you to check in a certain time ahead of the flight departure (usually two hours on international flights but longer on particularly security-conscious ones like El Al, the Israeli carrier). If you fail to check in on time and the flight is overbooked, the airline can cancel your reservation and give your seat to somebody else.

Confirmation Having a ticket written out with the flight and date on it doesn't mean you have a seat until the agent has confirmed with the airline that your status is 'OK' and has written or stamped that on your ticket. Prior to this confirmation, your status is 'on request'.

Courier Fares Businesses often send their urgent documents or freight through courier companies. These companies hire people to accompany the package through customs and, in return, offer cheap tickets that used to be phenomenal bargains but nowadays are just like decent discounted fares. In effect, what the courier companies do is ship their goods as your luggage on regular commercial flights; you are usually only allowed carry-on. This is a legitimate operation – all freight is completely legal. There are two drawbacks, however: the short turnaround time of the ticket (usually not longer than a month) and the limitation on your baggage allowance.

Discounted Tickets There are two types of discounted fares: officially discounted (such as Apex) ones and unofficially discounted tickets (see Bucket Shops). The latter can save you more than money – you may be able to pay Apex prices without the associated advance-purchase and other requirements. The lowest prices often impose drawbacks, such as flying with unpopular airlines, inconvenient schedules, or unpleasant routings and connections.

Economy Class Economy-class tickets are usually not the cheapest way to go, but they do give you maximum flexibility and they are valid for 12 months. If you don't use them, most are fully refundable, as are unused sectors of a multiple ticket.

Full Fares Airlines traditionally offer first class (coded F), business class (coded J) and economy class (coded Y) tickets. These days there are so many promotional and discounted fares available that the only passengers paying full fare are on expense accounts or at the gate and in a hurry.

Lost Tickets If you lose your ticket, an airline will usually treat it like a travellers' cheque and, after enquiries, issue you with a replacement. Legally, however, an airline is entitled to treat it like cash, so a loss could be permanent. Consider them as valuables.

MCO An MCO (Miscellaneous Charges Order) is a voucher for a given amount, usually issued by an airline as a refund or against a lost ticket. It can be used to pay for a flight with any IATA (International Air Transport Association) airline. MCOs, which are more flexible than a regular ticket, may satisfy the irritating onward ticket requirement, but some countries are now reluctant to accept them.

Open-Jaw Tickets These are return tickets that allow you to fly to one place but return from another, and travel between the two 'jaws' by any means of transport at your own expense. If available, this can save you backtracking to your arrival point.

Overbooking Airlines hate to fly with empty seats, and since every flight has some passengers who fail to show up, they often book more passengers than there are seats available. Usually the excess passengers balance those who fail to show up, but occasionally somebody gets bumped – usually the last passenger(s) to check in.

Promotional Fares These are officially discounted fares, such as Apex ones, which are available from travel agents or direct from the airline.

Reconfirmation If you break your journey, you must contact the airline at least 72 hours prior to departure of the ongoing flight to 'reconfirm' that you intend to fly. If you don't do this, the airline is entitled to delete your name from the passenger list.

Restrictions Discounted tickets often have various constraints placed on them, such as advance purchase, limitations on the minimum and maximum period you must be away, restrictions on breaking the journey or changing the booking or routing etc.

Round-the-World Tickets These tickets are very popular and basically come in two types: airline RTW tickets and agent (or "tailor-made') RTW tickets. An airline RTW ticket is issued by two or more airlines with reciprocal arrangements and allows you to fly around the world in *one continuous direction* on their combined routes. Other restrictions are that you (usually) must book the first sector in advance and cancellation penalties then apply. There may be restrictions on how many stopovers you are permitted. The RTW tickets are usually valid for from 90 days up to a year.The other type of RTW ticket is a combination of cheap fares strung together by an experienced travel agent. These may be much cheaper than airline RTW tickets, but the choice of routes will be limited.

Standby This is a discounted ticket where you only fly if there is a seat free at the last moment. Standby fares are usually only available directly at the airport, but may sometimes also be handled by an airline's city office. To give yourself the best possible chance of getting on the flight you want, get there early and have your name placed on the waiting list immediately. It's first come, first served.

Student Discounts Some airlines offer student-card holders 15% to 25% off on certain fares. The same often applies to anyone under the age of 26. These discounts are generally only available on normal economy-class fares; you wouldn't get one, for instance, on an Apex or an RTW ticket, since these are already discounted. Take a calculator and do the sums; discounted tickets – both the official and bucket-shop ones – are often better value than student fares.

Tickets Out An entry requirement for many countries is that you have an onward (ie out of the country) ticket. If you're not sure of your travel plans, the easiest solution is to buy the cheapest onward ticket to a neighbouring country or a ticket from a reliable airline that can be refunded later if you do not use it.

Transferred Tickets Airline tickets cannot be transferred from one person to another. Travellers sometimes try to sell the return half of their ticket, but officials can ask you to prove that you are the person named on the ticket. This may not be checked on domestic flights, but on international flights, tickets are usually compared with passports. remember that if you are flying on a transferred ticket and something goes wrong with the flight (hijack, crash), there will be no record of your presence on board.

Travel Periods Some officially discounted fares – Apex fares in particular – vary with the seasons. There is often a low (off-peak) season and a high (peak) season. Sometimes there's an intermediate (or shoulder) season as well. At peak times, when everyone wants to fly, both officially and unofficially discounted fares will be higher and discounted tickets may not be available. Usually the fare depends on your outward flight – if you depart in the high season and return in the low season, you still pay the high-season fare. ■

this with the airline at an early stage and, if necessary, with their doctor.

Guide dogs for the blind will often have to travel in a specially pressurised baggage compartment with other animals, away from their owner, though smaller guide dogs may be admitted to the cabin. All guide dogs will be subject to the same quarantine laws (six months in isolation etc) as any other animal.

Deaf travellers can ask for airport and in-flight announcements to be written down for them.

Children aged under two travel for 10% of the full fare (or free on some airlines) as long as they don't occupy a seat. They don't get a baggage allowance in this case. 'Skycots', baby food and nappies (diapers) should be provided by the airline if requested in advance. Prams and strollers can often be taken as hand luggage. Children aged between two and 12 can usually occupy a seat for half to two-thirds of the full fare. They do get a standard baggage allowance.

The USA

Flights to Germany from major cities in the USA abound and bargains are often available. Several airlines fly directly to Germany, most landing in Frankfurt, where you can catch a connecting flight to other cities in the country. Lufthansa connects Frankfurt with Chicago, New York, Los Angeles and other major US cities. American carriers serving Frankfurt include American Airlines, Delta Air and United Airlines. There are also direct flights to other German cities, including LTU's flights to Düsseldorf from Los Angeles, Phoenix and Daytona. Generally, though, flights to Frankfurt are the cheapest. One-way budget fares to Frankfurt in summer cost about US$330 from New York, US$400 from Los Angeles and US$450 from Chicago.

The *New York Times*, the *Los Angeles Times*, the *Chicago Tribune*, the *San Francisco Examiner* and many other major Sunday newspapers produce weekly travel sections in which you'll find lots of travel agents' advertisements.

Standard fares on commercial airlines are expensive and best avoided, especially since various types of discounts on scheduled flights are usually available. Besides advertised discount fares, options include charter flights, stand-by fares and courier flights. The US-based *Travel Unlimited* newsletter (PO Box 1058, Allston, Massachusetts 02134) publishes details of the cheapest airfares and courier possibilities for destinations all over the world from the USA and other countries, including the UK. It's a treasure trove of information. A single monthly issue costs US$5 and a year's subscription is US$25 (US$35 abroad).

Charter Flights These are often cheaper than scheduled flights. Reliable travel agents specialising in charter flights, as well as budget travel for students, include STA Travel and Council Travel, both of which have offices in major US cities.

STA Travel
- 2871 Broadway Ave, Columbia University, New York, NY 10025 (☎ 212-865 2700)
- 920 Westwood Blvd, Los Angeles, CA 90024 (☎ 310-824 1574)
- 51 Grant Ave, San Francisco, CA 94108 (☎ 415-391 8407)
- 429 S Dearborn St, Chicago, IL 60605 (☎ 312-786 9050)

Council Travel
- 148 West 4th St, New York, NY 10012 (☎ 212-254 2525)
- 205 East 42nd St, New York, NY 10017 (☎ 212-822 2700)
- 10904 Lindbrook Dr, Los Angeles, CA 90024 (☎ 310-208 3551)
- 530 Bush St, Ground Floor, San Francisco, CA 94108 (☎ 415-421 3473)
- 1153 N Dearborn St, 2nd Floor, Chicago, IL 60610 (☎ 312-951 0585)

Standby Fares These tickets are often sold at 60% of the standard price for one-way tickets. Airhitch specialises in standby tickets. You will need to give a general idea of where and when you want to go; a few days before departure, you will be presented with a choice of two or three flights. Airhitch has offices in three US cities:

Airhitch
  2641 Broadway, 3rd Floor, Suite 100, New York, NY 10025 (☎ 212-864 2000 or toll-free ☎ 800-326 2004)
  100 N Sepulveda Blvd, Los Angeles, CA 90245 (☎ 310-726 5000 or toll-free ☎ 800-397 1098)
  870 Market St, Suite 1056, San Francisco, CA 94109 (☎ 415-834 9192 or toll-free ☎ 800-834 9192)

Courier Flights Travelling as a courier means that you accompany freight to its destination, usually only on the outgoing flight. You don't have to handle any shipment personally, either at departure or arrival, and most likely will not even get to see it. All you need to do is carry an envelope with the freight papers with you on board and hand it to someone at your destination. The freight takes the place of your check-in luggage, so you will be restricted to what you are allowed to carry on the plane. You may have to be a US resident and present yourself in person before the company will take you on. Also keep in mind that only a relatively small number of these tickets are available, so it's best to call two or three months in advance and be somewhat flexible with the departure dates.

Most courier flights depart from New York, and a New York-Frankfurt return may cost as little as US$100 in the low season. Generally, you are required to return within a specified period (sometimes within one or two weeks, but often up to one month). Good sources of information on courier flights are Discount Travel International (☎ 212-362 3636) in New York City and the Worldwide Courier Association (☎ 716-464 9020 or toll-free ☎ 800-780 4359), 757 W Main St, Rochester, NY 14611.

Canada

Air Canada and Lufthansa offer flights to Frankfurt from Toronto, Vancouver and Montreal. Travel CUTS, which specialises in discount fares for students, has offices in major cities. Also check the travel sections of the *Toronto Globe & Mail*, *Toronto Star* and the *Vancouver Sun* for travel agents' ads. See the previous section for information on courier flights. The magazine *Great Expeditions* (PO Box 8000-411, Abbotsford, BC V2S 6H1) is a useful source as well.

Australia

Qantas flies from Melbourne and Sydney to Frankfurt via Singapore or Bangkok. STA Travel and Flight Centre are major dealers in cheap airfares, though your local travel agent may also offer some heavily discounted fares. Check the Saturday travel sections of the *Sydney Morning Herald* and Melbourne's *Age* newspapers for ads offering cheap fares to Europe, but don't be surprised if they happen to be 'sold out' when you contact the agents (who then offer you a more expensive fare) or if they turn out to be low-season fares on obscure airlines with lots of conditions attached.

Discounted return airfares on major airlines through reputable agents can be surprisingly cheap, with low-season fares around A$1399 and high-season fares up to A$2300. The following are addresses and contact numbers of agencies selling tickets at bargain prices.

STA Travel
  Level 4, Union Bldg, RMIT, Melbourne, Victoria 3000 (☎ 03-9660 2868)
  Shop 17, 3-9 Spring St, Chatswood, Sydney, NSW 2067 (☎ 02-9411 6888)
  222 Faraday St, Carlton, Vic 3053 (☎ 03-9349 2411)
  1st Floor, New Guild Bldg, University of Western Australia, Crawley, Perth, WA 6009 (☎ 09-380 2302)

Flight Centre
  Bourke Street Flight Centre, 19 Bourke St, Melbourne, Vic 3000 (☎ 03-9650 2899)
  Martin Place Flight Centre, Shop 5, State Bank Centre, 52 Martin Place, Sydney, NSW 2000 (☎ 02-9235 0166)
  City Flight Centre, Shop 25, Cinema City Arcade, Perth, WA 6000 (☎ 09-325 9222)

New Zealand

STA Travel and Flight Centre are popular travel agents in New Zealand. The cheapest fares to Europe are routed through the USA, and a round-the-world ticket may be cheaper than a simple return. Air New Zealand has flights from Auckland to Frankfurt, either with a stop-over in Asia or in Los Angeles. Otherwise, you can fly to Melbourne or Sydney to pick up a connecting flight there. Useful addresses include:

STA Travel
: 2nd Floor, Student Union Bldg, Princes St, Auckland University, Auckland (☎ 09-307 0555)

Flight Centre
: Auckland Flight Centre, Shop 3A, National Bank Towers, 205-225 Queen St, Auckland (☎ 09-309 6171)

The UK

London is the discount-flight capital of Europe and finding a cheap airfare to Germany should not be a problem. The main airlines are British Airways and Lufthansa, with flights several times a day to Frankfurt, Düsseldorf, Munich, Hamburg, Berlin and other cities. CityFlyer Express offers flights out of London-Gatwick, and Air UK flies from London-Stansted to Düsseldorf. Return tickets from Heathrow or Gatwick to Frankfurt in high season cost between UK£110 (with Air UK) and UK£128 (with British Airways/Lufthansa). Fares to other German cities are not significantly more expensive.

Bucket shops abound in London. They generally offer the cheapest tickets, though usually with restricted validity. However, many may not be registered with the ABTA (Association of British Travel Agents), which guarantees a refund or an alternative if you have paid for your flight and then the agent goes out of business.

The listings magazine *Time Out*, the weekend papers and the *Evening Standard* carry ads for cheap fares. Also look out for the free magazines and newspapers widely available in London, especially *TNT* – you can often pick them up outside main train and tube stations.

The Trailfinders head office in west London is a good place to go for budget airfares; it also has a travel library, bookshop, visa service and immunisation centre. STA Travel also has branches in the UK. Some useful addresses include:

STA Travel
: 86 Old Brompton Rd, London SW7 (☎ 0171-361 6161 for Europe, ☎ 0171-361 6262 for long-haul; tube: South Kensington)

Trailfinders
: 194 Kensington High St, London W8 (☎ 0171-937 5400; tube: High Street Kensington)

Council Travel
: 28a Poland St, London W1 (☎ 0171-437 7767; tube: Oxford Circus)

Continental Europe

Discount flights to various airports in Germany are available from many major cities in Continental Europe. Sometimes it may actually be cheaper – and faster – to catch a plane than to use ground transportation, especially on longer journeys. Smaller regional airlines, like Eurowings, are a good alternative to national carriers. They specialise in inexpensive short hops, often to regional airports, that may be more convenient than the big international hubs. Full-time students and those under 26 occasionally qualify for special discount rates.

LAND

Bus

In some cases, bus travel is a good alternative to the train if you're already in Europe and on your way to Germany. Especially for shorter distances, it's usually, though not always, cheaper than taking the train. The downside is, of course, that it's slower. Some of the coaches are quite comfortable, with toilet, air conditioning and snack bar. Advance reservations may be necessary at peak travel times. In general, return fares are markedly cheaper than two one-way fares.

Eurolines is the umbrella organisation of numerous European bus companies, with service between major cities across Europe. Their offices in Europe include those listed below, although information and tickets are also available from most travel agents.

France
: Gare Routière Internationale, 28 Ave du Général de Gaulle, 75020 Paris (☎ 01 49 72 51 51)

Germany
: Am Römerhof 17, 60486 Frankfurt/Main (☎ 069-790 35 0)

Netherlands
    Amstel Busstation, Julianaplein, 1097 DN Amsterdam (☎ 020-69 45 63 1)
UK
    52 Grosvenor Gardens, Victoria, London SW1 OAU (☎ 01582-404 511)

Buses connect major German cities like Düsseldorf, Cologne, Frankfurt, Hamburg, Munich and Aachen with London, Brussels and Amsterdam daily, with Paris up to six times a week, and with Prague three times a week. Sample one-way/return fares are: London-Frankfurt DM120/182, Paris-Hamburg DM102/188 and Amsterdam-Bremen DM60/95. If you're under 26 or a student, you get a 10% discount. For frequent travellers, there's the Eurolines Pass, offering unlimited travel between 18 cities for either 30 or 60 days, but you can only buy it from the Eurolines representative office in Frankfurt Hauptbahnhof. If you're under 26, it costs DM365/455 for 30/60 days in low season and DM465/505 in high season. If you're over 26, you pay DM455/575 for 30/60 days in low season and DM540/655 in high season.

An excellent budget option is travelling on Eurobus (☎ 0118-936 23 21; PO Box 3026, Wokingham, Berkshire, RG40 2YP), a British company that started up in 1995. In addition to hop-on, hop-off buses equipped with WC and video, the company's services include on-board guides and mail-forwarding. Buses complete a figure-eight loop of Europe every two days, taking in Berlin and Munich, plus Amsterdam, Brussels, Paris, Zürich, Prague, Vienna, Budapest and more. Tickets are valid for four months, but you're not allowed to repeat any route segment. Prices are divided in three zones. If you're under 26 years of age, you pay UK£119 for one zone, UK£199 for two and UK£269 for three. If you're over 26, the costs are UK£129 for one, UK£229 for two and UK£299 for three zones. Tickets are available from travel agents in many countries worldwide (eg from STA Travel in the UK), though you need to make your own way to a city on the loop to get started. In Germany, tickets are available from the travel agency Connections in Frankfurt (☎ 069-705 06 0). See the Frankfurt section for the address.

Train

The train is another good way to get to Germany if you're already in Europe, and it's more comfortable than the bus. It's not worth spending the extra money on a 1st-class ticket, since travelling 2nd class on German trains is perfectly comfortable.

Long-distance trains from major German cities to other countries are called EC (EuroCity) trains. Cologne has direct connections to Amsterdam, Basel, Brussels, Copenhagen, Paris and Rome. There are direct trains from Hamburg to Copenhagen and also an overnight service to Budapest. From Munich, trains travel to Rome, Milan, Florence, Verona, Prague, Paris, Strasbourg, Salzburg and Zurich.

Overnight international trains are increasingly made up of mostly sleeper carriages, and there may be only one or two carriages with seats. A berth in a four-person compartment will cost you a supplement of DM38, in a six-person compartment it's DM26. Supplements for single-bed sleepers are DM180, doubles are DM80 per person.

If you have a sleeper or sleeping berth on international train trips, the train conductor will usually collect your ticket before you go to sleep and hand it back to you in the morning. If you're in a regular seat, however, expect to be woken up by conductors coming aboard in each country to check your ticket (this is particularly annoying if your trip goes through several countries in the course of the night, ie Paris-Hamburg with passage through France, Belgium and Germany).

Be sure to make a seat reservation on EC trains, especially during the peak summer season and around major holidays. Trains get very crowded, and you may find yourself stuck in the narrow corridor for hours. Reservations cost DM3 and can be made as late as a few minutes before departure.

Examples of standard one-way 2nd-class fares from Germany are: Frankfurt-Paris DM139, Hamburg-London DM260, Berlin-

Rail Pass Specials

If you have a rail pass you're eligible for discounts on travel to Austria, the Czech Republic and Denmark. The deal is that you can go from the German border to any town within those three countries and back for an additional fee. It's a pretty good buy in 2nd class, which would let you, say, visit Prague from Munich for an extra US$25, or Copenhagen from Hamburg for an additional US$30.

And you don't have to limit yourself to capital cities – the supplement is for a round-trip ticket to anywhere in the neighbouring country.

For 2nd-class tickets, the supplement is US$25 to the Czech Republic, US$30 to Denmark and US$42 to Austria. ■

Amsterdam DM166. For the various rail passes on offer – both international and German – see the Getting Around chapter.

Security In recent years, the number of crimes committed on trains – especially at night – has increased. There have been horror stories of passengers being robbed after having been drugged or made unconscious with gas blown in through the ventilation ducts. While this should not stop you from using the train, it pays to be aware and to take a few precautions. Never leave your baggage out of sight, especially the bag holding your personal documents, tickets and money. Lock your suitcases, backpacks or bags; better yet, buy a lock and fasten them to the luggage rack. In general, travel in the daytime is safer, thought it's easier to catch some sleep (and save accommodation costs) on night trains. If you travel at night, at least try to lock the compartment, if possible.

Car & Motorcycle

Driving in Germany can be a lot of fun since the overall quality of the roads is very high and having your own vehicle provides you with the most flexibility to get off the beaten track. The disadvantage is that traffic in urban areas can be horrendous, and parking in the cities is usually restricted to expensive car parks. See the Getting Around chapter for more detailed coverage (roads, road rules, motoring organisations etc) of driving in Germany.

If you're taking your own vehicle, you should always carry proof of ownership. Driving licences from most countries are valid in Germany for one year. You must also have third-party insurance to enter the country. It is compulsory to carry a warning (hazard) triangle and first-aid kit in your car at all times.

If you're coming from the UK, the quickest option (apart from the Channel Tunnel) is to take the car ferry or Hovercraft from Dover, Folkestone or Ramsgate to Calais in France; you can be in Germany in three hours from there. The main gateways to southern Germany are Munich, Freiburg and Passau. Heading for Poland and to the Czech Republic, you may encounter long border delays.

For information about car rental and purchase while in Germany, see the Getting Around chapter.

Bicycle

Cycling is a cheap, convenient, healthy, environmentally sound and above all fun way of travelling. One note of caution if you are bringing your bicycle to Germany: before you leave home, go over your bike to check for wear and tear and fill your repair kit with every imaginable spare. As with cars and motorcycles, you won't necessarily be able to buy that crucial gizmo for your machine when it breaks down somewhere in the back of beyond.

Bicycles can travel by air, which can be surprisingly inexpensive, especially with some charter airlines. The independent charter airline LTU, for instance, charges only DM30 to transport a bicycle. You *can* take them to pieces and put them in a bike bag or box, but it's much easier simply to wheel your bike to the check-in desk where it will (or should) be treated as a piece of baggage. You may have to remove the pedals and turn the handlebars sideways so that it takes up less space in the aircraft's hold;

check all this with the airline well in advance, preferably before you pay for your ticket. For information about transporting your bicycle by train in Germany, see the Bicycle section in the Getting Around chapter.

Hitching & Ride Services

Lonely Planet does not recommend hitching (see the warning in the Hitching section of the Getting Around chapter). However, travellers who do decide to hitch should not have too many problems getting to and from Germany via the main autobahns and highways.

Aside from hitching, the cheapest way to get to Germany is as a paying passenger in a private car. Leaving Germany, or travelling within the country, such rides are arranged by *Mitfahrzentralen*, ride-share agencies that can be found in all major cities and many smaller ones as well. For local listings of Mitfahrzentralen see the Getting There & Away section in the individual cities and towns. Most agencies belong to umbrella Mitfahrzentrale networks like Arbeitsgemeinschaft Deutscher Mitfahrzentralen (ADM; ☎ 194 40 in most cities) or Citynetz Mitfahr-Zentrale (☎ 194 44).

The fare you pay comprises a commission to the agency and a per-km charge to the driver. Expect to pay about DM29 for a one-way Hamburg-Berlin trip, DM50 for Hamburg-Frankfurt and DM71 for Hamburg-Munich. From Berlin to Paris will cost about DM84, to Budapest DM90.

The people answering the phone at Mitfahrzentrale offices usually speak good English. If you arrange a ride a few days in advance, it's best to call the driver the night before and again on the morning of departure just to make sure they are still going.

SEA

Germany's main ferry ports are Travemünde and Kiel in Schleswig-Holstein, and Sassnitz on Rügen Island in Mecklenburg-Western Pomerania, all with service to Scandinavia. Ferries to the UK leave from Hamburg. Return tickets are often cheaper than two one-way tickets. Also keep in mind that prices fluctuate dramatically according to the season, the day and time of departure and, for overnight ferries, cabin amenities. All prices quoted below are for one-way fares. For more details see Getting There & Away in the individual port towns.

The UK

Hamburg-Harwich The car ferry run by Scandinavian Seaways (☎ 040-389 03 71 in Hamburg) operates year round at least twice weekly and takes 20 hours. One-way fares range from DM93 for a berth in an inner four-bed cabin in low season to DM493 for a one-bed outer suite with private bath in high season. Cars up to 6m long are an additional DM59 to DM121.

Hamburg-Newcastle Scandinavian Seaways also operates the ferry between Hamburg and Newcastle. It sails every four days from May to August. The crossing takes 24 hours and costs DM133 to DM513.

Sweden

Sassnitz-Trelleborg DFO HansaFerry (☎ 0180-534 34 43 or ☎ 038392-641 80 in Sassnitz) operates a quick ferry to Sweden, popular with day-trippers. There are five departures daily. The trip takes four hours and costs DM20/10 in summer/winter. Cars are DM140 to DM160, including all passengers.

Travemünde-Trelleborg Up to four TT-Line ferries (☎ 040-360 14 42 in Hamburg) make the 7½-hour trip daily, which costs from DM70 to DM100. Cars, including driver, are DM100 to DM250. Students get a significant discount.

Travemünde-Malmö Two daily ferries are offered by Nördo Link (☎ 04502-805 89 in Travemünde). The daytime ferry costs DM77, the overnight one DM115 (sleeping berth not included). The trip takes nine hours.

Kiel-Gothenburg The daily overnight ferry run by Stena Line (☎ 0180-533 36 00 or

(☎ 0431-9099 in Kiel) takes 14 hours and costs up to DM196 on some peak dates. Between November and April, fares are as low as DM66. Special tickets for those under 26 are available. Sleeping berths start from DM30 in four-bed cabins.

Denmark

Sassnitz-Rønne Three ferries operated by DFO HansaFerry (☎ 0180-534 34 43) make the journey daily to this town on Bornholm Island. The trip takes four hours and costs DM30 in summer, DM15 in winter each way. If you return the same day, you travel back for free.

Kiel-Langeland Two to three ferries a day make the trip to Bagenkop on the Danish island of Langeland. The crossing takes 2½ hours and costs DM9.50 in peak season. Cars are DM39, including the driver. Fares are lower in winter (no service from January to mid-February). The ferry company is simply called Langeland-Kiel (☎ 0431-974 15 0 in Kiel).

Norway

Kiel-Oslo Color Line (☎ 0431-974 09 0 in Kiel) makes this 19½-hour journey almost daily. The fare, including a berth in the most basic two-bed cabin, is DM136 and about 30% more in summer. Student discounts are available on some days.

Finland

Travemünde-Helsinki Finnjet-Silja Line (☎ 0451-589 92 22 in Lübeck) makes several trips weekly which take between 22 and 36 hours and cost from DM210 in the cheapest cabin in summer and about DM125 during low season. Students get about a 20% discount.

Poseidon Passagierdienst (☎ 0451-150 74 43 in Lübeck) also makes the run to Helsinki year round at least once a week. The price per person in a three-bed cabin is DM320 in low season and DM450 in peak season. It also goes to Turku (34½ hours).

LAKE

Switzerland

The Friedrichshafen-Romanshorn ferry provides the fastest way across Lake Constance from Germany to Switzerland. It's operated by Bodensee-Schiffsbetriebe (☎ 07541-201 38 9 in Friedrichshafen) year round (hourly in daylight), takes 45 minutes and costs DM8.80 (students DM5.40). Cars, including two passengers, are DM28 to DM36 depending on the size.

DEPARTURE TAX

Since May 1997, applicable departure taxes and airport security fees have been included in the price of any airline ticket purchased in Germany. You should not have to pay any more fees at the airport. There's no tax if you depart by sea or land.

Getting Around

The Germans are whizzes at moving people around, and the nation's transportation network is among the best in Europe. Though it's not cheap, it's usually good value.

The two best ways of getting around are car and train – probably in that order. While air connections are very good, they're aimed at the business market and priced accordingly; in any case, Germany is compact enough to make surface travel a better way to go. Buses tend to be far less convenient than trains, though regional bus service is crucial in the rare places not yet adequately served by the rail network.

AIR

There are lots of flights within Germany, but costs can be prohibitive compared with the train. Lufthansa, together with its Team Lufthansa partners (Augsberg Airways, Cimber Air and Contact Air), is by far the most popular airline in the country, flying a total of 3400 domestic flights a week. Team Lufthansa members are franchise partners that fly under their own livery under contract to Lufthansa. Foreign airlines also offer services between major cities, and two major competitors for Lufthansa are now Deutsche BA, a subsidiary of British Airways, and Eurowings, a regional airline that connects major European cities with regional and international airports in Germany.

Several small airlines offer service between regional cities, as well as to and from the North Frisian Islands.

There is only 'tourist' (economy) and business class on Lufthansa domestic flights. While discount tickets are available through travel agents, Lufthansa City Center offices and even direct from Lufthansa itself, the cheapest scheduled prices for economy travel (with a 14-day advance purchase excursion ticket) between any two points in the country ranges from DM222 to DM260. This fare would apply, for example, to a ticket from Munich to Hamburg, Berlin to Stuttgart or Frankfurt to Dresden. But you can do much better than these 'officially discounted' fares.

Infants generally travel on an adult passenger's lap for a 90% discount of the applicable fare. Children aged two to 11 travel at a 33% to 50% discount of the applicable fare. Unaccompanied children (over five years old only) can travel at the same 33% to 50% discount off the applicable fare, plus a handling fee of DM50.

European Air Service

European air service was in a state of flux as we went to press. From April 1997, any airline in a European Union country was permitted to set up domestic service within any other EU member state. This is expected to transform the European air market dramatically.

By mid-1997, competition was heating up, and it's no wonder – Germany is the highest-yield air market on the continent, and Germans travel and spend more on travel than anyone in Europe.

The impact existing and new carriers will have on the industry will no doubt be great news for air travellers. As competition and services increase, airfares are expected to fall. At the same time, in-flight service will most likely decline. ■

Information & Reservations

Call Lufthansa (☎ 0180-380 38 03 or ☎ 333 66 33) for reservations.

Tickets & Check-In

Full-fare tickets are valid for one year from the start of travel. You do not have to reconfirm domestic flights.

Check-in for domestic flights is generally at least 30 minutes before departure, though in Frankfurt (Main) and Berlin passengers without baggage may check in as late as 20 minutes before departure time.

To/From the Airport

There are frequent Lufthansa bus shuttles between the airport and city centre in Munich, Frankfurt, Heidelberg, Mannheim, Saarbrücken and Nuremberg. The fare is generally around DM10. There are also buses running – for more money and in conjunction with local bus companies – between the following:

Augsberg-Munich airport. Buses depart from Bahnhofstrasse in Augsberg; 1¼ hours; call ☎ 0821-502 25 34 for reservations
Heilbronn-Frankfurt airport. Buses depart from the Reisebusbahnhof, Karlstrasse; two hours; call ☎ 07131-150 93 0 for reservations

There's also bus service between Frankfurt airport and Strasbourg in France, with pick-up points at the Grand Hotel Concorde, Place de la Gare, and the Hilton Hotel. Call Lufthansa in Strasbourg (☎ +33 89-49 06 21) for information and reservations.

BUS

The bus network in Germany is excellent and comprehensive but not a popular mode of transport. For trips of any distance the train is faster and generally just as cheap. Buses are better geared towards regional travel in areas where the terrain makes train travel more difficult or impossible, and in this book we only list bus services if they're a viable and sensible option.

Each city in Germany has a central bus station *(Busbahnhof)*, from where almost all bus service originates. It is generally very close or adjacent to the central train station *(Hauptbahnhof)*. Tickets can be bought directly from the bus companies, which often have offices or kiosks at the bus station, or from the driver on board.

Since the privatisation of most regional bus services run by Deutsche Bahn (German National Railway), a slew of companies has sprung up to provide regional service. They include:

BRN (Busverkehr Rhein-Neckar)
☎ 0621-120 03 81
BVO (Busverkehr Ostwestfalen)
☎ 0521-520 70 66
BVR (Busverkehr Rheinland)
☎ 02461-520 36
ORN (Omnibusverkehr Rhein-Nahe)
☎ 06131-671 02 6
OVF (Omnibusverkehr Franken)
☎ 0911-244 01 61/62
RBO (Regionalbus Ostbayern)
☎ 0991-327 84
RBS (Regionalbus Stuttgart)
☎ 666 07 36
RKH (Regionalverkehr Kurhessen)
☎ 0561-200 98 33
RMV (Rhein-Mosel Verkehregesellschaft)
☎ 0261-173 83
RSW (Regionalbus Saar-Westpfalz)
☎ 0681-301 55 5
RVA (Regionalverkehr Schwaben-Allgäu)
☎ 089-551 64 13 0
RVH (Regionalverkehr Hannover)
☎ 0511-338 00 0
RVK (Regionalverkehr Köln)
☎ 0221-124 41 2
RVO (Regionalverkehr Oberbayern)
☎ 089-551 64 13 1
RVS (Regionalbusverkehr Südwest)
☎ 0721-695 87 1
WB (Westfalen Bus)
☎ 0251-490 00

Europabus, the bus network of Europe's railways, still operates within Germany as Deutsche Touring, a subsidiary of Deutsche Bahn (DB). Europabus services include the Romantic and Castle roads in southern Germany, as well as organised bus tours of Germany lasting a week or more. See the Frankfurt and Romantic Road sections for details, or contact the Deutsche Touring main booking office (☎ 069-790 30), Römerhof 17, 60486 Frankfurt/Main.

TRAIN

Operated almost entirely by the recently privatised Deutsche Bahn, the German train system is arguably the most efficient in Europe. A wide range of services and ticket options are available, making travelling by rail the most attractive way to get around the country, sometimes even better than car.

There's rail service to almost every place you could think of going in Germany –

41,000km of track make the network Europe's most extensive, and over 7000 cities and towns are served. Service is usually excellent.

The future of rail in the former GDR is glowing. DB has been shovelling money into the eastern part of the country's rail system like coal into a steam engine; the infrastructure has been renovated, and the country's decrepit rolling stock has been upgraded or replaced. While prices continue to rise, services have improved to the point that it's approaching the levels of western Germany. Apart from new rolling stock and track, the smaller narrow-gauge steam lines in more remote regions are still operating, and even regional services are continuing despite predictions of their imminent demise.

Train Passes

Eurail Pass Eurail passes can be a great deal if you're covering lots of territory in a very limited time. But if you're spending more than a week in Germany, the pass probably doesn't pay: you'll burn through the allotted time on routes that would cost you less if you paid the full fare.

For example, if you're under 26 you could qualify for a Youth pass – valid for 15 days of unlimited travel from the time you validate it – for $US418. Look at where you want to go in Germany. If you were to travel from Munich to Berlin, then on to Hamburg, Hanover, Frankfurt, Stuttgart, back to Munich and then along the Romantic Road with Europabus (with the 10% student discount), it all adds up, at the exchange rate as we write, to a grand total of $US385. That, plus not having to rush to do it all in 15 days, makes it worth skipping the pass.

Even if you're over 26 years of age, the same thing applies; within Germany for any length of time you're far better off with a DB BahnCard (see Discount Tickets below) than a Eurail pass.

If you're spending more time in other European countries, consult Lonely Planet's *Western Europe*, *Central Europe* or *Mediterranean Europe* guides for more details on the Eurail pass, along with information on Inter-Rail passes for European residents.

German Rail (Deutsche Bahn) Pass A German Rail pass can be a cheaper way of getting around the country and allows you to avoid the often long ticket queues. Passes can be obtained in most non-European countries including Australia, Canada, the USA and Mexico, and at most major train stations in Germany itself (passport required). The pass is valid on all trains, and some river services operated by the Köln-Düsseldorfer Line.

The standard German Rail pass is available to any non-German citizen not resident in Germany, and entitles you to unlimited 1st or 2nd-class travel for five/10/15 days within a one-month period. The 2nd-class German Rail pass costs US$188/304/410.

You must validate your rail pass before using it. If you haven't done so by the time you arrive in Germany, do so at any DB train station in the country.

German Rail Youth Pass Similar to the German Rail pass is the German Rail Youth pass, limited to 2nd-class travel for those aged between 12 and 25. It costs US$146/ $200/252 for five/10/15 days of travel.

German Rail Twin Pass Two adults travelling together should check out the German Rail Twin pass which costs US$282/456/615 for five/10/15-day passes in 2nd class.

Discount Tickets

There are youth, student and senior discounts available on certain DB fares to those with proper identification. Travellers with a physical disability can get a certificate entitling them to discounted or free DB services. Contact Deutsche Bahn for a copy of its excellent free access guide *Information für behinderte Reisende* (German only).

In addition there are various permanent and temporary reduced-rate ticket offers available.

BahnCard If you plan to travel within Germany for more than a month, the BahnCard

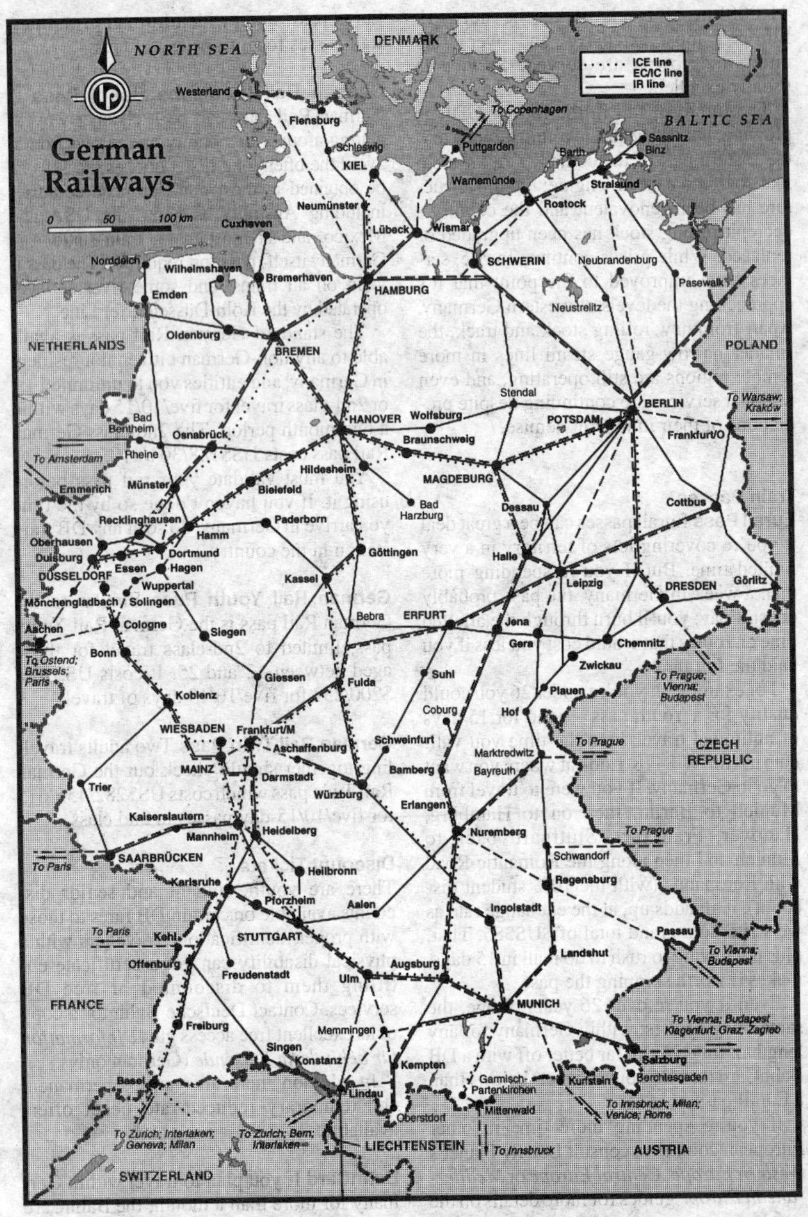
German Railways
NORTH SEA
BALTIC SEA
DENMARK
NETHERLANDS
POLAND
CZECH REPUBLIC
FRANCE
SWITZERLAND
LIECHTENSTEIN
AUSTRIA
ICE line
EC/IC line
IR line
0
50
100 km
Westerland
Flensburg
Schleswig
KIEL
Neumünster
Lübeck
Puttgarden
To Copenhagen
Warnemünde
Barth
Sassnitz
Binz
Stralsund
Rostock
Wismar
SCHWERIN
Neubrandenburg
Pasewalk
Neustrelitz
HAMBURG
Cuxhaven
Norddeich
Wilhelmshaven
Bremerhaven
Emden
Oldenburg
BREMEN
Stendal
BERLIN
POTSDAM
To Warsaw; Kraków
Frankfurt/O
HANOVER
Wolfsburg
Braunschweig
Bad Bentheim
Osnabrück
Rheine
To Amsterdam
Hildesheim
MAGDEBURG
Emmerich
Münster
Bielefeld
Bad Harzburg
Dessau
Cottbus
Recklinghausen
Paderborn
Oberhausen
Hamm
Duisburg
Dortmund
Göttingen
Halle
Essen
Hagen
DÜSSELDORF
Wuppertal
Kassel
Leipzig
DRESDEN
Görlitz
Mönchengladbach
Solingen
Bebra
ERFURT
Aachen
Cologne
Jena
Siegen
Gera
Chemnitz
Bonn
To Ostend; Brussels; Paris
Giessen
Suhl
Zwickau
Fulda
To Prague; Vienna; Budapest
Plauen
Koblenz
Coburg
Hof
WIESBADEN
Frankfurt/M
Schweinfurt
To Prague
Aschaffenburg
Marktredwitz
MAINZ
Darmstadt
Bamberg
Bayreuth
Trier
Würzburg
Erlangen
Kaiserslautern
Mannheim
Heidelberg
Nuremberg
To Prague
To Paris
SAARBRÜCKEN
Schwandorf
Heilbronn
Karlsruhe
Regensburg
Pforzheim
Aalen
Ingolstadt
To Paris
Kehl
STUTTGART
Passau
Landshut
To Vienna; Budapest
Offenburg
Freudenstadt
Augsburg
Ulm
MUNICH
To Vienna; Budapest Klagenfurt; Graz; Zagreb
Freiburg
Memmingen
Singen
Konstanz
Salzburg
Berchtesgaden
Kempten
Basel
Lindau
Garmisch-Partenkirchen
Kufstein
Mittenwald
To Innsbruck; Milan; Venice; Rome
Oberstdorf
To Zurich; Interlaken; Geneva; Milan
To Zurich; Bern; Interlaken
To Innsbruck

may be a cheaper option than just buying tickets at the counter. Once you pay what amounts to a sign-up fee, you're allowed to buy train tickets (including InterCity and InterCity Express, but *not* S-Bahn or U-Bahn ones) and many regional bus tickets for half-price. A 2nd-class BahnCard costs DM240 (DM120 for those between 17 and 22 years of age, students under 27, anyone over 60 and card holders' spouses) and is valid for one year. People aged 17 or under pay only DM60 for the BahnCard.

Sparpreis The Sparpreis, a return ticket between any two stations in Germany, costs DM209, and accompanying passengers pay only DM105. It is valid for 30 days but the return trip cannot be completed within a single Monday-to-Friday period. The Sparpreis is not valid on InterCity Express (ICE) trains.

Guten-Abend-Ticket If arriving very late is not a problem, the Good-Evening-Ticket is good value. It's valid for unlimited train travel from 7 pm until 7 am (from 2 pm Saturdays), and costs DM59 in 2nd class (DM69 in 2nd class on an ICE train). There are blacked-out periods around Easter and Christmas – check with DB for detailed information. A flat DM15 surcharge is levied at the weekend.

Schönes-Wochenende-Ticket Without much fanfare, DB has instituted one of the finest train deals in Europe – the so-called Nice Weekend Ticket. This allows you and up to four accompanying passengers to travel anywhere in Germany from midnight Saturday until 2 am Monday for just DM35. The catch is that you have to use local trains and *not* ICE, IC, ICN (InterCity Night) or IR trains. That's not so bad, though – you can get clear across the country on the slower trains (and no German train is *that* slow).

InterCity Express

DB's InterCity Express (ICE) trains offer ultra-rapid service aboard space-age bullet trains, and special fares apply. Travelling at speeds of up to 280km/h, ICE trains now dominate some long-distance routes between large cities, such as Frankfurt-Berlin (DM178, 4½ hours) and Hamburg-Munich (DM239, six hours).

Services aboard ICE trains are challenging those of domestic air travel. There are restaurants and bistros, telephones, computer data ports, huge picture windows and generally great service. All ICE trains – and some toilets and compartments – are wheelchair accessible. Smoking is permitted only in the first (1st-class) and last (2nd-class) carriages of the trains, and prohibited in restaurant and buffet cars.

ICE service is expanding all the time, but representative services include: Hamburg-Frankfurt (DM170, three hours); Frankfurt-Basel (DM107, 2¾ hours); Berlin-Hanover (DM68, three hours).

ICE trains also run along other major routes, such as Cologne-Nuremberg, but these are still mainly serviced by other train categories. In fact, the Cologne-Nuremberg ICE service is actually slower than the regular InterCity service.

InterCity & EuroCity

These are less rapid intercity trains than the ICEs. All run between 6 am and 10 pm; InterCity (IC) trains go between German cities and EuroCity (EC) trains between German cities and cities throughout Europe. They're still comfortable and relatively fast, but ICE trains they ain't.

InterRegio & Regional Express

InterRegio (IR) and Regional Express (RE) trains generally run regional and, on some lines, infrequent night services. These are the trains you'll need to take from the pastures to a major rail link.

Local Services

DB runs local services that rate just above, and sometimes complement, metropolitan public transport networks. One case in point are the SchnellBahn (S-Bahn) services, essentially suburban-metropolitan shuttle lines. These originate in a Hauptbahnhof and reach far-flung suburbs; in the case of Munich, Frankfurt, Stuttgart and Berlin, the S-Bahn also serves as the main city-to-airport train link.

StadtExpress (SE) is the S-Bahn in cities not large enough to really have one, and RegionalBahn (RB) offers local regional services. RBs are the next tier below REs.

Narrow-Gauge & Cog-Wheel Trains

There are several narrow-gauge steam trains still in operation in Germany, mainly in the east. Notable services include the Molli, running between Bad Doberan and the towns of Heiligendamm and Kühlungsborn, and the Rasender Roland between Putbus and Göhren (see the Mecklenburg-Western Pomerania chapter). Another popular steam-powered service is the *Harzquerbahn* from Wernigerode in the Harz Mountains (see that chapter).

Zahnradbahnen are privately run cog-wheel railways, with trains that grind their way up some of Germany's steepest mountains, mainly in the Bavarian Alps. They're a wonderful trip back in time, and if you get a chance to ride one, jump aboard! You can usually take a Zahnradbahn up the mountain and a cable car down.

Sleepers

Standard sleeper services are available on longer routes in Germany and have one to three-bed compartments or four to six-bed couchettes. Sleeping on a train is a great way to save on accommodation – though the cost of the bed is not included in the fare, and supplements are charged for sheets and towels. There are no showers, and you may feel a little uncomfortable about sleeping in a room with strangers. It may help to know that this is a very common method of travel, and it's perfectly safe and pretty comfortable. The surcharge for the simplest 2nd-class sleeping bunk is DM26 with sheets and other services; more expensive sleeping-car fares are available for three or two-bed compartments, and also one-bed compartments in 1st class.

A relatively new arrival, InterCity Night (ICN) trains, on limited services between major German cities, have one and two-person compartments complete with showers and toilets in 'comfort class', and aeroplane-style reclining seats in 'tourist class'. There's also a new type of couchette available on ICN trains called *Kajütliegwagen*. Prices (eg Berlin-Munich DM154) include breakfast. This could be worth it if you have a BahnCard (see Rail Passes), which would bring the 1st-class fare down to DM184.

Information & Schedules

The most straightforward way of finding out a train's schedule and price is at the station, where large yellow posters show all trains departing each hour (but not fares). Once you know the time you want to go, write down the information and ask at the ticket window. If you can't speak German, write down the train number, time, destination, class desired and slide it through the window.

Single tickets of over 100km are valid for up to four days, and there's normally no problem breaking your journey (though you should advise the conductor). Return tickets cost exactly double, but if the combined distance is more than 100km they're valid for one month (two months for international return tickets). Long-distance train tickets and passes are also valid on the S-Bahns.

There are travel centres *(Reisezentrum)* in most larger train stations where staff will help you plan an itinerary, though English is sometimes a problem.

For ticket and timetable information (available in English) by telephone you can ring ☎ 194 19 from anywhere in Germany for the cost of a local call. Timetable and/or fare information is available from several sites on the Internet, including Deutsche Bahn.

Reservations

On holidays and in the busy summer season, reservations are recommended for longer journeys or sleeping compartments. The reservation fee is a flat DM3, regardless of the number of seats booked. Most night trains are equipped with 1st-class (two-berth) and 2nd-class (four or six-berth) sleeping compartments, which must be booked at least one day in advance; otherwise turn up on the platform and ask the conductor (see Buying Tickets below).

Supplements For all EC and IC trains a supplementary reservation charge applies (DM6, or DM8 if bought from the conductor), though holders of Eurail, Inter-Rail and German Rail passes do not pay supplements on ICE or IC trains. There's never a surcharge on IR or RE trains.

Costs

The average per-km price of 2nd-class train travel in western Germany is currently DM0.26 and in eastern Germany DM0.24; for 1st class the average is DM0.38 and DM0.34 per km, respectively. In this book we round train fares to the nearest DM0.50, and list only 2nd-class fares. Children three and younger travel free, children from four to 11 pay half-price.

Though train travel in Germany does offer good value, without a rail pass or a ticket bought through a special offer, it can get expensive: it costs about DM90 for a Munich-Frankfurt ticket on non-ICE service and DM120 on an ICE train. Read the Rail Passes and Discount Tickets sections for more information, and shop around.

Buying Tickets

Tickets can usually be bought from the conductor for a surcharge of DM5 (or DM10 for ICE trains), but an increasing number of services (generally slower, regional ones) operate without a conductor. For these trains passengers are required to buy a ticket *before* boarding, so ask if you are in doubt. Anyone caught without a valid ticket is liable for a fine of DM60.

At many train stations passengers must buy tickets from vending machines for distances under 100km – it's generally more convenient anyway. If you're travelling further than anywhere indicated on the machine, press button 'X' for the maximum fare and contact the conductor on board. Holders of the BahnCard (see Rail Passes) should press the '½' or 'Kind' (child) button for a half-price ticket.

Left & Checked Luggage

All large (and many small) train stations in Germany have coin-operated, 24-hour left-luggage lockers (DM2/4 for small/large lockers). *Gepäckaufbewahrung* (left-luggage offices) are sometimes more convenient and charge similar rates.

Suitcases, bags or backpacks weighing up to 30kg can be sent door to door by KurierGepäck (☎ 0180-332 05 20) between any two train stations in Germany for DM28; overweight luggage (over 30kg), bicycles or skis cost DM46. KurierGepäck can also be used to send luggage to other Western European destinations. The list of countries that are serviced is small but growing though Spain, Portugal and Italy are not included at present.

The Car & Motorcycle and Bicycle sections in this chapter include information about transporting your bicycle, motorcycle or car by train.

CAR & MOTORCYCLE

Most German roads are excellent, and as a result, motoring can be a great way to tour the country. *Autobahnen* (motorways) run throughout Germany. Road signs (and most motoring maps) indicate national autobahn routes in blue with an 'A' preceding the number while international routes have green signs with an 'E' and a number. Though very efficient, the autobahns are often busy, and literally life in the fast lane. Tourists often have trouble coping with the very high speeds (there are no speed limits on autobahns) and the dangers involved in overtaking – don't overestimate the time it takes for a car in the rear-view mirror to close in at 180km/h.

Secondary roads, dubbed 'B' highways, are easier on the nerves, much more scenic, and still present a fairly fast way of getting from place to place.

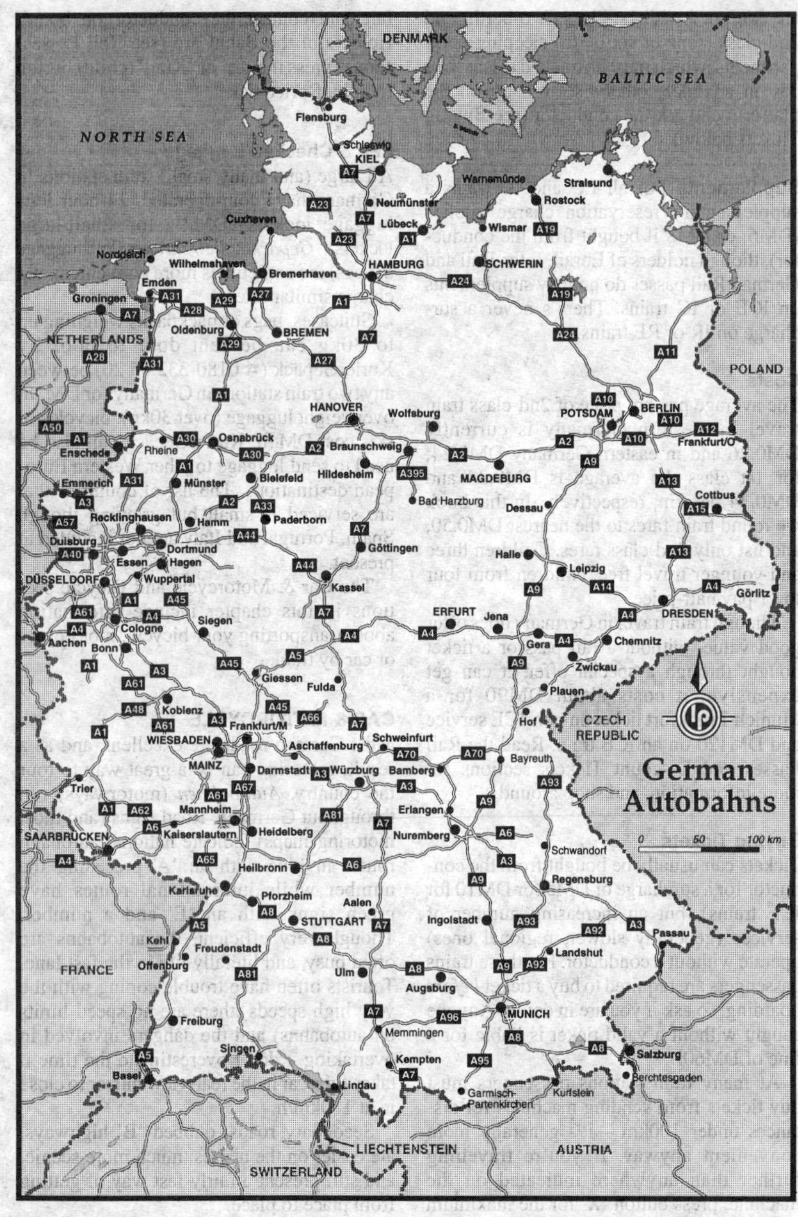
German
Autobahns
0
50
100 km
DENMARK
BALTIC SEA
NORTH SEA
NETHERLANDS
POLAND
CZECH
REPUBLIC
FRANCE
SWITZERLAND
LIECHTENSTEIN
AUSTRIA
Flensburg
Schleswig
KIEL
Neumünster
Lübeck
Cuxhaven
HAMBURG
Norddeich
Wilhelmshaven
Bremerhaven
Emden
Groningen
Oldenburg
BREMEN
Warnemünde
Stralsund
Rostock
Wismar
SCHWERIN
HANOVER
Wolfsburg
POTSDAM
BERLIN
Frankfurt/O
Enschede
Rheine
Osnabrück
Braunschweig
MAGDEBURG
Hildesheim
Bad Harzburg
Emmerich
Münster
Bielefeld
Cottbus
Dessau
Recklinghausen
Hamm
Paderborn
Duisburg
Dortmund
Göttingen
Essen
Hagen
Halle
Leipzig
DÜSSELDORF
Wuppertal
Kassel
Görlitz
DRESDEN
Cologne
ERFURT
Jena
Aachen
Bonn
Siegen
Gera
Chemnitz
Zwickau
Giessen
Fulda
Plauen
Koblenz
Hof
Frankfurt/M
WIESBADEN
Schweinfurt
Aschaffenburg
Bayreuth
MAINZ
Darmstadt
Würzburg
Bamberg
Trier
Mannheim
Erlangen
Kaiserslautern
Heidelberg
SAARBRÜCKEN
Nuremberg
Schwandorf
Heilbronn
Regensburg
Karlsruhe
Pforzheim
Aalen
STUTTGART
Ingolstadt
Passau
Kehl
Freudenstadt
Landshut
Offenburg
Ulm
Augsburg
MUNICH
Freiburg
Memmingen
Salzburg
Singen
Kempten
Berchtesgaden
Basel
Lindau
Garmisch-
Partenkirchen
Kufstein

Road Rules

Driving is on the right. Road rules are easy to understand and standard international signs are in use. Pedestrians at zebra crossings have absolute right of way over all motor vehicles; whether the light is green for you or not, you must yield. Similarly, you must give right of way to cyclists in bicycle lanes when you're turning – they won't even look so you'd better be prepared.

The usual speed limits are 50km/h in built-up areas (in effect as soon as you see the yellow town sign as you enter to the same sign with a red line through it as you leave) and 100km/h on non-autobahn highways. There is no speed limit on the autobahns.

The highest permissible blood-alcohol level for drivers is 0.08%. Obey the road rules carefully: the German police are very efficient and issue stiff on-the-spot fines; speed and red-light cameras are in widespread use, and notices are sent to the car's registration address wherever that may be.

Note that in eastern Germany, a fixed green arrow on a traffic signal means that even when the signal is red, you are still permitted to make a right turn – after you have come to a full stop.

There are emergency phones every kilometre or so along most autobahns, even in the east, to be used in the event of breakdown. Lift the metal flap and follow the (pictorial) instructions on it and help will arrive.

Traffic Jams German traffic jams *(Staus)* deserve special mention. Traffic jams are a subject of intense interest to motorists in Germany and are the focus of typical German thoroughness: you can actually get an annual Traffic Jam Calendar from the ADAC (see Motoring Organisations following).

German radio stations broadcast a special tone that interrupts cassette and CD players during traffic reports. Ask the rental agent to disable it unless you want all your music peppered with poetic phrases like, 'Die Autobahn von Frankfurt nach Stuttgart ist gebumper-zu-bumper...'

Normal Stau, however, are nothing when compared with the astounding *Stau aus dem Nichts* – the 'Traffic Jam from Nowhere'. You can be sailing along at 180km/h and suddenly find yourself screeching to a halt and taking the next eight, 10... even *30km* at a crawl. Most frustrating is that in the vast majority of cases, you'll just speed back up again and never see what caused the backup in the first place. These Traffic Jams from Nowhere are so prevalent that the government actually funded a study of the phenomenon!

Motoring Organisations

Germany's main motoring organisation, the Allgemeiner Deutscher Automobil Club (ADAC; ☎ 089-767 60; fax 089-767 62 80 1), Am Westpark 8, 81373 Munich, has offices in all major cities and many smaller ones, including a highly reassuring presence in eastern Germany. In this book we list ADAC offices under Information in many city sections.

The ADAC provides some of the best on and off-road services of any motoring club in the world. Members (DM75 annually

The Finger & Other Banned Gestures

German drivers are known for their aggressive road behaviour. It comes, says Oliver Bengl, a professional driver and commentator on things roadworthy, from the average German's belief that (a) they are excellent drivers while everyone else on the road is an execrable one, and that (b) the average German's highly conservative daytime role creates a 'King of the Road' mentality after leaving the workplace.

Road rage in Germany became so serious that German authorities stepped in and made any sort of offensive gesture illegal. If you give another driver 'the finger' (both British and American styles apply), tap your temple with your index finger, wave an inward-turned open palm up and down in front of your eyes, raise a fist or even give an Italian-style under-the-chin finger flick, the person at whom the gesture is directed can write down your registration number and report you to the police. You can be fined up to DM1500. ■

domestic, DM110 Europewide) can get help planning trips, free road maps, discounts on auto insurance and even international health insurance from any ADAC office in the country, as well as roadside breakdown assistance *(Pannenhilfe)* 24 hours a day.

ADAC's services, including their roadside assistance programme, are available to members of participating motoring organisations around the world – including American or Australian AAA, Canadian CAA and British AA. Call the ADAC road patrol (☎ 0180-222 22 22) if your car breaks down. Technicians probably won't speak English, but gestures work very well – impersonate the sound your heap was making before it died, and the mechanic will probably figure it out directly. ADAC mechanics also carry a multilingual auto-part dictionary, so they can tell you if it's your brake lining or fuel pump.

Petrol

Fuel prices in Germany are quite stiff, even by European standards, costing a little more than in the UK and a bit less than in Scandinavia. Prices vary from DM1.60 to DM1.65 per litre for unleaded regular, DM1.65 to DM1.70 for unleaded super, and DM1.30 to DM1.40 per for diesel. Autobahn filling stations are slightly more expensive than high-street ones, and can be found every 40km or so throughout the country. Most stations in Germany are open late; the major players – Aral, BP, Elf and Agip – usually run 24-hour operations complete with mini-markets selling soggy, overpriced sandwiches, Shaun Cassidy cassettes and porno magazines.

Sending Your Car by Train

All ICN and some other night trains are also auto trains, serving many major German cities as well as cities in France, Switzerland, Italy, Austria and Hungary. Service to France is limited to Narbonne, at the Spain/France border; to Italy at Bolzano; and in Hungary to Siófok. Prices vary, especially on international services, and dates are very limited. You must accompany your vehicle.

Parking

Cars are less practical in the centre of most German cities because one-way streets and extensive pedestrian zones are common. A *Parkschein* is a vending machine – often solar-powered – selling parking vouchers that must be displayed clearly in the windscreen, but it's usually more convenient to leave your car at a central *Parkhaus* (car park) and proceed on foot. Most cities have automated car parks with signs indicating available space; rates are roughly DM2.50 per hour or DM20 per day.

Rental

In general, to rent a car in Germany you'll need to be at least 21 years old and hold a valid driving licence (an international licence is not necessary) and a major credit card. Amex, Diners Club, Visa, and Euro Card/MasterCard are almost always accepted; JCB (Japan Credit Bank) is good only sometimes at airports, and they'll almost never take a Discover card unless you've pre-paid in the USA. There may be a supplement for additional driver(s).

Safety seats for children under four are not required by law but are highly recommended. Bring one from home or be prepared to shell out at least DM10 per day for one from the car-rental firm. Ski and luggage racks are available from rental companies for about DM50 per rental.

Rental Companies Germany's main rental companies are Avis (☎ 06171-68 18 80), Europcar (☎ 069-697 97 0), Hertz (☎ 0130-212 1) and Sixt (☎ 089-666 95 0), but there are a number of smaller local ones too. Alamo (☎ 069-690 72 36 0) has recently been expanding its operations in Germany and generally has lower prices than the others.

The four major outfits listed above and Alamo have offices in so many German cities that printing them here is folly. Suffice to say that wherever you are – from Aachen to Zwickau – there's a rental office nearby, usually at the airport and often in the city or town centre.

Rental rates are usually rather high if you simply walk up to the counter, even taking into account special weekend rates and discounts. It's generally more economical to make reservations ahead of time with the central reservation office in your country. If you haven't done that in advance, make sure you shop around. Check out the smaller agencies in particular, though the larger firms, feeling the crunch, often have some exceptional deals on offer. For example, a three-day weekend rental of a budget car – an Opel Corsa, say, or a Ford Fiesta – can cost as little as DM99.

One rental agency offering some of the best deals around is Auto Europe, a US company with offices around the world that you can simply call up on their toll-free numbers. If you're already in Germany, dial ☎ 0130-822 19 8. In the US, it's ☎ 800-223 5555; in Australia ☎ 1-800-126 409; in New Zealand ☎ 0800-440 722; in France ☎ 0590 1770; and in the UK ☎ 0800-899 893. The smallest car available costs around US$80 for three days (the minimum rental period), including unlimited km, value-added tax (or VAT equivalent) *and* third-party insurance.

Insurance You could seriously screw yourself by driving uninsured or even underinsured. Germans are very persnickety about their cars, and even nudging another car at a red light could lead to months of harassing phone calls until you pay for an entire new rear bumper and paint job if you're uninsured.

Liability insurance covers you for legal action filed against you when you crash your car against anyone or their property. This is generally not included in the rental price but available at extra charge.

Collision damage waiver (CDW) is protection for the car. It reduces the amount you'll have to reimburse the rental company (if you get their car stolen or bash it to bits) to DM300 if you're over 24 years old and DM1000 if under. It is available for an extra DM20 to DM50 per day.

American Express and some Visa and EuroCard/MasterCard holders are automatically covered for CDW on renting a car if they decline the policy on offer from the rental company. Check with your company to see what coverage they offer in Germany before assuming it will cover you, and note that CDW is *not* liability coverage.

Personal accident insurance (PAI) covers you and your passenger(s) for medical costs incurred as the result of an accident. If your health insurance from home does this as well, save yourself the DM10 to DM20 per day the rental firm will charge you.

Fly/Drive Packages Fly/drive deals can be excellent value for money; Lufthansa offers deals from around US$25 per day if you book for longer than three weeks. You may also get a better deal by calling the rental company's reservations number in the USA or the UK – even from within Germany – and asking the price for a rental in your home country. It often results in better deals. Otherwise, shop around upon arrival.

No-Go Areas Generally speaking, you're allowed to drive cars rented in Germany pretty much anywhere in Western Europe, and pretty much nowhere in Eastern Europe (except eastern Germany). Countries specifically forbidden include: Albania, Belarus, Bosnia, Bulgaria, Croatia, Czech Republic, Estonia, Hungary, Latvia, Lithuania, Macedonia, Poland, Romania, Russia, Slovakia, Slovenia, Turkey and Yugoslavia.

If you enter these places with a rental car, you're insurance is revoked, the rental agreement rendered void and the rental company could even report the car as stolen.

Purchase

Unless you're going to stay put in Germany for a while, buying a car here tends to be an unwise decision due to the costs and paperwork hassles involved. If you are an EU national, you must register the car with the Ordnungs- und Strassenverkehrsamt (Public Order & Traffic Office), a branch of which can be found in most larger towns. You will need proof of ownership, proof of insurance and a passport or ID. You're also subject to a motor vehicle tax. The vehicle also has to pass a safety inspection by the Technical Supervision Agency (TÜV) every two years in order to be kept legally on the road.

If you are not an EU national it is generally not possible to buy and register a car in Germany, since you have to be a resident to do so. The only way to get around that requirement is to have a friend or relative buy the car for you, though they may not feel comfortable about jeopardising their driving record and insurance rates in the event that you have an accident.

If you still want to buy a car, be warned: experienced car dealers from Eastern Europe get to the real bargains first, so it's a lot easier purchasing (and reselling) a vehicle in other Western European countries, especially Holland and Belgium.

Berlin and Munich are the best places in Germany to shop around for used cars if you know what to look for. And don't buy any vehicle without checking first that it has its *current* TÜV certificate of roadworthiness. The Berlin newspaper *Zweite Hand* has a separate car edition with thousands of listings each week. Opel Corsas with more than a few km on the clock can sometimes be snapped up for as little as DM3000.

BICYCLE

Bicycle touring *(Radwandern)* is very popular in Germany. In urban areas the pavement/sidewalk is often divided into separate sections for pedestrians and cyclists – be warned that this division is taken very seriously. Even outside towns and cities there are often separate cycling routes so you don't have to use the roads and highways. Of course, cycling is strictly *verboten* on the autobahns.

In Germany, the northern flatlands are especially suitable for long bike explorations, but you need to be in excellent shape to tackle the central highlands and certainly the mountainous areas of the south. Favoured routes include those along the Rhine, Moselle and Danube rivers and in the Lake Constance area.

Hostel-to-hostel biking is an easy way to go, and route guides are often sold at DJH hostels. There are well equipped cycling shops in almost every town, and a fairly active market for used touring bikes.

You can take a bicycle with you on most trains in Germany though you'll have to buy a separate ticket for it. For information, check the Deutsche Bahn Radfahrer-Hotline (☎ 0180-3 194 194). On IR trains with the special bike compartment, the charge is DM12, advance bookings necessary. The cost on IR trains for less than 100km is DM6.

Germany's main cyclist organisation is the Allgemeiner Deutscher Fahrrad Club (ADFC; ☎ 089-553 57 5), Landwehrstrasse 16, 80336 Munich. There's another office at Postfach 107747, 28077 Bremen (☎ 0431-346 29 0; fax 0431-346 29 50). See also Activities in the Facts for the Visitor chapter.

Rental & Purchase

Simple three-gear bicycles can be hired from train stations for around DM12/56 a day/week, and more robust mountain bikes from DM15/90; holders of rail passes or valid train tickets sometimes get a small discount. See DB's *Fahrrad am Bahnhof* brochures for lists of stations offering this service. If you plan to spend longer than several weeks in the saddle, buying a second-hand bike works out cheaper than renting a bike or bringing your own; good reconditioned models go for DM300 to DM400.

HITCHING

Hitching is never entirely safe in any country in the world, and we don't recommend it. Travellers who decide to hitch should understand that they are taking a small but potentially serious risk. However, many people do choose to hitch, and the advice that follows should help to make the journey as fast and safe as possible.

Hitching *(Trampen)* is considered an acceptable way of getting around in Germany and average waits are short. Don't waste time hitching in urban areas: take public transport to the main exit routes. It's illegal to hitchhike on autobahns or their entry/exit ramps, but service stations can be very good places to pick up a ride. Prepare a sign clearly showing your intended destination in German (eg 'München', not 'Munich' though 'Hanover' will probably get you to 'Hannover'). You can save yourself a lot of trouble by arranging a lift through a *Mitfahrzentrale* (see Hitching & Ride Services in the Getting There & Away chapter).

WALKING

Walking and hiking are hugely popular weekend activities throughout the country. Locals don *Wanderkleidung* (hiking clothes) and take to the well marked paths that are almost always found in the woods just outside cities. All tourist offices sell *Wanderkarten* (hiking maps), usually from between DM5 and DM12, and can give information on local hiking clubs which almost always run organised hikes on weekends.

BOAT

Boats are mostly used for basic transport when travelling to or between the Frisian Islands, though cruises along the Rhine and Moselle rivers are also popular.

In summer there are frequent services on Lake Constance but, except for the Constance-Meersburg and the Friedrichshafen-Romanshorn car ferries, these boats are really more for sightseeing than actual transport. From April to October, excursion boats ply the lakes and rivers of eastern Germany and are an excellent, inexpensive way of seeing the country. Paddle-wheel steamers operating out of Dresden are a fine way to tour the Elbe River. Cruises are popular between Berlin and Potsdam.

LOCAL TRANSPORT

Local transport includes buses, trams, S-Bahn (see Local Services under Train earlier) and/or U-Bahn (underground train system). Most public transport systems integrate buses, trams and trains; fares are determined by the zones or the time travelled, or sometimes both. Multi-ticket strips or day passes are generally available and offer far better value than single-ride tickets. See town and city Getting Around sections for details.

Bus & Tram

Cities and towns operate their own local bus, trolleybus and/or tram services. In most places you must have a ticket before boarding, and validate it aboard (or risk paying a fine of around DM60). Tickets are sold mainly from vending machines at train stations and tram or bus stops. Bus drivers usually sell single-trip tickets as a service to forgetful passengers, but these are more expensive than tickets bought in advance.

Train

S-Bahn Most large cities have a system of suburban train lines called the S-Bahn. Trains on these lines cover a wider area than buses or trams, but tend to be less frequent. S-Bahn lines are often linked to the national rail network, and sometimes interconnect urban centres. Rail passes and conventional train tickets between cities are generally valid on these services.

U-Bahn The larger cities, such as Berlin, Munich, Hanover and Frankfurt, have a fast and efficient underground/subway system known as the U-Bahn.

Taxi

Taxis are expensive in Germany and, given the excellent public transport systems, not recommended unless you're in a real hurry. (They can actually be slower if you're going to or from the airport.) Look up 'Taxi Ruf' in the local telephone directory to find the nearest taxi rank. Taxis are metered and cost up to DM4 at flag fall and DM3 per km; in some places higher night tariffs apply.

BahnTaxi Deutsche Bahn has put together an exceptional deal for travellers heading from major city train stations between 5 and 1 am: BahnTaxi, a flat-rate taxi ride for two people from the station to most city destinations.

The cities served and costs per two people are: Frankfurt/Main DM12, Nuremberg

DM12, Hanover DM15, Munich DM15, Hamburg DM17 and Cologne DM17.

You can order a BahnTaxi at all Reisezentrum offices in the station, or in advance by calling the city area code plus ☎ 194 19 (for example: Munich ☎ 089-194 19). See the appropriate city sections (under Getting Around/Taxi) for the location of BahnTaxi stands at each station.

ORGANISED TOURS

Local tourist offices offer tour options, from city sightseeing trips lasting an hour or two to adventure, spa-bath and wine-tasting packages over several days. Other good sources for organised tours both in and around Germany are Deutsche Bahn and Europabus.

There are many other international and national tour operators with specific options. Your travel agent should have details. It's also worth contacting the German National Tourist Office in your home country (see the Facts for the Visitor chapter under Tourist Offices for a list of offices outside Germany). Many airlines also offer tour packages.

Berlin

Berlin, the largest city in Germany, has more to offer visitors than any other destination in the country. Divided by the 165km Berlin Wall (see boxed text) until it was finally dismantled in June 1990, east and west Berlin remain separate and will continue to be so until the sentiments and associations of the past half-century are put aside. Even though the national government will return to its erstwhile capital early in the new millennium, it will be years before the wounds of the Cold War are fully healed.

The centre of 19th-century Prussian military and industrial might, Berlin finally reached maturity in the 1920s, only to be bombed into rubble in WWII – some 28.5 sq km of utter ruin remained, prompting the returning Bertolt Brecht to describe the city as 'a pile of rubble next to Potsdam'. Today, despite having lost a large part of its prewar population, Berlin counts almost 3.5 million people. A large percentage of them are 'outsiders' – born in other parts of Germany or abroad and attracted to the city for economic reasons or simply to witness a metropolis in transition. As a result, Berlin is the most cosmopolitan – and '*undeutsche*' – city in Germany.

Berlin has everything – history, green spaces, some of the world's finest museums, and a wonderful international and slightly edgy feel. And what many travellers don't seem to be aware of before they get to this *Weltstadt* is that Berlin is Europe's most uninhibited 'party city' – and it goes on seven nights a week till late, late, late (the surfeit of cafés serving breakfast daily till as late as 6 pm gives you an idea of just how late).

For centuries the bear has been the symbol of Berlin – some say that its name comes from the German word *Bärlein* (meaning 'little bear') or that the furriers' guild used it as a symbol when the town first made it on the map in the 13th century – you can visit the city's three ursine mascots in a pit behind the Märkisches Museum in Mitte. We're not

HIGHLIGHTS

- The ancient Greek Pergamon Altar and the Ishtar Gate from Babylonia in the Pergamon Museum
- View of the Postdamer Platz engineering project from Infobox
- The South Seas collection at the Ethnology Museum in Dahlem
- A stroll along Unter den Linden to the Brandenburg Gate
- The Bröhan Museum in Charlottenburg (Art Nouveau and Art Deco)
- Berlin's Love Parade in July, one of the world's great parties
- A classical-music concert at the Konzerthaus
- The Soviet monument in Treptower Park
- A cruise from Jannowitzbrücke in Mitte to Schlossbrücke near the Charlottenburg Palace
- An evening in the Tacheles cultural centre followed by an early (or late) breakfast at one of the cafés along Oranienburger Strasse

• **Population:** 3.5m • **Capital:** Berlin • **Area:** 884 sq km • **Area Code:** ☎030

Berlin Luminaries: Marlene Dietrich, Frederick the Great, Walter Gropius, George Grosz, Alexander von Humboldt, Nina Hagen, Max Liebermann, Gerhard Marcks, Leni Riefenstahl, Gustav Stresemann, Margarete von Trotta, Kurt Tucholsky, Katharina Witt about to tussle with tradition but if we had our way, Berlin's mascot would be the duck. Bear with us – as it were – and we'll explain.

One warm and dusty spring day in Berlin – because of all the rebuilding and construction it's always dusty in Berlin these days – one of us stood at the base of the Infobox at Leipziger Platz, peering down at a large pool that was taking in yet more groundwater sucked out by those pipes that snake and creep above the streets all over town. Out of the dusty blue flew a mallard, skimming the surface and coming to a sudden halt in the centre of the makeshift pond. Haughtily rejecting a bit of banana, she preened and moved over to an undoubtedly tastier bit of flotsam she spied floating by. Graceful, she was, and inventive, imperious, resilient and, well, a little quackers. To us, that's Berlin – the once and future capital of united Germany.

HISTORY

The first recorded settlement (1237) at present-day Berlin was a place named Cölln founded on marshland around the Spree River south of Museumsinsel (Museum Island), although Spandau, at the junction of the Spree and the ponded Havel River, and Köpenick, to the south-east, were Slavic fortresses at least as early as the 10th century. Medieval Berlin developed as a *Handelsstadt* (trade centre) on the banks of the Spree around the Nikolaikirche and spread north-east towards today's Alexanderplatz. In 1432, Berlin and Cölln merged.

In the 1440s, Elector Friedrich II (Frederick the Irontooth) of Brandenburg solidified the supremacy of the Hohenzollern dynasty, begun by his brother Friedrich Hohenzollern, which would last until Kaiser Wilhelm II's abdication and escape from Potsdam to Holland in 1918. Berlin's importance increased in 1470 when the elector moved his residence here from Brandenburg and built a palace near the present Schlossplatz, which stood until the GDR demolished the war-damaged ruin in 1950. By 1486 Berlin was the capital of the Mark (March) of Brandenburg.

During the Thirty Years' War (1618-48) Berlin's population was decimated, but the city was reborn stronger than before under the so-called Great Elector Friedrich Wilhelm of Brandenburg (the Soldier King, ruled 1640-88) and it experienced an unprecedented cultural and economic boom. His vision was the basis of Prussian power, and he invited immigrants, notably Jews (who had been banished from Berlin and Brandenburg in 1572) and Huguenot refugees from France, to settle in the city. Some 5000 of the latter arrived after 1685 when King Louis XIV revoked the Edict of Nantes, which had granted the Protestants religious freedom. Berlin's population swelled by 25%, and French superseded German in some districts. Some French words – or corruptions thereof – can still be heard in *Berlinisch: Feez* for *fête*; *Budiker* for *boutiquier*; *Milljöh* for *milieu*; and of course *Boulette*, the 'meatball' that is arguably Berliners' favourite food.

The Great Elector's son, Friedrich I, the first Prussian king, made the fast-growing Berlin his capital in 1701, and his daughter-in-law Sophie-Charlotte encouraged the development of the arts and sciences and presided over a lively and intellectual court. Friedrich II – better known to English speakers as Frederick the Great (1740-86) and to his subjects as 'Der alter Fritz' (Old Freddy) – sought greatness through building and was known for his political and military savvy. Berlin flourished as a great cultural centre and became known as *Spree-Athen*, the 'Athens on the Spree'.

The Enlightenment arrived with some authority in the persons of the playwright Gotthold Ephraim Lessing, the thinker and publisher Christophe Friedrich Nicolai, and the philosopher Moses Mendelssohn, grandfather of the composer Felix Mendelssohn-Bartholdy; all helped make Berlin a truly international city.

Prussia went into a downward spiral after the death of Friedrich II, culminating with the defeat of the Prussian army by Napoleon's forces at Jena south-east of Weimar in 1806. The French occupied Berlin for the next seven years. In 1848 a bourgeois democratic revolution was suppressed, stifling the political development that had been set in motion by the Enlightenment and had swept across Europe. From 1850 to 1870 the population more than tripled to just under 500,000 as the Industrial Revolution, spurred on by such companies as Siemens and Borsig, took hold. In 1871 Chancellor Otto von Bismarck united Germany under Kaiser Wilhelm I, marking the start of the *Gründerzeit* (literally 'Foundation Time'). The population of Berlin was almost two million in 1900.

Before WWI Berlin had become an industrial giant, but the war and its aftermath led to revolt throughout Germany. On 8-9 November 1918, following the abdication of Wilhelm II, the Social Democratic Party (SPD) proclaimed the German Republic from a balcony of the Reichstag (Parliament) with their leader, Friedrich Ebert, at the head; hours later Karl Liebknecht, the founder of the German Communist Party (then known as the Spartacus League) proclaimed a free Socialist republic from a balcony of the Berlin Schloss (City Palace). In January 1919 Liebknecht and his fellow Spartacist Rosa Luxemburg were murdered by the Freikorps, remnants of the old imperial army (allied with Ebert), which entered the city and brought the socialist revolution to a bloody end. Ebert was elected president later that month and the new republic moved to Weimar.

Berlin gained the reputation as a centre for both tolerance and indulgence in the 1920s, and outsiders – including the English writers WH Auden and Christopher Isherwood – flocked to this city of cabaret, dada and jazz. In 1920 eight towns and dozens of small communities were amalgamated to form *Gross Berlin* (Greater Berlin).

But not all was right in Berlin – as elsewhere in Germany crippling war reparations, strikes and the worst hyperinflation the world has ever known brought poverty and discontent.

On the eve of the Nazi takeover in 1933, the Communist Party under Ernst Thälmann was the strongest single party in 'Red Berlin', having polled 31% of the votes in the 1932 elections (almost the same as the 30% polled by Communists in the municipal elections in East Berlin in May 1990).

Berlin was heavily bombed by the Allies in WWII and, during the Battle of Berlin (November 1943 to March 1944), Allied bombers hammered the city every night. Most of the buildings you see today along Unter den Linden were reconstructed from the resultant ruins. The Soviets shelled Berlin from the east and, after the last terrible battle, buried 18,000 of their own troops. By the end of the war in May 1945 some 125,000 Berliners had lost their lives; of the 160,000 Jews who had made the capital their home in the early 1930s, only 7000 remained.

In August 1945, the Potsdam Conference sealed the postwar fate of Berlin by agreeing that each of the victorious powers – the USA, Britain, France and the Soviet Union – would occupy a separate zone. In June 1948 the city was split in two when the three western Allies introduced a western German currency and established a separate administration in their sectors. The Soviets then blockaded West Berlin, but an airlift kept it in the western camp. In October 1949 East Berlin became the capital of the German Democratic Republic.

The construction of the Berlin Wall in August 1961 prevented the drain of skilled labour (between 1945 and 1961 three million East Germans were lured westward by higher wages). So great was the animosity and mistrust on both sides of the Wall that even as late as 1987, when Berlin marked its 750th anniversary, separate celebrations were held in the East and West.

In September 1989, when Hungary cut away the electrified wire fence separating it from Austria, the move released a wave of East Germans holidaying in Hungary into the West and the gap attracted thousands more. The collapse of the communist regimes in the region – including the GDR – was now unstoppable. On 9 November 1989 the Wall opened, and on 1 July 1990, when West Germany's currency was adopted in the GDR, the Wall was being hacked to pieces.

I am a Doughnut

West Berlin had pulled off the PR coup of the Cold War. It was August 1963, exactly two years since the Wall separating East and West Berlin had been put up by the GDR, and the Leader of the Free World and everybody's favourite blue-eyed boy, John Fitzgerald Kennedy, 35th president of the United States, had agreed to speak.

From the steps of the Rathaus Schöneberg, the silver-throated orator flayed the forces of darkness to the east and applauded the powers of light in the west, concluding with the now famous words: 'All men free, wherever they live, are citizens of Berlin, and therefore, as a free man, I take pride in the words "Ich bin ein Berliner."' Looking at the old film footage of that momentous event, it's difficult to determine whether the crowd of 500,000 was smiling and cheering in support of the president's sentiments or laughing and jeering at his words. JFK had just told them: 'I am a doughnut.'

Unlike English, German does not use the indefinite article ('a' or 'an') before professions, nationalities etc. Thus *Ich bin Student* is 'I am (a) student' in English, while 'I am a Berliner' is rendered *Ich bin Berliner* in German. *Ein Berliner* in German is short for *ein Berliner Pfannkuchen*, a round jam-filled bun sprinkled with powdered sugar and very popular in the capital.

There's no record of what happened to JFK's chief of protocol or his linguistic advisors after the speech. Everyone probably had a good laugh and forgot about the 'doughnut debacle'. But not in Berlin. You can still buy little plastic Berliners at souvenir shops everywhere in Berlin emblazoned with the words 'Ich bin ein Berliner'. ■

The Unification Treaty between the two Germanys designated Berlin the official capital of Germany, and in June 1991 the Bundestag voted to move the seat of government from Bonn to Berlin over the next decade at a cost of between DM60 and DM80 billion.

ORIENTATION

Berlin sits in the middle of the region known from medieval times as the Mark (March), and is surrounded by the new *Bundesland* (federal state) of Brandenburg. The state of Berlin measures some 892 sq km while the municipal boundaries encompass 234 sq km. Roughly one third of the municipal area is made up of parks, forests, lakes and rivers; in spite of WWII bombing, there are more trees here than in Paris and more bridges than in Venice. Much of the natural beauty of rolling hills and quiet shorelines is in the south-east and south-west of the city.

Of course, the improvement and maintenance of these natural features was imperative in order to give people recreational areas after the erection of the Berlin Wall, when West Berlin became an 'island' in the GDR 'sea'; as Berliners used to say, 'No matter whether you go north, south, east or west from Berlin, you're still going East'. But it remains a very ecologically minded city, with bicycle lanes everywhere, recycling bins even in U/S-Bahn stations and solar-powered machines from which to buy your parking ticket.

The Spree River wends its way across the city for over 30km, from the Grosser Müggelsee, the city's largest lake, in the east to Spandau in the west. North and south of Spandau the Havel River widens into a series of lakes, from Tegel to below Potsdam. A network of canals links the waterways to each other and to the Oder River in the east on the Polish border, and there are beautiful walks along some of them.

Berlin has 23 independent administrative districts *(Bezirken)*, although most travellers will end up visiting only the eight 'core' ones. They are (clockwise from the west): Charlottenburg, Tiergarten, Mitte, Prenzlauer Berg (locals say Prenz'lberg), Friedrichshain, Kreuzberg, Schöneberg and Wilmersdorf. Kreuzberg itself, quite different in its eastern and western sections, is split here into Kreuzberg 36 and Kreuzberg 61 for clarity.

You can't really get lost within sight of the monstrous Fernsehturm (TV Tower) on Alexanderplatz in Mitte (Map 4). Unter den

Linden, the fashionable avenue of aristocratic old Berlin, and its continuation, Karl-Liebknecht-Strasse, extend east from the Brandenburg Gate to Alexanderplatz, once the heart of socialist East Germany. Some of Berlin's finest museums are here, on boot-shaped Museumsinsel in the Spree. The cultural centre of eastern Berlin is around Friedrichstrasse, which runs perpendicular to Unter den Linden.

South of here, in areas once occupied by the Wall, the largest construction site in Europe is taking shape. What used to be Checkpoint Charlie, where non-Germans once passed between the two Berlins, is now the new DM1.1 billion American Business Center designed by Philip Johnson. A new district, to be dominated by futuristic high-rises built by international corporations, is being erected all around Potsdamer Platz. But the Wall, Berlin's macabre erstwhile landmark, won't be forgotten altogether; sections of it will be left for public view around the city (see boxed text entitled The Berlin Wall).

The ruin of the shattered Kaiser-Wilhelm-Gedächtniskirche (Kaiser Wilhelm Memorial Church; Map 6), on Breitscheidplatz in Charlottenburg, a block away from the Zoologischer Garten (usually referred to as just 'Zoo' and pronounced 'Zoe') train station, is the most visible landmark in west Berlin. The tourist office and hundreds of shops are in the Europa-Center at the eastern end of the square. The Kurfürstendamm, the main thoroughfare here (known as the 'Ku'damm'), runs 3.5km south-west from Breitscheidplatz to Halensee.

To the north-east, between Breitscheidplatz and the Brandenburg Gate, is Tiergarten (Map 3), a district named after the vast city park that was once a royal hunting domain. The area adjacent to the park, along the bend in the Spree (the so-called Spreebogen) and between Lehrter Stadtbahnhof and Bellevue S-Bahn stations, is being transformed into a futuristic government/diplomatic district. The Lehrter Stadtbahnhof itself will become the capital's main station by 2002 for long-distance and suburban train travel. For what Berlin will look like in the future, visit the Infobox on Leipziger Platz next to Potsdamer Platz or the huge relief map and exhibit on the ground floor of the Staatsrat (Council of State) building on Museumsinsel.

While in central Berlin, keep in mind that the street numbers usually run sequentially up one side of the street and down the other (important exceptions are Unter den Linden and, in Schöneberg, Martin-Luther-Strasse and Lietzenburger Strasse). Although number guides appear on most corner street signs, this is not always true in eastern Berlin. Be aware, too, that a continuous street may change names several times, and that on some streets (eg Kurfürstendamm, Kantstrasse, Knesebeckstrasse etc) numbering sequences continue after interruptions caused by squares. The names of some streets and other landmarks have been changed for political reasons and more will follow; recently renamed are Dimitroffstrasse (now Danziger Strasse) in Prenzlauer Berg and central Marx-Engels-Platz on Museumsinsel, which has become Schlossplatz in honour of the City Palace, which stood here until September 1950.

The multi-coloured pipes with the company name Pollem that you see everywhere in Berlin these days are supplying building sites with gravel, sand and cement and removing groundwater. When massive reconstruction began after the *Wende* (the 'change' of 1989), the city ruled that construction sites could only be supplied by river, train or these pipes to avoid massive traffic jams and tie-ups.

Maps

The best maps of Berlin are the ones from Falkplan – either the standard sheet map (DM6) or the Falk Megaplan with a patented folding system (DM12.80), ADAC's 1:25,000 map (DM9.80), or the RV Verlag Euro City 1:27,500 version (DM8.80). The last is very user-friendly with an additional 14 1:10,000 and 1:20,000 maps of the centre, suburbs and Potsdam, along with an up-to-date street index.

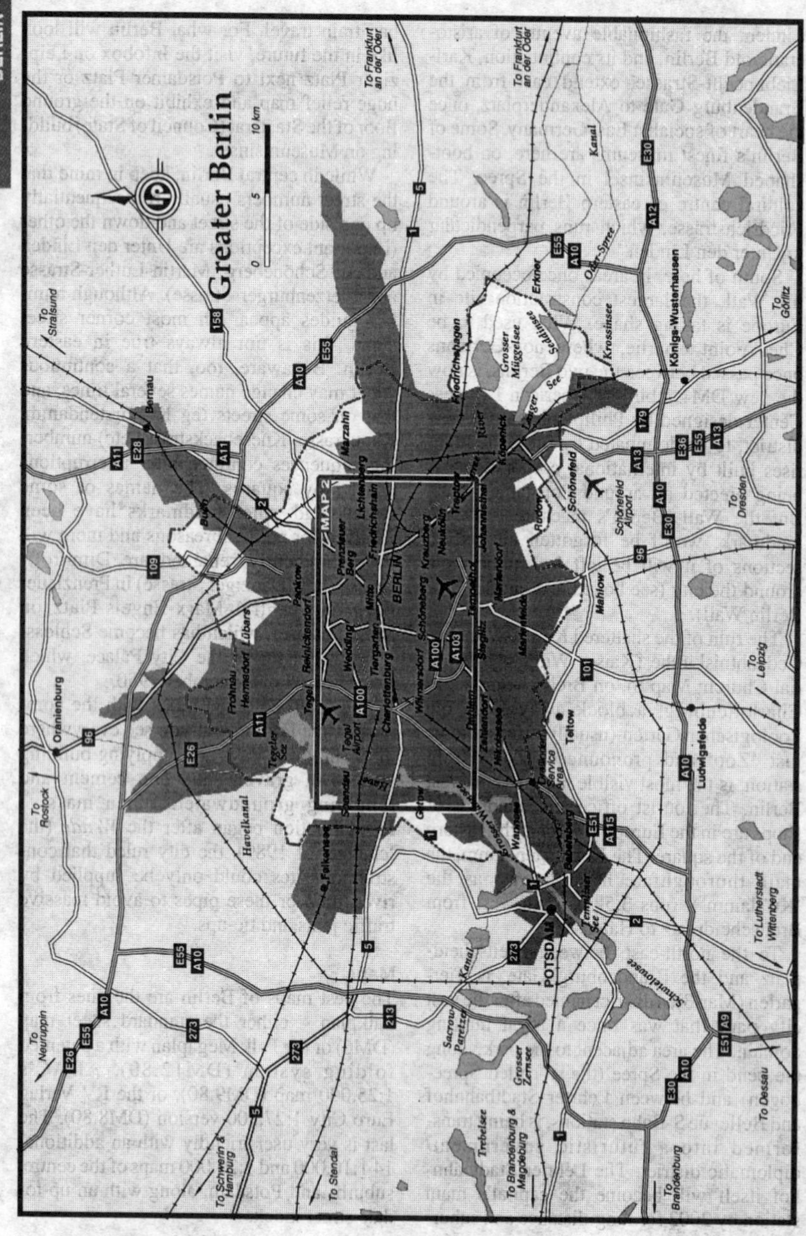
Greater Berlin
0
5
10 km
To Stralsund
Bernau
To Frankfurt an der Oder
To Frankfurt an der Oder
Buch
Marzahn
MAP 2
Lichtenberg
Friedrichshain
Prenzlauer Berg
Pankow
Reinickendorf
Wedding
Mitte
BERLIN
Kreuzberg
Neukölln
Treptow
Tiergarten
Charlottenburg
Schöneberg
Wilmersdorf
Tempelhof
Steglitz
Dahlem
Zehlendorf
Nikolassee
Wannsee
Grosser Wannsee
Havel
Spandau
Gatow
Tegel
Tegel Airport
Tegeler See
Frohnau
Hermsdorf
Lübars
Oranienburg
To Rostock
Havelkanal
Falkensee
Dreilinden Service Area
Teltow
Babelsberg
POTSDAM
Templiner See
Schwielowsee
Sacrow-Paretzer Kanal
Grosser Zernsee
Trebelsee
To Neuruppin
To Schwerin & Hamburg
To Stendal
To Brandenburg & Magdeburg
To Brandenburg
To Dessau
To Lutherstadt Wittenberg
Ludwigsfelde
To Leipzig
Mahlow
Marienfelde
Mariendorf
Rudow
Johannisthal
Schönefeld
Schönefeld Airport
To Dresden
Köpenick
Spree River
Friedrichshagen
Grosser Müggelsee
Langer See
Seddinsee
Krossinsee
Erkner
Oder-Spree Kanal
Königs-Wusterhausen
To Görlitz

If you plan to explore the city thoroughly or stay more than a week or so, invest in a street atlas, such as the one published by RV Verlag (DM24.80). It has more than 150 detailed maps (1:20 000) of the city, suburbs and Potsdam; an index with all the new street names; all public transport routes; and descriptive information and listings (in German).

Although most bookshops and even newsagents stock a decent supply of maps to the city and surrounding area, the best place to go is the enormous Kiepert bookshop (Map 6; ☎ 311 88 167), Hardenbergstrasse 4-5 on the corner of Knesebeckstrasse and Schillerstrasse. It has the widest selection in town.

INFORMATION

Tourist Offices

The main office of Berlin Tourismus Marketing (BTM; ☎ 250 02 5; fax 250 02 42 4) is in the Europa-Center (Map 6) at Budapester Strasse 45 in Tiergarten. It is open Monday to Saturday from 8 am to 10 pm, Sunday from 9 am to 9 pm.

This office also handles hotel (but not private) room reservations (same telephone number; email: reservierung@btm.de). There's a tourist office branch (Map 4; same telephone & fax numbers) in the south wing of Brandenburg Gate in Mitte, open daily from 9.30 am to 6 pm. In addition there are information points (same telephone & fax numbers) in the Dresdner Bank building at Unter den Linden 17 in Mitte (Map 4), open weekdays from 8.30 am to 2 pm (plus on Tuesday and Thursday from 3.30 to 6 pm), and in the main hall of Tegel airport at the left-luggage office opposite Gate O, open daily from 5 am to 10 pm. There may be a new branch in Zoo station by the time you read this.

The tourist offices sell maps, books (including the excellent *Berlin for Young People*, DM9.90) and the Berlin WelcomeCard (DM29), which entitles one adult and up to three children to 72 hours of unlimited transport within the Berlin-Brandenburg area and free or discounted admission to major museums, shows, attractions, sightseeing tours and boat cruises. The Welcome Card is also available at hotels and public-transport ticket offices.

The ADAC car club (☎ 868 60) has two offices in Berlin: one at Bundesallee 29-30 in Wilmersdorf and the other at Alexanderplatz 5 (Map 4).

Information for disabled people is available from Service-Ring-Berlin (☎ 859 40 10), weekdays from 10 am to 6 pm. The Verband Geburts- und anderer Behinderter (Disabled Persons' Association; ☎ 341 17 97) has wheelchairs available for free during your stay in Berlin.

Museums

Berlin has four main museum groups – on Museumsinsel, at the Dahlem complex, around Schloss Charlottenburg and in the Kulturforum in Tiergarten – plus many other smaller ones. State museums – those run by the Staatliche Museen Preussischer Kulturbesitz (State Museums of the Prussian Cultural Foundation) and denoted in this chapter with 'SMPK' – cost DM4/2 per entry or DM8/4 for a day card which is valid at all SMPK museums. A card valid for unlimited visits over a year costs DM60/30; if you're going to do a museum a day over a two-week period, it would be worth the price. Most state museums are open Tuesday to Sunday from 9 am to 5 pm (weekend hours are sometimes from 10 am to 5 or 6 pm). Admission is free on the first Sunday of every month.

Foreign Consulates & Embassy Branches

The main diplomatic missions of most countries will remain in Bonn until the transfer of the German capital to Berlin is complete, probably in 1999; see the Facts for the Visitor chapter for a listing. In the meantime, the following maintain consulates and/or embassy branches in Berlin, where the area code ☎ is 030:

Australia
Uhlandstrasse 181-183, 10623 Berlin (☎ 880 08 80; Map 6)

Austria
Wilhelmstrasse 64, 10117 Berlin (☎ 609 38 65)
Bulgaria
Leipziger Strasse 20, 10117 Berlin (☎ 201 09 22)
Canada
Friedrichstrasse 95, 23rd Floor, 10117 Berlin (☎ 261 11 61; Map 4)
China
Heinrich-Mann-Strasse 9, 13156 Berlin (☎ 480 01 61)
Czech Republic
Wilhelmstrasse 21, 10117 Berlin (☎ 220 04 81)
France
Rue Montesquieu 31, 13469 Berlin (☎ 414 30 72)
Hungary
Unter den Linden 76, 10117 Berlin (☎ 220 25 61)
Ireland
Ernst-Reuter-Platz 10, 10587 Berlin (☎ 348 00 82 2)
Japan
Wachtelstrasse 8, 14195 Berlin (☎ 832 70 26)
Netherlands
Friedrichstrasse 95, 10117 Berlin (☎ 201 20 23)
Poland
Unter den Linden 72-74, 10117 Berlin (☎ 220 25 51)
Romania
Matterhornstrasse 79, 14129 Berlin (☎ 803 30 18)
Russia
Unter den Linden 63-65, 10117 Berlin (☎ 229 11 10; Map 4)
Slovakia
Leipziger Strasse 36, 10117 Berlin (☎ 204 45 38)
South Africa
Douglasstrasse 9, 14193 Berlin (☎ 825 01 1)
Switzerland
Fürst-Bismarck-Strasse 4, 10557 Berlin (☎ 394 40 21)
UK
Unter den Linden 32-34, 10117 Berlin (☎ 201 84 0; Map 4)
Ukraine
Kurfürstenstrasse 56, 10785 Berlin (☎ 229 16 18)
USA
Neustädtische Kirchstrasse 4-5, 10117 Berlin (☎ 238 51 74; Map 4)

If you require passport-sized photographs for visas to the countries listed above, there are photo booths in many U/S-Bahn stations throughout the city, including Wittenberg-platz (Map 6), and on the ground floor of the KaDeWe department store (Map 6; see Things to Buy).

Money

Among the most central exchange offices *(Wechselstuben)* is the Reisebank (☎ 881 71 17) at Hardenbergplatz outside Zoo station, open seven days a week from 7.30 am to 10 pm. There's a Reisebank branch at the Hauptbahnhof (Map 2; S-Bahn: Hauptbahnhof). The Euro-Change office on Breitscheidplatz buys and sells banknotes of most any country without commission charge, and you can easily compare the daily rate with the banks and other exchange services around Zoo station. Euro-Change is open weekdays from 9 am to 6 pm and on Saturday to 4 pm.

A good place on Alexanderplatz is Alex Exchange (near the entrance to the S-Bahn), open weekdays from 9 am to 6 pm and to 2 pm on Saturday. The Optimus Bank on the 6th floor of the KaDeWe department store (Map 6) charges DM2 per exchange transaction and keeps the same hours as the department store (see Things to Buy).

Branches of the main German banks are plentiful around Breitscheidplatz and Kurfürstendamm and almost all of them have ATMs. Main post offices exchange travellers' cheques at the rate of DM6 per cheque.

American Express (Map 6; ☎ 884 58 82 1), at Uhlandstrasse 173 in Charlottenburg (open weekdays from 9 am to 5.30 pm, Saturday to noon), cashes its own travellers' cheques without charging commission but gives a very ordinary rate. There's an Amex branch (Map 4; ☎ 201 74 01 2) opposite the Galeries Lafayette department store at Friedrichstrasse 172 in Mitte (open weekdays from 9 am to 5.30 pm, Saturday from 10 am to 1 pm), and another branch (Map 6; ☎ 214 98 36 3) at Bayreuther Strasse 23 (open weekdays from 9 am to 6 pm, Saturday from 10 am to 1 pm). Thomas Cook (Map 6; ☎ 201 72 20) has an exchange office at Friedrichstrasse 56.

Post & Communications

There are dozens of post offices in Berlin, but most have restricted opening hours. The post office on the ground floor of Zoo station is open from 6 am to midnight (Sunday and holidays from 8 am). The poste restante is here; letters should be clearly marked 'Hauptpostlagernd', and addressed to Bahnhof Zoo, Hardenbergplatz, 10612 Berlin. You can send a fax with a telephone card from here and buy boxes of various sizes (DM2.90 to DM5.50) but you cannot send your package from here; for that service you must go to the post office (Map 6) at Goethestrasse 12. Remember that most photocopy shops also have fax facilities.

The main American Express office (☎ 884 58 82 1) at Uhlandstrasse 173 offers a client-mail service to those with an American Express card or travellers' cheques. The sender should make sure that the words 'Client's Mail' appear somewhere on the envelope. The office will hold mail for 30 days but won't accept registered post or parcels.

You can make international phone calls from just about any post office, but it's cheaper and more convenient to use phone cards (DM12 for 40 units or DM50 for 200 units). These allow you to make calls of any length to anywhere in the world from any phone booth that accepts these cards and nowadays most – if not all – do.

Online Services

There's a great deal of information on Berlin, its culture, institutions etc, on the Internet. Most of the sites listed here also provide useful cross links.

www.berlin.de
General tourist information on the city.

www.tagesspiegel.de
Daily news and events in the capital.

www.is.in-berlin.de
Information on the city's museums and educational services.

cityscope.icf.de
Panoramic view of Potsdamer Platz and work in progress.

www.dhm.de
Web site of the Museum of German History.

The Alpha Café (☎ 447 90 67), Dunckerstrasse 72 in Prenzlauer Berg (S-Bahn No 8 or 10 to Prenzlauer Allee), is a fun place; send email and surf the net free with any purchase of food or drink. For those who don't know the Internet from an intercom but would like to keep in touch with folks back home in this easy and cheap way, there are Internet and PC lessons from 1 to 3 pm on Sunday (DM15 per person). Other cybercafés include the Virtuality Café (☎ 327 51 43) on Lewishamstrasse in Charlottenburg (U-Bahn No 7 to Adenauerplatz) and *Pl@net* (☎ 427 80 62 9) at Petersburger Strasse 76 in Friedrichshain (U-Bahn No 5 to Petersburger Strasse).

Travel Agencies

Travel agencies offering cheap flights advertise in the *Reisen* classified section *(Kleinanzeigen)* of the popular city magazines *Zitty* and *Tip* (see Listings in the Entertainment section). One of the better discount operators is Alternativ Tours (Map 6; ☎ 881 20 89), Wilmersdorfer Strasse 94 in Wilmersdorf (U-Bahn No 7 to Adenauerplatz), which specialises in unpublished, discounted fares to anywhere in the world (open weekdays from 9 am to 6 pm, Saturday to 1 pm).

The big Atlas Reisewelt chain of travel agencies has several offices in Berlin, with the most convenient branch (Map 4; ☎ 242 73 70) at Alexanderplatz 5. It is open weekdays from 9 am to 6 pm and on Saturday to 2 pm. Others are at Münzstrasse 14 (Map 4; ☎ 247 76 48), at Schönefeld airport (☎ 609 15 65 0) and at Bahnhofstrasse 18 (☎ 657 12 24) to the south-east in Köpenick. These are good places to buy train tickets very cheaply or make bus, ferry and package-tour reservations.

Especially good deals on air tickets, bus travel and car hire are available at Kilroy Travel (Map 6; ☎ 310 00 43 3 for information, ☎ 313 94 66 for bookings), Hardenbergstrasse 9 in Charlottenburg, open weekdays from 10 am to 6 pm and Saturday from 10 am to 2 pm. Other branches are at Nollendorfplatz 7 in Schöneberg (U-Bahn No 2, 4 or 15 to Nollendorfplatz) and at Takustrasse 47 on the corner of Königin-Luise-Strasse in Dahlem (open on weekdays only; U-Bahn No 1 to Dahlem-Dorf). Kilroy also sells the GO25 card issued by the Federation of International Youth Travel Organisations (FIYTO) and ISIC student cards (DM15; one photo and ID required).

Another travel service catering largely to young people is STA Travel (Map 4; ☎ 285 98 26 4), near Friedrichstrasse station at Marienstrasse 25, open weekdays from 10 am to 7 pm. There are branches at Goethestrasse 73 (Map 6; ☎ 311 09 50; S-Bahn: Savignyplatz) and at Dorotheenstrasse 30 (☎ 201 65 06 3; U/S-Bahn: Friedrichstrasse). ISIC cards are issued here as well, provided you have proper and recognisable student and personal ID.

Flugbörse (☎ 216 30 61), at Nollendorfstrasse 28 in Schöneberg, is good for discounted air tickets, including student and youth fares. There's a branch (☎ 448 54 37) at Schönhauser Allee 184 in Prenzlauer Berg (U-Bahn No 2 to Rosa-Luxemburg-Platz). Over the Rainbow (☎ 695 12 65 2) is a gay and lesbian travel agency at Tempelhofer Damm 1-7 at Tempelhof airport (U-Bahn No 6 to Platz der Luftbrücke), open weekdays from 9 am to 9 pm.

On Budapester Strasse north-east of the zoo are several agencies specialising in exotic destinations, including the Middle East. LOT Polish Airlines (☎ 678 82 50 or ☎ 261 15 05) is at No 18 of Budapester Strasse and Malév Hungarian Airlines (☎ 264 95 45) at No 10.

Tourist information on Eastern Europe is available from Čedok Czech Republic; ☎ 204 46 44) at Leipziger Strasse 60; Ibusz (Hungary; ☎ 238 60 78), in Haus Ungarn at Karl-Liebknecht-Strasse 9; and Polorbis (Poland; ☎ 294 90 31 5) at Warschauer Strasse 5.

The Aeroflot office (☎ 226 98 10) at Unter den Linden 51, near the corner of Friedrichstrasse, has information about Russia.

Bookshops

Books in Berlin at Goethestrasse 69 (open weekdays from noon to 8 pm, Saturday from 10 am to 4 pm) has a good selection of both new and used English-language books. For both fiction and non-fiction paperbacks in English, try the Marga Schoeller Bücherstube (Map 6; ☎ 881 11 12), Knesebeckstrasse 33-34 in Charlottenburg, or the British Bookshop (Map 4; ☎ 238 46 80; open weekdays from 10 am to 6 pm, Saturday to 4 pm) at Mauerstrasse 83-84 in Mitte.

The enormous Kiepert (Map 6; ☎ 311 00 90), Hardenbergstrasse 4-5 on the corner of Knesebeckstrasse and Schillerstrasse, has many departments, from guidebooks (including the full range of Lonely Planet) and foreign-language dictionaries to maps, maps and more maps. It is open weekdays from 9 am to 6.30 pm and on Saturday to 4 pm. They have four more branches in Berlin, including a convenient one (Map 4; ☎ 208 25 11) at Friedrichstrasse 63 on the corner of Mohrenstrasse, open weekdays from 10 am to 8 pm, Saturday to 4 pm.

Berliner Universitätsbuchhandlung (Berlin University Bookshop; Map 4; ☎ 240 94 31), at Spandauer Strasse 2 in Mitte, has a huge selection of everything from glossy art books, German travel guidebooks and maps to cultural and historical material about Berlin and surrounds. It is open weekdays from 9 am to 8 pm, Saturday to 4 pm.

For international papers and magazines in most known languages, try the BHG Presse Zentrum in the main hall of Zoo station (Map 6); the International Reisebedarf newsagent just outside the station on the corner of Joachimstaler Strasse and Hardenbergstrasse; or the Europa Presse Center on the ground level of the Europa-Center (Map 6) on Budapester Strasse.

Libraries

The Amerika-Gedenkbibliothek (America Memorial Library; Map 3), built to commemorate the Berlin Airlift of 1948-49, is the largest circulating library in Germany. It is on Blücherplatz (U-Bahn No 6 or 15 to Hallesches Tor) and is open weekdays from 11 am (from 4 pm on Monday) to 8 pm.

The State Library (Map 4; ☎ 201 51 36 9) at Unter den Linden 8 is open from Monday to Saturday. There's a free tour in German every first Sunday of the month. The State Library branch (Map 3; ☎ 266 23 16) at

Potsdamer Strasse 33 is open most days from 9 am to between 5 and 9 pm depending on the department. There are free guided tours conducted on the third Saturday of every month at 10.30 am.

Campuses
Berlin counts three universities and 17 colleges with a total of 165,000 students. Humboldt Universität Berlin (Map 4; ☎ 209 30) is at Unter den Linden 6 in Mitte; the Freie Universität Berlin (☎ 838 1) is at Kaiserswerther Strasse 16-18 in Zehlendorf; and the Technische Universität (☎ 314 1) is at Hardenbergstrasse and Strasse des 17 Juni in Mitte.

International Centres
Amerika Haus Berlin (Map 6; ☎ 313 27 32), at Hardenbergstrasse 22-24 in Charlottenburg, is open weekdays from 11 am to 5.30 pm (to 8 pm on Tuesday and Thursday) and from 11 am to 4 pm on Saturday. The British Council (Map 6; ☎ 311 09 93 0) is next door at Hardenbergstrasse 20. There's an Institut Français (Map 6; ☎ 885 90 20) at Kurfürstendamm 211.

Laundry
The Schnell und Sauber chain has laundrettes at Uhlandstrasse 53 in Charlottenburg (Map 6); at Hauptstrasse 127 in Schöneberg; and at Wiener Strasse 15 on the corner of Lausitzer Strasse in Kreuzberg 36 (Map 5; U-Bahn No 15 to Görlitzer Bahnhof). They are normally open from 6 am to 9 or 10 pm. A load of wash costs DM6 to DM7 including soap powder; the dryer is DM1 per 10 minutes. In most laundrettes you select your machine and deposit the coin(s) in a central machine with numbers corresponding to the washers and dryers. The panel also distributes the soap powder so have one of the plastic cups strewn around the laundrette at the ready.

The Waschcenter (Map 6) at Leibnizstrasse 72 near Kantstrasse is open daily from 6 am to 10 pm, and the Öko-Express (Map 4), Rosenthaler Strasse near the corner of Torstrasse (U-Bahn No 8 to Rosenthaler Platz), is open daily from 6 am to 11 pm. A wash here normally costs DM5 but is DM1 cheaper between 6 and 10 am.

Medical Services
For 24-hour medical aid, dial ☎ 310 03 1; there's a doctor on call round the clock at ☎ 01805-304 50 5. If you need a pharmacy (or a vet, for that matter) after hours, dial ☎ 011 41. For information on where to find an emergency dentist *(Zahnarzt)*, dial ☎ 829 01 or ☎ 890 04 33 3. Charité Hospital (Map 4; ☎ 280 20), at 20-21 Schumannstrasse just off Luisenstrasse (U-Bahn No 6 to Oranienburger Tor), has an emergency/casualty department. This central facility, which started out as a plague hospital in the 18th century, is now operated by Humboldt University and open 24 hours a day. If you can't make it to here, you should call the emergency number.

Emergency
Call ☎ 110 for police emergencies only. Otherwise, there are police stations all over the city, including the City-Wache (Map 6) at Joachimstaler Strasse 14-19 just south of Zoo station. In eastern Berlin, there's a station (Map 4) at Otto-Braun-Strasse (formerly Hans-Beimler-Strasse) 27-37. For mishaps on trains, your first recourse should be the *Bahnpolizei*, located at ground level inside Zoo station.

The main police centre (☎ 699 5) and city lost & found office (☎ 699 36 44 4) is at Platz der Luftbrücke 6 beside Tempelhof airport. The latter is open Monday and Tuesday from 7.30 am to 2 pm, Wednesday from noon to 6.30 pm and on Friday from 7.30 am till noon. If you've lost something on public transport, contact the BVG (☎ 751 80 21) at Lorenzweg 5 in Tempelhof (U-Bahn No 6 to Ullsteinstrasse), weekdays from 9 am to 6 pm (to 2 pm on Friday).

The general emergency number for the fire brigade *(Feuerwehr)* throughout Berlin is ☎ 112. If your car breaks down, help is available at ☎ 01802-222 22 2.

Dangers & Annoyances

Berlin is among the safest and most tolerant of European cities. Walking alone at night on city streets should not be considered dangerous for anyone, bearing in mind the caveat that there is always safety in numbers in any urban environment.

You may want to avoid the area along the Spree south of the Hauptbahnhof, which has become the haunt of occasionally violent punks, urban drifters and druggies – but why would you be hanging out here in the first place? There are lots of drunks and mostly harmless unsavouries around Zoo station, Hardenbergplatz, Breitscheidplatz and Görlitzer Bahnhof. The little park just opposite the Metropol Theatre in Mitte (Map 4) attracts some real down-and-outers. Avoid eastern districts like Marzahn, Niederschönhausen and Lichtenberg – again, what *are* you doing here? – and their horrible grey housing blocks. If you see any 'white skins' (skinheads wearing jackboots with white boot laces) run the other way – and fast.

Berlin has an estimated 5000 prostitutes who are harmless but annoying with their solicitations ('You datin' tonight, honey?' – or words to that effect). On Friday and Saturday night the Ku'damm is crawling with day-tripping Polish whores. Other stomping grounds after dark include Kurfürstenstrasse, Lietzenburgerstrasse and Strasse des 17 Juni. Kantstrasse in Charlottenburg is the centre of the Russian and Ukrainian Mafia, responsible for a great deal of crime since the Wende.

Most U/S-Bahn stations are equipped with electronic information and emergency devices labelled 'SOS/Notruf/Information' and illustrated with a large red bell. If you require emergency assistance push the 'SOS' button. The Information button allows you to speak directly with one of the station masters.

Hardly dangerous but annoying *in extremis* are the guards and caretakers in most Berlin museums who follow you from room to room and watch your every move lest you breathe too closely on the Picasso or touch the pharaoh's death mask (God forbid). And there are so *many* of them… A walk through any museum will have you convinced that Berlin's museums single-handedly solved the mass unemployment problem after the Wende.

ALEXANDERPLATZ AREA (Map 4)

All the following sights are within walking distance of the U/S-Bahn Alexanderplatz station. Soaring above Berlin is the 365m **Fernsehturm** (TV Tower, 1969), a monumental eyesore perpetually under renovation. If it's a clear day and the queue isn't too long, it's worth paying the DM8/4 to go up the tower (open daily from 9 am to 1 am, 10 am to midnight November to March) or have a drink at the 207m-level Telecafé, which makes a complete revolution twice an hour. The complex also houses nine radio and two TV stations. You might consider going up just to be in the only place in Berlin where this dreadful structure is *not* visible. After the Wende there was talk of dismantling it, but *nostalgie de la boue* had already set in on both sides of the city for the dirty, shoddy old days of the GDR and the move was rejected. Pity.

On the opposite side of the elevated train station from the tower is **Alexanderplatz** (or 'Alex'), the mammoth, soulless square named after Tsar Alexander I, who visited Berlin in 1805. It's a mere shadow of the low-life district described so evocatively by Alfred Döblin in his realistic novel *Berlin Alexanderplatz* (1929). The area was redesigned several times in the late 1920s, but nothing was ever actually done because of the Depression. It was bombed in WWII and completely reconstructed in the 1960s. The **World Time Clock** (1969) is nearby in case you want to check the time before making a telephone call home. Don't use the subterranean men's loo nearby unless you want to be stared down by 101 homosexuals on the prowl around the clock.

MUSEUMSINSEL (Map 4)

South-west of the TV Tower, on Museum Island (S-Bahn: Hackescher Markt), between two arms of the Spree River and facing

Schlossplatz, is the GDR's **Palast der Republik** (Palace of the Republic, 1976), on the site of the war-damaged baroque City Palace, which was demolished in 1950. During the Communist era, the Volkskammer (People's Chamber) used to meet in this glitzy pile of concrete and golden mirrors dubbed the 'Show-off Palace' by locals. In 1990 it was discovered that asbestos had been used in the construction, so this 'palace' too is expected to be demolished. In 1993-94, one step ahead of Christo and his wrapped Reichstag, a French artist clad the ill-fated structure with plastic sheets designed to look like the old City Palace, sparking some interest in rebuilding the original structure.

Just in front of the palace is a golden pyramid-shaped tent containing the **Gästebuch Berlin** (Berlin Guestbook), which is 4.36m tall, 3.76m thick, weighs three tonnes and contains 1300 parchment pages for one million entries; yes, it's headed full tilt for the *Guinness Book of World Records*. But guess what? They charge you DM5/3 to enter and sign the thing. Gives a new meaning to 'be our guest', *night wahr*?

On the southern side of the square near the Spree bank is the former **Staatsrat** (Council of State) building (1964), with a portal from the City Palace incorporated in the façade. In the foyer is an interesting exhibit (in English and German) called 'Hauptstadt Planung für Berlin/Planning for the Capital City of Berlin' that is much more enlightening than the one at the Infobox on Leipziger Platz. Immediately to the east of the Staatsrat is the turn-of-the-century **Neue Marstall** (New Royal Stables) housing the State Archives and Library as well as the studios of Spree-radio (105.5 on your FM dial).

North of Schlossplatz looms the great neo-Renaissance **Berliner Dom** (Berlin Cathedral, 1905), the former court church of the Hohenzollern family, which can be visited (enter on the west side between portal Nos 3 and 8) daily from 9 am to 7.30 pm (admission DM5/3). There are daily organ recitals; see Classical Music in the Entertainment section for details.

Museumsinsel Museums

The imposing edifice north-west of the Berliner Dom is Karl Friedrich Schinkel's 1830 neoclassical SMPK **Altes Museum** (Old Museum), one of the first purpose-built museums in Europe, with its famed rotunda area featuring Roman statues of the Greek gods. It is currently used for rotating exhibitions only (open Tuesday to Sunday from 10 am to 6 pm).

The **Neues Museum** (New Museum) behind it is being rebuilt, but you can visit the adjacent SMPK **Alte Nationalgalerie** (Old National Gallery) with art from the 18th and 19th centuries, including sculpture by Christian Daniel Rauch and Johan Gottfried Schadow – note his *Tomb of Graf Alexander von der Mark* (1788-90) portraying the nine-year-old count sleeping next to a Roman helmet. Besides the Renoirs, Monets, Manets, Cézannes and Constables, you can take in the brooding and Romantic death images of Arnold Böcklin and Anselm Feuerbach, the Prussian military scenes of Adolph Menzel and, in the 'Berlin' rooms, the works of Max Liebermann, Max Beckmann, Max Slevogt and Lovis Corinth.

The huge SMPK **Pergamon Museum** is a feast of classical Greek, Babylonian, Roman, Islamic and Middle Eastern art and architecture and will wear you out if you're not careful. 'Listening wands' with a running commentary on the exhibits are provided.

The Pergamon consists of three sections: the Collection of Classical Antiquities, the Museum of Near Eastern Antiquities and the Museum of Islamic Art. You can probably skip the miniatures and Oriental carpets of the third museum (though the 8th-century Mshatta Palace from Jordan is worth a look), but the first two collections include at least three musts. In Room 2 of the Collection of Classical Antiquities is the reconstructed Pergamon Altar from Asia Minor (165 BC), a gargantuan raised marble altar with a 120m frieze of the gods doing battle with the giants, and in Room 6 the Roman Market Gate from Miletus, built under Emperor Hadrian in the early 2nd century AD. But the Museum of Near Eastern Antiquities contains the *pièce de résistance*: the world-renowned Ishtar Gate from Babylon built during the reign of Nebuchadnezzar II (605-562 BC). It is fronted by a 30m-long 'Processional Way' made of the same blue and ochre glazed bricks with reliefs of lions, horses, dragons and unicorns. It's so awesome you can almost hear the fanfare (though whether the trumpet flourishes are from ancient Babylonia or a Cecil B DeMille film set is debatable). One of us, who has visited more museums over the past five years for Lonely Planet than he's had hot dinners, can't think of anything much more impressive than this colossus.

The old-fashioned SMPK **Bodemuseum** at Museuminsel's northern tip houses collections of paintings from the 15th to 18th centuries, late-Gothic and Renaissance sculpture, Greek and Roman coins and Egyptian art and papyrus. In general the collection of the Egyptian Museum near Charlottenburg Palace (see Schloss Area Museums) is richer and better displayed than the one here though there is a fine exhibit of papyrus and early writing, including a 6th-century Coptic codex that might have been written by an unknown Christian Evangelist, and some excellent mummy portraits from the 2nd and 3rd centuries. An acoustic guide is available for DM6/4.

NIKOLAIVIERTEL (Map 4)

Across the Spree to the east between Rathausstrasse and Mülendamm is the rather twee oldy-worldy **Nikolaiviertel** (Nicholas Quarter; U-Bahn No 2 to Klosterstrasse), irreverently dubbed 'Disneyviertel' by some wags. The rebuilt 13th-century **Nikolaikirche** here, conceived and executed under the GDR's Berlin restoration programme, contains exhibits of early Berlin-Cölln, the Mark of Brandenburg and the remains of the church's original interiors (open Tuesday to Sunday from 10.30 am to 5.30 pm; admission DM3/1). Another medieval church, the **Marienkirche** (open Monday to Thursday from 10 am to noon and 1 to 5 pm, Saturday from noon to 5 pm, Sunday from 1 to 4 pm; admission free), is due north on Karl-Liebknecht-Strasse. Inside is the faint, 23m-long *Totentanz* (Dance of Death) fresco portraying a shrouded Death in 14 guises leading people from all walks of life to their graves. The line-up includes a peasant, a merchant, a burgher, a noble, a doctor, an abbot, a king and a pope. Ghoulish and strange though the Dance of Death may appear to be at first, it carries a simple message – we are all equal in the eyes of God no matter how important we (or others) think we are in this mortal life. It was a radical concept for the 15th century and remains a sobering and thought-provoking one today.

The Marienkirche stands near the monumental **Rotes Rathaus** (Red Town Hall) on Rathausstrasse, a neo-Gothic red-brick structure from 1860, which has been proudly restored and now houses Berlin's municipal government. Across Grunerstrasse on the corner of Littenstrasse, the medieval remains of the **Heiliger-Geist-Kapelle** (Chapel of the Holy Spirit) mark the spot of the former Spandauer Tor and the earliest town wall. Between Littenstrasse and Klosterstrasse is the bombed-out shell of the late 13th-century **Franziskaner Klosterkirche** (Franciscan Abbey Church). It was destroyed in 1945 and, like the Kaiser-Wilhelm-Gedächtniskirche in west Berlin, the shored-up remains (1951) were left as a war memorial.

MÄRKISCHES UFER (Map 4)

Several interesting sights can be covered from the Märkisches Museum U-Bahn (line No 2) station. The permanent exhibits of the **Märkisches Museum** (Mark of Brandenburg Museum; open Tuesday to Sunday from 10 am to 6 pm; admission DM3/1), a red-brick, cathedral-like pile at Am Köllnischen Park 5, include examples of Berlin painting and sculpture up to the neoclassical period, applied arts from the 17th to the 20th centuries and a look at some of the city's long-defunct theatres and colourful cabaret, stage and magic shows of the 1920s and 1930s through costumes, sets and posters. Best of all are the *Automatophone*, 18th-century mechanical musical instruments that are wound up and made to go through their

Berlin Transport Map overleaf

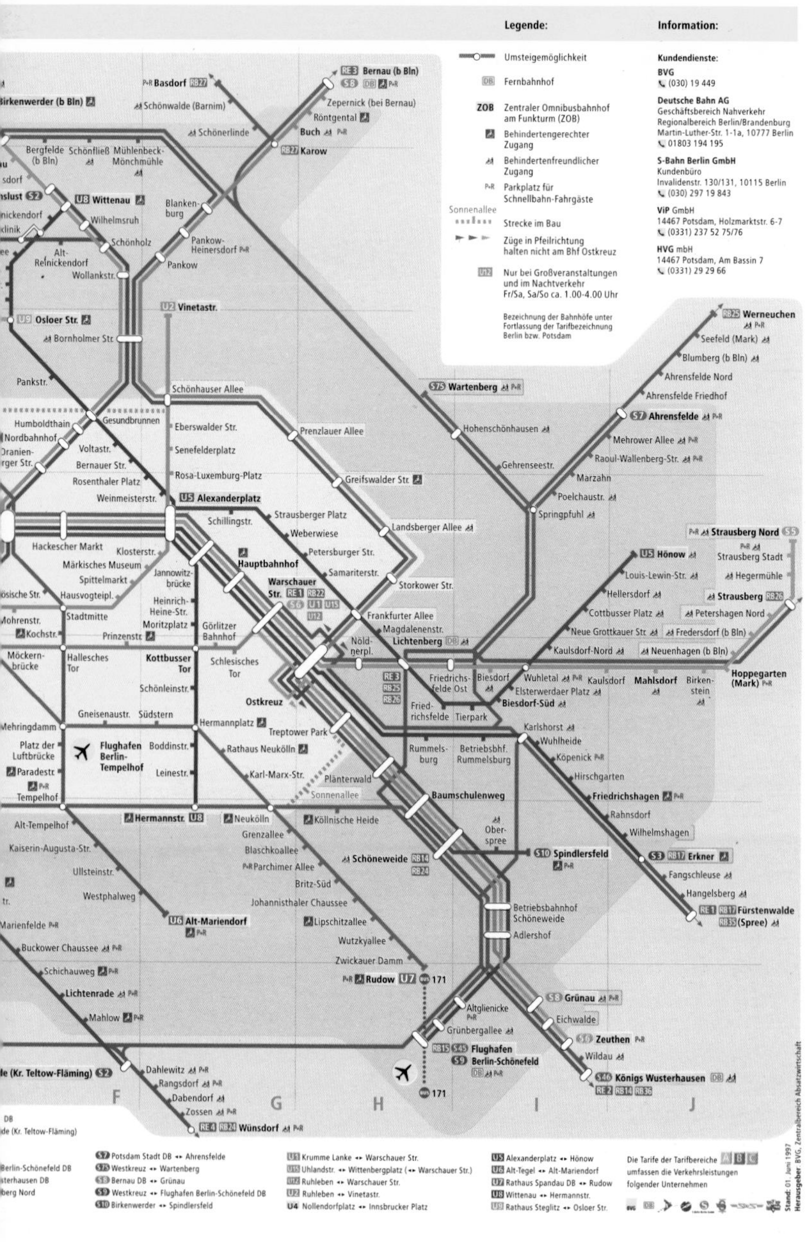

Legende:
Umsteigemöglichkeit
DB Fernbahnhof
ZOB Zentraler Omnibusbahnhof am Funkturm (ZOB)
Behindertengerechter Zugang
Behindertenfreundlicher Zugang
P+R Parkplatz für Schnellbahn-Fahrgäste
Sonnenallee Strecke im Bau
Züge in Pfeilrichtung halten nicht am Bhf Ostkreuz
U12 Nur bei Großveranstaltungen und im Nachtverkehr Fr/Sa, Sa/So ca. 1.00-4.00 Uhr
Bezeichnung der Bahnhöfe unter Fortlassung der Tarifbezeichnung Berlin bzw. Potsdam
Information:
Kundendienste:
BVG
(030) 19 449
Deutsche Bahn AG
Geschäftsbereich Nahverkehr
Regionalbereich Berlin/Brandenburg
Martin-Luther-Str. 1-1a, 10777 Berlin
01803 194 195
S-Bahn Berlin GmbH
Kundenbüro
Invalidenstr. 130/131, 10115 Berlin
(030) 297 19 843
ViP GmbH
14467 Potsdam, Holzmarktstr. 6-7
(0331) 237 52 75/76
HVG mbH
14467 Potsdam, Am Bassin 7
(0331) 29 29 66
Birkenwerder (b Bln)
P+R Basdorf RB27
Schönwalde (Barnim)
Schönerlinde
RE3 Bernau (b Bln)
S8 DB P+R
Zepernick (bei Bernau)
Röntgental
Buch P+R
RB27 Karow
Bergfelde (b Bln)
Schönfließ
Mühlenbeck-Mönchmühle
U8 Wittenau
Wilhelmsruh
Schönholz
Blankenburg
Pankow-Heinersdorf P+R
Pankow
Alt-Reinickendorf
Wollankstr.
U9 Osloer Str.
Bornholmer Str.
U2 Vinetastr.
Pankstr.
Schönhauser Allee
Humboldthain
Gesundbrunnen
Nordbahnhof
Oranienburger Str.
Voltastr.
Bernauer Str.
Rosenthaler Platz
Weinmeisterstr.
Eberswalder Str.
Senefelderplatz
Rosa-Luxemburg-Platz
U5 Alexanderplatz
Prenzlauer Allee
Greifswalder Str.
Landsberger Allee
Storkower Str.
Frankfurter Allee
Schillingstr.
Strausberger Platz
Weberwiese
Petersburger Str.
Samariterstr.
Hackescher Markt
Klosterstr.
Märkisches Museum
Spittelmarkt
Hausvogteipl.
Jannowitzbrücke
Hauptbahnhof
Warschauer Str. RE1 RB22 S6 U1 U15 U12
Heinrich-Heine-Str.
Moritzplatz
Stadtmitte
Mohrenstr.
Kochstr.
Prinzenstr.
Görlitzer Bahnhof
Möckernbrücke
Hallesches Tor
Kottbusser Tor
Schlesisches Tor
Schönleinstr.
Gneisenaustr.
Südstern
Mehringdamm
Hermannplatz
Ostkreuz
Nöldnerpl.
Magdalenenstr.
Lichtenberg DB
RE3 RB25 RB26
Treptower Park
Platz der Luftbrücke
Flughafen Berlin-Tempelhof
Boddinstr.
Rathaus Neukölln
Paradestr.
Tempelhof P+R
Leinestr.
Karl-Marx-Str.
Plänterwald
Sonnenallee
Alt-Tempelhof
Hermannstr. U8
Neukölln
Köllnische Heide
Grenzallee
Blaschkoallee
Parchimer Allee
Britz-Süd
Johannisthaler Chaussee
Lipschitzallee
Wutzkyallee
Zwickauer Damm
P+R Rudow U7
171
Kaiserin-Augusta-Str.
Ullsteinstr.
Westphalweg
U6 Alt-Mariendorf P+R
Marienfelde P+R
Buckower Chaussee P+R
Schichauweg P+R
Lichtenrade P+R
Mahlow P+R
Dahlewitz P+R
Rangsdorf P+R
Dabendorf
Zossen P+R
RE4 RB24 Wünsdorf P+R
(Kr. Teltow-Fläming) S2
S75 Wartenberg P+R
Hohenschönhausen
Gehrenseestr.
Springpfuhl
RB25 Werneuchen P+R
Seefeld (Mark)
Blumberg (b Bln)
Ahrensfelde Nord
Ahrensfelde Friedhof
S7 Ahrensfelde P+R
Mehrower Allee P+R
Raoul-Wallenberg-Str. P+R
Marzahn
Poelchaustr.
P+R Strausberg Nord S5
P+R Strausberg Stadt
Hegermühle
Strausberg RB26
Petershagen Nord
Fredersdorf (b Bln)
Neuenhagen (b Bln)
Hoppegarten (Mark) P+R
U5 Hönow
Louis-Lewin-Str.
Hellersdorf
Cottbusser Platz
Neue Grottkauer Str.
Kaulsdorf-Nord
Wuhletal P+R
Elsterwerdaer Platz
Biesdorf-Süd
Kaulsdorf
Mahlsdorf
Birkenstein
Friedrichsfelde Ost
Biesdorf
Friedrichsfelde
Tierpark
Karlshorst
Wuhlheide
Köpenick P+R
Hirschgarten
Friedrichshagen P+R
Rahnsdorf
Wilhelmshagen
S3 RB17 Erkner
Fangschleuse
Hangelsberg
RE1 RB17 Fürstenwalde RB35 (Spree)
Rummelsburg
Betriebsbhf. Rummelsburg
Baumschulenweg
Oberspree
S10 Spindlersfeld P+R
Schöneweide RB14 RB24
Betriebsbahnhof Schöneweide
Adlershof
Altglienicke P+R
Grünbergallee
RB15 S45 Flughafen S9 Berlin-Schönefeld DB P+R
171
S8 Grünau P+R
Eichwalde
S46 Zeuthen P+R
Wildau
S46 Königs Wusterhausen DB
RE2 RB14 RB36
F
G
H
I
J
DB
(Kr. Teltow-Fläming)
Berlin-Schönefeld DB
Oranienburg... Wartenberg / ...sterhausen DB
...berg Nord
S7 Potsdam Stadt DB ↔ Ahrensfelde
S75 Westkreuz ↔ Wartenberg
S8 Bernau DB ↔ Grünau
S9 Westkreuz ↔ Flughafen Berlin-Schönefeld DB
S10 Birkenwerder ↔ Spindlersfeld
U1 Krumme Lanke ↔ Warschauer Str.
U15 Uhlandstr. ↔ Wittenbergplatz (↔ Warschauer Str.)
U12 Ruhleben ↔ Warschauer Str.
U2 Ruhleben ↔ Vinetastr.
U4 Nollendorfplatz ↔ Innsbrucker Platz
U5 Alexanderplatz ↔ Hönow
U6 Alt-Tegel ↔ Alt-Mariendorf
U7 Rathaus Spandau DB ↔ Rudow
U8 Wittenau ↔ Hermannstr.
U9 Rathaus Steglitz ↔ Osloer Str.
Die Tarife der Tarifbereiche A B C umfassen die Verkehrsleistungen folgender Unternehmen
Stand: 01. Juni 1997
Herausgeber: BVG, Zentralbereich Absatzwirtschaft

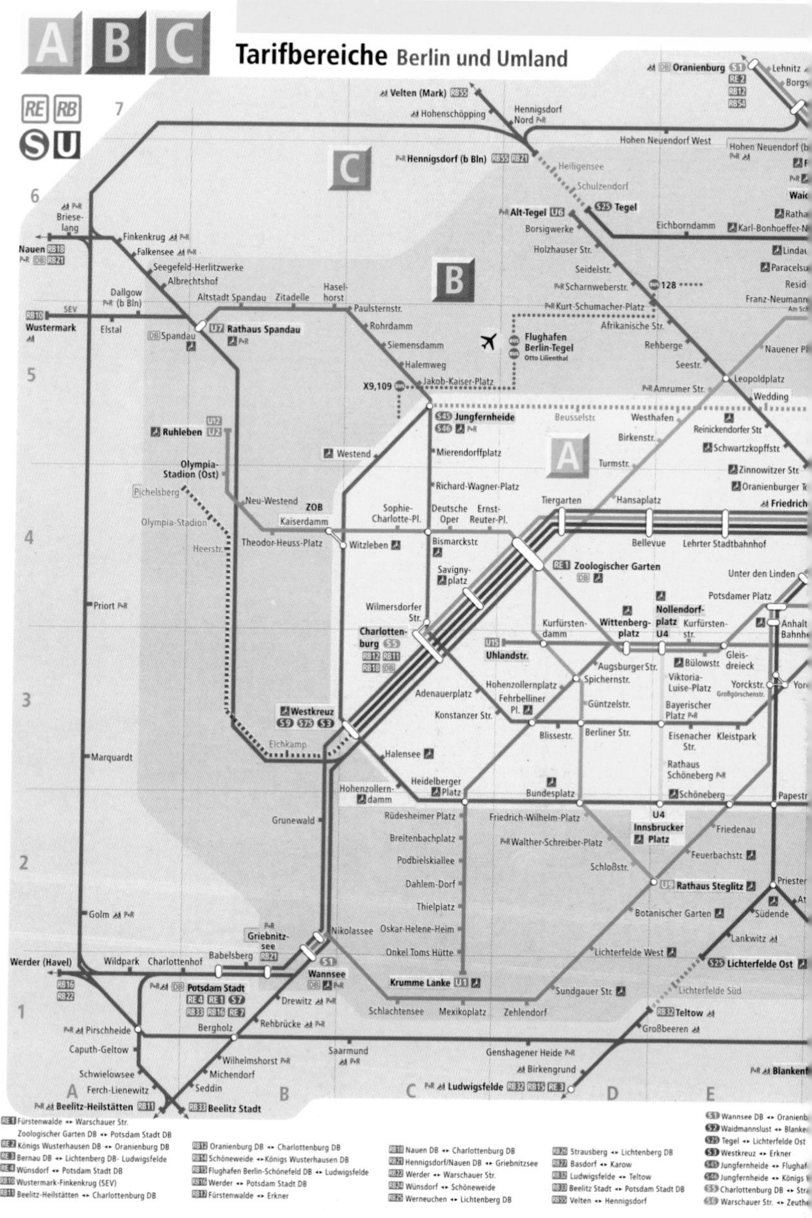

A B C
Tarifbereiche Berlin und Umland
RE RB
S U
7
6
5
4
3
2
1
C
B
A
Oranienburg
Velten (Mark)
Hohenschöpping
Hennigsdorf Nord
Hennigsdorf (b Bln)
Hohen Neuendorf West
Heiligensee
Schulzendorf
Tegel
Alt-Tegel
Borsigwerke
Holzhauser Str.
Seidelstr.
Scharnweberstr.
Kurt-Schumacher-Platz
Afrikanische Str.
Rehberge
Seestr.
Leopoldplatz
Wedding
Amrumer Str.
Eichborndamm
Karl-Bonhoeffer-Nervenklinik
Franz-Neumann-Platz
Nauener Platz
Briese-lang
Nauen
Finkenkrug
Falkensee
Seegefeld-Herlitzwerke
Albrechtshof
Dallgow (b Bln)
Wustermark
Elstal
SEV
Altstadt Spandau
Zitadelle
Hasel-horst
Paulsternstr.
Rohrdamm
Siemensdamm
Halemweg
Jakob-Kaiser-Platz
X9,109
Flughafen Berlin-Tegel
Otto Lilienthal
128
Rathaus Spandau
Spandau
Ruhleben
Olympia-Stadion (Ost)
Pichelsberg
Olympia-Stadion
Heerstr.
Neu-Westend
Westend
Jungfernheide
Beusselstr.
Westhafen
Birkenstr.
Reinickendorfer Str.
Schwartzkopffstr.
Turmstr.
Zinnowitzer Str.
Mierendorffplatz
Richard-Wagner-Platz
Tiergarten
Hansaplatz
ZOB
Kaiserdamm
Sophie-Charlotte-Pl.
Deutsche Oper
Ernst-Reuter-Pl.
Theodor-Heuss-Platz
Witzleben
Bismarckstr.
Bellevue
Lehrter Stadtbahnhof
Zoologischer Garten
Savigny-platz
Unter den Linden
Potsdamer Platz
Wilmersdorfer Str.
Charlotten-burg
Kurfürsten-damm
Wittenberg-platz
Nollendorf-platz
Kurfürsten-str.
Uhlandstr.
Gleis-dreieck
Augsburger Str.
Bülowstr.
Spichernstr.
Viktoria-Luise-Platz
Yorckstr.
Großgörschenstr.
Hohenzollernplatz
Adenauerplatz
Fehrbelliner Pl.
Güntzelstr.
Bayerischer Platz
Konstanzer Str.
Westkreuz
Blissestr.
Berliner Str.
Eisenacher Str.
Kleistpark
Eichkamp
Halensee
Rathaus Schöneberg
Hohenzollern-damm
Heidelberger Platz
Bundesplatz
Schöneberg
Priort
Marquardt
Grunewald
Rüdesheimer Platz
Friedrich-Wilhelm-Platz
Innsbrucker Platz
Friedenau
Breitenbachplatz
Walther-Schreiber-Platz
Feuerbachstr.
Podbielskiallee
Schloßstr.
Dahlem-Dorf
Rathaus Steglitz
Thielplatz
Botanischer Garten
Südende
Golm
Griebnitz-see
Nikolassee
Oskar-Helene-Heim
Lankwitz
Onkel Toms Hütte
Lichterfelde West
Lichterfelde Ost
Werder (Havel)
Wildpark
Charlottenhof
Babelsberg
Wannsee
Krumme Lanke
Potsdam Stadt
Drewitz
Sundgauer Str.
Lichterfelde Süd
Schlachtensee
Mexikoplatz
Zehlendorf
Teltow
Pirschheide
Bergholz
Rehbrücke
Großbeeren
Caputh-Geltow
Saarmund
Genshagener Heide
Wilhelmshorst
Birkengrund
Schwielowsee
Michendorf
Ferch-Lienewitz
Seddin
Ludwigsfelde
Beelitz-Heilstätten
Beelitz Stadt
RE1 Fürstenwalde ↔ Warschauer Str. Zoologischer Garten DB ↔ Potsdam Stadt DB
RE2 Königs Wusterhausen DB ↔ Oranienburg DB
RE3 Bernau DB ↔ Lichtenberg DB- Ludwigsfelde
RE4 Wünsdorf ↔ Potsdam Stadt DB
RB10 Wustermark-Finkenkrug (SEV)
RB11 Beelitz-Heilstätten ↔ Charlottenburg DB
RB12 Oranienburg DB ↔ Charlottenburg DB
RB14 Schöneweide ↔ Königs Wusterhausen DB
RB15 Flughafen Berlin-Schönefeld DB ↔ Ludwigsfelde
RB16 Werder ↔ Potsdam Stadt DB
RB17 Fürstenwalde ↔ Erkner
RB18 Nauen DB ↔ Charlottenburg DB
RB21 Hennigsdorf/Nauen DB ↔ Griebnitzsee
RB22 Werder ↔ Warschauer Str.
RB24 Wünsdorf ↔ Schöneweide
RB25 Werneuchen ↔ Lichtenberg DB
RB26 Strausberg ↔ Lichtenberg DB
RB27 Basdorf ↔ Karow
RB32 Ludwigsfelde ↔ Teltow
RB33 Beelitz Stadt ↔ Potsdam Stadt DB
RB55 Velten ↔ Hennigsdorf
S2 Waidmannslust ↔ Blankenfelde
S25 Tegel ↔ Lichterfelde Ost
S3 Westkreuz ↔ Erkner
S5 Charlottenburg DB ↔ Strausberg

Berlin-Tegel Airport
WEDDING
Volkspark Rehberge
Volkspark Jungfernheide
Saatwinkler Damm
Afrikanische Strasse
Rehberge
Seestrasse
Leopoldplatz
Wedding
Amrumer Strasse
Reinickendorfer Strasse
Westhafen
Birkenstrasse
Jakob-Kaiser-Platz
Halemweg
Siemensdamm
Jungfernheide
See Schloss Charlottenburg map
Schlossgarten Charlottenburg
Mierendorffplatz
Kaiserin Augusta Allee
MAP 3
Turmstrasse
Alt Moabit
Fritz-Schloss-Park
Hansaplatz
TIERGARTEN
Strasse des 17 Juni
Richard-Wagner-Platz
Otto-Suhr-Allee
Sophie-Charlotte-Platz
Bismarckstrasse
Deutsche Oper
E-Reuter Platz
Kaiserdamm
Theodor-Heuss-Platz
Kantstrasse
Wilmersdorfer Strasse
Zoologischer Garten
Kurfürstendamm
Uhlandstrasse
Wittenbergplatz
Adenauerplatz
Augsburger Strasse
Nollendorfplatz
Kurfürstenstrasse
Bülowstrasse
Hohenzollernplatz
Spichernstrasse
Viktoria-Luise-Platz
Konstanzer Strasse
Güntzelstrasse
MAP 6
Fehrbelliner Platz
Kleistpark
Berliner Strasse
Bayerische Platz
Eisenacher Strasse
Blissestrasse
Rathaus Schöneberg
SCHÖNEBERG
SCHMARGENDORF
Heidelberger Platz
Bundesplatz
Innsbrucker Platz
Rüdesheimer Platz
Friedrich-Wilhelm-Platz
Breitenbachplatz
Podbielskiallee
W-Schreiber-Platz
To Dahlem Museum Complex

See Prenzlauer Berg Map

MAP 3

MAP 4

MAP 5

WEISSENSEE
PRENZLAUER BERG
MITTE
FRIEDRICHSHAIN
LICHTENBERG
KREUZBERG 61
KREUZBERG 36
TREPTOW
NEUKÖLLN
TEMPELHOF
EDDING

Sophienkirch II
Humboldthain
Jüdischer Friedhof
Volkspark Prenzlauer Berg
Friedrichshain
Görlitzer Park
Treptower Park
Berlin-Tempelhof Airport

Vinetastrasse
Elsa-Brändström Strasse
Am Steinberg
Bornholmer Strasse
Wisbyer Strasse
Gust-Adolf-Strasse
Pistoriusstrasse
Berliner Allee
Prinzenallee
Pankstrasse
Gesundbrunnen
Schönhauser Allee
Ostseestrasse
Greifswalderstrasse
Michelangelo Strasse
Voltastrasse
Eberswalder Strasse
Danzigerstrasse
Bernauer Strasse
Kastanian Allee
Choriner Str
Strasse
Kniprodestrasse
Hohenschönhauser
Schwartzkopff-strasse
Zinnowitzer Strasse
Senefelder-platz
Rosenthaler Platz
Tor Str
Tor Strasse
Prenzlauer
Landsberger Allee
Am Friedrichshain
Oranienburger Tor
Rosa-Luxemburg-Platz
Weinmeister-strasse
Friedrich strasse
R. Luxemburg
Liebknecht-Str
Moll Strasse
Otto-Braun-Strasse
Frieden Strasse
Friedrichstrasse
Karl-Liebknecht-Str
Alexanderplatz
Alexanderstr
Schillingstrasse
K-Marx-Allee
Strausberger Platz
Unten den Linden
Spand Str
Mühlend Gruner Str
Klosterstrasse
Weberwiese
Frankfurter Allee
Samariterstrasse
Wilhelm Strasse
Französischer Strasse
Französischer Str
Werder Str
Breite Str
Hausvogteiplatz
Fischerstrasse
Jannowitzbrücke
Lichtenbergerstr
Petersburger Strasse
Boxhagenerstrasse
Grünbergerstrasse
Stadtmitte
Mohrenstr
Leipziger Strasse
Potsdamer Platz
Gertrauden
Spittelmarkt
Markisches Museum
H-Heine Strasse
Holzmarktstr
Der Pariser Kommune
Mühlenstrasse
Warschauerstrasse
Stressemannstr
Kochstrasse
Oranien Strasse
Warschauer Strasse
Moritzplatz
Oberbaum
Stralauer Allee
Möckenbrücke
Kottbusser Tor
Görlitzer Bahnhof
Skalitzerstrasse
Schlesisches Tor
Gitschiner Str
Prinzenstrasse
Hallesches Tor
Mehringdamm
Schönleinstrasse
Pushkin Allee
Am Treptower Park
Busser Damm
Gneisenaustrasse
Südstern
Hermannplatz
Duden Str
Platz der Luftbrücke
Columbia Damm
Hermannstr
Rathaus Neukölln
Flughafenstrasse
Boddinstrasse
Paradestrasse
Leinestrasse
Karl-Marx-Strasse
Sonnen Allee
Hermannstrasse
Karl-Marx-Strasse
Tempelhof
100
Neukölln
Lahnstrasse
Silbersteinstr
Allee
Tempelhof
Germaniastr
Boelckestrasse

MAP 3
Tiergarten, Schöneberg & Kreuzberg 61
To Museum of Contemporary Art
SPREEBOGEN
TIERGARTEN
MITTE
KREUZBERG 61
SCHÖNEBERG
TEMPELHOF
Zoologischer Garten
Viktoriapark Kreuzberg
Volkspark
Tempelhof Airport
0
0.5
1 km

PLACES TO STAY
23 Jugendgästehaus Berlin
24 Hotel Auberge
34 Hotel Sachsenhof
46 Pension Kreuzberg; Zynkali Club
52 Hotel Riehmers Hofgarten & Noodle Company
54 Hotel Transit
58 Studentenhotel Berlin

PLACES TO EAT
1 Tiergartenquelle Restaurant
27 Café Einstein
32 Café Sidney
37 Carib Restaurant
39 Habibi Takeaway
40 Fisch & Vegetables; Rani Imbiss
41 Café M
42 Maharaja Imbiss
44 Gargano Restaurant
45 E&M Leydicke
49 Lone Star Taqueria
50 Naturkost Vegetarische Buffet & Mississippi Pub
51 Café Lebensart

OTHER
2 Arts Academy
3 Grips Theater
4 Schloss Bellevue
5 Victory Column
6 Flea Market
7 Spreefahrt Boats
8 House of World Cultures
9 Carillon
10 Tempodrome
11 Reichstag
12 Soviet Memorial
13 Brandenburg Gate
14 Infobox
15 Musical Instruments Museum
16 Berliner Philharmonie
17 Arts & Crafts Museum
18 Copperplate Etchings Gallery
19 Museum of Design & Bauhaus Archives
20 St Mattäus Kirche
21 New National Gallery
22 State Library Branch
25 Andreas Kneipe
26 Post Office Museum
28 Wintergarten-Das Varieté
29 Made in Berlin
30 German Technical Museum
31 90° Grad Club
33 Metropol Disco
35 Tom's Bar & Hafen Pub
36 Pour Elle Club
38 Connection Disco
43 Mister Hu Bar
47 America Memorial Library
48 Rathaus Kreuzberg & Rathaus Casino Cafeteria
53 Kreuzkeller Sports Bar
55 Gay Museum
56 Zoulou Bar
57 Café Mirell
59 Rathaus Schöneberg
60 Odeon Cinema
61 Golgatha Club

DAVID PEEVERS

Reichstag, Berlin

PLACES TO STAY
2 Backpacker Hostel
4 Hotel Novalis
5 Hotel-Pension Merkur
13 Hotel-Pension Die Loge & Sushi-Bar
18 Hotel-Pension Amadeus & Bärenschänke Pub
36 Forum Hotel
39 Circus Hostel
43 Hotel Albrechtshof
44 Künstlerheim Luise Hostel
64 Hotel Unter den Linden
72 Hotel Adlon
76 Grand Hotel Berlin
111 Berlin Hilton
112 Hotel Gendarm

PLACES TO EAT
7 Burger King
10 Brazil Restaurant
12 Beth Café
20 Lautaro Restaurant
23 Kamala Thai Restaurant
24 Fressco Imbiss
25 Las Cucarachas Mexican Restaurant
28 Oren Restaurant
41 Kartoffelkeller Restaurant
54 Café Haus Ungarn & Ibusz
67 Café Einstein Unter den Linden
86 Food Stalls
92 Zur Letzten Instanz
94 Kartoffelaube Restaurant
95 Zum Nussbaum
116 Bräustübl Restaurant
117 Restaurant Indonesia & Hitler's Chancellory

OTHER
1 Natural History Museum
3 Brecht-Weigel House
6 Boudoir Club
8 Öko-Express Laundrette
9 Post Office
11 Delicious Doughnuts Research
14 Charité Hospital
15 Obst und Gemüse Pub
16 Tacheles Cultural Centre
17 Oscar Wilde Irish Pub
19 Deutches Theater
21 Friedrichstadtpalast
22 Kalkscheune Club
26 Café Orange
27 New Synagogue & Museums
29 Sophienklub
30 Firlefanz Puppet Theatre
31 Hackesche Höfe Bike Rental
32 Atlas Reisewelt
33 Police Station
34 Europcar
35 Atlas Reisewelt & ADAC Office
37 World Time Clock
38 Kilkenny Irish Pub
40 Berliner Ensemble
42 STA Travel
45 Bruno Winkler Boats
46 Tränenpalast
47 Metropol Theatre
48 Flea Market
49 Bodemuseum
50 Pergamon Museum
51 Neues Museum
52 Old National Gallery
53 Berlin University Bookshop
55 TV Tower
56 Marienkirche
57 Stern und Kreis Boats
58 Berliner Dom
59 Altes Museum
60 Maxim Gorki Theater
61 Canadian Embassy
62 Humboldt University
63 State Library
65 UK Embassy
66 US Embassy
68 Reichstag
69 Wall Victims Memorial
70 Flea Market
71 Brandenburg Gate & Tourist Office Branch
73 Russian Embassy
74 Meissener Porzellan
75 Komische Oper
77 Dresdner Bank & Tourist Office Branch
78 Old Royal Library
79 Deutsche Staatsoper
80 Neue Wache
81 Zeughaus & Museum of German History
82 Crown Prince's Palace
83 BWTS Water Taxis
84 Food Stalls & Berlin Guestbook
85 Palace of the Republic
87 Post Office
88 Hekticket
89 Heiliger-Geist-Kapelle Ruins
90 Franciscan Abbey Church Ruin
91 Podewil
93 Rotes Rathaus
96 Nikolaikirche
97 Neue Marstall
98 Staatsrat
99 Bike City
100 Friedrichswerdersche Kirche
101 Church of St Hedwig
102 Bürgel Keramik
103 American Express
104 Französischer Dom & Hugenottenmuseum
105 Galeries Lafayette
106 Konzerthaus (Concert Hall)
107 Stern und Kreis Boats
108 Berlin Congress Centre
109 Märkisches Museum & City Bears
110 Deutscher Dom
113 Planet Hollywood
114 Kiepert Bookshop
115 Tresor Disco
118 Hitler's Bunker
119 Infobox
120 British Bookshop
121 Thomas Cook
122 Former Checkpoint Charlie
123 Goethe Institute & Café Adler
124 Haus am Checkpoint Charlie
125 Martin-Gropius-Bau
126 Topographie des Terrors

Kreuzberg 36

0 400 800 m

1 Trash Club
2 Schnabelbar
3 O-Bar
4 Flammende Herzen Bar
5 Bierhimmel
6 Roses Bar
7 SO 36 Club
8 Franken Kneipe
9 Café Kafka
10 Café Anal
11 Abendmahl Restaurant
12 Baraka Restaurant
13 Jolesch Restaurant
14 Café Kloster
15 Oberbaum-Eck
16 MS Sanssouci
17 Food Stalls
18 Bagdad Restaurant
19 Posst Restaurant
20 Mini Café
21 Café Morena
22 Kuds Imbiss
23 Advena Café
24 Weisse Taube; Schnell und Sauber Laundrette
25 Spreewaldplatz Baths
26 Alte Berliner Kneipe
27 Tunnel Bar
28 Die Fabrik Hostel & Café Eisenwaren
29 Europa Language School
30 Guernika Basque Restaurant
31 Arena
32 KitKat Club

MAP 4
Köpenicker
Strasse
Waldemarstrasse
Wrangelstrasse
Muskauer
Oranienstrasse
Adalbert
Naunynstrasse
Manteuffelstr
Eisenbahnstrasse
Str
Zeughofstrasse
Skalitzer Strasse
Görlitzer Bahnhof
Kottbusser Tor
Mariannenstrasse
Kottbusser
Görlitzer
Wiener Strasse
Reichenberger
Strasse
Görlitzer Park
Schlesisches Tor
Oberbaum
Stralauer
Warschauer-strasse
Oppelner Strasse
Falckensteinstrasse
Schlesische Strasse
Cuvry Strasse
To Treptower Park
Paul-Lincke-ufer
Maybachstrasse
Schönleinstrasse
Hobrechtstrasse
Friedelstrasse
Pflügerstr
Glogauer Str
Ratiborstr
Urbanstrasse
Graefestr
Hasenheide
Wissmannstrasse
Hermannstrasse
Karl-Marx-Strasse

JONATHAN SMITH

Panorama of eastern Berlin at sunrise

MAP 6
Charlottenburg
& Wilmersdorf
0
300
600 m
PLACES TO STAY
4 Jugendgästehaus am Zoo
13 Pension Knesebeck
24 Hotel-Pension Cortina
26 Hotel Crystal
28 Pension Peters
34 Hotel Palace Berlin
44 Hotel-Pension Majesty
47 Pension Grossman & Kalkutta Indian Restaurant
55 Pension Fischer & Hotel-Pension Nürnberger Eck
56 Steigenberger Hotel Berlin
63 City-Pension Alexandra
66 Hotel-Pension Modena
70 Hotel Auberge
72 Hotel-Pension Pariser Eck
74 Pension Elton
75 Jugendgästehaus Central
PLACES TO EAT
8 Samadhi Vegetarian Restaurant
23 Dicke Wirtin
27 Café Hegel
29 Schwarzes Café
38 Marché Restaurant; Hekticket
39 Pizzeria Amigo
40 Café Kranzler
41 Zillemarkt
42 Café Bleibtreu
46 Don Quijote Spanish Restaurant
48 Einhorn Buffet
59 Café Möhring
61 Novo Skopje Macedonian Restaurant
65 Kim Chi Korean Restaurant
68 Piccola Taormina
OTHER
1 Kiepert Bookshop
2 Kartenservice (Ticket Service)
3 Kilroy Travel
5 Technical University Mensa
6 College of Arts Concert Hall
7 Post Office
9 Books in Berlin
10 STA Travel
11 Sack + Pack
12 Aldi Supermarket & Waschcenter
14 British Council
15 Amerika Haus
16 Reisebank
17 BVG Information Kiosk
18 Filmzentrum Zoo-Palast
19 Zoo & Aquarium
20 Aldi Supermarket
21 Erotik Museum
22 Theater des Westens & Quasimodo Jazz Café
25 A-Trane Jazz Club
30 Olympia Cinema
31 Kaiser-Wilhelm-Gedächtniskirche
32 Euro-Change
33 Tourist Office
35 Europa-Center
36 Hertz & Avis
37 Berlin Coach Tours
43 Die Kurbel Cinema
45 Salsa Club
49 Marga Schoeller Bookshop
50 Australian Embassy
51 Wertheim Department Store
52 Kaiser's Supermarket & Einhorn Buffet
53 American Express
54 KaDeWe Department Store
57 Synagogue
58 City-Wache (Police Station)
60 Institut Français
62 Kaiser's Supermarket
64 Alternativ Tours
67 Big Eden
69 American Express
71 Aldi Supermarket
73 Schnell und Sauber Laundrette
Deutsche Oper
Ernst-Reuter-Platz
Tiegarten
Zoologischer Garten
Steinplatz
Savignyplatz
Kurfürstendamm
Uhlandstrasse
Wittenbergplatz
Augsburger Strasse
Adenauerplatz
Olivaer Platz
Spichernstrasse
Konstanzer-strasse
Hohenzollern Platz
Innsbrucker Platz
To Bus Station (ZOB); Charlottenburger Hof Hotel; Café Voltaire
To Far Out & Halensee
To Zehlendorf

noisy paces every Wednesday and Sunday from 3 to 4 pm. The three brown bears *(Ursus arctos)* housed in a pit in Köllnischer Park behind the museum are the official mascots of the city. As much as we like Schnute (1981-), Maxi (1986-) and Tilo (1990-), we think ducks should live here (see introduction to this chapter).

UNTER DEN LINDEN (Map 4)

A stroll west of Museumsinsel along fashionable Unter den Linden ('Under the Linden Trees') takes in the greatest surviving monuments of the former Prussian capital. After crossing the lovely **Schlossbrücke** (Palace Bridge), with its eight clusters of marble statues tracing the training and development of a Greek warrior, the very first building on the right at Unter den Linden 2 is the **Deutsches Historisches Museum** (Museum of German History), in the former Zeughaus (Armoury, 1706, by Andreas Schlüter). The first floor contains an extensive and fascinating collection of objects, paintings, maps and photos tracing German history from 900 AD till the present day. On the ground floor are excellent rotating exhibits, focusing particularly these days on the GDR. The museum is open from 10 am to 6 pm Thursday to Tuesday; free entry. Be sure to see the baroque building's interior courtyard with Schlüter's famous 22 masks of dying warriors. The Chinese-American architect IM Pei has designed a glass roof for the original baroque building and a wonderful modern extension to the west that will surely become an Unter den Linden landmark. Opposite the Museum of German History is the beautiful colonnaded **Kronprinzenpalais** (Crown Prince's Palace, 1732), also called the Unter den Linden Palace.

To the west of the history museum is Schinkel's restored **Neue Wache** (New Guardhouse, 1818), Germany's central memorial to the victims of fascism and militarism, which harbours the tombs of an unknown soldier, resistance fighter and concentration camp victim, as well as Käthe Kollwitz's sculpture *Mother and Her Dead Son* (open daily; free). **Humboldt University** (1753), the next building to the west, was originally a palace of Prince Heinrich, brother of Friedrich II of Prussia. It was converted to a university building in 1810. Beside this is at No 8 is the massive **Staatsbibliothek** (State Library, 1914). An equestrian **statue of Friedrich II** usually stands in the middle of the avenue in front of the university but was removed in October 1997 for a two-year renovation.

Across the street from the university, beside the baroque **Alte Königliche Bibliothek** (Old Royal Library, 1780), now part of the legal faculty of the university, is Wenzeslaus von Knobelsdorff's **Deutsche Staatsoper** (German State Opera House, 1743). Behind this site is the **Church of St Hedwig** (1783), which was partly modelled on the Pantheon in Rome. It was the only Catholic church in Berlin until 1854 and the church of Blessed Bernhard Lichtenberg, who died on his way to Dachau in 1943. Students burned books on the Nazi 'index' in the square here on 10 May 1933 and there is a memorial marking the spot.

A short distance east along Französische Strasse and then Werderstrasse is the SMPK **Friedrichswerdersche Kirche**, which contains a permanent exhibit on the architecture and sculptures of Karl Friedrich Schinkel.

Just south-west of St Hedwig's Church is the **Gendarmenmarkt** (also called the Platz der Akademie), once a thriving market and now a lovely, quiet square framed by a trio of magnificent buildings. The **Deutscher Dom** (German Cathedral), at the southern end of the square, was originally constructed in 1708 and rebuilt in 1785, 1882 and again in 1995. Today it houses an excellent exhibit on German history from 1800 to the present (open Tuesday to Sunday from 10 am to 5 or 6 pm). At the square's northern end, the **Französischer Dom** (French Cathedral), so called because it was once the seat of French Huguenots, contains the **Hugenottenmuseum** (Huguenot Museum; open Tuesday to Saturday from noon to 5 pm, from 11 am on Sunday; DM3/2), which covers the contributions made by 18th-century French

Bertolt Brecht

Bertolt Brecht (1898-1956), the controversial poet and playwright who spent the last seven years of his life in East Berlin, wrote his first play, *Baal*, while studying medicine in Munich in 1918. His first play to reach the stage, *Trommeln in der Nacht* (Drums in the Night, 1922), won the coveted Kleist Prize and two years later he moved to the Deutches Theater in Berlin to work with the Austrian director Max Rheinhardt. Over the next decade, in plays like *Die Dreigroschenoper* (The Threepenny Opera, 1928), he developed his theory of 'epic theatre' which, unlike 'dramatic theatre', forces its audience to detach themselves emotionally from the play and its characters and to reason intellectually.

With the rise of Hitler in 1933, Brecht – by this time a Marxist – went into exile with his wife, the actress Helene Weigel, 'changing countries more often than (his) shoes' as he later wrote – from Switzerland to Denmark and Finland and then the USA. He wrote most of his best plays during this time: *Mutter Courage und ihre Kinder* (Mother Courage and Her Children, 1941), *Leben des Galilei* (The Life of Galileo, 1943), *Der gute Mensch von Sezuan* (The Good Woman of Sezuan, 1943) and *Der kaukasische Kreidekreis* (The Caucasian Chalk Circle, 1948).

After having to testify before the House Un-American Activities Committee in 1947, Brecht left for Europe, arriving in East Berlin in 1949. There he founded the Berliner Ensemble at the Theater am Schiffbauerdamm with Weigel, where adaptations of his plays were (and still are) staged.

During his lifetime Brecht was both suspected in the East for his unorthodox aesthetic theories and scorned (and often boycotted) in much of the West for his communist principles. A staple of left-wing directors throughout the 1960s and 70s, Brecht's plays are now under reassessment though his influence in freeing the theatre from the constraints of a 'well made play in three acts' is undeniable. The superiority of Brecht's poetry, so little known in English, remains undisputed. ■

Protestants to Berlin life. For a great view, climb the tower (daily 9 am to 7 pm; DM3/2). There's a guided tour of the cathedral's *Glockenspiel* hourly between noon and 4 pm on Saturday.

Between the two cathedrals is the opulent **Konzerthaus** (Concert Hall), designed by Schinkel in 1819.

ORANIENBURGER TOR AREA (Map 4)

Of particular interest in this area – once the 'Latin Quarter of Berlin' because of all the students living here – is the so-called **Scheunenviertel** district, the lively Jewish quarter up to WWII and once again coming into its own. Here stands the lovingly restored **Neue Synagoge** (New Synagogue) at Oranienburger Strasse 29 (S-Bahn No 1 or 2 to Oranienburger Strasse or U-Bahn No 6 to Oranienburger Tor). Built in the Moorish-Byzantine style in 1866 as the nation's largest synagogue (3200 seats), it was tragically destroyed – along with Berlin's 13 other synagogues – during Kristallnacht in November 1938. It recently re-opened as 'centrum judaicum', with a permanent exhibit called 'Open the Gates: The New Synagogue 1866-1995'. The fact that original furnishings and liturgical objects – a dented eternal lamp found in the concrete flooring, a rusted doorknob, a shard of broken glass – have been retrieved from the wreckage and put on display is both heartbreaking and exhilarating. Hushed 'sound fragments' of the synagogue's construction and destruction, as well as murmurings of prayer and everyday life in the quarter before the Holocaust, heighten the mood. The Schwedler Dome, all silver and gold and once again a Berlin landmark, is a glorious work of art.

The synagogue is open Sunday to Thursday from 10 am to 6 pm, Friday from 10 am to 2 pm; admission costs DM5/3 but donations are accepted also; give generously in memory of the thousands from this house of prayer who met their death in Nazi concentration camps. Guided tours (DM3/1.50) leave at 4 pm on Wednesday and at 2 and 4 pm on Sunday. Expect a lot of security checks – for all the right reasons.

Beside the synagogue, at Oranienburger Strasse 31, is the **Jewish Art Gallery**, open Monday to Thursday from 12.30 to 6.30 pm,

Friday from 1 to 5 pm and Sunday from 11 am to 3 pm. There are five other functioning synagogues in Berlin including two within walking distance of Zoo station: at Pestalozzistrasse 12 and Joachimstaler Strasse 13 (Map 6). Services are usually held on Friday at 6 or 7 pm and on Saturday at 9.30 am.

A short walk north-west of Oranienburger Tor station (and served by U-Bahn No 6 to Zinnowitzer Strasse) is the **Brecht-Weigel Gedenkstätte** (Brecht-Weigel Memorial) at Chausseestrasse 125, where the socialist playwright Bertolt Brecht (see boxed text) and his actress wife Helene Weigel lived from 1948 until his death in 1956. It's open Tuesday to Friday from 10 am to noon, on Thursday also from 5 to 7 pm, and on Saturday from 9.30 am to noon and 12.30 to 2 pm. Guided tours of the seven rooms leave every half-hour, and admission is DM4/2. Go into the rear courtyard and up the stairs to the right.

Behind the house is **Dorotheenstädtische Friedhof** (Dorotheenstadt Cemetery), with tombs of such notables as the architect Schinkel, the philosopher Georg Friedrich Hegel, the writer Heinrich Mann and the poet Johannes Becher as well as Brecht and Weigel. Don't look for the grave of Marlene Dietrich here; her final resting place is in the Friedenaur Friedhof (Friedenau Cemetery) on Fehlerstrasse in Friedenau and reached on U-Bahn No 9 to Friedrich-Wilhelm-Platz.

Nearby at Invalidenstrasse 43, Humboldt University's **Museum für Naturkunde** (Natural History Museum, 1810) has a good collection of dinosaurs (including one 12m tall) and prehistoric birds as well as minerals and meteorites. It is open Tuesday to Sunday from 9.30 am to 5 pm (admission DM5/2.50). On the same street, in the former Hamburger Bahnhof at No 50-51, is the new SMPK **Museum für Gegenwart** (Museum of Contemporary Art), which picks up where the New National Gallery at the Kulturforum leaves off.

TIERGARTEN (Maps 4 & 3)

Unter den Linden ends at the **Brandenburger Tor** (Brandenburg Gate), designed by Karl Gotthard Langhans in 1791 (S-Bahn No 1 or 2 to Unter den Linden). Once the boundary between East and West, it is now the very symbol of Berlin – the BTM uses a stylised drawing of the gate as its logo. The gate is crowned by the winged Goddess of Victory and a quadriga (a two-wheeled chariot drawn by four horses) by Schadow, and for nigh on three decades West Berliners only got to see the horses' arses. The gate's north wing contains the **Raum der Stille** (Room of Silence), which sounds like something out of the old US sitcom *Get Smart* but is actually where the weary and/or frenzied can sit and contemplate peace. The south wing contains a tourist office branch (see Information).

At the open-air stalls on **Pariser Platz** to the east of the gate you can buy GDR and Soviet military souvenirs, Russian dolls and ever-smaller painted pieces of the Wall. Compare prices before buying, and bargain. And mind the traffic – Pariser Platz is now full of tour buses and vehicles of all sorts and is a dangerous place to cross or to take photographs. At the south-east corner of the square is the recently rebuilt **Hotel Adlon**, the once – and doubtless future – grande dame of Berlin caravanserais. The American, British and French embassies were all here before WWII and are now being rebuilt.

If you continue a short distance east along Unter den Linden, you can't miss the **Russian Embassy** (1950), a white-marble Stalinist behemoth that stretches seemingly forever at No 63-65.

Beside the Spree River, just north of the Brandenburg Gate, is the **Reichstag** (1894), the German Parliament until it was burned down on the night of 27-28 February 1933 (see History in the Facts about the Country chapter). At midnight on 2 October 1990 the reunification of Germany was enacted here. After the artist Christo wrapped the edifice in fabric for two weeks in June/July 1995, (see boxed text entitled It's a Wrap), construction began that, by 1999, will turn the building once again into the seat of the German Federal Parliament. The incomparable British architect Sir Norman Foster is in charge, and his new glass dome promises to be a masterpiece.

It's a Wrap

Call him bogus, call him a quack, call him a brilliant businessman, but the 'environmental sculptor' Christo (born Christo Javacheff in Gabrovo, Bulgaria, in 1935) sure knows how to put on a good show. In 1976, the man who would later create pink plastic 'islands' in Biscayne Bay, Florida (1983), and cover Paris' Pont Neuf in beige fabric (1985), approached the president of the Bundestag (lower house of the West German Parliament) with his plan to wrap the Reichstag. Herr Präsident waffled and later politely declined, as did his successors in 1981 and 1987, the year of Berlin's 750th anniversary.

Cut. Scene change. It's 1994. The Berlin Wall has been down for almost five years, the country is united and Berlin has been voted the new seat of government. About that wrapping job, Herr Christo... The Bundestag debates and votes its go-ahead for the *Projekt Verhüllter Reichstag* (Wrapped Reichstag Project).'

For two weeks in late June/early July 1995, the Reichstag was enveloped in 100,000 square metres of metallic-silver fabric. By all accounts it was a complete success, putting Berlin in its best mood since the euphoria of the *Wende*.

Historians and symbolists will be out to lunch for years trying to decide what it all meant. Did the fragile, undulating shroud 'reveal the essence' of a structure that has gone through so many ups and downs this century? Did it 'signify closure' for a city torn asunder for more than four decades? Did it 'wrap up years of confusion and conflict' over the transfer of Germany's capital from Bonn to Berlin? Or was it just a great big Ringling Brothers-Barnum & Bailey circus enjoyed by one and all? We'll go with the last. *Schönen Dank* for the memories, Christo. ■

Just south of the Reichstag near the start of Scheidemannstrasse is a small **memorial** to some of the 191 people who died trying to cross the Wall – one as recently as February 1989, only nine months before the Wall came tumbling down. The city plans a more ambitious – and permanent – memorial around Checkpoint Charlie (see that section).

If you head west on Scheidemannstrasse and its continuation John-Foster-Dulles Allee to No 10 you'll reach the **Haus der Kulturen der Welt** (House of World Cultures, 1957), nicknamed the 'pregnant oyster' for its shape but looking more like a beached (and somewhat contorted) stingray. In 1980, the arched roof of this strikingly ugly structure collapsed; sadly, some bureaucratic Philistine decided it should be rebuilt and so it was. The photo and art exhibits inside – usually from Africa, Asia or Latin America – are worth a look (open Tuesday to Sunday from 10 am to 7 pm; free entry). The soft seats here will provide some welcome rest, and you can board excursion boats behind the building during the summer months (see Cruises). There are chime concerts from the 68-bell **Carillon** of black marble and bronze – the largest in Europe – to the south-east in the warmer months (see Classical Music in the Entertainment section for details).

The huge city park called **Tiergarten** stretches west from the Brandenburg Gate clear to Zoo station in Charlottenburg. It became a park in the 18th century and in the mid-19th century was landscaped with lakes and streams; during the frigid winter of 1946-7 impoverished local residents chopped down virtually all the trees for firewood. **Strasse des 17 Juni**, named by the West Berlin government in honour of the 1953 workers' uprising in East Berlin, leads west from the Brandenburg Gate through the park. It was known as the East-West Axis during the Nazi era, Hitler's showy entrance to Berlin. On the northern side of this street, just west of the gate, is a **Soviet war memorial** flanked by the first two Russian tanks (Nos 200 and 300) to enter the city in 1945. The brown marble is said to have come from Hitler's chancellory, which once stood on Wilhelmstrasse. (More of this recycled marble was used to face the walls of the Mohrenstrasse U-Bahn station and build the Soviet Monument in Treptower Park.)

Farther west along Strasse des 17 Juni, on the Grosser Stern (Big Star) roundabout, is the 69m-tall **Siegessäule** (Victory Column,

1873), which commemorates 19th-century Prussian military adventures and was moved here by the Nazis in 1938 from Königsplatz (now Platz der Republik) in front of the Reichstag. It is crowned by a gilded statue of Victory (Victoria), which is visible from much of Tiergarten. A spiral staircase (285 steps) leads to the top and affords a worthwhile view (open Monday from 1 to 6 pm, Tuesday to Sunday from 9 am to 6 pm; DM1.50/1).

Just north-east is **Schloss Bellevue** (1785), built for Prince Ferdinand, the youngest brother of Friedrich II, and now the official Berlin residence of the German president. Kaiser Wilhelm II, who disliked the building, used it as a school for his children. The Nazis turned it into a Museum of German Ethnology.

POTSDAMER PLATZ AREA (Map 4)

One of Berlin's biggest tourist attractions – and effectively off-limits for the time being – is the monumental construction site around Potsdamer Platz and Leipziger Platz to the east (U/S-Bahn: Potsdamer Platz). Over the next decade or so, an entire city will be built on the space once occupied by the Wall, including corporate headquarters, futuristic-looking shopping and apartment complexes and a hypermodern train station. Berliners say that the square, a no-man's land when the Wall was up, will soon become what it was in the early part of this century when the first traffic light in Germany was installed here – a terrible bottleneck.

The much touted **Infobox** at Leipziger Platz 21, a gleaming red three-storey structure on stilts, houses a free multimedia exhibit called 'See the City of Tomorrow Today' that explains this gigantic project in a rather boring, overly commercial way; you'll learn more about how the Berlin of the 21st century will look by examining the enormous relief map in the foyer of the Staatsrat (see the earlier Museumsinsel section). Infobox is open daily from 9 am to 7 pm, Thursday to 9 pm, and admission is free. There are hourly guided tours of the Infobox for DM6/4.

From Infobox's outside walkway, accessible only by lift (open daily 9 am to 8.45 pm; DM2), you have a view of the dusty spectacle created by a phalanx of sledgehammers, cranes and bulldozers building new headquarters for Daimler-Benz, Sony and other multinationals. Speaking of Sony, if you look carefully north-west towards Potsdamer Platz you'll see a much older building standing forlornly amidst all the steel and concrete. It's the café of the old **Hotel Esplanade**, the erstwhile *belle* of Bellevuestrasse to the north-west, which Sony moved with the help of some space-age technology when the hotel was demolished in 1996. It will be incorporated into the new Sony centre.

South-east of Potsdamer Platz at Stresemannstrasse 110 is the **Martin-Gropius-Bau** (MGB), containing three museums: the **Deutscher Werkbund**, dedicated to the German Jugendstil (Art Nouveau) movement; the sensational **Berlinische Galerie** of Berlin art from 1870 to the present, and the **Jüdische Museum** (Jewish Museum). The MGB is open Tuesday to Sunday from 10 am to 8 pm. Admission is DM8/4 except during special exhibits when the price jumps to DM12/6 (or DM20 for two people, good for two visits). The Jewish Museum will have moved south-east next to the renovated **Berlin Museum** at Lindenstrasse 14 (U-Bahn No 6 to Kochstrasse) by the time you read this.

Behind the MGB is the site of the former SS and Gestapo headquarters where the **Topographie des Terrors** (Topography of Terror) exhibition (open Tuesday to Sunday from 10 am to 6 pm; admission free) documents Nazi crimes. Much is made of the suffering of the Jewish and Rom peoples during the Holocaust, but there's not a word about the thousands of homosexual men and women who were persecuted, tortured and murdered by Nazi brutes. A booklet in English costs DM2. The exhibit opened shortly after the Wende and is very much showing its age. A new visitors' and documentation centre is planned on the tract of land to the east of the MGB facing Niederkirchnerstrasse. A long stretch of the Wall –

The Berlin Wall

There has been a lot of debate over this symbol of the Cold War, especially since the *Wende.* The Russians did not build what the West Germans simply called *Die Mauer* (the Wall) in August 1961; the East Germans themselves did, but construction was only made possible by Nikita Khrushchev's decision to hand over responsibility for security within the Soviet sector to GDR leader Walter Ulbricht and his Socialist Unity Party (SED) earlier that year. Until then many East Berliners worked in the West and attended concerts, films etc, returning at night.

But the allure of the more prosperous West was too great, and by the summer of 1961 up to 20,000 East Germans a month were quitting the GDR via West Berlin. The GDR actually built its so-called Anti-Fascist Protection Barrier to keep workers in and the GDR economy from haemorrhaging.

There it stood for more than 28 years, some 165km of ugly prefab concrete slabs that you could reach out and touch (or paint or spray) on the Western side but was protected by a 'no man's land' of barbed wire, land mines, attack dogs and watch towers in the East. This folly, this ribbon of shame, this affront to civilisation, claimed the lives of 80 would-be escapees during its lifetime, and it's difficult to imagine anything that more deserves to be consigned to the rubbish tip of history.

But *nostalgie de la boue* and the tourism industry has kept stretches of the wall standing in various parts of Berlin, including the following:

Mühlenstrasse in Friedrichshain (S-Bahn to Warschauer Strasse, U-Bahn No 1 or 15 to Schlesisches Tor) The longest (1300m) surviving stretch of the Wall, running along Mühlenstrasse from Oberbaumbrücke to Strasse der Pariser Kommune, has been painted on the east-facing side by a number of artists and is now the East Side Gallery.

Niederkirchnerstrasse in Mitte (U/S-Bahn to Potsdamer Platz) This 160m section runs along Niederkirchnerstrasse from Martin-Gropius-Bau to Wilhelmstrasse near the former Preussischer Landtag (Prussian State Parliament).

Leipziger/Potsdamer Plätze (U/S-Bahn to Potsdamer Platz) A short section of the Wall can be seen near the Infobox, at the corner of Leipziger Platz and Stresemannstrasse.

Checkpoint Charlie in Mitte (U-Bahn No 6 to Kochstrasse) Remains of the Wall and concrete lookout towers that occupied the site have been moved a short walk east to where Zimmerstrasse meets Charlottenstrasse.

Invaliedenfriedhof in Mitte (U-Bahn No 6 to Zinnowitzer Strasse) This cemetery, just north of the Museum of Contemporary Art in the former Hamburger Bahnhof, has two sections measuring about 150m in total.

Bernauer Strasse in Mitte (S-Bahn to Nordbahnhof) The new Gedenkstätte Berliner Mauer (Berlin Wall Memorial), composed of a lengthy section of the Wall plus border installations and perhaps the most appropriate site to visit, will stand at the corner of Bernauer Strasse and Gartenstrasse. ■

in fact the longest in Mitte – runs along Niederkirchnerstrasse from the MGB to Wilhelmstrasse (see boxed text entitled The Berlin Wall).

KULTURFORUM AREA (Map 3)

West of Potsdamer Platz is the warren-like gold and silver **Berliner Philharmonie** (by Hans Scharoun, 1963), housing the modern concert hall.

The SMPK **Musikinstrumenten-Museum** (Musical Instruments Museum) is in the north-east wing of the Philharmonie at Tiergartenstrasse 1. Harpsichords from the 17th century, medieval trumpets and shepherds' bagpipes may not be everyone's cup of tea, but the museum displays them in a unique and wonderful way. Historical paintings and porcelain figurines portray people playing them, and there are earphones sprinkled throughout the museum to hear what they sound(ed) like. Pride of place goes to the Gray Organ (1820) from Bathwick, Somerset, but our favourite is the 'mighty Wurlitzer' organ (1929) with more buttons and keys than a Beefeater guard. Guided tours (DM3) at 11 am on Saturday culminate with a recital on this white and gold confection. On Sunday at 11 am there are concerts of ancient music played on the original instruments (admission DM12).

The red-brick **St Mattäus Kirche** (Church

of St Matthew, 1846), open Wednesday to Sunday from noon to 6 pm, stands to the south of the Philharmonie in the centre of Berlin's **Kulturforum**, another complex of museums on Matthäikirchplatz.

The never-ending SMPK **Kunstgewerbemuseum** (Arts & Crafts Museum) has applied arts from the Middle Ages right up to our day – from 16th-century chalices of gold-gilded silver made in Nuremberg to Art Deco ceramics and 21st-century appliances. Don't miss Carlo Bugatti's crazy suite of furniture (1885) upstairs, with elements of Islamic, Japanese and Native American design all in one.

Across the plaza is the SMPK **Kupferstichkabinett** (Copperplate Etchings Gallery) – you can safely miss this one – and, to the south-east at Potsdamer Strasse 50, the SMPK **Neue Nationalgalerie** (New National Gallery, 1968), with a collection of 19th and 20th-century paintings and sculptures including works by Klee, Munch, Miró, Max Ernst, Juan Gris and Henry Moore. The main emphasis here, however, is German expressionism, and you can't miss the works of Otto Dix (eg *Old Couple*, 1923), Max Beckmann's triptychs and the wonderful 'egghead' figures of George Grosz. The sculpture garden in the back is a great place to put your feet up and catch a few rays if the sun is shining. The **State Library** branch (1976) across the street contains reading, periodical and exhibition rooms.

About 1km to the west along the Landwehr Canal is the **Museum für Gestaltung** (Museum of Design), in the Bauhaus Archives at Klingelhöferstrasse 14. It is devoted to the artists of the Bauhaus School (1919-33), who laid the basis for much contemporary architecture. The collection, including works by Klee, Wassily Kandinsky and Oskar Schlemmer, is housed in a building with distinctive glass-panelled gables designed by the school's founder, Walter Gropius (1883-1969), whose uncle was the architect Martin Gropius. The museum is open Wednesday to Monday from 10 am to 5 pm; admission is DM4/2 (Monday free).

CHECKPOINT CHARLIE AREA (Map 4)

Almost nothing remains of the famous **Checkpoint Charlie** on Friedrichstrasse (U-Bahn No 6 to Kochstrasse), gateway for foreigners between the two Berlins during the Cold War and now the site of the new American Business Center. The city plans to build an open-air museum nearby honouring those murdered by GDR border guards for the onerous crime of 'attempting to flee the republic' (as it actually appeared on the books). If you want to see where the barrier actually stood, walk north along Friedrichstrasse – traditionally the city's 'commercial street' where Berliners went to shop – from Kochstrasse station to the corner of Zimmerstrasse. Because of the construction, the remains of the Wall and concrete lookouts that occupied the site have been moved a short walk east to where Zimmerstrasse meets Charlottenstrasse.

The modern structure at Friedrichstrasse 207-208 next to the Goethe Institute was, until 1990, the headquarters of all Western intelligence organisations in Berlin, and from here photos were taken of everyone crossing the border. The history of the Wall is commemorated nearby in the **Haus am Checkpoint Charlie**, an interesting private museum of Wall memorabilia and photos at Friedrichstrasse 43-44 (open daily from 9 am to 10 pm; admission DM7.50/4.50, half-price for citizens of the erstwhile Soviet bloc, excluding the GDR).

North-west of here, on the corner of Wilhelmstrasse (Berlin's 'street of government') and Vossstrasse, stood the **Reichskanzlei**, Hitler's chancellory built by Albert Speer in 1938. It was completely effaced in the late 1980s when the Communists built the apartment complex and kindergarten that now occupy the site. **Hitler's bunker**, where the madman shot and killed himself on 30 April 1945, was farther to the west along Vossstrasse just north-east of Potsdamer Platz. A sandy mound overgrown with weeds marks the spot.

KURFÜRSTENDAMM (Map 6)

On Breitscheidplatz, at the start of the long

and broad Kurfürstendamm, stand the stark ruins of the **Kaiser-Wilhelm-Gedächtniskirche** (Kaiser Wilhelm Memorial Church; 1895; U/S-Bahn: Zoologischer Garten), engulfed in roaring commercialism and flashiness. This is the heart and formal centre of western Berlin. The Allied bombing of 22 November 1943 left only the broken west tower of the church standing. The **Gedenkhalle** (Memorial Hall, 1987) below the tower, which contains original mosaics on the ceiling, marble reliefs, liturgical objects and photos before and after the bombing, may be visited Monday to Saturday from 10 am to 4 or 5 pm.

The ugly modern **church** (1961), with its overwhelmingly bluer-than-blue stained glass, is open to visitors from 9 am to 7.30 pm daily, except during services. English-language tours of the church depart at 3 and 3.30 pm on Thursday and Friday. The modern hexagonal **bell tower** contains the Third World Shop at the bottom, with hand-made articles and books from Asia, Africa and South America.

On the eastern side of Breitscheidplatz opposite the memorial church is the **Europa-Center** (1965), a shopping and restaurant complex that wouldn't look out of place in Los Angeles or Singapore. Among the outlets, eateries and main tourist office is a weird **Flow of Time Clock** that measures hours, minutes and seconds via a series of vials and spheres that fill up with vile, radio-active-looking green liquid. It seems to fascinate the local Teutons.

North-east of the Europa-Center, at Budapester Strasse 34, is the Elephant Gate (complete with a chinoiserie-style roof) entrance to Germany's oldest **zoo** (1844) and **aquarium**. It contains some 14,000 animals representing 1500 different species and is open daily from 9 am to dusk (6.30 pm at the latest), the aquarium till 6 pm. Both the zoo and the aquarium charge an admission of DM11/9/5.50 for adults/students/children; a combined ticket is DM18/14.50/9. During the war most of the animals were killed in bombing raids though the last elephant, Siam, is said to have been driven insane by the pandemonium and trumpeted nonstop in terror.

To the west and adjacent to Zoo station on the corner of Kantstrasse and Joachimstaler Strasse is the **Erotik Museum**, which displays erotic sculptures, drawings and objects from around the world and has welcomed 'more than 350,000 customers!' in its short and happy life (open daily from 9 am to midnight; DM10/8). You have to be 18 or over to get in.

SCHLOSS CHARLOTTENBURG

Built at the end of the 17th century as a summer residence for Queen Sophie-Charlotte (1668-1705), Charlottenburg Palace is an exquisite baroque pile on Spandauer Damm 3km north-west of Zoo station. Along with several important buildings in the **Schlossgarten** (Palace Garden), there are also four fine museums nearby.

To get to the palace take U-Bahn No 2 to Sophie-Charlotte-Platz and then bus No 110 for three stops (or walk north about 1km from the station along Schlossstrasse to the entrance).

Huge crowds are often waiting for the guided tour of Charlottenburg Palace, and it may be difficult to get a ticket. This is especially true on weekends and holidays in summer. If you can't get into the main palace, content yourself with the façades and gardens. The palace buildings all charge separate admissions, but you can buy a day card for DM15/10 (family DM25). However, this does not allow entry to the state museums in and around the palace. For those you have to pay separately (DM4/2) or buy a SMPK day card for DM8/4.

The palace was bombed in 1943 but was completely rebuilt between 1950 and 1966. In front of the main entrance is an equestrian statue of Friedrich Wilhelm (1620-1688), the so-called Great Elector and Sophie-Charlotte's father-in-law. Along the Spree River behind the palace are extensive French and English-style gardens (free admission).

In the central **Nering-Eosander Building** of the palace are the former royal living quarters, which must be visited on a boring,

50-minute guided tour in German (Tuesday to Friday from 9 am to 5 pm, Saturday and Sunday from 10 am to 5 pm; DM8/4). The tour takes in 21 rooms and, as in most baroque palaces, they seem to be trying to outdo one another in brocade, gilt and overall opulence. Among the highlights are the Hall of Mirrors (Room 118); the lovely Oval Hall (Room 116), with views of the French gardens and distant Belvedere; the wind gauge in Friedrich I's bedchamber (Room 96); the fabulous Porcelain Chamber (Room 95), covered from floor to ceiling in Chinese blueware and figures; and the Eosander Chapel (Room 94) with its *trompe l'oeil* arches.

To the east of the Nering-Eosander Building is the **New Wing** (or Knobelsdorff Wing, 1746), containing some of the most beautiful rooms in the palace (same opening hours; DM5/3). Upstairs to the left are the confection-like White Hall with its elaborate concave ceiling; the Golden Gallery, a rococo extravaganza of mirrors and gilding; and the Concert Hall. To the right of the staircase are the recently reopened **Winterkammern** (Winter Chambers) of Friedrich Wilhelm II.

On the ground floor of the New Wing is the SMPK **Galerie der Romantik** (Gallery of the Romantics), which contains works by Caspar David Friedrich *(Abbey in the Oak Wood)*, the Gothic fantasies of Karl Friedrich Schinkel and Carl Blechen, as well as some fine examples of neoclassical and Biedermeier art.

Buildings within the Palace Garden include the 1824 **Schinkel Pavilion** (open Tuesday to Sunday from 10 am to 5 pm, with shorter hours between late October and late March; DM3/2), with Schinkel art and bric-a-brac; the rococo **Belvedere** folly (same hours and admission), built in 1788 and containing an impressive collection of Berlin porcelain; and the neoclassical **Mausoleum** (open late March to October Tuesday to Sunday from 10 am to 5 pm; DM2/1), which contains the tomb of Queen Luise (1776-1810) and her husband Friedrich Wilhelm III (1770-1840), among others.

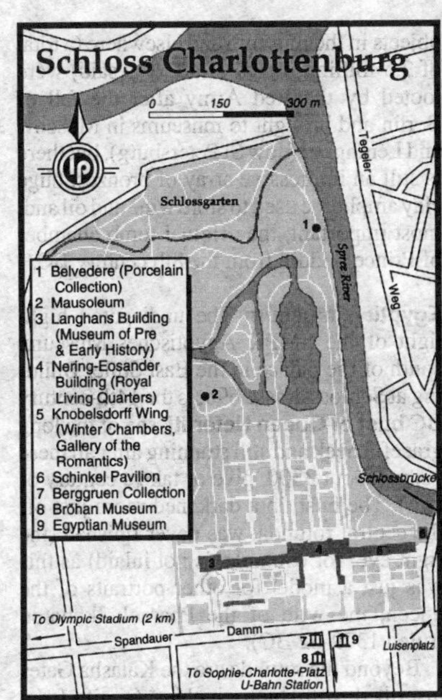

Schloss Area Museums

In addition to the splendour of the royal palace and its outbuildings, there are four museums in the immediate area well worth visiting. Three of them are state museums and one is private, so get your wallet or day card ready.

Museum of Pre & Early History The SMPK Museum für Vor- und Frühgeschichte occupies the west wing (or Langhans Building) of the Schloss Charlottenburg and contains archaeological artefacts from Stone, Bronze and Iron Age cultures in Europe and the Middle East. The most outstanding collection is that of Trojan antiquities upstairs in the **Schliemann Saal**, named after the archaeologist Heinrich Schliemann (1822-90) who pursued his life-long ambition to discover a historical basis for Homer's *Illiad*. In 1871, during excavations at Hissarlik in Turkey, he literally struck pay dirt – he discovered the site of ancient Troy. Many of the objects in the museum and elsewhere (a total of 2.5 million works of art, it is said) were looted by the Red Army after the fall of Berlin and brought to museums in Moscow and Leningrad (now St Petersburg), but there is still an impressive array of bronzes, huge clay amphorae used to store wine and oil and, most important, the original tomb chamber of Prince Seddin from the 8th century BC.

Egyptian Museum The undisputed highlight of the SMPK Ägyptisches Museum, south of the palace in the East Stüler Building at Schlossstrasse 69b, is the 14th-century BC **bust of Queen Nefertiti**, she of the long graceful neck and still stunning after all these years (about 3300, give or take a century or two). The bust, in a darkened room just off the central rotunda, was never finished (the right eye, for example, is not inlaid) as this was just a model for other portraits of the queen, the wife of the Pharaoh Ikhnaton (ruled 1379-62 BC).

Beyond the rotunda are the Kalasha Gates inscribed with hieroglyphics (a gift from Egypt for Germany's assistance in saving archaeological treasures during the construction of the Aswan Dam, 1960-70) and two rooms crammed with items from everyday life, totemic animal figurines (look for the baboon and the horse) and busts and statues of the Egyptian high and mighty, all with an enigmatic smile and their left foot jauntily placed forward. Head upstairs for a look at this wonderful museum's second-most cherished object: the **Berlin Green**. It's a small bust (500-400 BC) of a man carved from green stone and is almost expressionistic in style, with its broken nose, crow's feet and wrinkles.

Berggruen Collection In the West Stüler Building, opposite the Egyptian Museum, is the SMPK Sammlung Berggruen, entitled 'Picasso and His Time' and on loan for a decade from one Dr Heinz Berggruen, art connoisseur and FOP (Friend of Picasso). It focuses on the work of Picasso and his contemporaries and contains some 65 paintings, drawings and sculptures by the master himself as well as works by Cézanne, Braque, Klee and Giacometti. The works are interspersed with African woodcarvings from the Ethnology Museum at Dahlem, which obviously inspired Picasso. There's an excellent 50-minute cassette tour in German (DM6/4) partly narrated by Dr Berggruen himself.

Bröhan Museum This lovely museum, just south of the Berggruen Collection at Schlossstrasse 1a, focuses on applied arts and design from 1889 to 1939 and was donated to the city by Karl Bröhan in 1982. Some of the Art Nouveau and Art Deco suites of furniture (eg by Hector Guimard and Émile Ruhlmann) are outstanding – easily leaving the collection of the Arts & Crafts Museum at the Kulturforum in the dust; the collection of silver, glass, porcelain and enamelware seems endless but astonishes at every turn. The Bröhan is open Tuesday to Sunday from 10 am to 6 pm. Admission costs DM5/2.50 or DM3/1.50 with a state museums day card.

Olympic Stadium

The Olympia-Stadion, built by Hitler for the 1936 Olympic Games in which the African-American runner Jesse Owens won four gold medals and put paid to the Nazi theory that Aryans were the all-powerful *Übermenschen*, lies south-west of Schloss Charlottenburg. The 85,000-seat stadium, one of the best examples of Nazi-era neoclassical architecture, is still very much in use for track and other sporting events, but you can visit it daily when there isn't something on from 9 am to sunset (DM3/1.50). To reach it take U-Bahn No 2 to Olympia-Stadion Ost; from there it's a 15-minute signposted walk along Olympische Strasse to Olympischer Platz.

A short distance to the west is the 77m **Glockenturm** (Clock Tower), which offers superb views over the stadium, the city and the Havel. Check out the Nazi bell – it weighs 2.5 tonnes and is inscribed with the words: 'Ich rufe die Jugend der Welt' ('I call upon the youth of the world'). The tower is open daily May to October from 10 am to 5.30 pm (DM3/1.50).

DAHLEM MUSEUM COMPLEX

The SMPK Dahlem Museum complex, a group of museums all under one roof that is perhaps worth all the others in Berlin combined, is in the leafy south-western suburb of Dahlem in the district of Zehlendorf (U-Bahn No 1 to Dahlem-Dorf and then a five-minute walk south on Iltisstrasse). You could spend an entire day (preferably a rainy one) here, moving from 17th-century Flemish portraits to pre-Columbian gold jewellery and giant Melanesian outriggers. But choose carefully; it is a phenomenally rich collection. The normal state museum entry fee of DM4/2 gets you into everything here so a day card is unnecessary.

The complex consists of seven museums with almost as many subdivisions. The **Gemäldegalerie** (Picture Gallery) houses the better part of the Prussian art collection amassed by Friedrich II, evacuated from the Museumsinsel during WWII and never returned to East Berlin. There are rooms devoted to the works of Italian, German, Dutch, Flemish, French and English masters from the 13th to the late 18th centuries. The **Skulpturensammlung** (Sculpture Collection) contains works in wood, stone and plaster from the early Middle Ages to the 19th century. There are also specific museums devoted to Indian, East Asian, Islamic and late-classical and Byzantine art.

The **Museum für Völkerkunde** (Ethnology Museum) alone is divided into four huge departments – pre-Columbian American, South Seas (ie Australasian), African and South Asian – with two small touchy-feely rooms in the basement reserved for children and blind visitors.

It would take a dozen pages to point out the best things this complex has on show – we aren't kidding – but do not, under pain of death, miss any of the following highly subjective favourites: the reconstructed temple room and 8th-century frescos from Turfan in north-west China (Indian Art); the enormous outriggers (especially the one built in 1890 on Luf Island in Micronesia) in the boat hall (Australasian Ethnology); the treasury of pre-Columbian gold jewellery and other objects, especially the helmets (pre-Columbian American Ethnology); the reconstructed 16th-century *mihrab* (prayer nook) from Iran (Islamic Art); the 19th-century carved teak wall from a house in central Java (South Asian Ethnology); the Qing Dynasty red-lacquer screens (East Asian Art); the 18th-century woodcarving of St Michael the Archangel doing battle with Satan (Sculpture Collection); and Pieter Bruegel the Elder's *Dutch Proverbs*, illustrating 100 aphorisms (see if you can find the man 'armed to the teeth', someone 'crying over spilt milk', a 'bird in the hand' etc).

If you haven't had enough, the **Museum für Volkskunde** (Folklore Museum), a branch of the Dahlem Museum complex with objects from everyday life from the 16th century to the present, is at Im Winkel 6-8, a short walk east of Dahlem-Dorf station along Königin-Luise-Strasse, the main thoroughfare through the village. A couple of blocks farther on at No 6-8 is the 43-hectare **Botanischer Garten** (Botanical Garden), with over 20,000 plant species on display (open Monday to Saturday from 9 am to dusk; DM5/2.50).

TREPTOWER PARK

It is appropriate that the city's largest **Sowjetisches Ehrenmal** (Soviet Monument, 1949) should remain very much intact in east Berlin; after all, with the possible exception of Bulgaria, the GDR was Moscow's most faithful lackey, ready to do Big Brother's bidding at every turn for over four decades. But do remember that this is a grave site – some 5000 Soviet soldiers are buried here – and act with all the decorum and solemnity that such a place demands. To get here take any S-Bahn to Treptower Park or U-Bahn No 15 to Schlesisches Tor then bus No 265. It is easiest to enter from Pushkin Allee, on the park's northern side.

The memorial site starts with a statue of Mother Russia, grieving for her dead children. From here a wide plaza, flanked on either side by eight marble blocks with reliefs portraying scenes from the war and quotes from Stalin (in Russian and German), leads south-east to an enormous statue of a Russian soldier holding a child, his great sword resting on a shattered swastika. In the plinth is a socialist-realism mosaic of grateful Soviet citizens, including workers, peasants and some Central Asian minorities. The monument is always open.

OTHER MUSEUMS

Along with the four major museum groups – Museumsinsel, the Dahlem complex, Schloss Charlottenburg and the Kulturforum – there are smaller collections sprinkled throughout Berlin that cater to every taste, interest and visitor – from gays and lesbians to those with a sweet tooth. The following is a selective list.

Arts Academy (Map 3)
: The Akademie der Künste at Hanseatenweg 10 (U-Bahn No 9 to Hansaplatz) hosts exceptionally fine revolving exhibits, often in conjunction with other museums (eg the very successful 'Goodbye to Berlin: 100 Years of the Gay Movement' with the Gay Museum in the first half of 1997). Open daily from noon to 8 pm; DM8/4 (Wednesday free).

Dog
: The Hundemuseum at Alt-Blankenburg 33 in Weissensee (S-Bahn No 8 or 10 to Blankenburg) has more than 20,000 canine-related exhibits. Open Tuesday, Thursday and Saturday from 3 to 6 pm, Sunday from 11 am to 5 pm; DM2/1.

Marlene Dietrich
: The Marlene Dietrich Collection at Streitstrasse 15-17 in Spandau (bus No 131, 231 or 331) is only open the first Thursday of every month at 3.30 pm; DM10/6.

Gay (Map 3)
: The Schwules Museum, Mehringdamm 61 (U-Bahn No 6 or 7 to Mehringdamm), has hit-or-miss special exhibits, from the stupendous 'Goodbye to Berlin: 100 Years of the Gay Movement' in cooperation with the Arts Academy during the summer of 1997, to rather offensive ones on flagellation and that master fraud, the late William Burroughs. Open Wednesday to Sunday from 2 to 6 pm with a guided tour at 5 pm on Saturday; DM7/4.

GDR Design (Prenzlauer Berg map)
: The Sammlung Industrielle Gestaltung in the north wing of the Kulturbrauerei, Knaackstrasse 97 (U-Bahn No 2 to Eberwalder Strasse), is a sorry collection of East German 'designed' clothing, appliances and furnishings that illustrates all too well the sham that was the GDR: leopard-skin plastic raincoats, 1950s-style hairdryers the size of vacuum cleaners, plastic typewriters. Open Tuesday to Sunday from 9 am to 5 pm; free.

German Technical (Map 3)
: The Deutches Technikmuseum at Trebbiner Strasse 9 in Kreuzberg 61 (U-Bahn No 15 to Möckernbrücke or Gleisdreieck) examines technology through the ages – from printing and transport to information technology. The new Spectrum annexe displays more than 200 historical machines in operation. Open Tuesday to Friday from 9 am to 5.30 pm, Saturday and Sunday from 10 am to 6 pm; DM5/3.

Gründerzeit
: One of the main reasons for visiting the Foundation Time Museum, dedicated to the Berlin of 1870 to 1910, was to be hosted by its developer Charlotte von Mahlsdorf, the GDR's most famous transvestite. Alas, like Britain's Quentin Crisp *(The Naked Civil Servant)*, who saw greener pastures in New York, *Die Charlotte* has flown the coop to Sweden. The famous pack rat's collection, however – including, in the basement, the complete contents of the famous Mulack-Ritz bar from the Scheunenviertel – remains open. It's at Hultschiner Damm 333 in Hellersdorf (S-Bahn No 5 to Mahlsdorf then tram No 62 for two stops). Tours – on Sunday only at 11 am and noon – are often booked out so call ☎ 527 83 29 first; free entry.

Hairdressing (Prenzlauer Berg map)
: The Friseurmuseum at Husemannstrasse 8 in Prenzlauer Berg (U-Bahn No 2 to Senefelderplatz) has an odd assortment of barbers' scissors and knives, a wigmaker's workshop from the 18th century etc. Open Tuesday to Sunday from 10 am to 6 pm; DM2/1.

Post Office & Communication
: Philatelists may be interested in having a look at the stamp collections (from 1849) of the Museum für Post und Kommunikation at Haus der Urania, An der Urania 15 (U-Bahn No 2, 4 or 15 to Nollendorfplatz). There's also a fair bit on telecommunications. Open Monday to Thursday from 9 am to 5 pm, Saturday and Sunday from 10 am; free.

Stasi
: The Forschungs- und Gedenkstätte on Normannenstrasse, at the one-time headquarters of the Stasi (East German secret police), has cunning surveillance devices, Communist paraphernalia and blood-chilling documents about postwar

GDR internment camps. It's at Ruschestrasse 59 (house No 1) in Lichtenberg (U-Bahn No 5 to Magdalenenstrasse). Open Tuesday to Friday from 11 am to 6 pm, Saturday and Sunday from 2 to 6 pm; DM5/3.

Sugar

The Zucker Museum at Amrumer Strasse 32 in the northern suburb of Wedding (U-Bahn No 9 to Amrumer Strasse) has all you could possibly want to know about the sweet stuff – dietetics, technology, economic aspects, how sweet it is. Open Monday to Wednesday from 9 am to 5 pm, Sunday from 11 am to 6 pm; DM4.50/2.

ACTIVITIES

Cruises

Central Berlin may be crowded with roads, office buildings and apartment blocks, but the south-eastern and south-western sections of the city are surprisingly green, with forests, rivers and lakes. In the warmer months, tourist boats cruise the waterways, calling at picturesque villages, parks and castles. Food and drink are sold on board, but they're quite expensive, so take along something to sip or nibble.

Stern und Kreis Schiffahrt (Map 4; ☎ 536 36 00) operates many different cruises, except in winter (November to March). A 3½-hour cruise from Jannowitzbrücke near the Märkisches Museum in Mitte through Tiergarten to Schlossbrücke near Charlottenburg Palace and back costs DM23/14.50 and is offered twice daily, at 11 am and 3 pm, from late March to mid-October. A one-hour spin around Museumsinsel from the Nikolaiviertel (11 daily departures) will set you back DM13.50, while a four-hour voyage from just south of the Eisenbrücke in Treptow (S-Bahn to Treptower Park) east along the Spree and down the Havel to the castle of Cecilienhof in Potsdam is DM22/33 one way/return. Other cruises cover the Havel lakes from Wannsee and various canals.

Reederei Bruno Winkler (☎ 391 70 70) has sightseeing cruises on the Spree River or the Landwehr Canal from March to October. The main landing stage is at Schlossbrücke at Charlottenburger Ufer, just east of the Charlottenburg Palace. Three-hour tours leave twice daily at 10.20 am and 2.20 pm and cost DM10/20 one way/return. You can also hop aboard at the Friedrichstrasse landing at the Reichstagufer, which cuts down the travelling time to two hours and the round-trip cost to DM18.

Spreefahrt (☎ 364 10 68) has one-hour cruises through historical Berlin for DM10, leaving from behind the House of World Cultures (Map 3) just west of the Reichstag in Tiergarten. The cruises run between 11 am and 6 pm (no cruise at 1 pm); two-hour trips for DM15 depart on Saturday at 1 pm; and a 3½-hour tour called 'Old Berlin Bridges' costs DM13/20 one way/return.

BWTS (Map 4; ☎ 658 80 20 3), a water-taxi service just north of the Schlossbrücke across from Museumsinsel, has one-hour spins (DM9/12) up and down the Spree, leaving every half-hour between 10 am and 4.30 pm.

Swimming

Just about every district in Berlin has its own indoor *and* outdoor swimming pools but our ab faves are the Art Nouveau Stadtbad Neukölln (☎ 680 92 65 3) at Ganghoferstrasse 3-5 in Neukölln (U-Bahn No 7 to Rathaus Neukölln) and the Art Deco Bad am Spreewaldplatz (Map 5; ☎ 258 85 81 3), Wiener Strasse 59, in Kreuzberg 36. The latter, which has a sauna and wave machine, is open daily from 8 am to 10 pm, with some days or times reserved exclusively for men or women. Admission is DM3.50/2.

Casino

Spielbank Berlin (☎ 250 08 90), a casino at the Europa-Center on Breitscheidplatz in Charlottenburg, has 10 roulette tables (stakes DM5 to DM20,000), blackjack (minimum bet DM10) and baccarat (minimum bet DM50). It is open daily from 3 pm to 3 am and is a fairly informal place – men don't have to wear ties. You must be over 21 to enter, though.

LANGUAGE COURSES

The Goethe Institute (Map 4; ☎ 25906 3; fax 259 06 40 0), Friedrichstrasse 209, has intensive eight-week courses starting at around

DM2700. Course information can be obtained from German embassies or consulates abroad, from branches of the Goethe Institute or from its central registration office (☎ 089-15 92 10; fax 089-159 21 450; email: esb@goethe.de), Helene-Weber-Allee 1, 80637 Munich.

A private school teaching German to foreigners that seems to get high marks is the Europa Sprachenschule (Map 5; ☎ 618 88 63; fax 618 95 57), at Taborstrasse 17 in Kreuzberg 36 (U-Bahn No 15 to Schlesisches Tor). It offers 20-unit (a unit is a 45-minute classroom 'hour') weekly intensive courses at beginner and advanced levels for DM66 to DM180 depending on the class size, and a monthly course of 80 units for between DM264 and DM720. Lessons are held for four hours in the morning/early afternoon (9 am to 1.15 pm) and afternoon/early evening (3 to 7.15 pm).

ORGANISED TOURS

Bus Tours

You can see a great many of Berlin's most important – and interesting – sights from the upper deck of bus No 100 for the price of a BVG ticket (see Public Transport in the Getting Around section for details).

Eick's Rundfahrten Berlin (Map 6; ☎ 264 84 71 2) runs 1½-hour double-deck bus tours of both the eastern and western parts of Berlin year round from 10.30 am to 4.30 pm. A seat costs DM25 on the upper deck (DM15 below), and buses leave from outside the Kaiser Wilhelm Memorial Church on Kurfürstendamm.

Top-Tour-Berlin (Map 6; ☎ 256 24 74 0) is a jump-on, jump-off circular tour run by the BVG from mid-April to October. Buses also leave from outside the Kaiser Wilhelm church every half-hour from 9.30 am to 5 pm and make 22 stops. Tickets (DM35/29 for adults/children aged six to 14) bought after 3 pm are valid for the entire next day.

A similar tour is City Circle Sightseeing offered by BBS (☎ 351 95 27 0) in – count 'em – eight languages. Buses stop on Kurfürstendamm, on the corner of Rankestrasse *opposite* the Kaiser Wilhelm Memorial Church, every half-hour between 10 am and 6 pm. A full-day ticket costs DM30; if you don't mind starting after 2.30 pm, you only pay DM20.

Walking Tours

Among the best walking tours we've ever been on are the ones from Berlin Walks (☎ 301 91 94), who run English-language walking tours daily from late March to late December. They take between two and three hours and cost DM15/10 for those over/under 26 (children under 14 are free).

Their Discover Berlin tour covers the heart of the city and gives good historical background and architectural information; it leaves daily at 10 am and 2.30 pm from late March to October (extra departure at 9.15 am between June and August), and at 10 am only from November to late December. The Infamous Third Reich Sites tour runs on a more limited schedule, with between one and five departures a day at 10 am, depending on the season. Our favourite, the Jewish Life in Berlin tour, takes in the sights of the Scheunenviertel, including the New Synagogue, and departs on Sunday at 10 am (with an extra tour on Wednesday at the same time from May to October).

All tours by Berlin Walks leave from outside the main entrance of Zoo station (Map 6) at the top of the taxi rank. You must be armed with a BVG *Langstrecke* ticket (DM3.60; see Public Transport in the Getting Around section), though rail-pass holders don't need one for the Discover Berlin and Jewish Life tours as the S-Bahn is used.

Two other operators offering a larger choice of topical walking tours between April/May and October but in German only include StattReisen Berlin (☎ 455 30 28; DM15/12) and Gangart Berlin (☎ 327 03 78 3; DM18/12).

SPECIAL EVENTS

Berlin's calendar is loaded with annual fairs, festivals, concerts and parties; the following is just a small sampling.

Berlin Film Festival
: The Berliner Filmfestspiele, the world's second-largest film festival (after Cannes), is held over 12 days in February.

Festival Days
: The Festtage is a week-long music event in March celebrating Wagner and his operas.

Christopher Street Day
: The biggest annual gay event in the city takes place in late June with a parade from Savignyplatz in Charlottenburg to the eastern end of Unter den Linden.

Love Parade
: Berlin's top annual techno event held in early July attracts some 750,000 people; the parade itself marches from Brandenburg Gate along Strasse des 17 Juni to the Siegessäule.

Berlin Festival Weeks
: The Berliner Festwochen is a two-month theatre festival held throughout September.

JazzFest Berlin
: This four-day jazz festival at various venues around the city takes place in October.

Christmas Markets
: Christmas markets are held from late November to 21 December at several locations around Berlin, including Breitscheidplatz in Charlottenburg (daily 11 am to 9 or 10 pm); Schlossplatz in Mitte (daily 1 to 9 or 10 pm); and Reformationsplatz in Spandau (Saturday and Sunday from 10 am to 7 pm; U-Bahn No 7 to Altstadt Spandau).

PLACES TO STAY – BOTTOM END

Things are tight east of Tiergarten, as hotels close, are demolished or renovated into the exclusive class. This has diverted the attention of budget travellers to the west until the accommodation scene settles down. The tourist office has an excellent free booklet imaginatively called *Hotel Verzeichnis* (Hotel List), with a fairly comprehensive listing of hotel and pension options.

Camping

Camping facilities in Berlin are not plentiful or particularly good. There are several camping grounds charging DM8.50 per person plus from DM5.50 to DM8.50 per tent site and DM0.50 per shower, but they're far from the city centre, crowded with caravans and often full. They cater almost exclusively to permanent campers who use their caravans as weekend and holiday getaways all year. Although you may be admitted if you're persistent *and* polite, they aren't really set up to receive casual tourists.

The only camping ground convenient to public transport is *Campingplatz Kohlhasenbrück* (☎ 805 17 37), Neue Kreisstrasse 36, in a peaceful location overlooking the Griebnitzsee in the far south-west corner of Berlin, 15km from the centre. It's a 10-minute walk from the Griebnitzsee S-Bahn station, or get off at the previous stop, Wannsee, and take bus No 118, which runs directly there. If the gate is locked when you arrive, just hang around until someone with a key arrives, and then ask for the manager at the caravan near the gate. It is open from April to September.

If Kohlhasenbrück is full, 2km to the east along the Teltow Canal is *Campingplatz Dreilinden* (☎ 805 12 01), at Albrechts-Teerofen (open from March to October). It's 20 minutes on foot from the Griebnitzsee S-Bahn; bus No 118 from Wannsee station also stops here. Other camping grounds, such as *Campingplatz Kladow* (☎ 365 27 97) at Krampnitzder Weg 111-117 in Kladow, 18km to the west, and *Campingplatz Am Krossinsee* (☎ 675 86 87), Wernsdorfer Strasse 45 in Köpenick, 35km to the south-east, are much too complicated to reach by public transport.

DJH Hostels

Berlin's three official DJH hostels are all members of Hostelling International and require an HI or DJH membership card; it's usually possible to join the DJH for an annual fee of DM21/34 juniors/seniors when checking in. The hostels fill up fast on weekends and throughout summer; until early July, they are often booked out by noisy school groups. None of them offer cooking facilities, but breakfast is included in the overnight charge, and lunch and dinner are usually available. The hostels stay open all day year round, and all have curfews.

It is a good idea to book DJH hostels several weeks in advance in writing to the Deutsches Jugendherbergswerk (☎ 264 95 20; fax 262 04 37), Tempelhofer Ufer 32, 10963 Berlin. State precisely which nights you'll be in Berlin and enclose an international postal reply coupon so they can send back confirmation. This office in Kreuzberg 61 (U-Bahn No 7 or 15 to Möckernbrücke) sells DJH cards and is open Monday, Wednesday and Friday from 10 am to 4 pm and Tuesday and Thursday from 1 to 6 pm.

The only DJH hostel within walking distance of the city centre is the impersonal 364-bed *Jugendgästehaus Berlin* (Map 3; ☎ 261 10 97), which costs DM31/40 for juniors/seniors. It's at Kluckstrasse 3 in Schöneberg near the Landwehr Canal (U-Bahn No 15 to Kurfürstenstrasse). Curfew is at midnight.

The most pleasant location among the three hostels belongs to the modern 264-bed *Jugendgästehaus am Wannsee* (☎ 803 20 34), Badeweg 1, on the corner of Kronprinzessinnenweg on Grosser Wannsee, a lake south-west of the city. The hostel is at most an eight-minute walk from the Nikolassee S-Bahn station. Walk west from the station over the footbridge, turn left at Kronprinzessinnenweg, and the hostel will be in sight on the right. The cost is DM31/40 for juniors/seniors, and the key deposit is DM20. The curfew is at a raging 1 am.

Jugendherberge Ernst Reuter (☎ 404 16 10), Hermsdorfer Damm 48-50, is in the far north-west of Berlin. Take the U6 to Alt-Tegel, then bus No 125 right to the door. The 110 beds cost DM25/32 for juniors/seniors; there's a midnight curfew.

Independent Hostels

The handiest of the non-DJH hostels, where you usually don't require a hostel card, is *Jugendgästehaus am Zoo* (Map 6; ☎ 312 94 10), Hardenbergstrasse 9a, three blocks from Zoo station in Charlottenburg (U-Bahn No 2 to Ernst-Reuter-Platz), which charges DM47 for singles, DM85 for doubles and DM35 per person in rooms with four beds (breakfast not included). It's limited to people aged under 27, but the location is great if you get in.

The enormous, 450-bed *Jugendgästehaus Central* (Map 6; ☎ 873 01 88), at Nikolsburger Strasse 2-4 in Wilmersdorf, offers bed & breakfast for DM36 per person in double and multi-bed rooms; the DM7 sheet charge applies to the first two nights only. To get to the Central take U-Bahn No 1 to Hohenzollernplatz or U-Bahn No 9 to Güntzelstrasse.

The *Studentenwohnheim Hubertusallee* (☎ 891 97 18) at Delbrückstrasse 24 in Wilmersdorf (bus No 129) offers discounts to students with a recognised card (singles/doubles/triples DM45/70/90 per room), otherwise you pay DM80/110/126 (all prices include breakfast). This establishment operates only from March to October.

The *Studentenhotel Berlin* (Map 3; ☎ 784 67 20), Meininger Strasse 10 (U-Bahn No 4 to Rathaus Schöneberg), offers bed & breakfast for DM41 per person in a double room, DM37 in a quad. It's often full.

In July and August you can sleep in a big tent at the *Internationales Jugendcamp* (☎ 433 86 40) in north-west Berlin. From the U-Bahn station at Alt-Tegel (line No 6) take bus No 222 (direction Lübars) four stops to the corner of Ziekowstrasse and Waidmannsluster Damm.

The tents are behind the *Jugendgästehaus Tegel* (☎ 433 30 46), a huge, red-brick building opposite the bus stop at Ziekowstrasse 161. Beds in large communal tents are about DM10 per person (blankets and foam mattresses provided) and check-in is after 5 pm (no curfew). Officially this place is only for those aged 14 to 27, but they don't turn away foreigners who are a little older. The maximum stay is three nights, and no reservations are taken. Self-catering facilities are available. A bed in the Jugendgästehaus Tegel's four-bed room goes for DM37.50, including breakfast.

The Jugendgästehaus Tegel's sister hostel, the *Jugendgästehaus Nordufer* (☎ 451 99 11 2), at Nordufer 28 in Wedding, has 130 beds in 38 rooms and charges the same rates. Take U-Bahn No 9 to Westhafen and then bus No 126 to Sylter Strasse.

Even More Independent Hostels

In recent years a handful of new – and much more convivial – independent hostels have opened in more central locations in Berlin.

The managers are almost all ex-backpackers who have travelled extensively, know what people want and need, and are extremely friendly and well informed about their city. They never require a hostel card.

Mitte Beg, borrow and/or steal to secure a bed at *Circus – The Hostel* (Map 4; ☎ 283 91 43 3) at Am Zirkus 2-3 in Mitte, a few minutes' walk from the Friedrichstrasse U/S-Bahn station, the Oranienburger Tor U-Bahn station (line No 6) and the Oranienburger Strasse nightlife area. Comfortable, clean rooms with from one to five beds cost DM38 to DM25 per person (plus a one-off DM3 for sheets). The staff are particularly friendly and helpful; we watched the front-desk crew comfort and assist hot, tired and sometimes short-tempered backpackers again and again and would give them a '10' every time. Highly recommended. (In case you're wondering about the neat name, this is where the circus was held in the 19th century.)

The *Backpacker* (Maps 3 & 4; ☎ 262 51 40 or ☎ 283 90 96 5), at Chausseestrasse 102 (U-Bahn No 6 to Zinnowitzer Strasse or S-Bahn to Nordbahnhof), has 60 beds and a charming owner/manager who is as welcoming as a port in a storm. He'll take care of your laundry for DM5, and can arrange bike rental. There's a kitchen and TV room. Prices range from DM25 per person in a room with five or six beds to DM35 per person in a double. Sheets cost DM3 or DM4 extra. Breakfast costs between DM5 and DM10. You can check in as early as 7 am or as late as 11 pm.

Die Loge (Map 4; ☎ 280 75 13), Friedrichstrasse 115 on the corner of Torstrasse, is an 'artist hotel-pension' (how you prove that is a mystery), with hostel accommodation costing DM30 to DM40 depending on the size of the room (DM25 to DM30 if you stay for more than three nights).

If you're desperate, the – well, let's just say 'distressed-looking' – *Künstlerheim Luise* (Map 4; ☎ 280 69 41), just south of the Charité Hospital at Luisenstrasse 19 (S-Bahn: Friedrichstrasse), has seven rooms with beds costing DM30 to DM35 per person. Look upon it as an interesting GDR experience.

Kreuzberg 61 Two moderately priced hotels in Kreuzberg 61 (U-Bahn No 6 or 7 to Mehringdamm) that have dormitory accommodation include the friendly *Pension Kreuzberg* (Map 3; ☎ 251 13 62), Grossbeerenstrasse 64, with beds costing DM42 per person, and *Hotel Transit* (Map 3; ☎ 785 50 51), Hagelberger Strasse 53-54, which has multi-bed rooms with shower for DM33 per person, big breakfast included. The Transit tends to fill up with school groups from March to May and in September/October, but in other months it should have beds available.

Kreuzberg 36 *Die Fabrik* (Map 5; ☎ 611 71 16), in a huge converted machinery and telephone-components factory at Schlesische Strasse 18 (U-Bahn No 15 to Schlesisches Tor), has multi-bed rooms for DM30 per person.

The downstairs café called *Eisenwaren* serves up breakfast (DM7.50 to DM12.50), other cheap meals (soups from DM6, main courses from DM10) and attitude by the metric measure.

Private Rooms & Long-Term Rentals

The tourist office no longer books private rooms, but you can try the private agency ALGV (☎ 399 95 18 3) at Zinzendorfstrasse 8 (U-Bahn No 9 to Turmstrasse), which has double rooms for DM35 and apartments for four/six people for DM140/160. Other private agencies with similarly priced rooms are Agentur Last Minute (☎ 308 20 88 5); Berliner Zimmer (☎ 312 50 03); and Best Bed & Breakfast (☎ 693 84 66).

An excellent way to find inexpensive private rooms is through the various *Mitwohnzentralen*, or accommodation-finding agencies. Most of these have singles from DM35, doubles from DM60 and apartments from DM80 a day, and there is usually no minimum stay. Monthly rates for rooms range from DM350 to DM550 and apartments start at DM500. Depending on the length of stay, it may work out cheaper to pay the monthly rent, even if you don't stay the whole time.

Erste Mitwohnzentrale (☎ 324 30 31), at Sybelstrasse 53 in Charlottenburg (U-Bahn No 7 to Adenauerplatz), is open weekdays from 9 am to 8 pm and Saturday from 10 am to 6 pm. *Mitwohnagentur Kreuzberg* (☎ 786 20 03), on the 3rd floor of Mehringdamm 72 in Kreuzberg 61 (U-Bahn No 7 to Mehringdamm), is open Monday to Friday from 10 am to 7 pm and Saturday from 11 am to 4 pm. Another *Mitwohnzentrale* (☎ 194 30) in Kreuzberg 61 is at Yorckstrasse 52 (U/S-Bahn: Yorckstrasse).

If you're looking for long-term rentals, also check the *Wohnungen* classified section in *Zitty* or *Zweite Hand*. If you're staying for under a month, you may end up sharing a flat with others, a good way to meet people.

Hotels

Charlottenburg & Wilmersdorf There are a few inexpensive places near Zoo station and north of the Ku'damm. The excellent *Pension Knesebeck* (Map 6; ☎ 312 72 55), Knesebeckstrasse 86, just off Savignyplatz, has basic singles/doubles from DM60/120 or DM85/140 with facilities (triples available, breakfast included). Nearby, *Hotel-Pension Cortina* (Map 6; ☎ 313 90 59) at Kantstrasse 140 has plenty of rooms, starting at DM60/100 or DM100/150. To the south-west, *Hotel-Pension Majesty* (Map 6; ☎ 323 20 61), Mommsenstrasse 55, is one of the least expensive at DM60/80 or DM95/150, including breakfast.

Pension Fischer (Map 6; ☎ 218 68 08), on the 2nd floor of Nürnberger Strasse 24a, charges DM50/80 (or DM70/100 with facilities). Breakfast costs DM8 to DM10 extra. *Hotel-Pension Pariser Eck* (Map 6; ☎ 881 21 45), Pariser Strasse 19, has singles/doubles from DM40/80 or DM70/110; three to five-bed rooms are also available.

Mitte *Hotel-Pension Amadeus* (Map 4; ☎ 282 93 52), next to the Bärenschänke pub at Friedrichstrasse 124, is about as cheap as you're going to find in Mitte, with singles/doubles/triples/quads costing DM69/98/120/152.

Die Loge (Map 4; ☎ 280 75 13), Friedrichstrasse 115 on the corner of Torstrasse, has singles/doubles for DM70/120 and a four-person apartment for DM200; the prices go down to DM60/100/160 if you stay for more than three nights. This hotel-pension is run by an affable young couple who serve up some mighty fine – wait for it – candlelit breakfasts for DM10.

Kreuzberg & Schöneberg You'll find lots of low-priced accommodation in the lively quarter of Kreuzberg 61. Try the small but welcoming *Pension Kreuzberg* (Map 3; ☎ 251 13 62), Grossbeerenstrasse 64, which has singles/doubles without bath for DM65/85 (or DM70/95 with facilities).

In Kreuzberg 36, *Die Fabrik* (Map 5; ☎ 611 71 16), more of a hostel than a pension at Schlesische Strasse 18, has singles/doubles/triples/quads for DM66/94/120/144 on five floors (no lift). It's a big cavernous place with too-cool-by-half staff whose English is *nicht so gut*.

The budget option in Schöneberg is the large and dumpy *Hotel Sachsenhof* (Map 3; ☎ 216 20 74) at Motzstrasse 7, which has depressing rooms but a good breakfast buffet (DM10). Rooms start at an affordable DM57/99 (DM95/156 with facilities).

Spandau A budget pension north-west of the centre out in Spandau, and handy to the Altstadt Spandau U-Bahn station (line No 7), is *Hotel Hamburger Hof* (☎ 333 46 02), at Kinkelstrasse 6, where singles are DM50 to DM60 and doubles DM95 to DM110.

PLACES TO STAY – MIDDLE

Mid-priced pensions and hotels garnis – essentially smaller places without restaurants – are plentiful in Berlin, but most are small, plain and uncommercial, so expect no luxury. Rooms in this category cost a minimum of about DM70/100 for singles/doubles with shared facilities. Breakfast and even a shower can cost extra. Many are upstairs from shop fronts or in apartment blocks, and some are hard to find; often you must ring to enter. There are a few big places, but most have 20 beds or less.

Charlottenburg & Wilmersdorf

Pension Peters (Map 6; ☎ 312 22 78; fax 312 35 19), on the 1st floor of Kantstrasse 146, is one of the smallest pensions in the area, but good value with rooms starting at DM80/100 (DM110/130 with shower), including breakfast buffet. *Hotel Crystal* (Map 6; ☎ 312 90 47; fax 312 64 65), across Savignyplatz at Kantstrasse 144, is much larger but reasonably priced from DM70/90 or DM120/150.

Pension Grossmann (Map 6; ☎ 881 64 62; fax 883 74 76), in a wonderful old building with folk reliefs on the façade at Bleibtreustrasse 17, charges DM90/135 (or DM105/150 with facilities), including breakfast.

Nearby, the attractive *City-Pension Alexandra* (Map 6; ☎ 885 77 80; fax 885 77 81 8) at No 32 of quiet Wielandstrasse, has simple singles/doubles for DM95/125 or DM155/185 with full facilities; prices include a generous breakfast buffet. It's just a few steps north of Kurfürstendamm.

Among the best offers around the Ku'damm is *Hotel-Pension Modena* (Map 6; ☎ 885 70 10; fax 881 52 94), Wielandstrasse 26, with singles/doubles starting at DM70/120 and ranging up to DM120/170 with all facilities and breakfast. South of Breitscheidplatz at Nürnberger Strasse 24a (in same building as Pension Fischer) is the *Hotel-Pension Nürnberger Eck* (Map 6; ☎ 218 53 71; fax 214 15 40), with rates at DM80/130 (DM100/160 with shower).

Pension Elton (Map 6; ☎ 883 61 55; fax 883 61 56), at Pariser Strasse 9 in Wilmersdorf, charges from DM100/130.

Farther afield the *Hotel Charlottenburger Hof* (☎ 329 07 0; fax 323 37 23), Stuttgarter Platz 14, just south of the intersection of Kantstrasse and Lewishamstrasse, is large and conveniently located opposite the Charlottenburg S-Bahn station, but it's far from the action and the square is full of used cars for sale and Russian discount shops. Singles/doubles cost DM85/130 or DM90/170, depending on the room type and season.

Mitte

The family-operated *Hotel-Pension Merkur* (Map 4; ☎ 282 95 23; fax 282 77 65), Torstrasse 156, charges from DM75/125 for a single/double to DM110/150 with bath and breakfast. It's a little overpriced for what you get, but it has a few moderate family rooms. The small but excellent *Hotel Novalis* (Map 4; ☎ 282 40 08; fax 283 37 81), at Novalisstrasse 5 just off Torstrasse, is fairly central and ranges from DM125/165 to DM155/190 for a single/double with all facilities.

Kreuzberg & Schöneberg

Hotel Transit (Map 3; ☎ 785 50 51; fax 785 96 19), Hagelberger Strasse 53-54, a hotel usually crowded with backpackers, offers singles/doubles from DM90/105. It's close to a lot of nightlife, and we've heard good things about the Transit, but they were downright unfriendly the last time we visited.

The *Hotel Auberge* (Map 3; ☎ 235 00 20; fax 218 52 30), in an interesting old building at Bayreuther Strasse 10, has large singles/doubles from DM90/140 (DM120/160 with shower).

PLACES TO STAY – TOP END

You can't get more central than the business-style 302-room *Hotel Palace Berlin* (Map 6; ☎ 250 20; fax 262 65 77) at the Europa-Center on Budapester Strasse in Tiergarten, with singles/doubles from DM280/330. The breakfast buffet is a pricey DM29 but very lavish indeed. For another splurge option, consider the *Steigenberger Hotel Berlin* (Map 6; ☎ 212 70; fax 212 71 17) at Los-Angeles-Platz 1 in Charlottenburg. This pleasant 397-room hotel offers all the mod cons and is one minute away from the Ku'damm and the Kaiser Wilhelm Memorial Church. Rates start at DM290/340 (rising to DM455/505); the breakfast buffet is an extra DM29 per person.

In Mitte, the 324-room *Hotel Unter den Linden* (Map 4; ☎ 238 11 0; fax 238 11 10 0), south of Friedrichstrasse station at Unter den Linden 14, is a boxy concrete GDR leftover and God only knows who would want to stay here and why – but the location is pleasant. Singles/doubles go for DM145/185 or DM220/270, depending on the season. Instead check into the classy, 358-room *Grand Hotel Berlin* (Map 4; ☎ 202 70; fax 202 73 41 9), nearby at Friedrichstrasse 158-164, with singles/doubles from DM325/380. If your budget can really s-t-r-e-t-c-h – or the rich uncle or aunt are treating – head for the new *Hotel Adlon Kempinski* (Map 4; ☎ 226 10; fax 226 12 22 2), Unter den Linden 77, which re-opened to great fanfare in mid-1997 after a hiatus of more than a half-century. Among its 337 rooms, singles/doubles start at DM420/490 (not including the DM36 breakfast buffet).

The 502-room *Berlin Hilton* (Map 4; ☎ 202 30; fax 202 34 26 9), at Mohrenstrasse 30, has the usual Hilton-standard singles/doubles from DM345/375. A more moderately priced and smaller (26 rooms) alternative just opposite is the *Hotel Gendarm* (Map 4; ☎ 204 46 26; fax 298 24 82), Charlottenstrasse 60, overlooking the Deutscher Dom on Gendarmenmarkt. It's a bit pricey (from DM140/150 singles/ doubles) for its condition and facilities, but you can't beat the view.

The monstrous *Forum Hotel Berlin* (Map 4; ☎ 2 38 90; fax 238 94 30 5), with over 1000 rooms, dominates Alexanderplatz. Prices start at DM195/285 (breakfast buffet included). Don't stay here if you suffer from vertigo. The attractive and well located *Hotel Albrechtshof* (Map 4; ☎ 308 86 0; fax 308 86 10 0), with 99 rooms at Albrechtstrasse 8, starts at DM195/245 for a single/double with all facilities.

Over in Kreuzberg 61, the intimate 25-room *Hotel Riehmers Hofgarten* (Map 3; ☎ 781 01 1; fax 786 60 59), Yorckstrasse 83, is one up-market (but affordable) hotel that deserves special attention. Singles/doubles cost DM160/200 or DM200/240, including a big breakfast buffet. Bus No 119 from the Ku'damm stops right in front. This elegant, eclectic-style edifice (1892) will delight romantics, and it's a fun area in which to stay – though Yorckstrasse is a pretty busy and noisy street.

PLACES TO EAT

There are restaurants offering every cuisine under the sun in Berlin. In fact, there are so many *Spezialitäten* that you will soon regard German fare as unusual. Surprisingly, along with all the variety, the best food is generally available at (by local standards) reasonable prices. A full lunch or dinner at an unpretentious restaurant can easily cost less than DM20.

If you want a wider selection of restaurants and other eateries than we are able to provide here, consult the Berlin foodie's bible, the 688-page *Berlin von 7 bis 7* (Berlin from 7 to 7) by Monika & Dieter Wien (DM29.80) or the much cooler *Zitty Spezial* annual *Essen, Trinken, Tanzen in Berlin* (Eating, Drinking, Dancing in Berlin), available at newsagents for DM8.50. We've provided telephone numbers for restaurants where you should book ahead.

Berlin specialities to watch out for include *Bouletten* (meatballs), *Eisbein mit Sauerkraut/Erbsenpüree* (pork knuckle with sauerkraut/mushy peas), *Currywurst* (curried sausage), *Schusterjungen* ('cobbler's kids'; bread rolls made with rye flour) and *Soljanka*, a Ukrainian sour bean soup that has arrived via the GDR. Wash it down with any of these three beers: Berliner Kindl, Schultheiss or Berliner Weisse (a light, fizzy lager with fruit juice added).

Restaurants

German & Austrian One of Berlin's better local restaurants, *Posst* (Map 5; ☎ 618 24 50), at Skalitzer Strasse 54 (U-Bahn No 15 to Görlitzer Bahnhof), actually specialises in south German and Swabian cuisine. Starters, including Maultaschen (German ravioli), go for DM6 to DM12; main courses include Sauerbraten (marinated braised beef) for DM19.50 and an intriguing Swabian lentil plate prepared with several cuts of pork for DM20.

Tiergartenquelle (Map 3; ☎ 392 76 15), at Bachstrasse 6 (U-Bahn No 9 to Hansaplatz), comes highly recommended not only for its authentic and excellent German dishes (try the Eisbein) but its colourful clientele as well. Definitely a place with cult status.

Dicke Wirtin (Map 6), Carmerstrasse 9 off Savignyplatz, is an earthy Berliner Kneipe (typical Berlin pub) offering goulash soup (DM5.90) and beer (six on draft from DM4.50).

The *Bärenschänke* (Map 4), Friedrichstrasse 124 (U-Bahn No 6 to Oranienburger Tor), is an unpretentious neighbourhood pub serving local specialities from 10 am (11 am on Sunday) to 11 pm. Typical are the Schlachtersplatte mit Blut- und Leberwurst (a mixed meat 'butcher's plate') and the Wildsuppe (venison soup). There's a long bar where you can chat with Berliners as you swill your beer.

For a step back in time – and to the east – try the *Bräustübl* (Map 4; ☎ 229 9436) at Mohrenstrasse 66 (U-Bahn No 2 to Mohrenstrasse). The menu of typical Berlin dishes (from DM12) goes on forever, and it's open daily to 11.30 pm.

Restaurants serving potato dishes in all their incarnations are popular in Berlin. Two to try are *Kartoffellaube* (Map 4) at Probststrasse 1 in the twee Nikolaiviertel (dishes from DM7.50 to DM15) and *Kartoffelkeller* (Map 4) at Albrechtstrasse 14b in Mitte.

Jolesch (Map 5; ☎ 612 35 81), at Muskauer Strasse 1 in Kreuzberg 36, is an Austrian-style bistro. The menu changes regularly – they were serving masses of Beelitz asparagus main courses (from DM20) when we were last there – but most people come for the excellent goulash (large/small for DM16/8), served with baguette or potatoes, and their famous strudel (DM8). Service is slow, though.

Italian *Pizzeria Amigo* (Map 6), Joachimstaler Strasse 39-40 near Zoo station (open daily from 11 to 1 am), serves a wicked spaghetti or pizza for only DM7.50. It's a self-service place, but the food is good and there's a fine place to sit down. *Piccola Taormina* (Map 6), on Uhlandstrasse 29 in Charlottenburg, is a noisy blue-walled labyrinth of snugs serving fast, good-value pizzas (from the DM2 mini-variety up to a quite filling DM15) and pastas (DM5.50 to DM11); it's possible to escape for DM10 (including coffee). Locals like the style, and the aromas wafting along the street can be irresistible.

The *Gargano* (Map 3), at Goltzstrasse 52 on the corner of Grunewaldstrasse (U-Bahn No 7 to Eisenacher Strasse), is a comfortable Italian eatery – one of our favourites – with lots of specials like homemade vegetarian ravioli with tomato and basil (DM13) and saltimboca romana (DM18). It's open daily for lunch and dinner to 1 am (dinner only on Sunday). An exceptional place for authentic Italian food is *Hostaria del Monte Croce* (☎ 694 39 68), at Mittenwalder Strasse 6 in Kreuzberg 61 (U-Bahn No 7 to Gneisenaustrasse). But order a course or two off the menu and eschew the menù a sorpresa (DM89) of eight monstrous courses and all the wine you can drink; you'll be eating till the new millennium. It's open Tuesday to Saturday for dinner only.

Highly recommended is *Fressco* (Map 4), at Oranienburger Strasse 48-49, a non-smoker Imbiss with huge daily Italian specials for about DM11 and an outrageous fruit cake for DM6 per piece. It's open to 12.30 am (2 am on Saturday and Sunday).

Latin American & Spanish The *Brazil* (Map 4; ☎ 208 63 13), a cavernous, informal place at Gormannstrasse 22 where everybody is dressed in black, has specialities like frango estufado (chicken braised in wine) for DM18 and churrasco (grilled meats and sausages) for DM21.50, and huge nacho platters and salads from DM10.

Las Cucarachas (Map 4) is a so-so Mexican restaurant at Oranienburger Strasse 38 in Mitte; we just hope the cucarachas stay on the signboard and out of the kitchen. The Mexican – or rather, Tex-Mex – is much better at *Lone Star Taqueria* (Map 3) at Bergmannstrasse 11 in Kreuzberg 61.

Lautaro (Map 4), a simple restaurant specialising in South American dishes at Reinhardtstrasse 8, is a short distance from the Oranienburger Tor U-Bahn station. It charges only DM12 for all dishes from Monday to Wednesday.

Don Quijote (Map 6; ☎ 881 32 08), at Bleibtreustrasse 41 in Charlottenburg, serves excellent tapas. It's open for dinner on weekdays and for lunch as well at the weekend. *Guernika* (Map 5), at Görlitzer Strasse 42 (U-Bahn No 15 to Görlitzer Bahnhof), is a Basque restaurant with excellent tapas (from DM5) and some unusual main courses (from DM17.50).

Russian & Eastern European *Pasternak* (☎ 441 33 99), at Knaackstrasse 22-24 in Prenzlauer Berg, revives Russian nostalgia with updated versions of traditional Russian dishes (main courses around DM20); there's live Russian music on Tuesday night and shady characters most nights. For a much more authentic Russian evening, head for the *Café Hegel* (Map 6) at Savignyplatz 2, the preferred watering hole of the more cultured members of Berlin's Russian community.

Café Haus Ungarn (Map 4; ☎ 241 57 15), Karl-Liebknecht-Strasse 9 (S-Bahn: Alexanderplatz) is where to go if you crave Hungarian goulash, microwaved (we're convinced of it) palacsinta and the Soviet bloc aesthetic of the early 1970s. It's open daily to 1 am. *Novo Skopje* (Map 6), a Macedonian restaurant at Kurfürstendamm 38, specialises in meaty things (from DM16.50) like a dozen kebabs cooked on a wood-fired grill or things in a Pfanne (skillet). Vegetarians can order the filling bean soup. There's a lunch menu for DM15.

Indian & Middle Eastern *Kalkutta* (Map 6; ☎ 883 62 93), at Bleibtreustrasse 17 in Charlottenburg and open daily from noon to midnight, serves some of the best Indian food in town (especially the tandoori dishes), with dishes starting from DM12. Cheaper Indian fare is available at a couple of Imbisse on Goltzstrasse in Schöneberg: *Rani* (Map 3) at No 33 and *Maharaja* (Map 3) opposite at No 20, with huge main courses from DM7.50. Avoid the *Lahore* around the corner at Hohenstaufenstrasse 69; it's cheap (dosa masala from DM7, chicken biryani DM10) but nasty.

For authentic couscous (from DM8 for vegetarian) and Egyptian specialities (DM6 to DM15) try *Baraka* (Map 5), a neighbourhoody place at Lausitzer Platz 6 in Kreuzberg 36 (U-Bahn No 15 to Görlitzer Bahnhof). It looks like the Flintstones conspired with King Tut to decorate the place: stalactites, ogee arches and pharaoh's heads abound.

Bagdad (Map 5), at Schlesische Strasse 1, a stone's throw from the Schlesisches Tor station, has Turkish and Iraqi mains (DM16 to DM20) and salads from DM4.

East Asian *Fisch & Vegetables* (Map 3) is a simple Imbiss at Goltzstrasse 32 with cheap and very good Thai dishes. Another immensely popular and always crowded Thai place is the *Kamala* (Map 4; ☎ 283 27 97), downstairs at Oranienburger Strasse 69 in Mitte, with tom yom gung (DM8.50), curries (DM15.50 to DM19.50), noodle dishes (DM12.50 to DM14.50) and the like. It's open daily from 11.30 am to midnight.

Restaurant Indonesia (Map 4), on the site where Hitler's chancellory once stood at Vossstrasse 1, is more Chinese than Indonesian, but you'll still be able to get nasi goreng and a half-dozen satays. Starters/main courses – rather difficult to distinguish here – are from DM9.95/11.95.

The *Sushi-Bar* (Map 4), a Japanese Imbiss at Friedrichstrasse 115, open daily from noon (2 pm at the weekend) to 10 pm, has sushi by the piece for DM4 to DM6 and sushi plates for DM15 to DM20. It's always fresh and excellent. The *Kim Chi* (Map 6; ☎ 881 21 21), at Kurfürstendamm 165, has a Korean buffet Monday to Saturday from noon to 3 pm for only DM10, which makes it a popular lunch place for workers in the nearby office buildings. Main courses grilled à table include kalbi (DM19.50) and bulgogi (from DM20.50), served with all the usual Korean side dishes.

Vegetarian An excellent and very central option for a cheap vegie meal is the *Marché*

(Map 6), a Mövenpick-chain establishment at Kurfürstendamm 14-15, with excellent salads for DM4.10 to DM8.50 and pastas from DM9. Meat main courses are also available for DM4.10 to DM12, and there's a café (coffees from DM2.50), with tables inside and on the pavement terrace.

Vegetarians hankering after an Asian fix should head for *Samadhi* (Map 6) at Goethestrasse 6 in Charlottenburg. It has dishes seldom seen outside Thailand, like bami (soup noodles), with starters/main courses from DM8/16. The daily lunch menu is DM11.50.

Always open and a good café and restaurant for any purpose is the *Café Voltaire*, below the Hotel Charlottenburger Hof at Stuttgarter Platz 14 opposite Charlottenburg S-Bahn station. The speciality is fresh food prepared while you wait, which is not hard to do as this restaurant attracts an interesting crowd from across the spectrum of Berlin cultural life. The vegie menu is quite respectable and tasty. Good breakfasts (DM6 to DM9) are also served.

The most up-market – and expensive – vegetarian restaurant in town is *Abendmahl* (Map 5) at Muskauer Strasse 9 in Kreuzberg 36, with an inventive menu that includes fish dishes. Starters are from DM8, main courses from DM25 in this quite stylish place, all bizarrely watched over by a statue of the Sacred Heart of Jesus. As its name suggests, the Abendmahl serves meals in the evening only.

The *Advena Café* (Map 5), at Wiener Strasse 11 in Kreuzberg 36, has excellent vegetarian specials (DM8.50 to DM10.50), salads (DM6) and soups (DM5.50). It's open daily from 10 am (breakfast buffet served till 4 pm).

For simple vegetarian fare, try the *Einhorn* buffet, on the northern side of Wittenbergplatz in Schöneberg (Map 6), or the one at Mommsenstrasse 2 near Bleibtreustrasse in Charlottenburg (Map 6), with salads from DM2.60 per 100g and main dishes from DM6.

Another good place is *Naturkost Vegetarische Buffet* (Map 3), Mehringdamm 47 in Kreuzberg 61 (U-Bahn No 6 or 7 to Mehringdamm), with takeaway or eat-in choices. It's open weekdays from 9 am to 7 pm, Saturday from 10 am to 4 pm.

Kosher *Beth Café* (Map 4), at Tucholskystrasse 10 in Mitte (take U-Bahn No 6 to Oranienburger Tor), is an inexpensive kosher café-bistro with a pretty inner courtyard and entertainment by the Rosenthal and Ginsburg klezmer duo on the first Sunday of every month. It is open Sunday to Thursday from 11 am to 10 pm, Friday from 10 am to 6 pm. A bit more pricey and up-market is the stylish *Oren* (Map 4; ☎ 282 82 28), at Oranienburger Strasse 28, where the dishes (main courses around DM18) are not just kosher but meatless (they do serve fish).

Other Restaurants The *Noodle Company* (Map 3), at Yorckstrasse 83 in Kreuzberg 61, offers international noodle dishes such as Nudelomelette (DM11.80) and Sesamspätzle (DM13.80) for good value in tasteful surroundings. It's open Monday to Saturday from 5 pm to 1 am, on Sunday from noon.

The *Mississippi* (Map 3), Mehringdamm 45 in Kreuzberg 61 (U-Bahn No 6 or 7 to Mehringdamm), is essentially a pub with an all-you-can-eat spareribs deal for DM17.50 and happy hour from 4 to 7 pm. The *Carib* (Map 3; ☎ 213 53 81), at Motzstrasse 30 in Schöneberg, will transport you – sort of – to the West Indies on a dark and chilly Berlin night.

If it's views you're after, try the *Wintergarten* on the top (7th) floor of the KaDeWe department store (Map 6) at Tauentzienstrasse 21, or the *Turmstuben* (☎ 229 93 13) in the tower of the Französischer Dom (Map 4) on Gendarmenmarkt (open from noon to 1 am).

Cafés

Café Kranzler (Map 6), at Kurfürstendamm 18-19 near Zoo station, is one of Berlin's oldest coffee houses and a traditional Konditorei (cake shop). Popular with grandmas and tourists, it has a nice terrace for people-watching. It's open daily from 8 am to midnight; the breakfast buffet is available till noon. Another fine café on the Ku'damm is *Café Möhring* at No 42.

Berlin's most elegant and stylish café is *Café Einstein* (Map 3), a Viennese-style coffee house on Kurfürstenstrasse 58 in Tiergarten (U-Bahn No 15 to Kurfürstenstrasse). It's open daily from 10 to 2 am. This is a good place to go with friends if you want to natter. There's a full menu, with starters from DM6.50 and main courses for about DM28. Another, less popular branch called *Einstein Unter den Linden* (Map 4) is at Unter den Linden 42.

Café Adler (Map 4), Friedrichstrasse 206, across from where Checkpoint Charlie once stood and facing the famous sign 'You Are Now Leaving the American Sector', remains a popular place for afternoon Kaffee und Kuchen or a drink.

Another great place with very good cakes is *Café Lebensart*, with branches at Joachimstaler Strasse 41 in Charlottenburg and Mehringdamm 40 in Kreuzberg 61 (Map 3). They're open daily to 7 or 7.30 pm.

Breakfast Cafés

Breakfast *(Frühstück)* cafés are a Berlin institution, catering to the city's hungover, idle rich or just late risers. You can get a calorific brunch of yoghurt, eggs, meat, cheese, bread, butter and jam for around DM12; coffee is usually extra. Some of the breakfasts are huge, so consider sharing one between two people. Many restaurants serve these 'breakfasts' until the cows come home (especially at the weekend); they make an excellent lunch.

On Bleibtreustrasse in Charlottenburg (S-Bahn: Savignyplatz), you'll find two such establishments. At No 45 is *Café Bleibtreu* (Map 6), which serves breakfast from 9.30 am to 2 pm (weekend breakfast buffet: DM11) and at No 48 is the old-style *Zillemarkt* (Map 6), where you can indulge until 4 pm (weekend buffet: DM15). Another longtime favourite in Charlottenburg is the *Schwarzes Café* (Map 6) at Kantstrasse 148 east of Savignyplatz. It serves breakfast (from DM8.50) any time and is open around the clock from 11 am Tuesday to 3 am the following Tuesday (in other words, it's closed eight hours a week). This is one place to get off the street if you happen to roll into Berlin in the middle of the night – except the wee hours of Tuesday morning!

Café Sidney (Map 3), with an Aussie theme and owners who can't spell, at Winterfeldtstrasse 40 in Schöneberg (corner of Maassenstrasse), provides front-row seats to watch the trendy crowds, with breakfast served till 5 pm. *Café M* (Map 3), a short distance to the south-west at Goltzstrasse 33, is always full of people wanting breakfast – whether or not they've been to bed. It never seems to close.

Café Kloster (Map 5) is a baroque kitsch café at Skalitzer Strasse 75 in Kreuzberg 36 (U-Bahn 15 to Schlesisches Tor), which serves breakfast until 6 pm. The *Café Morena* (Map 5), a Spanish place nearby at Wiener Strasse 60, has great breakfasts (especially the pancakes with fruit) served daily till 5 pm. Beer – well, it's almost 5 o'clock! – comes in Stiefel, huge boot-shaped glasses, at the Morena.

Student Cafeterias & Canteens

On weekdays, you can enjoy a hot subsidised meal (DM5 to DM10) in a government cafeteria where you clear your own table. The *Kantine* in the Rathaus Charlottenburg, Otto-Suhr-Allee 100 close to Schloss Charlottenburg (U-Bahn No 7 to Richard-Wagner-Platz), is in the basement. What's available is usually written on a blackboard at the far end of the counter.

The *Rathaus Casino* cafeteria (Map 3), on the 10th floor of Rathaus Kreuzberg, Yorckstrasse 4-11 in Kreuzberg 61 (U-Bahn No 6 or 7 to Mehringdamm), is open weekdays from 7.30 am to 3 pm and offers cheap lunch specials, vegetarian dishes and great views. Everyone is welcome.

Almost any *Arbeitsamt* (employment office) will have a cheap Kantine. A good one is in Arbeitsamt IV at Charlottenstrasse 90 (U-Bahn No 6 to Kochstrasse); it's open weekdays from 9 am to 1 pm. Just walk

JONATHAN SMITH

JONATHAN SMITH

DAVID PEEVERS

JONATHAN SMITH

erlin

op left: Schlossbrücke (Castle Bridge)
ottom left: Victory Column

Top right: Sculpture on Schlossbrücke
Bottom right: Kaiser Wilhelm Memorial Church

JONATHAN SMITH

JONATHAN SMITH

DAVID PEEVERS

JONATHAN SMITH

JONATHAN SMITH

DAVID PEEVERS

A	B
C	D
E	F

Berlin

A: Französischer Dom on Gendarmenmarkt
B: Pariser Platz & Brandenburg Gate
C: The Kurfürstendamm at night
D: Old National Gallery
E: Marienkirche & TV Tower
F: New Synagogue

straight in and take the lift on the left up to the 5th floor.

If you have a valid student card there's a Mensa (student cafeteria) at the *Technical University* (Map 6), upstairs at Hardenbergstrasse 34 in Charlottenburg, three blocks from Zoo station (U-Bahn No 2 to Ernst-Reuter-Platz). It's open weekdays from 11.15 am to 2.30 pm and you can fill up a tray for under DM10. The *café* on the ground floor is open from 8 am to 7.45 pm and has main courses for under DM4. Other Mensas open the same hours are at *Humboldt University* (Map 4), Unter den Linden 6 in Mitte (S-Bahn 1 or 2 to Unter den Linden) and at the *Free University* at Kiebitzweg 26 in Zehlendorf (U-Bahn No 1 to Thielplatz).

Snacks & Fast Food

Berlin is paradise for the snacker on the go, with Turkish, Greek, Middle Eastern, Italian, Chinese – you name it – specialities available at Imbiss stands and stalls throughout the city. Good areas to look for this sort of thing are along Budapester Strasse in Tiergarten, the eastern end of Kantstrasse near Zoo station in Charlottenburg, on Schlossplatz in front of the hateful Palace of the Republic in Mitte, and around Schlesisches Tor station in Kreuzberg 36.

One of the most popular places in Berlin for doner kebabs, felafel and shwarma is *Habibi* (Map 3), at Winterfeldtplatz 24 in Schöneberg. It's open till 3 am (5 am at the weekend) and is especially popular with night-time crowds emerging from the surrounding pubs and bars. A smaller place – but just as good – is the *Kuds Imbiss* (Map 5), at Wiener Strasse 69 in Kreuzberg 36, with felafel (DM4) and other Middle Eastern goodies served daily from 10 to 1 or 2 am.

Substantial German snacks are sold at the many Imbiss stands around Wittenbergplatz in Schöneberg. In addition to German standbys like Rostbratwurst (from DM2.20), Currywurst (DM2.40) and pairs of Wiener, most Imbiss stands also have doner kebabs (usually DM4, though a mini-doner here and there costs about DM2.50) and mini-pizzas (often advertised for DM2). Many also offer barbecued half-chickens for DM3 to DM5.

Another place for a quick, cheap meal is the *Nordsee* chain, with an outlet at Karl-Liebknecht-Strasse 6 (corner of Spandauer Strasse) in Mitte. It specialises in fish and seafood (deep-fried fish sandwich DM3.50) that is filling and locally popular.

Self-Catering

To prepare your own food, start your shopping at the discount Aldi or Penny Markt supermarket chains, which have outlets throughout Berlin, or the less common Tip stores. You sometimes have to wait in long checkout queues, and the variety of goods can occasionally be lacking, but you will pay considerably less for basic food items. Handy travelling food such as powdered fruit drinks and soups, dried and fresh fruit, bread, cheese, packaged salads, sandwich meats and chocolate bars are among the worthwhile items. These are also the cheapest places to buy beer and table wines. Other big chains are Spar and Kaiser's.

Aldi is on Joachimstaler Strasse (Map 6), on the 1st floor opposite Zoo station, at Uhlandstrasse 42 (Map 6) and at Leibnizstrasse 72 (Map 6) near Kantstrasse in Charlottenburg. Tip and Penny Markt are side by side near the corner of Hohenstaufenstrasse and Martin-Luther-Strasse. Plus is another discounter – with more outlets and a slightly bigger range of goods – often competing with the others on price. There's a Kaiser's on Wittenbergplatz (Map 6) and at Bleibtreustrasse 19 (Map 6). Spar outlets are everywhere.

For good-quality fruit and vegetables, consider the various street markets (see the Things to Buy section). The 6th floor of the *KaDeWe* department store (Map 6) has pubs, wine bars and wonderful food halls with fresh produce and picnic-style food.

ENTERTAINMENT

Much of Berlin's nightlife is concentrated in five main areas: around Mehringdamm, Gneisenaustrasse and Bermannstrasse in 'clean' Kreuzberg 61; along Oranienstrasse and Wiener Strasse in 'dirty but cooler' Kreuzberg 36; the Oranienburger Strasse-Rosenthaler Platz-Hackescher Markt area (including the Scheunenviertel) in Mitte; south and south-west of Nollendorfplatz between the Ku'damm and Goltzstrasse in Schöneberg; and around Käthe-Kollwitz-Platz in Prenzlauer Berg north-east of Alexanderplatz. A lot of the action takes place in cultural centres which offer a rainbow of entertainment – concerts, discos, readings, theatre, cafés etc – all under one roof. What's on varies, so it is best to ring ahead, check the events listings in the city magazines mentioned below, or drop by and check the programmes usually posted at the door. The price of admission depends on the event.

Listings

An excellent source of both general information and the latest news about Berlin is the bilingual quarterly *Berlin: The Magazine* (DM3.50), published by the BTM and available at newsstands and tourist offices. To find out what's on, check out *Berlin Programm* (DM2.80), *Zitty* (DM3.60) or *Tip* (DM4). All offer comprehensive listings (in German only) of all current events, including concerts, theatre, clubs, gallery exhibits, readings, movies etc.

Tickets

Most of the best theatres are conveniently clustered in Mitte and Charlottenburg, and all performances are listed in the various events magazines. Many theatres are dark on Monday and from mid-July to late August.

Good seats can usually be obtained on the evening of a performance as unclaimed tickets are sold an hour before curtain time. Some theatres (such as the Metropol in Mitte) give students and pensioners a 25% to 50% discount on unsold tickets 30 minutes or one hour before the show. The best way to get in is simply to start making the rounds of the box offices at about 6 pm. If there's a big crowd waiting at one theatre, hurry on to the next. Berlin's not stuffy, so you can attend theatre and cultural events dressed as you please.

There are ticket outlets throughout the city; try Hekticket (☎ 883 60 10), at Kurfürstendamm 14 (Map 6) or Rathausstrasse 1 (Map 4) near Alexanderplatz; the Theaterkasse Centrum (☎ 882 76 11), just off the Ku'damm at Meineckestrasse 25; or the Erlebnis Berlin ticket booth (☎ 265 55 64 0), on the ground floor of the Europa-Center (Map 6; open weekdays from 10 am to 8 pm, Saturday to 4 pm). Another ticket service, convenient to the Jugendgästehaus am Zoo hostel, is Kartenservice (Map 6; ☎ 312 70 41) at Hardenbergstrasse 6. It's open weekdays only from 8 am to 4.30 pm. There are also ticket counters in the KaDeWe (Map 6; ☎ 218 10 28) and Wertheim (Map 6; ☎ 882 53 54) department stores.

Cinemas

Films are quite expensive in Berlin; tickets on Saturday night can cost as much as DM17. Admission is cheaper on Tuesday or Wednesday and before 5 pm, when tickets are DM8 to DM11. The *Filmzentrum Zoo-Palast* (Map 6; ☎ 254 14 77 7), at Hardenbergstrasse 29a near Zoo station, contains nine cinemas (the Berlin Film Festival is held here in February). There are many other movie houses along the Ku'damm, but foreign films are usually dubbed into German. (If the film is being shown in the original language with German subtitles it will say 'O.m.U.' on the advertisement. If it's in English, the ad will read 'engl. OV' or just 'OV'.)

Die Kurbel (Map 6; ☎ 883 53 25), Giesebrechtstrasse 4 in Charlottenburg (U-Bahn No 7 to Adenauerplatz), usually has at least one film in English (seats DM12, DM9 on Tuesday and Wednesday). You can also see movies in the original English at the *Odeon* (Map 3; ☎ 787 04 01 9), Hauptstrasse 116 (U-Bahn No 4 to Innsbrucker Platz or S-Bahn No 1, 45 or 46 to Schöneberg). There are three shows daily. The *Olympia* (Map 6; ☎ 881 19 78), at Kantstrasse 162 near Zoo station in Charlottenburg, also shows films in English.

Discos & Clubs

Berlin has a reputation for unbridled and very late nightlife – nothing happens until 10 pm at the very earliest. As in every major city, the club scene changes quickly, and it's hard to keep up. Before stepping out, call ahead to make sure the club's still there or consult any of the what's-on rags (see Listings). Berliners know their DJs and tend to follow them from club to club. Ask who's hot and who's not these days and check the '*Tanztermine*' schedule in *Zitty*. Cover charges (when they apply) range between DM5 and DM20. There are a lot of illegal 'squat' clubs too – a recent favourite was in the public loos below Rosenthaler Platz – but for details on those you'll have to rely on the kindness, and knowledge, of strangers.

You'll find lots of discos around the Ku'damm, such as the touristy *Big Eden* (Map 6; ☎ 882 61 20) at No 202 (U-Bahn No 15 to Uhlandstrasse). Other than Friday and Saturday nights there's no cover charge between 8 and 9 pm, but they make up for it with the price of the drinks. The 'Big Eden of the East' is the *Franz Club* (☎ 442 82 03), in the south wing of the Kulturbrauerei (see Prenzlauer Berg map) at Schönhauser Allee 36-39 (U-Bahn No 2 to Eberswalder Strasse), with rock, jazz, blues and funk concerts, and house and jungle dance music. Sunday is gay and lesbian night.

Far Out (☎ 320 00 72 3) is beneath the bowling alley around the side of the building at Kurfürstendamm 156 (U-Bahn No 7 to Adenauerplatz); the portrait of disco hero Bhagwan Rajneesh at the entrance points the way. Far Out is open daily except Monday from 10 pm, with theme nights on Tuesday (non-smoking) and Wednesday (Latin or techno).

Several nightclubs have perfected the fine art of the rave, and techno music has become quintessentially Berlin, as evidenced by the Love Parade held every year in July. Among the pioneering clubs has been the giant *E-Werk*, in a former electricity plant at Wilhelmstrasse 43 in Mitte (U-Bahn No 2 to Mohrenstrasse) but now, apparently, on the move. Check with *Zitty* or *Tip* when you're in town.

Tresor (Map 4; ☎ 609 37 02), nearby at Leipziger Strasse 126a, is a techno haven inside the actual money vault of a former department store. It opens at 11 pm but things don't get humming until well past midnight.

One of the best-known clubs in Berlin is *Delicious Doughnuts Research* (Map 4; ☎ 283 30 21), a café-bar-club at Rosenthaler Strasse 9 (U-Bahn No 8 to Weinmeisterstrasse). It's near Humboldt University and therefore popular with students. *SO 36* (Map 5; ☎ 615 26 01), a perennial favourite at Oranienstrasse 190 (U-Bahn No 15 to Görlitzer Bahnhof), has theme nights: from gay and hip hop to house, techno and hardcore.

Tränenpalast (Map 4; ☎ 238 62 11), at Friedrichstrasse station (Reichstagufer 17), is really better known these days for its cabaret, theatre and concerts, but it's still a disco with some great parties. It's called the 'Tears Palace' because this was as far as East Berliners could go on the S-Bahn (the next stop was Lehrter Stadtbahnhof in West Berlin) when saying goodbye to visiting friends and family from the West in the GDR days.

The *Akba Lounge* (☎ 441 14 63), at Sredzkistrasse 64 in Prenzlauer Berg (U-Bahn No 2 to Eberswalder Strasse), is a quiet café downstairs and a club upstairs playing the loudest music in Berlin – from Latino house to acid jazz. *Icon* (no telephone) is a drums and brass club nearby to the north-west at Cantianstrasse 15. *Kalkscheune* (Map 4; ☎ 283 90 06 5) is a great dance club upstairs at Johannisstrasse 2 near the Friedrichstadtpalast. Monday night is gay night.

Cultural Centres

Podewil (Map 4; ☎ 247 49 6), at Klosterstrasse 68-70 in Mitte (U-Bahn No 2 to Klosterstrasse), offers a mixed bag of film, theatre and live music as well as a café, all in a historic building dating from 1704. The popular café is open Monday to Friday from 11 am to 6 pm and for all performances. The beer garden is open in summer to 9.30 pm.

An adventure playground for adults is *Tacheles* (Map 4; ☎ 282 61 85), housed in a dilapidated, graffiti-covered building at Oranienburger Strasse 54-56 (S-Bahn No 1 or 2 to Oranienstrasse or U-Bahn No 6 to Oranienburger Tor). Its post-atomic look – it was a Jewish-owned department store before the war and later left to crumble by the East Berlin authorities – belies its active cultural programme that includes dance, jazz concerts, the *Café Camera*, cabaret, readings, workshops, weird art galleries, a theatre etc; the *Gartenhaus* club and beer garden is great in summer. There's an ongoing debate on whether Tacheles will remain what it is today; watch this space.

Another multi-media culture club, though a bit more tame, is the *UFA-Fabrik* (☎ 755 03 0), housed in the former UFA film studios at Viktoriastrasse 10-18 in Tempelhof (U-Bahn No 6 to Ullsteinstrasse). The hot spot in Prenzlauer Berg is the *Kulturbrauerei* (☎ 441 92 69) on Knaackstrasse 97 (or Schönhauser Allee 36-39), where artists from around the world work in a space of 8000 square metres; it's more 'easterly orientated'. The building was once the largest brewery in Europe and even had its own U-Bahn station.

Opera & Cabaret

The *Deutsche Staatsoper* (Map 4), Unter den Linden 5-7 in Mitte, hosts lavish productions with international talent. The box office (☎ 208 28 61) is open weekdays from 10 am to 6 pm and weekends from 2 to 6 pm; tickets cost between DM6 and DM190. Nearby, at Behrenstrasse 55-57 on the corner of Glinkastrasse (S-Bahn No 1 or 2 to Unter den Linden or U-Bahn No 6 to Französischer Strasse) is the *Komische Oper* (Map 4), with classic opera and operetta. The box office (☎ 202 60 36 0), at Unter den Linden 41, is open Monday to Saturday from 11 am to 7 pm, Sunday from 1 pm until 90 minutes before curtain. Tickets cost DM11.50 to DM103.

In Charlottenburg, at Bismarckstrasse 35, you'll find the *Deutsche Oper* (U-Bahn No 2 to Deutsche Oper), a glass and steel behemoth dating from 1961. Its box office (☎ 341 02 49) is open Monday to Saturday from 11 am to 7 pm, Sunday from 10 am to 2 pm; tickets range from DM15 to DM140.

Worn-out musicals (like My Fair Lady and West Side Story) and operettas are presented at the *Metropol Theater* (Map 4) at Friedrichstrasse 101-102 in Mitte, directly in front of Friedrichstrasse station. It's not as famous as the opera houses, so tickets are easier to obtain. The box office (☎ 202 46 11 7) opens Monday to Saturday from 10 am to 6 pm; tickets are DM7.50 to DM85. (Don't confuse this Metropol with the Metropol disco in Schöneberg; see Gay & Lesbian Berlin).

Seats at Charlottenburg's *Theater des Westens* (Map 6), Kantstrasse 12 near Zoo station, cost DM19 to DM75 most days, DM23 to DM84 on Friday and Saturday. The box office (☎ 882 28 88) across the street is open Tuesday to Saturday from noon to 8 pm, Sunday from 2 to 6 pm. Though this beautiful old theatre (1896) has style and often features excellent musicals, it's hard to see much from the cheapest seats.

Back in Mitte, the *Friedrichstadtpalast* (Map 4), at Friedrichstrasse 107, offers vaudeville musical revues, but it's often sold out and packed with coach tourists. The box office (☎ 232 62 47 4) is open Monday from 1 to 6 pm, Tuesday to Friday from 1 to 7 pm, Saturday and Sunday from 2 to 7 pm; tickets cost from DM19 to DM85 (DM24 to DM95 on Friday and Saturday). Tickets are also hot at the cool *Wintergarten-Das Varieté* (Map 3), Potsdamer Strasse 96, which features a kitsch 1920s-style cabaret-variety show updated for the tacky 1990s from Wednesday to Sunday at 8.30 pm. You can get in for DM48 to DM98. The box office (☎ 230 88 23 0) is open daily from 10 am to 8 pm. The original Wintergarten (1887-1944) was in the Hotel Central on Friedrichstrasse.

Theatre

Berlin counts some 30 theatres so there is something for everybody. The once staid *Deutsches Theater* (Map 4), at Schumannstrasse 13a near Friedrichstrasse station, goes from strength to strength with its fine productions, both classic (from Sophocles to

Ibsen) and modern (Klaus Chatten, Werner Schwab). The box office (☎ 284 41 22 5) is open Monday to Saturday from noon to 6 pm, Sunday from 3 pm.

Even if you speak little or no German, the *Berliner Ensemble* (Map 4), Bertolt Brecht's original theatre at Bertolt-Brecht-Platz 1 also near Friedrichstrasse station, is worth visiting for its architecture and the musical interludes, as well as the classic (some say dated) Brecht plays. The Threepenny Opera, Brecht's first great popular success, premiered here in 1928. The box office (☎ 282 31 60) opens Monday to Saturday from 11 am to 6 pm, Sunday from 3 to 6 pm; tickets cost from DM11 to DM56.

The *Maxim Gorki Theater* (Map 4) at Am Festungsgraben, north of Unter den Linden and the Neue Wache in Mitte, offers an interesting array of productions from works by 20th-century Russian and Eastern European playwrights, as well as the likes of Harold Pinter and Tennessee Williams. The box office (☎ 202 21 11 5) is open Monday to Saturday from 1 to 6.30 pm and Sunday from 3 pm.

For more avant-garde theatre check out what's on at the *Grips Theater* (Map 3), at Altonaer Strasse 22 (U-Bahn No 9 to Hansaplatz), which specialises in contemporary theatre for children and young adults. The box office (☎ 391 40 04) is open weekdays from noon to 6 pm, Saturday and Sunday from 11 am to 5 pm; tickets range in price from DM10 to DM26.

The *Puppentheater Firlefanz* (Map 4; ☎ 283 35 60), Sophienstrasse 10 in Mitte, stages both puppet and marionette shows for adults and children. Tickets cost from DM15/10 for adults/children.

Classical Music

Try to hear at least one concert at the *Berliner Philharmonie*, Matthäikirchstrasse 1 (U-Bahn No 15 to Kurfürstenstrasse, then bus No 148). All seats are excellent, so just take the cheapest (DM24 to DM78). The box office (☎ 261 43 83) opens weekdays from 3.30 to 6 pm, Saturday and Sunday from 11 am to 2 pm. Another treat is a concert at the extravagant *Konzerthaus* (Map 4) on Gendarmenmarkt in Mitte, formerly the Schauspielhaus and home to the renowned Berlin Symphony Orchestra. The box office (☎ 204 43 70), below the main staircase, is open Monday to Saturday from noon to 6 pm, Sunday to 4 pm.

The concert hall at the *Hochschule der Künste* (HDK; College of Arts; Map 6), at Hardenbergstrasse 33, is also busy in season. The box office (☎ 318 52 37 4) is open Tuesday to Friday from 3 to 6.30 pm, Saturday from 11 am to 2 pm.

Organ and other concerts are held in many of the city's churches, museums and other venues, including the *Marienkirche* (Map 4) on Rathausstrasse in Mitte (May to October, Sunday at 4.30 pm); the *Carillon* (Map 3) near the House of World Cultures in Tiergarten (April to September, Sundays and holidays at 2 pm); *St Mattäus Kirche* (Map 3) on Matthäikirchplatz in Tiergarten (Sunday at 8 pm); the *Berliner Dom* (Map 4) on Museumsinsel (Monday to Saturday at 3 pm, Sunday at 2 pm); the *Französischer Dom* (Map 4) on Gendarmenmarkt (first Thursday of the month at 7.30 pm); the *Kaiser Wilhelm Memorial Church* (Map 6) in Charlottenburg (Saturday at 6 pm); and the *Eosander Chapel* (see Charlottenburg map) of Charlottenburg Palace (Saturday at 7 pm, Sunday at 8 pm).

Rock

Many pubs and bars offer live music. A cover charge of up to DM20 may be levied but most places only charge admission on Friday and Saturday nights.

The *Arena* (Map 5; ☎ 533 20 30), in an old bus depot at Eichenstrasse 4 in Treptow (U-Bahn No 15 to Schlesisches Tor or the S-Bahn to Treptower Park), is a big party place with frequent concerts. On Saturday and Sunday from 2 to 10 pm there's all-day reggae music and tropical cocktails there at the *Yaam* (as the complex is known during these reggae sessions).

Berlin's largest outdoor venue for rock and pop concerts, seating 22,000 people, is the *Waldbühne* (Forest Theatre; ☎ 230 88 23 0), on Glockenturmstrasse in Charlottenburg (U-Bahn No 2 to Olympia-Stadion Ost).

Trash (Map 5; ☎ 614 23 28), at Oranienstrasse 40-41, is the 'dinosaur of Kreuzberg 36', with hard-rock still sending boppers into convulsions after all these years and live music two or three times a week.

Salsa (Map 6; ☎ 324 16 42), a 'Musik-Kneipe-Café' at Wielandstrasse 13 in Charlottenburg, features Latin and Caribbean music. It opens at 7 pm and has live music most nights from 10.30 pm, when the cover charge is between DM6 and DM12. The *Plantation Club* (☎ 262 55 76), on Stresemannstrasse in Kreuzberg 61 (S-Bahn No 1 or 2 to Anhalter Bahnhof), offers 70s music and a nice garden in summer.

Tempodrome (Map 3; ☎ 394 40 45), in a big tent in the Tiergarten, has concerts in the warmer months from Wednesday to Saturday. It's a great place, particularly in summer when urban folk music takes over, but be prepared, it's scheduled to move to Anhalter Bahnhof.

A nice comfortable place with soul music some nights is *90° Grad* (Map 3; ☎ 262 89 84), at Dennewitzstrasse 37 in Tiergarten (U-Bahn No 15 to Kurfürstenstrasse). Thursday is gay night.

Duncker (☎ 445 95 09), at Dunckerstrasse 64 in Prenzlauer Berg (S-Bahn No 8 or 10 to Prenzlauer Allee or U-Bahn No 2 to Eberswalder Strasse), plays old stuff – mostly rock. Spend a couple of hours here and move on to something more lively.

Jazz

The *A-Trane* (Map 6; ☎ 313 25 50), at Bleibtreustrasse 1 in Charlottenburg, is still *the* place in Berlin for jazz.

The *Sophienklub* (Map 4; ☎ 282 45 52), Sophienstrasse 6 off Rosenthaler Strasse (U-Bahn No 8 to Weinmeisterstrasse), has jazz nightly from 9 pm, with a special programme on Tuesday and Saturday nights. *Quasimodo* (Map 6; ☎ 312 80 86), Kantstrasse 12a near the Theater des Westens and in front of the Delphi Cinema (open from 9 pm, music from 10 pm), is a jazz café with live jazz, blues or rock every night. There are cover charges for 'name' acts. *Flöz* (☎ 861 10 00), at Nassauische Strasse 37 in Wilmersdorf (U-Bahn 7 or 9 to Berliner Strasse), has jazz that attracts an older crowd.

The *MS Sanssouci* (Map 5; ☎ 611 12 55), a café-bar and restaurant on a boat moored in the Spree just north of Oberbaum Brücke in Kreuzberg 36 (U-Bahn No 15 to Schlesisches Tor), has live jazz on Wednesday from 9 pm. It's a great place for a sundowner in the warmer months (it opens Wednesday to Sunday from 6 pm). It's also a good spot for viewing the East Side Gallery, the longest remaining section of the Wall in Berlin (see boxed text entitled The Berlin Wall), which is just across the Spree in Friedrichshain.

Folk Music

If you feel like spending the day back in Limerick or Birmingham, hang out with the Oirish lads working on the Potsdamer Platz and other construction sites around the city at the *Oscar Wilde* Irish pub (Map 4; ☎ 282 81 66), at Friedrichstrasse 112a. There's music at 10.30 pm from Thursday to Saturday but watch out, things can get pretty rough (say nice things about Gerry Adams). There's another, more subdued Irish pub called the *Kilkenny* (Map 4; ☎ 283 20 84), below the Hackescher Markt S-Bahn station. Both places are open to 2 or 3 am.

Pubs & Bars

If it's chi chi you're after, you'll find a couple of cocktail bars in Schöneberg that tend to be packed with primpers and preeners nightly. *Mister Hu* (Map 3), on Goltzstrasse 39 (U-Bahn No 7 to Eisenacher Strasse), is one such place. The *Zoulou Bar* (Map 3), at Hauptstrasse 4 (U-Bahn No 7 to Kleistpark), is another trendy establishment. There are lots of interesting pubs and cafés nearby on Crellestrasse, include *Café Mirell* (Map 3) at No 46.

A counterculture pub-café and home to the anarchistic Autonom crowd is *Café Anfall*, at Gneisenaustrasse 64 in Kreuzberg 61 (U-Bahn No 7 to Südstern). Anfall opens at 6 pm (9 pm on Monday) and has wild décor that changes every month or so and good, but loud, music. Another place, filled with punks and Autonomen in all their finery, is the *Weisse Taube* (Map 5) at Wiener Strasse 15. It's a great place to hang out on a Sunday afternoon while your wash tumbles away at the Schnell und Sauber laundrette next door.

There's a branch of the *Planet Hollywood* bar-restaurant chain (Map 4; ☎ 209 45 80 0), at Friedrichstrasse 68 (enter from Mohrenstrasse), complete with handprints of Sylvester Stallone, Kurt Russell and Kim Basinger.

The *Kreuzkeller Sports Bar* (Map 3), at Grossbeerenstrasse 32 in Kreuzberg 61 (U-Bahn No 6 or 7 to Mehringdamm), is the place to go if you want to do 'manly' – *Zitty*'s word, not ours – things like watch football on big-screen TVs and eat all the barbecued spareribs you can hold (Sundays only; DM14.50 with two litres of Warsteiner). *Jawohl*!

Zynkali (Map 3), nearby at Grossbeerenstrasse 64, has an unusual glass bar with odd trinkets and curios on display; a spliff before you visit will have you gazing at it for hours. There are also old-fashioned GDR-era vending machines with flowers and assorted junk for sale. *Boudoir* (Map 4), Brunnenstrasse 192 in Mitte (U-Bahn No 8 to Rosenthaler Platz), is tough to find but well worth the effort. It's an intimate bar in a flat and always fun.

Popular café-pubs with outdoor tables in warm weather are clustered around Käthe-Kollwitz-Platz in Prenzlauer Berg (U-Bahn No 2 to Senefelderplatz). They include *Weitzmann*, at Husemannstrasse 2 and, opposite at No 1, the historic *Restauration 1900*, which is also a fine German restaurant.

Berliner Kneipen Typical Berlin pubs have their own tradition of hospitality – good food (sometimes small courses or daily soups only), beer, humour and *Schlagfertigkeit* ('quick-wittedness'). You can find this atmosphere in a few unassuming, backstreet places, where a handful of fine establishments maintain a living, evolving tradition (eg the tendency to add modern music).

Stories abound about the historic *Zur letzten Instanz* ('The Final Authority'; Map 4), at Waisenstrasse 14 in Mitte (U-Bahn No 2 to Klosterstrasse). The pub, which claims traditions dating back to the 1600s, is next to a chunk of medieval town wall. The place got its present name 150 years ago, we are told, when a newly divorced couple came in from the nearby courthouse. By the time they were well oiled and ready to leave, they'd decided to remarry – at which one of those present exclaimed, 'This is the court of final authority!' It's open Monday to Saturday from noon to 1 am, to 11 pm on Sunday.

E&M Leydicke (Map 3), just off Goebenstrasse at Mansteinstrasse 4 in Schöneberg (U-Bahn No 1, 2 or 7 to Yorckstrasse), is one of Berlin's oldest surviving pubs (founded in 1877) and bottles its own flavoured schnapps on the premises. It is open for lunch daily except Sunday and then from about 4 pm to midnight, but it's primarily a drinking place and Brennerei (distillery).

The *Zum Nussbaum* (Map 4), associated in the past with artist Heinrich Zille and humorist Otto Nagel, has been re-established as part of the Nikolaiviertel; it's beside the Nikolaikirche on the corner of Propststrasse near Mühlendamm. You can enjoy the good, reasonably priced fare while examining some of Zille's sketches on the walls.

Not all Kneipen are as congenial as these three, though; some are as hospitable as a snake pit. For a true Berliner Kneipe experience, try the *Alte Berliner Kneipe* (Map 5), at Schlesische Strasse 6 in Kreuzberg 36. Another pretty authentic Kneipe nearby is the *Oberbaum-Eck* (Map 5), on the corner of Oberbaumstrasse and Bevern Strasse (U-Bahn No 15 to Schlesisches Tor), with good drinks, hearty dishes like smoked fish platters (DM13.50) and a large selection of steaks (from DM21.50). The restored bridge nearby crossing the Spree to Friedrichshain – the Oberbaumbrücke – was used during the Cold War for spy exchanges.

On Oranienstrasse, still in Kreuzberg 36 (U-Bahn No 15 to Görlitzer Bahnhof), try the *Schnabelbar* (Map 5) at No 31 which has great music and atmosphere and a dance floor in back; the *Flammende Herzen* (Flaming Hearts; Map 5) at No 170; and the stylish *Café Kafka* (Map 5), on the corner of Oranienstrasse and Skalitzer Strasse. A Kneipe with a difference is *Franken* (Map 5), opposite the *SO 36* at Oranienstrasse 190; it attracts Hell's Angels bikers (the nice ones, we've been assured). The *Mini Café* (Map 5), nearby at Spreewaldplatz 14 just off Wiener Strasse, is a friendly little place with intimate rooms where pleasures often go up in smoke. It's open daily to 6 am.

There are loads of comfortable bars and pubs along Oranienburger Strasse in Mitte, including the *Café Orange* (Map 4) near the New Synagogue at No 32, with a pleasant atmosphere and great salads, and *Obst und Gemüse* – that's Fruit & Veg (Map 4) – opposite Tacheles at No 48-49.

A great place in summer is the open-air *Golgatha* (Map 3), in Viktoriapark at Dudenstrasse 48-64 in Kreuzberg 61 (U-Bahn No 6 or 7 to Mehringdamm or U-Bahn No 6 to Platz der Luftbrücke). You can dance in your Birkenstocks here, ya rascal.

Gay Berlin

If you're reading this, you probably don't need to be told that Berlin is about the gayest city in Europe. As Christopher Isherwood wrote in his autobiography *Christopher and His Kind* (covering the period from 1929 to 1939): 'For Isherwood Berlin meant Boys'. For some of us, it still does – but nowadays it's spelled 'boyz'. It's estimated that up to 500,000 gays and lesbians call Berlin their home; the numbers were augmented mostly by Ossies before the Wende, since East Berlin was the only place in the GDR where one could have any semblance of a lifestyle.

Anything goes in the gay Berlin of the 1990s – and we mean *anything* – so please take the usual precautions. Discos and clubs are everywhere but don't really get going till about midnight. Before clubbing you can eat at a gay-owned and/or operated restaurant and nurse a drink at one of the dozens of gay cafés and bars. For listings check the gay and lesbian freebie *Siegessäule* or the strictly gay *Sergej Szene Berlin*. *Zitty* and *O30* also have listings. If you require even more information and listings than we or they are able to provide, get a copy of the bilingual *Berlin von Hinten* (Berlin from Behind; Bruno Gmünder Versand; DM19.80). You can also seek advice and/or information from the Mann-O-Meter service (☎ 216 80 08) at Motzstrasse 5 in Schöneberg (U-Bahn No 2, 4 or 15 to Nollendorfplatz).

There are three main gay areas in Berlin: around Nollendorfplatz in Schöneberg; Oranienstrasse in Kreuzberg 36 (U-Bahn No 15 to Görlitzer Bahnhof); and Prenzlauer Berg, particularly around Gleimstrasse (U-Bahn No 2 to Schönhauser Allee).

Around Nollendorfplatz Isherwood lived right in the thick of things at Nollendorfstrasse 17, so who are we to question tradition? *Hafen* (Map 3; ☎ 214 11 18), at Motzstrasse 19, is full of guppies fortifying themselves before they move on to (some say sneak into) *Tom's Bar* (Map 3; ☎ 213 45 70), next door on the corner of Eisenacher Strasse, with its cavernous and very dark and active cellar. Hafen opens at 8 pm, Tom's at 10 pm (but if you're OFB – out for business – don't get to the latter before midnight). *Connection* (Map 3; ☎ 218 14 32), north of Motzstrasse at Fuggerstrasse 33, is arguably the best gay disco in town (DM10, first drink free) and has a huge darkroom (a Berlin feature, according to the author Alfred Döblin, that goes back to some of the sleazier – and straight – Konditoreien (patisseries) of the 19th century). *Andreas Kneipe* (Map 3), at Ansbacher Strasse 29, is where everyone starts the evening; it's a convivial pub with lots of locals and lots of cruising. The *Metropol* disco (Map 3; ☎ 217 36 80), at Nollendorfplatz 5, has a gay tea dance on Sunday afternoon.

Kreuzberg 36 Interesting places here include the *O-Bar* (Map 5), with a good mixed crowd, at Oranienstrasse 168; *Roses* (Map 5), at No 187, with over-the-top baroque, queeny décor; and *Bierhimmel* (Map 5), a rather subdued and friendly bar at No 181-183. *Café Anal* (Map 5), a gay and lesbian Berlin fixture at Muskauer Strasse 15, is an artsy-fartsy café and very low-key.

Gay bars include the *KitKat Club* (Map 5; ☎ 611 38 33) at Glogauer Strasse 2 where, *030* tells us, there's not blood but S-E-X on the dance floor. The *Tunnel Bar* (Map 5), at Schlesische Strasse 32, is a friendly local, and the *MS Sanssouci* boat (Map 5; see Pubs & Bars) hosts a gay tea dance on Sunday at 8 pm.

Prenzlauer Berg The *Schall und Rauch*, at Gleimstrasse 23, has designer prices and attracts a 'young and beautiful' crowd. We came and we went. It's open daily to 3 am. *Café Amsterdam*, at No 24 of the same street, is much more down-to-earth – we stayed – and is open to 6 am at the weekend. The ever-changing DJs here play great music. *Pick Ab* (☎ 445 85 23), nearby at Greifenhagener Strasse 16, is a friendly neighbour pub with a darkroom. Age-wise, it's a mixed bag.

Other Areas Across the Spree in Friedrichshain, at Mühlenstrasse 11-12 (U-Bahn No 15 or S-Bahn to Warschauer Strasse), is *Die Busche* (☎ 589 15 85), the biggest gay place in east Berlin and a meat market popular, they say, with hairdressers. *Eimer* (☎ 282 20 74), at Rosenthaler Strasse 68 in Mitte, is a big club on two floors. It has truly bizarre music and different happenings and parties throughout the week.

Saunas Berlin counts about a half-dozen gay saunas but the biggest, cleanest and most active are *Gate Sauna* (☎ 229 94 30), south-east of the Brandenburg Gate at Wilhelmstrasse 81 in Mitte (open from 11 am to 7 am and nonstop over the weekend); and the *Treibhaus Sauna* (☎ 448 45 03), at Schönhauser Allee 132 in Prenzlauer Berg (open from 3 pm to 7 am, weekend nonstop).

Lesbian Berlin

The *Lesbenberatung* (Lesbian Advice Bureau; ☎ 215 20 00) is at Kulmer Strasse 20a in Schöneberg. Women's centres include the *EWA* (☎ 442 55 42), Prenzlauer Allee 6 in Prenzlauer Berg, and *Frieda* (☎ 442 42 76), at Proskauer Strasse 7 in Friedrichshain.

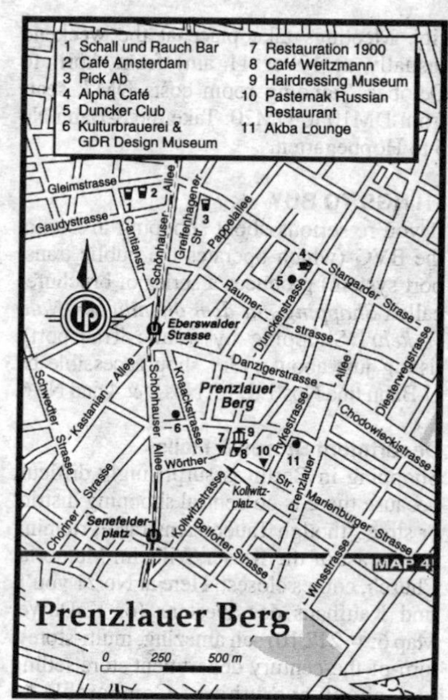

A good lesbian café is the smoke and alcohol-free *Café Seidenfaden* (☎ 283 27 83), at Dircksenstrasse 47 in Mitte, which is open Tuesday to Sunday from 11 am to 10.30 pm. The oldest lesbian bar-club (1973) in the city is *Pour Elle* (Map 3; ☎ 218 75 33), at Kalckreuthstrasse 10 in Schöneberg, open daily from 9 to 5 am. The *Sonntags Club* (☎ 449 75 90), at Rhinower Strasse 8 in Prenzlauer Berg, also has lesbians-only nights.

SPECTATOR SPORT

For a city of its size and prominence, Berlin's sporting calendar is pretty thin. There's the Berlin Marathon every September and the German Open women's tennis tournament in May (which Steffi Graf has won umpteen times). Berlin's soccer team, BSC Hertha, plays in the second division.

Berlin's racecourse, the Galopprennbahn Hoppegarten (☎ 03342-389 30), is in Dawlwitz-Hoppegarten north-east of the city. Meetings take place at the weekend (usually at 10 or 11 am) from April to October. Standing room costs DM7, seats from DM10 to DM20. Take the S-Bahn No 5 to Hoppegarten.

THINGS TO BUY

If you're serious about shopping in Berlin, the BVG (which operates the public transport system) produces a series of brochures called *Shopping mit dem öffentlichen Nahverkehr* (Shopping by Public Transport), listing just about every shop accessible by U-Bahn line Nos 1 & 15, Nos 2 & 4 and No 6.

Department Stores & Malls

Shopping in Berlin is surprisingly difficult because there is no central shopping district or street, though Tauentzienstrasse, running south-east of the Kaiser Wilhelm Memorial Church, comes closest. Here at No 21 you'll find Kaufhaus des Westens (or KaDeWe; Map 6; ☎ 212 10), an amazing, multi-storey, turn-of-the-century department store selling just about everything. Comparable to Harrods in London or Paris' La Samaritaine, it is open weekdays from 9 am to 6.30 pm and on Saturday to 2 pm. Reach it via U-Bahn No 2 or 15 to Wittenbergplatz.

Berlin's second-largest department store, Wertheim (Map 6; ☎ 882 06 1), at Kurfürstendamm 231, is less pretentious and expensive than KaDeWe. The French chain Galeries Lafayette (Map 4; ☎ 209 48 0) has opened an outlet on Friedrichstrasse (U-Bahn No 6 to Französische Strasse), which has an interesting interior. The Europa-Center (Map 6), opposite the memorial church on Breitscheidplatz, stays open late and has a large supermarket, newsstands, boutiques and restaurants.

Cars & Bicycles

Second-hand cars are lined up on Stuttgarter Platz in Charlottenburg (just west of the S-Bahn station) most days of the week. Prices start at about DM1500, but most of the respectable-looking Golfs and Corsas are in the DM3000-DM5000 range. Varied information appears on the windscreens and, although some offer service histories, it seems very much a case of *caveat emptor*. Perhaps it is better to ring around using *Zweite Hand* if you want a wide choice or a particular car or features.

You can buy solid second-hand bicycles (from about DM120) through the listings in *Zweite Hand*, although used touring models start at about DM250. Mehring Hof Fahrrad Laden (☎ 691 60 27), at Gneisenaustrasse 2a in Kreuzberg 61, is a handy showroom for good second-hand makes; solid, three-gear models cost from about DM300.

Outdoor & Camping Goods

For outdoor gear and camping equipment, have a look at the range at Der Aussteiger (☎ 441 04 14), Schliemannstrasse 46 in Prenzlauer Berg, and compare it with Bannat (☎ 882 76 01) at Lietzenburger 65 (corner of Fasanenstrasse), south of the Ku'damm in Wilmersdorf. Sack + Pack (Map 6; ☎ 312 13 15), at Kantstrasse 48 in Charlottenburg, has backpacks and bags galore, including Hedgrens, Jack Wolfskins and Tatonkas. Step by Step (☎ 784 84 60), at Kaiser-Wilhelm-Platz 4 in Schöneberg, has an excellent selection of hiking boots and other outdoor equipment.

Other Stores

Meissener Porzellan (Map 4), Unter den Linden 39, sells the famous Meissen porcelain. It's lovely to look at but, with prices starting at DM100 for an unpainted piece (an ashtray measuring 7cm by 10cm will set you back DM275), it's an expensive purchase. For something different, check out the Bürgel Keramik outlet (Map 4) at Friedrichstrasse 166 and its striking navy blue porcelain. It's open Monday to Saturday from 9 am to 8 pm.

Shops selling discount cameras can be found along Augsburger Strasse south-east of the Ku'damm. For funky, second-hand attire, try Made in Berlin (Map 3) at Potsdamer Strasse 106 in Schöneberg.

Markets

Berlin has over 100 weekly markets and

some 15 flea markets with a hotchpotch of produce, clothing, toiletries, books and other wares. The one at Rathaus Schöneberg (Map 3), where John F Kennedy once said, 'Ich bin ein Berliner' (see boxed text), is hard to beat for its range and quality (Tuesday and Friday to 1 pm).

A visit to the market on Winterfeldtplatz (Map 3) in Schöneberg (Wednesday and Saturday to 2 pm) should be rounded out with crowd-watching during a lavish breakfast in one of the surrounding cafés.

There's an outdoor flea market *(Flohmarkt*; Map 3) every Saturday and Sunday from 8 am to 3 pm on Strasse des 17 Juni at the Tiergarten S-Bahn station. Don't buy any GDR *Trödel* (junk) here, as you can get it much cheaper from the stands around Brandenburg Gate (Map 4) or from the market at Am Kupfergraben near the Pergamon Museum (Map 4; Saturday and Sunday from 11 am to 5 pm).

The Graf Hacke antique market, at the Spandauer Brücke on the corner of Dircksenstrasse (S-Bahn: Hackescher Markt), takes place daily from 11 am to 6 pm. The Berlin Antique and Flea Market, under the arches of the Friedrichstrasse U/S-Bahn station, is held at the same time daily except Tuesday.

GETTING THERE & AWAY

Air

Most Eastern European and Third World carriers use Berlin-Schönefeld airport (SXF; ☎ 609 10), next to Flughafen Berlin-Schönefeld S-Bahn station, just outside the south-eastern city limits some 22km from the centre.

Berlin-Tegel (TXL; ☎ 410 11), Berlin's main commercial airport, 8km north-west of Zoo station, receives most flights from Western Europe. There's a baggage-storage office (open from 5.30 am to 10 pm), a BTM tourist information counter, a post office and a bank in the main hall of the airport.

Berlin-Tempelhof airport (THF; ☎ 695 10), south of the centre, receives mostly domestic flights.

The Lufthansa City Centre (☎ 887 53 80 0) is at Kurfürstendamm 220 in Charlottenburg. Contact numbers for other airlines serving Berlin airports include:

Aeroflot
  ☎ 226 98 10
Alitalia
  ☎ 210 18 1 or ☎ 410 12 65 0
British Airways/Deutsche BA
  ☎ 01803-340 34 0 or ☎ 01803-333 44 4
Delta Airlines
  ☎ 410 13 44 1
El Al
  ☎ 201 37 45
Air France
  ☎ 01805-360 37 0 or ☎ 410 12 71 5
KLM
  ☎ 01805-214 20 1 or ☎ 410 13 84 4
LOT Polish Airlines
  ☎ 678 82 50 or ☎ 41013 67 0
Malév Hungarian Airlines
  ☎ 264 95 45 or ☎ 410 12 84 2

Bus

The Zentraler Omnibus Busbahnhof (ZOB; Central Bus Station), at Masurenallee 4-6 in Charlottenburg opposite the spindly Funkturm radio tower (U-Bahn No 2 to Kaiserdamm or S-Bahn No 45 to Witzleben), is open from 5.30 am to 10 pm. The Reisebüro ZOB (☎ 301 80 28 for information, ☎ 302 52 94 for reservations) is open weekdays from 6.30 am to 6 pm, Saturday to noon, Sunday to 10 am (though tickets are available from many travel agencies in Berlin). The left-luggage office at the station is open daily from 5.30 am to 9.30 pm.

Many bus lines operate out of the ZOB, with services both within Germany and abroad. The three main ones are BerLinien Bus, Gulliver's and Eurolines.

BerLinien Bus (☎ 860 96 0 or toll-free ☎ 0130-831 14 4) runs daily buses between Berlin and Munich (9½ hours) via Leipzig, Bayreuth, Nuremberg and Ingolstadt; single/return SuperSpar tickets, for passengers under 26 or over 60, cost DM75/139, full-fare tickets are DM129/149.

Other BerLinien Bus destinations and their frequencies, durations and SuperSpar and full fares include :

Destination	Frequency	Duration (hrs)	Fare (DM)
Amsterdam	daily	9	77/147 97/177
Bad Harzburg	thrice weekly	4¼	35/67 61/67
Bremen	daily	6½	55/98 84/98
Budapest	four weekly	14¾	113/180 130/210
Copenhagen	daily	7¾	65/100 70/115
Frankfurt/Main via Magdeburg & Göttingen	daily	9¼	76/143 110/143
Hamburg	six times daily	3¼	40/55 40/65
Hanover	twice daily	4½	33/65 58/65
Košice	weekly	19	99/180 110/200
London	daily	20½	159/279 179/299
Oslo via Gothenburg	twice weekly	15	155/255 (full fare price only)
Paris via Brussels	daily	13½	132/227 152/267
Prague	twice weekly	6	54/90 60/100
Rügen Island (including Sellin Baabe and Göhren)	weekly	4½	31/61 55/99
Sofia	weekly	35½	108/207 120/230
Tallinn via Riga	daily	3	126/234 140/260
Vienna	four weekly	10¾	79/149 99/179
Warsaw	thrice weekly	11½	63/108 70/120

Gulliver's (☎ 781 02 1), which has SleeperSeats (practically full beds) on some of its routes for DM10 to DM40 extra, offers students as well as the under 26s and over 60s discount fares and will transport a bike for DM50/80 return. Destinations include :

Destination	Frequency	Duration (hrs)	Fare (DM)
Amsterdam	four weekly	9	79/149 99/179
Barcelona	daily in summer	35½	199/329 239/389
Bratislava via Vienna	four weekly	13½	89/159 109/189
Budapest	four weekly	15	109/179 119/199
Freiburg im Breisgau via Strasbourg	twice weekly	12½	89/159 109/199
London	thrice weekly	21	139/259 169/299
Malaga via Brussels, Valencia and Granda	weekly	56	279/459 319/539
Moscow	twice weekly	34	149/269 159/299
Paris	daily	13	109/199 139/249
Vienna	four weekly	11	79/149 99/179

Eurolines (☎ 301 80 28 or ☎ 069-790 32 88 in Frankfurt), the umbrella organisation of numerous European bus companies, has service to most of the international destinations above as well as to Athens (weekly, 61 hours, DM282/517), Bucharest (twice weekly, 42 hours, DM220/390), Sarajevo (twice weekly, 27½ hours, DM223/357) and Zagreb (daily, 17 hours, DM176/281). If you're under 26 or a student, you get a 10% discount on Eurolines. There's also a Eurolines Pass for frequent travellers. For more information see the Getting There & Away chapter.

Other bus companies serving Berlin include Sperling (☎ 331 03 1), with buses to Bremen, Goslar, Hamburg, Kiel, Lübeck and other cities in northern Germany; BVB (☎ 683 89 10), with service to Bavarian towns as far as Freyung via Leipzig; ČSAD (☎ 238 48 08), with buses to towns in the northern Czech Republic including Liberec via Dresden; and DSB busser (☎ +45-32-53 66 31 in Copenhagen), with daily departures to about 10 cities and towns in Denmark, including Copenhagen and Århus.

Train

Berlin's main train station will be Lehrter Stadtbahnhof (Map 3) when it is completed in 2002; you can see how it will look and feel via a virtual-reality video in Infobox (see Potsdamer Platz Area). The station will be the centre of the Stadtbahn, a 12km, four-track railway line forming part of the Paris-Berlin-Warsaw-Moscow express line.

Until then train services to/from Berlin will remain confusing because the extensive construction around town affects several stations. Trains scheduled to leave from or arrive at one station may be spontaneously re-routed to another, so it's best to check in advance; call ☎ 194 19 for information about trains to/from any of the stations.

You may also find that services arriving at one station link with services leaving from another. To connect, take the U-Bahn or S-Bahn (DM2.50 or DM3.90, depending on the distance), but allow ample time for this transfer.

Conventional train tickets to and from Berlin are valid for all train stations on the city S-Bahn, which means that on arrival you may use the S-Bahn network (but not the U-Bahn) to connect or to proceed to your destination. Conversely, you can use the S-Bahn to go to the station from where your train leaves for another city, if you have a booked ticket. Rail passes are also valid on the S-Bahn.

Bahnhof Zoologischer Garten (or more commonly Bahnhof Zoo; Maps 3 & 6) on Hardenbergplatz, which has been completely renovated but continues to attract drunks, druggies and down-and-outers, is the main station for long-distance trains to cities in the west, including Hanover, Frankfurt and Cologne, as well as Paris, Amsterdam and Brussels. There's also frequent service to Hamburg and Munich and a direct train to Leipzig. Coin lockers cost DM2 or DM3 depending on the size, and the left-luggage office (open 5 am to 11 pm) charges DM4 per item per day. There's a large Deutsche Bahn Reisezentrum (reservation and information office) with quick service, open 5.15 am to 11 pm, and outside the main entrance on Hardenbergplatz is the BVG local transport information kiosk (Map 6), where you can get information and tickets. Downstairs near the lockers is a spick-and-span establishment called McClean where a shower costs DM10. DB also maintains an information and reservations kiosk on Alexanderplatz, open weekdays from 7 am to 7.30 pm and Saturday and Sunday from 8.30 am to 5.30 pm.

The Hauptbahnhof in Friedrichshain, which is undergoing extensive renovation, handles only a few trains now: those going east and south-east to Frankfurt/Oder and Warsaw as well as a daily train to Malmö in Sweden.

Bahnhof Lichtenberg, on Weitlingstrasse in Lichtenberg, handles trains to Stralsund, Rostock and other cities in Mecklenburg-Pomerania, as well as services to Cottbus, Dresden, Erfurt, Halle, Magdeburg, Vienna, Moscow, Prague and Budapest. The reservation office is open on weekdays from 6 am to 8 pm, on weekends from 8 am to 6 pm. The left-luggage room is always open (DM2 per piece per day), and there are coin lockers.

Car & Motorcycle

The A10 ring road around the city links Berlin with other German and foreign cities in every direction, including the A11 to Szczecin (Stettin) in Poland; the A12 to Frankfurt/Oder; the A13 to Dresden; the A9 to Leipzig, Nuremberg and Munich; the A2/A7 to Hanover; and the A24/A1 to Hamburg.

Hitching & Ride Services

You can hitch to Dresden, Hanover, Leipzig, Munich, Nuremberg and beyond from the Dreilinden service area on the A115. Take S-Bahn No 1, 3 or 7 to Wannsee, then walk east less than 1km up Potsdamer Chaussee and follow the signs to Raststätte Dreilinden. There's always a bunch of hitchhikers here, but everyone gets a ride eventually. Bring a sign showing your destination in German, and consider waiting until you find a car going right where you want to go.

There are several *Mitfahrzentrale* agencies, which charge a fixed amount payable to the driver plus commission ranging from DM7 for short distances to DM20 for trips abroad. Generally, a ride to Leipzig costs DM19, Frankfurt/Main is DM49, Munich DM53, Cologne DM50, Budapest DM90 and Paris DM84. All prices include the commission.

One central agency is Mitfahrzentrale im Bahnhof Zoo (☎ 194 40), on the Vinetastrasse platform of the U-Bahn No 2. It is open weekdays from 9 am to 8 pm and weekends from 10 am to 6 pm. Also open daily are Mitfahrzentrale im U-Bahnhof Alexanderplatz (☎ 241 58 20), as you cross from U-Bahn No 2 to No 8, and the CityNetz Mitfahr-Service, which has offices at Joachimstaler Strasse (☎ 194 44), in the Kurfürstendamm U-Bahn station (☎ 882 76 04) and the Südstern station (☎ 693 60 95).

Other ride-service agencies include the Mitfahrzentrale Prenzlauer Berg (☎ 448 42 75), at Oderberger Strasse 45, and ADM Mitfahrzentrale Berlin (☎ 194 20), at Yorckstrasse 52. The Mitfahrzentrale Berlin für Lesben und Schwule (☎ 216 40 20), also at Yorckstrasse 52, is for gay and lesbian hitchhikers.

The people answering the phone in these offices usually speak English well. If you arrange a ride a few days in advance, be sure to call the driver the night before and again on departure morning to make sure they're still going.

GETTING AROUND

The Airport

Berlin's three airports can all be reached by train and/or bus. S-Bahn No 9 runs from Zoo station to Schönefeld airport via Alexanderplatz every 20 minutes between 4 am and midnight (or take U-Bahn No 7 to Rudow and bus No 171, also every 20 minutes). The more infrequent S-Bahn No 45 links Schönefeld and Tempelhof airports.

For Tegel airport, take bus No 109 from Zoo station, which goes via Kurfürstendamm and Luisenplatz, or express bus X9 from Lützowplatz at Kurfürstenstrasse, which goes via Budapester Strasse and Zoo station. These buses, which also stop at Jakob-Kaiser-Platz U-Bahn station (line No 7), operate every 15 minutes from 5 am to midnight. You can also take U-Bahn No 6 to Kurt-Schumacher-Platz and then board bus No 128 for Tegel. A taxi to Tegel costs about DM35.

For Tempelhof airport take U-Bahn No 6 to Platz der Luftbrücke or bus No 119 from Kurfürstendamm via Kreuzberg.

Public Transport

Apart from the suburban trains (S-Bahn), the Berliner Verkehrsbetriebe (BVG; ☎ 194 49) operates an efficient network of metros (U-Bahn), buses and a ferry, reaching every corner of Berlin and the surrounding areas. At the moment, however, the extensive construction around town is causing frequent delays and schedule changes.

Trams exist only in east Berlin. The BVG ferry from Kladow to Wannsee operates hourly all year, weather permitting, with regular tickets, passes and transfers accepted. Bus stops are marked with a large 'H' (for *Halt)* and the name of the stop; some of the newer buses show the name of the street being travelled and the next stop on a light board inside. Drivers can give change.

The S-Bahn, which rail-pass holders can use for free, differs from the U-Bahn in that more than one line uses the same track. Destination indicators on the platforms tell you where the next train is going. Route maps are posted in all stations and carriages or you can pick one up from the information kiosks.

The system is relatively easy to use, but you have to pay attention at times. When trying to locate your line, remember that the little inverted triangle indicates the destination (eg Warschauer Strasse) while the arrow is pointing out which staircase or corridor to follow. Because of all the renovations and reconstructions, some stations in the east (especially Friedrichstrasse) are a nightmare when it comes to changing lines.

The next station (including an *Übergang*, or transfer point) is announced on most U-Bahn (but not S-Bahn) trains and even displayed at the end of carriages on some new trains. The recorded voice also tells you which side of the carriage from which to deboard. It's best, though, to know the name of the station before the one you need. Potentially confusing U/S-Bahn stations are

Kurfürstendamm (U-Bahn Nos 9 and 15) and Kurfürstenstrasse (U-Bahn Nos 1 and 15) and – to those who read German – Zoologischer Garten (or 'Zoo') and Tiergarten, which are side by side and mean about the same thing.

Fares A single DM2.50 *Kurzstrecke* ticket will take you three stops (with one change permitted) on a train or half a dozen stops on a bus or tram; if in doubt, ask. The DM3.60 *Langstrecke* ticket allows unlimited transfers on all forms of public transport for two hours within two of the three zones (AB or BC); the DM3.90 *Ganzstrecke* ticket allows the same in all three zones, which will get you as far afield as Potsdam and Oranienburg.

A day ticket good till 3 am the following day costs DM7.50/8.50 for two/three zones. If two adults (and up to three children) are travelling together, a group card valid for a day (DM20/22.50 two/three zones) is the best value. The WelcomeCard (DM29) includes 72 hours' unlimited travel in the Berlin-Brandenburg area plus lots of discounts (see Tourist Offices in the Information section for details). There's also a *Wochenende Ticket* (Weekend Ticket) valid over the weekend for five people for DM35. The DM40, seven-day, two-zone pass (DM45 for three zones) is a good buy if you are travelling a lot. Monthly passes cost DM93/104 for two/three zones, but they are based on the calendar month and are *not* 30-day passes as such. If you have a two-zone pass and want to travel into the third (eg from Zoo station to Potsdam or Oranienburg), you must buy a supplementary ticket *(Ergänzungsfahrschein)* for DM2.50.

Bus drivers sell single and day tickets, but other multiple, weekly or monthly tickets must be purchased in advance. Most types of ticket are available from the orange ticket-vending machines (instructions in English) in U/S-Bahn stations, as well as the ticket window at the stations' entrances and the BVG information kiosk (Map 6), open daily from 8 am to 10 pm, on Hardenbergplatz in front of Zoo station.

Validate your own ticket in a red machine *(Entwerter)* at the platform entrances to S-Bahn and U-Bahn stations or at bus stops so, if using a timed ticket like the Langstrecke, validate it as your train or bus arrives to ensure full value. If you're caught by an inspector without a ticket (or even an unvalidated one), there's a DM60 fine. If you do get nabbed, do us all a favour, shut up and pay up. The inspectors – and your fellow passengers – hear the same bogus stories every day of the week.

You can take a bicycle in specially marked carriages of the S-Bahn or U-Bahn for a DM2.50 fare or for free if you hold a monthly ticket. You can only take a bike on U-Bahn trains between 9 am and 2 pm and from 5.30 pm till closing time on weekdays (any time at the weekend). Dogs and one piece of luggage are free.

Double-deck buses offer great views from the upstairs front seats. Among the most popular routes is from Grunewald to Platz der Luftbrücke via the Ku'damm and Kreuzberg on bus No 119. An even better option is bus No 100, which passes 18 major sights on its way from Bahnhof Zoo to Michelangelostrasse in Prenzlauer Berg via Alexanderplatz, providing you with a great overview and cheap orientation to Berlin. The BVG even puts out a special brochure describing the route and its sights. Immediately after the Wall came down the 'Old Faithful' No 100 was the first transport link between the divided halves of the city. It runs every 10 minutes from 4 to 12.30 am.

The S-Bahn and U-Bahn lines close down between 1 and 4 am, though certain S-Bahn lines, including Nos 7 and 75, run limited service (about two trains an hour) throughout the night at the weekend. Also, some 70 bus lines run every 30 minutes all night from Zoo station to key points such as Rathaus Spandau, Alt-Tegel, Hermannplatz, Rathaus Steglitz etc. Regular fares apply.

Car & Motorcycle

Berlin is probably easier to drive around than many other big cities in Europe, but you will still run into roadworks in the eastern parts for some time yet. The A10 ring road gets you easily around the urban perimeter.

You can park immediately west of the zoo for DM20 a day; the per-hour rate is about DM2. Underground parking at similar rates is available on Augsburger Strasse, not far from Breitscheidplatz, and in the Europa-Center. Above-ground parking is easier to find in eastern districts and is generally cheaper. Outside parking is always on a 'pay and display' system in Berlin.

Rental All the large car-rental chains are represented in Berlin, and their standard rates for the cheapest car begin at around DM99 daily or DM449 weekly, including tax and unlimited km. Some arrangements also include collision insurance which can save up to DM40 a day. There are also special weekend tariffs for rental from Friday at noon to Monday 9 am, starting at around DM120. Rental cars are often fully booked in Berlin, so advance reservations are advisable, and you'll probably get a better rate by booking from abroad. Weekends are usually the best (and cheapest) times to rent.

Hertz (☎ 261 10 53), opposite the entrance to the Zoo at Budapester Strasse 39, has Volkswagen Polos or Ford Fiestas for DM119 a day on weekdays, including theft and collision insurance; ask for the 'city-hit' rate. On weekends, the same money will let you keep the car from Friday through to Monday, but insurance is extra. Weekly rentals are perhaps the best deal, starting at an all-inclusive DM549.

Avis (☎ 261 18 81), next door, offers pretty much the same deal, with an Opel Corsa or VW Polo for three days costing DM243 all inclusive. There's also a Sixt Rent-a-Car (☎ 212 98 81 1) outlet nearby at the Holiday Inn Crowne Plaza, Nürnberger Strasse 65, and a Europcar (Map 4; ☎ 240 79 00) near Alexanderplatz at Karl-Liebknecht-Strasse 19. Another Europcar branch (☎ 306 95 90) is near the ZOB (bus station) at Messedamm 8. You must be at least 21 years old to rent a car, and practically all credit cards are accepted by these companies. For small companies offering discount car rentals, check the 'PKW – Vermietung' section of the classified newspaper *Zweite Hand*.

One company that is sure to offer a better deal than the biggies (from DM439 a week) is Holiday Autos, whose cars are booked through travel agents including Kilroy (see Travel Agencies in the Information section) and can be picked up/dropped off at several locations, including Tegel Airport and at Düsseldorferstrasse 18 in Wilmersdorf.

For motorcycle rentals try American Bike Rent (☎ 03301-701 55 5), at Magnus-Hirschfeld-Strasse 26, north of Berlin in Lehnitz (S-Bahn No 1 to Lehnitz). Daily weekday/weekend rates for Harley-Davidsons range from DM139/163 to DM168/176 and the first 90km are free. Weekly rates, including the first 720km, are DM815 to DM985. There is a deposit of DM1500 on cash rentals. They're open weekdays from 2 to 7 pm. Another possibility is G Passeckel (☎ 781 18 73), at Eisenacher Strasse 79 in Schöneberg (U-Bahn No 7 to Eisenacher Strasse), which has Suzukis, Yamahas, Kawasakis and Hondas from as low as DM60 a day.

Taxi

There are taxi stands with 'call columns' *(Rufsäule)* beside all main train stations and throughout the city; just look for the sign nearest you. Flag fall is DM4 then it's DM2.10 for each of the first 6km and DM1.90 thereafter. Night and weekend km charges are higher by DM0.20 and a fifth passenger costs DM2.50 on top of the fare. If you've ordered a taxi by telephone, flag fall is DM6 then DM2.50/1.80 for the first/subsequent km.

Sample fares: Nollendorfplatz to Schlesisches Tor is DM21.50; Hermannplatz to Schlesisches Tor is DM11.50.

If you need to travel quickly over a short distance, you can use the DM5 flat rate, which entitles you to ride for five minutes or 2km, whichever comes first. This deal only applies if you flag down a moving taxi and ask for the DM5 rate before getting into the car. You can call a taxi at ☎ 210 10 1, ☎ 210

20 2 and ☎ 690 22, though for faster response try the *Taxi-Ruf* listings for your area in the telephone directory.

New to Berlin are Velotaxis (☎ 304 66 55), pedicabs that seat two people and follow three routes: along the Ku'damm from Adenauerplatz to Wittenbergplatz; from Zoo station to the Brandenburg Gate; and along Unter den Linden. The cost is DM2 per person per km.

Bicycle

Berlin is a very user-friendly city for cyclists, and it's probably the best way to get to know the city; there are bike lanes everywhere. In fact, once you've survived a few near-collisions after inadvertently stepping onto the special red-clay or painted lanes and then got the dressing-down of your life from an irate so-and-so on two wheels, you may think it's *too* user-friendly. Just pay attention and watch where you're going.

Bicycles can be rented from the Fahrradstation at the left-luggage office in Zoo station (☎ 297 49 31 9); at the one in Hof VI in the Hackesche Höfe (Map 4; ☎ 285 99 89 5) at Rosenthaler Strasse 40-41 in Mitte; and the station (☎ 216 91 77) at Möckernstrasse 92 in Kreuzberg 61. This company offers carefully inspected and maintained bikes from DM18 to DM23 a day during opening hours (weekdays from 10 am to 6 pm, Saturday to 2 pm), from DM23 to DM28 till noon the following day, from DM45 to DM55 for the weekend and from DM70 to DM95 per week.

Another outfit renting bikes is Bike City (Map 4; mobile ☎ 0177-210 66 61), with some stations open daily year round from 7 am to 9 pm, including one on Schlossplatz in front of the Staatsrat building and another at the Hansaplatz U-Bahn station (line No 9). The daily (24-hour) charge is DM10.

AROUND BERLIN

Most everything worth seeing 'around Berlin' is in the new, and very independent-minded state of Brandenburg. See that chapter for details on day and weekend trips to Potsdam (24km), Brandenburg (60km), the Sachsenhausen concentration camp at Oranienburg (35km), the Spreewald (80km), Cottbus (115km), Buckow (50km), Frankfurt an der Oder (80km), Rheinsberg (90km), Chorin (60km) and Niederfinow (55km).

Brandenburg

The state of Brandenburg, with a land mass the size of Belgium and just as flat, seems to be a hard act to follow Berlin, which lies at its very centre, but it has more than its share of attractions. It is a region of lakes, marshes, rivers, and canals connecting the Oder and Elbe rivers (utilising the Havel and Spree rivers, which meet at Spandau west of Berlin). Brandenburg is prime boating, fishing, hiking and cycling territory. The Spreewald, a wetlands area near Lübben and Lübbenau, has become the capital's playground since the *Wende* and is still the centre of Germany's Sorbian minority, a Slavic people who have lived here since at least the 6th century (see boxed text titled The Sorbs).

Brandenburg's biggest draw is Potsdam, the 'Versailles of Germany', but visitors should not ignore places like Brandenburg, a lovely baroque city and once the capital of the Mark (March) of Brandenburg, Rheinsberg with its graceful lakeside palace and summer concerts, the fine Gothic Cistercian monastery at Chorin, the impressive ship's lift at Niederfinow or the hilly Märkische Schweiz region, where the playwright Bertolt Brecht once spent his summers.

Brandenburg was originally settled by the Wends – the ancestors of the Sorbs – but they were overpowered in 1157 by Albrecht der Bär (Albert the Bear), who became the *Markgraf* (margrave) of Brandenburg. The Hohenzollern Friedrich I arrived in the early 15th century and by 1618, the electors of Brandenburg had acquired the eastern Baltic duchy of Prussia, merging the two states into a powerful union called the Kingdom of Prussia. This kingdom eventually brought all of Germany under its control, leading to the establishment of the German Empire in 1871.

Many Berliners will warn you about the 'Wild East', advising you not to stray too far afield in what they consider to be a backward and sometimes violent region. But Brandenburgers, ever *korrekt* in the Prussian style, sniff and ask what you can expect from a bunch of loud-mouthed and brash upstarts like the Berliners. It's a New York-Connecticut dichotomy that was inscribed in stone in May 1996 when a referendum to merge Brandenburg, which had only come back into existence after the Wende, with the city-state of Berlin failed. Brandenburgers voted overwhelmingly to remain independent.

Perhaps the best advice is that of the 19th-century novelist Theodor Fontane (see boxed text on Fontane later in this chapter): 'If you wish to travel around Brandenburg,' he wrote in his four-volume *Wanderungen*

HIGHLIGHTS

- The Chinese Teahouse in Sanssouci Park at Potsdam
- Rheinsberg and its magnificent Schloss
- Sachsenhausen Concentration Camp Memorial & Museum at Oranienburg
- View of the ship's lift in Niederfinow from the upper platform
- Hiking through the Spreewald Biosphere Reserve to the Freilandmuseum of traditional Sorbian architecture

• **Population:** 2.5m • **Capital:** Potsdam • **Area:** 29,060 sq km

Brandenburg Luminaries: Theodor Fontane, Heinrich von Kleist, Karl Friedrich Schinkel, Friedrich August Wolf

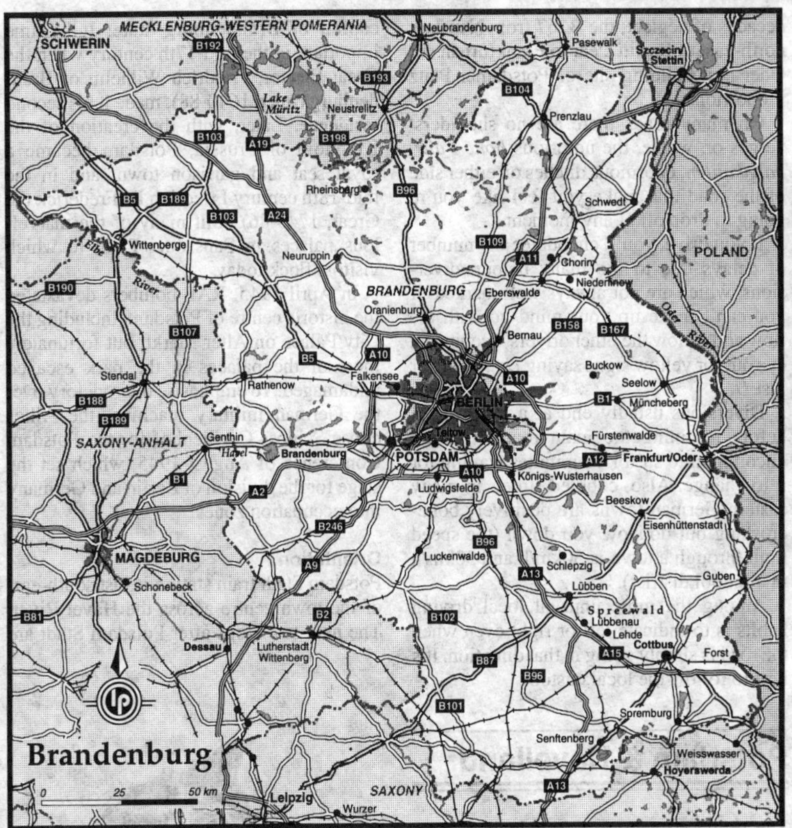

durch die Mark Brandenburg (Travels through the March of Brandenburg), 'you will first of all need to love these parts and the people who inhabit them … to have the magnanimity to recognise the good for what it is ... I have roamed around the March and found it richer than I dared to hope.' In a funny sort of way, so did we.

Organised Tours

BBS (☎ 030-351 95 27 0), the people who brought you City Circle Sightseeing in Berlin, has a couple of bus tours from Berlin to destinations in Brandenburg, including a four-hour tour to Potsdam and Sanssouci (Friday and Saturday at 2 pm, Sunday at 10.30 am; DM59) and, from May to early October, a seven-hour tour of the Spreewald (Wednesday and Sunday at 9.30 am; DM57), which includes a punt ride on the canals.

Getting There & Around

All destinations covered in this chapter are adequately served by train (and in some cases by bus) from Berlin, and we recommend using them.

Driving in eastern Germany can be a nightmare as roads are being repaired after decades of neglect; the B167 from Neustadt north-east of Berlin clear to Frankfurt an der Oder is a building site of Potsdamer Platz proportions.

On many roads there are no shoulders/verges or, worse, the notorious *hohe Fahrbahnkanten*, enormous ditches on either side of the road that make you feel like you're going to drop off at any moment.

If you drive, you'll encounter any number of delays due to the many detours/diversions, which are not always well marked. If you can't make up your mind go with the flow and follow the other drivers, keeping an eye out for yellow signs saying *Umleitung* or just *U*.

Diversions usually end at a traffic light before rejoining the main road; it is not uncommon to sit for 10 minutes waiting for it to change. Also, cobbled streets in many eastern German towns are positively bone-crushing but do slow you down (the speed limit through a town is 50km/h and 30km/h in a school district).

Among the more unusual local driving habits is to indicate left or right even when the road is simply going in that direction. It's best to follow the local custom.

Potsdam & Havelland

The prime attraction of Brandenburg state and the most popular day trip from Berlin is Potsdam, a mere 24km south-west of the capital and easily accessible by S-Bahn. But if time allows, try to make it to Brandenburg, the centre of the watery Havelland region another 36km west and the state's namesake. An attractive, untouristed city, it offers an interesting introduction to life in the new eastern Germany beyond the razzle-dazzle of Berlin.

POTSDAM

- *pop 142,000*
- *area code* ☎ 0331

Potsdam, on the Havel River just beyond the south-western tip of Greater Berlin, is the capital of Brandenburg state. It became important in the mid-17th century when the Great Elector, Friedrich Wilhelm of Brandenburg (ruled 1640-88), made it his second residence. Later, with the creation of the Kingdom of Prussia, Potsdam became a royal seat and garrison town, and in the mid-18th century Friedrich II (Frederick the Great, 1740-86) built many of the marvellous palaces in Sanssouci Park, to which visitors flock today.

In April 1945, RAF bombers devastated the historic centre of Potsdam, including the City Palace on Alter Markt, but fortunately most of the palaces in the park escaped undamaged. To emphasise their victory over the German military machine, the Allies chose Schloss Cecilienhof for the Potsdam Conference of August 1945, which set the stage for the division of Berlin and Germany into occupation zones.

Orientation

Potsdam Stadt train station is just south-east of the town centre across the Havel River. The next two stops after Potsdam Stadt are

Friedrich II (the Great) made Potsdam a cultural centre in the 18th century by stocking it with several sumptuous palaces.

Potsdam Charlottenhof and Potsdam Wildpark, which are closer to Sanssouci Park and all the palaces but are served only by RegionalBahn (RB) trains, not the Regional Express (RE) or S-Bahn Nos 3 and 7, which is how most people get here from Berlin. You can walk from Schloss Cecilienhof to Glienicker Brücke (and bus No 116 to Wannsee) in about 10 minutes. From Potsdam Stadt station to Charlottenhof is just under 4km. Do not confuse any of these stations with the Hauptbahnhof, an underutilised station serving destinations to the south.

Information

Potsdam-Information (☎ 275 58 16; fax 293 01 2), beside the Alter Markt at Friedrich-Ebert-Strasse 5, sells a variety of maps and brochures, but the office can get crowded. Its opening hours vary with the season: from April to October it is open from 9 am to 8 pm on weekdays, 10 am to 6 pm on Saturday, and 10 am to 4 pm on Sunday. From November to March its weekday hours are from 10 am to 6 pm and weekends from 10 am to 2 pm. A smaller branch (same telephone number) is at Brandenburger Strasse 18 and opens weekdays from 10 am to 6 pm and Saturday from 10 am to 2 pm. In both places you can buy the joint Berlin-Potsdam WelcomeCard (see the Information section of the Berlin chapter), which entitles you to unlimited transport and free or discounted admission to many attractions in both cities for 72 hours (DM29). Sanssouci-Information (☎ 969 42 00), with information on the palaces in the park, is near the old windmill opposite the Schloss Sanssouci. It's open daily April to October from 8.30 am to 5 pm and from 9 am to 4 pm the rest of the year.

The Dresdner Bank, on Brandenburger Strasse 28, at the corner of Jägerstrasse has an ATM. Euro-Change has an outlet at No 29 of the same street, open weekdays from 9.30 am to 6 pm and on Saturday to 2 pm. The post office is on Am Kanal north of the Alter Markt.

The bookshop Das Internationale Buch, on Friedrich-Ebert-Strasse (open weekdays from 9 am to 7 pm and Saturday to 4 pm), stocks maps and some English-language publications.

Sanssouci Park

This large park west of the city centre is open from dawn till dusk with no admission charge. The palaces and outbuildings all keep separate hours and charge separate admission prices. A day ticket allowing entry to all palaces and other sights in the park ('according to capacity', we are warned) costs DM20/15 adults/children and a family card is DM25. But you have to work pretty fast to make it pay off. There's a 50% student discount on all separate admissions.

Sanssouci Park is one of the worst signposted sights in Germany; take along the free map provided by the tourist office or you'll find yourself up the wrong path at almost every turn. With the palaces spaced fairly far apart – it's 2km, for example, between the Neues Palais and the Schloss Sanssouci and about 15km to complete the entire circuit – a bicycle (see Getting Around later in this section) is without doubt the best way to get around, particularly if you're determined to squeeze in as many palaces as you can in a day. You can ride on the tracks in the park but not along the footpaths.

Sanssouci is on UNESCO's World Heritage List but apparently almost lost the prestige recently when the city council decided to build a shopping mall in full view of the Schloss. That ill-conceived plan now appears to have been put on hold if not scuttled altogether.

Schloss Sanssouci Begin your tour of the park with Georg Wenzeslaus von Knobelsdorff's **Schloss Sanssouci** (1747), the celebrated rococo palace with glorious interiors. You have to take the guided tour, so arrive early and avoid weekends and holidays, or you may not get a ticket (DM10/5) at all. A maximum of 2000 visitors a day are allowed entry (UNESCO's rule) so tickets are usually sold out by 2.30 pm – even in the shoulder seasons. You might consider taking the tour sponsored by Potsdam-Information

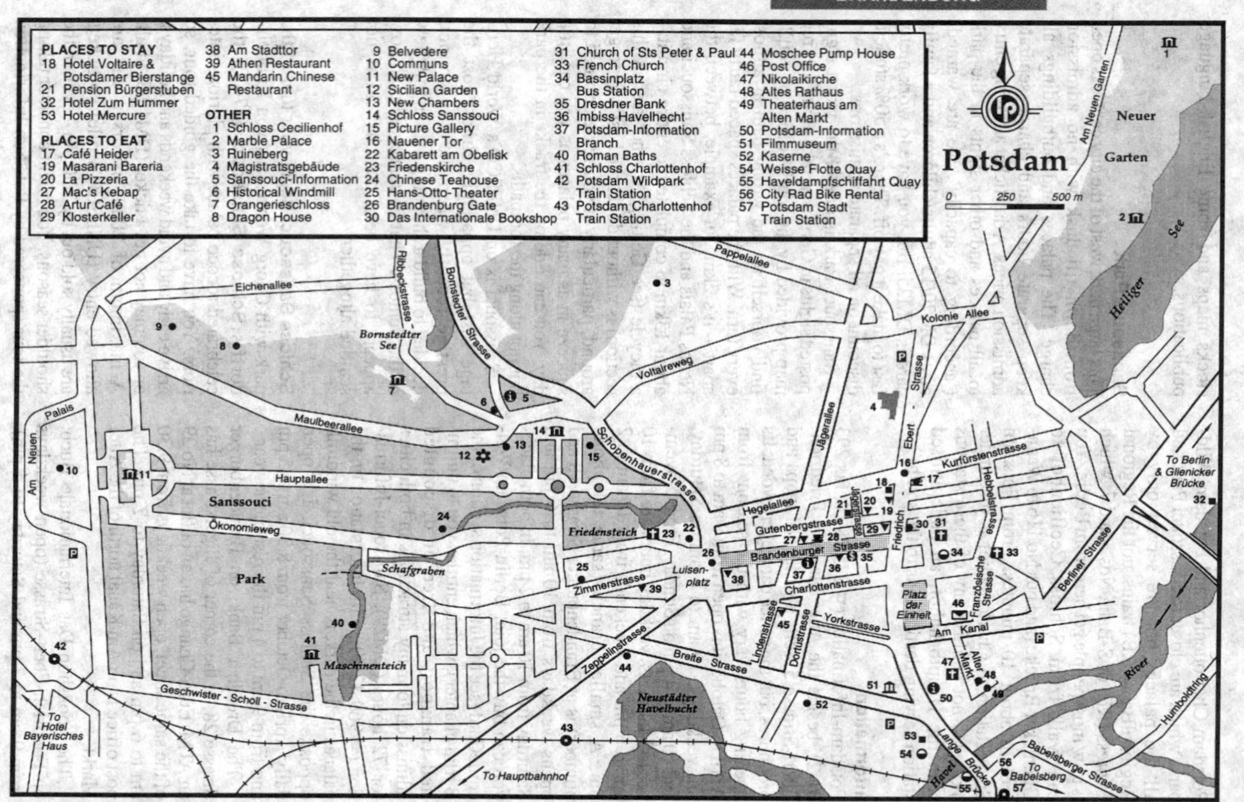
PLACES TO STAY
18 Hotel Voltaire & Potsdamer Bierstange
21 Pension Bürgerstuben
32 Hotel Zum Hummer
53 Hotel Mercure
PLACES TO EAT
17 Café Heider
19 Masarani Bareria
20 La Pizzeria
27 Mac's Kebap
28 Artur Café
29 Klosterkeller
38 Am Stadttor
39 Athen Restaurant
45 Mandarin Chinese Restaurant
OTHER
1 Schloss Cecilienhof
2 Marble Palace
3 Ruineberg
4 Magistratsgebäude
5 Sanssouci-Information
6 Historical Windmill
7 Orangerieschloss
8 Dragon House
9 Belvedere
10 Communs
11 New Palace
12 Sicilian Garden
13 New Chambers
14 Schloss Sanssouci
15 Picture Gallery
16 Nauener Tor
22 Kabarett am Obelisk
23 Friedenskirche
24 Chinese Teahouse
25 Hans-Otto-Theater
26 Brandenburg Gate
30 Das Internationale Bookshop
31 Church of Sts Peter & Paul
33 French Church
34 Bassinplatz Bus Station
35 Dresdner Bank
36 Imbiss Havelhecht
37 Potsdam-Information Branch
40 Roman Baths
41 Schloss Charlottenhof
42 Potsdam Wildpark Train Station
43 Potsdam Charlottenhof Train Station
44 Moschee Pump House
46 Post Office
47 Nikolaikirche
48 Altes Rathaus
49 Theaterhaus am Alten Markt
50 Potsdam-Information
51 Filmmuseum
52 Kaserne
54 Weisse Flotte Quay
55 Haveldampfschiffahrt Quay
56 City Rad Bike Rental
57 Potsdam Stadt Train Station
Potsdam
0 250 500 m
Neuer Garten
Heiliger See
Am Neuen Garten
Bornstedter See
Sanssouci
Park
Friedensteich
Schafgraben
Maschinenteich
Neustädter Havelbucht
Havel
River
To Berlin & Glienicker Brücke
To Babelsberg
To Hauptbahnhof
To Hotel Bayerisches Haus

(see Organised Tours later in this section), which guarantees entry.

Our favourite rooms include the over-the-top rococo Konzertsaal (Concert Room) and the bed chambers of the Damenflügel (Ladies' Wing), including a 'Voltaire slept here' one. From the northern terrace of the palace you can see **Ruineberg**, a group of classical 'ruins' that look like they've been there for time immemorial but actually make up a folly built by Frederick the Great in 1754. Schloss Sanssouci is open April to mid-October, Tuesday to Sunday from 9 am to 5 pm, to 4 pm in late October, February and March, and to 3 pm (with a half-hour break at 12.30 pm) from November to January.

Just opposite the palace is the **Historische Mühle**, the 'historical windmill' designed, like the Queen's Hamlet at Versailles, to give the palace grounds a rustic, rural air. On either side of the palace are the twin Neue Kammern (New Chambers) and the Bildergalerie (Picture Gallery). Highlights of the **Neue Kammern** (open all year Saturday to Thursday from 10 am to 5 pm; DM4/2), which was used both as a guesthouse and an orangery, include the large Ovidsaal, with its gilded reliefs and green and white marble floor, and the Meissen porcelain figurines in the last room to the west. The **Bildergalerie** (open mid-May to mid-October Tuesday to Sunday from 10 am to 5 pm; DM4/2) was completed in 1764 as Germany's first purpose-built art museum. It contains a rich collection of 17th-century paintings by Rubens, Van Dyck, Caravaggio and others.

Just west of the Neue Kammern is the **Sizilianischer Garten** (Sicilian Garden) of subtropical plants laid out in the mid-19th century.

Orangerieschloss The Renaissance-style Orangery Palace (open mid-May to mid-October, Friday to Wednesday from 10 am to 5 pm with a break from noon to 12.45 pm; DM5/3), built in 1864 as a guesthouse for foreign royalty on the go, is the largest of the palaces at Sanssouci but hardly the most interesting. It contains six sumptuous rooms, including the Raphaelsaal, with copies of the Italian Renaissance painter's work done by 19th-century German painters and a tower on the west side that can be climbed (DM2) for great views over the Neues Palais and the park. Part of the Orangery's west wing is still used to keep some of the more sensitive plants alive in the cold north German winter.

Around Orangerieschloss Two interesting buildings west of the Orangery and within easy walking distance are the pagoda-like **Drachenhaus** (Dragon House, 1770), housing a café-restaurant, and the rococo **Belvedere**, the only building in the park to suffer serious damage during WWII but now fully restored.

Neues Palais The late-baroque New Palace (1769), summer residence of the royal family, is one of the biggest and most imposing buildings in the park and the one to see if your time is limited. It keeps the same hours as the Schloss Sanssouci but closes on Tuesday instead of Monday and from 12.45 to 1.15 pm between November and January. The tour (DM6/4) takes in about a dozen of the palace's 200 rooms, including the Grottensaal (Grotto Hall), a rococo-phile's delight of shells, fossils and semi-precious stone set into the walls and ceilings; the Marmorsaal, a large banquet hall of white Carrara marble with a wonderful ceiling fresco; the Jagkammer (Hunting Chamber) with lots of dead furry things and fine gold tracery on the walls; and several chambers fitted out from floor to ceiling in rich red damask (they provide a sample so you don't have to resist the temptation to touch it). Note the *Fahrstuhl*, an electric 'stair lift' dating from 1899 that transported aging royals from the ground to the 1st floor. The **Schlosstheater** in the south wing has classical music concerts at the weekend; see the Entertainment section. Opposite the New Palace is the **Communs**, originally built to house the palace servants and kitchens and now part of Potsdam University.

Schloss Charlottenhof Karl Friedrich Schinkel's main contribution (1826) to the park must be visited on a 30-minute German-language tour (DM6/3), but don't wait around too long if the queues are long. In truth, the exterior of this mansion modelled after a Roman villa is more interesting than the interior, especially the Doric portico and the bronze fountain to the east. Charlottenhof is open mid-May to mid-October, Thursday to Tuesday from 10 am to 5 pm.

Around Schloss Charlottenhof A short distance to the north-east on the edge of the little Maschinenteich (Machine Pond) are the **Römische Bäder** (Roman Baths), built in 1836 by a pupil of Schinkel and never used. The floor mosaics and caryatids inspired by the baths at Herculaneum are impressive, but we liked the fountain of a flounder spitting into a clamshell near the entrance. The Roman Baths are open mid-May to mid-October, Friday to Wednesday from 10 am to 5 pm with a half-hour break at noon (DM3/2). If you follow the path crossing the Schafgraben, the narrow canal feeding the pond, to the north and then east, you'll come to what many consider to be the pearl of the park: the stunning **Chinesisches Teehaus** (Chinese Teahouse, 1757), a circular pavilion of gilded columns, palm trees and figures of Chinese musicians and animals (one of the monkeys is said to have the features of Voltaire). It keeps the same hours as the Roman Baths except it is closed on Friday instead of Thursday and for a half-hour from 12.30 pm (DM2).

Altstadt

The baroque **Brandenburger Tor** (Brandenburg Gate), on Luisenplatz at the western end of the old town, pales in comparison with its namesake in Berlin but is older (1770). From this square, pedestrian Brandenburger Strasse runs due east to the **Sts Peter und Paul Kirche** (Church of Saints Peter & Paul, 1868). The **Französische Kirche** (French Church), to the south-east on Charlottenstrasse and once the seat of the town's Huguenots, was built in 1753.

North-west of here, on Friedrich-Ebert-Strasse, is the **Nauener Tor** (Nauen Gate, 1755), another monumental arch. The **Holländisches Viertel** (Dutch Quarter) to the south-east and bounded by Friedrich-Ebert-Strasse, Hebbelstrasse, Kurfürstenstrasse and Gutenbergstrasse, has some 134 gabled red-brick houses built for Dutch workers who came to Potsdam in the 1730s at the invitation of Friedrich Wilhelm I.

South-east of central Platz der Einheit is the great neoclassical dome of Schinkel's **Nikolaikirche** (1850) on Alter Markt. On the eastern side of the square is Potsdam's old **Rathaus** (1753), which now contains several art galleries upstairs (open Tuesday to Sunday; free) and an elegant restaurant in the cellar.

West of the Alter Markt on Breite Strasse and housed in the **Marstall**, the former royal stables designed by Knobelsdorff in 1746, is the **Filmmuseum** (open weekdays from 10 am to 5 pm and on Saturday and Sunday to 6 pm; DM1). It contains exhibits on the history of the UFA and DEFA movie studios in Babelsberg and some excellent footage of Nazi-era and postwar Communist propaganda films.

Across Breite Strasse and farther to the west on Henning-von-Tresckow-Strasse is the former **Kaserne** (military barracks, now the Finanzamt) where, according to local lore, the plot by Colonel Claus von Stauffenberg and other officers to assassinate Adolf Hitler in July 1944 was hatched. A short distance beyond the 'bay' of the Havel to where Breite Strasse meets Zeppelinstrasse is the wonderful **Moschee** (mosque), a Moorish structure built in 1842 to house the palace waterworks. It can be visited from May to October on Saturday and Sunday from 10 am to noon and 1 to 5 pm (DM4/2).

Due north of this Moorish pump house on the south-eastern edge of Sanssouci Park is the **Friedenskirche** (Church of Peace), a neo-Romanesque pile completed in 1854 and containing the mausoleum of Friedrich Wilhelm IV (ruled 1840-61).

Neuer Garten

This winding lakeside park on the west bank of the Heiliger See and north-east of the city centre is a fine place to relax after all the baroque-rococo and high art of Sanssouci Park. The **Marmorpalais** (Marble Palace, 1792), by Carl Gotthard Langhans right on the lake, is being carefully restored and will be under wraps for at least two more years. Farther north is **Schloss Cecilienhof**, an English-style country manor contrasting with the rococo palaces and pavilions in Sanssouci Park. Cecilienhof is remembered as the site of the 1945 Potsdam Conference, and large photos of the participants – Stalin, Truman and Churchill – are displayed inside. The conference room can be visited on a guided tour daily except Monday year round from 9 am to noon and 12.30 to 5 pm. Admission costs DM6/4.

Babelsberg

The **UFA film studios** (☎ 721 27 55), Germany's one-time response to Hollywood, are located east of the city centre on August-Bebel-Strasse (enter from Grossbeerenstrasse). This is where such silent-movie epics as Fritz Lang's *Metropolis* were made, along with some early Greta Garbo films. Babelsberg is the most aggressively marketed sight in the Greater Berlin area; it doesn't seem to matter that most people under the age of 60 have never heard of – much less seen – most of the films celebrated here. Talk about resting on your Laurels and Hardys! For a look behind the scenes you can take the rather commercial and very expensive daily studio tour from March to October between 10 am and 6 pm (DM25/18, family ticket DM60).

It costs a mere DM3/2 to visit Schinkel's neo-Gothic **Schloss Babelsberg** near the lakes (open May to October, Tuesday to Friday from 10 am to noon and 12.30 to 5 pm, and on Saturday and Sunday only for the rest of the year), and you can also stroll in the pleasant park past Schinkel's **Flatowturm** (open mid-May to mid-October on Saturday and Sunday only from 10 am to noon and 1 to 5 pm; DM3/2). A DM5 combination ticket will get you into both the palace and the tower.

Cruises

Weisse Flotte (☎ 275 92 10) operates boats on the Havel and the lakes around Potsdam, departing from the dock below the Hotel Mercure near Lange Brücke regularly from April to early October between 9 am and 4.45 pm. There are frequent boats to Wannsee (DM14.50 return). Other popular trips are to Werder (DM12) and Spandau (DM22). Haveldampfschiffahrt (☎ 270 62 29) has steamboat tours (DM18/10) of the same areas leaving from the southern end of

Brandenburg on My Mind

Like the US state of Georgia, the German state of Brandenburg has strong musical associations, though they're a bit more highbrow in content than 'midnight trains' and 'rainy nights'. Even Philistines have at least heard of the *Brandenburg Concertos*. They are the six *concerti grossi* composed by Johann Sebastian Bach in 1721 for Margrave Christian Ludwig of Brandenburg, the youngest son of Elector Friedrich Wilhelm I, based at Köthen in Saxony-Anhalt.

In 1747 Friedrich II (Frederick the Great) managed to lure Bach to Potsdam, where the great composer wrote *The Musical Offering* on a theme proposed by the king himself.

And how many people know *The Wedding March* was first performed here? No, not the catchy 'Here Comes the Bride' number; that's from Wagner's opera *Lohengrin* and is played when the bride walks *down* the aisle. We mean the one played for the exit of the married couple. It's the sixth number of Felix Mendelssohn's incidental music to *A Midsummer Night's Dream* (1842). The vogue for the piece started in 1858 when Queen Victoria's daughter, the Princess Royal (affectionately known as Vicky), had it played at her wedding at Windsor to Crown Prince Frederick of Prussia (later Kaiser Frederick III of Germany). So the next time you watch a couple of newlyweds make their way up the aisle and hear Mendelssohn's rather stirring tune, you should have Brandenburg on your mind. ■

Lange Brücke *(opposite* the Weisse Flotte quay) daily except Monday and Friday from mid-April to late September.

Organised Tours

City tours (DM15), sponsored by Potsdam-Information, leave from the Filmmuseum on Breite Strasse daily (except Monday) at 11 am from April to October and at 11.30 am from Thursday to Sunday the rest of the year. There's also a Sanssouci Park/Schloss Sanssouci tour for DM39 (DM49 for both tours).

Special Events

The biggest annual events in Potsdam are the Musikfestspiele Potsdam Sanssouci (☎ 293 85 9 for tickets) during the second and third weeks of June; the Filmfestival Potsdam held in mid-June; and the Potsdamer Knoblauchfest (Potsdam Garlic Festival) on the last weekend in May.

Places to Stay

Accommodation is tight (particularly single rooms), hotels are expensive, and the closest hostel is the Jugendgästehaus am Wannsee on Grosser Wannsee (see Places to Stay in the Berlin chapter). Potsdam-Information (☎ 289 15 87 for bookings) can arrange private rooms from DM20 to DM25 per person and apartments from DM25 to DM50 per person a day. TourBu (☎ 888 10 12; fax 888 10 14), at Saarmunder Strasse 60, is a private room-booking service with singles/doubles for around DM40/50.

Campingplatz Sanssouci-Gaisberg (☎ 03327-556 80), open April to October, is the closest camping ground to Potsdam. Located south-west of the centre at An der Pirschheide 41, it can be reached by bus No 631 (direction Werder). It costs DM2.50/9.90 for a small/large tent site and DM9.50/3.90 per adult/child.

In the centre of Potsdam at Jägerstrasse 10 is *Pension Bürgerstuben* (☎ 280 11 09; fax 280 48 54), which also has a restaurant. Rooms with facilities go for DM90/170 a single/double. The renovated *Hotel Voltaire* (☎ 231 70; fax 231 71 00), at Friedrich-Ebert-Strasse 88, has singles/doubles for DM199/258 while the big, soulless *Hotel Mercure* (☎ 244 63 1; fax 293 49 6), on Lange Brücke, is slightly cheaper, charging from DM195/215.

Hotel Bayerisches Haus (☎ 973 19 2; fax 972 32 9), at Im Wildpark 1, is on the pricey side, with singles from DM125 and doubles from DM195, but it boasts a lovely location. Rooms at the three-star *Schlosshotel Cecilienhof* (☎ 370 50; fax 292 49 8), on Am Neuer Garten, are even higher at DM165 to DM245 for singles and DM280 to DM450 for doubles, but you get to sleep in one of Potsdam's most famous buildings.

If you want to be near the UFA film studios, the *Hotel Zum Hummer* (☎ 619 54 9; fax 707 39 8) is beautifully located at Park Babelsberg 2 and has singles/doubles with private bath for DM85/110.

Places to Eat

Klosterkeller, at Friedrich-Ebert-Strasse 94 (almost at the corner of Gutenbergstrasse), has a restaurant, wine bar, beer garden and cocktail bar. The restaurant serves traditional regional dishes at moderately expensive prices (from DM20). *Am Stadttor*, by the gate at the western end of Brandenburger Strasse, has good lunch specials and offers a pleasant view.

Bacchuskeller is a rather elegant eatery in the Rathaus on the Alter Markt. *Mandarin*, at Lindenstrasse 44, has reasonable Chinese dishes from about DM12 and is open daily from 11.30 am to midnight. *Athen Restaurant*, at Zimmerstrasse 15, has Greek starters from DM5, and gyros, souvlakia and grills from DM15. It is open daily from 11 am to midnight.

Young people congregate at *Artur Café*, a café-cum-antique shop at Dortustrasse 16, where small dishes cost under DM10. The airy décor of the two-floor *Potsdamer Bierstange* at the Hotel Voltaire, Friedrich-Ebert-Strasse 88, matches the contemporary menu that includes generous fish dishes at DM15. There's a lovely garden terrace. *Café Heider*, another lively meeting place, is just up the street at No 29 and adjacent to Nauen Gate.

The King of Vegetables

If you happen to be in Brandenburg in May and you like asparagus, get yourself down to Beelitz (pronounced 'bay-LEETS'), the capital of the 'king of vegetables' since the 19th century. This sleepy little town (pop 5900), 20km south-west of Potsdam, produces more asparagus than any other place in Germany – some eight million of the succulent stalks each year – and in season it enters into a feeding-frenzy of *Spargel* in soup, with ham, with schnitzel and, of course, *natur*.

Remember, though, that the season is short: *Kirschen rot, Spargel tot* ('When the cherries are red, the asparagus is dead'). The climax marking the end of the season is the Beelitzer Spargelfest, held over the first weekend in June.

Asparagus, prized by epicures since Roman times, is difficult to grow and prefers light, sandy soil – just the crop for an area once called the 'sandbox of the Holy Roman Empire'. Today, some 200 hectares are given over to cultivation of the noble vegetable, up from the nine hectares allowed under the GDR, which despised anything aristocratic (even vegetables). White asparagus, preferred for its tenderness and delicate flavour, is grown under the soil to inhibit the development of chlorophyll.

Despite the huge amounts produced at Beelitz these days, there never seems to be enough asparagus for Germans – and Berliners in particular – who would eat it year round if they could. Michael Habbel of the Habbel distillery family has come up with a possible solution: asparagus schnapps. The ratio, he says, is 3.5kg of asparagus to a half-litre of alcohol (42%). And the taste? Well, most liquor stores in Brandenburg sell *Kräuter*, a vile herbal concoction. Have a slug of that, and you'll get the picture. Then switch to beer. ■

BRANDENBURG

La Pizzeria, Gutenbergstrasse 90, is popular with locals for its well priced pizzas and pastas. *Masarani Bareria*, next door to the Hotel Voltaire at Friedrich-Ebert-Strasse 92, has cheap pizzas, pastas and salads from DM6.

Two places on pedestrian Brandenburger Strasse for a quick bite are *Imbiss Havelhecht*, at No 25, and *Mac's Kebab*, at the corner of Lindenstrasse. There's a large *Kaiser's* supermarket next to the bus station on Bassinplatz.

Entertainment

The box office (☎ 275 71 0) at *Theaterhaus am Alten Markt* (open Monday to Thursday from 10 am to 6 pm and Friday and Saturday to 1 pm) has tickets for performances there and at its decrepit parent, *Hans-Otto-Theater* at Zimmerstrasse 10. It also sells tickets for concerts held at the *Schlosstheater* in the Neues Palais in Sanssouci Park (usually Friday at 5.30 pm, Saturday at 4.30 pm and Sunday at 7 pm).

From May to late October, there are organ concerts at various churches in Potsdam, including the *Friedenskirche*; ask Potsdam-Information for the locations. *Kabarett am Obelisk*, Schopenhauerstrasse 27, presents satirical programmes (in German) with contemporary themes from Tuesday to Sunday. The box office (☎ 291 06 9) is open Tuesday to Friday from 4 to 8.30 pm, Saturday from 6 to 8.30 pm and Sunday from 5 to 7.30 pm. Tickets cost DM10 to DM25.

Getting There & Away

Bus Potsdam's bus station, on Bassinplatz, is accessible from the Rathaus Spandau in Berlin on bus No 638 (hourly from 5 am to 9 pm) and from Schönefeld on bus No 602. If you're headed for Schloss Cecilienhof, take bus No 116 from Wannsee to Glienicker Brücke in Potsdam and walk from there.

Train S-Bahn train Nos 3 and 7 link central Berlin with Bahnhof Potsdam Stadt near the centre of town about every 10 minutes. Some regional (RB) trains from Berlin-Zoo stop at all three train stations in Potsdam. There is no direct service to Berlin-Schönefeld airport, but you can take S-Bahn No 3 or 7 from Potsdam Stadt to Westkreuz in western Berlin and change to S-Bahn No 45 (or take bus No 602, see Bus above). Berlin transit passes must cover Zones A, B and C to be valid for the trip to Potsdam by either S-Bahn or BVG bus.

Many trains between Hanover and Berlin-Zoo also stop at Potsdam Stadt. Train connections from Potsdam Stadt south to Leipzig are poor, and most require a change in Magdeburg. Going to Dresden means changing trains at Berlin-Lichtenberg.

To reach Babelsberg from Berlin, take S-Bahn No 3 or 7 to Babelsberg station (one stop before Potsdam Stadt) and then bus No 692 to the Ahornstrasse stop. You can also get off the S-Bahn at Griebnitzsee station and take bus No 696 to the Drewitz stop.

Getting Around

Potsdam is part of Berlin's S-Bahn network but has its own local trams and buses; these converge on Lange Brücke near Potsdam Stadt train station. To reach Schloss Charlottenhof and the Neues Palais from Lange Brücke, take bus No 606; tram No 96 is also good for the former. Bus No 695 goes past Schloss Sanssouci, the Orangerieschloss and the Neues Palais. From the bus station on Bassinplatz, bus No 610 will get you almost as far as the Neues Palais. Tram No 92 heads north from Lange Brücke for the city centre and points beyond. For a taxi ring ☎ 810 404.

City Rad (☎ 619 05 2) rents bikes from Bahnhofsplatz just north of the Potsdam Stadt train station. It's open from May to September on weekdays from 9 am to 7 pm and on weekends to 8 pm. In winter, ring ☎ 280 05 95. Rental fees (plus DM100/US$50 deposit) are DM15/10.50/7 for adults/students/children per day (opening hours); DM20/14/10 for 24 hours; DM35/24.50/17 for two days; and DM50/35/25 for three days. They also offer a four-hour guided bike tour (called Tour Alter Fritz after Frederick the Great) on Saturday at 10 am for an additional DM20 per person.

BRANDENBURG AN DER HAVEL

- *pop 93,000*
- *area code* ☎ 03381

Brandenburg is the oldest town in the March of Brandenburg, with a history going back to at least the 6th century when Slavs settled near today's cathedral. It was an important bishopric from the early Middle Ages and the seat of the Brandenburg *Markgrafen* until they moved to Berlin in the 15th century. Though it suffered some damage during WWII, Brandenburg is being restored and is once again becoming a lovely baroque town with many half-timbered houses and a few interesting sights. Though hardly a compulsory stop, it's a good place to break away from wild and crazy Berlin.

Orientation & Information

Brandenburg is split into three sections by the Havel River, the Beetzsee and their canals: the Neustadt, on an island in the centre; Dominsel (Cathedral Island), to the north; and the Altstadt, to the west. There are worthwhile sights in all three areas, which are connected by six bridges. The train station is on Am Hauptbahnhof, 1.5km south of central Neustädtischer Markt.

The tourist office (☎ 194 33; fax 223 74 3), at Hauptstrasse 51, is open weekdays from 9 am to 7 pm (to 8.30 pm on Thursday) and from 10 am to 2 pm on Saturday. There's a Deutsche Bank branch with an ATM at Neustädtischer Markt 10. The post office is due west at Molkenmarkt 29.

Walking Tour

Begin a stroll through Brandenburg at the Romanesque **Dom St Peter und Paul** (Cathedral of Saints Peter & Paul) on the northern edge of Dominsel.

Begun in 1165 by Premonstratensian monks and completed in 1240, it contains the wonderfully decorated Bunte Kapelle (Coloured Chapel), with a vaulted and painted ceiling; the carved 14th-century Böhmischer Altar (Bohemian Altar) in the south transept (which may be still under renovation); a fantastic baroque organ (1723) in the choir loft; and the **Dommuseum** of liturgical treasures upstairs (DM3/2).

Much of the cathedral is being rebuilt so some items may have been moved around – or disappeared altogether! The cathedral is open Monday to Saturday from 10 am to 6 pm (only to noon on Wednesday) and from 11 am on Sunday. The museum is open Tuesday to Saturday from 10 am to 4 pm (to noon only on Wednesday) and from noon to 4 pm on Sunday.

From the cathedral walk south on St Petri to Mühlendamm. Just before you cross the Havel to the Neustadt, look left at the **Hauptpegel**, the 'city water gauge' erected to measure the river's height. On the other side is the **Mühlentorturm**, the Mill Gate Tower that once marked the border between the separate towns of Dominsel and Neustadt.

Molkenmarkt, the continuation of Mühlendamm, and running parallel to Neustädtischer Markt, leads to the **Pfarrkirche St Katharinen** (Parish Church of St Catherine), a Gothic hall church dating back to the early 1400s and currently under renovation. South-west of the church at the end of Steinstrasse is the impressive **Steintorturm**, the second of four city towers still standing. To the east along St Annen Promenade are sections of the **city wall** dating from the 14th and 15th centuries and among the best preserved in Europe. St Annen Promenade leads to the ruins of the 14th-century **St Pauli-Kloster**, a Dominican monastery.

To reach the Altstadt, walk back up Steinstrasse to pedestrianised Hauptstrasse and then west over the Havel to the **Museum im Freyhaus** at Ritter Strasse 96. It's a local history museum with much emphasis on the EP Lehmann factory, which produced mechanical toys here in the late 19th century, and the distinctive blue and white pottery from the town of Görzke to the south. The museum is open Tuesday to Friday from 9 am to 5 pm and on Saturday and Sunday from 10 am to 6 pm (DM4/2).

A short distance north-east is the red-brick Gothic **Altstädtischer Rathaus**, with a 'signature' **statue of Roland** (1474) in front symbolising the judicial independence of the town.

Cruises

A number of boat companies offer cruises along the Havel from Am Salzhof in the Altstadt, including Weisse Flotte (☎ 223 95 9) and Bollman Flotte (☎ 663 59 0). The latter has everything – from two-hour spins up and down the river (DM10) to full-day trips to Spandau and disco cruises (every second and fourth Saturday from 6 pm to midnight; DM20).

Special Events

Brandenburg's two big-ticket events are the Havelfest Brandenburg, a folk festival held throughout the Altstadt in mid-June, and the Musiktage der Havelstadt Brandenburg (Music Days of the Havel City of Brandenburg), with an emphasis on 20th-century works, in the first half of September. Tickets can be purchased from the Brandenburger Theaterkasse (☎ 222 59 0) at Steinstrasse 42.

Places to Stay

Accommodation is relatively expensive in Brandenburg, though the tourist office can arrange private rooms from about DM35 per person. The closest camp sites are on Breitlingsee, a large lake about 5km to the west, including *Campingplatz Malge* (☎ 663 13 4) and *Campingplatz Insel Kiehnwerder* (mobile ☎ 0161-630 54 64); both are open from April to October. The DJH *Jugendherberge Brandenburg* (☎ 521 04 0), almost opposite the cathedral at Hevellestrasse 7 (walk through the courtyard), charges juniors/seniors DM18/23 for bed & breakfast. Reception is open from 7 am to 6.30 pm on weekdays and from 5 to 6.30 pm on Saturday and Sunday. You can book by phone, and there's no curfew.

Central places to stay in Brandenburg include *Pension Blaudruck* (☎ 225 73 4), at Steinstrasse 21, with basic singles/doubles for DM40/80, and *Am Beetzseeufer* (☎ 303 31 3), a guesthouse north of Dominsel at Beetzseeufer 6. Singles/doubles with all facilities at this place start at DM78/130. A slightly more central place for a splurge is *Hotel Am St Gotthard* (☎ 529 00; fax 529 03 0), at Mühlentorstrasse 56, with singles/doubles from DM90/130. The poshest place in town is *Hotel Sorat Brandenburg* (☎ 59 70; fax 597 44 4). Singles/doubles with all the mod cons start at DM180/210.

Places to Eat

Dom Café, at Burghof 11, just west of the cathedral, has salad platters from DM5.50 and main courses for about DM15. It's open from April to September between 11 am and 6 pm. For potatoes in just about any form imaginable (soups from DM5.50, main courses from DM6.50 to DM13), try *Kartoffelkäfer* at Steinstrasse 56. *Blaudruck Café*, at No 21 of the same street, has breakfast (DM6.50) and lunch (under DM10) menus. At night it opens its snazzy wine cellar.

Places for a quick, cheap bite include *Pizzeria No 31*, at Steinstrasse 31; *Pizzeria Avanti*, at the corner of Hauptstrasse and Wollenweberstrasse; *Orient Grill*, at Steinstrasse 43; and *Ewald's Imbiss*, on Molkenmarkt. You'll find a *Spar* supermarket at Hauptstrasse 35.

Entertainment

There are organ concerts in the *Dom St Peter und Paul* and *St Katharinen Kirche* in summer; consult the tourist office for times and dates. *Chapeau Claque* is a café-bar at Steinstrasse 26; the *Altstadt* pub, at Ritter Strasse 98, next to the Freyhaus Museum, has live music some nights. *Galerie*, a café-bar with terrace along the Havel on Kommunikation Strasse, has a 'Live Keller' called the *Donna Lee* downstairs.

Getting There & Around

Regional Express RE 1 trains link Brandenburg with Berlin-Zoo station (40 minutes, DM23.30) hourly via Potsdam. From Potsdam the more frequent RB 16 also goes to Brandenburg.

Tram Nos 6 and 9 run from Brandenburg Hauptbahnhof to Hauptstrasse via Steinstrasse and Neustädtischer Markt. A single ride is DM1.90, four tickets cost DM7.60. There's a Fahrradstation (☎ 289 39 8) at the Hauptbahnhof renting bicycles for DM13 a day during opening hours (weekdays from 10 am to 6 pm and Saturday to 2 pm), DM18 until noon the following day, DM35 for the weekend and DM55 per week.

BRANDENBURG

Spreewald

The Spreewald, the watery 'Spree Forest' (287 sq km) of rivers, canals and streams 80km south-east of Berlin, is the closest thing the capital has to a playground. Day trippers and weekend warriors come here in droves to punt on more than 400km of waterways, hike the countless nature trails and fish in this region declared a 'Biosphere Reserve' by UNESCO in 1990. The focal points of most of this activity are the twin towns of Lübben and Lübbenau. The Spreewald is also home to most of Germany's Sorbian minority (see The Sorbs boxed text later in this section), who call the region the Błota. Its unofficial capital is Cottbus, 30km farther to the south-east.

LÜBBEN & LÜBBENAU

- *pop 15,000 & 23,800*
- *area code* ☎ 03546 & ☎ 03542

There's an ongoing debate among Berliners over Lübben (Lubin in Sorbian) and Lübbenau (Lubnjow), which lie 13km apart. Which is the more historical/touristy/picturesque 'Spreewald capital'? Lübben, a tidy and attractive town and the centre of the drier Unterspreewald (Lower Spreewald), has a history going back at least two centuries further than Lübbenau, boasts more interesting architecture and feels like a 'real' town. Lübbenau in the Oberspreewald (Upper Spreewald) is equally picturesque but positively crammed year round with tourists trying to get out onto the canals on *Kähne* (punt boats), once the only way to get around in these parts. A visit to both towns has its merits.

Orientation & Information

Lübben Hauptbahnhof is south-west of the central Markt on Bahnhofstrasse. To reach the centre of town walk north-east along Friedensstrasse and then through the Hain, a large park. The train station in Lübbenau is on Poststrasse, about 600m south of the tourist office.

Lübben's tourist office (☎ 309 0; fax 254 3),

more like a shop than an information centre, is in the Schloss Lübben at Ernst-von-Houwald-Damm 14 and opens weekdays from 10 am to 6 pm, Saturday to 4 pm and Sunday to 3 pm (shorter hours in winter). The tourist office in Lübbenau (☎ 366 8; fax 467 70) is at Ehm-Welk-Strasse 15. From March to October it is open weekdays from 9 am to 6 pm and on Saturday and Sunday to 4 pm. During the rest of the year it's open only on weekdays from 9 am to 4 pm. If you want to learn more about the Spreewald Biosphere Reserve, go to Haus für Mensch und Natur (☎ 892 11 1; fax 892 14 0) at Schulstrasse 9. It's open weekdays from 10 am to 5 pm and, between April and October, at the same times on Saturday and Sunday.

Banks with ATMs on Hauptstrasse in Lübben include a Sparkasse at No 9-10 and a Dresdner Bank at No 13. Both banks also have branches, each with an ATM, in Lübbenau, facing one another on the Topfmarkt. The Dresdner Bank is at No 5 and the Sparkasse at No 8.

Hiking

The Spreewald has hiking and walking trails to suit everyone. The tourist offices sell the 1:25 000 *Oberspreewald* (No 4) and *Unterspreewald* (No 1) maps in the Landesvermessungsamt Brandenburg series for DM9.75 each. These maps are a must if you take your hiking seriously.

From Lübben an easy trail follows the Spree south to Lübbenau (13.2km) and north to Schlepzig (12.3km). From Lübbenau you can follow a nature trail (30 minutes) west to Lehde, the 'Venice of the Spreewald', with its wonderful **Freilandmuseum** (DM6/4) of traditional Sorbian thatched houses and farm buildings. The Leipscher Weg, which starts near the Grosser Hafen on Dammstrasse in Lübbenau, is part of the E10 European Walking Trail from the Baltic to the Adriatic and leads south-west to Leipe, accessible only by boat as recently as 1936. Another popular walk is the 3km one from the Topfmarkt north-east to the Wotschofska restaurant, crossing 14 small bridges.

Boating

The Kahnfahrhafen in Lübben, where you can board punts (DM5 to DM6 per person per hour), is along the Spree south-west of the tourist office. Bootsverleih Gebauer (☎ 719 4) rents one/two-person kayaks for DM7/8 for the first hour and DM4/5 for each additional hour. Day rates are DM28/35 during the week and DM32/40 at the weekend. Canoes cost DM10/7 for the first hour/subsequent hour and DM49/56 per day during the week/weekend.

In Lübbenau there are two 'harbours': the Kleiner Hafen on Spreestrasse, about 100m north-east of the tourist office, and the Grosser Hafen, 300m south-east on Dammstrasse. From the former you can go on a two-hour tour of the canals for DM10; or

BRANDENBURG

The Sorbs

The ancestors of the Sorbs, Germany's only indigenous minority (pop 70,000), were the Slavic Wends, who settled between the Elbe and Oder rivers in the 5th century in an area called Lusatia (Luzia in Sorbian, from *luz* or 'meadow').

Lusatia was conquered by the Germans in the 10th century, subjected to brutal Germanisation throughout the Middle Ages and partitioned in 1815. Lower Sorbia, centred around the Spreewald and Cottbus (Chosebuz), went to Prussia while Upper Sorbia around Bautzen (Budessin), 53km north-east of Dresden, went to Saxony. Upper Sorbian, closely related to Czech, enjoyed certain prestige in Saxony while the Kingdom of Prussia tried to suppress Lower Sorbian, which is similar to Polish. The Nazis tried to eradicate both.

Sorbian has been taught in schools since 1948. ■

paddle as far as Lehde (DM15) and Leipe (DM35). The large Grosser Hafen has any number of punt and boat companies vying for business throughout the year.

Organised Tours

From late April to mid-October the Berlin-based BVB bus company (☎ 030-683 89 10) runs a bus daily to Lübbenau from the central bus station (ZOB) at 7.45 am and from Kurfürstendamm 225 at the corner of Meinekestrasse at 8 am, returning to Berlin at 5.30 pm. The DM40/30 return fare for adults/children includes a ride on a punt.

Lübbenau-based Ewald Pohle (☎ 367 9), Berliner Strasse 23, has tours by van of the Spreewald for DM18 per person.

Special Events

The highlight of the Spreewald Summer (Sommer in German) festival of cultural events is the Tage der Sorbischen Kultur/Dny serbskeje kultury (Days of Sorbian Culture), held in the Markt in Lübben during the first week in June. The Spreewaldfest, with its colourful *Kahnkorso* (punt competition), is held in Lübben in late September.

Places to Stay

The DJH *Jugendherberge Lübben* (☎ 304 6) is at Zum Wendenfürsten 8, about 2.5km south of the centre. It charges juniors/seniors DM18.50/22 for bed & breakfast. The DJH *Jugendherberge Burg* (☎ 035603-225), at Weg zur Jugendherberge 220 in Burg, south-east of Lübbenau, charges the same rates.

Spreewald-Camping (☎ 705 3 or ☎ 333 5) in Lübben, across the Spree from the tourist office at Am Burglehn, charges DM5/3/7/3 per tent/car/adult/child. They also rent caravans accommodating two/three/four people for DM25/30/40. *Campingplatz Am Schlosspark* (☎ 353 3) is a short distance east of the Schloss Lübbenau.

Lübben and Lübbenau have plenty of private rooms from DM25 per person; the tourist offices can organise one for you for a DM5 booking fee.

In Lübben, the central *Pension Am Markt* (☎ 457 6; fax 327 2), at Hauptstrasse 5, has singles/doubles from DM50/70. The lovely *Hotel Spreeufer* (☎ 800 3; fax 806 9), near the bridge just south of Hauptstrasse at Hinter der Mauer 4, has singles/doubles from DM80/100.

In Lübbenau, the *Pension Spreewald-Idyll* (☎ 225 1), at Spreestrasse 13, is quiet and has a good restaurant. Singles/doubles cost DM50/80. The *Ebusch* (☎ & fax 367 0), at Topfmarkt 4, is a dumpy pension with a restaurant. Singles/doubles start at DM60/90. *Pension Höhn* (☎ 457 22; fax 468 88), at Dammstrasse 38, is a fairly basic place with doubles for DM80. For a real splurge check in at the *Hotel Schloss Lübbenau* (☎ 873 0; fax 873 66 6), east of the centre at Schlossbezirk 6. Singles/doubles start at DM150/200.

Places to Eat

Goldener Löwe, a somewhat touristy but decent place at Hauptstrasse 15 in Lübben, has a lovely beer garden and serves fresh-water fish dishes from DM12. There are a number of cheap *Imbiss* (snack) stands just opposite the NKD Citykauf department store at the start of Hauptstrasse.

One of the nicest places for a meal in Lübbenau is the cosy *Lübbenauer Hof*, at Ehm-Welk-Strasse 20, with main courses from DM17. The restaurant at the *Pension Spreewald-Idyll*, at Spreestrasse 13, is also quite good, with salads from DM4 and main courses from DM12. If you want to try eel, pike or tench *(Aal, Hecht, Schleie)* pulled from the Spree, try *Strubel's* at Dammstrasse 3, where main courses are about DM20. A much cheaper alternative is *Heuschober*, two doors from the tourist office at Ehm-Welk-Strasse 13, where a bowl of fish stew is DM6.50. The *butcher shop* at Ehm-Welk-Strasse 3 (open weekdays from 8 am to 6 pm and Saturday until noon) has the usual ready-to-eat *Wurst* (DM2) and half-chickens. Pizzas at *Café Fontane*, Ehm-Welk-Strasse 42, start at DM6.50.

Getting There & Around

The Regional Express RE 2 train serves

DAVID PEEVERS

Brandenburg
Sanssouci Park, Potsdam

DAVID PEEVERS

DAVID PEEVERS

DAVID PEEVERS

DAVID PEEVERS

A	B
	C
	D

Thuringia

A: Typical onion decorations, Weimar

B: Aerial view of Erfurt

C: Medieval Festival, Kapellendorf Castle

D: Wartburg Castle, Eisenach

Lübben/Lübbenau every two hours from Berlin-Lichtenberg and Berlin-Schöneweide (about one hour, DM31.30/35.70) en route to Cottbus. The regional RB 14 also serves the two towns from Berlin-Schöneweide.

The tourist office in Lübben rents bicycles for DM10 a day as does K-Heinz Oswald (☎ 406 3), at An der Spreewaldbahn 6, north-west of the centre.

In Lübbenau, try Kretschmann (☎ 343 3) at Poststrasse 16.

COTTBUS

- *pop 125,700*
- *area code* ☎ 0355

Cottbus (Chošebuz in Sorbian) is a pretty town with some wonderful architecture and a decent number of cultural offerings.

The tourist office (☎ 242 54; fax 791 93 1) is at Berliner Strasse 1; the Sorbischen Kulturinformation Lodka (☎ 791 11 0), in the Wendisch Haus at August-Bebel-Strasse 82, provides information about the Sorbs – and serves excellent (and authentic) Sorbian specialities at its café.

Those who are interested in Sorbian culture should check out the **Wendsiches Museum/Serbski muzej** at Mühlenstrasse 12, which thoroughly examines this Slavic people's history, language and culture. It's open weekdays from 8.30 am to 5 pm and Saturday and Sunday from 2 to 6 pm. Admission costs DM4/2.

Other places worth inspection in Cottbus include the 15th-century **Oberkirche** on Oberkirchplatz west of the central Altmarkt; the Jugendstil **Staatstheater** on Schillerplatz to the south-west; and **Branitzer Park** to the south-east, with its lovely 18th-century baroque Schloss and the Seepyramide, a curious grass-covered pyramid 'floating' in a little lake nearby.

The RE 2 leaves Berlin-Lichtenberg for Cottbus, via Lübben and Lübbenau (1½ hours, DM48.50), about every two hours. You can also reach Cottbus from the Spreewald twin towns on the RB 41. Cottbus is linked with Frankfurt an der Oder (1¼ hours) by the RE 1.

Märkische Schweiz & Oderbruch

For a region where the highest 'peak' reaches a mere 129m (Krugberg, north of Buckow), 'Switzerland of the March of Brandenburg' is a rather grandiose label. But it is a lung for Berlin – a land of clear streams, lakes and beautiful, low-lying hills. The lovely town of Buckow, the 'pearl of the Märkische Schweiz', has long been a popular place for rest and recreation for Berliners. The Oderbruch region to the south couldn't be more different: it is flat, marshy, prone to flooding and has as its centre the dull city of Frankfurt an der Oder.

BUCKOW

- *pop 1800*
- *area code* ☎ 033433

In 1854 Friedrich Wilhelm IV's physician advised His Majesty to visit this village, where 'the lungs go as on velvet', and Fontane praised its 'friendly landscape' in *Das Oderlands* (1863), the second book in his four-volume travelogue. But Buckow really only made it on the map in the early 1950s, when Bertolt Brecht and Helene Weigel spent their summers here, away from the hot and humid capital of the new GDR.

Orientation & Information

Buckow, in the centre of the 205-sq-km Märkische Schweiz Nature Park, is surrounded by five lakes, the largest of which is Schermützelsee (146 hectares in area, 45m deep). Wriezener Strasse, the main street where you'll find the tourist office (☎ 659 81; fax 659 20) at No 1a, runs parallel to the lake before becoming Hauptstrasse, at the end of which is the train station (about 800m). The tourist office is open weekdays from 9 am to noon and 1 to 5 pm, Saturday from 10 am to 5 pm (to 2 pm November to March) and Sunday (April to October only) from 1 to 4 pm.

There's a Sparkasse with an ATM just west

of the tourist office at Wriezener Strasse 2. The post office is at Hauptstrasse 84.

Things to See

Brecht-Weigel-Haus, where the GDR's first couple of the arts spent their summers from 1952 to 1955, is at Bertolt-Brecht-Strasse 29. The easiest way to reach it is to walk due west on Werderstrasse, but it's much more fun strolling along Ringstrasse and Bertolt-Brecht-Strasse admiring the posh villas and mansions that once housed the elite of the GDR. Brecht's house is a relatively simple affair with an overhanging roof, geometric patterns outside and a relief of Europa riding a bull over the front door.

Among the photos, documents and original furnishings inside is Mother Courage's covered wagon; outside in the fine gardens are copper tablets engraved with Brecht's words. The Brecht-Weigel-Haus is open April to October, Wednesday to Friday from 1 to 5 pm and to 6 pm on Saturday and Sunday. During the rest of the year it's open Wednesday to Friday from 10 am to noon and 1 to 4 pm and on Sunday from 11 am to 4 pm. Admission is DM3/1.50.

The **Eisenbahnmuseum** (Railroad Museum) at the train station is open May to October on Saturday and Sunday from 10 am to 4 pm (DM2/1). Much is made of the Buchower Kleinbahn, the little forest train that has been running for 100 years between here and Müncheberg to the south.

The **Ehemaliges Rechenzentrum der Nationale Volksarmee** (Former Computer Centre of the GDR National People's Army) is in a huge 70-room bunker some 15m underground at Gladowshöher Strasse 3 in Garzau, 12km south-west of Buckow. It can be visited on a two-hour tour (DM15/5). Ring ☎ 033435-742 01 to book. Unfortunately, Garzau is not served by public transport from Buckow. Don't forget to bring some warm clothes – it's a chilly 12°C down there in summer and 8°C in winter.

Activities

Buckow is paradise for hikers and walkers; there are marked trails fanning out in every direction. You can follow the Panoramaweg from north of Buckow clear around the Schermützelsee (7.5km), the Drachenkehle north to Krugberg (5km), the Poetensteig to the north-east above the Kleiner Tornowsee, the Grosser Tornowsee to Pritzhagener Mühle (9km), or the Alter Schulsteig to Dreieichen (10km). The tourist office sells two useful maps with marked walks: *Märkische Schweiz Reisegebiet Karte* (DM6.50) and the 1:25,000 *Märkische Schweiz Topographische Karte* (DM9.75). The Kneipp- und Heimatvereins Märkische Schweiz (☎ 575 00), in the same building as the tourist office, organises walking tours in the area on some Saturday mornings from April to October.

There's a Strandbad (beach) with a raft and diving board on the north-east tip of Schermützelsee. Entry is DM3. At the dock just south you can rent rowing boats or go on a cruise with Seetours (☎ 232). In season, the large MS *Scherri* sails hourly from Tuesday to Sunday between 10 am and 5 pm while the little MS *Seeadler* sails Saturday and Sunday only from 10.30 am to 5.30 pm.

A trip to the Pension Buchenfried and Fischerkehle restaurant at the south-western end of the lake and back is DM7/3.50, or you can go just one way for DM5/2.50 (taking a bike along costs DM2). If you want to do some angling, stop in at Fred Schüler (☎ 571 28), at Wriezener Strasse 54. Four-hour/day-long fishing trips cost DM10/15. A permit is DM6 a day.

The Kurbahn, a mini-coach made up to look like a train that you wouldn't be caught dead on at home for fear of embarrassment, twirls around the nature park from in front of the Strandbad on Saturday and Sunday between noon and 6 pm (DM7/5).

Places to Stay

The DJH *Jugendherberge Buckow* (☎ 286) is south-west of the tourist office at Berliner Strasse 36; to reach it from the train station walk north on Hauptstrasse and turn left (west) onto Berliner Strasse. It charges juniors/seniors DM20/25 for bed & breakfast.

The tourist office can organise private rooms from DM30 per person plus DM2 booking fee, or you can make your own deal by going directly to the source; Königstrasse and Lindenstrasse (east and north-east of the travel office) have the richest pickings. One of the most central places is *Rosemarie Krüger* (☎ 296), Königstrasse 55 at the corner of Wallstrasse, with singles/doubles for DM30/50.

Pensions close to the centre of town include *Zur Märkische Schweiz* (☎ 464), near the post office at Hauptstrasse 73, with rooms from DM55 per person, and the very central *Schlossburg* (☎ 385), at Wriezener Strasse 59, with singles/doubles for DM80/100.

Pension Buchenfried (☎ 575 63; fax 575 62) enjoys an enviable position on the south-western shore of Schermützelsee at Am Fischerberg 9, but it's a bit away from whatever action there is in Buckow and costs DM76/110 for singles/doubles. Much closer to town but still near the water is *Pension Strandcafé* (☎ 279; fax 680 6), with rooms for DM55 per person.

The palatial *Bergschlösschen* (☎ 573 12; fax 574 12), at Königstrasse 38-41, could once lay claim to being the swankiest place in town (singles/doubles with full facilities cost DM110/160), but it must now take a back seat to the *Stobbermühle* (☎ 668 66; fax 668 44), a very chi-chi 'apartment hotel' (suites from DM148, breakfast DM12 extra).

Places to Eat

The restaurant at the *Stobbermühle* (see Places to Stay above) is superb, with inventive starters/main courses (from DM6.50/19) – worthy of a hotel in a world-class city, not pokey (but pretty) little Buckow. Try the potato and cress soup with lox (a kind of smoked salmon) and any of the fabulous duck dishes. A popular place with tourists is the 85-year-old *Fischerkehle* on the south-west shore of the lake at Am Fischerberg 7.

Buckow boasts a Vietnamese restaurant – the *Minh Hoa* at Königstrasse 33. There's a stylish Chinese place called *Chao'sche* in a lovely old villa at Bertolt-Brecht-Strasse 9, open daily from 11.30 am to 11.30 pm.

A very central place for a quick pizza is the *Café Am Markt* in the Markt where Wriezener Strasse meets Hauptstrasse. It's open Tuesday to Sunday. *Mini Grill* on Wriezener Strasse, almost opposite the tourist office, sells kebabs and takeaways daily from 11 am to 8 pm. There's an *Edeka* supermarket on Wriezener Strasse, next to the Sparkasse, open weekdays from 7.30 am to 6 pm and Saturday from noon. An open-air *market* sets up every Thursday morning on the Markt.

Special Events

In July and August the open-air theatre in the Schlosspark behind the tourist office stages plays for children. Contact the Schlosspark Sommer Theater (☎ 562 97) at Neue Promenade 30-31 for details.

Getting There & Around

There are two ways to reach Buckow from Berlin. The RB 26 leaves hourly from Berlin-Lichtenberg for Müncheberg, where you change to the toy train RB 29 for two stops (total travel time one hour, DM23.30). Buses connect Müncheberg with Buckow four times a day on weekdays. A slower but cheaper alternative is to take the S-Bahn No 5 to Strausberg and board the bus there (11 departures on weekdays, three on Saturday and Sunday) to Buckow via Hohenstein and Bollersdorf.

The Haus Wilhelmshöhe (☎ 246), a hotel at Lindenstrasse 10-11, has bicycles for rent.

FRANKFURT AN DER ODER

- *pop 84,000*
- *area code* ☎ 0335

It's difficult to imagine a city in all of Germany less welcoming than Frankfurt an der Oder. It's the kind of place where staff at a café will refuse to bring you a cup of coffee because 'we're not serving outside today', a query at the tourist office as to whether any of the staff speak English or French will be met with a resounding *Nee* (that's dialect for

Nein), and you'll almost certainly get a parking ticket.

Frankfurt has had more than its share of troubles, despite its early successful start. As the easiest place at which to cross the Oder, it prospered as a centre of trade from the early 13th century and within 150 years had become a member of the Hanseatic League. For centuries the town was known for its three annual fairs. During WWII the city, with some 750 medieval houses, was evacuated. In the last few days before Germany's surrender in May 1945, a holdout group of Nazi guerrillas engaged in hand-to-hand combat with Polish soldiers. Frankfurt was burned to the ground in the process, with only five of the old houses left standing. In the summer of 1997, Frankfurt and the surrounding area was struck by the 'flood of the century', causing millions of Deutschmarks worth of damage.

Frankfurt is an easy gateway to Poland and points beyond; Slubice, a town that seems to exist only to supply Frankfurters with cut-rate tobacco and booze, is five minutes away over the Oder.

Information

Frankfurt's tourist office (☎ 325 21 6; fax 225 65) is at Karl-Marx-Strasse 8a, a stone's throw from the unspeakable, 23-storey, shoebox-like Oderturm (Oder Tower, 1976). It opens on weekdays from 10 am to 6 pm (with a half-hour break at noon) and from 10 am to 12.30 pm on Saturday. There's a Sparkasse ATM on Schmalzgasse off Karl-Marx-Strasse, and a Commerzial Bank with an ATM on the corner of Karl-Marx-Strasse and Logenstrasse. Just opposite, in the splendid Haus der Künste (1902), is the post office.

Things to See & Do

There's not much in the way of sights in this town. You might have a look inside the **St Gertraudkirche**, at Gertraudenplatz 6 off Lindenstrasse, whose treasures were all brought from the ruined **Marienkirche** on Grosser Scharrnstrasse. The 14th-century **Rathaus**, just north on Bischofstrasse, has a golden herring (Frankfurt had the trading monopoly on this salt-laden commodity) hanging from its lovely south gable. Inside is the **Museum Junge Kunst** of GDR art – but don't tarry.

Places to Stay & Eat

The tourist office can organise private rooms from DM35 per person plus a DM5 booking fee. The closest affordable pension to the Stadtbrücke (City Bridge), allowing you an early morning getaway, is *Pension Wagner* (☎ 238 90; fax 533 98 8), in the Kleistpark at Humboldtstrasse 14, with doubles for DM100.

Should you get hungry near the combined train and bus stations, *Broilereck*, to the south-west at Tunnelstrasse 48, serves chicken and salad (of sorts) for well under DM10, daily from 11 am to 11 pm. There are a number of *Imbisse* next to the *Kaiser's* supermarket on Heilbronner Strasse. Closer to town there's a *Mensa* (student cafeteria) on Kellenspring near the river (open 8.30 am to 3.30 pm), or try the *Studenten Passage* takeaway place on Schmalzgasse, open weekdays from 8.30 am to 7.30 pm, to 2 pm on Saturday. *Café Calliope*, in the Haus der Künste at Lindenstrasse 5, has pizzas and pasta from DM8. *Kartoffel Haus*, with potato-based specialities, or *Das total unmögliche Gasthaus* (The Totally Ridiculous Inn) are trendy places on Holzmarkt, just north of the Kleist Museum.

Getting There & Around

Frankfurt is served hourly by regional RE 1 trains from Berlin-Hauptbahnhof (one hour, DM27.30); they carry on from Frankfurt to Cottbus (1¼ hours). There are also good connections via the RB 60 to Eberswalde via Niederfinow. To reach the centre of town from the bus and train stations, walk north on Bahnhofstrasse and east on Heilbronner Strasse or jump on tram No 1 or 3 (or bus A, B, D or G) and get off at Schmalzgasse (DM1.50).

A Fahrradstation (☎ 564 24 44) at the Hauptbahnhof rents bicycles for DM13 a day during opening hours (weekdays from 10 am to 6 pm and Saturday to 2 pm), DM18 until noon the following day, DM35 for the weekend and DM55 per week.

Northern Brandenburg

SACHSENHAUSEN CONCENTRATION CAMP

In 1936 the Nazis opened a 'model' *Konzentrationslager* (concentration camp) for men in a disused brewery in Sachsenhausen, near the town of Oranienburg (pop 28,000), about 35km north of Berlin. Inmates (political undesirables, gays, Jews, Gypsies – the usual Nazi targets) were forced to make bricks, hand grenades and weapons, counterfeit dollar and pound banknotes (to flood Allied countries and wreak economic havoc) and even to test out boot leather for days on end on a special track. By 1945 about 220,000 men from 22 countries had passed through the gates of Sachsenhausen KL – labeled, as at Auschwitz in south-western Poland, *Arbeit Macht Frei* ('Work Sets You Free'); about 100,000 were murdered here, their mortal remains consumed by the fires of the horrible ovens.

After the war, the Soviets and the Communist leaders of the new GDR set up *Speziallager No 7* (Special Camp No 7) for political prisoners, rightists, ex-Nazis, monarchists or whoever didn't happen to fit into *their* mould. An estimated 60,000 people were interned at the camp between 1945 and 1950, and up to 12,000 are believed to have died here. There's a mass grave of victims at the camp and another one 1.5km to the north.

You should visit Sachsenhausen, a place of hatred, violence and death, to remind yourself that such things did not fly away with the war. It's an easy day – or even half-day – trip from Berlin.

Orientation & Information

The triangular shaped, walled camp (31 hectares) is about 2km north-east of Oranienburg train station, but it's an easy, signposted 20-minute walk. Follow Stralsunder Strasse north and turn east (right) onto Bernauer Strasse. After about 600m turn left at Strasse der Einheit and then right on Strasse der Nationen, which leads to the main entrance. If you're really weary, you can catch bus No 804 or 805 as far as the corner of Bernauer Strasse and Strasse der Einheit.

A short distance north of the train station, at Stralsunder Strasse 31, is the Touristik-Information Oranienburg (☎ & fax 03301-535 38 5), open weekdays from 8 am to 4 pm. There's also an information office (☎ 03301-803 71 5; fax 803 71 8) in the camp itself, selling maps, brochures and books.

Gedenkstätte und Museum Sachsenhausen

The Sachsenhausen Memorial and Museum consists of several parts. As you approach the entrance, along a quiet tree-lined lane, you'll see a memorial to the 6000 prisoners who died on the *Todesmarsch* (Death March) of April 1945, after the Nazis emptied the camp of its 33,000 prisoners and tried to march them to the Baltic in advance of the Red Army.

At the end of this road, past a mass grave of 300 prisoners who died in the infirmary after liberation on 22-23 April 1945, the camp commandant's house and the so-called Green Monster (where SS troops were trained in the finer arts of concentration-camp maintenance), is the **Neues Museum** (New Museum), with excellent exhibits, including a history of anti-Semitism and audiovisual material.

East of the New Museum are **Barracks 38 & 39**, reconstructions of two typical huts housing most of the 6000 Jewish prisoners brought to Sachsenhausen after Kristallnacht (9-10 November 1938). They are now being rebuilt after having been burned to the ground by neo-Nazis in September 1992 just days after a visit by the late Israeli Prime Minister Yitzhak Rabin.

Just north of Barracks 38 & 39 is the **prison**, where particularly brutal punishment was meted out, and prisoners were placed in stifling blackened cells. Nearby is a memorial, bearing the pink triangle, to the homosexuals who died here, one of the few monuments you'll see anywhere to these 'forgotten victims' (there's another one at the Nollendorfplatz U-Bahn station in Berlin).

To get to the **Lagersmuseum** (Camp Museum), with moth-eaten and dusty exhibits which focus on both the Nazi concentration camp and Special Camp No 7, walk north along the parade ground where endless roll calls took place, past the site of the gallows. The museum is housed in the building on the right, once the camp kitchen. In the former laundry room opposite, a particularly gruesome film of the camp after liberation is shown throughout the day. Steel yourself before entering.

To the left of the tall, ugly monument – erected by the GDR in 1961 in memory of political prisoners interned here – is the **crematorium** and **Station Z extermination site**, a pit for shooting prisoners in the neck and a wooden 'catch' where bullets could be retrieved and re-used. A memorial hall on the site of the **gas chamber** is a fitting visual metaphor for the 'glorious' Third Reich and the 'workers' paradise' of the GDR: subsidence has caused it to sink, its paving stones are cracked and the roof is toppling over an area containing, we're told, 'considerable remains from corpses incinerated in the crematorium'.

To the north-east, beyond the wall, are **stone barracks** built to house Allied POWs in 1941. From 1945 German officers and others sentenced by the Soviet military tribunal were imprisoned here. To the north is a mass grave from the latter period.

When you've had a look around this silent, almost antiseptic place, make your way to the central parade ground and try to imagine a roll call lasting up to 26 hours, with prisoners on either side of you shitting in their pants from dysentery or fear, the smell of disease and death. And the hunger, always the hunger… Then the trampling on the stones begins – to test, for God's sake, the soles of the boots for the soldiers of the glorious, 1000-year Reich. Let your eyes stray up to the open sky and do something the inmates here could not do… Don't say but shout: 'Never! Never! Never again!' Whoever wasn't listening 50 years ago just might have tuned in by now.

The Sachsenhausen Memorial & Museum are open from April to September, Tuesday to Sunday from 8.30 am to 6 pm (to 4.30 pm the rest of the year). Admission is free.

Places to Eat

Food will probably be the last thing on your mind when you leave Sachsenhausen, but if you need a cup of coffee or a fortifying schnapps to bring you back to the 'saner' late 20th century, there's a café called *Lena* at Bernauer Strasse 60. Opposite the tourist office, at Stralsunder Strasse 3, *Kro-El No 1* and its adjoining *Imbiss* have pizzas/pasta/salads from DM6/6.50/4. Between 5 and 7 pm all drinks here are half price.

Getting There & Away

The easiest way to get to Sachsenhausen from Berlin is to take the S-Bahn No 1 to Oranienburg (50 minutes, DM3.90), which runs every 20 minutes.

RHEINSBERG

- *pop 5500*
- *area code* ☎ 033931

A moated castle stood on the shores of the Grienericksee from the early Middle Ages to protect the March of Brandenburg's northern border from the marauders of Mecklenburg. But the Schloss Rheinsberg as we see it today only began to take shape in 1566, when its owner, Achim von Bredow, had it rebuilt in the Renaissance style. Friedrich Wilhelm I purchased it in 1734 for his 22-year-old son, Crown Prince Friedrich (the future Frederick the Great), and expanded the palace and cleaned up the town – paving roads, plastering house façades and tiling roofs. The palace and town remained a favourite of the royal family until the early 19th century.

Today Rheinsberg has much to offer visitors: concerts in the palace, walks in the lovely Schlosspark to the south, boating on the lake and Rhin River, some top-notch restaurants and affordable accommodation.

Orientation & Information

Rheinsberg hugs the south-eastern shore of Grienericksee, a large lake with boating and fishing possibilities. The centre of town is the Markt, where you'll find the friendly tourist office (☎ & fax 205 9) in the Kavalierhaus. It is open year round from Monday to Saturday between 9.30 am and 5 pm and on Sunday from 10 am to 2 pm. Buses stop on Mühlenstrasse just south of Schlossstrasse. The train station is about 1km south-east of the Markt on Berliner Strasse.

Sparkasse has a branch at Berliner Strasse 16, and there's an ATM booth in Kirchplatz in front of the 13th-century Kirche St Laurentius (Church of St Lawrence). The post office is at the corner of Schlossstrasse and Poststrasse.

Schloss Rheinsberg

Crown Prince Friedrich said the four years (1736-40) he spent here studying and preparing for the throne were the happiest of his life. He oversaw much of the remodelling of the palace, by Johann Gottfried Kemmeter and Knobelsdorff; some say this was his 'test', on a minor scale, of the much grander Schloss Sanssouci (1747) in Potsdam. After he left for Berlin, Friedrich handed the palace keys to his brother Prince Heinrich, who lorded over the estate until his death in 1802.

During WWII art treasures from Potsdam were stored at Schloss Rheinsberg, which was somehow spared in the bombings. Alas, the palace was looted in 1945 and used as a sanatorium by the Communists from 1953. Today, Schloss Rheinsberg is a mere shadow of its former self, but it is being renovated at a furious pace. No doubt you'll see restorers touching up frescos and gilding as you walk around.

A tour of the palace takes in about two dozen, mostly empty, rooms on the 1st floor, including the oldest ones: the Hall of Mirrors, where young Friedrich held flute contests; the Tower Chamber, where the future king studied and which he recreated in the Berlin Schloss in 1745; and the Bacchus Room, with a ceiling painting of a very old-looking Ganymede. Among our favourites, though, are the Lacquer Room, with its *chinoiserie*; Prince Heinrich's bedchamber, with an exquisite *trompe l'oeil* ceiling; and the rococo Shell Room.

The ground floor of the north wing contains the **Kurt Tucholsky Gedenkstätte**, a small memorial museum dedicated to the life and work of writer Kurt Tucholsky (1890-1935). He wrote a popular novel called *Rheinsberg – ein Tagebuch für Verliebte* (Rheinsberg – A Lovers' Diary) in which the young swain Wolfgang traipses through the Schloss with his beloved Claire in tow, putting the palace and the town of Rheinsberg firmly on the literary map.

The palace and museum are open April to October Tuesday to Sunday from 9.30 am to 5 pm with a half-hour break at 12.30 pm. During the rest of the year it opens at 10 am and closes at 4 or 5 pm.

Admission to the palace is DM6/4 (family card DM15), and to the museum it costs DM2/1.

Activities

Reederei Halbeck (☎ 386 19), next to the tourist office at Markt 11, offers a number of lake and river cruises – from two hours for DM14 to 12 hours for DM35. The Untermühle guesthouse (☎ 204 2), at Untermühle 2, rents horses for DM15 an hour and canoes and two-person kayaks for DM50/200 a day/week. They also have canoe and kayak day tours of the Rhin River for DM80.

Ponyhof Fatima (☎ 279 7), at Schlossstrasse 35, offers pony rides and short treks for DM5/9 per half-hour/hour daily at 3 pm.

Special Events

The Rheinsberger Musiktage (Rheinsberg Music Days) is a three-day festival of music round the clock – from jazz and chamber music to children's cabaret. It takes place around Whitsun/Pentecost in May/June. Ring ☎ 205 7 for information. The Musikakademie Rheinsberg (☎ 205 7), in the Kavalierhaus, performs opera and classical music in the Hall of Mirrors, the palace courtyard and St Lawrence Church from late June to mid-August. Tickets (DM15 to DM55) are available from the tourist office or, in Berlin, from the TAKS ticket agency (☎ 030-341 02 03).

Places to Stay

The closest hostel and camp sites are at Zechlinerhütte, about 6km north of Rheinsberg. The DJH *Jugendherberge Prebelow/ Zechlinerhütte* (☎ 033921-222), Prebelow 2, charges juniors/seniors DM18/23 for bed & breakfast; lunch/dinner is available for DM6/5.50. *Campingplatz Berner Land* (☎ 033921-702 83), at Am Bikowsee 4, is open all year. Only two buses a day on weekdays (6 am and 1.55 pm) connect Rheinsberg with Zechlinerhütte.

There are no end of private rooms available (from DM20 per person) in Rheinsberg; just walk along Lange Strasse (eg at Nos 9, 11, 43 and 45), Paulshorster Strasse (Nos 9 and 31) and Menzerstrasse (No 2), which is the continuation of Schlossstrasse, looking for *Zimmer Frei* signs.

The cheapest guesthouse is the *Goldener Stern* (☎ 217 9), at Mühlenstrasse 4, with singles/doubles for DM50/80, but it's a dump; instead try *Pension Butschak* (☎ 275 3), Menzerstrasse 6, with spick-and-span singles/doubles in a quiet garden for DM60/ 80. *Zum Jungen Fritz* (☎ 409 0; fax 409 34), near the Church of St Lawrence at Schlossstrasse 8, is a lovely little guesthouse with singles/doubles from DM80/115.

Pension Am Rheinsberger Schlosspark (☎ 392 71; fax 392 70), due south of the palace in the park at Fontaneplatz 2, is surprisingly affordable with singles/doubles from DM90/120. If you really want to break the bank, head for the *Deutsches Haus Atrium Hotel* (☎ 390 59; fax 390 63), at Seestrasse 13, with singles/doubles from DM120/200.

Places to Eat

Among the excellent new restaurants in Rheinsberg is the popular *Seehof*, just up from the boat dock at Seestrasse 18. If you're not inclined to eat here, at least have a beer in the lovely back courtyard. The *Schloss Rheinsberg* restaurant at the Deutsches Haus Atrium Hotel is the town's silver-service restaurant, with prices to match. *Zum Alten Fritz*, at Schlossstrasse 11, is an excellent place for north German specialities like Schlesisches Krustenbraten (ham with beans and parsley potatoes, DM17), Märkische Rinderrouladen (beef olives à la March, DM18) and Hasenpfeffer (jugged hare, DM13.50). Fish dishes (mostly trout) cost around DM18. It's open daily from 11.30 am to 11 pm.

Al Castello, in the Rhin Passage, a mall on Rhinstrasse, has pizzas/pastas from DM7/ 8.50. If you crave something Asian, walk a few steps over to the *Garden* Chinese restaurant with starters/main courses from DM4/ 15. They have good-value weekday lunches for DM12. *Orient*, at Mühlenstrasse 13, has cheap takeaway kebabs and pizzas and is popular with Rheinsberg's young bloods, who race their souped-up Trabis around the Markt. You'll find a *Spar* supermarket on Schlossstrasse.

Entertainment

When was the last time you watched a movie at a *drive-in*? There's one (☎ 033923-704 26) at Zempow, about 15km north-west of Rheinsberg, charging DM1 per car and DM7 per person. Obviously you'll need a car.

Things to Buy

Rheinsberg is a traditional centre of faïence and ceramics; you can visit the Rheinsbergische Keramik Manufaktur (RKM) in the Rhin Passage seven days a week from 10 am (9 am on Saturday) to 6 pm. Not surprisingly, there's a large outlet with RKM wares for sale.

Getting There & Around

Rheinsberg can be reached from Berlin (two hours, DM35.70) on the regional RB 54 train from Oranienburg, which is on the S-Bahn No 1 from Friedrichstrasse. Two buses a day make the trip between Oranienburg train station and Rheinsberg, stopping at Mühlenstrasse south-east of the Markt. Deutsche Bahn runs steam trains from Berlin to Rheinsberg on certain Sundays throughout

Brandenburg's Fontane of Knowledge

In 1859, Theodor Fontane (pronounced 'foon-TAH-neh'), a Huguenot writer from Neuruppin in north-west Brandenburg, set out on a series of walking tours of the March. To the eternal gratitude of the Tourismusverband Land Brandenburg (Tourism Association of the State of Brandenburg), Fontane wrote all about these experiences in his four-volume *Wanderungen durch die Mark Brandenburg* (Travels through the March of Brandenburg), published between 1862 and 1882. His name is everywhere nowadays – in travel brochures, on 'Fontane Slept Here' plaques and in bookshop display windows. Wherever you find yourself, Fontane was there first.

Moving around the state, you might get the impression that Fontane (1819-98) was just an old travel hack who 'did' Brandenburg, and not the greatest master of the social novel German literature has known. But he did say a lot of nice things about the March – from Rheinsberg and Chorin to Buckow and the Spreewald.

Fontane is buried in the Französischer Friedhof (French Cemetery) in Berlin's Mitte district. But prepare for company; he still enjoys a wide following, and there are always pilgrims milling about his modest tombstone. ■

the year, leaving Berlin-Lichtenberg station at 9.09 am and Rheinsberg station for the return journey at 2.53 pm. Ask DB or the tourist office for details.

The Fahrradhaus Thäns (☎ 262 2), also called Sporthaus, at Schlossstrasse 16, rents bicycles for DM10/63 a day/week and mountain bikes for DM15/95. It's open weekdays from 9 am to 12.30 pm and 2 to 6 pm and on Saturday from 9 am to noon.

CHORIN

- *pop 522*
- *area code* ☎ 033366

Kloster Chorin (Chorin Monastery), in this little town 60km north-east of Berlin, is considered to be one of the finest red-brick Gothic structures in northern Germany, and the classical-music festival held here in summer is world-class. There's no tourist office, but the reception desk at the Hotel Haus Chorin (☎ 447 or ☎ 500) acts as a sort of de facto information centre.

Chorin was founded by Cistercian monks in 1273, and 500 of them laboured over six decades to erect their monastery and church of red brick on a granite base (a practice later copied by the Franciscans at the Nikolaikirche and Marienkirche in Berlin). The monastery was secularised in 1542 following Elector Joachim II's conversion to Protestantism and, after the Thirty Years' War, it fell into disrepair. Renovation of the structure (instigated by Schinkel) has gone on in a somewhat haphazard fashion since the early 19th century.

The entrance to the monastery is through the bright red and ornate western façade and leads to the central cloister and ambulatory, where the summer concerts are held. To the north is the early-Gothic **Klosterkirche** with its wonderful carved portals and long lancet windows in the apse. Have a look along the walls at floor level to see the layer of granite supporting the porous handmade bricks. The monastery is open daily from April to October between 9 am and 6 pm and to 4 pm the rest of the year. Admission is DM3/1.50 and you have to pay DM3 to park.

The celebrated Choriner Musiksommer takes place in the monastery cloister from June to August on most Saturdays and Sundays at 3 pm; expect to hear some top talent. For information contact the Chorin Music Summer organisers (☎ 03334-657 31 0), Schickelstrasse 5, in Eberswalde Finow. Tickets are available through ticket agencies in Berlin. There are chamber music concerts in the church, said to have near perfect acoustics, on certain Sundays at 4 pm from late May to August.

Getting There & Away

Chorin is served from Berlin-Lichtenberg

(one hour, DM27.30) about every two hours by the RE 3. The train station in Chorin town is about 3km north-west of the monastery, but you can reach it via a marked trail in less than a half-hour. Buses link Chorin with Eberswalde Hauptbahnhof, which is served by the RE 3 from Berlin as well as the RB 60 to/from Frankfurt an der Oder (1¾ hours). They stop close to the monastery entrance along the B2.

NIEDERFINOW

- *pop 700*
- *area code* ☎ 033362

The Schiffshebewerk (ship's lift) at Niederfinow, south-east of Chorin, is one of the most remarkable feats of engineering from the early 20th century. It's also fun, especially for kids. A mechanical hoist (1934) allows barges to clear the difference of 36m in height between the Oder River and the Oder-Havel Canal. This being Germany, technical data about the structure is posted everywhere ('60m high, 27m wide, 94m long' etc), but it's still an amazing sight watching 1200-tonne Polish barges laden with coal being hoisted in a watery cradle up from the Oder and deposited in the canal.

The lift can be viewed from Hebewerkstrasse for free, but it's much more fun to pay the DM2/1 and climb the steps to the upper platform to view the 10-minute operation from above. It's open daily from May to September between 9 am and 6 pm, to 4 pm the rest of the year.

There's supposed to be a tourist information point (☎ 701 95) in the car park on Hebewerkstrasse next to the lift, but you'll be lucky to find it open. Instead contact the Eberswalde tourist office (☎ 03334-231 68) in the Pavillion am Markt.

Oder-Havel Schiffahrt (mobile ☎ 0171-551 80 85) has 1½-hour boat trips (DM8/4) along the Oder-Havel Canal and down onto the Oder via the Schiffshebewerk a couple of times a day between April and October. The embarkation point is along the canal about 3km west of the lift.

Niederfinow is not difficult to reach from Berlin (DM27.30), but the journey involves a change of trains. First you must take the RE 3 from Berlin-Lichtenberg to Eberswalde Hauptbahnhof (45 minutes) and then transfer to the RB 60 for one stop (15 minutes). The Schiffshebewerk is about 2km to the north, and the way is signposted.

Saxony

Saxony (Sachsen) is the most densely populated and industrialised region in eastern Germany.

Saxon tribes originally occupied large parts of north-western Germany, but in the 10th century they expanded south-east into the territory of the pagan Slavs.

The medieval history of the various Saxon duchies and dynasties is complex, but in the 13th century the duke of Saxony at Wittenberg obtained the right to participate in the election of Holy Roman emperors. Involvement in Poland weakened Saxony in the 18th century, and ill-fated alliances, first with Napoleon and then with Austria, led to the ascendancy of Prussia over Saxony in the 19th century.

In the south, Saxony is separated from Czech Bohemia by the Erzgebirge, eastern Germany's highest mountain range. The Elbe River cuts north-west from the Czech border through a picturesque area known as 'Saxon Switzerland' towards the capital, Dresden. Leipzig, a great educational and commercial centre on the Weisse Elster River, rivals Dresden in historic importance, and upstages it in accessibility and fun. Quaint little towns like Weesenstein, Görlitz and Meissen punctuate this colourful, accessible corner of Germany.

HIGHLIGHTS

- The Stasi Museum, shopping centres and all-night cafés, bars and discos in Leipzig
- Dresden's Zwinger, Semperoper and Staatsoperette
- Meissen's porcelain factory and festivals
- The undervisited Weesenstein palace, and the tourist-packed ones at Pillnitz and Moritzburg

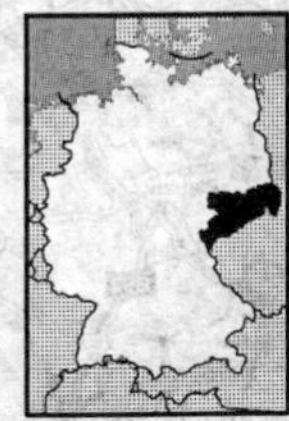

- **Population:** 4.6m • **Capital:** Dresden
- **Area:** 18,340 sq km

Saxony Luminaries: JC Bach, Paula Becker-Modersohn, Hanns Eisler, Johann Gottlob Lehmann, GW Leibniz, Gotthold Ephraim Lessing, Karl Liebknecht, Friedrich Wilhelm Nietzsche, Richard Wagner, Robert Schumann, Clara Wieck-Schumann, Heinrich Schütz

LEIPZIG

- *pop 480,000*
- *area code* ☎ 0341

In Goethe's *Faust* a character named Frosch calls Leipzig 'a little Paris'. He was wrong – Leipzig is more fun.

Among the first participants in the democratic revolution of 1989, Leipzigers began protests in May and by early October were taking to the streets by the hundreds of thousands, placing candles on the front steps of the Runde Ecke (Round Corner) and Stasi headquarters, and attending peace services at St Nikolai Church.

By the time the secret police got round to turning their secret documents to papier-mâché, Leipzigers were partying in the streets, and they still haven't stopped – from late winter, sidewalk cafés begin pouring out into the streets, and trendy and underground music clubs thud through the night.

That's not to say it's *just* a party town. Leipzig is home to some of the finest classical music and opera in the country; its art and literary scenes are flourishing. It was home to Bach, Wagner and Mendelssohn, and to Goethe, who set a key scene of *Faust* in the

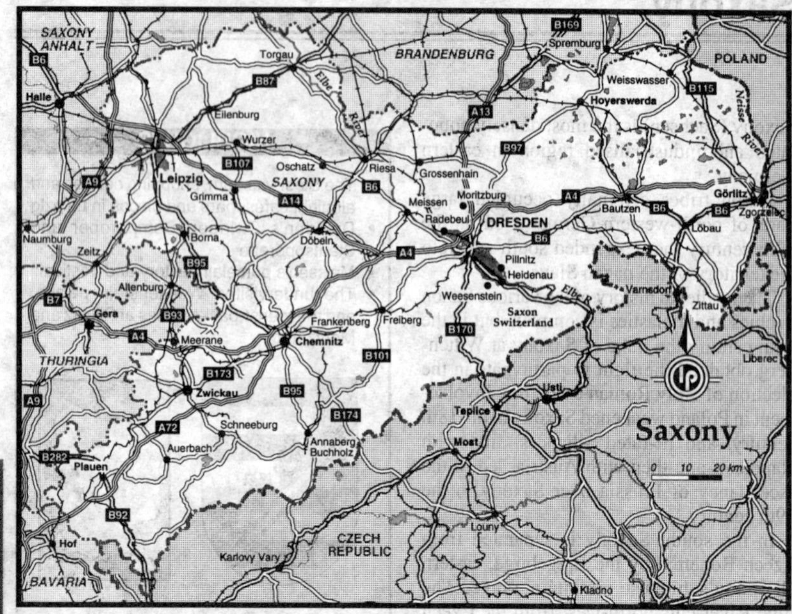

cellar of his favourite watering hole. And Leipzig's university attracts students from all over the world.

This all adds up to a lively, cosmopolitan city that's making great strides to throw off its GDR dust.

Leipzig has hosted annual trade fairs since medieval times. During the communist era these provided an important exchange between East and West. After reunification, the city spent a huge sum of money on a new ultra-modern fairground with the intention of re-establishing its position as one of Europe's great fair cities.

Since the discovery of rich silver mines in the nearby Erzgebirge (Ore Mountains) in the 16th century, Leipzig has enjoyed almost continual prosperity. Today it's an important business and transport centre, and the second-largest city in eastern Germany. Its strong cultural tradition still offers much for book and music lovers – Bach's time here is celebrated by a museum and an active choir.

Leipzig is pronounced 'LAH-iptsh' in the local Saxon dialect.

Orientation

Leipzig's city centre, called the Innenstadt (or Inner City), is within a ring road that lies on the boundaries of the town's medieval fortifications. To reach the city centre from the Hauptbahnhof, head through the underpass below Willy-Brandt-Platz and continue south along Nikolaistrasse for five minutes; the central Markt is just a couple of blocks south-west.

The impressive, 26-platform Leipzig train station (1915) is the largest in Europe. This massive structure is undergoing total renovation, including the construction of a large underground shopping and services complex. This should be completed by the time you read this. Outside the southern entrance is the central tram stop.

The wide Augustusplatz, three blocks east of the Markt, is ex-socialist Leipzig, with the space-age lines of the university and Neues Gewandhaus concert hall juxtaposed against the functional opera house. The main post office is also here.

Leipzig's dazzling new trade fairgrounds (Neue Messe) are 5km north of the Hauptbahnhof (take tram No 16).

Information

Tourist Offices The excellent Leipzig Tourist Service (☎ 710 42 60/26 5; fax 710 42 71; email lipsia@aol.com) is at Richard-Wagner-Strasse 1, between the Hauptbahnhof and the Altes Rathaus. It's open Monday to Friday from 9 am to 7 pm and weekends from 9.30 am to 2 pm. Useful pamphlets include *Visitor Guide* and *Guide to Leipzig as a City of Music*. The state of Saxony publishes the superb *Museums In Saxony's Major Cities*.

The LVB transport office at Nikolaistrasse 59 is another key location, where you can buy the one or three-day Leipzig Card (DM9.90/21) allowing free or discounted admission to the city's museums and the zoo as well as free travel on trams and buses.

The ADAC has an office (☎ 211 05 51) at Augustusplatz 5-6, inside the Hotel Mercure.

Foreign Consulates The US consulate (☎ 213 84 0), Wilhelm-Seyfferth-Strasse 4, provides commercial support for American business in Thuringia and Saxony but only emergency consular services.

Money There's a DVB bank at Nikolaistrasse 42. For the locations of major banks in the city centre, see the Banks section – they're as much sights as exchange offices.

Post & Communications The main post office is at Augustusplatz 1, with a large branch inside the Hauptbahnhof.

Online Services There are several Internet cafés. Film Café-Intershop, at Burgstrasse 9, is a very popular one; access is DM4 per 20 minutes, DM8 per hour for students between 6 and 9 pm. Also try Media Treff (☎ 301 18 42) at Karl-Liebknecht-Strasse 117.

Travel Agencies There are several bucket shops in Leipzig, including Kilroy Travel (☎ 303 09 0) at Augustusplatz 9, and Messe Service (☎ 564 05 82) at Berliner Strasse 34. For specials, check ads in *Fritz* and *Kreuzer* (see Listings in the Entertainment section).

Bookshops & Libraries Buch & Kunst (☎ 960 42 42), Am Brühl 8, and Franz-Mehring-Haus (☎ 711 84 0), Goethestrasse 3-5 have good book selections, as do the newsstands in the Hauptbahnhof.

Leipzig has long been a major publishing and library centre, and the Deutsche Bücherei (☎ 227 10), Deutscher Platz 1, is one of the largest German-language libraries in the world. It houses millions of books (including almost every title published in German since 1913) and runs a book and printing museum (free entry). The university library (☎ 973 05 77) at Beethoven Strasse 6 has periodicals and foreign-language books.

Campuses Universität Leipzig (☎ 971 08; email info@leipzig.de), formerly Karl Marx University, has 21,200 students studying languages, medicine, law and economics. The main campus is just south of the Hauptbahnhof, with satellites throughout the city.

International Centres There are several bastions of international cooperation here, including Amerika Haus (☎ 213 38 42 0) and Amnesty International (☎ 211 10 40), both at Wilhelm-Seyfferth-Strasse 4, and the British Council (☎ 564 67 12) and Institut Francais (☎ 564 22 39), both at Lumumbustrasse 11-13.

Phone Numbers

A huge percentage of Leipzig telephone numbers have been changed in the last year. Unfortunately, there's no real system to the distribution of new numbers. We have given the latest available numbers for all sights, attractions, restaurants and places to stay, but note that they are subject to change. ■

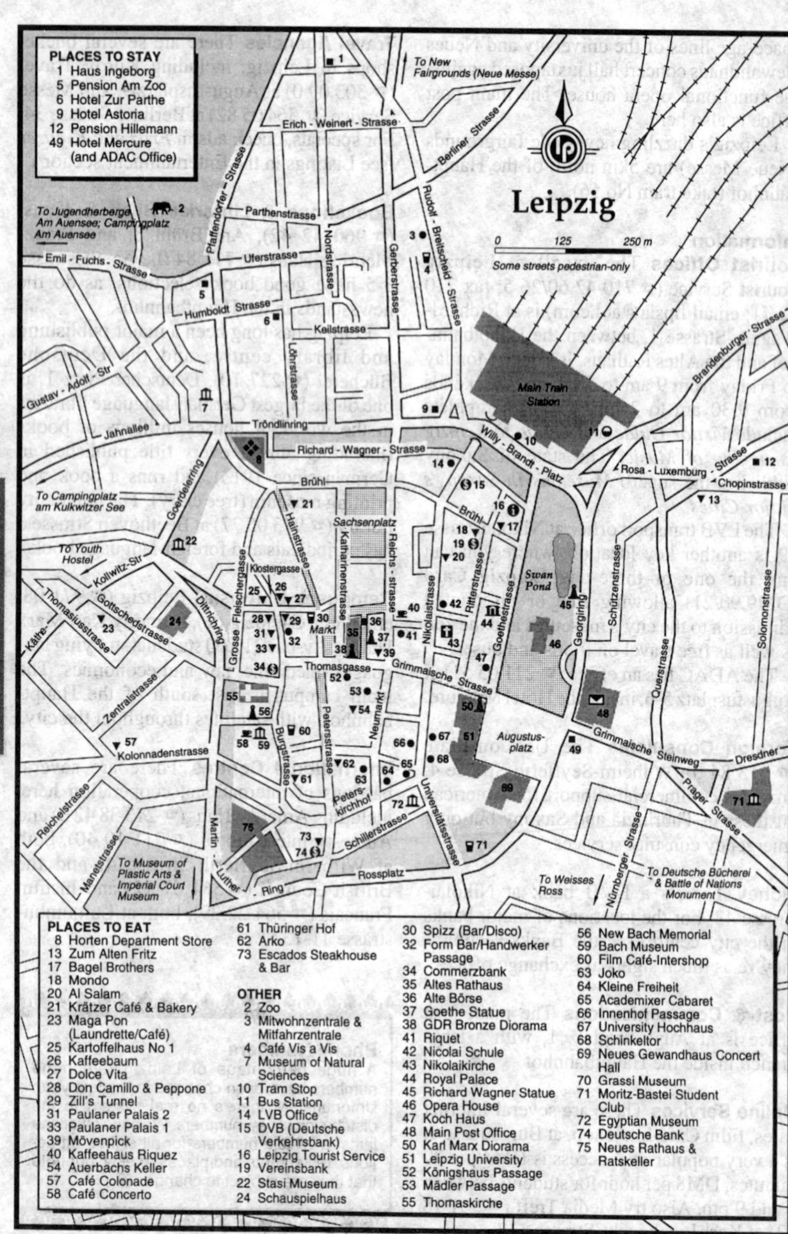
Leipzig
0 125 250 m
Some streets pedestrian-only
PLACES TO STAY
1 Haus Ingeborg
5 Pension Am Zoo
6 Hotel Zur Parthe
9 Hotel Astoria
12 Pension Hillemann
49 Hotel Mercure (and ADAC Office)
To New Fairgrounds (Neue Messe)
To Jugendherberge Am Auensee; Campingplatz Am Auensee
To Campingplatz am Kulkwitzer See
To Youth Hostel
To Museum of Plastic Arts & Imperial Court Museum
To Weisses Ross
To Deutsche Bücherei & Battle of Nations Monument
Main Train Station
Swan Pond
Sachsenplatz
Augustusplatz
Markt
Erich - Weinert - Strasse
Berliner Strasse
Parthenstrasse
Uferstrasse
Emil - Fuchs - Strasse
Humboldt Strasse
Keilstrasse
Gustav - Adolf - Str
Jahnallee
Tröndlinring
Richard - Wagner - Strasse
Willy - Brandt - Platz
Rosa - Luxemburg - Strasse
Chopinstrasse
Brandenburger Strasse
Brühl
Goerdelerring
Kollwitz-Str
Gottschedstrasse
Thomasiusstrasse
Käthe-
Dittrichring
Klostergasse
Thomasgasse
Grimmaische Strasse
Grimmaische Steinweg
Dresdner
Prager Strasse
Zentralstrasse
Kolonnadenstrasse
Reichelstrasse
Manetstrasse
Martin Luther Ring
Rossplatz
Schillerstrasse
Universitätsstrasse
Peterskirchhof
Nürnberger Strasse
Querstrasse
Schützenstrasse
Solomonstrasse
Georgiring
Goethestrasse
Ritterstrasse
Nikolaistrasse
Reichsstrasse
Katharinenstrasse
Hainstrasse
Grosse Fleischergasse
Burgstrasse
Petersstrasse
Neumarkt
Pfaffendorfer Strasse
Nordstrasse
Löhrstrasse
Gerberstrasse
Rudolf - Breitscheid - Strasse
PLACES TO EAT
8 Horten Department Store
13 Zum Alten Fritz
17 Bagel Brothers
18 Mondo
20 Al Salam
21 Krätzer Café & Bakery
23 Maga Pon (Laundrette/Café)
25 Kartoffelhaus No 1
26 Kaffeebaum
27 Dolce Vita
28 Don Camillo & Peppone
29 Zill's Tunnel
31 Paulaner Palais 2
33 Paulaner Palais 1
39 Mövenpick
40 Kaffeehaus Riquez
54 Auerbachs Keller
57 Café Colonade
58 Café Concerto
61 Thüringer Hof
62 Arko
73 Escados Steakhouse & Bar
OTHER
2 Zoo
3 Mitwohnzentrale & Mitfahrzentrale
4 Café Vis a Vis
7 Museum of Natural Sciences
10 Tram Stop
11 Bus Station
14 LVB Office
15 DVB (Deutsche Verkehrsbank)
16 Leipzig Tourist Service
19 Vereinsbank
22 Stasi Museum
24 Schauspielhaus
30 Spizz (Bar/Disco)
32 Form Bar/Handwerker Passage
34 Commerzbank
35 Altes Rathaus
36 Alte Börse
37 Goethe Statue
38 GDR Bronze Diorama
41 Riquet
42 Nicolai Schule
43 Nikolaikirche
44 Royal Palace
45 Richard Wagner Statue
46 Opera House
47 Koch Haus
48 Main Post Office
50 Karl Marx Diorama
51 Leipzig University
52 Königshaus Passage
53 Mädler Passage
55 Thomaskirche
56 New Bach Memorial
59 Bach Museum
60 Film Café-Intershop
63 Joko
64 Kleine Freiheit
65 Academixer Cabaret
66 Innenhof Passage
67 University Hochhaus
68 Schinkeltor
69 Neues Gewandhaus Concert Hall
70 Grassi Museum
71 Moritz-Bastei Student Club
72 Egyptian Museum
74 Deutsche Bank
75 Neues Rathaus & Ratskeller
SAXONY

Laundry Wash your dirties at Maga Pon (☎ 960 79 22), a combination laundry and hip café at Gottschedstrasse 3. There's a more traditional option at the modern Schnell und Sauber laundrette just south-east of the city centre at Dresdner Strasse 19.

Medical Services St Georg Krankenhaus (☎ 909 00), Delitzscher Strasse 141, is the largest in the area; take tram No 17 in the direction of Neue Messe. The University Clinic (☎ 971 08) at Liebigstrasse 21 in the centre is both a hospital and a clinic for everyday problems.

In an emergency call (☎ 192 92) from 7 pm to 7 am for a doctor.

There are pharmacies throughout the city. In emergencies the Löwenapotheke (☎ 292 01 4 or ☎ 292 12 6), Grimmaische Strasse 19, is the place to contact.

Dangers & Annoyances The area around the Hauptbahnhof is as sleazy as can be expected; you should use caution at night.

Parking in the centre can be dangerous; there have been plenty of smash-and-grab incidents in the last year. Don't leave any valuables in your car, even if it's parked right in front of the tourist office.

Markt

The Renaissance **Altes Rathaus** (1556), one of Germany's largest town halls, houses the **City History Museum** (open Tuesday to Friday from 10 am to 6 pm, Saturday and Sunday to 4 pm, closed Monday; DM4, discount DM2).

Behind it is the **Alte Börse** (1687), with a **monument to Goethe** (1903), who studied law at Leipzig University. Today the Alte Börse is a cultural centre, with concerts, plays and readings throughout the year; see the Entertainment section for more information.

At the southern end of the square is one of our favourite monuments – a wonderful **GDR bronze diorama** depicting the march of history from the downtrodden medieval workers slaving away with pickaxes (at the left), through the granting of the market and other historical markers (centre) to the apex of civilisation (at the far right), socialist man and woman hugging; their muscles, taut and toned from lifting wheat and swinging sickles, rippling in the pleasure of building world communism.

Königshaus Passage Across the street, the orange baroque number with the lovely bay windows is the **Apelshaus** (1606-07). It's now a shopping mall, popularly known as the Königshaus Passage, but in its heyday its impressive list of overnight guests included Peter the Great and Napoleon. Walk in and 10m ahead on the left is a steel door. Open it and walk into the stone spiral staircase's stairwell. Stand at its base, look straight up and think of James Bond.

Saxon Speak

The Saxons speak a dialect as incomprehensible to non-Saxons as Bavarian is to outsiders. Many visitors may find themselves saying 'Huh?' more often than usual. It's as if the Saxons learned German from the Scots, with their very soft pronunciation of consonants. For example, when a Saxon says 'LAH-iptsch', he means Leipzig. And the 'ü' sound is pronounced like an English short 'i' – BIT-nershtrazze for 'Büttnerstrasse'.

But Saxon speak is far from an odd off-shoot of German; on the contrary, it was from Saxony that the German language developed (as many a Saxon will proudly tell you). Martin Luther's translation of the Bible into the Saxon language laid the foundation for a standard German language.

Saxons might also hark back to a 1717 Dutch reference to the Saxon dialect as 'the purest, most comprehensible, charming and delightful to the ear of all German dialects'. ■

Mädler Passage The Königshaus Passage leads directly into the Mädler Passage which, despite the claims of Sydney's Queen Victoria Building, is the most beautiful shopping centre in the world. A mix of neo-Renaissance and Art Nouveau, it opened as a trade hall in 1914. Today it's home to chi-chi shops, restaurants, cafés and the **Auerbachs Keller** (see Places to Eat). There are Faust-related statues (students, Mephistopheles and Faust) at the eastern exit, where stairs lead down to the restaurant.

Specks Hof Passage Yet another delightfully renovated passage/shopping mall is Specks Hof Passage, off Schumacher Gässchen, which contains a great New York diner (see Places to Eat) and a beautiful series of tile and stained-glass reliefs by Halle artist Moritz Götze.

SAXONY

Augustusplatz

At the east end of the inner city, Augustusplatz is a centre of Leipzig's cultural life. Flanked at the north by the **Opernhaus** (1956-60), and to the south by the **Neues Gewandhaus** (1981), home to the city's classical-music and jazz concerts; it's an area you'll definitely become familiar with. North of the Opernhaus (Opera House) in the park is a **statue of Richard Wagner** (1813-83), who was born in Leipzig.

Just north-west of the square on Goethestrasse is the neoclassical **Royal Palace**, now a university building, and south of that are two skyscrapers of note: the 11-storey **Koch Haus**, Leipzig's first skyscraper (1920s), topped by a large clock and bell ringers that bash the huge bell hourly, and farther south, the GDR-built **Universitäts Hochhaus** (1970), a towering thing that tries to take the shape of an open book standing on its end. At its northern end is another revolting bronze diorama depicting Karl Marx with – we would swear to it – Lenin's forehead.

Continuing farther south brings you to the **Moritz-Bastei**, perhaps Europe's largest student club. It was renovated over an eight-year period by students and volunteers; see the Entertainment section for more details. On the western side of the university building is the **Schinkeltor**, a mid-19th century gate that was one of the few bits of the original university to survive WWII and the GDR.

Southern Inner City

Step into **Café Richter** (☎ 960 52 35), Petersstrasse 43, not a café but the oldest coffee seller in town (since 1879). The spectacular eclectic building, with its golden iron spiral staircase, is worth seeing, and the coffees (DM7.50 per half-kg) are wonderful too. Outside the Thüringer Hof (see Places to Eat) is a renovated, working **well pump**. It eventually gives you non-potable water, but it's fun.

Innenhof Passage One block west of the university is the Innenhof Passage; go through the gate and pass the Kaiser Maximilian restaurant and you'll come to a courtyard. This area was formerly a cloth exchange (Gewandhaus) and later the site of the city's first concert house, which is why the city's concert hall is called Neues Gewandhaus. The courtyard was also home to a music school set up by composer Felix Mendelssohn; there are free concerts here in summer.

Neues Rathaus Although the building's origins date back to the 16th century, the baroque Neues Rathaus, with its impressive 108m-high tower, was completed in 1905. Recently renovated, the interior of the new town hall makes it one of the finest municipal buildings in Germany, with a grand staircase out of a Donald Trump dream.

It's open on weekdays from 6.45 am to either 4.30 or 6.30 pm; entry is free. In the lobby are rotating art exhibitions, generally featuring something to do with the city's history or architecture.

Banks

In 1991, when the German government offered a 1:1 exchange rate for Ostmarks, tonnes of cash was shipped to the east, and

Dr Jurgen Schneider: Leipzig's Big Swinging Dick

In *Liar's Poker*, Michael Lewis' tale of 1980s Wall Street excess, the term Big Swinging Dick was applied to financial high rollers willing to take risks to seize huge profits. If that's the criterion, Dr Jurgen Schneider is the biggest, swingingest dick of them all.

In 1990, just as Germany was talking reunification, the Frankfurt-born Schneider was planning his reconstruction of central Leipzig. Over the next few years, he managed to convince dozens of German banks – including Deutsche Bank, Dresdner Bank, Bayerische Hypotheken and Landesbank – to lend him a total of DM300 million for Leipzig's development and an estimated DM6 billion for property development in the new federal states.

Schneider's properties included such Leipzig landmarks as the Mädler Passage, Königshaus Passage, Bartels Hof and what's now the Hotel Kempinski.

As time went on, Schneider skimmed off the top, effectively creating his own mini-pyramid scam with German banks as the dupes. When the inevitable crash came in 1994, Schneider fled the country for Miami.

Located after a year-long Interpol search, Schneider was extradited by US authorities and now resides in a Frankfurt prison. Even in disgrace Schneider had style. He was flown 1st class – at government expense – on his extradition flight.

Leipzigers tend to find the whole matter distasteful, but if you press them they come down harder on the banks than on Schneider – it was, after all, the banks' fault for having been fooled so easily.

And Deutsche Bank gained no sympathy at all when former spokesman Hilmer Kopper characterised the losses as negligible, saying that the DM1.2 billion it lent the wayward investor amounted to (and he used the English word) 'peanuts' – which became a national buzzword for the next two years.

Deutsche Bank, though, says it is confident it can recoup half of the money it lent the good doctor through the liquidation of his assets.

Good luck, guys. ■

Leipzig held a lot of it in its safes, particularly the main **Deutsche Bank** at the corner of Schillerstrasse and Petersstrasse. Looking at the bank's Italian-Renaissance headquarters today, you might suspect they held back a little: gilded gold ceiling mouldings, spectacular furnishings, marble pillars, etched glass and a skylight so large it illuminates the entire teller area. Given all this grandeur, it seems only natural that the bank hosts art exhibitions and literary readings. There's even a flashy restaurant in the former vaults downstairs (see Places to Eat).

Other banks in town appear inordinately prosperous, too. The **Commerzbank**, at the corner of Thomas Kirchhof and Klostergasse, has a façade that drips so much gold that the bank itself complained to the building's owner. Also not too shabby is the **Vereinsbank** on Ritterstrasse just south of Brühl, with its aquamarine Art Nouveau tiles and copper-plated doors. All three of these banks are most happy to exchange your foreign currency for Deutschmarks.

Churches

St Nicholas Church Located between the Markt and Augustusplatz, Nikolaikirche (1165), has a remarkable history. Begun in Romanesque style, it was enlarged and converted to late Gothic, with an amazing classical interior. But the church stands out as the central gathering point for peaceful demonstrators from May 1989. The church's pamphlet tells, in many languages, the story of 600 loyal party members being sent into the church to break up the services, but in the end listening to the sermon and joining the protesters. The church still runs its 'Swords to Ploughshares' services on Monday at 5 pm.

St Thomas Church Just south-west of the Markt is Thomaskirche (1212), with the tomb of composer Johann Sebastian Bach in front of the altar. The church was extended and converted to the Gothic style in 1496, and was the site of the baptisms of Richard Wagner, Karl Liebknecht and all of Bach's children.

Bach worked here as a cantor from 1723 until his death in 1750. Outside the church is the **New Bach Memorial** (1908) showing the composer standing against an organ, with his left-hand jacket pocket turned inside-out (he always claimed to be broke and with 20 children from two marriages ...).

The St Thomas Choir, once led by Bach, is still going strong and now counts 80 boys aged eight to 18. See the Entertainment section for more information. Church services are held at 9.30 am on Sunday.

Museums

The city's excellent Museum of Plastic Arts is in constant danger of closing, but it was still going strong when we visited. Keep your fingers crossed. And a visit to the city's fascinating Stasi Museum is a mandatory stop.

Bach Museum Opposite St Thomas Church, in a baroque house at Thomaskirchhof 16, is the Bach Museum, which has exhibitions focusing on the composer's life in Leipzig – where he wrote, among many other works, *Matthaus Passion, Johannes Passion, Weinachts Oratorium, H-Moll Messe* and numerous cantatas and organ works. There are portraits, manuscripts and other Bach memorabilia. It's open daily from 10 am to 5 pm, and guided tours in German are given at 11 am and 3 pm. Admission is DM4/2.50.

Museum of Plastic Arts The Museum der Bildenden Künste is housed in the former buildings of the Supreme Court of the Reich (1888). An excellent collection of works by old masters is downstairs. Upstairs you'll find the Historische Räume im Reichsgericht (Imperial Court Museum), where the communist Georgi Dimitrov was tried and acquitted in the 1933 Reichstag Fire trial. The museum is open from 1 to 9.30 pm on Wednesday and from 9 am to 5 pm other days, closed Monday; entry costs DM5. Unfortunately, the Federal Administrative Tribunal plans to relocate to these premises, which – if the move goes ahead – would force the museum to relocate.

Stasi Museum At No 24 of Dittrichring, where it intersects with Goerdelerring, is the former headquarters of the East German Ministerium für Staatssicherheit (or Stasi), the secret police. It's in the building known as the Runde Ecke (Round Corner) and is now a museum (☎ 961 24 99).

At the front are photographs of demonstrations in October and November of 1989, and of Lt General Manfred Hummitsch, the former head of the Stasi in Leipzig. Inside are exhibits on propaganda, preposterous Stasi disguises, surveillance photographs (while we were visiting someone said 'Hey, that's a friend of mine!') and, in the back, samples of the mounds and mounds of the papier-mâché Stasi created when they shredded and then soaked secret documents before the fall of the GDR – grab a chunk and take it home; it's free and there's plenty of it.

The museum is open Wednesday to Sunday from 2 to 6 pm, closed Monday and Tuesday; admission is free.

Egyptian Museum This museum at Leipzig University (☎ 973 70 10), Schillerstrasse 6, has a 9000-piece collection of Egyptian antiquities, making it one of the most important such collections in Europe. Among the items on display are stone vessels from the first half of the third millennium BC, Nubian decorative arts and ceramics, and sarcophagi. The museum is open Tuesday to Saturday from 1 to 5 pm, Sunday from 10 am to 1 pm. Admission is DM3/1.50.

Grassi Museum Complex There are three museums within the Grassi complex at Leipzig University, Taübchenweg 2 and 2c, all charging separate admissions and closed Monday: the **Museum für Völkerkunde** (Ethnological Museum; ☎ 214 20), an enormous collection of cultural exhibits from around the world (admission DM5/2, open Tuesday to Friday from 10 am to 5.30 pm, Saturday and Sunday from 10 am to 4 pm); the **Musikinstrumenten-Museum** (Musical Instrument Museum; ☎ 214 21 20), with a collection of almost 1000 instruments from around the world (DM5/2, free guided tour

Sundays at 10 am, open Tuesday to Saturday from 10 am to 5 pm, Sunday from 10 am to 1 pm); and the **Museum für Kunsthandwerk** (Arts & Crafts Museum, ☎ 214 20), DM4/2, open Tuesday to Friday from 10 am to 6 pm (to 8 pm on Wednesday), Saturday and Sunday from 10 am to 5 pm.

Zoo

Leipzig's zoo, north-west of the train station, is renowned for its breeding of lions and tigers. It's open from 8 am to 7 pm during summer (entry DM7).

Battle of Nations Monument

South-east of the centre is Leipzig's most impressive sight, the Völkerschlachtdenkmal (Battle of Nations Monument, 1913), a 91m-high monument commemorating the decisive victory here by the combined Prussian, Austrian and Russian forces over Napoleon's army 100 years earlier (DM3.50, open daily from 10 am to 5 pm). You can climb the tower for a good view of the city and surrounding area.

Organised Tours

Leipzig Tourist Service runs guided tours every day from the meeting point in front of its office. The 1½ hour city-orientation tour costs DM10 and leaves on weekdays at 10.30 am. More in-depth, two-hour tours leave every day at 1.30 and 4.30 pm, and cost DM12.

Special Events

Leipzig's annual events calendar includes the following:

Book Fair
: Late March. Second biggest in the country after Frankfurt. Lots of readings and book-related events.

Leipzig during the Napoleonic invasion of 1813.

Strassemusik Festival
  Early May. Rock, folk, country and world-music groups from around the country.
Wochenende Summertheater
  July and August weekends. In the courtyard behind the Paulaner Palais.
Leipziger Jazztage
  Late September/early October. Jazz performers from Europe and the USA.
Leipziger Literarischer Herbst
  Early November. More readings than you can shake a stick at.
euro scene leipzig
  Early November. International modern-theatre and dance-theatre performances.

Places to Stay

During fairs many of Leipzig's hotels raise their prices, and it can be hard to find a room. The Leipzig accommodation scene is rapidly changing – in six months, three great pensions and a major hotel closed – so expect changes to the following.

Camping The *Campingplatz Am Auensee* (☎ 461 19 77), Gustav-Esche-Strasse 5, is in a pleasant wooded spot on the city's north-western outskirts (take tram No 10 or 28 to the end of the line at Wahren, then walk for eight minutes). Camping is DM8 per person plus DM5 for a car/tent site. A-frame cabins/bungalows are also available for singles/doubles at DM50/90 per night. Not quite so nice is the *Campingplatz am Kulkwitzer See* (☎ 941 15 14) on Seestrasse, south-west of the city centre in Miltitz.

Hostels Leipzig's main *hostel* (☎ 983 45 07) is at Käthe-Kollwitz-Strasse 62-66 in the city's south-west. This large prewar mansion with a pleasant back garden has four and six-person dorms at DM22/27 for juniors/seniors, plus DM6 for linen. Book in summer as it fills up quickly; take tram No 1 or 2 from the Hauptbahnhof. It has prison-like showers in the dungeon ... er ... cellar, but a great breakfast buffet.

Another, smaller and less central hostel is *Jugendherberge Am Auensee* (☎ 571 89), Gustav-Esche-Strasse 4 on the lake near the camping ground, which charges DM20/24 for juniors/seniors.

Private Rooms Leipzig Tourist Service runs a free room-finding service (☎ 710 40), with singles/doubles from around DM45/80. You can reserve by faxing or mailing your requirements and a credit card number, c/o Saxonia Touristik International Travel Agency (fax 710 42 51), Leipzig Tourist Service, Richard-Wagner-Strasse 1, 04109 Leipzig.

Hotels – bottom end There's a great deal on simple rooms at the *Beyers SPÄT Centre* (☎ 585 29 38), Georg-Schumann-Strasse 102, north of the city centre, with very basic singles/doubles (without breakfast) for DM50/90, and DM40/80 at weekends. Surrounded by idle GDR-era factories south-west of the centre in Plagwitz (tram No 2 or bus No 52 evenings and weekends) is *Elster Pension* (☎ 479 80 39), Giesserstrasse 15, which charges DM65/90 for singles/doubles with semi-private (shared with one other room) shower and WC. The *Pension Am Listplatz* (☎ 688 05 92) has about the same for a bit more (DM65/95).

Hotels – middle North-west of the Hauptbahnhof is the *Pension Am Zoo* (☎ 960 24 32), Pfaffendorfer Strasse 23, which charges DM60 for simple singles and DM90/130 for single/double rooms with private shower. Not far away is *Haus Ingeborg* (☎ 960 31 43), Nordstrasse 58, with basic rooms with shared bath for DM70/100 and with private bath for DM130/140. Other reasonable options include the newly renovated *Weisses Ross* (☎ 960 59 51), Rossstrasse 20, which offers rooms for DM70/110 with shower or DM65/95 without, and the *Pension Prima* (☎ 688 34 81) at Dresdner Strasse 82, with simple rooms for DM55/95 (without breakfast). It's 2km east of the centre, but easily reached from Willy-Brandt-Platz by tram No 4, 6 or 20.

Hotels – top end At the airport, about 20km from town, the *Treff Hotel Leipzig* (☎ 254 0; fax 254 15 50), at Schongauer Strasse 39, has singles/doubles from DM129/179 and is the cheapest of the up-market places, but the perfectly central *Hotel Mercure Leipzig* (☎ 214 60; fax 960 49 16), Augustusplatz 5-6, is probably the best value in the range, with rooms from DM130/180.

Also not too shabby is the *Holiday Inn Garden Court* (☎ 125 10; fax 1251 10 0), Rudolf-Breitscheid-Strasse 3, with rooms from DM155/200.

Moving north at a jaunty clip, you'll find the rest of the city's high-end places, including *Hotel InterContinental Leipzig* (☎ 988 0; fax 988 12 29), Gerberstrasse 15, with rooms from DM295/325; and the very luxurious, if exorbitant *Kempinski Hotel Fürstenhof Leipzig* (☎ 140 0; fax 140 37 00), Tröndlinring 8, the former Schneider property, clocking in at a brisk DM320/390.

Long-Term Rentals The Mitwohnzentrale (☎ 980 50 00) at Rudolf- Breitscheid-Strasse 39 can arrange flat rental (from DM20 to DM50 per person per day). The office is open daily from 9 am to 8 pm.

Places to Eat

If you're here during asparagus season in May, don't miss a bowl of Allerlei, a soup made from all the vegies that grow around that time, served with crêpes. Lerche (or 'lark') is a small marzipan-filled tart, made after the ban on the shooting of the little songbirds in the 19th century.

Restaurants – bottom end Students clean up at one of the two *Paulaner Palais* restaurants (☎ 211 31 15 or ☎ 960 00 00) at Klostergasse 3 and 5. The student menu of spare ribs, Leberkäse or Nürnburger sausage with sauerkraut, bread and salad is DM7.80, and from 3 pm the 'Futtern wie bei Muttern' (eating like at mother's) menu has dishes from DM3.50; after 9 pm students get a 10% discount on everything.

The *Kantin* in Room 163 on the 1st floor of the Neues Rathaus is a superb deal if you don't mind all the bureaucrats: beautiful salad bar from DM4 and sandwiches or even full meals for about DM7.50.

Zum Alten Fritz (closed weekends), Chopinstrasse 6, is a simple tavern that offers good-sized meals from around DM15.

Maga Pon (☎ 960 79 22) at Gottschedstrasse 13, the laundry-café, is probably better as the latter than the former: great atmosphere, friendly staff, high ceilings and healthy foods. Menu with soup and special of the day is DM10, daily soups are DM6, and there's a great wine selection. It's open daily from 9 am and to 3 am most nights.

Restaurants – middle *Mövenpick* (☎ 211 77 22), Am Naschmarkt 1-3, offers outstanding value with a nightly buffet where you can help yourself to imaginative salads, casseroles and desserts for DM19.50 per person. A Leipzig eating house with a long culinary tradition is the *Thüringer Hof* (☎ 994 49 99), Burgstrasse 19; Luther's favourite pub, it was completely destroyed in WWII and what you see today is entirely new. There's a traditional vaulted-ceiling restaurant in front and an atrium in back. It has great food and decent prices: vegie dishes from DM13 to DM16, fish from DM18 to DM23 and meat from DM19 to DM23. Another place with a long tradition is *Zill's Tunnel* (☎ 960 20 78), Barfussgässchen 9, with typical German specialities from about DM18.

At the *Ratskeller* (☎ 123 62 02) in the Neues Rathaus, try the cream goulash with red cabbage and dumplings for DM12.90.

Kartoffelhaus No 1 (☎ 960 46 03), Barfussgässchen 12 in Mr Drinks Beerhouse, was opened by a former employee of the Mövenpick; it serves great potato dishes in a somewhat absurd Bavarian décor. Main courses range from DM15 to DM22.

NYC New York City (☎ 211 07 07), in Specks Hof Passage, looked authentic enough to this New Yorker, who greedily eyed the excellent-looking omelettes (DM7.70 with toast and chips/French fries, plus DM2 per filling), good vegetarian dishes from DM8.50 to DM14, and huge burgers with real Heinz ketchup (DM8 to DM14). No cell phones allowed. Cocktails are outrageously overpriced – still, it's a great place.

Restaurants – top end Founded in 1525, *Auerbachs Keller* (☎ 216 10 40), just south of the Altes Rathaus in the Mädler Passage, is one of Germany's classic restaurants. Goethe's *Faust – Part I* includes a scene at Auerbachs Keller, in which Mephistopheles and Faust carouse with students before they leave riding on a barrel. In summer, you may be able to join a tour of the historic section of the restaurant, including the Goethe room (where the writer constantly drank – excuse us, gleaned inspiration), the Weinfass and, beneath that, the genuinely spooky Hexenküche, where the witches brewed up the dreaded Verjüngungstrunk. Note the wood carvings above the table in the Weinfass, featuring witches, Faust riding off on the barrel and Mephisto, complete with hooves, in pursuit. The tour includes a drink, buffet or fixed-menu dinner and the chance to, Faust-like, climb atop the large barrel that spews Sächsische Unstrut wine for DM9 a glass. The tours cost DM100 per person.

Escados Steakhouse & Bar (☎ 960 71 27), in the vault section of Deutsche Bank, is certainly pricey, but the atmosphere is so suave and the food so good that it's worth a shot. The place is tropical-meets-classical with palm trees and rattan amidst the columns, and the food (DM28 to DM50) is mainly meat and potatoes: chicken, Argentinian beef and steaks.

Cafés Klostergasse, one block west of the Markt, is a wonderful street that's chock-a-block with outdoor tables when the weather warms up. Along here you'll find two excellent pizzerias, *Dolce Vita* and the spanking new and up-market *Don Camillo & Peppone*, though the latter has dry pizza. A bit farther on is Leipzig's oldest coffee bar, *Kaffeebaum*, established around 1700; it was under renovation during our last visit but should be open again when you read this.

Mondo, Am Brühl 52, is a very small, very Italian and very smoky café with great coffees (DM3.50) and sandwiches (DM4.50 to DM6), and an absolutely awesome wood carving on the wall. The *Café Colonade*, at the corner of Max-Beckmann-Strasse and Kolonnadenstrasse, serves sound dishes for less than DM15; there's a small beer garden out the back.

The *Kaffeehaus Riquez*, a somewhat up-market café in a superb Art Nouveau building (identifiable by the two enormous bronze elephant heads above the entrance), stands at the corner of Reichsstrasse and Schuhmachergässchen. Other good cafés include the *Bachstübl* and the *Café Concerto* on Thomaskirchhof next door to the Bach Museum.

There's also a very popular café in the Neues Szene theatre (see Entertainment).

Snacks & Fast Food Always good for a filling feed is the cafeteria on the 5th floor of the *Horten* department store on Trondlinring, where a meal costs around DM10. The *Krätzer* is a cheap stand-up café and bakery on Hainstrasse. In the Hauptbahnhof there are the usual offerings, with the addition of an itty-bitty *McDonald's* and a larger *Pizza Hut*.

The best Middle Eastern food we've had in ages was at *Al Salam*, at Nikolaistrasse 33. They have enormous felafel (DM4) and doner (DM5), bursting-fresh salads and excellent hot dishes; everything is under DM10. The vegetarian platter is DM7.50, and there's a huge range of sweets.

Inside the Königshaus Passage, there's another doner place, a couple of bakeries and a crêperie as well, all with snacks for under DM5.

Entertainment

Live theatre and music are major features among Leipzig's cultural offerings. The classical music, ballet and opera seasons here run from September to July. Buy tickets at the venues themselves or at Leipzig Tourist Service, but don't let travel agencies do it for you – you get a better deal on your own. The city is a constant host to rock and jazz concerts, the latter enough to warrant a separate monthly jazz calendar published by the city.

Leipzigers, unlike many of their western German counterparts (Berlin excluded, of course) party till they drop at 7 or 8 the next morning. There are no city-imposed closing hours, and on warm summer nights the narrow cobblestone streets of the inner city are filled with thousands sipping Freyburger or Australian wine or cappuccino at sidewalk tables. It makes you wonder for a moment if you're in Germany at all.

Listings *Kreuzer* is the best magazine for what's on in Leipzig, with great listings, the best events calendar, a great travel section and more. It's DM2.50 at newsstands and restaurants around the city.

Leipzig Im is a monthly pamphlet available from the Leipzig Tourist Service. As is often the case in eastern German cities, the two leading free listings magazines are *Fritz* and its thicker but inferior cousin *Blitz*, with listings and what's-on guides, available practically everywhere. The *Litfassäule* section of the daily *Leipziger Volkszeitung* has a good what's-on guide.

Gay & Lesbian The city publishes *Leipzig Stadtplan für Schwule*, a map of bars, discos, saunas and helpful organisations, including RoseLinde (☎ 484 15 11) at Lindenauer Markt 21, an advocacy group for gays and lesbians. The *Buntes Archiv Lesbengruppe* holds meetings every Thursday at 7.30 pm in *Lesecafé TIAN* (☎ 479 74 75), Könneritzstrasse 67.

Cinema *Kino Im Grassi* (☎ 960 48 38) at the Grassi Museum Complex, Täubchenweg 2d, screens films in the original language with German subtitles. Features start at 6 pm daily with main showings at 8 pm. Children's films are at either 10 am or 3 pm.

Discos & Clubs The two most popular discos in town are at the Moritz-Bastei and *Spizz* (see Rock & Jazz), but two others are *You Too* (☎ 960 59 62), Fleischergasse 12 right near the Thomaskirche (with a room for Top 20 and a second section for African and world beat) and the nearby and also popular *Lips Disco* (☎ 960 48 18), Barfussgässchen 12 (enter from Kleine Fleischergasse).

Opera Composer Udo Zimmermann, the director of the Opernhaus, favours Wagner and Albert Lortzing because, of course, of their Leipzig connections. But he's also very dedicated to modern opera, especially by Stockhausen, as well as electronic music and Görg Herchet. Tickets range from DM12 to DM65, averaging DM30 to DM35.

Theatre The largest theatre in town is the *Schauspielhaus* (☎ 126 80), a few blocks west of the Markt at Bosestrasse 1. Despite a programme of classics, it concentrates heavily on modern theatre. Modern performances are held at the Schauspielhaus' *Neue Szene* at Gottschedstrasse 16 (tram No 1 or 2 to Gottschedstrasse). Downstairs is the screamingly popular café *Metropol*.

Theater der Jungen Welt (☎ 477 29 90), at Lindenauer Markt 21, specialises in plays with themes that appeal to young audiences (late teens to early 20s) but also has puppet theatre and other children's performances.

Cabaret The best known cabaret theatres are *Leipziger Pfeffermüle* (☎ 960 32 53) at Thomaskirchhof 16; *Leipziger Akademixer* (☎ 960 48 48) at Kupfergasse, and *Sanftwut – Boccaccio* (☎ 301 01 12) at Kurt-Eisner-Strasse 43. All three hold highly satirical performances poking fun at most aspects of Germany and German life, especially east-west relations.

Readings The *Literaturcafé* (☎ 995 41 51) in the Haus des Buches is open on weekdays from 9 am to 11 pm. Throughout the month it hosts various readings and other literature-related events. There are also readings at the Alte Börse, the Altes Rathaus, all the libraries, Amerika Haus, Institut Français and the British Council.

Classical Music The *Neues Gewandhaus* concert hall on Augustusplatz has Europe's longest-established orchestra with a tradition dating back to 1743 – Mendelssohn was one of its conductors. Today the Gewandhaus Orchestra performs every conceivable type of classical music, with guest appearances by soloists, conductors and orchestras from around the world. Tickets range from DM20 to DM60.

Bach There are free concerts every Monday at 6 pm in front of the Bach statue near the Thomaskirche. Every Sunday in July and August at 3 pm there are concerts in the courtyard of the Bach Museum. Tickets are from DM10 to DM15.

Organ & Choral Concerts There are free organ concerts in St Thomas and St Nicholas churches on Saturday in July and August; at St Thomas they're at 6 pm and at St Nicholas at 5 pm. The St Thomas Choir performs year round on Friday at 3 pm and Saturday at 6 pm, and during Sunday services.

Rock & Jazz See the earlier Listings section for calendars of what's on. Large rock concerts are held in the *Neue Messe Leipzig* (☎ 678 0; tram No 16); *Zentral Stadion* (no telephone; 10 minutes from the city centre near Jahnallee; take tram No 5 or 15 to Miltitz); *Easy Auensee* (☎ 461 28 77; tram No 10 or 28 to Wahren); and sometimes in the *Messe Halle 7*, in the old trade fair area near Philipp-Rosenthal-Strasse; take tram No 15 or 21 to the Altes Messegelände stop.

One of the best student clubs in Germany, *Moritz-Bastei*, at Universitätsstrasse 9 in a spacious cellar below the old city walls, has live bands or disco on most nights, and movies in summer outside on top (you'll see what we mean when you're there). It's incredibly popular, with cheap eats and a good, young crowd.

Spizz (☎ 960 80 43) at Markt 9 is a very slick place, one of the coolest bars in town. Up-market but relaxed, it attracts a good crowd and has good drinks. Downstairs there's excellent live jazz and disco – check with the pub or any listings magazine: it's in all of them.

The best places for jazz are *Spizz* and *Moritz-Bastei* as well as *naTo* (☎ 328 20 6), Karl-Liebknecht-Strasse 46, a cultural house, meeting spot and general cool hang-out. There's also jazz at the *Neues Gewandhaus* and at the *Opernhaus*. Check the Leipzig Jazz Kalender, printed monthly and available at Leipzig Tourist Service.

Ballet The Leipzig Ballet performs at the Opernhaus. The performances feature classics as well as modern dance programmes. Ticket prices range from DM12 to DM35.

Pubs & Bars *Film Café-Intershop*, Burgstrasse 9, is a café-pub popular among young Leipzigers. Its name derives from the defunct chain of GDR-run hard-currency shops.

The bar at the *Mövenpick* (see Places to Eat) is great – grab peanuts from the huge barrel by the bar, shell 'em, eat 'em and throw the shells on the floor. There's free food from 5 to 7 pm daily. *Spizz* is a very chic place to hang out, with three levels, slow service and a good range of wines and beers.

A small but fun place is *Form Bar* (☎ 960 05 72), Handwerker Passage at Markt 10, an intimate bar by night and a jewellery shop during the day. It draws an interesting crowd, but the WC is next door.

Gay & Lesbian *Café Vis a Vis*, just north of the Hauptbahnhof at Rudolf-Breitscheid-Strasse 33, draws a largely gay clientele (open 24 hours). Other popular gay bars include the *Black Horse* (☎ 284 01 6), Rossstrasse 12, a gay-friendly Irish pub, and *Markt NEUN*, on Barfussgässchen.

Getting There & Away

Air The enormous and ever-expanding Leipzig-Halle airport, which serves the two cities (it's practically equidistant from both) is served by several airlines including British Airways (☎ 224 18 96), Aeroflot (☎ 224 18 61), Lufthansa (☎ 224 16 00) and Condor (☎ 224 22 49).

Most airlines have their offices in Terminal B at the airport but there are offices in town, including Aeroflot (☎ 960 00 01), Kolonnadenstrasse 8-10, and British Airways (☎ 211 07 77), Reisebüro Arcadia, Dittrichring 1.

SAXONY

Train Leipzig is an important link between eastern and western Germany, with connections to all major cities in the country. There's regular and frequent service between Leipzig and Frankfurt every two hours (DM93, 3¾ hours), Munich hourly (DM122, 5½ hours), Dresden hourly (DM28, 1½ hours), Berlin twice an hour (DM43, two to three hours), Hanover hourly (DM63, three hours), Hamburg hourly (DM114, 4½ hours), Rostock hourly with change required (DM94, about five hours) and Stuttgart hourly with one direct night train (DM94, about five hours).

Ride Services There are two local Mitfahrzentrale. One, combined with the Mitwohnzentrale (see Places to Stay above), is at Rudolf-Breitscheid-Strasse 39 (☎ 194 40 or ☎ 211 42 22). The other, Campus Mitfahrzentrale (☎ 973 78 55), is at Augustusplatz 9-10. Fares (including booking fee) include: Berlin DM20, Munich DM40 to DM50, and Frankfurt DM45.

Getting Around

The Airport Zubringerbusse Leipzig shuttles the 20km between Leipzig-Halle airport and the Hauptbahnhof (DM9 adults, DM4.50 for children aged six to 14), running from the airport every half-hour from 5.45 am to 8 pm, and from the Hauptbahnhof every half-hour from 3.45 am to about 10 pm.

Public Transport Trams are the main form of public transport in Leipzig, with the most important lines running via Willy-Brandt-Platz in front of the Hauptbahnhof. The S-Bahn circles the city's outer suburbs. Fares are time-based (not zone-based), with DM1.40 (15-minute) and DM2 (60-minute) adult tickets available. A 24-hour ticket – if stamped on Saturday, it's valid all day Sunday – costs DM7, while strip-tickets valid for four journeys cost DM5 for 15-minute rides, or DM7.50 for 60-minute rides.

Car & Motorcycle Be extremely careful of trams at all major intersections, but especially at Tauchnitz Strasse at Martin-Luther-Ring.

Taxi Taxi rates in Leipzig are DM3.50 flag fall and DM2 per km. Taxis line up outside the Hauptbahnhof and at taxi ranks; you can order one through Funktaxi (☎ 488 4) or Löwen Taxi (☎ 982 22 2). From 10 pm to 7 am, any bus or tram driver will arrange for a taxi to meet you at the bus or tram stop – the reservation is free, the taxi is not.

Bicycle The ADFC has an office (☎ 306 51 82) at Bernhard-Göring-Strasse 52. Bicycle rental is available at several locations, including:

Berger (☎ 941 03 00), Am Sandberg 26, from DM10 per day, reserve three days in advance
Bike Department Ost (☎ 689 33 34), Rosa-Luxemburg Strasse 45, from DM10 per day
Fahrrad Ossi (☎ 302 57 57), Holzhäuser Strasse 60, DM15 per day plus DM100 deposit
Eckhardt Zweiräder (☎ 512 40), Georg-Schumann-Strasse 75, from DM15 per day plus DM150 deposit

ZWICKAU

- *119,000*
- *area code* ☎ 0375

Once a major centre of GDR industry, Zwickau, one hour south of Leipzig, is perhaps best known as the place from where the mighty Trabants rolled ... slowly ... very slowly ... off their assembly lines.

First mentioned in 1118, Zwickau began life as a trading and silver-mining town, but it's been a seat of the German auto industry since 1904, when the Horst factory churned out roadsters. Horst was nationalised by the GDR, and when it had been sufficiently devolved, Trabant production began.

These days, the Trabi grounds have been completely renovated and taken over by the company Trabant always tried to emulate, Volkswagen.

Zwickau was also the birthplace of composer Robert Alexander Schumann (1810-56), and his house is now open as a museum. This, plus a lovely city centre and an impressive cathedral, make Zwickau worth a stop.

Orientation & Information

The Altstadt is surrounded by the circular Dr-Friedrichs-Ring. The Hauptbahnhof is west of the Altstadt, connected to it by Bahnhofstrasse and Schumann-Strasse. Leipzigstrasse is the main road jutting north from Dr-Friedrichs-Ring; it becomes the B175/B93, which splits off north of the city. Stay on the B93 to get to Leipzig. There's a serious lack of street signs throughout the city.

The tourist information office (☎ 293 71 3/14) is at Hauptstrasse 6, right in the centre of the city. The staff are very friendly and have a huge range of pamphlets, books and magazines on the city and the region; they also book private rooms and sell theatre tickets. It's open Monday to Friday from 9 am to 4 pm, Saturday from 9 am to noon. Lufthansa has an office (☎ 294 41 4) right next door.

The central post office is opposite the Hauptbahnhof. There's a Schnell und Sauber coin-operated laundrette at Leipzigstrasse 27. The lovely Löwenapotheke pharmacy is on Hauptmarkt.

SAXONY

City Centre

The narrow, twisting streets of Zwickau's Altstadt are a joy to walk. At Hauptmarkt, the southern end of Hauptstrasse, sits the **Rathaus**, looking for all the world like a theatre, and next door is the city **theatre**, looking like a city administration building. Behind the theatre is the **Kleine Bühne Puppet Theatre** and **Theater im Malsaal am Gewandhaus** (see Entertainment).

Behind Hauptmarkt (though the address is Hauptmarkt 5) is the **Schumann Haus** (☎ 215 26 9), open Tuesday to Saturday from 10 am to 5 pm, closed Sunday and Monday (admission DM5, discount DM3, children DM1.50). It contains exhibits on the composer and his wife, Clara, a noted pianist.

Also behind Hauptmarkt is an **archaeological dig** on the site of the Gasthof zum Weissen Hirsch – the plans of the hotel are on permanent display outside, and you can watch digs from Monday to Friday.

The city's **Marienkirche** (1219), where Schumann was baptised, is justifiably a place of pride. It was converted to the late-Gothic style from 1453 to 1565, the steeple added between 1671 and 1679. Inside, the church has an impressive stone **font** (1538, cover

The Inevitable Trabi Joke

The Trabant (1949-89) was the GDR's answer to Volkswagen. Intended to be economical, convenient and ubiquitous, it succeeded in being only the latter. Despite production times from hell (the *average* Trabant owner waited nine years to get their lemon), the Trabi, as it was affectionately dubbed, is still one of the most common cars on the road in eastern Germany.

Each Trabi took so long to build because its plastic pieces (most of the vehicle's parts, aside from the frame, bonnet and other necessarily strong sections were plastic) were moulded by workers running hand-operated moulding systems.

A plastic car with a two-stroke engine that you had to wait years to own? That reminds us of a little joke.

A Texas oil man heard that there were cars in East Germany so popular that buyers had to wait years to take delivery of one. He immediately sent a cheque to the Trabi factory.

The directors sensed a propaganda coup in the making and arranged to send him the very next car off the line.

Two weeks later the oil man was in a bar, speaking with some friends.

'I ordered me one o' them Trabis that folks over there wait 12 years to get,' he drawled, 'and you know, them East Germans are so efficient. Why, just last week they sent me over a little plastic model so I can know what to expect.' ■

1689), restored in 1960, and a wonderful **high altar shrine**.

On Dr-Friedrichs-Ring, at the corner of Schillerstrasse and just in front of the Westsächsische Hochschule, is the **Solar Anlage**, an enormous orange solar-powered sculpture that shows the date, time and temperature.

Automobile Museum

The best thing about Zwickau's Automobilmuseum (☎ 205 21 8), Walter-Rathenau-Strasse 51, isn't the excellent exhibition on Zwickau auto production (from Horst through Audi and all makes of Trabant), but rather the gift shop, where for DM5 you can buy plastic wind-up toy Trabants, advertising posters and other Trabi trinkets. The car exhibitions are fantastic, with lots of different Trabant models and prototypes – you're really stylin' in a three-cylinder IFA-F9 Trabant Cabrio (1949-53).

Upstairs, the Horst and Audi-Sachsen Ring cars are classic, sleek limousines, fire engines and other great cars, plus there's a cutaway Trabant and samples of Trabi manufacturing equipment.

Admission is DM5/3.50, tours in German are DM5, and you'll have to pay DM1 to take photographs (DM3 for video).

Places to Stay

There's no hostel or camping ground in Zwickau yet, but a strange entry is the *Beherbergungsgewerbe Karin Kretzschmar* (☎ 441 33 72 or ☎ 215 41 0), a stark place in the middle of nowhere with spooky, if clean, dorm beds for DM25 or singes/doubles for DM30/50. Your co-residents will probably be foreign workers in Germany for factory gigs. The place is at Leipzigstrasse 240, the last stop on tram No 4 way north of the Altstadt, set back about 150m from the main road.

About 5km north of town in Crossen, the *Etap Hotel Zwickau-Crossen* (☎ 0375-475 88 6) at Rudolf-Ehrlich-Strasse 9 has very clean, modern rooms in cubicle-like comfort for DM50/60 (DM50 for all on weekends).

Back in town, the clean enough *Hotel-Sachsenring* (☎ 216 25 1), Leipzigstrasse 160, has rooms from DM60/85.

The *Achat Hotel* (☎ 297 11 1; fax 297 88 8), Gleisstrasse 8/1 (actually Leipzigstrasse north of the Altstadt) is an absolutely spotless, totally modern place with large, comfortable singles/doubles from DM140/180 (including breakfast) on weekdays; all rooms DM109 from Friday to Sunday. If you're staying in town for a while they have two-room apartments for DM70 a day.

Places to Eat

There's a *Burger King* on Hauptmarkt, and a *Nordsee* at Hauptstrasse 23. The *Stadt Café*, Hauptstrasse 14-16, is a blast from the past (the tiles in the men's room are absolutely hysterical). The *Jugendcafé City Point* (☎ 213 70 0), Hauptstrasse 44, is a very cool place, and a bit farther up the road is *Italian Eisspezialitäten Gianno* at Hauptstrasse 62.

There's good Chinese food at *China Restaurant Mou Tai* (☎ 212 12 5), Leipzigstrasse 40, with lunch specials of a main course plus egg roll or soup for DM10. At other times main courses run from DM10 to DM12.

The *Bistro Basilicum* at the Achat Hotel is a nice, modern place with great desserts and friendly, if slow, service.

Right down the street from the Schnell und Sauber laundrette is *Pizzeria Pinocchio*, with a wonderful atmosphere and hushed but attentive service. Pizzas are from DM8 to DM12, pastas from DM8 to DM11 and risotto from DM9 to DM13.

Entertainment

Kommunales Kino at the *Kleine Bühne* (☎ 215 87 5), just behind Hauptmarkt, shows English-language films. There's lots of theatre, dance, concerts and puppet shows at *Theater Zwickau* (☎ 216 00 9), *Kleine Bühne Puppentheater* (☎ 215 87 5) and *Theater im Malsaal am Gewandhaus* (☎ 216 00 9), all just behind or on Hauptmarkt. There's also an interesting theatre programme at *Sero – Theater im Hauptbahnhof* (☎ 296 66 2).

The *Jugendclub Roter Oktober*, Kolpingstrasse 54 at the corner of Leipzigstrasse, open daily from 7 pm to 1 am, is a scream: a tiny bar dedicated to all things GDR, with posters of Communist luminaries, propaganda, flags and drink specials like Intershop Weissbier and Castro Libre. The *Tullamore Pub* is an Irish pub at Leipzigstrasse 26, with live music on Fridays.

There's cheap beer (DM2.70 per half litre of Mauritius, the local pils) and a pool table at the *Café am Rathaus* opposite the Rathaus on Hauptmarkt.

Getting There & Away

There are direct trains every two hours, or hourly service with one change, from Leipzig's Hauptbahnhof (DM19, 1¼ hours). By car, it's about a 1½-hour drive from Leipzig on the B93.

Getting Around

Trams (DM1.80 or five rides for DM9) serve outlying areas, but it's easy to walk in the Altstadt.

SAXONY

DRESDEN

- *501,500*
- *area code* ☎ 0351

In the 18th century the Saxon capital, Dresden, was famous throughout Europe as 'the Florence of the north'. During the reigns of Augustus the Strong (ruled 1694-1733) and his son Augustus III (1733-63), Italian artists, musicians, actors and master craftsmen, particularly from Venice, flocked to the court at Dresden.

The Italian painter Canaletto depicted the rich architecture of the time in many paintings, which now hang in Dresden's Alte Meister Gallery alongside countless masterpieces purchased for Augustus III with income from the silver mines of Saxony.

In February 1945 much of Dresden was devastated by Anglo-American firebombing raids. At least 35,000 people died in the attack, which happened at a time when the city was jammed with refugees and the war was almost over. There is great debate about the bombing of Dresden, which was inspired more by vengeance than strategic necessity.

In the postwar years quite a number of Dresden's great baroque buildings were restored, but the city's former architectural masterpiece, the Frauenkirche, is still in the early stages of a laborious and enormously expensive reconstruction.

The Elbe River cuts a curving course between the low, rolling hills, and in spite of modern rebuilding in concrete and steel, this city invariably wins the affection of visitors. With its numerous museums and many fine baroque palaces, a stay of three nights is the minimum required to appreciate Dresden.

Orientation

Dresden is a sprawling city. The Elbe River cuts through it in a rough V-shape that separates the northern section of town from the southern. The southern contains most of the main attractions, but the north has lots of its own, too.

Most of Dresden's priceless art treasures are housed south of the Elbe in two large buildings, the Albertinum and the Zwinger, which are at opposite sides of the largely restored Altstadt. From Dresden Hauptbahnhof, the Prager Strasse pedestrian mall leads north into this old centre. Major redevelopment is planned for the area around the Hauptbahnhof and Prager Strasse, including a dozen new high-rise buildings as well as pedestrian and traffic underpasses.

North of the Elbe, the main draws are the Albertplatz, Neustadt and Anton Stadt areas. The beautiful pedestrianised Hauptstrasse, relatively undamaged by bombing and far more charming than Prager Strasse, connects Albertplatz with Augustusbrücke.

Train & Boat Stations Dresden has two important train stations: the main Dresden Hauptbahnhof, on the southern side of town, and the nicer Dresden-Neustadt north of the river. Most trains stop at both, but the Hauptbahnhof is more convenient unless you're staying in Neustadt. Tram Nos 3 and 11, S-Bahn trains and many other trains make the 10-minute run between the two stations regularly.

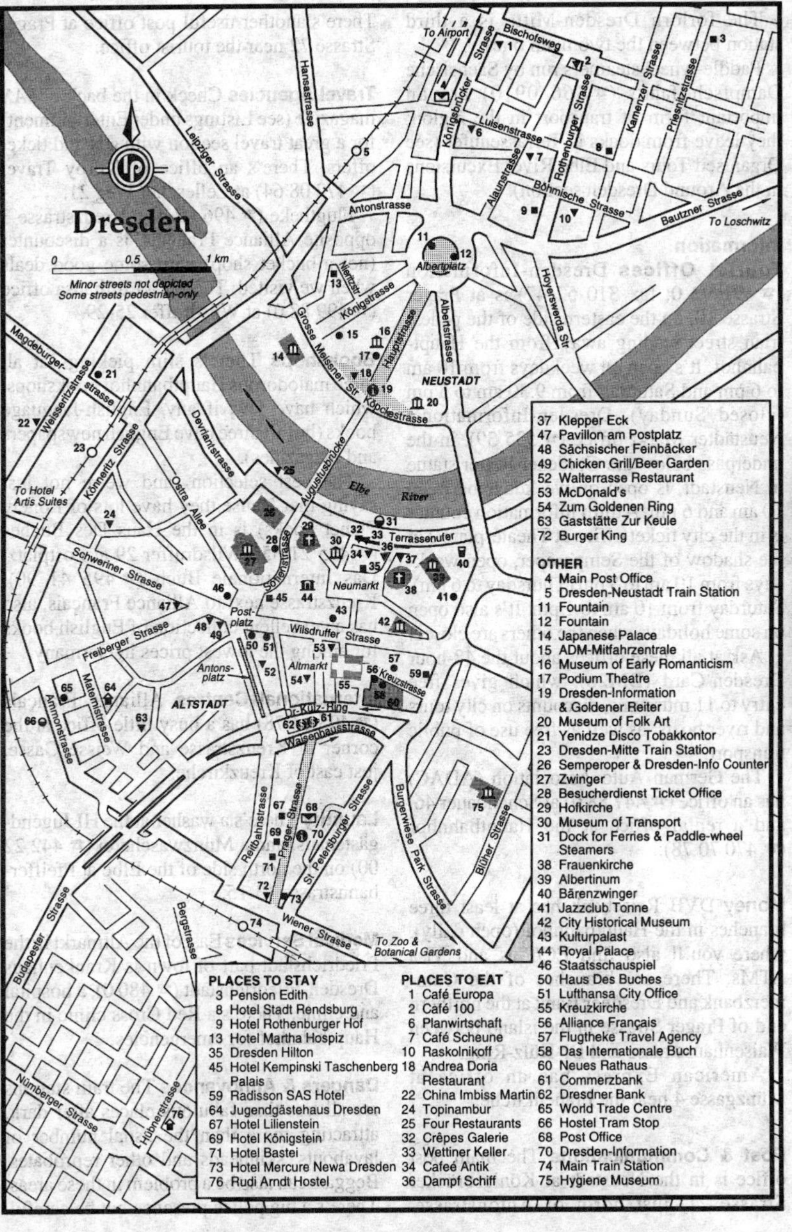
Dresden
0
0.5
1 km
Minor streets not depicted
Some streets pedestrian-only
To Airport
Bischofsweg
Hansastrasse
Königsbrücker Strasse
Rothenburger Strasse
Kamenzer Strasse
Prießnitzstrasse
Luisenstrasse
Alaunstrasse
Böhmische Strasse
Bautzner Strasse
To Loschwitz
Leipziger Strasse
Antonstrasse
Albertplatz
Nieritzstr
Königstrasse
Grosse Meissner Str
Hauptstrasse
Albertstrasse
Hoyerswerda Str
NEUSTADT
Köpckestrasse
Magdeburger-strasse
Weisseritzstrasse
Devrientstrasse
Könneritz Strasse
Ostra-Allee
Augustusbrücke
Elbe
River
To Hotel Artis Suites
Terrassenufer
Sophienstrasse
Schweriner Strasse
Neumarkt
Post-platz
Wilsdruffer Strasse
Freiberger Strasse
Antons-platz
Altmarkt
Kreuzstrasse
Marienstrasse
Ammonstrasse
ALTSTADT
Dr-Külz-Ring
Waisenhausstrasse
Reitbahnstrasse
Prager Strasse
St Petersburger Strasse
Burgerwiese Park Strasse
Blüher Strasse
Budapester Strasse
Bergstrasse
Wiener Strasse
To Zoo & Botanical Gardens
Nürnberger Strasse
Hübnerstrasse
PLACES TO STAY
3 Pension Edith
8 Hotel Stadt Rendsburg
9 Hotel Rothenburger Hof
13 Hotel Martha Hospiz
35 Dresden Hilton
45 Hotel Kempinski Taschenberg Palais
59 Radisson SAS Hotel
64 Jugendgästehaus Dresden
67 Hotel Lilienstein
69 Hotel Königstein
71 Hotel Bastei
73 Hotel Mercure Newa Dresden
76 Rudi Arndt Hostel
PLACES TO EAT
1 Café Europa
2 Café 100
6 Planwirtschaft
7 Café Scheune
10 Raskolnikoff
18 Andrea Doria Restaurant
22 China Imbiss Martin
24 Topinambur
25 Four Restaurants
32 Crêpes Galerie
33 Wettiner Keller
34 Cafeé Antik
36 Dampf Schiff
37 Klepper Eck
47 Pavillon am Postplatz
48 Sächsischer Feinbäcker
49 Chicken Grill/Beer Garden
52 Walterrasse Restaurant
53 McDonald's
54 Zum Goldenen Ring
63 Gaststätte Zur Keule
72 Burger King
OTHER
4 Main Post Office
5 Dresden-Neustadt Train Station
11 Fountain
12 Fountain
14 Japanese Palace
15 ADM-Mitfahrzentrale
16 Museum of Early Romanticism
17 Podium Theatre
19 Dresden-Information & Goldener Reiter
20 Museum of Folk Art
21 Yenidze Disco Tobakkontor
23 Dresden-Mitte Train Station
26 Semperoper & Dresden-Info Counter
27 Zwinger
28 Besucherdienst Ticket Office
29 Hofkirche
30 Museum of Transport
31 Dock for Ferries & Paddle-wheel Steamers
38 Frauenkirche
39 Albertinum
40 Bärenzwinger
41 Jazzclub Tonne
42 City Historical Museum
43 Kulturpalast
44 Royal Palace
46 Staatsschauspiel
50 Haus Des Buches
51 Lufthansa City Office
55 Kreuzkirche
56 Alliance Français
57 Flugtheke Travel Agency
58 Das Internationale Buch
60 Neues Rathaus
61 Commerzbank
62 Dresdner Bank
65 World Trade Centre
66 Hostel Tram Stop
68 Post Office
70 Dresden-Information
74 Main Train Station
75 Hygiene Museum

SAXONY

The forlorn Dresden-Mitte is a third station between the two main ones.

Paddle-wheel steamers run by Sächsische Dampfschiffahrts (☎ 866 09 0) are an important form of transport in the region; they leave from docks at Terrassenufer (see Organised Tours and Elbe River Excursions in the Around Dresden section).

Information

Tourist Offices Dresden-Information (☎ 491 92 0; fax 310 52 47) is at Prager Strasse 10, on the eastern side of the pedestrian street leading away from the Hauptbahnhof. It's open on weekdays from 10 am to 6 pm and Saturday from 9.30 am to 5 pm (closed Sunday). Dresden-Information's Neustädter Markt office (☎ 535 39), in the underpass below the Goldener Reiter statue in Neustadt, is open on weekdays between 10 am and 6 pm. A third information counter is in the city ticket office at Theaterplatz 2 in the shadow of the Semperoper, open weekdays from 10 am to 5 pm (Thursday to 6 pm), Saturday from 10 am to 1 pm. It's also open on some holidays when the others are closed.

Ask at all these offices about the 48-hour Dresden-Card (DM26), which gives free entry to 11 museums, discounts on city tours and river boats, as well as free use of public transport.

The German Auto Association (ADAC) has an office (☎ 447 88 0) at Schandauer 46, and a rental office at the Hauptbahnhof (☎ 470 70 78).

Money DVB Reisebank has at least three branches in the Hauptbahnhof (open daily), where you'll also find EC/Plus and Visa ATMs. There are branches of the Commerzbank and Dresdner Bank at the northern end of Prager Strasse in the island between Waisenhausstrasse and Dr-Külz-Ring.

American Express has an office at Münzgasse 4 near the Frauenkirche.

Post & Communications The main post office is in the Neustadt at Königsbrücker Strasse 21, just north of Antonstrasse. There's another useful post office at Prager Strasse 72 near the tourist office.

Travel Agencies Check in the back of *SAX* magazine (see Listings under Entertainment) for a great travel section with ads and ticket offers. There's an office of Kilroy Travel (☎ 472 08 64) at Zellescher Weg 21.

Flugtheke (☎ 496 02 48), Kreuzstrasse 3 opposite Alliance Français, is a discounter (not a bucket shop) with some good deals when we visited. There's a Lufthansa office (☎ 499 88 0) at Wilsdruffer 25-29.

Bookshops There's slim pickings at all three malodorous Hauptbahnhof bookshops, which have few, if any, English-language books (but all three have English newspapers and magazines).

The best selection (and we're not just saying that 'cause they have lots of Lonely Planet books) is in the Haus Des Buches (☎ 495 21 35), Wilsdruffer 29 at Postplatz. Das Internationale Buch (☎ 495 41 90), Kreuzstrasse next to Alliance Français, also has an excellent collection of English books for among the lowest prices in Germany.

International Centres Alliance Français (☎ 495 14 78) has a busy little office at the corner of Kreuzstrasse and Weisse Gasse, just east of Kreuzkirche.

Laundry There's a washer at the HI Jugendgästehaus, and a Münzwascherei (☎ 442 22 00) on the north side of the Elbe at Pfeifferhannstrasse 13-15.

Medical Services East of the Altmarkt in the Friedrichstadt part of town is Krankenhaus Dresden-Friedrichstadt (☎ 480 0), a hospital and clinic. There's a Red Cross clinic in the Hauptbahnhof for emergencies.

Dangers & Annoyances The train stations are all less than fabulous places after dark, attracting more than the usual number of layabouts, skinheads and other reprobates. Beggars can also be a problem in these areas. There's a big police presence but be careful.

Be very cautious at night in the area around Dresden-Mitte station and Yenidze disco.

Altstadt

A 10-minute walk north along Prager Strasse from the main train station brings you into the Altmarkt area, the historic centre of Dresden. Today it looks and feels just like Warsaw did a few years back. They seem to have used the same decorator, resulting in lots of granite, socialist-realism statues and an impractically wide area that's sometimes filled with a market.

Many restaurants have set up sidewalk cafés, and when the markets aren't operating it's nice to sit outside and gaze across the square.

On the east is the rebuilt **Kreuzkirche** (1792). Originally the Nikolaikirche, the church was renamed for a cross *(Kreuz)* found floating in the Elbe River by fishermen. The church is famous for its 400-strong boys' choir, the Kreuzchor, which performs every Saturday at 6 pm (free, donations suggested).

Behind the Kreuzkirche stands the neo-Renaissance **Neues Rathaus** (1905-10), topped by a shining golden statue of Hercules. Today it's the offices of the city administration, and while you can enter and gawk at the lobby, there are no scheduled tours of the building.

Cross the wide Wilsdruffer Strasse to the **City Historical Museum** (closed Monday; entry DM3, discount DM1.50) in a building erected in 1775. It contains exhibits on the city's history up to 1989. Due west of here, opposite the Altmarkt and the hugely popular McDonald's restaurant, is a centre of the city's cultural life, the obnoxiously squat **Kulturpalast**, home to a huge range of concerts and performances year round. When they replace the air-conditioning system it should sound (and feel) great.

Neumarkt

The **Frauenkirche** (Church of Our Lady), at the eastern end of Neumarkt, was built under the direction of George Bähr from 1726 to 1738. Until 1945 it was Germany's greatest Protestant church, its enormous dome known as the 'stone bell'. The church was destroyed in the bombing raids of 13 February 1945, and it was decided to leave it in rubble as a war memorial. But the movement to rebuild the church was overwhelming, and an enormous archaeological dig and reconstruction project began. Today you can see sorted pieces of the building arranged on huge steel inventory counters as the painstaking reconstruction, expected to last almost two decades, proceeds. To view the progress, take a one-hour guided tour (several daily, German only) of the Frauenkirche site; it's free, but donations are greatly encouraged, especially so from British and American visitors, who are actively made, through literature and guide talks, to feel more than a little guilty for blowing it up in the first place.

Leading north-west from Neumarkt is Augustusstrasse with the 102m-long *Procession of Princes* mural depicted on the outer wall of the former **Royal Stables**. The scene, a long row of horses, was first painted in 1876 by Wullhelm Walther and then transferred to some 24,000 Meissen porcelain tiles, which make up the mural. Join the crowds standing across the street and squinting.

Here you'll also find the interesting **Verkehrsmuseum** (Museum of Transport; closed Monday; DM4/2), with very cool turn-of-the-century transport including a railway car, huge-wheeled bicycles, dirigibles and carriages.

Brühlsche Terrasse

One of Europe's most spectacular promenades, the Brühlsche Terrasse, which has been called the balcony of Europe, is an elevated sidewalk above the southern embankment of the Elbe. In summer it's a must for strolling, with expansive views of the river, the paddle-steamers and, across the river, the Goldener Reiter statue and Neustadt.

Beneath the promenade is the **Dresden Fortress**, a Renaissance brick bastion. The museum inside is open daily and admission is DM6/4. For an extra DM2 you can get a tape player and a cassette in English (or six other languages).

Schlossplatz

Augustusstrasse leads directly to Schlossplatz and the baroque Catholic **Hofkirche** (1755), whose crypt contains the heart of Augustus the Strong. Just south of the church is the neo-Renaissance **Royal Palace**, which is being reconstructed as a museum. The restoration work is well advanced, and the Hausmannsturm (tower) and an exhibit on the reconstruction are now open to the public (DM3/1.50, closed Monday).

Theaterplatz

On the western side of the Hofkirche is Theaterplatz, with Dresden's glorious neo-Renaissance **Semperoper**. The first opera house on the site opened in 1841 but burned down in 1869. Rebuilt in 1878, it was again destroyed in 1945 and only reopened in 1985 after the Communists invested millions in restoration. The Dresden opera has a tradition going back 350 years, and many works by Richard Strauss, Carl Maria von Weber and Richard Wagner premiered here.

SAXONY

Zwinger The baroque Zwinger (1728) occupies the southern side of Theaterplatz and houses five museums. The most important are the **Old Masters Gallery** (Tuesday to Sunday from 10 am to 6 pm; entry DM7, discount 3.50), which features the works of numerous old masters, including Raphael's *Sistine Madonna*; and the **Historical Museum** (same hours; DM3/1.50), with its superb collection of ceremonial weapons.

There are also the **Mathematics Salon** (open from 9.30 am to 5 pm, closed Thursday; DM3/1.50) with old instruments and timepieces; the **Museum für Tierkunde** (Tuesday to Sunday from 9 am to 4 pm; DM2/1), with natural history exhibits, and the dazzling **Porcelain Collection** (open from 10 am to 6 pm, closed Thursday; DM3/1.50), all housed in opposite corners of the complex with separate entrances. The grey porcelain bells of the clock on the courtyard's eastern gate chime on the hour.

In the Long Gallery in the Zwinger is the **Zoological Museum** (open Tuesday to Sunday from 9 am to 4 pm; DM2/1), with an exhibition entitled 'It's Their Earth, Too.'

Albertinum

To reach the Albertinum (☎ 495 30 56), on Brühlsche Garten just off Terrassenufer, stroll east along the promenade overlooking the river. Here you'll find the **New Masters Gallery**, with renowned 19th and 20th-century paintings, and the **Grünes Gewölbe** (Green Vault), one of the world's finest collections of jewel-studded precious objects; both are closed Thursday and admission is DM7/3.50. Eventually the Grünes Gewölbe will be relocated to its original site in the Royal Palace.

Tobakkontor

As your train came into town at Dresden-Mitte station, you probably noticed a large building looking very much like a gaudy mosque, bearing the words *Yenidze* on its stained-glass onion dome. In 1907, the place opened as a tobacco factory, manufacturing a cigarette they ever so tastefully named Salaam Alakhem, and modelled the place after a mosque to incite awe of its foreign intrigue and allegedly Turkish tobacco. It didn't work.

An American tobacco company is said to be in talks to take it over, but now there's an interesting disco in the basement.

Neustadt

Neustadt is an old part of Dresden largely untouched by the wartime bombings. After unification Neustadt became the centre of the city's alternative scene, but as entire street blocks are renovated it's gradually losing its hard-core bohemian feel.

The **Goldener Reiter** statue (1736) of Augustus the Strong stands at the northern end of the Augustusbrücke, which leads to Hauptstrasse, a pleasant pedestrian mall with the **Museum of Early Romanticism** (closed Monday and Tuesday; DM3) at No 13.

On **Albertplatz** at its northern end there's an evocative marble **monument to Schiller**, and two lovely **fountains** flanking the walkway down the centre.

Museums in the vicinity of the Goldener Reiter include the **Museum für Volkskunst** (Museum of Folk Art; closed Monday; DM3/1.50) at Grosse Meissner Strasse 1, and the **Japanese Palace** (1737), Palaisplatz, with Dresden's famous **Ethnological Museum** (closed Friday; DM4/2).

Grosser Garten
South-east of the Altstadt is the Grosser Garten (Great Garden), enchanting in summer and home to the excellent **zoo** (☎ 478 06 0; open daily; DM7/3, family passes DM12 to DM19), with 2600 animals representing more than 400 species. At the garden's north-western corner are the **Botanical Gardens** (admission free). The hothouse is especially lovely during a freezing Dresden winter.

Other Museums
In a park just west of the Grosser Garten is the unique **Hygiene Museum** (closed Monday; DM4/2), Lingnerplatz 1, established by Odol-mouthwash mogul Karl August Lingner. It'll appeal to anyone with a healthy interest in the human body – cutaway models, the transparent man and other health related exhibits, including a good one on STDs and AIDS.

On the south-eastern outskirts of town on the way to Pillnitz is the interesting **Carl Maria von Weber Museum** (☎ 261 82 34), Dresdner Strasse 44 (bus No 85 to Van-Gogh-Strasse in Pillnitz), the summer home of the composer and conductor who lived and worked here for several years before his death in England in 1826 at age 39. Staff are very keen, and there are regular concerts here as well. The museum is open Wednesday to Sunday from 1 to 6 pm; admission is DM3/1.50.

As (perhaps more) impressive is the **Richard Wagner Museum** (☎ 482 29) in a positively serene setting at Richard-Wagner-Strasse 6 in Graupa (bus No 83). Dedicated staff talk you through each detail of the stormy composer's life in GDR-style mind-numbing thoroughness. (The maestro's favourite breakfast food? We won't give it away.) But there are some very nice exhibits and again, the grounds are lovely.

Organised Tours
Dresden-Information, Prager Strasse 10, books tours of its own and with the following organisations.

Get off the beaten track with thematic tours from Igeltour (☎ 804 45 57), starting at DM6. River tours are run by Sächsische Dampfschiffahrts (☎ 866 09 0) – which prides itself on having the world's oldest fleet of paddle-wheel steamers – on rebuilt steam ships that lower their smokestacks to clear bridges. The tours run daily at 10 am and noon and 2 and 4 pm and cost DM16, discount DM9. (See also Elbe River Excursions in the following Around Dresden section).

The Hamburger Hummelbahn Dresden (☎ 498 95 19) runs double-deck buses, 'choo-choo' trains and other touristy vehicles around the city, stopping at all the major sights (at clearly marked 'Hummelbahn' stops). Tours leave from Postplatz from April to October daily at the same hours as the boats (though no 4 pm tour in winter), take 1½ hours and cost DM20/16.

Special Events
Dresden's International Dixieland Festival is enormous and takes place every year in the first half of May. May's a very busy month; in addition to Pfingsten (Pentecost/Whitsun) festivals throughout the city and surrounding area, there's also the Dresden Music Festival, with 40 days of concerts and celebrations of music throughout the city.

Places to Stay
Accommodation in Dresden can be expensive, particularly hotels, with average room rates among the highest in Germany and few genuine budget places near the centre.

Camping There are two camping grounds near Dresden. The closest is *Camping*

Mockritz (☎ 471 82 26, open March to December), 5km south of the city (take the frequent No 76 Mockritz bus from behind the Dresden Hauptbahnhof). It has bungalows which, like the camping ground itself, are often full in summer.

A more appealing, if distant, choice is the spacious *Camping Mittelteich Moritzburg* (☎ 035207-423; open April to mid- October) on a lake called Mittelteich, a 10-minute walk beyond Schloss Moritzburg (see Around Dresden).

Hostels Six cheers for the best and most central hostel in town, the spotless and enormous *Jugendgästehaus Dresden* (☎ 492 62 0), in a former Communist Party training centre 15 minutes walk north-west of the Hauptbahnhof at Maternistrasse 22. Beds cost DM33/38 for juniors/seniors in basic twin or triple rooms, or DM38/45 in better twins with private shower and WC. You can make any room a single by paying an additional DM15. They have a cafeteria, games room, stellar staff and generally make a great hostel experience – one of the best in the country. Too bad the breakfast is lousy. From the Hauptbahnhof, take tram No 7, 9, 10 or 26 to the corner of Ammonstrasse and Freiberger Strasse (look for the World Trade Centre building) and walk one block north-east.

The non-DJH *Rudi Arndt Hostel* (☎ 471 06 67), Hübnerstrasse 11, is a 10-minute walk south of the Hauptbahnhof and offers dorm beds for DM22/27 juniors/seniors.

On the outskirts of Dresden are two other hostels. *Jugendherberge Radebeul* (☎ 830 52 07), Weintraubenstrasse 12 in Radebeul, makes a lot of sense – it's quiet and pleasant, and there's a public pool nearby. Take the S-Bahn towards Leipzig (every half-hour, DM4.60, 20 minutes); it's a stone's throw from the Radebeul-Weintraube stop. The *Jugendherberge Oberloschwitz* (☎ 366 72) is at Sierksstrasse 33. Both hostels charge DM24/29 for juniors/seniors.

Private Rooms Dresden-Information, Prager Strasse 10, finds private rooms priced from around DM35 per person (plus a fee of DM5 per person).

Deutscher Zentraler Simmernachweis (☎ 830 90 61; fax 830 90 79), in the northern side of the Hauptbahnhof, is a private accommodation agency that's worth checking out. They book rooms in private flats from DM30, pensions from DM35, hotels outside the centre for DM70/110 singles/doubles, or inside the centre from DM99/110.

For private rooms in the Radebeul area, contact Zentraler Zimmernachweis/IG Touristik (☎ 830 90 61; fax 830 90 79), which books rooms for between DM22 and DM50.

Hotels & Pensions – South of the Elbe *Artis Suites* (☎ 864 50), Berliner Strasse 25, 1km west of the centre, offers basic singles/doubles from DM60/90 (without breakfast).

The *Hotel Cosel* (☎ 471 94 95), August-Bebel-Strasse 46, is 2km south-east of the centre and charges DM65/100 for similar rooms.

New on the scene is *Berg-Hotel Freital* (☎ 648 48), Am Langen Rain 15-17, 6km east of the centre in the suburb of Freital, with clean rooms from DM109/119 including breakfast – fine if you're driving, but if not, it'll cost you DM25 in a taxi from the Hauptbahnhof.

Along Prager Strasse are three almost identical 1960s-style Ibis hotels: the *Hotel Bastei* (☎ 485 63 88), the *Hotel Königstein* (☎ 485 64 42) and the *Hotel Lilienstein* (☎ 485 64 89). Rates are lower in the Bastei (but staff at all three are as identical as the hotels themselves), with singles/doubles from DM112/145. At the Königstein and Lilienstein they're DM125/170.

The *Mercure Newa Dresden* (☎ 481 41 09), St Petersburger Strasse 34, is perfectly located right at the southern foot of Prager Strasse, a minute's walk from the Hauptbahnhof. Clean, perfectly fine rooms cost from DM178/188.

There are three notable expensive places. Squeaking by with the 'cheapest' expensive bed in town is the *Dresden Hilton* (☎ 864 20; fax 864 27 25), with very mod, very '60s singles/doubles from DM310/345. They rent bikes here.

Opening just as we went to press was the *Radisson SAS Gewandhaushotel* (☎ 494 90; fax 494 94 90), Ringstrasse 1 just south of Wilsdruffer Strasse, with room rates at a very Scandinavian DM320/380 (without breakfast, believe it or not).

Dresden's most elegant place is the *Hotel Kempinski Taschenberg Palais* (☎ 491 20; fax 491 28 12), Taschenberg 3 opposite the Zwinger. In a restored 18th-century mansion, it is serious luxury: swimming pool, health club, business centre, sauna and solarium. Rooms are DM395/455, and if you've just fled with the treasury of a large central African country, remember that the Kronprinzen Suite is from DM1300 to 4590 *plus* DM32 – per person – for the breakfast buffet.

In July and August, there are special rates of DM295 per room including all the extras and breakfast.

Hotels & Pensions – North of the Elbe Over in Neustadt, *Hotel Stadt Rendsburg* (☎ 804 15 51), built in 1884, is at Kamenzer Strasse 1, and offers basic singles/doubles with shared bath for DM65/95 including breakfast. The *Pension Edith* (☎ 802 83 42), in a quiet back street at Priesnitzstrasse 63, has doubles with private shower for DM103 (singles DM78); it only has a few rooms, so book well ahead.

Hotel Martha Hospiz (☎ 817 60), Nieritzstrasse 11 near Neustadt train station, has recently expanded. Under friendly family management, it offers very cheerful, simple single rooms for DM90, but most rooms are singles/doubles with private WC and shower costing DM140/230.

The *Rothenburger Hof* (☎ 812 60 17), Rothenburger Strasse 15-17, has single/double rooms with shared bath for DM105/165.

Want a view? Head for the *Bellevue Dresden* (☎ 812 00), Grosse Meissner Strasse 15 just south of the Japanese Palace, with unparalleled views across to the Brühlsche Terrasse, the ferry terminal, Neues Rathaus and the Kreuzkirche for DM230/270.

Hotels & Pensions – East of the Centre A reasonable option in the suburb of Blasewitz, several km from the centre, is the *Waldparkhotel* (☎ 344 41), Prellerstrasse 16, with basic singles/doubles from DM70/100. The nearby *Pension Andreas* (☎ 337 77 6), Mendelssohnallee 40-42, whose rooms all have private facilities, charges DM90/140 per single/double.

Places to Eat

Restaurants – bottom end & middle South of the Elbe, Terrassen Gasse, beneath the Brühlsche Terrasse at the back of the Hilton hotel, is a great place in summer for cafés and sidewalk cafés, with several places offering cheap options for sitting and watching the world go by, including *Crêpes Galerie* (☎ 864 29 46), with crêpes from DM8 to DM12 and drinks from DM3.

In the Hilton itself is *Kunst und Antiquitäten an der Frauenkirche* (☎ 864 29 48), an antique shop and café where you can sit among really expensive furniture and have arrogant staff bring you good coffee (DM3 to DM9). Farther east, at the corner of Münz Gasse, are two places, *Dampf Schiff* and *Klepper Eck*, both sidewalk beer gardens with good beer and great views of people walking up to the Brühlsche Terrasse.

Interesting restaurants are scattered pretty thinly around the Altstadt. A pleasant but unexciting place is *Walterrasse*, on Wallstrasse overlooking Antonsplatz. Drinks and meals are brought to tables on its spacious 1st-floor terrace. Also reasonable is the *Zum Goldenen Ring* at Altmarkt 18 opposite the Kreuzkirche, with main courses for around DM13.

The *Gaststätte Zur Keule* (☎ 495 15 44), below a cabaret at Sternplatz 1, is a lively beer hall that offers good, solid meals.

Dresden's down-to-earth Volk eat at *Topinambur*, Schützengasse 18 (next to the environment centre), where menu favourites include wholemeal noodles with gorgonzola sauce (DM11.50) and tofu schnitzels with baked vegies (DM14.50).

North of the Elbe, a great place to sit outside with a pils is *Andrea Doria* (☎ 803 29 49), Hauptstrasse 1a in the shadow of the Goldener Reiter statue. Service is super. Lunch main courses range from DM14 to DM20; it's open from 11 to 2 am.

Worth another mention is *Rothenburger Hof* (see Places to Stay), whose restaurant has alternating evening menus for around DM12.50 (closed Monday). For something special, dine at the *Kügelgenhaus* (☎ 527 91, open daily), Hauptstrasse 13, below the Museum of Early Romanticism in Neustadt. It has a good range of local Saxon dishes, and there's a beer cellar below the restaurant.

Neustadt's selection of late-night restaurant-bars includes the *Planwirtschaft*, in a beer cellar at Luisenstrasse 20 (through the small courtyard); *Café 100*, another cellar pub at the corner of Alaunstrasse and Bischofsweg; and the *Café Scheune*, Alaunstrasse 36, whose tasty five-course Indian menu is amazingly good value at just DM35 for two people. The bohemian *Raskolnikoff* at Böhmische Strasse 34 has cheap Russian dishes like borscht (beetroot soup) and wareniki (dough baked with potatoes and mushrooms).

SAXONY

Café Europa at Königsbrücker Strasse 68 in Neustadt is a convenient place to drop in for a meal or a drink; it only closes for one hour every day (from 5 to 6 am).

Restaurants – top end It's worth a trip out of Dresden to get to the top-end food at the restaurant in Schloss Weesenstein (see Around Dresden).

The *Sophienkeller* (☎ 497 226 0), under the Hotel Kempinski Taschenberg Palais, is a very interesting place, with good local specialities and wines and excellent service, even if they do have a tendency to burst into song (they sing good German and folk songs, they don't beg for tips, and you can tell them to leave you alone). Full dinners are DM25 to DM40, main courses are DM16 to DM28.

The *Four Restaurants*, opposite the Semperoper, offers stylish surroundings and varied food, from Italian to German specialities, at equally stylish prices. Nice for drinks before or after a performance.

Snacks & Fast Food The three markets in the Hauptbahnhof are good for stocking up before a trip. The *Asia Markt* is the best of the lot; the *Markt im Hauptbahnhof* has a better selection but is older than the *Reise Point Market*, which is much more expensive. For fast food, there are two branches of *Pizza Hut* and several Wurst stands, and breakfast at *Kaffee Mit* is never a bad idea if you're in a rush.

In Dresden-Neustadt station, stock up on food at the *Nimm's Mit*, which is larger than usual. There's also a *Burger King* and a *Le Cro Bag*, which does croissants and good coffee.

If you're stuck at Dresden-Mitte station, hit *China Imbiss Martin* (☎ 490 58 88), across the road at Weisseritzstrasse 38, which does enormous fried noodle dishes for DM7.50 to DM9.50 and stays open to 9 pm.

South of the Elbe, the city's several *Burger King* and *McDonald's* outlets are quite the scene, packed with people and spilling outdoors in summer.

In the Post Platz/Theaterplatz section, there are several fast-food options, though clientele at some is, shall we say, scruffy. The *Pavillon am Postplatz* is the nicest of these, with good doner (DM4 to DM6), Grillhaxe with sauerkraut (DM8.50) and half chickens for DM4.50. Next door there's a good *Sächsischer Feinbäcker* with pastry, cheese bread and the like. Be careful at the *chicken grill* on the west side of Post Platz; it's a pleasant enough beer garden and has half chickens for DM3.80, but lots of unsavoury characters, too.

Entertainment

Listings Without a doubt, the finest all-round listings guide to Dresden is *SAX* (DM2.50), available at newsstands around the city. It has listings for clubs, restaurants, schools, cafés, travel agencies and cheap tickets, and a whole lot more. Less useful freebies include *Blitz* and *Spot*; they're available at clubs, restaurants and bars.

Tickets Tickets for all theatres in town can be bought at the following three places: the *Besucherdienst* office at Theaterplatz 2 (at the side of the palace opposite the Semperoper); Dresden-Information; or at the theatre box office an hour before each performance. Tickets for the Semperoper cost from DM30, but they're usually booked out well in advance. In fact, the Besucherdienst office suggests that for major performances – *The Magic Flute*, *Der Freischutz*, *Fidelio* etc – you should reserve as far as a *year* in advance by writing them at Besucherdienst Theaterkasse Anrechtsbüro, Theaterplatz 2, Postfach 120712, 01008 Dresden.

Many theatres close for holidays from mid-July to the end of August.

Cinema Undubbed English films are shown at Programmkino Ost (☎ 310 37 82), Schandauer Strasse 73, and less frequently at Quasimodo (☎ 866 02 11), Adlergasse 14.

Discos & Clubs *Yenidze – Die Diskotek* (☎ 494 00 94), Weisseritzstrasse 3 near Dresden-Mitte station, is a hip place in the basement of this weird former tobacco company. It gets a mixed crowd (aged 25 to 40). On Friday night women get in free and get a DM10 coupon for drinks.

Hollywood (☎ 502 24 51), Bautzner Strasse 118, is a very popular spot with hip hop, acid jazz and some techno.

Speaking of techno, that's pretty much all that's on offer at *Mega Drome* (☎ 837 12 21), Meissner Strasse 507 in Radebeul. Older crowds find solace at *Banana Diskotek* (☎ 842 04 0), Lommatzscher Strasse 82, in the Elbepark/Stadthaus.

Gay *Down Town* (☎ 801 18 52), Katherinenstrasse 11-13, is gay on Monday only. Gerede Lesben, Schwule und alle Anderen (☎ 464 02 20) is a resource centre that also runs a gay and lesbian-friendly café.

Theatre There's an active theatre scene in Dresden, with many small companies playing throughout the city; the best bet is to check in *SAX* . Dresden's two great theatres are the *Staatsschauspiel*, near the Zwinger, and the *Staatsoperette*, at Pirnaer Landstrasse 131, in Leuben in the far east of the city.

The *Landesbühnen Sachsen* (☎ 895 42 14), Meissner Strasse 152 in Radebeul, has a good range of drama, music and cabaret, along with some ballet and opera. *Podium* (☎ 804 32 66), upstairs at Hauptstrasse 11, is a very cool alternative theatre. A couple more alternative places are *Theater in der Fabrik* (☎ 421 45 05), Tharandter Strasse 33, and, especially convenient if you're staying in the Jugendgästehaus Dresden, *theater 50* (☎ 495 41 23), in the former GDR business centre near the World Trade Centre. Inside the latter is *Komödie Dresden* (☎ 866 41 0), geared more to comic plays than stand-up acts.

Classical Music Dresden is synonymous with opera, and performances at the spectacular *Semperoper*, opposite the Zwinger, are brilliant. Performances by the renowned Philharmonic also take place in the Semperoper but mainly in the *Kulturpalast*.

Rock & Jazz A variety of musical events are presented in the *Kulturpalast* (☎ 486 63 06), which changes its programmes daily.

The *Jazzclub Tonne* (☎ 495 13 54), Tzschirnerplatz 3, has live jazz five nights a week (entry DM12 to DM20).

There's a fun jazz and Dixieland cruise on paddle-steamers every Friday and Saturday from 7 to 10 pm with music, food and drinks during a swing up the Elbe; the cost is DM24/12 for adults/children up to 14.

Pubs & Bars The best area to head to for a drink is the southern end of Königstrasse and Hauptstrasse, where lots of combination bar/restaurants can be found (see Places to Eat).

The *Bärenzwinger* (☎ 495 14 09) is a cheap students' bar in an old cellar at Brühlscher Garten in front of the Albertinum. It has pantomime, cabaret or live music most nights.

Getting There & Away

Air Dresden-Klotzsche airport, 9km north of the city centre, is served by Lufthansa and other major airlines.

Bus Dresden's bus station is attached to the Hauptbahnhof; regional buses depart for more remote Saxon destinations.

Train Dresden is just over two hours south of Berlin-Lichtenberg (DM45) by fast train. The Leipzig-Riesa-Dresden service (DM28, 1½ hours) operates hourly. The double-deck S-Bahn trains run half-hourly to Meissen (DM6.50, 30 minutes). There are also direct trains to Frankfurt (DM120, 5½ hours), Munich (DM135, seven hours), Vienna (DM89/58 for those over/under 26, an additional DM8 for EuroCity trains, eight hours), Prague (DM30/20/8, 2½ hours), Budapest (DM106/67/9.50, via Prague, 10½ hours), Warsaw (DM60/37, via Görlitz and Kraków, 10 hours) and Wrocław (Breslau in German, DM39/37, 4½ hours).

Car & Motorcycle To/from Leipzig, take the A14/A4. From Berlin, take the A113 to the A13 south. To the Czech Republic, take the B170 south. From Munich, take the A9 to the A72 and on to the A4.

Ride Services There's an ADM-Mitfahrzentrale (☎ 194 40) at Königstrasse 10. Some destinations and prices (including fees) are: Berlin DM23, Hamburg DM50, Prague DM15 to DM20 and Munich DM49.

Getting Around

The Airport The Airport City Liner runs between Dresden-Klotzsche airport and Dresden-Neustadt station (DM6) and the Hauptbahnhof (DM8). It runs weekdays from 7.30 am to 8.45 pm, Saturday from 8.30 am to 1 pm and 2.30 to 9 pm, Sunday from 10 am to 1 pm and 2.30 to 9 pm.

Public Transport Fares for Dresden's bus and tram-based transport network are charged by the time travelled – there are no zones. Seven-ride strip tickets cost DM8.50; stamp once for 10 minutes of travel (but no more than four stops), or twice for 60 minutes' travel. Day/weekly tickets cost DM8/22. Bicycles or dogs cost DM1.

Car & Motorcycle All major car-rental firms have offices at the airport. Driving in town is a cinch; signs are good and parking is easy. Note that there are Parkshein ticket machines in use in the centre.

Taxi Taxis line up in ranks outside the Hauptbahnhof and Dresden-Neustadt stations. To call a taxi ring ☎ 459 81 12; a ride between the two main stations is about DM15; from the Hauptbahnhof to the Jugendgästehaus Dresden is about DM8.

Bicycle The luggage counters at both the Hauptbahnhof and Dresden-Neustadt stations rent spanking new bicycles, all with baskets and some with child seats, for DM10 per day.

AROUND DRESDEN

Sächsisches Schweiz (Saxon Switzerland), the area south of Dresden near the Czech border, is a wonderfully sprawling land, dotted with castles and tiny towns. Get information on hiking in the Sächsisches Schweiz National Park from Dresden-Information (☎ 491 92 0; fax 310 52 47) at Prager Strasse 10.

You can follow the hordes and head for the beautiful castles at Moritzburg and Pillnitz, or go off the tourist route to the unheralded and absolutely lovely castle and gardens at Weesenstein. Whatever you do, though, don't miss a visit to Meissen, the porcelain capital of Germany and a lovely little city in its own right.

Weesenstein

In Weesenstein, a charming, untouched town 20km south-east of Dresden, **Schloss Weesenstein** is one of the most under-visited and untouched extant medieval castles in Germany.

Built by the margraves of Dohna, who owned land stretching into Bohemia, the castle was begun in the 13th century as a fortification along busy trade routes.

In 1385, a feud began when a son of the margraves' family danced too closely to the wife of Jeschka, a knight from Colbitz. Over the next 20 years the feud escalated into full-scale battle between the families, and the margrave of Meissen was called in to be an impartial judge in the conflict.

Impartial as he was, he awarded the castle to himself, and then gave it to his cronies in the Bühnau family, who lived here for the next 360 years.

The castle today is a mixture of Gothic, Renaissance and baroque architectural styles. It expanded in concentric circles, and by the time they got round to adding a beer cellar, the only place to put it – the castle is built atop a hill – was *upstairs* from the living quarters.

The castle was later the home of King Johann who, from 1860 on, actually ran the Saxon court from here rather than from Pillnitz.

Exhibits are designed to let you really see how royalty and servants lived here – down to the toilets. The **Bier Keller**, where they brewed Weisenstein beer from the 16th century (they expect to begin brewing again in 1999) is open to visitors, as is the lovely **chapel**, which hosts regular concerts.

Manuscripts of music by the Bühnau family's court composers have just been rediscovered in state archives, and a CD of recordings of the music is available (DM33) at the cashier.

Behind the castle are the story-book baroque **gardens**, open to the public and bisected by a stream fed by a waterfall.

The castle is open Tuesday to Sunday from 9 am to 6 pm. Admission is DM6, discount DM4, and it's an extra DM5 to take photos. There are Sunday services in the chapel at 8.30 am.

Special Events In mid-May during the Pfingsten (Pentecost or Whitsun holiday), the town holds its **Mittel Alter Fest** (Middle Ages Festival; DM10/5), which features jousting, medieval crafts, local speciality foods and freshly brewed beer. During fine weather it's some of the most fun you can have in Germany and not at all on the tourist track.

Places to Eat The *Schloss Café*, on a balcony overlooking the formal gardens, serves coffee (DM2 to DM4), beer (DM3 to DM4.50) and ice cream (DM6.50). There's a lovely view.

Dresdeners drive to the *Krönigliche Schlossküche* (☎ 035027-537 8) for nice dinners out, and so should you. It has excellent Saxon specialities and very nice touches like flower petals in the Lauch (leek) soup. Superb game and beef dishes with local mushrooms and other vegetables run from DM21 to DM31 for main courses, DM9.50 to DM12.50 for starters.

Getting There & Away There are five trains a day (DM5, 20 minutes) from Dresden's Hauptbahnhof to Weesenstein's train station, about 500m south of the castle – follow the road up the hill and you can't miss it. By road, a lovely way to go is to head east out of Dresden along the B172 to Prohlis, turning right at the Bahr Baumarket (direction: Borthen), turn right again in Röhrsdorf (direction: Dohna), head through Dohna and follow the signs.

Pillnitz Palace

From 1765 to 1918, this palace on the Elbe, about 10km directly south-east of Dresden, was the summer residence of the kings and queens of Saxony. The most romantic way to get there is on one of Dresden's old steamers. The cost for round-trip passage (six departures a day from the Sächsische Dampfschiffahrts dock in Dresden) is DM20; the journey takes 1¾ hours.

Otherwise, take tram No 14 from Wilsdruffer Strasse, or tram No 9 from in front of the Dresden Hauptbahnhof, east to the end of the line, then walk a few blocks down to the riverside and cross the Elbe on the small ferry, which operates year round. The museum at Pillnitz (open from May to mid-October) closes at 5.30 pm, but the gardens (which stay open till 8 pm) and the palace exterior with its Oriental motifs are far more interesting than anything inside, so don't worry if you arrive too late to get in.

Schloss Moritzburg

This palace rises impressively from its lake 14km north-west of Dresden. Erected as a hunting lodge for the duke of Saxony in 1546, Moritzburg was completely remodelled in baroque style in 1730, and it has an impressive interior. Entry costs DM6 (students DM4), and it's open Tuesday to Sunday from 10 am to 5.30 pm (until 3.30 pm in winter). Behind the palace is lovely parkland ideal for strolling. There are buses to Moritzburg from Dresden's Hauptbahnhof, as well as five trains a day. The 45-minute trip's price was under review as we went to press.

Elbe River Excursions

From May to November Sächsische Dampfschiffahrts (☎ 0351-866 09 0; see Organised Tours under Dresden) has frequent services upriver from Dresden via Pirna (DM24) and Bad Schandau (DM27) to Schmilka (DM27). Here the Elbe River has cut a deep valley through the sandstone, producing abrupt pinnacles and other striking rock formations. Local trains return to Dresden from Schmilka-Hirschmühle (opposite Schmilka) about every half-hour until late in the evening (DM10.50, 54 minutes), with stops all along the river. On weekends, boats also run downriver as far as Meissen (DM27).

MEISSEN

- *pop 35,600*
- *area code* ☎ 03521

Some 27km north-west of Dresden, Meissen is a perfectly preserved old town and the centre of a rich wine-growing region. Its medieval quarter, Albrechtsburg, crowns a ridge high above the Elbe River, and contains the former ducal palace and Meissen Cathedral, a magnificent Gothic structure. Augustus the Strong of Saxony created Europe's first porcelain factory here in 1710.

Orientation

Meissen straddles the Elbe, with the old town on the western bank and the train station on the eastern bank. The train/pedestrian bridge behind the station is the quickest way across and presents you with a picture-postcard view of the river and the Altstadt.

From the bridge, continue up Obergasse then bear right through Hahnemannsplatz and Rossplatz to the Markt, the town's central square. A new road bridge is being built a km downriver; from 1998 or 1999 it will replace the vehicle-choked Elbbrücke and divert traffic from the historic centre.

Sächsische Dampfschiffahrts boats arrive and depart from the landing on the west side of the Elbe, about 300m east of the Markt. Very helpful pointer signs throughout the city make it hard to get lost.

Information

The helpful Meissen-Information (☎ 454 47 0), in an old brewery at An der Frauenkirche 3 just off the Markt, charges a service fee of DM5 per person for finding accommodation in private rooms. In summer the office is open weekdays from 10 am to 6 pm and weekends from 10 am to 3 pm. Winter opening hours are weekdays only from 9 am to 5 pm.

Change money at the Commerzbank in the Hauptbahnhof or at the Sparkasse (with an ATM outside), at the corner of Dresdner Strasse and Bahnhof Strasse.

Things to See & Do

On the Markt are the **Rathaus** (1472) and the 15th-century **Frauenkirche** (open 10 am to 4 pm daily from May to October). The church's tower (1549) has a porcelain carillon, which chimes every quarter-hour – this, along with the church's traditional bells, makes an interesting acoustic contrast: *bink* ... BONG ... *pi-bink* BONG. It's well worth climbing the tower (DM2) for fine views of Meissen's Altstadt; pick up the key in the church or from the adjacent Pfarrbüro (parish office).

Various steeply stepped lanes lead up to the **Albrechtsburg**, whose towering medieval **cathedral** (open daily; DM3.50 or DM2.50 for students), with its **altarpiece** by Lucas Cranach the Elder, is visible from afar. Beside the cathedral is the remarkable 15th-century **palace** (open daily but closed in January; DM6, discount DM3), constructed with an ingenious system of internal arches.

Meissen has long been renowned for its chinaware, with its trademark insignia of blue crossed swords. The Albrechtsburg palace was originally the manufacturing site, but the **porcelain factory** is now at Talstrasse 9, a km south-west of town. There are often long queues for the workshop demonstrations (DM7/5), but you can view the fascinating porcelain collection in the museum upstairs at your leisure (another DM7/5). Even if you're not interested in buying anything, it's still worth having a look at the factory's porcelain shop downstairs.

There are two lovely carved-stone **drinking fountains**. The one in the Markt is new (1995); the other, at the northern end of Burgstrasse in Platz am Café Zieger, dates from 1884.

Organised Tours

There are 1½-hour guided tours of the town in German daily at 1 pm (meet at the tourist office), which include visits to (but not inside) the porcelain factory. The cost is DM6, discount DM3.

Places to Stay

Budget accommodation is fairly scarce, but Meissen-Information can often find private rooms from around DM30 per person (plus a service fee of DM5 each).

Camping Rehbocktal (☎ 452 68 0) is in a beautiful forest at Scharfenberg on the banks of the Elbe, 3km south-east of Meissen. Charges are DM3 per car, DM5 per tent plus DM6.50 per person. The four-person bungalows are good value at DM17.50 per person for the first night, DM12.50 thereafter; take bus No 404 from the station.

The very crowded, non-DJH *Jugendgästehaus* (☎ 453 06 5), Wilsdrufferstrasse 28, about 20 minutes walk south of the Markt, offers beds in small dorms for DM20. Call first – if they're full they say so on their answering machine.

The *Pension Burkhardt* (☎ 458 19 8), in a renovated building about halfway between Rossmarkt and the porcelain factory at Neugasse 29, offers fair value for money. It has attractive rooms all with WC, shower, phone and TV from DM60/90 a single/double. The *Pension Schweizerhaus* (☎ 457 16 2), off Talstrasse at Rauhentalstrasse 1, has seven double rooms, all with private shower and WC, from DM90. A similar deal is offered by the *Haus Hartlich* (☎ 452 50 1), on the southern edge of town at Goldgrund 15.

A new entry with a wonderful location (but petulant staff) is the shining *Hotel Am Markt 6* (☎ 400 41 0), with very clean rooms, all with satellite TV and bathroom, from DM95/145.

Places to Eat

Meissen's cheapest surprise is the *Meissner Hof*, Lorenzgasse 7 (closed weekends). A bowl of vegetable stew costs DM3, a steaming serving of Soljanka (Russian sour soup) with bread is DM2.80, and half-litre mugs of frothy beer go down the hatch for just DM3 – definitely lower than average prices. The *Kellermeister*, a simple pub at Neugasse 10, has daily set-meals from DM7.40.

For cheap snacks, look for outlets of the chain bakery *Sächsisches Bäckerhaus Meissen*, with several locations around town including one opposite the Hauptbahnhof. They have good pastry, pizza and snacks.

On the way up to the Albrechtsburg is the *Gaststätte Winkelkrug*, Schlossberg 13 (closed Monday and Tuesday). It's in a quaint old building with many cosy corners, and you can eat from as little as DM8. The *Rabener Keller*, in an old arched wine cellar below at Elbstrasse 4, offers local specialities from around DM15.

The *Weinschänke Vincenz Richter*, An der

Frauenkirche 12 (closed Sunday and Monday), is rather expensive but it's in an old house with plenty of atmosphere (the interior looks more like a museum – check the torture chamber). The food menu is short but the wine list long. A better place to sample Meissen's fine fermentations is the *Probierstube* (☎ 735 53 3), 10 minutes walk north-east of the train station at Bennoweg 9. It's run by the local wine growers' cooperative and dishes up hearty food to complement the excellent wines.

Café Antik (☎ 451 38 8), Burgstrasse 6 in the courtyard, is a fine place on summer days, with a very nice atmosphere, drinks from DM2 to DM5 and light meals from DM8 to DM12.

Pizzeria Gallo Nero (☎ 452 73 5), Elbstrasse 10, comes highly recommended, with pizzas averaging DM7 to DM10 and pastas from DM10 to DM12.

SAXONY

Getting There & Away

Meissen is most directly accessible from Dresden by the half-hourly S-Bahn trains from the Hauptbahnhof and Dresden-Neustadt train stations (DM6.50, 30 minutes), but a more interesting way to get here is by steamer (between May and September). Boats leave from the Sächsische Dampfschiffahrts dock in Dresden at 9.30 am for the two-hour journey, which costs DM27 return. Boats head back to Dresden at 3.15 pm.

GÖRLITZ

- *pop 75,000*
- *area code* ☎ 03581

Some 100km east of Dresden on the Neisse River, Görlitz emerged from WWII with its beautiful old town virtually unscathed, though the town was split in two under the Potsdam Treaty, which used the Neisse as the boundary between Germany and Poland.

A major trading city and cultural bridge between east and west and north and south, Görlitz's wealth is obvious from its buildings, which have survived wars but not, unfortunately, three great fires over the years. Sections destroyed in successive fires were rebuilt in the style of the day, and today the city's Renaissance, Gothic and baroque architecture is better preserved than that of any city its size in Saxony. After receiving UNESCO protection for some 3500 buildings, Görlitz is receiving special federal funding to restore its entire Altstadt.

The locally made pils, Landskron, is out of this world.

Görlitz is a surprisingly cosmopolitan place, and it makes for a very nice side trip from Dresden, or an overnight stopover between Germany and Poland.

Orientation & Information

The Altstadt spreads to the north of the Hauptbahnhof; Berliner Strasse and Jacob Strasse connect the two. There are several market squares; at the northern end of Jacob Strasse is Postplatz, containing the main post office. North of here is Damianiplatz/Marienplatz, home to the Karstadt department store and the town's main bus stop and tram stop; north of here is Elisabethstrasse, where a lively market takes place on Saturday, and north of that is Obermarkt, for all intents and purposes, the main town square.

East of Obermarkt is Untermarkt, which leads to Neissestrasse and finally to the Neisse River. The Polish town of Zgorzelec ('zgo-ZHE-lets'), part of Görlitz before 1945, is on the east side of the river; see Lonely Planet's *Poland* or *Eastern Europe* guides for more information on this and the beautiful city of Wrocław ('VROTS-wuf'), 30 minutes east.

West of the city towers is – get this – the dormant volcano of Landeskrone. There's a viewing tower at the top.

The tourist office, Görlitzinformation (☎ 475 70; fax 475 72 7), is at Obermarkt 29. It's open Monday to Friday from 10 am to 6 pm, Saturday from 10 am to 4 pm and Sunday (except in January and February) from 10 am to 1 pm.

Change money at the Deutsche Bank on Damianiplatz or the Dresdner Bank at Postplatz.

Fun fact – the city sits on 15° longitude, the dividing line for Central and Eastern

European time. Technically, then, it should take you an hour to walk from the Untermarkt to the river, but the whole town is on CET.

Obermarkt & Southern Altstadt

The tourist office is interesting for its brochures as well as for the fact that Napoleon stayed here in 1813 and addressed his troops from the balcony above the entrance. At the eastern end of Obermarkt is the 16th-century **Dreifaltigkeitskirche**, a former salt house, cloister and guard house.

At the western end of Obermarkt are the remains of town fortifications, two structures now open as museums (Tuesday to Sunday from 10 am to 5 pm; admission DM3, discount DM2). The **Reichenbacherturm**'s seven floors were used until 1904 by 'tower families' entrusted to keep a watchful eye out for fires in the town. The **Kaisertrutz** (1490) is now home to temporary art exhibitions.

Behind the latter is the city **theatre** and the **Blumenuhr**, a flower clock handy as a meeting point.

A bit south of Postplatz is the newly restored **Strassburg Passage**, connecting Berliner Strasse and Jacob Strasse. It's at least as impressive as the Art Nouveau **Karstadt** department store at Damianiplatz/Marienplatz, once a hotel. Walk into its centre, look up and gawk at its amazing **skylight**.

At the northern end of Damianiplatz/Marienplatz is the **Dicke Turm**, also known as the Frauenturm and Steinturm, and almost 5.5m thick in some places.

Untermarkt

Perhaps the most beautiful section of town, Untermarkt is built around a fountain of Neptune and contains the **Rathaus**, begun in 1537 and built in three sections and three styles. The oldest is at the south-western corner of the square and its tower features a spectacularly restored clock, astrological clock and gold-plated lion (which roars occasionally). Concerts are held here in summer. Heading east on Neissestrasse brings you past the **Barokhaus/Library** at No 30, a museum (DM3/2) in the town's only purely baroque house; the **Biblischehaus** next door, whose façade is adorned with reliefs of Old and New Testament scenes; and finally to the river and the **Technical Museum** (free entry) beneath the easternmost restaurant in the country (see Places to Eat).

North from Untermarkt, walk along Peterstrasse to the Gothic **Peterskirche** (1497), containing a fascinating 'sun organ' built by Silesian-Italian Eugenio Casparini and his son, with pipes shooting off like rays. It's to be reinstalled here soon.

Organised Tours

Walking tours (DM5) leave from in front of Görlitzinformation every Saturday at 2 pm and every Sunday at 11 am.

Places to Stay

The grim *DJH hostel* (☎ 406 51 0), south of the station at Goethestrasse 17, charges juniors/seniors DM21/25. Exit the Hauptbahnhof via the Südliche Ausgang, turn left and follow the road to Goethestrasse.

Book private rooms at Görlitzinformation; rooms average DM25 to DM50 per person.

There are few things as pleasant to write about as wonderfully run family hotels; *Zimmervermietung Annette Münch* (mobile ☎ 0170-947 02 16), Büttnerstrasse 8, is one of these. In a beautifully restored house, rooms (singles/doubles are DM40/60, including breakfast) are very comfortably appointed, have satellite television and are as romantic as you'd like. Breakfast, downstairs in the sunny breakfast nook, is great, too. The street is unmarked and just north-west of Ubermarkt.

The next best bet in town is the charming *Gasthaus Zum Flyns* (mobile ☎ 0172-861 53 38), Langenstrasse 1 just west of Untermarkt, another lovely restoration, with similar prices, very friendly and helpful staff and a good restaurant downstairs.

The central *Gästehaus Lisakowski* (☎ 400 53 9), Landeskronstrasse 23, offers simple singles/doubles for DM60/90.

The most central hotel in town is the newly renovated *Sorat Hotel Görlitz* (☎ 406 56 67), Struvestrasse 1 at the north-east corner of Marienplatz, with modern rooms going for DM145/175. Claiming a view (neglecting to say it's a view of Poland) is the always dependable *Hotel Mercure* (☎ 662 0; fax 662 66 2), Uferstrasse 17f, a modern place on the river with rooms from DM162/204.

Places to Eat

If you don't mind a little proselytising with your food, you're in for a treat at the *Mission Soup Kitchen*, Langenstrasse 43 (entrance on Fleischerstrasse), which serves bowls of hot soup daily from 11 am to 1 pm for DM1.

There's a *Nimm's Mit* grocery shop and a *doner kebab takeaway* in the Hauptbahnhof; service at both reminds one of past administrations.

Inside the Strassburg Passage is a good *Becker's Backhaus*, the very popular *Eiscafé Lisotto* and a huge *Spar* supermarket.

As well as a lovely interior with vaulted ceilings, the restaurant in the *Gasthaus Zum Flyns* has nice wines and local specialities like Flyns Steak – pork cutlet with baked banana, curry sauce and croquettes – for DM15.

The easternmost restaurant in Germany is the *Vierradenmühle* (☎ 406 66 1), at the site of one of the bridges that spanned the Neisse before WWII. Today there's a main filtration station here, the works of which are beneath the restaurant, making it a double whammy: easternmost restaurant and technical museum. Ask the owner, Dietmar Dörfer, for a tour; he'd be happy to show you around. If you're not in the mood for all that action, walk inside and look down through the glass floor at the pump station.

Food, by the way, is excellent here, with main courses for lunch from DM5 to DM8 and dinner mains from DM12 to DM22. The terrace over the Neisse is a requirement for any visitor.

Getting There & Away

Over a dozen daily trains run in either direction between Görlitz and Dresden (1½ to three hours, DM24). There are also about the same number of connections between Görlitz and Berlin (DM60, 2½ to four hours).

Görlitz is an important border crossing; daily Frankfurt-Warsaw and Berlin-Kraków trains make a stop here before heading into Poland via the historic Neisseviadukt bridge (1847), a 450m-long, 35m-high span with 35 arches.

Trains run from Görlitz to Wrocław at 12.30 and 8.04 am and 8.24 pm (DM14, 2½ hours). The latter train continues to Warsaw (DM34.50, eight to nine hours).

Thuringia

The 'green heart' – as Thuringia (Thüringen) is widely known – is an integral part of German tourism these days. Much of Thuringia's appeal lies in its natural landscape: large, lush forests and sprawling valleys cover much of the state and offer limitless opportunities for outdoor activity.

But it is the state's cultural heritage that draws most visitors to Thuringia. It was here that Johann Wolfgang von Goethe and Friedrich Schiller penned most of their best-known works. Johann Sebastian Bach was born in Thuringia, and the Hungarian composer Franz Liszt founded a music school here. The Bauhaus architectural movement originated in this state, whose countryside inspired painters like the American Lyonel Feininger. The reformer Martin Luther preached here and took refuge in Wartburg castle. His nemesis, the revolutionary Thomas Müntzer, led the Peasants' War on Thuringian soil, and the 19th century saw the founding of the German workers' movement. In a grotesque irony, Weimar – the centre of the German Enlightenment, where nearly every house bears a plaque in a testament to the luminary who lived or worked within – exists scant km from the horrors of the Buchenwald concentration camp.

No other German state has been characterised by territorial fragmentation as much as Thuringia. The Kingdom of Thuringia was decidedly short-lived, existing only from the 4th century to the year 531, when Frankish troops quashed King Herminafried and began converting the locals to Christianity. After the 13th century, the area splintered into countless duchies and principalities – a squabbling patchwork of microstates that is commemorated today by the stars on the state flag.

Only in 1920 was Thuringia reconstituted as a state within something ap- proaching its original borders. Under communism, it was again split into separate districts before being reunited for the third time in 1990.

HIGHLIGHTS

- Goethe House in Weimar
- Hiking the Goethe Trail or the Rennsteig, German's oldest and most famous trail
- The Kyffhäuser Monument and Panorama Museum in Bad Frankenhausen
- Wartburg Castle, Martin Luther's hideout, in Eisenach
- The cathedral in Erfurt

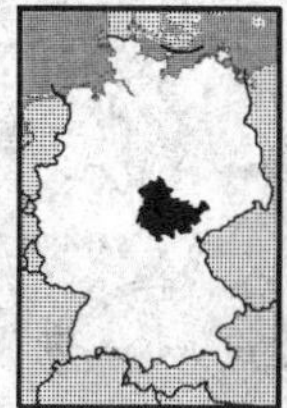

• **Population:** 2.5m • **Capital:** Erfurt • **Area:** 16,250 sq km

Thuringia Luminaries: Ernst Abbe, Johann Sebastian Bach, Karl Philipp Emanuel Bach, Max Weber, Carl Zeiss

With 16,250 sq km Thuringia is the smallest of the five new German states. With 2.6 million people, it is rather densely populated although there are no big cities. Even the capital, Erfurt, has only 215,000 people.

Compared with other states of the former GDR, Thuringia's touristic infrastructure is fairly well developed because, along with the coastal resorts along the eastern Baltic, it was one of the top holiday areas for East Germans before the Wall came down.

Travelling within Thuringia is relatively easy, certainly by eastern German standards; trains connect most towns. One of the most scenic rides is from Erfurt to Meiningen through the Thuringian Forest. There's also

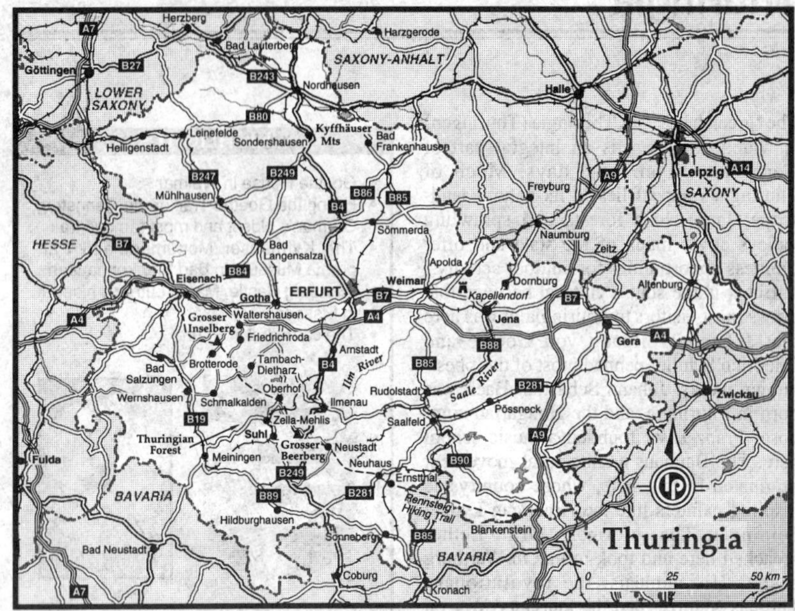

a bus system, though it is usually slow, infrequent and often restricted to weekdays. Despite the relatively short distances, if travelling by car or motorcycle be prepared for long hours on tedious – though usually scenic – country roads.

State-of-the-art hotels have mushroomed since unification, though they tend to charge top Deutschmark. Budget options, on the other hand, are depressingly scarce. Besides hostels and camping grounds, your best bets are private rooms, though standards vary widely.

Central Thuringia

Thuringia's main towns – Eisenach (known for Wartburg castle), charming Gotha (with its perfectly preserved baroque palace filled with wonderful art treasures), Erfurt, Weimar and Jena – are strung like pearls on the A4 autobahn bisecting Thuringia.

ERFURT

- *pop 215,000*
- *area code* ☎ 0361

Erfurt, the capital of Thuringia, was founded by St Boniface as a bishopric in 742. In the Middle Ages the city catapulted to prominence and prosperity due to its location on the Via Regia, an important trade route from Paris to Kiev, and to the local production of a much desired blue pigment from the woad plant. The Altstadt's many well preserved buildings attest to that period's wealth.

Erfurt's university was founded in 1392 and soon became a centre of humanism that counted the young Martin Luther among its students. Erfurt was also known as the 'Thuringian Rome' because it contained some 90 churches within its walls; 20 of them are still standing. Later on, it was governed successively by the bishop of Mainz,

Napoleonic troops (1807-14), Prussia (1815-1945) and the GDR until 1990. During WWII, damage was extensive, but since the *Wende*, restoration and modernisation efforts have picked up and made Erfurt an extremely attractive, lively town that deserves a day or two of exploration.

Orientation

Most of the car traffic is routed around the Altstadt via two ring roads, making it a pleasure to walk between the main sights (do watch out for the fast-moving trams, though). The train and bus stations are just beyond the south-eastern edge of the town centre. It's a five-minute walk from here north along Bahnhofstrasse to Anger, the main shopping and business artery. The little Gera River bisects the Altstadt, spilling off into a number of creeks. Erfurt's landmark, the Dom St Marien, is at the western end of the Altstadt.

Information

Tourist Office The main tourist office (☎ 562 34 36; fax 655 11 19) is at No 3 right on the historic Krämerbrücke and is open weekdays from 10 am to 6 pm, Saturday to 4 pm and Sunday to 1 pm. A second branch is at Schlösserstrasse 44 (☎ 562 62 67) near the Rathaus (open weekdays 10 am to 6 pm, Saturday to 1 pm), but it will probably have moved to Fischmarkt 27 by the time you read this.

Both offices sell the ErfurtCard (DM25), which buys admission to most museums in town, a few castles in the vicinity, and unlimited public transport for 72 hours. A one-day pass to the city's museums is good value too at DM5.

Money A number of banks with regular business hours cluster at the intersection of Bahnhofstrasse and Juri-Gagarin-Ring near the Hauptbahnhof. Your best bet, though, may be the Reisebank inside the train station itself which is open to 7.30 pm Tuesday to Friday and to 4 pm Saturday and Monday.

Post & Communications The main post office on Anger has a public fax-phone and a copy machine. Poste-restante mail is delivered here; letters should be clearly marked as *Hauptpostlagernd* and to 99084 Erfurt.

Medical Services & Emergency The general phone number for medical emergencies is ☎ 115. After hours (between 7 pm and 7 am and on weekends), you can go directly to the clinic (☎ 262 64) at Espachstrasse 2. For dental problems, call ☎ 516 18. There's a police station (☎ 662 0) at Andreasstrasse 38.

Walking Tour

Unless noted otherwise, museums mentioned below are open from 10 am to 5 pm from Tuesday to Thursday and on Sunday, to 1 pm on Friday and 1 to 5 pm on Saturday. Students get a 50% discount on all admissions.

Though a state capital, Erfurt is surprisingly small, and most sights are conveniently grouped together in the Altstadt. This walking tour begins at the train station and ends at Fischmarkt in the heart of the city. It takes you to all the major sights and will last anything from two hours to a full day, depending on how many places you choose to visit.

From the Hauptbahnhof head north on Bahnhofstrasse. Just after crossing Juri-Gagarin-Ring, you'll come upon the 14th-century **Reglerkirche** on the eastern side of the street. The portal and the southern tower of the former Augustinian monastery church are Romanesque, and the large carved altar dates back to 1460.

Bahnhofstrasse intersects with Anger, which is lined by houses from seemingly different historical periods but most of them are only about 100 years old. The quince-yellow, richly stuccoed **Angermuseum** (DM3) immediately to your left, however, is original baroque (1706-12). The rooms that once housed a packing and weighing station now harbour extensive collections of medieval arts and crafts, 19th and 20th-century landscape paintings and 18th-century Thuringian faïences (glazed earthenware).

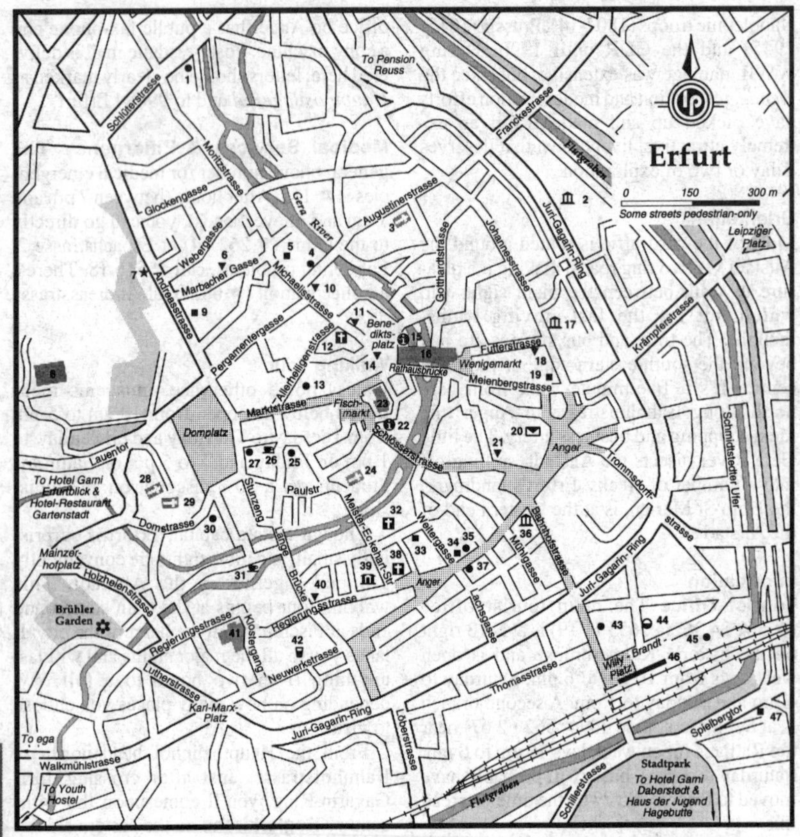

As you head west on Anger, pay attention to the opulent façades at No 28 and No 37-38. You'll also pass the **Bartholomäusturm**, a tower that is all that remains from the 15th-century court church of the counts of Gleichen.

Head down Regierungsstrasse for a few steps to the part-Renaissance, part-baroque **Statthalterpalais**, once home to city governors and now the office of the Thuringia state governor. Turn north on Meister-Eckehart-Strasse past the Catholic **Wigbertikirche** to the haunting ruins of the **Barfüsserkirche**, a medieval gem left as a memorial after it was destroyed by WWII bombs. Only the choir was restored and now houses a small museum of medieval art (open May to October, closed between 1 and 2 pm; DM2).

Farther north along Meister-Eckehart-Strasse is the 13th-century **Predigerkirche**, a basilica with a reconstructed baroque organ. From the church head west on Paulstrasse and Kettenstrasse to the giant Domplatz, presided over by the stunning **Severikirche** and the imposing cathedral itself, joined by a flight of 70 stone steps.

PLACES TO STAY
- 5 Pension & Pizzeria Don Camillo
- 9 Hotel zum Bären
- 19 Dorint Hotel
- 33 Hotel Ibis
- 34 Hotel Zumnorde
- 47 Hotel Spielbergtor

PLACES TO EAT
- 6 Double B
- 10 Zum Augustiner
- 11 Wirtshaus Christoffel
- 14 Gaststätte Feuerkugel
- 18 Gasthaus zum Rebstock
- 21 Anger Maier
- 26 Barock-Café
- 31 Altstadt Café
- 40 Suppengrün
- 42 Dubliner Irish Pub

OTHER
- 1 Rotplombe
- 2 Museum für Thüringer Volkskunde; Museumskeller
- 3 Augustinerkloster
- 4 Georgenburse
- 7 Police Station
- 8 Petersberg
- 12 Michaeliskirche
- 13 Studentenclub Engelsburg
- 15 Tourist Office Krämerbrücke
- 16 Krämerbrücke
- 17 Haus zum Stockfisch (City History Museum)
- 20 Main Post Office
- 22 Tourist Office Schlösserstrasse
- 23 Rathaus
- 24 Predigerkirche
- 25 Haus zum Sonneborn
- 27 Theater Waidspeicher; Die Arche Cabaret
- 28 Severikirche
- 29 Dom St Marien
- 30 Spar Supermarket
- 32 Barfüsserkirche
- 35 Bartolomäusturm
- 36 Angermuseum
- 37 Jazzkeller
- 38 Wigbertikirche
- 39 Statthalterpalais
- 41 Schauspielhaus
- 43 Rewe Supermarket
- 44 Central Bus Station
- 45 Rewe Supermarket
- 46 Main Train Station

Dom St Marien

Looming at the western end of Domplatz, St Mary's Cathedral had its origins as a simple chapel from 752 but wasn't completed until the 14th century. In order to build the choir, the hillside occupied by the earlier church had to be artificially extended, creating the enormous substructure on which the cathedral now perches. This also required construction of the stone staircase, which you must climb to enter the church via the richly ornamented triangular portal.

Perhaps the single most impressive sight inside are the bright **stained-glass windows** dating from between 1370 and 1420 and showing scenes from the Old and New Testaments. Other interior highlights are the **Wolfram** (1160), a bronze candelabrum in the shape of a man, the **Gloriosa bell** (1497), the Romanesque **stucco Madonna** and the 14th-century **choir stalls**. Tours are available but you can guide yourself with the help of a free pamphlet, available as you enter.

Around the Dom

Adjacent to the cathedral is the **Severikirche** (1280), a five-aisled hall church boasting a stone Madonna (1345) and a 15m-high baptismal font (1467), as well as the sarcophagus of St Severus, whose remains were brought to Erfurt in 836.

North of the Dom complex, on a little hill, is the **Petersberg**, the site of a former citadel which can be entered through a baroque portal. The remains of the Romanesque **Peterskirche** grace the plateau with especially fine views of the Altstadt. The main tourist office offers tours of the Petersberg at 2 pm on Saturdays.

Back on the Domplatz, take a look at the ornate façades of the houses at its eastern side, then duck into the tiny Mettengasse. Immediately to your right is the **Waidspeicher**, now a puppet theatre and cabaret but formerly a storage house for *Waid* (woad), a plant that produced blue dye and brought wealth to Erfurt in the Middle Ages. A few metres farther is the **Haus zum Sonneborn** (1536) with its richly ornamented portal, now the city's wedding office.

Andreas Quarter

At the end of Mettengasse, turn north into Grosse Arche, cross Marktstrasse and head north-east on Allerheiligenstrasse. You're now in the former university quarter, which is undergoing a badly needed restoration.

Amid the rubble, you'll find the **Haus zur Engelsburg** at Allerheiligenstrasse 20, where a group of humanists met between 1510 and 1515 to compose at least two of the contentious *Dunkelmännerbriefe* (Obscurantists' Letters). These were a series of satirical letters mocking contemporary theology, science and teaching practices. It is now a students' club.

Beyond lies the Gothic **Michaeliskirche**, where Martin Luther preached in 1522. Across the street is the arched portal of the **Collegium Majus**, the only remaining section of the old university building (1512-15) destroyed in 1945. The university was founded in 1392 and for centuries was so prominent that Luther himself called it 'my mother to which I owe everything'. It closed in 1816, but plans to reopen it in a new location are currently under way. To see where Luther lived as a student, take your next left into Michaelisstrasse and a right turn on Augustinerstrasse to get to the **Georgenburse**, a 15th-century student residence that was later a prison.

Farther along is the austere **Augustinerkloster**, where Luther was a monk from 1505 to 1511. Enter either via Kirchgasse or Comthurgasse. The monastery, where Luther was ordained as a priest, can only be seen on a guided tour (DM4.50, discount DM3) which takes in the church (note the 14th-century stained-glass windows), the cloister, an exhibit on Luther and his cell. From the monastery, Gotthardtstrasse leads south to the best view of the lovely medieval **Krämerbrücke** (merchant bridge), an 18m-wide curiosity lined by two rows of houses and buttressed by six arches spanning the Gera River.

THURINGIA

Fischmarkt

From the western end of Krämerbrücke, walk down Marktstrasse to **Fischmarkt**, the medieval market square with a gilded statue of a Roman warrior at its centre. It is flanked by several noteworthy buildings, including the **Haus zum Breiten Herd** (1584), festooned with a rich Renaissance façade. The frieze depicting the five human senses continues with the four virtues on the adjacent **Gildehaus**. Also note the **Haus zum Roten Ochsen** (1562), another Renaissance gem (and now a gallery) opposite the neo-Gothic **Rathaus** (1870-75). It's worth taking a look inside the town hall for the series of murals along the stairwell depicting scenes from the *Tannhäuser* and *Faust* legends, as well as for the extravagant festival hall on the 3rd floor.

Museums

At Johannesstrasse 169, at the eastern end of the Altstadt, is the late-Renaissance **Haus zum Stockfisch**, once the home of a woad merchant and now containing the **City History Museum** (DM3). Highlights here include an ornate reliquary shrine, a medieval bone carver's workshop and insignia from the former university. For insight into the history of Thuringian folk art, visit the **Museum für Thüringer Volkskunde** (DM3) at Juri-Gagarin-Ring 140a, where you can see the reassembled workshops of a glass blower, toy carver, mask maker and other craftspeople as well as the products they made, including pottery, carvings, painted furniture and folk clothes.

West of the city centre is the **ega**, which stands for Erfurter Gartenausstellung, a huge garden show centred around **Cyriaksburg** castle (tram No 2 from Anger). For a complete assault on nose and eyes, visit in spring. It is open daily from 9 am to 6 pm; entry is DM4.

Organised Tours

The tourist office at Krämerbrücke offers a two-hour walking tour of the historical Altstadt at 1 pm daily from April to October and on weekends only the rest of the year (DM6, discount DM3). A city tour by tram leaves weekends at 11 am and 2 pm from the eastern end of the Domplatz (DM16, children DM12, family card DM40).

Places to Stay

The availability and quality of rooms in Erfurt has improved significantly in recent years. Top-quality accommodation, though, has its price, and if you can't spend big, you may have to put up with less comfort or stay outside the city centre. For DM5, the tourist office (☎ 194 33) will book you into a hotel or find you a private room (around DM30/60 for singles/doubles). Options are also listed in the *Erfurt magazin* (see Entertainment below). Unless mentioned, all prices quoted here include breakfast.

Camping The nearest camping ground is *Ferienpark Hohenfelden* (☎ 036450-420 81) in the scenic Ilmtal about 15km south of Erfurt (bus No 155 from the central bus station to Hohenfelden Stausee; DM5 one way). It's one of Thuringia's largest and most modern facilities and is open all year. Charges are DM7.50 per person, DM3.50 per tent and DM4 per car.

Hostels Erfurt's newly renovated *DJH hostel* (☎ 562 67 05) is about 2km south of the city centre at Hochheimer Strasse 12 (tram No 5 from the train station to Steigerstrasse, then a five-minute walk). Bed & breakfast is DM24/28 for juniors/seniors; sheets are DM7. A pleasant alternative is the independent *Haus der Jugend Hagebutte* (☎ 423 30 00) at Hagebuttenweg 47a (tram No 6 to Färberwaidweg). Beds in double rooms go for DM15/30, breakfast is DM6, and sheets DM5.

Hotels All prices quoted are for rooms with shower and WC.

Pension Reuss (☎ 740 63 55) at Spittelgartenstrasse 5, north of the city centre, is a great bargain with singles for DM45 and doubles for DM85. Budget options in the suburb of Daberstedt, just south-east of the Altstadt, include *Hotel Garni Daberstedt* (☎ 373 15 16) at Buddestrasse 2 with singles ranging from DM50 to DM85 and doubles topping out at DM90. West of the Altstadt is the family-run *Hotel Garni Erfurtblick* (☎ 220 66 0), Nibelungenweg 20, with rooms for DM90/130, and the cute *Hotel-Restaurant Gartenstadt* (☎ 210 45 12), which charges from DM95/125.

Among the row of hotels and pensions along Andreasstrasse just north of the Domplatz, the traditional *Hotel zum Bären* (☎ 562 86 98; fax 562 86 98) at No 26 stands out. Rooms with all facilities cost DM155/185. One of the best bargains in town is *Pension Don Camillo* (☎ 642 29 23) at Michaelisstrasse 29. Huge, modern rooms with kitchenette cost DM100/120. The pizzeria downstairs is great too (see Places to Eat). Right next to the Barfüsserkirche ruin at Barfüsserstrasse 9, is a branch of the *Ibis* (☎ 664 10; fax 664 11 11) chain of hotels. These are good, reliable business hotels charging a flat DM130 per room, plus DM15 per person for breakfast. If they're not busy on weekends, you may be able to get a double room for only DM79. Behind the train station, at Spielbergtor 20, is *Hotel Spielbergtor* (☎ & fax 348 10), with singles in the DM110 to DM195 range and doubles costing between DM165 and DM210.

One of Erfurt's finest hotels, with lots of comfortable facilities and character, is *Hotel Zumnorde* (☎ 568 00; fax 568 04 00) at Anger 50-51 (enter from Weitergasse). The German president and celebrities like it for its classy atmosphere and large rooms, which go for DM185/210 singles/doubles. Another winner is the central *Dorint Hotel* (☎ 594 90; fax 594 91 00) at Meienbergstrasse 26-28, which has all the amenities of a state-of-the-art business hotel. Ask for a room in the historical wing. Singles/doubles range from DM170 to DM220.

Places to Eat

Restaurants & Cafés Rubble may be piling up on the pavement as the Andreasviertel undergoes a face-lift, but the bars and restaurants along Michaelisstrasse and its side streets already hint at the rebirth of this former university quarter as Erfurt's entertainment strip. Lots of cosy restaurants serve traditional Thuringian cuisine, including *Gaststätte Feuerkugel* at No 4, which has main dishes from DM13 served in a large wood-panelled dining room with picture windows and lace curtains. At *Zum Augustiner*, a warmly lit restaurant at No 32 with a fake oak tree 'growing' through the ceiling, you can fill up from DM10. The rustic

Wirtshaus Christoffel at No 41 has a pricier menu with main dishes for between DM20 and DM35.

For a change from hearty German food, go to *Pizzeria Don Camillo* at No 29, where Aldo from Turin serves killer pizza and pasta dishes. Nearby, at Marbacher Gasse 10, is *Double B*, a student pub serving about two dozen varieties of cooked breakfasts all day.

Vegetarians should try *Suppengrün*, a clean, cafeteria-style soup kitchen at Regierungsstrasse 70 with an organic menu that changes every day (open until 6 pm). In summer, try to grab a terrace table above the little canal of the *Altstadt Café* in Fischersand, just west of Lange Brücke. A stylish place for traditional coffee and cake is the *Barock-Café* on the corner of Grosse Arche and Mettengasse. The tunnel-like *Anger Maier*, at Schlösserstrasse 8, is an Erfurt institution. It's always crowded – no wonder with snack prices starting at DM5 and daily specials from DM11.

A good place to meet people over a pint of Guinness and hearty fare is the *Dubliner Irish Pub*, Neuwerkstrasse 47a, next to a construction site the size of several football pitches. For dining in a highly civilised atmosphere at surprisingly civil prices, go to *Gasthaus zum Rebstock* in the historic wing of the Dorint Hotel (enter from Futterstrasse).

Self-Catering There's a Rewe supermarket in the InterCity Hotel east of the train station and another on Bahnhofstrasse, about two minutes' walk north of the station. You'll also find a large Spar market behind the Dom at the south-western corner of Domplatz.

Entertainment

Be sure to pick up a copy of the free monthly events publication *Erfurt magazin* which is available from the tourist office.

For classical theatre, Erfurt has its *Schauspielhaus* on Klostergang, south of the Domplatz. The ticket office (☎ 223 31 55) is at Dalbergsweg 2. The *Theater Waidspeicher* (☎ 598 29 24) is a popular puppet theatre – and not just for children – on the ground floor of the medieval building at Domplatz 18 (in a courtyard reached via Mettengasse east off Domplatz). Upstairs is the home of the satirical cabaret *Die Arche* (☎ 598 29 24).

Popular with young people is the historic *Studentenclub Engelsburg* (☎ 562 90 36) at Allerheiligenstrasse 20-21, a dance club with live concerts most nights after 9 pm (student discounts available, Thursday night free). Another live-music venue is the *Rotplombe* (☎ 210 91 0) on Schlüterstrasse, at the corner of Amploniusstrasse (entrance downstairs in the alley on the left). Most concerts cost under DM10. Both clubs are closed on Monday.

The *Museumskeller* (☎ 562 49 94), in the same building as the Museum für Thüringer Volkskunde at Juri-Gagarin-Ring 140a, has live concerts on Friday and Saturday nights. For jazz, go to the *Jazzkeller* (☎ 561 25 35) at Anger 28-29, open only on Thursday after 8 pm.

Getting There & Away

Air Erfurt's small airport (☎ 656 22 00) is in the suburb of Bindersleben, about 5km west of the city centre. Apart from some holiday charters, it has mostly domestic flights.

Bus Because it's so well connected by rail, bus service to/from Erfurt is fairly limited. Most lines make the rounds of outlying villages and are of little interest to the visitor. There's one bus weekdays to Schmalkalden in the Thuringian Forest (No 618) and several to Rudolstadt (No 13) on the Saale River. Buy your tickets from the driver.

Train Erfurt's Hauptbahnhof (☎ 194 19 or ☎ 562 48 22/23 for information) has direct InterCity (IC) trains every two hours to Berlin-Lichtenberg (DM72, 3½ hours), Leipzig (DM28, 1½ hours), Dresden (DM57, three hours) and Frankfurt (DM68, 2½ hours). There's also direct service to the Thuringian Forest towns of Meiningen (DM21.80, two hours) and Schmalkalden (change in Zella-Mehlis; DM20, two hours). Trains to Weimar (DM6.80, 20 minutes) and

Eisenach (DM13.20, 30 minutes) run several times hourly.

Car & Motorcycle Erfurt is just north of the A4 (exits Erfurt-West or Erfurt-Ost) and crossed by the B4 (Hamburg to Bamberg) and the B7 (Kassel to Gera). Most major car-rental agencies have offices at the airport. Avis can be reached at ☎ 656 24 25, Hertz at ☎ 656 24 69 and Europcar at ☎ 656 24 44.

Getting Around

Bus No 891 runs four times daily from the Hauptbahnhof to the airport. You can also take tram No 1 to Hauptfriedhof, then change to bus No 91/92 to Flughafen. The trip takes about 30 minutes and costs DM2. A taxi should cost around DM20.

The Erfurt Verkehrsbetriebe (☎ 194 49) operates an efficient tram and bus system covering practically every corner of the city. The suburban area is divided into three zones (yellow, red, blue), and the entire city centre is within the yellow zone. Buy your tickets from orange ticket vending machines at all stations and also directly on the trams and buses. Single tickets for one zone cost DM2, a five-ticket block DM7.50 and day passes are DM5. A one-zone day pass for up to five people (no more than three over age 14) costs DM12. To order a taxi ring ☎ 511 11 or ☎ 666 66 6.

EISENACH

- *pop 45,000*
- *area code* ☎ 03691

The birthplace of Johann Sebastian Bach, Eisenach is a small, industrial town on the edge of the Thuringian Forest with a long tradition as a car-manufacturing centre. Its main attraction is Wartburg castle. Richard Wagner based his opera *Tannhäuser* on a minstrel's contest taking place in the castle in 1206-07. It was the residence of the much revered Elisabeth, the wife of the landgrave of Thuringia, who was canonised shortly after her death in 1235 for rejecting a pompous court lifestyle in favour of helping the poor and disadvantaged. In 1521-22 the reformer Martin Luther went into hiding in the Wartburg under the assumed name of Junker Jörg after being excommunicated and put under papal ban. The town itself is not without appeal, though decades of neglect during the GDR regime have left scars that are only now being smoothed over.

Orientation & Information

The Markt, Eisenach's central square, can be reached on foot from the train station by following Bahnhofstrasse west to Karlsplatz, then continuing west via the pedestrianised Karlstrasse shopping street (about 15 minutes). Except for the Wartburg, which is 2km south-west of town, most sights are close to the Markt. Eisenach has two bus stations, one right outside the train station and another on Müllerstrasse one block to the west.

The tourist office (☎ 670 26 0; fax 670 96 0) is at Markt 2 and is open Monday from 10 am to 6 pm, Tuesday to Friday from 9 am, and Saturday from 10 am to 2 pm. The EisenachCard (DM24) provides unlimited public transportation and free access to all attractions for 72 hours. There's a Volksbank at Schillerstrasse 16 to change money. The main post office is at the south-western corner of the Markt at No 16. There's a police station at August-Bebel-Strasse 6 (☎ 261 0).

Wartburg

This superb medieval castle, perched high above the town on a wooded hill, supposedly goes back to Count Ludwig der Springer who in 1067, upon seeing the craggy hillside, exclaimed: 'Wart, Berg, du sollst mir eine Burg werden' (literally 'Wait, mountain, you shall be a castle for me'). Martin Luther translated the New Testament from Greek into German while in hiding here, contributing enormously to the development of the written German language. His modest, wood-panelled study is part of the guided tour (in German), which is the only way to see the interior. The tour also takes in the museum and the amazing Romanesque Great Hall.

Tours run frequently between 8.30 am and 5 pm (9 am to 3.30 pm in winter) and cost

Wartburg: Martin Luther's famous hide-out.

DM11, discount DM6; arrive early to avoid the crowds. A free English-language translation sheet that follows the tour is available. To get to the Wartburg from the Markt, walk one block west to Wydenbrugkstrasse, then head up Schlossberg through the forest. From May to October, bus No 10 runs to the castle roughly every 1½ hours (DM2.50 return) from outside the train station.

City Centre
The Markt is dominated by the galleried **Georgenkirche**, where members of the Bach family, including Johann Sebastian himself, served as organists between 1665 and 1797. Its collection of ancient tombstones includes the one of Ludwig der Springer, the legendary founder of the Wartburg. A few steps south, at Lutherplatz 8, is the half-timbered **Lutherhaus** (open daily 9 am to 5 pm and from 2 pm on Sunday in winter; entry DM5, discount DM2), where Martin Luther lived as a schoolboy between 1498 and 1501. The exhibit traces important stages in the reformer's life as well as his accomplishments through paintings, manuscripts and illustrated works, as well as through a series of interactive multi-media terminals (in German and English).

South of here, at Frauenplan 21, stands the **Bachhaus** (open daily 9 am to 5.45 pm and in winter to 4.45 pm, closed Monday morning; entry DM5, discount DM4). It contains a memorial exhibit on the composer who was born in 1685 in a now demolished house nearby. Each visit concludes with a little concert played on antique instruments.

The first nationwide proletarian movement, the Social Democratic Workers Party, was founded in Eisenach by August Bebel and Wilhelm Liebknecht in 1869. The **Gedenkstätte 'Goldener Löwe'** (literally 'Golden Lion Memorial Site'; open weekdays from 9 am to 4 pm) at Marienstrasse 57, has an interesting exhibit on the 19th-century workers' movement in Germany.

In the **Predigerkirche** on Predigerplatz you'll find an exhibit on medieval art in Thuringia (open daily, except Monday, from 10 am to 8 pm, in winter to 5 pm; DM5, discount DM3). Eisenach's car-manufacturing tradition is the subject of the **Automobilmuseum** (open 9 am to 5 pm, closed Monday; DM4, discount DM1) at Rennbahn 8 where you can admire such GDR relics as the Dixi and the Wartburg 1.3.

Places to Stay

Camping The nearest camping ground is *Campingplatz Altenberger See* (☎ 215 63 7), 7km south of town in Wilhelmsthal (take the bus in the direction of Bad Liebenstein from the Müllerstrasse station). Charges are DM5 per tent, plus DM6 per person and cars are DM2 extra.

Hostels Of Eisenach's two DJH hostels, the 65-bed *Jugendherberge Bornstrasse* (☎ 732 01 2) at Bornstrasse 7, is more central but fairly dilapidated (bus No 3 from the station to Ernst Abbe Schule, then a 10-minute walk). Beds cost DM20/24 for juniors/seniors. A better alternative is the *Jugendherberge Artur Becker* (☎ 203 61 3) at the foot of the Wartburg at Mariental 24, which charges DM23/27 (bus No 3 from the train station to Liliengrund). Just off the Markt, at

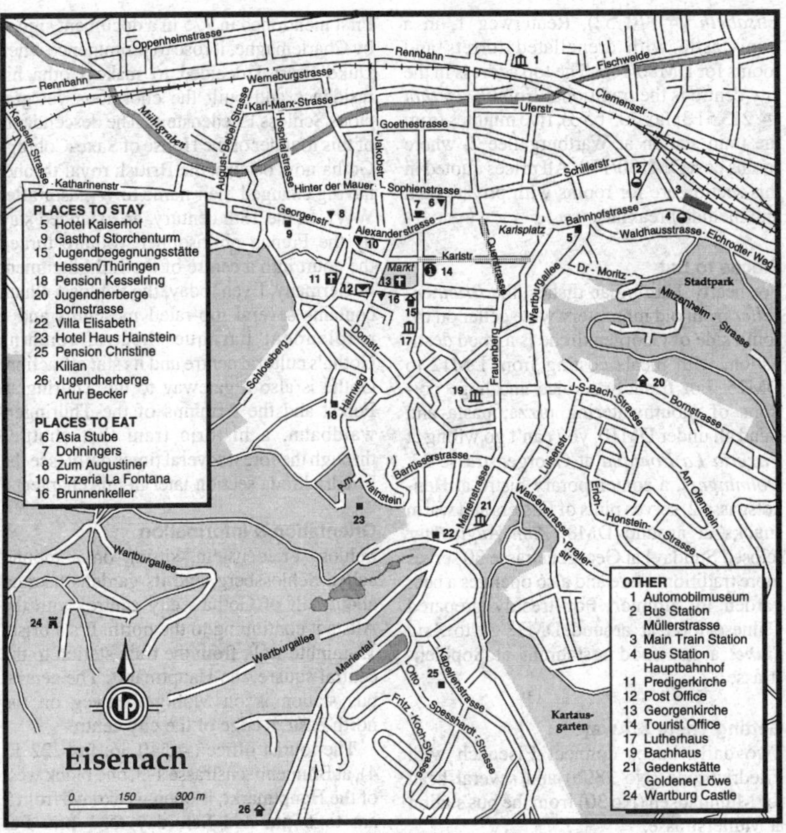

Auf der Esplanade, is *Jugendbegegnungsstätte Hessen/Thüringen* (☎ 214 13 3), which charges DM18/25 per bed (no breakfast but there is kitchen access), plus a one-off laundry fee for sheets and towels of DM8.

Hotels The tourist office has a free room-finding service. Private rooms start at DM30/50 a single/double. Otherwise, for cheap stays in central Eisenach try the hostel-like *Gasthof Storchenturm* (☎ 215 25 0), Georgenstrasse 43, whose modern but tiny and very basic doubles cost DM70.

Most smaller hotels are located among the cluster of charming Art Nouveau villas in Eisenach's hilly south. The small *Pension Christine Kilian* (☎ 211 12 2) at Kapellenstrasse 8 has rooms from DM40/80. *Pension Kesselring* (☎ 732 04 9), just a 10-minute walk up from the Bachhaus in a petite yellow villa at Hainweg 32, offers nice rooms for DM60/90; it's very popular and often full.

Farther up the hill, at Am Hainstein 16, is the sprawling *Hotel Haus Hainstein* (☎ 242 0; fax 242 10 9) with great views of the Wartburg and quiet, stylish rooms for DM95/130. Nonsmokers might like *Villa*

Elisabeth (☎ 770 52), Reuterweg 1, in a mini-castle with crenellated turrets and rooms for DM80/160. The top address in the city centre is the traditional *Hotel Kaiserhof* (☎ 213 51 3; fax 203 65 3), five minutes from the train station at Wartburgallee 2, where rooms cost DM130/170. All prices quoted in this section are for rooms with private bath and include breakfast.

Places to Eat

For hearty Thuringian dishes, the *Brunnenkeller* in an old monastery wine cellar on the south side of Georgenkirche is a good destination, with meals costing from DM12 to DM25. For friendly service and huge portions of mouthwatering pizza, pasta and salad all under DM10, you can't go wrong at *Pizzeria La Fontana* at Georgenstrasse 22. *Dohningers*, a contemporary bistro at Henkelsgasse 2, serves pints of Fosters and warm snacks at around DM8. *Zum Augustiner* (closed Sunday) at Georgenstrasse 30 serves more traditional fare and also operates a beer garden in summer. For freshly prepared Chinese food at around DM7, go to *Asia Stube*, a fast-food restaurant at Sophienstrasse 12.

Getting There & Away

Two daily buses connect Eisenach with Friedrichroda (No 280b) and several head for Mühlhausen (No 30) from the bus station at Müllerstrasse.

Frequent direct trains run to Erfurt (DM13.20, 30 minutes), Gotha (DM6.80, 15 minutes) and Weimar (DM17.60, one hour) as well as to Meiningen (DM14.80, one hour) in the Thuringian Forest. IC trains to Frankfurt/Main and IR (InterRegio) regional trains to Berlin-Lichtenberg also stop here. If you're driving, Eisenach is right on the A4 (exits Eisenach Ost or Eisenach West) and crossed by the B7, B19 and B84.

GOTHA

- *pop 54,000*
- *area code* ☎ 03621

Gotha is a pleasant provincial town between Eisenach to the west and Erfurt to the east. First mentioned in 775 in a document signed by Charlemagne, it rose to prominence when Duke Ernst I decided to make Gotha his residence and built the enormous yet gracious Schloss Friedenstein. The descendants of this founder of the House of Saxe-Coburg-Gotha now occupy the British royal throne, having changed their name to Windsor after WWI. In the 18th century, an extended stay by the French philosopher Voltaire turned the court into a centre of the Enlightenment in Germany. Even today, the Schloss, which contains several top-rated museums and a resplendent baroque theatre, remains Gotha's cultural centre and its star attraction. Gotha is also a gateway to the Thuringian Forest and the terminus of the Thüringerwaldbahn, a historic tram that shuttles through the forest several times daily (see the Friedrichroda section later in this chapter).

Orientation & Information

Schloss Friedenstein, sitting on a mound called Schlossberg, and its gardens take up about half of Gotha's city centre, with the Altstadt continuing to the north. It's a brisk, 15-minute walk from the train station to the central square, the Hauptmarkt. The central bus station is on Mühlgrabenweg on the north-eastern edge of the city centre.

The tourist office (☎ 540 36; fax 222 13 4), at Blumenbachstrasse 1-3, one block west of the Hauptmarkt, is open weekdays from 9 am to 6 pm and Saturday to 1 pm. For information on the Thuringian Forest, there's also the Fremdenverkehrsverband Thüringer Wald (☎ 363 11 1; fax 361 11 3) in Margarethenstrasse 2-4 (same opening hours as the tourist office, plus Sunday from 10 am to noon from June to August). The GothaCard (DM15 for one adult and one child up to age 12) is good for 72 hours of unlimited public transport and admission to most museums. The Touristenticket (DM8, children DM5) entitles you to free transport (including the Thüringerwaldbahn) and reduced admissions for one day.

The main post office on Ekhofplatz 1 has a public fax-phone and also exchanges currency.

THURINGIA

Schloss Friedenstein

Built between 1643 and 1654, this horseshoe-shaped palace was never destroyed, so its early baroque exterior remains largely unchanged. Note the two characteristic towers, one round, the other square. Among the museums it contains, the **Schlossmuseum** deserves top billing, in fact it's worth visiting Gotha only to tour its lavish baroque and neoclassical royal apartments and the eclectic collections they hold. Expect to spend at least two hours to see it all, though you could easily spend an entire day.

The absolute highlight of the medieval collection is the ethereal *Gothaer Liebespaar* (1484). This depiction of two lovers is considered the first double portrait in German painting. Also of note are several works by Lucas Cranach the Elder, including the haunting *Verdammnis und Erlösung* (Damnation and Deliverance, 1529).

On the 2nd floor, you'll find the **Festsaal**, an exuberantly decorated hall of stuccoed ceilings, walls and doors that reflect the tastes of the more flamboyant successors to the palace.

The less flashy neoclassical wing contains a collection of sculptures, of which the Renaissance work by Conrad Meit called *Adam and Eve* deserves special mention. The **Kunstkammer** is jammed with small-scale curiosities and treasures, including engraved ostrich eggs and a cherry pit graced with the carved portrait of Ernst the Pious. Highly unusual too are the cork models of ancient buildings, a craft in vogue in 18th-century Italy. Towards the exit look out for the fake Egyptian 'tomb' containing several real mummies.

At the end of the palace's western wing is the entrance to the **Museum of Regional History and Folk Art**, incorporating the recently refurbished **Ekhof-Theater** (1681-83), one of the oldest baroque theatres in Europe, which is still used for performances.

The **Schlosskirche** occupies the north-eastern corner, while the east wing contains a **research library** with more than half a million books spanning 12 centuries.

Behind the Rose Garden to the south, along Parkallee, is the **Museum der Natur** (Nature Museum) with lots of stuffed animals grouped in dioramas and a new exhibit on dinosaurs.

All Schloss museums are open daily from 9 am to 5 pm. Admission to the Schlossmuseum and the Regional History Museum is DM8, discount DM4. The Ekhof-Theater costs DM3. The Nature Museum is DM4, discount DM2. A combination ticket for all museums costs DM10, discount DM5. Guided tours of the research library take place from May to September on weekdays at 2.30 pm and cost DM3, discount DM1.

Hauptmarkt

The burgundy-coloured **Rathaus** and its 40m-tall tower command the large rectangular Hauptmarkt, the focal point of the Altstadt. Built as a *Kaufhaus* (department store) in 1567, the structure was later inhabited by Duke Ernst I until Schloss Friedenstein was completed and finally turned into the town hall in 1665. Its northern end sports a gorgeously restored Renaissance façade, which is complemented by several other buildings framing the square.

Note the late 16th-century houses at Nos 40 and 41. Martin Luther stayed briefly at No 42 in 1537. Feeling in poor health and faced with possible death, it was here that he dictated the first version of his last will and testament.

Places to Stay

Camping The nearest camping ground is *Am Schwimmbad Georgenthal* (☎ 036253-413 14), about 15km south-west of Gotha at Am Flössgraben 3 (take bus No 864 from the central bus station). It's open April to October and costs DM6.50 per person, DM5 per tent and DM2.50 per car.

Hostel Gotha's *DJH hostel* (☎ 540 08) is a convenient five-minute walk north of the train station at Mozartstrasse 1. It costs DM20 for juniors and DM24 for seniors, breakfast included.

Hotels The tourist office can help with

THURINGIA

private accommodation (DM25 to DM40 per person), but Gotha also has a number of budget options in the city centre. At the foot of the palace, at Bergallee 3, is *Am Schloss* (☎ 853 20 6) where singles/doubles with shared bath cost DM40/70. Near the train station, at Bebelstrasse 8, you'll find the tiny *Café Suzette* (☎ 856 75 5), which has singles with private bath for DM70 and doubles for DM120.

The *Pannonia Hotel am Schlosspark* (☎ 442 0; fax 442 45 2), Lindenauallee 20, ranks among the town's top hotels and costs DM165/235. All prices include breakfast.

Places to Eat

Old-world coffee-house culture reigns in Gotha's Altstadt, and there's a café every 50m or so. Especially fine are *Cassignoel* at Querstrasse 5 and the *Hof-Café Harmonie* upstairs in a little arcade at Hauptmarkt 8. Be aware that cafés usually close at 6 pm, as does the *Gockelgrill* at Hauptmarkt 26, which has decent grilled half chickens for DM4.50.

For more variation and a casual atmosphere, head for the whimsical *Firlefanz* at Klosterstrasse 5, where you can spend as little as DM4 for a snack or up to DM20 for a full meal. For proper dining surrounded by historical ambience, there's the *Ratskeller* at Hauptmarkt 3 and the *Weinschänke* in Gartenstrasse 28.

Getting There & Away

Gotha is easily reached by train from Eisenach (DM6.80, 15 minutes), Erfurt (DM6.80, 25 minutes) and Weimar (DM11, 40 minutes). It's also an IR train stop (every two hours) to Berlin-Lichtenberg (DM80, 3¾ hours) and Düsseldorf (DM110, 4½ hours). There's also direct train service to Frankfurt. Gotha is just north of the A4 (exit Gotha) and is crossed by the B247 and B7.

For easy access to the Thuringian Forest, take the Thüringerwaldbahn (tram No 4) which makes regular trips to Friedrichroda and Tabarz.

WEIMAR

- *pop 61,000*
- *area code* ☎ 03643

Neither a monumental city nor a medieval one, Weimar appeals to cultural and intellectual tastes. Its position as the centre of German humanistic tradition, and the source of much that is considered great in German thought and deed, is unrivalled. But these traditions are not always apparent to visitors in a hurry. The parks and small museums (most closed on Monday) should be savoured, not downed in one gulp.

Many luminaries lived and worked in Weimar, including Lucas Cranach the Elder, Johann Sebastian Bach, Christoph Martin Wieland, Friedrich Schiller, Johann Gottfried Herder, Johann Wolfgang von Goethe, Franz Liszt, Friedrich Nietzsche, Walter Gropius, Lyonel Feininger, Vasili Kandinsky, Gerhard Marcks and Paul Klee. The Bauhaus movement, which laid the foundations of modern architecture, flourished in the city from 1919 to 1925. Weimar remains a centre for architecture as well as music studies.

Weimar is best known abroad as the place where Germany's republican constitution was drafted after WWI (hence, the 1919-33 Weimar Republic), though there are few reminders of this historical moment here. The ruins of the Buchenwald concentration camp near Weimar, on the other hand, still provide haunting evidence of the terrors of the Nazi regime.

Because of its historical significance, Weimar has received particularly large handouts for the restoration of its many fine buildings. It has been declared the European Capital of Culture for 1999 and a range of generously funded cultural activities are planned.

Orientation & Information

The centre of Weimar is just west of the Ilm River and a 20-minute walk south of the train station. Buses run fairly frequently between the station and Goetheplatz, from where it's a short walk east along small streets to Herderplatz or the Markt.

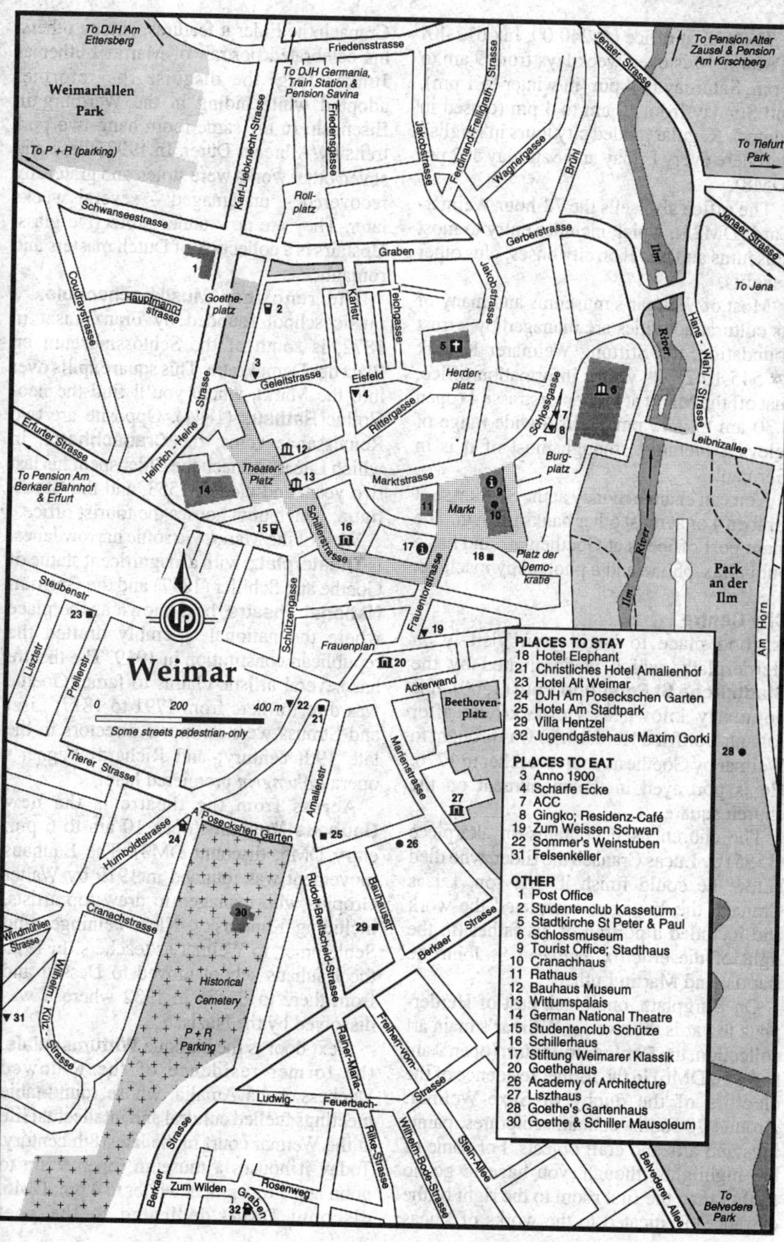
Weimar
To DJH Am Ettersberg
Weimarhallen Park
To P + R (parking)
To DJH Germania, Train Station & Pension Savina
To Pension Alter Zausel & Pension Am Kirschberg
To Tiefurt Park
To Jena
To Pension Am Berkaer Bahnhof & Erfurt
To Belvedere Park
Friedensstrasse
Friedensgasse
Karl-Liebknecht-Strasse
Jakobstrasse
Ferdinand-Freiligrath-Strasse
Wagnergasse
Brühl
Jenaer Strasse
Rollplatz
Schwanseestrasse
Gerberstrasse
Graben
Coudraystrasse
Hauptmannstrasse
Goetheplatz
Karlstr
Teichgasse
Herderplatz
Geleitstrasse
Eisfeld
Rittergasse
Schlossgasse
Hans-Wahl-Strasse
Leibnizallee
Burgplatz
Erfurter Strasse
Heinrich-Heine-Strasse
Theaterplatz
Marktstrasse
Markt
Schillerstrasse
Platz der Demokratie
Frauentorstrasse
Schützengasse
Steubenstr
Lisztstr
Prellerstr
Frauenplan
Ackerwand
Beethovenplatz
Ilm River
Park an der Ilm
Am Horn
0 200 400 m
Some streets pedestrian-only
Trierer Strasse
Amalienstr
Marienstrasse
Humboldtstrasse
A Poseckshen Garten
Rudolf-Breitscheid-Strasse
Bauhausstr
Berkaer Strasse
Cranachstrasse
Windmühlen Strasse
Wilhelm-Külz-Strasse
Historical Cemetery
P + R Parking
Freiherr-vom-Stein-Allee
Rainer-Maria-Rilke-Strasse
Ludwig-Feuerbach-Strasse
Wilhelm-Bode-Strasse
Belvederer Allee
Berkaer Strasse
Zum Wilden Graben
Rosenweg
PLACES TO STAY
18 Hotel Elephant
21 Christliches Hotel Amalienhof
23 Hotel Alt Weimar
24 DJH Am Poseckschen Garten
25 Hotel Am Stadtpark
29 Villa Hentzel
32 Jugendgästehaus Maxim Gorki
PLACES TO EAT
3 Anno 1900
4 Scharfe Ecke
7 ACC
8 Gingko; Residenz-Café
19 Zum Weissen Schwan
22 Sommer's Weinstuben
31 Felsenkeller
OTHER
1 Post Office
2 Studentenclub Kasseturm
5 Stadtkirche St Peter & Paul
6 Schlossmuseum
9 Tourist Office; Stadthaus
10 Cranachhaus
11 Rathaus
12 Bauhaus Museum
13 Wittumspalais
14 German National Theatre
15 Studentenclub Schütze
16 Schillerhaus
17 Stiftung Weimarer Klassik
20 Goethehaus
26 Academy of Architecture
27 Liszthaus
28 Goethe's Gartenhaus
30 Goethe & Schiller Mausoleum

The tourist office (☎ 240 00; fax 612 40) at Markt 10 is open weekdays from 9 am to 6 pm, Saturday to 4 pm (in winter to 1 pm), and Sunday from 10 am to 4 pm (closed in winter). Regular guided city tours in English start here every Friday and Saturday at 2 pm (DM8).

The office also sells the 72-hour Weimar-Card (DM25), which includes entry to most museums and travel on city buses, plus other benefits.

Most of Weimar's museums and many of its cultural activities are managed by a trust foundation, the Stiftung Weimarer Klassik (☎ 545 10 2). Its visitor information office, just off the Markt at Frauentorstrasse 4 (open 8.30 am to 4.45 pm), sells a wide range of relevant literature, though most of it is in German.

You can change money at the Sparkasse at Graben 4 or at most other banks in town. The main post office is at Goetheplatz and has a public fax-phone and a photocopy machine.

City Centre

A good place to begin your visit is on Herderplatz, which is dominated by the **Stadtkirche St Peter und Paul** (1500). It is popularly known as Herderkirche after Johann Gottfried Herder who was brought to Weimar by Goethe as court preacher in 1776. He is portrayed in the monument on the church square.

The church itself contains an altarpiece (1555) by Lucas Cranach the Elder, who died before he could finish it. His son, Lucas Cranach the Younger, completed the work and included a portrait of his father (to the right of the crucifix, between St John the Baptist and Martin Luther).

On Burgplatz, one block east of Herderplatz towards the river, is Weimar's main art collection, the **Schlossmuseum** (open 9 am to 6 pm; DM6) in the former residence of the electors of the duchy of Saxe-Weimar. Around 70 rooms contain sculptures, paintings and arts and craft objects. For some of the highlights, though, you have to go no farther than the first room to the right of the entrance. Dedicated to the works of Lucas Cranach the Elder it features, among others, his celebrated portrait of Martin Luther as Junker Jörg, the disguise the reformer adopted while hiding in the Wartburg in Eisenach. In the same room hang two portraits by Albrecht Dürer. In 1992, these and seven other works were stolen and gratefully recovered – undamaged – several weeks later. They are now under protective glass. Upstairs is a collection of Dutch masters and romanticists.

The renowned **Musikhochschule**, a music school founded by Franz Liszt in 1872, is south of the Schlossmuseum on Platz der Demokratie. This square spills over into the Markt, where you'll find the neo-Gothic **Rathaus** (1841). Opposite are two Renaissance gems, the **Cranachhaus**, in which Lucas Cranach the Elder spent his last two years and died in 1553, and the **Stadthaus**, which now houses the tourist office.

West of the Markt, via some narrow lanes, is **Theaterplatz**, with a magnificent statue of Goethe and Schiller (1857) and the **German National Theatre**, best known as the place where the national assembly drafted the republican constitution in 1919. The theatre has several artistic claims to fame: Goethe was director here from 1791 to 1817; Liszt and Strauss were its music directors in the late 19th century; and Richard Wagner's opera *Lohengrin* premiered here.

Across from the theatre is the new **Bauhaus Museum** (open 10 am to 6 pm; entry DM5, discount DM3). The Bauhaus movement was founded in 1919 by Walter Gropius who managed to draw top artists, including Kandinsky, Klee, Feininger and Schlemmer, to Weimar as teachers. In 1925 the Bauhaus school moved to Dessau and from there to Berlin in 1932 where it was dissolved by the Nazis.

Next door is the baroque **Wittumspalais**, the former residence of the widowed Duchess Anna Amalia, whose round-table meetings fuelled cultural and intellectual life at the Weimar court in the late 18th century. Today it houses a museum (open 9 am to noon and 1 to 5 pm, in winter to 4 pm; DM6, discount DM4) dedicated to the poet

Christoph Martin Wieland (1733-1813), who first translated Shakespeare's works into German.

In the southern part of the city centre, at Marienstrasse 17 by the edge of the Park an der Ilm (see Parks & Palaces), is the **Liszthaus** (open 9 am to noon and 1 to 5 pm; entry DM4, discount DM3). Liszt resided in Weimar in 1848 and again from 1869 to 1886, and he composed his *Hungarian Rhapsody* and *Faust Symphony* here.

In the yellow complex across the road from the Liszthaus, Walter Gropius laid the groundwork for all modern architecture with his Bauhaus movement. The buildings themselves were erected by the architect Henry van de Velde between 1904 and 1911 and now house the **Academy of Architecture**.

A new museum of contemporary and modern art, the **Neues Museum Weimar**, is currently being built at Rathenauplatz, north of the centre. It is expected to open at the end of 1998 and will house the extensive collection of Paul Maenz, a gallery owner and avid collector from Cologne who is now resident in Berlin.

Goethe House

No other individual is as closely associated with Weimar as Johann Wolfgang von Goethe, who lived here from 1775 until his death in 1832. In 1792 his sponsor and employer, Duke Carl August, gave him the **Goethehaus** on Frauenplan as a gift, and it was here that he worked, studied, read, researched, and wrote such immortal works as *Faust*.

The house has been a museum since 1885 and features Goethe's living quarters on the 1st floor, pretty much in their original shape. You reach them via an expansive Italian Renaissance staircase decorated with sculpture and paintings brought back from his travels to Italy. From the top of the stairs you wander through a series of rooms, each painted in a different shade, set up according to Goethe's own colour theories. The highlight is his study and the adjacent simple room where he died.

The Goethehaus is open from 9 am to 5 pm (in winter to 4 pm); admission is DM8, discount DM5. Because demand often exceeds capacity, you will be given a time slot during which you're allowed to enter the house. Once inside, you may stay as long as you want. During peak season in spring and autumn, you may also prefer to buy your tickets in advance at the Stiftung Weimarer Klassik (see Information).

The re-opening of the Goethe Nationalmuseum next to the Goethehaus is scheduled for January 1999. In addition to extensive exhibits on Goethe's life and work, it will also be dedicated to the other names of Weimar's classic era, notably Schiller, Wieland and Herder.

Schiller House

The dramatist Friedrich von Schiller lived in Weimar from 1799 until his early death in 1805 but, unlike Goethe, he had to buy his house with his own money. You'll find the **Schillerhaus** at Schillerstrasse 12. The little study at the end of the 2nd floor contains the desk where Schiller wrote *Wilhelm Tell* and other works, as well as the bed where he died. His wife's quarters are on the 1st floor and the servants lived on the ground floor. The house is open from 9 am to 5 pm (in winter to 4 pm) and closed on Tuesday. Admission is DM5, discount DM3; enter through the modern building on Neugasse.

Both Goethe and Schiller are interred in a neoclassical crypt along with Duke Carl August in the **Historischer Friedhof** (Historic Cemetery; open 9 am to 1 pm and 2 to 5 pm, closed Tuesday and at 4 pm in winter; admission is DM4, discount DM3).

Parks & Palaces

Weimar boasts three large parks, each replete with monuments, museums and attractions. Most accessible is **Park an der Ilm**, which runs right along the eastern side of Weimar and contains **Goethe's Gartenhaus**. This simple cottage was an early present (1776) from Duke Carl August and was intended to induce Goethe to stay in Weimar. He lived in this building until 1782 and also helped landscape the park. Today, house and garden still bear witness to Goethe's love of nature during his early days in Weimar. It is open from 9 am to noon and 1 to 5 pm, closed Tuesday. Admission is DM4, discount DM3.

Several km farther south is the **Belvedere Park**, with its baroque castle housing the **Rokokomuseum** and the **Orangery Coach Museum** (both open April to October from 10 am to 6 pm; admission DM4). The surrounding park is beautiful and spacious, and it could absorb hours of your time. Bus No 12 runs hourly from Goetheplatz to Belvedere.

Tiefurt Park, a few km east of the train station, is a similar but smaller park (palace closed Monday, and also Tuesday from November to February; admission DM6, discount DM4). This is the place where Duchess Anna Amalia held her intellectual round-table gatherings. To get here take bus No 3, which leaves hourly from Goetheplatz.

Places to Stay

Accommodation options have improved significantly in Weimar, but true budget choices are still hard to come by. From Easter to October, the town is often busy with school groups and business travellers, while on weekends and public holidays it's crawling with tour groups. For DM5, the tourist office can arrange private rooms (from DM25 to DM35 per person). Unless noted, all prices below include breakfast and, except camping grounds and hostels, rooms have private shower and WC.

Camping The closest camping ground is the *Campingplatz Oettern* (☎ 036453-264, open May to November) at Oettern, 7km south-east of Weimar, but it's badly in need of a make-over. Charges are DM4.50 per person, DM2 per vehicle, plus DM5 per tent. A much better option, but about 25km south of town, is *Ferienpark Hohenfelden* (see Places to Stay in the earlier Erfurt section).

Hostels At last count Weimar had four DJH hostels. The *Jugendherberge Germania* (☎ 850 49 0), at Carl-August-Allee 13 near the train station, is a wonderfully modern facility charging juniors/seniors DM22/26. Most central is the hostel *Am Poseckschen Garten* (☎ 850 79 2) at Humboldtstrasse 17 near the Historischer Friedhof, where beds cost DM22/26. It was scheduled for a badly needed face-lift in 1997. *Jugendgästehaus Maxim Gorki* (☎ 347 1) is on the hilly southern side of town at Zum Wilden Graben 12 (bus No 8 from the station to Rainer-Maria-Rilke-Strasse), while the *Jugendgästehaus Am Ettersberg* (☎ 347 1) at Ettersberg-Siedlung is north of town (bus No 6 from the station to Obelisk). Both offer beds for DM24/28. Reservations for both must be made at the DJH Maxim Gorki.

Pensions Near the train station at Meyerstrasse 60 is *Pension Savina* (☎ 866 90), which has singles/doubles with kitchenette from DM50/90. *Pension Am Kirschberg* (☎ 619 68), Am Kirschberg 27, offers doubles at DM110 and triples for DM150. *Pension Alter Zausel* (☎ 501 66 3), Carl-Von-Ossietzky-Strasse 13, has one single for DM95 and doubles for DM120. West of the centre, but still conveniently close to town, is the *Am Berkaer Bahnhof* (☎ 202 01 0), Peter-Cornelius-Strasse 7, with singles/doubles for DM75/90 and triples costing DM120.

Hotels Hotels in Weimar are not inexpensive. Good value for money is the stylish and quiet *Christliches Hotel Amalienhof* (☎ 549 0; fax 549 11 0) in a neoclassical villa with matching interior at Amalienstrasse 2, about a minute's walk from the Goethehaus. Rooms here cost from DM120 for singles and DM160 for doubles. On the same street at No 19, *Hotel Am Stadtpark* (☎ 248 30; fax 511 72 0) asks from DM165 for a twin room. A better bet is the contemporary and friendly *Villa Hentzel* (☎ 865 80; fax 865 81 9) at Bauhausstrasse 12, whose 13 large, individually designed rooms cost DM110/160. Those who like their décor minimalist should try *Hotel Alt Weimar* (☎ 861 90; fax 861 91 0), at the corner of Prellerstrasse and Steubenstrasse, which charges DM155/190. Weimar's classic hostelry, the historic *Hotel*

Elephant (☎ 802 0; fax 653 10) at Markt 19, often gets top billing but charges an excessive DM225/310 and up.

Places to Eat

Weimar's selection of eateries has improved enormously over the past five years and now satisfies just about every taste and budget. Despite its slightly posh ambience, the *Anno 1900*, in a restored turn-of-the-century winter garden at Geleitstrasse 12a, offers quite good value. On the menu are Thuringian dishes (from DM10 to DM18) and almost a dozen vegetarian dishes (DM11 to DM16). Nearby, at Eisfeld 2, you'll find the *Scharfe Ecke* (closed Monday), with home-cooked cuisine from DM11 and a wide range of beers.

The *Ginkgo* (whose name alludes to Goethe's fascination for the East Asian trees) is upstairs at Grüner Markt 4 and serves Chinese food. Downstairs is one of Weimar's most popular haunts, the *Residenz-Café* ('Resi' to the cognoscenti), whose soft décor and lighting, café tables and plump sofas attract a literary crowd. The food is inexpensive and delicious and the portions are super-sized. Around the corner, at Burgplatz 1, is *ACC*, a restaurant-cum-gallery popular with students. It serves simple but good food, including many vegetarian options.

Cosy too are the small, wood-panelled rooms at *Sommer's Weinstuben*, Humboldtstrasse 2, where you can go for a beer and a chat or a full meal (dishes from DM12). If you want to dine where Goethe, Schiller and Liszt did, you must go to the historical *Zum Weissen Schwan*, across from the Goethemuseum on Frauenplan, and pay accordingly (from DM25).

Another Weimar institution is the *Felsenkeller* at Humboldtstrasse 37, run by the local Felsenbräu brewery. The atmosphere is great, the beer cheap, the food good and well priced – no wonder it's often full.

Entertainment

The *German National Theatre* on Theaterplatz is the main stage of Weimar's cultural activities. It offers a grab-bag of performances: classic and contemporary plays (often in an avant-garde format), occasional ballet and opera performances, and classical concerts by the Staatskapelle Weimar. Tickets range from DM12 to DM45 and can be bought at the tourist office or by calling ☎ 755 33 4.

A Weimar classic of a different sort is the *Kasseturm* in the historic round tower on Goetheplatz, which has three floors of live music, disco or cabaret most nights (open after 8 pm). The *Studentenclub Schütze*, just off Theaterplatz at Schützengasse 2, is a lively student bar that also serves cheap drinks and food. Admission to both venues varies according to the event; from free to as high as DM10.

Getting There & Away

Train Weimar is an IC train stop on the route from Frankfurt to Leipzig (DM21.80, one hour) and Dresden (DM52, 2¾ hours), leaving every two hours. Very few other long-distance trains stop at Weimar, so for longer trips changing in Erfurt (just 22km and 15 minutes away) may be quicker.

There's direct IR service to both Berlin-Lichtenberg (DM67, three hours) and Eisenach (DM16.60, one hour). Berkaer Bahnhof is a second station west of the city centre, but only trains to the suburbs depart from it.

Car & Motorcycle Weimar is on the B7 from Kassel to Gera and 5km north of the Weimar exit off the A4. Unless you're staying in a hotel in Weimar's Altstadt, you must park your vehicle in one of the two big lots west and south of the city centre. Look for the signs saying 'P+R'. Parking is free, and there are shuttle buses (DM2.50 one way) into town. Otherwise it's a 15 to 20-minute walk.

BUCHENWALD

The Buchenwald concentration camp museum and memorial are on Ettersberg Hill, 10km north of Weimar. You first pass the memorial erected atop the mass graves of some of the 56,500 victims from 18 nations, including German antifascists, Jews, and

Soviet and Polish prisoners of war. The concentration camp and museum are 1km beyond the memorial. Many prominent German Communists and Social Democrats, Ernst Thälmann and Rudolf Breitscheid among them, were murdered here. After 1943, prisoners were exploited in the production of weapons. Many died during medical experimentation. Shortly before the end of the war, some 28,000 prisoners were sent on death marches. Between 1937 and 1945, more than one fifth of the 250,000 incarcerated here died. On 11 April 1945, as US troops approached and the SS guards fled, the prisoners rebelled (at 3.15 pm, and the clock tower above the entrance still shows that time), overwhelmed the remaining guards and liberated themselves.

After the war, the Soviet victors turned the tables by establishing Special Camp No 2, in which another 7000 (alleged) anti-communists and former Nazis were literally worked to death. Their bodies were found, after unification, in mass graves north of the camp and near the train station.

The main Buchenwald museum and concentration camp are open from 9.45 am to 5.15 pm (8.45 am to 4.15 pm in winter). In 1997, a museum dealing with the post-1945 oppression at Buchenwald also opened. Admission to all exhibits is free, and there are pamphlets and books in English and French for sale at the bookstore. From Weimar's centre take bus No 6 which runs via Goetheplatz and the train station roughly every 40 minutes.

THURINGIA

JENA

- *pop 106,000*
- *area code* ☎ 03641

Jena will probably forever be associated with the optical precision technology developed at the turn of the century by Carl Zeiss, Ernst Abbe and Otto Schott. Its university (1558) is still strong in the sciences.

About 23km east of Weimar, Jena's scenic location in the Saale River valley has been somewhat tainted by industry and hideous GDR architecture. Since the Wende, though, it has undergone major structural and architectural changes and stands to become an attractive place to visit once again – especially after the forest of construction cranes disappear. Flanked by limestone hills, Jena is blessed with an unusually mild climate that allows the growth of vines and wild orchids.

Orientation & Information

Jena is long and narrow, but with a compact centre whose main attractions are all within walking distance of each other. The city has three train stations: Saalbahnhof in the north (take bus No 15 to get to the centre); Westbahnhof in the south-west and Paradiesbahnhof next to the Saale right in the centre.

The tourist office (☎ 586 30; fax 586 32 2) is at Holzmarkt 8 and is open weekdays from 9 am to 6 pm and to 2 pm on Saturday. It sells the JenaCard (DM25), which gives free admission to most attractions as well as unlimited public transport and other benefits for 72 hours.

Dresdner Bank at Am Holzmarkt 9 stays open till 7 pm Monday to Thursday and to 4 pm on Friday. The main post office is at Engelplatz 8.

There's no self-service laundrette in Jena, but the Waschsalon (☎ 244 05) at Bachstrasse 33 offers same-day service for DM2.50 per kg. The police headquarters is at Käthe-Kollwitz-Strasse 1 (☎ 810). For an ambulance, call ☎ 112 or ☎ 444 44 4.

Around the Markt

The Markt is one of the few places in Jena that still reflects some of the city's medieval heritage. At its southern end stands the **Rathaus** (1380) whose most interesting feature is the 15th-century clock in its baroque tower. On the hour every hour, a little door opens and a devil/fool called Schnapphans appears, trying to catch a golden ball – representing the human soul – dangling in front of him. The Schnapphans is one of the 'Seven Wonders of Jena', things designated as curiosities by the town's students.

The statue in the square centre represents Johann Friedrich the Magnanimous, founder of Jena's university and popularly known as 'Hanfried'. The handsome building with the half-timbered upper section at the western end is the **Göhre** and contains the **Stadtmuseum** (closed Monday; DM5, discount DM3), with an interesting local history collection. A walkway beneath the museum leads to the Gothic **Stadtkirche St Michael**, which contains the original engraved tombstone of Martin Luther. Another one of the 'Seven Wonders' is the passageway right under the altar, which cannot be noticed from the inside.

Jena University

The city's university was founded in 1588 and currently has about 12,000 students. Several buildings around town contain the various faculties. You'd have to be blind to miss the 120m-tall **Universitätshochhaus** (called *phallus Jenensis* by locals), yet another striking example of GDR aesthetics. In the early 1970s, Jena's most beautiful square, the Eichplatz, was razed to make room for this concrete behemoth, which was meant to house a research facility for the Zeiss optics factory. It was given to the university when it turned out to be unsuitable for that purpose. Recent discussions about tearing it down have polarised the population, and its fate is still in the balance.

South of this eyesore, in Kollegienstrasse, is the **Collegium Jenense**, where the original university was founded in a former Dominican monastery. The most striking feature of its quiet courtyard is the colourful Renaissance coat of arms of Johann Friedrich the Magnanimous and his family, the Ernestine line of the House of Wettin.

The main building of the university is in a turn-of-the-century structure on the north-eastern edge of the Altstadt at Fürstengraben 1. Its assembly hall contains a monumental painting by the Swiss artist Ferdinand Hodler, featuring Jena students going off to fight in the Wars of Liberation in 1813 against Napoleon.

Goethe & Schiller

Weimar is not the only town where these two literary giants left their marks. As minister for the elector of Saxe-Weimar, Goethe spent five years in Jena. When not busy regulating the flow of the Saale, building streets, designing the botanical garden or cataloguing the university library, he crafted his *Faust* and *Wilhelm Meister*. He also discovered some obscure jaw bone in the so-called **Anatomieturm**, the tower at the corner of Teichgraben and Leutragraben, which once formed part of the medieval fortifications. Most of time he lived in the building at Fürstengraben 26, which now contains the **Goethe Gedenkstätte** (closed Monday and Tuesday; free entry), a memorial exhibit focusing on his accomplishments as a natural scientist. It was Goethe himself who planted the giant gingko tree just west of it.

Goethe was also responsible for bringing Schiller to Jena university. Schiller gave his first lecture as a history professor in the yellow building at the corner of Löbdergraben and Saalstrasse. He liked Jena and spent 10 years here, more than anywhere else. In his **Gartenhaus** (closed Sunday and Monday; DM2, discount DM1), a small cottage at Schillergässchen 2, you can get a glimpse of how he and his family lived. More interesting perhaps is the garden with the little wooden hut where he wrote *Wallenstein*, as well as the oval stone table where he liked to wax philosophical with his buddy Goethe.

Carl Zeiss & Ernst Abbe

Two others responsible for putting Jena on the map are these scientists. Zeiss opened his first mechanical workshop here in 1846 and began building fairly primitive microscopes. In 1866, he enlisted the help of the physicist Ernst Abbe, and together they developed the first scientific microscope. In cooperation with Otto Schott, the founder of Jenaer Glasswerke, they pioneered the production of optical precision instruments that catapulted Jena to international prominence in the early 20th century.

Their life stories and the evolution of optical technology are showcased in the **Optisches Museum** (closed Monday and holidays; DM8, discount DM5), on Carl-Zeiss-Platz 12. In addition to microscopes, cameras, binoculars and other instruments, there's a collection of spectacles through the ages, plus an interactive room with various simplified eye tests. Ask to borrow the English-language pamphlets describing the exhibits. The reconstructed Zeiss workshop, dating from 1866, is in the adjacent Volkshaus and may be visited on request.

The octagonal Art Nouveau pavilion outside the museum, designed by Henry van de Velde, dates from 1911 and contains a marble bust of Abbe. The **Zeiss-Planetarium** (1926), at Am Planetarium 5 in the northern city centre, was the world's first public planetarium; today it boasts a huge state-of-the-art telescope. There are several shows daily (DM8, discount DM6).

Successful urban re-engineering was achieved with the former Zeiss factory complex west of the Universitätshochhaus. The company was largely dismantled after unification, and its halls have been converted into a series of airy, light-flooded buildings now used primarily by the university.

Places to Stay

Camping Closest to Jena is *Campingpark Rabeninsel* (☎ 036427-222 56) in Porstendorf. It is open from May to October and costs DM4 to DM6 per tent site, DM5 per person and DM3 per car. There are also cabins for between DM40 and DM80.

Hostels Jena's *Jugendgästehaus* (☎ 625 0) is part of a recently renovated hotel in the hills at Am Herrenberge 9, with great views over the town. From Saalbahnhof in Jena take bus No 1 to Holzmarkt, then bus Nos 10, 11, 33 or 40 to Mühlenstrasse; from there it's a 10-minute walk uphill. Beds in double rooms cost DM33.50 for juniors and DM37.50 for seniors. A second facility is the *Internationales Jugendgästehaus* (☎ 687 0) next door at Am Herrenberge 3, which charges DM34 for the first night in a three-bed room and DM24 for each subsequent night.

Hotels The tourist office operates a room-booking service at ☎ 586 32 1 (no fee for hotels, DM3 for private rooms). All prices below are for rooms with private bath and include breakfast. The cheapest of the centrally located hotels is *Hotel Jenaer Hof* (☎ 443 85 5), Bachstrasse 24, which charges from DM75/100 for singles/doubles. At *Gasthof Zur Schweiz* (☎ 449 35 5; fax 449 35 4), Quergasse 15, you can expect to pay DM80/140. Not as central but in a historic house (with a brewery attached to it) is *Hotel Papiermühle* (☎ 459 80; fax 459 84 5) at Erfurter Strasse 102, where singles cost DM90 and doubles DM126.

For long-term stays, there's a *Mitwohnzentrale* (☎ 820 93 9) at Leutagraben 2-4, open Monday to Thursday.

Places to Eat

One of the cheapest options is the *Turmeck* student cafeteria inside the Universitätshochhaus (enter from Johannisstrasse). One of the best places for Thuringian food is *Roter Hirsch* (closed Sunday), an old-fashioned restaurant on Holzmarkt 10, where daily specials cost DM10 to DM18 (try to get a table upstairs). For a drink and perhaps a snack, the snug and quiet *Museumskneipe Philisterium* (closed Monday) inside the Stadtmuseum is hard to beat. After 5 pm, you must ring the bell and wait till someone answers the door.

For an introduction to Jena's active student scene, go to the *Rosenkeller*, a historic student club in the cellars of Johannisstrasse 13. It has occasional live music.

Getting There & Away

The regional bus station is slightly north of Paradiesbahnhof, though for buses bound for Weimar (DM6.80, 1¼ hours) you have to go to Westbahnhof. IC trains to Berlin-Zoo (DM66, three hours) and Hamburg-Altona (DM139, six hours) depart every two hours from Saalbahnhof. Regional services to Weimar (DM9, 35 minutes) and Erfurt (DM11, 50 minutes) leave several times hourly from here as well, as do trains to Halle. To travel down the Saale Valley to

Rudolstadt/Saalfeld, you can board either at Saalbahnhof or Paradiesbahnhof.

Jena is on the A4 from Dresden to Frankfurt and just west of the A9 from Berlin to Munich. It's also crossed by the B7 (east-west) and B88 (north-south). The Mitfahrzentrale (☎ 194 40) is at Fürstengraben 30.

AROUND JENA

Dornburger Schlösser

An excursion not to be missed takes in this magnificent trio of palaces from different eras, built on a steeply sloping hillside about 15km north of Jena.

The southernmost is the Renaissance palace, frequently visited by Goethe, who sought to regain his inner peace here after the death of his patron, Duke Carl August. The rooms he stayed in have been restored more or less to their state in 1828.

The central palace is a late-rococo confection and beautifully blends with the garden. The uppermost structure is a mix of Romanesque, late Gothic, Renaissance and baroque elements and may only be viewed from the outside.

The complex is closed on Monday in summer, and also on Tuesday in winter. Admission is DM6, students DM2.

Take the train from Saalbahnhof to Dornburg (DM4.20, 10 minutes) from where it's a steep 20 to 30-minute climb uphill. Bus No 407 leaves every two hours on weekdays (less frequently on weekends) from Jena's central bus station.

Kapellendorf

This moated castle, halfway between Weimar and Jena and just north of the B7, makes for another worthwhile excursion, but unfortunately it cannot be reached by public transport. The classic 9th-century castle was fortified with a moat in the 14th century and, in 1806, was used as the Prussian military headquarters in the Battle of Jena-Auerstedt against Napoleon. The museum inside is open Wednesday to Sunday and admission is DM3, discount DM1.50.

Northern Thuringia

North of the A4 are the towns of Bad Frankenhausen and Sondershausen, which hug the edge of the legendary Kyffhäuser Mountains.

BAD FRANKENHAUSEN

- *pop 9500*
- *area code* ☎ 034671

About 55km north of Erfurt, this quiet spa town at the southern threshold of the low, forested Kyffhäuser range is in good hiking and biking territory and provides the best access to two of the region's most heavily visited and impressive sights, the Kyffhäuser Monument and the Panorama Museum.

Orientation & Information

Bad Frankenhausen's train station is on Bahnhofstrasse, a five-minute walk south of the town centre. The bus station is on Esperstedter Strasse just west of the centre.

The tourist office (☎ 717 16; fax 717 19) is housed in the town's oldest half-timbered house at Anger 14 and is open from 9 am to 6 pm weekdays (in winter to 5 pm), 10 am to 3 pm on Saturday (in winter to noon) and 10 am to noon on Sunday (closed in winter). The post office on Poststrasse also exchanges money.

Kyffhäuser Monument

Above the dense forests and steep ravines of the 457m-high Kyffhäuser mountain looms this bombastic memorial (1896) to Emperor Wilhelm I. A statue showing him on horseback stands below a 60m-high tower and above the stone throne of Emperor Friedrich I (1125-90) – better known as Barbarossa – whom he considered his spiritual predecessor.

He found justification for this belief in a bizarre legend connected with the Kyffhäuser mountains. It goes like this ... after Barbarossa failed to return from the crusades, his subjects refused to believe that the popular emperor was dead. Instead, they thought that a spell had been cast that would confine him to live in the depth of a mountain – the Kyffhäuser – until he would one day return to earth to unite all the German people.

For centuries, Barbarossa whiled away the time in half slumber in his mountain prison. Every hundred years, however, he woke up and sent a boy outside to check whether the ravens (a symbol for calamity) were still flying around the mountain. If the answer was yes, the emperor fell back asleep for another century. If the ravens were gone, however, the moment had come to return. So when the German people were united in 1871 under Emperor Wilhelm I, he considered himself – a tad immodestly – as the reincarnation of the beloved Barbarossa. And, incidentally, there are no more ravens on the Kyffhäuser.

The monument stands on the foundations of the Oberburg (Upper Castle) of the medieval Burg Kyffhausen, Germany's largest castle complex (608m long, 60m wide) before its destruction in 1118. Today, only the ruins of the Unterburg (Lower Castle), as well as a gate and a 172m-deep well survive.

The remote monument is best reached by car (12km from the town centre), but there's also infrequent bus service from the bus station in Bad Frankenhausen.

The complex is open daily from 9 am to 5 pm between October and April and to 7 pm the rest of the year. Admission is DM6, discount DM3.

Panorama Museum

On the Schlachtberg north of the city centre, where the final battle in the Peasants' War took place (see boxed text titled Thomas Müntzer & the Peasants' War), stands a cylindrical concrete monstrosity that harbours a painting of truly epic proportions and content. Called *Frühbürgerliche Revolution in Deutschland* (Early Civil Revolution in Germany), the oil painting measures 14m by 123m and was created in a style called 'fantastical realism' reminiscent of such classical artists as Bruegel and Hieronymus Bosch. More than 3000 figures, assembled in numerous scenes, metaphorically depict the tumultuous transition from the Middle Ages to the modern era in 15th and 16th-century Europe.

It took artist Werner Tübke and his five assistants five years to complete this complex and allegorical *theatrum mundi* (theatre of the world), which opened in 1989 as one of the last official acts of the GDR government. The work's artistic merit and political context have been questioned, but its sheer size and ambitious themes do not fail to impress.

The museum is open daily, except Monday, between April and September from 10 am to 6 pm, October to March to 5 pm. In July and August, it is also open on Monday from 1 to 6 pm. Entry is DM10, students DM7, children DM2. There are guided tours

Thomas Müntzer & the Peasants' War

In 1524-25, central and southern Germany were rocked by a series of peasant uprisings that culminated in May 1525 with the final bloody battle on the Schlachtberg in Bad Frankenhausen.

Motivated by extreme poverty and a dearth of rights, more than 8000 rebels banded together in their fight for freedom and justice. They were joined by the priest and radical reformer Thomas Müntzer, who served as their spiritual leader. In the war he preached, 'The lord of hosts will overthrow the tyrants and place the power in the hands of the faithful'.

The rebels' chance of winning against the superior forces of the princes' army was nil, however, and few survived the slaughter. Müntzer himself was captured, tortured and killed 12 days later outside the gates of Mühlhausen.

The government of the GDR saw an opportunity for its own legitimisation in this historical insurrection. Its interpretation of history regarded the Peasants' War as a precursor to the proletarian revolution that finally came to fruition 450 years later in the founding of the 'Workers' and Peasants' State'. Müntzer was given national-hero status. ■

(in German) on the hour. English-language brochures are available.

Barbarossahöhle

The Barbarossa Cave on the southern edge of the Kyffhäuser range is one of the largest accessible gypsum caverns in Europe. Crystalline underwater lakes reflect the bizarre ceiling formations. Guided tours last 45 minutes and leave daily from 9 am to 5 pm (October to April) and to 7 pm the rest of the year. Admission is DM5, children DM3.

Kreisheimatmuseum

This regional history museum is housed in the Renaissance castle on Schlossstrasse. Its numerous exhibits provide detailed insights into the Kyffhäuser's history as a salt-producing centre as well as the area's culture, geology, flora and fauna. The museum is open from 10 am to 5 pm, closed Monday; admission is DM3, children DM2.

Places to Stay & Eat

The nearest camping ground is *Stausee Kelbra* (☎ 034651-631 0) at Lange Strasse 150 on a large reservoir in Kelbra, about 17km north of Bad Frankenhausen. The *DJH hostel* (☎ 201 8) is right in town at Bahnhofstrasse 6, only a five-minute walk from the train station. It has 118 beds and charges DM20 for juniors and DM24 for seniors. *Pension Krieg* (☎ 774 69) at Kyffhäuserstrasse 36, has singles/doubles with shower and WC for DM60/90. Slightly more upmarket is the central *Hotel Grabenmühle* (☎ 798 82; fax 798 83) at Am Wallgraben 1, which has rooms with private bath for DM60/120. For private accommodation, ask at the tourist office.

For casual Italian food head for *Pizza Pasta* at Kyffhäuserstrasse 28. At No 27 on the same street, you'll find *Akropolis* with – surprise, surprise – Greek food. For a decent glass of wine, there's the *Weinlokal Zum Schwan* at Erfurter Strasse 9.

Getting There & Around

Getting to Bad Frankenhausen by train requires a change in Sondershausen, but connections are fairly good. From Erfurt, the trip takes 1½ hours and costs DM17.60. The town is about an hour's drive from Erfurt via the B4, B86 and then the B85, and about the same distance from Weimar (B85).

To reach the outlying sights, it's best to be under your own steam. For bike rental, try Fahrradhaus Gerhard Ritter (☎ 271 8) at Kräme 30.

SONDERSHAUSEN

- *pop 23,000*
- *area code* ☎ 03632

Set in the Wipper River valley about 20km west of Bad Frankenhausen, Sondershausen was once the residence of the counts of Schwarzburg-Sondershausen. It's a pretty little town with a big tradition in music; a court orchestra existed here as early as 1637. The Lohorchester was founded in 1801 and soon attracted such musical luminaries as Franz Liszt and Max Reger. It continues to thrive to this day.

Orientation & Information

The train station is west of the town centre. Heading east on August-Bebel-Strasse will take you to the Markt where, at No 9, you'll find the tourist office (☎ 788 11 1; fax 600 38 2). Opening hours are from 9 am to 5 pm (closed from 12.30 to 1.30 pm) and to 11 am on Saturday.

Schloss Sondershausen

The former palace of the counts of Schwarzburg-Sondershausen (1534) is a harmonious hotchpotch of architectural styles – Renaissance, baroque and neoclassical. The interior, just as eclectic, is occupied by a museum, a small theatre fitted out in the early 19th-century Biedermeier style and a chapel, in addition to the living quarters reflecting the various tastes of the generations of counts who lived here. Surrounding the castle is an English garden with a baroque octagonal building used as a concert hall by the Lohorchester. The Schloss can be visited daily except Monday between 10 am and 5 pm (4 pm in winter). Entry is DM4, discount DM2.

Places to Stay & Eat

At the *Hotel Zum Erbprinzen* (☎ 750 33 6) near the castle park at Im Loh 1, rooms with shower and WC start at DM40 per person. Right next door, at No 1b, is the four-room *Pension Schweizer Haus* (☎ 601 11 1), which has doubles with shower and WC on the same floor for DM80.

Thuringian food is the fare at the *Ratskeller* at Markt 7 in the city centre and at *Hotel Thüringer Hof* at Hauptstrasse 30-32. More up-market is the restaurant inside the west wing of the Schloss.

Getting There & Away

There's regular train service from Erfurt (DM13.20, one hour). Sondershausen can be reached by car from Erfurt via the B4.

MÜHLHAUSEN

- *pop 42,000*
- *area code* ☎ 03601

About 30km north of Eisenach, in the picturesque Unstrut River valley, lies Mühlhausen, which experienced its greatest glory as a 'free imperial city' in the Middle Ages. Its historical core, crisscrossed by cobbled alleyways, reflects 800 years of architectural styles. There's a good selection of half-timbered houses with gorgeous carved and painted doors.

Information

The tourist office (☎ 452 33 5; fax 452 31 6) is at Ratsstrasse 20 and is open from 9 am to 5 pm weekdays and 10 am to noon on Saturday.

There are several banks on Untermarkt, including a Deutsche Bank branch at No 27. The post office is on Bahnhofsplatz 1. There's a police station at Karl-Marx-Strasse 4 (☎ 500). For an ambulance and in medical emergencies call ☎ 332 3.

Things to See

Mühlhausen's historical core is encircled by its 12th-century **town wall**, just under 3km long. Two of the gates and three towers, which contain exhibits on the fortifications (DM2, discount DM1), still stand.

For sweeping views of the town and surrounding area, climb the **Rabenturm**. Mühlhausen's skyline is characterised by the steeples and spires of 13 churches, of which the **Marienkirche** at Am Obermarkt, with its neo-Gothic steeple, is the most noticeable and notable.

The five-nave construction makes it the second-largest church in Thuringia after the Dom in Erfurt. In 1525, Thomas Müntzer preached here to the rebels before the Peasants' War on the Schlachtberg (see Bad Frankenhausen above), which is why it now houses a memorial to the reformer (DM3, discount DM2).

A museum dedicated to the history of the Peasants' War is nearby in the **Kornmarktkirche** (DM2, discount DM1).

At the **Divi-Blasii Kirche**, just south of the Altstadt on Felchtaer Strasse, Johann Sebastian Bach – followed by his cousin and then by his fourth son – worked as organist and inaugurated a new organ in 1709. Also worth a look is the **Rathaus** (DM1, discount DM0.50), a sprawling cluster of buildings from several centuries built around a Gothic core.

Places to Stay & Eat

The *DJH hostel* (☎ 813 32 0) is at Auf dem Tonberg 1, about 2km from the city centre (bus Nos 5 or 6 from the train station to Blobach, then a 500m walk). Beds are DM20/24 for juniors/seniors, breakfast included; sheets are DM7.

For an in-town budget place, try *Pension An der Harwand* (☎ 420 96 1), Hinter der Harwand 3, where private singles with bath are DM40, doubles DM80.

More up-market is the traditional *Hotel Stadt Mühlhausen* (☎ 455 0; fax 455 70 9) at Untermarkt 18, with rooms for DM80/120.

Healthy portions of local food for between DM12 and DM20 are served at the *Postkeller* at No 6 on the pedestrianised Steinweg. In the building behind (walk to the end of the tiled walkway) is the *Postkeller Club*, a pub with occasional live music. Thuringian fare is on the menu at *Zum Luftbad* at Goetheweg 90, next to the park.

Getting There & Away
Travelling to Mühlhausen by train from Erfurt (DM13.20, 1½ hours) almost always requires a change in Bad Langensalza. If you're coming from Eisenach (DM14.80, 1¾ hours) expect to make an additional change in Gotha. Mühlhausen is at the crossroads of the B249 from Sondershausen and the B247 from Gotha.

Thuringian Forest

South of the A4 is the Thuringian Forest, a mountainous area roughly bordered by the Werra River in the west and the Saale River in the east. The tallest peaks are just under 1000m and provide good opportunities for winter sports. The Rennsteig, one of Germany's most popular trails, runs along the mountain ridges for 168km.

Not all of the forest is idyllic, however. Many beautifully situated towns, like Ilmenau and Suhl, have been ravaged by industry or blighted by the bleak concrete high-rise apartment blocks typical of GDR architecture. Despite these drawbacks, its climate, dense woods, unhurried lifestyle and relative lack of commercialism still make the Thuringian Forest a wonderful place to explore.

FRIEDRICHRODA
- *pop 6000*
- *area code* ☎ 03623

Friedrichroda is scenically located on the northern edge of the Thuringian Forest about 20km south of Gotha. During the days of the GDR, residents of the 'workers' paradise' were shipped in droves to holiday in this small town. As the GDR's second-most popular resort, it claimed more than one million overnight stays a year. Because of its mild climate, Friedrichroda has been a popular health resort since 1837 and saw its first tourist heyday around the turn of the century. Many of its stately Art Nouveau villas date back to this time.

Orientation & Information
Friedrichroda has two train stations: Bahnhof Friedrichroda in the east of town, and Bahnhof Reinhardsbrunn north of the centre, which is the stop for the Thüringerwaldbahn tram to/from Gotha.

The tourist office (☎ 304 57 5; fax 200 69 4) is at Marktstrasse 13-15 (enter from Kirchgasse) and is open Monday to Thursday from 9 am to 5 pm, Friday to 6 pm and Saturday to noon. There's a Sparkasse bank at Hauptstrasse 35. The post office is northwest of the tourist office at Lindenstrasse. In medical emergencies, dial ☎ 112 or ☎ 365 50.

Things to See & Do
Among Friedrichroda's prime attractions is the **Marienglashöhle** (guided tours daily from 9 am to 5 pm in summer, to 4 pm in winter; entry DM7, children DM4), a large gypsum cave whose highlights include an underwater lake and a crystal grotto. You enter the latter in the dark, then – just to give you that otherworldly feel – a variation on the theme of the film *Close Encounters of the Third Kind* plays in the background as the light gradually brightens, unveiling a sparkling universe. Most of the crystallised gypsum here has been harvested and used to decorate statues of the Virgin Mary and altars in the region and beyond.

The cave is about a 20-minute walk from the city centre and is also a stop on the unique **Thüringerwaldbahn**, a colourful and historic tram making the run between Gotha and Tabarz several times hourly (DM1.50 one way, one hour). The most scenic stretch begins right after Friedrichroda through the forest to Tabarz.

In the northern part of town, in the midst of a lavish English park with ancient trees, stands the neo-Gothic **Schloss Reinhardsbrunn** on the foundations of a medieval Benedictine monastery founded by Wartburg builder Ludwig the Springer (see the earlier Eisenach section). The palace was built in 1828 by Duke Ernst I of Coburg and Gotha. Queen Victoria of England was a frequent guest in the early 19th century and it was here that she met her cousin, Duke Albert of Saxe-Coburg-Gotha, who she married in 1840. The palace, which is being restored, can only be viewed from the outside, except for the parts housing a hotel.

For leisurely excursions into the forest surrounding Friedrichroda, there's the **Thüringer Wald-Express** (DM7, return DM12; children DM5/8), a bus that takes passengers up the mountain to the Heuberghaus, a stop on the Rennsteig long-distance trail.

Places to Stay

The nearest camping ground is *Campingplatz Paulfeld* (☎ 036253-251 71) in Catterfeld, a few km south-west of Friedrichroda. The *DJH hostel* (☎ 304 41 0) is at Herzogsweg 25 on the outskirts of town, a five-minute walk from the Friedrichroda stop on the Thüringerwaldbahn and 20 minutes from Reinhardsbrunn train station. Beds here cost DM17 for juniors, DM21 for seniors; sheets are DM7. *Cabins* on the Heuberg mountain along the Rennsteig trail must be booked at the hostel (same prices).

The more reasonable hotel options in town include *Pension Zur Alten Backstube* (☎ 361 70) at Lindenstrasse 3, which charges DM80 for doubles and has a restaurant with vegetarian food. The central *Hotel Phönix* (☎ 200 88 0; fax 200 88 1) at Tabarzer Strasse 3 has cosy singles/doubles for DM70/110.

Getting There & Away

There's regular local train service between Gotha and Bahnhof Reinhardsbrunn. The Thüringerwaldbahn (tram No 4) makes the trip from Gotha several times hourly. If you're driving, take the Waltershausen/Friedrichroda exit off the A4. The town is also on the B88 to Ilmenau.

SCHMALKALDEN

- *pop 18,000*
- *area code* ☎ 03683

Hugging the south-western slopes of the Thuringian Forest, Schmalkalden is about 17km south of Friedrichroda. Historically, the little town will forever be tied to the Reformation because, in 1530, the Protestant princes formed the Schmalkaldic League to counter the central powers of Catholic Emperor Charles V. The league met eight times in Schmalkalden until 1545, and it was here in 1537 that Martin Luther presented the Schmalkaldic Articles of Faith which sealed the separation of the Catholic and Protestant churches in Germany. Charles V retaliated and beat the league in the Schmalkaldic Wars that same year, but he couldn't keep the Reformation movement down for long; with the Peace of Augsburg in 1546, each German state was allowed to choose its own religion. Schmalkalden today offers few reminders of those tumultuous and eventful times, but it has preserved its medieval feel, with narrow streets lined by wonderfully restored half-timbered houses and a beautiful castle thrown in for good measure.

Orientation & Information

Schmalkalden's train station lies beyond the south-western edge of the old city centre, near the central bus station. It's about a 10-minute walk from here to Altmarkt, the town's central square.

The tourist office (☎ & fax 403 18 2) is at Mohrengasse 2 and is open from 9 am to 1 pm and 2 to 5 pm weekdays and 10 am to 3 pm on Saturday (to 1 pm in winter). There's a Sparkasse bank in Weidebrunner Gasse. The post office is at the southern end of Altmarkt.

In medical emergencies call ☎ 112 or ☎ 694 00. The police station is in Weidebrunner Gasse (☎ 681 0).

Things to See

Towering above the city centre to the west is the well preserved late Renaissance-style **Schloss Wilhelmsburg** (open from 10 am to 4 pm November to January and 9 am to 5 pm the rest of the year, closed Monday; entry DM4, discount DM3). It was built between 1585 and 1590 by Landgrave Wilhelm IV of Hessen as a hunting lodge and summer residence. Lavish murals and stuccowork decorate nearly all the rooms, of which the **Riesensaal** with its coffered and painted

THURINGIA

ceiling is the most impressive. Notable, too, is the playful **Schlosskirche**, the palace chapel whose ornate white and gilded decorations tend to reflect secular rather than religious themes. The rare wood organ still works.

A dank basement room intended for use as a crypt now contains a copy of a 13th-century mural depicting scenes from the *Iwein legend*, a variation on the King Arthur myth written by German 12th-century poet Hartmann von Aue. The original is in the Hessenhof in the city centre but not accessible to the public.

On Altmarkt in the city centre is the **Rathaus** (1419), meeting place of the Schmalkaldic League. The two incongruous towers of the late-Gothic **St Georgenkirche**, where Luther once preached, also look out over the square. The **Lutherhaus**, where the reformer stayed, is a stately half-timbered building at the northern end of Steingasse on Lutherplatz.

Places to Stay & Eat

One of the most original places to stay in Schmalkalden is the *Grünes Tor* (☎ 608 11 1) at Weidebrunner Gasse 12. Each room in this galleried converted barn is furnished differently, but with much imagination and taste. Rates are reasonable: DM80 for a single and DM120 for a double. There's also a charming restaurant with healthy portions of German food and lots of nooks and crannies.

If they're full, you might try *Hotel Jägerklause* (☎ 600 14 3), located on the outskirts of town at Pfaffenbach 45 with doubles only for DM100 to DM120 and a decent restaurant.

Getting There & Away

To reach Schmalkalden by train from Eisenach requires a change in Wernshausen (DM11, one hour). From Erfurt, change in Zella-Mehlis (DM20, 1¾ hours). Schmalkalden is about 5km east of the B19, which connects Eisenach and Meiningen.

MEININGEN

- *pop 27,000*
- *area code* ☎ 03693

Meiningen lies about 30km south of Schmalkalden, tucked between the Thuringian Forest and the Rhön mountain range. This idyllic town on the Werra River was once the residence of the dukes of Saxe-Meiningen and owes its continuing reputation as a regional cultural centre to the vision of Duke Georg II (1826-1914), an avid supporter of both theatre and music.

Orientation & Information

Two large parks, the Schlosspark to the west and the English Garden to the north, fringe Meiningen's town centre. The train and bus stations are on the eastern side of the English Garden, which also contains Meiningen's theatre. It's about a 10-minute walk to the Markt from here.

The friendly tourist office (☎ 446 50; fax 446 54 4) is at Bernhardstrasse 6, almost opposite the Meininger Theater, and is open weekdays from 9 am to 6 pm and Saturdays from 10 am to 3 pm. The main post office is at Eleonorenstrasse 1-3. There's a police station (☎ 591) at Friedenssiedlung 9.

Meininger Theater

On the western edge of the English Garden stands the palatial Meininger Theater, its Corinthian columns facing Bernhardstrasse, an elegant boulevard lined by banks and villas. Constructed in 1909 after a fire destroyed the original, the theatre is home to a large permanent ensemble that enjoys a fine reputation throughout Germany. The original resident troupe, founded by Georg II in 1866, was the first to take its lavish productions on tour, travelling as far as Moscow and London. All in all, they gave 2591 performances in 38 cities. The duke also catapulted the court orchestra, the Meininger Hofkapelle, to international fame by appointing the pianist-conductor Hans von Bülow as musical director. Later, Richard Strauss and Max Reger also held this position. The Theatre Festival takes place annually in spring; contact the tourist office for information.

Schloss Elisabethenburg

The handsome baroque Schloss Elisabethenburg at the north-western end of the town centre was built immediately after the founding of the duchy of Saxe-Meiningen in 1680 and served as ducal residence until 1918. It now contains several permanent exhibits highlighting the town's accomplishments in theatre and music. Among the prized items of the **Theater Museum** are 275 original stage backdrops from the early days of the Meininger Theater, some of which are on permanent display. There are also accomplished sketches of set designs and costumes drawn by Georg II himself and historic photographs of well known actors.

Another wing holds the **Music Museum**, a series of rooms dedicated to the musical directors of the Meininger Hofkapelle. A medieval and Renaissance **art collection** rounds out the exhibits.

The palace is open daily except Monday from 10 am to 6 pm between May and September (9 am to 5 pm in winter). Admission is DM6, discount DM4.

Places to Stay & Eat

The tourist office can help with reservations for hotels and private rooms. One of the cheaper options is *Pension Pelzer* (☎ 442 10) at No 8 in quiet Georgstrasse where singles/doubles cost DM60/100. The historic *Gasthof Schlundhaus* (☎ 427 76) at Schlundgasse 4 has charming rooms for DM95/140 and a restaurant popular with locals. This is supposed to be the place where Thuringian potato dumplings, a regional speciality, were invented. *Henneberger Haus* in Georgstrasse is a charming restaurant-bistro with a beer garden open in fine weather. The beautiful baroque *Turmcafé* in Schloss Elisabethenburg is a great place for afternoon coffee and cake.

Getting There & Away

Direct trains travel from Meiningen to Eisenach (DM14.80, one hour) and Erfurt (DM21.80, 1¾ hours). Scheduled buses link Meiningen with Suhl, Zella-Mehlis and other towns in the Thuringian forest. The town lies along the B19 from Eisenach to Schweinfurt in Bavaria, and is also on the B89 to Sonneberg in southern Thuringia.

RENNSTEIG

The Rennsteig, one of Germany's most popular long-distance walks, has its origins in medieval times as a natural border between the states of Thuringia and Hesse and Franconia to the south.

It wends through largely uninterrupted forest from Hörschel near Eisenach to Blankenstein on the Saale River, 168km to the south-east. Along this ridge there are beautiful views of dreamy valleys, snug villages and medieval hill-top castles. The trail is well maintained and signposted with markers bearing the letter 'R'. The best hiking time is May/June and September/October, though summers are tolerable too because most of the walking is done at elevations above 700m.

Locals say that, in order to enjoy a smooth hike, before starting out you must dip your walking stick into the Werra and pick up a pebble from its waters. Upon leaving the Rennsteig, the pebble must be given back to the forest.

The entire stretch may be explored by mountain bike, but there's no separate trail. Two warnings – the trip, though enjoyable, is not very challenging and it is generally discouraged because of the damage to the environment.

Information

The tourist offices in all communities on the Rennsteig – such as Hörschel, Oberhof and Neustadt – will be able to furnish you with detailed information on the trail, including overnight options, restaurant information and, of course, maps.

The travel agency Gothaer Reisebüro (☎ 03621-305 70) in the train station in Gotha has package deals and can also help you put together a trip.

THURINGIA

Rennsteig Hike
This is a basic outline for a five-day hike along the entire length of the Rennsteig, beginning in Hörschel and ending in Blankenstein. To cover the distance in this time, you should be moderately fit, but otherwise these medium-high mountains do not require extensive hiking experience or special equipment. Spending more time to cover the trail is no problem, since there are plenty of overnight accommodation options along the way. Make sure you are adequately dressed – especially in spring and autumn – and be prepared against cold and rain.

The following is intended only as a guide; you should get Kompass Wanderkarte's 1:50,000 map *Der Rennsteig* (No 118) before setting off. Any section of the Rennsteig, especially between Hörschel and Oberhof, makes for a good day hike, too.

Day One The first stretch is 33km long and runs from Hörschel to Grosser Inselsberg. It has a steady elevation gain over a total of 700m. The trail picks up about 100m above the junction of the Hörsel and Werra rivers. At Vachaer Stein, a marker points out a mountain pass via which Napoleon retreated from the Prussians in 1812-13. At Hohe Sonne, there are gorgeous views of the Wartburg. Heading on, the trail passes the site where Martin Luther was 'captured' and brought to Wartburg castle to protect him from his detractors. At Dreiherrenstein, the territories of three duchies abutted in the 18th century. From the Oberer Beerberg, you have great views into the steep valley of the Inselsberger Loch. The trek ends at Grosser Inselsberg (916m).

Day Two The second day covers a distance of 31km from Grosser Inselsberg to Oberhof and includes one steep ascent, but otherwise little elevation gain. Grenzwiese marks the former border of the duchies of Saxe-Gotha and Schmalkalden. The Ebertswiese is a marshy meadow where the Spitter Stream has its source; after heavy rains, it turns into a small waterfall. Farther on, between Neuhöfer Wiesen and Wachserasen, an atypical Rennsteig landscape of moors and lakes awaits; this is the result of decades-long Soviet tank exercises. The day ends in Oberhof (853m), the centre of winter sports in Thuringia.

Day Three This 35km trek from Oberhof to Masserberg is characterised by a moderate hill and dale pattern. It passes by the Rennsteiggarten, a botanical garden featuring plants indigenous to the forest. The trail climbs to the Grosser Beerberg, at 982m the tallest mountain in the Thuringian Forest. Mordfleck (literally 'murder spot') has nothing to do with death but is a lovely wildflower meadow. Grosser Dreiherrenstein is the halfway mark of the Rennsteig.

The trail then leads right through the main street of Neustadt, which once divided the duchies of Saxe-Meiningen and Schwarzburg-Sondershausen. Masserberg is a town of 900 people (elevation 800m) at the transition point between the Thuringian Forest and the Thuringian Slate Mountains.

Day Four Leading from Masserberg to Ernstthal, this is a relatively brief day of hiking (25km) with only two short steep climbs. The trail passes through numerous small communities, but first you can enjoy excellent 360-degree views from the Rennsteigwarte on the Eselsberg. Friedrichshöhe is Thuringia's smallest community with just 26 inhabitants. The Dreistromstein marks the watershed of the Weser, Elbe and Rhine rivers. The town of Limbach has a tradition in porcelain manufacturing. After passing through Neuhaus, today's trip concludes in Ernstthal (770m).

Day Five This is the longest stretch, 45km from Ernstthal to Blankenstein on the Saale River, but overall it's a steady, easy walk. Between Ernstthal and Kalte Küche an educational nature trail runs along the Rennsteig. At Laubeshütte, take the 100m detour for worthwhile views from Frankenwaldblick. The Rennsteig now runs close to the former GDR border, crossing the 'death strip' several times. The final destination,

Blankenstein, is right at the confluence of the Saale and Selbitz rivers. The town itself, with its smoking chimneys and paper industry, cannot be called scenic. It has an elevation of 415m.

Places to Stay

Numerous *DJH hostels* can be found on or near the Rennsteig. There are ones in Brotterode (☎ 036259-232 9), in Friedrichroda (☎ 03623-304 41 0), in Tambach-Dietharz (☎ 036252-361 49) and in Neuhaus am Rennweg (☎ 03679-722 86 2). Small guesthouses also dot the trail and can be found in each of the communities just off it.

The *Berggasthof Ebertswiese* (☎ 03683-606 45 1) is in a lovely meadow with a little waterfall nearby (see Day Two). *Gasthaus Dreiherrenstein* (☎ 036784-502 02) is a romantic overnight stop that uses only oil lamps after 8 pm. Expect to pay from DM30 to DM40 per person at these guesthouses.

Getting There & Away

To get to the trailhead in Hörschel from Eisenach, take bus No 93 (direction Oberellen) from the bus station on Müllerstrasse, which is one block west of the Hauptbahnhof. There are also occasional trains to Hörschel. If you hike the entire distance to Blankenstein, you can then catch a train to Saalfeld and on to Jena.

OBERHOF

- *pop 3000*
- *area code* ☎ 036842

Oberhof is Thuringia's top winter resort, but its location right on the Rennsteig hiking trail makes it also an ideal summer base for forays into the forest. During the GDR days, the little town absorbed more than 100,000 visitors a year and was an athletic training centre. As any resident will tell you with pride, members of the local sports club have brought home 38 Olympic medals and 85 gold medals in European and world championships.

Today, Oberhof continues to be a training ground for top athletes from united Germany. In addition, regional, national and even international competitions take place throughout the year, especially in the biathlon stadium (in summer with rollerblades or mountain bikes) and on the artificially iced luge track (1113m); there are also two ski jumps with ice, mat and ceramic start runs.

Orientation & Information

Oberhof's train station is about 4km south of town at an elevation of around 700m. Regular shuttle buses take you into town, but if you have a hotel reservation, you may arrange to be picked up.

The tourist office (☎ 221 43; fax 223 32) is at Crawinkler Strasse 2 and is open weekdays from 9 am to 6 pm, to 3 pm on Saturday and from 10 am to 1 pm on Sunday. Plenty of trail maps are available and the staff are usually full of ideas for activities. The Snow Telephone (☎ 036874-706 23) provides updates on snow conditions. The post office on Poststrasse also exchanges money.

Activities

Many visitors to Oberhof come to watch top athletes during their training sessions and competitions (schedules available from the tourist office). Those who want to be active themselves can explore the forest on 35km of cross-country skiing tracks. There are also two downhill slopes, but at 150m and 250m in length, they are only suitable for beginners. Rental skis go for around DM15 a day at the Treff-Hotel Panorama or Sport-Luck on Gräfenroder Strasse.

In summer, Oberhof is ideal hiking country. You can start your exploration right from the town or have the Rennsteiglinie bus, which runs parallel to the Rennsteig between Oberhof and Masserberg, take you to a different trailhead. To stay oriented, pick up the 1:30,000 *Wanderkarte Oberhof und Zella-Mehlis*, which features hiking and biking trails as well as cross-country skiing tracks.

Goethe Trail This lovely, at times challenging, 18.5km day hike follows in the footsteps of Goethe who travelled in this area many times in the employ of the duke of Saxe-Weimar. It's a versatile hike, encompassing level forest terrain, steep climbs and everything in between. Like most routes in the Thuringian Forest, it is well marked. Highlights are the **Amtshaus** in Ilmenau, where Goethe lived and worked; the **Schwalbenstein** rock, where he wrote the fourth act of *Iphigenie on Tauris*; the **Kickelhahn Mountain** with a replica of Goethe's little forest cabin, where he wrote the poem *Wayfarer's Night Song*; the **Jagdhaus Gabelbach**, which contains a museum on his nature studies; and finally the **Goethehaus** in Stützerbach, where he often stayed.

The classic route begins in Ilmenau and runs south to Stützerbach. From Oberhof you can do it the other way around, but it's a little bit longer (22km). Take the Rennsteiglinie bus to Bahnhof Rennsteig and head north on the Panoramaweg which joins the Goethe Trail after about 3km. From Ilmenau, you can take bus No 300 back to Oberhof (change in Suhl).

Places to Stay

Oberhof's hotels and pensions are still in the process of being modernised, and you may find some of them of GDR standard or closed for renovation.

Try *Hotel Thüringenschanze* (☎ 2 22 67) at Theo-Neubauer-Strasse 19, which has singles for DM55 and doubles for DM90. Practically next door, at No 29 of the same street, is the new *Treff-Hotel Panorama* (☎ 500; fax 225 54), where doubles cost DM170 and quads DM210.

For hostels in the vicinity, look under Places to Stay in the earlier Rennsteig section.

Getting There & Away

There are direct buses to Oberhof from Gotha, Suhl and Meiningen, and direct trains from Erfurt (DM13.20, one hour).

Oberhof lies on the B247 between Gotha and Suhl.

THURINGIA

Saxony-Anhalt

The state of Saxony-Anhalt (Sachsen-Anhalt) comprises the former East German districts of Magdeburg and Halle.

Originally part of the duchy of Saxony, medieval Anhalt was split into smaller units by the sons of various princes.

In 1863 Leopold IV of Anhalt-Dessau united the three existing duchies, and in 1871 his realm was made a state of the German Reich.

The mighty Elbe River flows north-west through Saxony-Anhalt, past Lutherstadt-Wittenberg and Magdeburg on its way to the North Sea at Hamburg. Halle is on the Saale River south of Magdeburg.

The Harz Mountains, the most touristed part of the state, occupy its south-west corner and spread westward into Lower Saxony to Goslar. Quaint historical towns like 1000-year-old Quedlinburg and Wernigerode hug gentle, wooded slopes (see the Harz Mountains chapter for more information on these towns).

In the south-east, the Saale Valley's wine region makes for wonderful wine-tasting trips, using Naumburg – with its spectacular cathedral – as a base; alternatively, you could camp or stay in hostels along the way.

The extreme south-east is entirely undertouristed. That has kept prices a fair bit lower than in better known areas.

As investment into and renovation of this area chugs on at a slower pace, it provides travellers with the chance to see a bit of what's left of the GDR in eastern Germany. For the most part, this translates to small, untouristed and relatively unchanged villages that are just beginning to acquire higher-end hotels and restaurants.

Don't miss Ferropolis, the state's fascinating historical preservation of GDR-era strip coal-mining equipment, gathered together in Europe's largest open-air technical museum. Built on one of the ugliest spots on earth, it's now the coolest concert space and recreation area you're ever likely to see.

HIGHLIGHTS

- The bizarre concert space at Ferropolis
- Lutherstadt-Wittenberg for its associations with Luther and its Trabants for rent
- Wörlitz Park near Lutherstadt-Wittenberg
- The Vineyard Road in the Saale-Unstrut region
- The Cathedral of Saints Peter & Paul and wine tasting in Naumburg
- Leaving Magdeburg

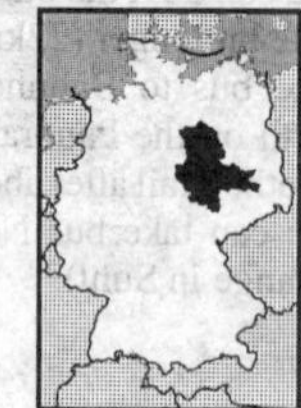

• **Population:** 2.8m • **Capital:** Magdeburg • **Area:** 20,455 sq km

Saxony-Anhalt Luminaries: Otto von Bismarck, Dorothea Erxleben, Hans Dietrich Genscher, George Frideric Händel, Friedrich Gottlieb Klopstock, Martin Luther, Georg Philipp Telemann, Christa Wolf

MAGDEBURG

- *pop 270,000*
- *area code* ☎ 0391

Magdeburg, on the Elbe River, lies at a strategic crossing of transport routes from Thuringia to the Baltic Sea and Western Europe to Berlin.

On 16 January 1945 a 39-minute bombing raid left 90% of the city destroyed. Magdeburg was rebuilt under the GDR and they did a terrible job, using steel and concrete for everything.

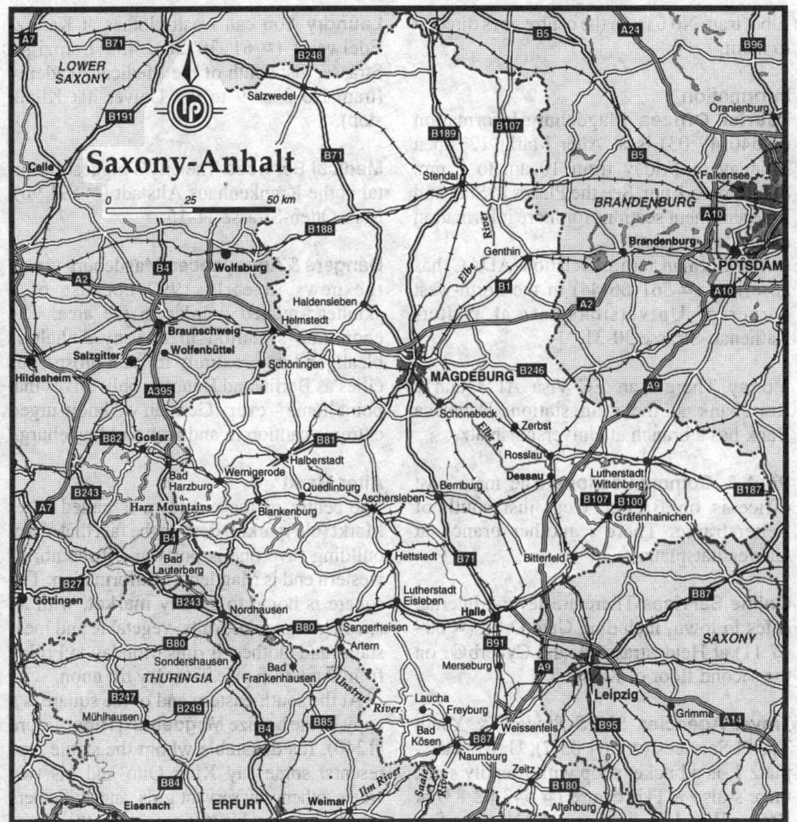

These days, Magdeburg is a lively city struggling to come out from under its ham-fisted architecture. It's nice to see little touches, like the former traffic-police perch at the north-east corner of Breiter Weg and Ernst-Reuter-Allee now finding use as a bill-board.

The city centre has generous boulevards lined with lovely, refurbished 19th-century buildings, a Gothic cathedral and a few Romanesque churches.

Magdeburg has a lively cultural scene, with its own philharmonic and plenty of opera and ballet on offer.

Orientation

From the broad square in front of the train station, Ernst-Reuter-Allee leads east to the Neue Strombrücke that crosses the Elbe. Alter Markt, home to the tourist office, is a block back on the left.

The main shopping street is the pedestrianised section of Breiter Weg, which runs north-south between Universitätsplatz and Ernst-Reuter-Allee. The main attractions are at the southern end of the Altstadt, between the Elbe and Otto-von-Guericke-Strasse.

Herrenkrug Raceway, the Stadthalle and Stadtpark Rotehorn are on the east side of the

Elbe; tram No 6 from the centre goes directly to them.

Information

Tourist Offices Magdeburg-Information (☎ 540 49 03) is at Alter Markt 12, open Monday to Friday from 10 am to 6 pm, Saturday to 1 pm. See the Places to Stay and Entertainment sections for more information about its services.

The German auto association (ADAC) has an office (☎ 561 66 44) in the north-west corner of Universitätsplatz at Walter-Rathenau-Strasse 30-31.

Money There's an EC-Visa ATM and a Reisebank at the train station. Deutsche Bank has a branch at Universitätsplatz.

Post & Communications The main post office is on Breiter Weg, just south of Leiterstrasse. There's another branch at Universitätsplatz.

Online Services There are several Internet cafés in town, including Café Orbit (☎ 609 17 11) at Heidestrasse 9, and Cyberb@r on the second floor of Karstadt.

Travel Agencies SYTS Student & Youth Travel Services (☎ 564 03 7), Universitätsplatz 1, is a bucket shop with friendly staff; there's also a TUI centre (☎ 543 02 83) at Breiter Weg 113, right near the Nordsee fish restaurant.

Bookshops & Libraries There's a good selection of English-language books at HD Presse und Buch Im Hauptbahnhof at the train station. The main library is the Stadtbibliotek (☎ 540 48 21), north of the centre at Weitlingstrasse 1a.

Campuses Otto-von-Guericke University, a technical and medical school and teaching college, has about 8000 students. The main campus is just north of the Altstadt, and the medical school is south-west of the centre, on Leipziger Strasse just south of Fermersleber Weg.

Laundry You can wash clothes at Karutz-Edelweiss (☎ 61 30 28), 45a Leipziger Strasse, just south of the Medical Academy (tram No 3 or 9 to the Universität Klinik stop).

Medical Services The city's biggest hospital is the Krankenhaus Altstadt (☎ 591 90), Max-Otten-Strasse 11-15.

Dangers & Annoyances Magdeburg was in the news in early 1997 because of a skinhead-related murder in the area. The economic situation in Saxony-Anhalt is bleak, and its proximity to such prosperous cities as Berlin and Hanover only drives that point home – every German we know urged extreme caution in and around Magdeburg.

Alter Markt

The centre of the old town is called Alter Markt (old market) despite the fact that every building save one is postwar. At the north-western end is Magdeburg-Information. The square is home to a daily **market**, with an excellent range of fruits, vegetable and meat stalls, and clothes. It runs Monday to Friday from 9 am to 6 pm, Saturday till noon.

At the south-eastern end of the square is a copy of the bronze **Magdeburg Rider** figure (1240). It's debatable whom the statue represents: some say King Otto and his two wives, others say servant girls, and still others say it's just any king approaching the city.

The door to the **Rathaus** (1698) is one of many bronze works by local artist Heinrich Apel (1936-), and it depicts the history of the city from King Otto to the apex of civilisation, the GDR in 1969. Note the representation of Till Eulenspiegel, a 14th-century trickster who charged admission to the square so people could watch him 'fly from the balcony' of the Rathaus. They paid, he vanished through a back door and was never seen here again (he pulled a similar stunt in Halle).

North of the Alter Markt is a **statue of Otto von Guericke** (1602-86), a mayor and scientist who worked on vacuum technology. Behind it, the lavish Art Nouveau

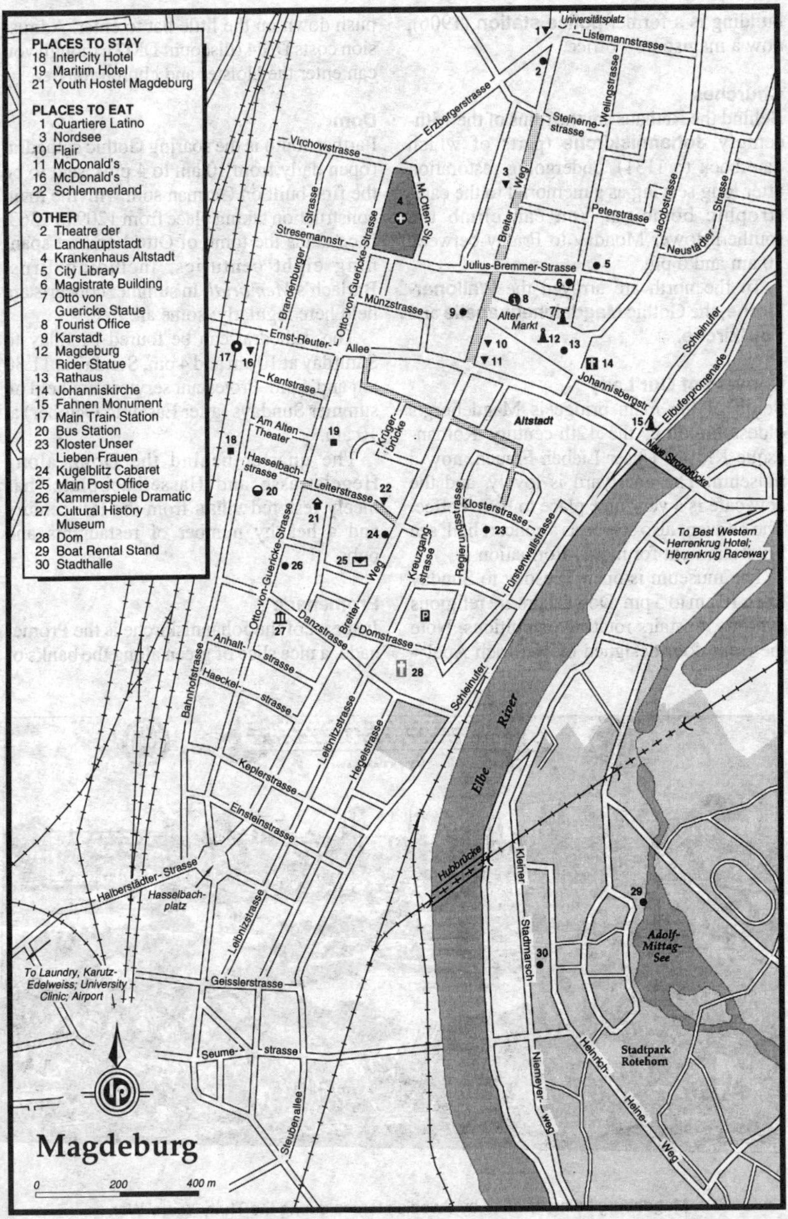

PLACES TO STAY

18 InterCity Hotel
19 Maritim Hotel
21 Youth Hostel Magdeburg

PLACES TO EAT

1 Quartiere Latino
3 Nordsee
10 Flair
11 McDonald's
16 McDonald's
22 Schlemmerland

OTHER

2 Theatre der Landhauptstadt
4 Krankenhaus Altstadt
5 City Library
6 Magistrate Building
7 Otto von Guericke Statue
8 Tourist Office
9 Karstadt
12 Magdeburg Rider Statue
13 Rathaus
14 Johanniskirche
15 Fahnen Monument
17 Main Train Station
20 Bus Station
23 Kloster Unser Lieben Frauen
24 Kugelblitz Cabaret
25 Main Post Office
26 Kammerspiele Dramatic
27 Cultural History Museum
28 Dom
29 Boat Rental Stand
30 Stadthalle

To Best Western Herrenkrug Hotel; Herrenkrug Raceway

To Laundry, Karutz-Edelweiss; University Clinic; Airport

Magdeburg

0 200 400 m

building is a former **police station** (1906), now a magistrate's office.

Churches

Behind the Rathaus are the ruins of the 15th-century **Johanniskirche** (parts of which date back to 1131), undergoing restoration after long serving as a memorial to the catastrophic bombing. You can climb the southern tower Monday to Friday between 10 am and 6 pm.

To the north are arrayed the **Wallonerkirche**, the Gothic **Magdalenenkapelle** and **Petrikirche**.

Convent of Our Lady

South of the main bridge is Magdeburg's oldest building, the 12th-century Romanesque Kloster Unser Lieben Frauen, now a museum. The courtyard is lovely, and the new café is a very nice place to have coffee. The convent also serves as a concert hall; see Entertainment for more information.

The museum is open Tuesday to Sunday from 10 am to 5 pm. Downstairs are religious exhibits, upstairs rotating exhibitions. Note the front door designed by Heinrich Apel – push down on the little hat to enter. Admission costs DM4 (discount DM2), though you can enter the cloister and church for free.

Dom

Farther south is the soaring Gothic cathedral (open daily from 10 am to 4 pm), said to be the first built on German soil, with the main construction taking place from 1209 to 1363. It contains the tomb of Otto I and art spanning eight centuries, including Ernst Barlach's *Memorial*. In summer concerts are held here regularly; some are free.

The cathedral can be toured Monday to Saturday at 10 am and 4 pm, Sunday at 11.30 am and 4 pm. Protestant services are held on summer Sundays (after Easter to October) at 10 am.

The quarter behind the Dom, along Hegelstrasse and Hasselbachplatz, has nicely restored **villas** from the last century and a healthy number of restaurants and pubs.

Promenade

Just east of the Johanniskirche is the Promenade, a nice slice of green along the banks of

Magdeburg being invaded by Swedish forces during the Thrity Years' War.

the Elbe. At its southern end is an atrocious GDR-era statue entitled *Fahnen* (flags), dubbed 'the corkscrew' by locals for obvious reasons.

Cultural History Museum
The Kulturhistorisches Museum (☎ 326 45), Otto-von-Guericke-Strasse 68-73 at the corner of Danzstrasse, houses the original *Magdeburg Rider* statue along with a good collection of graphic arts and furniture. It's open Tuesday to Sunday from 10 am to 6 pm, to 8 pm on Thursday. Admission is DM2/1.

Stadtpark Rotehorn
On the east side of the Elbe, south of the Hubbrücke, is Stadtpark Rotehorn, with playgrounds, picnic areas and **Adolf-Mittag-See**, where you can rent rowing boats. Tram No 6 stops about 300m north of the lake. This city park is also the site of outdoor concerts in summer; they're attracting bigger and bigger names here – see the Entertainment section.

Horse Racing
There's horse racing from April to October on Saturday or Sunday from 3 pm at Herrenkrug Raceway. Take tram No 6 to the last stop, and you're at the racecourse.

Organised Tours
There are German-language tours (DM5) Monday to Saturday at 11 am leaving from in front of Magdeburg-Information. English tours can be booked on one day's notice (DM65 for up to 15 people).

Places to Stay
Magdeburg's budget accommodation scene is just getting off the ground. While a new hostel has recently opened, most of the other options are out of town. Otherwise, you're at the mercy of business-class hotels.

Camping There's camping at *Campingplatz Barleber See* (☎ 503 24 4), 8km north of town and the last stop on tram No 10. It costs DM4/7 per person/car, and it's a nice if simple place right on a lake; there's a swimming beach as well.

Much more upscale is *Heide-Camp Colbitz* (☎ 039207-291), a totally modern camping ground/holiday resort with cranky staff but a swimming pool, cabins and organised activities for the kids. Tent sites are DM6 plus DM4.50 per car and DM7 per person in high season, DM4/5/5 in low season. Cabins, which sleep up to six, cost DM110/90 per day without linen, DM10 extra for linen. It's 18km north of Magdeburg and difficult to reach without a vehicle. Take the A2 north (direction: Stendal) to Colbitz and it's 2km off the exit and well signposted. By public transport take the S-Bahn to Wolmirrstedt (10km away). A taxi from there averages DM20.

Hostels The DJH *Jugendgästehaus Magdeburg* (no telephone at the time of writing) is between Otto-Von-Guericke Strasse and Breiter Weg at Leiterstrasse 10. This wheelchair-accessible hostel plans a huge dining area on the 1st floor and a fitness centre and table tennis area in the basement. It's DM27 for juniors, DM32 for seniors, plus DM6 for linen and DM6 for breakfast. It has a perfect location and very friendly management.

The DJH *Gommern* (☎ 039200-514 91), Manheimer Strasse 21, is about 20km southeast of the centre. Take bus No 1 from the Magdeburg bus station in the direction of Gommern (DM3.20 for adults, DM1.80 for kids; 40 minutes). The stop is about 200m from the hostel.

Private Rooms You can get good private rooms for DM40 to DM75 (average DM55) from Magdeburg-Information. It's a free service.

Hotels Adjacent to the InterCity Hotel at the Hauptbahnhof, there's a sign offering rooms at the *Pension am Hauptbahnhof* (☎ 0171-235 70 30), Bahnhofstrasse 68, but when we entered staff said it was closed. It might be worth checking as it looked clean and cheap.

Several hotels with reasonable prices are also close to the town centre. Among them is the *Bildungshotel* (☎ 223 43 0), Lorenzweg 56, which charges DM71/95 for singles/doubles. The *Uni-Hotel* (☎ 551 14 4), Walther-Rathenau-Strasse 6 near the university, has rooms for DM105/140. The *Hotel Stadtfeld* (☎ 738 06 0), Maxim-Gorki-Strasse 57, has rooms with breakfast and lunch for DM130/160. Rooms at all these hotels have shower, toilet, phone and TV.

At the top end, the *InterCity Hotel* (☎ 596 20; fax 596 24 99) attached to the train station has singles/doubles from DM190/230. While the admittedly chic *Maritim Magdeburg* (☎ 594 90; fax 594 99 90), Otto-von-Guericke-Strasse 87, is perfectly located, has large rooms (DM229/278 singles/doubles) and a pool, watch out: it also has unforgivable telephone prices (DM3 per minute to Berlin, for example), exorbitant restaurant prices (DM40 for a lunchtime buffet) and, for all that, service is lacking.

It's also utterly outclassed by the Art Nouveau *Best Western Herrenkrug Hotel* (☎ 850 85 00; fax 850 85 01). This may well be the best hotel in eastern Germany, and it's great value. Staff are very friendly, rooms are large and spotless, there's a fitness centre and the restaurants (see Places to Eat) are superb. It's in a park 15 minutes east of the centre via tram No 6, which stops right in front. Room rates are DM170 to DM195 for singles, DM205 to DM235 for doubles. It's about 25% less on weekends, there are lots of specials, and it's cheaper if booked through a travel agent.

Places to Eat

Restaurants & Cafés The café at the *Kloster Unser Lieben Frauen* is a lovely place for breakfast (DM 5 to DM10) or lunch (light meals from DM8 to DM10). It's in the refectory at the western end of the building, open the same hours as the convent.

Flair (☎ 561 89 95), at the corner of Ernst-Reuter-Allee and Breiter Weg next to the McDonald's, is popular and rightly so. Great food, good portions and fair prices: snacks and sandwiches from DM7 to DM10, pastas from DM10 to DM12, huge salads from DM5 to DM13, vegetarian stuff from DM12 to DM15, and full meat dishes average DM15. They do a great breakfast buffet from 10 am on Saturdays for DM10, and there's mellow live music on some Fridays from 7.30 pm.

The *Quartiere Latino* (☎ 543 97 39) on Universitätsplatz is cheaper than it looks, and it's a good spot for lunch. The enormous menu includes pasta dishes from DM8 to DM13, pizza (about 30 varieties) from DM8 to DM12, and main courses averaging DM15. Attached is an ice-cream café and a takeaway pizza place.

The best places for a blow-out meal are both at the Best Western Herrenkrug Hotel. Its great *Die Saison* restaurant has a seasonally changing menu and a spectacular Art Nouveau setting. Main courses range from DM24 to DM33, soups start at DM8 and a few vegie items are there as well from DM17. In summer the tables spill outside toward the *Beer Garden*, which hosts regular jazz and classical-music concerts.

The setting is as nice in the hotel's second restaurant, the *Eiskeller*, in a genuine ice cellar (ask to sit inside the 19th-century brick ice vault). Prices are about DM10 higher than at Die Saison.

Snacks & Fast Food There's a good *food shop* in the Hauptbahnhof with fruits and breads, and downstairs *Ditsch* does pizza and pretzels for under DM3.50. There are two *McDonald's*: at the Hauptbahnhof and at the corner of Ernst-Reuter-Allee and Breiter Weg. Opposite the latter, in the ground floor of the Karstadt department store, are several snack options, including *Steinecke's Heidebrot Bäckstube* with sandwiches and pizzas from DM2 to DM5, a *Bratwurst stand* (from DM2) and, at the northern end of the shop one block up, *Happy Happy Grill* with doner kebabs and the like at around DM5. Farther up Breiter Weg towards Universitätsplatz is *Nordsee* at No 118.

At the western end of the market on Alter Markt there's a great *roast chicken truck* (DM3.50 for a half), and *Bodo's Nudeln* has spag bol for DM5.50 to DM8 and Bratwurst for DM2.

Opposite the DJH youth hostel on Leiterstrasse is *Schlemmerland*, with a great selection of breads and pastries, sausage from DM2, huge fruit and mixed salads for DM4, and soups for DM3.

Entertainment

Listings *StadtPASS* is a free monthly calendar printed by the city. The two biggest privately published listings guides are both excellent – *DATEs* is free and has great listings and articles, *Citadel* is thicker and costs DM2.

Clubs *Mekka* (☎ 401 50 75), Halbstädter Strasse 110, is – despite its techno thudding – a pretty mellow place packed with PIB (People In Black) and students. They do 'black music' on Friday night and teeny parties on Saturday from 4 to 8 pm. There's also techno at the more popular *Space* (☎ 343 73 5), Wilhelm-Kobelt-Strasse 10.

Cabaret There's cabaret at *Der Kugelblitz*, next to the post office on the corner of Leiterstrasse and Breiter Weg.

Theatre & Classical Music The *Kloster Unser Lieben Frauen* also serves as a concert hall, featuring the music of Magdeburger Georg Phillipp Telemann, the Magdeburger Kammerchor, the energetic Gruppe M (chamber music from Debussy, Ravel, Ligeti and others) and other performances.

The Magdeburg Philharmonic plays at the *Theater der Landeshauptstadt Magdeburg* (☎ 543 47 66), at Universitätsplatz, which also hosts opera and ballet performances from September to July, and theatrical performances year round.

Dramatic performances are staged at *Kammerspiele Dramatic* (☎ 598 82 26), Otto-von-Guericke-Strasse 64, which also puts on free open-air theatre performances at various places around the city from the end of June to mid-July.

Kids flock in droves to the *Puppentheater* (☎ 404 24 29), Warschauerstrasse 25, for puppet shows and other children's theatre.

Rock & Jazz Magdeburg is on the itinerary of most visiting big-name bands. The *Stadthalle* (☎ 593 45 29) is a 2000-seat arena at Stadtpark Rotehorn, which is also a huge open-air concert area. Other big concerts take place at *AMO Kultur- und Kongresshaus* (☎ 543 30 23), Erich-Weinert-Strasse 27.

Pubs & Bars Bars in town are kind of dire. *Café Orbit* (see Online Services) has happy hour on Wednesday from 7 to 8 pm. There's a somewhat tropical feel at *Kingston Town* (☎ 733 99 22), Grosse Diesdorfer Strasse 65, a Jamaican-themed place with reggae night on Saturday. *The Lion* (☎ 620 17 74), Halberstädter Strasse 137, calls itself a 'public inn', and serves English beer on tap.

Gay & Lesbian *Couraje* (☎ 404 80 89), Porsestrasse 14, is a bar for lesbians only. *GummiBärchen* (☎ 543 02 99), Leibigstrasse 6, is exclusively gay, and *Music Bar FEZ* (☎ 561 36 94), Mittagstrasse 32-33, attracts a mixed crowd.

Getting There & Away

Air Flugplatz Magdeburg (☎ 622 78 77) is a regional airport with limited scheduled and charter services and not popularly used by non-business travellers. Bus No 57 (DM3) runs between the airport and the Hauptbahnhof. There's a Lufthansa office (☎ 561 63 10) at Ernst-Reuter-Strasse 7-11.

Train Trains to/from Berlin-Hauptbahnhof (DM34) take about 1½ hours. Magdeburg is on the main route from Rostock (DM65, 3¼ hours) and Schwerin (DM45, two hours) to Leipzig or Erfurt (DM45, 2¼ hours). There are hourly, or even more frequent, direct trains to Leipzig (DM29, 1½ hours).

Car & Motorcycle From Berlin take the A10 west to the A2, continue west, then take exit 70, just north of the centre. From Hanover, follow the A2 east. From Wernigerode take the B81 all the way.

Getting Around

The Airport By public transport, take bus No 57 from the bus station and transfer to tram No 3 or 9. A taxi to the centre should cost about DM30.

Public Transport Magdeburg has a good system of buses and trams. You can buy single tickets (DM2.30 for adults, DM1.80 for children and bicycles) at the Hauptbahnhof or bus station or, for a DM0.20 surcharge, on board. Much better value is the Tageskarte (DM5), valid for 24 hours, and the 9-Uhr Tageskarte (DM4), valid from 9 am to midnight.

Car & Motorcycle Free street parking gets easier north and south of the centre. Watch out for parking near the Hauptbahnhof and bus station, which is by permit only. The parking garage under the Maritim Hotel charges DM18 per day. There's free parking in the lot in front of the Dom.

Taxi Taxis clump, in true GDR style, by the several dozen outside the Hauptbahnhof. To order a cab, call Taxi Ruf (☎ 737 37 3) or Taxi Zentrale (☎ 568 88 8). Flag fall is DM3.50 and each additional km costs DM1.90.

Eastern Saxony-Anhalt

LUTHERSTADT-WITTENBERG

- *pop 53,000*
- *area code* ☎ 03491

Lutherstadt-Wittenberg is most famous as the place where Martin Luther did most of his work, but the Renaissance painter Lucas Cranach the Elder also lived here for 43 years. Wittenberg was a famous university town and the seat of the elector of Saxony until 1547. It was from here that Luther launched the Reformation in 1517, an act of the greatest cultural importance to all of Europe.

Wittenberg can be seen in a day from Berlin, but it is well worth a longer look – especially to note the names on the ceramic plaques attached to buildings that indicate past residents both famous and infamous.

Orientation

There are two train stations: Hauptbahnhof Lutherstadt-Wittenberg is the stop for all the fast trains to/from Berlin, Leipzig, Magdeburg and Halle. Bahnhof Wittenberg-Elbtor is a minor stop for local trains. From the main station, the city centre is a 15-minute walk away, between the two train lines and then under the tracks and into Collegienstrasse.

All of the city's sights are within a stone's throw of the hostel at the western end of the Altstadt. The city's main street, Collegienstrasse, runs east-west through the Markt. At its western end, Collegienstrasse becomes Schlossstrasse.

Information

Wittenberg-Information (☎ 402 23 9) is at Collegienstrasse 29 but will probably have moved by the time you read this. It will relocate (☎ 498 61 0; fax 488 61 1) to Schlossstrasse 2, opposite the Schlosskirche. It's open weekdays from 9 am to 6 pm, Saturday from 10 am to 2 pm, and Sunday from 11 am to 3 pm. The regional tourist office (☎ 402 61 0) is at Mittelstrasse 33. *The Historic Mile* (DM4.80) is a very good English-language guide to the city.

Money The best rates in town are at the Commerzbank at Markt 25.

Post & Communications The main post office is at Friedrichstrasse 1, with a monument to Wilhelm Weber, inventor of the telegraph.

Bookshops & Libraries Buchhandlung Christoph Franzke at Collegienstrasse 82 (☎ 402 82 8) has a small collection of English-language books. The main city library (☎ 402 16 0), Schlossstrasse 1, has a collection of English books you can read there.

SAXONY-ANHALT

Medical Services The biggest hospital is the Paul-Gehrhardt Stifftung (☎ 420 0), Paul-Gehrhardt-Strasse 42, 500m north-east of the centre. There's also a polyclinic inside for everyday matters.

Dangers & Annoyances Some tourists have been subjected to angry shouting by radical teens, but the city authorities say that there have been no violent incidents. That said, the Hauptbahnhof, near a school, can get a little hairy during school hours.

Luther House

The Lutherhaus is a museum devoted to the Reformation. It's inside a former Augustinian monastery at Collegienstrasse 54 (DM6, discount DM3; closed Monday). Luther stayed here in 1508 when he came to teach at Wittenberg University and made the building his home for the rest of his life after returning in 1511. The house contains an original room furnished by Luther in 1535 and a copy of the papal bull threatening his excommunication (yes, a *copy*; the original is in the state archives in Stuttgart). The **Luthereiche**, the site where Luther burned (yet another) copy of the document, is at the corner of Lutherstrasse and Am Bahnhof.

Melanchthon House

Philipp Melanchthon was born in 1497 at Breton, near Heidelberg. A humanist and a master of ancient languages, he became a close friend of Martin Luther, and eventually a reformer. He came to town in 1518 as a university lecturer, and stayed until his death in 1560. Melanchthon's idea of reform went far beyond religious matters – his primary goal was the reform of the German education system, which at that time taught entirely in Latin.

Melanchthon helped Luther translate the Bible into German from Greek and Hebrew sources. Later, he was heavily recruited by other universities, and to keep him in town, the last local elector gave him his house, at Collegienstrasse 60, in 1536.

Today the house functions as a museum. It was scheduled to reopen following extensive renovation just after we went to press, so hours and new prices had not yet been set.

Stadtkirche St Marien

The large altarpiece in this church was designed jointly by Lucas Cranach the Elder and his son, and completed in 1547. It shows Luther, Melanchthon and other Reformation figures, as well as Cranach the Elder himself,

Luther Lore

Martin Luther's '95 Theses' questioned Roman Catholic practices of the time, especially the selling of indulgences (or simony) to forgive sins and give the buyer reduced time in purgatory for past or even future sins. Luther's theses and questions created the Protestant church (the first one was in Wittenberg and the first service in 1522) and led to the Reformation, which changed the face of Europe.

Today hundreds of thousands make what amounts to a pilgrimage to see where Luther worked.

Local lore and some guidebooks claim that in 1517, Luther hammered a copy of his 95 Theses to the door of the Schloss Kirche for all to see. There's no proof either way, but he probably didn't.

Believers point to the fact that the door was used as a bulletin board of sorts by the university; that the alleged posting took place the day before the affluent congregation would pour into the church on All Saints' Day (1 November), and the fact that at Luther's funeral, Philipp Melanchthon himself said he personally witnessed the deed.

But Melanchthon didn't arrive in town until 1518 – the year *after* the alleged posting. It's suspicious that Luther, whose writings were voluminous to say the least, never once mentioned in them what would have been a highly radical act.

While it's known that he wrote and sent the theses to the local archbishop to begin a discussion, some locals argue that it would have been entirely out of character for a devout monk, interested principally in an honest discussion of his points, to challenge the system so publicly and flagrantly without first exhausting all his options. ■

in Biblical contexts. On 13 June 1525 Luther married an ex-nun named Katherina von Bora in this church, where he also preached. Note the octagonal bronze baptismal font from the Fischer foundry. The church's altar is painted on two sides. On the back at the bottom is a representation of heaven and hell. Medieval students etched their initials and the date into the heaven section if they passed their final exams and in the hell part if they failed.

There are also many fine paintings here; note especially *The Lord's Vineyard* by Cranach the Younger behind the altar in the south-east corner of the church.

Jewish Memorial

Outside the south-east corner of the Stadtkirche is a deplorable example of early German anti-Semitism.

In 1304, to commemorate the first known expulsion of Jews from Wittenberg, the town's elders inscribed on the church façade a German interpretation of the most holy Hebrew words for God, partially covered by reliefs of pigs, placed there to mock the words. Though the church has been renovated several times, this blatantly racist mockery has remained.

On the ground below, placed here by the local church community in 1988, is a memorial to persecuted Jews and those murdered during the Holocaust. On the left and right, in Hebrew and German, is the opening line of Psalm 130: 'Out of the depths I cry unto you, O Lord'. The plaque's representation of broiling water beneath a cross indicates guilt and reconciliation. Nearby stands a cedar tree, donated by the Children of Israel.

Kleine Kapelle

Just south of the Stadtkirche is the tiny 'Little Chapel', where, from April to September, English-language services are scheduled on Saturdays at either 5.30 or 6.30 pm.

Lucas Cranach House

On one corner of the Markt, at Stillest 1, is the house of Lucas Cranach the Elder, with a picturesque courtyard you may enter. On the walls of the courtyard are photographs showing the shocking condition the house had been allowed to fall into by the GDR. Inside, the **Gallerie im Cranach Haus** (☎ 410 91 2) has rotating art exhibitions.

Schloss Wittenberg

At the western end of town is Wittenberg Castle (1499) with its huge, rebuilt **Schlosskirche** (free; DM2 with a German-language tour by church custodians) onto whose door Luther allegedly nailed his 95 Theses on 31 October 1517. The door itself was destroyed by fire in 1760 and has been replaced by a bronze memorial (1858) inscribed with the theses in Latin. Luther's tombstone lies below the pulpit, and Melanchthon's is opposite.

Markt

On the northern side of the Markt is the **Rathaus** (1523-40), a banner example of an affluent central-German Renaissance town hall. In front of the Rathaus are two large statues. The one in the centre (1821) is of Luther, and on his right side is Melanchthon's (1855).

Organised Tours

From April to October two-hour tours of the city leave every day at 2 pm from in front of the Schlosskirche. The cost is DM10, including admission to both the Schlosskirche and Stadtkirche. One-hour tours in English cost DM75 for a group of up to 25 people.

Places to Stay

Camping The nearest camping ground is *Bergwitz* (☎ 034921-282 28), in the village of Kemberg some 11km south of town on Bergwitzsee, an artificial lake in a flooded mine pit. From the Hauptbahnhof trains leave every hour (DM2.80, eight minutes). Go under the tunnel to Bahnhofstrasse, and follow this to Walkstrasse, turn right, go to the end, turn right, and you'll see the lake. From there it's 400m ahead on the right. Look for signs indicating 'Zum See'.

Hostels The 104-bed *DJH hostel* (☎ 403 25 5) is housed upstairs in Wittenberg Castle (DM19/25 for juniors/seniors, sheets DM6.50). It's a fun place with table tennis and comfortable rooms.

Private Rooms Book private rooms through Wittenberg-Information (room reservations number ☎ 414 84 8) from about DM35 to DM70 per person (plus a DM3 fee). The regional tourist office (☎ 402 61 0), Mittelstrasse 33, also books accommodation in and around the city.

Hotels *Gasthaus Central* (☎ 411 57 2), Mittelstrasse 20, has bathless singles for DM58 and doubles with shower and WC for DM92. Up the same street at No 7 is *Pension An der Stadtkirche*, which charges DM60/80. The 34-room *Hotel Goldener Adler* (☎ 410 14 7), Markt 7, starts at DM70/80 for singles/doubles without bath.

At the higher end of the middle range is the charming *Pension Am Schwanenteich* (☎ 410 10 30; fax 280 7), Töpferstrasse 1 at the corner of Mauerstrasse, with rooms for DM70 to DM80/125.

About 10 minutes' drive north-west of town on the B107 is the lovely *Hotel Grüne Tanne Braunsdorf* (☎ 629 0; fax 629 25 0). It's quiet and well organised, with good service and clean rooms. Singles range from DM78 to DM98, doubles from DM148 to DM180. There's a good restaurant downstairs.

The *Alba Hotel Park Inn* (☎ 461 0; fax 461 20 0), Neustrasse 7-10, is a very modern business hotel with singles/doubles from DM135/165. It has a nice bar, a weird breakfast buffet and is the town's Trabant rental place (see Getting Around).

Places To Eat

Much of the town's food scene is along Collegienstrasse. Try Speckkuchen, a pizza-like edible topped with bacon and eggs scrambled with cream and onions. Lutherbrot is a scrumptious gingerbread-like concoction with chocolate and sugar icing.

Great fishy snacks can be had at *Kruse's Fischeck*, Collegienstrasse 37, with lots of smoked fish from DM2 to DM2.50 per 100g, and hot fast food at around DM3.50. The GDR-style concrete café opposite the Schlosskirche is now home to *Eis Café Lido*, with snacks, fast food and ice cream from the simple (DM2 to DM3) to large banana splits (DM9).

There's pub food like Irish stew and meat pies for under DM8 at the *Irish Harp Pub*, Collegienstrasse 71.

The *Wittenberger Kartoffelhaus* (☎ 412 00), Schlossstrasse 2, is a great place for snacks (Bratkartoffeln DM4 to DM7), salads (DM6 to DM9) or pizzas (the ominous sounding Kartoffel Pizza is DM13); there's a cool pub in the back.

Crêperie Lorette (☎ 404 04 5), Collegienstrasse 70, is a charming little place with OK crêpes, great salads and very friendly service – meat and fish-filled crêpes are DM7 to DM12.50, vegetarian ones DM8.50 to DM10.

Entertainment

Listings *Die neue Brücke* is a free biweekly magazine published by the city. The *Wochenspiele*, *Freizeit Magazine* and *Wittenberger Sonntag* also are magazines listing a variety of entertainment. *Wittenburg In* is another monthly cultural magazine.

Clubs & Bars The place to be is the *Irish Harp Pub* (see Places to Eat), with live music most weekends, great crowds and draught Guinness. *Music Café No 1* (☎ 106 96 9), Collegienstrasse 51, has live music on Friday and Saturday nights. *Klapsmühle*, Fleischstrasse 4, is a meat market of a barn with admission most nights under DM4 (DM0.99 on Wednesday and Sunday at 7 pm).

Theatre & Classical Music Buy tickets at the tourist office or at the venues. The *Mitteldeutsches Landestheater* has operettas, classical music, Christmas concerts and the like and there's cabaret in the *Brettl-Keller*.

Wittenberger Kantorei is a church choir that performs at the Stadtkirche during services and at special concerts throughout the year. There is also a choir at the Schlosskirche, where there are regular organ concerts.

Getting There & Away

Wittenberg is on the main train line to Halle and Leipzig, 90 minutes south of Berlin-Lichtenberg. All the Berlin-bound trains stop at Schönefeld airport. For train tickets and times, go to the Hauptbahnhof or to Reise Welt at Markt 12.

Getting Around

Bus You probably won't have to take a bus here, but it's nice to know they're there – the bus station is along Mauerstrasse just west of Neustrasse; single tickets are DM1.50/0.90 for adults/children, blocks of 10 tickets are DM12/9.60.

Car & Motorcycle Parking enforcement is stringent, especially in the Altstadt. There's a guarded car park under the Alba Hotel Park Inn at Neustrasse 7-10.

You can rent a like-new Trabant at the Alba Hotel Park Inn, whose owner bought 18 of the things. The cost is DM100 a day for just the car, or DM349 per person as part of a three-day 'Trabi Safari' through the region including accommodation at the Alba Hotel, breakfast and lunch and two dinners. You ain't lived till you've driven a plastic car.

AROUND LUTHERSTADT-WITTENBERG

Ferropolis

Some 24km south-west of the city is Ferropolis, one of eastern Germany's most fascinating destinations and absolutely worth the trip; it's more than likely the weirdest thing you'll ever see.

Built on Golpa North, one of the world's ugliest open-pit lignite coal mines, Ferropolis is now a technology museum and an outdoor concert venue for up to 25,000 people set against the backdrop of some of the most monstrous and hideous equipment ever devised.

Coal mining has played an enormous role in Saxony-Anhalt's history. The idea, conceived and executed by the Bauhaus school in Dessau (where it was based from 1925-32), was to create a monument to the bravery of the miners, point out the ecological impact of the operations, and symbolise the changes wrought by industrial society. Today it's billed as a display of Europe's largest steel sculptures and Germany's largest open-air technical museum.

The pitted moonscape created by the strip mining will, by the year 2000, be filled in with water diverted from the Elbe, transforming one of the world's ugliest holes into one of its most interesting swimming holes.

The equipment alone is worth the trip. The monstrous machines (with charming names like Mad Max, Big Wheel and Medusa) are so large they defy description, and mere statistics just don't do them justice. The rusting machinery looks as if it's been sent back through a time warp from some post-apocalyptic nightmare. If things go as planned, you'll be able to climb all over it by the time you read this.

Organised Tours For information on organised tours of the site, call Ferropolis' office (☎ 034953-351 20) or the Bauhaus (☎ 0340-650 82 40). For concert information, check with Wittenberg-Information.

Getting There & Away If driving, take the B100 to its junction with the B107 in Gräfenhainichen and turn north; the entrance is on the right. There's a footpath/bicycle track from Gräfenhainichen to the grounds. Direct train service from Lutherstadt-Wittenberg to the site is planned.

Wörlitz Schloss & Park

Some 15km west of Lutherstadt-Wittenberg is Schloss Wörlitz (1769-73) and its absolutely charming English-style park. The rambling park is a wonderful place to get away from it all, with bike tracks and footpaths, and gondola-like rowing boats making quick jaunts (DM0.50) across the lake throughout the summer.

The park was constructed between 1764 and 1800 by Leopold Friedrich Franz, a duke of Saxony-Anhalt. Centred on a large lake, the park has formal gardens, including the **Schloss**, **Neumarks** and **Schochs** gardens. Admission is free.

There are park tours from May to September at 1.30 pm leaving from a meeting point just inside the southern gate.

Getting There & Away Getting here by public transport is a pain; by train you need to go to Dessau, change from the Dessau Hauptbahnhof to the Dessau Wörlitzer Bahnhof and then connect with another train. The journey takes two hours and costs DM19! If you're under your own steam, take the B187 west to the B107 and turn south, which brings you right into town. The park entrances are all well signposted.

HALLE

- *pop 277,000*
- *area code* ☎ 0345

Saxony-Anhalt's former state capital and its largest city, Halle is, at first glance, as romantic as a crime scene in a coal field. Grimy and crumbling buildings, dilapidated roads and smog-filled air are about what you'd expect of a city that was the centre of the GDR's chemical industry – and we were warned by Wessis, Ossis and even a couple of normally unflappable Lonely Planet authors that the place was a pit.

But there's a spark of life in Halle that, given the chance, reveals to visitors a vibrant university city with plenty of history, and a firm commitment to culture and the arts. The city's keen preservation of historical landmarks – including those from the GDR days – reflects an administration with both restraint and a sense of humour. Halle, on the river Saale, is worth a visit.

First mentioned in 806, Halle was a powerful religious and financial centre – home to an archbishop, an important market town and finally a major salt producer. Halle's university merged with and finally absorbed the one in Lutherstadt-Wittenberg in 1817. Halle was the capital of Saxony-Anhalt from 1947 to 1952, but after reunification that status was awarded to Magdeburg.

Orientation

All the city's main sights are within spitting distance of the Ringstrasse, which marks the boundary of the former city walls. The Hauptbahnhof is to the south-east of the city, west of Riebeck Platz. The Altstadt – the centre of town – is bordered by a rough ring with various names but collectively referred to as the Stadt Ring (city ring).

To walk to the city centre from the Hauptbahnhof, head through the underpass (Der Tunnel) and along pedestrianised Leipziger Strasse past the 15th-century Leipziger Turm to the Markt, Halle's central square.

Information

Tourist Office Halle-Information (☎ 202 33 40; email NLHalle@avstudio.de) is in the unmistakable elevated gallery built around the Roter Turm in the middle of the Markt. It's open weekdays from 9 am to 6 pm (from 10 am on Wednesday), on Saturday from 9 am to 1 pm, and on Sunday (April to October only) from 10 am to 2 pm. The office sells the HalleCard, one and three-day transport and museum passes, for DM9/25.

The German Automobile Association (ADAC) has an office (☎ 202 64 93) at Joliot-Curie-Platz 1a.

Money There's a Reisebank at the Hauptbahnhof and a Commerzbank at Leipziger Strasse 11.

Post & Communications The central post office is at Hansering 19, at the north-east corner of the Altstadt. There's a branch at the Hauptbahnhof.

Online Services There's an Internet café (☎ 208 99 90) at Kaulenberg 5.

Bookshops A huge collection of cheap (DM3.95 apiece) English-language classics was available at the time of writing at Wort und Werk (☎ 551 57 0), Leipziger Strasse 73.

Campus Halle's main campus is Martin-Luther- Universität Halle-Wittenberg (☎ 557 0), with about 12,000 students in faculties of medicine, philosophy, law, business and agriculture.

Laundry Das Waschhaus (☎ 522 06 11) is a coin-operated laundrette at the corner of Richard-Wagner-Strasse and Böckstrasse.

Medical Services Ärztekammer Sachsen-Anhalt (☎ 388 09 36) is a clinic at Am Kirchtor 9. There are pharmacies at the Hauptbahnhof and the Markt.

Dangers & Annoyances A fair number of undesirables hang around the Hauptbahnhof at all hours. Use common sense when in Der Tunnel, which runs between the station and the eastern end of Leipziger Strasse.

Protected Eyesores

The city is casting, well, an interesting light on several GDR-era eyesores that it's decided to preserve. The legalisation of graffiti in **Der Tunnel** has attracted artists – some excellent – from all over the country. At the eastern end of Der Tunnel in Riebeck Platz is ***Die Faust*** (The Fist), a goofy GDR-era monument to workers' pride that looks like a pulled tooth. Artists have wrapped it in canvas, painted it and, when we visited, three people were abseiling down its sides.

There's a **Trabant** atop the Neues Theater building, best viewed from the eastern side.

And you can visit the **Stasi Archives** (☎ 644 06 3 or ☎ 661 07 4), Gemritzer Damm 4, weekdays from 9 am to 4 pm (Tuesday to 6 pm). Entry is free.

Markt

Halle's large Markt is punctuated by several notable monuments, but two immediately grab your attention: the 19th-century **statue of Georg Friedrich Händel**, the celebrated composer born in Halle in 1685, and the **office of Halle-Information** in what has got to be the most monstrous GDR construction ever perpetrated on a medieval tower. That tower is known, despite its sooty colour, as the **Roter Turm** (Red Tower; 1506). The tower was once a courthouse (denoted by the **statue of Roland** just in front of it). The red, then, would be the blood of those executed here. Today it's an art gallery.

Just south, in the Christian-Wolff-Haus at Grosse Märker Strasse 10, is the **City Historical Museum** (☎ 202 62 43) open daily from 10 am to 5 pm (to 8 pm on Thursday).

Marktkirche

The four tall towers of the Marktkirche (1529) loom above the western end of the Markt. The towering late-Gothic church has a folding altar painted at the workshop of Louis Cranach the Elder. There's a Romanesque bronze baptismal font, and two spectacular organs (Händel first doodled his *Messiah* on the smaller one). But the treasure of the church's collection is the **death mask of Martin Luther** (cast when Luther's body was placed here for the night on its way back to Wittenberg for burial), locked in the chamber behind the altar (ask to see it during a city tour).

The church is open daily. There are organ concerts on Tuesday and Thursday at 4 pm, and services on Sunday at 10 am.

Händel House

The Händelhaus (☎ 500 90 0), at Grosse Nikolai Strasse 5-6, was the composer's birthplace and now houses a major collection of musical instruments. Händel left Halle in 1703 and, after stays in Hamburg, Hanover and Italy, spent the years from 1712 to his death in 1759 in London, where he achieved his great fame. There are concerts in the courtyard in summer, inside year round; some are free, some not. There's a Händel Festival during the first week of June. Admission to the house and museum is DM4/2. It's open daily from 9.30 am to 5.30 pm (to 7.30 pm on Thursdays, when admission is free).

Triebsch Mural

On the side of the building at the corner of Kleine Ulrich Strasse and Grosse Klausstrasse, one block south of the Händelhaus, is another enduring GDR-era (1988) work of art, this one very noteworthy. It's a mural by local artist Joachim Triebsch depicting, from left to right, a *Prostitute* and *John* in front of a glass door, behind which is the silhouette of a *Stasi Officer* listening in; *Till Eulenspiegel* walking the tightrope between buildings above the *Café Haase* and a generic *Demonstration* – note the *Wall* behind the demonstrators and the *Mountain* of freedom beyond. The Coca-Cola ads were added in 1992.

Schloss Moritzburg

Nearby the Triebsch mural, on Friedemann Bachplatz, is the 15th-century Moritzburg castle (DM5/3, closed Monday), a former residence of the archbishops of Magdeburg that now contains a museum of 19th and 20th-century art, including some impressive German expressionist works by artists such as Edvard Munch and Johanna Schutz-Wolff, as well as a sculpture collection. The **Maria Magdelienien Kapelle** across the courtyard is also worth a look, and if you're lucky you'll hear a choral recital.

Organised Tours

Halle-Information runs guided city tours (DM8.50/5, times vary), but the town is easily explored independently on foot.

Places to Stay

Camping The closest camping ground is the municipal *Am Nordbad Campingplatz* (☎ 523 40 85), near the Saale River on the northern edge of town at Am Nordbad 12; it's open from early May until late September. Sites are DM2 plus DM8 per person and DM8 per car. Take tram No 2 from the Hauptbahnhof and tram No 3 from the Markt to Am Nordbad.

Hostel The 72-bed *DJH hostel* (☎ 202 47 16) at August-Bebel-Strasse 48a, in the town centre, charges DM23/29 for juniors/seniors (including breakfast).

Private Rooms For private rooms (from DM30 per person plus a DM5 service fee), contact Halle-Information's booking department (☎ 202 83 71). Otherwise, it's lean pickings for budget accommodation in Halle.

Hotels The small *Kaffeehaus Sasse Hotel* (☎ 202 30 88), near the Thalia Theater at Geiststrasse 22, has rooms with shower and WC for DM95/135, while *Pension Am Markt* charges DM95/135. The brand new *Steigenberger Esprix Hotel* (☎ 693 10), Neustädter Passage 5, is the 'budget' version of the business-class hotel chain, with rooms costing DM120/150.

If the very clean *City Hotel Am Wasserturm* (☎ 512 65 42), Lessingstrasse 8, were better situated it would be an exceptional deal, but it's still worth considering, with singles/doubles from DM99/140.

The nicely located *Congresshotel Rotes Ross* (☎ 372 71), Leipziger Strasse 76, has a few rooms for DM90/130, but those with private bath cost a steep DM150/180.

Just across from the Hauptbahnhof is the new *Maritim Hotel Halle* (☎ 510 10; fax 510 17 77), an expensive option with smallish rooms with shower modules from DM197/298.

Places to Eat

Restaurants & Cafés For a bit of atmosphere, try the *Zum Schad*, a brewery-restaurant at Reilstrasse 10, with a menu of hearty meat dishes. You can get smaller portions (around DM10) of most meals.

Strieses Biertunnel, around the corner from the Neues Theater on Schulstrasse, serves Bohemian food until midnight and has many beers on tap. Also historic – and popular with students – is *Gasthof zum Mohr*, right on the Saale River across from Giebichstein castle. Another favourite haunt is the lively *Café Nöö* at Grosse Klausstrasse 11, near the old cathedral.

In summer, other popular cafés that spill out onto the sidewalk include *Café Diex* (☎ 522 71 61), Seebener 175, and the pubby *Gosenschänke* (☎ 523 35 94), Burg 71.

Our favourite place in town is the *Drei Kaiser* (☎ 203 18 68), Berg 1, with main courses from DM9 to DM15. The speciality here is Ofenfrische Brotlaib, a cholesterol fest of pork, bacon, white wine and crème fraîche baked into a sort of pie (DM18).

Snacks & Fast Food Fast-food offerings are mostly along Leipziger Strasse: a *Burger King* at No 11, *Nordsee* at No 20, and the hugely popular *Eis Café Venezie*, which spills out onto the sidewalk. Near the eastern end of the street, at Martin-Strasse 15, is the great *Kim Yen Asia Bistro* (no telephone), a cheap place with soups from DM3 to DM3.50, spring rolls for DM3.50, fried noodles with chicken and/or vegetables for DM5.50, beef or excellent pork for DM7.50 and awesome bean-sprout salad for DM3. It's open to 10 pm daily.

Entertainment

Listings *Fritz* is the most popular free monthly magazine, and rightly so: great articles, listings and even a club and record-shop map. *Halle Blitz*, its competitor, includes art, travel, clubs and straightforward ads for prostitutes.

Cinema *Kommunales Kino 188* (☎ 503 92 5), Böllberger Weg 188, is an arty movie house with lots of English-language options and a café. Admission is DM6. There's also a children's film series for kids up to 12 years old, screening daily at 9 or 10 am; admission is DM3.

Clubs Most disco-goers in Halle begin their night at *Objekt 5* (☎ 522 00 16), Seebener Strasse 5, a very popular place with Tango Totale on Friday and Saturday, and on other nights a healthy mix of salsa, 70s music, acid jazz etc. Then, around 3 am, when Objekt 5 closes, they all head over to *Eisenstein* (☎ 121 33 90), Markt 2 at Schmeerstrasse, for acid jazz and hip hop, with funk and 'black music' every Friday. It's open to 6 or 7 am.

Students flock to *Turm*, with oldies on Wednesday, Friday and Saturday, and a smattering of other styles on other days. *Easy Schorre* (☎ 212 24 0), Philipp-Müller-Strasse 77-78, has techno and a younger crowd; on Friday (Ladies Night) women enter free from 9 to 10 pm, and drinks for everyone cost DM1 from 9 to 10.30 pm.

Gay *Pierrot Gay-Bar* (☎ 202 94 61), Grosser Sandberg 10, is open Thursday to Sunday. There's free entry and a very cruisey atmosphere.

Theatre The two best options in town are the *Neues Theater* (☎ 205 02 22/23), Grosse Ulrichstrasse 50, and *Steintor Variete Halle* (☎ 208 02 05), Am Steintor, with variety and visiting shows. There's alternative theatre at *Theater am Volkspark* (☎ 522 06 88), Burgstrasse 27 in Halle-Süd (S-Bahn No 8 to Volkspark).

Classical Music Large concerts and opera performances are held at the *Opernhaus Halle* (☎ 510 0), Universitätsring 24, and at the *Konzerthalle Ulrichskirche* (☎ 202 89 36), Kleine Brauhausstrasse 26, home to the city's philharmonic. Most of the churches, especially the Marktkirche, host opera regularly and organ music on Sundays.

Rock & Jazz There's live rock music and jazz at *Easy Schorre*, *Objekt 5* and *Turm* (see Clubs), and at *Miller's American Bar* (see Pubs & Bars). Huge concerts fill the *Eissporthalle* (☎ 690 22 74), Gimmritzer Damm 1, and there are still more at the *Capitol* (☎ 444 34 44), Lauchstädter Strasse 1a, and *Wunder Tüte* (☎ 550 04 63), Wörmlitzer Strasse 109.

Pubs & Bars *Miller's American Bar* (☎ 202 53 33), Franckesstrasse 1, is what it sounds like, with the addition of live music. There's copious beer-guzzling at the *Paulaner Keller* (☎ 208 37 09), Waisenhausring 3, and also at *Strieses Biertunnel* (see Places to Eat).

Getting There & Away

Air Leipzig-Halle airport is just that; the two cities, only 40km apart, share the ever-expanding airfield that sits about smack between them. Because of Leipzig, the airport is a major link with connecting international services from Frankfurt and

Munich, as well as services to major German and European cities.

Train Leipzig and Halle are linked by hourly StadtExpress shuttle trains. Halle is also on the route of fast trains from Rostock (DM85, 4¼ hours) and Magdeburg (DM19, one hour) to Leipzig (DM8.50, 30 minutes) or Erfurt (DM25, 1½ hours), and also from Berlin-Lichtenberg (DM41, two hours) and Frankfurt/Main (DM91, 3¾ to six hours). Trains also come from Dresden (DM37, 2¾ hours), direct or via Leipzig. Between Lutherstadt-Wittenberg and Halle, you may have to take a local train (DM14, 45 minutes).

Car & Motorcycle From Leipzig, take the A14 west to the B100, and then west again to the B91. The B71 runs directly between Halle and Magdeburg. The B91 runs south from Halle and connects with the A9, which connects Munich and Berlin.

Getting Around

The Airport Bus No 300 runs every 30 minutes during the day and less frequently at night between the airport and the Hauptbahnhof. The fare is DM10. Taxis will cost about DM50.

Public Transport If you're not getting run over by Halle's trams they can be handy; bus and tram tickets cost DM1.50 for short rides of under 10 minutes, DM2.30 for others, and DM7 for day tickets. All public transportation is included when you buy a one or three-day HalleCard (see Information).

Car & Motorcycle This is a nightmare. Watch out for trams, which will run you down like a dog in the street and then yell at you for messing up their paintwork! Street signs are awful and hotel indicators peter out before the crucial last turn. The best bet is to follow signs to the Hauptbahnhof, look for parking (avoiding the pay lot behind the Maritim but checking the free one in front of it, behind the bus stop) and walk.

Saale-Unstrut Region

The Saale and Unstrut (pronounced 'ZAH-leh' and 'OON-shtroot') rivers converge in a valley just north of Naumburg. The valley is Germany's northernmost wine-growing area, and in summer it's a breathtakingly quaint region. Its bicycle and hiking paths meander through rolling, castle-topped hills, there's horseback riding along the Saale, and the Vineyard Road that runs through here makes an irresistible one or two-day stopover for exploring and wine and *Sekt* (sparkling wine) tasting.

The vineyards – many of them tiny family-owned operations – make some very good tipple, and if you're here between June and September you'll almost certainly run into a wine festival. Freyburg's do, which takes place on the second weekend in September, is the largest in eastern Germany.

You can find accommodation throughout the region, but it makes sense to use Naumburg as a base; it has the most hotels, restaurants, camping sites and hostels, and it's within 8km of all the major sights and attractions, with frequent bus and train service to everything of interest.

This is the real eastern Germany, as yet relatively untouched by rampant Westernisation. Things move slower, prices stay lower and the people take the time to open up and welcome you. Although they're renovating and cleaning up the place, it's still going to be about five or 10 years before you stop seeing crumbling buildings along cobblestone lanes in towns and villages that are still heated by coal and wood stoves.

NAUMBURG

- *pop 31,500*
- *area code* ☎ 03445

Naumburg is one of those pretty little medieval towns for which Germany is so famous. Once a powerful market town and member of the Hanseatic League, it's best known for its exquisite cathedral. Naumburg's charms lie in its lovely buildings, friendly people and general accessibility. Its claims to fame are

Wine & Apples

The Saale-Unstrut region has more than 750 vineyards, producing excellent, crisp white wines and, well, let's just say 'tangy' reds.

The Saale-Unstrut Weinbauverband (☎ 034462-202 12) has come up with the *Weinstrasse* (Vineyard Road). In any *Weingut* (vineyard) along it, you can sample the local product free. Or, for a fee of between DM5 and DM15, you can drink up to six large glasses accompanied by bread and cheese and a history of the vineyard. From tourist offices in the region pick up copies of *Weinstrasse – Land der Burgen* (DM6.80), a regional map that indicates the Vineyard Road as well as bicycle paths, and *Weinbau Saale-Unstrut* (DM1), a vineyard guide with tour and tasting prices.

There's something magical about riding a bike and stopping for wine tasting – you can rent bikes in Naumburg or Freyburg. If you plan to do some serious tasting, there's a ferry running from the Blütengrund camping site to Freyburg (see the Freyburg section).

The Saale-Unstrut region is also locally famous for its apples, and in the autumn they are everywhere.

The best apples (DM1.70 a kg) and honey in the region are available from August to June, along with potatoes, other vegies and fruit juices at the recently privatised *Agrar-und Absatzgenossenschaft eb Naumberg* (☎ 702 97 6), at the northern end of Naumberg on the road out to Henne. ■

brief visits by Luther (he stayed, preached, drank and taught here twice), and the fact that it was, for several years, the residence of Friedrich Nietzsche.

The town goes absolutely barking on the last weekend in June with the Kirsch Fest, held at the Vogelwiese at the south-east end of town. It celebrates the unlikely story, dating from the Middle Ages, of the lifting of a blockade by Czech soldiers when their leader, Prokop, gave in to requests by the town's children, dressed in their Sunday finest, to please leave and let the townsfolk eat again.

Naumburg is a perfect base for exploring the region, but even if you can only make it a day trip from Halle or Leipzig, it's definitely worth putting on your itinerary.

Orientation & Information

The Hauptbahnhof is 1.5km north-west of the old town. You can walk into town along Rossbacher Strasse, visiting Naumburg's famous cathedral along the way. Alternatively, bus Nos 1 and 2 run frequently from the Hauptbahnhof to the Markt, Naumburg's central square. The Zentral Omnibus Busbahnhof (ZOB), or bus station, is at the north-eastern end of town on Hallesische Strasse.

Naumburg's tourist office (☎ 194 33 or ☎ 201 61 4), Markt 6, is open from 9 am to 6 pm on weekdays, and from 10 am to 4 pm on Saturday (closed Sunday).

There's a privately run tourist information service called Naumburg-Tourist (☎ 202 51 4) – more of a souvenir shop, really – in the shadow of the Dom at Steinweg 3 (open daily). They book tours of the region and are sometimes the meeting place for city tours. The main post office is just north of Marientor.

Marientor & Markt

The ruins of the city's medieval defence system are crowned by the impressive Marientor, at **Marienplatz**, the northern end of the city. The brick tower has a walled-in area that's today used in summer for concerts, puppet shows, and, coolest of all, outdoor evening films.

Admission prices range from free to DM7, and beer, wine, soft drinks and snacks are sold.

Walking south down Marienstrasse, passing the **Marien-Magdalen-Kirche**, on the right you'll see the 16th-century **Simson-Portal** at No 12a, a doorway with carvings of Samson and the Lion (above) and Saints Peter & Paul (below).

Marienstrasse twists to the right and leads into the Markt, which is dominated by the

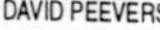

DAVID PEEVERS

DAVID PEEVERS

DAVID PEEVERS

DAVID PEEVERS

A	B
C	D

Saxony-Anhalt

A: View of Quedlinburg

B: Schlosskirche, Lutherstadt-Wittenberg

C: Wernigerode market square

D: Renaissance facade, market square, Quedlinburg

ANTHONY HAYWOOD

ANTHONY HAYWOOD

ANTHONY HAYWOOD

Harz Mountains
Top: Facade of the Rathaus in Wernigerode
Left: Pharmacy entrance in Clausthal-Zellerfeld
Right: Marktkirche in Clausthal-Zellerfeld

picturesque **Rathaus** (1528) on the western side. The **Schlösschen**, home to the tourist office, is on the southern side, and the **Portal von 1680** is at the eastern end. All three are examples of a style known as Naumburg Renaissance. Closest to the southern side is a **statue of St Wenzel**.

The late 15th-century **Hohelilie**, the white gabled Gothic structure at the north-western end of the Markt along Herrenstrasse, is under renovation and will reopen as the town's history museum.

Stadtkirche St Wenzel

This Gothic church, built between 1218 and 1523, has a 76m-high tower that rises above the southern end of the Markt. Inside, surprisingly enough, is a baroque interior complete with a Hildebrand baroque organ (under reconstruction), a bronze Gothic baptismal font, and two paintings by Cranach the Elder: *The Adoration of the Three Magi* (1522) and *The Blessing of the Children* (1529).

Just outside is the entrance to **Jüdengasse**, a backwards L-shaped alley running into Jakobstrasse. It was home to the town's Jewish community until they were chased out and their homes burned in 1494; a memorial on the southern side of the alley depicts the townsfolk chasing the (bearded) Jews out, and a *Lebensbaum* (tree of life) stands as a penitent reminder of the horrible deed.

Dom

In the ancient western quarter of town stands the magnificent late-Romanesque/early-Gothic Cathedral of Saints Peter & Paul. The cloister, crypt, sculptures and four tall towers of this great medieval complex are unique; the west rood screen and choir are adorned with a series of sculptures by the anonymous Master of Naumburg, and the choir includes the celebrated 13th-century **statues of Uta and Ekkehard** along with the other founders of the cathedral – note Uta's crafty little smile.

The first, fourth and fifth stained-glass windows here date to 1250-60, some of the most valuable in Germany.

On the staircases at the east and west sides of the crypt both kids and adults fall in love with the **banisters** by Magdeburg artist Heinrich Apel, a series of delightful brass characters, animals and footprints on long brass snakes.

An informative, if droning, tour (in German)' is included in the admission price (DM6, DM4/3 for students/children), but you can also walk around on your own.

Nietzsche House

Fans of Friedrich Nietzsche will want to make a pilgrimage to the Nietzsche Haus at Weingarten 18, which contains a permanent exhibition on his days in Naumburg. Nietzsche attended school here, and his mother and sister lived here.

Special Events

The annual Kirsch Fest, five days around the last weekend of June, is huge. The main focus of the festival is at the Vogelwiese, a meadow at the north-eastern edge of town, with about 15 tents run by local organisations, each with live music every night, lots of regional food, wine and beer and, on Saturday, an enormous fireworks display. On Sunday a large parade at 2 pm runs from the Marientor to the Markt and on to the Vogelwiese.

At Marienplatz and into Marienstrasse, the Peter Paul Messe sets up – it's an emulation of a medieval market, with goods that are half genuine handicrafts, half tourist kitsch.

Places to Stay

If you're after a private room, get in touch with Naumburg-Information; expect to pay from DM20 to DM50 per person (plus a 5% service fee) for somewhere central.

Camping *Camping Blütengrund* (☎ 202 71 1) in the Blütengrund park, 1.5km north-east of Naumburg at the confluence of the Saale and Unstrut rivers, charges DM2 for a tent site and DM5 per person; there are also bungalows with private facilities from DM30 per night. It's a family fun area, and your fellow campers most likely will be locals on holiday. There's a swimming area as well as a cinema.

Hostels Naumburg's large and well equipped *DJH hostel* (☎ 703 42 2), 1.5km south of the town centre at Am Tennisplatz 9, has multi-bed rooms for DM21/27 juniors/seniors, and double rooms for DM26/30. There's another, better hostel 5km southwest of Naumburg in Bad Kösen (see that section later this chapter).

Pensions & Hotels *Gasthaus St Othmar* (☎ 201 21 3) is a recently restored historic hotel with rooms from DM40/80.

Gasthaus Zum Alten Krug (☎ 200 40 6), at Lindenring 44 halfway between the cathedral and the Markt, has lovely furniture, a great atmosphere and rooms for DM80/110. *Zur Alten Schmiede* (☎ 245 60), almost next door at Lindenring 36-37, has really friendly staff, rooms from DM85/110, and a good restaurant.

The *Hotel Stadt Aachen* (☎ 247 0), nicely tucked away behind Markt 11, is more expensive (DM100/155 singles/doubles).

If you're going to spend that amount of money, you may as well stay at the excellent *Hotel Garni St Marien* (☎ 201 52 2), Marienstrasse 12. It has hugely friendly staff, a free locked car park, spotless rooms and arguably the best morning coffee in Germany. Rates are DM80 to DM110 for singles, DM110 to DM130 for doubles, and a very large triple room for DM160.

Places to Eat

Besides our favourite Italian place, the best restaurants in town are all typically German, with no surprises in what they serve. The good news, though, is the excellent locally produced wines that are available everywhere, with large glasses for DM5 or DM6.

Restaurants *Gritti* (☎ 200 35 4), Rosengarten 8-10 just north of Lindenring, is an excellent and comfortable Italian place with friendly staff and lovely food at reasonable prices. Huge salads cost DM6.50 to DM11, pastas from DM7.50 to DM12.50, soups from DM6 to DM8, main meat dishes are around DM17, and fish ones cost DM15 to DM17. They do a brunch with jazz on Sunday from 11.30 am to 2.30 pm (DM35, kids up to age seven DM9.50, up to age 13 DM17.50).

Zur Alten Schmiede, in the hotel of the same name, does good stuff from DM15 to DM20. *Carolus Magnus* (☎ 205 57 7), downstairs at the Hotel Stadt Aachen, is a flashy, comfortable place, while *Landgasthof Gieckau*, outside of town towards the autobahn, is the place to take that special someone. It's expensive but said to be well worth it.

Snacks & Fast Food Doner kebabs (DM5) are great at *Anatolen* (☎ 201 77 4), on Herrenstrasse between the Markt and Lindenring; burgers are DM3.50 and pizzas from DM4 to DM6. They'll do splendid vegie sandwiches for DM3 if you ask.

There's an excellent *Bäckerei-Konditorei* at Marienplatz.

A *market* sets up on the Markt, Monday and Wednesday from 8 am to 5 pm, Saturday from 8 am to noon.

Stock up on essentials for the camp site at the discount *Supermarket* at the corner of Thainburg and Marienmauer.

Entertainment

Kö Pi is a great little Irish pub just behind the Rathaus with live music on weekends, draught Guinness and Kilkenny and a good, young crowd.

Alt Naumburg at Marienplatz is a cosy, comfortable place with a good bar and local wines and beers.

Across the square *Larifari* goes for a more upscale, slick crowd, and down Marienstrasse through the alley opposite the (so-so) Greek restaurant is *Kaktus*, another very comfortable neighbourhood hang-out with good local wine and beer.

In summer, the Markt is *the* place to be at night, as tables from the local bars and ice-cream places spill outside.

Kanzlei is a yuppie hang-out; downstairs, its *Nachtschwärmer* disco has a similar crowd on Friday and Saturday nights.

Nach Acht gets a good mixed crowd (early 20s to 40ish), looking to flirt and dressed to kill.

Getting There & Around

There are fast trains to Naumburg from Halle (DM10.50, 45 minutes), Leipzig (DM12.50, 45 minutes), Jena (DM8.50, 30 minutes) and Weimar (DM10.50, 30 minutes).

A local line runs to Artern (DM28, 2½ hours) via Laucha (DM4.50, 20 minutes) and Freyburg (see below).

There are IC trains to/from Frankfurt/Main (DM80, 3½ hours) and Leipzig, Berlin (DM54, three hours) and Munich (DM118, 4¾ hours).

By road from Halle or Leipzig, take the A9 to either the B87 or the B180 and head west; both lead right into town – the B87 is less direct and more scenic, though it's the first exit from the A9.

You can rent bicycles at the Radhaus (☎ 203 119), Rosengarten 6, for DM12/20 a day/weekend.

FREYBURG

- *pop 5000*
- *area code* ☎ 034464

Eight km north-west of Naumburg, Freyburg lies right in the heart of the lovely Unstrut Valley.

The enthusiastic tourist office (☎ 272 60) on the Markt is open weekdays from 7 am to 6 pm, Saturday from 7 am to 2 pm (closed Sunday). They offer tours of the town in German on advance notice for DM50 for groups up to 20, but you can join one if one's running for DM3. They include the Rotkäppchen Sekt Kellerei (Rotkäppchen sparkling wine cellar) and the castle. The tourist office also sells a huge range of locally produced wines, with bottles from DM6 to DM14.

The large medieval **Neuenburg castle** (☎ 280 28), now undergoing major restoration, stands on the wooded hill top directly above (ie south-east of) the town (admission DM5). The adjacent tower (DM2) offers splendid views. Both are open April to October, Tuesday to Sunday from 10 am to 6 pm, closing an hour earlier from November to March.

One very sunny attraction is the **Rotkäppchen Sekt Kellerei** (☎ 272 33), at Sektkellereistrasse 5. The sparkling-wine maker, established in 1856 and the most famous in the GDR, has restored its facilities and is once again producing about a dozen varieties of the bubbly stuff.

Tours are run daily at 11 am and 2 pm, but to be certain of joining one you must book a couple of weeks in advance. If you're lucky enough to find one going when you arrive you can join it for DM2 (DM5 if you taste). Standard sekt is DM6.95 a bottle, reserve brut is DM12, and quarter-bottle splits are from DM2.

Classical concerts called (get ready) *Sektivals* are held in the factory once a month from March to September; tickets range from DM20 to DM40.

Getting There & Around

Trains run every two hours (DM2.80, nine minutes), and buses every hour (DM1.80, 15 minutes) between Naumburg's Hauptbahnhof/ZOB and Freyburg's Markt. The bicycle route *(Radwandern)* between the two cities is very well marked and makes for a wonderful ride. Rental bikes are available at Baldur Müller (☎ 273 02), Braugasse 1a.

Perhaps the most scenic way to get to Freyburg is by boat from Blütengrund, at the confluence of the Saale and Unstrut rivers just outside Naumburg.

The *MS Fröliche Dörte* (☎ 03445-202 80 9) tootles its way up the Unstrut at 11 am and 1.30 and 4 pm between March and September. It's more of a tour – it goes past Freyburg and then back to it.

The journey takes 70 minutes and costs DM10/6 for adults/children one way, DM14/8 return. It runs back from Freyburg at 12.15, 2.45 and 5.15 pm.

SCHULPFORTE

Between Naumburg and Bad Kösen is

Schulpforte, a quiet little village worth a stop. The **Landesschule Pforta** (Stateschool Pforta) was founded by Cistercian monks in 1137; in 1543 it was converted to a high school (grades 9 to 12, or pupils aged from about 14 to 18), which by the middle of the 19th century was one of Germany's finest.

Students here have included Friedrich Nietzsche (from 1858-64) and the philosopher JG Fichte (1774-80).

Today it's still one of the finest schools in eastern Germany, specialising in music, art and language. Students good enough to get in are blessed with subsidised tuition – including books, room and board – of around DM210 per month.

You can roam on the romantic grounds, and the great park behind the main campus is perfect for a picnic.

On campus is the state-owned *Landesweingut Floster Pforta* (☎ 034463-300 0), a very pleasant little wine bar and shop open daily from 10 am to 6 pm. You can try all two dozen varieties of their wine for free, or order by the glass (DM2 to DM5). Bottles range from DM7 to DM10, though *Eiswein*, a lateseasonal wine, runs in excess of DM110 per half-litre bottle.

Across the Saale is the main **vineyard**, with its spectacular **Fasskeller**, a wine cellar where you can taste and buy.

Buses running between Naumburg and Bad Kösen stop in Schulpforte.

BAD KÖSEN

- *pop 5200*
- *area code* ☎ 03446

The spa town of Bad Kösen isn't exactly a bastion of young, energetic folk, but there's a great hostel and a couple of very interesting sights, including the oldest secular building in central Germany.

The town straddles the Saale, and its main sights are on the east side. So too is the city's stunningly unhelpful tourist office (☎ 282 89), on the Loreleypromenade east of the bridge.

The **Romanisches Haus** (open Tuesday to Friday from 9 am to noon and 1 to 4 pm, weekends from 9 am to noon, closed Monday; admission DM4, discount DM3) was built in 1037.

Today it's teamed up with the **Kunsthalle** behind it to form a local history museum and a museum of dolls, the latter highlighting the locally made and marvellous stuffed animals from Spielseug Bad Kösener.

West of the Saale, follow the signs towards the hostel, past the train station, up the hill, past the hostel and on to the lookout at **Himmelreich**.

This peers down on a scene of such wondrous beauty – fairy-tale castle ruins at **Saaleck** and **Rugelsburg** towering over rolling hills, the Saale River and the little village of Saaleck – that you'll think you're looking at a children's pop-up book. There's a café at the lookout.

Places to Stay & Eat

The tourist office can book private rooms for between DM30 and DM50, and will give you a list of the spa-town accommodations, none too cheap.

Camping An der Rugelsburg (☎ 287 05) is south of town on the east side of the Saale; they hadn't set prices when we visited.

The excellent *Jugendherberge Bad Kösen* (☎ 275 97), at Bergstrasse 3, 1.5km uphill from the train station, has beds for DM18/21 for juniors/seniors, plus DM6 for linen. The complex has three buildings and great food (barbecue in summer). Lunch is an extra DM8, dinner DM7. They also sell beer (DM1.50) and local Bad Kösener wines, and can arrange wine tastings and tours throughout the area. There's even a pool table (DM1).

One of the best pastry shops in eastern Germany is the *Schoppe Café*, right at the foot of the bridge in the centre of town. They have absolutely spiffing cakes, pies, tortes and cookies for very cheap prices (huge piece of cake DM3), as well as a small selection of snacks. Service, however, can be dreadful.

Things to Buy

Other than wine, there's a factory outlet

selling Kösen animals – wonderful pigs, giraffes, squirrels, guinea pigs and elephants – at far below retail prices.

It's at Rudelsburgpromenade 22, on the way out to the hostel.

Getting There & Away

Bad Kösen is a five-minute train ride from Naumburg (hourly; DM2.80). Bus service between the two towns (DM2) is also frequent.

Harz Mountains

The Harz Mountains rise picturesquely from the North German Plain and cover an area some 100km long and 30km wide. Until the *Wende* – the dramatic 'change' of 1989 – they were shared by West and East Germany. Although a far cry from the dramatic peaks and valleys of the Alps, the Harz region is a great year-round sports getaway, with plenty of opportunities for hiking, cycling and skiing.

The Brocken (1142m) is the focal point of the Harz. Goethe set 'Walpurgisnacht', an early chapter of his play *Faust*, on the Brocken, and Heinrich Heine spent a well oiled night here, described in his *Harzreise* (Harz Journey) in 1824. Narrow-gauge steam trains run to the peak and link major towns in the eastern Harz.

The eastern Harz is in the state of Saxony-Anhalt; the western Harz lies in Lower Saxony. Hochharz National Park was established in eastern Germany immediately after the Wende; Harz National Park in western Germany followed in 1994. These two parks form the region's heartland. Good entry points are Schierke, Drei Annen Hohne (Hochharz National Park), Bad Harzburg, Torfhaus and St Andreasberg (Harz National Park).

The Harz once had large deposits of silver, lead, copper and zinc. Mining began around the 10th century and continued up to 1988. All that remains of this industry today are several interesting mining museums and a system of dams and aqueducts that once supplied the mines with water. From 1945 to 1990 the Harz region was a frontline in the Cold War and the Brocken was used by the Russians as a military base.

HIGHLIGHTS

- Trekking to the Brocken on Walpurgisnacht with the pagan masses
- A sunny morning in the empty Gernrode Stiftskirche while the organist practises
- Hexentanzplatz and the Bode Valley hike from Thale to Treseburg
- Wernigerode Castle at dusk
- 1000-year-old Quedlinburg
- The openness of the Harz people and the bizarre stories bus drivers tell
- Cross-country skiing in the Hochharz

- **Population:** 185,000
- **Location:** shared by the states of Lower Saxony, Saxony-Anhalt and Thuringia

Information

The main information centre for the Harz Mountains is the Harzer Vekehrsverband (☎ 05321-340 40) in Goslar, but information on the eastern Harz is best picked up in towns there, particularly in Wernigerode. For details see the Information sections under the individual towns.

Make sure you get the excellent *Grüner Faden* (Green Thread) booklet (DM5), available from most tourist offices in the Harz region and at many hotels. It is especially useful for activities and equipment hire, but many telephone numbers and prices are outdated.

For information on camping ask any tourist office for the free *Campingführer* brochure (in German), which lists major camping grounds and facilities open all year.

The *Ganze Harz Freizeitkarte* map

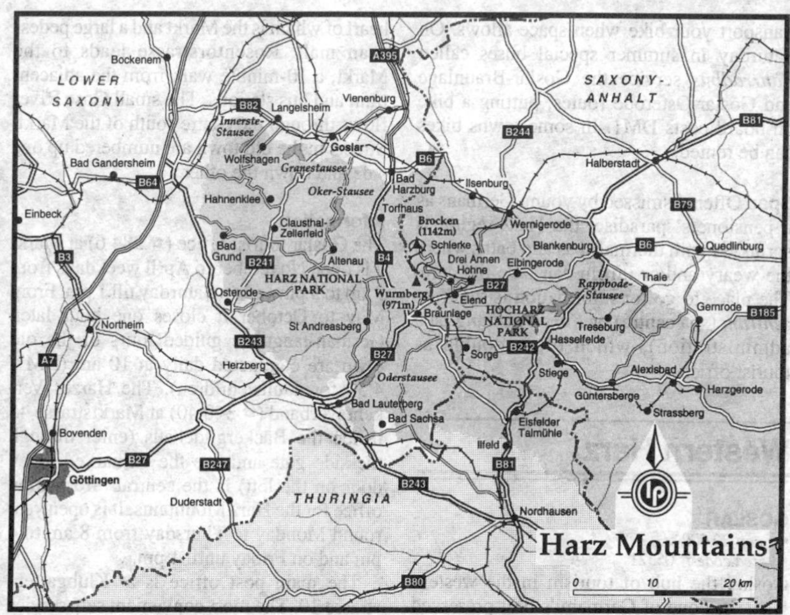

(DM10.80) provides the best general overview of sights and trails (cycling and hiking) for the entire Harz.

Activities

Skiing The main centres for downhill skiing are Braunlage, Hahnenklee and St Andreasberg, with many other smaller runs dotted throughout the mountains, though the quality of the slopes might disappoint real enthusiasts. Conditions for cross-country skiing can be excellent, with lots of well marked trails and equipment-hire shops. For weather reports and snow conditions ring the Harzer Verkehrsverband (☎ 05321-340 40) in Goslar. A German-language information service can be reached on ☎ 05321-200 24.

Hiking The main attraction in summer is hiking. Every town has its own short trails, which often link up to long-distance ones, and there are usually traditional restaurants along the way to quell hunger pains. Trail symbols are colour coded in red, green, blue and yellow on a square or triangular plate. Maps put out by the Harzclub hiking association also show trail numbers. The 1:50,000 Harzclub maps are the best for hikers. Harzclub offices in mountain towns are also good sources of information: hiking tips, itineraries, the availability of hiking partners and guides. Tourist offices usually stock the club's leaflets. Most trails are well marked and maintained, but it doesn't hurt to ask occasionally to make sure you are heading in the right direction. Weather conditions can change quickly throughout the year; be prepared.

Cycling Anyone seeking a challenge will enjoy cycling or mountain-biking in the Harz. The *Harzrundweg* map (DM19.80), available at tourist offices, covers the whole Harz and has cycling routes marked. The *Radtourenkarten* map (DM12.80) is another possibility for serious cyclists. Buses will transport your bike when space allows. On Saturday in summer special buses called *Fahrradbus* service the Goslar-Braunlage and Goslar-Osterode routes; putting a bike on board costs DM1. In some towns bikes can be rented.

Spas Often dismissed by young Germans as a pensioners' paradise, the Harz region is sprinkled with thermal spas and baths where the weary and/or infirm can take the cure. The place to go for information is the *Kurzentrum* (spa centre) or *Kurverwaltung* (spa administration), which often double as tourist offices.

Western Harz

GOSLAR

- *pop 50,000*
- *area code* ☎ 05321

Goslar, the hub of tourism in the western Harz, has one of Germany's best preserved medieval town centres, with plenty of elaborately carved half-timbered buildings oozing old-world charm.

In 1992 the town and nearby Rammelsberg mine were included on UNESCO's World Heritage List of cultural sites, and Goslar's Kaiserpfalz is one of Germany's best restored Romanesque palaces. Things can get crowded on summer weekends, when it is advisable to book ahead.

Founded by Heinrich I in 922, Goslar's early importance centred on silver and the Kaiserpfalz, the seat of the Saxon kings from 1005 to 1219. Largely due to its mines, Goslar enjoyed a second period of prosperity in the 14th and 15th centuries, after which it fell into decline, reflecting the fortunes of the Harz as a whole. The town temporarily lost its mine to Braunschweig in 1552 and its soul to Prussia in 1802. It then changed hands several times before being incorporated into the state of Lower Saxony.

Orientation

Goslar has a medieval circular layout, the heart of which is the Markt and a large pedestrian mall. Rosentorstrasse leads to the Markt, a 10-minute walk from the adjacent train and bus stations. The small Gose River flows through the centre south of the Markt. Streets in the old town are numbered up one side and down the other.

Information

The Goslar tourist office (☎ 284 6) at Markt 7 is open November to April weekdays from 9 am to 5 pm and on Saturday till 1 pm. From May to October it closes one hour later. German-language guided tours of the old town are conducted daily at 10 am (DM7/4.50 for adults/children). The Harzer Verkehrsverband (☎ 340 40) at Marktstrasse 45 inside the Bäckergildehaus (enter through the side gate and use the unmarked green door on the left) is the central information office for the Harz Mountains. It is open year round Monday to Thursday from 8 am to 4 pm and on Friday until 1 pm.

The main post office is at Klubgartenstrasse 10. The most convenient self-service laundry is City-Textilpflege at Petersilienstrasse 9 (a load costs DM9 plus DM5 for the dryer).

For medical attention, try Harz Kliniken (☎ 555 0) at Kösliner Strasse 12. Call ☎ 130 3 in emergency cases. The police station (☎ 791) is at Heinrich-Pieper-Strasse 1.

Around the Markt

There are some fine half-timbered houses on or near the Markt. The building housing the **Hotel Kaiserworth** (see Places to Stay) at No 3 was erected in 1494 to house the textile guild. The impressive late-Gothic **Rathaus** comes into its own at night, when its stained glass windows light up the town square. The **Huldigungssaal** inside the Rathaus, which may still be closed for restoration, has a beautiful cycle of religious paintings.

In front of the Rathaus is a replica of the **Elle**, the local yardstick for cloth. A pillory for debtors who couldn't (or wouldn't) pay up once stood here; a local custom required the poor devils to drop their trousers before being led off for the next round of abuse.

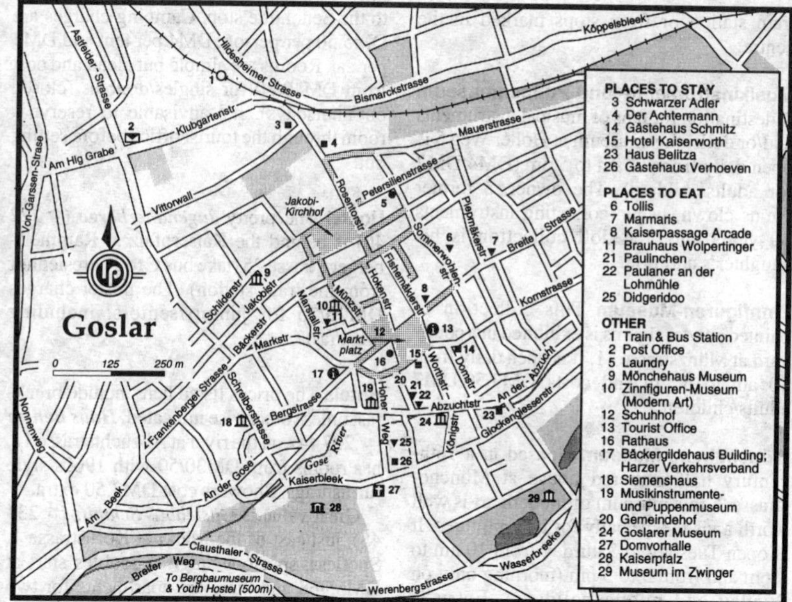

The **market fountain**, crowned by an eagle symbolising Goslar's status as a free imperial city, dates from the 13th century, but the eagle itself is a copy of the original. Opposite the Rathaus is the **Glockenspiel**, a chiming clock depicting four scenes of mining in the area. It 'plays' at 9 am, noon and 3 and 6 pm.

The baroque **Siemenshaus** at Schreiberstrasse 12 is the ancestral home of the Siemens industrial family and can be visited on Tuesday and Thursday between 9 am and noon (admission free). **Brusttuch**, at Hoher Weg 1, and the **Bäckergildehaus**, on the corner of Marktstrasse and Bergstrasse, are two fine early 16th-century houses.

Kaiserpfalz

This reconstructed 11th-century Romanesque palace at the top of Hoher Weg is Goslar's pride and joy. The interior frescos of idealised historical scenes date from the 19th century. On the south side is **St Ulrich Chapel**, which houses a sarcophagus containing the heart of Heinrich III. Below the Kaiserpfalz is the recently restored **Domvorhalle**, which displays the 11th-century Kaiserstuhl, the throne used by Salian and Hohenstaufen emperors. In the pleasant gardens behind the palace you can track down an excellent sculpture by Henry Moore, the **Goslarer Krieger** (Goslar Warrior). The Kaiserpfalz is open daily from 10 am to 5 pm (to 4 pm from November to March). Entry is DM3.50, discount DM2.

Museums

Rammelsberger Bergbaumuseum About 1km south of the town centre along Rammelsberger Strasse, this 1000-year-old mine (now a museum) is where visitors descend into the shafts and delve into the area's mining history. It is open daily from 9 am to 6 pm (last admission 4 pm).

Entry is DM6 (from DM9 with a German-language guided tour). Take bus C from the train station or from stops marked in the centre.

Musikinstrumente- und Puppenmuseum A destination for fans of musical instruments and/or dolls, this museum at Hoher Weg 5 is open daily from 11 am to 5 pm (DM4/DM2 for adults/children). The owner, a former circus clown, began collecting instruments 40 years ago; the doll collection is his daughter's addition.

Zinnfiguren-Museum This collection of painted pewter figures is exhibited in a courtyard at Münzstrasse 11. It is open daily from 10 am to 5 pm and costs DM3.50/DM2 adults/children.

Mönchehaus Museum Housed in a 16th-century half-timbered house at Mönchestrasse 3, this museum of modern art is well worth a visit, especially for its sculptures. It is open Tuesday to Saturday from 10 am to 1 pm and from 3 to 5 pm (morning only on Sunday and public holidays). Entry is DM3.50.

Goslarer Museum This museum at Königstrasse 1 provides an excellent overview of the history of Goslar and the geology of the Harz Mountains. It is open Tuesday to Sunday from 10 am to 5 pm (to 4 pm November to March). Admission is DM3.50.

Museum im Zwinger Set in gardens south of the Markt at Thomasstrasse 2, the 16th-century Zwinger, a tower that was once part of the ramparts, has a collection of such late-medieval delights as torture implements, coats of armour and weapons used during the Peasant Wars. It is open daily March to mid-November from 9 am to 5 pm (to 4 pm the rest of the year). Entry is DM3.

Places to Stay

Camping A year-round option for campers and non-campers alike is the *Hotel & Campingplatz Sennhütte* (☎ 225 02), at Clausthaler Strasse 28, 3km south of Goslar via the B241. Take bus No 434 from the train station to the Sennhütte stop. Camping charges are DM5.50 per person, DM4 per tent and DM3 per car. Rooms are simple but clean and cost from DM40/80 for singles/doubles (closed on Thursdays). It's advisable to reserve a room through the tourist office before setting out.

Hostel The pretty *Jugendherberge* (☎ 222 40) is behind the Kaiserpfalz at Rammelsberger Strasse 25 (take bus C to Theresienhof from the train station). The hostel charges DM20/25 for juniors/seniors, including breakfast.

Hotels The prices listed here include breakfast unless otherwise indicated. *Haus Belitza* (☎ 207 44), on the river at Abzuchtstrasse 11, has rooms from DM30/50 with 1960s-style furnishings. Showers cost DM3.50 extra.

Great value is *Gästehaus Schmitz* (☎ 234 45), just east of the Markt at Kornstrasse 1. Spotless, spacious singles/ doubles start at DM55/68 and there are apartments for two for DM80 (without breakfast). The resident tortoiseshell cat is called Micky.

The recommended *Schwarzer Adler* (☎ 240 01), a stone's throw from the train station at Rosentorstrasse 25, has rooms without bathroom from DM60/90.

Gästehaus Verhoeven (☎ 238 12), near the Kaiserpfalz at Hoher Weg 12, has basic but clean singles/doubles for DM50/80 (DM55/90 with shower).

For a dash of luxury, *Hotel Kaiserworth* (☎ 211 11), in a magnificent 500-year-old building at Markt 3, has singles/doubles from DM95/190 with bath and WC. Larger rooms are from DM120/210, and good-value weekend package deals are available. *Der Achtermann* (☎ 210 01), at Rosentorstrasse 20, has rooms from DM159/268, including use of the pool and whirlpool (saunas half-price at DM7).

Places to Eat

Goslar has many surprisingly good-value restaurants, and plenty of places with cheap weekday lunch menus for DM10 or less.

Some traditional restaurants are closed on Mondays.

The Kaiserpassage shopping arcade on Breite Strasse has several good options, including *Dolce Vita*, an Italian café open until 8 pm that serves excellent pasta for around DM13, and the *Altdeutsches Kartoffelhaus*, which serves generous portions of north German potato dishes for between DM5.50 and DM23.50. *Pizzeria Dolomiti* at the Breite Strasse entrance is a bargain, with tasty small pizzas from DM4 to DM6.

Tollis, off Breite Strasse at Sommerwohlenstrasse 5, is a no-frills and friendly place, with many dishes for less than DM10. Back on Breite Strasse, *Marmaris* at No 90 is a stylish Turkish restaurant with main courses for DM20 to DM30.

Of the beer halls serving food, *Brauhaus Wolpertinger*, in a brewery courtyard (a beer garden in summer) at Marstallstrasse 1, is the most rustic, serving dishes from DM14 to DM28. In a similar vein are *Paulinchen* at Gemeindehof 6 (on the south side of the Markt between Worthstrasse and Hoher Weg) and *Paulaner an der Lohmühle*, next door at No 3-5. The latter has south German cuisine for DM12 to DM17. *Didgeridoo*, at Hoher Weg 13, is an oddity that serves Australian cuisine. Open for lunch and dinner, it doesn't close till 2 am. Kangaroo burgers cost from DM6 to DM11, barbecue meals around DM16. It has a good Australian wine selection.

Things to Buy

Hoher Weg is packed with shops selling souvenirs, mostly of the tacky variety. A few quality establishments sell local crafts such as ceramics, puppets and marionettes, many of them portraying witches. The better ones go for about DM200. Approach the local Harz fruit wines and herbal schnapps with caution – some of it will leave you the worse for wear. Try the Harzer Roller, a local, if somewhat bland, sour-milk cheese.

Getting There & Away

Bus The Regionalbus Braunschweig (RBB) office (☎ 343 10) at the train station, from where buses also depart, has free timetable leaflets for services in the Harz region. Bus Nos 408 and 61/432 run between Goslar and Altenau. Bus No 61/432 continues on to St Andreasberg (DM10.40, one hour). Bus Nos 408 and 434 (via Hahnenklee) run to Clausthal-Zellerfeld (DM6.80). For Bad Harzburg, where you can change buses for Torfhaus, take bus No 62/407 (DM3.60). The Berlinienbus BEX runs three times weekly to Berlin (DM61) via Magdeburg. For timetables and bookings, refer to DER-Reisebüro (☎ 288 4) at the train station.

Train The frequent Bad Harzburg-Hanover train (via Hildesheim) stops at Goslar, as does the Braunschweig-Göttingen train. There's a direct service to Wernigerode and a more frequent service via Vienenburg, but you must change.

Car & Motorcycle The B6 runs north to Hildesheim and east to Bad Harzburg, Wernigerode and Quedlinburg. The north-south A7 is reached via the B82. For Hahnenklee, take the B241. The car-rental chain Europcar (☎ 251 38) has a branch at Lindenplan 3.

Getting Around

Local bus tickets cost DM2.20 or can be bought in batches of 10 for DM16 from the Presseladen im Achtermann newsagent, next to Der Achtermann hotel on Rosentorstrasse. To book a taxi ring ☎ 131 3. Mountain bikes can be hired from Harz Bike (☎ 820 11) at Bornhardtstrasse 3-5, about 2km north of the station at the end of Hildesheimer Strasse. They cost DM35 per day.

AROUND GOSLAR

Oker Valley

The Oker Valley, which begins at Oker, a small industrial town now part of Goslar, is one of the prettiest in the western Harz. An 11km hike (red triangle) follows the course of the Oker River and leads to a 47 million cubic metre dam, constructed in the 1950s to regulate water levels and generate power. Along the way you'll pass the 60m-high

Römkerhalle waterfall, which was created in 1863. The B498 leads to the dam. If travelling by bus, take No 407 from Goslar to the stop marked Okertalsperre.

HAHNENKLEE

- *pop 2200*
- *area code ☎ 05325*

This small thermal spa some 15km southwest of Goslar is one of the more tasteful ski resorts in the Harz Mountains and a good base for summer hikes in the western Harz.

Orientation & Information

If arriving by bus, disembark at the Post stop opposite the small post office on Rathausstrasse. The tourist office (☎ 510 40) is in the Kurverwaltung building off Rathausstrasse at Kurhausweg 7, about 50m past the cable-car station. It is open weekdays from 9 am to 5 pm, on Saturday from 10 am to noon. There's a police station (☎ 215 4) in the same building. The nearest hospitals are in Goslar and Clausthal-Zellerfeld; see Information under those towns for details.

Gustav-Adolf-Kirche

Tucked away at the top of Rathausstrasse, this Norwegian-style wooden stave church was built in 1907. Its attractive interior, a blend of Byzantine and Scandinavian styles, can be viewed free of charge on weekdays from 10.30 am to 4.30 pm (closed from noon to 1.30 pm) and on Saturday from 1.30 to 4 pm.

Thermal Baths

The Kurzentrum (☎ 235 2) at Kurhausweg 10, actually in the tourist office building, offers a whole range of services including sauna (DM12) and swimming pool (DM5). To book a session, drop by or phone on weekdays between 8 am and noon.

Skiing

Hahnenklee has several good downhill pistes, all on Bocksberg, the mountain overlooking the town. Day tickets for the cable car and lifts cost DM30. Skikeller in der Seilbahnstation (☎ 218 6), at Rathausstrasse 6, hires downhill ski equipment for DM20 a day, cross-country gear for slightly less. Wehrsuhn (☎ 223 5), at Rathausstrasse 19 and Berghotel (☎ 250 5), at An der Buchwiese 1, are other options. Snow-Fun (☎ 217 2 or ☎ 304 5) at Hindenburgstrasse 4 has snowboards and skis for hire. Ice skates can also be rented at these places for when the Kranicher Teich (a large pond) freezes over.

DSV-Ski-Schule Hahnenklee (☎ 218 6), at Rathausstrasse 19, has weekend ski courses for DM60.

Hiking

The tourist office can help with hiking suggestions. The car park near the Gustav-Adolf-Kirche is the starting point for several loop trails and for paths to Bocksberg. Taking the cable car for one leg to the mountaintop restaurant is another option. Other trails lead through the forest to/from Goslar (trail 2G; blue dot; 11km) via Windsattel and Glockenberg. Be sure to take the Harzclub 1:50,000 walking map and be prepared for changing weather conditions.

Special Events

Hahnenklee's annual Walpurgisnacht festival is a highlight for both visitors and locals. Based on a medieval myth, the festival is held throughout the Harz on 30 April. Locals dress up as witches and warlocks and engage in all manner of bacchanalia.

Places to Stay

Hahnenklee levies a nightly resort tax of DM3.50 per person – keep your resort card for discounts. A reduced tax is charged on hostel and camping accommodation.

Hahnenklee is full of hotels. Of the cheaper options, *Campingplatz am Kreuzeck* (☎ 257 0), on the B241 at the turn-off to Hahnenklee, has modern facilities and is open year round. Take bus No 434 from Hahnenklee to the Kreuzeck stop. The *Jugendherberge Bockswiese* (☎ 225 6), at Steigerstieg 1, costs DM20/25 per night for juniors/seniors. Take the bus from the Post stop to the Bockswiese stop.

Places to Eat
Restaurants are mainly concentrated on Rathausstrasse, but you might like to try *Steffens Café Restaurant* at Kurhausweg 6. The *Bauernstübchen*, at No 1 of the same street, has basic north German cuisine priced from DM8.50 to DM21. *Al Vulcano*, at Rathausstrasse 4, has pasta and pizza from DM9.50 to DM16.50 and meat dishes from DM20.

Getting There & Away
Bus No 434 from Goslar to Bad Grund via Clausthal-Zellerfeld stops in Hahnenklee. The Berlinienbus BEX to Berlin stops daily at Hahnenklee. Hahnenklee is just west of the B241, between Goslar and Clausthal-Zellerfeld.

BAD HARZBURG
- *pop 25,000*
- *area code ☎ 05322*

This pretty town is a thermal spa with a high incidence of fur coats and rheumatism among its visitors. Unless you fit into one of these categories, its main attraction will be the nearby Harz National Park and trails. The town's proximity to Goslar (9km) makes it possible to stay in one town and commute to the other.

Orientation
Bad Harzburg is shaped like a wedge, rising towards the northern edge of the Harz Mountains and narrowing to an apex as it follows the valley of the Radau River southward. Herzog-Wilhelm-Strasse and its continuation Bummelallee form the main axis. The latter is a pedestrian mall that ends at Kurpark, a 15-minute walk from the train station.

Information
The tourist office (☎ 753 30) is in the Kurzentrum at Herzog-Wilhelm-Strasse 86. It's open weekdays from 8 am to 8 pm and on Saturday from 9 am to 4 pm.

The Harzclub-Zweigverein (☎ 133 7), Kleine Krodostrasse 1, has brochures on many mountain walks and activities. Two-hour guided walks around town in German (DM2 or free with the resort card, issued on payment of the resort tax) leave from the tourist office on Friday at 10 am.

The post office is at Herzog-Wilhelm-Strasse 80. The Fritz-König Stift hospital (☎ 760) is at Ilsenburger Strasse 95. The police station (☎ 228 0) is at Herzog-Wilhelm-Strasse 47. Many shops are closed during the early afternoon *Ruhestunden*, a German siesta.

Grosser Burgberg
This mountain above Bad Harzburg has the ruins of an 11th-century fortress built by Heinrich IV. The 481m-long cable car to the fortress costs DM4/6 one way/return for adults. It operates daily year round from 9 am to dusk, which makes it a good after-dinner option in summer. You can reach it by continuing up Bummelallee to the Kurpark. Not far from the fortress is a traditional café-restaurant.

Haus der Natur
The Harz National Park information centre at Berlinerplatz in the Kurpark has audio-visual material, lots of brochures on the park, and a collection of stuffed wild animals that does – despite your misgivings about taxidermy – allow you to view some of the rarer Harz Mountains creatures in the flesh (almost). It is open daily except Tuesday from 10 am to 5 pm.

Thermal Baths
The baths in Bad Harzburg are recommended for rheumatism and sports injuries – anything, in fact, to do with joints. A full list of prices is available from the Kurzentrum (☎ 753 30) at Herzog-Wilhelm-Strasse 86. A day ticket for the thermal baths costs DM18 or you can drink the stuff at the beautiful **Trink- und Wandelhalle**, a restored late 19th-century building in Badepark, east of the Kurzentrum and Herzog-Wilhelm-Strasse. A glass costs DM0.50 (free with a resort card).

Hiking & Skiing

Marked trails lead into the national park from Berlinerplatz and Grosser Burgberg, the latter just over 3km from Berlinerplatz on foot. Among the many walks are those to Sennhütte (1.3km), Molkenhaus (3km) and to scenic Rabenklippe (7km), overlooking the Ecker Valley. All have restaurants; a blackboard inside the valley cable-car station indicates which ones are open. From Grosser Burgberg you can take the Kaiserweg trail, which leads to Torfhaus and connects to the Brocken. A marked trail also leads to the 23m-high Radau Waterfall, some 7km from Grosser Burgberg. The Harzclub-Zweigverein (see Information) conducts various guided hikes in German, some led by park rangers. If snow conditions are good, it is possible to ski cross-country to/from Torfhaus, which has equipment-hire facilities. (See Brocken & Torfhaus in the Eastern Harz section.)

Special Events

Bad Harzburg has plenty of concerts, though most are fairly staid affairs. Nevertheless, it pays to check out the tourist office's events calendar. An annual music festival is held in June. The July Gallopp-Rennwoche horse race, a notable bright spot for punters, is held just outside town at the Pferde-Rennbahn racecourse (bus No 62/407 to the Silberbornbad stop).

Places to Stay

A nightly resort tax of DM4 per night is charged on all hotel stays.

Campingplatz am Wolfstein (☎ 358 5), about 3km east of town at Ilsenburger Strasse 111, can be reached by bus Nos 74 and 77 from the train station. Another camping option is *Campingplatz Stadtteil Göttingerode* (☎ 812 15), about 4km west of town along the B6 (bus No 62/407 from the train station).

The *Braunschweiger Haus* hostel (☎ 458 2), at Waldstrasse 5 (bus No 73 from the station to the Lärchenweg stop), has beds for DM20/23 juniors/seniors.

You will find several good hotels west of the tourist office on Am Stadtpark; follow the small path below the tennis courts.

Places to Eat

The *Europa-Grill*, a Hungarian-Balkan eatery at Herzog-Wilhelm-Strasse 24, is a good bet, with main courses from DM12.50 to DM25, including several trout dishes. *Bella Roma*, below the tourist office at Goslarsche Strasse 1, has reasonable pizzas from DM8, pasta for DM10 to DM17 and meat dishes for DM24 to DM34. *Hexenhaus*, in the Kurpark near the cable car, serves up a full range of traditional German dishes, with mains from DM17 to DM30 (closed Tuesday).

Getting There & Away

The train station and adjacent bus station are on the northern side of town, a 10-minute walk from the pedestrian mall. Bus No 62/407 leaves regularly for Goslar, and bus No 77 heads for Wernigerode (DM4.70, one hour). Bus No 63/422 shuttles almost hourly to Braunlage (DM6.80) via Radau Waterfall and Torfhaus. Frequent train services link Bad Harzburg with Goslar, Hanover, Braunschweig and Wernigerode. Bad Harzburg is on the A395 to Braunschweig. The B4 and B6 lead to Torfhaus and Wernigerode respectively.

Getting Around

Long-distance buses double as local town buses in Bad Harzburg. The number to ring for a taxi is ☎ 262 6.

BRAUNLAGE

- *pop 6000*
- *area code* ☎ 05520

Though your first impression of Braunlage, situated some 23km south of Bad Harzburg and just a few kilometres from the former GDR border, may be less than favourable, winter sports and summer hiking draw the crowds here. Skiing in Braunlage is usually the best in the Harz Mountains, and the town itself is possibly the northernmost point where you'll see the Bavarian Dirndl being worn.

Orientation & Information

Braunlage's heart is the junction of Elbingeröder Strasse and Herzog-Wilhelm-Strasse, the latter a thoroughfare that changes names several times. The tourist office (☎ 194 33) is in the Kurverwaltung building at Elbingeröder Strasse 7. It is open weekdays from 7.30 am to 12.30 pm and 2 to 5 pm, Saturday from 9.30 am to noon. The post office is off Elbingeröde Strasse at Marktstrasse 3. The police station (☎ 553) is on Herzog-Johann-Albrecht-Strasse.

Skiing

A cable car will take you up the 971m Wurmberg, from where you can ski down or use the three lifts on the mountain itself. Day tickets cost DM32 (DM3 extra for closed cabins on the cable car). Downhill ski equipment can be rented at Café-Restaurant Zur Seilbahn (☎ 600) from DM20 a day, including boots and stocks/poles, or from one of the many ski shops dotted around town. Skischule Braunlage (☎ 828 0), on Herzog-Johann-Albrecht-Strasse, has five-day group lessons starting on Monday for DM130 per person. Braunlage has several smaller pistes, groomed cross-country trails, and a ski jump where high flyers can land on the former East German border.

Plenty of places in town offer cross-country skis for hire. Rosy's Souvenir Ecke (☎ 322 4), at Elbingeröder Strasse 8a, has gear for DM12 per day.

Ice Skating

Eisstadion Braunlage (☎ 219 1), an ice rink on Harzberger Strasse, rents skates from DM4.50 per two-hour session. It is open all year Tuesday to Saturday from 10 am to noon and 2 to 4 pm, and on Sunday from 1.30 to 3.30 pm and 4 to 6 pm.

Hiking

The tourist office has a free leaflet, *Wandervorschläge Rund Um Braunlage* (Hiking Suggestions around Braunlage), covering trails in the area and showing restaurant stops in capital letters. Its *Wanderwege Braunlage* (Hiking Trails Braunlage) is also free and also good. If you are heading east, a trail follows the B27 to Elend (red triangle; 7km), where you can pick up the narrow-gauge railway to Wernigerode.

Horse Riding

Waldgaststätte Ponystuben (☎ 352 0), off the B27 near the camping ground at An der Waldmühle 4, has horse and pony riding from DM25 an hour. Individual lessons cost DM35 an hour and guided group tours (minimum two people) cost from DM25 per person for one hour. It also rents holiday flats accommodating two people from DM110 for one night or DM70 per night for longer stays.

Places to Stay

A resort tax of DM3 is charged nightly on hotel stays in Braunlage, less for camping grounds and hostels.

The nearest camping ground is *Campingplatz Ferien vom Ich* (☎ 413), 1.5km south of Braunlage, off the B27 to Bad Lauterberg. The *Jugendherberge* (☎ 223 8) hostel is a 15-minute walk from the centre at Von-Langen-Strasse 28. Prices for juniors/seniors are DM20/25.

Getting There & Away

Bus No 65 runs to St Andreasberg (DM3.60) from the Von-Langen-Strasse stop. For Torfhaus and Bad Harzburg, take bus No 63/422 from the bus station, which is south of the centre, where Herzog-Wilhelm-Strasse becomes Bahnhofstrasse. The B4 runs north to Torfhaus and Bad Harzburg. The B27 leads south-west to the St Andreasberg turn-off and north-east to the eastern Harz.

ST ANDREASBERG

- *pop 2500*
- *area code* ☎ 05582

Known for its mining museums, clean air and hiking and skiing options, this small hill-top spa sits on a broad ridge surrounded by mountains, some 10km south-west of Braunlage. A silver-mining centre from the late 16th century until 1910, St Andreasberg has seen its fair share of disasters – first the bubonic plague, which wiped out most of its inhabitants in the 14th century, then an 18th-century fire that dispensed with two thirds of its mostly timber houses. It's wonderful to visit St Andreasberg during a warm snowless spring or a 'golden October'.

Orientation & Information

The tourist office (☎ 803 36) is in the Kurverwaltung building at Am Glockenberg 12, a southern extension of Dr-Willi-Bergmann-Strasse, the main thoroughfare. It is open weekdays from 9 am to 12.30 pm and 2 to 5 pm, on Saturday from 10 am till noon. Information on Harz National Park can be picked up in the Kurhaus (☎ 135 7) at Am Kurpark 9. It has audiovisual shows, and is open daily from 8 am to 6.30 pm.

The post office, at Dr-Willi-Bergmann-Strasse 28, is open weekdays from 8.30 to 11.30 am and 2.30 to 5 pm, on Saturday from 8.30 to 11.30 am. The police station (☎ 714) is on Silberstrasse. Most shops close for several hours around noon.

Grube Samsan

To reach this mining museum, follow the signs from Dr-Willi-Bergmann-Strasse. German-language tours, which take you 20m down into the tunnels to view early forms of mine transportation, leave Monday to Saturday at 11 am and 2.30 pm and cost DM5.50. Previous visitors include Goethe, who descended the shafts for a look-see in 1777. The nearby Catharina Neufang tunnel includes a mining demonstration and can be seen on the same days at 1.45 pm (DM3).

Skiing

St Andreasberg has some decent pistes; the closest one serviced by lifts is on Mathias-Schmidt-Berg. A single ride to the top costs DM2; day tickets for adults are DM28. Signs point the way from Wäschegrund, near the post office. The Skischule Pläschke (☎ 260), at Dr-Willi-Bergmann-Strasse 10, rents ski equipment from DM25 a day and also has some good three-day deals. Hiring a snowboard costs DM15. A lift also operates from nearby Jordanshöhe; a day ticket costs DM28.

A smaller, easier ski slope with equipment hire is at Sonnenberg, which can be reached in 10 minutes on the infrequent bus No 445 from the tourist office.

Cross-country skiers should pick up the *Wintersportkarte* map (DM4) from the tourist office, which shows groomed and ungroomed trails. An option for experienced skiers is the 12km return hike, partly through the national park, between Dreibrode and Sonnenberg. Hotel Altes Forsthaus (☎ 495), at Sonnenberg 2, hires alpine and cross-country skis and boots from DM25/20 per day.

Hiking

The tourist office has free, detailed hiking leaflets in German. The Rehberger Grabenweg leads into the Harz National Park and to Rehberger Grabenhaus, a forest café 3km from St Andreasberg and only accessible by foot. Start from Hotel Tannhäuser, at Am Gesehr (gold/blue, then blue, triangle). This beautiful trail follows the Rehberger Graben aqueduct to Oderteich (9km from the trailhead), an historic dam built in the early 18th century to drive the mines' wheels. The café is open for coffee and cakes Tuesday to Sunday from 9 am to 6 pm. From Oderteich a pretty trail leads west alongside the B242 to Sonnenberg, where weary trampers can get the bus back to town. Be sure to check the timetables first.

Other Activities

The Kurmittelhaus (☎ 522), at Am Kurpark 8, has some good-value sauna/massage packages from DM30. It is open weekdays from 8 am to noon and 2 to 6 pm (closed Wednesday afternoon). Saturday visits must be arranged in advance. The sauna section is open on Tuesday (men only), Thursday (women only) and Friday (mixed) from 2 to 7 pm. There is also a moderately priced restaurant.

Kids will enjoy the 540m-long Rutschbahn (slide) down Mathias-Schmidt-Berg. It is open May to October daily in dry weather from 10 am to 5.30 pm, and costs DM5/4 for adults/children (including the chair-lift ride).

Special Events

St Andreasberg is popular among families for its Walpurgisnacht celebrations on 30 April. Tickets for various events can be bought from the tourist office.

Places to Stay & Eat

A small resort tax is charged in St Andreasberg. The nearest camping ground is *Campingplatz Erikabrücke* (☎ 143 1), 8km south of St Andreasberg on the B27. The *Jugendherberge* (☎ 269) hostel is at Am Gesehr 37 and costs DM25 for both juniors and seniors.

La Capri, uphill from the post office at Dr-Willi-Bergmann-Strasse 27, is a recommended eat-in and takeaway Italian restaurant with pizzas from DM7 to DM15, good pasta dishes, and meat main courses from DM17 to DM27. *Adria*, at Schützenstrasse 35, has a pleasant atmosphere and Balkan dishes starting at DM13.50 for kebabs, rising to about DM25 per head for grill platters. The restaurant at *Hotel Tannhäuser*, Clausthaler Strasse 2a, has a good selection of traditional dishes from DM18.50 and wholefood dishes from DM14 to DM20.

Getting There & Away

Bus No 65 runs between St Andreasberg and Braunlage. Bus No 432 offers direct services several times daily to/from Goslar and Bad Lauterberg. The less frequent bus No 445 runs to/from Clausthal-Zellerfeld.

St Andreasberg can be reached by the B27, which winds along part of the scenic Oder Valley from Bad Lauterberg to Braunlage. The L519 (Sonnenberg) leads north to the B242 and Clausthal-Zellerfeld, to the B4 and Bad Harzburg, and to Goslar (B241 or the B498 along the Oker Valley).

CLAUSTHAL-ZELLERFELD

- *pop 17,000*
- *area code* ☎ 05323

Actually two settlements that were united in 1924, this small university town was once the region's most important mining centre. Its main attractions are mineral and spiritual: an excellent mining museum and a spectacular wooden church. But outdoors enthusiasts will feel at home here too, with 66 lakes and ponds, mostly created for the mines, in the immediate area.

Orientation

Clausthal-Zellerfeld is spread for approximately 2km along the B241. As in many similar linear towns in the Harz, the main street changes names several times, with Kronenplatz as the hub. Clausthal lies to the south while Zellerfeld begins just beyond Bahnhofstrasse, roughly 1km to the north.

Information

The tourist office (☎ 810 24), a 10-minute walk north of Kronenplatz, is in the former train station at Bahnhofstrasse 5a (turn left off Zellbach). It is open weekdays from 9 am to 5 pm, and on Saturday from 10 am to noon. The building also houses the Kurverwaltung (same telephone number and hours) as well as the Harzclub (☎ 817 58). The latter is open on weekdays from 9 am to noon. The post office is at Kronenplatz 2. For medical services go to the Robert-Koch-Krankenhaus (☎ 714 0) at Windmühlenstrasse 1. There's a police station (☎ 709 7) at Berliner Strasse 10.

Mines

The **Oberharzer Bergwerksmuseum** at Bornhardtstrasse 16 has an interesting open-air exhibition of mine buildings and mining methods, including a model of a horse-driven carousel used to convey minerals. There are lots of mineral exhibits and artefacts in the museum building, and tours take you down into the depths. The museum is open daily from 9 am to 5 pm (the last tour leaves at 4 pm); entry costs DM7. Tours are in German, but if you ask beforehand, someone will translate for you.

The **Mineralogische Sammlung**, south of Kronenplatz at Adolph-Roemer-Strasse 2a, is a geologist's dream, with Germany's largest collection of mineral samples. It is open on Monday from 2 to 5 pm, and Tuesday to Friday from 9 am to noon. Entry is DM1.

Marktkirche Zum Heiligen Geist
This impressive baroque church dedicated to the Holy Spirit and consecrated in 1642 seats over 2000 people, making it Germany's largest wooden house of worship. Its onion-shaped domes and lightness are a welcome change from the Harz's more stolid structures. The church is in Clausthal at Hindenburgplatz 1, off Adolph-Roemer-Strasse. Its decorative interior can be viewed Monday to Saturday from 9.30 am to 12.30 pm and from 2 to 5.30 pm, on Sunday and public holidays from 1 to 5 pm.

Activities
Clausthal-Zellerfeld has a good network of cross-country trails. Angelsport Gerhard Krause (☎ 142 4), at Zellbach 82, hires cross-country skis from DM12 a day. Ski-Verleih Menzel (☎ 812 25), in Zellerfeld towards the camping ground at Spiegeltaler Strasse 23a, has the same equipment available for between DM10 and DM15.

Experienced skiers might like to do a ski hike in the area. The tourist office can help you with trail information and maps.

The Harzclub-Verein (see Information) has leaflets in German with suggested day and half-day walks, many of which can be combined with a dip in one of the lakes. Don't forget to pack a Harzclub map.

Places to Stay & Eat
A nightly resort tax of DM1.50 is charged by hotels, less at camping grounds and hostels. *Campingplatz Waldweben* (☎ 817 12), about 1km west of Zellerfeld at Spiegeltaler Strasse 31, is open year round. Costs are DM6.50 per person, DM4 for a tent and DM4 per car. Over-heated cyclists can cool off in the lakes nearby. The *Jugenherberge* (☎ 842 93) hostel is set in a forest about 2km from town at Altenauer Strasse 55. To get there take bus No 408 (the Goslar-Altenau bus) from Kronenplatz and disembark at the Jugendherberge stop. The price for juniors/seniors is DM20/25. The hostel is usually closed on the first weekend of the month from mid-September to mid-May.

Lilienbrunnen (☎ 835 23), at Marktstrasse 13 in Zellerfeld near St Salvatoris Church, has clean singles/doubles with facilities from DM65/95, and an average-priced traditional restaurant. *Friese Hotel* (☎ 331 0), behind the Marktkirche at Burgstätter Strasse 2, has rooms with facilities from DM70/100 and two restaurants, one serving pasta. *Goldene Krone* (☎ 930 0), centrally located at Am Kronenplatz 3, has tasteful singles/doubles with shower and WC from DM98/150. Its restaurant is highly recommended, with plenty of game dishes. Most dishes cost DM25 to DM30.

Clausthal-Zellerfeld has lots of good Italian cafés and Eiscafés (ice-cream parlours), most around Kronenplatz.

Getting There & Away
Regular bus services leave 'Bahnhof', the former train station, and Kronenplatz for Goslar and Bad Grund. Catch bus No 445 for St Andreasberg and bus No 408 for Altenau. The B241 leads north to Goslar and south to Osterode, the B242 east to Braunlage and St Andreasberg. To reach the A7, take the B242 west. Long-distance buses double as town buses in Clausthal-Zellerfeld. The number to ring for a taxi is ☎ 222 9.

Eastern Harz

WERNIGERODE
- *pop 35,000*
- *area code* ☎ 03943

Wernigerode is flanked by the foothills of the Harz Mountains. A romantic ducal castle rises above the old town, which counts some 1000 half-timbered houses spanning five centuries in various states of repair. In summer this busy tourist centre attracts throngs of German holiday-makers. It is also the northern terminus of the steam-powered narrow-gauge Harzquerbahn, which has chugged the breadth of the Harz for almost a century. The line to the summit of the Brocken, the highest mountain (1142m) in northern Germany, also leaves from here.

Orientation

The bus and train stations are adjacent on the northern side of town. From Bahnhofplatz, Rudolf-Breitscheid-Strasse leads south-east to Breite Strasse, which runs south-west to the Markt.

The roads Burgberg (where a path begins), Nussallee and Schlosschaussee all lead to a fairy-tale castle on a hill at Agnesberg to the south-east.

Information

The tourist office (☎ 194 33) is at Nicolaiplatz 1, just off Breite Strasse near the Markt. From October to April, it is open on weekdays from 9 am to 6 pm, weekends from 9 am to 3 pm. From May to September it closes one hour later on weekdays and is open on weekends from 10 am to 4 pm. Its excellent map, *Stadtplan Wernigerode* (DM4.90), includes hiking trails in and around Hochharz National Park.

You'll find several banks on Nicolaiplatz, and the post office is on the corner of Marktstrasse and Kanzleistrasse. A hospital, Harz-Klinikum Wernigerode (☎ 610), is at Ilsenburger Strasse 15. The police station (☎ 653 0) is at Nicolaiplatz 4.

Altstadt

On the Markt, the towered **Rathaus** began life as a theatre around 1277, but what you see today is mostly late Gothic from the 16th century. Legend tells us that the artisan who carved the town hall's 33 wooden figures fell out with authorities – and added a few mocking touches. The neo-Gothic **fountain** (1848) was dedicated to charitable nobles, whose names and coats of arms are immortalised on it.

The colourful 15th-century **Gothisches Haus**, now a hotel, took its name from the 19th-century habit of calling anything old 'Gothic'. Nearby, the quirky **Schiefes Haus**, at Klintgasse 5 (reached via Marktstrasse), owes its appearance to a brook below what was once a mill. Downstairs you will find a good music venue (see Entertainment).

In Oberpfarrkirchhof, which surrounds the **Sylvestrikirche** nearby, you will find **Gadenstedtsches Haus** (1582), with its Renaissance oriel. The **Harz Museum**, a short walk away at Klint 10, focuses on local and natural history. It is open Monday to Saturday from 10 am to 5 pm; entry is DM3/2 for adults/children.

Narrow-Gauge Railways

Fans of old-time steam trains or anyone who likes train travel will be in their element on any of the three narrow-gauge railways crossing the Harz. This 132km integrated network – the largest in Europe – is served by 25 steam and 10 diesel locomotives, which tackle gradients of up to 1:25 (40%) and curves as tight as 60m in radius. Most locomotives date from the 1950s, but eight historical models, some from as early as 1897, are proudly rolled out for special occasions. Timetables indicate which trains have steam locomotives.

The network, a legacy of the GDR, consists of three lines. The Harzquerbahn runs 60km on a north-south route between Wernigerode and Nordhausen. The serpentine 14km leg from Wernigerode to Drei Annen Hohne includes 72 bends and will drop you on the edge of Hochharz National Park.

From the junction at Drei Annen Hohne, the Brockenbahn train begins the steep climb to Schierke and the Brocken. Direct services to the Brocken can also be picked up from the terminuses in Wernigerode and Nordhausen, or at stations en route.

The third service is the Selketalbahn, which begins in Gernrode and runs to Eisfelder Tal or Hasselfelde. At Eisfelder Tal, you can change trains for other lines. The picturesque Selketalbahn initially follows Wellbach, a creek with a couple of good swimming holes, through deciduous forest to Mädgesprung, before joining the Selke Valley and climbing past Alexisbad to high plains around Friedrichshöhe, Stiege and beyond.

Passes for three/five/seven days cost DM70/80/100 for adults and DM35/40/50 for children. Timetables, information and books on the network can be picked up from Harzer Schmalspurbahnen (☎ 03943-55 81 43; fax 03943-55 81 48) at Marktstrasse 3, 38855 Wernigerode. ■

Cross the Markt to Breite Strasse. The pretty **Café Wien** building (1583) at No 4 is a worthwhile stopover both for architectural and gastronomical reasons. Elements of the carved façade of the **Krummelshes Haus**, at Breite Strasse 72, depict Africa and America – the latter portrayed as a naked woman riding an armadillo. At No 95 you can visit the **Krell'sche Schmiede** (1678), a blacksmith museum in an historic workshop built in the south German baroque style. It is open Wednesday to Sunday from 10 am to 4 pm (DM3/1 for adults/children).

Schloss

First built in the 12th century, Wernigerode Castle has been restored and enlarged over the centuries. It got its fairy-tale façade from Count Otto of Stolberg-Wernigerode in the last century. The museum (DM8 adults, DM7/4 concessions/children) includes portraits of Kaisers, beautiful panelled rooms with original furnishings and the opulent **Festsaal**.

The stunning **Schlosskirche** (1870-80) has an altar and pulpit made of French marble. For an extra DM2 you can climb the castle tower, but the views over town from the castle or restaurant terrace (best appreciated late, when the grounds are empty of visitors) are free and just as spectacular. The museum is open May to October daily from 10 am to 6 pm (last admission at 5 pm), in November on weekends only, and from December to April from Tuesday to Sunday at the same times. You can walk (1.5km) or take one of the two Bimmelbahn wagon rides (adults/children DM3/2 one way) from stops at Marktstrasse (near Schiefes Haus) or Breite Strasse (near Grosse Bergstrasse). In summer horse-drawn carts make the trek from the Markt.

Activities

Highly recommended for picnickers, hikers and cyclists is the beautiful deciduous forest behind the castle, which is crisscrossed by trails and *Forstwege* (forestry tracks). The marked nine-minute walk to town from the castle meets Blumenweg, which leads to Erbgrafenweg and a traditional restaurant, beer garden and children's playground at Christianental (about 2km from the castle).

Wernigerode is also a good starting point for hikes and bike rides into Hochharz National Park (see Getting Around for bike-hire places). More serious hikers might tackle the 30km route marked by blue crosses from Mühlental (south-east of the town centre) to Elbingerode, Königshütte (with its 18th-century wooden church) and the remains of medieval Trageburg castle at Trautenstein. Popular too are short walks to the waterfall and inn at Steinerne Renne, south-west of Wernigerode. Take all necessary precautions for changing weather conditions and pack a map.

Special Events

The Harz-Gebirgslauf, an annual fun run and hike programme held on the second Saturday in October, includes a Brocken marathon (☎ 632 83 2 for information). A festival of music and theatre is held in the castle each year from 19 July to 30 August. Contact the tourist office for programmes.

Places to Stay

The nearest camping ground is *Camping am Brocken* (☎ 039454-425 89), 10km south in Elbingerode. The city of Wernigerode runs two hostel-like guesthouses, both in town. *Jugendgästehaus* (☎ 632 06 1), at Friedrichstrasse 53, handles bookings for both of them (DM23 per person, breakfast included). Take bus No 1 or 4 from the train station to the Kirchstrasse stop. You can also take the narrow-gauge railway to the Wernigerode Kirchstrasse stop. The other guesthouse, *Schanzenhaus* (☎ 633 10 1), at Zwölfmorgental 30, can be reached by bus No 2 from the train station.

Hotel zur Tanne (☎ 632 55 4), at Breite Strasse 59, has singles/doubles with shared facilities from DM40/60. The nearby *Hotel am Anger* (☎ 923 20), at Breite Strasse 92, has free parking, and spotless, pleasant rooms from DM70/120 with shower and WC. Small groups should consider its holiday flats costing from DM120. *Hotel*

Schlossblick (☎ 632 00 4), at Burgstrasse 58, has rooms with bathroom from DM55/75. *Pension Schweizer Hof* (☎ 632 09 8,) at Salzbergstrasse 13, should be the first choice for those keen on hiking, with route information and rooms from DM65/100. This is also a branch of the Harzclub.

The historic *Gothisches Haus* (☎ 675 0), at Am Markt 1, is an up-market option with singles/doubles from DM110/165 off-season. Their package deals are good value, and the hotel has a sauna and gym. The adjoining *Nonnenhof* (same telephone number) is no less historic (with rooms for the same price) and has a traditional restaurant with Harz specialities from DM11 to DM20. The *Hotel und Restaurant zur Post* (☎ 690 40), Marktstrasse 17, has singles/doubles for DM95/160.

Places to Eat

The Markt is a good hunting ground for restaurants. *Da Filippo* at Markt 9 has pizzas from DM8.50 to DM12.50 and pasta dishes for around DM13. Most pasta dishes are reduced to DM8 on Tuesdays. Next door is *Konditorei und Café am Markt*, with a chic interior and tall windows. Light meals cost DM8.50 to DM14, larger main courses average DM14. It is also popular for ice cream (from DM5 to DM7). *Meeres Buffet*, Breite Strasse 50, has seafood dishes with Bratkartoffeln (fried potato) from DM7 to DM9 and Matjes Brödchen (fish rolls) from DM2.50 (daytime only).

The Schäfer family will take care of your gastronomic needs at *Hotel und Restaurant zur Post* (see Places to Stay), where main courses average DM14.

Entertainment

A highly recommended pub is *d.a.g.-Guinnesskniepe*, hidden away at Kleine Bergstrasse 13 (off Burgstrasse; look for the lantern). This small, friendly place (closed Monday) began life as a gallery-café shortly after the Wall came down, and it combines *Ost-Charme* ('eastern charm') with Irish conviviality. It serves snacks, occasionally has live music, and has been known to celebrate St Patrick's Day twice. The cellar of *Schiefes Haus*, south of the Markt, is a quality bar and music venue for night owls. *Karussell*, inside the passage at Breite Strasse 44, is a similar place. It serves food and has a beer garden on warm summer evenings.

Filmkneipe Capitol, at Burgstrasse 1, is a modern bar and restaurant with movie-theme décor and standard dishes from DM8.

Getting There & Away

Direct buses run to major towns in the region. Consider buying the WVB bus timetable (DM2) from the office (☎ 564 13 4) at the train station if you plan to explore the eastern Harz; it includes a train schedule as well. Bus No 253 runs to Blankenburg and Thale while bus No 257 serves Drei Annen Hohne and Schierke, both on the edge of Hochharz National Park.

There are frequent trains to Goslar and Halle. Change at Halberstadt for Quedlinburg and Thale, at Vienenburg for Goslar. Less frequent direct services go to Braunschweig. Tickets on the narrow-gauge trains to the Brocken via Schierke cost DM25/40 one way/return. By car or motorcycle, Wernigerode can be reached from Quedlinburg in the east and Bad Harzburg in the west by the B6. The B244 leads south-west to Braunlage and the B81 north to Magdeburg from the B6.

Getting Around

Bus Nos 1 and 2 run from the bus station, in front of the train station, to the Rendezvous stop, just north of the Markt, connecting with bus No 3. Tickets cost DM1.30. For car hire, go to Avis (☎ 498 14), at Otto von Guerecke Strasse 1-3; for a taxi, call ☎ 411 44. Hallermann (☎ 632 50 8), at Breite Strasse 27, rents mountain bikes for DM15 a day. Zweirad John (☎ 63 32 94), north-east of the train station at Zaunwiese 2, does the same at a similar price.

RÜBELAND CAVES

Rübeland, a small, rather claustrophobic town 13km south of Wernigerode, has two of Germany's more beautiful caves. **Baumannshöhle** was formed about 500,000 years ago, and the first tourists visited in 1646, just over a century after its 'rediscovery'. Human presence in the caves dates back 40,000 years. The **Goethesaal**, which has a pond, is sometimes used for concerts and plays.

Hermannshöhle was formed 350,000 years ago and was rediscovered during 19th-century roadworks. Its stalactites and stalagmites are just as spectacular, especially in the transparent Kristallkammer. Cave-dwelling salamanders, introduced from southern Europe by researchers, inhabit one pond. Both caves are open daily July to October from 9.30 am to 5.15 pm (last entry). During the rest of the year only one cave is open (last entry at 3.15 pm). Admission, which includes a guided tour in German, is DM7/3.50 for adults/children.

WVB bus No 258 leaves Wernigerode and Blankenburg for Rübeland hourly. Bus No 265 from Wernigerode to Hasselfelde (on the Selketal train line) goes via the Wendefurth stop, where you can join the magnificent Bodetal trail (blue triangle; 16km) to Thale. You can also start the trail from Rübeland itself and cross the Rappbodetalsperre, a 106m-high dam wall across the Harz's largest reservoir, on foot.

Frequent trains ply a small branch line connecting Rübeland with Blankenburg and Königshutte.

If driving from Wernigerode, take the B244 south to Elbingerode, then the B27 east towards Blankenburg.

SCHIERKE

- *pop 1000*
- *area code* ☎ 039455

Schierke, 16km south-west of Wernigerode, is the last stop for the Brockenbahn before it climbs to the summit. It's also the perfect base for exploring Hochharz National Park. Once located inside the GDR exclusion zone, this former border town has shaken off its isolation since unification, has upgraded tourist facilities and, quite rightly, has become a favourite with outdoors enthusiasts.

Orientation & Information

Nestled in a narrow valley of the Kalte Bode River, Schierke consists of an upper town around Brockenstrasse, its main street, and a lower town in the valley proper. The tourist office (☎ 310) is at Brockenstrasse 10, a 10-minute walk west of the train station (by bus, get off at the Rathaus stop). It is open on weekdays from 9 am to noon and from 1.30 to 4.30 pm, on weekends from 10 am to noon, and sells a wide range of maps. Nationalpark Info (downstairs from the tourist office, same telephone number) is open daily from 8.30 am to 4.30 pm. It has good material in English on the parks, and lots of hiking suggestions.

The post office is on Brockenstrasse next to the Rathaus.

Activities

Climbing Climbers will find all levels of difficulty on the cliffs nearby.

The Climbing-Center-Schierke (☎ 868 12), downstairs from the tourist office, has a practice/ learner's wall. It costs DM20/15/10 for adults/students/children, including equipment. Courses are also offered. For the real thing, complete climbing gear rents for DM25/20/15 a day. The equipment is modern, and you can join a group.

Skiing Cross-country and alpine ski equipment rentals start at DM17 a day (cheaper for subsequent days), and you will find 70km of groomed trails in and around the park. Downhill skiing is very average.

Hiking The Brocken can be reached via the bitumen Brockenstrasse (12km), which is now closed to private cars and motorcycles.

More interesting is the 7km hike via Eckerloch. This steep trail leads off from Brockenstrasse, winding through a range of typical Harz vegetation. Pick up the free *Wanderführer 2* hiking guide from Nationalpark Info. Marked hiking trails also lead to the rugged rock formations of Feuersteinklippen (half an hour from the tourist office) and Schnarcherklippen (1½ hours). From Hotel Bodeblick (see Places to Stay & Eat), an easy trail runs along the valley to Elend in about 30 minutes.

Horse-Drawn Rides Horse-drawn coaches go from Schierke to the Brocken and cost DM40/20 return for adults/children under 10. Bookings should be made through Reiterhof Mühlental (☎ 03943-241 44) or Reiterhof Schierke (☎ 512 12). Both companies also operate horse-drawn sleigh services in winter.

Special Events

On the night of 30 April, Walpurgisnacht, Schierke attracts about 25,000 visitors, many of whom set off on walking tracks to the Brocken. Book rooms early or prepare for a long, sleepless night.

Places to Stay & Eat

Schierke levies a nightly resort tax of DM4, less in hostels. The *Jugendherberge* (☎ 510 64) hostel is at Brockenstrasse 48 and costs DM27/32 for juniors/seniors.

Finding single rooms can be difficult at peak times in Schierke. *Pension Barbara* (☎ 869 0), at Brockenstrasse 1, has bright singles/doubles with full facilities from DM55/70, and holiday flats sleeping four from DM100. Equally pleasant rooms at *Pension Schmidt* (☎ 333), nearby at No 13, start at DM60/90 with shared facilities. *Pension Andrä* (☎ 512 57), next door at No 12, is spacious and stylish, with rooms from DM80/120 and holiday flats from DM90. The traditional restaurant downstairs has meals for DM15 to DM25. *Hotel König* (☎ 383), at Kirchberg 15, has a beautiful foyer, basic singles/doubles from DM60/80, and very classy rooms with facilities from DM90/120. It also has a good restaurant, with hearty dishes from DM13 to DM20.

Getting There & Around

WVB bus No 76 runs six times daily between Braunlage and Schierke via Elend. The frequent WVB bus No 257 runs between Wernigerode and Schierke, connecting with bus No 76. Narrow-gauge railway services between Wernigerode and Schierke cost DM8/13 one way/return. Tickets for the Brockenbahn cost DM25/40 one way/return from all stations. If driving from the west, take the B27 from Braunlage and turn off at Elend. From Wernigerode, take Friedrichstrasse.

The Climbing-Center-Schierke (☎ 868 12), downstairs from the tourist office, hires mountain bikes for DM20 per half day (DM15 for children), and has 24-hour rentals at DM35/25 for adults/children (helmets and locks DM5, child seats also extra).

BROCKEN & TORFHAUS

- *area code* ☎ 039455 (Brocken)
- *area code* ☎ 05320 (Torfhaus)

There are prettier landscapes and hikes in the eastern Harz, but the Brocken is what draws the crowds – about 50,000 on a warm summer's day. The view from northern Germany's highest peak has changed only marginally since Heinrich Heine's time. Goethe, when he wasn't exploring mines, also scaled the mountain – in stockings.

Brocken Museum

Here on top of Brocken you'll find national park information and exhibits on the natural, social and folkloric history of the Brocken from earliest times to the present. It is open year round daily from 9.30 am to 5 pm and costs DM3/2 for adults/students.

Brockenkuppe Trail

This 2.5km trail loop around the summit traces the path of the concrete wall, now removed, that once protected Soviet military installations here. Free German-language tours of the **Brockengarten**, which contains alpine plants, are conducted on weekdays at 11 am and 2 pm.

Goetheweg from Torfhaus

The 8km Goetheweg trail to the Brocken from the western Harz starts at Torfhaus, about mid-way between Bad Harzburg and Braunlage on the B4. The Goetheweg, which is easier than other approaches, initially takes you through bog, follows an historic aqueduct once used to regulate water levels for the mines, then crosses the Kaiserweg. Anyone who has begun their sweaty Brocken ascent via the 11km Kaiserweg from Bad Harzburg to Torfhaus will probably feel a prickle of excitement here. Unfortunately, your next stop will be a dead forest, killed by several species of beetle that lay eggs under the bark, weakening the trees' immune systems. The trail becomes steep and more interesting as you walk along the former border; you then hike alongside the train line on a ramp above soggy moorland. On the last stretch you'll be joined by horse-drawn carriages that have trundled up from Schierke along the Brockenstrasse. Enjoy the view, the pea soup and Bockwurst that's served at the top, and think of Goethe and Heine.

The **Nationalparkhaus** (☎ 263), at Torfhaus 21, has information on the parks and is open daily from 9 am to 5 pm. From November to March its reduced weekend hours are from 10 am to 4 pm.

Torfhaus is a good starting point for cross-country skiing or winter ski treks. Downhill skiing is limited to 1200m (two pistes). Lift prices start at DM17 for half-day passes. One recommended ski hike is the 11km Kaiserweg trail to Bad Harzburg. Make sure you pack a good map and take all precautions.

There is no shortage of outlets for ski-equipment rental. Café Hubertus (☎ 203), opposite Grossparkplatz, has alpine and cross-country skis from DM20 per day. Prices are similar at Sporthotel Brockenblick (☎ 248), on Grossparkplatz. The latter has basic singles/doubles for DM35/70. The *Jugendherberge* (☎ 242) is at Torfhaus 3. Prices are DM23/27 for juniors/seniors, and the hostel runs nature programmes, including hikes into the park.

Getting There & Away

Bus No 63/422 stops frequently at Torfhaus on the Bad Harzburg-Braunlage route.

QUEDLINBURG

- *pop 26,000*
- *area code* ☎ 03946

Unspoiled Quedlinburg, which recently celebrated its 1000th birthday, is a popular year-round destination, especially since it was added to UNESCO's World Heritage List of cultural sites in 1992. Almost all the buildings in the historic town centre are half-timbered – street after cobbled street of them – and they are slowly being restored. The history of Quedlinburg is closely associated with the Frauenstift, a medieval collegiate foundation for widows and daughters of the nobility that enjoyed the direct protection of the Kaiser.

The Reich was briefly ruled in the 10th century from here by two women, Theophano and Adelheid, successive guardians of the child-king Otto III.

Orientation

The circular, medieval centre of the old town is a 10-minute walk from the train station along Bahnhofstrasse. To reach the Markt, turn left into Heiligegeiststrasse after the post office. Hohe Strasse, off the Markt, leads south to the castle. The Bode River flows north-east through the town near the train station.

Information

The tourist office (☎ 773 01 2) is at Markt 2. It is open May to September weekdays from 9 am to 8 pm, weekends from 9 am to 6 pm. In October and from March to April it is open on weekdays from 9 am to 6 pm and on weekends from 10 am to 3 pm. From November to February it is open on weekdays from 9 am to 5 pm (closed weekends). The accommodation service here is free. Book well in advance in summer.

There are several banks on the Markt, and the post office is on Bahnhofstrasse. A hospital, Dorothea Christiane Erxleben (☎ 909 0), is at Ditfurter Weg 24. The police station (☎ 97 70) is at Schillerstrasse 3.

Around the Markt

The **Rathaus** (1310) has been expanded over the years. It received its Renaissance façade in 1616. Quedel, the small hound above the entrance, is the city's symbol and is said to protect those who enter. Inside, the beautiful **Festsaal** is decorated with a cycle

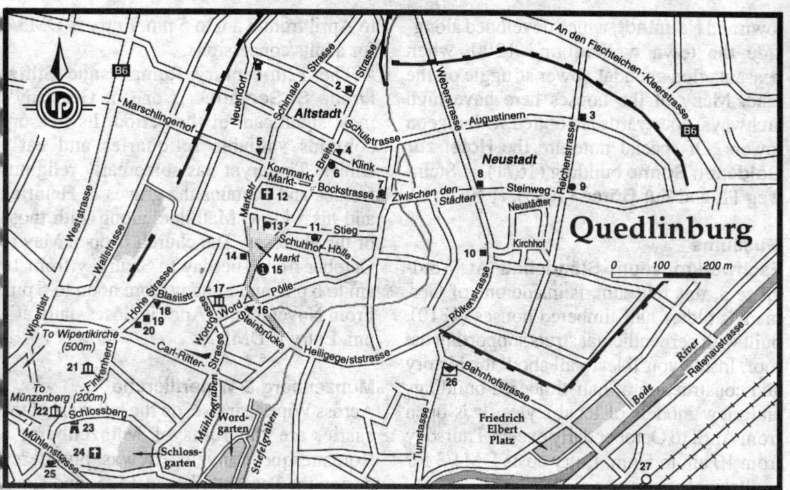

PLACES TO STAY
1 JuBa Hostel
2 Hotel am Dippeplatz
3 Zum Augustinern
8 Hotel zur Goldenen Sonne
10 Zum Alten Fritz
14 Hotel Theophano
19 Zimmervermietung Her Borchardt
20 Familie Klindt

PLACES TO EAT
4 Kartoffelhaus
5 Buntes Lamm bei Max
16 Pasta Mia
18 Brauhaus Lüdde
25 Café Romanik

OTHER
6 Gildehaus zur Rose
7 Hagensches Freihaus
9 Zur Börse
11 Alter Klopstock
12 Marktkirche St Benedikti
13 Rathaus
15 Tourist Office
17 Fachwerkmuseum Ständebau
21 Lyonel-Feininger-Galerie
22 Klopstockhaus
23 Schloss
24 Stiftskirche St Servatius
26 Post Office
27 Train & Bus Station

of frescos focusing on Quedlinburg's colourful history. A German-language tour of the Rathaus (DM4) is conducted daily at 1.30 pm from April to October. The Roland statue (1426) in front of the Rathaus dates from the year Quedlinburg joined the Hanseatic League.

The late-Gothic **Marktkirche St Benedikti** is behind the Rathaus. On the tower you'll see a small house used by town watchmen until 1901. The mausoleum nearby survived the relocation of the church graveyard in the 19th century. There are some fine half-timbered buildings in Marktkirchhof and Kornmarkt. At Breite Strasse 39 is the **Gildehaus zur Rose** (1612), arguably the city's most spectacular half-timbered house. The richly carved and panelled interior is the town's best night-time haunt (see Entertainment).

Return to the Markt and walk through Schuhhof, a shoemakers' courtyard on the east side, with shutters and stable-like 'gossip doors'. **Alter Klopstock** (1580), at Stieg 28, has scrolled beams typical of Quedlinburg's 16th-century half-timbered houses. Also worth a peek is the Renaissance **Hagensches Freihaus** (1564), an impressive stone mansion at Klink 11. Zwischen den Städten, an old bridge, connects the old town and **Neustadt**, which developed alongside the town wall around 1200, when peasants fled a feudal power struggle on the land. Many of the houses here have high archways; courtyards are dotted with pigeon towers. Of special note are the **Hotel zur Goldenen Sonne** building (1671), at Steinweg 11, and **Zur Börse** (1683), at No 23.

Museums

Fachwerkmuseum Ständebau At Wordgasse 3, this museum, is inside one of Germany's oldest half-timbered houses (1310), built with perpendicular struts supporting the roof. Inside you'll learn all about the history and construction of half-timbered buildings and view models of local styles. It is open from April to October daily except Thursday from 10 am to 5 pm. Entry costs DM4/3 for adults/concession.

Klopstockhaus This museum, inside a 16th-century house at Schlossberg 12, is the birthplace of the early classicist poet, Friedrich Gottlieb Klopstock (1724-1803). Closed for restoration at the time of writing, it usually contains exhibits on Klopstock and Dorothea Erxleben (1715-62), Germany's first woman doctor.

Lyonel-Feininger-Galerie This gallery, at Finkenherd 5a, is devoted to the work of influential Bauhaus artist Lyonel Feininger (1871-1956). It has been undergoing renovations; contact the tourist office for more information.

Schlossberg

The castle district, perched above Quedlinburg on a 25m-high plateau, was established during the reign of Heinrich I, from 919 to 936. The present-day Renaissance **Schloss**, partly built upon earlier foundations, dates from the 16th century and offers good views over town from its gardens. The **Residenzbau** in the north wing houses the **Schloss Museum**, with a few interesting exhibits on the natural and social history of the area. The museum is open May to September daily except Monday from 10 am to 6 pm, October to April from 9 am to 5 pm. Entry is DM5/3 for adults/concessions.

The 12th-century Romanesque **Stiftskirche St Servatius** is one of Germany's most significant of the period. Its treasury contains valuable reliquaries and early Bibles. The crypt has some early religious frescos and contains the graves of Heinrich and his widow, Mathilde, along with those of the abbesses. The church is open May to October from Tuesday to Saturday from 10 am to 6 pm, and Sunday from noon to 6 pm. From November to April it closes daily at 4 pm. Entry is DM5/3.

Münzenberg & Wipertikirche

Across Wipertistrasse, on the hill west of the castle, are the ruins of Münzenberg, a Romanesque convent. It was plundered during the Peasant Wars in 1525, and small houses were later built among the ruins. The settlement then became home to wandering minstrels, knife grinders and other itinerant tradespeople.

The crypt of the Wipertikirche dates from around 1000, and the church itself was used as a barn from 1812 until its restoration in the 1950s. The only way to see the church is by taking a tour (DM6/4 for adults/children), conducted by the tourist office daily at 11 am from May to October.

Special Events

A programme of classical music is held in the Stiftskirche St Servatius each year from May to September. For tickets and information, contact the tourist office.

Places to Stay

One drawback to Quedlinburg is its relative shortage of budget accommodation.

The closest camping ground is *Am Bremer Dammteich* (☎ 039485-608 10), along a forest lake approximately 7km south of Gernrode, near Haferfeld. The *hostel* there (same telephone number) charges DM15 per person (no breakfast).

JuBa (☎ 308 5), a large hostel and youth encounter centre at Neuendorf 28, has beds in twin dorms from DM36 without breakfast.

The central *Familie Klindt* (☎ 702 91 1), at Hohe Strasse 19, has reasonable singles/doubles with shower and WC for DM30/50. *Zimmervermietung Herr Borchardt* (☎ 702 91 2), next door at No 18, does a bit less for slightly more at DM35/50.

Zum Augustinern (☎ 701 23 4), at Reichenstrasse 35a, has tasteful rooms with full facilities from DM70/110; there's a traditional restaurant downstairs. Rooms at the *Hotel am Dippeplatz* (☎ 705 02 2), Breite Strasse 16, are bright and clean, starting from DM80/100 with facilities. The historic *Hotel zur Goldenen Sonne* (☎ 962 50), at Steinweg 11, has a spacious and suitably wooden interior, with rooms from DM90/140.

The marginally less historic *Zum Alten Fritz* (☎ 704 88 0), nearby at Pölkenstrasse 18, has pleasant rooms from DM95/125.

Highly recommended for a night of baroque luxury is *Hotel Theophano* (☎ 963 00), at Markt 13/14. It has rooms from DM110/150 (parking costs DM12), a few four-poster beds, a good restaurant (see Places to Eat) and a vaulted wine bar in the cellar.

Places to Eat

Finding a reasonable place to eat in Quedlinburg shouldn't be a problem. *Kartoffelhaus*, at Breite Strasse 37 (enter from Klink), is difficult to beat for its filling potato dishes, priced from DM6 to DM20. The Italian *Buntes Lamm bei Max* (☎ 700 38 6), on Kornmarkt, has tasty pizzas from DM5.50. Meat main courses cost around DM20, pasta dishes DM12. *Pasta Mia* (☎ 212 2), at Steinbrücke 23, is a trendier Italian café and eatery with slightly higher prices. The *Brauhaus Lüdde* brewery, at Blasiistrasse 14, has hearty lunches and dinners for DM13 to DM22 and fine beers brewed on the premises. It stays open till midnight most nights.

The restaurant at *Hotel Theophano* has traditional dishes for DM20 to DM30. It is closed on Sunday and, from November to March, on Monday too. *Café Romanik*, behind the castle at Mühlenstrasse 21, is highly recommended for tea and cakes, and has a comfortable old-world ambience.

Entertainment

After-dark options in Quedlinburg are extremely limited. Drop into the *Gildehaus zur Rose*, Breite Strasse 39, which has a dance venue off the main room. The pub area, which serves light meals, is good for a tipple (closed Sunday).

Getting There & Away

The QBus office (☎ 223 6) inside the train station has timetables and information on its frequent regional services, which leave from the train station for most towns in the eastern Harz. For trains to Wernigerode, change at Halberstadt. A branch line runs to Gernrode; other frequent trains go to Thale.

The Romanesque Road (Strasse der Romanik) leads south to Gernrode. The B6 runs west to Wernigerode, Goslar, the A395 (for Braunschweig) and the A7 between Kassel and Hanover. For Halle take the B6 east, and for Halberstadt the B79 north.

Getting Around

Infrequent city buses ply the ring road, but you probably won't need them. Cars can be hired from Avis (☎ 880 5), at Schillerstrasse 10. For a taxi call ☎ 707 07 0 or ☎ 888 8.

GERNRODE

- *pop 4000*
- *area code* ☎ 039485

Gernrode, 8km south of Quedlinburg, is ideal for a day trip. Its Stiftskirche St Cyriakus is one of Germany's finest churches. Hikers, picnickers and steam-train enthusiasts will also enjoy this pretty town.

Information

The tourist office (☎ 354) is a 10-minute walk from the train station on Suderode Strasse. It's open weekdays from 9 am to 5 pm (weekends by arrangement).

Stiftskirche St Cyriakus

This church is one of the purest examples of Romanesque architecture from the Ottonian period. Construction of the basilica was begun in 959, based on the form of a cross. Especially noteworthy is the early use of alternating columns and pillars, later a common Romanesque feature. The octagonal **Taufstein** (Christening stone), whose religious motifs culminate in the Ascension, dates from 1150. In the south aisle you will find **Das Heilige Grab**, an 11th-century replica of Christ's tomb in Jerusalem. The 19th-century organ is both visually and aurally impressive. St Cyriakus is open April to October on weekdays from 9 am to 5 pm and on Saturday from 10 am. On Sundays it stays open after the 10 am service. Winter hours are from 10 am to 4 pm. Tours cost DM3 and are conducted at 3 pm daily, when the church is closed for an hour to general visitors. The tourist office has information on summer concerts here.

Stiftskirche St Cyriakus: one of the finest churches in Germany and one of the purest examples of the Romanesque style.

Activities

Especially picturesque is the 30-minute ride on the narrow-gauge railway from Gernrode to Mägdesprung (DM2 per person). The trip can be broken at Sternhaus Ramberg, where a short trail leads through the forest to Bremer Teich, a pretty swimming hole with a camping ground and hostel (see Places to Stay in Quedlinburg). You can also walk from Gernrode along paths beside the train track.

From the corner of Bahnhofstrasse and Marktstrasse marked trails lead east to Burg Falkenstein (11km), the historic castle in the Selke valley, and west to Thale (about 13km).

Getting There & Around

Regular QBus services stop at the train station, and link Thale, Quedlinburg and Gernrode. Three night buses also stop here, including the Nacht3 to Thale. Small trains chug almost hourly across the plain from Quedlinburg. Gernrode is the railhead for the Selketalbahn (see boxed text titled Narrow-Gauge Railways earlier in the Eastern Harz section). Tickets and information can be picked up from staff at the train station (☎ 624 23), where you can also hire bicycles (DM18 a day).

THALE

- *pop 15,000*
- *area code* ☎ 03947

Situated below the northern slopes of the Harz Mountains, Thale is blessed with a sensational landscape of rugged cliffs and a lush river valley that makes for ideal hiking. On the two cliffs at the head of the valley are Hexentanzplatz and Rosstrappe, both Bethlehems for postmodern pagans, who gather in grand style and numbers each year on 30 April to celebrate Walpurgisnacht.

Thale's mainstay was once its steelworks, the Eisen- und Hüttenwerk Thale, which in GDR times employed some 8000 workers. That number has now dropped to 500, but Thale has kept its identity as a workers' town.

Orientation

Thale's two main shopping and service streets are Poststrasse, which runs diagonally off Bahnhofstrasse (go left on leaving the train station), and Karl-Marx-Strasse, which begins north of the train station across the tracks and runs north-east to the Bode River.

Information

The tourist office (☎ 259 7) is opposite the train station at Rathausstrasse 1. It is open January to April weekdays from 9 am to 5 pm. From May to October it closes an hour later and is also open on Saturday from 10 am to 3 pm. In November and December it is open weekdays from 9 am to 4 pm.

Pick up from the tourist office the free English-language brochure *Thale Fabulous*.

The post office, at Poststrasse 1, is open weekdays only. A Sparkasse bank is near the train station at the top of Karl-Marx-Strasse.

The police station (☎ 460) is at Wotanstrasse 11.

Hexentanzplatz & Rosstrappe

These two rugged outcrops flanking the Bode Valley once had Celtic fortresses and were used by Germanic tribes for sacrifices and occult rituals (see boxed text titled Witches & Warlocks). The name of the Bode River is said to derive from a myth. Brunhilde, who symbolises the 'unnaturally' powerful woman, refuses to marry the uncouth Bohemian prince, Bodo. Unhappily crowned and dressed to the nines for the wedding, she flees on horseback, springing across the gorge, hotly pursued by Bodo. The impact of Brunhilde's (successful) landing leaves an imprint of the horse's hoof in the stone (which you can see, of course), on Rosstrappe; the crown, however, topples into the valley. Meanwhile, Bodo, who isn't

Witches & Warlocks

The area around the mouth of the Bodetal once contained Celtic fortresses built to fend off tribes descending from the north. The Celts had been driven out by 500 BC, when Germanic tribes took over the fortresses and turned them into sites for meetings and ritual sacrifices. These played an important role in the 8th-century Saxon Wars, when Charlemagne embarked upon campaigns to subjugate and Christianise the local population. The mythology surrounding the sites blends these pagan and Christian elements.

One popular – but misleading – explanation for the Walpurgisnacht festival is that it was an invention of the tribes who, pursued by Christian missionaries, held secret gatherings to carry out their rituals. They are said to have darkened their faces one night and, armed with broomsticks and pitchforks, scared off Charlemagne's guards, who mistook them for witches and devils. A similar explanation appears in Goethe's *Faust*. The name 'Walpurgisnacht' itself probably derives from St Walpurga (or Walburga), who was born in England around 710 and became a Benedictine abbess at Hildesheim. Her name day is 1 May.

Originally considered benevolent, witches were only ascribed evil traits in the Middle Ages. A turning point came with the book *Hexenhammer*, published by two Dominican clerics in Strasbourg in 1486, which drew a connection between heresy and witchcraft. Natural disasters, disease, childlessness and impotence were blamed on heretics – mainly women. *Hexenhammer* described how witches met secretly in covens at night, renounced Christianity and paid homage to the devil. This was followed by a feast, often on the flesh of babies and children, and orgies between witches and warlocks. These orgies were said to represent copulation with the devil. The region's most notorious inquisitor was Duke Heinrich Julius of Braunschweig. In Quedlinburg, 133 people were convicted of sorcery in 1574, many ending up burnt at the stake.

According to local mythology, witches and warlocks gather on Walpurgisnacht at locations throughout the Harz Mountains before flying off to the Brocken on broomsticks or goats. There they recount the year's evil deeds and top off the stories with a bacchanalian frenzy. Frightened peasants used to hang crosses and herbs on stable doors to protect their livestock. Ringing church bells or cracking whips was another way to prevent stray witches from dropping by.

One of the best places to celebrate Walpurgisnacht is Thale. Schierke, also popular, is a starting point for Walpurgisnacht treks to the Brocken. ■

much chop at hurdling gorges, plunges into the valley, mysteriously turns into a black dog, and is destined to guard Brunhilde's crown there for evermore. It is worth a climb or ride up for the magnificent views alone.

An ultramodern cable car runs to Hexentanzplatz (DM5/8 one way/return), or you can take a chair lift to Rosstrappe for DM4/6. (Check on discounts for families and children.) Both run daily May to September from 9.30 am to 6 pm, the cable car also daily October to April from 10 am to 4.30 pm, and the chair lift also in October from 9.30 am to 6 pm. From November to April the chair lift runs on weekends and public holidays only from 10 am to 4.30 pm. Signs direct you from the train station. Go early or late in the day to Hexentanzplatz and Rosstrappe if you want to avoid crowds.

The wooden **Walpurgishalle** museum on Hexentanzplatz has exhibitions and paintings on matters heathen, including the **Opferstein**, a stone once used in Germanic sacrificial rituals. It is open daily April to October from 9 am to 5 pm. Entry is DM2. The 10-hectare **Tierpark** nearby has lynx, wild cats and other animals and is open daily May to October from 8 am to 7 pm (to 5 pm the rest of the year). Entry is DM4 (DM3/2 for students/children).

Hiking

The tourist-office brochures *Wanderführer* and *Führer durch das Bodetal* (DM3 each) are excellent if your German is up to it – the latter for natural history, flora and fauna. Highly recommended is the Bode Valley walk between Thale and Treseburg (10km one way; blue triangle). If you take the bus from Thale to Treseburg (QBus No 18 or WVB 272; check your timetable or with the tourist office as the service is restricted), you can walk downriver and enjoy the most spectacular scenery at the end. Another 10km trail (red dot) goes from Hexentanzplatz to Treseburg; combine with the valley walk to make a round trip.

Special Events

The open-air Harzer Bergtheater on Hexentanzplatz has a summer programme of music and plays, and a performance on Walpurgisnacht, when some 35,000 people flock to Thale. Tickets are sold at the venue or in advance from the tourist office (refunds/swaps are possible if performances are cancelled due to bad weather). You can also buy tickets in Quedlinburg from Theaterkasse Quedlinburg (☎ 03946-962 22), Marschlingerhof 17-18.

Places to Stay & Eat

Book extremely early for Walpurgisnacht. The number of cheap private rooms is limited, but the tourist office can help, especially in finding holiday flats, a good option if you plan to stay a few days.

The *Jugendherberge* (☎ 282 1) hostel is nestled in the lush Bode Valley, five minutes from the train station at Bodetal-Waldkater, and costs DM22/27 for juniors/seniors. To reach it, go south along Hubertusstrasse from the top of Friedenspark. The Bode Valley trail begins at the door.

The friendly *Kleiner Ritter* (☎ 257 0), a small pension across the Bode River at Marktstrasse 2, is best reached via Karl-Marx-Strasse (across the bridge and right into Rosstrappenstrasse). Singles/doubles are DM35/70. Double rooms for DM90 (with bathroom) are the main option at *Pension Schröder* (☎ 239 2/246 3), Karl-Marx-Strasse 10. Singles are marginally cheaper. Ask inside the Reform Haus shop downstairs during business hours.

Pension Am Steinbach (☎ 935 0), at Poststrasse 9 near the train station, has cosy singles/doubles for DM70/90. *Wilder Jäger* (☎ 950 0), at Poststrasse 18, has rooms with facilities from DM80/125. *Zur alten Backstube* (☎ 498 0), at Rudolf-Breitscheid-Strasse 15 (a continuation of Poststrasse), has fine rooms for DM115/160, as well as holiday flats and free parking. Mains in the traditional restaurant downstairs cost around DM20. The rustic *Kleiner Waldkater* (☎ 282 6), in the valley alongside the hostel, is good value at DM70/100 for singles/doubles with shower and WC. The location alone makes its restaurant a good place to drop in.

You will find restaurants and hotels on Hexentanzplatz and Rosstrappe. The friendly *Grüne Tanne*, across the Bode River at Rosstrappenstrasse 10-11, is about as traditional as you can get, with a horsemeat patty and other dishes from DM7 to DM15.

Getting There & Around

The bus station in Bahnhofstrasse is alongside the train station and tourist office. For Wernigerode, take WVB 253. For Treseburg, take QBus No 18 or WVB 272 (both services have season restrictions). Night buses N3 and N4 go via Thale (and Hexentanzplatz) to Harzgerode and Quedlinburg respectively.

Frequent trains travel to Halberstadt, Quedlinburg and Magdeburg. Karl-Marx-Strasse leads to the main junction for roads to Quedlinburg, Wernigerode and Blankenburg.

For a taxi telephone ☎ 243 5 or ☎ 553 5. Fahrradhaus Wagner (☎ 915 46), Bodestrasse 4, has bikes for hire from around DM25 per day.

Mecklenburg-Western Pomerania

MECKLENBURG

Mecklenburg-Western Pomerania (Mecklenburg-Vorpommern) is a low-lying, post-glacial region of lakes, meadows, forests and the beaches of the Baltic Sea (German: Ostsee), stretching across northern Germany from Schleswig-Holstein to the Polish border. Most of the state is historic Mecklenburg; only the island of Rügen and the area between Stralsund and Poland traditionally belong to Western Pomerania.

In 1160 the duke of Saxony, Heinrich der Löwe (Henry the Lion), conquered the region (under the guise of introducing Christianity) and made the local Polish princes his vassals. Germanisation gradually reduced the Slavic element, and in 1348 the dukes of Mecklenburg became princes of the Holy Roman Empire. Sweden became involved in the area during the Thirty Years' War (1618-48). In 1867 the whole region joined the North German Confederation and, in 1871, the German Reich.

Some of the offshore islands, such as Poel and Hiddensee, are still undiscovered paradises, while others, including Rügen, are becoming increasingly popular with tourists. Just keep in mind the very short swimming season (July and August only). Spring and autumn can be cold.

In the centre of the state, the Mecklenburg Lake Plains (Mecklenburger Seenplatte) are wide open to hikers, cyclists and sailors, especially in the vast Müritz National Park. The medieval walled city of Neubrandenburg and its surrounding area is delightful. And the maritime cities of Rostock and Wismar are accessible and welcoming.

HIGHLIGHTS

- The beaches on Rügen and Poel islands
- Hiking the Höhenuferweg on Rügen from Binz to Sellin
- A ride on Rügen's historical Rasender Roland steam train
- Smoked fish along the Alter Strom in Warnemünde
- Kayaking and hiking in Müritz National Park

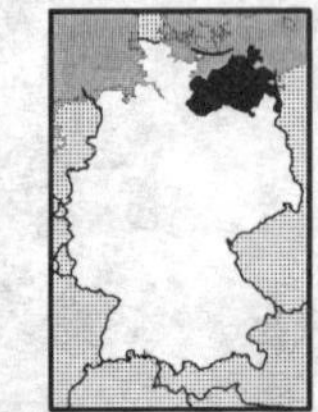

• **Population:** 1.8m • **Capital:** Schwerin • **Area:** 23,840 sq km

Mecklenburg-Western Pomerania Luminaries: Ernst Moritz Arndt, Ernst Barlach, Caspar David Friedrich, Philipp Otto Runge, Max Schmeling

Accommodation

In addition to an excellent range of hostels and camping grounds, especially within the Mecklenburger Seenplatte area, dozens of the state's more than 2000 castles are open as castle hotels *(Schlösser und Herrenhäuser)*. Some are used as spas, others as resorts and executive retreats. Prices start at about DM75 per person per night.

For a comprehensive list of castle hotels, contact Tourismusverband Mecklenburg-Vorpommern (☎ 0381-448 42 5; fax 448 42 3), Platz der Freundschaft 1, 18059 Rostock. They'll send you a free catalogue.

Food & Drink

Much of the truly regional cooking is traditional German with a sweet-and-sour twist. Prime examples are *Rippenbraten*, rolled roast pork stuffed with lemon, apple and plums, and *Eintopf*, a stew-like potato soup

NICK SELBY

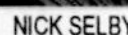

NICK SELBY

DAVID PEEVERS

DAVID PEEVERS

DAVID PEEVERS

MARIE OAMEK

A	B
C	D
E	F

Mecklenburg-Western Pomerania

A: Neuer Markt, Rostock
B: Elaborate facade, Rostock
C: Rügen sunset, Rügen Island
D: Port scene in Warnemünde
E: Schloss Schwerin
F: Lighthouse, Kap Arkona, Rügen

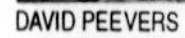
DAVID PEEVERS

NICK SELBY

DAVID PEEVERS

DAVID PEEVERS

DAVID PEEVERS

DAVID PEEVERS

DAVID PEEVERS

A		B
C	D	E
F	G	

Bavaria

A: Befreiungshalle, outside Kelheim
B: Oktoberfest, Munich
C: View of the Frauenkirche, Munich
D: Grounds of Schloss Linderhof
E: Guesthouse, Schloss Nymphenb
F: Country idyll near Munich
G: Neuschwanstein Castle

served with vinegar and sugar on the side. Fresh fish, cooked in every conceivable way, is very popular, as is *Heringe in Sahnestipp*, herring in cream sauce. In Wismar, try *Wismarer Spickaal*, young eel smoked in a way unique to the area.

Local firewaters include the powerful (45% alcohol) Rostockerkümmel, an after-dinner drink made from caraway, and the wheat-based Rostockerkorn. The most popular beers are Rostocker Pils, slightly bitter, and Rostocker Dunkles, a dark beer.

ROSTOCK

- *pop 230,000*
- *area code* ☎ 0381

Rostock, the largest city in sparsely populated north-eastern Germany, is a major Baltic port and shipbuilding centre. First mentioned in 1161 as a Danish settlement, the city began taking shape as a German fishing village around 1200.

In the 14th and 15th centuries, Rostock was an important Hanseatic city, trading with Riga, Bergen and Bruges. Rostock University, founded in 1419, is the oldest in northern Germany, and the city's distinctive Marienkirche received its unique astrological clock in 1472.

The city centre, especially along Kröpeliner Strasse, retains the flavour of this period. Rostock has all the charm and flair of other northern maritime cities: the remote feeling of Murmansk, the cobblestone streets and playful façades of Copenhagen, and the ancient town squares and little side streets of Tallinn and Helsinki.

As a major shipbuilding and shipping centre of the GDR, the city was pummelled by socialist architectural 'ideas', and the old city is surrounded by sprawling developments hastily thrown up to accommodate throngs of workers brought in to the shipyards along the Warnow River. But even these places are sparkling and the city itself looks great. Much is being redeveloped, including the remains of the old city walls, medieval churches and the now excellent local transit system.

Today Rostock is as much a tourist as a business centre, and the very lively and popular beach resort of Warnemünde is only 12km to the north.

Orientation

The city begins at the Südstadt (Southern City), south of the Hauptbahnhof, and extends north to Warnemünde on the Baltic Sea. Much of the city is on the western side of the Warnow River, which creates a long shipping channel from the Altstadt practically due north to the sea.

The Altstadt – the city centre – is a circular area about 1.5km north of the Hauptbahnhof. Bücher Strasse runs north from the station to Steintor, which unofficially marks the southern boundary of the Altstadt; the northern and eastern boundary is formed by the Warnow inlet; the western boundary is Kröpeliner Tor.

Following the western bank of the Warnow from south to north takes you through several neighbourhoods: Bramow, Marienehe, Evershagen, Schmarl, Lütten Klein, the notorious Lichtenhagen (see Dangers & Annoyances), Gross Klein and, finally, Warnemünde.

Information

Tourist Office The very helpful Rostock-Information (☎ 194 33 or 497 99 0; email rostock@compuserve.com) is at Schnickmannstrasse 13-14, about 2km from the train station. Take tram No 11 or 12 outside the station and get off at the Lange Strasse stop.

Money There's a DVB bank in the Hauptbahnhof. The main post office has a Postbank. There's a Citibank just north of Universitätsplatz on Kröpeliner Strasse, and

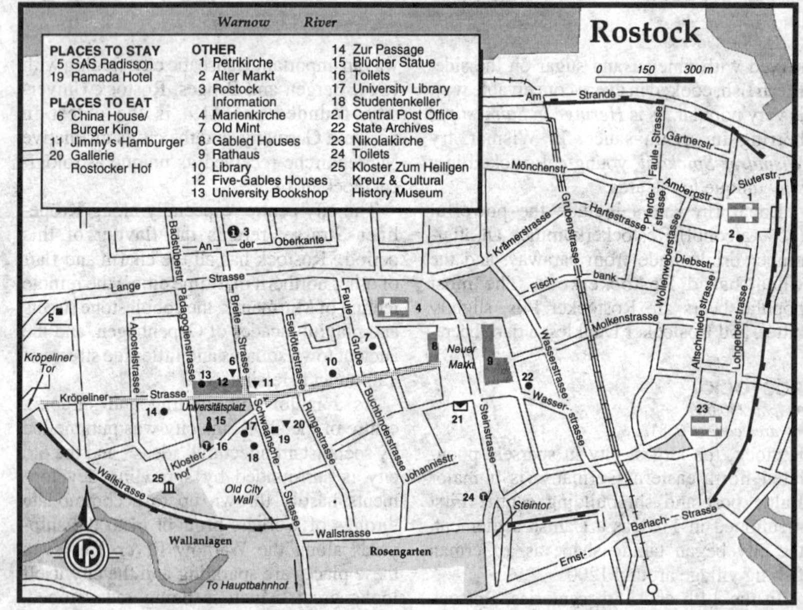

it's always fun to change money in the beautiful BfG Bank in the former city mint (see Neuer Markt).

Post & Communications Rostock's main post office is opposite the Rathaus, on the southern end of Neuer Markt.

Travel Agencies Atlas Reisewelt, at Lange Strasse in front of the Radisson SAS Hotel, does last-minute and discount tickets as well as train tickets. Zimmerbörse Reisecenter Delphini, at Lange Strasse 19 (☎ 454 44 4), books rooms and package tours.

Bookshops Pressezentrum (☎ 490 80 72) on the ground floor of Gallerie Rostocker Hof, the shopping mall at Kröpeliner Strasse 26, has a good selection of English-language books and a huge foreign-press section. The Universitäts Buchhandlung in Five-Gables Houses (☎ 492 26 03) also stocks foreign-language books.

Libraries The University's Amerikanistic-Anglistic Library (☎ 498 26 08), August-Bebel-Strasse 28, has English books; call when you're in town and they'll open it up for you (no regular business hours). The main city library, at Kröpeliner Strasse 82, has a great reading room and cocoa and tea available in the front entrance.

Campus Established in 1419, Rostock University is the oldest in northern Germany. It has 9000 students, concentrated mainly in faculties of medicine, law and theology. The main campus is in the city centre, at Universitätsplatz.

Laundry The laundrette (☎ 442 03 8) at Rudolf-Diesel-Strasse 1 in the Südstadt is inconvenient but nice. Walk under the Hauptbahnhof, turn right on the walkway in front of the Büro Hotel to Südring, south one block, turn right, go one block to Rudolf-Diesel-Strasse and it's on the left.

Medical Services In an emergency, call ☎ 444 11 for an ambulance, or Klinikum Süd (☎ 440 10) at Südring (there's no street number, but everyone knows it). Call the Ärztehause (☎ 456 16 22), Paulstrasse 48, for less serious matters during regular business hours.

Dangers & Annoyances In 1992 the Rostock suburb of Lichtenhagen was the site of a neo-Nazi arson attack on a hostel for foreigners. The attack was met with outrage by local residents as well as the mainstream German and world press, which roundly condemned it. A second attack in January 1996 killed 10 people.

So far the targets of these attacks have been foreign workers, not tourists, but the areas outside the Altstadt can be very intimidating. Use common sense and be neither paranoid nor careless. Don't flash cash, drink to excess, travel alone at night or in other ways make yourself a target.

Marienkirche

Rostock's greatest single sight is the 13th-century Marienkirche (1290, reconstruction completed 1440), and its unique, functioning and fascinating astrological clock, all of which somehow survived WWII unscathed – the only one of Rostock's four main churches to do so. The long transept running north-south was added after the ceiling collapsed in 1398; this gave the building its unique shape, and strengthened its structure. As you enter (DM2, children under 11 free) the main altar is to the right, the lavish Renaissance pulpit (1574) to the left.

The 12m-high astrological clock (1470-72), hand-wound every morning, is behind the main altar. At the very top are a series of doors; at noon and midnight the farthest right door opens and six of the 12 apostles pass from the right-hand door all the way over to the left-hand one – though Judas is locked out.

Astrological Clock There are two main sections. The upper section, with 24 Roman numerals on its outer edge, uses only one hand to tell the time. The gold pointer indicates the hour – the upper half of the clock indicates day, the bottom half night. The two astrological pointers, Sun and Moon, rotate on their own disks; the more accurate moon pointer changes astrological signs every 27⅛ days, the sun progresses round the entire dial in exactly a year. The disk shows light for full moons and dark for new moons – during a full moon the moon and sun indicators are opposite one another.

The lower section of the clock is a disc that tells the day and date as well as the exact day on which Easter, a moveable feast day, falls in any given year. The discs are replaceable; each is accurate for 130 years. The current one (the fourth) was installed in 1885 and expires in 2017 – the university already has the new one ready. The calendar man on the left side phallically points at today's date and, in the centre, the dates on which Easter will next fall.

Other Highlights Other highlights of the church include the Gothic bronze baptismal font (1290), the baroque organ (1770) and, on the northern side of the main altar, fascinating tombstones in the floor. Ascend the 207 steps of the 50m-high church tower for the view.

There are Protestant services on Sunday at 10 am; the church is open to visitors Monday to Saturday from 10 am to 5 pm, Sunday from 11.30 am to noon.

Kröpeliner Strasse & Universitätsplatz

Kröpeliner Strasse, a broad, lively, cobblestone pedestrian mall lined with 15th and 16th-century burghers' houses, runs from Neuer Markt west to Kröpeliner Tor.

At the centre of the mall is Universitätsplatz, positively swarming with people year round, but more so in summer, and its centrepiece, the **Brunnen der Lebensfreude** (Fountain of the Joy of Life).

At the south side of the square's triangular grassy area stands an impressive bronze **statue of Field Marshal Blücher von Wahlstatt**, Rostock's most beloved military hero who helped defeat Napoleon at Waterloo. On the statue's rear is a poem by Goethe himself, though *Faust* it ain't; on the statue's north is a relief depicting the battle at Waterloo.

At the northern side of Universitätsplatz are the **Five Gables Houses**, modern interpretations of the gabled houses that lined the square before WWII.

Cultural History Museum

At the south-western end of Universitätsplatz is the **Kloster Zum Heiligen Kreuz**, a convent established in 1270 by Queen Margaret of Denmark. Today it houses the Cultural History Museum (☎ 454 17 7), with an excellent permanent collection including several sculptures by Ernst Barlach and a collection of Victorian furniture. There are rotating exhibitions as well. The museum is open Tuesday to Sunday from 9 am to 5 pm. Admission is DM4 (discount DM2).

City Walls & Gates

The wall that surrounded the Altstadt once contained 23 city gates. Today only two main gates and a small section of wall remain. **Steintor** is at the southern end of the Altstadt surrounded by tram tracks. Its Latin inscription, *Sit intra te concordia et publica felicitas*, means 'Within these walls, let unity and general prosperity prevail'.

At its west is **Wallstrasse**, which takes you past a remaining section of wall; the street continues to the western side of the Altstadt and the 55m-high **Kröpliner Tor**, containing the city's very good **Regional History Museum** (Wednesday to Sunday from 10 am to 6 pm; admission DM4/2). The top floor is dedicated to the GDR days, including a leather jacket given in 1980 by West German rocker Udo Lindenberg to GDR strongman Erich Honecker. There's a great view from up here, though there's no lift.

Neuer Markt

The splendid and very pink 12th-century **Rathaus** is at the eastern side of this square, just north of the Steintor. The baroque facade was added in 1727 after the original brick Gothic structure collapsed in 1725. The newly restored Gothic turrets on the roof shine brightly. Hensellmann, the architect of the northern addition to the Rathaus, was a GDR favourite; his works grace other eastern German cities with equal style and tact. Just behind the Rathaus is the intricate, Gothic **State Archives building**.

Opposite the Rathaus is a lovely series of restored **gabled houses**, and the northern end of the square leads to the Marienkirche. Just behind the Marienkirche is the gorgeous Renaissance doorway on the former city **Mint**, now a BfG Bank branch.

Maritime Museum

Rostock's good Maritime Museum (☎ 492 26 97), at August-Bebel-Strasse 1, on the corner of Richard-Wagner-Strasse near the Steintor, has displays on the history of Baltic navigation, coins and medallions and rotating exhibitions. From October to March, it's open Tuesday to Sunday from 9 am to 5 pm. From April to September hours are 10 am to 6 pm. Admission is DM4.

Petrikirche

The 117m-high steeple – a mariner's landmark for centuries – on the Gothic Petrikirche at Alter Markt was restored in 1994; the steeple had been missing since WWII. It's open from April to October daily from 10 am to noon and 2.30 to 4 pm.

Just next door, the **Slueter monument** honours Joachim Slueter, a reformer who preached in the *niederdeutschem* (Low German) dialect outside the church, and three blocks south is the **Nikolaikirche**, Rostock's oldest church.

Rostock Zoo

Rostock's zoo (☎ 371 11) has been renovated and is constantly getting better. Its 2000 animals seem happy, and kids absolutely love the place. From the centre of the Altstadt, take tram No 11 or bus No 39 directly there. Admission is DM5/4. From April to September it's open from 9 am to 5 pm; from October to March between 9 am and 4 pm.

Activities

Neptune Schwimmbad (☎ 456 25 00) is a 24m-long indoor pool at Kopernikus-Strasse. It's open every day; Saturdays from 8 to 10 pm it's for women only. Admission is DM5/2.50 for the first hour, DM2.50/2 each additional hour.

Organised Tours

Guided tours lasting 1½ hours depart two to three days a week at 11 am and/or 2 pm, depending on season, from the Rostock-Information office. The cost is DM7, kids under 12 free. English-language tours can be arranged for DM85 for up to 15 people.

Special Events

Every June to August, the classical Festspiele Mecklenburg Vorpommern is held at various venues in town and throughout the region. Tickets (from DM18 to DM90) can be reserved by telephone (☎ 040-410 79 29) Monday to Friday from 10 am to 5 pm year round.

Places to Stay

Accommodation in Rostock is in a state of flux, with newer entries generally being very expensive, and older, cheaper options, like hostels, in danger of closing. Private accommodation fills the gap. See the Warnemünde section for more options.

Camping The city-run *Baltic Freizeit Camping- und Ferienpark* (☎ 038206-580), in Markgrafenheide, on the east side of the Warnow River, is enormous. Tent sites range from DM20 to DM48, including two people, a tent and a car. Take tram No 4 from the Hauptbahnhof to Dierkower Kreuz, then bus No 18 (direction: Markgrafenheide). The trip takes 45 minutes. If you have a car, head up to Warnemünde and catch the ferry (DM4.50 for car and driver, DM1 each additional passenger) for the quick trip across the Warnow to Hohe Düne. From there, take the only road straight up to the camp site.

Hostels The cheery *Jugendgästeschiff Traditionsschiff* (☎ 716 22 4) is in a converted freighter on the harbour at Schmarl-Dorf, between Rostock and Warnemünde. Take the S-Bahn to Lütten Klein station, then walk east past the apartment blocks for 25 minutes, turn left at the three-way intersection and past the small lighthouse and the two car parks to the far gangway. Whilst the hostel is a long way out, it's a fun place and a good deal at DM26/32 for juniors/seniors. The rooms and setting are very pleasant, and it's run more like a pension. Rumour has it that the hostel might be closing so call before you head out.

There's a second hostel nearby in Warnemünde; see that section.

Private Rooms Rostock-Information can book private rooms from around DM30 per person plus a DM5 fee. If you arrive after hours, you can call ☎ 194 14 for a recorded message (in German only) about all vacant rooms in the city.

Hotels Small but central and worth trying is *City-Pension* (☎ 4590829) at Krönkenhagen 3, with singles/doubles with private facilities from DM85/150. *Landhaus Immenberg* (☎ 776 93 0), Gross Kleiner Weg 19, has rooms with facilities for DM108/158. The *Ramada Hotel* (☎ 497 00) at Universitätsplatz has great service and rooms for DM185/203. Pricey (DM175/210) but nice is the nine-storey *Radisson SAS Hotel*, Lange Strasse 40.

Rooms at the *Inter-City Hotel*, at the Hauptbahnhof, are spotless and comfortable, (DM129 to DM183 for singles, DM129 to DM206 for doubles), but they feel a bit like 1st-class sleeper compartments on a train.

Places to Eat

Restaurants Restaurants are cheaper here than in western Germany. Expect to pay DM4 to DM5 for soups; DM10 to DM13 for simple local fish dishes with potatoes; and DM15 to DM25 for more elaborate main courses or ones in more up-market places.

It's hard to beat the *Rostocker Ratskeller* in the Rathaus building on Neuer Markt, where everything is half-price between 3 and 5 pm on weekdays.

Pull up a lifeboat and sing a sea shanty in the over-the-top *Zur Kogge* (☎ 493 44 93), Wokrenterstrasse 27, complete with life preservers on the walls and very good seafood. We had an awesome meal at *China House* (☎ 459 10 03), underneath the Burger King at Universitätsplatz 7, and got out for almost exactly DM20 per person with drinks.

Out by the zoo, the *Jäggerhütte* (☎ 400 15 52), a hunting lodge in the Barnstorfer Wald, is a very good local hang-out specialising in Wild (game). Another spot for regional specialities is the *Altstädter Stuben* (☎ 459 09 1), Altschmiedestrasse 25.

The expensive *Gastmahl des Meeres*, opposite the Maritime Museum on August-Bebel-Strasse, specialises in seafood.

Snacks & Fast Food Just outside the Hauptbahnhof are two great options for cheap (DM3.40 to DM4.50) pizza: *Die Brezelbäckerei*, in a little kiosk, and a *Pizza Hut Express*. For a veritable feast of quick snacks of fruit, fish, pizza, sandwiches, quiche and the like, head to the ground floor of *Gallerie Rostocker Hof*, on Universitätsplatz beneath the Ramada Hotel. The *Stadtbäckerei* (☎ 492 32 97) there makes good sandwiches for under DM5, and just down the hall *Vino Veritas* lets you sample any of its hundreds of wines for DM4.50 to DM9 per glass.

A local standby is *Jimmy's Hamburger*, on the corner of Breite Strasse at Universitätsplatz, with good burgers and big coffees for DM2.30.

Kartoffelhaus No 1, Am Strande 3a, serves delicious potato-based dishes at reasonable prices.

Entertainment

Listings Section 2 of the daily *Ostseer Zeitung* is the *Rostocker Zeitung*, with detailed listings of attractions, what's on and emergency phone numbers. The city puts out a free tri-monthly pamphlet, *Die Stadt Erleben*, listing everything from car repairs to concerts and events. The much flashier, privately published *Rostock Live* has a useful map in the centrefold. Both are available free at Rostock-Information and at tourist attractions, bars and restaurants around the city.

Szene, a super-useful free monthly, is geared more to music and concerts but also includes useful listings, articles, reviews and classified ads.

Rat + Tat eV (☎ 453 15 6), Gerberbuch 13, publishes *Rostocks Verein für Schwule und Lesben*, a what's-on pamphlet available at gay-friendly locations around town.

Discos & Clubs Many of the smaller places on Universitätsplatz are worth checking out. Disco cover charges average DM7 to DM10. The *Studentenkeller* (☎ 455 92 8) has been rocking on for years. Enter through the main university building at the eastern side of Universitätsplatz, go through the tunnel and it's on the left-hand side downstairs. There's live music and lots of nightly partying in summer and on weekends in winter.

Disco Fun/Lollipop (☎ 768 37 82), Rigaerstrasse 5, has two dance floors, one haunted by the 20-to-40 crowd, the other dedicated to techno and other teeny stuff; take bus No 39 or the S-Bahn to Lütten Klein.

Speicher-Discotek (☎ 492 30 31), Am Strande 3a, a small venue in an old warehouse in the old port, has live jazz, rock, blues, etc, as well as oldies parties, techno and reggae nights.

Theatre & Classical Music *Volkstheater Rostock* (☎ 244 0), Doberaner Strasse 134, puts on a very good range of ballet, drama, opera and concerts, and it's home to the *Norddeutsche Philharmonie*, which performs classical concerts year round.

Cultural Centre The *Stadthalle* (☎ 440 00) at Platz der Freundschaft, just south of the train station, is an enormous events arena that caters to a huge array of performances and events (there's also a bowling alley!). Concerts range from classical to jazz to rock and everything in between.

Getting There & Away

Air Flughafen Rostock-Laage (☎ 038454-313 0), about 30km south of the city, is served by smaller private airlines, with direct charter connections to Hamburg, Hanover and Dortmund.

Bus Regionalverkehr Kueste (☎ 405 60 18) runs services throughout the region, leaving from the central bus station behind the Hauptbahnhof. There's regular bus service from Rostock to Wismar, Güstrow and Neubrandenburg but not to Schwerin, Stralsund, Lübeck, Hamburg or Kiel.

Train There are frequent direct trains to Rostock from Berlin-Lichtenberg (DM55, 2¾ hours), and trains run several times daily to Stralsund (DM16.60, 55 minutes), Wismar (DM12.60, 1½ hours) and Schwerin (DM19, 1½ hours). Atlas Reisewelt at Lange Strasse, in front of the Radisson, sells train tickets, as does the main station's ticket office.

Car & Motorcycle From Berlin, head north or south out of the city to the B10; follow that north-west to the A24 (direction: Hamburg), which leads directly into the A19 that runs straight north to Rostock (2½ hours). From Neubrandenburg, take the B104 west to the A19 and turn north (1½ hours).

Ride Services For a lift, get in touch with the Mitfahrzentrale im DeTe 64 (☎ 493 44 38), Am Kabutzenhof 21. It's open Monday to Friday from 8 am to 6 pm.

Boat Several ferry companies, chiefly TT-Line ferries (☎ 670 79 0; fax 670 79 80) and DFO Vogelfluglinie (☎ 673 12 17; fax 673 12 13), offer crossings to Trelleborg (Sweden) and Gedser (Denmark) from Rostock Seaport on the east side of the Warnow. The A19 runs right into the port. From the Hauptbahnhof take tram No 4 to Dierkower Kreuz, then change for bus No 19 or 20 (once an hour) to the port.

All boats are wheelchair accessible.

Sweden The crossing takes three hours on TT-Line and six hours on DFO Vogelfluglinie. TT-Line charges DM46/50 in winter/summer. Bicycles are DM10 extra. Cars, including driver, are DM120/210. On DFO, one way costs DM15/30 in winter/summer, children aged four to 11 pay half price. Cars, including five passengers, cost DM120/160 and motorcycles DM50/70.

Denmark DFO also runs to Gedser, in Denmark eight times a day. Tickets for the two-hour trip cost DM5/8 in winter/summer; cars (with up to five people) cost DM120/155; motorcycles DM40/50. There's a faster boat (by 50 minutes) as well; prices are DM10/16 for pedestrians, DM145/180 per car, and the same price for motorcycles.

Getting Around

The Airport There's no public transport from the airport to town, but there are taxis (about DM40) and car-rental offices.

Public Transport Buses and trams run 24 hours a day; services are infrequent after midnight.

The Rostock area, which includes Warnemünde, is zoned; for a single trip you pay DM2 for one zone, DM2.80 for two or more zones. Day cards are DM7.50, and the discounted after-9 am day card is excellent value at DM3.80 (one zone) and DM5 (two or more zones).

A *Familien Tageskarte* (Family Day Card), costing DM12 for two or more zones, covers up to three adults and two kids for travel from the moment you first stamp it until the following day at 3 am.

Tram Nos 2, 11 and 12 travel from the Hauptbahnhof up Steinstrasse, around Marienkirche and down Lange Strasse. Take tram No 11 or 12 to get from the Hauptbahnhof to the university; to the hostel, it's tram No 12.

Car & Motorcycle With complicated one-way systems, confusing street layouts and dedicated parking-ticket police, Rostock is not a driver-friendly city. *Parkschein* ticket machines are in place throughout the city and you can park in the lot next to the InterCity Hotel at the south end of the Hauptbahnhof for DM12 a day.

Taxi Taxi rates at the time of writing were DM4 flag fall plus a varying per kilometre rate; prices actually go *down* at night. From Warnemünde to the Hauptbahnhof will cost about DM25.

Bicycle Cycling isn't the best within the city of Rostock because of very heavy (and crazy) traffic, but just outside the city it quickly improves.

You can rent bicycles from Express-Guthalle (☎ 240 11 53), at the southern end of the Hauptbahnhof; in Warnemünde from Wilhelm Meyer Touristen Service Mobil (☎ 519 19 55) at Am Leuchtturm 16, and at the camping ground in Markgrafenheide (see Places to Stay in the Rostock section). Get parts or buy second-hand bikes (from DM30) at Fahrradhandel (☎ 490 20 50), Grosser Katthagen 2-4, near the Kröpeliner Tor.

AROUND ROSTOCK

Warnemünde

- *pop 10,000*
- *area code* ☎ 0381

Warnemünde, at the mouth of the Warnow River on the Baltic Sea just north of Rostock, is among eastern Germany's most popular beach resorts. S-Bahn trains connect Warnemünde to Rostock every 15 minutes on weekdays, every 30 minutes in the evenings, and hourly from midnight to dawn. Warnemünde can easily be used as a base for day trips to Rostock, Wismar, Stralsund and even Schwerin: it's a good choice if you want to enjoy the comforts of city life while staying in what is essentially a small fishing village on the beach.

Orientation & Information The Hauptbahnhof is at the eastern end of town, east of the Alter Strom, the main canal on which all the fishing and tour boats moor. The Alter Strom runs almost straight as an arrow from north to south. To the east of the Hauptbahnhof is the Neuer Strom, across which is the Hohe Düne section and, further east, the camping ground at Markgrafenheide.

The main action takes place along the promenade, which fronts the wide, surprisingly white beach. The town's main drags are Am Strom (the walkway along the Alter Strom), and Kirchenstrasse, which leads west from the bridge over the Strom to Kirchenplatz and finally on to Mühlenstrasse, lined with cafés, chic shops and cheap bistros.

Warnemünde Tourist-Information (☎ 511 42), on the corner of Wachtler Strasse and Heinrich-Heine-Strasse, is open weekdays from 10 am to 5 pm and in summer also on Saturday morning. Outside you'll find an information board with push-button screen and a coin telephone.

For currency exchange, DVB/Reisebank, Am Bahnhof in the station area, is open Monday to Friday from 8.30 am to 6 pm, Saturday from 9 am to noon. There are ATMs in the station and throughout the town.

Harbour Am Strom is a picturesque street lined with quaint fishers' cottages. The **Heimatmuseum** (Local Folklore Museum; open Wednesday to Sunday from 11 am to 6 pm; DM3), a converted fishers' cottage, is on Alexandrinenstrasse just south of Kirchenstrasse, the church and the main square. Lining the inlet on the west side are tempting restaurants, while boats moored at the quay below sell fish and rolls, offer cruises (DM9 to DM15 all year, weather permitting), or present themselves as restaurants (some manage all three).

The crowded **promenade** to the north, on the sea, is where tourists congregate. Warnemünde's broad, sandy beach stretches west from the **lighthouse** (1898), and is chock-a-block with bathers on hot summer days.

Places to Stay Warnemünde is a resort town and budget accommodation is not easy to find. Apart from the hostel, the camping site at Markgrafenheide (see Places to Stay in the Rostock section), and private rooms, reasonably priced accommodation is basically non-existent.

Hostels & Private Rooms The friendly *hostel* (☎ 548 17 00) at Park Strasse 46 charges DM20/24 for juniors/seniors, including breakfast. For private rooms, turn to Warnemünde Tourist-Information (☎ 511 42) or Warnemünde Zimmervermittlung und Reiseservice (☎ 591 76) at Am Bahnhof 1 just outside the Hauptbahnhof. Expect to pay DM25 to DM50 per person in winter, DM50 to DM75 in summer. Otherwise, look for the 'Zimmer frei' (room available) signs in the windows along Parkstrasse. You should book well in advance if you're planning to visit between mid-May and September; spur-of-the-moment rooms are expensive.

Pensions & Hotels *Pension Katy* (☎ 543 94 0), Kurhausstrasse 9, has doubles with private bath for DM55 to DM75. *Hotel am Alten Strom* (☎ 525 81), Am Strom 60, has rooms starting at DM45/70 (shared baths), ranging up to DM100/160. *Hotel Stolteraa* (☎ 543 20), Strandweg 17, offers doubles for DM130 to DM220.

Top of the pops here are two hotels managed by the same company, Arkona Hotels. In the enormous *Hotel Neptun* (☎ 777 77 77; fax 777 80 0), built in 1972 by the GDR, every room – yes, *every* one – has a great view of the beach. The place has been completely renovated (with an excellent spa) and though the lobby feels a little like Moscow's Cosmos Hotel, the rooms are very comfortable. The hotel offers has some good deals: weekends from DM105 per person in the off season, DM160 in high season. Standard rates are DM200 to DM300 (singles) and DM300 to DM400 (doubles) in high season.

The *Strand-Hotel Hübner* (☎ 543 40; fax 543 44 44), Sistra's 12, has newly renovated and very stylish rooms for DM195/235.

Places to Eat Lovers of smoked fish will be in heaven here, as many of the boats lining the Alter Strom smoke their catches on site and sell them cheaply. There's a *Nimms Mit* convenience shop at the Hauptbahnhof.

Café zur Traube, Alexandrinenstrasse 72, is cosy but pricey. You can find better prices at *Zur Gemütlichkeit*, Mühlenstrasse 25, where many dishes go for around DM12. Also affordable are the daily fish specials at *Kettenkasten*, Am Strom 71. Lots of Italian cafés and restaurants prepare similar fare for the same prices; pizzas from DM8 to DM10, pastas from DM7 to DM11, bigger meals from DM12 to DM18. *Mamma Mia* (☎ 519 28 31), Am Strom 101, definitely looked worth a try.

Getting There & Away The sleek double-deck S-Bahn has frequent services from Rostock with 1st (DM5.60) and 2nd class (DM2.80) fares. Be careful which class you get into: tickets are almost always checked.

Molli Steam Railway

About 15km west of Rostock, the former summer ducal residence of Bad Doberan is the starting point for a ride on the Molli Schmalspurbahn, a narrow-gauge steam train that runs between here and the towns of Heiligendamm and Kühlungsborn.

The train service, which everyone refers to simply as 'Molli', began huffing and puffing its way to Heiligendamm in 1886, carrying three wagons and one luggage car. Today it's operated by Mecklenburger Bädebahn (☎ 038203-240 0; fax 212 6).

Trains depart year round from Bad Doberan's Hauptbahnhof 10 times a day from Monday to Friday, slightly less frequently on weekends and holidays. There's a bar car on some journeys, and on all trips the lovely scenery. The one-way/return fare is DM4/6.50 (discount DM2/3, family tickets DM9.90/ 15.90).

Trains leave Rostock's Hauptbahnhof every hour or more (DM5/7.50, 20 to 25 minutes) for Bad Doberan. By car take the B105 in the direction of Wismar.

WISMAR

- *pop 50,000*
- *area code* ☎ 03841

Wismar, about halfway between Rostock and Lübeck, became a Hanseatic trading town in the 13th century – the first one east of Lübeck. For centuries Wismar belonged to Sweden, and traces of that rule can still be seen. Less hectic than Rostock or Stralsund, Wismar is definitely worth an overnight stay – it's a very pretty little town, with some interesting museums, fine restaurants and a cool Irish pub.

Wismar is also the gateway to Poel Island, a lovely little piece of green to the north that, in addition to being a bird sanctuary, offers hiking, cycling, riding and, in summer swimming.

Orientation

The Altstadt is the city centre, built up around the Markt – said to be the largest medieval town square in Germany. The Hauptbahnhof is at the north-eastern corner and the Alter Hafen port is at the north-western corner of the Altstadt; a canal runs from Alter Hafen almost due east across the northern half of the Altstadt. The streets around the Markt are pedestrianised. The main night-time entertainment area is around Alter Hafen.

Information

Wismar-Information (☎ 251 81 5; fax 251 81 9; email info@wismar.de), at Am Markt 11, is open daily from 9 am to 6 pm, and definitely has its stuff together. Change money on the Markt, at the Sparkasse (No 15) or Deutsche Bank (No 16).

The main post office is south of the Markt on the east side of Mecklenburger Strasse.

There are showers (DM2), toilets and a coin operated washer-dryer in the little house in the harbour at Am Alten Hafen.

The town's medical clinic (☎ 330) is at Am Dahlberg, south of the centre.

Markt

It's hard to believe that Wismar's **gabled houses** were badly bombed. Busy **markets** are held here on Tuesday and Thursday from 8 am to 6 pm, and Saturday to 1 pm. Also on Saturday, a lively fish market takes place at **Alter Hafen**. The **Rathaus** (1817-19) is at the square's northern end.

The **Alter Schwede**, a building with an outlandish brick Gothic façade and now home to one of the city's most popular restaurants, is at the south-eastern side of the square, in front of the **Waterworks** (*Wasserkunst*, or 'water art'), an ornate, 12-sided well, completed in 1602, that was the source of the town's drinking water until 1897.

Wismar's excellent new **Historical Exhibition**, housed in the basement of the Rathaus, displays original 17th-century *Wandmalerei* (wall paintings), recently uncovered by archaeologists; maps and models of the city; and, in the back, a glass floor over a medieval well – stand over it if you dare.

The museum is open daily from 10 am to 6 pm; admission is DM2 (discount DM1).

Churches

Wismar was a target for Anglo-American bombers just a few weeks before the end of WWII. Of the three great red-brick churches that once rose above the rooftops, only **St Nikolaikirche** (1380-1415), containing a font from 1335, is intact.

The massive red shell of **St Georgenkirche** is being restored for future use as a church, concert hall and exhibition space (completion is planned for somewhere between 2005 and 2010).

In 1945, a freezing populace was driven to burn what was left of a beautiful wooden statue of St George and the dragon. Cars now park where the 13th-century **St Marienkirche** once stood, although its great brick steeple (1339), now partly restored, still towers above the city.

The 14th-century Gothic **Heilige Geist Kirche**, in the courtyard west of the Markt (entered on Neustadt between Heide and Lübsche Strasse), contains the city **Music School**, and is a concert venue in summer.

Prison & Fürstenhof

Just west of the Marienkirche is the city **prison**, also called the *Kittchen*, or 'clink'. Across the street from it is the Kittchen restaurant and pool hall, decorated with huge caricatures of prisoners laughing and pointing at the real ones across the street.

Around a little corner from the prison is the Italian Renaissance **Fürstenhof** (1512-13), currently the city courthouse. The façades are slathered in terracotta reliefs depicting the history of the town and, under the arch in the courtyard, biblical scenes.

Historical Museum

The town's historical museum is in the Renaissance **Schabbelhaus** in a former brewery (1571) at Schweinsbrücke 8, just south of the Nikolaikirche across the canal. The museum's pride and joy is the large tapestry called *Die Königin von Saba vor König Salomon* (The Queen of Sheba before King Solomon; 1560-75).

There are also displays on the history of

Ossi v Wessi

The differences between *Ossis* ('Easties') and *Wessis* ('Westies') are manifold. One of the many subtle differences emerged when one of the authors was walking through Wismar with a *Wessi* and an *Ossi* guide. We saw a sign that read *Volkseigener Betrieb*, abbreviated VEB, which is a GDR-era term for 'people-owned company.'

The *Wessi* mentioned a local pun on the initials: locals call VEBs *'Vaters ehemaliger Betrieb'* – 'Father's former company'. We all laughed.

But after a moment it became clear that the *Ossi* and *Wessi* were laughing at two totally different interpretations. While the *Wessi* thought the joke meant that this company was owned by someone's father and then nationalised by the GDR government after WWII, the *Ossi* believed that it meant her father worked in this company until post-reunification budget cuts forced it out of business!

The misunderstandings, though, are usually that subtle. East and West Germans, though separated by the Cold War and so recently reunited, still both tell the same jokes about Austrians. ■

Wismar as a Hanseatic power and a Swedish garrison town. It's open Tuesday to Sunday from 10 am to 4.30 pm (Thursday to 6 pm). Admission is DM3/ 1.50 for adults/students, free for children.

Regional artist Christian Wetzel's four charming **pig statuettes** grace the nearby **Schweinsbrücke**.

Scheuerstrasse

About 400m north-west of the Markt is Scheuerstrasse, a street lined with charming gabled houses, especially No 15, with its towering façade, and No 15a, with the cargo crane. No 17 is the charming O'Donohoes Irish Pub (see Places to Eat).

Activities

From May to September, Clermont Reederei operates hour-long harbour cruises five times daily (DM10) from Alter Hafen. By arrangement, boats also go to Poel Island.

Organised Tours

In summer there are 1½-hour walking tours of the city, leaving at 11 am from Wismar-Information (DM7/3.50). English-language tours can be arranged for up to 15 people on one day's notice (or less).

Special Events

In mid-June, the annual Harbour Festival (Hafenfest) includes old and new sailing ships and steamers, music and food.

Places to Stay

With no hostel in town, private rooms fill much of the city's accommodation needs. Wismar-Information can arrange private singles/doubles from DM30/75 per person (DM5 booking fee). The nearest *camping ground* (☎ 03841-642 37 7) is at Am Strand 19c in Zierow and can be reached on bus No 320.

The nearest hostel is the *Beckerwitz Hostel* (☎ 0384-283 62), Haus Nr 21 in Beckerwitz. Take bus No 240 (direction: Boltenhagen) from the Hauptbahnhof.

Hotel Gothia (☎ 734 15 6), Sella-Hasse-Strasse 11, is a good deal at DM75 for singles and from DM45 per person for apartments. Also affordable is *Hotel Lippold* (☎ 283 57 7), Poeler Strasse 138, which has doubles only for DM60 to DM80.

The historic *Hotel Altes Brauhaus* (☎ 211 41 6), Lübsche Strasse 37, has singles/doubles from DM85/120. The elegant *Hotel Alter Speicher* (☎ 214 76 1), Bohrstrasse 12, has rooms starting at DM110/160.

Hotel Stadt Hamburg (☎ 239 0; fax 239 23 9), Am Markt 24, is a very flash place in a beautifully renovated building with rooms starting at DM145/185.

Places to Eat

The local speciality is a sparkling wine. Hanse-Sektkellerei Wismar (☎ 484 80), a champagne factory at Turnerweg 4, south of the city centre, produces several varieties, from dry (Hanse Tradition) to extra dry (Hanse Selection). You can tour and sample by prior arrangement.

There's a *Nur Hier Café* and lots of *Steh-cafés* in and around the Markt. The *Grill-master* budget grill is at Lübsche Strasse 49; meals are fast and filling for DM8 or less.

Wismar's 'restaurant row' is along the pedestrianised Am Lohberg, near the fishing harbour. The string of atmospheric restaurants and bars includes *Brauhaus*, the town's first brewery. *Kartoffelnhaus Nr 1* (☎ 200 03 0), Frische Grube 31, does 'international dishes centred around the potato', like Budapester gratin potatoes, Hungarian potato soup, and Himmel und Erde (Heaven and Earth – potatoes and apples). It's worth trying and good value.

Zum Weinberg (☎ 283 55 0), Hinter dem Rathaus 3, is a wine restaurant in a lovely Renaissance house.

Possibly the best situated restaurant is the historic and exclusive *Alter Schwede*, Am Markt 18, though the food isn't all that hot – you're paying for the atmosphere and service.

Hanse Keller (☎ 409 08), with its vaulted ceilings, on two subterranean levels in St Marien Passage, Lübsche Strasse, is another lovely place.

The *Bayernstadl* (☎ 212 82 0), ABC-

Strasse 17, is set up like a Bavarian beer hall without the Bavarian price tag; main courses cost from DM10 to DM18.

To'n Zügenkrog (pronounced 'tun TSAY-gencrokh'; ☎ 282 71 6), Ziegenmarkt 10 near the harbour, prepares excellent fish dishes, with main courses from DM9 to DM23.

O'Donohoes Irish Pub, a great, fun place, is open from 5 pm and has Guinness on tap (though it's pricey at DM5.50 a pint).

The new Italian place, *Ristorante/Pizzeria Rialto* (☎ 285 00 5), at Dankwartstrasse 40a, is said to be very good.

Getting There & Away

Trains travel every hour to/from Rostock (DM12.60, 1¼ hours) and Schwerin (DM8.40, 30 minutes). Most trains to/from Berlin-Lichtenberg (DM57, 3½ hours), Lübeck (DM18.50, 1¼ hours) and Hamburg (DM39, two hours) travel via Bad Kleinen. There are no lockers at the Hauptbahnhof.

POEL ISLAND

- *pop 2000*
- *area code* ☎ 038425

The beaches on Poel Island, in Mecklenburg Bay inlet north of Wismar, are relatively undiscovered. It's a good spot for cycling, windsurfing and horse riding, and in high summer its beaches accommodate everyone.

Orientation

The island's main road access is just north-west of the village of Gross Strömkendorf. Most of the action takes place in Kichdorf, in the centre of the island and home to Poel's main fishing port and marina, which are at the southern end of the city. Kichdorf's brick **Gothic church** (Protestant services on Sunday in summer at 10 am) is at the southern end of town; the **local history museum** (☎ 207 32; closed Monday) is just north of the port at Möwenweg 5. The post office is at the plaza at the junctions of Möwenweg, Wismarsche Strasse and Ernst-Thälmann-Strasse.

Information

The local tourist office (☎ 203 47), Wismarsche Strasse 3, hands out excellent street plans and cycling and hiking maps of the island. Change money at the Sparkasse next to the tourist office at Wismarsche Strasse 1d. Its ATM takes EC and MasterCard/EuroCard but *not* Visa. There's also an ATM at the Raiffeisenbank just next door.

Beaches

High summer here means late June to late August; at other times it's pretty chilly. Note that the island can get very windy year round. Families should head for the beaches at **Am Schwarzen Busch** (almost due north of Kichdorf) and **Gollwitz** (at the island's north-east corner), where the water is shallow and calm. Nude bathing is permitted at **Hinter Wangern** and sections of Gollwitz. There are lifeguards at Am Schwarzen Busch but not at the other beaches.

Cycling

The island is flat and perfect for riding. Get maps at the tourist information office and rent bicycles for DM8 to DM12 per day at the Poel Island Kurverwaltung (☎ 203 47), Wismarsche Strasse 2.

Horse Riding

There's horse riding at Neuhof, west of Kichdorf, and at Timmendorf. Horses cost DM20 per hour from Reiterhof Plath (☎ 207 60) in Timmendorf.

Places to Stay & Eat

You can camp in Timmendorf, near the beach and the lighthouse, from April to October at *Campingplatz Leuchtturm* (☎ 202 24); the high-season rate applies from June to August. Tent sites are DM5 in low season, DM6 in high season, plus DM5/6 per person and DM2/3 for children. Showers are an additional DM1. Tempting as it may be, camping wild is prohibited.

There are two ways through which you can book private rooms on the island, both free: the Kurwaltung Insel Poel (☎ 203 47; fax 404 3), which also reserves rooms in hotels and pensions; or the privately run Ferienhausverwaltung und Zimmervermittlung Hanni Evers (☎ 209 94), Krabbenweg 5 in Kichdorf. Private rooms range from DM20 to DM40 per person per night with breakfast.

Hotels are more expensive. In Kichdorf there's the four-room *Pension Bernd Holst* (☎ 203 97), Möwenweg 3, with rooms for DM32 per person, and *Pension Seemöwe* (☎ 205 80), at DM60 to DM85 per person. In Gollwitz, the *Inselhotel Poel* (☎ 240), with its golf course, swimming pool and lots of amenities, has rooms from DM55 to DM85 per night.

There are restaurants at most of the hotels and pensions. Poel's restaurants sell mainly seafood and Mecklenburg specialities. In Niendorf, *Poeler Forellenhof* has sweeping views over Kichdorf harbour.

Getting There & Away

Bus & Train From Wismar's Hauptbahnhof, take the hourly bus No 460 (30 minutes) directly to the island; one-way tickets are DM4.

Car & Motorcycle From Wismar, take Poelerstrasse due north and follow the yellow signs to 'Insel Poel', through the village of Gross Strömkendorf and over a little bridge to the island. This lovely drive takes about 20 minutes.

Boat As we went to press, the Wismar to Poel ferry service had been discontinued, but there's talk of service aboard the *Mecklenburg*, which will travel from Wismar's old harbour to Kichdorf. Check with Wismar-Information for the latest information.

Mecklenburger Seenplatte

The Mecklenburg Lake Plains is a band of wilderness spreading across the centre of the state. The area may well become one of the most popular outdoor and sport destinations for foreign visitors looking for peace, quiet and reasonably pristine wilderness.

The plains are crisscrossed by roads and highways that make getting around very easy. The roads (many of them canopied by trees planted by medieval fish merchants to shield wagons from the heat of the summer sun) meander through charming little villages and hamlets – many of them untouched by changes in government either after WWII or the *Wende*. In some places, like Penzlin, it's as if you've stepped back in time.

But in others, like Schwerin and Neubrandenburg, you'll have a chance to see eastern Germany in a state of flux that will be gone in just a few years' time. Get here fast; it's one of the country's most rewarding destinations.

SCHWERIN

- *pop 115,000*
- *area code* ☎ 0385

Schwerin, the state capital and oldest city (established 1160) in Mecklenburg-Western Pomerania, is one of the most picturesque towns in eastern Germany. It has so many lakes that locals and officials can't even agree on the number. Whatever the number, the city's charm is certainly infectious.

The town gets its name from a Slavic castle known as Zaurin ('animal pasture') on the site of the present Schloss. This former seat of the Grand Duchy of Mecklenburg is an interesting mix of 16th, 17th and 19th-century architecture. The centre is small enough to explore on foot, but if you can spare the time, two to three days is best to really explore the city and its environs.

Orientation

The centre of Schwerin is the Altstadt, the heart of which is a 10-minute walk south from the Hauptbahnhof along Wismarsche Strasse. Just east of the Hauptbahnhof is the almost rectangular Pfaffenteich, a man-made pond marked (or marred, depending on your sense of humour) on its south-west corner by the wacky Arsenal building, a blend of

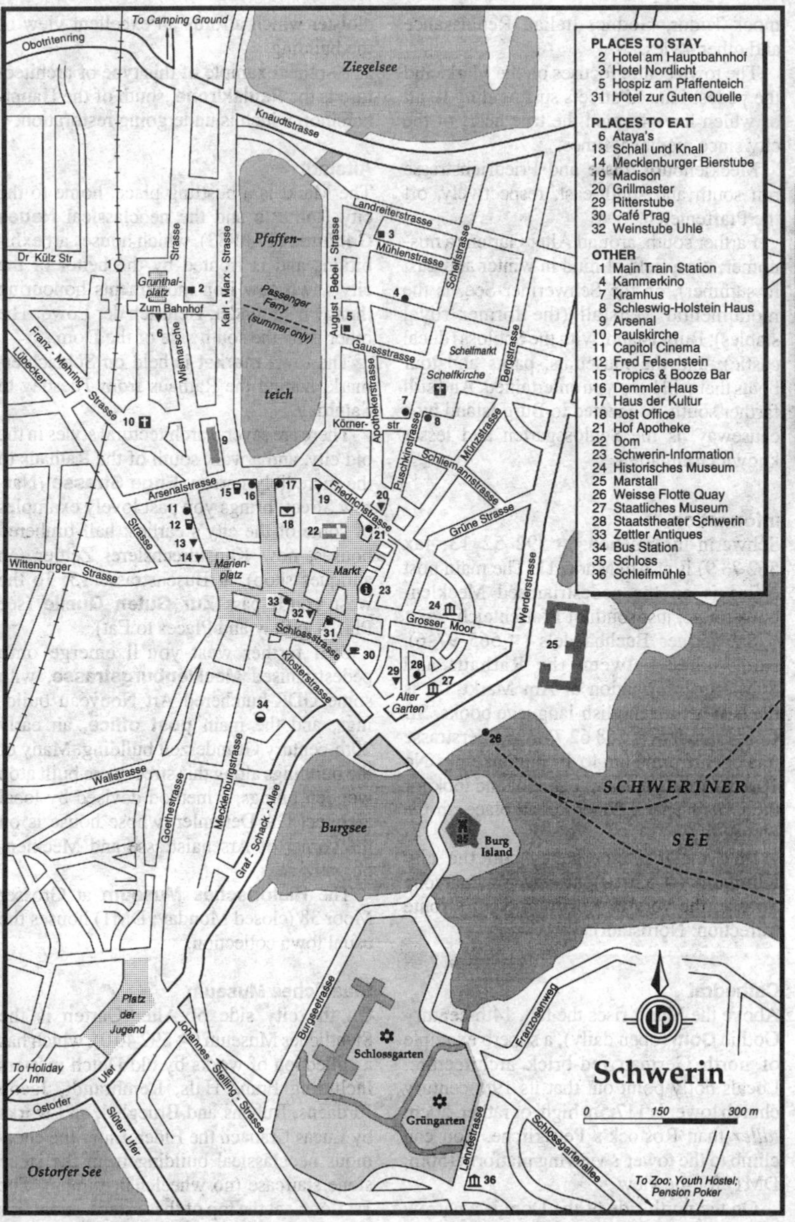
PLACES TO STAY
2 Hotel am Hauptbahnhof
3 Hotel Nordlicht
5 Hospiz am Pfaffenteich
31 Hotel zur Guten Quelle
PLACES TO EAT
6 Ataya's
13 Schall und Knall
14 Mecklenburger Bierstube
19 Madison
20 Grillmaster
29 Ritterstube
30 Café Prag
32 Weinstube Uhle
OTHER
1 Main Train Station
4 Kammerkino
7 Kramhus
8 Schleswig-Holstein Haus
9 Arsenal
10 Paulskirche
11 Capitol Cinema
12 Fred Felsenstein
15 Tropics & Booze Bar
16 Demmler Haus
17 Haus der Kultur
18 Post Office
21 Hof Apotheke
22 Dom
23 Schwerin-Information
24 Historisches Museum
25 Marstall
26 Weisse Flotte Quay
27 Staatliches Museum
28 Staatstheater Schwerin
33 Zettler Antiques
34 Bus Station
35 Schloss
36 Schleifmühle
To Camping Ground
Obotritenring
Ziegelsee
Knaudtstrasse
Pfaffen-
teich
Passenger Ferry (summer only)
Landreiterstrasse
Mühlenstrasse
Schelfstrasse
August - Bebel - Strasse
Karl - Marx - Strasse
Wismarsche Strasse
Dr Külz Str
Grunthal-platz
Zum Bahnhof
Franz - Mehring - Strasse
Lübecker
Gaussstrasse
Schelfmarkt
Schelfkirche
Bergstrasse
Apothekerstrasse
Körner- str
Puschkinstrasse
Münzstrasse
Schliemannstrasse
Friedrichstrasse
Arsenalstrasse
Grüne Strasse
Werderstrasse
Wittenburger Strasse
Marien-platz
Markt
Grosser Moor
Schlossstrasse
Klosterstrasse
Alter Garten
Wallstrasse
Goethestrasse
Mecklenburgstrasse
Graf - Schack - Allee
Burgsee
Burg Island
SCHWERINER SEE
Platz der Jugend
To Holiday Inn
Ostorfer Ufer
Johannes - Stelling - Strasse
Slüter Ufer
Burgseestrasse
Schlossgarten
Grüngarten
Lennéstrasse
Franzosenweg
Schlossgartenallee
Ostorfer See
Schwerin
0 150 300 m
To Zoo; Youth Hostel; Pension Poker
MECKLENBURG

mock-Tudor, Gothic, Italian Renaissance and other styles.

The town centre focuses on the Markt and the pedestrianised streets surrounding it, all of which have formed the true heart of the city since medieval times.

Mecklenburgstrasse and Friedrichstrasse run south and south-east, respectively, off the Pfaffenteich.

Farther south, around Alter Garten (a misnomer; it's a field of mud in winter and dust in summer), on the Schweriner See, is the monumental Marstall (the former royal stables); Burg Island, with the Schloss (ducal castle); and the museums, parks and tour boats that will keep you entertained. And still farther south, connected to Burg Island by a causeway, is the Schlossgarten and lesser known Grüngarten.

Information

Schwerin-Information (☎ 592 52 13; fax 562 73 9) is at Am Markt 11. The main post office is on the pedestrianised Mecklenburgstrasse, just south of Pfaffenteich.

Schweriner Buchhandels (☎ 565 97 6), sandwiched between the Rathaus and Schwerin-Information at Am Markt 13, is the best bet for English-language books. SB Coin Laundry (☎ 568 62 7) at Werderstrasse 6 is open from 6 am to 10 pm; take bus No 10 or 11 from the Hauptbahnhof and look for the Orient Snack doner kebab place on the corner.

In a medical emergency call the city Klinikum (☎ 520 0) at 397 Wismarsche Strasse, the very end of tram No 1's route (direction: Nordstadt).

Cathedral

Above the Markt rises the tall, 14th-century Gothic **Dom** (open daily), a superb example of north German red-brick architecture. Locals hotly point out that its 19th-century church tower is 117.5m high, or rather, 50cm *taller* than Rostock's Petrikirche. You can climb to the tower's viewing platform (50m; DM1) for the view.

On the north side of the Dom is a narrow cloister which affords an excellent view of the building.

Another example of this type of architecture is the **Paulskirche**, south of the Hauptbahnhof, which is undergoing restoration.

Altstadt

The Markt is a bustling place, home to the city **Rathaus** and the neoclassical **Neues Gebäude** (1780-83), which houses art exhibitions and is fronted by the better of the city's two new lion monuments honouring the town's founder, Heinrich der Löwe. The other is on the south side of the Dom.

The town **market** is held on Schlachtermarkt behind the Rathaus from Tuesday to Saturday.

There are several architectural styles in the old city, and a walk south of the Rathaus to the incredibly narrow **Enge Strasse** (Narrow Street) brings you past lovely examples of some of the city's earliest half-timbered houses, now Kunstdrechslerei Zettler (an antiques shop), at Buschstrasse 15. To the west you'll pass **Zur Guten Quelle** (see Places to Stay and Places to Eat).

Still farther west you'll emerge onto pedestrianised **Mecklenburgstrasse**, with some GDR-butchered Art Nouveau buildings, and the main **post office**, an early 20th-century Gründerzeit building. Many of the buildings along this street were built atop wooden pilings, a method devised by local architect GA Demmler, whose house is on the corner of Arsenalstrasse and Mecklenburgstrasse.

The **Historisches Museum** at Grosser Moor 38 (closed Monday; DM1) houses the usual town collection.

Staatliches Museum

On the city side of Alter Garten is the Staatliches Museum (☎ 592 40 0), which has a collection of works by old Dutch masters including Frans Hals, Rembrandt, Jacob Jordaens, Rubens and Brueghel, and works by Lucas Cranach the Elder. Enter the enormous neoclassical building from the steep stone staircase (no wheelchair ramps). The 1st floor – at the top of these steps – contains the permanent Dutch collection; an exhibit of every school of Dutch painting from the 17th to the 18th centuries, including the museum's favourite, Frans Hals' *Bust of a Laughing Boy with A Flute*.

The ground floor has rotating exhibitions of modern works, and a hip café which sometimes hosts concerts in its night-time incarnation as a bar (see Entertainment).

The museum is open Tuesday from 10 am to 8 pm, and Wednesday to Sunday from 10 am to 5 pm. Tours in German are given on Wednesday and Saturday at 3 pm, Sunday at 11 am and 3 pm. Admission is DM7 (discount DM4).

Schelfstadt

Up Puschkinstrasse north of the Markt is Schelfstadt, a planned baroque village that was autonomous until the expansion of Schwerin in the mid-19th century. Today it is home to the spectacularly restored Schleswig-Holstein Haus (1737, with additions throughout the 19th century). The house, which was allowed to fall into an equally spectacular state of disrepair under the GDR, contains a gallery (☎ 555 52 4/70) which houses temporary exhibitions. Admission is DM6/4.

Just across the street at Puschkinstrasse 15 is the **Kramhus**, another restoration and home to a private art gallery and a wonderful little café, the Mäkelborger Kramhus (see Places to Eat). Just north of here is the baroque **Schelfkirche** (also known as St-Nikolai-Kirche; 1708-1713), and **Schelfmarkt**, the former town market.

Schloss

South-east of Alter Garten over the causeway and on Burg Island is Schwerin's neo-Gothic **Schloss** (closed Monday), which is in turn connected to the **Schlossgarten** by another causeway. The castle, built around the chapel of a 16th-century ducal castle, is guarded by a foreboding equestrian **statue of Herzog Niklot**, a Frenchman defeated by Heinrich der Löwe. Admission to the superb interior costs DM6/3.

Schloss & Grün Gardens In summer, the gardens' walkways, along with its **Kreuzsee** lake, are lined with flowers, lovely against the accompanying reproductions of Greek statues. **Grüngarten**, on the east side of the canal separating it from the Schlossgarten proper, is a very peaceful place indeed. For a serene workout (a pleasant walk along smooth paths for 5km or so), pick up the Franzosenweg at the Grüngarten's north-east end and follow this lovely promenade all the way down to Zippendorf (see the Zippendorf section below) – but only if you're up to it!

Schleifmühle

South-east of the Schlossgarten is the historic Schleifmühle, a museum in a restored 19th-century mill (DM3/1.50).

Zoo

Continue south-east from the Schlossgarten on Schlossgartenallee, which leads to the surprisingly interesting zoo (☎ 208 03 0), home to a great variety of denizens, including pheasants and ostriches, great reptiles such as anacondas and boa constrictors, rare bison, polar bears and big cats. The zoo is open May to September Monday to Friday from 9 am to 5 pm; from October to April it closes an hour earlier; weekend hours are from 9 am to 6 pm year round. Admission is DM5/2. It is about 3km south-east of Alter Garten (bus No 15 from the bus station to the terminus). Note that the terminus, on a little loop, is very close to the hostel.

Zippendorf

In summer you can catch ferries from the piers off the Alter Garten to Zippendorf, a nice beach area with white sand and lots of kids. The area is pleasant to walk through, and the zoo is nearby. This is also a smart way to get from the centre to the hostel.

Activities

From May to September, excursion boats operate every 30 minutes on the Schweriner See from the Weisse Flotte (☎ 581 15 96) quay between the castle and the Marstall. Cruises lasting one hour/90 minutes/two hours cost DM12.50/15/18. There are three cruises daily in March and April, but none in winter. Ask about booze cruises and twilight cruises in the high season.

In summer you can rent a boat at Ruderboote am Burgsee, at the piers off the Alter Garten.

Organised Tours

There are walking tours (in German) of the city every day of the year. Leaving at 11 am from Schwerin-Information, the 1½-hour tours cost DM6 (discount DM3).

Two-hour tours in English for up to 30 people cost DM115; reserve one or two days in advance.

Places to Stay

Camping *Campingplatz Seehof* (☎ 512 54 0), 10km north of Schwerin on the western shore of Schweriner See, is easily accessible on bus No 8 from the bus station. There aren't any bungalows, and in summer it's crowded, but the snack bar stays open to 9 pm.

Hostel *Jugendherberge Schwerin* (☎ 213 00 5) is on Waldschulenweg, just opposite the entrance to the zoo, about 4km south of the city centre (bus No 15 from the bus station or Platz der Jugend). Dorm-only accommodation (93 beds) costs DM17.50 for juniors, DM21 for seniors.

Private Rooms Inexpensive hotel beds are rare so private rooms (from DM35/65 singles/doubles) are a good option; book them at the Zimmervermittlung (☎ 592 52 12; fax 555 09 4).

Hotels Among the more reasonably priced hotels is the charming and central *Hotel zur Guten Quelle* (☎ 565 98 5), Schusterstrasse 12, where singles/doubles are DM98/140. The hotel has an excellent restaurant (see Places to Eat).

In the same historic vein, *Hotel Nordlicht* (☎ 558 15 0) on Apothekerstrasse 2 offers singles/doubles for DM97/145. Another option is *Pension Poker* (☎ 550 71 60), Am Tannenhof, with rooms for DM80/100. At *Hotel am Hauptbahnhof* (☎ 565 702), opposite the station, you will pay about DM75/150, and at *Hospiz am Pfaffenteich* (☎ 565 60 6), Gaussstrasse 19, near the small ferry landing on the Pfaffenteich, rooms are DM80/140.

At the top end of the accommodation spectrum, the *Holiday Inn Crowne Plaza* (☎ 575 50; fax 575 57 77) is arguably the best modern hotel in Mecklenburg-Western Pomerania. Service is excellent, beds comfortable, and rooms range from DM190 to DM220 away from the lake, DM205 to DM235 on the lake, plus DM19 for the breakfast buffet.

Places to Eat

Restaurants & Cafés We loved the atmosphere in *Mäkelborger Kramhus* (☎ 581 31 05), a bistro-café packed with 19th-century wood furnishings at Puschkinstrasse 15, across the street from Schleswig-Holstein Haus. Lunch specials are under DM10 (the fried potatoes are out of this world) and service is very friendly.

If you don't mind dropping DM10 on coffee and cake, *Café Prag*, Schlossstrasse 17, has a chi-chi atmosphere and is a great place for excellent pastries or a small meal (closes at 6 pm).

At the restaurant in *Zur Guten Quelle*, where the service is great and the atmosphere pleasant, we had a great pepper steak for DM12.

An eclectic clientele congregates at *Schall und Knall* (☎ 563 01 6), a brewery and restaurant at Wismarsche Strasse 128, where lunch specials (served until 5 pm) start at DM7 and include a glass of beer. There's a small snack menu. Soups, salads and burgers are a great deal at the really fun *Madison* (☎ 555 31 5), Friedrichstrasse 1 on the corner of August-Bebel-Strasse.

The moderately expensive *Ritterstube*, Ritterstrasse 3 in the old town, serves a good selection of regional and German dishes (closed Monday).

What an atmosphere at the *Weinstube Uhle* (☎ 193 0) opposite Zur Guten Quelle!

It has vaulted portrait ceilings in the downstairs restaurant and a lovely Weinstube upstairs. Fine food too.

Snacks & Fast Food *Orient Snack* (☎ 568 46 3) at Werderstrasse 6, open to midnight daily, is a good Turkish place with cheap pizza, salads, doner and lots of other meaty stuff. Service is friendly. The *Mecklenburger Bierstube*, Wismarsche Strasse 104, serves barbecued half and quarter-chickens till midnight. The *Grillmaster* snack bar on the corner of Puschkinstrasse and Friedrichstrasse has daily lunch specials such as cutlets & chips for under DM10.

The *Stadt Kantine* in the Rathaus, Puschkinstrasse 44, opens its doors to the public at lunchtime (11 am to 2 pm). A heaped plate of whatever's being served is just DM6.50.

Good and reasonably priced (DM6 to DM9) pizza comes from *Ataya's* (☎ 557 47 81), Zum Bahnhof 10. Delivered pizzas cost from DM6 to DM15 for one person, up to DM21.80 for two people.

Entertainment

Listings *Piste* is a free culture and listings publication. It, along with *Schwerin Magazin*, is available at bars, restaurants and the tourist information office.

Cinema *Kammerkino* (☎ 555 07 8), Röntgenstrasse 22, is an arty foreign-movie house in a baroque building at one block west of Schelfmarkt.

Clubs Cover charges in town range from DM5 to DM10. Large pop and rock concerts are held at the *Sport- und Kongresshalle* (☎ 761 90 0), 2km west of the centre along Wittenburger Strasse; take bus No 5, 10 or 11 from the Hauptbahnhof. Farther west, on Neumullerstrasse, *8-Eck* (☎ 760 86 0) draws a very young crowd with house, techno and rave.

Tropics (☎ 562 15 4), Arsenalstrasse 16, is a hot new place in the centre that is packed with ever so fabulous types. Attached to it is the stylish *Booze Bar*, which we list here merely for its name.

Sternschnuppe, at the back of the Holiday Inn Crowne Plaza, plays a range of music including soul and blues.

Theatre & Classical Music The *Staatstheater Schwerin* (☎ 530 00), across the Alter Garten from the Staatliches Museum, hosts an impressive range of concerts and theatrical performances; check with Schwerin-Information or in *Schwerin Magazin* to see what's on. There is theatre, comedy, music and cabaret at *Freies Theater Studio Im Tik* (☎ 562 40 1) in the Haus der Kultur, Mecklenburgstrasse 2, on the corner of Arsenalstrasse.

In summer, evening concerts are held in the courtyard behind the Kammerkino (see Cinema).

Rock & Jazz *Schall und Knall*, Wismarsche Strasse 128, has good beer and gets pretty crowded. It's especially popular on Friday and Saturday, when they have live local bands. Next door is *Fred Felsenstein*, whose wacky, grotto-like interior was inspired by the Fred Flintstone cartoon character.

There's live music on weekends at the *Nacht Bar* in the Staatliches Museum, and also at *Phillies* (☎ 713 10 1), which does jazz and oldies on weekends. It's at Wittenburger Strasse 51, west of the centre.

Getting There & Away

Bus Regional buses depart for Wismar and Lübeck from Grunthalplatz outside the Hauptbahnhof; tickets are available from the driver.

Train Trains arrive regularly from Rostock (DM19, one hour), Magdeburg (DM45, two hours) and Stralsund (DM37, 2¼ hours). Direct trains to/from Wismar (DM8.50, 30 minutes) leave frequently throughout the day. Trains from Hamburg, Lübeck and Berlin-Lichtenberg travel via Bad Kleinen. You can buy train tickets and get train information at Atlas Reisewelt, Grosser Moor 9, as well as at the station.

Car & Motorcycle From Rostock, head south-west on the B105 (E22), then follow the signs in Wismar.

There's perpetual construction on this road and it's busy as well, so count on a total travel time of about 1½ hours.

Getting Around

The city's buses and trams cost DM2; *Mehrfahrtenkarten* cost DM1.70 each in blocks of at least five, and *Tageskarten*, good for 24 hours from the first use, are DM6.

In summer a ferry plies the Pfaffenteich from east to west.

AROUND SCHWERIN

Lewitz

The Lewitz is a series of canals about halfway between Schwerin and Ludwigslust. *Lewitzboot* (☎ 03861-740 5), a kayak and canoe rental company, arranges independent or guided tours (kayaks DM35 a day, DM210 a week, canoes DM40/255), including overnight stays throughout the region. The office is in the town of Banzkow; take bus No 119 (four a day, DM6, 30 minutes) from Schwerin's Hauptbahnhof to Banzkow.

GÜSTROW

Some 50km south of Rostock and 75km from Schwerin is the charming city of Güstrow. The city's Renaissance Schloss, a ducal residence of Herzog Ulrich III and once the home of sculptor Ernst Barlach (1870-1938), still towers above the city. It's definitely worth a day trip to view the impressive castle and the Barlach museums.

Orientation & Information

The city's Markt is at the centre of the Altstadt; the Schloss Museum is south-east, the Dom south-west, and the Barlach Museum north-west of the Altstadt.

The helpful Gustrow tourist office (☎ 03843-681 02 3; fax 682 07 9; email guestrow@twfg.de) is at Domstrasse 9. It's open Monday to Friday from 9 am to 6 pm, and Saturday from 9.30 am to 1 pm. From May to September it's open on Sunday as well.

Things to See & Do

There has been a castle of some sort at Franz-Parr-Platz since 1556, but the **Schloss** (☎ 752 0) on the site today was completed in 1599.

Today it's a museum (open Tuesday to Sunday in summer from 10 am to 6 pm, in winter from 9 am to 5 pm; DM5, discount DM2) with art exhibitions, a cultural centre and occasional concerts.

The city's Gothic **Dom** (☎ 682 07 7), begun as early as 1225, was completed in the 1860s. It contains Ernst Barlach's *Hovering Angel*.

On the **Markt**, the Renaissance **Rathaus** competes with the **Pfarrkirche** for prominence.

There are two museums in the city dedicated to sculptor, dramatist and graphic artist Ernst Barlach.

Barlach's expressionist work in bronze and wood carvings reflects the influence of his time spent in Russia – chunky forms borrowing from Russian peasant and medieval styles. He was born and worked here, and died just as Nazi bans of his work were reaching their peak. His **studio** (Artelierhaus; ☎ 822 99) is 4km south of the city at Inselsee (an hour's walk or 15 minutes on bus No 4) and is open March to October, Tuesday to Sunday from 10 am to 5 pm, in winter from 11 am to 4 pm; admission DM3, discount DM2. In town, the **Gertrudenkapelle** (☎ 683 00 1) is open the same hours.

Getting There & Around

Buses (DM14.50 return, 1¼ hours) leave for Rostock's bus station at 5.15 am and 12.15 and 4.20 pm, returning at 6.40 am and 2 and 5.40 pm.

Trains leave once or twice an hour from Rostock's Hauptbahnhof (DM8.40, 30 minutes) and hourly from Schwerin (DM16.50, one hour).

You can rent bikes for DM12.50 a day from Zweiradhaus Dräger, at both Lange Strasse 49 and Plauer Strasse 71.

NEUBRANDENBURG

- *pop 79,000*
- *area code* ☎ 0395

At the eastern end of the Mecklenburger Seenplatte and the north-eastern end of the Tollensesee sits the charming city of Neubrandenburg. While the old city dates back to the 13th century (the 2.5km-long wall that encircles it dates to the 14th century), it's surrounded by modern urban sprawl.

Writer and satirist Fritz Reuter (1810-74) lived for two years in a house (now a café) at Stargarder Strasse 35.

Orientation

The Altstadt is a circular cluster in the very centre of the city; the satellite cities surrounding it are called Oststadt and Südstadt.

The Hauptbahnhof is at the northern end of the Altstadt, the bus station 100m west of it. The Altstadt's wall effectively creates the largest roundabout outside Britain; it's circled by Friedrich-Engels-Ring.

Inside the walls is a grid of north-south and east-west streets. The main shopping street is Turmstrasse, pedestrianised between Stargarder Strasse (the main north-south thoroughfare, which leads right to the Hauptbahnhof) and the eastern wall.

All the main sights and attractions are found within the walls.

Information

The tourist office (☎ 194 33; fax 582 22 67) is tucked away in the little alley to the left as you walk east past the Radisson SAS Hotel on the Markt, east of the corner of Treptowerstrasse and Stargarder Strasse. It's open Monday to Friday from 9 am to 6 pm, and Saturday and Sunday from 10 am to 2 pm. See Organised Tours for more information.

The ADAC has an office (☎ 422 65 24) at Demminer Strasse 10, close to the hostel.

Money Change money and use the ATM at the Deutsche Bank, on the south-west corner of Treptowerstrasse and Stargarder Strasse.

Post & Communications The main post office (☎ 558 40) is at Poststrasse 6, two blocks south of the Hauptbahnhof.

Library The foreign-language library (or Fremdsprachenbibliotek; ☎ 707 29 39) is in the Oststadt at Einsteinstrasse 4 (closed Monday).

Laundry There's a laundrette on the south side of Ziolkowskistrasse between Leibnizstrasse and Keplerstrasse. Take bus No 8 from the Hauptbahnhof to the Lindetal Centre stop on Juri-Gagarin-Strasse, north of Ikarusstrasse, and walk east on Ziolkowskistrasse.

Medical Services In an emergency, call the Klinikum Neubrandenburg at ☎ 775 0. For more minor complaints, there's a medical clinic (Ärztehaus; ☎ 544 26 34) behind (east of) the Marienkirche.

Altstadt

The best way to see the Altstadt is to walk around the interior wall and then cycle around the exterior pathways. The inside is more interesting visually; while the outside is also nice, the traffic on Friedrich-Engels-Ring is hellish and the dust atrocious in summer.

Enter from the north, walk straight south on Stargarder Strasse to the Stargarder Tor and work your way anti-clockwise along the inside wall, then concentrate on the centre. You can walk the whole Altstadt in three hours.

City Gates When the city was founded in 1248 by Herbord von Raven, a Mecklenburg knight granted the land by Brandenburg Margrave Johann I, the town progressed in the usual manner: defence system, church, town hall, pub. The security system was the enormous stone wall, breached by four main gates.

The **Friedländer Tor**, begun in 1300 and completed in 1450, was first. The **Treptower Tor**, at the western end of the Altstadt, is the largest, and contains what's billed as the **Regional History Museum** (☎ 582 65 57)

MECKLENBURG

but it's really more of an archaeological collection. It's open Tuesday to Friday from 9 am to 5.30 pm, Saturday and Sunday from 1 to 5.30 pm. Admission is DM2, discount DM1.

At the southern end of the city is the gaudy **Stargarder Tor**, and the simple brick **Neues Tor** fronts the east side of the Altstadt.

Churches Neubrandenburg's centrepiece was the once-enormous Gothic **Marienkirche** (1270), seriously damaged in WWII. Since then major portions have been rebuilt, notably the steeple, which crowns the church's 89.4m-high tower; there has, however, been heated debate about just how to restore the interior. It hasn't been a consecrated church since the early 1970s.

Renovations under the GDR were halted when the project ran short of money. Eventually, it was decided to make the place an enormous concert hall.

Inside is a small exhibit of photographs of the church at different stages of construction and information on archaeological digs after the GDR took over. You can get into the church by getting the key from the tourist office.

Every summer, concerts and outdoor events are held in the yard on the south side of the church.

Also worth mentioning is the late-Gothic **Johanniskirche** (begun 1260), with its adjacent **cloister**.

Wiekhäuser The city wall had 56 sentry posts built into its circumference. After the spread of firearms rendered such fortifications obsolete around the 16th century, the guard houses were converted into *Wiekhäuser*, homes for the poor, handicapped and elderly. Some 26 of these remain today; some – like Wiekhaus No 6 just east of the northern end of Stargarder Strasse – are in the original guardhouse form, while others – such as Wiekhaus No 45, now a pub – were rebuilt with white stucco and half-timber fronts.

Mill Outside the Treptower Gate stands the region's oldest flour mill (1287). Stand on the little bridge west of the mill and look to the south-west and you'll see a trail leading out to Tollensesee (see Around Neubrandenburg), an eight-minute walk away.

Fangelturm West of Johanniskirche is the Fangelturm, once the city dungeon. Ask for the key (free) to the padlock at the tourist office. Inside you can climb the 74 steps of the very steep and narrow staircase to the top, or just peer down through the grating to see the dungeon. At the top, kick the door to break the bird-crap seal and you will get a good view – invisible from the street – of a side of the Johanniskirche.

Grosse Wollweberstrasse The only row of houses to survive WWII line Grosse Wollweberstrasse, at the south-western section of the city. The must-see house on the street is the very blue one at **No 25**, owned by graphic artist Gerd Frick. When he's home he'll give visitors a tour for the asking.

House of Culture & Education The saving graces of the city's **Haus der Kultur und Bildung**, with its obnoxious 56m-high tower and bunker-like foundation, are the viewing platform on the roof (DM1), with great views of the region on clear days; Bar No 14 (see Entertainment); and the Turm Café on the 13th floor (see Places to Eat).

Neubrandenburg's last **statue of Karl Marx** is in the beer garden adjacent to the building's north side; kids now put ice cream cones (and sometimes condoms) in the statue's hand.

Activities

Cycling The tourist office publishes the very good *11 Radtouren rund am Neubrandenburg* (11 Bicycle Tours Around Neubrandenburg). For rental outlets, see Getting Around.

Hiking Several moderate and clearly marked routes are near the town. There are cheap overnight accommodation possibilities on routes south of the city, either camping at Gat Scheck on the western side of Tollensesee or in the hostel at Burg Stargard (see Around Neubrandenburg).

Trail maps (DM2), or a detailed free pamphlet called *Auf Wanderschaft durch das Neubrandenburger Tollensebecken*, are available at the hostel or tourist office.

Horse Riding & Children's Activities

There's horse riding at the very hip *Zentrum für Kinder-, Jugend- und Sozialarbeit* (☎ 769 59 0), in a converted mill at Hinterste Mülle 2. Various classes is fun stuff for kids – like arts and crafts – are available here, and there's a zoo where you can pat the animals. This is a great place to find out about other stuff as well, like organised nature hikes.

Organised Tours

The tourist office (☎ 194 33) offers guided tours of the Altstadt from May to August daily at 10 am. The tours take 1½ hours and cost DM3.50 (discount DM1.50). The office can also arrange tours at any time – just walk in and ask. A 1½-hour tour for up to 20 people costs DM70, two hours is DM80.

Places to Stay

Camping & Hostel You can camp at Gat Scheck, on the west side of Tollensesee; see Around Neubrandenburg for more information. The good, if hard to find, *Jugendherberg Neubrandenburg* (☎ 422 58 01) is on Ihlenfelder Strasse, 1.5km north-east of the Hauptbahnhof. From the station on weekdays, take bus No 7 and ask the driver for the Jugendherberg. On weekends, take bus No 9 to Deminer Strasse at Reitbahnweg and it's right there. If you're walking (20 to 30 minutes) or driving, cross the bridge (B96) just east of the Hauptbahnhof, turn right onto Torgelowerstrasse, then left onto Ihlenfelder Strasse; it's two very long streets from that point.

The hostel is a little ramshackle, but everything's clean and staff are cheerful. Excellent and enormous buffet breakfasts, and other meals, are served in the building across the compound, where there's also a pool table. Dorm beds are DM19/22 for juniors/seniors.

Private Rooms The tourist office books private rooms. Expect to pay DM50 to DM100 per night per couple – it's still cheaper than the hotels – without breakfast.

Hotels Little *Hotel Weinert* (☎ 581 23 0; fax 581 23 11), Ziegelbergstrasse 23, about three blocks west of the Altstadt, is a very modern, if uninspired, place with friendly service and clean rooms. Singles/doubles are DM98/130.

The *Hotel Borchert* (☎ 544 20 03; fax 544 20 04) is pricey but absolutely spotless, with lovely staff and comfortable singles/doubles for DM104/126 to DM120/135.

The *Radisson SAS Hotel* (☎ 558 60; fax 558 66 25) is typically Radisson SAS in every way: predictably business-style rooms are pricey at DM155 to DM195 (singles) and DM185 to DM225 (doubles). There's a cool bar and a restaurant downstairs.

Places to Eat

Cafés & Restaurants Cheap meals – main courses from DM6 to DM12 – in great surrounds can be had at *Boulevard Bistro* (☎ 582 64 69), Turmstrasse 8. There's no smoking between 11 am and 2 pm.

For a more, um, interesting atmosphere, pull up a stool at the *Police Department Canteen* (☎ unavailable – scared to ask), at the rear of the police station; the entrance is on the east side of Darrenstrasse, just north of Pontanusstrasse. It's open Monday to Friday from 11 am to 3 pm, and full meals are under DM9. There's a similar canteen – open the same hours but also early in the morning for breakfast – in the Rathaus, outside the Altstadt walls due east of Turmstrasse.

Several steps up from the police canteen is the very nice *Café im Reuterhaus*, Stargarder Strasse 35, serving light snacks and appetisers from DM5 to DM7, soups from DM4 to DM5 and main courses from DM12 to DM20. It's a nice place to sit and have coffee. If it's something stronger you're after, the *Bierstube im Reuterhaus* is the ticket, with beers from DM3 to DM5, and soups and snacks from DM4 to DM10. Next door (south), the *Furstenkeller* has all that and a little more.

The *Turm Café* (☎ 559 61 68), on the 13th floor of the House of Culture and Education, Markt 1, is a fun place for a drink and a snack.

The *Tor Café*, in the Friedländer Tor, has a very comfortable atmosphere and nice staff. Coffee & cake costs about DM6; full meals are DM9 to DM15. *Wiekhaus 45* (☎ 566 77 62), 4-Ringstrasse 45, is a lovely example of a renovated Wiekhaus, and a comfortable pub as well. They do a really good tomato cream soup for DM5, and have some specials for under DM10 but mains average DM13 to DM20.

The *Vier Tore Restaurant* (☎ 558 60), at the Radisson SAS Hotel, has an international menu with main courses averaging DM20 to DM35, and theme nights.

Snacks & Fast Food For quick snacks, head for the pedestrian mall along Turmstrasse, where the Kaufhof department store has let out its street-level windows to several purveyors of tasty treats. On the corner of Turmstrasse and Stargarder Strasse, in the entry to the shop itself, is a Bratwurst stand, selling decent sausages with bread and mustard for under DM3. Just east is the excellent *Grillstation*, selling roasted chickens; small ones cost DM3.50, larger ones DM6.50. And still farther east is *Die Brezelbäckerei*, which does pizza pretzel for DM3.50, plain pretzels for DM0.80.

Entertainment

Listings *Belvedere* , a free monthly covering the entire Mecklenburg Lake Plains area, has a cultural calendar and club and pub listings. It's available at clubs, pubs and restaurants around the area.

Cinema *Latücht – Das Kulturlicht* (☎ 581 36 0), in the old church at Krauthöferstrasse 16, due east of the Friedländer Tor, is home to *Latücht Kommunales Kino*, which screens alternative films from around the world.

Discos & Clubs Mix it up at the *Alter Schlachthof*, a disco in a former abattoir at Rostocker Strasse 33. It gets a great mixed crowd – from 18 to 80. Several dance floors, a couple of restaurants and a pizzeria attract the multi-generation crowd, and it's fun.

Disco Colosseum (☎ 778 21 05), An der Hochstrasse 4, gets a young teenage crowd, while the thirty-somethings go for *Joy* (☎ 422 63 30) at Demminer Strasse 49.

Theatre The city's *Kammertheater* (☎ 544 26 17/18; fax 582 61 79), Pfaffenstrasse 22 in the *Shauspiel Haus*, is host to a variety of generally alternative entertainment, including children's theatre, puppetry and shows by solo performers from around the world. Performances start at 10 am and 3 and 8.15 pm, closed Sunday.

Classical Music The *Neubrandenburger Philharmonie* (☎ 581 95 0) performs classical concerts and chamber music at Zigelbergstrasse 5a, just outside the south-east edge of the Neues Tor; and at the *Haus der Kultur* during its September to June concert season. There's also a programme for children, with concerts and classes; check with the Philharmonic for details.

Cultural Centre In addition to films, the *Latücht* (see Cinema) hosts a range of theatrical performances, concerts and festivals.

Rock & Jazz Big rock concerts are held at *Jahnsportforum Neubrandenburg* (☎ 559 51 00), a 5000-seat arena south of the Altstadt, west of Neustrelitzer Strasse; take bus No 2 from the train station to the Schwedenstrasse stop and walk west for about 10 minutes – you can't miss it.

There are two good bars for live music, mostly jazz, blues and rock: *Die Pauke* (☎ 421 34 10), on Heidenstrasse, and *Konsulat* (☎ 544 16 31), at Jahnstrasse 12.

Pubs & Bars *Bar No 14* (☎ 582 36 20), open from 6 pm, is on the 14th floor of Haus der Kultur. Turn right as you get out of the lift. It's pricey but the view is worth it for one or two drinks. *Up To Date* (☎ 422 62 60),

Pasewalker Strasse 4, and *Destille* (☎ 582 54 85), Fritz-Reuter-Strasse 1a, are both more mellow drinking and talking spots, with lots of graphics and pictures on the walls.

Getting There & Away

Train From Berlin's Hauptbahnhof, trains leave every two hours (DM35, one hour). There's an hourly service to/from Rostock (DM28, two hours) and Stralsund (DM19, 1¼ hours).

Car From Berlin take the A10 north-west (direction: Hamburg) to Neuruppin. At Neuruppin, head east towards Löwenberg, where you catch the B96 and head north; follow the signs for Stralsund. From Stralsund or Greifswald, head south on the B96. From Rostock, take the A19 south to Güstrow and follow the B104 east all the way.

Getting Around

Single-trip tickets from city buses cost DM2 on board, DM1.30 at the bus station. Eight rides will cost DM10.

Bike-rental outlets include Fahrradhaus Leffin (☎ 58 16 60), at Friedrich-Engels-Ring 23; Kolping-Initiative Sozialwerkstatt (mobile ☎ 0171-217 47 16), at the Youth Centre, Lindenstrasse 12; and Thomas Behn (see Tollensesee in the Around Neubrandenburg section). Generally, bike rental costs DM8 to DM10 per day.

AROUND NEUBRANDENBURG

South and west of the city lies a wonderful region of wilderness (and oddities, including a witch museum) that's great for day trips, hikes or bike trips. Though most people stay in Neubrandenburg, there's camping in Müritz National Park, a great hostel in Burg Stargard, a castle hotel at Prillwitz and small guesthouses here and there.

Tollensesee

In summer, people flock to Tollensesee, a lake south-west of Neubrandenburg, for swimming, boating, camping and sunbathing.

The best swimming places are both free and fun: **Strandbad Broda** at the north-west tip of the lake and **Augustabad** on the north-eastern side. Both have lifeguards and organised play and swim areas for kids. You can rent paddle, rowing, electric and motor boats from **Thomas Behn** (☎ 0395-566 51 22; mobile ☎ 0171-217 47 16) at the northern end of the lake. Rentals range from DM7 to DM15 per hour.

Just south-east around the bend from Behn's place are the departure points for two touring ships: the *De Lütt* does one to two-hour tours for DM4 to DM15, and *Mudder Schulten* (☎ 368 21 95) tootles round the lake in summer from 10 am to noon, 1 to 2.30 and 3 to 5 pm. Tickets for 1½/two-hour tours cost DM7/9.

Place to Stay *Camping Gat Scheck am Tollensesee* (☎ 566 51 52), on the western side of the lake, is a simple place with basic facilities. Camping sites cost DM15 per couple.

Penzlin

The main attractions at Penzlin, about 15km south-west of Neubrandenburg, are its generally weird atmosphere and witch museum. Penzlin is so drab it feels as if you've just walked into a B&W WWII movie.

The **Alte Burg Hexenkeller** (☎ 03962-210 49 4), with displays on the Penzliner witches of the late 17th century, is worth a look. The museum is in the old city **Burg**, a massive castle up a hill from the town's main **Markt**. A nice beer garden opens in summer, on Thursday and Friday from 5 to 10 pm, and on Saturday and Sunday from 11 am to 10 pm. The museum has just undergone renovation so prices and hours weren't available at press time.

From the Markt, with its enormous **Marienkirche**, walk west to Alteburg Strasse and then north up the little hill to the Hexenkeller.

By car or motorcycle, take the B104 west out of Neubrandenburg and turn south on the B192, which leads right into the Markt. An excursion to Penzlin shouldn't take more than an hour if you go by car.

MECKLENBURG

Burg Stargard

About 12km south-east of Neubrandenburg is tiny Burg Stargard, in the middle of a lovely wilderness that's great for hiking and cycling. The town is a good base for trips into Müritz National Park.

Burg Stargard is about half recovered from GDR rule – half is shiny and the other half dilapidated: together they make an interesting contrast. Burg Stargard is used as a stopover on hikes or bike trips, or it can be a short day trip from Neubrandenburg to check out the old Burg and the town's tiny zoo.

Orientation & Information The Hauptbahnhof is at the western end of town. The main post office is diagonally opposite. Bahnhofstrasse, the main drag, leads east to the Markt and then off to the hostel. The hostel is just over 1km east of the station, and a great source for information on the whole area. The town's tourist office (☎ 039603-208 95), at Kurze Strasse 3, has lists of private rooms for rent in its window.

Things to See & Do Marked hiking and cycling **trails** lead out of town throughout the region; the hostel here or in Neubrandenburg can help plan your trip.

The **Klüschenberg Zoo** is a big drawcard for the town (open May to September from 8 am to 6 pm, October to April to 4 pm; DM4, discount DM2); it's across the pass along the east side of the pond.

The chunky brick ducal **Burg** at the top of the hill and visible throughout the town has incredibly frustrating opening hours. Inside, there's a **regional history museum**.

Places to Stay & Eat The *Jugendherberg Burg Stargard* (☎ 202 07) is at the eastern end of Hauptstrasse. Like its counterpart in Neubrandenburg – it's under the same management – it is clean and comfortable but looks more than a tad institutional. Dorm beds are DM19/22 for those under/over 26. The hostel prepares three meals daily; breakfast is included in the overnight rate, lunch and dinner are DM4 and DM6.50 respectively. There's an Aldi supermarket next door to the hostel. The *Bäckermeister*, Bahnhofstrasse 5, opposite the Soviet war memorial, is a discount bakery with loaves from DM1 and cake from DM0.50 a slice.

Burg Tenne, a new restaurant two doors down from the tourist office at Kurze Strasse 1, looked very promising; cheap lunches for DM5, soups from DM4 to DM6, main courses up to DM17; it's open Monday to Friday from 1 pm to midnight. *Pub Zurlinde*, Marktstrasse 9, has good soups (DM4.50 to DM6.50) but it's really more of a pub.

Getting There & Away There's an infrequent bus service (No 8) from the bus station at Neubrandenburg. Trains make the six-minute journey from Neubrandenburg (DM3) every two hours or so. By road, take the B96 south from Neubrandenburg and turn left, following signs for Gross Nemerow and Burg Stargard; this brings you right into the centre of town, about 3km past the turning.

Müritz National Park

• *area code* ☎ 03981

The two main sections of lovely Müritz National Park sprawl over 300 sq km to the east and (mainly) west of Neustrelitz. Declared a protected area in 1990, the park consists of bog and wetlands and is home to a wide range of waterfowl, mainly ospreys, white-tailed eagles and cranes. It has over 100 lakes, and countless other ponds, streams and rivers. The network of rivers and lakes is vast – dedicated boaters can make their way from here clear to Hamburg – and working with a good set of maps and information from rangers, you can make a great trip paddling and camping between Neustrelitz and Lake Müritz, at the park's western end.

The park's territory is divided into three categories: developed, active management and protected core areas. The most pristine areas are around the western end, east of Lake Müritz.

Orientation & Information The park's waterway begins on the Zierker See west of

Neustrelitz, and continues west through a series of rivers, streams and canals leading to Lake Müritz. The main information centre is the national park office (Nationalparkamt, An der Fasanerie 13, 17235 Neustrelitz; ☎ 458 90), south of Speck in the western half of the park, about 3km east of Lake Müritz. Tourist offices, hostels and camping grounds in Neubrandenburg, Neustrelitz and Burg Stargard also have trail and park maps.

Activities The national park office arranges regular tours and excursions throughout the park. Contact the office for information about ranger-led tours. Hiking is permitted on marked trails.

Havel Tourist (☎ 247 90; fax 247 99 9) rents one or two-person kayaks for DM7.50/45/190 per hour/day/week. It has offices at camping grounds throughout the park (see Places to Stay). Rowing boats (DM5/35/200) and sailing boats (from DM20/95/520) are available from Santana Yachting (☎ 205 89 6), at the eastern end of the Zierker See, which is west of Neustrelitz.

Places to Stay You must use designated camping grounds, of which there are over a dozen within the park. The biggest operator is *Havel Tourist* (☎ 247 90; fax 247 99 9), with camping grounds at Leppinsee-Schillersdorf, Rätzee Drozedow, Havelberge am Ziernsee Priepert, Grossen Pülitzsee Strasen, Grossen Labussee, Zwenzkow and Weissen See Wesenberg. Rates at all sites in high season (from 21 June to 30 August)/low season are DM7/5.50 per tent plus DM4/6 per person.

Neustrelitz

- *pop 20,000*
- *area code* ☎ 03981

Neustrelitz, 28km south of Neubrandenburg, is worth an afternoon's excursion. The city's tourist information office (☎ 253 119; fax 20 54 43) is at Markt 1, open May to September Monday to Friday from 9 am to noon and 1 to 5 pm, Saturday and Sunday from 10 am to 1.30 pm (shorter weekday hours and closed on the weekend in winter).

Private rooms are the best bet in Neustrelitz. They're available for a DM2 service fee at the tourist office; rooms average DM25 to DM30 per person without breakfast, DM35 to DM40 with.

Things to See & Do The first thing you'll notice in the enormous circular Markt is the klunky, square spire of the **City Church** (church 1768-78, spire 1831), dubbed the 'Butter Churn' by locals. You can climb the 174 steps to the viewing platform (DM1) atop this, well, interesting piece of ecclesiastic architecture to get a panoramic view of the town.

The **Rondteil** at the centre of the Markt was once home to two memorials. The first (1866) was a bronze statue of Duke Georg, who was instrumental in the development of the city. After WWII, it stood next to the inevitable Soviet war memorial for a short time, but proletarian concerns eventually removed the duke. The Soviet memorial was unceremoniously removed in 1995.

The duke's statue was rediscovered in the 1980s, and brought to its current resting place, between the **Schlossgarten** and the **Schlosskirche**, just south-west of the centre. The Schloss itself was destroyed, but you can still walk through the gardens and into the mid-19th century church.

Getting There & Away There's a hourly train from Neubrandenburg (DM8.50, 25 minutes). By road, follow the B96 south from Neubrandenburg and you'll head straight into the Markt.

Western Pomerania

STRALSUND

- *pop 64,000*
- *area code* ☎ 03831

Stralsund is an enjoyable city on the Baltic Sea, about 70km east of Rostock. The Altstadt, which is still undergoing heavy restoration, is almost surrounded by lakes and the sea – a position which once contributed significantly to the town's security and defence. In the Middle Ages, Stralsund was the second most powerful member, after Lübeck, of the Hanseatic League. The fair degree of prosperity enjoyed by its citizens is still evident in the graceful town hall, massive churches and elegant town houses.

After the decline of the league, Stralsund was absorbed into the Duchy of Pommern-Wolgast in 1612. In 1648, as a result of the Thirty Years' War, Stralsund – along with Rügen and Pomerania – came under the control of the Swedes, who had helped in their defence. It remained Swedish until it was incorporated into Prussia in 1815.

The town's importance grew a bit with the completion of the Rügendamm, the causeway to Rügen across the Strelasund channel, in 1936. Though it suffered a fair amount of damage in WWII, Stralsund became the third-largest port in the GDR.

Today, Stralsund is an attractive, historic town with fine museums and buildings, pleasant walks and a restful, uncluttered waterfront.

Orientation

The Altstadt is connected by causeways to the surrounding areas. The centre's main hubs are Alter Markt in the north and Neuer Markt in the south. A few blocks south of the latter is the central bus station. The train station is across the Tribseer Damm causeway, west of the Neuer Markt. The harbour is on the Altstadt's eastern side.

Information

The tourist office (☎ 246 90; fax 246 94 9) is at Alter Markt 9 next to the Rathaus. Between May and mid-October, opening hours are weekdays from 9 am to 7 pm, weekends to 2 pm. Winter hours are 10 am to 6 pm, closed on Sundays. Ask about the Touristenpass, which has six coupons that

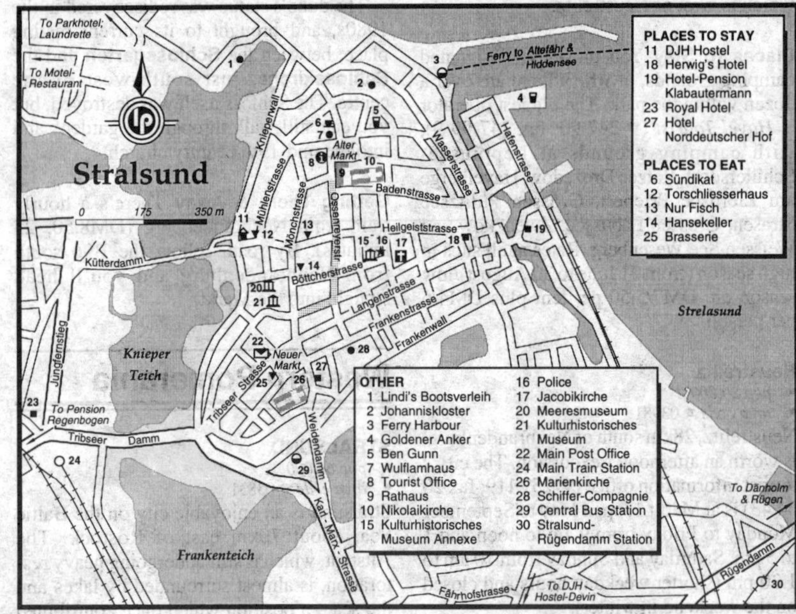

you can exchange for admission to a variety of attractions, including museums, harbour tours, theatre performances and organ concerts. It costs DM19, discount DM9 in summer (DM15/9 in winter).

The Sparkasse at Neuer Markt 7 and the Dresdner Bank at Tribseer Strasse 20 are among the banks that offer exchange services. The post office, at Neuer Markt 4, has a public fax-phone and photocopier.

The Weiland bookshop at Ossenreyerstrasse 14 has a small selection of English-language novels. There's a Schnell & Sauber laundrette in the modern shopping mall in the suburb of Knieper-West , about 3km north of the centre (bus No 4 to Hans-Fallada-Strasse). A police station is at the corner of Böttcherstrasse and Jacobistrasse.

Northern Altstadt

The heart of the northern Altstadt is Alter Markt, dominated by the Nikolaikirche and the splendid **Rathaus** with its late-Gothic decorative façade. Its upper portion consists of a row of slender copper turrets alternating with small gables that each sport a circular opening to prevent strong winds from blowing over the free-standing façade. This ornate design was Stralsund's answer to its rival city Lübeck, whose town hall has a similar exterior. Walking through a vaulted walkway gets you to the sky-lit atrium that links the two separate buildings of the Rathaus. It has a gallery held aloft by a row of shiny black pillars perched on carved and painted bases.

Exit through the eastern walkway to find yourself outside the main portal of the **Nikolaikirche** (1270), modelled after the Marienkirche in Lübeck, and filled with art treasures. Restoration of the medieval church's magnificent painted interior is ongoing, but it's open Tuesday to Saturday from 10 am to 4 pm, and Sunday from 11 am to 2 pm. The flamboyant **main altar** (1708), designed by the baroque master, Andreas Schlüter, shows the eye of God flanked by cherubs, capped with a depiction of the Last Supper. Also worth a closer look is the **high altar** (1470), 6.7m wide and 4.2m tall, showing Jesus' entire life cycle, from his childhood, in the predella, to the crucifixion. Some of the carved figures were damaged or destroyed during WWII. Behind the altar, in the ambulatory, is the **astronomical clock** (1394), allegedly the oldest in the world. It still has the original clockwork, but apparently it never worked very well. Also note the fine alabaster reliefs on the **pulpit** supported by a sculpture of Moses.

Opposite the Rathaus, at Alter Markt 5, you'll find the **Wulflamhaus**, a beautifully restored 15th-century town house that once belonged to a mayor called Wulflam. Its turreted step gable somewhat mirrors the Rathaus façade. Take a short stroll down Mühlenstrasse off Alter Markt where other historic houses are being restored.

On Schillstrasse, reached via Külperstrasse north off the Alter Markt, is the **Johanniskloster** (open mid-May to mid-October from 10 am to 6 pm, closed Monday; DM3, discount DM2), a former Franciscan monastery, founded in 1254. It's famous for its unusual smoking attic (there was no chimney), chapter hall and cloister. The ruins of the destroyed church are now a concert venue.

Southern Altstadt

The southern Altstadt is anchored by Neuer Markt and dominated by the massive 14th-century **Marienkirche**, another example of typical north German Gothic red-brick architecture. The church's main attraction is the huge organ (1659), built by F Stellwagen, festooned with music-making cherubs. You can climb (DM2) the 350 steps of the tower (and brave a daunting network of near vertical wooden ladders towards the end) for a sweeping view of Stralsund over to Rügen island.

The church is open daily from 10 am to 5 pm (in winter to 4 pm); it is not open to tourists during Sunday morning services.

North of Neuer Markt are two excellent museums. The highlight is the **Meeresmuseum**, an oceanic aquarium complex in a 13th-century convent church at Katharinenberg 14-17. There's a large natural history section and much information on the fishing industry here. Some aquariums in the basement contain tropical fish and coral, others display creatures of the Baltic and North seas. The museum is open daily from 10 am to 5 pm (closed Monday in winter). In July and August, opening hours are 9 am to 6 pm Monday to Thursday and to 5 pm Friday to Sunday. Admission is DM7.50, discount DM3.50.

The **Kulturhistorisches Museum** (Cultural History Museum) is nearby in the cloister of the former St Catherine convent at Mönchstrasse 25-27. It has a large collection on the history of Stralsund and the Pomerania region, including paintings by Caspar David Friedrich and Philipp Otto Runge, faïences (tin-glazed earthenware), playing cards and Gothic altars. The museum is open from 10 am to 5 pm, closed Monday; DM4, discount DM1.50. Part of the exhibit is housed in a historical warehouse at Böttcherstrasse 23. One ticket allows entry to both.

East of Neuer Markt, at Frankenstrasse 9, is the **Schiffer-Compagnie** (open weekdays from 9 to 11.30 am and 1 to 3.30 pm; DM3, discount DM1.50), a small museum run by a sailors' association displaying model ships and paintings.

Activities

Ferries to the scenic fishing village of Altefähr on Rügen's southern coast operate every 30 minutes in high season and cost DM3 each way; bikes are DM2. One-hour harbour cruises depart daily at 11 am and 2.30 pm (DM8). Buy your tickets from the kiosk on the quay. The ferry harbour is on the northeastern edge of the Altstadt.

To do some paddling of your own on the lakes encircling the Altstadt, you can rent boats at Lindi's Bootsverleih (☎ 383 04 5) daily between 9 am and 6 pm (DM4.50 per person per hour).

Between May and September, the **Hanse-Bahn**, a miniature motorised train, travels to the town's sights at irregular intervals. The 40-minute tour starts after 11 am (on Saturday after 1.30 pm). It does not run on Sunday. The trip costs DM7, discount DM5. Stops are at Neuer Markt, Alter Markt and the ferry terminal.

Places to Stay

Camping The nearest *camping ground* (☎ 038306-75483) is in the fishing village of Altefähr on the southern shore of Rügen Island. It's at Klingenberg 15 and open April to October. You can get there by bus No 413 or by taking the ferry (see Activities above).

Hostels Stralsund's 180-bed *DJH hostel* (☎ 292 16 0) is inside an actual 17th-century town gate at Am Kütertor 1 (bus No 4 or 5 to Kütertor or 15 minutes' walk from the train station). Bed & breakfast costs DM20/24 for juniors/seniors. A second *DJH hostel* (☎ 490 28 9) is at Strandstrasse 21, off the road to Greifswald in nearby Devin (20 minutes on bus No 3 from the train station).

Private Rooms & Hotels The tourist office handles reservations for private rooms (from DM30 per person) and hotels and may charge a DM5 fee (sometimes waived for foreigners). Prices below are for the main season (May to September). Some hotels charge around 10% less the rest of the year. True budget hotels are virtually nonexistent, but most places have been recently refurbished (rooms with private bath) and now offer a fairly high standard.

One of the cheapest options is *Pension Regenbogen* (☎ 497 67 4) at Richtenberger Chaussee 2a, about 2km from the centre. Singles/doubles cost DM70/90. Also outside the centre (about 15 minutes' walk) is *Motel-Restaurant* (☎ 390 13 5), An den Bleichen 45b, where rooms go for DM90/120. *Hotel-Pension Klabautermann* (☎ 293 62 8; fax 280 61 2), at Am Querkanal 2, near the port, has a view back to the city and charges DM80/140. Nearby at Heilgeiststrasse 50 is the small family-run *Herwig's Hotel* (☎ 293 95 4; fax 266 82 3), whose rooms cost DM120/150.

A more stylish mid-priced option is the Art Nouveau *Royal Hotel* (☎ 295 26 8; fax 292 65 0), at Tribseer Damm 4 near the train station, with rooms for DM125/155. Traditional, too, is *Hotel Norddeutscher Hof* (☎ & fax 293 16 1), centrally located at Neuer Markt 22, which charges DM120/160.

Top of the line is the business-class *Parkhotel* (☎ 474 0; fax 474 86 0), at Lindenallee 61, where large singles/doubles with all the amenities range from DM135/195 to DM155/215, though it's worth calling for special weekend rates. It's at the edge of town with good bus connections to the centre.

Places to Eat

Right next to the hostel is the cosy *Torschliesserhaus*, which sells steaks and fish, as well as snacks for under DM10. In an old guild house at Mönchstrasse 48, the *Hansekeller* serves hearty regional dishes at moderate prices (DM15 to DM20) in the earthy atmosphere of a vaulted brick cellar. *Nur Fisch*, near the corner of Mönchstrasse and Heilgeiststrasse, is a clean cafeteria-style restaurant with – as its name suggests – 'only fish' for DM10 or less (open to 6 pm, Saturday to 2 pm). For a more sophisticated meal, head to the *Brasserie*, a brass and wicker café-restaurant with a large bar on Neuer Markt. It has a moderately priced menu of salads, baguette sandwiches, steaks and fish.

Entertainment

Between May and September, organ recitals take place on Wednesday at 8 pm, alternating between the Marienkirche (DM8, discount DM5) and the Nikolaikirche (DM7, discount DM4).

For a throw-back to GDR days, give the *Goldener Anker*, at the far northern end of Hafenstrasse in the harbour, a try. This is a great pub if you don't mind tattered old furniture. It's heated by a tile stove and the music comes out of a juke box. Only the prices are post-Wende.

Another place popular with young people is the pub *Ben Gunn*, at Fährstrasse 27, and the nearby *Sündikat*, at Knieperstrasse 15.

Getting There & Away

Bus Buses travel to Bergen and Sassnitz on Rügen several times daily from the central bus station.

Train Regional trains make the trip to/from Rostock (DM17.60, one hour), Berlin-Lichtenberg (DM61, three hours) and Hamburg (DM66.80, 3½ hours) at least every two hours. There's less frequent service to Leipzig (DM104, 5½ hours). There are about 20 trains daily to Sassnitz (DM13.20, one hour) from Stralsund or Stralsund-Rügendamm, and at least 10 daily to/from Binz (DM13.20, 50 minutes), also on Rügen.

International trains between Berlin and Stockholm or Oslo use the car-ferry connecting Sassnitz Hafen on Rügen Island with Trelleborg and Malmö in Sweden. Some trains to/from Sassnitz Hafen don't stop at Stralsund's Hauptbahnhof but instead call at Stralsund-Rügendamm south-east of the city (some stop at both). Boarding for Sweden, use the cars labelled for Sassnitz Hafen and Malmö, as the train will split at Sassnitz Hauptbahnhof.

Car & Motorcycle If you're coming from the west – Lübeck, Wismar or Rostock – at all costs avoid travelling on the B105, a tortuously slow, jammed and dangerous country road. What rare open road you encounter will be cleverly speed-trapped. For an alternate route, leave Rostock on the B110 to Sanitz, then continue via Bad Sülze, Tribsees and Richtenberg to the B194 and head north. Coming from Greifswald or points east, you will come in on the B96.

Boat From late March to September, Reederei Hiddensee ferries (☎ 0180-321 21 50) depart up to three times daily from the ferry terminal for Hiddensee Island. Trips to Neuendorf cost DM13, return DM22; to Vitte and Kloster it's DM16/24. Bikes are an extra DM10. You can also buy tickets from the kiosk at the quay.

Getting Around

In Stralsund's Altstadt you'll only need your feet to get around. To get to the outlying areas, there's a fairly comprehensive bus system. You can also rent a bicycle from Fahrradgeschäft Bremer (☎ 396 63 5) at Lindenstrasse 26, on the corner of Vogelwiese, or at ALV (☎ 280 15 5) at Bahnhofstrasse 10.

GREIFSWALD

- *pop 64,000*
- *area code* ☎ 03834

The old university town of Greifswald, birthplace of the Romantic painter Caspar David Friedrich (1774-1840), lies about 35km east of Stralsund on the Ryck River. Greifswald went through a rather steep evolution from Cistercian monastery in 1199 to Hanseatic city only a century later. It's justly famous for its university, the second oldest (1436) in northern Europe after the one in Rostock.

Like Stralsund and the rest of Pomerania, the town became Swedish in 1648 and Prussian in 1815. It escaped WWII largely unscathed thanks to a courageous German colonel who surrendered to Soviet troops in the final days of the war, a move usually punished with summary execution. As a result, Greifswald has preserved its handsome Altstadt, which announces itself through its three distinctive church spires. It's a provincial but fairly lively place, due to its student population.

Orientation

Greifswald's Altstadt is in the north of town, right on the southern bank of the Ryck. It's partly encircled by a road, partly by railway tracks. On its south-western edge lies the train station, with the bus station across on the other side of Bahnhofstrasse. The mostly pedestrianised Lange Strasse bisects the Altstadt from east to west and is quickly reached via Karl-Marx-Platz, a short walk north of the train station.

Information

The tourist office (☎ 346 0; fax 378 8) is at Schuhhagen 22, a continuation of Lange Strasse, and is open weekdays from 9 am to 6 pm (in winter to 5 pm) and in summer also on Saturday from 9 am to noon. Guided walking tours in German are offered on Monday, Wednesday and Friday (DM9). To exchange money or travellers' cheques, you can go to the Commerzbank at Markt 7-8 or to the Sparkasse next door. Also here is the post office. The Weiland bookshop at Markt 5 has a small selection of English-language books.

Marienkirche

Locals teasingly call this red-brick church on Brüggstrasse 'Fat Mary' for its corpulent dimensions, compounded by a single square tower trimmed with incongruously dainty turrets. She's an elderly lady, too, born in the 12th century as a three-nave hall church. The rectangular interior is rather modest except for one jewel – the awesome Renaissance **pulpit** (1587), an intricate masterpiece for which Rostock carver Joachim Melekenborg used 60 types of wood. The church is open weekdays from 10 am to noon and 2 to 4 pm and on Sunday after services.

Markt & Around

The large size of the Markt and the many historical buildings that flank it hint at Greifswald's stature in the Middle Ages. The **Rathaus**, at the western end, had an earlier incarnation as a 15th-century department store with characteristic arcaded walkways. The red-brick gabled houses on the eastern side are worth a closer look too. Note especially the one at No 11, a good example of a combined living and storage house owned by Hanseatic merchants. The house next door (No 13) dates from 1450 and sports a high late-Gothic step gable.

Walk one block east on Mühlenstrasse which runs from the south-eastern corner of the Markt, to Thomas-Pyl-Strasse. At No 1-2 is the **Museum der Stadt Greifswald** housed in a former Franciscan monastery (open Wednesday to Sunday from 10 am to 6 pm, in July and August also on Monday and Tuesday; DM3, discount DM1.50). Displays focus on the history of the town and the university; the prized exhibit is a small collection of paintings and drawings by local boy Caspar David Friedrich.

Dom St Nikolai and University Area

West of the Markt, the spires of Greifswald's **Dom** rise above a row of historic façades. Nicknamed 'Long Nicholas' for its 100m-tall tower topped by an onion dome, it has a light-flooded, completely whitewashed interior whose austerity is accentuated by a large and solitary golden cross. The Greifswalder Bachwochen, a concert series, has been taking place in the Dom since 1946. The cathedral is open May to October from 10 am to 4 pm (Sunday only to 1 pm after the service). Its tower can be climbed (DM3, discount DM1.50) and, yes, there is a great view from the top.

Half-timbered, single-storey buildings in a sea of red brick make up the former **St Spiritus Hospital**, clustered around a small courtyard. It's an alternative cultural centre now, with a beer garden and a small stage for concerts in summer. For maximum visual effect, enter via the building at Rubenowplatz 12-14.

Rubenowplatz, to the west, is the heart of the university area. The **monument to Heinrich Rubenow** in the middle of the little park is dedicated to the university's founder. The university's main building flanks the square's south side. Only the former library, used as the assembly hall since 1881, is worth a closer look. A dozen pillars support a gallery, sumptuously decorated with vases and cherubs. On the walls are paintings by former professors.

On the western side of the square is the **Jacobikirche**, affectionately called 'Little Jacob' as it is the smallest of the town's churches.

Kloster Eldena & Wieck

Among the painter Friedrich's favourite motifs were the ruins of the Kloster Eldena, the very monastery that shepherded Greifswald into this world. There isn't much to see, but what's left – a few façades and walls – hints at the spacious dimensions of the complex. It's all in a lovely park with giant trees and is certainly a good place to come to relax or have a picnic. You'll often find art students with their sketch pads gathered here. Bus No 40 makes regular trips here from the central bus station.

A few minutes' walk north of the ruins leads you to the Ryck River and the equally peaceful fishing village of Wieck. Many of the reed-thatched cottages are listed buildings, but the main attraction is the late-19th century wooden drawbridge (it costs DM5 to cross it by car). Take bus No 60 from the bus station to get here.

Places to Stay

Greifswald does not have a hostel. Private rooms are the cheapest option at around DM30 per person (the tourist office can help you find accommodation).

Hotels are not too plentiful. The less expensive ones are in Wieck, including the small *Schipp In* (☎ 346 0) at Am Hafen 2, which has singles/doubles for DM60/80, breakfast not included. At the *Hotel Nordland* (☎ 872 21 5), Pappelallee 1, very basic rooms with shared facilities start at DM35/60; a bit more comfort can be had for DM75/110. Another option is *Zur Fähre* (☎ 840 04 9), Fährweg 2, which charges from DM70 for doubles.

At the upper end of the spectrum is the large *Hotel Am Gorzberg* (☎ 540 0), with singles/doubles for DM140/ 170.

Places to Eat

One of nicest places for dinner is the *Braugasthof*, in a step-gabled Gothic building at Markt 13. The food is hearty, the portions big, the service friendly, the atmosphere lively and the house brew smooth. A major winner is the Sunday all-you-can-eat brunch (DM13.50). The *Brasserie* at Lange Strasse 22 serves breakfast from 8 am and bistro fare for under DM12. Traditional German food is on the menu at *Gerberstube*, also on Lange Strasse. The historical *Zur Falle*, predominantly a pub, in the cavernous cellars at Schuhagen 1, is popular with students. There's a small menu with simple dishes. A number of nice fish restaurants, such as *Zur Brücke* and *Fischerhütte*, are on the harbour at Wieck.

Getting There & Away

Bus Greifswald is well connected by bus to other communities in Mecklenburg-Western Pomerania, though service is either restricted or suspended on weekends.

To get to Stralsund or Rostock, take bus No 300. Bus Nos 508, 514 and 518 all go to Wolgast. Bus No 300 makes runs to Neubrandenburg. The express bus from Rügen to Berlin also stops here.

Train There's regular train service from Rostock (DM25, 1½ hours), Stralsund (DM9, 20 minutes) and Berlin-Lichtenberg (DM53, 2½ hours).

Car & Motorcycle Greifswald is on the notorious B105 to/from Rostock. Another slow country road is the B96, which leads south to Berlin.

Getting Around

It's easy to get around Greifswald's centre on foot, but to reach the outlying sights, you may want to make use of the fairly comprehensive bus system. Single tickets cost DM2 and an eight-ticket block is DM13.

AROUND GREIFSWALD

Usedom Island

Usedom lies in the delta of the Oder River, about 30km east of Greifswald, and is separated from the Pomeranian mainland by the wide Peene River. The island's greatest asset is its 42km stretch of beautiful beach; sandy, festooned with dunes and facing the Baltic Sea. Tourism arrived relatively late in Usedom, and ironically its first resort – Swinemünde, founded in 1821 – is located in the far eastern section which now belongs to Poland. By the turn of the century Usedom was so popular – especially among Berliners – that it earned the nickname 'Badewanne Berlins' (Berlin's Bathtub). In GDR days, it was a much sought-after holiday spot as well. Since the Wende, Usedom has been somewhat overshadowed by neighbouring Rügen, but as the sprucing-up process continues, it is coming into its own. Elegant white villas with wrought-iron balconies from the 1920s grace many of the traditional resorts, including Zinnowitz and Koserow in the western half and Bansin, Heringsdorf and Ahlbeck further east.

Usedom's central tourist information office (☎ 038375-234 10; fax 234 29) is at Bäderstrasse 4 in Ückeritz, a resort between Koserow and Bansin.

The island's only *DJH hostel* (☎ 038378-223 25) is in Heringsdorf, just west of the border at Ahlbeck. It charges DM20 to DM22 for juniors and DM24 to DM27 for seniors.

Peenemünde Usedom's only attraction of historical importance is Peenemünde on the island's western tip. It was here that Wernher von Braun developed the V2 rocket, first launched in October 1942. It flew 90km high and over a distance of 200km before plunging into the Baltic. This marked the first time in history that a flying object had exited the earth's atmosphere. The research and testing complex was destroyed by the Allies in July 1944, but the Nazis continued their research in mine shafts in Nordhausen in the southern Harz region.

The **Historisch-Technisches Informations-Zentrum** (Historical and Technological Information Centre), located at Bahnhofstrasse 28, commemorates this era, immodestly billing Peenemünde as the 'birthplace of space travel'; Von Braun went on to lead the US space programme, which ultimately put astronauts on the moon in 1969. The museum is open April to October from 9 am to 6 pm, in winter to 4 pm, closed Monday. Admission is DM6, discount DM4.

Getting There & Away Wolgast is the gateway to Usedom. From Greifswald, take bus No 508, 514 or 518 here, then connect to island-bound buses leaving from the bus station at Wolgast-Hafen. Wolgast can also be reached by train from Stralsund and Greifswald and local trains continue the journey on to Peenemünde, Zinnowitz, Heringsdorf and the other resorts. Note that local trains leave from a second station located on the island itself (after the bridge, on the left), about a five-minute walk east of the station in Wolgast. If you're driving, you have to cross the Peene, either via the bridge in Wolgast or the one about 25km further south between Anklam and the town of Usedom.

Rügen Island

Rügen's tourist tradition reflects Germany's recent past and the people who shaped it or played a role in it. In the 19th century, such luminaries as Einstein, Bismarck and Thomas Mann came to unwind here in the fashionable coastal resorts. During the Third Reich, Hitler picked one of the island's most beautiful beaches on which to build a barbaric holiday resort to accommodate 20,000 of his loyal troops at any one time. In the days of the GDR, Rügen became the holiday choice for millions of comrades, not to mention the top apparatchik himself, Erich Honecker. Today, Rügen looks poised to become one of the most popular destinations, after the Wende, in the Baltic.

What is the appeal of Germany's largest island? An incomparable, somewhat untamed, landscape for one, with its gleaming white-chalk cliffs spilling into a deep green sea, thick beech forests with fragrant displays of wildflowers and mushrooms, roads shaded by leafy canopies, long white sandy beaches. Then there's an old-time narrow-gauge steam train, a hunting castle of fairy-tale proportions, historic lighthouses, fishing villages ... the list goes on.

Much of Rügen and its surrounding waters are either national park or protected nature reserve. The Bodden inlet area is a bird refuge and popular with bird-watchers. The main resort area is around the settlements of Binz, Sellin and Göhren on Rügen's east coast.

Information

Fremdenverkehrsverband Rügen (☎ 03838-807 70; fax 254 44 0), the head office for all the local tourist offices on the island, is located at Am Markt 4 in Bergen. It provides information only, no room reservations; these are handled by the local tourist offices and a number of private agencies.

The latter include Rügen-Besucher-Service (☎ 038301-605 13; fax 613 95) at Bahnhofstrasse 2 in Putbus, and Touristik Service Rügen (☎ 038306-616 0; fax 616 66) in Altefähr. In Binz, there's also Boy's Touristinformation (☎ 038393-325 15; fax 321 14) at Proraer Chaussee 2. See Information under the individual towns for the addresses and contact numbers of the local tourist offices.

For emergency medical attention, ring ☎ 03838-802 30.

Dangers & Annoyances

Driving on Rügen roads is a horrific experience. The island males of this formerly sequestered society have apparently discovered 'muscle cars', and they've wasted no time turning them into weapons of intimidation. Along some of the most beautiful – and narrow – roads in Germany, these hooligans will appear out of nowhere at extremely dangerous speeds and play their little macho games. We've seen them nearly run cyclists into the ditches, and their favourite tactic – on roads where there is no escape – is to tailgate. Do *not* provoke them. The local police are not a presence on Rügen's roads; your best bet is somehow to pull over as quickly as possible and not let these morons ruin your visit.

Getting There & Away

Bus BerLinien Bus (toll-free ☎ 0130-719 10 7) runs a regular service between Berlin and the resort towns of Binz, Sellin, Baabe and Göhren. Trips cost DM55/99 one way/return. If you're under 26, you pay DM31/61. Reservations are essential.

Train Local trains run almost hourly from Stralsund to Sassnitz and also to Binz (DM13.20, one hour). Both services pass

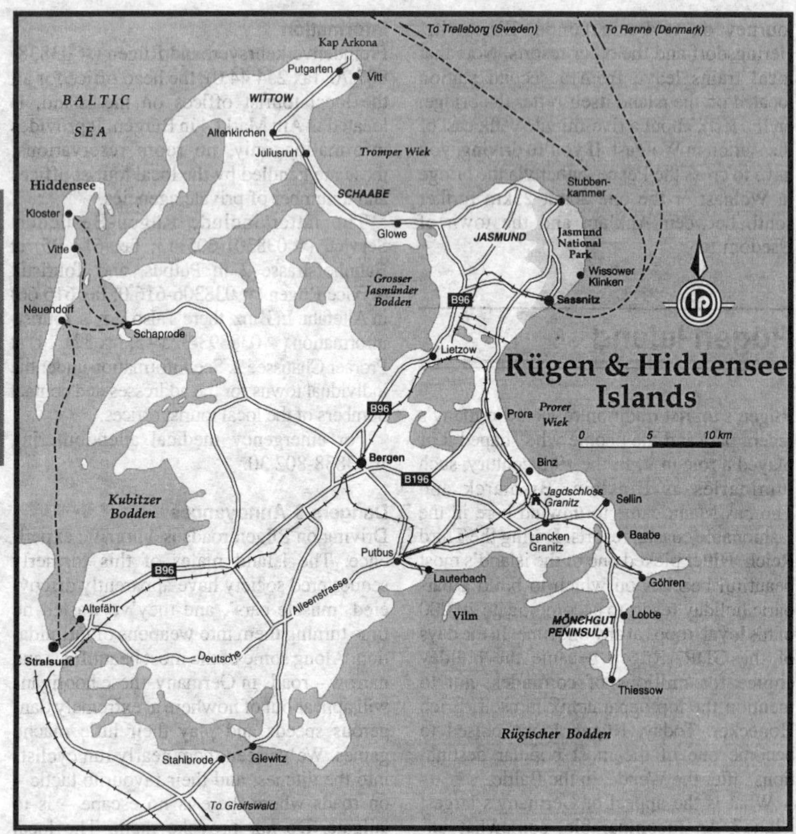

Lietzow, 13km before Sassnitz, where you may have to change trains. To get to Putbus and Lauterbach, change in Bergen. To get to Sellin, Baabe and Göhren, you can catch the Rasender Roland historic train in Putbus or in Binz (see the Getting Around section).

Car & Motorcycle The most obvious way to get to Rügen is via the Rügendamm, the causeway across the Strelasund channel from Stralsund. However, during rush hour or in peak season, it becomes a bottleneck with traffic piled up for kilometres. To make things worse, in order to let major ships pass through the channel, the causeway opens five times daily for 20 minutes at 2.30 and 7.20 am and again at 12.50, 6.20 and 9.30 pm. So unless you're travelling out of season or during off-peak hours, be prepared to wait. The only way to avoid the Rügendamm altogether is by taking the car ferry from Stahlbrode.

Boat Rügen is a stop for both domestic and international ferries.

The Mainland An excellent alternative to the Rügendamm are the ferries. A small passenger ferry shuttles between Stralsund and Altefähr on Rügen's south-western shore every 30 minutes in high season (DM3 one way, bikes DM2).

If you want to take your car onto the island, you must drive to Stahlbrode, about 15km south-east of Stralsund (direction: Greifswald). Between April and October, Weisse Flotte ferries (☎ 038328-805 13) to Glewitz on Rügen leave every 20 minutes between 6 am and 9.40 pm. From November to March, departures are every 30 minutes from 7 am to 6.45 pm. There's a DM6 charge per car up to 4m long, plus DM2 per person. Vehicles weighing up to three tonnes cost DM12 (including driver), DM15 for those weighing up to five tonnes. Bikes are DM2.

Hiddensee Reederei Hiddensee (☎ 0180-321 21 50) runs ferries between Schaprode on Rügen's western shore and Neuendorf, Kloster and Vitte several times daily between late March and mid-September. One-way/return fares to Neuendorf are DM10/17.50 and to Kloster and Vitte DM12/20.50. Children under 11 get a 30% discount. Bikes are DM10 return.

Sweden DFO HansaFerry runs five ferries daily from Sassnitz to Trelleborg and back. The crossing takes just under four hours and costs DM20 from June to mid-September and DM10 the rest of the year. Cars are DM140 to DM160 in summer, otherwise DM120; motorcycles are DM35/25. Prices are return and include all passengers. For bookings, call ☎ 038392-641 80 or ☎ 0180-534 34 43, or visit a travel agent or the ticket kiosk on Trelleborger Strasse between Sassnitz train station and the harbour.

If you are taking the train to the Sweden-bound ferry, find out whether it ends at Sassnitz's main station or goes right to the quay at Sassnitz Hafen (in the case of a split train, you need to be in the appropriately labelled carriage). It's about a 10-minute walk downhill from the station to the harbour. Generally, local trains from Stralsund end at the main station, while through services to/from Malmö connect with the ferry.

Denmark From June to mid-September, DFO HansaFerry runs three services daily between Sassnitz and Rønne on Bornholm Island. The trip takes almost four hours and costs DM30 each way. Same-day return tickets also cost DM30. The rest of the year, the price is DM15 each way and there are only two daily crossings. For booking details, see Sweden above.

Getting Around

Bus Rügen has a fairly comprehensive bus system, with links to practically all communities. Service, however, is sporadic with sometimes just a few daily departures. The main hub is Bergen. The local tourist offices have bus schedules and maps, or you can call ☎ 03838-194 49. Most buses will let you transport your bicycle.

Train The Rasender Roland steam train is not just a tourist attraction but an integral part of Rügen's public transport system. It shuttles between Putbus and Göhren – stopping in Binz, Jagdschloss Granitz, Sellin and Baabe – daily between 6 am and 11 pm. The route is divided into four zones, each costing DM3 (ie Putbus to Binz two zones, Putbus to Göhren four zones). Bikes are a flat DM3.50.

Car & Motorcycle If you don't have much time, the car is the best mode of transport on Rügen – though see the Dangers & Annoyances section. The main artery cutting through Rügen is the B96. Parking meters abound, so carry a lot of change.

Bicycle Rügen's network of bicycle paths has not yet been completed so sharing roads with cars cannot always be avoided. Ask for the *Fahrrad & Nahverkehrskarte Insel Rügen* at tourist offices: besides being a map, it includes route recommendations and a list of bike rental and repair places.

DEUTSCHE ALLEENSTRASSE

After crossing the Rügendamm, if you turn east instead of continuing north on the B96, you will soon be driving beneath a lush canopy of chestnut, oak, elm and poplar trees which line the two-lane, sealed road for the next 60km to the coastal resort of Sellin. This stretch is the first segment of the Deutsche Alleenstrasse, an ambitious project aiming to construct a route of leafy boulevards through Germany from here all the way south to Lake Constance. On Rügen, it leads through the island's largely agricultural, thinly populated south, where brilliant yellow fields of rape alternate with potato fields and meadows.

Putbus

- *pop 5000*
- *area code* ☎ 038301

Having passed through the modest farming villages that surround it, Putbus will seem like a mirage. Some 16 large white neoclassical buildings surround a gigantic **circular plaza** like candles on a birthday cake. Eight pie-shaped grassy areas, framed by low hedges, converge in the centre, from where an austere grey stone **obelisk** rises skyward. Nearby stands a **theatre** with a Pantheon-like façade decorated with a baby-blue frieze of mythological figures. The 75-hectare **English park** – filled with gingkos, cypress, Japanese spruce and other exotic trees – lets you take a botanical journey around the world.

Putbus is an oddity, conceived and realised in the 19th century by an overly ambitious local prince, Wilhelm Malte I of Putbus (1783-1854). The prince was late to latch onto the early-19th century fashion for building geometrically designed towns, so Putbus stands as the last purpose-planned residence in Europe.

Today, Putbus prides itself on being Rügen's cultural centre, with the island's only theatre (currently under renovation and scheduled to reopen in 1998) and the annual Rossini Festival held around May/June.

Putbus is the western terminus of the Rasender Roland (see Getting Around). The old-time steam train used to plough on for another 40km west to Altefähr near the Rügendamm, but this stretch is now covered with a wonderful bike trail including sections leading right through the forest.

Putbus' tourist office (☎ 870 60; fax 271) is at Markt 8 and is open weekdays from 8 am to 6 pm (in winter to 4 pm) and Saturday from 9 am to 2 pm.

Putbus has only a few overnight options. Private rooms start at DM30 per person. In town at Bahnhofstrasse 9 is *Hotel Koos* (☎ 278), which charges DM40 to DM65 per person. In Neukamp, a few km south on the coast, is *Hotel Nautilus* (☎ 830) with rooms from DM60 per person. Their restaurant, built to look like the guts of a U-boat, is worth a visit too, though it's often filled with coach tourists.

Lauterbach

Two kilometres south but still a part of Putbus is Lauterbach, the departure point for excursions to the tiny nearby island of **Vilm**. During GDR days, its primeval natural splendour was enjoyed only by the political elite. These days it can be visited, but because of its delicate ecology, only one naturalist-guided tour for up to 30 people is offered daily (DM25). Reservations are mandatory (☎ 618 96). Alternatively, you can take a 90-minute cruise (DM14) around Vilm, offered twice daily during high season.

Lauterbach is also the springboard for fast catamaran trips to **Swinemünde**, a resort town on the Polish island of Usedom. Boats leave several times weekly, and the return price ranges from DM12 to DM48, depending on the time of day you travel. For details, call ☎ 0180-321 21 20.

Sellin

- *pop 2700*
- *area code* ☎ 038303

The seaside resort of Sellin is the gateway to the Deutsche Alleenstrasse. The main artery of this 700-year-old fishing village is the rather sophisticated **Wilhelmstrasse**, a broad boulevard bordered by white-painted villas, most of which are now hotels and pensions. The road leads you right to the beach. Also here is the **Seebrücke** pier (1905), which is currently being restored to its original condition.

Sellin's tourist office (☎ 305; fax 860 75)

is at Wilhelmstrasse 40 and is open weekdays from 9 am to 6 pm, Saturday from 9.30 am to noon and 2 to 5 pm and Sunday from 10 am to 2 pm (shorter hours in the low season).

Sellin has a good selection of accommodation. Expect to pay about DM40 per person for a private room in peak season. At Wilhelmstrasse 18, perhaps the town's most handsome villa, is the family-run *Pension Ingeborg* (☎ 292), where rooms with private bath cost DM65 per person. The GDR elite used to stay at the *Cliff Hotel* (☎ 848 4; fax 849 5), Siedlung am Wald; it has its own lift to the beach but charges a steep DM190/235 for singles/doubles with all the amenities. You'll find a number of restaurants along Wilhelmstrasse, including *Waldfrieden* at No 5, which serves reasonably priced, home-cooked meals.

MÖNCHGUT PENINSULA

The Mönchgut Peninsula in Rügen's southeast has a wildly irregular coastline, deep bays, sandy beaches, softly rising hillsides and stretches of forest. Much of the land is protected as a nature preservation area. The Mönchgut was first settled by monks in the 14th century. Because the monks prevented the people who settled with them from mixing with the other islanders – who were pagan Slavs – they developed their own traditions over the centuries. Some of these, such as costumes and dances, have survived to this day.

Göhren

- *pop 1200*
- *area code* ☎ 038308

Insight into the lifestyle of the Mönchgut people can be gained at the local history museums in Göhren. In addition to the **Heimatmuseum**, which has exhibits on the area's ethnography, history, geography and tourism, there's the **Museumshof**, a historic farm; the **Rauchhaus** (smoke house), a chimney-less, 18th-century fishing cottage; and the **Museumschiff**, a motorised sailing boat from 1906. In the neighbouring village of Middelhagen is the **Schulmuseum**, a one-room school house with adjacent teacher's quarters. All museums are closed on Monday except in July and August. Only the Heimatmuseum is open between November and March. Admission is DM3 per museum.

Göhren itself is a pleasant and laid-back resort town, squatting on the Nordperd, a spit of land that juts into the sea like Pinocchio's nose. The beach is split into the quieter Südstrand and the livelier and more developed Nordstrand, with a pier, park and a promenade that leads to the neighbouring village of **Baabe**. Göhren is also the eastern terminus of the Rasender Roland steam train.

The tourist office (☎ 259 10; fax 259 11) is at Schulstrasse 8 and is open weekdays from 7 am to 6 pm (closed Friday from 12.30 to 4 pm) and weekends from 4 to 6 pm. Hours are restricted between October and mid-May.

Places to Stay Camping is king on the Mönchgut Peninsula. There are at least five sites to choose from: *Campingplatz Baabe* (☎ 038306-142 99), partially open year round; *Campingplatz Göhren* (☎ 038308-212 2), open Easter to October; *Campingplatz Gager* (☎ 821 0), open April to October; *Campingplatz Thiessow* (☎ 822 6), open December to October; and *Freizeit-Oase Rügen* (☎ 231 4), open May to September.

Private rooms in Göhren cost from DM20 per person. *Pension Franz* (☎ 234 0) is about 250m from the beach at Thiessower Strasse 23 and charges DM40 to DM50 per person. *Waldhotel Göhren* (☎ 253 87), Waldstrasse 7, charges DM65 to DM85 per person.

For food, try the huge *Ristorante Al Mare* right on the north beach promenade, or the *Caprice* at Thiessower Strasse 32, which has local fish dishes priced from DM15 to DM20.

BINZ

- *pop 6300*
- *area code* ☎ 038393

Binz is Rügen's largest and most celebrated seaside resort. It lies along one of the island's best beaches, fringed by dunes and forest with glorious views of Prorer Wiek bay.

Thanks to heavy restoration, Binz has once again blossomed into a fully-fledged beach town.

Information The tourist office (☎ 374 21) is at Heinrich-Heine-Strasse 7 and is open weekdays from 9 am to 6 pm and Saturday from 9 am to noon (also on Sunday in July and August). There's a branch office (☎ 278 2) at Schillerstrasse 15.

Things to See & Do Binz is known for its **collection of houses** built in the late 19th-century, Romantic style called *Bäderarchitektur* (spa architecture). Typical of this style are the large covered balconies, decorated with white filigree lattice work fashioned from wood and wrought-iron. Most of these elegant villas have recently been renovated, including the superb quartet gracing the intersection of Schillerstrasse and Margaretenstrasse.

Binz has a 4km-long **beach promenade** whose focal points are the long pier and the palatial Kurhaus.

At the northern end of the promenade is the IFA holiday park with the state-of-the-art **Vitamar** pool, with slides, whirlpool, saunas and waterfalls (open daily to 9.30 pm; DM6 for one hour and DM14 for three hours).

Jagdschloss Granitz (1723), a hunting palace built on top of the Tempelberg (at 107m the highest elevation in the Granitz Forest), was significantly enlarged and altered by Wilhelm Malte I, whose flights of fancy also gave Rügen the grandiose Putbus (see that section). Malte added the 38m-tall central tower, the palace's main attraction. To get to its top you have to climb up a cast-iron spiral staircase.

The palace is open year round from 9 am to 5.30 pm (October to March to 4 pm) and closed Monday, except from July to September. Admission is DM4.50, discount DM3.50.

From Binz, you can either walk to the Schloss (one hour, see the following paragraph for details) or catch the motorised mini-train that regularly shuttles between the pier and the palace (DM9 return, high season only). You can also travel on the Rasender Roland train and get off at Garftitz or Jagdschloss from where it's a 30-minute walk. If you're driving, you must pay to leave your car or motorcycle in a parking lot and pay again for the shuttle up to the palace – unless you prefer to walk.

Binz is an excellent base for hiking. One of the nicest walks is along the rocky coastline to Sellin, 6km south on the **Höhenuferweg**. It's a moderately tiring walk through the beech forest above the shore, but there are fantastic views over the bay. Binz borders the Granitz, a hilly forest with an extensive network of hiking trails. The **Südweg** leads right through to the Jagdschloss Granitz and ends in Sellin after about 7km. If you don't want to walk back to Binz, jump aboard the Rasender Roland steam train.

Places to Stay & Eat Accommodation is plentiful here. Binz also has one of Rügen's two *DJH hostels* (☎ 325 97), right on the Strandpromenade at No 35, charging DM24/29.50 for juniors/seniors. Book ahead during the summer months. Private rooms in Binz start at DM25 per person. Among the cheapest hotels is *Pension Nymphe* (☎ 257 0), at Strandpromenade 28, which has doubles from DM70. *Hotel Zur Promenade*, Strandpromenade 46, charges from DM80/ 140 for singles/doubles. *Pension Marion* (☎ 231 1) is less central at Bahnhofstrasse 42 and charges from DM110 for doubles.

You'll find a number of nice restaurants along Strandpromenade, including the *Strandcafé* at No 29, where you can have coffee and cake or a pizza. You'll need deeper pockets for the *Brasserie* in the stylish Villa Salve at No 41, once visited by Chancellor Helmut Kohl.

Prora

Prora lies just north of Binz, along almost 5km of uninterrupted fine white-sand beach. Running parallel to this beautiful stretch of coast is a wall of hideous six-storey buildings, each 500m long. This eyesore, begun in 1936, was the Nazis' idea of a holiday resort for 20,000 people. The outbreak of

WWII stopped its completion. After the war, Soviet troops tried to blow up the existing structures, but failed; after all, they had been built 'to last 1000 years.' So instead the troops moved in, along with their buddies from the GDR army. Later the military barracks were joined by an officer training school.

What to do with Prora today is still the focus of much debate. Tearing it down is too costly though it's a blatant reminder of two hated regimes. Plans to turn it into a multipurpose complex of apartment buildings, holiday flats, hotels and so on are being considered. The **Museum zum Anfassen** (loosely translated as 'Hands-On Museum') has a multimedia exhibit chronicling the various stages of the life of Prora and is complemented by 'period rooms' from the Nazi and GDR eras. The museum is at Objektstrasse, Block 1, and is open daily from 10 am to 6 pm (October to March to 3 pm). Admission is DM5, children under 12 pay DM4.

Camping Prora (☎ 208 5) is at Proraer Chaussee and is open from the end of March to the end of October. Rügen's only other *DJH hostel* (☎ 328 44) is also here at An der Jugendherberge, Haus 1, and costs DM22/27 for juniors/seniors. It's a five-minute walk from the train station at Prora-Ost.

JASMUND NATIONAL PARK

The rugged beauty of Jasmund National Park in Rügen's north-east has inspired a long line of artists, led by the Romantic painter Caspar David Friedrich. The **Stubbenkammer**, an area at the northern edge of the park where jagged white-chalk cliffs plunge into the jade-coloured sea, was his favourite.

The most famous attraction is the **Königstuhl** (king's chair), at 117m Rügen's highest elevation. Unfortunately, most of the time, one's enjoyment of the scenery is marred by the masses trying to do the same thing. On busy summer weekends, up to 10,000 people visit the Königstuhl, each shelling out DM2 for the privilege of pushing through the turnstile that separates them from the viewing platform. Fortunately, few make the trek a few hundred metres east to the equally impressive **Victoria-Sicht** (Victoria View), which provides the best view of the Königstuhl itself. And it's free.

Bus No 419a goes to the Stubbenkammer from Sassnitz. If you're driving, you must pay to leave your vehicle in the parking lot in Hagen, then either pay for the ride on a shuttle bus or walk 2.5km past the legendary Herthasee (Hertha Lake) through the forest. At the time of writing, it was possible, and free, to take a car all the way to the Königstuhl after 6 pm. The nicest way to approach the area, though, is by making the 10km trek from Sassnitz along the coast through the ancient forest of Stubnitz. The trail also takes you past the **Wissower Klinken**, another vista painted by Friedrich.

Though once a popular resort town, most people today only go to **Sassnitz** to board one of the ferries headed for Denmark or Sweden (see the Getting There & Away section).

The tourist office (☎ 516 0; fax 516 16), at Seestrasse 1, is open weekdays from 8 am to 7 pm (in winter to 5 pm) and weekends from 3 to 7 pm (closed in winter). It also has information on the delights of the Jasmund National Park.

WITTOW

Wittow, the northernmost area on Rügen, began life as an island of its own. It was later connected to the main island after enough sand had washed up to form the Schaabe. It's a thinly populated, windswept stretch of land used mostly for agriculture.

Schaabe

This narrow strip of land, connecting the Jasmund Peninsula with Wittow, has arguably the nicest beach on the island. It's a 10km-long crescent of fine white sand bordered by fragrant pine forest. The fact that it's practically devoid of infrastructure (no life guards, beach wicker chairs, snack bars etc) only adds to its untamed charm. There are parking lots with beach access on both sides of the road that traverses it.

You'll find a *camping ground* (☎ 038391-237; open May to mid-October) at Wittower Strasse 1-2 in Juliusruh at the northern end of the Schaabe.

Kap Arkona

Rügen ends at the rugged cliffs of Cape Arkona, with its famous pair of lighthouses. The older of the two, designed by Karl Friedrich Schinkel, was completed in 1827. The so-called **Schinkel-Leuchtturm** (DM5, discount DM4) is square and squat and 19.3m high. Inside are exhibits by Rügen artists, and from the viewing platform there's a wonderful view over a colourful quilt of rape fields, meadows and white beaches, all set off against the dark blue Baltic Sea. The views are better still from the 36m-high **Neuer Leuchtturm** (DM6, discount DM5) immediately adjacent, which has been in business since 1902.

A few metres east of the lighthouses is the **Peilturm**, which used to be a radio directional tower for shipping and now contains a museum (DM5, discount DM4). It stands right next to the **Burgwall**, a complex that harbours the remains of a *Tempelburg*, a Slavic temple and fortress built for the four-headed god Svantevit. The castle was taken over by the Danes in 1168, paving the way for the Christianisation of Rügen.

Vitt If you follow the coast for about 1.5km in a south-easterly direction, you will reach the charming fishing village of Vitt. The toy-sized village has 13 snug reed-thatched cottages and a few restaurants and snack bars. Have a look inside the whitewashed octagonal chapel with its black shutters at the village entrance. It's open daily and contains a copy of an altar painting by Philipp Otto Runge (the original is in the Kunsthalle in Hamburg).

Getting There & Away The gateway to Kap Arkona is the village of Putgarten, served infrequently by bus No 403 from Altenkirchen. If you're staying in the northern half of Rügen and you're not driving, it's probably best to travel by bicycle.

If you are in a car or motorbike, you have to leave the vehicle in a pay parking lot in Putgarten about 1.5km south of the lighthouses. The walk through the village to the cape is pleasant, though you can also cover the distance aboard a motorised mini-train. A second train services Vitt. The stretch between Kap Arkona and Vitt is covered by horse-drawn carriage. Any single trip costs DM3, two trips DM5 and the round trip (meaning parking lot-Kap Arkona-Vitt-parking lot) is DM8. A special DM9 pass entitles you to two trips and admission to one of the lighthouses. An alternative is to rent a bike (DM2.50/10 an hour/day).

HIDDENSEE ISLAND

- *pop 1250*
- *area code* ☎ 038300

Hiddensee is a narrow island off Rügen's west coast, 17km long and 1.8km at its widest point. It's a quiet and peaceful place with no cars and little infrastructure. Locals, in their dialect, affectionately refer to their island as 'Dat söte Länneken', which translates as 'The sweet little land'. In the 19th and early 20th centuries, Hiddensee bewitched artists like Thomas Mann, Asta Nielsen, Max Reinhardt and Bertolt Brecht and, of course, the writer Gerhart Hauptmann, who is buried here.

There's no mass tourism on Hiddensee and its three villages – Kloster, Neuendorf and Vitte – have preserved an innocent charm rarely found these days. Hiddensee is best explored by bike, and rental places abound.

The tourist office (☎ 642 26/27/28; fax 642 25) is at Norderende 162 in Vitte. It's open weekdays from 8 am to 5 pm. From July to mid-September it's also open on weekends from 10 am to noon.

There are no camping grounds or hostels on Hiddensee. A number of private rooms from DM20 in high season are available in all three villages, which is a good thing since there are basically no hotels either. One of the least expensive places is *Zur Boje* (☎ 296) at Königsbarg in Neuendorf, which charges DM60/120 for singles/doubles with shared facilities. *Haus am Hügel* (☎ 234), at Hügelweg 8 in Kloster, charges DM77/104. At *Hotel Godewind* (☎ 235), Süderende 53 in Vitte, prices start at DM50 per person for bathless rooms.

Hiddensee is served by ferries from Schaprode on Rügen and from Stralsund. For details, see the earlier Getting There & Away sections under Stralsund and Rügen Island.

Bavaria

For many visitors to Germany, Bavaria (Bayern) is a microcosm of the whole country. Here you will find German stereotypes in spades: *Lederhosen*, beer halls, oompah bands and romantic castles. Yet the Bavarians themselves are proudly independent and pursue a separate course from the rest of Germany in a number of ways, not the least being the refusal of most hostels to accept any guests over the age of 26.

Bavaria was ruled for centuries as a duchy under the dynasty founded by Otto I of Wittelsbach. It became a kingdom in 1806, with no small amount of interference by Napoleon in the establishment of its territorial boundaries. The region suffered through numerous power struggles between Prussia and Austria and was finally brought into the German Reich in 1871 by Bismarck.

The last king of Bavaria was Ludwig II (1845-86), who earned the epithet the 'mad monarch' due to his obsession with building fantastic fairy-tale castles and supporting cantankerous (but brilliant) composers, all at enormous expense (see History in the Munich section for more on this fascinating character, and be sure to visit his most celebrated castle, Neuschwanstein, on the Romantic Road).

Bavaria draws visitors all year. If you only have time for one part of Germany after Berlin, choose Bavaria. Munich, the capital, is the heart and soul of the state. The Bavarian Alps, Nuremberg and the medieval towns along the Romantic Road are other important attractions. Try getting off the beaten track in a place like the Bavarian Forest for a glimpse of Germany away from the tourist coaches.

HIGHLIGHTS

- The Romantic Road, especially Wurzburg and Augsburg
- Neuschwanstein, the most romantic of all German castles
- Rafting along the Isar River
- Munich's nightlife and English Garden
- Regensburger sausages and beer
- Ingolstadt's markets
- Pedalling a boat around the Five Lakes near Starnberg
- Electric-boat ride on spectacular Königssee, near Berchtesgaden

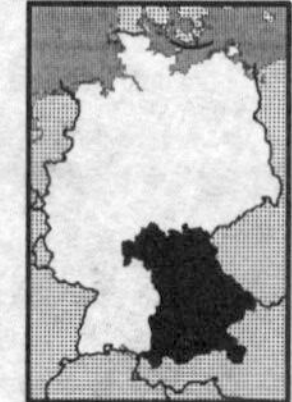

• **Population:** 12m • **Capital:** Munich • **Area:** 70,554 sq km

Bavaria Luminaries: Franz Beckenbauer, Bertolt Brecht, Lucas Cranach the Elder, Albrecht Dürer, Ludwig Erhard, Rainer Werner Fassbinder, Lion Feuchtwanger, Christoph Willibald Gluck, Werner Heisenberg, Hans Holbein the Elder, Petra Kelly, Ernst Ludwig Kirchner, Henry Kissinger, Franz Marc, Max Slevogt, Franz Josef Strauss, Richard Strauss, Patrick Süskind, Martin Walser

Orientation

Bavaria is Germany's largest state. It's made up of several counties, but the boundaries of tourist offices and governmental organisations don't mesh. So, for example, you can't get information on Franconia from Munich tourist offices. For tourism purposes, Bavaria is broken up into five regions:

Munich (München). The capital of Bavaria, Munich is located in the south-east of the state. A city of 1.3 million, Munich and its surrounding area is a separate region in itself.

Upper Bavaria (Oberbayern). This refers to the Bavarian Alps, at the southernmost point of the state.

East Bavaria (Ostbayern). This area includes Passau, the Bavarian Forest and Regensburg.

Franconia (Franken). The northernmost district of the state includes Nuremberg, Erlangen, Bayreuth, Bamberg, Würzburg and several Romantic Road cities including Rothenburg ob der Tauber.

Allgäu-Bavarian Swabia (Allgäu-Bayerische-Schwäbisch). Includes Augsburg, eastern Lake Constance and the heart-stopper of the Romantic Road: Neuschwanstein Castle.

Accommodation

While Bavarian hostels – even the HI-member hostels – generally prohibit stays by anyone over age 26, some don't.

While we can't, unfortunately, list all the hostels that welcome over 26s (because the hostels would risk their membership), we will say that even if they *say* they don't, many hostels will take in people aged over 26, if there's room available, for a slightly higher price.

Bavaria's parks, as well as certain popular rafting routes, are open to free camping, and it's a wonderful thing to do. While cruising down a river in a canoe or rubber raft, you're permitted – generally speaking – to stop along the bank and pitch a tent.

Be sure to follow the local code of ethics and common decency and pack up everything you brought along – litter, bottles, cans – and bury human waste in catholes at least 15cm deep before you leave.

Food & Drink

Prepare yourself: Bavarians enjoy beer, and one of the finer ways you can sample their brew is in beer gardens. In many places you can bring along a picnic lunch and just buy the beer; in some, though, outside food is forbidden.

You can be sure of one thing: travel in Bavaria involves a lot of stops in beer gardens, eating sausage and other meat, and drinking lots of glorious Bavarian beer – including some of the best brews in the world.

Munich

- *pop 1.3 million*
- *area code* ☎ 089

Munich (München) is the Bavarian mother lode. It's the capital of the state of Bavaria, home to its finest museums, dotted with castles and one of Germany's most prosperous cities. Only since reunification has it become the nation's second-most popular destination, after Berlin.

Munich has been the capital of Bavaria since 1503, but it really achieved prominence under the guiding hand of Ludwig I in the 19th century. It has seen many turbulent times, but this century has been particularly rough. WWI practically starved the city to death, and WWII (which in many ways began here with the infamous Munich Agreement) brought bombing and more than 200,000 deaths.

Whether you see the city during the tourist-packed summer, the madness of Oktoberfest or the cold stillness of a February afternoon, Munich offers the chance to see Bavarians and the values and attitudes that so dominate the exported image of 'Germany'.

History

There's evidence of settlements here as early as 525 AD, but it's generally agreed that the most important settlers were Benedictine monks around the 8th century; the city's name derives from *Munichen*, or 'monks' settlement'.

Heinrich der Löwe's rule through conquest was made official by the Imperial Diet in Augsburg in 1158, which is the city's official birthdate. Heinrich's control over the city was tenuous at best and was repealed just 30 years later. In 1240, the city was passed from the bishops of Freising to the House of Wittelsbach, which would run the city as well as much, or all, of Bavaria until the 20th century.

Munich became a ducal residence in 1255 under Ludwig the Stern. In the next century, Ludwig the Bavarian expanded the city,

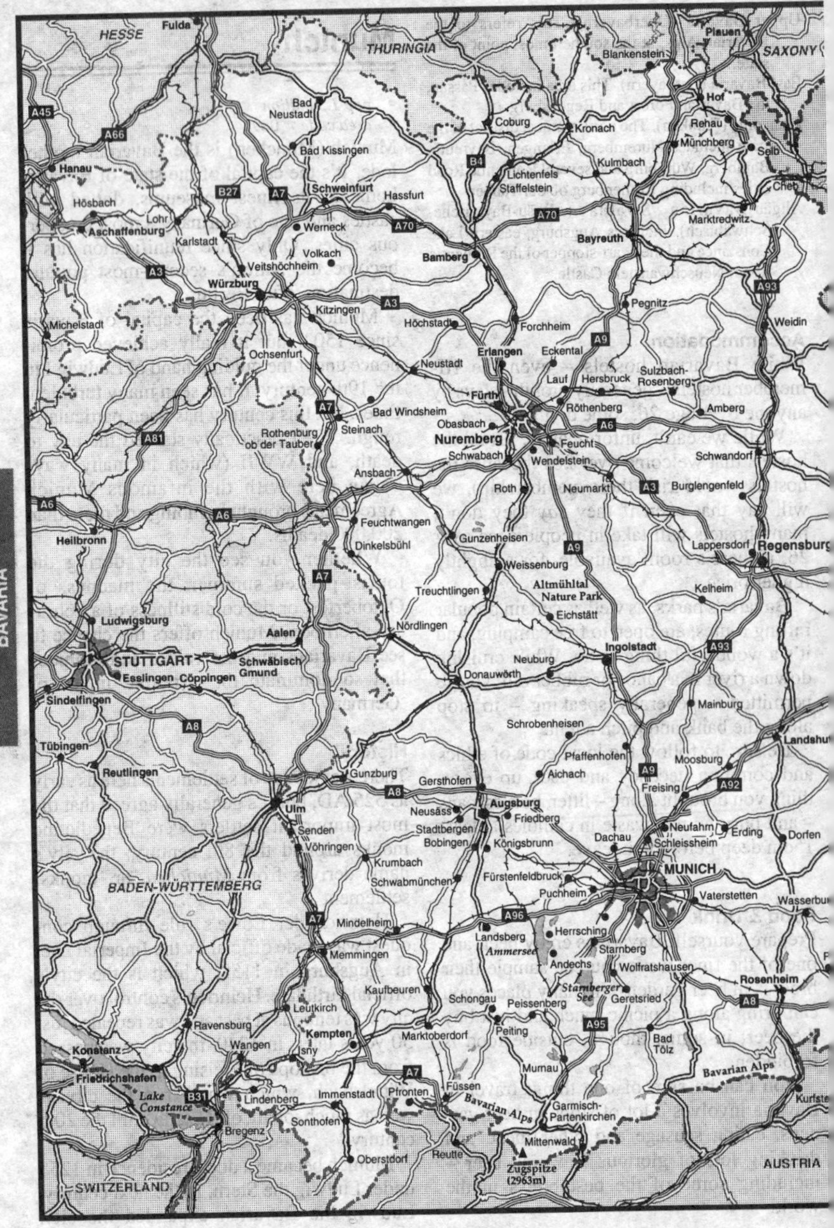
HESSE
Fulda
THURINGIA
Plauen
SAXONY
Blankenstein
Hof
Rehau
Selb
Münchberg
Cheb
Bad Neustadt
Coburg
Kronach
Kulmbach
Lichtenfels
Staffelstein
Bad Kissingen
Hanau
Hösbach
Aschaffenburg
Lohr
Karlstadt
Schweinfurt
Hassfurt
Werneck
Volkach
Veitshöchheim
Würzburg
Bamberg
Bayreuth
Marktredwitz
Kitzingen
Höchstadt
Forchheim
Pegnitz
Weidin
Michelstadt
Ochsenfurt
Erlangen
Eckental
Lauf
Hersbruck
Sulzbach-Rosenberg
Neustadt
Bad Windsheim
Fürth
Röthenberg
Amberg
Obasbach
Nuremberg
Feucht
Rothenburg ob der Tauber
Steinach
Schwabach
Wendelstein
Schwandorf
Ansbach
Roth
Neumarkt
Burglengenfeld
Feuchtwangen
Heilbronn
Gunzenheisen
Dinkelsbühl
Lappersdorf
Regensburg
Weissenburg
Treuchtlingen
Altmühltal Nature Park
Kelheim
Eichstätt
Ludwigsburg
Aalen
Nördlingen
Ingolstadt
STUTTGART
Schwäbisch Gmund
Esslingen
Cöppingen
Neuburg
Donauwörth
Sindelfingen
Mainburg
Schrobenheisen
Tübingen
Landshut
Pfaffenhofen
Moosburg
Reutlingen
Gunzburg
Aichach
Freising
Gersthofen
Ulm
Neusäss
Augsburg
Friedberg
Senden
Stadtbergen
Neufahm
Erding
Dorfen
Vöhringen
Bobingen
Königsbrunn
Dachau
Schleissheim
Krumbach
MUNICH
Schwabmünchen
Fürstenfeldbruck
BADEN-WÜRTTEMBERG
Puchheim
Vaterstetten
Wasserburg
Mindelheim
Landsberg
Herrsching
Ammersee
Starnberg
Memmingen
Andechs
Wolfratshausen
Rosenheim
Kaufbeuren
Starnberger See
Schongau
Peissenberg
Geretsried
Leutkirch
Ravensburg
Peiting
Kempten
Marktoberdorf
Bad Tölz
Konstanz
Wangen
Isny
Murnau
Bavarian Alps
Friedrichshafen
Füssen
Lake Constance
Lindenberg
Immenstadt
Pfronten
Garmisch-Partenkirchen
Bregenz
Sonthofen
Mittenwald
Reutte
Oberstdorf
Zugspitze (2963m)
AUSTRIA
SWITZERLAND
A45
A66
B27
A7
A70
B4
A3
A9
A93
A81
A6
A8
A92
A96
A95
B31

rebuilt areas destroyed by the Great Fire of 1328, built many of the fortifications that you can still see today, and ensured Munich's role as a power player by granting it a monopoly on the salt trade.

This established Munich as a wealthy trading city, and over the next 200 years it continued to prosper. By 1503, Munich had 13,500 residents and had become the capital of the Duchy of Bavaria.

Dozens of outbreaks of the plague began in 1349 and continued for the next 150 years, despite frantic efforts to cordon off the city. Reinforcements were constructed and improved sewage and sanitation systems introduced, but the city's population was ravaged. As the plague passed, the *Schäffler* (coopers) began a ritualistic dance in 1517, which they vowed to perform every seven years as long as the city was spared further outbreaks. The tradition continues today: the *Schäfflertanz* is re-enacted daily by the little figures on the city's *Glockenspiel* on Marienplatz.

The Reformation hit Munich particularly hard. Under Duke Wilhelm IV, Protestants were persecuted and by the outbreak of the Thirty Years' War local residents were resolutely Catholic. During the war, the city was invaded with little fanfare – Imperial General Tilly (1559-1632), realising he was hopelessly outnumbered and outflanked, wisely surrendered it to Swedish king Gustav Adolphus in 1632.

While the city's freedom was bought from the Swedes, it fell under Habsburg rule from 1705 to 1714. The 18th century saw a rejuvenation of Munich, with an explosion of spectacular baroque and Italianate architecture throughout the city.

In the 19th century, Napoleon's conquest of the territories and his rejigging of the German royal hierarchy elevated Bavaria to the rank of kingdom. The marriage in 1810 of Bavarian Crown Prince Ludwig I to the Saxon-Hildburghausen Princess Therese marked what would become the Oktoberfest.

In 1818, Bavaria became the first German state with a written constitution. The first half of the 19th century also saw runaway

BAVARIA

expansion under the rule of the now King Ludwig I, who was determined to transform his capital into a cultural and artistic centre. He hired architects including Leo von Klenze and Friedrich von Gärtner and commissioned the construction of such landmarks as Königsplatz, the Alte Pinakothek and Ludwigstrasse, as well as the Königsbau and Festsaalbau sections of the Residenz. It was during this period too that the university moved to Munich from Landshut, and the Theresienwiese (site of the Oktoberfest), with its Ruhmeshalle (Hall of Fame), was constructed.

Ludwig II took the reins of power after his father's death and immediately set about spending the family fortune on projects that were seen by other members of the royal family as, to put it mildly, nutty. Ludwig's bizarre shyness, predilection towards ever more grandiose and unmanageable construction projects and steadfast loyalty to those who also felt that the royal coffers were there to be emptied (especially Bismarck, the composer Richard Wagner and many of Ludwig's architects and planners) earned him the moniker of 'Loony Ludwig' (or various permutations of the same). Ironically, the very projects that bankrupted the government and royal house and earned Ludwig the scorn and hatred of his family are the very ones that today are the biggest money-spinners for the Bavarian tourism industry and indeed the country.

Arrested after being declared mentally unfit to rule, Ludwig and his doctor were found drowned in highly mysterious circumstances in Lake Starnberg (see Around Munich). His brother Otto, who was certifiably (as opposed to allegedly) insane, was unable to take the throne, and his regent, Prince Luitpold, took charge and embarked on yet another expansion of the city, including the construction of Prinzregentenstrasse.

By the turn of the 20th century, Munich had over 500,000 residents. Political turmoil

BAVARIA

Munich's Olympic Tragedy

Munich's bid for the 1972 Olympic Games came after official recognition of the GDR by the UN in 1965. The philosophy behind the move was that, through the Olympics, West Germany would put itself forward as a rebuilt nation, a model of international cooperation and the proud father of Munich, which had undeniably become a world-class city.

The Games got off to an auspicious start: these were the heady days of the Cold War, and much of the action was dominated by contests between East and West. The main attractions included the contest between the US and Soviet basketball teams and the brilliant individual performances by US swimmer Mark Spitz (who won a record seven gold medals) and Soviet gymnast Olga Korbut.

On Wednesday, 6 September, the Israeli athletes' dormitory in the Olympic Village was raided by Palestinian terrorists from the Black September movement. Nine athletes and coaches were kidnapped and two were killed immediately.

Black September demanded the release of prisoners from Israeli jails and threatened to kill the hostages if their demands weren't met immediately. German authorities frantically negotiated for the release of the athletes.

The Germans offered money – to no avail. They even offered a swap of the Israelis for 'substitute' hostages, including federal interior minister Hans-Dietrich Genscher, the former Munich mayor Han-Jochen Vogel and Bavarian interior minister Otto Merk, but this move was also rejected.

After hours of failed negotiations, and with every indication that the terrorists were about to start killing the hostages, the Germans decided to take military action. They arranged for three helicopters to fly the terrorists and hostages to a military airfield at Fürstenfeldbruck, west of Munich, where they were promised a plane that would fly them all to Cairo.

When the choppers arrived at Fürstenfeldbruck, police sharpshooters opened fire on the terrorists, who immediately began shooting hostages. One terrorist detonated a hand grenade inside a helicopter. The remaining nine Israelis, as well as four of the terrorists and a Munich police officer, were killed in the shootout. ■

and infighting, along with runaway inflation and economic collapse after WWI, created fertile ground into which Adolf Hitler planted the earliest seeds of his National Socialist movement; it was here, in the Hofbräuhaus in 1920, that Hitler addressed the party's first large meeting.

Hitler spent the next several years consolidating power and trying to raise money and gain supporters, with great success. On 8 November 1923, he and about 600 troops stormed Munich's Bürgerbräukeller and kidnapped officials of the Bavaria provincial government, who were there for a meeting. The caper was a fiasco: Hitler's troops fled the following day, and Hitler was arrested and jailed. While serving his sentence, he began work on what would become *Mein Kampf* (My Struggle).

Munich was severely damaged by Allied bombing during WWII, and on 30 April 1945 the city was occupied by US forces. Reconstruction seemed to have reached completion when the city was awarded the 1972 Olympic Games, though they ended in tragedy (see boxed text).

Today Munich is a thriving capital city, having come through the latest recession rather painlessly, thanks to the presence of such unshakable industries as Siemens (electronics and computers as well as industrial equipment), BMW, Bayer pharmaceuticals, and MAN (automotive and truck production), among many others. With the opening in 1992 of Franz-Josef Strauss airport, Munich became the second-most important air transport hub in the country after Frankfurt.

Orientation

The Hauptbahnhof is less than 1km west of the Altstadt, the centre of town. The Isar River flows through the eastern part of the city from south to north. Munich is officially divided into numerous districts; formerly separate villages, they have been absorbed into the greater metropolitan area.

Hauptbahnhof The area around the main train station is remarkably diverse. On its north side are expensive package-tourist hotels; to the east is the 'gizmotronics, computer and beeping stuff' district – dozens of shops selling everything the computer geek could possibly want; to the south is Ludwigs-Vorstadt, a lively area often mistaken as dangerous that's packed with Turkish shops, restaurants, cafés and relatively inexpensive (if grotty) pensions and hotels.

Altstadt The Altstadt is the city centre and Marienplatz is the heart of the Altstadt. Pedestrianised Kaufingerstrasse runs west from Marienplatz to Karlsplatz (also known as Stachus) at the western boundary of the Altstadt. The city's historical centre is encircled by a ring of roads in the position of the former city fortifications: Sonnenstrasse to the west, Oskar-Von-Miller-Ring and Von-der-Tann-Strasse to the north, Franz-Josef-Strauss-Ring, Karl-Scharnagl-Ring and Thomas-Wimmer-Ring – one road with three named sections – at the east, and Blumenstrasse and Frauenstrasse at the south.

North of Marienplatz is the Residenz (the former royal palace), with the National Theatre and Residenz Theatre. Just north is Odeonsplatz, home to the spectacular Theatinerkirche. East of Marienplatz is the Platzl quarter for pubs and restaurants, as well as Maximilianstrasse, a fashionable street that's fun for strolling and window-shopping.

Just south of the centre on Museumsinsel, an island in the Isar, is the Deutsches Museum and the Forum Der Technik.

Westend Once considered a dangerous slum area, Westend, south-west of the Hauptbahnhof, has experienced something of a renaissance and is now home to renovated houses, hip cafés and wine bars and some nicer hotels. It's also just west of the Theresienwiese, where trade fairs and the Oktoberfest are held.

Schwabing The centre of the city's university and its student life, Schwabing, north of Marienplatz, is bursting with energy.

The main stretch of chi-chi cafés is along

Central Munich (München)
To Olympiapark; BMW Museum; Schleissheim
To Schloss Nymphenburg; DJH Hostel
To Theresienwiese (Oktoberfest) & Jugendinformationszentrum
See Enlargement
Theresienstrasse
Schellingstrasse
Technische Universität
Gabelsbergerstrasse
Brienner Strasse
Königsplatz
Propyläen
Karolinenplatz
Odeonsplatz
Maximiliansplatz
Karlsplatz
Hauptbahnhof
Bahnhofplatz
Marienplatz
Viktualienmarkt
Sendlinger Tor
Sendlinger-Tor-Platz
Gärtnerplatz
U-Bahn
S-Bahn
0
200
400 m

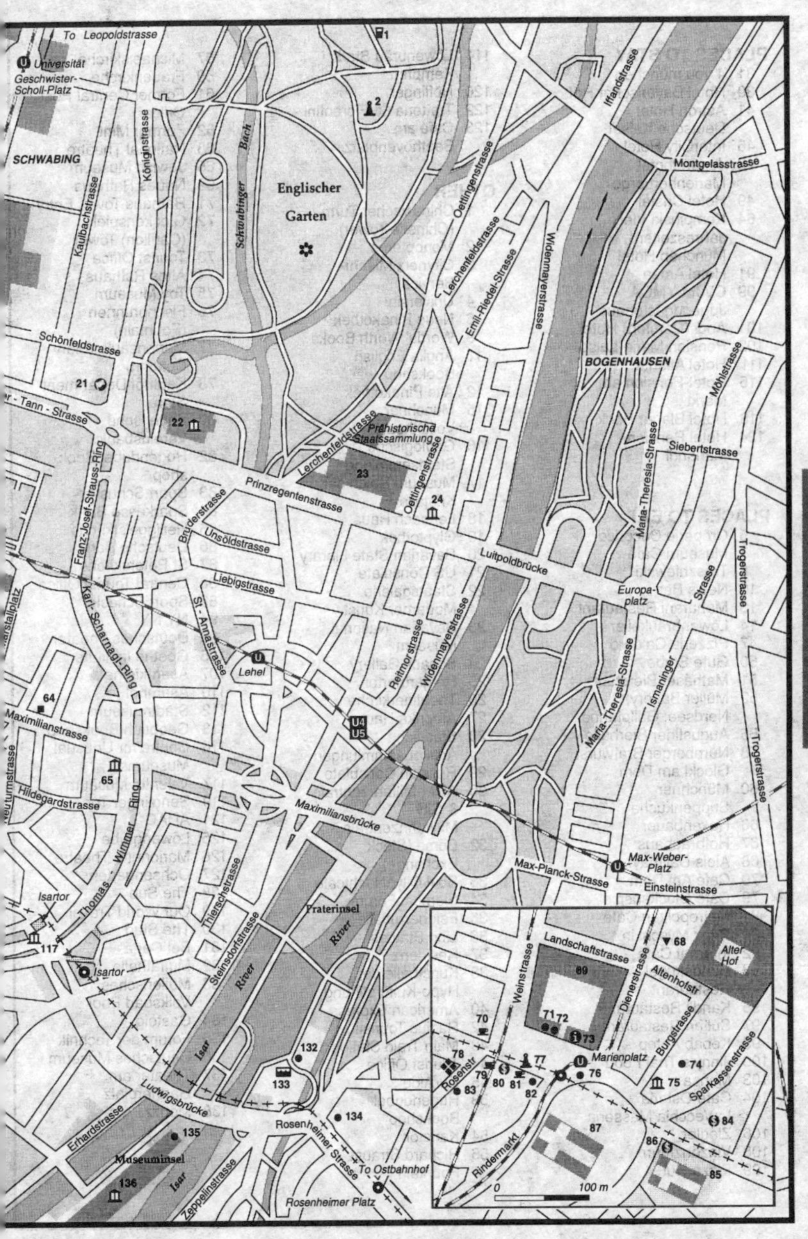
To Leopoldstrasse
Universität
Geschwister-Scholl-Platz
SCHWABING
Königinstrasse
Kaulbachstrasse
Schwabinger Bach
Englischer Garten
Oettingenstrasse
Iffandstrasse
Montgelasstrasse
Lerchenfeldstrasse
Emil-Riedel-Strasse
Widenmayerstrasse
Schönfeldstrasse
BOGENHAUSEN
Möhlstrasse
Tann - Strasse
Prähistorische Staatssammlung
Maria-Theresia-Strasse
Siebertstrasse
Franz-Josef-Strauss-Ring
Prinzregentenstrasse
Bruderstrasse
Unsöldstrasse
Luitpoldbrücke
Liebigstrasse
Europa-platz
Trogerstrasse
Karl-Scharnagl-Ring
St-Annastrasse
Lehel
Reitmorstrasse
Ismaninger
Strasse
U4
U5
Maximilianstrasse
Hildegardstrasse
Wimmer Ring
Thomas
Maximiliansbrücke
Max-Weber-Platz
Max-Planck-Strasse
Einsteinstrasse
Thierschstrasse
Isartor
Steinsdorfstrasse
Praterinsel
River
Isar
Landschaftstrasse
Altenhofstr
Alter Hof
Weinstrasse
Dienerstrasse
Burgstrasse
Marienplatz
Sparkassenstrasse
Rosenstr
Rindermarkt
Ludwigsbrücke
Erhardstrasse
Museuminsel
Zeppelinstrasse
Rosenheimer Strasse
To Ostbahnhof
Rosenheimer Platz
0
100 m

PLACES TO STAY

31 4 you münchen
39 Hotel Bayerischer Hof
41 Astron Hotel Deutsche Kaiser
46 InterCity Hotel
48 Jugendhotel Marienherberge
49 Hotel Cristal
64 Kempinski Vier Jahreszeiten München Hotel
91 Hotel Arosa
99 CVJM-YMCA Jugendgästehaus
101 Andi (Comfort) Hotel
102 Pension Marie-Luise
111 Hotel Atlanta
115 Hotel-Pension am Markt
118 Hotel Blauer Bock
124 Hotel Pension Mariandl

PLACES TO EAT

5 Crêperie Cocorico
7 Museum Café
8 Treszniewski
10 News Bar
13 Maharani Restaurant
14 Löwenbräukeller
47 Pizzeria Ca'doro
50 Gute Stube
51 Mathäser Bierstadt
52 Müller Bakery; Nordsee; Grillpfanne
55 Augustiner Bierhalle
58 Nürnberger Bratwurst Glöckl am Dom
60 Münchner Suppenküche
66 Haxenbauer
67 Hofbräuhaus
68 Alois Dallmayr
70 Café Am Dom
79 Café Glockenspiel
81 Metropolitan Café
90 Prinz Myschkin
92 Internet Café
93 Hundskugel Restaurant
95 Kandil Restaurant
97 Sultan Restaurant
98 Kebab Antep
100 Jinny's Thai Food
103 Mensa
104 Café Osteria LaVecchia Masseria
106 Ziegler
108 Vinzenzmurr
109 Pizza Hut
114 Löwenbräu Stadt Kempten
120 Höflinger
122 Trattoria La Fiorentini
123 Café am Beethovenplatz

OTHER

1 Chinesischer Turm (Chinese Tower)
2 Monopteros
3 Citynetz Mitfahr-Service
4 University
6 Neue Pinakothek
9 Words' Worth Books
11 Anglia English Bookshop
12 Alte Pinakothek
15 Münchner Volkstheater
16 Geologische Staatsammlung
17 Museum Reich der Kristalle
18 Lenbach Haus
19 Glyptothek
20 Bavarian State Library
21 US Consulate
22 Staatsgalerie Moderner Kunst
23 Bavarian National Museum
24 Schack Gallery
25 Hofgartnertor
26 Theatinerkirche
27 Amerika Haus
28 Staatliche Antikensammlungen
29 Russian Consulate
30 ADM-Mitfahrzentrale & City Mitwohnzentrale
32 Börse (Stock Exchange)
33 Soul City; Nachtcafé
34 SiemensForum
35 Feldherrnhalle
36 Lion Statues
37 Residenz
38 Kunsthalle der Hypo-Kulturstiftung
40 American Express
42 Radius Touristic
43 Main Train Station
44 Tourist Office
45 EurAide
53 Hugendubel Bookshop
54 Karlstor
56 Richard Strauss Fountain
57 Michaelskirche
59 Frauenkirche
61 Former Central Post Office
62 Former Mint
63 National Theatre
65 Jewish Museum
69 Neues Rathaus
71 Rathaus Tower Entry
72 Glockenspiel (Carillon) Tower
73 Tourist Office
74 Altes Rathaus
75 Toy Museum
76 Fischbrunnen (Fountain)
77 Mariensäule (Mary Column)
78 Kaufhof Department Store
80 Bayerische Vereinsbank
82 Hugendubel Bookshop
83 Sport Schuster
84 Sparkasse Bank
85 Heiliggeistkirche
86 Deutsche Bank
87 St Peterskirche
88 Central Tourist Office
89 Sport Scheck
94 NY NY
96 Deutsches Theater
105 Goethe Institute
107 Asamkirche
110 Asamhof
112 Stadtmuseum
113 Geobuch Bookshop
116 Centre for Unusual Museums
117 Valentin Musäum
119 Sendlinger Tor
121 ADAC
125 Löwengrube
126 Marionette Theatre
127 Ochsengarten
128 The Sub
129 Our World Travel
130 The Stud
131 Bei Carla
132 Muffathalle
133 Müllerisches Volksbad Pool
134 Gasteig
135 Forum der Technik
136 Deutsches Museum
137 Theater am Gärtnerplatz
138 Morizz

BAVARIA

Leopoldstrasse, just west of the English Garden, but west Schwabing, south and west of the university, is much more down-to-earth, with bookshops, cafés and restaurants more reasonably priced and with less flamboyant clientele.

Eastern Munich North-east of the Altstadt but on the west side of the Isar, the English Garden (Englischer Garten), Europe's largest city park, sprawls northward. On the east side of the Isar, near the Ostbahnhof (East Train Station) is an enormous nightlife attraction, the new Kunstpark Ost, a complex containing discos, restaurants, bars and cinemas.

Neuhausen North-west of the Hauptbahnhof is cosmopolitan Neuhausen, a more residential area that's home to the city's most popular hostel. The neighbourhood's hub, Rotkreuzplatz, is the terminus for U-Bahn No 1.

Western Munich Walking along Nymphenburger Strasse north-west from Rotkreuzplatz in Neuhausen brings you to Schloss Nymphenburg and its lovely gardens.

Northern Munich The main attraction north of the city is Olympiapark, site of the 1972 Olympic Games. The park today hosts a wide range of attractions, including the Tollwood Festival (see Special Events). The BMW Museum is just north of the park.

Information

Tourist Offices The excellent *Young People's Guide to Munich* (DM1) is available from all of the tourist offices listed here.

EurAide (☎ 593 88 9), near platform No 11 at the Hauptbahnhof, is the city's best source of information in English, is open year round, and is generally the best place to head for when you get into town. The office makes reservations and sells tickets on DB trains. It sells Eurail passes for the US price plus US$20 delivery charge (delivery 24 hours later), and it registers Eurail and other train passes.

EurAide's room-finding service (DM6 per booking) is at least as skilful as the city tourist office (see below). It's open from April to the end of Oktoberfest (early October) daily from 7.45 am to noon and 1 to 6 pm. From October to June it's open on weekdays from 7.45 am to noon and 1 to 4 pm, as well as Saturday morning.

EurAide's free newsletter, *The Inside Track*, is packed with practical info about the city and surrounding regions, and gives discounts on money-changing commissions (see the Money section).

The central city tourist office is at Sendlinger Strasse 1 (☎ 233 03 00; fax 233 30 23 3; email 100711.1505@compuserve.com) near Rindermarkt (upstairs in Room 213). It opens Monday to Thursday from 8.30 am to 4 pm and to 2 pm on Friday.

The city tourist office (☎ 233 30 25 6) at the eastern end of the Hauptbahnhof is open Monday to Saturday from 10 am to 8 pm, Sunday from 10 am to 6 pm. Expect to queue during summer, and staff can be stunningly rude.

The room-finding service offered by the tourist office costs between DM5 and DM9. You can apply in person or by writing to Fremdenverkehrsamt München, 80313 Munich.

A tourist office branch is at the Neues Rathaus (same telephone number as the Hauptbahnhof office) at the northern end of Marienplatz. It keeps the same hours but closes at 4 pm on Sunday.

The Munich airport tourist office (☎ 975 92 81 5) is open Monday to Saturday from 10 am to 9 pm, and from noon to 8 pm on Sunday and holidays.

The Jugendinformationszentrum (Youth Information Centre; ☎ 514 10 66 0), a couple of blocks south of the Hauptbahnhof at the corner of Paul-Heyse-Strasse and Landwehrstrasse, is open from noon to 6 pm Monday to Friday (until 8 pm on Thursday). It has a wide range of printed information for young visitors to Munich and Germany.

The German auto association (ADAC) has several offices here. The biggest one (☎ 767 60) is at Sendlinger-Tor-Platz.

Foreign Consulates Excellent consular representation (with the notable exception of the surly staff at the Russian and US consulates) as well as a superb rail and bus network make Munich a popular place to begin a journey into Eastern Europe or Asia.

Queues at consulates here are generally shorter than at embassies in Bonn. Consulates include:

Austria
  Ismaninger Strasse 136 (☎ 921 09 00)
Belgium
  Brienner Strasse 14 (☎ 286 09 0)
Bulgaria
  Böcklinstrasse 1 (☎ 155 02 6)
Canada
  Tal 29 (☎ 219 95 70)
Czech Republic
  Siedlerstrasse 2, Unterföhring (☎ 950 12 4/5/6)
Denmark
  Sendlinger-Tor-Platz 10 (☎ 545 85 40)
Finland
  Arabellastrasse 33 (☎ 910 72 25 7)
France
  Möhlstrasse 5 (☎ 419 41 10)
Greece
  Dingolfinger Strasse 6 (☎ 492 06 1)
India
  Petuelring 130 (☎ 359 36 27)
Indonesia
  Widenmayerstrasse 24 (☎ 294 60 9)
Ireland
  Mauerkircherstrasse 1a (☎ 985 72 3)
Italy
  Möhlstrasse 3 (☎ 418 00 30)
Japan
  Prinzregentenplatz 10 (☎ 471 04 3/4/5)
Netherlands
  Nymphenburger Strasse 1 (☎ 545 96 70)
Norway
  Promenadeplatz 7 (☎ 224 17 0)
Poland
  Ismaninger Strasse 62a (☎ 418 60 80)
Portugal
  Delpstrasse 8 (☎ 984 02 3)
Russia
  Seidlstrasse 28 (☎ 592 52 8)
Slovakia
  Vollmannstrasse 25d (☎ 910 20 60)
Slovenia
  Lindwurmstrasse 10 (☎ 543 98 19)
Spain
  Oberföhringer Strasse 45 (☎ 985 02 7/8/9)
Sweden
  Josephspitalstrasse 15 (☎ 545 21 21 5)
Switzerland
  Brienner Strasse 14 (☎ 286 62 00)
Thailand
  Prinzenstrasse 13 (☎ 168 97 88)
Turkey
  Menzinger Strasse 3 (☎ 178 03 10)
UK
  Bürkleinstrasse 10 (☎ 211 09 0)
USA
  Königinstrasse 5 (☎ 288 80; ☎ 28 88 72 2 fc
  American citizen services and passport issues)

Money Reisebank has two branches at th Hauptbahnhof; note that presenting a cop of EurAide's newsletter *The Inside Trac* (available when EurAide is closed from box outside the office) will get you a 50% reduction on commissions at those branches Otherwise there are branches of Deutsch Bank, Bayerische Vereinsbank and Spar kasse on Marienplatz (the Deutsche Ban has a currency-exchange machine outside) Deutsche Bank and Citibank both hav offices on Rotkreuzplatz, very close to th hostel.

Post offices offer good rates for cash, bu as usual charge DM6 per travellers' cheque You'll find American Express at Promenade platz 6 and Thomas Cook at Kaiserstrass 45. Money wired through American Expres using their MoneyGram service, or Wester Union (you can pick it up at Postbank o Reisebank branches) will reach you in abou 15 minutes from the time at which it's sent Both are very expensive ways to sen money, so use them as a last resort.

Post & Communications Munich's mai post office is at Arnulfstrasse 32, at th corner of Seidlstrasse, just behind th Hauptbahnhof. It's open on weekdays fro 8 am to 8 pm, Saturday till noon. The post restante address is Hauptpostlagernd (Post Restante), Arnulfstrasse 32, 80074 Munich.

The post office upstairs in the Hauptbahn hof is open weekdays from 7 am to 8 pm Saturday from 8 am to 4 pm, and Sunda from 9 am to 3 pm.

Online Services The Internet Café (☎ 26 78 15), Altheimer Eck 12 near Marienplatz is a fun place; send email and surf the net free with any purchase. There's a branch (☎ 129 11 20) at Nymphenburger Strasse 145 just east of Rotkreuzplatz near the hostel.

Travel Agencies EurAide (see Tourist Offices) is the best place to go with complicated rail-pass enquiries or to book train travel in Germany or elsewhere in Europe.

Munich is a great city for bucket shops and cheap airfares, with several helpful options. Council Travel (☎ 395 02 2), near the university at Adalbertstrasse 32, is one of the best around; take U-Bahn No 3 or 6 to Universität.

STA Travel (☎ 399 09 6), Königinstrasse 49, is also a good bet.

Travel Overland (☎ 272 76 10 0) is a great bucket shop with several locations, including a good one at Barerstrasse 73; we've used it many times with great results. Studiosus Reisen (☎ 235 05 20) at Oberanger 6 organises educational trips within Germany and abroad. The abr Reisebüro (☎ 120 40) in the Hauptbahnhof handles train tickets.

Our World Travel (☎ 260 55 71), near Sendlinger Tor at Müllerstrasse 43, offers standard booking services for full package trips aimed at gays and lesbians but not necessarily to exclusively gay and lesbian resorts and destinations.

Bookshops The best travel bookshop in town is Geobuch (☎ 265 03 0), opposite Viktualienmarkt at Rosental 6. The best cultural book range is available at Hugendubel (☎ 238 90), opposite the Rathaus at Marienplatz, with an enormous selection of Lonely Planet guides and tons of English-language offerings. You can sit on sofas and read before you buy.

In Schwabing, the wacky but well stocked – if you can find anything – Anglia English Bookshop (☎ 283 64 2) is at Schellingstrasse 3. Down the street in the courtyard at Schellingstrasse 21a is Words' Worth Books (☎ 280 91 41).

The more expensive and limited but handy Sussmann international bookshop in the Hauptbahnhof has books in English and French, newspapers, magazines and Calvin & Hobbes collections (check their 'bargain' basket for books for DM10).

EurAide, also in the Hauptbahnhof, has a small selection of used English-language paperbacks for sale.

Max&Milian (☎ 260 33 20), Ickstattstrasse 2 south-east of Sendlinger Tor, is the best established gay and lesbian bookshop in Munich. You might also try Apacik & Schell (☎ 483 64 9), Ohlmühlertstrasse 18 (enter from Etenbachstrasse).

Libraries There are branches in Munich of *Stadtbüchereien* (city libraries), where you will usually find some books in English. You can get a library card with some identification.

Branches include those at Rosental 16 (☎ 265 24 4) in the Altstadt, at Winthirstrasse 10 (☎ 160 18 0) in Neuhausen and at Hohenzollernstrasse 16 (☎ 336 01 3) in Schwabing.

University libraries include the Universitätsbibliothek (☎ 218 00), Geschwister-Scholl-Platz 1, and the Technical University Library (☎ 210 5), opposite the Alte Pinakothek, at Arcisstrasse 21.

The libraries at the British Council (☎ 223 32 6), Bruderstrasse 7, and Amerika Haus (☎ 595 36 7), Karolinenplatz 3, both specialise in books about culture and business in those countries.

Campuses With over 63,000 students, the Ludwig-Maximilians-Universität München (☎ 218 00), at Geschwister-Scholl-Platz 1, is Germany's largest single university. The top three faculties are medicine, economics and law.

The Technischen Universität München (☎ 289 01), Arcisstrasse 21, has about 22,000 students studying mainly mathematics, physics, chemistry, biology and earth sciences.

International Centres Cultural organisations abound; the *München im...* publication (see Listings in the Entertainment section) has the complete list. The city has active branches of Amerika Haus (☎ 595 36 7),

Karolinenplatz 3; the British Council (☎ 223 32 6), Bruderstrasse 7; the Institut Français (☎ 286 62 80), Kaulbachstrasse 13; and the Goethe Institute (☎ 551 90 30), Sonnenstrasse 25.

Laundry The best laundrette close to the centre is Der Wunderbare Waschsalon, Theresienstrasse 134, open 6 am to midnight every day. It's spotless, has café-style tables, drinkable coffee and a pleasant atmosphere. A load of laundry costs DM6.

Close to the Hauptbahnhof but swarming with layabouts is Prinz Münz-Waschsalon at Paul-Heyse-Strasse 21, open daily from 6 am to 10 pm. Loads cost DM7, dryers are DM1 for 15 minutes, and the last wash must be in by 8 pm.

Close by in Westend, there's the nicer SB Waschsalon at Schwanthalerstrasse that's the cheapest in town (just DM5 per load).

In Neuhausen, there's a 24-hour Waschsalon on the west side of Landshuter Strasse at No 77, on the corner of Volkartstrasse, about 10 minutes from the hostel. There's a tanning salon downstairs, lest you leave sallow.

Medical & Emergency Services The US and UK consulates can provide lists of English-speaking doctors on request.

Medical help is available through the Kassenärztlicher Notfalldienst; call ☎ 557 75 5 and help will arrive. For an ambulance ring ☎ 192 22. Most pharmacies will have some English-speaking staff on hand, but there are several designated 'international' ones with English-speaking staff: at the airport (☎ 975 92 95 0); Bahnhof-Apotheke (☎ 694 11 9), Bahnhofplatz 2; and Ludwigs-Apothek at Neuhauser Strasse 11 (☎ 260 30 21). To find an open pharmacy in an emergency, call ☎ 594 47 5. For an emergency dentist call ☎ 516 00.

There's a police station at the Hauptbahnhof on the Arnulfstrasse side.

Dangers & Annoyances Crime and staggering drunks leaving the beer halls are major problems in Munich. This can get very dangerous at closing time during Oktobe fest, especially near the southern end c Hauptbahnhof (it's no joke: drunk people i a crowd trying to get home can get violen and there are about 100 cases of assault ever year). Leave early or stay very cautious, not sober, yourself.

Watch valuables carefully around tourist areas, especially when on guided walkin tours. A common trick is to steal your gear you strip off in the English Garden (that's nc to discourage stripping off, mind you, bu keep an eye on your kit).

The *Föhn* (pronounced 'foon') is weather-related annoyance peculiar t Munich's location in a valley. Static-charge wind from the south brings both exquisit views clear to the Alps as well as an area c dense pressure that sits on the city. Asthma ics and others sensitive to rapid pressu changes claim it gives them headache Münchners claim it makes them all cranky

Marienplatz

This is usually the start of most people's tou of Munich, and rightly so: it's the centre c the action in the Altstadt and the true heart c the city, punctuated by the glowing **Marien säule** (Mary Column), erected in 1638 t celebrate the removal of Swedish forces. A its top is the golden figure of the Virgin Mary carved in 1590 and originally located in th Frauenkirche. Our tour of the square start under the towering spires of the Neue Rathaus.

Neues Rathaus The late-Gothic new tow hall (1867-1908) surrounds six courtyards including the **Prunkhof**; there are festival and events in them throughout the year. Th building's blackened façade is festoone with gargoyles and statues, including, at th corner, a wonderful dragon climbing th turrets.

The highlight of the building is, of course its incessantly photographed **Glockenspie** (carillon), which has three levels. Tw portray the **Schäfflertanz** (see the Histor section) and the **Rittertunier**, a knights' tour nament held in 1568 to celebrate a roya marriage. The Glockenspiel springs into action at 11 am (November to April only), noon and 5 pm. The night scene, featuring the **Münchner Kindl** and **Nachtwächter**, runs at 9 pm. See Places to Eat (under Cafés & Bistros) for information on the two best cafés from which to watch the spectacle.

You can take a lift to the top of the 85m-tall tower (DM3 adults, DM1.50 concession) Monday to Friday from 9 am to 7 pm, and from 10 am on Saturday, Sunday and holidays. The cashier is on the 4th floor; take the lift inside or, for a look at the workings of the building, take the stairs.

Fischbrunnen The Fish Fountain was used to keep river fish alive during medieval markets; later it was used as the ceremonial dunking spot for butchers' apprentices, and today it's a good meeting spot. Local legend says that dipping an empty purse into the water here on Ash Wednesday guarantees it will always be full.

Altes Rathaus The Bavarian-Gothic old town hall building (1474) stands forlornly at the eastern end of the square; destroyed by fire and bombs, it was rebuilt with far less fanfare after WWII. In its south tower is the city's Toy Museum (see Other Museums).

Churches Several important churches are on or near Marienplatz. At the southern end is the **Alter Peter** (also known as St Peterskirche), which was the city's first parish church in the 11th century. The Gothic building you see today was begun in the 14th century. You can climb its unique rectangular 92m-tall tower (297 steps; entry DM2.50/1.50) for spectacular views of the city. The flamboyant rococo interior was restored after WWII.

Behind the Altes Rathaus, the **Heiliggeistkirche** (1392, interior 1724-30) is Munich's largest Gothic hall church. It first appears almost economical in design until you look up to see the Asam brothers' amazing rococo ceiling.

At the western end of the square, walk north one block on Weinstrasse and left down the alley and you'll come upon Munich's trademark, the oxidised copper onion domes atop the twin spires of the clunky late-Gothic **Frauenkirche** (Church of Our Lady, 1468-88), the metropolitan church of the archbishopric of Munich-Freising. The monotonous red brick is very Bavarian in its simplicity. Also simple, but elegant, are its highlights: the magnificent **St Nepomuk Altar** by Cosmas Damian Asam and Johan Michael Ernst, and the **tomb of Emperor Ludwig the Bavarian**. You can climb the south tower (98m; DM4/2) April to October, Monday to Saturday from 10 am to 5 pm.

Just south-west of the Frauenkirche and back on Neuhauser Strasse is **Michaelskirche**, Germany's grandest Renaissance church.

Sendlinger Strasse

At Marienplatz, follow Sendlinger Strasse south-west to No 32, St Johann Nepomuk-Kirche, called simply the **Asamkirche** (1733-46), a remarkable church designed and built by the Asam brothers. It shows a rare unity of style, with scarcely a single unembellished surface. The interior is jaw-dropping (note, as you enter, the **golden skeleton** of Death trying to cut the string of Life to the right).

At the south-western end of the street is **Sendlinger Tor**, the 14th-century southern city gate. As you walk back towards Marienplatz, turn right into Rosental, which leads to St-Jakobs-Platz and the **Stadtmuseum** (closed Monday; DM5), where the outstanding exhibits cover brewing, fashion, musical instruments, photography and puppets. There are films shown nightly here as well; see Cinema in the Entertainment section.

Viktualienmarkt

The Viktualienmarkt is one of Europe's great food markets. It's crowded throughout the year: in summer the entire place is transformed into one of the finest and most expensive beer gardens around; in winter people huddle for warmth and schnapps in the small *Kneipen* (pubs) around the square.

The merchandise and food are of the finest quality, but bargains don't exactly abound (see Self-Catering in Places to Eat for some suggestions).

From Marienplatz to Max-Joseph-Platz
From the central **Sparkasse** building, Sparkassenstrasse leads north past some exceptional buildings. At the northern end of the street is the **Alter Hof**, the Wittelsbach residence until they outgrew it and built the Residenz. Turn right into Ledererstrasse and walk one block, make a left onto Orlandostrasse (teeming with tourist crap shops) and one block up on the right-hand side is Munich's celebrated **Hofbräuhaus**, crawling with tourists from opening time at 11 am. The ballroom upstairs was the site of the first large meeting of the National Socialist Party on 20 February 1920; you can visit it if the rooms aren't being used for a function. As you guzzle from a *Mass* (litre mug) of beer (DM11 to DM13) downstairs, remember that the city is getting 25% of the take.

BAVARIA

Just north of the Hofbräuhaus is a formerly lovely building that's destined (or doomed) to become another Munich landmark: the Planet Hollywood bar-restaurant should be open when you read this.

Another notable building in this area (a block north of the Alter Hof) is the former **Mint**. An inscription on the west side of the building reads *Moneta Regis* (Money Rules).

Max-Joseph-Platz
Broad **Maximilianstrasse**, Munich's most glamourous shopping street with splendiferously expensive designer shops and the grand Kempinski Vier Jahreszeiten Hotel, runs into the southern end of Max-Joseph-Platz, home to some of Munich's most beloved buildings, among them the **Nationaltheater**, the five-tiered **Opera House**, and the grand daddy of them all – the Residenz. The square's focal point is a statue of Bavarian king Max I Joseph, who promulgated Germany's first constitution in 1818.

At the southern end of the square is the old **central post office**, on the site of a former palace, with a frescoed Italianate arcade. The building is still a post office; enter at the west side.

Residenz
This huge palace housed Bavarian rulers from 1385 to 1918, and contains more than 400 years of architectural history. The building was begun in 1571 with the wing that now fronts Max-Joseph-Platz. Expansions were added gradually until the northern wings created several interior courtyards, including the Emperor, Apothecary and Fountain courtyards and the smaller Chapel and King's Tract ones. The enclosed Grotto Court, one of the first places you'll see when you enter, features the wonderful **Perseus Fountain**. The west side of the building fronts Residenzstrasse and has the entrance to the Egyptian Art Museum and the Altes Residenztheater; the south side of the building, fronting Max-Joseph-Platz, holds the entrance to the Residenzmuseum and the Schatzkammer.

Residenzmuseum Within the palace, the Residenzmuseum (☎ 290 67 1) has an extraordinary array of over 100 rooms displaying treasures of the Wittelsbach dynasty. The museum is so large that the tours (in German only) are broken into two sessions of two hours each. To do it on your own is better; pick up a copy of the excellent English-language guide *Residence Munich* (DM6, at the cash desk), which has room-by-room tours with photographs and explanations.

Highlights include the **Ancestral Gallery**, remodelled in 1726-30 and including 121 portraits of the rulers of Bavaria (note, in the centre, the larger paintings of Charlemagne and Ludwig the Bavarian); the **Schlachtensäle** (Battle Halls); **Porcelain Chambers**, containing 19th-century porcelain services from factories in Berlin, Meissen and Nymphenburg; and the **Asian Collections** with Chinese and Japanese lacquerware, tapestries, carpets, furniture and jewellery.

The museum is open Tuesday to Sunday from 10 am to 4.30 pm; admission is DM6 (free for children). Two-hour tours (DM8) in

German are held on Sunday and Thursday at 11 am, and Thursday and Saturday at 2 pm; each tour views half the collection.

Schatzkammer The Residenzmuseum entrance is also the entrance to the Schatzkammmer der Residenz (Treasury; separate admission of DM6/free), which exhibits an enormous quantity of jewels, ornate goldwork and other precious objects. The mind-boggling treasures in this Aladdin's Cave include portable altars, the ruby jewellery of Queen Therese, amazing pocket watches, and 'exotic handicrafts', including applied art from Turkey, Iran, Mexico and India. It's definitely worth the admission price; the English-language guide to the collection, *Treasury in the Munich Residence*, is another DM6. The Schatzkammer is open Tuesday to Sunday from 10 am to 4.30 pm.

Altes Residenztheater The Old Residence Theatre, also known as the Cuvilliés Theater, is perhaps Europe's finest rococo theatre, with a stunning, lavish interior. While the building was destroyed during bombings in 1944, the interior furnishings had been removed so what you see today is original. You can visit, except during state opera and theatre company rehearsals, Monday to Saturday from 2 to 5 pm and Sunday from 10 am to 5 pm; admission is DM3/free. The entrance is at Residenzstrasse 1.

Egyptian Art Museum At the south side of the Hofgarten and the north side of the Residenz, the Staatliche Sammlung Ägyptischer Kunst (☎ 298 54 6) – at Hofgartenstrasse 1 but enter at the north side of the Residenz at the Obelisk – has an excellent display of Egyptian antiquities, artwork, monuments and statues from the Old, Middle and New Kingdoms (2670-1075 BC). It's open Tuesday to Friday from 9 am to 4 pm and 7 to 9 pm; Saturday, Sunday and holidays from 10 am to 5 pm; closed Monday. Admission is DM5/3.

Lion Statues At the entrance to the theatre and the Egyptian Art Museum on Residenzstrasse, note the two lions guarding the gates. Rubbing one of the lions' shields (look for the one that's been buffed to a gleaming shine) is said to bring wealth to the rubber.

Odeonsplatz

Residenzstrasse leads north from Max-Joseph-Platz to the **Feldherrnhalle** (Field Marshal's Hall) at the south end of Odeonsplatz. This square is the starting point of Ludwigstrasse, a broad Parisian-style boulevard, which shoots north past the university to the **Siegestor** (Triumphal Arch), which itself marks the starting point of chic Leopoldstrasse.

Odeonsplatz was the site of one of the earliest putsch attempts by Nazis in 1923, the so-called Beer Hall Putsch which landed Hitler in jail. The Feldherrnhalle, dedicated to the field marshals under the Wittelsbachs, has several statues, including one of General Tilly, who surrendered Munich to the Swedes during the Thirty Years' War.

At the west side of the square is the landmark **Theatinerkirche St Kajetan** (1663-90), built to commemorate the conception (after a lengthy period of trying by Henriette Adelaide) of Prince Max Emanuel. Designed by Agostino Barelli, the church's massive twin towers around a giant cupola are another landmark of Munich's skyline. Inside, the intensely stuccoed high dome stands above the Fürstengruft, containing the remains of Wittelsbach family members.

South of the Theatinerkirche, on fashionable Theatinerstrasse at No 15, is the **Kunsthalle der Hypo-Kulturstiftung** (☎ 224 41 2; U-Bahn No 3, 4, 5 or 6 to Odeonsplatz or tram No 19 from the centre), which has excellent rotating exhibitions. Check with EurAide or the tourist offices as to what's on when you're in town.

At the east side of Odeonsplatz, the neoclassical **Hofgartentor** (1816) leads the way to the **Hofgarten**, the former royal gardens, with lovely paths around a **temple**. At the eastern end is the modern **Bayerische Staatskanzlei** (city chancellor's office), in front of which is the city's **WWI memorial**.

Karlsplatz
At the Altstadt's western end is Karlsplatz, punctuated by the medieval **Karlstor** (the old west city gate), and an enormous **fountain**, a favourite meeting point. One of the city's largest department stores, Karstadt, has a huge branch here; it's also a major tram, bus, U-Bahn and S-Bahn connection point. Just north is the city **Börse** (stock exchange) and east of the gate, the **Richard Strauss Fountain**.

Königsplatz
North-west of the Altstadt is Königsplatz (U-Bahn No 2 or tram No 27), a Greek-revivalist pile created under Ludwig I to house several art museums. The square is flanked by the **Glyptothek** at the north and the **Staatliche Antikensammlungen** opposite, designed in the centre like a Corinthian temple. The centrepiece of the square is the Doric-columned **Propyläen** gateway.

The Glyptothek and the Antikensammlungen are worth a look; either museum costs DM6/3.50; to visit both costs DM10/6. Try to go on a Sunday when they're free; both are closed on Monday.

Glyptothek The Glyptothek (☎ 286 10 0), Königsplatz 3, contains a fascinating collection of Greek and Roman sculpture and portraits of Greek philosophers and leaders and Roman kings. It's open Tuesday to Sunday from 10 am to 5 pm (to 8 pm on Thursday).

Antikensammlungen The Staatliche Antikensammlungen (☎ 598 35 9), Königsplatz 1, features one of Germany's best antiquities collections, including vases, gold and silver jewellery and ornaments, bronzework, and Greek, Roman and other sculptures and statues. It's open Tuesday to Sunday from 10 am to 5 pm (to 8 pm on Wednesday).

Lenbach House Portraitist Franz von Lenbach (1836-1904), a leading *Gründerzeit* painter, used his considerable fortune to construct a residence in Munich between 1883 and 1889. It was sold to the city by his widow in 1924, and she threw in a bunch of his works as part of the deal. Today his fabulous residence is open as the Museum im Lenbach Haus (☎ 233 03 20), Luisenstrasse 33, featuring a staggering range of 19th-century masterpieces by Munich and other German masters and space for exhibitions of international modern art. A whole section upstairs is devoted to *Blaue Reiter* (Blue Rider) painters, members of a movement begun in 1911 by Franz Marc (1880-1916) and Wassily Kandinsky (1866-1944), widely acknowledged to be the first abstract painter. The group, which also included Paul Klee, Alexej Jawlenski, August Macke and Gabrielle Münter, is acknowledged as the high point of German expressionism (see Expressionism in the Painting & Sculpture section of the Facts about the Country chapter). Entry to the museum is DM8/4. Outside the museum is a beer garden and a lovely courtyard with fountains.

Mineral Museums Rock fans should head for the nearby **Geologische Staatssammlung** (☎ 520 31), Luisenstrasse 37, with exhibitions on the earth's crust and mineral wealth. Admission is free. Also popular is the **Museum Reich der Kristalle** (☎ 239 44 31 2), Theresienstrasse 41 (entrance at Barer Strasse, across the street from the Alte Pinakothek), with excellent exhibitions on the formation of minerals and crystals. It's open Tuesday to Friday from 1 to 5 pm and Saturday and Sunday from 1 to 6 pm; admission is DM2/1.

Alte Pinakothek The Alte Pinakothek (☎ 238 05 0), at Barer Strasse 27 (north entrance), is a veritable treasure house of the works of European masters between the 14th and 18th centuries, including Albrecht Dürer's Christ-like *Self-Portrait* and his *Four Apostles*; Rogier van der Weyden's *Adoration of the Magi*; and Botticelli's *Pietà*. Unfortunately it has been closed for renovations the past several years. Stay tuned.

Neue Pinakothek Just opposite the Alte

BAVARIA

Pinakothek at Barer Strasse 29 is the Neue Pinakothek (☎ 238 05), entrance on Theresienstrasse. During the researching of this book it contained selections from the Alte Pinakothek, in addition to an abbreviated showing of its own wonderful works, mainly 19th-century painting and sculpture. It's open Tuesday to Sunday from 10 am to 5 pm (to 8 pm Tuesday and Thursday). Entry is DM7/4, free on Sunday.

English Garden

The Englischer Garten is nestled between the Altstadt, Schwabing and the Isar River. The **Chinesischer Turm** (Chinese Tower), now in the centre of the city's best known beer garden, was constructed in 1789, which also marked the beginning of the park's construction. The largest city park in Europe, this is a great place for strolling, drinking, sunbaking and paddle-boating.

In balmy summer weather, nude sunbathing is the rule rather than the exception here. It's not unusual for hundreds of naked people to be in the park on a normal working day, with their coats, ties and frocks stacked primly on the grass. It's a lovely way to spend a sunny afternoon, but keep an eye firmly on your stuff (see Dangers & Annoyances).

Check out one of the three beer gardens here (see Places to Eat), or head out for a little paddle on the lake. Just south of the Chinesischer Turm is the heavily photographed monument **Monopteros** (1838).

If you like the park so much you'd like to spend the night, remember that police patrol frequently, and muggers, junkies, proselytisers and other colourful characters are everywhere. In other words, forget it.

Deutsches Museum

Said to be the world's largest science and technology museum, the Deutsches Museum (☎ 217 91), Museumsinsel 1 near Isartor to the east of the city centre, takes up eight floors: the basement is devoted to mining and automobiles; the ground floor to tunnel construction, railways and aeronautics. The 1st floor has a flimsy and dated section on physics and chemistry, and a wonderful section on musical instruments. The 2nd floor has the Altamira cave exhibit. The 3rd floor ranges from geodesy and weights & measures to microelectronics and telecommunications. The 4th to 6th floors are dedicated to astronomy and amateur radio.

The museum is open from 9 am to 5 pm daily; admission is DM10, discount DM4. It's free for children under six and a family ticket costs DM22. A visit to the planetarium is DM3 extra. To reach it take any S-Bahn to Isartor, U-Bahn No 1 or 2 to Fraunhoferstrasse, or tram No 18 almost to the door.

Forum der Technik In the north-east corner of the museum complex on Museumsinsel, near Rosenheimer Strasse, is the Technical Forum (☎ 211 25 18 3), with a Zeiss planetarium show and an IMAX (big-screen) cinema. Offerings generally look at nature and it's absolutely worth the admission price of DM11.90/8.90 (a combination ticket for the planetarium and IMAX is DM20.50/15.50). Several days a week, there are late-night performances of a Pink Floyd laser show (DM18.90/14.90). Programmes for children run on weekdays (DM6.50) and prices are reduced on Monday, 'cinema day' (DM8.50).

Modern Art Gallery

The Staatsgalerie Moderner Kunst (☎ 211 27 13 7), Prinzregentenstrasse 1 in the Haus der Kunst (bus No 53 from the centre), displays some great German and international contributions to modern art, including wild paintings by Munch, Picasso and Magritte, as well as funky sculpture and some pop art. It's open Tuesday to Sunday from 10 am to 5 pm (to 8 pm on Thursday); entry is DM6/3.50.

Bavarian National Museum

At the eastern end of Prinzregentenstrasse, at No 3 (U-Bahn No 4 or 5 to Lehel or tram No 17 or bus No 53 almost to the door), the formidable Bayerisches Nationalmuseum (☎ 211 24 1) has the city's biggest collection of Bavarian and other German art, as well as artwork from around the world, modern and industrial art and prehistory. In the main building, there's folk art and history, including religious and folk costumes and artefacts.

The ground floor has early-medieval, Gothic, Renaissance, rococo, baroque and neoclassical works; and the 1st floor has applied arts, including clocks, ceramics, jewellery and stained glass. The Fine Art Collection has sculptures, carvings and paintings up to the 14th century. It's open Tuesday to Sunday from 9.30 am to 5 pm; admission is DM3/2.

The **Neue Sammlung** (New Collection; ☎ 227 84 4) holds rotating exhibitions from its huge collection of applied and industrial art.

At the northern section of the complex, the **Prähistorische Staatssammlung** (Prehistoric Collection; ☎ 293 91 1), Lerchenfeldstrasse 2, is packed with archaeological goodies, including artefacts from the city's first Roman and Celtic residents. It's open Tuesday to Sunday from 9 am to 4 pm (to 8 pm Thursday); DM5/3.

Schackgalerie

This little gallery (☎ 238 05), at Prinzregentenstrasse 9 (bus No 53), houses a fine collection of 19th-century German paintings from the collection of a Count Schack. It's open daily except Tuesday from 10 am to 5 pm; admission is DM4/2.50.

Schloss Nymphenburg

If the Residenz hasn't satisfied your passion for palaces, visit the amazing Schloss Nymphenburg north-west of the city centre (tram No 17 or bus No 41). Begun in 1664 as a villa for Electress Adelaide of Savoy, the castle and formal gardens were continually expanded and built upon over the next century to create the royal family's summer residence. Today the castle, porcelain factory and grounds (the surrounding park is worth a long stroll) are open to the public, and the grounds are also home to the Museum Mensch und Natur (Museum of Man and Nature), all definitely worth it if you're here with kids.

A combined ticket to everything except the Museum of Man and Nature costs DM8/7. Admission to the Schloss and the Schönheitengalerie is DM4/3; to Amalienburg or Badenburg DM3.

Palace The main palace building (☎ 179 08) consists of two wings to the north and south of the main villa. You can visit Tuesday to Sunday from 9 am to 12.30 pm and from 1.30 to 5 pm. The rooms are all sumptuously decorated, but our favourite is Ludwig's **Schönheitengalerie** (Gallery of Beauties). in the southern wing, formerly the apartments of Queen Caroline. It's now the repository of 38 portraits of women, all of social standing, whom Ludwig I considered beautiful; most famous of these is *Schöne Münchnerin*, the portrait of Helene Sedlmayr, daughter of a shoemaker.

Also in the south wing is the **Marstallmuseum** (☎ 179 08), with the coaches and riding gear of the royal families. It's open Tuesday to Sunday from 9 am to noon and 1 to 5 pm. Admission is DM3/2.

Tours of the palace are only offered to groups; pick up a copy of the unintentionally hilarious English-language translation of the guide *Nymphenburg* for DM5 at the cash desk.

Porcelain Museum The former factory of Nymphenburg Porcelain, on the 1st floor of the Marstallmuseum, is now the Nymphenburger Porzellan Sammlung Bäuml (☎ 179 08 0), which has the exhibit 'Treasures of Porcelain', spanning 250 years of porcelain manufacturing here. Entry is DM3/2.

Gardens The royal gardens are a magnificently sculpted English park. In front (east) of the palace is a long canal, on which locals can be seen ice skating in winter. Behind (west of) the castle, the royal gardens ramble on around the continuation of the Nymphenburger Canal.

The whole park is enchanting, and home to several smaller buildings, four of them notable and open to the public.

Electress Amelia had the **Amalienburg**, a

small hunting lodge with a large domed central room, built between 1734 and 1739. Don't miss the amazing Spiegelsaal (Mirror Hall). Amalienburg is open daily from 9 am to 12.30 pm and 1.30 to 5 pm. The two-storey **Pagodenburg** (1717-19) was built as a Chinese teahouse by Prince Max Emanuel; the building is closed for renovation. Opposite it, the **Badenburg**, by the lake of the same name, was also built by Max Emanuel, as a sauna and bathing house. You can visit it Tuesday to Sunday from 10 am to 12.30 pm and 1.30 to 5 pm.

Museum Mensch und Natur This natural history and science museum (☎ 176 49 4) is a fun place to bring the kids. Interactive, if aged, displays in German let kids take quizzes, but mostly they'll be racing to the upstairs exhibits on animals and the earth. There are rotating exhibitions in addition to the permanent collection, and a nice café downstairs. It's open Tuesday to Sunday from 9 am to 5 pm. Admission is DM3/1.50, kids under six free.

Olympic Park

A quarter century after the Olympics for which it was built, Olympiapark (☎ 306 70) is still an integral part of life in the city. The centrepieces are the 290m-high Olympiaturm (Olympia Tower) and the 75,000-sq-m transparent 'tented' roof covering the west side of the Olympic Stadium, Olympic Hall and the swimming centre.

Today the complex is open as a collection of public facilities, and the grounds are the site of celebrations, concerts, fireworks displays and professional sporting matches throughout the year. The swimming hall is open to the public, as is the ice arena.

There are two tours daily from April to October (meet at the information booth at the park's north-east): a soccer tour at 11 am, which visits the Olympic Stadium, VIP area and locker rooms (one hour; DM 8 for adults, DM6 for children under 15), and an adventure tour which covers the entire Olympiapark on foot and in a little train (1½ hours; DM13/8).

Olympia Tower If you like heights, go to the top of the Olympiaturm, which is open daily from 9 am to midnight, with the last trip up at 11.30 pm (DM5/2.50).

At the top, when the weather's good, you'll have stunning views of the city and, if you're feeling cashed up and hungry, you can have a meal at the revolving restaurant (☎ 308 10 39).

BMW Museum

Opposite Olympic Park at Petuelring 130 is the popular BMW Museum (☎ 382 23 30 7). Behind the museum, the BMW (Bayerische Moteren Werke) headquarters building (1970-73), with its striking steel cylinders, is an architectural attraction in its own right.

The museum is as immaculate as you'd expect. Exhibits include many BMW cars, motorcycles, planes, concept cars and, near the top, simulators and interactive displays. It's open daily from 9 am to 5 pm (last entry at 4 pm). Admission is DM5.50/4.

Take the U-Bahn No 2 to Scheidplatz and then the U-Bahn No 3, or take the No 3 direct from Marienplatz to Olympiazentrum. Look for the huge silver towers.

The BMW factory (☎ 382 23 30 6), adjacent to the headquarters and museum, discontinued its free tours of the factory line in 1997 but you might telephone to see if they have been resumed.

Other Museums

Jewish Museum The Jüdisches Museum München (☎ 297 45 3), Maximilianstrasse 36 (tram No 19), is an under- visited exhibition on the history of Jews in Munich and Bavaria.

Admission is free, but the hours are severely limited due to budgetary constraints, so donations are encouraged. It's open Tuesday and Wednesday from 2 to 6 pm and Thursday from 2 to 8 pm.

Bavaria Film Museum Tour An often-missed treasure in Munich is the Bavaria Film Tour (☎ 649 92 30 4) of the Bavaria Film Museum, at Bavariafilmplatz 7 in the suburb of Geiselgasteig (U-Bahn No 1 or 2 to Silberhornstrasse then tram No 25 to Bavariafilmplatz). You'll see sets of *Enemy Mine*, *Das Boot*, *Cabaret* and *The Never-Ending Story*, all of which were filmed here. German TV series and films are still shot here as well. It runs from March to October; admission is DM15/10.

Valentin Musäum Dedicated to one of Bavaria's most beloved comic actors, this museum (☎ 223 26 6) celebrates the life and work of Karl Valentin and his partner, Liesl Karlstadt. It's in Isartor, the southernmost gate of the medieval fortifications and itself a work of 14th-century art, bearing an impressive fresco of King Ludwig's triumphant return to the city in 1322.

The museum's uproarious opening hours are Monday to Wednesday and Friday and Saturday from 11.01 am to 5.29 pm, Sunday from 10.01 am to 5.29 pm, closed Thursday. The admission prices are DM2.99/1.99. At night it's also a bar with folk music. Take any S-Bahn to Isartor.

Centre for Unusual Museums We could make lots of jokes about this place, but to paraphrase Groucho Marx, it doesn't need our help. The Zentrum für Ausergewöhnliche Museen (☎ 290 41 21), Westenriederstrasse 26 (any S-Bahn to Isartor or tram No 17 or 18), is a gathering of bizarre and unusual collections, including bottles, Easter bunnies, chamber pots, corkscrews and locks. There's also a collection of items associated with Sissy (that's Empress Elisabeth of Austria to you). It's open daily from 10 am to 6 pm and entry costs DM8/5 – a bargain at twice the price.

SiemensForum The SiemensForum (☎ 234 3), Prannerstrasse 10, has fascinating exhibits on electronics and microelectronics from the telegraph to the multimedia personal computer. It's a fun, hands-on kind of place, open Monday to Friday and Sunday from 10 am to 5 pm. Entry is free, so why not? Take any S-Bahn to Karlsplatz, U-Bahn No 4 or 5 to Odeonsplatz or tram No 19.

Toy Museum In the tower of the Altes Rathaus, the most amusing thing about the city's **Spielzeugmuseum** (☎ 294 00 1) is right in front: the wind-powered sculpture that releases pent-up energy every few minutes by clanging and banging. That's a free exhibit. Inside (admission DM5/1) you'll stare at case after case of dolls. Unless you're a big doll fan, give this one a wide berth.

Theresienwiese

The Theresa Meadow, just south-west of the city centre (U-Bahn No 4 or 5 to Theresienwiese, or bus No 31 or 32), is the site of the annual Oktoberfest (see Special Events) as well as trade shows throughout the year. At the western end of the meadow, just near Theresienhöhe, is the **Ruhmeshalle** (Hall of Fame) containing statues of Bavarian leaders and the *Bavaria* statue, whose cunning design makes it seem as if the thing is solid. It isn't – and you can climb to the head to get a so-so view of the city or a great view of the Oktoberfest for a mere DM3 (free for kids), Tuesday to Sunday from 10 am to noon and 2 to 5.30 pm.

Zoo

The Hellabrunn Zoo (☎ 625 08 0), Tierparkstrasse 30, south of the centre in Thalkirchen, was the first 'geo-zoo' (one with distinct sections dividing animals by continents). Today it has about 5000 animals representing 460 different species, including rhinos, elephants, deer, bucks and gazelles. It's absolutely worth the DM10/5 admission if only to gain access to the petting zoo, crawling with sheep, deer and lambs that you can feed. Perhaps the best exhibit, though, is the tropical bird that shouts, loudly, '*Arschloch!*' ('Asshole!') to giggling tourists. Take U-Bahn No 3 to Thalkirchen or bus No 52 almost to the entrance.

Activities

Munich makes a perfect base for outdoor activities. For information about hiking and climbing, contact the Deutscher Alpenverein

(German Alpine Club; ☎ 140 03 0), west of the centre at Von-Kahr-Strasse 2-4.

For gear, the Sport Schuster, Rosenstrasse 1-5, and the better Sport Scheck (☎ 216 60), nearby at Sendlinger Strasse 6, both have multiple floors of everything imaginable for the adventurer, from simple camping equipment to expedition wear, plus excellent bookshops. There's a discount Sport Scheck at the Ostbahnhof selling discontinued merchandise.

Swimming It's illegal to swim in the Isar River within the city limits. The Disneyland of German swimming pools is about an hour away at Alpamare; see Bad Tölz in the Around Munich section for more information.

The two best swimming pools in town are at Olympiapark and the spectacular Art Nouveau Müllerisches Volksbad (☎ 236 13 42 9), Rosenheimer Strasse 1. The latter is worth visiting even if you don't swim. It has a large pool, sauna, steam baths and public baths; the cost is DM3.50/2.50 per hour, or with a private cabin (in which to take a hot bath) DM7.50. It's open to women only on Tuesday and Friday, men only on Wednesday and Thursday.

The Olympic pool at Olympiapark is open to the public for varying sessions throughout the day. Admission is DM5/4; add a sauna and the price is DM15/11. Tanning beds (DM5) are available as well.

Boating There are several places in town to take a little tootle with a boat; the most popular spot is the English Garden's Kleinhesseloher See, where rowing/pedal boats cost DM10/12 per half hour for up to four people. Cheaper are the boats at Olympiapark, which rent for DM10/12 per hour for up to four people.

Rafting Rafting down the Isar River is a wonderful thing to do, and on warm days, many Munich residents take advantage of a little loophole in the law that allows free camping on the banks of the river (as long as you don't make a fire in protected areas).

The usual route is to begin between 25 and 50km south of Munich, at either Wolfratshausen or Bad Tölz, and make your way back with the current. There's a really easy starting point 100m from the Wolfratshausen S-Bahn station, and in good weather you'll just need to follow the crowds. There are several places along the river where you'll have to take the raft out of the water and carry it around dams or locks, but for the most part it's just a lazy, wonderful trip. For a couple it can be the most romantic part of a trip to Munich.

Nude bathing along the route is not only permitted, it would seem to be mandatory (though for some of the folks you'll see standing on the riverbank *clothing* should be mandatory!). Make sure to use plenty of sunscreen on places not ordinarily exposed to the sun.

To get started you'll need a reasonable quality inflatable rubber raft (available at Kaufhof, Sport Scheck or Schuster, though the first is cheapest) for about DM110 to DM125. Get on S-Bahn No 7 and head for Wolfratshausen (the last stop) or change trains for Bad Tölz. You'll need food, four litres of water per person per day plus something waterproof to hold all your gear (a second little kiddy raft tied to your raft works well, but make sure your sleeping bag and clothes are secure and in sealed plastic bags).

As evening approaches, find a nice quiet stretch of riverbank on which to bed down, take the raft out of the water and set up camp. It's quiet, peaceful and if you have a camping stove, you can probably get away with cooking dinner. It's usually not bug-infested, so you won't need a tent.

Do not attempt this if it's rained heavily in the previous three days. The Isar, while shallow, is very cold and swells to dangerous levels after rainstorms, creating fast and unstable currents. Call for weather reports (☎ 0190-116 95 8; DM1.20 per minute) and check the newspapers before heading out. The best rule of thumb is to watch the locals and follow warning signs along the route.

For more information on river trips and rowing possibilities in the area, contact the

Bayerische Kanu Verband (☎ 157 02 44 3), and ask them for a copy of their *Wanderführ-Bayern*, which lists routes and regional rental outlets.

Raft Tours Organised tours down the Isar aboard huge rafts are really fun, and if you're not into buying a raft and doing it all yourself, this is a great way to spend an afternoon. They're usually for groups (though individuals can join some), and they're a real hoot: usually accompanied by an oompah band and at least a keg of beer, the rafts stay out for several hours. The price (from DM50 to DM150 per person) includes transport, beer and lunch. To book, call or visit abr (☎ 120 42 37), the official Bavarian travel agency, at Promenadeplatz 12.

Skating The coolest thing in inline-skating is Skate 'n' Fun (☎ 490 01 31 3), in Kunstpark Ost at Grafingerstrasse 6 behind the Ostbahnhof. It's a safe and clean indoor stunt park with ramps, shells and skating areas for people of all ages. Rented gear, including complete protection (pads, helmets and the like), costs from DM8, plus the DM5 entry fee. You can also rent standard skates/those with extra stunt protection for DM10/15 a day or DM30 for the weekend. Courses are run daily.

Billiards There's a great pool hall in the Ostbahnhof called Billiard World (☎ 485 64 9). Open to 1 am, it has dozens of pool and snooker tables, with playing costs ranging from DM13 to DM15 per hour, depending on the time of day.

Organised Tours

Among the best organised walking tours in Germany are those with Munich Walks (mobile ☎ 0177-227 59 01), which runs English-language tours daily from May to December (two to 2½ hours; DM15/10 for adults/children). The Discover Munich tour covers the heart of the city and gives good historical background and architectural information; it leaves at 10 am and 3 pm from May to October, at 10 am only from November to 22 December. The Infamous Third Reich Sites tour covers exactly that, and runs on a more limited schedule. All tours leave from in front of the city tourist office at the east side of the Hauptbahnhof. Bring transport tickets.

Mike's Bike Tours (☎ 651 42 75) runs 3½-hour guided city cycling tours in English (DM29). They depart every day at 11.30 am and 4 pm from the archway in front of the Toy Museum on Marienplatz.

Panorama Tours (☎ 598 16 0) runs about six coach tours to various places in the city (one to 2½ hours; from DM15/8 to DM100 per person). They're all right but the commentary is given in two languages so everything takes twice as long to explain. They leave from in front of the Hertie department store opposite the Hauptbahnhof.

You can hire English-speaking private guides from the city tourist offices for groups of up to 25 people from DM140.

Special Events

Oktoberfest Try to get to Munich for the Oktoberfest, one of Europe's biggest and best parties (see also the boxed text). It runs from mid-September to the first Sunday in October. No entrance fee is charged but most of the fun costs something. Major Oktoberfest events include:

Grand Entry The parade through the city centre, from Sonnenstrasse to the fairgrounds via Schwanthalerstrasse, begins at 11 am on the first day of the festival. At noon, the lord mayor stands before the thirsty crowds at Theresienwiese. With due pomp, Hizzoner slams home a wooden tap with a mallet. When the tap breaks through the cask's surface and beer gushes forth, the mayor exclaims, '*Ozapft ist*!' ('It's tapped!').

Münchner Kindl A young girl on horseback carrying a litre of beer in one hand and a huge pretzel in the other leads 7000 performers from all over Europe (wearing pretzel bras and other traditional drunkenwear) through the streets of the city centre during the ceremonial opening.

BAVARIA

Oktoberfest

After the wedding on 12 October 1810 of Bavarian Crown Prince Ludwig I to the Saxon-Hildburghausen Princess Therese, an enormous party was held in front of the city gates. That was the beginning of what's now the largest beer festival in the world, Oktoberfest, a 16-day extravaganza that attracts over seven million people a year.

During the event, the Theresienwiese fairgrounds are practically a city of beer tents, amusements, rides – including a giant ferris wheel and roller coasters (just what beer drinkers need after several frothy ones) – and kiosks selling snacks and sweets.

The Oktoberfest, which runs from late September to early October, is Munich's largest and most economically important tourist attraction. Visitors and locals leave behind almost DM1.5 billion, and a lot of that will be in chunks of DM8 and DM12 (the prices, respectively, of a pretzel and a one-litre glass of Bavaria's finest).

There's not a whole lot you can do about the beer prices, but the food is where they really get you at the Oktoberfest tents. After a litre or two of amber liquid, the reluctance to part with DM20 for a beer and a chicken leg tends to waver, so make sure you eat before you arrive.

Self-catering is the cheapest way (see that section in Places to Eat for information on supermarkets and food halls). Avoid at all costs shops in the central train station, where prices for staple goods are 30 to 50% higher than in regular shops and markets.

Also, it's imperative that you reserve accommodation as early as you can (like a year in advance). Hotels book out very quickly, and their prices skyrocket, during the fair. If you show up during Oktoberfest, forget about finding a room in Munich.

Consider staying in the suburbs or nearby cities (eg Augsburg, Garmisch-Partenkirchen or Bad Tölz, all of which are under an hour away).

The festival is held at the Theresienwiese, a 15-minute walk from the Hauptbahnhof, and is served by its own U-Bahn station. If you're asking directions, say 'd'wies'n' (dee-VEEZEN), the diminutive nickname for the grounds. Trams and buses heading that way, however, sport signs reading '*Zur Festwiese*' ('to the Festival Meadow').

The Oktoberfest runs daily from about 10.30 am to 11:30 pm. It's best to leave the fair early, about 9 or 10 pm, as crowds can get a bit touchy when the beer and schnapps supplies are turned off.

Thursday is Children's Day, when all children's rides and attractions are half price. ■

Oktoberfest Folklore International Music, dance and folklore in the Circus Krone building at 8 pm on variable nights.

In addition, there's a big gay meeting the first Sunday of Oktoberfest at the Bräurosl tent, with legions of butch guys in leather pants. It is timed to coincide with a gay leather convention; it's huge fun and open to all.

Tollwood Festival Another fine Munich tradition is the summer Tollwood Festival, held each June and July at the Olympiapark complex. It's a world culture festival, with music, food, clothes and merchandise from around the world, and nightly world-music concerts, weather permitting. Admission is free but the concerts cost something (anywhere from DM5 to DM35).

Opera Festival The Munich Opera Festival is held every July at the Bayerische Staatsoper (Bavarian State Opera). Consisting mainly of shows staged during the past year, it always concludes on 31 July with *Die Meistersinger von Nürnberg*.

Places to Stay

Officially, no one older than 26 (unless travelling with children aged under 18) can stay in Bavarian hostels. This puts extra pressure on budget hotels and pensions, of which there are precious few in Munich. Reserve if possible and arrive early in the day. Remember that the EurAide and city tourist offices can book you into hotels and pensions.

Camping See Rafting under Activities for information about free camping along the Isar River.

The most central camping ground is *Campingplatz Thalkirchen* (☎ 723 17 07),

BAVARIA

south-west of the city centre at Zentralländstrasse 49, close to the hostel on Miesingstrasse. Open from mid-March to October, it can get incredibly crowded in summer, but there always seems to be room for one more tent. The price is DM7.80 per person plus DM5.50 per tent and DM8.50/4 per car/motorcycle. An extra charge is levied during Oktoberfest. There are laundry facilities on the grounds. Take U-Bahn No 3 to Thalkirchen and bus No 57 to Thalkirchen, the last stop (about 20 minutes from the city centre).

A bit farther from the city centre are *Waldcamping Obermenzing* (☎ 811 22 35) and *Langwieder See* (☎ 864 15 66); the latter has a great location but can only be reached by car on the autobahn towards Stuttgart. It is open from early April to the end of October.

DJH Hostels Munich's summer budget favourite is the *Jugendlager am Kapuziner Hölzl* (☎ 141 43 00) on In den Kirschen, north of Schloss Nymphenburg (U-Bahn No 1 to Rotkreuzplatz and then tram No 12 to the Botanischer Garten). Nicknamed 'The Tent', this mass camp is only open from mid-June to early September. There's no night curfew, but the usual 26-year age limit applies (with priority given to people under 23). The cheapest 'beds' (a thermal mattress and blanket in the big tent) cost DM13 with breakfast; showers are available. Normal beds are DM15.

Most central is the sparkling *Jugendherberge München* (☎ 131 15 6), north-west of the city centre at Wendl-Dietrich-Strasse 20 (U-Bahn No 1 to Rotkreuzplatz). One of the largest hostels in Germany, it is relatively loud and very busy, but very popular and friendly. Beds cost from DM25.50 (DM23 if you're willing to sleep in a room with 36 others!). There's no curfew or lock-out. The hostel has a restaurant, a garden and bicycles for rent (see Getting Around).

Still fairly accessible to the centre, and a better deal, is the more modern *Jugendgästehaus München* (☎ 723 65 50/60), south-west of the city centre in the suburb of Thalkirchen, at Miesingstrasse 4 (U-Bahn No 3 to Thalkirchen, then follow the signs). Costs per person are DM26 in dorms, DM28 in triples and quads, DM30 in doubles, and DM34 in singles. A 1 am curfew applies.

Jugendherberge Burg Schwaneck (☎ 793 06 43) at Burgweg 4-6 (S-Bahn No 7 to Pullach then a 10-minute walk) is in a great old castle in the southern suburbs. Dorm beds cost from DM19.50.

Independent Hostels Munich has quite a few non-DJH hostels or hotels that offer cheaper dormitory accommodation as well as simple rooms. The newest on the inner Munich budget scene is the ecologically inspired *4 you münchen* (☎ 552 16 60) at Hirtenstrasse 18. The downstairs 'hostel' section (where, unfortunately, the under-27 rule also applies) has dorm beds from DM27, as well as very nice singles/doubles from DM42/57. The wholemeal-organic breakfast costs an extra DM6. Guests over 26 can stay in the 'hotel' section upstairs for DM89/119 a single/double (including breakfast).

At the persnickety *CVJM-YMCA Jugendgästehaus* (☎ 552 14 10) at Landwehrstrasse 13, triples/doubles/singles are DM38/41/48 (or DM53 for a larger single), but prices are 15% higher for guests over 26. The staff are robotic.

The *Kolpinghaus St Theresia* (☎ 126 05 0) at Hanebergestrasse 8, a 10-minute walk north of Rotkreuzplatz (U-Bahn No 1), has beds for DM32/42/48 in triple/double/single rooms.

Women aged under 26 can try the *Jugendhotel Marienherberge* (☎ 555 80 5) at Goethestrasse 9, where beds start at DM25 and singles/doubles cost only DM35/60.

Somewhat scruffy but clean and pleasant the *Haus International* (☎ 120 06 0), at Elisabethstrasse 87 (tram No 12 to Barbara Strasse), is a 'youth hotel', not a hostel, so travellers of any age can stay. It has more than 500 beds in all; prices range from DM40 in five-person dorms to DM55/104 for small and simple singles/doubles, to DM85/144 for clean singles/doubles with all the moc cons. There's a pool, disco, beer garden and cafeteria.

Private Rooms & Long-Term Rentals In addition to the booking services of EurAide and the city tourist offices (see Information), *City Mitwohnzentrale* (☎ 194 30; fax 19 42 0), on the northern side of the Hauptbahnhof at Lämmerstrasse 4, lets furnished or unfurnished flats or rooms, from four days to indefinitely. The most you'll pay as a fee for long-term rentals is 1½ months' rent. Generally speaking, a room in a flat costs about DM500 per month, an apartment starts at DM800; some are cheaper, some more expensive. You'll need a credit card and your passport. They'll send you a form in English; fill it out and fax it back along with a photocopy of your ID/passport and credit card. Another agency is *Antje Wolf Bed & Breakfast Munich* (☎ 168 87 81), which arranges apartments and guest rooms with or without breakfast for anywhere from a day to a month.

Hotels – bottom end Prices in Munich are higher than in most other parts of Germany. Accommodation services (see Information and Private Rooms & Long-Term Rentals) can help, but even if you insist on the lowest price range, it's unlikely they'll find anything under DM55/90 for a single/double. Note also that prices in almost all city hotels rocket during Oktoberfest.

Hauptbahnhof There are plenty of fairly cheap, if sometimes seedy, places near the main train station. The best option is the cramped but reasonably clean *Pension Marie-Luise* (☎ 554 23 0), upstairs at Landwehrstrasse 35, which offers rooms from DM50/80. Phone for vacancies at the 11 am check-out time.

The staff are very nice and the rooms perfectly pleasant at the clean and cheerful *Andi (Comfort) Hotel* (☎ 552 56 0), Landwehrstrasse 33, with singles/doubles from DM95/130.

The somewhat run-down but friendly *Hotel Atlanta* (☎ 263 60 5), Sendlinger Strasse 58, is nicely located between Sendlinger Tor and the Asamkirche; go through the creepy door and up the creepy stairs to clean, simple, if brown, rooms from DM50/80, or DM75/85 with facilities.

Just north of the Hauptbahnhof in the package-tourist hotel area sits the *Amba* (☎ 545 14 0), Arnulfstrasse 20, which offers simple rooms from DM75/100 and standard rooms from DM140/160. (See Hotels – middle for more hotels along this strip.)

An ideal compromise of location, price and cleanliness is *Pension Haydn* (☎ 531 11 9), at Haydnstrasse 9, near the Goetheplatz U-Bahn station and within walking distance of the Hauptbahnhof. Rooms without bath start at DM50/80.

There's old-world charm, nice staff and clean, pleasant rooms at the *Hotel Pension Mariandl* (☎ 534 10 8), Goethestrasse 51; singles/doubles cost DM65/90, or DM60/85 if you book through the city tourist office (not EurAide) at the Hauptbahnhof. Downstairs, the restaurant has a jazz band every Sunday (see Places to Eat and Entertainment).

South of the Hauptbahnhof off Kaiser-Ludwig-Platz, *Pension Schubert* (☎ 535 08 7), upstairs at Schubertstrasse 1, has rooms without bath for DM50/85, while a fully equipped double isn't bad for DM95.

Around Marienplatz Another value-for-money deal is the *Hotel-Pension am Markt* (☎ 225 01 4) at Heiliggeiststrasse 6, just off the Viktualienmarkt. Simple rooms start at DM60/102; rooms with bath and toilet from DM110/150.

Clean, comfortable, central and reasonably spacious rooms can be found at *Hotel Blauer Bock* (☎ 231 78 0), Sebastiansplatz 9. Rooms with private shower and toilet start at DM95/150, or DM70/110 with communal facilities. A buffet breakfast is included and garage parking is available. Of a similar standard and price is *Hotel Arosa* (☎ 267 08 7), Hotterstrasse 2, with simple rooms from DM75/100, standard rooms from DM100/140.

Westend *City Pension* (☎ 540 73 86 4), Gollierstrasse 36, has simple, cheerful and bright rooms a whopping four flights up (no lift) for DM50 to DM70 (singles) and DM100 to DM120 (doubles) plus DM10 for breakfast, served around the corner at *Café Corner*.

The best deal out here is the *Hotel Petri* (☎ 581 09 9) at Aindorferstrasse 82. Rooms have distinctive old wooden furniture and a TV, and there's also a garden and a small indoor swimming pool. Singles/doubles with shower and WC start at DM110/170. Take U-Bahn No 4 or 5 to Laimer Platz.

Neuhausen Perhaps because it's a bit out of the way, the *CA Comfort Aparthotel* (☎ 159 24 0), Dachauer Strasse 195-99, is very good value, with modern, well appointed rooms and nice staff. Singles/doubles begin at DM97/134.

Hotels – middle 'Middle' in Munich can range from DM200 to DM350, but note that these are only the rack (ie listed) rates, and you may do far, far better by joining a package tour or buying the accommodation through a travel agent. Also, many places list these higher rates but will come down if you merely ask if they have anything cheaper.

In the Westend, right near the Theresienwiese, two places cater predominantly to the convention crowd and can therefore be bargained down if there's nothing happening at the Messe: the *Hotel Krone* (☎ 504 05 2), Theresienhöhe 8, and *Siebel* (☎ 514 14 20), next door at No 9, both with posted rates of DM199/299 for singles/doubles, but going as low as DM99/119.

Right in the main train station is the *Inter-City Hotel* (☎ 545 56 0), with about as convenient a location as you could wish for, and very clean, if somewhat aged, rooms from DM198/250.

North of the Hauptbahnhof is a veritable package-tourist ghetto, with several hotels lining Arnulfstrasse. All seem to offer the same thing: moderately clean, moderately well appointed rooms, and staff used to groups of up to 100; these can be an excellent bargain if you can get yourself booked into a group, so don't scoff at the idea. Rack rates for the hotels – the *Regent* (☎ 551 59 0), at Seidlstrasse 2; *REMA-Hotel Esplanade* (☎ 551 39 0), at Arnulfstrasse 12; and the *Astron Hotel Deutscher Kaiser* (☎ 545 30), at Arnulfstrasse 2 – all range from DM205 to DM350.

South of the Hauptbahnhof, but not too far south, are two options run by Best Western; we recommend only one of them: the *Hotel Cristal* (☎ 551 11 0), at Schwanthalerstrasse 36, with nice, clean rooms from DM209/240, and friendly staff.

Hotels – top end Hotels at the top of the heap are what you'd expect: clean, luxurious and very, very expensive. Of the chain hotels, the 'cheapest' may well be the nicest: the *Holiday Inn Crowne Plaza* (☎ 381 79 0; fax 381 79 88 8), Leopoldstrasse 194 in the heart of Schwabing, has nice singles/doubles and great service from DM324/353. Others include the *München Park Hilton* (☎ 384 50; fax 384 51 84 5), Am Tucherpark 7, with rooms from DM334/445, and the *München City Hilton* (☎ 480 40; fax 480 44 80 4), Rosenheimerstrasse 15, where singles/doubles cost DM383/493.

One of the grand dames of the Munich hotel trade is the lovely *Bayerischer Hof* (☎ 212 00), at Promenadeplatz 2-6, with singles/doubles for DM322/453, and suites from DM391/583. It boasts a lovely location, right behind Marienplatz, and a pool.

The most famous – and certainly the most expensive – hotel in town is the *Kempinski Vier Jahreszeiten München* (☎ 212 50; fax 212 52 00 0), Maximilianstrasse 17, with a grand façade featuring statues of the managers, the four seasons, and the four continents known at the time of original construction in 1857. Rooms here, with not as many amenities as you'd think (but enough), start at DM415/485, suites range from DM485 to DM755. There's a pool downstairs.

Places to Eat

Munich has a fine selection of restaurants in all price ranges, including some excellent top-end places. Especially good value is Italian food, and the city has several excellent Vietnamese and Thai places, and at least one fantastic Indian restaurant.

Eating cheaply in Munich is much like anywhere else in Germany: excellent Turkish fast food is the leader of the snack pack, especially in the area south of the Hauptbahnhof. Doner kebabs cost from DM5 to DM6 and are large enough to constitute a meal. For German food, it's best to go local, like the less touristy beer halls and restaurants, or one of the many markets.

Vegetarian Restaurants For imaginative vegetarian cuisine at acceptable prices, nothing beats *Prinz Myschkin* (☎ 265 59 6), Hackenstrasse 2. It offers gourmet vegetarian cooking, blending East Asian, Indian and Italian influences. Daily menus and main courses cost as little as DM16; pizzas are most expensive at DM15 to DM18, but there's a great business lunch – a superb deal at DM13.80.

Italian Restaurants Munich's proximity to Italy means that there are good and relatively inexpensive Italian options throughout the city. *Café Osteria LaVecchia Masseria* (☎ 550 90 90), Mathildenstrasse 3 south of Landwehrstrasse, is one of the best-value places in Munich, and perfect for a romantic evening. The beautiful atmosphere comes with great service and nice touches like fresh aniseed bread on ceramic tiles. Pizzas cost from DM9 to DM11, pastas from DM9 to DM14, all meat dishes are DM21, and all fish dishes are DM24. There's a beer garden outside, too.

Also south of the Hauptbahnhof is the small *Trattoria La Fiorentini* (☎ 534 18 5) at Goethestrasse 41, a local hang-out that does good pizzas from DM7 to DM12.50. The menu, which changes daily, has main courses that average DM14 to DM18. Staff can get snooty if it's crowded, but the food's good.

Cipriani (☎ 260 43 97), in the Asamhof, a small courtyard off Sendlinger Strasse behind the Asamkirche, has pastas from DM12 to DM14. The outside area is lovely in summer. Happy hour is daily from 5 to 9 pm, when cocktails are DM6.

Indian & East Asian Restaurants At Stiglmaierplatz, *Maharani* (☎ 527 19 2), diagonally opposite the Löwenbräukeller at Rottmannstrasse 24, is the best bet for dependable, authentic Indian food, and they'll make it spicy if you ask them to. Main courses average DM20 to DM30.

Bombay (☎ 272 44 54), south of the Hauptbahnhof at Geyerstrasse 22 in Isavorstadt, is a very small place with nice food.

It's hard not to rave too much about *Vinh's* (☎ 123 89 25), on Leonrodstrasse near the corner of Landshuter Allee (U-Bahn No 1 to Rotkreuzplatz or bus No 33 or tram No 12 to Albrechtstrasse). This tiny place (reservations essential) does spectacular Vietnamese food, with rice dishes from DM15 to DM18, and the house specialities range from DM21 to DM35 (don't miss the roast duck for DM22.50). If he likes the crowd, the eccentric owner will dress up in silver duds and perform magic tricks.

Maitoi (☎ 260 52 68), Hans-Sachs-Strasse 10 near the gay area south of Sendlinger Tor, is a very slick, simple Japanese restaurant with takeaway sushi. Special evening prices apply after 7 or 9 pm, when everything is 25% less.

You could also try *Mangostin Asia* (☎ 723 20 31), Maria-Einsiefel-Strasse 2 in Thalkirchen near the zoo; it's a very chi-chi place with Thai, Japanese and Indonesian food. It's popular, but service can be reprehensible, and the food varies from good to despicable depending on the night. The sushi buffet (all you can eat for DM45 per person) is a reasonable deal.

Shida (☎ 269 33 6), Klenzestrasse 32, is a very good and very intimate Thai place (it's small, so reservations are essential). Main courses range from DM20 to DM30.

Top-End Restaurants The top restaurants in Munich usually serve (what else?) French food but we've heard good things about *Hippocampus*, a trendy and upscale Italian place with a nice atmosphere and outside terrace right near the Prinzregententheater. Set menus range from DM60 to DM80, main courses from DM20 to DM30. *Hundskugel* (☎ 264 27 2), at Hotterstrasse 18 right in the centre, is Munich's oldest restaurant, founded in 1440. It's a famous place to go with family and friends, and the food's perfectly fine, if pricey.

Le Bousquerey (☎ 488 45 5), Rablstrasse 37 in Haidhausen, east of the Isar River, is a splendid French place that specialises in seafood. The restaurant is small and intimate (reservations suggested). There's a good French and German wine list; set menus are about DM60 to DM70 per person, main courses average DM20 to DM35.

Another very good but expensive French place is *Rue des Halles* (☎ 485 67 5), south of the centre at Steinstrasse 18 in Mittersendling, with a very light, modern interior, comfortable atmosphere, and slick but attentive service. Count on spending about DM150 per person without wine.

The restaurant upstairs at *Alois Dallmayr* (☎ 213 51 00), Dienerstrasse 14-15 near Marienplatz, is renowned for its excellent French and Continental food and great service; main courses range from DM30 to DM60.

Another well known top-end place is the *Garden-Restaurant* (☎ 212 09 93), behind the Hotel Bayerischer Hof at Promenadeplatz 2-6.

Airport Restaurants Security concerns have resulted in huge advance check-in times, and the airport has a number of restaurants to keep you going. While expensive, they're not at all bad. There are snack bars and cafés in each terminal, open from 5 am to 10 pm. *Trattoria Monaco* (☎ 975 92 87 0), Level 6, Terminal B, is fine for Italian food and wine – you can get a small main course for about DM10; the pasta dishes are good.

More expensive but also not at all bad is the *Zirbelstube* (☎ 975 92 86 0), Level 4, Central Area, with Bavarian specialities from DM15 to DM22, beer and Dirndl-clad staff.

Beer Halls & Gardens More people go to beer halls to drink than to eat – especially given the quality of the 'food' at places like the Hofbräuhaus – so see the Entertainment section.

Munich beer gardens allow you to pack food but no drinks, and everyone in town does just that: stock up (see Self-Catering) and show up for the evening. A few have live music (from oompah to Dixieland) but the main thing is being outside with the beer.

You sometimes have to pay a *Pfand* (deposit) for the glasses (usually DM5). Beer costs DM9 to DM12 per litre. Food includes roast chicken (about DM15 for a half), spare ribs (about DM20, and probably not worth it except in Taxisgarten), huge pretzels (about DM5) and Bavarian specialities including *Schweinebraten* and schnitzel (for DM17 to DM22). There's both self-service and waiters. *Radi* is a huge, mild radish that's eaten with beer; it's cut with a *Radimesser*, which sticks down in the centre and you twist the handle round and round, creating a radish spiral. Buy a Radimesser at any department store and buy the radish at a market, or buy prepared radish for about DM7. If you do it yourself, smother the cut end of the radish with salt until it 'cries' to reduce bitterness (and increase your thirst!).

Obazda (pronounced 'oh-batsdah') is Bavarian for 'mixed up' – this cream-cheese-like beer garden speciality is made of butter, Camembert and paprika (about DM7 to DM8). Spread it on Brez'n (a pretzel) or bread. If you hate it while sober, you may like it when pissed.

English Garden Here you'll find the classic *Chinesischer Turm* (☎ 950 28), at Englischer Garten 3, with a very weird crowd of businessfolk, tourists and junkies, all entertained by what has to be the world's drunkest oompah band (in the tower above the crowd, fenced in à la *The Blues Brothers*). The nearby *Hirschau* and *Seehaus* beer gardens (☎ 381 61 30), on the banks of the Kleinhesseloher See, are less crowded, though a more smug crowd abounds.

City Centre The large and leafy beer garden at the *Augustiner Keller* (☎ 594 39 3), Arnulfstrasse 52, near the Hauptbahnhof, has a laid-back atmosphere ideal for recreational drinking.

The *Viktualienmarkt* (☎ 297 54 5), Viktualienmarkt 6, is a wonderful place right in the city centre; see the earlier Viktualienmarkt section for more information.

Neuhausen We love the *Hirschgarten* (☎ 172 59 1), at Hirschgartenallee 1 (S-Bahn to Laim), just south of Schloss Nymphenburg. It's packed with locals and fewer tourists. The shady garden is enormous, and you can sit next to the deer that wander just on the other side of the chain-link fence.

The *Taxisgarten* (☎ 156 82 7), at Taxisstrasse 12 north of Rotkreuzplatz, is another peaceful place with mainly local families. Take bus No 177 from Rotkreuzplatz to Klugstrasse.

Northern Munich *Waldwirtschaft Grosshesselohe* (☎ 795 08 8), Georg-Kalb-Strasse 3 (S-Bahn No 7 to Grosshesselohe), is in one of the most expensive neighbourhoods in town. The wealthy residents decided that all the racket (Dixieland music, mainly) was too down-market for their taste and tried to shut it down. The resulting citywide brouhaha became headline news and the counter-movement is written in Munich history as the 'Beer Garden Revolution'. It was, of course, successful.

Cafés & Bistros Centrally located cafés cater largely to tourists and therefore tend to be rather expensive. Two cheap and central stand-up cafés that serve excellent home-made sweet and savoury pastries are *Höflinger*, at the corner of Sendlinger-Tor-Platz and Sonnenstrasse, and *Ziegler*, at Brunnstrasse 11. The *Stadtcafé* at the Stadtmuseum is a popular haunt for Munich's intellectual types, especially in summer when the lovely courtyard opens.

City Centre A newcomer is *Kandil Restaurant* (☎ 548 28 25 2), at Landwehrstrasse 8 near the Hauptbahnhof, which has a wide selection of full cafeteria-style but good meals from DM8.50 to DM11.90. They also serve breakfast (a simple one is DM5.50).

In Marienplatz, the best places to watch the Glockenspiel as it does its thing are the bistro at the *Metropolitan* (☎ 230 97 70), Marienplatz 22 on the 5th floor (*not* the 6th-floor restaurant, from where the views aren't as good), and next door at *Café Glockenspiel*, the same thing but far more down-market. Across the square on the west side is *Café Am Dom*, from where the view is just so-so but the atmosphere is nicer outside in summer.

On the Viktualienmarkt, seek out *Löwenbräu Stadt Kempten* at No 4 (closed Sunday). There, you'll get a half-litre of Löwenbräu for DM4.90, and the daily set-menus start at around DM13.

The speciality of *Nürnberger Bratwurst Glöckl am Dom*, in the shadow of the Frauenkirche at Frauenplatz 9, is the small Nuremberg-style sausages, served with sauerkraut (DM12). *Haxenbauer* (☎ 291 62 10 0), at Sparkassenstrasse 8 (look for the pig on a spit in the window) is a mid-range inner-Munich establishment offering hearty four-course menus for DM50 per person, and very cheap fast food like Schweinshax'n (pork thigh) for DM5.60 and Kalbshax'n (veal thigh) for DM6.20 in the stand-up area.

Neuhausen The *Löwenbräukeller* (☎ 526 02 1), in the brewery at Nymphenburger Strasse 2 on Stiglmaierplatz (U-Bahn No 1 to Stiglmaierplatz) is usually uncrowded, has great food and service, and the prices aren't bad either. Huge portions of Bavarian specialities (eg mushrooms in cream and anything with meat) are between DM12 and DM20.

Closer to Rotkreuzplatz, a really nice and totally untouristed place to sit and chat is *froh & munter* (☎ 187 99 7) at Artilleriestrasse 5. This welcoming café does excellent snacks, soups and great Spanish-style tapas, with offerings like rice balls with bacon and sweet-and-sour sauce from DM4.50 to DM7.50. It also serves up organically prepared Unertl

(DM5), some of the best Weissbier in town. The menu changes nightly. Food is served to 11 pm and the service is always friendly.

Schwabing Among the many lively student hang-outs in Schwabing are the *Vorstadt Café*, Türkenstrasse 83, and the *News Bar*, at the corner of Amalienstrasse and Schellingstrasse; both are open daily at least until 1 am, and the latter sells English magazines.

Crêperie Cocorico (☎ 264 37 2), Schellingstrasse 22, is very French and very nice, with excellent coffees, good salads (around DM12) and, of course, crêpes.

The cafés that line Leopoldstrasse are more for socialising, being seen and looking fabulous than eating, but food is available in spite of it all. Don't expect it to be good and do expect it to cost: they're all the same, but two notable entries are *Café Roxy* (☎ 349 29 2) at No 48, with burgers for DM14.50 and sandwiches from DM8.50 to DM13.50; and the nearby *Eis Boulevard*, No 52, with lots of ice cream.

Farther west, *Egger* (☎ 398 52 6), Friedrichstrasse 27, is a fine place with large plates and two-course lunch specials from DM10.80 to DM14.80. At dinner, vegetarian main courses average DM12 to DM15, meat dishes from DM14 to DM21.

Westend The nicely renovated *Stoa* (☎ 507 05 0), Gollierstrasse 38, is a fine place for lunch or dinner. It has a comfortable atmosphere, tapas from DM7.50 to DM15.50, and varied main courses like penne in a three-cream sauce from DM13.30 or chicken roulade with spinach in a mushroom cream sauce from DM10.50.

Breakfast Places When your train drops you at Hauptbahnhof at 7 am, and everyone in the station is drinking large glasses of beer and eating Currywurst, get out of there before you join them.

If you absolutely must eat in the station, the *bakery* on the ground level next to Sussmann's international bookshop is better than the one downstairs, and the kiosk at the head of Track 14 does fine cappuccinos for DM3. The *cafeteria* is somewhat pleasant, with boiled eggs for DM1.30. And there's always *Burger King*, upstairs in the main hall, which serves breakfast.

Outside the Hauptbahnhof, go south, where breakfast is cheaper than in the expensive hotels to the north and east of the station. Two good spots for breakfast here are *Sultan*, on the corner of Schwanthalerstrasse and Goethestrasse, and *Kandil Restaurant* at Landwehrstrasse 8. *Café am Beethovenplatz* (☎ 544 04 34 8), Goethestrasse 51 at the Hotel Pension Mariandl (see Places to Stay), does breakfast from 9 am for DM8.50 to DM17, and on Sunday mornings from 11 am (when prices are the same but there's live jazz as well).

In Schwabing, *News Bar* (☎ 281 78 7), Amalienstrasse 55 at the corner of Schellingstrasse, does big American breakfasts of eggs, pancakes, bacon and fried potatoes for DM11.50.

In Neuhausen, the painfully trendy *Café am Platz der Freiheit* (☎ 134 68 6), Leonrodstrasse 20, has very good Milchcafé (café au lait), served steaming hot in giant bowls, and three eggs with ham for DM8.50, but service is terrible.

Student Cafeterias & Fast Food Student-card holders can fill up for around DM4 in any of the university Mensas. The best of these is probably the one on Schillerstrasse just north of Pettenkoferstrasse. There are others at Leopoldstrasse 13, at Arcisstrasse 17, and at Helene-Mayer-Ring 9.

For quick snacks, any Müller bakery *Stehcafé* offers coffee for around DM2 and pretzels or bread rolls covered with melted cheese (about DM3) or with bacon or ham (DM3 to DM4).

Throughout the city, branches of *Vinzenzmurr* have hot buffet and prepared meals; a very good lunch (like Schweinbraten with knödel and gravy) can be as low as DM8, and pizza and hamburgers average about DM4.

Around Hauptbahnhof Doner and pizza rule the fast-food scene in Munich. Opposite the Hauptbahnhof on Bayerstrasse there are lots of tourist traps, but you can grab a quick cheap bite at *Pizzeria Ca' doro*'s street pizza window, where large slices are DM3.50. *Don't* go inside – it's a tourist trap.

Inside the central post office at Arnulfstrasse 32 opposite the north-west side of the Hauptbahnhof, there's a very good *Stehcafé* with Turkish and Greek specialities. It's very popular and crowded at lunchtime, with doner and gyro sandwiches going for DM6, and full plates with salad and bread from DM8 to DM10. There's a *bakery* here too.

Just south of the Hauptbahnhof are about a dozen places doing doner kebab; two favourites are the *Gute Stube* at the corner of Schwanthalerstrasse and Schillerstrasse, with great ones for DM6, and the tiny *Kebab Antep* (☎ 532 23 6), Schwanthalerstrasse 45 (entrance on Goethestrasse), where they cost DM5. There's also spinach pie and other vegetarian offerings.

Thai fans absolutely must head for *Jinny's Thai Food* (☎ 557 88 0), Schillerstrasse 27 just south of Landwehrstrasse, where exquisite soups (DM4.20) along with daily specials (DM9.90 to DM10.90) await. They're fantastic and the staff are really friendly, too.

You don't have to be staying at the CVJM-YMCA hostel to eat at the *Jugendrestaurant* at Landwehrstrasse 13; it's open until 11 pm on weekdays and Saturday.

Around Karlsplatz Cheap eating is also available in various department stores in the centre. Right opposite Karlsplatz, on the ground floor of Kaufhof, are three good options next to each other: a *Müller* bakery, *Nordsee* seafood and *Grillpfanne* doing sausages. Also at Karlsplatz is a seemingly always-crowded *McDonald's*.

The *Münchner Suppenküche*, north of the Frauenkirche at Schäfflerstrasse 7, has meat and vegetarian soups from DM3.50.

Schwabing *Reiter Imbiss*, at Hohenzollernstrasse 24, has heaps of meaty stuff for cheap prices, as well as changing daily specials. There are *McDonald's* outlets along Leopoldstrasse.

Right next to the Haus International youth hotel is the *BP filling station*, with excellent and cheap sandwiches.

Neuhausen A spectacular deal for lunch is *Vinh's* (see Indian & East Asian Restaurants) super set-lunch specials from DM7.50 (between 11.30 am and 2.30 pm).

Eis Ecke Sarcletti, at the southern end of Rotkreuzplatz, may well have the best Italian ice cream in the city, and the crowds know it. It's about DM1 per scoop, and there's a little outdoor café as well. It's a must.

Self-Catering In Neuhausen and reasonably convenient to the hostel is Munich's best bakery, the tiny Schneider's Feinbäckerei, Volkartstrasse 48, between Albrechtstrasse and Artilleriestrasse just east of Landshuter Allee. They bake indescribably good bread rolls, other breads and cake. Don't miss it if you have the chance.

Norma and Aldi supermarkets, with outlets throughout the city, are the cheapest places to buy staples. They also have great deals on French and Italian wines, starting at an amazing DM2.50 per bottle.

Aussies with Vegemite cravings should head for *Australia Service* (☎ 186 05 1), Dachauer Strasse 103, with the famous spread plus Aussie everything from beer and wine to Akubra hats and Lonely Planet Australia guides. In a similar vein, the *English Shop* (☎ 488 40 0), Franziskanerstrasse 14, has lots of British stuff.

The supermarket in the basement of the Kaufhof department store opposite Karlsplatz has a far more upscale selection, plus goodies like fresh mozzarella, superb sliced meats and cheeses, and a good bakery.

At *Viktualienmarkt*, just south of Marienplatz, you can put together a picnic feast of breads, cheeses and salad to take off to a beer garden for DM10 or less per person, but it's so good that chances are you'll get carried away and the price will soar. Make sure you figure out the price before buying, and don't be afraid to move on to another stall. *Nordsee* has simply awesome seafood from cheap to ridiculous; *Thoma* is a wonderful cheese and wine shop behind which you'll find the *Juice Bar*, with great fruity concoctions from DM3 to DM6, and right next to the maypole, look for the *Oliven & Essiggurken* stand, with olives and pickles plus pickled garlic and loads more.

More prosperous picnickers might prefer the legendary *Alois Dallmayr* at Dienerstrasse 14-15, one of the world's greatest (and priciest) delicatessens, with an amazing range of exotic foods imported from every end of the earth.

Entertainment

Munich's entertainment scene will keep you busy. Apart from discos, pubs and beer halls, try not to miss out on the city's excellent classical and opera scenes.

Not surprisingly, beer drinking is an integral part of Munich's entertainment scene. Germans drink an average of 250 litres of the amber liquid each per year, while Munich residents average some 350 litres! If you're keen to keep up with the locals, a key investment is Larry Hawthorne's *Beer Drinker's Guide to Munich*, available locally, which lists and rates many of Munich's better beer gardens and brews.

Munich nightclub bouncers are notoriously rude and 'discerning', so dress to kill (or look, as locals say, *schiki-micki)* and keep your cool.

Listings If you have even rudimentary German the best sources of information are the free *in München*, available at bars, restaurants, ticket outlets and other venues, and the tall, thin, yellow, city-published monthly *München im ....* (DM2.50), which is an A-to-Z listing of almost everything the city has to offer except discos. It's the best source of information on new museum exhibitions, festivals, concerts and theatre.

Another great German guide (available at any newsstand) is the monthly *Müchner Stadtmagazin* (DM4), which is probably the most complete guide to bars, discos, clubs, concerts and nightlife in the city.

Bigger newsstands and shops sell *Munich Found* (DM4), an English-language ci magazine with somewhat useful listings.

Gay & Lesbian Much of Munich's gay a lesbian nightlife is centred in the area ju south of Sendlinger Tor. Information for g men and lesbians is available throug Schwules Kommunikations und Kultu zentrum, dubbed 'the sub' (☎ 260 30 5 Müllerstrasse 43, open Sunday to Thursd from 7 to 11 pm, to 1 am on Friday a Saturday nights. It's a very cool gay a lesbian community centre, with two floors bar downstairs and a library upstairs) that a home to gay and lesbian resources, suppo groups etc. There's also a very lively bullet board. Also at the sub is the Münchn Schwul-Lesbische Gehörlosen-Gruppe, gay and lesbian deaf support group.

Lesbians can contact LeTra/Lesbe telefon (☎ 725 42 72), Dreimühlenstras 23, open Tuesday from 10.30 am to 1 p Wednesday from 2.30 to 5 pm and Thursd from 7 to 10 pm. A women-only teahous the *Frauentee-stube* (☎ 774 09 1), is at Dre mühlenstrasse 1 at the corner of Isartalstras south of the city centre (closed Wednesd and Saturday).

The *Rose Seiten* (Pink Pages; DM5) is t best guide to everything gay the city has offer; get it in shops like Weissblauer G Shop (☎ 522 35 2; U-Bahn No 2 to Ther sienstrasse) or Black Jump (☎ 448 10 73), Orleansstrasse 51 (U-Bahn to Sendling Tor). These places also hand out free copi of *Our Munich*, a monthly guide to gay a lesbian life in the city.

Tickets Tickets to entertainment venues a available at official ticket outlets *(Karte vorverkauf)* throughout the city, but th range of tickets at these is often limited to certain genre, like ballet, rather than th entire entertainment spectrum. The exce tion is the *Zentraler Kartenvorverka* (☎ 264 62 0), which sells tickets to ever thing in town, including theatre, balle opera, rock concerts and all special event Their office is very conveniently located the Marienplatz underground on the 1st lev of the S-Bahn station, and they have another outlet at Rosenstrasse 6 in the pedestrian zone.

Cinema Call or check any listings publications for show information; admission is between DM12 and DM14.

Two larger cinemas that show first-run (sort of) films in English daily are *Museum-Lichtspiele* (☎ 482 40 3) at Lilienstrasse 2 and the excellent *Cinema* (☎ 555 25 5) at Nymphenburger Strasse 31. Films are shown nightly in the *Filmmuseum* (☎ 233 55 86) at the Stadtmuseum, usually in the original language with subtitles.

Other cinemas that often have English-language movies include the *Atelier* (☎ 591 91 8), Sonnenstrasse 12; *Atlantis* (☎ 555 15 2), Schwanthalerstrasse 2; and *Cinerama* (☎ 499 18 81 9), Grafinger Strasse 6. *Amerika Haus* (☎ 552 53 70), Karolinenplatz 3, and the *British Council* (☎ 223 32 6), Bruderstrasse 7, both show movies in their original languages as well.

Discos & Clubs Cover prices for discos change often, sometimes daily, but average between DM5 and DM15.

The biggest recent arrival on the Munich nightlife scene is *Kunstpark Ost* (☎ 490 02 73 0), a multiple disco-restaurant-bar-cinema complex, at Grafinger Strasse 6 directly behind the Ostbahnhof in the former Pfanni factory. This place has become swarmingly popular, effectively Munich's disco and concert centre. Discos here, which often host live and sometimes very large concerts, include *Bongo Bar*, with 1950s style weirdness, go-go dancers and kitsch extraordinaire; *K41*, with a 30-plus crowd getting into pretty straightforward disco mixed in with acid jazz; and the enormous *Babylon*, the biggest place here, which holds big-name concerts and is home to 'party with thousands' nights at weekends. Friday nights are Fruit of the Room, with 70s and 80s stuff and Schlager, currently hip updates of German folk music.

Another large complex is the *Muffathalle* (☎ 458 75 07 5), Zellstrasse 4, which holds large concerts and, in summer, is an open-air disco on Friday with drum/bass, acid jazz and hip hop (always crowded, so expect long waits to get in). *P1* (☎ 294 25 2), at Prinzregentenstrasse 1, is *the* chic spot of the second, which means you can't get in and neither could we.

Tilt (☎ 129 79 69), west of the Hauptbahnhof and off Arnulfstrasse at Helmholzstrasse 12, is a fun place, with a young crowd but certain over-30s types feeling quite at home as well; they play underground, metal and, on Friday, oldies and Schlager.

Backstage (☎ 183 33 0), Helmholzstrasse 18, is another concert place and disco; cross-over, psychedelic, hip hop, trash and other freaky music is the rule.

Nachtwerk Club (☎ 578 38 00), Landsberger Strasse 186, next to Nachtwerk (see Rock), is another place with an over-30 crowd and middle-of-the-road house and dance-chart music.

Party on the rooftop in Schwabing at *Skyline* (☎ 333 13 1), Leopoldstrasse 82, with soul and hip hop up top of the Hertie department store; it's right next to the Münchener Freiheit U-Bahn station.

Far Out (☎ 226 66 1), Am Kosttor 2 near the Hofbräuhaus, does mixed theme nights daily; it attracts a slightly older crowd but is very fun.

Gay & Lesbian *The Stud* (☎ 260 84 03), Thalkirchner Strasse 2, is a leather-Levis place with a dark, coal mine-like interior and lots of butch guys with no hair. The clientele is gay and lesbian (in fact, they're always looking for more lesbians, so if that fits, head on over). The sound is mostly techno, and lots of different events are held – Sundays they put in a labyrinth.

Fortuna Musikbar (☎ 554 07 0), Maximiliansplatz 5 (in the Reginahaus), is a great place. Wednesday to Friday it's exclusively gay and lesbian; Wednesday is movie night; Thursday it's house and live-music parties; and on Saturday it's lesbians only.

At the two-level *Soul City* (☎ 595 27 2), Maximiliansplatz 5, there's a bar and café on the 1st level, while the 2nd level has a disco and dance floor with a young 20s crowd. While predominantly gay, it's definitely a mixed straight and gay crowd. They also do theme nights.

Together Again (☎ 263 46 9), Müllerstrasse 1, has live shows Sunday to Thursday from 10 pm, and disco on Friday and Saturday nights. *NY NY* (☎ 591 06 5), Sonnenstrasse 25, is a slick and very gay place with a bar on the ground floor, and a high-tech disco upstairs, with laser shows nightly at 11.30 pm and 1 am. It's a pretty 70s, mixed crowd.

Theatre Munich has a lively theatre scene. The two biggest theatre companies are the Staatschauspiel and the Kammerspiele. The Staatschauspiel performs at the *Residenztheater*, at the intimate rococo *Cuvilliés Theater* (also within the Residenz), and at the *Marstall Theater*, behind the Nationaltheater (see Classical Music).

The *Kammerspiele* (☎ 237 21 32 8), at Maximilianstrasse 26, stages large productions of serious drama from German playwrights or works translated into German. (These are the folks who said that Shakespeare sounded 'better' in German.)

The *Deutsches Theater* (☎ 552 34 36 0), Schwanthalerstrasse 13, is Munich's answer to the West End: touring road shows (usually light musicals) perform here.

The *Gasteig* (☎ 480 98 0), Rosenheimer Strasse 5 (S-Bahn to Rosenheimerplatz or tram No 18 or bus No 51), is a major cultural centre, with theatre, classical music and other special events in its several halls; theatre is performed here in the Carl-Orff-Saal and on the far more intimate Black Box stage.

Other large theatrical venues include the *Prinzregententheater* (☎ 218 52 95 9), Prinzregentenplatz 12 (U-Bahn No 4 or bus No 53 or 54); the *Modernes Theater* (☎ 266 82 1), Hans-Sachs-Strasse 12 (U-Bahn No 1 or 2 to Frauenhoferstrasse or tram No 17, 18 or 27); and the *Neues Theater München* (☎ 650 00 0), Entenbachstrasse 37 (U-Bahn No 1 or 2 to Kolumbusplatz).

There's regular comedy in the chic *Komödie im Bayerischen Hof* (☎ 292 81 0), Passage Promenadeplatz (tram No 19), and at the *Kleine Komödie am Max II* (☎ 221 85 9), Maximilianstrasse 47 (U-Bahn No 4 or 5 to Lehel, or tram No 17 or 19).

Children's Theatre A big hit with kids is *Circus Krone* (☎ 558 16 6), Marsstrasse 43, with performances from Christmas to April. For puppet theatre, try *Marionettenstudio Kleines Festspiel* (no telephone), Neureutherstrasse 12, entrance on Arcisstrasse (free admission; U-Bahn No 2 to Josephsplatz or tram No 27), or *Das Münchner Marionettentheater* (☎ 265 71 2), Blumenstrasse 29a (U-Bahn No 1, 2, 3 or 6 to Sendlinger Tor, or tram No 17, 18, 20 or 27). There are performances (including puppet shows and children's theatre) throughout the year at *Münchner Theater für Kinder* (☎ 595 45 4), Dachauer Strasse 46 (U-Bahn No 1 or tram No 20 or 21 to Stiglmaierplatz).

Classical Music The Munich Philharmonic Orchestra performs at the *Philharmonic Hall* within the Gasteig (☎ 480 98 0), which is Munich's premier classical-music venue. It's also the home of the Bayerischer Rundfunk's orchestra, which performs on Sunday throughout the year.

There are regular classical concerts at the *Theater am Gärtnerplatz* (☎ 201 67 67), Gärtnerplatz 3 (U-Bahn No 1 or 2 to Frauenhoferstrasse), but this is more an opera and operetta venue. There are always opera productions (some very good, some not) here.

Classical concerts are often held in the absolutely lovely *Altes Residenztheater*, within the Residenz.

The Bayerische Staatsoper (Bavarian State Opera) performs at the *Nationaltheater*, Max-Joseph-Platz 2, which is also the site of many cultural events, particularly during the opera festival in July. You can buy tickets at regular outlets, at the theatre box office at Maximilianstrasse 11 (from 10 am to 6 pm Monday to Friday, to 1 pm Saturday), or by telephone (☎ 218 51 92 0).

Rock Large rock concerts are staged at the

Olympiapark. Most other rock venues are also listed in Discos & Clubs, including the *Muffathalle* (☎ 458 75 00 0), Zellstrasse 4, which also holds jazz, salsa, African and world music and other concerts as well; *Nachtwerk Club* (☎ 578 38 00), Landsberger Strasse 186; and *Babylon* at Kunstpark Ost.

There are also concerts regularly at the *Schlachthof* (☎ 765 44 8), Zenettistrasse 9 (U-Bahn No 3 or 6 to Poccistrasse or bus No 31 to the door), which also hosts a regular TV show called *Live aus dem Schlachthof* with Marc Owen, and comedy nights. It attracts a thirty-something crowd.

There's country & western music at the *Rattlesnake Saloon* (☎ 150 40 35), Schneeglöckchenstrasse 91 (S-Bahn No 1 to Fasanerie Nord), and at the *Oklahoma Country Saloon* (☎ 723 23 47), Schäftlarnstrasse 156 (U-Bahn No 3 to Thalkirchen and take the Zennerstrasse exit). Both of them, as you might imagine, are Wild West-style bars, too.

Other concerts are held at the *Night Club* (☎ 212 09 94), in the Hotel Bayerischer Hof Hotel (see Jazz).

Jazz Munich is also a hot scene for jazz; *Jazzclub Unterfahrt* (☎ 448 27 94), at Kirchenstrasse 96 near the Ostbahnhof, is perhaps the best known place in town. It has live music from 9 pm (except Monday), and jam sessions open to everyone on Sunday nights. There are also daily concerts in Munich's smallest jazz club, *Mr B's* (☎ 534 90 1), Herzog-Heinrich-Strasse 38 (U-Bahn No 3 or 6 to Goetheplatz).

Go a bit more up-market with jazz shows at the *Night Club* (☎ 212 09 94), in the Hotel Bayerischer Hof, Promenadeplatz 2-6, which has regular jazz and other concerts including reggae, blues and funkabilly. An upscale spot for open-air concerts is in the *Brunnenhof der Residenz* (☎ 296 83 6), Residenzstrasse 1 in the Residenz, which hosts a broad range of concerts including rock, jazz, swing, classical and opera. There's a jazz brunch on Sunday at *Café am Beethovenplatz* (☎ 544 04 34 8), Goethestrasse 51, at the Hotel Pension Mariandl.

Backstage Aluminium (☎ 183 33 0), Helmholzstrasse 18 right at the S-Bahn Donnersberger Brücke station, is a very popular jazz venue, with lots of live performances.

Munich's most infamous Dixieland venue (it also plays jazz) is the *Waldwirtschaft Grosshesselohe* (☎ 795 08 8), Georg-Kalb-Strasse 3 (see Beer Halls & Gardens under Places to Eat), which plays it nightly to the consternation of local residents.

Folk Music The best bet for Bavarian folk music, other than at the café in the *Valentin Musäum* (☎ 223 26 6) in Isartor (see Other Museums), is the Chinesischer Turm beer garden in the English Garden. There's Irish folk music regularly in the city's Irish pubs (see Pubs & Bars).

Beer Halls Several breweries run their own beer halls; try at least one large, frothy litre of beer before heading off to another hall. Even in the touristy places, be careful not to sit at a Stammtisch, reserved for regulars (there will be a brass plaque).

Most celebrated is the enormous *Hofbräuhaus*, Am Platzl 9. A live band plays Bavarian folk music every night, but the place is generally packed with tipsy tourists.

The *Augustiner Bierhalle*, Neuhauser Strasse 27, has a less raucous atmosphere than the Hofbräuhaus (not to mention decent food), yet it's a more authentic example of an old-style Munich beer hall.

Also much less touristy is the *Mathäser Bierstadt* at Zweigstrasse 5, near the Hauptbahnhof. Run by the Löwenbräu brewery, it is Munich's main blue-collar beer hall. It has the best food, good prices and the menu is listed in Bavarian first, with High German translations below!

Pubs & Bars Right in the centre, the *Nachtcafé* (☎ 595 90 0), Maximiliansplatz 5, stays open until 6 am, but they won't let you in unless you're *très* chic, female and dressed in a tight black dress, or throwing Deutschmarks around. Far more down-home Bavarian is *Jodlwirt* at Alten Hofstrasse 4, in an alley just north of Marienplatz, a nice, relatively untouristed place with good Ayinger beer and a pleasant atmosphere.

Julep's (☎ 448 00 44), Breisacherstrasse 18 in Haidhausen east of the centre, is a Mexican place with great drinks and a very rowdy crowd.

Schwabing The area along and around Leopoldstrasse, between the university and Münchener Freiheit U-Bahn station, is the bar district; the backstreets are teeming with places, big and small, and there's something to fit every taste. *Lardy* (☎ 344 94 9), Leopoldstrasse 49, is a quasi-exclusive place, but the goons at the door don't really stop anyone from entering. There are DJs on Thursday and Friday night, and English-speaking staff.

Nearby, *Egger* (see Cafés & Bistros under Places to Eat) is a classic Munich bar, with high ceilings, lots of smoke and even good service. Near the technical university is the *News Bar*, very fun late at night (see Places to Eat).

Towards Königsplatz is *Treszniewski* (☎ 282 34 9), Theresienstrasse 72, a chic spot that attracts lots of people in black and intellectual types.

While *Munich's First Diner* (☎ 335 91 5), at Leopoldstrasse 82 (enter from Feilitzschstrasse), is truly a diner (complete with diner food and waiters on rollerblades), it's better known by the expat set as a great place for imported beer and cocktails. It's a fun flashback to the US of A, if that's what you're after.

Neuhausen This is a neighbourhood for little local, rather than tourist, pubs. *Krayttmayr's*, Krayttmaierstrasse just east of Erzgiesereistrasse, is a real bar crawler's bar: bar food, good drinks, a pool table, Kugel (sort of bowling), darts and pinball, and live music on Thursday (from Irish folk to jazz). It also has a beer garden in summer. *froh & munter* (see Cafés & Bistros under Places to Eat) is the best place for good Weissbier, with a great crowd of locals and good snacks as well.

The heavily advertised American bar *Ralph's* (☎ 186 76 4) is at Leonrodstrasse 85. Watch your bill: there have been complaints of padding the already outrageous cocktail bills.

Irish Pubs Munich has a huge Irish expatriate population; if you're out looking for friendly, English-speaking people, you're in luck. Most have live music at least once a week.

In Schwabing, two very cool underground cellar bars are *Günther Murphy's Irish Tavern* (☎ 398 91 1), Nikolaistrasse 9a, and *Shamrock* (☎ 331 08 1), Trautenwolfstrasse 6. Both are fun, loud, boisterous and crowded every night. Get ready to be jostled and get there early if you want a table.

Also in Schwabing, *Shenanigans* (☎ 342 11 2), Ungererstrasse 19, has karaoke. It's bigger and less crowded than most of the others, and also sometimes has live music.

A divey atmosphere prevails at *Paddy's* (☎ 333 62 2), Feilitzschstrasse 17 in Schwabing, with locals and other interesting folks with interesting smokes.

Gay & Lesbian Unless noted as exclusively gay or lesbian, all are welcome at the places described here. There's great service, good food and cocktails at *Morizz* (☎ 201 67 76), Klenzestrasse 43, which looks a lot like a Paris bar: lots of mirrors, very quiet early in the night with lots of theatre types from Gärtnerplatz, but the later it gets the more gay and rowdy it becomes (though it's always fashionable and sophisticated). Another very popular place is *Iwan* (☎ 554 93 3), Josephspitalstrasse 15, a once ultra-chic place that's 'democratised' its crowd. Its two floors host a very mixed crowd, and in summer there's a nice outside area.

A good exclusively lesbian bar is *Be Carla* (☎ 227 90 1), Buttermelcherstrasse 9 with a good mixed-age crowd. It serves snacks.

The *Ochsengarten* (☎ 266 44 6), Müllerstrasse 47, was Germany's first leather bar. It has a rustic interior, lots of boots hanging from the ceiling, and an older (mid-30s to mid-40s) crowd.

There's a mainly lesbian crowd at *Karotte* (☎ 201 06 69), just south of the centre at Baaderstrasse 13, which also serves food from a daily menu.

Leather lovers head straight (or rather, 'gaily forward') to *Löwengrube* (☎ 265 75 0), Reisingerstrasse 5, a small, exclusively gay place jammed with a leather, Levis and rubber crowd.

Things to Buy

Bavarian dress is the most distinctive of traditional German clothing. Loden-Frey, a specialist department store at Maffeistrasse 5-7 in the centre, stocks a wide range of Bavarian wear, but expect to pay at least DM400 for a good leather jacket or a women's Dirndl dress.

Also look out for optical goods (Leica cameras and binoculars), especially along Landwehrstrasse near Sonnenstrasse and at Sauter Photographic on Sonnenstrasse, just off Sendlinger-Tor-Platz.

The Christkindlmarkt (Christmas market) on Marienplatz in December is large and well stocked but often expensive. The Auer Dult, a huge flea market on Mariahilfplatz in Haidhausen, has great buys and takes place during the last weeks of April, July and October.

Beer steins and *Mass* glasses are available at all the department stores, as well as from the beer halls themselves.

Getting There & Away

Air Munich is second in importance only to Frankfurt for international and domestic flights. From here you can reach major destinations like London, Paris, Rome, Athens, New York and Sydney. Main German cities are served by at least half a dozen flights daily. The main carrier is Lufthansa (☎ 545 59 9), Lenbachplatz 1. For general flight information, call ☎ 975 21 31 3.

For some tickets, especially those to Asia or cheap flights to the USA, you need to reconfirm by telephone 24 to 48 hours before your flight.

Airlines serving Munich's Franz-Josef Strauss airport include:

British Airways/Deutsche BA
  Promenadeplatz 10 (☎ 292 12 1)
Delta Air Lines
  Maximiliansplatz 17 (☎ 0180-333 78 80)
El Al
  Maximiliansplatz 15 (☎ 210 69 20)
Finnair
  Oskar-von-Miller-Ring 36 (☎ 281 02 3)
Air France
  Theatinerstrasse 33 (☎ 01805-360 37 0)
Japan Air Lines (JAL)
  Prielmayrstrasse 1 (☎ 0180-222 87 00)
Sabena
  Schillerstrasse 5 (☎ 555 84 5)

Bus Munich is a main hub for Eurobus (see the Getting There & Away chapter), with daily service to and from France, Austria and Italy. Munich is also linked to the Romantic Road by the Europabus Munich-Frankfurt service (see Getting Around in the Romantic Road section later in this chapter). Enquire at Deutsche Touring (☎ 591 82 4) near platform No 26 at the Hauptbahnhof.

This is also the agent for Eurolines bus services to Budapest (DM110/165 one way/return, 10 hours), and other Central and Eastern European destinations.

BEX (BerLinien Bus; ☎ 0130-831 14 4 for travel to Berlin, ☎ 030-860 96 0 from within Berlin) runs daily buses between Berlin and Munich, via Leipzig, Bayreuth, Nuremberg and Ingolstadt; one way/return SuperSpar tickets, for passengers under 26 or over 60, cost DM75/139; full-fare tickets are DM129/149. See Getting There & Away under individual cities and towns for other fares and services.

Train Train services to/from Munich are excellent. There are rapid connections at least every two hours to all major cities in Germany, as well as frequent services to European cities such as Vienna (five hours), Prague (6½ hours) and Zürich (4¼ hours).

High-speed ICE services from Munich include Berlin-Zoo (DM250, 6¾ hours), Frankfurt (DM132, 3½ hours) and Hamburg (DM243, 5½ hours).

Prague extension passes to your rail pass (see the Getting Around chapter) are sold at the rail-pass counters (Nos 19 and 20) at the

Hauptbahnhof, or through EurAide (see Tourist Offices under Information).

Car & Motorcycle Munich has autobahns radiating on all sides. Take the A9 to Nuremberg, the A92/A3 to Passau, the A8 to Salzburg, the A95 to Garmisch-Partenkirchen and the A8 to Ulm or Stuttgart.

All major car-rental companies have offices at the airport. Sixt (Budget), Europcar and Hertz have counters on the 2nd level of the Hauptbahnhof; pick up and return the cars to the garage under the Maritim Hotel (enter from Senefelderstrasse).

If you're thinking about buying a car here (see Purchase under Car & Motorcycle in the Getting Around chapter) and you're not very technically minded, you should seriously consider having the vehicle vetted by the ADAC's Prüfzentrum Gebrauchtwagenuntersuching (testing centre for used cars; ☎ 519 51 88), Ridlerstrasse 35, which will run through the thing with a fine-toothed comb for DM85/110 for ADAC members/nonmembers.

Hitching & Ride Services In order to hitchhike from Munich, you should take public transport from the centre to the highway entrance and stand on the non-highway side of the blue sign, where it's legal. Some suggestions for getting to the best hitching spots by public transport include:

Salzburg, Vienna and the Brenner Pass via the A8
: Take U-Bahn No 1 or 2 to Karl-Preis-Platz.

Stuttgart via the A8
: U-Bahn No 1 to Rotkreuzplatz, tram No 12 to Amalienburgstrasse, then bus No 73 or 75 to Blutenburg.

Nuremberg via the A9
: U-Bahn No 6 to Studentenstadt; it's about 500m to the Frankfurter Ring entrance.

Garmisch-Partenkirchen via the A95
: U-Bahn No 6 to Westpark then bus No 33 to Luise-Kieselbach-Platz

For arranged rides, contact the ADM-Mitfahrzentrale (☎ 194 40), near the Hauptbahnhof at Lämmerstrasse 4. It's open daily to 8 pm. Charges (including booking fees) are: Vienna DM26, Berlin DM35, Amsterdam DM50, Paris DM54, Prague DM24 and Warsaw DM60.

The CityNetz Mitfahr-Service (☎ 194 44), at Amalienstrasse 87, is slightly cheaper.

Women can use the Frauen Mitfahrzentrale (☎ 01 46 90), Klenzestrasse 57b. There's also a gay and lesbian Mitfarhrzentrale at ☎ 0190-344 06 4 (DM1.20 per minute).

Getting Around

Even at the height of the summer tourist season, the central pedestrian zone leading from the Hauptbahnhof to Marienplatz makes for very pleasant walking.

The Airport Munich's new Flughafen Franz-Josef Strauss is connected by S-Bahn to the Hauptbahnhof (S-Bahn No 8, DM13.20 with a single ticket or eight strips of a *Streifenkarte)*. The service takes 40 minutes and runs every 20 minutes from 4 am until around 1 am.

The Lufthansa airport bus runs at 20-minute intervals from Arnulfstrasse near the Hauptbahnhof (45 minutes, DM15/25 one way/return) between 6.50 am and 8.50 pm. A taxi will cost at least DM80!

Public Transport Getting around is easy on Munich's excellent public-transport network (MVV). The system is zone-based, and most places of interest to visitors (except Dachau and the airport) are within the 'blue' inner-city zone *(Innenraum)*.

MVV tickets are valid for the S-Bahn, U-Bahn, trams and buses, but must be validated before use by time-stamping them in machines at entrances and on board buses and trams. Failure to validate puts you at the mercy of uniformed (sometimes plain-clothes) ticket inspectors who speak perfect English, who have seen and heard all possible excuses before, and who possess admirable Teutonic efficiency when it comes to handing out fines of DM60 for unauthorised travel.

The U-Bahn stops at around 12.30 am on weekdays and 1.30 am on weekends, but there are some night buses. Rail passes are valid on S-Bahn trains. Bicycle transport is free, but forbidden on weekdays during the morning and evening rush hours.

Short rides (over four total stops with no more than two U-Bahn or S-Bahn stops) cost DM1.70, longer trips cost DM3.40; children pay a maximum of DM5 per trip but usually DM3. It's cheaper to buy a strip-card of 10 tickets called a Streifenkarte for DM15, and stamp one strip (DM1.36) per adult on rides of two or less tram or U-Bahn stops, two strips (DM2.73) for longer rides. But the best value is in day passes for the inner zone, which cost DM8 (DM12 covering two adults and up to three kids), and three-day inner-zone passes, which are DM20/30.

A network of night buses *(Nachtbussen)* operates after standard hours – very convenient for disco and club-goers; the routes, hours and schedules change often. Pick up a copy of the latest schedule from any tourist office.

Car & Motorcycle It's not worth driving in the city centre; many streets are pedestrian-only, ticket enforcement is Orwellian and parking is a nightmare. The tourist office map shows city car parks, which generally cost about DM3 per hour.

Taxi Taxis are expensive (more than DM5 at flag fall, plus DM2.20 per km) and not much more convenient than public transport. For a radio-despatched taxi ring ☎ 216 10, ☎ 216 11 or ☎ 194 10. Taxi ranks are indicated on the city's tourist map.

The BahnTaxi stand (DM15 per couple; see the Getting Around chapter for details) is at the south-east end of the Hauptbahnhof near the Bayerstrasse exit.

Bicycle Guests of the Jugendherberge München can rent bikes for DM22/40/54 for one/two/three days. Radius Fahrradverleih (☎ 596 11 3), at the end of platform No 31 in the Hauptbahnhof, rents city bikes for DM25/95 per day/week, mountain and trekking bikes for DM35/140. Rail-pass holders get a 10% discount, and there's a 20% discount from Tuesday to Thursday.

Around Munich

DACHAU

'The way to freedom is to follow one's orders; exhibit honesty, orderliness, cleanliness, sobriety, truthfulness, the ability to sacrifice and love of the Fatherland'

Inscription from the roof of the concentration camp at Dachau

Dachau was the very first Nazi concentration camp, built by Heinrich Himmler in March 1933. It 'processed' more than 200,000 prisoners, and 31,531 were reported killed here. In 1933 Munich had 10,000 Jews. Only 200 survived the war.

The camp is now one of the most popular day trips from Munich, though the experience can be so disturbing that we don't recommend it for children under age 12.

Just outside the main exhibition hall is a monument, inscribed in English, French, Hebrew, German and Russian, that reads 'Never Again'. Nearby are large stakes onto which prisoners were hanged, sometimes for days, with their hands shackled behind their backs.

Inside the main hall, as you enter, is a large map showing camp locations throughout Germany and Central Europe. Indicators show which were the extermination camps. The exhibit inside shows photographs and models of the camp, its officers and prisoners and of horrifying 'scientific experiments' carried out by Nazi doctors. There's also a whipping block; a chart showing the system for prisoner identification by category (Jews, homosexuals, Jehovah's Witnesses, Poles, Rom and other 'asocial' types); documents relating to the camp and the persecution of 'degenerate' authors banned by the party; and exhibits on the rise of the Nazi party and the establishment of the camp system.

Also on the grounds are reconstructed bunkers and a (never used) crematorium and extermination gas chamber disguised as showers. Outside the gas chamber building is a statue to 'honour the dead and warn the living' and a Russian Orthodox chapel. Nearby are churches and a Jewish memorial.

Guided tours in English are essential if you don't understand German, and a good idea even if you do. Even if you take the tour, consider buying a copy of the catalogue, which has detailed descriptions of all the exhibits in the museum as well as a written history. The DM25 goes directly to the Survivors Association of Dachau. An English-language documentary is shown at 11.30 am and 3.30 pm. The camp is open from 9 am to 5 pm every day except Monday, and admission is free. Expect to spend two to three hours here.

Organised Tours

Dachauer Forum and Action Reconciliation runs two-hour tours in English on Saturday and Sunday at 12.30 pm, and has recently been experimenting with daily tours as well. They are excellent and informative, but the bigger the group the longer the tour.

Check to see if EurAide director Alan Wissenberg has resumed his intimate and excellent walking tours through Dachau.

BAVARIA

Getting There & Away

The S-Bahn No 2 to Dachau leaves Munich Hauptbahnhof three times an hour at 18, 38 and 58 minutes past. The trip takes 19 minutes and requires a two-zone ticket (or four strips of a Streifenkarte), including the bus connection.

In front of the Dachau train station change for local buses; bus No 726 (from Monday to Saturday) and bus No 724 (on Sunday and holidays) are timed to leave the station about 10 minutes after the train arrives. Show your stamped ticket to the driver. The driver will announce the stop (KZ-Gedenkstätte); then follow the crowds – it's about a five-minute walk from the bus stop to the entrance of the camp. Return buses leave from near the camp car park every 20 minutes. By car, follow Dachauer Strasse straight out to Dachau and follow the KZ-Gedenkstätte signs. Parking is free.

CHIEMSEE

Munich residents have a special place in their hearts for this lovely lake an hour east of Munich. So did Ludwig II, who liked it so much he built his homage to Versailles on an island in the centre.

The bizarre Neues Königsschloss, built up on Herreninsel, makes a very pleasant day trip from Munich, and getting here is about half the fun. A steam train connects the train station in Prien am Chiemsee with the ferry docks.

There's a good tourist office at the Prien am Chiemsee train station, open in summer only, and another at Alte Rathausstrasse 11 (☎ 08051-228 0); they are the central information centres for the entire lake district. There's bicycle rental (DM15 a day) at the station itself.

From the Prien am Chiemsee train station (hourly service from Munich, DM21.20, one hour), walk down the stairs and through the tunnel to Chiemsee Bahn station, where you catch a steam train (10 minutes, DM3.50/1.50 one way, DM5.50/2.50 return) to the ferry terminal at Prien/Stock (Hafen). From there, Chiemsee Schiffahrt (☎ 609 0), Seestrasse 108, operates boats that ply the waters of the lake with stops at Herreninsel, Gstadt, Fraueninsel, Seebruck and Chieming.

You can circumnavigate the entire lake and make all these stops (get off and catch the next ferry that comes your way) for DM20.50.

Beaches & Boat Rental

The most easily accessed swimming beaches are at Chieming and Gstadt. Boat rental, available at many beaches, costs between DM12 and DM20 per hour, depending on the type. Swimming is free.

Herreninsel

Begun in 1878 on the site of an Augustinian monastery and never completed, **Neues Königsschloss**, Ludwig's own copy of Versailles, is as good an insight as one can get into the king's bizarre motivations.

The palace is both a knock-off and an

attempted one-up of Versailles, with larger rooms, the immense Ambassador Staircase and a 77m-long Hall of Mirrors. There's a portrait of Louis XIV in a more prominent position than any of Ludwig himself, represented only by an unfinished statue. Ludwig spent less than a month in the palace.

Return ferry fare is DM14; admission to the castle is DM7/4. The castle is open from April to October daily from 9 am to 5 pm; in winter, from 10 am to 4 pm.

Fraueninsel

This island is home to the Frauenwörth, a 12th-century Benedictine monastery. Benedictine monks returned to the area in the 1980s and founded another monastery, which functions today. The island also contains a memorial to (and the remains of) Irmengard of Fraueninsel, the great-granddaughter of Charlemagne, and the **Torhall**, the gateway to the monastery (mid-9th century); inside is a chapel. Return ferry fare, including a stop at Herreninsel, is DM16.

STARNBERG

Once a royal retreat and still a pretty affluent neighbourhood, Lake Starnberg (Starnberger See), just 30 minutes by S-Bahn No 6 from Munich (two zones or four strips of a Streifenkarte), is a fast and easy way to get away from the urban bustle of Munich and out onto the water.

The city of Starnberg, at the northern end of the lake, is the heart of the Fünf Seen, the Five Lakes district. Starnberger See, about 22km long, 5km wide and between one 1m and 100m deep, is a favourite spot for Munich windsurfers, who also skittle over nearby Ammersee, and the much smaller Wörthsee, Pilsensee and Osterseen.

The tourist information office (☎ 08151-906 00) is at Wittelsbacherstrasse 9, open Monday to Friday from 8 am to 6 pm, and from June to October also on Saturday from 9 am to 1 pm. The office gives out and sells maps and hiking maps of the entire area, and can help you plan public transport between here and other lake towns, as well as to the heavily touristed kloster at Andechs.

Starnberg is best known, though, as the place where Ludwig II was found dead, along with his physician, in one metre of water. Ludwig had been brought here under arrest in an effort to remove him from power due to insanity. The circumstances of his death have remained a mystery to this day, and it was known both that Ludwig was not at all a bad swimmer, and that his doctor was perhaps the only person who could vouch for the king's sanity.

Conspiracy theorists have a ball with the story. The spot where Ludwig's body was found, near the **Votivkapelle** in Berg, is now marked with a cross erected in the water.

The Bayerische Seen Schiffahrt company runs electrically powered tour boats across the lake from their docks right behind the S-Bahn station. There are one-hour tours (DM12.50) to the five castles around the lake's circumference (daily in summer at 8.50, 9.30 and 10.35 am and 12.15, 1.15, 2.30 and 4.30 pm).

If that's too organised for your taste, head to one of the several boat-rental booths just west of the train station, where you can rent rowing/pedal/electric-powered boats for DM12/15/20 per hour. The electric boats have about enough power to get you a third of the way down the lake and back.

ANDECHS

A short bus ride from Herrsching, on the east side of the Ammersee (from Munich take S-Bahn No 5 to the last stop), is the Benedictine kloster of Andechs (☎ 08152-376 0), rebuilt in 1675 after the Thirty Years' War left it in ruins. The lovely hill-top rococo structure has always been a place of pilgrimage, but today an overwhelming majority of the visitors are after the beer that the monks here have been brewing for over 500 years. It's good beer, but the place is so overrun by tourists it's easy to forget that you're in a religious institution, pious as your love for beer may be.

From Herrsching train station, take the Rauner bus (DM2.50), which leaves at least once an hour between 7.55 am and 4.35 pm and returns from 9.55 am to 6.45 pm. Or take a 3km walk along the well marked footpaths.

SCHLEISSHEIM

Just north of Munich, the suburb of Schleissheim is home to two major castles that compete with anything in the heart of the city.

The **Neues Schloss Schleissheim** (☎ 089-315 87 20), in Oberschleissheim (S-Bahn No 1 in the direction of Freising to Oberschleissheim, then bus No 292, which runs weekdays only), is another spectacular castle modelled after Versailles, this one ordered by Emperor Max Joseph in 1701. The grounds are equally impressive (bring a picnic). Inside, you'll see the vaulted ceiling above the staircase, with frescos by Cosmas Damian Asam. It's open Tuesday to Sunday from 10 am to 12.30 pm and 1.30 to 5 pm; admission is DM2/1.50.

Nearby, the Renaissance **Altes Schloss Schleissheim** (☎ 315 52 72) is open as a museum of religion (DM5/3).

The third castle here, on the grounds of Altes Schloss park, is **Schloss Lustheim** (☎ 315 87 20), with amazing frescos and a stunning baroque interior, now home to the **Meissner Porzellan Sammlung**, said to be the largest collection of Meissen chinaware in Germany. It's open the same hours as Schloss Schleissheim; entry costs DM3/2.

Flugwerft Schleissheim

After Germany's defeat in WWI, the maximum power of German aircraft was heavily restricted. German engineers began a 'ground-up' approach to aerodynamics in an effort to increase performance and speed, and in doing so revolutionised the design of modern aircraft.

This museum (☎ 315 71 40), a 7800-sq-m display within three halls (including a renovated hangar built between 1912 and 1919), is the aviation branch of the Deutsches Museum and on the site of the birthplace of the Royal Bavarian Flying Corps in 1912. On exhibit are aircraft from around the world, including the USA, the former Soviet Union, Sweden, Poland and Germany, including a great collection of gliders 'alternative' flying kits.

The museum is open daily from 9 am to 5 pm; admission is DM5/3 for adults/students (kids under six free).

Getting There & Away

Take S-Bahn No 1 (direction: Freising) to Oberschleissheim. It's about a 15-minute walk from the station along Mittenheimer Strasse towards the palaces. By car, take Leopoldstrasse north until it becomes Ingolstadter Strasse. Then take the A99 to the Neuherberg exit, at the south end of the airfield.

BAD TÖLZ

Bad Tölz is a pleasant spa town that's a favourite day trip for Munich residents because of the good swimming at Alpamare, the alpine slide at Blomberg Mountain and rafting down the Isar River (see Activities in the Munich section). The resort's tourist office *(Kurverkersamt)* books accommodation, rents bikes and organises tours.

Churches

Not to be missed is Bad Tölz's hill-top **Kalvarienbergkirche**, best viewed from the bridge crossing the Isar. The enormous baroque church with its large central Holy Staircase is also the site of the tiny **Leonhardikapelle** (1718), which is the destination of the town's elaborate Leonhardifahrt annual pageant.

But the town's star attraction is the **Pfarrkirche Maria Himmelfahrt**, just south of Marktstrasse at the end of Kirchgasse. The enormous yellow Gothic building that stands today was built in 1466 (the neo-Gothic tower from 1875 to 1877) on the site of the 13th-century original, which was destroyed in 1453.

East of the pedestrian zone of Salzstrasse is the **Mühlfeld Kirche** (1737), now in its third incarnation after fire and bomb damage, with a baroque interior complete with a painting of the Plague Procession by rococo master Matthöus Günter.

Alpamare

The closest thing to an Orlando-style water park in Germany is just south of Bad Tölz at Alpamare (☎ 08041-509 33 4). This utterly fantastic complex for adults and kids has heated indoor and outdoor pools, a wave pool, a series of waterslides including the longest one in Germany (the 330m-long Alpabob-Wildwasser), saunas, solariums and its own hotel. They've managed, of course, to add things that allow some to write it off as a medical expense, like massage, a Turkish steam bath, water gymnastics classes and even an 'iodine inhalatorium'! Just in case...

Everything is included in one ticket price: four-hour passes for adults on weekdays/weekends and holidays cost DM29/35, and DM22/24 for children from five to 13. Day-long passes cost DM42/54 for adults, DM29/35 for children. Holders of a *Kurpass*, which overnight guests get when they pay their *Kurtaxe* (resort tax), get a DM5 discount on all tickets.

The park is open Sunday to Thursday from 8 am to 9 pm, Friday and Saturday from 8 am to 10 pm; it is closed 25-26 December and 1 January. From Bad Tölz take Umgehungstrasse (the B13) south in the direction of Lenggriess, then take the Stadt Krankenhaus exit and follow the signs.

Blomberg

South-west of Bad Tölz towers the Blomberg (1248m), a family-friendly mountain with a natural toboggan track in winter and fairly easy hiking and a really fun alpine slide in summer.

The chair lift (☎ 08041-372 6) runs from 9 am to 6 pm in summer and to 4 pm in winter, weather permitting. There's a station midway and at the top. A return ticket to the top/middle/alpine slide costs DM10/6/4 for adults, DM5/5/4 for children.

The summer alpine slide is a 1226m-long fibreglass track that snakes down the mountain from the middle station. You ride down on little wheeled bobsleds that have a joystick to control braking (push forward to go, pull back to brake). You can achieve speeds of about 40 to 50 km/h, but chances are if you do that you're going to either ram a rider ahead of you or, as one of us did, fly off the track and watch helplessly as the cart careens down the mountain (leaving our unfortunate author-rider with a massive friction burn and sore legs from walking back up the hill)! If you do try for speed, wear a long-sleeve shirt and jeans.

Getting There & Away

Bad Tölz has hourly train connections with Munich (DM14.50, one hour). Take S-Bahn No 7 to the end of the line at Wolfratshausen and connect from there.

The Romantic Road

The Romantic Road (Romantische Strasse) links a series of picturesque Bavarian towns and cities. It has so far been the most successful of Germany's marketing campaigns designed to get tourists away from the big cities and out into the countryside, and some two million people ply the route every year. That means, of course, lots of signs in English and Japanese, tourist coaches and kitsch galore.

Despite the tourists, it's worth falling for the sales pitch and taking time to explore this delightful route. You won't be alone, but you certainly won't be disappointed: the route travels through some of the most beautiful towns and cities in Germany.

Orientation & Information

The Romantic Road runs north-south through western Bavaria, from Würzburg in Franconia to Füssen near the Austrian border, passing through about a dozen cities and towns including Rothenburg ob der Tauber, Dinkelsbühl and Augsburg.

The Romantic Road tourist office (☎ 09851-902 71), Markt 1, 91550 Dinkelsbühl, can help you put together an itinerary and give you accommodation lists and prices. The office can also suggest excursions outside the Romantic Road towns. But the best places for information about the Romantic Road are the local tourist offices in Rothenburg (☎ 09861-404 92), at Markt 1, and in Dinkelsbühl (☎ 09581-902 40), at Markt 1 (in the same building as the Romantic Road tourist office).

Füssen's tourist office (☎ 08362-70 77) is at Kaiser-Maximilian-Platz 1 (closed for lunch, Saturday afternoon and Sunday).

Places to Stay

Considering the number of tourists, accommodation along the Romantic Road can be surprisingly good value. Tourist offices in most towns are very efficient at finding accommodation in almost any price range. Most of the DJH hostels listed here accept only people aged under 27, though some will in practice accept over 27s in 'emergencies', or when they have room.

Getting There & Away

Though Frankfurt is the most popular starting point for the Romantic Road, Munich is a good choice as well, especially if you decide to take the bus (the stop is at the north side of the Hauptbahnhof).

Bus Half a dozen daily buses connect Füssen and Garmisch-Partenkirchen (DM14.80, all via Neuschwanstein and most via Schloss Linderhof). There are also several connections between Füssen and Oberstdorf (via Pfronten or the Tirolean town of Reutte).

Train To start at the southern end, take the hourly train link from Munich to Füssen (DM34, 2½ hours, some services change at Buchloe). Rothenburg is linked by train to Würzburg and Munich via Steinach, and Nördlingen to Augsburg via Donauwörth (DM18.40).

Heidelberg Europabus runs a daily Castle Road coach service in each direction between Heidelberg and Rothenburg (DM47/94 one way/return, 4¼ hours).

Nuremberg OVF has a daily morning bus (No 8805) from Nuremberg Hauptbahnhof to Rothenburg, which returns late in the afternoon.

Zürich & Berlin BerLinien buses (☎ 0130-831 144) running between Zürich and Berlin pass through Rothenburg (DM96 one way, seven hours from Berlin).

Getting Around

Bus It is possible to do this route using train connections or local buses (see the individual town listings) or by car (just follow the brown '*Romantische Strasse*' signs), but most travellers prefer to take the Europabus. From April until October Europabus runs one coach daily in each direction between Frankfurt and Munich (12 hours), and another in either direction between Dinkelsbühl and Füssen (4½ hours). With either bus, you're seeing about half the route. The only way to see all of it is by car.

The bus makes short stops in some towns, but it's silly to do the whole trip in one go, since there's no charge for breaking the journey and continuing on the next day (you can reserve a seat for the next day before you disembark).

Reservations & Fares Tickets are available for short segments of the trip, and reservations are only necessary at peak-season weekends. For information and reservations, contact Deutsche Touring (☎ 069-790 32 81; fax 790 32 19) at Am Römerhof 17, 60486 Frankfurt/Main.

The full fare from Frankfurt to Füssen is DM126/252 one way/return (change buses in Dinkelsbühl, Nördlingen, Augsburg or Munich). Eurail and German Rail passes are valid. Inter-Rail pass-holders and people over 60 get a 50% discount, Europass holders get 30%, and students under 27 get 10% off. Here are the most heavily travelled circuits and the one-way/return fares from Munich:

Augsburg – DM29/58
Nördlingen – DM36/72
Rothenburg ob der Tauber – DM55/110
Würzburg – DM82/164
Frankfurt am Main – DM113/226

One-way/return fares from Frankfurt are:

Würzburg – DM32/64
Rothenburg ob der Tauber – DM58/116
Nördlingen – DM77/154
Augsburg – DM96/192

Bicycle With its gentle gradients and ever-changing scenery, the Romantic Road makes an ideal bike trip. Bikes can be rented from most large train stations. Tourist offices in all the towns keep lists of 'bicycle-friendly hotels' that permit storage, as well as providing information on public storage facilities. Radl-Tour (☎ 08191-471 77 or ☎ 09341-539 5) offers nine-day cycling packages along the entire route from Würzburg to Füssen for DM848, which covers bike rental, accommodation and daily luggage transport. You can transport bikes aboard Europabus buses for DM10 for fewer than 12 stops (DM20 for 12 or more stops).

WÜRZBURG

- *pop 97,000*
- *area code* ☎ 0931

Surrounded by forests and vineyards, the charming city of Würzburg (pronounced 'VURTS-bourg') straddles the Main River and is the official starting point of the Romantic Road. Although not very well known outside Germany, Würzburg is a centre of art, beautiful architecture and delicate wines.

Würzburg was a Franconian duchy when, in 686, three roving Irish missionaries – Kilian, Totnan and Kolonat – walked in one day and asked Duke Gosbert if he wouldn't mind converting to Christianity and – oh, yes – ditching his wife, the duke's brother's widow. Gosbert was said to be mulling it over when his wife, Gailana, had the three bumped off in 689. When the murders were discovered decades later, the three martyrs were canonised as saints and Würzburg became a pilgrimage city.

In 1720, the architect Balthasar Neumann was called in to design the new residence for the prince-bishops who had ruled the city from the hill-top fortress Marienberg since the early 13th century; he was joined by Giovanni Battista Tiepolo, who painted the frescos. Neumann's masterpiece is heralded around the world as containing the finest baroque staircase ever to stand under a fresco (and the fresco itself is not bad either!).

About 90% of Würzburg's centre was destroyed by fire bombing in WWII, but the city has rebuilt with a vengeance. If Würzburg's highlights seem familiar to you, it's because you're rich: you've seen them (and Neumann) on the DM50 note.

Orientation

The Hauptbahnhof is at the northern end of the Altstadt. The Main flows north through the western side of the Altstadt; the fortress, camping site, coin laundry and hostel are on the west bank; all the other sites are on the east. The boundaries of the Altstadt are roughly the river at the west and Friedrich-Ebert-Ring/Martin-Luther-Strasse, which runs in a rough circle around the east side and at the enormous roundabout at Berliner Platz, at the north-east corner of the Altstadt.

The stone footbridge, the Alte Mainbrücke, is the main route across the river; it leads right into Domstrasse and the pedestrianised heart of the Altstadt. The Residenz and the Hofgarten are on the Altstadt's east side.

Information

Tourist Offices There are three tourist offices in town. The head office is at the Congress und Tourismus Zentrum (☎ 373 33 35), on Pleichtorstrasse (open Monday to Thursday from 8.30 am to 5 pm, Friday to 1 pm). The one in the pavilion outside the Hauptbahnhof on Röntgenring (☎ 373 43 6), and the other at the rococo masterpiece Haus zum Falken (☎ 373 39 8), on Oberer Markt, are both open daily from 10 am to 6 pm (closed Sunday in winter).

Money Change money at the Postbank, next to the Hauptbahnhof at Bahnhofplatz 2, and at American Express (☎ 355 69 0), Haugerpfarrgasse 1, five minutes south of the Hauptbahnhof.

BAVARIA

Post & Communications The main post office is at Bahnhofplatz 2: there's another one at Paradeplatz.

Online Services Internetpoint Würzburg (☎ 353 42 93), near the Congress und Tourismus Zentrum at Pleichtorstrasse 2, is a business centre that offers free Internet access.

Travel Agencies STA Travel (☎ 521 76) is at Zwinger 6.

Bookshops & Libraries Buchhandlung am Dom (☎ 530 55) is at Kürschnerhof 2. The Stadtbucherei (city library; ☎ 373 29 4) is at Haus zum Falken, Oberer Markt, in the same building as the tourist office. The Universitätsbibliotek (☎ 888 59 43), Am Hubland, is at the eastern outskirts of the city.

Campus You can study just about everything at Julius-Maximilian Universität (☎ 310), Sanderring 2, at the southern end of the Altstadt, but most of the 20,000 or so students are there for medicine or related fields. It was established in 1582.

Laundry The SB-run Waschsalon Waschhaus (☎ 416 77 3), Frankfurter Strasse 13a, is on the west side of the Main and relatively close to the hostel.

Medical Services The biggest hospital in town is Juliusspital (☎ 393 0), Juliuspromenade 19, five minutes from the Hauptbahnhof.

BAVARIA

Schloss Marienberg

The Marienberg fortress, begun as early as 1201, has been rebuilt, expanded and renovated over the centuries in a variety of architectural styles. Built as the residence of the prince-bishops of Würzburg who lived here until 1718, it is today the symbol of the city, visible from most everywhere: the huge castle atop the splendid vine-covered hills.

There are two museums: the **Fürstenbau Museum** (☎ 438 38; DM4/3), featuring the episcopal apartments; and the regional **Mainfränkisches Museum** (☎ 430 16; DM3.50), the combined Lower Franconia and local history museum, including wine exhibits. Both museums (combined ticket DM6) are open Tuesday to Sunday.

Residenz

The Residenz, Neumann's baroque masterpiece, is spread along Balthasar-Neumann-Promenade. The DM5 admission (students DM3.50) is well worth it. As you enter, the **Grand Staircase** is to the left, a single central set of steps that splits into two and zigs up to the 1st floor, under Tiepolo's stunning fresco, *The Four Continents*, which depicts Europe as the cultural and financial capital of the world (they hadn't heard of Oz yet, so calm down). The **Imperial Hall** and **Spiegelsaal** upstairs, in the **Imperial Apartments**, are just as impressive.

Attached is the **Martin-von-Wagner Museum** (☎ 312 28 8) with graphics, 14th to 19th-century paintings and Greek masterworks. Admission is free but it's closed on Monday. Behind this, the **Hofgarten** (open dawn to dusk) has spectacular French and English-style gardens and is the site of concerts and special events throughout the year. Picnics are allowed.

Churches

In the Altstadt, the interiors of the **Dom St Kilian** and the adjacent **Neumünster**, which contains crypts said to hold the bodies of Saints Kilian, Totnan and Kolonat, continue the baroque themes of the Residenz. The city **Dom**, heavily damaged, has been rebuilt around the remaining sections of choir and transept in several styles – Romanesque, Gothic and modern. You either like it or you don't.

Röntgen Museum

Würzburg's most important non-architectural, proselytising or poetic son is Wilhelm Conrad Röntgen, discoverer of the X-ray. The Röntgen Gedächtnisstätte at Röntgenring 8 is a tribute to his life and work and is open from Monday to Friday (free).

Wine Tasting

Neumann's fortified Alter Kranen (old crane), which serviced a dock on the river south of Friedensbrücke, is now the **Haus des Frankenweins** (☎ 120 93), where you can sample and buy some of Franconia's finest wines (for around DM2 per glass). From March to September, every Friday at 3 pm you can go on an hour-long tour (DM7) of the splendid old wine cellars, rooms and courtyards of the **Juliusspital** (☎ 393 14 00), Juliuspromenade 19.

Organised Tours

From late March to late October the tourist office runs guided city walks (two hours; DM13/10, including admission to the Residenz) from Tuesday to Sunday at 11 am. Meet in front of the Haus zum Falken.

For DM10, you can rent a cassette player and tape from the tourist office in the Haus zum Falken, with an English-language tape guiding you through the major sights.

Special Events

Every September the Weinprämiierung festival is held at the Marienberg, during which the finest Franconian wines are judged. Tickets are sold out a year in advance, but to try the winners, head to Würzburg's Haus des Frankenweins.

Places to Stay

The nearest camping ground is *Kanu-Club* (☎ 725 36), on the west bank of the Main at Mergentheimer Strasse 13b (tram No 3 or 5 to Jugendbühlweg). Two/four-person tents are DM3/6 plus DM4 per person.

The *Jugendgästehaus Würzburg* (☎ 425 90), on Burkarder Strasse below the fortress, charges DM27 for beds (tram No 3 or 5 from the Hauptbahnhof).

Two places with absolutely no frills but clean rooms are *Pension Siegel* (☎ 529 41), Reisgrubenstrasse 7, with singles/doubles from DM46/90; and *Pension Spehnkuch* (☎ 547 52), Röntgenring 7, which charges DM50/90.

If you have a car, the best accommodation option is about 5km east of the centre on Nürnberger Strasse, where a new *Etap Hotel* is soon to open (with rooms for DM53/65); check with the tourist office.

The *Gasthof Goldener Hahn* (☎ 519 41), Marktgasse 7, offers perhaps the best value for a central location, with no-frills singles for DM55 and singles/doubles with bath and WC from DM85/140. *Hotel Dortmunder Hof* (☎ 561 63), at Innerer Graben 22, has comparable rooms from DM50/100.

Hotel Meesenburg (☎ 533 04) at Pleichtorstrasse 8 has various rooms, from simple singles (DM55) to fully equipped doubles (DM120). *Hotel Barbarossa* (☎ 559 53), at Theaterstrasse 2, charges similar rates.

Places to Eat

In the Hauptbahnhof there's good stuff at both *Cro Bag*, with broccoli and mozzarella-filled goodies for DM2.90, and outside at *Ditsch*, which has Asian vegie versions of the same thing for DM2.80. Doner fans should head for *Simsim Felafel* (☎ 161 53), Pleichtorstrasse 2, right around the corner from the tourist office in the Congress und Tourismus Zentrum. Run by friendly Palestinians, it has outstanding doner and felafel from DM5. *Café Haupeltshorfer* has a very young, energetic crowd, and good salads and sandwiches.

The *City Café*, Eichhornstrasse 21, serves just about everything that's easy to prepare, tastes good and doesn't cost (much) more than DM10, like salads, soups, pastas, pancakes, toasted sandwiches, vegetable dishes, baked Camembert, fried sausages etc.

One of Würzburg's most popular eating and drinking establishments is *Bürgerspital* (☎ 138 61), at Theaterstrasse 19 (closed Tuesday). Originally a medieval hospice, it offers a broad selection of Franconian wines (including its own vintages), and serves tasty house specialities from DM15.

Mosquito (☎ 510 22), Karmelitenstrasse 31, is a small Mexican place with good chilli con carne (DM10.50), nachos (DM11.50) and big burritos (DM15.50).

For the romantic evening out, the beautiful, overtouristed *Zum Stachel*, behind Unterer Markt (ask anyone), isn't as nice as the fabulous *Backlöfele* (☎ 590 59), Ursulinergasse 2, which has three very romantic rooms, sharp service and regional specialities from DM24 to DM36 (cheaper from 2 to 5.30 pm when they average DM10).

Entertainment

Trend, *Groschen Heft* and *Wox* are listings magazines. Two notable discos are *Airport* (☎ 237 71), Gattingerstrasse 17, which is huge and very trendy; and *Zauberberg* (☎ 519 49), Veitshöchheimer Strasse, which has a healthy mix of soul, dance tunes and other styles. *Brazil*, in the cellar at Sandestrasse 7 under *Robert's American Bar*, has theme nights (eg salsa on Wednesdays). *Omnibus* (☎ 561 21), Theaterstrasse 10, is the best place for live rock, jazz and folk music; there's almost always something going on.

The coolest street in town for pubs is Neubaustrasse, which has several popular student café-bars that stay open late and also serve good cheap food. They include *Gehrings* (☎ 129 07), at No 26; *Le Clochard Bistro*, at No 20, with good crêpes and a daily Schneller Teller (fast dish) for DM9.90; and the hugely popular *Uni-Café* (☎ 156 72), No 2, with two floors, cheap snacks and a fun crowd. The two most popular gay and lesbian places are *Sonderbar* (☎ 543 25), Bronnbachergasse 1, and the chic and all-friendly *Contrast*, Juliuspromenade 4, which also has a sidewalk café.

Getting There & Away

Würzburg is 70 minutes by train from Frankfurt (DM36) and one hour from Nuremberg (DM27); both Frankfurt-Nuremberg and Hanover-Munich trains stop here several times daily. It is also handily situated if you want to join Europabus Romantic Road tours – from Rothenburg by bus is DM26 and 2½ hours; by train via Steinach it costs DM15.40 and takes about one hour. The main bus station is next to the Hauptbahnhof off Röntgenring. BerLinien Bus (☎ 0130-831 144) runs daily from Berlin (DM87/95 one way/return, six hours).

AROUND WÜRZBURG

Veitshöchheim

- *pop 9000*
- *area code* ☎ 0931

Veitshöchheim (pronounced 'FIGHTS hoosh-hime'), 10km north of Würzburg c the Main River, was the 17th-century sun mer residence of the prince-bishops Würzburg. Its pavilion-packed rococo ga den may well be the most beautiful Europe.

The garden is open to the public fro dawn to dusk, while the castle is open f tours April to September from Tuesday Sunday from 9 am to noon and 1 to 5 pr The obligatory guided tour of the castle interior costs DM2.50. The ferry drops yo off about 150m east of the entrance to th garden. Kirchstrasse is the main drag, line with restaurants and cafés.

Getting There & Away The most comm way to get to Veitshöchheim and its castle by boat. Kurth & Schiebe (☎ 587 53) an Veitshöchheimer Personen-Schiffah (☎ 915 53) have boats hourly (from 10 a to 4 pm and 10 am to 5 pm respectively) fro the Alter Kranen (Haus des Frankenwein in Würzburg. There's heavy competitio between the companies, both of which hav snacks and drinks on board and charg DM8/13 one way/return for the 35-minu journey. Alternatively, take bus No 11 or 1 from the bus station at the Würzbu Hauptbahnhof (DM3.70, 30 minutes), whic leave every 20 minutes or so. By car, take th B27 north (direction: Fulda).

Volkach

- *pop 9000*
- *area code* ☎ 09381

With dozens of annual wine festivals, th sweet little town 25km north-east of Wür burg, at a loop in the Main River, is definite in danger of being overrun by tour buses. F now though, it's just a peaceful mediev town with lovely alleyways, nice wine ba and pretty houses.

From the bus stop, at the former tra station, walk east on Bahnhofstrasse and tu left (north) onto Hauptstrasse, through the late-Gothic Sommerach gate (formerly the town jail) with the stepped Renaissance gable. Once past it, you'll see the tower of St-Bartholomäus-Kirche.

The tourist office (☎ 401 12) is in the Rathaus on Markt. Change money at the Hypo Bank, right in front of the Sommerach. There's an Internet café at Der Keller (☎ 814 22 2), Hauptstrasse 30.

Things to See & Do Throughout the city are lovely buildings, especially along **Kreuzgasse**, which is lined with half-timbered houses. Don't miss the baroque **Schelfenhaus** (1720), now home to the city library and the **local history museum** (closed Monday).

Outside town is the 15th-century **Maria im Weingarten**, a pilgrimage church on top of the **Kirchberg** containing the wooden carved *Madonna im Rosenkranz* by Tilman Riemenschneider.

Volkach's **wine festivals** are held most weekends from May to October, when the place is awash with fairs, festivals and music performances. Everything takes place on Markt. Rent bicycles at Fahrrad Maier (☎ 162 9), Hauptstrasse 32.

Places to Stay & Eat Most people make Volkach a day trip, but nice singles/doubles are available at *Hotel Behringer* (☎ 245 3), Markt 5, which has (thank goodness) a no-smoking breakfast room. The very nostalgic *Bäckerei Gutbrot*, Hauptstrasse 26, has spectacular bread and bread rolls, and absolutely immense cakes for DM3 a slice. Two good wine and beer gardens are *Hinterhöfle* (☎ 814 20 0), Hauptstrasse 30, and *Weingut Zur Schwane*, at Hauptstrasse 12.

Getting There & Away From Würzburg, take one of the very frequent trains to Seligenstadt (15 minutes) and switch to bus No 8105, or take bus No 8163 from Würzburg's Hauptbahnhof directly to Volkach station (DM7). By car, take the B19 (direction: Schweinfurt); after about 9km, just after the exit for the autobahn, you'll see a big yellow sign pointing to a right turn onto a local road. Make the right, follow the signs and it's about 15km from the turn-off.

ROTHENBURG OB DER TAUBER

- *pop 12,000*
- *area code* ☎ 09861

Disney-park planners would probably dismiss it as too kitschy, but Rothenburg is probably the main tourist attraction along the Romantic Road.

Granted the status of a 'free imperial city' in 1274, Rothenburg is full of cobbled lanes and picturesque old houses and enclosed by towered walls, all of which are worth exploring. Crowded in summer, its museums are open for shorter afternoon hours from November to March. The most crowded months are May, September, October and December, when the city holds its Christmas market.

Orientation & Information

The train station and post office are about a five-minute walk east of the Altstadt along Ansbacher Strasse. The walled Altstadt's centre is based around the Markt, where you'll find the supremely helpful tourist office (☎ 404 92), at Markt 1, which provides a great range of services, including room bookings. The main shopping street in town is Schmiedgasse, and all display signs along it are old-fashioned gold or brass ones. Even McDonald's sports a pair of actual golden arches.

In the train station, Rothenburger Reiseburo (☎ 461 1) books onward transport on Europabus and trains. Wash clothes at the Waschsalon (☎ 277 5), Johannitergasse 9.

Rathaus

The town hall on the Markt was begun in Gothic style in the 14th century but completed during the Renaissance. The viewing platform of the **Rathausturm** (220 steps; DM1) offers a majestic view over the town and the Tauber Valley. According to legend, the town was saved during the Thirty Years' War when the mayor won a challenge by the Imperial General Count Tilly and downed more than three litres of wine at a gulp. It's pretty much accepted that the wine legend is hooey, and that Tilly was placated with hard cash. Nevertheless, the **Meister Trunk** scene is re-enacted by the clock figures on the tourist office building (year round every hour from 11 am to 3 pm and 8 to 10 pm) and in costumed ceremonies in the Kaisersaal in the Rathaus during Whitsuntide celebrations (mid to late May).

Jakobskirche

The Gothic Church of St James (1311-22; nave 1373-1436) has glorious stained-glass windows but the highlight is the carved *Heilige Blut* altar by Tilman Riemenschneider, made from 1499 to 1505. It depicts the Last Supper with Judas at the centre, taking bread from Christ, a bit left of centre; the other characters are set exactly as Tilman said they were in the Bible. There's an entry fee, except during services, of DM2.50, concessions DM2. Tours (in German only) run at 11 am and 2 pm.

Medieval Criminal Museum

The fascinating and extensive Mittelalterliches Kriminalmuseum, at Burggasse 3 south of the Markt, displays brutal implements of torture (sorry, 'interrogation') and punishment used in centuries past (DM5, students DM4; DM8 when combined with the Reichstadt Museum). The museum obtained its collections from various towns around the region; the building it's in today is a former hospital, not a former torture chamber. It's open April to October daily from 9.30 am to 6.30 pm, November to February from 2 to 4 pm, and during Christmas markets and in March from 10 am to 4 pm.

Town Walls and Peter & Paul Church

The intact city walls are a 3.5km ring around the city (2.5km are walkable) and on the west side of town they offer great views into the Tauber Valley. From this vantage point, you can see the double-deck **Doppelbrücke** in the valley below, which is the best place to watch fireworks displays during the Reichstadt Festtage (see Special Events). Fro here, too, you can see the head of a trail th leads down the valley and over to the lovel Peter und Paul Kirche in Detwang, whic contains another stunning Riemenschneid altar. There's a beer garden about halfwa along the trail. Also at the west side of th city is the **Burg Turm**, which now contair a **puppet theatre** (☎ 753 4), with show Monday to Saturday at 3 pm.

Reichstadt Museum

The Reichstadt Museum, in a forme convent (DM4/3, or DM8 for a combinatio ticket to this and the Medieval Crimin Museum), features the superb *Rothenburge Passion* (1494) in 12 panels by Martinu Schwarz and the **Judaica room**, with a co lection of gravestones with Hebrew ir scriptions. Outside, the convent **gardens** a a quiet place to shake off the throngs (until bus tour group walks through every now an then).

Other Museums

The **Puppen und Spielzeugmuseum** c dolls and toys, at Hofbronnengasse 13, is th largest private collection in Germany (DM students DM3.50). The **Handwerke Häuschen** (☎ 209 8), Alter Stadtgraben 2 is a reconstruction of medieval life in the city Admission is DM3/1.50.

Organised Tours

The tourist office holds English-languag walking tours year round daily at 2 pm fc DM6; meet in front of the Rathaus. Tour lasting 1½ hours in German (DM5) run at 1 am and 2 pm daily from Easter to Christmas A very entertaining walking tour of th Altstadt is conducted every evening by th town *Nachtwächter* (night watcher), dresse in his traditional costume. For the English language tour (DM6), meet at the Markt a 7.55 pm; the German-language versio (DM5) heads off at 9.30 pm.

Special Events

A play based on the Meister Trunk is com bined with the Meister Trunk Fest, a enormous outdoor festival on Whitsunday weekend featuring parades, shows and a huge beer festival. From May to July and September to October, the play is performed on its own. Performances always take place in the Kaisersaal in the Rathaus; tickets range from DM20 to DM30 and are available from the ticket booth on the Markt in front of the tourist office, or at the Kaisersaal cashier.

In September, the Reichstadt Festtage sees the whole town history re-enacted, with different eras portrayed in different city streets. It runs from Friday to Sunday, and there's a huge fireworks display, best seen from the Tauber Valley, 10 minutes on foot from the city centre.

The *Schaeffer* (traditional shepherd's) dances are held around seven or eight times a year in the Markt. Tickets range from DM5 to DM10.

Places to Stay

The camping options are a kilometre or two north of the town walls at Detwang, west of the road on the river. Signs point the way to *Campingplatz Tauber-Idyll* (☎ 317 7) and the larger *Tauber-Romantik* (☎ 619 1). Both are open from Easter to late October.

Rothenburg's heavily booked *DJH hostel* (☎ 941 60), housed in two enormous renovated old buildings at Mühlacker 1, has beds for DM20. Reserve ahead or else.

The tourist office can find singles/doubles in hotels and pensions from around DM35/50 (plus a fee of DM2).

Pension Eberlein (☎ 467 2), behind the Hauptbahnhof at Winterbachstrasse 4, offers excellent value, with basic singles/doubles from DM36/54. Inside the Altstadt are the *Pension Raidel* (☎ 311 5), at Wenggasse 3, which is only slightly more expensive, and the *Gasthof Butz* (☎ 220 1), at Kapellenplatz 4, where singles/doubles with bath cost from DM48/90.

The nicest views in town are from the expensive, family-run *Burghotel* (☎ 948 90; fax 948 94 0), Klostergasse 1, built right into the town fortifications. If you're looking for a romantic getaway and price is no object, this is it – the views are phenomenal. Large double rooms with ugly carpets are DM210 to DM270 in summer and at Christmas, DM160 to DM180 at other times.

Places to Eat

Bäckerei Striffler (☎ 678 8), at Untere Schmiedgasse 1, is an excellent bakery with pastries, breads and Schneeballen, a sugary Rothenburg speciality. Two cheap options in Hafengasse with sit-down and takeaway food are the imaginatively named *Doner Kebab* at No 2, where kebabs cost from DM6, and *Albig's Quick Restaurant*, just opposite at No 3, with German schnitzels from DM12 and burgers from DM5.

At *Gasthof zum Ochsen*, Galgengasse 26, you can fill up on local Franconian fare from DM12 (closed Thursday). The *Bräustüble*, Alter Stadtgraben 2, has daily set menus for around DM14.

The *Altfrankische Weinstube* (☎ 640 4), Klosterhof 7, is a cosy, romantic place with friendly staff and an open fireplace. In a half-timbered building, it has dried flowers, low lighting, good soups and light meals from DM10 to DM12, and full-on lunches for DM15.

Zur Höll (☎ 422 9), Burggasse 8, near the Medieval Criminal Museum, is a Weinstube and a great tavern with a lovely atmosphere. Good German and Franconian specialities cost from DM14 to DM20.

Things to Buy

A one-stop kitsch superstore that's built itself up from a local tourist stand to a powerful city industry, Käthe Wohlfahrt (☎ 409 0) has two main stores and four smaller outlets throughout the city, selling every Christmas trinket you could possibly imagine, and lots and lots of souvenirs. Prices are as you'd expect, but the tourists can't pass up those cuckoo clocks.

Getting There & Away

The Europabus stops in the main bus park at the south end of town. There's frequent train service from Würzburg (DM15.50, one hour) via Steinach, and Munich (DM71, three hours) via Augsburg.

Getting Around

You can rent bicycles at the Esso petrol station (☎ 670 6), Adam Hörber Strasse 38, for DM15 per day. Farther away and more expensive, but with a bigger selection, is Rad + Tat (☎ 879 84), Bensentstrasse 17, with bikes for DM5/15/20 per hour/half day/day. Horse-drawn carriage rides of 25 to 30 minutes through the city cost DM10 per person. You'll find them right in the centre of town.

DINKELSBÜHL

- *pop 11,000*
- *area code* ☎ 09851

Another walled town of cobbled streets about 40km south of Rothenburg, Dinkelsbühl has a far less contrived feel to it than its more famous neighbour, as well as fewer tourists and buses. It is a pleasant walk of about an hour around the town's fortification walls and its 16 towers and four gates. Don't miss the wonderful Museum of the 3rd Dimension, which is a real trip.

Orientation & Information

The city tourist office (☎ 902 40) is at Markt 1 and opens April to November weekdays from 9 am to noon and 2 to 6 pm, Saturday from 10 am to 1 pm and 2 to 4 pm, and Sunday from 10 am to 1 pm (closed Sunday in winter). This is also the main Romantic Road tourist information centre (☎ 902 71).

The main post office is next to the police station, just south of the Wörlitz Tor at the east side of the city. The tourist office rents bicycles for DM7/35 a day/week.

Weinmarkt

The city's main market square contains the Renaissance Gustav-Adolph and Deutsches Haus buildings, but its star attraction is the **St-Georg-Münster**, one of southern Germany's purest late-Gothic churches.

Museum of the 3rd Dimension

This museum (☎ 633 6) in Nordlinger Tor is probably the first museum dedicated entirely to simulating acid trips. It has three floors of entertainment, with holographic images, stereoscopic mind-blowers and lots of fun f the whole family. Watch a spiral and then s your hand turn concave; see lots of lovely 3 imagery (especially in the nude section c the 3rd floor); and much more. You ca easily spend an hour here; borrow the ta tered English-language guide and follow th numbers. It's open daily year round, but wi reduced hours in winter. Admission DM10/9 – expensive but worth it.

Organised Tours

There's a free night-watcher's tour in Ge man, daily from April to November at 9 p (Saturday and Sunday only in winter).

The city tourist office runs hour-long tou through the Altstadt (DM3.50) daily at 2.3 and 8.30 pm. They begin opposite the S Georg-Münster on Weinmarkt. Horse-draw carriage rides leaving from the same pla cost DM7.

Special Events

Dinkelsbühl celebrates the 10-day Kinde zeche (Children's Festival) in the third wee of July, commemorating a legend from th Thirty Years' War that the children of th town successfully begged the invadin Swedish troops to leave Dinkelsbühl undam aged. The festivities include a pageant, re enactments in the Stadt Festsaal, lots o music and other entertainment.

In summer the Jazz Festival Franken swing runs at weekends (the dates chang annually) and involves local and interna tional groups. It takes place throughout th Altstadt, and admission is DM10 per day o DM25 for the three days.

Places to Stay

DCC-Campingplatz Romantische Strass (☎ 781 7) is about 300m north-east of th Wörlitz Tor. It costs DM11.50/7/5 per sit person/car and is open all year.

Dinkelsbühl's *DJH hostel* (☎ 950 9), jus west of the centre at Koppengasse 1(charges DM17.50.

The tourist office books rooms (DM6 pe person fee) in private flats (about DM25 t DM30 per person including breakfast).

The small *Pension Lutz* (☎ 945 4) at Schäfergässlein 4 offers singles/doubles for DM35/70; the *Fränkischer Hof* (☎ 579 00) has similar rooms from DM41/76. The ornate façade of the *Deutsches Haus* (☎ 605 9), Weinmarkt 3, is one of the town's attractions, yet singles/doubles start at just DM80/120.

Places to Eat

Gasthof Sonne on Weinmarkt is a charming place that sets up a beer garden out front in summer; nice for people-watching. *Eisenkrug* is a much fancier place, with lunches from about DM16 to DM20, and three-course dinners from DM35 per person. For fast food, try *City Grill* (☎ 471 3), Nordlingerstrasse 8, with burgers from DM4.50, schnitzel and half chickens for DM4.70 and whole chickens from DM9. It attracts a sleazy crowd but has decent food.

NÖRDLINGEN

- *pop 19,000*
- *area code* ☎ 09081

First mentioned 1100 years ago, the town of Nördlingen is still encircled by its original 14th-century walls, measuring some 2.7km in diameter and dotted with five gates, 16 towers and two bastions – you can climb the tower of the St Georg Kirche for a bird's-eye view of the town. Nördlingen lies within the Ries Basin, a huge crater created by a meteor more than 15 million years ago. The crater – some 25km in diameter – is one of the best preserved on earth, and was used by US astronauts to train before the first moon landing. Find out more at the Rieskrater Museum.

Orientation

The train station is south-east of the city and outside the city walls, about a 15-minute walk from the city centre. The main post office is there as well. The city is almost perfectly round, with concentric rings emanating from Markt, and access through the city gates.

The Eger River runs west to east across the very top of the Altstadt. The north-east of the Altstadt is the Gerberviertel, the former leather workers' quarter, which is packed with charming old buildings.

Information

The city tourist office (☎ 438 0), behind the Rathaus at Markt 2, is open from Easter to November, Monday to Friday from 9 am to 6 pm, Saturday from 9.30 am to 12.30 pm. In winter it's open weekdays from 9 am to 5 pm, closed weekends.

Gates & Walls

You can circumnavigate the entire city by walking on top of its old walls (they're covered, so you can even do this in the rain). Admission is free. Climb up at any of the town's five gates; clockwise from the north, they are the **Baldinger Tor**, **Löpsinger Tor**, **Deininger Tor**, **Reimlinger Tor** and **Berger Tor**. They're all at the end of streets bearing their names.

St Georg Kirche

The late-Gothic Church of St George (1427-1519) is one of the largest in southern Germany. For a great view, climb to the top of the 90m-tall **Daniel Tower** (350 steps; DM2.50/1.50).

Rieskrater Museum

The Ries Crater Museum (☎ 841 43), Hinter den Gerbergasse 3, has examples of other craters, a genuine moon rock (on permanent loan from NASA) and a large display on the geology of the region. It's open Tuesday to Sunday; admission is DM5/2.50.

Other Museums

The Stadtmuseum right in the centre of town has costumes and displays on local history, while the **Stadtmauermuseum**, in the Löpsinger Tor, has an exhibition on the history of the town walls and fortification system, paintings of the city through history, and a model of the medieval city. They're both closed on Monday.

Organised Tours

Hour-long German-language tours (DM4)

leave daily at 2 pm from in front of the tourist office. English-language tours can be arranged from DM60 for up to 30 people. The Rieskrater Museum offers 1½-hour geological tours of the area in several languages for up to 30 people for DM50.

Special Events

The largest annual celebration is the 10-day Nördlinger Pfingstmesse at Whitsuntide/Pentecost (late May to early June). It's an exhibition of regional traders, with a huge market (tourists love it) featuring beer tents, food stalls and the usual entertainment.

There's also the Stadtmauerfest, a three-day blowout every third September (the next is in 1998) featuring medieval costumes, huge parades, medieval-style food and grog etc.

The Christmas market is held in the pedestrian zone, along Schrannenstrasse and Bei den Kornschrannen.

Places to Stay

The nearest camping ground, *Erwin & Else Vierkorn* (☎ 07362-350 2), 5km away in Riesberg-Utzmemmingen, is nice and romantic (near an old mill and a pond) but because it's actually in Baden-Württemberg, bus service is difficult, with daytime departures only from the Rathaus in Nördlingen. By car, take the B466 (direction: Ulm), turn right in Holheim and follow the signs. It's DM5 per site plus DM7 per person.

The *DJH hostel* (☎ 841 09) is at Kaiserwiese 1 and charges DM18 for juniors (it will admit seniors in 'emergency situations' for DM23.50). It's a 10-minute walk north of the centre and well signposted.

By the church at Hallgasse 15 is *Gasthof Walfisch* (☎ 310 7), with singles/doubles for DM30/60. The *Drei Mohren* (☎ 311 3), Reimlinger Strasse 18, has rooms from DM35/70 (and a more than passable restaurant). The renovated *Altreuter Garni* (☎ 431 9), Markt 11, has simple but nice singles/doubles for DM40/70, (DM75/105 with bathroom), including breakfast.

Places to Eat

Sixenbräu-Stüble (☎ 310 1), Berger Strasse 17, has typical Swabian specialities like Maultaschen (like ravioli) and Spätzle (flat noodles) for DM10 to DM12; meat dishes cost slightly more. Go downstairs to the vaulted-ceiling wine cellar at the *Hotel Sonne*. The restaurant there does daily lunch specials from DM12; in the evening main courses cost around DM20. The somewhat greasy *Kochlöffel*, Markt 9, does chips/French fries and roast chicken for about DM6.

Getting There & Away

The Europabus stops at the Rathaus. Hourly trains connect Nördlingen with Munich (DM35, two hours) via Augsburg (DM19, one hour) and Stuttgart (DM30, two hours). During festivals there's steam-train service between Nördlingen and Dinkelsbühl (DM20/14); check with the Eisenbahnmuseum (☎ 438 0) at the Nördlingen train station, or the tourist office.

Getting Around

You can rent bicycles at Radsport Böckle (☎ 801 04 0), Reimlinger Strasse 19, for DM15 per day, or at Zweirad Müller (☎ 567 5), Gewerbestrasse 16.

AUGSBURG

- *pop 260,000*
- *area code* ☎ 0821

Established by the stepchildren of Roman Emperor Augustus over 2000 years ago, Augsburg later became a centre of Martin Luther's Reformation: in 1530, the *Confessio Augustana* (Augsburg Confession) set forth the fundamentals of the Lutheran church.

A major trader in gold, silver and copper, Augsburg was an economic powerhouse in the Middle Ages. When Hans-Jakob Fugger arrived here around 1367 he was a weaver; within three generations the Fugger family was one of the wealthiest in Europe.

Today Augsburg is Bavaria's third most populous city, but its easily walkable Altstadt maintains an ambience and vitality matched by few other places in Germany.

For most visitors, Augsburg is a day trip from Munich, only a half-hour ICE-train ride away. But it is seldom used as an Oktoberfest accommodation option. It is also an ideal base for the Romantic Road.

All museums in Augsburg are closed on Monday and Tuesday.

Orientation

The Hauptbahnhof is at the eastern end of Bahnhofsplatz, which runs into Fuggerstrasse at Königsplatz, the city's main bus transfer point. The heart of the Altstadt is Rathausplatz, reached on foot by walking from Königsplatz up Annastrasse.

Information

Tourist Offices Augsburg's tourist offices are at Bahnhofstrasse 7 (☎ 502 07 0), open Monday to Friday only from 9 am to 6 pm, and on Rathausplatz (☎ 502 07 24) at Maximilianstrasse 4, open weekdays from 9 am to 6 pm, Saturday from 10 am to 4 pm in summer (10 am to 1 pm in winter) and Sunday in summer only from 10 am to 1 pm.

Money The Postbank at the Hauptbahnhof has the best commissions on travellers' cheques, and it's open Monday to Saturday. There's a Sparkasse on Königsplatz, and a Vereinsbank at Bahnhofstrasse 8.

Post & Communications The post office is opposite the Hauptbahnhof. Nexus is an Internet café at Maximilianstrasse 52.

Travel Agencies Fernweh (☎ 155 03 5), Dominikanergasse 10, is a representative office of STA Travel. Travel Overland (☎ 314 15 7) has an office at Zeuggasse 5.

Bookshops & Libraries Rieger und Kranzfelder Buchhandlung (☎ 349 08 10), in the Fugger Haus at Maximilianstrasse 36, is an enormous place with English-language books and everything else. There's another branch at Universitätsstrasse 10. Darsana (☎ 349 50 28), Auf dem Rain 2, near the Brecht Haus, has books on natural healing, astrology and other groovy subjects.

The Stadtbibliotek (☎ 324 27 39) is at Schaezlerstrasse 25; the Stadtbücherei (☎ 324 27 56) is right in the centre at Gutenbergstrasse 2.

Campuses Universität Augsburg (☎ 598 0), Universitätsstrasse 2, has two campuses at the southern end of the city. It is a liberal arts university with about 15,000 students.

Laundry The Waschcenter HSB (☎ 419 45 1), Wolfgangstrasse 1 (tram No 2), is open from 6 am to 11.30 pm; there's also Karkosch, at Vorderer Lech 27.

Medical Services The most central hospital is the Zweckverband (☎ 400 01), Stenglinstrasse 2. For a doctor or ambulance, call the Rotes Kreuz (Red Cross; ☎ 192 22).

Rathausplatz

The twin onion-dome topped spires of the city's town hall (1615-20) dominate the pedestrianised Rathausplatz. Destroyed in 1944, the Rathaus was reconstructed from 1947 to 1962. Topping the building, as is the case with many other Augsburg structures, is a pine cone, the city's symbol. Inside the lobby you can see the original **statue of Kaiser Augustus** that used to top the Renaissance **Augustus Brunnen** in the square (there's a copy on the fountain now). There's also a model of the old city here.

Upstairs, the **Goldener Saal** (open daily from 10 am to 6 pm; DM2), a dazzling restoration of the city's main meeting hall, is worth the price. They used only 2.6kg of gold to cover the whole place with a thin layer of gold leaf, and the 14m-high, 32m-long room is spectacular.

Next to the Rathaus is the **Perlachturm**, a former guard tower. You can climb to the top (DM2/1) mid-May to mid-October from 10 am to 6 pm for a great view of the city.

The square is thronged with people year round – at outdoor cafés in summer and for the Christkindlmarkt in December.

Dom

The Dom Mariae Heimsuchung (9th to 14th centuries), on Hoher Weg north of Rathausplatz, has amazing bronze doors at the south end, with 35 relief panels. The crypt, which dates to 1065, has a typical round Roman Madonna, and they say that passages leading from here went all the way to the Ulrich Kirche at the other side of town. In the centre of the church is the *Weingartner Altar* by Hans Holbein the Elder. While modern 1960s glass mars some of the windows, others of medieval glass, dating to at least the 11th century, are spectacular.

St Anna Kirche

This former Carmelite monastery (1321) was expanded over the centuries and finally converted to a Protestant church; appropriate, since Luther himself slept here when in Augsburg. Inside the church are artworks by Lucas Cranach the Elder. Closed Monday.

Fuggerei

One of the earliest welfare settlements, the charming little three-room houses and one-room widow's flats of the Fuggerei were established by Jakob Fugger in 1521 to provide homes for poor Catholics. The rent here is DM12.72 per *year*, plus utilities and a daily prayer. It's a very nice place to walk through. To see how Fuggerei residents of the past lived, stop into the **Fuggerei Museum** (March to October daily from 9 am to 6 pm; DM1/0.50), next door to the former home of Franz Mozart, Wolfgang Amadeus' great-grandfather, who lived here for 12 years. Gates close from 10 pm to 6 am (5 am in summer); residents returning after that are fined DM0.50, and after midnight a whole DM1! The chalk markings on the doors are placed there by priests blessing the houses on Epiphany (6 January).

Brecht House

The family home of the playwright and poet Bertolt Brecht, on the canal at Am Rain 7, is now the Bertolt-Brecht-Gedenkstätte, a museum dedicated to Brecht and the work of young artists (DM2.50/1.50). Brecht's work was banned by the Nazis for his communist leanings; he was later shunned by West Germans for the same reason, and it's only recently that the city has come round to honour one of its most heralded sons.

Maximilianstrasse

This grand boulevard is more conventionally styled than the rest of the city, although one of Luther's more unconventional anti-papal documents was posted here after he was run out of town in 1518. Highlights of the street include the cafés, the **Mercur Brunnen** (a fountain topped with a statue of Mercury – under renovation at the moment), and the restored **Fugger Haus** at No 36-38, the former residence of Jakob Fugger. Walk through the entrance near the signs for the Fugger Keller and through to the stunning Italian Renaissance **Damenhof**.

Right behind Maximilianstrasse, stop off for a beer in the beer garden next to the outrageous **Zeughaus** (1602-7), the former armoury that is now a trade school, cinema and beer garden. The statues on the front are of the Archangel Michael stomping Satan.

The **Schaezler Palais** (1765-70) is the rococo palace built for banker Liebert von Liebenhofen; today it's open as the German baroque art gallery and the Bavarian art gallery. Its inconceivably lavish ballroom makes the Goldener Saal in the Rathaus look shabby. It's open October to April from 10 am to 4 pm (to 5 pm in summer). Admission is DM4/2.50.

Synagogue

Synagogue Augsburg (☎ 513 65 8), Halder strasse 8, right behind the tourist informatio office on Bahnhofstrasse, is an Art Nouvea temple built from 1914-17. Inside is th excellent **Jewish Cultural Museum** (Tues day to Friday from 9 am to 4 pm, Sunday fror 10 am to 5 pm, closed Saturday and Monday DM3/2), with exhibitions on Jewish life i the region, Germany and Central Europ Tours are given most Wednesday evenings 6 pm; check with the tourist office to see one's on when you're in town.

Other Sights

The onion-shaped towers of the modest **St Maria Stern Kloster** in Elias-Holl-Platz started a fashion which spread throughout southern Germany after its construction in the 16th century.

The tower of **St Ulrich und Afra Basilika**, on Ulrichsplatz near the south edge of the Altstadt, is visible from throughout the city.

The Maximilianmuseum, at Philippine-Welser-Strasse 24 (DM4/2.50), houses a permanent collection on the history of gold and silversmithing in the city upstairs, with rotating exhibitions downstairs.

Places to Stay

Camping *Campingplatz Augusta* (☎ 707 57 5) is near the airport, half a km from the Augsburg Ost autobahn interchange north-east of the city. Apart from camping sites, it also has a few family rooms. Bus No 305 or 306 departs at least once an hour (DM4.80 each way) from the Busbahnhof, starting at 6.18 am, last bus at 11.45 pm.

Two km farther (on the same buses) in the town of Mühlhausen bei Augsburg is the nicer, family-run *Lech Camping* (☎ 08207-220 0), Seeweg 6, costing DM6.50/6/2/1.50 per person/tent/car/motorcycle and DM1 for rubbish removal.

Hostels At Augsburg's central *DJH hostel* (☎ 339 09), Beim Pfaffenkeller 3, you can get a bed (if you're under 27) for DM21 (plus DM5.50 for linen). From the station, take tram No 2 (direction: Kriegshaber) to Mozarthaus, then walk east on Mittleres Pfaffengässchen.

Hotels & Pensions Book pensions, which range from DM35 for singles and DM65 to DM80 for doubles, at the tourist offices. There's a charge of DM3 per room.

Behind the Hauptbahnhof at Thelott-strasse 2 is the *Lenzhalde* (☎ 520 74 5), with simple rooms from DM40/75.

Perhaps the best value in Augsburg is the *Jakoberhof* (☎ 510 03 0), Jakobstrasse 39-41, a simple place with a decent Bavarian restaurant downstairs, and simple rooms from DM45/65. Also in this range is the *Hotel von den Rappen* (☎ 412 06 6), Äussere Uferstrasse 3, where modern bathless singles/doubles go for DM50/80. Another good one is the pleasant *Georgsrast* (☎ 502 61 0), Georgenstrasse 31, run by a gaggle of older women, with simple rooms from DM58/85.

The *Privat Hotel Ost am Kö* (☎ 502 04 0), Fuggerstrasse 4-6, is a whole lot better inside than the 1960s cube architecture would have you believe. As well as very friendly service, it has large, clean singles/doubles without bath for DM70/130, and DM99/148 with bath & WC.

Right near the Hauptbahnhof are the *Ibis Beim Hauptbahnhof* (☎ 501 60), Halder-strasse 25, with modern if sparse rooms from DM104/119, and the *InterCity Augsburg* (☎ 503 90), nearby at Halderstrasse 29, with the usual InterCity rooms from DM140/160.

The *Steigenberger Drei Mohren Hotel* (☎ 503 60), Maximilianstrasse 40, is a stunning and very expensive place right next to the Fugger Haus.

Long-Term Rentals The Mitwohnzentrale (☎ 364 71) at Maximilianstrasse 14 specialises in long-term rental of private rooms.

Places to Eat

Cafés & Restaurants *Café bei den Barfüssern* (☎ 159 30 8), Kanalstrasse 2, next to the Protestant Barfüsser Kirche, is a wonderful place to sit; they make their own cakes and pastries, and you can sit outside next to the little canal. There are lots of cafés along Maximilianstrasse, including *Café Mercur*, just in front of the Mercury fountain, and *Café Stadler*, Maximilianstrasse 49, which has pastas for DM9 to DM9.50.

Die Pyramide, Johannesgasse 2, serves quite good Egyptian dishes, including vegetarian main courses from DM9, up to DM21 for fish cooked 'Suez Canal style'.

A big local favourite with enormous portions of good Bavarian food is the *Bauerntanz* (☎ 153 64 4), Bauerntanz Gässchen 1, which is a much better deal at lunchtime (when main courses average about DM14), than at dinner, when the prices shoot northward. There's outdoor seating in nice weather.

The Bavarian food is also good at the mellow *Fuggereistube* (☎ 308 70), Jakobstrasse 26 next to the north gate of the Fuggerei. Main courses range from DM15 to DM20.

Beer Gardens The city is filled with beer gardens; the three coolest are *Thing*, at Vorderer Lech 45; *Lug Ins Land*, in the park at the northern tip of the Altstadt at Herwartstrasse; and *3 Königinnen*, at Meister-Veits-Gässchen 32, south of the Fuggerei.

Snacks & Fast Food There are real *farmers' markets* Monday to Friday from 7 am to 6 pm (to 1 pm on Saturday) between Fuggerstrasse and Annastrasse. They have everything – from Thai to Bavarian and back.

The gleaming *Seval Imbiss* (☎ 395 18), Karrengässchen 1 near the Fuggerei, has absolutely splendid doners for DM6. Also try the *Türkische Grill*, Pfladergasse 20 near the Alte Silberschmeide, with small/large kebabs for DM4.50/6.50.

BAVARIA

Entertainment

Get a copy of *Szene*, a free listings magazine, from the tourist office.

There's a fledgling disco scene in Augsburg. Crowds flock to *Spectrum* (☎ 409 02 6), on Ulmer Strasse, with live music on some nights, and disco nights with rock and standard chart stuff on others. *Rockfabric* (☎ 412 00 1), Riedingerstrasse 24, is open Monday to Saturday and has theme nights: rock and classic, Gothic, grunge, alternative – check in *Szene* for weekly offerings.

The *Städtische Bühnen Augsburg* (☎ 324 45 27) runs a wide range of drama, musical and classical music productions.

The *Comödie* (☎ 324 45 27), Vorderer Lech 8, has comedy, cabaret and musicals, like *Rocky Horror*.

Join the queue to get into *König von Flandern* (☎ 158 05 0), Karolinenstrasse 12 in the Badenkeller, where they brew great beer and sell it for an astounding DM9 per *two litre* serving. *Peaches* (☎ 312 25 8), Maximilianstrasse 35, is a cocktail bar with 1960s music and a fun crowd. *Lucky's Club Afra*, Afrawald 2, does student parties on Tuesdays and sometimes live music.

The *Irish Inn* (☎ 155 02 1), Ludwigstrasse 32-34, has Irish folk and rock music and, of course, darts. Similar atmosphere can be found in *Murphy's Law* (☎ 951 05 4), Auf Dem Kreuz 2, and *Fuxi's Fuchsbau* (☎ 154 29 6), Bei St Ursula.

Getting There & Away

Augsburg Air (0180-333 34 34) is one of the movers and shakers of the deregulated skies over Germany, offering flights from the totally inconvenient Augsburg-Mühlhausen airport to Berlin, Dresden, Düsseldorf, Frankfurt/Main, Gdańsk in Poland, and other destinations.

Trains between Munich and Augsburg are frequent (30 minutes, DM15.40). Connections to/from Regensburg take two hours, either via Munich (DM51) or Ingolstadt (DM36). There are also main-line links to Stuttgart and Nuremberg. Augsburg is just off the autobahns north-west of Munich.

Getting Around

The Airport Bus Nos 3 and 5 servicing Augsburg-Mühlhausen airport offer lousy weekdays-only service. City-bound buses depart from the airport at 10.13 am and 2.09, 4.32 and 6.06 pm. From the centre to the airport, buses leave the Hauptbahnhof at 6.11 and 9.35 am and 4.03, 4.38 and 5.33 pm. A taxi will cost between DM25 and DM30.

The Lufthansa airport bus (☎ 502 25 34) runs between Bahnhofstrasse and Munich's airport at 3.20, 4.50, 6, 8.50 and 9.50 am and 12.30, 2 and 4.40 pm. The 50-minute ride costs DM25.

Public Transport Short rides in the centre cost DM1.70; two-zone rides are DM3.20. Family day cards are DM8, and a weekly pass is DM22 for two zones.

Bicycle Bäuml (☎ 336 21), Jakobstrasse 70, has a good range of bikes from DM10/60 per day/week for a touring bike, DM15/65 for a trekking bike, or DM30/120 for a tandem. If you have a rail pass or BahnCard you get a 20% discount. Bring a passport or photo ID.

FÜSSEN

- *pop 17,000*
- *area code* ☎ 08362

After passing through the 1000-year-old Donauwörth, at the confluence of the Danube and Wörnitz rivers, and Schongau, a lovely medieval town in the alpine foothills, the road continues to Füssen, just short of the Austrian border. Füssen has a monastery, a castle and some splendid baroque architecture, but it is primarily visited for the two castles in nearby Schwangau associated with mad King Ludwig II: Hohenschwangau and Neuschwanstein.

Orientation & Information

Füssen's train station is at the western end of the city, about a three-minute walk from the tourist office, the slick Kurverwaltung Füssen (☎ 707 7) at Kaiser Maximilian Platz 1, and behind the Sieben Stein Brunnen, an interesting stone fountain. The castles are about 8km east of Füssen.

Museums

Almost everyone who comes to Füssen is here for the castles, but a fair number of people visit the **Museum of Füssen** (closed Monday; DM2) in the Rathaus, and the **St Anne Kapelle**, the oldest wing of the monastery's church, which is entered through the museum. Above the town is the **Staatsgalerie im Hohen Schloss**, the former residence of the prince-bishops of Augsburg, now a museum of religious artwork. It's a long climb to the top (open April to October, Tuesday to Saturday from 11 am to 4 pm, in winter from 2 to 4 pm).

Castles

The castles provide a fascinating glimpse into Ludwig II's state of mind. Fortunately they're practically next to one another, so you can visit both on the same day. **Hohenschwangau** is where Ludwig lived as a child, but more interesting is the adjacent **Neuschwanstein**, which appears through the mountain-top mist like a kooky mirage. Ludwig's own creation, and never completed, it's perhaps the world's best known castle; the fantastic pastiche of architectural styles inspired Walt Disney's Cinderella Castle. Inside, there's abundant evidence of Ludwig's twin obsessions: swans and Wagnerian operas.

There's a great view of Neuschwanstein from the Marienbrücke over a waterfall and gorge just above the castle. From here you can hike the Tegelberg for even better vistas. Or better yet, get over to the Tegelberg, go up using the Tegelberg cable car and walk down to the castle.

Tickets & Tours You must visit the castles as part of a tour. These get awfully crowded after about 9.30 am, when those coming in from Munich by train arrive, so go early to avoid the crowds. Tickets to Neuschwanstein cost DM10/7, to Hohenschwangau they are DM7. When you reach the gate at Neuschwanstein, get in the line of the language of your choice; tours leave when there are enough people.

Neuschwanstein is open April to September from 9 am to 5.30 pm, October to March from 10 am to 4 pm. Hohenschwangau is open mid-March to mid-October from 8.30 am to 5.30 pm, and mid-October to mid-March from 9.30 am to 4.30 pm.

The extra expense of an organised tour (with transport included) is worth it, as it usually includes both castles and sometimes others. EurAide's excellent three-castle tours visit Linderhof, Neuschwanstein and Hohenschwangau, along with the Wieskirche. It's the best deal around – DM75 per person – and leaves every Wednesday in summer from the EurAide office in Munich. Sign up as soon as you get to town as it fills up fast.

Getting There & Away From Füssen, take the bus from the Hauptbahnhof (DM4.80 return), share a taxi (DM14) or walk the 5km. From the bus stop, it's a 20 to 30-minute walk up the hill to the castle entrance at

Neuschwanstein, or a slightly longer trip by horse-drawn carriage (DM7 uphill, DM3.50 downhill). You can also take bus No 9713 from Füssen train station to Tegelbergbahn, which goes right to the cable car. The cable car (☎ 983 60) runs in summer from 8.30 am to 5 pm, in winter from 9 am to 4.30 pm, and costs DM25. From the top, you can hike down to the castles (follow the signs to *Königschlosser*) in about two or three hours, or you can just ride down after getting a gander at the castle and the ubiquitous hang-gliders and parasailers.

From Munich (DM34, 2½ hours), the best train to catch to beat the crowds is the one that no one in their right mind would want: the No 4500 at 5.01 am, changing for the 6.10 am train at Buchloe, arriving at 7.23 am in Füssen. The most popular early train is the 6.50 am (No 3206), changing at Buchloe for the 7.46 am, arriving in Füssen at 8.57 am; subsequent trains include ones at 7.53, 8.53 and 10.53 am; return trains run at five minutes past the hour until at least 11.05 pm. Always check schedules before you go. Some fast and loose tourist information suggests train and bus travel between Linderhof, Neuschwanstein and Hohenschwangau in one day, but the connections are precarious and if you miss one, you're in the middle of nowhere – check with DB or EurAide before setting out on the route, which involves morning trains to Garmisch-Partenkirchen and buses between there and Füssen.

BAVARIA

Places to Stay

Camping There are several camping options near the castles; get the full list from the Schwangau tourist office, which is near the bus stop at the foot of the castles. From Schwangau, bus No 9715 takes you to *Campingplatz Bannwaldsee* (☎ 810 01), Münchner Strasse 151, with camping sites from DM13 right on the lake. They have bicycle and boat rentals and friendly staff. With a car, the best bet is *Brunnen am Forggensee* (☎ 827 3), Seestrasse 81 at the southern end of the Forggensee, where the cost is DM10.50 per person and DM10.50 per site.

Hostel The Füssen *DJH hostel* (☎ 775 4), Mariahilferstrasse 5, is by the train tracks, 10 minutes west of the station. Dorm beds cost DM20, curfew is at 10 pm and the hostel is closed from mid-November to Christmas. Reserve early – showing up without a reservation is really pushing your luck.

Hotels & Pensions The central *Hotel Alpenhof* (☎ 323 2), Theresienstrasse 8, has attractive singles/doubles from DM40/75. The tourist office has lists of private rooms from DM25 per person. In Füssen there's a resort tax of DM3 per person per night.

Places to Eat

Schinagl (☎ 613 9), Brunnengasse 20, is a great bakery with wonderful pastries and breads. *Infooday*, at Ritterstrasse 6 (open weekdays until 6.30 pm and Saturday until 1 pm), has excellent and cheap buffet food (including salads, pastas and desserts) to take away or eat in-house. The old *Franziskaner Stüberl* (☎ 371 24), at the corner of Ritterstrasse and Kemptener Strasse, specialises in delicacies like roast trotters served with beer sauce and rye bread (DM10.80), for which Bavaria is renowned.

Next to the fire station, *Gasthof am Schrannenplatz* (☎ 631 2) has great beer and Bavarian specialities served by really nice staff. House specials range from DM13 to DM17, Schweinebraten from DM12.50 and daily lunch specials from DM12 to DM14. It's closed on Friday.

Getting There & Away

As the terminus of the Romantic Road, Füssen is easily reached by bus or car. There are frequent trains from Munich.

AROUND FÜSSEN

Wieskirche

On 14 June 1743, a local farmer in Steingaden, a town on the Romantic Road north-east of Füssen, witnessed the miracle of his Christ statue crying. Over the next few years, so many pilgrims poured into the town that the local abbot commissioned the construction of a church in a nearby meadow specifically to house the weepy work.

Enter master craftsman Dominikus Zimmermann, from nearby Landsberg, who supervised the construction of what became known as the Wieskirche (1746-56). The church is an astounding festival of baroque. Admission is free.

At least three buses per day make the trip from Füssen. New schedules had not been set at time of press so check with EurAide in Munich for the latest information. By car from Munich, head west on the A96 to Landsberg, then turn south on the B17 towards Füssen. From Füssen, take the B17 north-east and turn right (east) at Steingaden. The church is very clearly signed.

Bavarian Alps

Stretching west from Germany's remote south-eastern corner to the Allgäu region near Lake Constance, the Bavarian Alps (Bayerische Alpen) take in most of the mountainous country fringing the southern border with Austria.

The year-round resort of Garmisch-Partenkirchen is Munich's favourite getaway spot, though nearby Mittenwald is a less hectic alternative. Other suitable bases from which to explore the Bavarian Alps are Berchtesgaden, the Tegernsee area, Füssen (see the previous Romantic Road section) and Oberstdorf.

While not as high as their sister summits farther south in Austria, the Bavarian Alps rise so abruptly from the rolling hills of southern Bavaria that their appearance seems all the more dramatic.

For those with the time, energy and money, the Bavarian Alps are extraordinarily well organised for outdoor pursuits, though naturally skiing (or its increasingly popular variant, snowboarding) and hiking have the biggest following.

The ski season usually begins in late December and continues into April. Ski gear is available for hire in all the resorts, with the lowest daily/weekly rates including skis, boots and stocks for around DM20/90 (downhill), DM12/60 (cross-country) and DM30/110 (snowboard). Five-day skiing courses (15 hours total) cost around DM190.

The hiking season goes from late May right through to November, but the higher trails may be icy or snowed over before mid-June or after October.

Large lakes are another feature of the landscape and are ideal for water sports. Rafting, canoeing, mountain biking and paragliding are popular summer activities.

Most of the resorts have plenty of reasonably priced guesthouses and private rooms, though it's still a good idea to ring ahead and book accommodation. Tourist offices can help you find a room; otherwise look out for *Zimmer frei* signs.

During the busy winter and summer seasons, some places levy a surcharge (usually at least DM5 per person) for stays of less than two or three days. In most resorts a local tax (or *Kurtaxe*, usually an extra DM3 per night) is levied, but as a tax-paying guest you're usually entitled to certain perks, like free tours, city bus service and entry to special events.

Getting Around

While the public transport network is very good, the mountain geography means there are few direct routes between main centres; sometimes a short-cut via Austria works out quicker (such as between Garmisch and Füssen or Oberstdorf). Road, rather than rail routes, are often more practical.

For those with private transport, the German Alpine Road (Deutsche Alpenstrasse) is a more scenic way to go – though obviously much slower than the autobahns and highways that fan out across southern Bavaria.

Regional (RVO) passes giving free travel (with certain route restrictions) on the upper-Bavarian bus network between Füssen and Salzburg are excellent value; the day pass is DM13/6.50 for adults/children and a pass giving five free days travel within one month costs DM40/20.

GARMISCH-PARTENKIRCHEN

- *pop 27,000*
- *area code* ☎ 08821

The combined resort towns of Garmisch-Partenkirchen were merged by Adolf Hitler to host the 1936 Winter Olympics. The reason they stayed merged is because their location is the best ski gateway in southern Germany. With access to four ski fields, including ones on Germany's highest mountain, the Zugspitze (2963m), the town is a favourite destination for skiers, hikers, snowboarders and mountaineers.

The huge ski stadium on the slopes right outside town has two ski jumps and a slalom course; it hosted more than 100,000 people for the 1936 Winter Olympics and is still used for professional competitions today.

About 20km west of town is Ludwig II's charming Schloss Linderhof (see the following Around Garmisch-Partenkirchen section). Garmisch can also serve as a base for excursions to Ludwig's extravagant castles, Hohenschwangau and Neuschwanstein, near Füssen (see the Romantic Road section for details); regular daily RVO buses from Garmisch to Füssen pass Neuschwanstein en route (two hours each way).

Orientation & Information

The railway tracks that divide the two towns run right down the centre to the Hauptbahnhof. From it, turn east on St Martin Strasse to get to Garmisch and west on Bahnhofstrasse to get to Partenkirchen.

The tourist office (☎ 180 6), on Richard-Strauss-Platz, is open Monday to Saturday from 8 am to 6 pm, and Sunday and holidays from 10 am to noon.

Activities

Skiing The tallest mountain peak in Germany, the Zugspitze, offers some of the most breathtaking views around. In winter, of course, it has some pretty amazing skiing. In summer, it offers spectacular hiking. Other than climbing the thing (see Hiking), there are two options for ascending – a cable car and a cog-wheel train *(Zahnradbahn)*, both a lot of fun.

On a standard day ticket, the cost for the two is the same; there are some discounts available for the train in conjunction with a train trip from Munich.

Both are spectacularly crowded at peak times in winter (around Christmas, New Year and festivals) and through much of the summer. Skiers may find it easier, if a little slower, to schlep their gear up on the train, which offers exterior ski-holders.

Ski Areas Garmisch is bounded by four separate ski-fields: the Zugspitze plateau (the highest area), the Alpspitze/Hausberg (the largest area), and the Eckbauer and Wank areas (yes, Wank residents do jokingly say '*Ich bin ein Wanker*').

Day ski passes cost DM59 for Zugspitze (though this includes the cable car or Zahnradbahn ride up to the top), DM46 for Alpspitze/Hausberg, DM33 for Wank and DM30 for Eckbauer. The Happy Ski Card covers all four areas, but it's available for a minimum of three days (DM139, DM184 for four days).

Cross-country ski trails run along the main valleys, including a long section from Garmisch to Mittenwald.

Ski Hire Flori Wörndle (☎ 583 00) has the cheapest rates for ski hire (and convenient outlets at the Alpspitze and Zugspitze lifts). For skiing information and instruction (downhill) you can contact the Skischule Garmisch-Partenkirchen (☎ 493 1), Am Hausberg 8, or (cross-country) the Skilanglaufschule (☎ 151 6), Olympia-Skistadion. Sport Total (☎ 142 5), at Marienplatz 18, also runs skiing courses and organises numerous outdoor activities like paragliding, mountain biking, rafting and ballooning, as well as renting a wide range of gear.

Ski Theft If your skis are stolen (it hardly ever happens) call ☎ 883 9. The Bayerische Grenzpolizei have a good chance of finding them!

Cable Car What a rush: the 10-minute journey aboard the Eibsee cable car is actually worth the admittedly high price (DM59 for adults, DM41 for teens aged 16 to 18, DM35 for kids), even if you're not skiing or hiking.

The car, packed to the brim with people, sways and swings its way up from the base to the **Panorama Observation Terrace**, and the ride is not for the fainthearted!

Zahnradbahn Built from 1928 to 1930, this charming narrow-gauge railway makes its way from the mountain base up to the Zugspitzplatt station, where you can switch for the Gletscherbahn cable car that takes you to the summit of the Zugspitze. Included in a day pass, this is the more scenic, but slower, way up the mountain.

Hiking The best way to get to the top of the Zugspitze is to hike (two days). A recommended hiking map is *Wettersteingebirge* (DM7.50) published at 1:50,000 by Kompass. For information on guided hiking or courses in mountaineering call at the Bergsteigerschule Zugspitze (☎ 58 99 9), Dreitorspitz-Strasse 13, Garmisch.

A great short hike from Garmisch is to the Partnachklamm gorge via a winding path above a stream and underneath waterfalls. Take the cable car to the first stop on the Graseck route and follow the signs.

Places to Stay

The camping ground nearest to Garmisch is *Zugspitze* (☎ 318 0), along highway B24. Take the blue-and-white bus outside the Hauptbahnhof in the direction of the Eibsee. Sites cost DM8, plus DM9 per person and DM5 per vehicle.

The *hostel* (☎ 298 0) is at Jochstrasse 10, in the suburb of Burgrain. Beds cost DM21 (including tourist tax) and there's an 11.30 pm curfew; it's closed from November until Christmas. From the Hauptbahnhof take bus No 3, 4 or 5 to the Burgrain stop.

Five minutes' walk from the station is the quiet *Hotel Schell* (☎ 957 50), Partnachauen Strasse 3 (*not* Partnachstrasse), with singles/doubles from DM45/90.

In the centre of Garmisch, *Haus Weiss* (☎ 468 2), Klammstrasse 6, *Gasthaus Pfeuffer* (☎ 223 8), Kreuzstrasse 9, and the nearby *Haus Trenkler* (☎ 343 9), at Kreuzstrasse 20, all offer simple but pleasant rooms for around DM35/70.

Places to Eat

Bistros & Restaurants Do stop in at *Chapeau Claque* (☎ 713 00) at Mohrenplatz 10, a very cosy and very French wine bar-bistro with soft lighting and great service. Good snacks include French onion or tomato soup (DM7.80), baked potato with bacon and onions (DM11.80) or with shrimp and curry sauce (DM12.80). There's also a good range of full dinners from DM18 to DM22.

A similar, if smaller and less flash, place is *Café Max* (☎ 253 5), Griesstrasse 10A. They do baguette sandwiches or baked camembert for DM11, snacks like mozzarella, basil and tomato on French bread for about DM12, and main courses from DM13 to DM16.

On the south side of the river near the Alte Kirche in Garmisch are two local favourites. The *Bräustüberl* (☎ 231 2), Furstenstrasse 23, is about as Bavarian as you can get, complete with enormous enamel coal-burning stove and Dirndl-clad (but sometimes curt) waitresses. The dining room is to the right, beer hall to the left; main courses (nary a vegetable to be seen) are DM10.50 to DM26.50, though the average is about DM17. Next door, *Zum Husar* is a four-star place, said to be excellent, if expensive.

Directly opposite the Cafeteria Sirch is the *Gasthaus zur Schranne*, an old tavern with three-course evening menus from just DM12.80. The *Hofbräustüberl* (☎ 717 16), at the corner of Chamonixstrasse and Olympiastrasse, has home-made Hungarian specialities like hajducki cevap (skewered and grilled meat with paprika; DM18).

One of the best restaurants in town is *Isi's Goldener Engel* (☎ 566 77; closed Wednesday), at Bankgasse 5, complete with outside frescos and stags' heads. The menu varies widely, from the game platter with deer loin and roast boar for two for DM80 to more modest dishes like Leberknödel (liver dumplings) with sauerkraut for DM14.50.

BAVARIA

Snacks & Fast Food *Bavaria Grill* (☎ 330 8), Am Kurpark 16 in Garmisch (entrance on the little alley), is a lot friendlier than it looks from the outside, and the food's good and cheap. Fill up on sausage dishes from DM6.90 to DM9.50, and add some excellent fries for DM4.50.

Also in Garmisch, *Konditorei Krönner* (☎ 300 7), Achenfeldstrasse 1 (entrance on Am Kurpark), is a beautiful if pricey place for coffee and cakes, but the attached take-away bakery is far more reasonable; try their speciality Mocca creme and almond Agnes Benaur torte for DM3.20.

Perhaps the best value in town is the excellent *Cafeteria Sirch* (☎ 210 9), Griesstrasse 1 (they have a sister restaurant, the *Grill*, in Partenkirchen). Not much to look at but excellent roast chicken with salad and bread costs DM4.60, whole chickens go for DM9.20, and bratwurst is DM2.70.

Schnönegger Käseversand (☎ 173 3), Mohenplatz 1, has really friendly staff and cheese sandwiches from DM2 to DM5; it also sells a range of delicious all-natural yoghurt (DM6/4.50 with/without fruit) as well as fresh butter and honey. Right next door, the *Andolue Restaurant* has doner sandwiches or goulash with bread for DM6, and a half-chicken with salad & fries for DM10.

BAVARIA

Getting There & Away

Garmisch is serviced from Munich by hourly trains (DM26, 1½ hours). A special return train fare from Munich or Augsburg for DM68 (DM84 on weekends) includes the trip up the Zugspitze (or a day ski pass). The A95 from Munich is the direct road route. Trains between Garmisch and Innsbruck pass through Mittenwald.

AROUND GARMISCH-PARTENKIRCHEN

Mittenwald

- *pop 8500*
- *area code* ☎ 08823

In the charming nearby town of Mittenwald, the tourist office (☎ 339 81) is at Dammkarstrasse 3; open weekdays from 8 am to noon and 1 to 5 pm. There's a second office at the train station, but its hours are useless.

Popular local hikes with cable-car access go to the Alpspitze (2628m), the Wank (1780m), Mt Karwendel (2384m) and the Wettersteinspitze (2297m). The Karwendel ski field has the longest run (7km) in Germany. Combined day ski passes covering the Karwendel and nearby Kranzberg ski fields cost DM38. For ski hire and instruction, contact the Vereinigte Skischule (☎ 808 0), Bahnhofstrasse 6.

Places to Stay The camping ground closest to Mittenwald is *Am Isarhorn* (☎ 521 6), 2km north of town off the B2 highway (bus No 9608 or 9610). The local *DJH hostel* (☎ 170 1) is in Buckelwiesen, 4km outside Mittenwald. It charges DM18 per night and closes from early November until late December. Impossible by public transport, take the road to Klais, bear left at the BMW dealer, up the hill, round the lake, follow the signs – it's about 4km.

Two good budget places in the middle of town are *Hotel Alpenrose* (☎ 505 5), Obermarkt 1, with singles/doubles for DM45/85, and *Gasthaus Bergfrühling* (☎ 808 9), at Dammkarstrasse 12, which has basic but bright rooms from DM30/60.

Places to Eat Bavaria's best pretzels are at *Café Zunterer*, Obermarkt 16, and they're only 80pf each. Nearby at Hochstrasse 14, the *Grillshop* does great roast chickens (DM5.30 for half).

Gasthof Alpenrose, in an ornate 18th-century building at Obermarkt 1, offers affordable old-style eating – there's nothing on the menu over DM18 – and live Bavarian music almost every night. *Gasthof Stern*, at Fritz-Brösl-Platz 2 (closed Thursday), also has local dishes at reasonable prices.

Oberammergau

- *pop 5400*
- *area code* ☎ 08822

Approximately 20km north of Garmisch-Partenkirchen is the unbelievably touristy town of Oberammergau, celebrated for its

Passion Play, performed every 10 years since the townsfolk say they made a deal with God in 1633. Minus some politically incorrect attacks on the Jews, the play is still performed, and tickets sell out years in advance. The next performance is in 2000, for which tickets go on sale in 1998. You can visit the Passionstheater (DM4) for a history of the play and a peek at the costumes and sets.

The city tourist office (☎ 102 1), Eughen-Papst-Strasse 9a, books accommodation, as well as horse-drawn carriage rides to Schloss Linderhof for DM30.

Throughout the town the highlights are the *Luftmalerei*, trompe l'oeil paintings on the façades of buildings designed to impart an aura of wealth. Several houses have fairytale motifs, like *Hansel & Gretl* and *Little Red Riding Hood*. The crowning glory of the town's Luftmalerei is that on the front of the Pilate's House, just off Dorfstrasse.

Getting There & Away Buses run regularly to/from Garmisch-Partenkirchen (DM4.80).

Schloss Linderhof

About 20km west of town is Schloss Linderhof (1870-78), Ludwig II's hunting palace. Nestled at the crook of a steep hillside, it is fronted by formal French gardens with fountains, pools and a grotto based on Wagner's *Tannhäuser*. The fountains play in summer.

Right in the front entrance is a statue of Louis XIV, the Sun King, with the inscription *Nec Pluribus impar*, 'I'm the Greatest'. The castle and the grounds are more Ludwig Francophilia, and the best part is that the sunnier the weather, the fewer the visitors.

It's open daily from 8.30 am to 5.30 pm. Admission costs DM8. A return bus fare from Garmisch-Partenkirchen costs DM11.

OBERSTDORF

- *pop 11,000*
- *area code* ☎ 08322

Over in the western part of the Bavarian Alps is the car-free resort of Oberstdorf. The tourist office (☎ 700 0), at Markt 7, is open weekdays from 8.30 am to noon and 2 to 6 pm. There's also a convenient room-finding service near the Hauptbahnhof.

Like Garmisch, Oberstdorf is surrounded by towering peaks and offers superb hiking. For an exhilarating day walk, ride the Nebelhorn cable car to the upper station, then hike down via the Gaisalpseen, two lovely alpine lakes.

In-the-know skiers value Oberstdorf for its friendliness, lower prices and generally uncrowded pistes. The village is surrounded by several major ski fields: the Nebelhorn, Fellhorn/Kanzelwand and Söllereck. Daily/weekly ski passes that include all three areas (plus the adjoining Kleinwalsertal lifts on the Austrian side) cost DM55/272.

For ski hire and tuition, try the Neue Skischule (☎ 273 7), which has convenient outlets at the valley stations of the Nebelhorn and Söllereck lifts.

The Oberstdorf Eislaufzentrum, behind the Nebelhorn cable-car station, is the biggest ice-skating complex in Germany, with three separate rinks.

BAVARIA

Places to Stay

The local *camping ground* (☎ 652 5) is at Rubinger Strasse 16, 2km north of the station beside the train line.

The *hostel* (☎ 222 5), at Kornau 8 on the outskirts of town near the Söllereck chair lift, charges DM20 per night; take the Kleinwalsertal bus to the Reute stop.

Geiger Hans (☎ 367 4), at Frohmarkt 5, has small rooms from DM35 per person. The *Zum Paulanerbräu* (☎ 234 3), at Kirchstrasse 1 right in the heart of the Altstadt, charges DM45/84 for simple rooms (or DM60/114 with private shower). Also central is *Gasthaus Binz* (☎ 445 5), in a quaint wooden inn at Bachstrasse 14, with simple rooms for DM40 per person.

Places to Eat

The large *Zum Paulanerbräu* (see Places to Stay) has a wide range of belly-filling selections priced from around DM12. The restaurant is closed on Tuesday. *Zum wilde Männle*, at Oststrasse 15, is a bit splashier, and the extra you pay is worth it.

Getting There & Away

The direct 'Alpenland' InterRegio train runs daily in either direction between Hamburg and Oberstdorf (via Hanover, Würzburg, Augsburg and Buchloe). There are several daily bus connections to Füssen (via Reutte in Austria or Pfronten).

BERCHTESGADEN

- *pop 8200*
- *area code* ☎ 08652

Berchtesgaden is perhaps the most romantically scenic place in the Bavarian Alps. Nestled in valleys that hug the Austrian border, and at the northern end of the beautiful Königssee, it's best known to non-Germans as the site of Hitler's retreat, the Eagle's Nest. Every year, tourists (including Americans in their tens of thousands) come on a sort of pilgrimage to catch a glimpse of the mountain-top retreat, open to visitors in summer only.

Orientation & Information

The Berchtesgaden tourist office (☎ 967 0), just across the river from the Hauptbahnhof at Königsseer Strasse 2, is open in summer on weekdays from 8 am to 6 pm, on Saturday from 8 am to 5 pm, and on Sunday and public holidays from 9 am to 3 pm. At other times of the year it is open on weekdays from 8 am to 5 pm and Saturday from 9 am to noon. The post office and bus station are at the train station.

Salt Mines

A tour of the **Salzbergwerk** (☎ 600 20) is a must. Visitors change into protective miners' gear before descending into the depths of the salt mine for a 1½-hour tour. It's open daily from 8.30 am to 5 pm between 1 May and 15 October, and from 12.30 to 3.30 pm Monday to Saturday during the rest of the year. Admission is DM17 for adults and DM8.50 for children.

Eagle's Nest

At Kehlstein, at 1834m atop the sheer-sided mountain of Obersalzberg that overlooks Berchtesgaden, is Hitler's former mountain retreat (open from late May to early October). Better known as the Eagle's Nest, this is one of the most scenic spots in Germany. Here Hitler established his holiday house (which he called 'Berghof'), complete with a maze-like bunker complex built into the alpine rock. Kehlstein is reached from Berchtesgaden by RVO bus to Hintereck, then by special bus to the Kehlstein car park, from where a lift goes 120m up to the summit. A combined return ticket from Berchtesgaden costs DM26.50. On foot it's a 30-minute brisk climb from the Kehlstein car park to the summit.

Königssee

The Berchtesgaden area's other great attraction is the 8km-long, 1.25km-wide, 200m-deep Königssee, a beautiful, crystal-clear alpine lake 5km to the south. There are frequent electric-boat tours (DM21; 1½ hours) in all seasons across the lake to the quaint chapel at St Bartholomä.

In summer, boats continue to the far end of the lake. If you're lucky, the boat will stop and the guide will play a trumpet to let you experience the amazing **Echo Wall**. In the valley about one hour's hike from the dock at St Bartholomä is the **Eis Kapelle** – as snow gathers in the corner of the rocks here, a dome is created that attains heights of over 200m; in summer, as the ice melts, the water digs tunnels and creates a huge opening in the solid ice.

National Park

The wilds of Berchtesgaden National Park unquestionably offer some of the best hiking in Germany. A good introduction to the area is a 2km path up from St Bartholomä beside the Königssee to the Watzmann-Ostwand, a massive 2000m-high rock face which has claimed the lives of scores of mountaineers attempting to climb it. Another popular hike goes from the southern end of the Königssee to the Obersee. The tourist office sells excellent topographical maps for DM10.80, and hiking maps from DM10 to DM15.

Skiing
Berchtesgaden's main ski field is the Jenner area (☎ 249 5) at Königssee. Daily/weekly ski-lift passes cost DM37/179. The lines are not huge, but good for families.

The Erste Skischule Mittenwald (☎ 854 8), Mathias-Klotz-Strasse 5, rents skiing and snowboarding equipment at good rates. The Outdoor Club (☎ 500 1), Ludwig-Ganghofer-Strasse 20½, organises a vast range of activities and courses, from hiking and mountaineering to paragliding and rafting.

Places to Stay
Camping Of the five camping grounds in the Berchtesgaden area, the nicest are at Königssee: *Grafenlehen* (☎ 414 0) and *Mühleiten* (☎ 458 4). Both charge DM10 per site plus DM8 per person.

Hostel The *hostel* (☎ 219 0), at Gebirgsjägerstrasse 52, charges DM22 (including tourist tax and breakfast) for a bed. From the Hauptbahnhof, take bus No 3 to Strub, then continue a few minutes on foot. The hostel is closed from early November to late December.

Hotels The *Hotel Watzmann* (☎ 205 5) is at Franziskanerplatz 2, just opposite the chiming church in the Altstadt. Simple singles/doubles cost just DM33/66 (DM39/78 in summer). The hotel closes in November and December. Only 15 minutes' walk from the station but with great views over the valley is the *Pension Haus am Berg* (☎ 505 9), Am Brandholz 9, which charges DM78 for doubles with bath & toilet.

Rooms at the *Gästehaus Alpina* (☎ 251 7), Ramsauer Strasse 6 near the train station, range from DM38 to DM45, and some have nice views to Kehlstein, Jenner, Göll and Brett.

Also near the station, the *Hotel Floriani* (☎ 660 11), Königsseer Strasse 37, has rooms with bath, cable TV and minibar from DM44.50 to DM87.50. Some rooms have balconies.

The *Silencehotel Rosenbichl* (☎ 560 0), Rosenhofweg 24 in the middle of the protected nature zone, is exceptional value with singles from DM55 to DM85 and doubles from DM75 to DM105. Nonsmokers find solace here. There's also a sauna, whirlpool, solarium and a library (mainly German stuff).

Hotel Geiger (☎ 965 3, ☎ 965 55 5), Berchtesgadener Strasse 103-115, has a huge range of rooms at a huge range of prices – from DM100 to DM600 for singles, DM130 to DM660 for doubles. It's on the south side of the Kälberstein and half the rooms have balconies with a view of the national park.

At Schönau am Königssee, the *Hotel-Pension Greti* (☎ 946 50), Waldhauserstrasse 20, a 15-minute walk from the lake, has well appointed rooms from DM59/79, all with bath and balcony.

The *Alpenhotel Zechmeisterlehen* (☎ 945 0), Wahlstrasse 35, about halfway between Berchtesgaden and Königssee, has rooms from DM79/108.

Places to Eat
There's a good local *market* at Rathausplatz (albeit only three times a year – on the last Friday of every month in summer), with an incredible array of fresh produce and meats. *Diemeter*, just off Rathausplatz, has delicious organic bread and pastries and other groovy things.

Hotel Watzmann (see Places to Stay) deserves another mention for its well priced dishes served to outside tables. The *Hubertus Stuben*, next door to Hotel Vier Jahreszeiten on Maximilianstrasse, offers vegetarian as well as hearty meat dishes from around DM18. *Gasthaus Bier-Adam*, Markt 22, has a good range of traditional fare to suit all budgets, and the nearby *Gasthaus Neuhaus* at Markt 1 has a beer garden.

Getting There & Away
For the quickest train connections to Berchtesgaden it's usually best to take a Munich-Salzburg train and change at Freilassing. It's a 2¾-hour train trip from Munich (DM46), but less than an hour from Salzburg, although from Salzburg it's more convenient

to take a bus or even a tour. Berchtesgaden is south of the Munich-Salzburg A8 autobahn.

Franconia

Franconia occupies the northern part of the state of Bavaria, and its lovely rolling hills are home to a beautiful wine region, stunningly beautiful parks and the absolutely unmissable cities of Nuremberg and Würzburg (for Würzburg, see the Romantic Road section earlier in this chapter).

The Franconian wine region, in the northwest of the state, produces some exceptional white and red wines, all served up in the distinctive Franconian bottle – the flattened teardrop-shape that is only used for these wines and for Mateus, the Portuguese table wine. The oldest variety of wine in Franconia is Bochbeuel Silvaner. Labelling of wines in the region is simple: yellow labels mean dry, green half-dry and red is somewhat sweet (locals say 'mild').

NUREMBERG

- *pop 500,000*
- *area code* ☎ 0911

Though the flood of tourists to this historical town never seems to cease, it's still worth the trip. Nuremberg (Nürnberg), capital of Franconia, is known for its spectacular (if now bordering on kitschy) Christmas Market, and infamous for its Nazi party rallies. By positioning Nuremberg as the 'secret' and symbolic capital of the Third Reich (the first laws that removed Jews' rights as citizens were enacted here and named for the city), the National Socialists ensured its complete destruction: Allied bombers reduced the city to rubble on the night of 2 January 1945, and soon after, American soldiers became the first to invade the walled city since fortifications were erected in the Middle Ages.

Of 10,000 Jews living in Nuremberg before the war, 10 survived. Allied bombing raids of the city killed about 2000. After the war, the city was the site of the War Crimes Tribunal, now known as the Nuremberg Trials.

The Marshall Plan and local dedication resulted in the reconstruction or recreation of almost all the city's buildings – including the castle and the three old churches in the Altstadt, which were painstakingly rebuilt using the original stone.

Fortunately for posterity, the Nazis had envisioned the devastating bombing raids and had removed all important works of art from the city's museums and churches and stored them in a bomb shelter. The city's churches – all of which converted to Protestantism in 1525, though the Frauenkirche converted back to Catholicism in 1916 – contain fantastically valuable artworks.

Today Nuremberg is one of Bavaria's most touristed destinations, and crowds get very thick in summer and during the Christmas Market. A compact city, it's easy to get around and makes a very enjoyable base for excursions into the Franconian wine country or the Romantic Road.

Orientation

Almost all the city sights are within the roughly rectangular-shaped Altstadt (old town), surrounded by reconstructed city walls and a dry moat. The shallow Pegnitz River flows from west to east right through the centre of the city.

The Hauptbahnhof is just outside the city walls at the south-east corner of the Altstadt. The Altstadt's main artery, the mostly pedestrian Königstrasse, takes you north from the Hauptbahnhof through Hauptmarkt and Rathausplatz and leads into Burgstrasse, which heads steeply uphill and brings you to the hostel and Kaiserburg.

The biggest attractions outside the Altstadt are the Reichsparteitagsgelände, the Nazi rally ground south-east of the centre, and the Justizgebaüde, the courthouse in which the Nuremberg Trials were held, west of the centre.

Information

Tourist Offices There are tourist information offices in the Hauptbahnhof's main hall

(☎ 233 61 31/32; open May to October, Monday to Saturday from 9 am to 7 pm), and at Hauptmarkt 18 (☎ 233 61 35; open the same days until 6 pm). During the Christkindlmarkt, both offices are also open Sunday from 10 am to 1 pm and 2 to 4 pm.

The ADAC has an office (☎ 232 59 9) at Frauentorgraben 43. The city lost & found service (☎ 261 07 0) is at Rothenburger Strasse 10 at the east end of the Hauptbahnhof.

Money Change money at the Reisebank in the Hauptbahnhof. There's a Commerzbank at Königstrasse 21, a Deutsche Bank at Fürtherstrasse 32, and a Bayerische Vereinsbank at Fürtherstrasse 38. American Express (☎ 232 39 7) has an office at Adlerstrasse 2 just off Königstrasse.

Post & Communications The main post office is at Bahnhofplatz 1 by the station.

Online Services Nuremberg has several Internet cafés. No 1 Internet Café (☎ 200 77 22) is at Königstrasse 57-59; Cyberthek (☎ 446 68 93) is at Pillenreuther Strasse 34; and Maximum is on Farberstrasse.

Travel Agencies Noricus Tours (☎ 222 86 8), Breite Gasse 22 on the 1st floor, is a good discount travel agent. Celtic Travel (☎ 439 89 28), Bulmannstrasse 26, specialises in travel to Ireland and Scotland. Plärrer Reisen (☎ 935 55 0) has a last-minute ticket desk at the airport.

Bookshops & Libraries Buchhandlung Edelmann (☎ 992 06 0), Kornmarkt 8, has Lonely Planet and other travel books upstairs and English novels and classics downstairs.

Männertreu Buchladen (☎ 262 67 6), Bauerngasse 14, is a gay-oriented bookshop. The research library at the German National Museum (see below), has 50,000 volumes and 1500 periodicals.

International Centres The Amerika Haus (☎ 230 69 0), Gleissbühlstrasse 13 near the Hauptbahnhof, runs a very impressive range of cultural and artistic programmes each month. There's an English-language discussion group and a resource library.

Laundry There's a very central laundrette on Obstmarkt. Schnell & Sauber has three coin laundries in the city that are open from 6 am to midnight: at Sulzbacher Strasse 86 (tram No 8 to Deichslerstrasse) in the north; at Allersberger Strasse 89 on the corner of Augustenstrasse (tram Nos 4, 7 and 9 to Schweiggerstrasse) in the south; and at Schwabacher Strasse 86 on the corner of Offstrasse (U-Bahn No 2, to St Leonhard) in the west.

Medical Services In a medical emergency, call the Bayerisches Rotes Kreuz, or Bavarian Red Cross (☎ 940 32 60).

Dangers & Annoyances Legions of reprobates hang out near the Hauptbahnhof. If you're American and homesick for nocturnal shouting, sleep in any of the hotels in that area on Friday and Saturday and leave the windows open to hear American servicemen and women representing their country this fine way.

Kaiserburg

It's a decent climb up Burgstrasse to the Kaiserburg castle area, but the location offers some of the best views of the city. The area was formerly two castles: the Kaiserburg, which stands today, and the Burggrafenburg, which faced it but was destroyed in 1420, leaving only its towers on either side. Between them was built the Kaiserstallung (Royal Stables), which today is the HI hostel.

Inside the palace complex, on a DM5 ticket (discount DM3.50), you can see the chapel, the tower (113 steps), and the amazing deep well (48m – they lower a platter of candles so you can see the depth) which still produces drinking water today.

The castle walls and dry moat spread west to the tunnel-gate of **Tiergärtnertor**, through which you can stroll behind the castle into its lovely **garden**.

At the foot of the castle's western end is

BAVARIA

Tiergärtnerplatz, with the **Albrecht Dürer Haus** (☎ 231 25 68), where Dürer, Germany's Renaissance draughtsman, lived from 1509 to 1528. The house survived WWII with moderate damage, and features a large number of Dürer artefacts, though no original works (entry DM5/3).

Opposite, in front of the **Pilatushaus** – marked by a knight in shining armour standing atop a dragon – is ***Der Hase*** (*The Hare*; an updated version of Dürer's *Junger Feldhase* of 1502), which shows the consequences of human meddling with nature. Nearby is the **Historischer Kunstbunker** (☎ 244 96 10), the bunker that housed th city's art treasures during the bombing raic of WWII. You can visit on tours (DM5) o Thursday, Saturday and Sunday at 2 and pm.

A few blocks south of the Dürer house Karlstrasse 13-15, the **Spielzeugmuseu** (☎ 231 31 64) displays toys from throughou the ages. It's open Tuesday to Sunday fro 10 am to 5 pm (Wednesday to 9 pm); admi sion is DM5/2.50.

The grassy hill just in front of the host and the castle is Am Ölberg, a favourite sp to sit and gaze out over the city's rooftop

PLACES TO STAY
1 Jugendgästehaus
8 Albrecht Dürer Hotel Garni
27 Pension Altstadt
39 Pfälzer Hof
41 Probst-Garni Hotel
46 Grand Hotel Nürnberg
47 Gasthof Schwänlein
51 InterCity Hotel

PLACES TO EAT
5 Burgwächter Restaurant
12 Alte Küch'n
18 Bratwursthäusle
22 Café am Trödlmarkt
23 Lotos Naturkost Imbiss
24 Heilig Geist Spital
28 Café Treibhaus
29 Pizza Sombrero
31 Stefansbäck
32 Wok Man
36 Kaufhof & Markthalle
38 Irish Castle Pub
42 Burger King
43 Berkin Imbiss
44 McDonald's
45 McDonald's

OTHER
2 Kaiserburg
3 Tiergärtnertor
4 Pilatushaus
6 Historischer Kunstbunker
7 *Der Hase* (The Hare)
9 Altstadthof Brewery
10 Albrecht Dürer Haus
11 Dürer Monument & Air Raid Shelter
13 St Sebalduskirche
14 Altes Rathaus
15 Laundrette
16 Tourist Office
17 Neues Rathaus
19 Spielzeugmuseum
20 Goldener Brunnen
21 Pfarrkirche Unsere Liebe Frau
25 Mach 1
26 American Express
30 Hugendubel Bookshop
33 Noricus Tours
34 St Lorenzkirche
35 Toleranz
37 Buchhandlung Edelmann
40 Germanisches Nationalmuseum
48 Handwerkerhof
49 Main Post Office
50 Tourist Office
52 Main Train Station

One fine place to do that is in the Burgwächter restaurant (see Places to Eat).

Just down the hill is the **City Museum Fembohaus** (☎ 231 25 95), a restored 16th-century merchant house with amazing stucco and wood panelling (entry DM4/2).

Dürer Platz

The **statue** of Albrecht Dürer in the square that bears his name was one of two things here that survived the bombing raid; the second, beneath the ground, is the city **air-raid shelter**, now open for tours daily at 11 am and 1, 3 and 5 pm (DM7/5).

St Lorenzkirche

On Lorenzer Platz is the St Lorenzkirche, noted for the 15th-century tabernacle which climbs a pillar like a vine, all the way up to the vaulted ceiling. Note also the many beautiful artworks.

Hauptmarkt

Bustling Hauptmarkt, site of daily **markets**, is also the site of the famous Christkindlmarkt (see Special Events).

At the square's eastern end is the ornate Gothic **Pfarrkirche Unsere Liebe Frau** (1350-58) or simply the Frauenkirche; the figures around the clock, seven electoral princes, walk clockwise three times around Charles IV, to glockenspiel accompaniment, every day at noon.

At the north-west corner of the square, the 19m **Goldener Brunnen** (Golden Fountain; aka the **Schöne Brunnen** or Pretty Fountain), a stunning golden vision of over 40 figures rising spire-like from the base, has been standing since 1396.

Rathaus

Just north of Hauptmarkt is the Altes Rathaus (1616-22), containing the *Lochgefängnisse* (torture chambers); pick up free explanatory information in English at the entrance. You must join a tour (DM4/2); they run daily every 30 minutes from 10 am to 4.30 pm.

Opposite the Neues Rathaus is the 13th-century **St Sebalduskirche**, Nuremberg's oldest church, with the shrine of St Sebaldus.

German National Museum

The Germanisches Nationalmuseum (☎ 133 10), Kartäusergasse 1 on Kornmarkt, is the most important general museum of German culture. It features works by German painters and sculptors, an archaeological collection, arms and armour, musical and scientific

BAVARIA

instruments and toys. It's open Tuesday to Sunday from 10 am to 5 pm (to 9 pm Wednesday). Admission costs DM6/3.

Handwerkerhof

The Handwerkerhof, a re-creation of the crafts quarter of old Nuremberg, is a walled tourist trap opposite the Hauptbahnhof. Open from March to December, it's about as quaint as a hammer on your thumbnail and the prices are about as painful, but if you're cashed up you'll find that there is some decent merchandise here. The Bratwurstglöcklein im Handwerkerhof (see Places to Eat) is also good, with friendly service and good sausages, but the other restaurants are a little cheesy – accordion versions of *In the Mood* and violinists assaulting your table. The yard closes at 10 pm.

Reichsparteitagsgelände

Nuremberg's role during the Third Reich is emblazoned in the minds of the world: the B&W images of over a million ecstatic Nazi supporters thronging the city's flag-lined streets as goose-stepping troops salute their *Führer*.

The rallies held in the city were part of a perfectly orchestrated propaganda campaign that began as early as 1929 to build support for the party. By 1933, the rallies had grown to such proportions that the party planned an entire complex south-east of the Altstadt to house the masses. It was to have included the **Zeppelinwiese**, a military parade ground; the never-completed **Deutsches Stadion**, which was to seat 400,000; and the **Luitpoldarena**, designed for mass SS and SA parades. Collectively, the area is officially called the Reichsparteitagsgelände, but it's commonly referred to as the Luitpoldhain.

A chilling documentary film, *Fascination and Force*, can be seen in the museum at the rear of the Zeppelin stand (on the Zeppelin field); the museum is open May to October, Tuesday to Sunday from 10 am to 6 pm (free entry); in an unbelievable show of bad judgment, the documentary inexcusably costs DM2/1.

Get there by S-Bahn No 2 to Frankenstadion (every 20 minutes); tram No 9 from the Hauptbahnhof to the Luitpoldhain-Volkspark; or tram No 4 or bus No 55 or 65 to Dutzendteich.

Justice Centre

The Justizgebaüde (☎ 321 26 79), Furthstrasse 110, is the state courthouse in which the war crimes trials were held at the conclusion of WWII. It's not normally open to visitors, though you can see the outside (U-Bahn No 1, direction: Furth). The trials, which were held in Room 600, were set in Nuremberg by the Allies as a symbolic final nail in the Nazi coffin. Indeed the very laws passed by the Nazis to justify the arrest and later extermination of Jews were called the *Nürnberger Gesetze* (Nuremberg Laws). Passed in 1935, they revoked Jewish citizenship.

The trials, which began shortly after the war and concluded on 1 October 1946, resulted in the conviction and sentencing of 177 Nazi leaders, and the execution by hanging of dozens. Among those convicted early on were Joachim von Ribbentrop, Alfred Rosenberg, Wilhelm Frick, Julius Streicher and Hermann Göring – Göring committed suicide in his cell. Those sentenced to life imprisonment included Rudolf Hess, Walter Funk and Erich Raeder.

Organised Tours

The tourist office operates walking tours that meet at the tourist office on Hauptmarkt. There are daily two-hour tours in German (DM8, under 14s free) at 10 am and 2.30 pm (Wednesday only at 2.30 pm, no tours on major holidays). English-language walking tours (2½ hours, DM12, under 14s free) run daily from May to October at 2 pm.

History For All (☎ 332 73 5) conducts two-hour tours of the Nazi rally area at Luitpoldhain from April to November on Saturday and Sunday at 2 pm (DM8/6). Meet at Luitpoldhain, the last stop of tram No 9.

The Nürnberger Altstadtrunfahhrten (☎ 421 91 9) is a tourist choo-choo that loops through the Altstadt for half-hour guided tours in German. The cost is DM7/6; they run daily from 10 am and start at Hauptmarkt.

Special Events

From the Friday before Advent to Christmas Eve, the Hauptmarkt is taken over by the most famous Christkindlmarkt in Germany. The location is noteworthy: this was Nuremberg's Jewish ghetto until the 'expulsion' (actually mass murder) of the Jews in 1349 under Kaiser Karl IV. Over 600 were killed when their homes, buildings and synagogues were razed while the people were trapped inside.

During the Christmas market, scores of stalls line the Hauptmarkt, selling mulled wine, strong spirits, roast sausages and other treats, as well as countless Christmas trinkets. Performances by choirs are a regular feature.

Places to Stay

Book rooms at the tourist information office for DM5 per room. The hardest time to get accommodation is during the (closed to the public) toy fair in late January to early February.

Camping *Campingplatz im Volkspark Dutzendteich* (☎ 811 12 2), Hans-Kalb-Strasse 56, is near the lakes in the Volkspark, south-east of the city centre (U-Bahn No 1 from the Hauptbahnhof takes you to Messezentrum, which is fairly close). It costs DM8 per person plus DM10 per site. It's open from early in May to the end of September.

Hostels The very good *Jugendgästehaus* (☎ 241 35 2) is in the historical Kaiserstallung next to the castle. Dorm beds including sheets cost DM27 (juniors only). The cheapest option for those aged over 26 is the *Jugend-Hotel Nürnberg* (☎ 521 60 92) at Rathsbergstrasse 300, north of the city (take U-Bahn No 2 to Herrnhütte, then bus No 21 north four stops). Dorm beds start at DM26, and there are singles/doubles from DM39/64; prices exclude breakfast.

Hotels & Pensions The most reasonable pension in the city centre is *Garni Probst Hotel* (☎ 203 43 3), on the 3rd floor in a creaky building at Luitpoldstrasse 9. The simple singles/doubles are minuscule but so are the prices, DM40/80, or DM70/100 with toilet and shower (including breakfast). The management is friendly.

Another good deal is *Pension Altstadt* (☎ 226 10 2), Hintere Ledergasse 4, with bathless singles/doubles from DM50/90. Near the station is *Gasthof Schwänlein* (☎ 225 16 2), Hintere Sterngasse 11, which has basic singles/doubles from DM45/80. The quiet and central *Pfälzer Hof* (☎ 221 41 1), at Am Gräslein 10 (near the Germanisches Nationalmuseum), has rooms from DM50/80. *Haus Vosteen* (☎ 533 32 5), just north-east of the Altstadt at Lindenaststrasse 12, charges from DM38/80 a single/double.

The *Albrecht-Dürer Hotel Garni* (☎ 204 59 2), Bergstrasse 25, has clean singles/doubles up by the castle for DM89/135 including breakfast.

The *InterCity Hotel* (☎ 247 80; fax 247 89 99), Eilgutstrasse 8 at the Hauptbahnhof, offers no surprises from the chain's usual standard, with rooms from DM185/235. Nicer is the *Holiday Inn Crowne Plaza* (☎ 402 90; fax 404 06 7), at Valzmnerweiherstrasse 200 south-east of the centre, with rooms from DM184. Probably the most luxurious top-end hotel is right in the centre – the recently renovated *Grand Hotel Nürnberg* (☎ 232 20; fax 232 24 44), opposite the Hauptbahnhof at Bahnhofstrasse 1-3. It features tonnes of amenities, great service and a good location; singles/ doubles cost from DM199/320.

Places to Eat

Restaurants & Bistros Probably the loveliest place to sit on a sunny day is the *Café am Trödelmarkt* (☎ 208 87 7), on an island overlooking the covered bridge and half-timbered houses that are now student dorms. They do continental breakfasts from DM7, Bratwurstl from DM6.

The *Burgwächter Restaurant* (☎ 222 12 6), Am Ölberg 10 in the shadow of the castle, is a great place to sit for drinks or meals of schnitzel and steak; main courses average DM14, and they have an outside section with wonderful views of the city.

A classic Nuremberg restaurant is the *Heilig Geist Spital* (☎ 221 76 1), Spitalgasse 16, whose large dining hall spans the river. There's an extensive wine list and Franconian specialities from DM17.

Pizza Sombrero, at Schlotfegergasse 2 (closed Sunday), offers Italian-Mexican arrangements from as little as DM12.50 per main course.

A tip for money-conscious diners is *Sabberlodd*, at Wiesentalstrasse 21 just north-west of the Altstadt in the backstreets of St Johannis (tram No 6). It offers generous plates of ravioli and mixed salads for around DM10, along with inexpensive house wines and draught beers.

Snacks & Fast Food Königstrasse is the place to head for fast-food options, which include two *McDonald's*, a *Burger King*, and the great *Berkin Imbiss*, with a special doner & drink deal for DM2.99.

At *Alte Küch'n*, Albrecht-Dürer-Strasse 3, the house speciality is Backers, a kind of savoury cake of grated potato served with apple sauce or bacon accompanied by sauerkraut (from DM8.50). The *Markthalle* in the basement of the Kaufhof department store is a very good deal, with Turkish meals for less than DM10. You'll also find here a baker, a butcher and a wine bar.

Wok Man (☎ 204 31 1), Breite Gasse 48, is a good fast-food Chinese place with beef fried noodles for DM4, mixed veg and beef with noodles for DM6.50 and big full meals for DM10. Nearby, *Stefansbäck*, at Breite Gasse 70, has awesome sandwiches from DM3.

Nuremberger Bratwurstl There's heated competition between Regensburg and Nuremberg over whose tiny sausages are the best. Judge for yourself: try 'em at the *Bratwursthäusle*, Rathausplatz 1 (closed Sunday), or at the *Bratwurstglöcklein im Handwerkerhof* (☎ 227 62 5); the little links cost DM9 for eight, DM11.60 for 10. The are served with potato salad, sauerkraut c horseradish.

Entertainment

Listings The excellent *Plärrer* (DM4) i available throughout the city and is heav enough with information to kill someon with.

The city tourist office publishes *Da Aktuelle Monats Magazin*, which also ha information on cultural events.

Gay & Lesbian *Männertreu* magazine is th biggest gay magazine in the city, available a the tourist offices (free). Old copies of *Ros. Piste* can sometimes be found – there's on at the tourist offices. It's a complete guide t bars, restaurants and businesses.

Cinema The *Roxy* (☎ 488 40), Am Sudfried hof, Julius Lossmannstrasse 116, show English-language first-run films. The *DA Cinema* (☎ 230 69 0) at the Amerika Hau (see International Centres) regularly screen first-run and classic American, English an Australian films.

Disco *Mach 1*, on Kaiserstrasse right in th centre of town (look for the big metal door) is a very cool basement club with house, hip hop, 70s-80s and soul music parties.

Kilian, Kilianstrasse 108-110 north of th centre near Freudenpark, is an enormous ha with house music and a good, friendl crowd. *Hirsch* (☎ 429 41 4), Vogelweihe strasse 66 (U-Bahn No 1 to Frankenstrasse) way down south in Gibitzen Hof Garden, i a great live alternative music scene.

Gay *Toleranz*, Katherinegasse 14, gets good crowd for nightly theme parties an special events.

Theatre & Classical Music The Schauspie Nürnburg performs a huge range of theatre including drama, comedy and youn people's performances, at the *Schauspiel haus* and the *Kammerspiel*, while classica music and opera are performed at th

BAVARIA

Städtische Bühnen. All these venues are on Richard-Wagner-Platz; for tickets to all performances, call ☎ 231 35 14. Home-grown plays and comedy are performed on the stage behind the *Altstadthof Brewery* (☎ 222 71 7), Bergstrasse 19, which is also a nice pub.

Pubs & Bars A popular student bar is *Café Treibhaus*, Karl-Grillenberger-Strasse, with filling baguettes from DM7. The crowded *Irish Castle Pub*, Schlehengasse 31, has typical pub food and Guinness on tap (DM6.20 a pint); there's live folk music most nights.

Getting There & Away

Air Nuremberg airport (☎ 350 60), 7km from the centre, is served by several regional and international carriers, including Lufthansa (☎ 266 11 5), Air Berlin (☎ 364 74 3), KLM (☎ 522 09 6) and Air France (☎ 529 85 22).

Bus Eurolines buses run daily between Nuremberg and Prague (DM63, 5½ hours). BEX BerLinien buses leave for Berlin daily at 12.10 pm and arrive from Berlin at 2.30 pm daily. The SuperSpar/standard cost for a one-way ticket is DM58/108; for a return ticket it's DM102/130.

Train Trains run approximately hourly to/from Frankfurt (DM63, 2¼ hours) and Stuttgart (DM52, three hours). There are connections several times daily to Berlin (DM125, 6¼ hours). Hourly trains run to/from Munich (DM66, 1¾ hours), and several daily trains travel to Vienna and to Prague (six hours each).

Car & Motorcycle Several autobahns converge on Nuremberg, but only the north-south A73 joins B4, the ring road.

Ride Services There's an ADM Mitfahrbüro (☎ 194 40) at Strauchstrasse 1.

Getting Around

The Airport Bus No 20 is an airport express shuttle (DM12) running every 20 minutes between the airport and the Hauptbahnhof from 5.30 am. A taxi to/from the airport will cost DM20 to DM25. Work on a U-Bahn connection to the airport is well under way and the station is expected to open in late 1998.

Public Transport In the mainly pedestrian-only city centre, walking is usually best. Tickets on the VGN bus, tram and U-Bahn system (☎ 270 75 99 for information; Monday to Thursday from 8 am to 3 pm, Friday from 8 am to 1 pm) cost DM2.50/3.30 per short/long ride in the central zone, and 24-hour weekday or all-weekend passes are DM7.40. A strip of 10 short-ride tickets costs DM12.90.

Taxi Flag fall is DM4.80, and it's DM2.20 per kilometre.

The BahnTaxi stand (DM12 per couple) is at the northern end of the Hauptbahnhof near the Mittelhalle exit.

Bicycle The Allgemeiner Deutscher Fahrrad Club (ADFC), with an office (☎ 396 13 2) at Rohledererstrasse 13, organises group rides throughout the year. Rent bicycles from Fahrradverlei (☎ 397 33 7), Bielingsstrasse 17, which has rinky dink/good/mountain/tandem bikes for DM6/9/12/20 per day. There's also Fahrradkiste (☎ 287 90 64), Knauerstrasse 9, which has kids' bikes/trekking and mountain bikes/tandems for DM7/15/30 per day. The city tourist office sells the ADFC's *Fahrrad Stadtplan* (DM8.50), a highly detailed map of the city and surrounding area.

The tourist office also hands out a list of 'bicycle friendly' hotels in town that can store bicycles.

ERLANGEN

- *pop 101,000*
- *area code* ☎ 09131

About 20km north of Nuremberg, the city of Erlangen ('AIR-longen') is a charming little university town and company town, with Siemens the major employer. Lined with quaint streets and ivy covered buildings and with a lovely little schloss right in the centre, it's definitely worth a day or two of exploration, especially in summer.

Orientation

The Regnitz River flows almost due north at the west side of the Hauptbahnhof. Just east of Bahnhof Platz is Hugenottenplatz, from where Universitätsstrasse and Obere Karlsstrasse run west to east. Friedrichstrasse is south of these two, running west-east as well. North of Hugenottenplatz is Schlossplatz and, of course, the Schloss, east of which is the Botanical Garden. The main post office is two blocks south-east of the Hauptbahnhof at the corner of Henkestrasse and Nürnberger Strasse; one long block south of there on Nürnberger Strasse is Rathausplatz.

Universität Erlangen's campus spreads to the east of Schlossplatz.

Information

The city tourist office (☎ 895 10) is in the Rathaus, Rathausplatz 1, open Monday from 8 am to 6 pm, Tuesday to Thursday from 8 am to 4.30 pm, and Friday from 8 am to 12.30 pm. The ADAC has an office (☎ 356 52) at Henkestrasse 26. Change money at the Vereinsbank at Hugenottenplatz or the Dresdner Bank at Schlossplatz.

Universität Erlangen's main office is at Schlossplatz 4. The Merkel Universitätsbuchhandlung, and next door, Merkel Jr, on Untere Karlsstrasse at Neustadter Kirchenplatz, have great maps and English books. Just east is the Universitätsbibliotek, at Schuhstrasse 1a.

Things to See & Do

The city's **Schloss** is now university offices. Behind it, the **Botanical Garden** (open 8 am to 6 pm daily) is a fabulous park; on any given day you can see concerts, theatre rehearsals, fencing or t'ai chi going on, and it's lovely in summer for a picnic. Speaking of lovely, the **Aromagarten**, near the Palmsanlage, is open March to October daily from 8 am to 7 pm. The walk up to the **Burgberg** (follow the main drag north out of town) is definitely worthwhile. The site of a major folk and beer festival, even when empty its enormity (thousands of long wooden benches and well-tended beer cellars) and its leafy setting are impressive.

Places to Stay

One of Germany's best-located camping grounds, the *Naturfreunde Erlangen* (☎ 253 03), is about a five-minute walk from the Hauptbahnhof right on the Regnitz. Walk into the tunnel away from Bahnhofplatz, head straight up two blocks and follow the signs. It's DM4 per tent, DM9 per car, DM7 per person. There's a nice beer garden, and staff are friendly. Outside the gate you may be able to rent canoes from the Marine-Heim restaurant, which has a lot of them and a launch site.

The city's *DJH hostel* (☎ 227 4; reservations ☎ 862 55 5) will actually allow people over 26 if there's room; beds are DM18/23 for juniors/seniors. It's in the Freizeitzentrum Frankenhof, which also has a swimming pool (DM5/3 per 1½-hour session), a nice courtyard, a restaurant that has dinner meals for DM9, and the *Jugendgästehaus* (same telephone number), with simple singles/doubles/triples from DM37/ 50/75 and singles/doubles with shower and toilet for DM47/74. It's at Südliche Stadtmauerstrasse 35, entrance at the corner of Holzgarten Strasse.

Right at Bahnhofplatz is the very nice *Bahnhof Hotel* (☎ 270 07), Bahnhofplatz 5, with clean and well appointed simple singles/doubles from DM55/115, and rooms with bath and toilet from DM80/150.

Places to Eat

There's a *bakery*, *butcher* and *imbiss* right downstairs from the Bahnhof Hotel, and a *McDonald's* at Hugenottenplatz. *Erlanger Teehaus Café* (☎ 229 11), Friedrichstrasse 14, is a wonderful place with teas, coffees, cakes, breakfasts (a Sunday breakfast buffet for DM17 from 10 am to 2 pm), snacks for under DM7 and full meals for around DM13. There are two large rooms and a beer garden and the staff are a treat.

Nearby, *Umberto Pizzeria* (☎ 209 52 9), on Schuhstrasse has cheap pasta from

DM8.50 to DM12.50, and pizzas from DM7.50 to DM10.

Another Bahnhofplatz offering is *Daddy's Diner* (☎ 205 08 0), Bahnhofplatz 6, with American diner food like burgers (DM10 to DM15) and submarine sandwiches (DM8.50 to DM13) and a jukebox; it's open to midnight.

The *Speisegastätte Römming Biergarten* behind the Schloss is a nice place to sit and munch on a vegetarian selection from the menu. Meals cost from DM11 to DM17.

Entertainment

E-Werk (☎ 800 55 5), Fuchsenwiese 1, is a combination jazz club, disco, culture and communication centre, cinema and 'cultural meeting pace' that always has something on. Theatre and cabaret is performed at *Fifty Fifty* (☎ 248 55), Südliche Stadtmauerstrasse 1 near the hostel.

Spruz, Weisse Herz Strasse 4 through the little courtyard, is a very cool local bar with a nice garden and a cool wood interior. Hostellers spend lots of time at *De Old Inn*, right around the corner on Holzgarten Strasse. *Route 66*, Helmstrasse 9 next to the Hanf Centre (which sells hats, clothing, spirits and other products made from hemp) is an American-style cocktail bar.

Getting There & Away

There are four trains an hour from Erlangen to Nuremberg's Hauptbahnhof (DM5.80, 25 minutes). You can rent bicycles at Fahrradkiste (☎ 209 94 0), Henkestrasse 59; prices are the same as in Nuremberg. Fahrrad Lang (☎ 241 44), Engelstrasse 14, rents bikes as well.

BAMBERG

- *pop 70,000*
- *area code* ☎ 0951

Tucked off the main routes in northern Bavaria, the 1000-year-old city of Bamberg is practically a byword for magnificence; an unwalled, untouched monument to Holy Roman Emperor Heinrich II (who conceived it), to its prince-bishops and clergy and to its patriciate and townsfolk. Recognised as perhaps the most beautiful city in Germany, Bamberg was declared a World Heritage City by UNESCO in 1993.

In the 17th century, some of Europe's finest architects, including Küchel, the Dientzenhofers and Balthasar Neumann, went on a baroque frenzy here, converting hundreds of buildings to the style, many of which stand intact because Bamberg escaped the wartime bombings that devastated other German cities.

The city's canals give Bamberg a Venice-of-the-north feel, and its dedication to culture and the arts is reflected in the renowned Bamberg Symphony Orchestra and the baroque ETA-Hoffmann Theatre – the Calderon Festival here draws thousands every year. The town's nine – and the region's 87 – breweries produce over 200 kinds of beer, including *Keller Bier*, a less fizzy variety designed to help you drink more beer faster, and *Rauchbier*, a dark-red ale with a smooth, smoky flavour. The hills surrounding the city are dotted with wonderful beer gardens, so in town or on the hills, walk, behold, drink the unique beers but experience Bamberg for at least a day.

Orientation & Information

Two waterways flow through the city from north-west to south-east: the Main-Danube Canal, just south of the Hauptbahnhof, and the Regnitz River, which flows through the centre of town. From the station, take Luitpoldstrasse south, turn right onto Obere Königstrasse and left over the Kettenbrücke into Hauptwachtstrasse and into Max Platz.

The tourist office (☎ 871 15 4) is at Geyerswörthstrasse 3 on the island in the Regnitz River, open Monday to Friday from 9 am to 6 pm and Saturday from 8 am to 3 pm. Ask there about the Bamberg*card* (DM13 for one person, DM24 for two), which gives free or reduced admission to city attractions and access to all city bus lines for 48 hours, plus a city tour. The tourist office also sells tickets to performances by the Bamberg Symphony Orchestra, which you will only be able to get in July. The main post office is at the Hauptbahnhof.

Wash clothes at Bamberger Waschsale (☎ 215 17), Untere Königstrasse 32 right in the centre, or in the coin laundry beneath the train station in the Atrium mall. Call ☎ 192 22 for a doctor.

Altstadt

The appeal of Bamberg's historic old town rests in its sheer number of fine buildings, their jumble of styles and the ambience this creates. Most attractions are spread either side of the Regnitz River, but the colourful **Altes Rathaus** (old town hall) is actually on it – or rather over it, built on twin bridges.

The princely and ecclesiastical district is centred on Domplatz, where the Romanesque and Gothic **Dom** (cathedral), housing the statue of the chivalric king-knight, the *Bamberger Reiter*, is the biggest attraction.

Diözesan Museum The highlight of the Diözesan Museum, in the cloister at Domplatz 5 (☎ 502 32 5), is Heinrich II's Blue Coat of Stars. It's open Tuesday to Sunday from 10 am to 5 pm; admission is DM4, discount DM2.

The adjacent courtyard, the **Alte Hofhaltung** (partly Renaissance in style), contains the secular **Historisches Museum** (☎ 871 14 2), with an interesting exhibit on the history of the region, and on 19th-century Bamberg. It's open May to October, Tuesday to Sunday from 9 am to 5 pm; admission is DM4/2.

Neue Residenz The episcopal Neue Residenz (☎ 563 51), though not as large as Würzburg's, is stately and superb, with its elaborate Kaisersaal and Chinese cabinet, and a collection of paintings from the Bavarian National Gallery. It's open from April to October, Tuesday to Sunday from 9 am to noon and 1.30 to 5 pm (in winter to 4 pm); admission is DM4/3.

The **Rosengarten** behind offers one of the city's finest viewing points. Another view is from the tower of the castle **Altenburg** a few kilometres away (take bus No 10 from Promenadestrasse and finish with a walk to the hill top).

Michaelsberg

Above Domplatz, at the top of Michaelsberg, is the former Benedictine **monastery** of St Michael. The **Kirche St Michael** is a must-see for its baroque art and the herbal compendium painted on its ceiling. The garden terraces grant another marvellous view of the city's splendours.

Up here too is the **Fränkisches Brauereimuseum** (☎ 530 16), which shows how the monks brewed their robust *Benediktiner Dunkel*, with exhibits from malt production to the final product. It's open April to October, Tuesday to Sunday from 1 to 4 pm; admission is DM3/1.50.

Places to Stay

The town is packed from May to September, so book ahead.

Camping Camping options are limited to *Campingplatz Insel* (☎ 563 20; bus No 18), at the interestingly named town of Bug on the west bank of the Regnitz a few kilometres south of the city. The camping ground is large and pleasant. Prices are DM12 per site plus DM6.50 per adult.

Hostel The juniors-only *Jugendherberge Wolfsschlucht* (☎ 560 02), Oberer Leinritt 70, is on the west bank of the Regnitz, closer to town than the camping ground; turn south off Münchener Ring near the clinic complex, then east at Bamberger Strasse, then north along the river. Beds cost DM20, plus DM5.50 for linen. The hostel is closed from mid-December to February.

Brewery Hotels Two interesting options in town are both brewery hotels – rooms upstairs and breweries downstairs – and both come highly recommended. The *Bamberger Weissbierhaus* (☎ 255 03), Obere Königstrasse 38, has simple singles/doubles for DM39/70, or doubles with a shower for DM80.

The *Fässla Gasthof* (☎ 229 98 or ☎ 265 16), Obere Königstrasse 19, has doubles for DM98.

Hotels & Pensions Good deals on simple but central hotels are at *Zum Alten Goldenen Anker* (☎ 665 05), Untere Sandstrasse 73 on the west side of town north of Michaelsberg with simple singles for DM45 and doubles with shower/WC for DM85), and at *Café-Gästehaus Graupner* (☎ 980 40 0), Lange Strasse 5 (singles/doubles without shower for DM50/80, with shower for DM60/90).

Hotel Garni Hospiz (☎ 981 26 0), Promenadestrasse 3, is highly recommended: DM66/88 for singles/doubles with all facilities (and budget singles for DM50). *Hotel Alt-Bamberg* (☎ 986 15 0), in a quiet location near the Rathaus at Habergasse 11, is more great value: DM58 for simple singles or DM68/115 for singles/doubles with all facilities.

Places to Eat

The city's brewery-restaurants should be the first stop for both local specialities (like stuffed Bamberger onion with beef in smoked beer sauce) and the unique beers. Try *Greifenklau* (☎ 532 19), Laurenziplatz 20, serving Keller Bier in summer and, from October to November, awesome bock beer. Also try the *Massbräukeller*, on Stephensburg, which serves Pils and Keller Bier, and the restaurant at the *Bamberger Weissbierhaus* (see Places to Stay). The 17th-century *Wirtshaus zum Schlenkerla* (☎ 260 60), Dominikanerstrasse 6, offers Frankonian specialities from DM12, along with its own house-brewed Rauchbier (just DM3.10 per half-litre mug).

Another of Bamberg's beautiful old half-timbered breweries is *Klosterbräu* (☎ 577 22), Obere Mühlbrücke 3, which has excellent beers to complement its solid standard specialities (between DM12 and DM18). *Dom Terrassen*, Untere Kaulberg 36, presents quite tasty pastas, salads and other vegetable-based dishes all for around DM10; sit outside on the scenic terrace looking across to the town cathedral.

Getting There & Away

The most regular train connections to Bamberg are twice hourly from Nuremberg (DM15.50; 45 minutes) or hourly from Würzburg (DM26, one hour), though several through-services run daily to Leipzig (DM63, three hours) and there are daily trains from Munich (DM68, 2¼ hours) and Berlin (DM107, 5¼ hours). The A73 runs direct to Nuremberg.

Getting Around

Walking is the way to go in the city, but you can rent bicycles for DM9 per day from Radinfo Rad in Hof Bredt (☎ 230 12), Untere Königstrasse 32, or for DM15 a day from Fahrrad Dratz (☎ 124 28), Pödeldorferstrasse 190. Cars are impossible in town, so park on the outskirts and walk or ride. For a taxi, call ☎ 150 15.

BAYREUTH

- *pop 72,000*
- *area code* ☎ 0921

Every year over 600,000 people vie, by computer drawing, for fewer than 60,000 seats to the Bayreuth (pronounced 'buy-ROYT') Richard Wagner Festival, started in 1876 by the cantankerous composer himself and now a pilgrimage for die-hard fans.

Bayreuth was first mentioned in 1194 as *Bairrute*, a name which roughly translated from old German means 'Bavarians clearing the forest'. It was the seat of margraves from 1514, but gained prominence after Margravine Wilhelmine, sister of Frederick the Great, was forced into a marriage to Margrave Friedrich, dashing her dreams of moving to London. Wilhelmine – herself a composer, artist, actress and writer – set to putting Bayreuth on the cultural map by inviting the finest artists, poets, composers and architects in Europe to come to court here.

Money was somebody else's problem, and by the time she finished, the city was home to some of the most spectacular (and spectacularly gaudy) examples of rococo and baroque architecture in Europe.

Orientation & Information

The train station is at the north-east corner of the Altstadt, which is ringed by the Hohenzollernring. The Festspielhaus, where the

Richard Wagner

Richard Wagner (1813-83) was born in Leipzig but spent the last years of his life in Bayreuth. He arrived on 24 April 1872 from Switzerland with his wife, Cosima. With the financial backing of loony Ludwig II, his biggest patron and protector, Wagner built his spectacular house, Villa Wahnfried.

Wagner's operas, including *Götterdämmerung*, *Parsifal*, *Tannhäuser*, and *Tristan and Isolde*, are powerful pieces supporting his grandiose belief that listening to opera should be work (*Ring of the Nibelungs* is literally four days long), not a social affair, and that music carries messages about life that are too important to ignore.

Wagner designed his own festival hall in Bayreuth. The acoustic architecture in the hall is as bizarre as his works are popular. The orchestra performs beneath the stage, and reflecting boards and surfaces send the sound up and onto the stage, where it bounces from the wall behind the singers and, mixed with the singers' voices, finally makes its way to the house. If you're scratching your head right now, visit the model of the stage and pit in the Wagner Museum.

Wagner is also well known for his reprehensible personal qualities: he was a notorious womaniser, an infamous anti-Semite and a hard-liner towards 'non-Europeans'. So extreme were these views that even fun-loving Friedrich Nietzsche called Wagner's works 'inherently reactionary, and inhumane'. Wagner's works – and by extension he himself – were embraced as a symbol of Aryan might by the Nazis, and even today there is great debate among music lovers about the 'correctness' of supporting Wagnerian music and the Wagner Festival in Bayreuth. ■

Wagner Festival is held, is on the hill north of the Altstadt. The city tourist information office (☎ 885 88) is at Luitpoldplatz 9, right in the centre of the Altstadt. The main drags are Richard-Wagner-Strasse and Maximilianstrasse, which is also the Markt.

The post office is next to the tourist office. Also in the tourist office are ticket agents for local concerts and opera (but not the Wagner Festival), and Bayreuth Travel which has good deals on cheap flights in addition to standard package offerings.

Things to See & Do

Visiting is a bit of a Catch-22: there's little happening outside the Wagner Festival in June-July, at which time the place is booked solid.

Always worth a look is the amazing **Markgräfliches Opernhaus** (☎ 759 69 22), on Opernstrasse. Built from 1744 to 1748, the stunning baroque masterpiece was Germany's largest opera house until 1871. Richard Wagner deemed the place too quaint for his serious work, and conducted here just once, a performance of Beethoven's 9th symphony. You can visit on guided tours only from April to September daily from 9 to 11.30 am and 1.30 to 4.30 pm, in winter from 10 to 11.30 am and 1.30 to 3 pm. Tours run every half-hour.

Wilhelmine's **Neues Schloss** (☎ 759 69 21) and the **Hofgarten** are now open as museums of the margraves' residence, open April to September from 10 to 11.20 am and 1.30 to 4.10 pm, in winter to 2.50 pm. This is the site of the annual opening celebrations of the Wagner Festival.

To find out more about Wagner, visit the **Richard Wagner Museum** (☎ 757 28), in Haus Wahnfried, Richard-Wagner-Strasse 48. The composer had this lovely home built with money sent by Ludwig II, and it was worth every pfennig. Inside is the composer's death mask, information about his alternative lifestyle (his many mistresses, his temper etc) and marks showing his true and stated height. It's open daily from 10 am to 5 pm (to 8.30 pm on Tuesday and Thursday); admission is DM4. CDs of Wagner's music are played at 10 am, noon and 2 pm. In the garden is a second house containing the **German Freemason's Museum**, open Tuesday to Friday from 10 am to noon and 2 to 4 pm, Saturday from 10 am to noon.

Outside the city (take bus No 2, which departs from Markt every 20 minutes) is the **Eremitage** and **Altes Schloss**, two lovely palaces and an enormous formal garden along with a 'pre-aged' grotto. The whole thing was a gift to Wilhelmine from her husband in 1735. The grounds had been built in 1714 by Margrave Georg Willhelm as a retreat, but Wilhelmine turned them into a pleasure palace.

Special Events

The Wagner Festival has been held every summer for over 120 years. The festival lasts 30 days, and a different Wagner opera is played every night for an audience of 1900. Demand is insane, and the board that runs the event has no mercy – the festival chairman, by the way, is Wolfgang Wagner, the composer's grandson. The enrolment process is quirky, and it takes an average of seven years to score tickets. To apply for ticket enrolment, send a letter (no phone, fax or email) to the Bayreuther Festspiele, Kartenbüro, Postfach 1 00262, 95402 Bayreuth, before September of the year before you want to attend. When you've done it once, you're (allegedly) automatically entered every year until you 'win'.

Places to Stay & Eat

Everything, even the hostel, is booked out well in advance of the Wagner Festival. The *DJH hostel* (☎ 251 26 2), Universitätsstrasse 28 south of the centre (bus No 11 or 18), is new and shiny; beds go for DM20, plus DM5.50 for linen. You can camp outside in summer.

Just north-east of the centre, *Gasthof Hammerstatt* (☎ 228 26), Friedrich-Ebert-Strasse 9, has simple singles/doubles for DM50/92. The perfectly located *Hotel Goldener Hirsch* (☎ 230 46), right in the centre at Bahnhofstrasse 13, has nice singles/doubles from DM90/130. Nearby, the *Akzent Hotel* (☎ 880 70) in the Kolpinghaus, Kolpingstrasse 5, has similar rooms from DM95/130.

Iskendel Kebab, a little kiosk around the corner from the tourist information centre, does good doner for DM4.50. *Hulinsky*, with branches at Richard-Wagner-Strasse 13 and 25, has incredible breads, pizzas, sandwiches and wine for dirt-cheap prices. The *Café* in the orangery at the Eremitage is a very nice place to sit and have pots of coffee (DM5.50, DM6.50 spiked with grappa). There's a beer garden at the southern end of the park, and an expensive restaurant, said to be very good.

Back in the centre, *Wolffenzacher* (☎ 645 52), Badstrasse 1, has enormous portions of Grillhax'n (barbecued thigh, usually pork) for DM13, and good salads.

Getting There & Away

Bayreuth is well served by rail connections from Nuremberg (DM23, one hour), Munich (DM89, three hours) and Regensburg (DM51, 2½ hours).

ALTMÜHLTAL NATURE PARK

In the south of Franconia, the Altmühl River very gently meanders through a region of little valleys and hills before joining the Rhine-Main Canal and emptying into the Danube at Kelheim. In 1969, a 3000-sq-km area was set aside as Germany's largest nature park; its main information centre is in the city of Eichstätt, a charming town at the southern end of the park that makes an excellent base for exploring.

German national parks are areas of highly controlled and extremely limited activity designed entirely to protect wildlife and its habitat. But nature parks are less protected areas designed to preserve the cultural heritage within their borders. For all intents and purposes, the parks are just well defined areas where you can enjoy the outdoors.

Altmühltal covers some of Bavaria's loveliest lands, but it's absolutely undiscovered by non-Germans. Some 90% of visitors are domestic, and about 5% more are from German-speaking countries.

You can explore on your own via extremely well organised and marked hiking and biking trails, or canoe for an hour or several days. There's free basic camping in several areas along the river, and camping grounds throughout the region, along with hotels, pensions, guesthouses and hostels.

Several companies offer services that allow you to pick up canoes in one part of the park and drop them off in another; if you feel like paying for it, they'll schlep your bags for you, too, so you can go without the weight. If you prefer company, you can sign on to any number of organised bike or canoe tours that include accommodation, transfers and itineraries.

Orientation
The park takes in the area just south-west of Regensburg, south of Nuremberg, east of Treuchtlingen and north of Eichstätt. The eastern boundaries of the park actually include the town of Kelheim and the Klosterschenke Weltenburg (see the Around Regensburg section later this chapter).

Eichstätt, about a half-hour train ride north of Ingolstadt, sits about halfway between Kelheim and Gunzenhausen (at the north-west end of the park and the start of the Altmühl canoe trails). The river flows from west to east. There are bus and train connections between Eichstätt and all the major milestones along the river, including, from west to east, Gunzenhausen, Treuchtlingen and Pappenheim.

North of the river, the activities focus around the towns of Kipfenberg, Beilngries and Riedenburg.

Planning a Trip
The Informationszentrum Naturpark Altmühltal (☎ 08421-987 60; fax 987 65 4), Notre Dame 1, 85072 Eichstätt, is a font of excellent information. They can put together an entire itinerary for free and send you (for face value) maps and charts of the area, information on bike, boat and car rental, and lists of hotels, camping sites and guesthouses throughout the park – but they won't reserve rooms.

The information centre is also a very good museum of the park's wildlife and habitats, complete with a recreation of landscapes in its garden. It also sells the incorrectly titled *Altmühl Valley National Park*, an English guidebook to the area for DM9.80; though it's dated in terms of contact information, it's good on basics. There's a German version as well.

Get in touch as soon as you know you'll be visiting, so you can plan the best way for you.

Activities
Canoeing The most beautiful section of the river is from Treuchtlingen or Pappenheim to Eichstätt or Kipfenberg, about a 60km stretch that you can do lazily in two to three days. There are lots of little dams along the way, as well as a few fun little pseudo-rapids about 10km north-west of Dollnstein. Signs warn of impending doom, but tourist officials say that if you heed the warning to stay to the right, these little canoe slides are pretty safe.

Tours San-Aktiv Tours (☎ 09831-493 6; fax 805 94), Nürnberger Strasse 48, 91710 Gunzenhausen, is the largest and best organised canoe-rental company in the park, with a network of vehicles to shuttle canoes, bicycles and people around the area. They run canoe packages through the park from April to October for three, five and seven days.

You can do it alone or join a group. Prices start at DM229 per person for three days including boats, maps, instructions, two nights lodging in guesthouses (DM299 if you stay in hotels) and transport from the meeting point.

Natour (☎ 09142-961 10), Am Schulhof 1, 91757 Treuchtlingen, is another package canoe-trip operator, with similar trips and prices.

Rental Friendly, English-speaking Frank Warmuth runs Fahrradgarage (☎ 08421-676 76 9; mobile ☎ 0161-290 74 65), Herzoggasse 3 in Eichstätt, which rents four-person canoes for DM50 per day including insurance, paddles, life-vests, and a waterproof box for your clothes, and will haul you and the boats for varying prices (for example, DM37.80 from Eichstätt to Dollnstein, about 25km upstream), or just the canoe for a flat DM1 per km between Eichstätt and the drop-off point. It's open daily, including Sunday.

There are canoe-rental stands in every

town within the park, and prices are uniform; you can get a list of rental outlets from the Informationszentrum Naturpark Altmühltal.

Cycling & Hiking Bicycle trails throughout the park are very clearly labelled with long, rectangular brown signs bearing a bike symbol. Hiking-trail markers are yellow, and perhaps even better marked.

Rental Fahrradgarage (see above) rents bicycles for DM12 per day, and *Trettroller*, sort of a super high-tech push-scooter with handlebars and brakes, for DM5 per hour. They'll bring the bikes to you or bring you with the bikes to anywhere in the park on the same conditions as for canoes (see above).

There are bicycle-rental stands in every town within the park, and prices are uniform; you can get a list of rental outlets from the Informationszentrum Naturpark Altmühltal. Most bike-rental agencies will also store bicycles; Fahrradgarage charges DM1 per hour or DM3 per day.

Camping

Bootrast Platz are absolutely bare-boned camping facilities along the Altmühl River and Rhine-Main Canal that have no services (no water, electricity, toilets or showers) but are usually within walking distance of a town centre or public transport connection. Ostensibly, there's a one-day limit on stays but that's half-heartedly enforced.

The camping grounds are clearly marked on better maps of the park, available from the Informationszentrum Naturpark Altmühltal. The information centre can also send you a booklet with contact information for privately owned camping sites throughout the park, which charge an average of DM5 to DM7 per tent and DM6 to DM8 per person.

Getting There & Away

Bus On Saturday, Sunday and holidays from May to October, regional bus companies offer a bicycle transport service between Regensburg, Ingolstadt, Riedenburg, Kelheim, Beilngries, Eichstätt Stadtbahnhof, Kipfenberg and Wellheim. All-day tickets cost DM15 for passengers with bicycles, DM10 for passengers without, or DM35 per family with bikes, DM25 without. The service is run by several companies; routes and the companies that serve them are:

Regensburg-Kelheim-Riedenburg: RBO (☎ 0941-999 08 0)
Ingolstadt-Riedenburg-Beilngries: RBA (☎ 0841-973 74 0)
Wellheim-Eichstätt-Kipfenberg-Beilngries: Jägle (☎ 08421-972 10)

Train Trains run between Eichstätt Bahnhof and Treuchtlingen hourly or better (DM7, 25 minutes), and between Treuchtlingen and Gunzenhausen hourly (DM7, 15 minutes). Trains from Munich that run through Eichstätt Bahnhof also stop in Dollnstein, Solnhofen and Pappenheim.

Eichstätt

- *pop 13,000*
- *area code* ☎ 08421

Home to Bavaria's largest Catholic university, Eichstätt's buildings and streets haven't been damaged since Swedes stormed and razed the place during the Thirty Years' War. With several pleasant attractions, in addition to a great hostel and several guesthouses, Eichstätt makes a perfect base for exploring Altmühltal as it lies completely within the park. Note that businesses in Eichstätt close between noon and 2 pm.

Orientation There are two train stations. The Bahnhof, 5km from the centre, is the hub for trains between the Stadtbahnhof (south of the Altmühl River near the city centre) and everywhere on earth. From the Stadtbahnhof, Willibaldsburg is due south up Burgstrasse, uphill for about 10 minutes. For the hostel, take Burgstrasse to Reichenaustrasse and turn right; it's about four minutes ahead on the left side of the road.

The city centre is on the north side of the Altmühl. From the Stadtbahnhof, walk north across the Spitalbrücke and you'll end up in Domplatz.

For the tourist and nature park information offices, continue east at Domplatz to

Ostenstrasse and then turn left on Kardinal-Preysing-Platz.

Information The city's fabulous tourist information office (☎ 988 00), Kardinal-Preysing-Platz 14, in the Kloster of Notre Dame, is open Monday to Saturday from 9 am to 6 pm, Sunday from 10 am to noon. It has more pamphlets and information than you'd think possible. The Informationszentrum Naturpark Altmühltal is in the same building. Change money at the Dresdner Bank, Westendstrasse 1 at Markt. The central (and only) post office is at Domplatz 7.

Universitäts Buchhandlung Sporer (☎ 153 8), Gabrielstrasse 4, has English books. The Universitätsbibliothek (☎ 931 41 4) is in the Ulmer Hof, Pater-Philipp-Jeningen-Platz 6.

Katholische Universität Eichstätt (☎ 930), Ostenstrasse 26 just east of the tourist office next to Café Fuchs, has about 4000 students studying theology, geography, languages and philosophy.

In an emergency, contact the regional hospital, the Kreiskrankenhaus (☎ 601 0), at Ostenstrasse 31.

Willibaldsburg The hill-top castle of Willibaldsburg (1355-1725) is home to two museums: the **Jura-Museum Eichstätt** (DM5, discount DM4), with a fascinating collection of fossils collected within the region as well as other geological and natural history exhibits, and the **Museum of Pre-History & Early History**. Don't miss the 76.5m-deep **well** downstairs – toss in a coin and listen for about 10 seconds for the ting or the plop. There are baroque and Renaissance concerts in the castle **courtyard** in summer.

Looking out over the valley, you'll see the **Kloster Rebdorf**, now also a boys' boarding school, which contains a splendid baroque church and some of Germany's most interesting arcades. At the hill top, you'll also see the **limestone quarry**, a favourite spot for locals to go looking for fossils.

If you happened to forget your hammer and chisel, fear not: rent them at the **Museum Bergér** (☎ 468 3), at the base of the quarry, which displays a lot of geological samples itself; it's open Monday to Saturday from 1 to 5 pm, Sunday from 10 am to noon and 1 to 5 pm. Chisel and hammer rental is DM2 per day.

Kloster St Walburga After the death of Walburga, sister of Eichstätt's first bishop, her body was brought back here and buried in the Heilige Kreuz Kirche, now the Kloster St Walburga. You can go inside the church, at the north-west end of town, on Westenstrasse just south of the city's spectacular **fortifications**, and see the crypt. About once a year, a mysterious oily substance oozes forth from the crypt; nuns here bottle the goo and give it away as balm. It's free – just ask for a little Walburgis Öl.

City Centre The highlight of the city, other than the spectacular churches and buildings designed by architects Gabriel de Gabrieli and Maurizio Pedetti, is the **Dom**, containing an enormous stained-glass window by Hans Holbein the Elder, and its prize, the **Pappenheimer Altar** (1489-97), intricately carved from sandstone and depicting a pilgrimage from Pappenheim to Jerusalem. The detail is so amazing it's worth an hour.

Behind the Dom, in **Residenzplatz**, crowned by a golden statue of Mary atop a 19m-high column, is the **Residenz** (1725-36), a Gabrieli building with a stunning main staircase and the **Spiegelsaal** with its mirrors and a fresco of Greek mythological figures. You can visit on free tours Monday to Thursday at 11 am and 2 pm, and there are concerts here about 10 times a year.

Walk through **Markt**, noting **Café Im Paradeis**, a beautifully restored building with elements from 1313 and 1453 that's open to the public as a museum – just walk through. Continue up Westenstrasse, past the **Maria-Hilfe-Kapelle**, and you'll pass a moss-covered **water wheel**; turn right on Kapellbuck and you'll find the little **carp pond**, with hundreds of carp being fattened up for pre-Easter celebrations. Feed them for 20pf a handful.

Organised Tours The tourist office gives 1½-hour walking tours (DM5, kids under 12 free) at 1.30 pm on Saturday from April to October.

The tourist office in Treuchtlingen (☎ 09142-312 1) runs a bus tour to the eastern Altmühle Valley every Tuesday (DM30) that leaves at 9.20 am from the police station, opposite the Stadtbahnhof. The bus goes to Kelheim, where you get on a boat to the Weltenburg Monastery (see the Around Regensburg section later in this chapter).

Places to Stay & Eat *Bootsrastplatz Aumühle* (no telephone), on the north side of the Altmühle River, is a free camping ground with toilets but no washing facilities. From the Stadtbahnhof take a Green, Yellow or Red Line bus to Römerstrasse (Krankenhaus stop) and walk south along Universitätsallee.

The *hostel* (☎ 980 40), Reichenaustrasse 15, is a modern place in a good location, with dorm beds for DM22, but you can only book from 8 am to noon and 5 to 7 pm Monday to Friday – and they're frequently booked out with schoolgroups. The hostel is closed December and January.

Gasthof Sonne (☎ 679 1), Buchtal 17, is a perfectly pleasant place with clean rooms (though they're stingy with soap and shampoo), friendly service and singles/doubles from DM60/100. The best thing about the place is the *restaurant*, where we had a really good steak for DM21.

There's a barbecue grill in the Zentrale Park Platz (Green, Yellow or Red Line bus lines to Volkfest Platz), where the city is considering placing a more formal camp site.

There's fast food on Markt at *Metzgerei Schneider*, which is open all day, and there are *markets* held here on Wednesday and Saturday mornings.

Getting There & Away There's hourly service or better between Ingolstadt and Eichstätt (DM7, 25 minutes). For more connections, see Getting There & Away earlier in this Altmühltal Nature Park section.

Eastern Bavaria

A cluster of romantic ancient cities lies in the north-east of the state, stretching from Regensburg to the Czech border. Regensburg is one of Germany's loveliest and liveliest cities, and a bicycle ride from there along the Danube to Passau (about 120km away), where it converges with the Inn and Ilz rivers, is a very rewarding journey.

REGENSBURG

- *pop 132,000*
- *area code* ☎ 0941

An undisturbed gem on the Danube River, Regensburg has relics of all periods yet it lacks the packaged feel of some other German cities. Romans settled here in 179 AD, and the city's Roman, medieval and later landmarks – over 1400 protected landmarks in the city alone – escaped the fate of carpet bombing. Here, as nowhere else in Germany, you enter the misty ages between the Roman and the Carolingian.

The patrician tower-houses in the city's centre are as arresting as the populace is friendly and unspoiled – even by the relatively large hordes of tourists they see each year. Oskar Schindler lived in the city for years, and now one of his houses bears a plaque to him and his recently celebrated accomplishments.

Regensburg is pretty much a must on any Bavarian itinerary, and if you do come you must not, under any circumstances, miss sampling one of the best food products in Germany: *Händlmaier's Susser Hausmachersenf*, the world's best sweet mustard, made to go with another city speciality, *Regensburger bratwurstl*. Wash it all down with a locally made Kneipinger Pils and you have the makings of a beautiful day in Regensburg.

Orientation

The city is divided by the east-flowing Danube, separating the Altstadt, on the southern side, from the newer northern banks. Islands in the middle of the river,

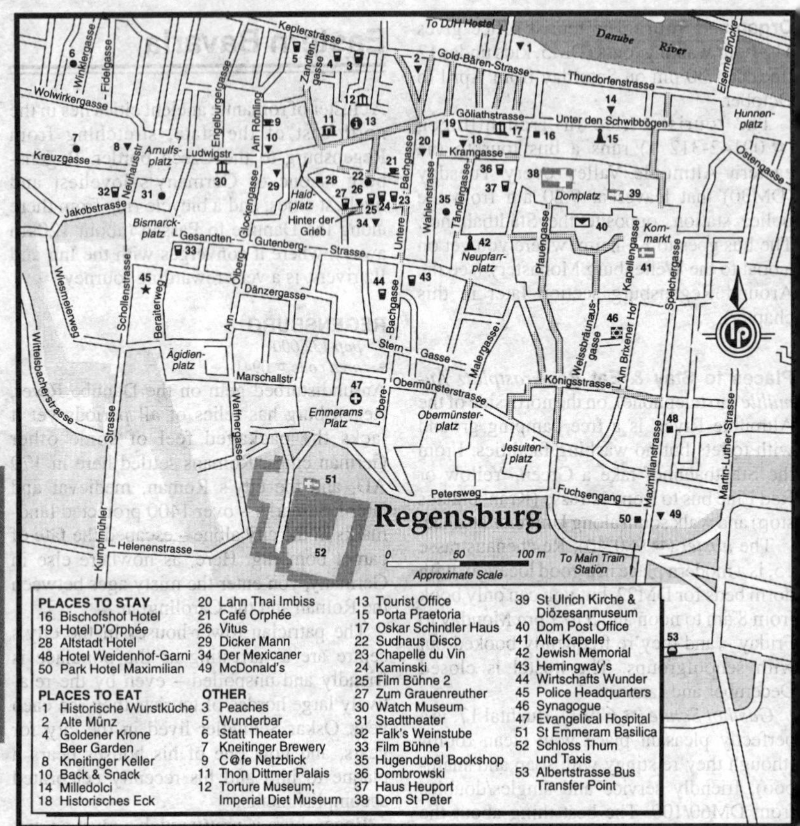

mainly Oberer and Unterer Wöhrd, are populated as well; the hostel is on Unterer Wöhrd, east of the Steinerne Brücke.

The Hauptbahnhof is at the southern end of the Altstadt. Maximilianstrasse leads straight north from there to Kornmarkt, at the centre of the historic district.

The twisting, pedestrianised streets of the Altstadt are closed to cars, but not buses.

Information

Tourist Offices The tourist office (☎ 507 44 10) is in the Altes Rathaus and is open Monday to Friday from 8.30 am to 6 pm, Saturday from 9 am to 4 pm, Sunday and holidays from 9.30 am to 2.30 pm (from April to October to 4 pm); closed New Year's Day.

Ask about the *Verbundkarte* (DM10, DM5 discount, DM20 per family), giving free entry to four of the city's main museums.

The ADAC has an office (☎ 0180-510 11 12) at Luitpoldstrasse 12.

Money Change money at the Postbank next to the Hauptbahnhof. There are also several banks along Maximilianstrasse, and a Vereinsbank at Pfarrplatz.

Post & Communications The central post office is adjacent to the Hauptbahnhof, but the de facto main branch is the lovely Dom post office at Domplatz, in the former ducal court opposite the south side of the Dom.

Online Services C@fe Netzblick (☎ 599 97 00), Am Römling 9, is a fun Internet café; surf or mail for DM5 per half-hour, DM10 per hour, DM79 per 10 hours. It's open from 10 am to 1 am in winter, 7 pm to 1 am in summer.

Bookshops & Libraries Get English books and magazines at the Hauptbahnhof's International Presse stand. Hugendubel (☎ 585 32 0), Wahlenstrasse 17 (with another entrance on Tändlergasse), has the usual good collection of English and travel books (including Lonely Planet titles) and a reading area. The Stadtbucherei (city library; ☎ 507 24 70) is at Haidplatz 8 in the Thon Dittmer Palais.

Campuses Viertelandes Universität (☎ 943 1) has its campus at the southern end of the city. Its approximately 20,000 students are enrolled in major schools including theology, economics, medicine, philosophy and mathematics. Take bus No 11 to the Universität stop.

International Centres The Deutsche-Americanisches Institute (☎ 524 76), Haidplatz 8 in the Thon Dittmer Palais, has a good range of cultural programmes and events.

Laundry There's a large and clean Schnell & Sauber coin laundry at Herrmann-Geib-Strasse 5, at the corner of Landshuter. Other laundrettes are at Winklergasse 14 and at Hoffgartenweg 4.

Medical Services The largest hospital close to the centre is the Evangelisches Krankenhaus (☎ 504 0) at Emmerams Platz, near the Schloss Thurn und Taxis and the Hauptbahnhof.

Dom St Peter

Dominating the skyline are the twin spires of Dom St Peter, considered one of Bavaria's most important cathedrals. Constructed, on the site of four previous churches, between 1275 and 1520, its distinctive jet-black grime layer was sandblasted in 1997 to reveal for the first time in centuries the green sandstone and limestone façade you now see.

Inside the dark, cavernous church, you'll immediately see the cathedral's most prized possessions, its richly hued original 13th and 14th-century **stained-glass windows**, above the choir on the east side. These, along with the 13th to 15th-century windows on the south side, positively embarrass the 19th-century glass at the west.

Just west of the altar are two more of the cathedral's prizes: the **statues** – *The Smiling Angel of Regensburg*, his charming mug beaming at *Mary* (on the north pillar) as he delivers the news that she's pregnant.

At the west exit (you'll have to look hard unless crowds of tourists beat you there), note the **statuettes:** *Satan* and *Satan's Grandmother*, both reminders that outside these walls bad things await. Especially if you don't make a donation.

Alte Kapelle

Around the corner from the Dom, the Alte Kapelle (8th to 15th centuries) has such an unbelievably lavish rococo interior that each person we saw walk in audibly gasped. Just emerging from renovations, it's amazing.

Schloss

The family castle, **Schloss Thurn und Taxis** (pronounced 'Torn und TAK-siss') has been handed down over the generations since Franz von Taxis (1459-1517) established the international postal system throughout Western Europe. Taxis ran the post until 1867 when ownership passed to Prussia.

The castle is near the Hauptbahnhof, and is divided into three expensive and separate sections: the castle proper (Schloss), the monastery (Kreuzgang) and the royal stables (Marstall). A combined ticket for all three

BAVARIA

costs DM17 (students DM12); you need to be a part of a guided tour except in the Marstall; tours, of course, are in German only. For tours in English (minimum of DM120 for up to 30 people) call ☎ 504 81 33. If you're happy about handing over up to DM17 to one of Germany's richest and most reclusive people – former brewer Duchess Gloria von Thurn und Taxis – this place is for you (photos of the duchess looking stern and businesslike are DM2 at the gift shop).

St Emmeram Nearby, St Emmeram Basilika is a baroque masterpiece of the Asam brothers containing untouched Carolingian and Episcopal graves and relics (free entry).

Jewish Memorials

Regensburg's Jewish community was well established by the early 16th century, and Jews found a 'protector' in Emperor Maximilian. But on Maximilian's death in 1519, the Jews were summarily expelled from the city; angry mobs burned the Jewish ghetto to the ground and destroyed, piece by piece, the synagogue, which had been in the area of today's Neupfarrplatz. The square was named for the church that was erected on the site of the synagogue practically before the fires had gone out.

The city has recently undertaken archaeological work and uncovered the foundation of the synagogue and several of the houses and is working to create a monument to Regensburg's Jewish community.

On the north side of the Steinerne Brücke is a memorial to concentration-camp victims.

Museums

Diözesanmuseum The painted medieval church of St Ulrich houses a collection of religious art. It's at Domplatz 2 (open from April to October, except Monday). Admission is DM3, or DM5 when combined with a visit to the cathedral's **treasury**.

Historical Museum The city's historical museum (☎ 507 24 48), Dachauplatz 2-4, houses exhibits ranging from the Stone Age to the Middle Ages, and an art collection focusing on 14th and 15th-century handicrafts, painting and sculpture. There's also a large collection of Bavarian folklore, under renovation when we visited. It's open daily except Monday; admission is DM4/2.

Imperial Diet Museum The Altes Rathaus was progressively extended from medieval to baroque times and remained the seat of the Reichstag for almost 150 years (tours in English take place at 3.15 pm Monday to Saturday; DM5). Today, Regensburg's three mayors rule the city from here. In the Imperial Diet Museum (☎ 507 44 11), above the tourist office, you can see the Imperial Chamber, supported by the enormous original centre beam. The museum is closed Monday; admission is DM4/2.

Torture Museum Just beneath the tourist office are perhaps the last surviving original torture chambers in Germany – the reconstructed museum in Rothenburg ob der Tauber notwithstanding. Walk into the old holding cell and look down to the **dungeon** before entering the **torture chamber** where interrogations were carried out using tools like the **rack**, the **Spanish Donkey** (a tall wooden wedge on which naked men were made to sit), spiked chairs and other charming objects.

Watch Museum This breezy little privately owned museum (☎ 599 95 95), Ludwigstrasse 3, has a fabulous collection of valuable and notable watches, including the obvious stuff, from companies like Jaeger-LeCouitre, Patek Phillippe ... ahem ... Swatch, and what is billed as the most 'complicated and expensive in the world', the Blancpain 1735. Also look out for the world's first digital watch, the 1972 Pulsar. Admission is DM8/4, worth it if you're a watch nut.

Danube Navigation Museum The Donau-Schiffahrts-Museum (☎ 525 10), Werftstrasse on Unterer Wöhrd not far from the hostel, is a historic paddle-wheel steam tugboat moored on the Danube with exhibits on the history of navigation on the river. Admission is DM4/3 or DM8 per family. The museum is open from April to October daily from 10 am to 5 pm.

Kepler Tower

The astronomer and mathematician Johannes Kepler lived and died in the house at Keplerstrasse 5, which is now the **Kepler-Gedächtnishaus** (☎ 507 34 42), closed Mondays; admission DM4/2. Of more immediate concern these days is the wonderful beer garden behind the house – see Entertainment.

Roman Wall

The Roman wall, with its seriously impressive **Porta Praetoria** arch, dates to 179 AD. It follows Unter den Schwibbögen onto Dr-Martin-Luther-Strasse and is the most tangible reminder of the ancient Castra Regina (Roman fortress), whence the name 'Regensburg' comes.

Stone Bridge

The Steinerne Brücke (1135-46), the oldest in Germany, remains one of the most flabbergasting accomplishments of medieval architecture: until recently the 850-year-old bridge supported vehicular traffic. Today, in an effort to conserve it, the city has banned all private vehicles, to the great consternation of car owners on the north bank of the Danube.

Canoeing & Kayaking

There are lots of canoeing and kayaking opportunities in the area. San-Aktiv Tours (☎ 09831-493 6; fax 805 94), Nürnberger Strasse 48, 91710 Gunzenhausen, runs full-blown canoe packages through the Altmühltal Nature Park – see the earlier Altmühtal Nature Park section.

Christian Platzeck of Nautilus Canoes (☎ 09401-512 95; mobile ☎ 0172 851 69 13; fax 655 2) can hook you up with a kayak, or a three or four-person canoe, and set you loose on any number of journeys along the Regen, Naab or Vils rivers for a day, weekend or week. The cost per day is DM30/50/60 per kayak/three-person canoe/four-person canoe, DM60/100/120 per weekend and DM120/200/240 per week including boat, paddles, life-vests, maps and advice. His address is Embacher Strasse 10, 93803 Niedertraubling, south-east of Regensburg on the B15 towards Landshut. Take one of the very regular trains (DM3, six minutes) to Obertraubling and he'll meet you.

Kanu Tours (☎ 09964-109 3), Irschenbach 50, 94353 Haibach, rents the same types of boats for DM30/60/70 per day.

Organised Tours

Walking tours of the Altstadt in German (DM8/4; 1½ hours) are run by the tourist office and take place all year Monday to Saturday at 2.45 pm (Saturday an extra tour at 10.15 am), Sunday and holidays at 10 am and 2 pm. Meet at the tourist office. From April to October they add an extra tour Monday to Friday at 10.15 am. English tours are available as well; call ☎ 341 3 for information.

Ferry cruises depart from the landing near the Steinerne Brücke from late March to late October hourly from 10 am to 4 pm; the fare is DM10/7.

BAVARIA

Places to Stay & Eat

Camping Camp at the *Azur-Campingplatz* (☎ 270 02 5), Am Weinweg 40 (adults DM10 plus DM13 site fee if you have a car, DM7 if you don't, DM4 per motorcycle). It's at the north-west end of the city just south of the Danube; from the Hauptbahnhof take bus No 6 right to the entrance.

Hostels The *DJH hostel* (☎ 574 02), at Wöhrdstrasse 60, on Unterer Wöhrd east of the Steinerne Brücke, costs DM22 (juniors only; closed all of December). Its location is perfect. From the station, take bus No 3 from the Albertstrasse stop to the Eisstadion stop.

Private Rooms Get a list of private flats from the tourist office. There's a city Mitwohnzentrale (☎ 220 24) as well.

Pensions & Hotels – bottom end *Hotel Spitalgarten* (☎ 847 74), at St-Katherinen-Platz 1, has singles/doubles from DM40/80. The *Diözesanzentrum Obermünster* (☎ 568 12 49) has simple rooms from DM50/80 to DM95; ring ahead if you can't arrive before 5 pm.

Gaststätte Roter Hahn (☎ 595 09 0), Rote-Hahnen-Gasse 10, and *Hotel Peterhof* (☎ 575 14), at Fröhliche-Türken-Strasse 12, have simple rooms from around DM48/80 a single/double.

Hotel D'Orphée (☎ 596 02 0), Wahlenstrasse 1 right around the corner from the tourist office, is a pleasure to recommend. Each room is unique and it's a lot cheaper than it should be: simple singles upstairs start at DM60, but the stunningly romantic room No 7 is DM90/105 and worth it. Downstairs rooms have baths (room No 5's bathroom entrance is hidden in a secret door) and range from DM125/140 to DM150/180. There's a very nice common room downstairs with a large terrace, and breakfast is a block away at the Café Orphée – see Places to Eat.

A friend recommended the cheerful *Hotel Weidenhof-Garni* (☎ 530 31), Maximilianstrasse 23. It's a recently renovated place with friendly staff and as good a location as the expensive Park Hotel (see below) at a fraction of the price: clean, simple singles start from DM65; rooms with bathrooms are DM90/135.

Another good deal on simple rooms is at the *Hotel Karmeliten* (☎ 546 58), Dachauplatz 1, east of the Dom. Simple rooms start from DM80/120; rooms with bath and toilet from DM120/170.

Hotels – middle The city's two *Ibis* hotels, the *Castra Regina* (☎ 569 30), Bahnhofstrasse 22, and the *Furtmayr* (☎ 780 40), Furtmayrstrasse 1, both at the Hauptbahnhof, post rack rates of DM104/119 and DM111/136 respectively, but you can get rooms from DM89 (for a single) by asking.

The *Bischofshof Hotel* (☎ 590 86), Krauterermarkt 3, looks dreary from the outside but rooms are nicer than you'd think and, for its location right by the Steinerne Brücke, cheaper, too: singles/doubles from DM110/195. Some rooms are located within the Roman walls – nice touch, eh?

The *Altstadt Hotel* (☎ 586 60), Haidplatz 4, is another city landmark that's been around forever; rooms range from DM115/160.

Hotels – top end The modern and shining *Sorat Insel-Hotel* (☎ 810 40; fax 810 44 44), Müllerstrasse 7 on Oberer Wöhrd, has a totally awesome location at the island's tip and great views of the town's skyline; rooms start from DM200/240.

The *Park Hotel Maximilian* (☎ 568 50; fax 529 42), Maximilianstrasse 28, employs old-world European charm. They'll charm you right out of DM218/268, too.

Places to Eat

Cafés & Restaurants The Historische Wurstküche (see boxed text titled Regensburg's No 1 Sausage Stop) may have a lock on the tourist trade in bratwurstl, but locals know that the best place to get the little links is the *Kneitinger Keller* (☎ 524 55), Arnulfsplatz 3. Walk around the corner onto Kreuzgasse for a peep into the window of their

Regensburg's No 1 Sausage Stop

The Historische Wurstküche, at the southern end of the Steinerne Brücke, has been serving up *Regensburger bratwurstl* on beds of sauerkraut since the Stone Age. Every tourist and local ends up here eventually, and while the sausages and kraut aren't nearly as good as they could be, and while the mustard isn't Handlmaier's but rather a generic brand, *and* while the place gets packed in summer, its lovely riverside setting and age-old tradition is still worth a shot.

Grab a bench outside and tell the waiter you want six (DM7.80) or eight (DM10.40). The delicious *schwarze gibferl* (rye and caraway seed) rolls that are on the table cost 70pf a pop, and they, along with the beer (DM4.40 for Pils, DM4.60 for Weiss), are the best thing about the place. Note the high-water marks on the walls inside and outside the outdoor kitchen. ■

brewery and then sit down to the best saussies around (DM8). There's a Bierstüberl here as well, though the atmosphere is a lot seedier.

The *Hinterhaus*, in a roofed-over lane at Rote-Hahnen-Gasse 2, serves vegetarian and meat dishes from DM10. *Der Mexikaner* (☎ 515 99), Hinter der Grieb 5, attempts Mexican – locals say it's good.

There's dependably good local food at the *Dicker Mann* (☎ 573 70), Krebsgasse 6, with real Bavarian dishes all averaging DM12 to DM15, good service and a little beer garden. Also great for solid Bavarian specialities (good steaks, too) is the *Alte Münz* (☎ 548 86), Fischmarkt 7. It has a friendly atmosphere – lots of wood and booze bottles – and nice service. The place smells heavenly.

Just across the river at Müllerstrasse 1, the *Alte Linde* (☎ 880 80; closed Wednesday) serves fairly routine, well prepared food but it's more of a beer garden – see Entertainment.

Café Orphée (☎ 529 77), Untere Bachgasse 8, is as French as De Gaulle; very nice breakfasts for two are DM16.80 and include fresh fruit, crêpes, croissant and coffee. Sweet crêpes are around DM8, meat and vegetable crêpes are DM11, and main courses start from DM15.

Vitus (☎ 526 46), Hinter der Grieb 8, is a hugely popular café-bar, with very big salads from DM5 to DM13, quiche from DM8.50, and expensive meat dishes from DM17.

Probably the finest restaurant in town is the *Historisches Eck* (☎ 589 20), Watmarkt 6, which does amazing (and amazingly expensive) French food in a lovely setting with fine service. An eight-course menu costs DM120 per person, and the entire menu changes seasonally. Count on prices averaging DM24 to DM27 per starter, DM39 to DM44 for fish main courses, and DM39 to DM74 for meat dishes. Too rich? Stop off for one of their signature desserts, like apple or apricot maultaschen served in a berry cream sauce for a mere DM17.

Snacks & Fast Food There are several *McDonald's* in town including one on Maximilianstrasse two blocks north of the Hauptbahnhof that serves breakfast. *Back & Snack*, Haidplatz 5, does good baked treats, as does the *bakery* in the Hauptbahnhof right next to the exit to the tracks – with huge ham and cheese sandwiches for DM3.90.

For an orgasmic taste treat, head to *Milledolci* (☎ 515 95), on Unter den Schwibbögen opposite the Porta Praetoria, for Italian coffee and pastries, including the scrumptious chocolate and ricotta cheesecake.

The very good *Lahn Thai Imbiss* (☎ 563 89 7), Untere Bachgasse 1, does good, cheap Thai meals, like red curry or sweet and sour chicken, from DM8.50, and soups and spring rolls for DM3. More Asian fast food is available nearby at *Little Saigon* (☎ 567 75 2), which despite its name does fast Chinese food.

The *Dampfnudelküche*, in a medieval tower at Am Watmarkt 4, serves steamed doughnuts with custard (DM7.80), a local speciality of Regensburg; it's closed after 6 pm, and all day Sunday and Monday.

Entertainment

Listings The city publishes a seasonal *Kultur in Regensburg* guide, available at the tourist office (free). For gay information contact Rosa Hilfe (☎ 514 41), a gay switchboard service; lesbians can contact the lesbian group Frauenzentrum (☎ 242 59).

Cinema English-language films are screened regularly at *Film im Dai* (☎ 524 76), at the Deutsche-Americanisches Institute, Haidplatz 8.

Disco The *Sudhaus Disco* (☎ 519 46), Untere Bachgasse 8, in the basement in the little alley, is a very popular place, straight except for gay Thursday night parties.

Theatre The Regensburg Städtische Bühnen (from September to July) runs the *Stadttheater*, Bismarckplatz 7, where drama and musicals are staged.

The *Theater Am Haidplatz*, at Haidplatz 8, is an open-air theatre venue in the courtyard of the Thon Dittmer Palais. The *Statt Theater*

(☎ 533 02), Winklergasse 16, is a privately owned venue that stages alternative dramas, plays and cabaret.

Classical Music Opera, operettas, ballet and classical-music performances are held at the *Stadttheater*. There are concerts of the Dom Spätzen boys' choir during Sunday services at the Dom, and classical concerts in lots of venues around town, including the baroque *Oswald-Kirche*, Weissgerbergraben 1 (just south of the pedestrian Eisener Steg bridge), the *Rathaus*, and the *Theater Am Haidplatz*.

Jazz The *Jazzclub Regensburg* (☎ 563 37 5), Bertoldstrasse 9, is open Tuesday to Sunday from 11 to 1 am and features regular live music.

Beer Gardens The city's loveliest beer garden is probably the tiny Keplergarten at the *Goldener Krone Biergarten* (☎ 560 63 5), Keplerstrasse 3. Walk through the long tunnel and emerge into a sweet little yard beneath a tower. The *Alte Linde* (also in Places to Eat) runs a large and leafy beer garden in view of the cathedral – lovely on summer evenings. *Zum Grauenreuther*, at the western end of Hinter der Grieb, has a nice beer garden; the same can be said for the *Bischofshof Hotel*, an excellent, if over touristed, choice.

Pubs & Bars *Haus Heuport* (☎ 599 92 97), Domplatz 7, is probably the most famous place in town. Visitors stop on the staircase to look (left) at the statuettes of a *Virgin* being tricked by *Temptation*; note Temptation's hollow robes in back – the Virgin is judging him only on appearance, not substance. On a lighter note, the bar is fun and friendly and has a great atmosphere. Next door, *Dombrowski* (☎ 573 88), Kramgasse 10-12, is a chic place with a nice sidewalk café.

Two well known but missable places are *Hemingway's* (☎ 561 50 6), Obere Bachgasse 6, and *Peaches*, on Keplerstrasse. Near Peaches is *Wunderbar*.

Wirtschafts Wunder, Obere Bachgasse 8, performs economic miracles Fridays from 8 pm, when all cocktails are DM6.50. There's a courtyard out back.

Three places worth crawling into or out of on Hinter der Grieb are the *Chapelle du Vin*, a wine cellar in the 13th-century Löblturm; *Kaminski*, sharp as a razor and peopled by a vain crowd; and the hugely popular *Vitus* (☎ 526 46).

Falk's Weinstube is in the lovely little white building next to the Stadttheater; across the street is one of the fiercely fashionable *Film Bühne*, where the elite meet.

Getting There & Away

Train Mainline trains run from Frankfurt through Regensburg on their way to Passau and Vienna (nine daily). Several Munich-Leipzig and Munich-Dresden services also pass through. Sample ticket prices are: Munich DM35 (1½ hours), Nuremberg DM37 (one hour), Passau DM42 (one hour).

Car & Motorcycle The A3 autobahn runs north-west to Nuremberg and south-east to Passau, while the A93 runs south to Munich and north towards Dresden.

Bicycle Regensburg is a key player on the Danube Bike Route; all approaches to the city are well signed along bike paths. There are bicycle lockers at the Hauptbahnhof on platform 1 (DM1 per day). Rent-a-Bike (☎ 0172-831 12 34), on Donaumarktplatz just east of the Dom, offers a variety of services, including bike storage and bike wash.

Ride Services For a lift, call the city Mitfahrzentrale (☎ 220 22).

Getting Around

Bus The main city bus transfer point is one block north of the Hauptbahnhof, on Albertstrasse. Other big transfer points include Arnulfsplatz, Domplatz and Neupfarrplatz. Bus tickets cost DM2.50/1.30; strip tickets cost DM10 for six rides (two strips per ride in the city).

Car & Motorcycle The Steinerne Brücke is

closed to private cars. To cross the river, you'll have to head east and work your way to Weissenburgstrasse, which becomes Nibelungenbrücke and leads to Nordgaustrasse. There's an exit from Nibelungenbrücke onto Unterer Wöhrd and the hostel.

The centre of the city is also closed to vehicles, but not buses and taxis. Car parks are very well signed.

Taxi Taxis cost DM4 flag fall plus DM2.50 per km. For a taxi, call ☎ 194 10, ☎ 570 00 or ☎ 520 52.

Bicycle Rent-a-Bike (☎ 0172-831 12 34), on Donaumarktplatz, has daily rental from Monday to Saturday. Children's bicycles cost DM10, touring bikes DM14, cruisers DM15, trekking bikes DM17 and tandems DM30. The seventh day is free. On Sundays and holidays there's also hourly rental, for DM3/5/6/7/10 per hour or DM7/10/11/12/20 for three hours. Staff also help plan bike trips along the Danube and in other regions.

Fahr Rad Laden (☎ 700 03 65), Furtmayrstrasse 12 two blocks south of the Hauptbahnhof, rents bikes for DM15 per day.

AROUND REGENSBURG

Weltenburg

- *pop 400*
- *area code* ☎ 09441

When you're this close to the world's oldest monastic brewery, there's just no excuse to miss out. Klosterschenke Weltenburg has been brewing its absolutely delicious dark beer since 1050. The hulking monastery (☎ 368 0), run by the Röhrl family since 1934, is set against the backdrop of the Danube Gorge, with dramatic hills and cliffs and rolling countryside. It also has a splendid baroque church built by the Asam brothers.

Only a half hour or so out of Regensburg, it's a favourite spot for Regensburgers (and now for hordes of tourists) at weekends in summer, who come by the boatload to sit in the beer garden and sample the beer (DM5 per half-litre and worth every pfennig). There are several beer halls, including a bierstube (the hard-to-get-into Asamstuberl), and one of the nicest beer gardens in the country.

The suds are served up daily from April to October from 8 am to 7 pm; in early November and late March hours are more limited.

Getting There & Away From Regensburg's Hauptbahnhof, grab one of the hourly trains to Kelheim (DM7, 24 minutes), which actually bring you to Saal (Danau), from where there's connecting bus service to Kelheim. In Kelheim, climb aboard one of the boats run by Personenschiffahrt Altmühltal (☎ 218 01); these travel from Kelheim to Kloster Weltenburg via Donaudurchbruch.

The schedule has four seasons within the March to November period, with more frequent service on weekends; suffice to say that between 10 am and 4 pm, there are boats at the very least every 1½ hours. The return fare is DM9, plus DM6 per bicycle. Family tickets are DM25 return.

INGOLSTADT

- *pop 100,000*
- *area code* ☎ 0841

Shunned by most as the industrial headquarters of the Audi car company, Ingolstadt is a fascinating little medieval city with beautiful streets and buildings, and a church museum with the largest flat fresco ever made, the masterpiece of Cosmas Damian Asam inside the Maria de Victoria church.

Ingolstadt is also home to one of the best hostels in Bavaria, a fascinating military museum, and the 'birthplace' of the Frankenstein monster, now the stunningly ghoulish Museum of the History of Medicine.

Local beer drinkers (read: the populace) are especially proud that Germany's Beer Purity Law of 1516 was issued in Ingolstadt. This demands an investigation, on the part of visitors, as to whether this claim to fame has affected the local brews, Herrnbräu, Nordbräu and Ingobräu.

Orientation

The Hauptbahnhof is 2.5km south-east of the city centre; bus Nos 10, 11, 15 and 16 make the trip every few minutes (DM2.70). The centre of the city is the Altstadt, roughly in the shape of a baseball diamond, with the Danube on the south side. The Altstadt's heart is formed at Am Stein, the convergence of its main north-south street, Harderstrasse, and its main east-west one, Theresienstrasse/Ludwigstrasse. Ludwigstrasse runs east from Harderstrasse to the Neue Schloss; Theresienstrasse runs west from Harderstrasse to the Kreuz Tor, west of which is the hostel.

The Audi factory is at the northern end of the city.

Information

The city-run tourist information office (☎ 305 10 98), Rathausplatz 4, has lots of pamphlets but staff won't tell you anything about the Audi museum or factory tour or any other 'private' information unless you insist. They also don't book private rooms.

Change money at the post offices next to the Hauptbahnhof, at Am Stein, or at one of the several banks (including Sparkasse, Raiffeisenbank and Dresdner Bank) at Rathausplatz.

Buy English books and copies of *Frankenstein* in any language (DM5 for English) at Schönhuber (☎ 934 50), Theresienstrasse 6. Menig Presse & Buch at the Hauptbahnhof also has a great selection. The city library is in the Alte Schloss, aka Herzog's Kasten, on Theaterplatz.

Maria de Victoria

Built as a conference centre from 1732 to 1736, the Maria de Victoria isn't a church – though that didn't stop it from becoming one of the favourites of the Asam brothers, who designed and built it. The building was turned over to the Bavarian government in the early 19th century, which has since maintained it as a museum.

Cosmas Damian Asam's trompe l'oeil ceiling (painted in just six weeks in 1737) is the largest fresco on a flat surface in the world, and it does things so trippy you can spend hours staring at it.

To see the thing in proper perspective, walk in six paces from the door and stand on the little circle in the diamond tile and look ahead. The illusions begin when you walk around. From the circle looking east, look over your left shoulder at the archer with the flaming red turban. Wherever you walk in the room the arrow points right at you. Focus on anything – the Horn of Plenty, Moses' staff, the treasure chest – and it will appear to dramatically alter when you move around the room. Asam took the secret methods he used in the painting to his grave.

Ask the caretaker, Herr Schuler, to let you into the side chamber to see the *Lepanto Monstrance*, a gold and silver depiction of the Battle of Lepanto (1571).

Buzz for Herr Schuler (an absolute hoot if you can understand Bavarian) next door if the front door is locked during opening hours, which are Tuesday to Sunday from 9 am to noon and 1 to 5 pm. Admission is DM2.50, discount DM1.50.

Medicine Museum

The Museum of the History of Medicine (☎ 305 49 3), Anatomiestrasse 18/20, just shouts 'body parts'. It was the main medical faculty of the university (which was moved to Landshut in 1803), and its operating theatre was where professors and students performed experiments on dead bodies and tissues. Mary Shelley (1797-1851) used the institute, in the lovely baroque building (1732-37), as the setting for the laboratory of the title character in her classic, *Frankenstein*, who combined harvested body parts and electrically 'animated' a 'son'.

The downstairs isn't too bad, but upstairs isn't for the fainthearted: maternity gear, dental equipment, surgery tools (note the saw, ladies and gentlemen) and real skeletons with preserved musculature. The grounds are lovely – bring a picnic if you still have an appetite.

It's open Tuesday to Sunday from 10 am to noon and 2 to 5 pm. Admission is DM4/2, an extra DM2/1 during special exhibitions (we shudder to think!).

Neues Schloss

Unhappy with his local lot upon his return

from wealth-laden France, Ludwig the Bearded ordered this Gothic castle built in 1418. It's a little ostentatious, what with the 3m-thick walls, Gothic net vaulting and individually carved doorways, but today it makes a fine home for the **Bayerisches Armee Museum** (☎ 937 70), a fascinating collection of armaments from the 14th century through to WWII, including a collection of 17,000 tin soldiers in the tower.

Its extension is the **Reduit Tilly** across the river, named for the Thirty Years' War general, with exhibits on the history of WWI and post-WWI Germany. Admission is DM5.50/4 for either, and DM7.50/5.50 for both.

Münster

The city's Münster is less fascinating for what it is – a reasonably impressive Gothic cathedral – than for what it isn't: finished. The city ran out of money several times during the construction, and a quick walk round reveals archways that were started and abandoned, bows that were left off and the towers left devoid of ornamentation and at a fraction of their intended height. Regular concerts and recitals are held here.

Kreuz Tor

The Gothic Kreuz Tor (1385) was one of the four main gates into the city until the 19th century. It and the main gate within the Neues Schloss are all that remain of the main city gates, but the former **fortifications**, now flats, still encircle the city. There's a terrific beer garden next to the Kreuz Tor.

Audi Factory

You can take free one-hour tours of the Audi factory (☎ 890) Monday to Friday at 9.40 am, noon and 1 pm; bus No 11 goes right there from the centre. Car nuts can't miss the Audi Historical Car Museum (☎ 891 24 1), Ettinger Strasse 40 just south of the factory, open Wednesday to Friday from 9 am to noon and 1 to 5 pm. Tours are held Monday to Friday at 2.15 pm, Saturday at 10.15 am. Admission is free.

Other Sights

The city's **Museum of Concrete Art** (☎ 305 72 8), Tränkorstrasse 6-8, which also has modern art exhibitions, was under renovation when we visited but should reopen soon. Admission is DM3/1.50.

The city's **Toy Museum**, on the top floor of the Alte Schloss, or Herzog's Kasten, has a selection of toys from the 18th to the 20th centuries. It's open daily; admission is DM2/1, free on Sunday.

Places to Stay

The huge *Campingplatz Auwaldsee* (☎ 961 16 16), at the Auwaldsee lake about 3km south-east of the city centre, has five season changes during the year – in high/low season sites are DM12/10 (DM6/5.50 without a car) plus DM9/7 per person. Bus service is screamingly inadequate; a taxi from the centre will cost about DM8.

The seriously nice *DJH hostel* (☎ 341 77) is in a renovated city fortification (1828). Rooms are a little crowded, with eight to even 12 beds, but staff are friendly and the place is incredibly clean. Beds are DM20 with breakfast, DM7 with half-pension. There's a nice little pub at the corner, called Corner. Walk west through the Kreuz Tor, out of the Altstadt, and the hostel is 150m ahead on the right.

Gästehaus Bauer Pension (☎ 670 86), Hölzstrasse 2, has simple singles/doubles from DM50/75, nicer ones from DM84/115. Much nicer and more central is the *Bayerischer Hof* (☎ 140 3), Münzbergstrasse 12, with clean rooms from DM90/140.

Places to Eat

Restaurants & Bistros It may look new but the *Herrnbräu Keller* (☎ 328 90), Dollstrasse 3, is the oldest brewery restaurant in town, and it's just gone through renovation. It serves excellent Weissbier and dependably good food, either inside or in the beer garden out back.

The best beer garden is *Glock'n am Kreutz Tor* (☎ 349 90), in the shadow of the Kreuz Tor near the hostel at Oberer Graben 1. Open from 10 am, it has lots of great food starting from under DM10. The aromas coming from the kitchen at *Daniel* (☎ 352 72), Roseneckstrasse 1, were good enough to recommend it highly, and it's the oldest pub in town, too. If Italian strikes your fancy, there's *Nudelstube Carrara* (☎ 340 43), Kanalstrasse 12, with well prepared pasta dishes from DM12 to DM15. It's closed Sunday and Monday.

Snacks & Fast Food The Wednesday and Saturday *markets* on Theaterplatz are wonderful.

The interesting *mensa*, perhaps appropriately located at Konviktstrasse 1, serves breakfast for DM2.50, lunch and dinner for DM6 to DM8; it's one block from the Maria de Victoria.

The chi-chi crowds at the *Mohrenkopf Café* (☎ 177 50), Donaustrasse 8, fill much of the sidewalk in summer, and maybe that's why the staff are so overworked and surly. They're nicer at *Bar Centrale*, right next door.

Getting There & Away

BEX BerLinien buses leave for Berlin daily at 10.55 am and arrive from Berlin at 3.45 pm daily. The SuperSpar cost for a one-way/return ticket is DM125/143; a standard ticket is DM73/133. Trains from Regensburg leave hourly and take one hour. From Munich, trains leave twice an hour and take 45 minutes.

Getting Around

Caritas (☎ 901 64 13) has placed recycled bright-yellow bicycles throughout the city. They are available free to anyone; just grab one, go where you're going and lean it up against a wall in a prominent spot.

PASSAU

- *pop 51,000*
- *area code* ☎ 0851

As it exits Germany for Austria, the Danube River flows through the baroque town of Passau, where it converges with the rivers Inn and Ilz. The Italian-baroque essence has not doused the medieval feel, which you will experience as you wander through the narrow lanes, tunnels and archways of the Altstadt and monastic district to Ortspitze, where the rivers meet.

Passau is not only at a confluence of inland waterways, but also the hub of long-distance cycling routes, eight of which converge here.

Orientation

The Altstadt is a narrow peninsula with the arms of the Danube and Inn rivers converging at the tip. The little Ilz River approaches from the north, the other two from the west. The Hauptbahnhof is at the western end of the city, about a 10-minute walk from the heart of the Altstadt. The Veste Ober-haus and the hostel are on the north side of the Danube, reached by crossing the Luitpoldbrücke and walking up the hill.

Information

There are two useful tourist offices: at Rathausplatz 3 (☎ 351 07) and opposite the train station at Bahnhofstrasse 26 (☎ 955 98 0; for tours ☎ 955 98 14). The latter is especially useful for bicycle and boat travel along the Danube. Staff provide maps, accommodation lists and help you plan your trip. Office hours are bewildering; if you have to go out of your way, call first.

The tourist offices both sell a coupon booklet (DM2) worth DM9 in discounts to local attractions plus one bus ticket plus, for some reason, a free drink at one of four hotels. The ADAC has an office (☎ 340 1) at Brunngasse 5.

Change money at the Postbank adjacent to the Hauptbahnhof, or across the street at the Dresdner Bank, Bahnhofstrasse 23.

The main post office is adjacent to the Hauptbahnhof and has a bank and telephone centre.

Fortress

Towering over the city is the 13th-century **Veste Oberhaus** (closed Monday and all February; DM6), containing the **Cultural History Museum**.

The fortress, built by prince-bishops for defence – and taken over by Napoleonic troops in the early 19th century – commands absolutely superb views over the city, either from the castle tower (DM1), or from the **Batallion Linde**, a lookout that gives the only bird's-eye view of the confluence of all three rivers. The Cultural History Museum includes a permanent exhibition of the work of local artist Hans Wimmer, whose 1970s social-realist bronze works recall a cold-war era long past. The hostel's up here as well.

From the city, cross the Luitpoldbrücke and follow the Ludwigsteig path right up the hill, or take a shuttle bus.

Dom

The baroque **Dom St Stephan** houses, along with fascinating scenes of heaven in the vaulted ceilings, the world's largest church organ (17,388 pipes). It also has a **treasury** and **museum**; the treasury has a display of gold and silver jewellery. The half-hour concerts held in the cathedral daily at noon (DM4) are acoustically stunning. Note, on the way out, the little cloth draped over the railing on top of the archway – said to have been left by one of the workmen.

Altes Rathaus

The glockenspiel in the colourful **Rathaus** (1399; tower 1891) chimes several times daily (the times are listed on the wall, which also shows historical flood levels). Inside, the **Kleine Rathaus Saal**, the **Registry** and the **Great Assembly Room** have wonderful paintings by local artist and crackpot Ferdinand Wagner. Wagner, who used to live in the huge building on the north bank of the Danube just to the right of where the Luitpoldbrücke suspension bridge is today, threatened to move out of town if the bridge was built. It was, he did, and after viewing the paintings, you wonder whether the city made the right choice. The fresco in the Small Assembly Room shows women representing the three rivers and the town.

Glass Museum

The Passau Museum of Glass (☎ 350 71) has a splendid collection of over 30,000 examples of Bohemian glasswork and crystal from over 250 years. If you charge through the place you'll need an hour to view all the 35 rooms containing Art Nouveau, baroque, classical and Art Deco pieces. The museum, in the Hotel Wilder Mann, is directly opposite the Rathaus. Admission is DM5/3; it's open in summer daily from 10 am to 4 pm, in winter from 1 pm.

Modern Art Museum

A constantly rotating exhibition of modern art passes through this museum (☎ 340 91), on Bräugasse just east of the Luitpoldbrücke. One of the nicest things about it is seeing the contrast between the building's Gothic architecture and whatever's on display at the moment. It's open Tuesday to Sunday from 10 am to 6 pm; admission changes with exhibits.

Roman Museum

In Kastell Boiotro, across the Inn footbridge from the city centre, is the Römermuseum (DM2/1), which covers Passau's original settlement by the Romans. It's open March to November, Tuesday to Sunday from 10 am to noon and 2 to 4 pm, in summer from 10 am to noon and 1 to 4 pm.

Activities

The enormous city Freibad (DM2) on the banks of the Ilz is probably going to close, but there's a free swimming area on the Ilz at Hochstein; take bus No 3 or 4 to Hochstein. From there, you can take a very pleasant, easy hike across the isthmus and through the tunnel to Zum Triftsperre (☎ 511 62), a very nice beer garden and restaurant along a peaceful section of the Ilz. Ask at the tourist office for hiking maps, or at the swimming area.

Places to Stay

Camping There's camping at *Zeltplatz an der Ilz* (☎ 414 57), Halser Strasse 34, with a DM9 fee per adult and no tent price. It's over the Ilz River bridge with bus No 1, 2 or 3; no campervans are allowed.

Hostels It's a wheezy climb up to the castle which contains the *hostel* (☎ 413 51), at

BAVARIA

Veste Oberhaus 125. The hostel only accepts juniors (DM16.50 including breakfast or DM24 with breakfast and dinner, plus DM5 for linen). There's a curfew from 11.30 pm to 7 am.

With its fewer restrictions, travellers of all ages may prefer the more central *Rotel Inn* (☎ 951 60), open from early May to late October. On the Danube at Donaugelände (just two minutes' walk from the train station), this place offers tiny yet clean rooms for an amazing DM25/50 per single/double, with reasonably private hall shower/toilet. Breakfast is not included, but only costs an extra DM8 in the cafeteria.

Hotels & Pensions The *Hotel Wienerwald* (☎ 330 69), Grosse Klingergasse 17, has basic singles/doubles from DM50/80 (but there's no hall shower and the kitchen is noisy until very late). The *Gasthof Blauer Bock* (☎ 346 37) on Fritz-Schäffer-Promenade has quieter rooms from DM49/98.

Though it's often packed with busloads of tourists, the *Hotel König* (☎ 385 0) has well appointed and clean rooms right on the Danube for DM60/80.

The *Hotel Wilder Mann* (☎ 350 71), home to the Glass Museum, has singles/doubles from DM77/117.

And right across the street from the Hauptbahnhof is the *Passau Holiday Inn* (☎ 590 05 25), Bahnhofstrasse 24, with standard HI rooms from DM85/115; there's a pool and sauna downstairs.

BAVARIA

Places to Eat

There are *markets* every Friday morning at Domplatz. For cheap eats, Ludwigstrasse is the place to head for, with a *Kochlöffel* at No 26, *Nordsee* at No 19, *Eis Café Fontanella* at No 20 (with great ice cream and outdoor tables) and the large *Müller* marketplace at No 16, complete with fruit stalls, meat and fish stand and a restaurant in back with full meals from DM7.50.

Café Nyhavn, Theresienstrasse 31, has light-style Danish food including yoghurt salads. *Peschl-Terrasse* (☎ 248 9) at Rosstränke 4, an old-style pub-brewery with a spacious dining terrace overlooking the Danube, offers generous servings of hearty fare. The *Weisses Kreuz*, in a back alley at Milchgasse 15, is popular with local students and serves big plates of cheesy wholemeal spätzle (flat noodles) for DM14 and half-litre glasses of local ale for DM3.80; it's open daily to 1 am.

For good food, nice atmosphere and terrible service at good prices, jump on bus No 5 or 190 which brings you right to the entrance of *Gasthaus Vogl*, a beer garden north of the castle that does typically Bavarian dishes for under DM15. It commands great views into the Ilz Valley.

Getting There & Away

Bus Regional buses to and from Zwiesel (DM16), Grafenau and Bayerisch Eisenstein stop at the Hauptbahnhof concourse outside the main post office. Buses to/from Plattling use the stop on the lower level.

Train Passau is on the main rail line linking Cologne, Frankfurt, Nuremberg, Regensburg and Vienna. Trains run direct to/from Munich (DM50), Regensburg (DM31) and Nuremberg (DM57); you change at Plattling for the Bavarian Forest.

Austria There are 11 direct train connections daily to/from Linz (DM28/AS188, 1½ hours) and at least 11 to/from Vienna's Westbahnhof (DM59/AS410, 3¼ to four hours).

Car & Motorcycle The A3 runs from Passau to Linz and Vienna, or back to Regensburg. The A92 from Munich connects with it.

Boat From April to October Wurm + Köck (☎ 929 29 2), Höllgasse 26, has a twice-daily boat service down the Danube to Linz in Austria, departing Passau at 9 am and 2 pm (DM34/AS235, five hours). Another line, DDSG (☎ 330 35), Im Ort 14a, runs boats downstream as far as Vienna (DM152/AS1075).

BAVARIAN FOREST

The largest continuous mountain forest in all of Europe, the Bavarian Forest (Bayerischer Wald) is a lovely landscape of rolling wooded hills interspersed with tiny, little-disturbed valleys. Being mostly visited by other Germans, the locals here speak little English. Go out of your way to do some hiking in this surprisingly wild and rugged region.

Orientation & Information

The ranges of the Bavarian Forest stretch north-west to south-east along the German-Czech border, and its wild frontier nature is still the region's chief attribute. At its heart is the town of Zwiesel, which makes an ideal base for exploring the Bavarian Forest. Zwiesel's helpful tourist office (☎ 09922-962 3) is in the town hall at Stadtplatz 27, about 1km from the Hauptbahnhof. It has lots of free brochures, maps and helpful hints for exploring the area.

The tourist office (☎ 08552-962 30) in Grafenau is at Rathausgasse 1. The best information about wildlife areas and trails is available from the Dr-Hans-Eisenmann-Haus (☎ 08558-130 0) in Neuschönau.

Things to See & Do

Zwiesel's **Waldmuseum** (Forest Museum) deals with forestry and the wood industry (open daily); the **Glasmuseum** covers local glass-making. Lindberg's **Bauernhaus-museum** features traditional Bavarian Forest houses, Regen has the **Landwirt-schaftsmuseum** (Agricultural Museum), and there's the **Handwerksmuseum** (Handicrafts Museum) at Deggendorf.

The **Museumsdorf Bayerischer Wald** (☎ 08504-848 2) in Tittling, just north of Passau, is a museum of East Bavarian farm life from the 17th to 19th centuries, with over 140 houses on 20 hectares. If you haven't been to one of these museums, it's really worth the trip. Admission is DM5, discount DM3; take the RDO bus to Tittling from Passau Hauptbahnhof.

The **Dampfbier-brauerei** (☎ 09922-140 9) at Regener Strasse 9-11 in Zwiesel has a brewery tour at 10 am every Wednesday (DM13), which includes generous samplings of its peppery local ales.

The **Bayerwald-Bärwurzerei** (☎ 09922-151 5), 2km out of Zwiesel at Frauenauer Strasse 80-82, produces some 26 Bavarian liqueurs that you can sample and purchase.

The production of superior-quality glass is another important local industry. You can buy wares and watch glass being blown in many places, such as the Glasbläserei Schmid (☎ 09922-946 2), Am Daiminger-strasse 24 in Zwiesel.

Activities

Hiking & Skiing South of Zwiesel is the 130-sq-km Bavarian Forest National Park, a paradise for the outdoors enthusiast. There are several superb long-distance hiking routes, with mountain huts along the way. The most famous is the 180km Nördliche Hauptwanderlinie or E6 trail, a 10-day trek from Furth im Wald to Dreisessel.

The Südliche Hauptwanderlinie or E8 is its shorter sibling at 105km, while the 50km trek from Kötzting to Bayerisch Eisenstein near the Czech border is the quickest way to experience the Bavarian Forest. A good walking map is the 1:50,000 *Mittlerer Bayerischer Wald* published by Fritsch (DM11.80).

Downhill skiing in the Bavarian Forest is relatively low-key, with the best resorts in the north around peaks such as Geisskopf (1097m), Grosser Arber (1456m), Pröller and Hoher Bogen (1079m). More exciting and popular here is cross-country skiing, with numerous routes through the ranges.

In Eukirchen b. Hl Blut, Freizeitzentrum Hoher Bogen (☎ 09947-464) runs a summer alpine slope (Rodelbahn) – see Blomberg in Bad Tölz (Around Munich section) for a description. It runs from April to the end of October daily from 9 am to 5 pm.

Canoeing Waldschrat's Adventure Company (☎ 09926-731), Flanitzmühle 9 in Fraueneau, rents three-person Canadian canoes for DM70 per day/DM300 for five days, and kayaks for DM30/120. Staff will transport the boats to a number of places within the forest for anywhere from DM50 to DM120. They have an agent at the booze-maker Bayerwald-Bärwurzerei (☎ 09922-151 5) in Zwiesel (see earlier this section).

Places to Stay

Zwiesel's camping ground is *Azur-Camping* (☎ 09922-184 7), 1km from the Hauptbahnhof, near public pools and sports facilities.

The local *hostel* (☎ 09922-106 1) is at Hindenburgstrasse 26, where beds are DM20. Other dormitory accommodation in the region includes the Frauenau *hostel* (☎ 09926-543), Hauptstrasse 29 (DM18), and the *Waldhäuser* (☎ 08553-600 0), at Herbergsweg 2 in Neuschönau (DM20). All these hostels close for at least a month in early winter, and only accept guests under 27 years of age.

Zwiesel is crammed with budget pensions and apartments; prices include resort tax. Excellent value is the *Pension Haus Inge*, (☎ 09922-109 4), Buschweg 34, which stands at the edge of the forest and has comfortable rooms with private shower and toilet from just DM36/61 for a single/double. The *Naturkost Pension Waldeck* (☎ 09922-327 2), at Ahornweg 2, is a nonsmokers' pension featuring organic vegetarian cooking. It costs from DM49 to DM58 per person for half-board. Two quiet places in the hills at nearby Rabenstein are the *Pension Fernblick* (☎ 09922-940 9), Brücklhöhe 48, and the smaller *Berghaus Rabenstein* (☎ 09922-124 5), Grosses Feld 8, which both charge around DM35 per person.

Grafenau's central *Gasthof Schraml* (☎ 08552-122 9), at Stadtplatz 14, has basic rooms for DM26 per person (excluding breakfast). Nearby at Stadtplatz 8 is *Gasthof Kellermann* (☎ 08552-121 3), with better rooms for DM35/65 a single/double.

Places to Eat

In Zwiesel, *Bistro Flair*, Dr-Schott-Strasse 16, has schnitzels from just DM7.80. Another good option in Zwiesel is the *Musikantenkeller*, a live-music pub at Stadtplatz 42, where a pork cutlet served with chips and salad costs DM11.50; wash it down with a half-litre glass of local draught beer for DM3.80. The *Zwieseler Hof Hotel-Restaurant*, Regener Strasse 5, has a comfortable ambience despite the plastic plants. The extensive menu (DM12 to DM25) includes fish, lamb and Bavarian dishes.

Two good restaurants in Grafenau are the *Gasthof Jägerwirt*, Hauptstrasse 18, and *Zum Kellermann*, at Stadtplatz 8.

Getting There & Away

From Munich, Regensburg or Passau, Zwiesel is reached by rail via Plattling; most trains continue to Bayerisch Eisenstein on the Czech border, with connections to Prague. The direct buses between Zwiesel and Passau work out cheaper than a change of trains at Plattling, and run several times daily (DM13, 2⅓ hours).

Two scenic narrow-gauge railways from Zwiesel go to Grafenau (DM4.60 one way) and to Bodenmais (DM3.10).

BAVARIA

Baden-Württemberg

Baden-Württemberg is one of Germany's main tourist regions. With recreational centres like the Black Forest (Schwarzwald) and Lake Constance (Bodensee), and medieval towns such as Heidelberg and the health spa of Baden-Baden, it's also one of the most varied parts of the country.

Tübingen and Heidelberg are laid-back university towns. Stuttgart – the corporate base of Mercedes-Benz and Porsche – has some fascinating museums and an a wealth of city parks and green spaces. Surrounding Stuttgart is one of Germany's lesser-known wine-growing regions, producing excellent whites and some very good reds.

The Lake Constance area, encompassing sections of Baden-Württemberg, Bavaria and Switzerland, is justifiably one of the biggest draws, but don't skip the less travelled regions of the Schwäbisch Alb, especially the lovely town of Schwäbisch Hall.

The prosperous modern state of Baden-Württemberg was created in 1951 out of three smaller regions: Baden, Württemberg and Hohenzollern. Baden, the first to be unified, was made a grand duchy by Napoleon, who was also responsible for making Württemberg a kingdom in 1806. Both areas, in conjunction with Bavaria and 16 other states, formed the Confederation of the Rhine under French protection, part of Napoleon's plan to undermine Prussia. Baden and Württemberg sided with Austria against Prussia in 1866, but were ultimately drafted into the German Empire in 1871.

HIGHLIGHTS

- Everything about Heidelberg
- A ride on the cog-wheel train and tram No 15 in Stuttgart
- Wine tasting in and around Stuttgart
- The Freilichtspiele (open-air summer theatre) in Schwäbisch Hall
- The Goethe plaque and most everything else in Tübingen
- Ulm's magnificent Münster, with the highest spire in Europe
- Hiking through the Wutach Gorge
- A ride on the scenic Schwarzwaldbahn between Offenburg and Villingen
- Mainau Island, especially the Butterfly House
- Baden-Baden spas, especially Friedrichsbad and Caracalla-Therme
- A visit to the Pilgrimage Church of Birnau

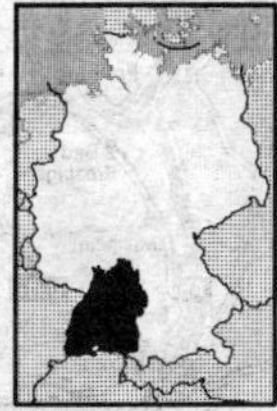

• **Population:** 10.3m • **Capital:** Stuttgart • **Area:** 35,750 sq km

Baden-Württemberg Luminaries: Boris Becker, Karl Benz, Johann Christoph, Gottlieb Wilhelm Daimler, Friedrich Ebert, Albert Einstein, Steffi Graf, Georg Wilhelm Friedrich Hegel, Herman Hesse, Friedrich Hölderlin, Johannes Kepler, Kurt Georg Kiesinger, Jürgen Klinsmann, Philipp Melanchthon, Erwin Rommel, Friedrich von Schiller, Hans & Sophie Scholl, Christoph Martin Wieland, Max Wolf, Graf Ferdinand von Zeppelin

STUTTGART

- *pop 630,500*
- *area code* ☎ 0711

Stuttgart is known primarily as the home of Mercedes-Benz (even the train station sports a Mercedes logo), and most travellers imagine it is an industrial city. Nothing could be further from the truth. It's set in a valley just west of the Neckar River, and Stuttgart residents go to great pains to keep their city as green as possible. From the moment you leave the train station in the city centre and

BADEN-WÜRTTEMBERG

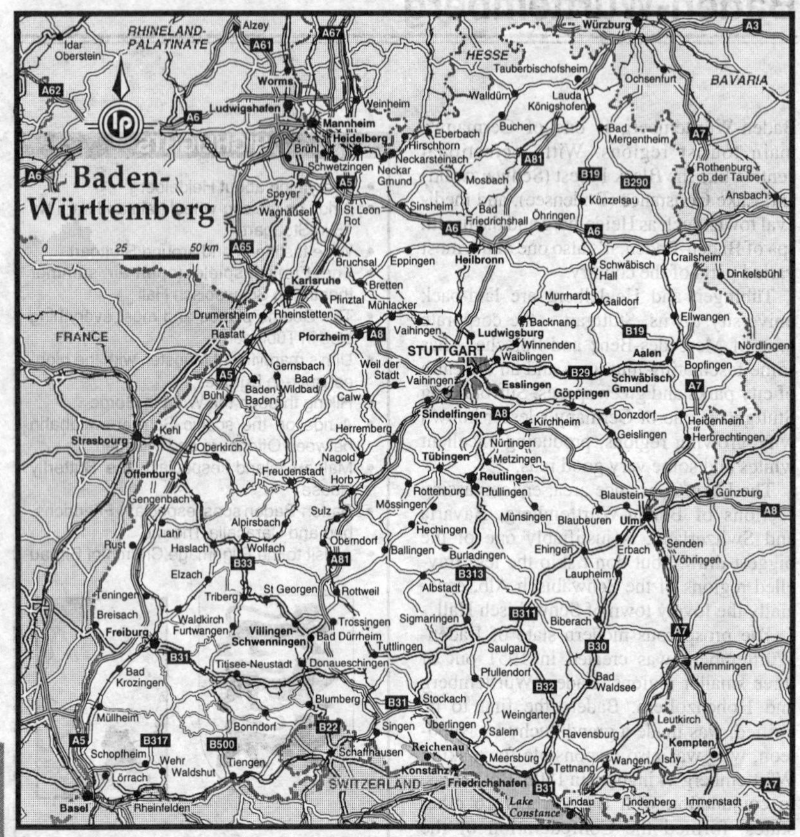

see the working Kriegsberg vineyard just to your right, everything about Stuttgart seems captivating.

Nestled in a U-shaped belt of thick hillside forests and surrounded by parks, Stuttgart could be the greenest city in Europe. Over half its area is covered with orchards, vineyards, meadows and forest – you're never more than 15 minutes from dense woods. Over 500 vineyards turn out some excellent wines, many kept and consumed locally.

The city began as a stud farm (*Stuotgarten*, from where it derives its name) on the Nesenbach Stream around 950. By 1160 it had become a booming trade centre and by the early 14th century, Stuttgart was the seat of the royal family of Württemberg.

It is also the birthplace of two gadgets that have changed the world: Gottlieb Daimler's petrol-powered, high-speed engine and Robert Bosch's spark plug. The Mercedes-Benz factory began automobile production here in 1926. (Daimler patented the motor coach, and Karl Benz the motor car, in 1886). Not to be outdone, Ferdinand Porsche set up shop here as well.

After WWII, the city's architectural treasures were painstakingly reconstructed;

today, Stuttgart attracts almost a million visitors a year with its impressive museums and air of relaxed prosperity.

Orientation

The city sits in a valley surrounded to the south by hills, ranging in height from 50m to 300m, which are covered with vineyards, parks and public-access forest. Steep grades – of 15 to 18% – are common on city streets and over 500 city streets end in staircases – *Stäffele* – that lead to the top of the hills.

The Hauptbahnhof is just north of the central pedestrian shopping street, Königstrasse. The tourist office, i-Punkt, is just opposite the station. There's a shopping-mall underpass beneath the station called Die Klett Passage.

The Schlossgarten, which stretches almost 4km south-west from the Neckar River to the city centre, is divided into three sections – Unterer, Mittlerer and Oberer – complete with swan ponds, street entertainers and modern sculptures.

The Mercedes museum is east of the Neckar River, about 15 minutes by tram from the centre; and the company's factory is in the suburb of Sindelfingen, south-west of the centre. Bad Cannstatt, home to a large beer festival, is east of the city's excellent zoo and botanical gardens at Wilhelma.

Information

Tourist Offices The i-Punkt tourist office (☎ 222 82 40), Königstrasse 1a, has multilingual staff who make room reservations for no fee. It can sell tickets to everything in town and is open Monday to Friday from 9.30 am to 8.30 pm, Saturday to 6 pm and Sunday and holidays from 11 am to 6 pm (1 to 6 pm between November and April).

Stuttgart-Marketing (☎ 222 82 46/48; fax 222 82 51), which runs i-Punkt, offers a number of very good deals during festivals that include hotel, train fares, passes etc. See Places to Stay for the excellent Young & Fun deal, or write to: Lautenschlagerstrasse 3, 70173 Stuttgart.

ADAC has a huge office (☎ 280 00) at Am Neckartor, north of the Hauptbahnhof.

Passes The three-day Stuttgarter City-Pass (DM27.50), available at the i-Punkt office, gives you free transport on the U-Bahn, buses and trams, and discounted or free admission to almost every tourist attraction in the city.

Alternatively, the three-day transport pass costs DM12 for the city centre and airport, or DM19 to cover the entire region.

The three-day Night-Pass (DM12) gives you admission to most clubs and discos and discounts on drinks, but with about a million exceptions, caveats and exemptions.

Foreign Consulates Consulates in Stuttgart include the following:

Denmark
  Bolzstrasse 6 (☎ 290 13 7)
France
  Richard-Wagner-Strasse 53 (☎ 237 47 0)
Greece
  Firnhaberstrasse 5a (☎ 221 05 6)
Italy
  Lenzhalde Strasse 46 (☎ 256 30)
Netherlands
  Hardweg 60 (☎ 297 08 0)
Norway
  Nord Bahnhofstrasse 41 (☎ 256 89 49)
Spain
  Lenzhalde Strasse 61 (☎ 226 20 01)
Sweden
  Rotebühlstrasse 77 (☎ 667 29 99)
USA
  Urbanstrasse 7 (☎ 210 08 0 ☎ 242 56 5)

Money There's a Reisebank at the Hauptbahnhof, and an American Express office (☎ 162 49 20) across the street. You can also change money at the Deutsche Bank at Königstrasse 1a, and the Dresdner Bank at Königstrasse 9.

Post & Communications The main post office is at Lautenschlagerstrasse 17, and there's a branch at the Hauptbahnhof.

Online Services A surprising number of Internet cafés have popped up in the city. The most central are at Karstadt (☎ 208 20),

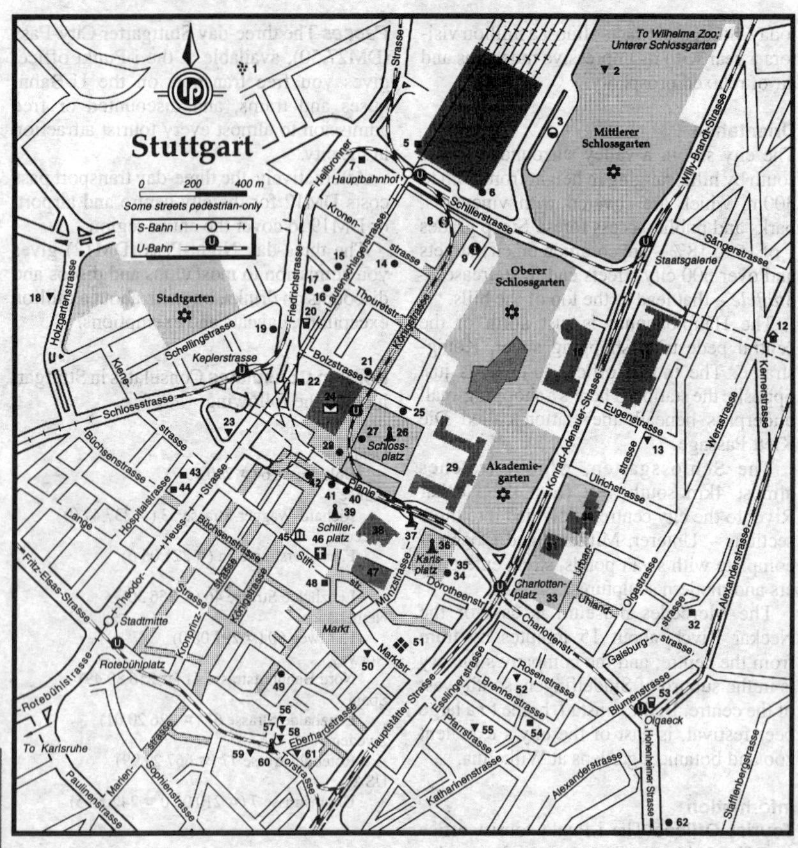

Königstrasse 1, and Galeria Kaufhof (☎ 203 60), Königstrasse 6.

Travel Agencies Reisefieber (☎ 649 80 94), Tübinger Strasse 72, is a good bucket shop. Fun Point (☎ 211 15 40), at Breuninger Sports in the Breuninger Passage shopping centre (see Things to Buy), runs periodic deals on odd travel plans, like 28 hours in Paris for DM99. Discount Travel (☎ 794 20 55) is a last- minute ticketing service at Stuttgart airport.

Bookshops Lindemann Books (☎ 245 32 3), Nadlerstrasse 4-10, south of the Rathaus, has English-language books, plus a great travel section with Lonely Planet titles. Wittwer (☎ 250 70), Königstrasse 30, has great foreign-language and travel sections (even more LP titles). It also runs the excellent Internationale Presse stand at the Hauptbahnhof, with newspapers, magazines and books.

Libraries There are several libraries right on Konrad-Adenauer-Strasse near the Staatsgalerie. The Landesbibliothek (☎ 212 0), at Konrad-Adenauer-Strasse 8, is by far the

PLACES TO STAY

5 InterCity Hotel
7 Steigenberger Graf Zeppelin Hotel
12 DJH Hostel
14 Hotel Unger
22 Pension Märklin
32 Wirt am Berg
43 Museumstube
44 Gasthof Alte Mira
48 Holl's Arche
54 Hotel Dieter

PLACES TO EAT

2 Beer Garden
13 Urbanstuben
18 University Mensa
23 Stuttgarter Kellerschenke
35 Beer Garden
47 Markthalle
50 iden
52 Weinstube Stetter
53 Café & Waschsalon
55 Pica Pao
56 Paddock
57 Max and Moritz
58 Deli
59 Hans im Glück
61 Ali's Brasserie

OTHER

1 Kriegsberg Vineyards
3 Bus Station
4 Main Train Station
6 Entrance to Die Klett Passage
8 American Express
9 Tourist Office
10 Staatstheater
11 Staatsgalerie
15 Laura's Club
16 Kommunales Kino
17 Lufthansa City Centre
19 Varieté im Friedrichhaus
20 Palast de Republic
21 Palais Disco
24 Main Post Office
25 Kunstverein (Municipal Art Gallery)
26 König Wilhelm Column
27 Börse (Stock Exchange)
28 Alexander Calder's *Mobile*
29 Neues Schloss
30 City Library & Archives
31 Stadtbücherei
33 Musikbücherei
34 James F Burns Institute
36 Wilhelm I Statue
37 Cobes Nazi Memorial
38 Altes Schloss; Württemberg State Museum
39 Friedrich Schiller Statue
40 Alte Kanzlei
41 Wittwer Books
42 Amex Travel
45 Instrumenten Museum
46 Stiftskirche
49 Lindemann Books
51 Breuninger Shopping Centre
60 Hans im Glück Statue
62 Waschsalon

largest. Nearby, the Stadtbücherei (☎ 216 57 0), at No 2, is the city library. Next door at No 4 is the Staatsarchive (☎ 212 43 35), which houses the original *Bannandrohungsbulle*, the papal bull that threatened Martin Luther with excommunication for heresy.

The excellent Musikbücherei (☎ 216 57 81), Charlottenstrasse 1, has books on music along with a large collection of sheet music.

Campuses Universität-Stuttgart has 130 institutes, 14 faculties and 21,000 students; its most important schools are of architecture, agriculture, economics and engineering. The Universität Hohenheim, in the castle in the suburb of Hohenheim, has over 6000 students, with important schools of biology, chemistry and physics, agriculture and economics.

International Centres The James F Burns Institute (Deutsch-Amerikanisches Zentrum; ☎ 228 18 0), Charlottenplatz 17, has American resource materials. The Institut Français (☎ 239 25 0) is in a villa at Diemarshaldenstrasse 11.

Laundry There's a brand new Waschsalon with a café-pub at Charlottenstrasse 27 on the corner of Olgaeck, and another at Hohenheimer Strasse 33. There's also a washing machine at the Tramper Point Stuttgart hostel (see Places to Stay).

Medical Services For a doctor in an emergency call ☎ 262 80 12 or ☎ 280 21 1. There are over 20 hospitals; the largest are the Katharinen Hospital (☎ 278 0), Kriegsbergerstrasse 60, and the Marienhospital (☎ 648 90), Böheimstrasse 37.

Dangers & Annoyances Stuttgart is a remarkably safe city, but there are some rather sleazy characters in the Hauptbahnhof, especially at Die Klett Passage, underneath, after dark.

Schlossplatz

This square provides a crash course in architecture. Stand in the middle, beneath the **König Wilhelm Jubilee column**, flanked by fountains representing the eight rivers of Baden-Württemberg, then look straight

Coolest, Cheapest Orientation Tour
The best way to get oriented in Stuttgart is to go to Marienplatz (U-Bahn No 4) and get on the city's charming little Zahnradbahn (cog-wheel train, Germany's first, built in 1884) up the steep hills to the top. From the station there, take a 15-minute walk north through lovely countryside to the TV Tower. Ride on up to the observation level and marvel at the view.

Leave the tower, walk to the tram stop about five minutes away and take the wonderful tram No 15 back towards the city through thick forest.

Jump off at Eugene Platz and stand with the crowds at the large statue *Die Schöne Galathea*. While contemplating her once scandalous exposed buns, you'll have a great view down to Schlossplatz. Get back on tram No 15 to return to the centre. ■

ahead and spin clockwise. The classical **Königsbau**, with its 30 columns, is a focal point of nightlife in the city. On warm evenings crowds of thousands gather to watch buskers and other street performers. Downstairs are shops; upstairs, the city's **Börse** (stock exchange).

To the right of that is a fine example of 1950s architecture in the **Olgabau**, home to the Dresdner Bank. Farther right is the Art Nouveau **Kunstverein**, which contains the municipal art gallery and the Württemberg Art Society. The late-baroque/neoclassical front section of the **Neues Schloss**, once the residence of kings Friedrich I and Wilhelm I, now houses the city's finance and culture ministries.

Continue to turn clockwise and across the street in Schillerplatz you'll see the late-Gothic **Stiftskirche Steeple** and the Renaissance **Alte Kanzlei** (old chancellery).

At the western end of Schlossplatz is Alexander Calder's controversial ***Mobile***, a modern sculpture the city bought in 1981 for DM950,000. Stuttgarters – known for a quality that other Germans might call 'miserliness' but which they themselves refer to as 'thriftiness' – went ballistic over the cost, but now they're proud of it (it's tripled in value since the installation). There are concerts every Sunday in summer at the **Musik Pavillon** at the north-west corner of the square.

Schillerplatz

Opposite Schlossplatz is Schillerplatz – named for poet-dramatist Friedrich Schiller, whose statue stands in the centre. In its south-western corner, in the **Stiftsfruchtkasten**, a former wine storehouse (note the Bacchus statue on top), is the (musical) **Instrument Museum** component of the Württemberg State Museum. Next to it is a reconstruction of the city's **Stiftskirche**, with its twin 61m-high towers (city law says no building can be taller than these).

Through the tunnel to the east is **Altes Schloss**, with a large statue of Eberhard, Württemberg's first duke and the founder of the university at Tübingen. The reconstructed old palace now holds the **Württemberg State Museum** (closed on Monday; DM5/3 including entry to the Instrument Museum), containing exhibitions on the Württemberg crown jewels. Watch the deer above the restored clock on the tower, they ram their horns together on the hour.

There are concerts and opera in the courtyard here in summer.

Museums

Staatsgalerie The State Gallery (☎ 212 40), Konrad-Adenauer-Strasse 30-32, contains Stuttgart's best art collection, divided between two buildings. The new section, housed in the spectacular postmodern Neue Staats-Galerie (1984), designed by James Stirling, concentrates on modern art and has one of Europe's largest Picasso collections. It is also home to rotating exhibitions that recently included a huge Robert Mapplethorpe show. The old section features art works from the Middle Ages to the 19th century.

The museum is open Tuesday to Sunday from 10 am to 5 pm, to 8 pm on Tuesday and Thursday. Admission is DM5/3.

Beer Museum If you like beer, it's worth a

BADEN-WÜRTTEMBERG

trip to the suburb of Vaihingen (S-Bahn No 1, 2 or 3) for a peep into the Schwäbisches Brauereimuseum (☎ 737 02 01), a complete history of beer-making with displays on brewing technology and methods throughout the world. It's open Tuesday to Sunday from 10.30 am to 5.30 pm, entry is free. From the Vaihingen train station, walk west on Vollmoellerstrasse to Robert-Koch-Strasse and the museum is ahead on the left.

Motor Museums & Factory Tours The pioneers of the motor car were Gottlieb Daimler and Karl Benz, who began separately to make cars at the end of the 19th century.

The impressive **Mercedes-Benz Museum** (☎ 172 25 78), about 2km east of the Neckar, tells the story of their partnership and achievements via recorded commentary and numerous gleaming vehicles. It's open Tuesday to Sunday from 9 am to 5 pm; entry is free (take S-Bahn No 1 to Gottlieb-Daimler-Stadion).

Though smaller and less fun, the **Porsche Museum** (☎ 827 56 85), Porschestrasse 42 (open Monday to Friday from 9 am to noon and 1 to 4 pm, free entry), definitely has the sexier cars. To get to the Porsche Museum take S-Bahn No 6 to Neuwirtshaus.

Better than either museum is a **factory tour**, where you can view the whole production process. Porsche (☎ 827 53 84) does a free daily tour in English at 10 am. It's often possible to join at short notice, but it's best to book at least six weeks ahead. Write to Porsche Besucherservice, Frau Schlegl, Postfach 400640, 70435 Stuttgart.

Mercedes-Benz also runs free tours of its Sindelfingen plant at 8.50 am and 2.05 pm on weekdays (kids under 14 years are not allowed), but you're strongly advised to call beforehand (☎ 07031-907 52 7).

Linden Museum The state ethnological museum (☎ 202 24 56), Hegelplatz 1, has a large collection of exhibits of life in South America, Asia and Africa. Admission and tours are free; it's open Tuesday to Sunday from 10 am to 5 pm (Wednesday to 8 pm, Friday to 1 pm). Take bus No 40, 42 or 43 from the city centre to Hegelplatz/Lindenmuseum, west of the Hauptbahnhof.

Weissenhof Estate

In the mid-1920s, 16 esteemed architects from five European countries – including Charles Le Corbusier, Hans Sharoun, Ludwig Mies van der Rohe and Walter Gropius – joined forces to build the Weissenhof Housing Estate, a collection of 21 Bauhaus dwellings that were intended to exemplify functional architecture. The houses, unveiled in 1927, used ground-breaking ideas and techniques to increase flexibility inside (like moveable walls to allow room reconfiguration), and had features like increased window space to improve natural light and flat roofs to provide large terraces. But they were deemed 'degenerate' by the Nazis, who moved to tear them down. Allied bombing took care of most of them, but today there are still 11 buildings standing. More information is available at the **Architecture Museum** (☎ 257 91 87), Am Weissenhof 20, open Tuesday to Sunday from 10 am to 2 pm, Sunday to 3 pm, entry free. The estate is at the north-west corner of the city, very close to the Stuttgart Messe; take U-Bahn No 5 or 6 to Löwentorbrücke.

Parks & Zoo

Royal Gardens All three parts of the Schlossgarten – Unterer, Mittlerer and Oberer – are exceptional. Right in the centre of the city, they're filled with meandering walkways, fountains and sunbathing folk watching the world – and the inline skaters – go by. There's a very good beer garden in the Unterer Garten, about seven minutes' walk north-east of the Hauptbahnhof.

Rosensteinpark At the north end of Unterer Garten you probably won't even know that you've crossed into the Rosensteinpark, which jigs west to its main entrance, on the corner of Nord-Bahnhof Strasse and Pragstrasse, through the **Löwentor**.

Within the park is the amazing **Schloss Rosenstein**, now the city's **Natural History Museum** (open Tuesday to Friday from 9 am to 5 pm, Saturday and Sunday to 6 pm; DM4/2).

Wilhelma At the northern edge of Rosensteinpark is the Wilhelma zoo and botanical gardens (open daily; DM12, discount DM6), an enormously popular place. It has animals from around the world in an amazing botanical garden on the grounds of the Schloss Rosenstein. The favourite here is the polar bear area where you get right up next to the ferocious beasties, behind glass.

Lapidarium Almost unknown to tourists – and even to many locals – the Lapidarium der Stadt Stuttgart is a breathtaking, though tiny, park on a hillside near Marienplatz. Nestled amid the park's lush greenery are fragments of buildings destroyed in WWII: doorways, portals, façade ornamentation, statues, gargoyles and parts of fountains. It's like coming across a lost civilisation, in a thrilling, serene sort of way. You can enter (free) from April to mid-September on Wednesday and Saturday from 2 to 5 pm. At other times, peep through the fence; walk up the Willy-Reichert-Stäffel from the base to the top of Karlshöhe Park. The address is Mörikestrasse 24/1; the entrance is guarded by a statue of a royal sentry.

Karlshöhe At the top of the hill just north-east of Marienplatz and the Lapidarium is Karlshöhe, another great park with sweeping views of the city and lovely hillside vineyards. Walk up the path through the vineyards to the beer garden at the top of the hill.

Karlshöhe is accessible either by taking the Willy-Reichert-Stäffel or by following Humboldtstrasse up the steep hill from its intersection with Mörikestrasse and Hohenzollernstrasse.

That yeasty smell is coming from the nearby **Dinkel Acker Brewery** (☎ 648 10), Tübinger Strasse 46; call ahead and you may be able to join free tours (and tasting) at the brewery, though you'll have to join a group.

Weissenburg Park Another lovely hillside park offering great views of the city is Weissenburg (U-Bahn No 5, 6 or 7 to Bopser then walk south). At the top of the hill is the spectacular **Teehaus** (see Places to Eat).

On the Grapevine

Stuttgart's – and the region's – vineyards are losing that charming terraced look in favour of straight rows of grapevines grown on wire fences, which allows automated harvesting.

This is in keeping with the trend of regional wine producers to consolidate into cooperatives and share techniques and technology to increase vintage quality and lower labour costs. The removal of the terraces has been going on for the last 20 years, and by the turn of the century you probably won't see them anywhere.

So if you're walking through or near one of the city's terraced vineyards and you notice people looking as if they're picking grapes, they're probably Greek or Turkish immigrants collecting grape leaves to stuff with rice and vegetables or meat and serve with olive oil, a dish the Greeks call *dolmades* and the Turks call *dolmus*. ■

TV Tower

At the southern end of the city is the 217m-high TV Tower (Fernsehturm; ☎ 288 30 37), the first to be built with pre-stressed concrete. It was erected between 1954 and 1956. Lifts zoom you up to the viewing platform (DM5/3), which is 450m above the centre of the city. The views are extraordinary. The restaurant, one level down, doesn't rotate but you can simulate rotation by having a *Viertel* (quarter litre) of local wine (DM5.50 to DM7.50) or a beer (DM5). Getting here is half the fun.

Planetarium

On the east side of the Mittlerer Schlossgarten is the Carl Zeiss Planetarium (☎ 162 92 15), a pyramid-shaped building that houses one of the best planetariums in the country. Admission prices to the star shows vary. They run Tuesday to Friday at 10 am and 3 pm (extra 8 pm shows on Wednesday and Friday), Saturday and Sunday at 2, 4 and 6 pm (most U-Bahn lines: Staatsgalerie).

Organised Tours

Bus The city runs 2½-hour bus tours every day from April to October, Monday to Saturday at 1 pm, Sunday and holidays at 11 am. The DM32 charge includes admission to the TV Tower. They're fine if your German is good, overpriced if you only understand English. The i-Punkt office can arrange a great variety of walking tours as well.

Taxi It's a rare thing indeed to see taxi tours mentioned in a Lonely Planet guide, as they tend to be pricey – and this is no exception. But if you're willing to invest DM200 for four people (DM250 on Saturday, Sunday and holidays), we highly recommend a 2½-hour taxi tour (in English, French or German) with official city guide Anselm Vogt-Moykopf (☎ 01072-740 11 38).

Herr Moykopf is a very knowledgeable and easy-going fellow who really loves the city, its architecture, his job and taking people to out-of-the-way, beautiful regions nearby.

Boat Between March and October, Neckar Personen Schiffahrt (☎ 541 07 3) runs one and two-hour Neckar River tours (DM9.50/15) from its dock opposite Wilhelma in Bad Cannstatt. They take place Monday to Friday at 9 and 11 am; Saturday, Sunday and holidays at 11 am.

Special Events

The city organises a number of notable annual events:

Sommerfest (August)
: Open-air festival with live music and food, at Schlossplatz.

Weindorf (late August)
: Stuttgart's biggest wine festival; hundreds of booths sell the year's vintages. Very chic affair. At Schlossplatz and Oberer Schlossgarten.

Cannstatt Folk Festival (late Sept/early Oct)
: A large beer festival. Stuttgart's version of the Oktoberfest has better-behaved crowds, lower prices and better beer. Held at venues throughout the city.

Weihnachtsmarkt (late November to Christmas)
: Christmas market on Markt and Schillerplatz.

Places to Stay

Camping You can camp at *Campingplatz Stuttgart* (☎ 556 69 6), by the river at Mercedesstrasse 40, just 500m from the Bad Cannstatt S-Bahn station on the small river called Cannstatter Wasen.

Hostels If you're between 16 and 27, the best deal in town is *Tramper Point Stuttgart* (☎ 817 74 76), Wiener Strasse 317, open late June to early September. Beds are DM10. Breakfast is DM5, but there's a kitchen where you can cook, and a washing machine. Check-in is from 5 to 11 pm, and there's a three-night maximum stay. Take U-Bahn No

Besenwirtschaft

For one month in autumn and in spring, wine growers throughout the region attach brooms to the front of their homes to indicate that they're a *Besenwirtschaft*, a small restaurant that allows people to come in and taste the new vintage (around DM4 for a quarter-litre). They open from 11 am and also serve lunch and dinner featuring typical Swabian dishes like *Kartoffelsuppe*, *Gaisberger March* (a stew of sliced potatoes, noodles and beef), and the evil-sounding *Schlachtplatte* (sauerkraut with pork belly, liver, lard sausage and smoked meat, with peas and other vegetables).

Some Besenwirtschaft open every year, but most don't. Check in *Lift Stuttgart* or *S-Trip*, published in the *Stuttgarter Zeitung* on the last Wednesday of the month during vintage times.

Besenwirtschaft that operate annually include the home of *Jürgen Krug* (☎ 859 08 1), Wildensteinstrasse 24 in Feuerbach, which also holds free art shows and performances by artistes – singers, cabaret performers, variété types etc (take tram No 6 to Feuerbacher Krankenhaus). The *Family Ruoff* (☎ 321 22 4), Uhlbacher Strasse 31, Obertürkheim, is in a fabulous house built in 1550 (S-Bahn No 1 to Obertürkheim). In Untertürkheim, *Helmut Zaiss* (☎ 331 14 9), Strümpfelbacher Strasse 40, has a romantic vaulted wine cellar. Bus Nos 60 and 61 (direction: Rotenberg/Fellbach) stop right in front. ■

6 to Sportpark Feuerbach north-west of the centre.

The *DJH hostel* (☎ 241 58 3), Haussmannstrasse 27, is a signposted 15-minute walk east of the Hauptbahnhof. Beds cost DM23/27 for juniors/seniors, and the curfew is midnight.

The non-DJH *Jugendgästehaus* (☎ 241 13 2), south-east of the centre at Richard-Wagner-Strasse 2, charges DM35/60 for singles/doubles (take U-Bahn No 15, the Heumaden tram, and get off seven stops from the train station).

Private Rooms & Long-Term Rentals Stuttgart offers two Mitwohnenzentrale offices: AMB-Mitwohnbüro (☎ 194 22), at Hauptstätter Strasse 154, and the Home Company (☎ 221 39 2), at Frank-Korn-Lerchenstrasse 72.

Hotels & Pensions The Surprise deal from Stuttgart-Marketing (see Tourist Offices under Information) costs DM88 and includes a hotel room with breakfast, a City-Pass, Night-Pass and three-day transport ticket.

You'll need to book ahead for the plain but central *Pension Märklin* (☎ 291 31 5), Friedrichstrasse 39, which charges DM45/80 for singles/doubles (without breakfast). The Greek-run *Hotel Dieter* (☎ 235 16 1), Brennerstrasse 40, has spartan rooms for DM50/90 (but try bargaining). Rooms at the *Gasthof Alte Mira* (☎ 295 13 2), Büchsenstrasse 24, start at DM60/100 or DM75/130 without/with private shower. Just around the corner at Hospitalstrasse 9 is the smaller *Museumstube* (☎ 296 81 0), with simple rooms from DM55/82 and doubles with bath from DM104 to DM120.

The best value in the city centre is offered by *Holl's Arche* (☎ 245 75 9), an old tavern just off Markt at Bärenstrasse 2. Here, singles/doubles with private shower and toilet cost only DM80/130.

The *Pension Schaich* (☎ 602 67 9), at Paulinenstrasse 16, has large and sunny rooms (soundproofed to combat the noisy overpass outside) for DM65/100, or DM75/110 with shower cubicle in the room.

Service is excellent at the *Hotel Köhler* (☎ 166 66 0), Neckarstrasse 209 (U-Bahn Nos 1, 11 and 14 stop right in front at Metzstrasse), where simple rooms without bath range from DM68/110, and with shower and toilet from DM95/140.

The *Wirt am Berg* (☎ 262 20 08), in a quiet backstreet at Gaisburgstrasse 12a, has simple rooms for DM70/110. *Hotel Unger* (☎ 209 90; fax 209 91 00), Kronenstrasse 17, is very central, with a quiet location just south of the i-Punkt office; it's also the outlet for bicycle rentals (see Getting Around). It has pleasant singles/doubles from DM179/209.

The *InterCity Hotel* (☎ 225 00; fax 225 04 99) at the west end of the Hauptbahnhof has rooms from DM190/240.

Business travellers' current favourite is the curvy *Inter-Continental* (☎ 202 00; fax 202 01 2), Willy-Brandt-Strasse 30, with the usual spotless rooms (all with bay windows overlooking the Unterer Schlossgarten) from DM294/323.

Looming over the Hauptbahnhof is the priciest hotel, the *Steigenberger Graf Zeppelin* (☎ 204 80; fax 204 85 42), Arnulf-Klett-Platz 7, which had better be pretty luxurious indeed for rooms that start at DM305/405.

Places to Eat

Some other good eating places are listed under Pubs & Bars in the Entertainment section.

Restaurants – bottom end Join the shoppers and office workers gathered at *iden*, Eberhardstrasse 1. It's a spacious, vegetarian, cafeteria-type restaurant with a healthy spread of wholefood selections from salads to sweets. It's open weekdays until 8 pm (or 9 pm on Thursday) and Saturday until 4 pm.

Stuttgart is a good place to sample the special Swabian flavours of central Baden-Württemberg. The *Weinstube Stetter* (☎ 240 16 3), at Rosenstrasse 32, has simple Swabian specialities like Linsen und Spätzle (lentils with noodles) or Maultaschen (meat and spinach 'ravioli') for under DM8. There's also a great assortment of regiona wines at down to earth prices. It's open weekdays until 11 pm, and Saturday until 4 pm.

The *Stuttgarter Kellerschenke* (☎ 294 44 5) is downstairs in the unpretentious trade union hall at Theodor-Heuss-Strasse 2a, and offers daily three-course Swabian menus from DM12.50. It's open Monday to Friday from 10 am to midnight. The cosy *Urbanstuben*, on the corner of Urbanstrasse and Eugenstrasse, has predominantly vegetarian dishes from around DM20 and some excellent local wines.

Restaurants – middle *Ali's Brasserie*, at Eberhardstrasse 49, is popular with young Stuttgarters, and serves very good Turkish cuisine. More adventurous is *Pica Pao*, Pfarrstrasse 7, open to 2 am, which features Latin American-inspired combinations like maize pancakes (DM12.50) and cauliflower with avocado cream (DM14.50) along with the more predictable tortillas.

If you can get past the unattractive entrance and climb down the creepy stairs to get into *China Restaurant Asia* (☎ 261 84 2), Neckarstrasse 220, you're in for a good meal, though the evening prices – from DM17 to DM22 for most dishes, are a little high for what you get. It's better to come at lunchtime when several specials cost under DM12. It's close to the zoo and just opposite the Hotel Köhler.

Restaurants – top end For a blow-out meal in a great restaurant with a fantastic view, bring lots of cash to *Wielandshöhe* (☎ 640 88 48), directly opposite the Wielandshöhe U-Bahn station at the top of the hill. The menu is a mixture of German and European specialities, but it leans heavily to French and French-influenced Continental European – in other words, a good place for a romantic evening, but expect to drop DM75 to DM125 per person including drinks and dessert.

Beer Gardens Of Stuttgart's many beer gardens, the best three we know of are in the Unterer Garten, Karlshöhe and the courtyard of the James F Burns Institute on Karlsplatz. You'll need to put down a DM3 deposit *(Pfand)* on your glass. They all sell Dinkel Acker beer and other brands, along with great food. Main courses cost from DM9 to DM18, salads under DM10.

The *Altes Schutzenhaus* (☎ 649 81 57), Burgstallstrasse 99 at Südheimer Platz, is a very popular place packed with students who sit outside this old castle-like building. There's a disco on Saturdays as well.

Snacks & Fast Food The *Marktstation* in the Hauptbahnhof is a stylish, but cheap food court with fruit stalls, a McDonald's, a pizza place and a Wurst-Bratkartoffeln. In the main terminal there are four good pretzel and sandwich places, too.

The *Markthalle*, a superb Art Nouveau-style market gallery on Dorotheenstrasse, is the perfect place to pick up delicatessen goodies for your picnic in the nearby parks; it's open weekdays from 7 am to 6 pm and to 2 pm on Saturday.

For a really cheap lunch, though, try the university *Mensa* at Holzgartenstrasse 11. The upstairs dining hall is officially reserved for students but the ground-floor cafeteria and the small *Mensa Stüble* in the basement, where meals cost only around DM7, are open to all.

Entertainment

Listings *Lift Stuttgart* is a good publication that distributes two versions: a free version called a 'free uni-guide to Stuttgart and the region', and its twice-as-hefty *Stadt Magazine* (DM4.50). Both available throughout the city, they are spectacularly indexed and easy-to-use German-language practical guides to the city.

Prinz (DM5) is another listings magazine that does about the same thing but not quite as well.

Rosa Telefon (☎ 194 46) is a gay information and help line; Lesbenberatung im Fetz (☎ 285 90 02), Obere Strasse 2, is the same for lesbians.

You can get tickets to almost everything that's on in the city at the i-Punkt office.

Cinema There's English-language cinema at the *Lupe*, *Artilier* and at the *Kommunales Kino* (☎ 221 32 0), Friedrichstrasse 23a in the old Amerika Haus building. Check in *Lift Stuttgart* and *Prinz* for details.

Discos & Clubs Once a snooty, exclusive place, *Boa* (☎ 226 31 13), Südheimer Platz 99, seems to open and close all the time these days. It was open and not so snooty when we last visited, and it's very big on Monday nights, when the rest of the city is relatively dead. It attracts a youngish crowd; the music is soul, funk and house.

If you like thudding music, *M1*, Wagenladungstrasse 30, is the place for you: two dance floors filled with crazy, pierced people wearing few clothes. It's a big techno scene.

The biggest and best known club in town is *Perkins Park* (☎ 256 00 62), Stresemannstrasse 39, massive place with two dance floors, a restaurant, a pool table and a very well mixed crowd aged from 16 to 60. There's techno, Brazilian, rock 'n' roll, soul, hip-hop ... you name it.

Palais (☎ 226 32 52), Königstrasse 22, is a mainstream disco and cocktail bar right near Schlossplatz. It has a ladies-only male stripper show on Friday from 10 to 11 pm.

Gay & Lesbian The *King's Club* (☎ 226 45 58), Gymnasiumstrasse 21, is predominantly gay but there are some women here as well; most are lesbian. *Laura's Club* (☎ 290 16 0), Lautenschlagerstrasse 20, is a lesbian disco that's also an information centre.

Theatre & Classical Music The Stuttgart area has 40 theatres and dozens of music venues. The *Staatstheater* (☎ 221 79 5), in the Oberer Schlossgarten just near Konrad-Adenauer-Strasse, holds regular orchestral, ballet and opera performances; the Stuttgart Ballet is renowned as one of the best in Europe.

The *Stuttgart Variété im Friedrichhaus* (☎ 778 57 77), Friedrichstrasse 24, is locally famous for its excellent variety shows and cabaret productions.

The *Theaterhaus* (☎ 402 07 0), at Ulmer Strasse 241, east of the centre in Wangen (take U-Bahn No 4 or 9 and get off at the Im Degen stop), stages anything from serious theatre productions to jazz concerts and cabaret. The *Laboratorium* (☎ 341 14 66), east of the centre at Wagenburgstrasse 147 (take bus No 42 from Schlossplatz), has live bands most nights. See the tourist office for reservations and tickets.

Rock & Jazz Check in *Lift Stuttgart* and at the tourist office for special events. Live music is a regular fixture at *Longhorn/LKA* (☎ 409 82 90), Heiligenwiesen 6, and at *Ali's Litfass* (see Pubs & Bars). There's also regular jazz and rock at the *Theaterhaus* (see Theatre & Classical Music).

Pubs & Bars On the corner of Friedrichstrasse and Lautenschlagerstrasse is the grandly named *Palast de Republic*, a busy bar that's grown from a kiosk to an institution. Probably the coolest place for bars is tiny Geissstrasse, just a block from Eberhardstrasse, where there are several little café-pubs that pour out onto what's unofficially called Hans-im-Glück Platz – a little square with a fountain depicting the German fairy-tale character 'Lucky Hans'.

The café-pubs include the chi-chi *Paddock*, the very friendly *Max and Moritz*, which also does great pasta and pizzas; *Deli*, a local favourite; and *Hans im Glück*, which is probably the best-known cocktail bar in Stuttgart.

The *Waschsalon* (☎ 236 98 96) at Charlottenstrasse 27 (see Laundry under Information) is doing its best to become a night spot too.

Ali's Litfass (☎ 243 03 1), Schwabenzentrum, just around the corner from Ali's Brasserie and down the steps, is a really fine courtyard pub with drinks, great coffee (large ones, served in bowls) and, on weekends, live music.

Things to Buy

There are a number of weekly markets in Stuttgart; the biggest are the food markets on Markt and the flower markets on Schiller,

BADEN-WÜRTTEMBERG

which take place on Tuesday, Thursday and Saturday from 7 am to 12.30 pm. There's a large flea market every Saturday at Karlsplatz.

Even if you aren't into shopping, it's worth browsing in the nearby Breuninger Passage shopping centre, south of Markt, the most expensive department store in the city.

While all styles and types of German wines are produced in the region, the most popular locally produced wine is Trollinger, a full-bodied – and very drinkable – red made from a variety of grape originally brought to the region from the South Tirol in Austria.

Stuttgarters account for twice the national average consumption of wine, so while it's readily available here, they're not really exporting a lot. See Wine in the Facts for the Visitor chapter for basic descriptions of German wine and labels. Locally the big players include:

Stuttgarter Mönchhalde Trollinger – The most popular red, accounting for about 25% of all wine produced in the region

Rotenberger Schlossberg Herold – A cross between Portugieser and Lemberger reds, it's light and fruity

Cannstatter Zuckerle Lemberger – The rich soil and sunshine in Cannstatter produces a sweeter, fruity, dark red

Stuttgarter Mönchhalde Müller Thurgau – A cross between Riesling and Sylvaner

You can buy local wines in liquor shops, at the Wine Museum (see Uhlbach in the Around Stuttgart section) or during the annual Weindorf celebration (see Special Events), but the most fun is going round by bicycle or car to wine growers and tasting there. Call ahead to see if they're open for tastings (they change their schedules and hold special events constantly) and for directions.

Wine producers include Weingärtnergenossenschaft Bad Cannstatt (☎ 542 26 6); Weingärtnergenossenschaft Fellbach (☎ 578 80 30); and Weingärtnergenossenschaft Untertürkheim (☎ 331 09 2).

Getting There & Away

Air Stuttgart's busy international airport (☎ 948 0), south of the city, is served by domestic and international airlines. Airline offices here and in the city include:

Austrian – Lautenschlagerstrasse 20 (☎ 221 11 1)
British Airways – airport (☎ 299 47 1)
Delta – Arnulf-Klett-Platz 3 (☎ 293 44 1)
Finnair – Calwer Strasse 23 (☎ 229 09 0)
Iberia – Königstrasse 31 (☎ 221 02 8)
Lufthansa – airport (☎ 223 00)
Singapore – Arnulf-Klett-Platz 3 (☎ 221 87 4)

Bus Eurolines runs international buses to numerous cities in Europe from the bus station next to the Hauptbahnhof.

Train There are frequent departures for all major German and many international cities, including ICE and IC trains to Frankfurt (DM77, 1⅓ hours), Berlin (DM229, six hours) and Munich (DM76, 2¼ hours). There's also a very frequent regional service to Tübingen (DM15.50, one hour), Schwäbisch Hall (DM27, 1½ hours), Ravensburg (DM57, two hours) and Ulm (DM23, one hour).

Car & Motorcycle The A8 from Munich to Karlsruhe passes Stuttgart, as does the A81 from Würzburg south to Lake Constance.

Ride Services An ADM-Mitfahrzentrale (☎ 636 80 36) is at Lerchenstrasse 65.

Getting Around

The Airport S-Bahn Nos 2 and 3 run frequently between the airport and the Hauptbahnhof. The ride takes about 30 minutes. A taxi from the airport to the centre of town will cost between DM40 and DM45.

Public Transport On Stuttgart's public transport network single fares are DM1.80/2.70 for short/long trips within the central zone. A four-ride strip ticket costs DM9.80, but a three-day central-zone ticket is better value at DM12, and includes the airport.

Car & Motorcycle The city is a pleasure to drive in – great roads and excellent street signs. There's underground parking throughout the centre costing about DM3.50 for the first hour and DM3 per hour after that.

There are Avis, Sixt and Europcar car-rental offices at the airport and in the Vermietungzentrum in the Hauptbahnhof.

Taxi Taxis cost DM4.70 at flag fall and DM2.60 per kilometre, plus DM2 for calling a taxi (☎ 194 10 or ☎ 566 06 1).

Bicycle You can rent bicycles (DM8/18/25/65/100 per hour/half-day/day/weekend/week) at Rent a Bike (☎ 209 90), which has branches throughout the area. The most central outlet is at the Hotel Unger on Kronenstrasse just west of Königstrasse.

You can travel on the S-Bahn with a bike Monday to Friday from 8.30 am to 4 pm and from 6.30 pm onward, and all day on Saturday, Sunday and holidays. The U-Bahn allows bikes only after 7.30 in the evening Monday to Friday, from 2 pm on Saturday and all day Sunday and holidays. No bikes are allowed on buses.

The Zahnradbahn tows a special cabin for bicycles. The ADFC has an office (☎ 636 86 37) in Stuttgart at Breitscheidstrasse 82. Call for bike maps, information on organised rides etc.

AROUND STUTTGART

The entire region around Stuttgart is worth exploring and it's easy to get there on bus, tram, S-Bahn, U-Bahn, or, better still, by bicycle. All the following places are within 20 minutes of the centre of the city by S-Bahn or U-Bahn.

Don't miss the spectacular vineyards and lovely paths along the Neckar, or the castles at Ludwigsburg.

Uhlbach

The best way to get into the spirit of the region is to head for the **Weinbaumuseum Uhlbach** (☎ 325 71 8), Ulbacher Platz 4, in an old pressing house; look for the statue of the *very* happy-looking fellow outside. There are exhibits on the history of wine making, but the tasting room is the big draw, with up to 16 wines available for tasting at any given time.

Tastes, in glasses large enough to cost A$7 at those chi-chi Sydney yuppie holes, cost DM2. You can learn an awful lot about the region's wines here. Admission is free.

Opposite the museum is the late-Gothic/Renaissance **Andreaskirche**, with an interesting steeple and, next to it, a **WWII monument** to locals who died.

Getting There & Away Take tram No 4 or S-Bahn No 1 to Obertürkheim and then catch bus No 62 to the museum.

Württemberg

When Conrad von Württemberg established the Württemberg family dynasty, he sensibly built the family castle on this absolutely breathtaking hill south-east of Stuttgart. The hill is covered with vines and the castle has sweeping views down into a gorgeous valley.

Katherina Pavlovna (1788-1819), the daughter of a Russian tsar and the wife of Wilhelm I of Württemberg (1781-1864), reputedly told her husband that she'd never seen such a beautiful place and that she hoped to be buried here when she died. When she did, Wilhelm tore down the Württemberg family castle and in its place built a **Russian Orthodox chapel**. The iconostasis of this chapel is not as impressive as the cornerstone (all that remains of what's believed to be Germany's oldest palace chapel) but downstairs is amazing. The tombs of Wilhelm and Katherina are at the east, and their daughter, Marie, at the south.

The chapel is open from March to October, Wednesday from 10 am to noon, Friday to Sunday and holidays from 10 am to noon and 1 to 5 pm. The grounds outside afford lovely views of the countryside and are a perfect place for a picnic.

Getting There & Away Bus No 61 runs here from the Obertürkheim S-Bahn station.

BADEN-WÜRTTEMBERG

Max-Eyth-See & River Ride

Bring a bicycle on this little excursion north-east of Stuttgart along the most beautiful stretches of the Neckar. On warm summer days, young Stuttgarters head for the public recreation areas at the Max-Eyth-See (U-Bahn No 14), a pleasant place for barbecues and picnics – though the water in the lake isn't too pristine. Ride or take the U-Bahn one stop north to Seeblickweg, then bicycle down to the river bank.

There's a large, well maintained bike path along this spectacular stretch of river bank. The steep hills still have some of the older terraced-style vineyards, and many of the little *Weingerter Häuschen* – tool sheds – that dot the hillside are over 200 years old and protected landmarks. You can follow the river all the way back into town.

Ludwigsburg

- *pop 83,000*
- *area code* ☎ 07141

Ludwigsburg is named for Duke Eberhard Ludwig, who built the Residenzschloss in this lovely baroque city – childhood home of Friedrich Schiller – a 20-minute train ride north of Stuttgart.

Orientation & Information The S-Bahn station is at the south-western end of town. Follow Myliusstrasse north-east to Arsenalstrasse and wend your way through the pedestrian centre to the Markt.

Ludwigsburg-Information (☎ 910 25 2) is at Wilhelmstrasse 10, one block south of the Markt, and open Monday and Thursday from 9 am to noon and 2 to 5.30 pm. On Tuesday, Wednesday and Friday it's open from 8.30 am to noon and 2 to 5.30 pm; on Saturday from 9 am to noon.

The main sights – the Residenzschloss and grounds, and Hunting Palace Favorit – are at the eastern end of town.

Things to See & Do The 18 buildings and 452 rooms comprising the **Residenzschloss** (1704-33) are now a museum but you can only view them on a guided tour. The tours leave every 30 minutes and cost DM8, discount DM4. In summer, the castle (☎ 186 44 0) is open daily from 9 am to noon and 1 to 5 pm. In winter tours take place Monday to Friday at 10.30 am and 3.30 pm, and every half hour on Saturday, Sunday and holidays from 10 am to noon and 1 to 4 pm.

In 1758, Duke Karl Eugen established a porcelain factory in the castle. It had its heyday in the late 18th century and you can see samples of what was made, as well as the porcelain that's still being made today, in the **Porzellan-Manufaktur im Residenzschloss**.

The amazing **Blühendes Barok** (baroque in bloom) floral festival is held in the gardens of the castle from April to September. The grounds are yet another fabulous picnic area.

There are two more castles of the former Württemberg rulers in the city. Just north of the Residenzschloss is the **Hunting Palace Favorit**, today in the centre of a nature preserve. The other, east of the city, is the lakeside **Monrepos.**

The **Städtisches Museum** (☎ 910 29 0), Wilhelmstrasse 9/1, has exhibits on the town's history and industry and regional life. It's open Wednesday to Sunday from 10 am to noon and 1 to 5 pm; admission is free. It's especially agreeable here at Christmas, during the Weihnachtsmarkt (Christmas fair).

Getting There & Away S-Bahn Nos 4 and 5 go directly to Ludwigsburg train station. Alternatively, take a two-hour ferry ride (DM26.60) from Bad Cannstatt to Ludwigsburg Hoheneck aboard a Neckar Personen Schiffahrt boat (☎ 541 07 3).

SCHWÄBISCH HALL

- *pop 30,500*
- *area code* ☎ 0791

The site of ancient Celtic saltworks, the city of Reichstadt Hall became known as Schwäbisch Hall in 1806 when it was granted to the district of Swabia.

The city is celebrated for its open-air theatre and its ancient buildings along the Kocher River. It is also known for the

Schwäbisch Hall banking and insurance company.

But the reason to come here is to see a German town that really does look like the ones portrayed in tourist brochures, on calendars and on chocolate boxes – a settlement of colourful half-timbered houses surrounded by rolling hills and covered bridges.

Because of its good hostel and camping grounds, it's also a cheap way to explore the area of the Schwäbisch Alb – a series of plateau-like hills crisscrossed with hiking and biking trails.

Orientation & Information

There are two main train stations: trains from Stuttgart arrive at the Hessental station; those from Heilbronn go to the Schwäbisch Hall one. Trains and buses run regularly between the two stations. The Kocher River runs south through the city separating the Altstadt (on the east) from the Neustadt. The bus station (Zentraler Omnibus Bahnhof, or ZOB) is on the east side of the Kocher, north of Neue Strasse, the main shopping drag.

The Hauptbahnhof is south-west of the Altstadt; cross the bridge, walk down the stairs and follow the path, which will lead you across Roter Steg Bridge and finally into Markt.

The tourist office (☎ 751 24 6), on the Markt, is open Monday to Friday from 9 am to 6 pm, Saturday from 10 am to 3 pm. The main post office is just west of the Markt.

Markt

The centrepiece of the Markt isn't the **Rathaus**, reconstructed in baroque style after a town fire in 1728 and again after WWII bombing, but rather the **Stadtkirche St Michael**, begun in 1156 but mainly constructed during the 15th and 16th century in late-Gothic style. Note the classical **net vaulting** on the ceiling of the choir. You can climb the **tower** (DM1) for a good view of the city.

Outside the church, the **staircase** has been used every summer since 1925 as the **Freilichtspiele**, or open-air theatre (see Entertainment).

Next to the tourist office is the **Gotischer Fischbrunnen** (1509), a large tub used for storing river fish for markets. There are still **markets** here every Wednesday and Saturday morning.

Just south of the Markt, at the end of Pfargasse, is the massive **Neubausaal**, built as an arsenal and granary and now a theatre; walk up the stone staircase on its south side for a wonderful view of the city. Looking down to the river you can see the former **city fortifications** and, crossing the river, the covered **Roter Steg Bridge** and the **Hangman's Bridge** connecting Neue Strasse to the west side of the Kocher.

Hällisches-Frankisches Museum

Housed in several buildings in the old city, the Hällisches-Frankisches Museum (☎ 751 28 9) covers the history of Swabia and Franconia. Exhibits include the houses themselves as well as artwork and crafts from the 17th century.

The museum's most important new addition won't be in place until 1999. It's an original **synagogue** (1738-39) from the town of Steinbach, near where the camp site is today. It was torn down piece by piece by the Nazis and placed into storage, but apparently forgotten. It was rediscovered recently by a local man when he was renovating his house and will be reconstructed and opened as a documentation of Jewish life in the region.

The museum is open Tuesday to Sunday from 10 am to 5 pm, to 8 pm on Wednesday. Admission is free.

Activities

For a very nice day-long hike, pick up maps from the tourist office which give details for walking along the river, past the former monastery at Comburg (see Around Schwäbisch Hall) and up to the Einkorn tower, on a hilltop 25km outside the city. There are rest areas with barbecue grills and playgrounds along the way. Unfortunately, there's no public transport back to town; a taxi ride (☎ 252 6 or ☎ 611 7) will cost you between DM45 and DM65.

Rent **rowing boats** just north of Roter Steg Bridge for DM5/8 per half hour/hour. Horse riding from Reit- und Fahrverein Schwäbisch Hall (☎ 837 0) costs DM30 per hour (DM15 for kids), or DM125 for five hours.

Places to Stay

Camping The idyllic *Campingplatz Steinbacher See* (☎ 298 4; open April to mid-October) charges DM9 per site plus DM7/5 per adult/child. There's a good restaurant, plus a washer/dryer and communal kitchen. Take bus No 4 to Steinbach Mitte.

Hostel The pristine *DJH hostel* (☎ 410 50), at Langenfelder Weg 5, charges juniors/seniors DM22/27 for dorm rooms or the same price in private two and three-bed rooms with showers and toilets (reserve early). Located in a large, recently renovated former retirement home, the hostel is antiseptically clean, and service is warm and friendly. There's a barbecue grill and picnic tables right outside, and it's 10 minutes on foot from the Markt.

Hotels & Pensions The *Krone* (☎ 602 2), next to the Stadtkirche St Michael at Klosterstrasse 1, offers singles/doubles from DM70/100 with shower and toilet, and from DM55/85 without. The *Gasthof Hirsch* (☎ 232 2), near the Hessental train station at Sulzdorfer Strasse 14, has simple rooms from DM40/75.

The *Hotel Garni Scholl* (☎ 975 50), just behind St Michael at Klosterstrasse 2-4, has very clean and newly renovated rooms from DM95/150.

Places to Eat

Zum Grünen Baum, at Gelbinger Gasse 33, serves main courses priced from around DM10 (closed Sunday). There's excellent pizza at *Da Cesare* (☎ 857 626), with enormous, scrumptious, truly New York-style slices for DM3.50 plain, DM5 with lots of toppings. There's a takeaway window, a sit-down restaurant doing full Italian meals from DM9 to DM15, an ice-cream parlour and an outdoor café.

Entertainment

The open-air theatre season is from June to September, when there are at least three, sometimes four, plays. Tickets, which range from DM27 to DM60, are available at the tourist office. And you can't peek: all the streets around the square are sealed off. Shows begin at sunset.

Getting There & Around

There's hourly (or more frequent) train service to Stuttgart (DM21, 1½ hours), one that leaves every two hours for Heilbronn (DM14, 45 minutes) and, via Crailsheim, a service to Swäbisch Gmund which goes every hour (DM23, 1¼ hours). The best way to go to Ulm is via Crailsheim; trains run at least hourly (DM29, 1½ hours). From Crailsheim, catch the regular service back to Schwäbisch Hall-Hessental and a connecting service to Schwäbisch Hall Hauptstadt.

Outfits renting bikes for DM10 a day include 2-Rad Zügel (☎ 890 66), Johanniterstrasse 55; Radsport Fiedler (☎ 930 24 0), Kirchstrasse 4 in Hessental; and MHW-Radsport (☎ 484 10), Schmollerstrasse 43.

AROUND SCHWÄBISCH HALL

Comburg

This former Benedictine monastery at the top of the hill just 5km south of Schwäbisch Hall was established in a baron's castle in 1078. Today it's a teacher's college, but its **Stiftskirche St Nikolaus** is a functioning Catholic church that's open to the public from mid-March to November, Tuesday to Saturday, from 10 am to noon and 1 to 5 pm, Sunday from 1.30 to 5 pm. Admission is DM2, discount DM1, free during church services on Sunday mornings. From here the views are terrific, especially across the way at **Kleine Comburg,** now a low-security prison for prisoners on work-exchange programmes. Take bus No 4 to Comburg.

Hohenloher Freiland Museum

For an easy immersion into the countryside

take bus No 7 to the front entrance of this open-air farming museum (☎ 840 61), in the town of Wackershofen, 10km west of Schwäbisch Hall. The ancient farmhouses have been taken from throughout the region and reconstructed here to show as closely as possible what farming life was like before the 20th century. There are fascinating demonstrations of farming and equipment.

Another big reason to come here is the **Weindorf**. Every weekend winemakers from throughout the region set up shop and give talks and tastings and sell snacks. Good fun and good prices.

The farming museum and wine village are open from April to October, Tuesday to Sunday from 10 am to 6 pm, daily in July and August. Admission is DM4/2.50.

Places to Stay & Eat The *Sonneck Hotel* (☎ 970 67 0), at Fischweg 2 in Gottwollshausen, is a very nice family-run place with clean rooms from DM60/90 and good service. There's a restaurant downstairs and a games room with pool tables.

Gasthof zum Roten Ochsen, at the entrance to the farming museum, has good local specialities from DM14 to DM16 and local beers from DM2.50 to DM5.

SCHWÄBISCH GMUND

- *pop 56,000*
- *area code* ☎ 07171

At the northern end of the Schwäbisch Alb, this little city has a fine collection of old buildings and churches, but it doesn't offer visitors much to do. Most people here are coach tourists stopping off for an hour or so on their way to somewhere else, or exchange students – the city has a University of Maryland campus.

The situation is different during Euro Weeks in July and August, when musicians from around the world perform at a number of venues. Ditto during the Guggenmusik Festival, the week before Fasching, when about 35,000 people descend on the city to watch Swiss performers, carrying home-made instruments and wearing outlandish costumes, storm through the city.

Orientation & Information

The Hauptbahnhof is a five-minute walk from the centre of the Altstadt at Markt. All the city's sights are within the Altstadt. The tourist office (☎ 603 45 5) is in the Kornhaus at the southern end of Markt, open Monday to Friday from 9 am to 5.30 pm, Saturday from 9 am to noon. Staff here can have an unhelpful attitude sometimes but be persistent. The post office is at the Hauptbahnhof, and there's a branch on the Markt. The stunningly restored city library is in the Spitalplatz complex at the northern end of Markt.

Things to See & Do

The city's Gothic **Münster**, said to be the largest long-hall cathedral in southern Germany, is very impressive, with amazing stained glass. The blue and red stained-glass windows (1951) represented Germany at Expo 1953 in Osaka. There are organ concerts every Friday evening. As you exit note the carvings of the Last Judgment in the south portal: depicting a bishop being sent to hell!

The **Lapidarium** in the Johanniskirche (DM1, discount DM0.50) contains old statues and gargoyles from the church tower and parts of demolished buildings from throughout the town.

Check at the tourist office for hiking and biking maps (or take bus No 4) if you want to get up to **Hohenrechberg**, the 707m hill just outside town. At the top, past the privately owned castle, now under restoration, and up the trail lined with icons, is the lovely baroque **Pfarrkirche St Maria** (1760). Look north over the hill for a spectacular view of Schwäbisch Gmund.

Places to Stay & Eat

There's a *camping ground* (☎ 97165-819 0) at Schurrenhof, in a beautiful hillside area. Bus No 4 will get you there, but if it's late, the owner will pick you up at the train station at no extra charge. The cost is DM6 per person and DM7.50 per tent in winter, DM7.50 per person and DM10 per tent in summer. There's a washer/dryer and a tiny swimming pool, and a little café as well.

The *hostel* (☎ 26 0), Taubenthalstrasse 46/1 at the top of the hill, has dorm beds for DM20/24, including breakfast. Book ahead in summer.

There are lots of snack food outlets in Markt, including a *Kochlöffel*. Two good restaurants in the centre are the *Restaurant Fuggerei* (☎ 300 03), Münstergasse 2, and the comfortable *Stube am Münster* (☎ 656 90), Münsterplatz 12.

At the top of Hohenrechburg is the *Gaststube Haus Rechburg* (☎ 445 49), a nice enough place with decent food costing from DM12 to DM16 and friendly staff.

Getting There & Away

There's no direct service to anywhere from Schwäbisch Gmund, but with one or two train changes, you'll get to Schwäbisch Hall (change in Crailsheim or Waiblingen, DM28, two hours), Ulm (change at Aalen, DM23, 1¾ hours) and Stuttgart (DM14, 40 minutes).

TÜBINGEN

- *pop 8000*
- *area code* ☎ 07071

In this picturesque university town, just 40km south of Stuttgart, wander through winding laneways and enjoy views of half-timbered houses and old stone walls. It's very popular with student travellers, but Tübingen's tourist office is seriously reaching in pointing out that Tübingen University – founded in 1477 by Duke Eberhard – is not just the region's oldest university but also 'Germany's oldest university established by a member of the lower ranks of the aristocracy'.

The city is famous for its university, which has over 25,000 students, as well as for the Stift, one of the earliest post-Reformation theological institutes. It is equally known for being a favourite haunt of Goethe (his first works were published here), and is a centre of student life, a lovely city in which to chill out for a few days, grab some great Swabian specialities and wines, hit some pubs and canoe or paddle your way around in the Neckar River.

Orientation

The Neckar flows from east to west in a boomerang shape through the town; the Altstadt and all important sights are at the north. The metre-wide Ammer River, a tributary, flows through the town north of the Neckar. The Hauptbahnhof is on the south side, a five-minute walk from the Neckarbrücke, which connects the north and the south banks with an exit onto the Platanenallee, a long, thin island in the middle of the Neckar extending to the west of the bridge. The hostel is on the north bank of the river, east of the bridge.

Information

The tourist office (☎ 91 36 0) is on An der Neckarbrücke beside the bridge. It's open Monday to Friday from 9 am to 7 pm, Saturday from 9 am to 5 pm. ADAC has an office (☎ 527 27) at Wilhelmstrasse 3.

Money There's a Post Bank right opposite the Hauptbahnhof with an ATM, and other banks throughout the city.

Post & Communications The main post office is in the Altstadt at the corner of Hafen Gasse and Neue Strasse.

Online Services There's a very cool Internet café called H@ckers (☎ 219 19) at Neustadtgasse 11, which stays open to 1 am.

Bookshops & Libraries Buchhandlung Heckenhauer Antiquariat, Holzmarkt 5, is a national landmark: Hermann Hesse worked here from 1895 to 1899.

The Frauenbuchladen Thalestris (☎ 265 90), Bursagasse 2, has an enormous assortment of women's books – no men are allowed inside. It's also a women's information centre and meeting place. The Brit Corner (see Things to Buy) has cheap used books in English.

The city library (☎ 204 54 0) is at Nonnengasse 19. The university library is at Wilhelmstrasse 32.

Laundry Try the Steinlach-Waschsalon (☎ 720 67), at Albrechtstrasse 21, or the Waschsalon im Stedentenwerk, at Rümelinstrasse 8.

Dangers & Annoyances Tübingen is a very safe town, but for some reason it has a high percentage of homeless people who flog newspapers. They can be persistent (they seem to hone in on backpackers), and they're everywhere.

North River Bank

Walking from the Neckarbrücke west beside the bank and the old city fortifications will bring you past the one-room **Zimmer Theater**, the fraternity **gondolas** and the **Hölderlinturm**, where the poet Friedrich Hölderlin (1774-1843) was treated for mental illness until his death. Today it is open as a museum dedicated to his life and work.

Up the little hill is the **Burse**, the first university building (1477), and the centre of academic life in the city; today the university campus is spread throughout the city. West of the Burse is the **Stift**, the central Lutheran clerical training college from 1536. It's still a theology school today and about half its students are women.

Schloss

From the heights of the Renaissance Schloss Hohentübingen (now part of the university), there are fine views over the steep, red-tiled rooftops of the Altstadt. The Schloss now houses an **Egyptology & Archaeology Museum** (open Wednesday to Sunday from 10 am to 6 pm, to 5 pm in winter; DM4/2). Walk through the tunnel at the west side of the courtyard, past 'lovers' lane' and follow the path down through the narrow winding streets of the Altstadt and eventually onto Haaggasse.

Markt

On Markt, the centre of town, which overflows with geraniums in summer, is the **Rathaus** (1433), with a riotous 19th-century baroque façade. At the top of the building is a glorious **clock**, **astronomical clock** and **moon-phase indicator** (1511). The four women of the **Neptune Fountain** represent the seasons, and the city council members who approved finance for the fountain modestly placed silhouettes of them- selves in the decorative ironwork.

At the northern side of Markt stands the **Lamm**, once a watering hole for many of Tübingen's well known figures; today it's owned by the Protestant church. Walk through the little passageway and there's a beer garden behind.

Stiftskirche

The late-Gothic Stiftskirche (1470) nearby is where university lectures were held before the main university buildings were erected. The church, which houses tombs of the Württemberg dukes and has excellent, original medieval stained-glass windows (some date to the early 15th century), is open daily from 9 am to 5 pm, to 4 pm from November to January. Admission is DM1/0.50.

Cotta Haus & Goethe Plaque

Opposite the western side of the Stiftskirche is the former home of Johann Friedrich Cotta, who first published the work of both Schiller and Goethe. Goethe stayed here for over a week in September 1797. Herr Goethe, who was known to glean inspiration from sampling most of the stock of the local pubs, apparently staggered back one night, missed the front door and wrote a Technicolour Poem on the wall next door. If you look up at the 1st floor window on that house, now a student dorm, you'll see a little sign: '*Hier Kotzte Goethe*' ('Goethe Puked Here').

Other Sights

The **Platanenallee**, the long sliver of an island in the middle of the Neckar, is especially pleasant in late June, when the fraternities hold their wildly popular gondola races, which draw thousands of spectators.

Misbehaving students (as young as 14) were given the choice of losing their wine ration or being sent to the city's **Karzer**, the student jail on Münzgasse. If you've seen the one in Heidelberg you can skip this one. If not, it can be part of a city tour at no extra cost if you specifically request it.

When shows are on at the **Kunsthalle** every couple of years, people arrive in droves. They're run by a Professor Götz Adriani, who has exceptional skills at talking big museums into lending their masterpieces to Tübingen. Some 250,000 people came here to see the Cézanne exhibition in 1993, and there's talk of a Van Gogh exhibition in the near future; check with the tourist office.

Organised Tours

The city tourist office conducts a German-language walking tour of the city every Saturday at 2 pm, starting at the Rathaus. The cost is DM6. It also arranges other tours, including one in Latin.

Places to Stay

Camping There is a convenient *camping ground* (☎ 431 45) at Rappenberghalde 61. The cost is DM5.50 to DM7 per tent plus DM9.50 per person (DM6 per child).

Hostel The *DJH hostel* (☎ 230 02) is at Gartenstrasse 22/2 on the north bank of the Neckar, just east of the tourist office. Dorm beds cost DM20/26 for juniors/seniors, including breakfast.

Private Rooms & Long-Term Rentals The Mitwohnzentrale Tübingen (☎ 551 02 0), Wilhelmstrasse 3/2, books rooms in private flats from DM35 to DM70 per person per day. The tourist office does the same; complete apartments with kitchens for three people go for DM100.

Familie Gellert (☎ 525 83), Gartenstrasse 35, has single and double rooms in their house for DM35 per person.

Hotels The *Hotel Am Schloss* (☎ 929 40), at Burgsteig 18, in the shadow of the castle, has a few simple singles/doubles from DM50 per person – very reasonable considering the central location and superb service. Ask for room No 26, which has views in all four directions. There's also a great restaurant here – see Places to Eat.

The *Hotel Hospiz Tübingen* (☎ 924 0), very close to the Markt at Neckarhalde 2, has rooms without baths from DM50/68, with bath from DM105/130. It's OK, but nothing to jump up and down about.

Places to Eat

The best chips/French fries (DM2) in Baden-Württemberg are at *X*, at the bottom of Kornhausstrasse – just follow the crowds. It also has Bratwurst and burgers from DM3 to DM4.

For super coffee, *Hanseatica*, at Hafengasse 2, can't be beaten and the coffee is only DM1.70 per cup; follow your nose.

Naturgabe Backstube, on the corner of Froschgasse and Kornhausstrasse, has organic bread products and lovely outdoor tables; cross the little bridge over the Ammer River to the entrance.

The *Markthalle Kelter*, on the corner of Kelternstrasse and Schmiedtorstrasse, is a food hall with cheap takeaway and restaurants, many selling organic products. The university *Mensa*, Hafengasse 6, has full meals from DM4, but student IDs are often checked.

Inside the shopping mall at the Nonnenhaus, at the northern end of Neue Strasse, are *Losterla* (☎ 279 49) and *Eis Café San Marco*; the former has excellent home-made pasta costing from DM6 per portion and both have great outdoor cafés.

The *Collegium*, on the corner of Lange Gasse and Collegiumsgasse , has good-sized main courses costing from DM13.

For a blow-out meal, the restaurant at the *Hotel Am Schloss* (☎ 929 40) is the place. It literally wrote the book on the local speciality, a ravioli-like stuffed pasta called Maultaschen; the owner, Herbert Rösch, published *Schwäbisches Maultaschen Buche* which is available around town. The restaurant serves 28 types of Maultaschen costing from DM12.90 to DM18; salad plates and light meals range from DM8 to DM15.

Sit on the back terrace for great views. Service is excellent.

Entertainment

English-language films are shown at the *Atelier* (☎ 212 25), Vor dem Haagtor 1, and at the *Museum* (☎ 133 55), Am Stadtgraben 2. *Cinderella* (☎ 335 57) is a mainstream disco; *Patty* (☎ 516 12), Schlachthofstrasse 9, does Turkish nights on Friday and Latin sounds on Saturday. *Tangente Jour* (☎ 245 72), Münzgasse 17, is the local *Szene* bar – and not to be confused with *Tangente Night* (☎ 230 07), Pfleghofstrasse 10, a big disco and nightclub.

Club Voltaire (☎ 512 14), Haaggasse 26b, at the end of the little alley, has gay and lesbian discos and cabaret. Check with the tourist office to see what's on at the *Zimmer Theater* (☎ 927 30), Bursagasse 16, and at the *LTT Landestheater* (☎ 931 31 49), Eberhardstrasse 6.

The *JazzKeller* (☎ 276 85), Haaggasse 15/2, has live jazz and 'funky soul'; *Tapas* (☎ 550 89 5), Bursagasse 4, has flamenco music and serves tapas costing from DM5 to DM9 and tortillas from DM8 to DM11. Good bars include the *Alt Tübingen*, opposite the JazzKeller; *H@ckers* (see Online Services), which stays open to 1 am; and, quite convenient to the hostel, *Neckar Müller* (☎ 278 48), Gartenstrasse 4 on the north side of the Neckarbrücke, a microbrewery and restaurant with a beer garden.

Things to Buy

Vinum (☎ 520 52), Lange Gasse 6, has over 400 wines from around the region and the world, and samples are free. It also sells fine sherries and spirits and a wonderful selection of olive oil.

The Brit Corner (☎ 272 63), Schmiedtorstrasse 13, is about as well stocked as the average (small) supermarket. It also buys and sells used English books, priced from DM3 to DM5, and (Aussie) Vegemite (DM8).

Getting There & Away

Tübingen can be easily visited on a day trip from Stuttgart. Direct trains link the two twice hourly (DM31 return, one hour). There's a Mitfahrzentrale (☎ 194 40) at Münzgasse 6 and a Mitfahrzentrale für Frauen (☎ 265 90) at the women's bookshop at Bursagasse 2.

Getting Around

You can book a taxi on ☎ 243 01. Rent bicycles (DM18 for the first day, DM14 each additional day) from FahrRadladen Am Rathaus, Haaggasse 3. Rent rowing boats/pedal boats/canoes at Bootsvermietung Märkle Tübingen (☎ 315 29) for DM10.50/16/9 per hour. It's just east of the bridge, behind the tourist office down the little stairs.

A more stylish way of cruising down the river is aboard one of the university fraternities' gondolas; count on DM100 per boat, which holds about 20 people. They're on the north bank of the river, west of the bridge.

HEIDELBERG

- *pop 140,000*
- *area code* ☎ 06221

Although Heidelberg was devastated in 1622 during the Thirty Years' War (1618-48) and all but destroyed by invading French troops under Louis XIV in 1689 and 1693, the city's magnificent castle and medieval town are irresistible drawcards for most travellers.

The American novelist and humourist Mark Twain (1835-1910) began his European travels here and recounted his comical observations in *A Tramp Abroad*. Britain's JMW Turner (1175-1851) loved Heidelberg too, and it inspired him to paint some of his greatest landscapes.

With a sizable student population (attending the oldest university in Germany), Heidelberg is a lively city. This is the place for a serious pub crawl. There are dozens of earthy, enjoyable bars and pubs, with good beer, friendly local people and heaps of tradition. But be warned: Heidelberg is perhaps the most popular city in the state, with over three million visitors passing through its narrow, twisting streets annually. It is chock-a-block with tourists during the high season of May and June and again in autumn.

Orientation

The modern and less interesting western side

of the city starts near the train station. To find out what this city is really all about head down Kurfürsten-Anlage to Bismarck Platz, where the romantic old Heidelberg begins to reveal itself. The Neckar River runs east-west just north of the Altstadt; streets that go from east to west (ie those parallel to the Neckar) are called 'strasse', and north-south ones are called '-gasse'. Hauptstrasse is the pedestrian thoroughfare, leading 1600m – the so-called Royal Mile – eastwards through the heart of the old city from Bismarck Platz via Markt to Karlstor.

Two main bridges cross the Neckar from the Altstadt: at the western end, north of Bismarck Platz, is the Theodor-Heuss-Brücke; north of the Markt is the Alte Brücke (also known as Karl-Theodor-Brücke).

On the north side of the Neckar is Heiligen Berg (Holy Hill); half way up is Philosophenweg (Philospher's Walk).

The castle (Schloss) is at the southern end of the city up the hill. The DJH hostel is north of the Neckar, west of Theodor-Heuss-Brücke.

The US military communities of Mark Twain Village and Patrick Henry Village, with about 15,000 residents, are south-west of the Altstadt.

Information

Tourist Offices Heidelberg's main tourist office, (☎ 194 33; fax 167 31 8; email cvbhd@info.hd.eunet.de), outside the train station, has exceptionally friendly staff and mountains of good advice, though queues can get long. It's open from 9 am to 7 pm Monday to Saturday throughout the year, plus Sunday from 10 am to 6 pm between mid-March and mid-November. There are tourist office branches open from May to October at the funicular station near the castle and on Neckarmünzplatz.

All the offices sell the Heidelberg Card (DM19.80), valid for 24 hours and including use of all public transport and discounts to museums, theatres and even some hotels and restaurants.

The ADAC has an office (☎ 720 98 1) at Carl-Diem-Strasse 2-4.

Money There's a Deutsche Verkehrsbank at the train station and other moneychangers throughout the city. American Express (☎ 912 70) has an office at Brückenkopfstrasse 1-2.

Post & Communications The main post office is in the huge white building just to the right as you leave the train station.

Online Services There's a new Internet Café (☎ 303 02 0) at Plöck 101.

Bookshops & Libraries Wetzlar (☎ 241 65), at Plöck 79-81, specialises in foreign-language books. There are English-language books and Lonely Planet titles at Koesters Akademische Buchhandlung (☎ 298 69), Hauptstrasse 72.

The university library (☎ 542 38 0), Plöck 107-109, has books in English, as does the Stadtbücherei (☎ 583 61 3/4), Poststrasse 15.

Campus The Ruprecht-Karl-Universität (☎ 540) is the oldest university in Germany, established in 1386 by Count Palatinate Ruprecht I, one of the seven imperial prince-electors.

The original university consisted of four faculties: philosophy, law, medicine and theology. Today it has more than 29,000 students from 80 nations in 18 faculties. Women, first admitted in 1900, now make up 51% of the student body.

Universitätsplatz is the historic centre of the university, but today the main campus is on the north side of the Neckar, west of the city.

International Centres The Deutsches-Amerikanisches Institut (☎ 247 71), Sofienstrasse 12, holds cultural events and has a library.

There's an Institut Français (☎ 252 88) at Seminarstrasse 3, offering French-language courses, a library, cultural events, concerts and cheese-smelling contests.

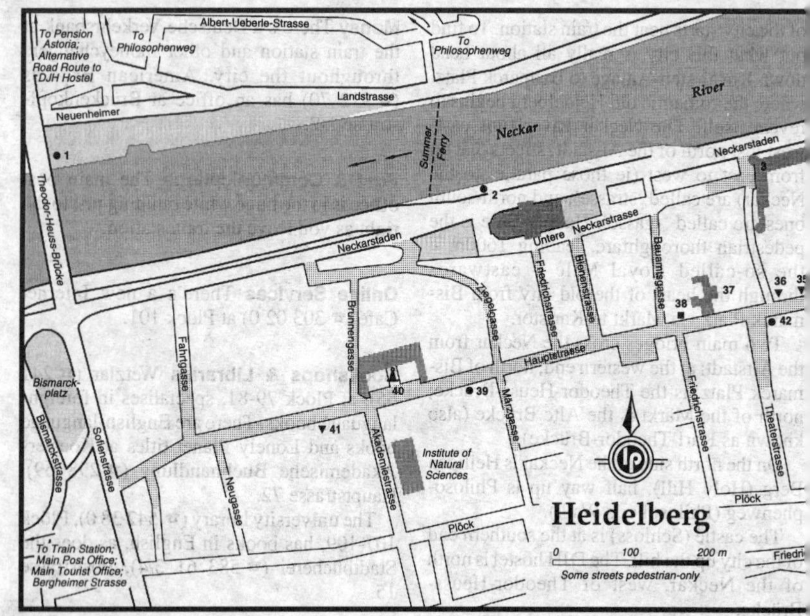

PLACES TO STAY

6 Hotel Vier Jahreszeiten
9 Hotel Goldener Hecht
30 Hotel Am Kornmarkt
31 Jeske Hotel
33 Hotel Zum Ritter
38 Hotel Futterkrippe
53 Hotel Zum Pfalzgrafen

PLACES TO EAT

12 Zur Herrenmühle
14 Sudpfanne
21 Starfish
22 Cafe Knössel
32 McDonald's
35 Zum Güldenen Schaf
36 Viva Italia/Viva Mexico
41 Nordsee
43 Riegler
49 Simplicissimus
52 University Mensa

OTHER

1 Boat Rental
2 Rhein-Neckar Fahrgastschiffahrt (River Boats)
3 Marstall
4 Karl-Theodor Statue
5 Monkey Statue
7 Napper Tandy's Irish Pub
8 Schnookeloch

Laundry There's an SB laundrette at Poststrasse 50. Or drop off your dirty smalls at Waschsalon Wojtala (closed Sunday), a fast and economical laundry service at Kettengasse 17.

Medical Services There's an American hospital (☎ 170) on Römerstrasse near Mark Twain Village.In an emergency, contact the Ärtzlicher Notdienst (☎ 192 92). For an ambulance call ☎ 192 22.

Schloss (Heidelberg Castle)

Heidelberg's large ruined castle is one of Germany's finest examples of a Gothic-Renaissance fortress and the city's chief attraction. Begun in the 13th century, its oldest remaining structures date from 1400. It was a residence of a branch of the Wittelsbachs, a noble family from Bavaria. Over the years, family and court intrigues led to many changes in ownership; the place was first sacked in 1623 by forces representing

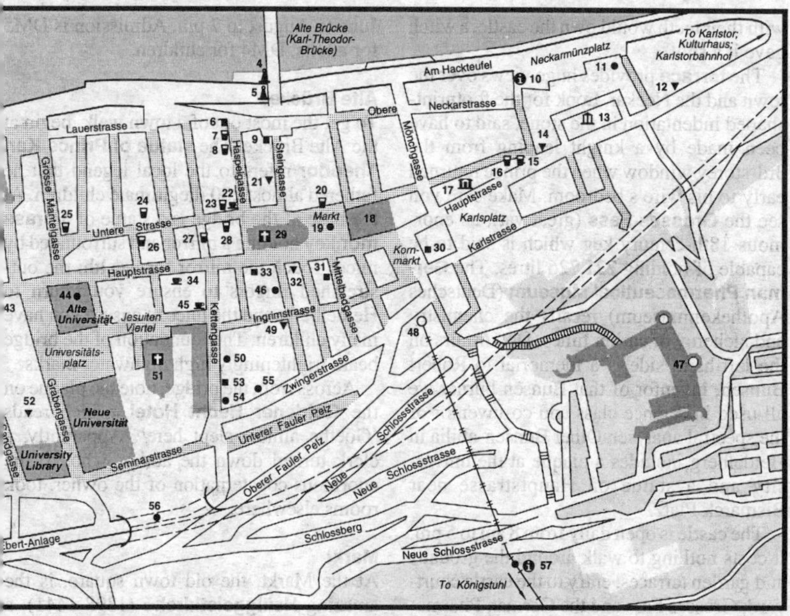

10	Tourist Office	25	Gasthaus Zum Mohren	45	Drugstore Café
11	Transport Exhibition	26	DeStille	46	Cave
13	Ethnology Museum	27	Palmbräu Gasse	47	Schloss
15	Zum Roten Ochsen	28	i Punkt	48	Funicular Railway (Kornmarkt Station)
16	Zum Sepp'l	29	Heiligkeitskirche		
17	Palais Boisserie	34	Café Journal	50	Waschsalon Wojtala
18	Town Hall	37	Palatinate Museum	51	Jesuit Church
19	Hercules Fountain	39	Koesters Books	54	Tangente – Disco
20	Cafe Max	40	Bunsen Statue	55	Zwinger3
23	Goldener Reichsapfel	42	Harmonie Cinema	56	Tunnelkult
24	Weinloch	44	Studentenkarzer	57	Tourist Office

the Catholic Wittelsbachs against Protestants within the castle. At the end of the Thirty Years' War the castle was rebuilt, but it was destroyed again in 1693, along with most other buildings in the city save for some 16 structures.

The building's half-ruined condition actually adds to its romantic appeal. Seen from anywhere in the Altstadt, the striking, red, sandstone pile dominates the hillside. There are several places to eat up here (see Places to Eat). The Renaissance **castle courtyard** is amazing. Outside, just east of the entry, is the **Pulver Turm** (gunpowder tower), destroyed by French forces in 1693. The half-destroyed wall and chimney behind it is worth a look.

As you walk through the outside fortifications and gates, look to the left at the tiny door with the iron ring. The ring is cracked; legend says that when Ludwig V announced that anyone who could bite through the ring with their teeth would own the castle, a witch gave it a shot.

The **terrace** provides huge views over the town and the Neckar. Look for the footprint-shaped indentation in the stone, said to have been made by a knight leaping from the 3rd-storey window when the prince returned early to his wife's bedroom. Make sure you see the **Grosses Fass** (great vat), an enormous 18th-century keg which is said to be capable of holding 221,726 litres. The **German Pharmaceutical Museum** (Deutsches Apothekenmuseum) recalls the chemistry and alchemy of earlier times. Downstairs on the left-hand side is a memorial to Robert Bunsen, inventor of that Bunsen burner we all used in science class and co-inventor of the spectral analyser. Other Bunsen-abilia in Heidelberg includes a plaque at the university and a statue on Hauptstrasse near Bismarck Platz.

The castle is open daily from 8 am to 5 pm. It costs nothing to walk around the grounds and garden terraces; entry to the castle courtyard, Grosses Fass and the German Pharmaceutical Museum is DM3/1.50, or sign up for the rather dull guided tour of the interior (DM4/2), which includes everything. For DM2 you can buy an English-language guide and map to the place.

To get to the castle, high on a hillside south of the town centre, either take the funicular railway from the lower Kornmarkt station (DM2.50, discount DM1.60 each way), or make the 'invigorating' 10-minute walk up steep cobbled lanes. If you walk, it's nice to start from the less-touristed path beginning at the east side of Karlplatz, which brings you past the statue of Goethe near the fountain.

Königstuhl & Fairy-Tale Park

The funicular continues up to the Königstuhl, where there's a TV Tower; the return fare from Kornmarkt, with a stop at the castle, is DM7. Also at the top of the hill is the Fairy-Tale Park (☎ 234 16), a wonderful playground with fairy-tale characters, hobby horses and other kiddie stuff. It's open March to October daily from 10 am to 6 pm, from June to August to 7 pm. Admission is DM5 for adults, DM4 for children.

Alte Brücke

To get the most out of a town walk, begin at the Alte Brücke. The **statue of Prince Karl Theodor** refers to the local legend that he fathered almost 200 illegitimate children. At the base of the bridge is a statue of a **brass monkey** holding a mirror and surrounded by mice. Touch the mirror for wealth; the outstretched fingers to ensure you return to Heidelberg; and the mice to ensure you have many children. The foundation of the bridge bears frighteningly high highwater marks.

Across from the bridge, note the plaque on the **Goldener Hecht Hotel**, which reads 'Goethe almost slept here'. Apparently, a clerk turned down the author who, to the enormous consternation of the owner, took rooms elsewhere.

Markt

At the Markt, the old town square, is the amazing **Heiliggeistkirche** (1398-1441), a Gothic cathedral with a baroque roof. There was, for a long time, a wall between one part used by Protestants, and that used by Catholics, but it was torn down in 1936. Today, it's a Protestant place of worship.

You can climb the 204 steps to the top of the church spire (DM1) Monday to Saturday from 11 am to 5 pm, from 1.30 pm on Sunday.

The **market stalls** surrounding the church are a Heidelberg tradition. Across the street, on the south side of the square, the lavishly decorated former **royal pharmacy** has been reborn as a McDonald's.

In the centre of the Markt is a **Hercules fountain**; in medieval times petty criminals were chained to the fountain and left to face the townsfolk.

Palais Boisseree

This former palace at Hauptstrasse 235, east of the Markt, is said to be the cradle of the Romantic movement. It once housed a collection of medieval altars and artworks that attracted poets, writers and artists (including

Goethe and the Brothers Grimm, among many others).

Ethnology Museum

This museum (open Tuesday to Friday from 3 to 5 pm, Sunday from 1 to 5 pm; DM3/2) contains, in the blockhouse behind the main building, an exhibit on the Asmat tribe of south-west Irian Jaya (now part of Indonesia). On the river side of the building, you can look through the glass to see the wonderful collection of boats and canoes.

Jesuiten Viertel

East of Universitätsplatz is Jesuit Quarter, a little square containing the city's former **Jesuit church** (1712-50), fronted by statues including **St Ignatius Loyola**, **St Francis Xavier**, **Christ** at the façade's top centre, and **Faith** on the rooftop. The church is still Catholic but not Jesuit.

Universitätsplatz

Dominating University Square are the 18th-century **Alte Universität** (Old University) and the **Neue Universität** (New University) buildings. Head south down Grabengasse to the **University Library** and then down Plöck to Akadamiestrasse and the old **Institute of Natural Sciences** where Robert Bunsen taught for more than 40 years.

Student Jail

From 1778 to 1914 the Studentenkarzer (student jail) was used to incarcerate university students guilty of such infractions as playing practical jokes, singing, womanising, drinking and goofing off. Sentences were generally a minimum of three days, during which they were fed only bread and water; during longer sentences, prisoners were permitted to have food delivered to them after the first three days. A stint in the jail was considered *de rigueur* to prove one's manhood. Women, who were only allowed entry to the university from 1900, were never imprisoned here.

The jailbirds passed their time by carving inscriptions and drawing on the walls (which you can still see).

The jail (☎ 542 33 4) is on Augustinergasse and opens daily from Tuesday to Saturday (admission DM1.50/1).

Palatinate Museum

The Palatinate Museum (☎ 583 40 2), tucked behind the courtyard at Hauptstrasse 97, contains regional artefacts and works of art, plus a copy of the jawbone of the 600,000-year-old Heidelberg Man. The original – the whole skeleton and not just the jaw – is held across the river at the specialised palaeontology centre, which is closed to the public.

The museum is open Tuesday to Sunday; admission is DM5/3.

Philosophenweg

A stroll along the Philosophenweg, north of the Neckar River, provides a welcome respite from the tourist hordes. Leading through steep vineyards and orchards, the path offers those great views of the Altstadt and the castle that were such an inspiration to the German philosopher Hegel. It's a well known lovers' haunt, and many young locals are said to have lost their hearts (and virginity) along the walkway. A little closer to the river bank is a meadow on which people gather to watch the tri-annual fireworks displays (see Special Events). There are also many other hiking possibilities in the surrounding hills.

You can rent rowing and pedal boats at the stand on the north side of Theodor-Heuss-Brücke. Charges are DM9/15 per half hour/hour for up to three people.

Organised Tours

The tourist office arranges several tours of the city each week. There are daily guided tours (DM10) in English and in German at 2 pm from April to October, and in German only from January to March; they depart from the Lion Fountain in Universitätsplatz.

Rhein-Neckar Fahrgastschiffahrt (☎ 201 81), at the docks on the south bank of the Neckar, offers a huge range of tours and trips throughout the Neckar Valley. Boats leave for three-hour river cruises daily at 9.30 and 11 am and 2 and 2.40 pm (extra trips are sometimes available). Return tickets are DM16.50/9.50. See Around Heidelberg for more information.

Special Events

Heidelberg has many annual festivals. The most popular are Heidelberger Herbst, the huge autumn festival during which the entire pedestrian zone is closed off to non-ticket-holders for a wild party on the last Saturday in September, and the fireworks festivals, held three times a year (on the first Saturday in June and September, and the second Saturday in July).

During these festivities the castle is specially lit and the whole town, plus members of the US military communities, show up to watch the magic. Best viewing sites are from the northern bank of the Neckar and from Philo- sophenweg.

The city's Christkindlmarkt, held at the Markt throughout December, is also very special.

Places to Stay

You don't get very good value for money when it comes to accommodation in Heidelberg and in the high season finding *any* place to stay can be difficult. Arrive early in the day or book ahead – especially for the hostel.

Camping *Camping Neckartal* (☎ 802 50 6), about 4.5km east of the city by the river, costs DM8 per site and DM7.50 per person. Take bus No 35 from Bismarck Platz and get off at the Orthopädische Klinik. It's open from Easter to October.

Camping Haide (☎ 02663-211 1), across the river and back towards town about 1km, has sites for DM6 plus DM8 per adult, DM2/1.50 per car/motorcycle. You can also rent a place in the dormitory lofts – like bunk barns – for DM9.50 per person, or in more private log huts for DM16.50/33/58 for one/two/four people. Take bus No 35 to the Schwäbische Brücke stop, cross the bridge and walk east along the river.

Hostels The local *DJH hostel* (☎ 412 06 6) is across the river from the train station at Tiergartenstrasse 5. The rates are DM22/27 for juniors/seniors (including breakfast). To get there from the station or Bismarck Platz, take bus No 33.

The veteran *Jeske Hotel* (☎ 237 33) is ideally situated at Mittelbadgasse 2. Frau Jeske offers beds in simple rooms for just DM24 without breakfast.

Private Rooms & Long-Term Rentals It's very difficult to book private rooms in the city. The tourist office represents a very limited number of private flats in town that cost from about DM65 to DM80 per double, but they book out very quickly and well in advance.

However, the office can easily book rooms in the DJH hostel and in hotels and pensions. The service is free, but you have to make a 7% deposit on the room at the tourist office when you book it. Pay the balance when you check in.

The tourist office (☎ & fax 800 64 9) in Ziegelhausen, 4km east of the city, books private rooms from DM35/65 a single/double, including breakfast. Bus No 33 or 34 from Bismarck Platz goes there every 20 minutes.

If you want to stay at least a month in Heidelberg, contact the Home Company (☎ 194 45).

Hotels & Pensions With a few notable exceptions, the cheap places are well outside the old part of town. Many places have rates that vary according to the season.

The *Kohler* (☎ 970 09 7), east of the train station at Goethestrasse 2 and within walking distance, has singles/doubles from DM66/118. The tiny *Astoria* (☎ 402 92 9), Rahmengasse 30, in a quiet residential street north of the river just across Theodor-Heuss-Brücke, has rooms for DM65/110. At the *Hotel Elite* (☎ 257 34), Bunsenstrasse 15, all rooms come with private shower; it charges DM75/95.

Near the Alte Brücke (Karl-Theodor-Brücke) is the *Hotel Vier Jahreszeiten* (☎ 241 64), Haspelgasse 2, with singles/doubles varying from DM85/135 in low

BADEN-WÜRTTEMBERG

season to DM130/165 in high season. It's claimed that Goethe himself once creased the sheets here. One place we know he didn't sleep in is the *Goldener Hecht* (☎ 166 02 5), Steingasse 2, where the author would have been happy to fork out DM115/170 for a single/double had the clerk not been so uppity (see the Alte Brücke section).

Another lower-budget hotel in Heidelberg's Altstadt is *Hotel Am Kornmarkt* (☎ 243 25), Kornmarkt 7, where the rates are DM120/175 for rooms with shower and toilet or DM90/120 without. Similar is the *Hotel Zum Pfalzgrafen* (☎ 536 10), Kettengasse 21, where fully equipped rooms cost from DM100/150 a single/double.

The *Renaissance Heidelberg Hotel* (☎ 908 0; fax 908 50 8) has rooms from DM155/255. It's at Vangerowstrasse 16, north of the train station, and it's the drop-off/pick-up point for the Lufthansa Airport Express bus.

The ornate 16th-century *Romantik Hotel-Zum Ritter St Georg* (☎ 135 0; fax 135 23 0), Hauptstrasse 178 on Markt, is one of the few buildings in Heidelberg to have survived the French attacks of 1693. Standard singles/doubles cost DM160/265.

Places to Eat

You might expect a student town to have plenty of cheap eating options, but free-spending tourists seem to outweigh frugal scholars in Heidelberg.

Restaurants & Cafés The *Güldenen Schaf*, a large old tavern at Hauptstrasse 115, has an extensive menu, with vegetarian fare from DM13 and local specialities priced from around DM20. The *Sudpfanne*, at Hauptstrasse 223, has similar cuisine.

For fine dining, head to *Simplicissimus* (☎ 183 33 6; closed Tuesday), at Ingrimstrasse 16, where main courses start at DM32.

If you want to impress someone, take them to the super-deluxe *Zur Herrenmühle* (☎ 129 09), Hauptstrasse 237-39, east of the Ethnology Museum. Service is superb but slow, and you get smallish portions of outstanding nouvelle cuisine (don't blink or you'll miss it). You'll need loads of time and lots of dosh; main courses here cost from DM46 to DM60.

Cafés Heidelberg's current favourite café is the *Starfish* (☎ 125 87), Steingasse 16a, which has quality 'natural food' like vegetarian Balinese curry with basmati rice for DM15.50. The place is small, so it fills up quickly.

Up at the castle, there's a *café* outside near the cashier that's fine for snacks, but the *bistro* inside is truly good and a good deal, with local specialities from DM10 to DM13 – definitely don't miss the pasta pockets (a bit like big ravioli) and, if they have it on the menu, the turkey Bratwurst with cabbage cooked in wine.

For a quick sugar fix, head for the somewhat stuffy *Café Knösel* (☎ 223 45), Haspelgasse on the corner of Untere Strasse, which sells 'student kisses' (chocolate-covered wafers) and other tasty things, along with very good coffee and cocoa.

At the Markt's north side, *Café Max* is a big favourite, and it's a bit more democratic than the more posey 'intellectual' cafés. One of the best of those is *Café Journal* at Hauptstrasse 162, where you can linger for hours over a cup of coffee and read the English-language papers. Serious chess players (and other quiet guests) gather at the small *Drugstore Café*, Kettengasse 10, and at *DeStille* on Untere Strasse.

Snacks & Fast Food For students, a viable option is the *Mensa*, at Universitätsplatz, where a meal costs only about DM4. For takeaways seek out fast-food places along Hauptstrasse, including the *McDonald's* in the Markt (with another branch at the railway station); the *Nordsee* at Hauptstrasse 40; the awesome pastry, pizza and bread offerings at *Riegler*, at No 118 of the same street; and the double-whammy of Italian and Mexican food at *Viva Italia/Viva Mexico* (☎ 285 86), No 113a, with excellent pizzas (DM2 for itty-bitty ones, DM4 to DM8 for larger ones) and some of the best Mexican food in

Germany. That doesn't say a *whole* lot, but it's pretty good and very cheap: burritos, tortillas and, for some reason, that old Mexican favourite, doner kebab.

For cheaper sit-down meals, Bergheimer Strasse, west of Bismarck Platz, isn't a bad place to look. There are also many student pubs (see Entertainment) with main courses priced from around DM8 to DM14, soups from DM5, and salads and cheese plates for between DM7 and DM9, though it's the lively atmosphere rather than the food that tends to attract the customers.

One exception to that is *Brauhaus im Schöneck* (☎ 165 85 0), Steingasse 9, which has good soups, salads and light dishes all under DM10, along with their own microbrewed beer (see Pubs & Bars).

Entertainment

Listings *Meier* (DM2) is a monthly publication with information on clubs, pubs, restaurants and gay and lesbian haunts.

Espresso (DM9.80) is *the* guide to the region's nightlife, but it only comes out twice a year. The city prints *Heidelberg Aktuell*, available at the tourist office.

Cinemas *Gloria und Glorietta* (☎ 253 19), Hauptstrasse 146, shows English-language films regularly. *Harmonie*, on the corner of Hauptstrasse and Theaterstrasse, shows them less regularly.

Discos & Clubs *Nachtschicht* (☎ 164 40 4), near the train station at Bergheimerstrasse 147, has top-40 canned music on weekends, live music on weekdays and, on Thursday, soul and hip-hop. The *Schwimmbad Musik Club* (☎ 470 20 1), Tiergartenstrasse 13, near the hostel, has lots of live music, and the programme changes constantly – 1980s and 90s music, heavy metal and sometimes techno. Trendoids flock to *Tangente* (☎ 277 63), Kettengasse 23, one of the town's most popular places.

Theatre & Classical Music *Zwinger3* (☎ 583 54 6) has a series of plays for children and young adults.

The biggest theatres in town are *Theater der Stadt Heidelberg* (☎ 583 52 3), Theaterstrasse 4, and the smaller *Zimmertheater* (☎ 210 69), Hauptstrasse 118.

Organ concerts are held weekdays from 6 to 6.30 pm for DM5 at the *Heiliggeistkirche* on the Markt. There are also concerts at the castle, and in the Kulturhaus Karlstorbahnhof (see Cultural Centre).

From time to time there are concerts at the *1935 Amphitheatre* on Heilige Berg; there are signposts along Philosophenweg and schedules available from the tourist office.

Cultural Centre The former train station at Karlstor, east of the centre, has been converted to the *Kulturhaus Karlstorbahnhof* (☎ 978 14), Am Karlstor 1, a cultural centre with a wide range of theatrical, cinematic and musical offerings as well as art shows and special events. Call when you're in town for more information.

Rock, Jazz & Folk Music There's live music at the *Schwimmbad Musik Club* (see Discos & Clubs) and occasionally at *TunnelKult*, in the traffic tunnel underneath Friedrich-Ebert-Anlage at the southern end of the Altstadt; check when you're in town to see if anything's on. *Cave* (☎ 278 40), Krämergasse 2, is said to be the oldest jazz club in Germany, opened in 1954 (Louis Armstrong played here). It's open daily, and famous for the Sunday jam sessions from 9 pm to 3 am.

The only folk music in town is Irish, heard at some of the city's fine Irish watering holes: *Napper Tandy's Irish Pub* (☎ 259 79), at Haspelgasse 4; *Scruffy Murphy's* (☎ 183 47 3), Ingrimstrasse 26a; and *O'Reilly's* (☎ 410 14 0), Brückenkopfstrasse 1, across the river from Bismarck Platz.

Pubs & Bars Backstreet pubs and cafés are a feature of the nightlife in this thriving university town. We went seriously overboard with the microbrewed beer at *Vetter im Schöneck* (☎ 165 85 0), Steingasse 9, which has a very comfortable atmosphere, friendly service and shiny beer vats.

The *Zum Roten Ochsen* (☎ 209 77), at

Hauptstrasse 217, and *Zum Sepp'l* (☎ 230 85), next door at No 213, are very cool-looking, historical, student pubs decorated with graffiti and street signs collected through the centuries. Nowadays most students avoid these touristy joints.

Better places are the *Gasthaus Zum Mohren*, at Untere Strasse 5-7 (or its little sibling, *Kleiner Mohr*, next door), and the *Schnookeloch* (☎ 144 60) at Haspelgasse 8, which first opened its doors in 1407. Some nights you'll catch fraternity members singing.

The *Goldener Reichsapfel* (☎ 279 50), Untere Strasse 35, is one original student hang-out that hasn't quite gone the way of the others. There's noisy chat, even louder music and nowhere to sit just about every night. Also popular with young locals is the modern *i Punkt* (☎ 124 41), diagonally opposite at No 30. *Weinloch*, Untere Strasse 19, is a wine bar whose customers spill out onto the street every weekend.

With an entrance next door to i Punkt, in the passage running between Untere Strasse and Hauptstrasse, is *Palmbräu Gasse* (☎ 285 36), Hauptstrasse 185, an amazing place with medieval feel and stonework, wooden benches, a great crowd and good service. It's always packed. *Mata Hari* (☎ 181 80 8), Oberbadgasse 10 on the corner of Zwingerstrasse, is a popular gay bar.

Getting There & Away

Bus From mid-May until the end of September, the Europabus has a daily coach service, with one bus in either direction, between Heidelberg and Rothenburg ob der Tauber (DM47/94 one way/return, 4¼ hours). The bus from Heidelberg leaves at 8 am and the stop is in front of McDonald's at the train station. You can buy tickets on the bus, or enquire at Deutsche Touring (☎ 069-790 30), Am Römerhof 17 in Frankfurt.

Train There are frequent train connections to/from Frankfurt (DM21, one hour), Stuttgart (DM30, 45 minutes), Baden-Baden (DM21, one hour), Munich (DM91, three hours) and Nuremberg (via Frankfurt or Stuttgart, DM81, 3½ hours).

Car & Motorcycle The north-south A5 links Heidelberg with Frankfurt and Karlsruhe.

Ride Services You can arrange a lift through the local Citynetz Mitfahr-Service (☎ 194 44) at Bergheimer Strasse 125.

Getting Around

The Airport There's a Lufthansa airport shuttle bus from Terminal B of Frankfurt airport to the Renaissance Heidelberg Hotel; you can check in for any Lufthansa flight at the hotel, too. The one-hour ride costs DM36.

Public Transport Bismarck Platz is the main transport hub. The bus and tram system in and around Heidelberg is extensive and efficient. Single tickets are DM3.20 and a 24-hour pass costs DM10. Bus Nos 11, 21, 34, 41 and 42, and tram No 1, run between Bismarck Platz and the train station.

Car & Motorcycle There are well marked underground parking garages throughout the city. They cost DM2 to DM3 per hour.

Taxi Flag fall is DM4.20 plus DM2.20 per km. Taxis line up outside the train station, or you can order one by ringing ☎ 302 03 0. It's about DM12.50 from the train station to the Alte Brücke.

Bicycle Bicycle rental is no longer available at the train station, but you can rent bikes at Per Bike (☎ 161 14 8), south-west of Bismarck Platz at Bergheimer Strasse 125, for DM25/20/55/120 per day/subsequent day/weekend/week.

AROUND HEIDELBERG

Excursions to the Neckar Valley offer a good introduction to the surrounding countryside. Check with Touristikverband Neckarland-Schwaben (☎ 07131-785 20), Lothorstrasse 21, 74072 Heilbronn, for information on cycling opportunities in the region, and for its guide to bike trails.

Rhein-Neckar Fahrgastschiffahrt (☎ 201 81), on the south bank of the Neckar in Heidelberg, offers the most scenic and some of the cheapest ways to get around the Neckar Valley, with boats to the main destinations (eg the castles at Neckarsteinach and Hirschhorn). See Other Sights for more information.

Heilbronn

- *pop 117,500*
- *area code* ☎ 07131

Pummelled virtually out of existence by Allied bombs, Heilbronn is a pale shadow of its former self. There is practically nothing old left except the Gothic **Kiliankirche**, which has an amazing carved altar. These days the town is much more of a gateway between Frankfurt and Heidelberg (DB's steam trains run through here) than an attraction in its own right. The tourist office (☎ 562 27 0) in Markt hands out information on the sights, including the **Stadtische Museum** (a free local history museum) and the **Rathaus** (opposite the tourist office), with an astrological clock. Frequent trains for Heilbronn depart from Heidelberg's main station.

Other Sights

An excellent excursion is a trip upriver to **Neckarsteinach** and its four castles which were built by four brothers between 1100 and 1250 as a result of a family feud. Two of the castles are still residences of members of the family. Take Bahnhofstrasse west and it will become Hauptstrasse; a path running north is marked '*Zu dem Vier Bergen*' ('To the Four Castles'). The tourist office (☎ 06229-920 00) is in the Altes Rathaus, Hauptstrasse 7.

From April to October, Rhein-Neckar Fahrgastschiffahrt boats (DM16.50/9.50 adults/children, three hours return) leave from Heidelberg up to six times daily.

There are many castles in the Neckar Valley, such as the **Hirschhorn Castle** and, outside Neckarzimmern, **Burg Hornberg**. Deutsche Bahn has introduced scheduled services aboard steam-powered trains on several routes on weekends between Frankfurt and the Neckar Valley, through Heilbronn, Heidelberg and up to Neckarsteinach.

ULM

- *pop 165,000*
- *area code* ☎ 0731

On the Danube River at the border between the states of Baden-Württemberg and Bavaria, Ulm is famous for its Münster tower – the highest cathedral spire in Europe – and as the birthplace of Albert Einstein.

Ulm was a trading city as early as the 12th century and the *Ulmer Schachten*, flat barges with box-like cargo carrying local fabrics and goods, floated down the Danube as far as the Black Sea. The city's trade guilds – mainly composed of shipbuilders, fisherfolk and tanners – achieved political power through a new city charter in 1397.

Ulm is also technically the place in which the hang-glider was invented in 1802 by Albrecht Berblinger (1770-1829). A highly sceptical public watched as Berblinger attempted to fly across the river after leaping (some say he was kicked) from the city wall. He made a splash landing, but his design worked, and it is the clear prototype of the modern hang-glider.

Greater Ulm is actually two cities in two *Länder*, a state of affairs that dates back to Napoleon's influence on the region – it was he who decreed that the middle of the river would divide Baden-Württemberg and Bavaria. On the south side of the Danube, the Bavarian city of Neu Ulm, with a population of 50,000, is a rather bland, ugly and modern city that was formerly home to the US Army's Wiley Barracks, now used as low-income housing and a cultural and entertainment complex.

On the north side of the river is Ulm, which counts 115,000 people and contains all the main attractions. The two cities share transport systems and important municipal functions.

Orientation

The Danube (Donau) River bisects Ulm. All

the major sights are within the area south of Olga Strasse and the Danube and west of Münchner Strasse and the Gänstor Brücke, the main bridge between Ulm and Neu Ulm. The Hauptbahnhof is at the eastern end of the city.

The hostel and university are south-west of the centre; the Wiley Barracks are south-east of the centre.

Information

Tourist Offices Tourist Information Ulm/Neu Ulm (☎ 161 28 39; fax 161 16 14; email unt@extern.uni-ulm.de), at Münsterplatz 50 in the Stadthaus building, is open Monday to Friday from 9 am to 6 pm, Saturday from 9 am to 12.30 pm.

The ADAC has an office (☎ 666 66) at Neue Strasse 40.

Money Change money at the Hauptbahnhof or at the Vereinsbank across the street. There's a Deutsche Bank on Münsterplatz.

Post & Communications The main post office is at the Hauptbahnhof at Bahnhofplatz 2.

Online Services Albert's (☎ 153 02 2) is an Internet café in the city high school at the Einsteinhaus, Kornhausplatz 5. Internet access is free with any purchase, like coffee or tea (DM2).

Bookshops & Libraries Bartz am Münster (☎ 624 85), Münsterplatz 75, is a travel bookshop which has Lonely Planet titles and dozens of other travel books and maps. There's a Wittwer Internationale Presse in the Hauptbahnhof. The main city library (☎ 161 41 40) is in the Schwörhaus at Weinhof 12.

Campus Universität Ulm is the smallest in Baden-Württemberg, with about 6000 students. It's a technical university south of the city, with specialities in computer science, electronics, engineering and other technical fields.

Laundry There are several laundrettes in town; the expensive but central City-Wash is at Schützenstrasse 46 (entrance around the corner). Otherwise there's the Waschsalon Kaiser, Memminger Strasse 72; Haus 235, at the former Wiley Barracks (bus No 42 to Memminger Strasse); or Waschsalon Grill, Weinbergerweg 257, near the university.

Medical Services For a doctor or an ambulance in an emergency, call the Deutsches Rotes Kreuz (☎ 622 22), Frauenstrasse 125.

Dangers & Annoyances Ulm is dubbed the 'London of Germany' for its pea-soup fog which shrouds the steeple of the Münster in winter.

Münster

The reason for coming to Ulm is to see the huge Münster, celebrated for its 161.6m-high steeple – the tallest anywhere in the world. Though the first stone was laid in 1377, it took over 500 years for the entire structure to be completed. There's a permanent renovation and construction team on call, with an annual budget of about DM1.5 million. Only by climbing to the viewing platform (DM3) at 143m, via the 768 spiralling steps, do you fully appreciate the tower's astonishing height – on clear days you can see the Alps.

As you enter the cathedral you'll see over the west door the ***Israelfenster***, a stained-glass window intended to serve as a memorial to Jews killed during the Holocaust.

Note the carved **pulpit canopy**, as detailed as lace, which eliminates echoes during sermons. On the canopy is a tiny spiral staircase leading to a mini pulpit for the Holy Spirit.

The church's important **stained-glass windows** in the choir, dating from the 14th and 15th centuries, were removed for the duration of the war; they are now back in place. The oldest window (1385), to the right of centre, depicts the church as it used to be at that time.

Also in the choir you'll see the original 15th-century oak **choir stalls**; the top row of figures is from the Old Testament, the middle from the New Testament, while the figures on the bottom and on the sides are historical figures, including the Roman playwright Seneca, Nero's tutor (who committed suicide by slashing his wrists), as well as Pythagoras, who strums a lute.

On your way out, note the **Gebetswand** ('prayer wall'), a sort of bulletin board on which the faithful write invocations or place votives.

Throughout the church, note the **hallmarks** on each ston, placed there by stone cutters who were paid by stone. Allow about half an hour to climb up to the top, though the last entry to the top of the tower is an hour before closing time.

Services are held on Sundays at 8 and 9.30 am (10 am from January to Good Friday) and at 6 pm. There are also free daily organ concerts (see Entertainment).

Münsterplatz

The other highlight of Münsterplatz is the **Stadthaus** (1993), designed by American architect Richard Meier. He caused a scandal for putting a postmodern building next to the city's Gothic gem but the result is gorgeous and functional. It is open to the public for exhibitions and special events and is also home to the tourist office, and a very expensive café. Just south of the Münster is the **Münster Bazaar**, a beaten-up little shopping mall with about a dozen shops.

Rathaus

The nearby town hall also demands inspection. It was a commercial building until 1419. The eastern side of the Rathaus has a very ornate Renaissance façade along with ornamental figures and an amazing **astrological clock** (1520). There's a standard clock with Arabic numbers above it. Not accurate enough? Check the **sundial** above that or listen for the bells, which count off every quarter-hour. Inside the Rathaus you can see a replica of **Berblinger's flying machine**.

In the Markt, at the south, is the **Fischkasten Brunnen**, a tank where fishmongers kept their river fish alive on market days.

City Wall & Towers

On the north bank of the Danube you can walk along the **Stadtmauer**, the former city wall. Its height was reduced in the early 19th century after Napoleon decided that a heavily fortified Ulm was against his best interests. Note the **Metzger Turm**, leaning 2m off true to the north.

North-east of the Gänstor Brücke is a monument at the spot where Berblinger attempted his flight.

Fischerviertel

Stroll past the **Schwörhaus** (Oath House) and between the buildings whose roofs almost touch in **Kussgasse**. Cross the **Liar's Bridge** into the charming **Fischerviertel**, the old city's fishing and shipbuilding quarter, built along the tiny and sparkling clear Blau River, which runs into the Danube.

Einstein Monument

In front of the city's health ministry at Zeughausgasse 14, north-east of the Münster, is a fiendishly funny fountain, a memorial to Albert Einstein, who was born in Ulm but left when he was a year old. Before WWII he was granted 'honorary citizenship', but the Nazis revoked it. After the war, when Ulm asked the physicist if he wanted this honour reinstated, he declined. The ministry building bears a single stone attached to the wall entitled *Ein Stein* (one stone).

Museums

The **Ulmer Museum** (☎ 161 43 00), Markt 6, contains a well respected collection of ancient and modern works of art. These include icons and other religious paintings, sculptures and the 20th-century **Kurt Fried Collection**, with works from artists including Paul Klee, Wassily Kandinsky, Pablo Picasso, Roy Lichtenstein and August Macke. It's open Tuesday to Sunday from 11 am to 5 pm (to 8 pm on Thursday); admission is DM5/3, free on Friday.

The **Deutsche Brotmuseum** (☎ 69 55), Salztadelgasse 10, north of Münsterplatz, celebrates bread as the staff of life in the Western world. Apart from some interesting exhibits on the history of bread making, it also works with universities to develop new strains of wheat and other grain for use in developing countries. It's open Tuesday to Sunday from 10 am to 5 pm.

Organised Tours

The tourist office arranges daily 1½-hour walking tours in German through the city from May to November at 10 am (11 am on Sundays and holidays) and 2.30 pm; during the rest of the year, only the morning tour is held. The cost is DM7/3.50.

You can take two to three-hour canoe tours on the Danube for DM31/21 per adult/child under 14. Book at the tourist office.

There are also cruises (DM9/4.50) up the Danube daily at 2, 3 and 4 pm, with extra ones at 11 am and 5 pm on Saturday and Sunday. The docks are on the Ulm side, just south-west of the Gänstor Brücke.

Places to Stay

Hostel The *DJH hostel* (☎ 384 45 5) at Grimmelfinger Weg 45 charges juniors/seniors DM22/27 with breakfast. From the train station, take S-Bahn No 1 to Ehinger Tor, then bus No 4 to Schulzentrum, from where it's a five-minute walk, or you can take bus No 8.

Hotels & Pensions Across the river in Neu Ulm at Kasernstrasse 42a the *Rose* (☎ 778 03) has singles/doubles for DM40/80.

In the centre, the *Hotel Anker/Spanische Weinstube* (☎ 632 97), right beside the Münster at Rabengasse 2, has simple rooms from DM45/80. There's a good restaurant and it's a very popular stop for cyclists doing the Danube. The *Münster Hotel* (☎ 641 62), Münsterplatz 14, has the same standard of accommodation, from DM45/90. The family-run *Hotel am Rathaus* (☎ 968 49 0; fax 968 49 49), right behind the Rathaus at Kronengasse 10, has very clean and comfortable rooms from DM70/100. There's an *InterCity Hotel* (☎ 965 50; fax 965 59 99) attached to the Hauptbahnhof at its southern end; rooms start at DM146/164.

One of the nicest hotels in all of Baden-Württemberg is the *Hotel Schiefes Haus* (☎ 967 93 0; fax 967 93 33), Schwörhausgasse 6. The half-timbered house (1443) claims to be in the *Guinness Book of Records* as the 'most crooked hotel in the world' (the building, that is). The hotel, which appears to be collapsing, was renovated in 1994. The rooms are as crooked inside as they are outside, but the beds have specially-made individual height adjusters and spirit levels. The renovation is unbelievable and the house as romantic as you can ask for. Downstairs, a terrace hovers just above the Blau River – watch the trout! Singles/doubles start at DM185/245.

Places to Eat

Restaurants In the Fischerviertel, three cheers for *Hans Malknecht* (☎ 644 11), Fischergasse 3, a typical Swabian place (run by a typical Austrian) that has enormous portions of food from DM16 to DM20, and a good selection of vegetarian dishes and specials (DM14 to DM18), along with local beers and great service. The *Allgäuer Hof* at Fischergasse 12 has basic dishes for around DM15, while the more up-market *Zunfthaus*, at Fischergasse 31, offers local Swabian specialities.

It's really nice at the *Drei Kannen* (☎ 677 17), Hafenbad 31, north of Münzerplatz, with a courtyard next to a beautifully decorated former patrician's home and good Swabian food at very reasonable prices.

Out at the Wiley Barracks, there are two good, if pricey, options: the *Yu Japanese Restaurant* (☎ 838 11), Memminger Strasse 72/220, with good food and an excellent atmosphere in a vaulted former arsenal; and the *Wiley Club*, Memminger Strasse 72, in the former officers' casino and club, right near the former main entrance (bus No 42 to Memminger Strasse stops right outside). The latter is a chic and yuppie-filled renovated place with an American-style bar that goes on forever.

Forelle (☎ 639 24), Fischergasse 25, is widely held to be the most expensive and the best seafood restaurant in town. Note the cannonball lodged in the wall outside!

Snacks & Fast Food At the Hauptbahnhof's Markt Im Bahnhof there's a *Pizza Hut*, a *Kaffee Mit,* a butcher, fruit market and *La Mare*, which has fish specialities. There's also a great bakery in the main entry hall. The *McDonald's* is right across the street.

Good pizza slices for DM3.50 are available at the little *Pizza* bar on the south side of Markt. Right on Münsterplatz, the *Café Kassmeyer* bakery is open seven days a week, as is *Nudelmacher*, a kind of Pizza Hut that has an all-you-can-eat pasta bar for DM9.90 from 3 pm daily and all day on Sunday.

Out at the Wiley Barracks, right in front of the bus No 42 stop at Algauer Ring, is the *Markthalle*, with 30 or so food shops.

Entertainment

The *Roxy* (☎ 968 620), Schillerstrasse 1, is a huge, multi-venue centre with a concert hall, cinema, disco, bar and special-event forum. It's popular throughout the year.

Tangente (also called *The Hole)*, 500m north-east of the Münster at Frauenstrasse 20, has been around for over 25 years; it's open from 10 pm to 2 am. Closer to the cathedral is *Aquarium*, Kohlgasse 20, a flashy night bar with a small stage for live music. The *Wiley Club*, Memminger Strasse 72, hosts huge live concerts, jazz, rock and disco. Also on the former military base is *Arts & Crafts* in the former US Army gym, now a concert hall for everything from Brahms to head-banging.

Don't pass up some of the city's better beer gardens, especially *Zunfthaus der Schiffleute* (☎ 773 90), Fischergasse 31, and the *beer garden* on the south bank of the Danube west of the Gänstor Brücke.

Getting There & Away

Ulm is on the main Stuttgart-Munich train line – trains cost DM23/38 respectively and take one hour/1¼ hours. It's an hour from Ravensburg (DM21).

The B311 runs from Tuttlingen to Ulm, and the B16 from Ulm to Regensburg.

Getting Around

Buses leave from the Zentrale Omnibus Busbahnhof (ZOB) at the Hauptbahnhof, and there's a major transfer point at the Rathaus. Bus tickets cost DM2.70 for a single ride, DM7.50 for a day pass or DM9.50 for a four-ride strip ticket.

Rent bicycles at the Schiefes Haus Hotel (if it has any left) for DM15 per day.

RAVENSBURG

- *pop 42,500*
- *area code* ☎ 0751

Ravensburg, a pleasant medieval town half an hour's drive north of Lake Constance (Bodensee), will certainly entertain you for a day or so. Its hostel – in the former stable of a castle – still retains some of its original atmosphere and the views are marvellous.

Orientation & Information

The train station and central post office are at the western end of the city, a five-minute walk down Eisenbahnstrasse to Marienplatz, the centre of the Altstadt. The hostel is at the south-eastern end of the Altstadt on the top of the hill near the Mehlsack tower.

The tourist office (☎ 823 24) is in the Weingartner Hof building, Kirchstrasse 16, just east of Marienplatz. It's open Monday to Friday from 8 am to 12.30 pm, Tuesday to Friday from 2 to 5.30 pm, Saturday from 9 am to noon. Free walking tours run from 2 to 3.30 pm every Saturday, leaving from Holzmarkt.

W4 is an Internet café at Rossbachstrasse 8. Get English-language books and maps at Ravensbuch, Marienplatz 34.

Things to See & Do

The central **Marienplatz** is the site of bustling weekly **markets** from 6 am to 1 pm on Saturdays. It's a regional event and thousands come to buy farm goods and watch the buskers. At the western end of the square the

Renaissance **Lederhaus** (1574) has an outrageous façade. The teeny Flattbac River peeps through on its north side and people sit beside the little canal on sunny days to listen to the burbling water.

The stepped gable of the large, late-Gothic **Gewandhaus** (1498) dominates the eastern side of the square. Nearby is the impressive **Blaserturm**, part of the original city fortifications. The **Rathaus** doesn't look like much from the front, but the northern side is full of stained glass.

Ravensburger Publishing is one of Germany's largest manufacturers of board games; its **Toy Museum** (open Thursdays from 2 to 6 pm; free) has an exquisite baroque door and shining brasswork.

The 41m-high Gothic **Obertor** at the south-eastern corner of the city is overshadowed by the 51m-high **Mehlsack**, the city's tallest tower, nicknamed the 'Flour Sack' because of its white colour and bulky shape. You can climb the tower (free) from 10 am to noon every third Sunday between March and October (except in July) for a view over the city. To the north is the **Grüne Tor** (Green Tower), with its intricate tiled roof, and the large, late-Gothic **Liebfrauenkirche** (1362-90). The tower was constructed as a defence against soldiers who invaded from the hilltop town **Veitsburg** (1088), believed to be the birthplace, in 1130, of Heinrich der Löwe. Today the castle houses the hostel and a chic restaurant.

Next to the Liebfrauenkirche is a hideously ugly bronze **column** (1967), a war memorial on which the word 'peace' is spelled out in 20 languages.

Places to Stay & Eat

There's no camping in town. The *DJH Jugendherberge* (☎ 253 63) in Veitsburg castle is a pretty severe place: check-in is from 5 pm; the hostel is closed from 9.30 to 11.30 am and from 2 to 5 pm. There's a 10 pm lockout; showers are open only from 7 to 8 am and 5.30 to 9 pm. Dorm beds are DM14.80 for DJH members, DM16 for HI members; sleeping bags cost DM18.50.

There's a good deal at the historic *Hotel Residenz* (☎ 369 80), Herrenstrasse 16, which has fine rooms and good service: simple singles/doubles cost from DM42/51, rooms with baths are DM79/108. Downstairs in the Weinstube you can taste Ravensburger; the family that owns the hotel is the last wine maker in the area.

Hotel Garni Bauer (☎ 256 16), Marienplatz 1, is central and has very reasonable rooms from DM50/65. The *Obertor Hotel* (☎ 366 70), right next to the tower at Marktstrasse 67, has well worn rooms from DM85/100.

Vegetarians will be thrilled with *The Up Town Shop* (☎ 166 89), Rossbachstrasse 16, with samosas, pakoras, vegie pockets and tofu burgers from DM3 to DM4, and full meals from DM7.

The *Ravensburger Kebap Stube*, Marktstrasse 14, has doner kebab and vegetarian sand- wiches for DM5.

Tom's Elefant, Kirchstrasse 21, has good Thai food, and the downstairs bar is very popular.

Getting There & Away

Trains leave hourly for Stuttgart (DM57, two hours) via Ulm (DM21, one hour). From Markdorf, near Meersburg, trains run hourly (DM7, 30 minutes); from Friedrichshafen the ride takes 20 minutes and costs DM6.

Northern Black Forest

Resort Tax

If you're spending more than one night almost anywhere in the Black Forest, you will be subject to a *Kurtaxe*, a resort or visitors' tax of usually DM1.50 to DM3 per day. But unlike other places in Germany that also levy such a tax, here you'll be given a *Gästekarte* (guest card) that is valid in 178 towns and villages. Whenever you present this card, you will be entitled to discounts on museum admissions, boat trips, cultural events, public pools, bike rental, major attractions like the Europa Park Rust and the Black Forest Open-Air Museum and lots

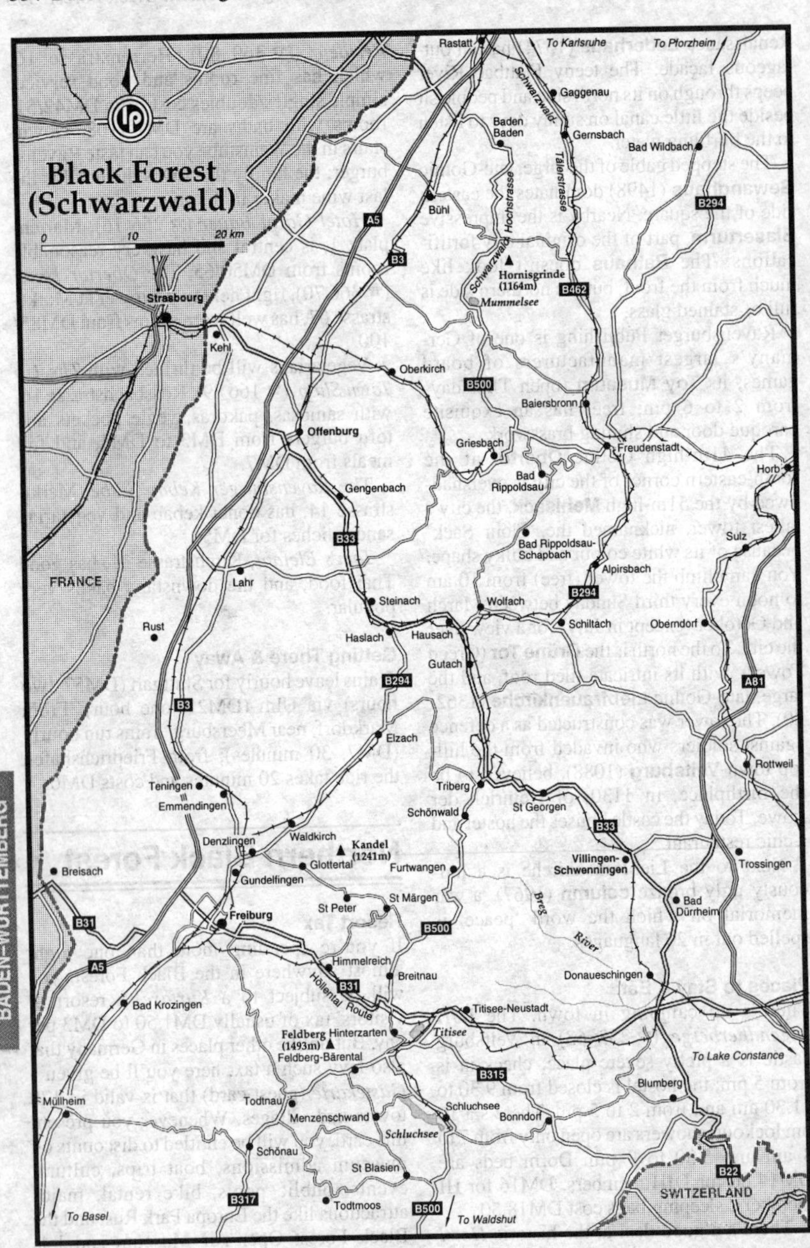
Black Forest (Schwarzwald)
0 10 20 km
Rastatt
To Karlsruhe
To Pforzheim
Schwarzwald-Tälerstrasse
Gaggenau
Baden Baden
Gernsbach
Bad Wildbach
Bühl
Schwarzwald Hochstrasse
Hornisgrinde (1164m)
Mummelsee
Strasbourg
Kehl
Oberkirch
Baiersbronn
Offenburg
Griesbach
Freudenstadt
Bad Rippoldsau
Horb
Gengenbach
Bad Rippoldsau-Schapbach
Sulz
Alpirsbach
FRANCE
Lahr
Steinach
Wolfach
Schiltach
Oberndorf
Rust
Haslach
Hausach
Gutach
Elzach
Rottweil
Teningen
Emmendingen
Triberg
St Georgen
Schönwald
Denzlingen
Waldkirch
Kandel (1241m)
Villingen-Schwenningen
Trossingen
Breisach
Glottertal
Furtwangen
Gundelfingen
St Märgen
St Peter
Bad Dürrheim
Freiburg
Breg River
Himmelreich
Breitnau
Donaueschingen
Höllental Route
Bad Krozingen
Titisee-Neustadt
Titisee
Feldberg (1493m)
Hinterzarten
Feldberg-Bärental
To Lake Constance
Blumberg
Müllheim
Todtnau
Schluchsee
Bonndorf
Menzenschwand
Schönau
St Blasien
SWITZERLAND
Todtmoos
To Basel
To Waldshut
A5
B3
B294
B462
B500
B33
A81
B31
B315
B317
B22
BADEN-WÜRTTEMBERG

more. Details can be found in the small Schwarzwald Gästekarte booklet available at most tourist offices.

KARLSRUHE

- *pop 274,000*
- *area code* ☎ 0721

Karlsruhe, which literally means 'Carl's Rest', was dreamed up in 1715 by Margrave Karl Wilhelm of Baden-Durlach as a residential retreat. The purpose-built town is laid out like the spokes of a wheel: at its centre is the horseshoe-shaped Schloss which is surrounded by the circular Schlosspark. From this inner circle emanate 32 spokes – completely straight streets, of which more than half culminate in a second ring road.

Imaginative as this is, were it not for the Schloss and some stellar museums, there would be little reason to visit Karlsruhe. Blown to bits in WWII, it was not rebuilt in an attractive way, and the unusual layout gets lost amid modern concrete (despite a few surviving neoclassical buildings around Markt).

These days, Karlsruhe is a centre of industry and chiefly known as the location of two of the country's high courts, the Bundesgerichtshof (Federal Supreme Court) and the Bundesverfassungsgericht (Federal Constitutional Court).

Orientation & Information

The Hauptbahnhof is on the southern edge of the city centre, with the Schloss 2km due north (tram No A, B or 3 to Markt). The tourist office (☎ 355 30; fax 355 34 3) is opposite the train station at Bahnhofplatz 6 and is open weekdays from 8 am to 7 pm and Saturday to 1 pm. A branch office (☎ 355 32 0; fax 355 32 1) is at Karl-Friedrich-Strasse 22 with the hours on weekdays from 9 am to 6 pm, Saturday to 12.30 pm. The Reisebank in the train station is open daily. The main post office is at Kaiserstrasse 217.

Schloss & Badisches Landesmuseum

The single most compelling reason to come to Karlsruhe is to visit the Schloss, which houses the superb collections of the Badisches Landesmuseûm. The Schloss itself was completely destroyed in the war, but fortunately the city custodians at the time had enough sense – and money – to rebuild it in the original style, which represents the transition from the baroque to the neoclassical periods. Be sure to climb the tower, really the only point from which to appreciate the eccentric town layout. The Schloss surroundings reflect its purpose as both a residence and a retreat. While the gardens facing the city are laid out in a strictly formal – thus public – way, the huge park north of the palace is done in a natural 'English style'. In fine weather, the latter is a popular gathering spot for students of the nearby university.

The museum occupies most rooms in this large structure and deserves at least a couple of hours. Right by the entrance is the **antiquity collection** with fascinating statues, jewellery, objects and even some mummies from extinct cultures in Mesopotamia, Anatolia and Egypt. The opposite wing is filled with altars, statues and paintings from the Middle Ages. On the 1st floor you'll find an interesting assembly of booty brought back by Margrave Ludwig Wilhelm of Baden from his 17th-century military campaigns against the Turks, including guns, knives, saddles and clothing. Adjacent is the **Zähringer Saal** whose *pièces de résistance* are the dazzling diadem and gem-encrusted crown and sceptre of that ruling family. Museum hours are 10 am to 5 pm, Wednesday to 8 pm, closed Monday. Admission is DM5, discount DM3.

Kunsthalle

The private collections of the margraves of Baden form the basis of this extensive art collection, which was first exhibited in 1846, making it one of the oldest public museums in Germany. On view is the full range of European masters from the 14th to the 20th centuries. A highlight is the **Gallery of Old German Masters** on the top floor, with good works by Matthias Grünewald (look for the masterful *Crucifixion)* and Lucas Cranach the Elder *(Frederick the Wise in Adoration* *of the Mother of God)*, as well as Hans Holbein and Hans Baldung. Much of the ground floor is occupied by 19th-century paintings by French artists like Manet, Degas and Delacroix and Germans like Corinth, Liebermann and Slevogt. The impressive large-scale murals covering the walls of the central staircase are by Moritz von Schwind and show the consecration of the Freiburg Minster. The Kunsthalle is open Tuesday to Friday from 10 am to 5 pm, weekends to 6 pm. Admission is DM8, discount DM5.

Places to Stay & Eat

Camping Turmbergblick (☎ 440 60) is at Tiengerer Strasse 40 in the eastern suburb of Durlach. Karlsruhe's *DJH hostel* (☎ 282 48) is at Moltkestrasse 24 east of the Schloss (take tram No 3 from the Hauptbahnhof to Europaplatz, then 10 minutes on foot) and charges DM22/27 juniors/seniors. The tourist office can help you find a *private room*. As for pensions and hotels, one budget option is *Pension am Zoo* (☎ 336 78) at Ettlinger Strasse 33, which has basic singles for DM55 and doubles for DM100. Very central is *Pension Stadtmitte* (☎ 389 63 7), Zähringer Strasse 72, which charges DM75/120 for rooms with private bath. The upmarket *Hotel Barbarossa* (☎ 372 50; fax 372 58 0), at Luisenstrasse 38, has singles with shower from DM88 and doubles from DM128.

Karlsruhe has a decent selection of eateries. Near the Kunsthalle at Waldstrasse 3 is *Ril*, a bubbly bistro with simple fare from DM5. Several student haunts cluster a few blocks south of here on Ludwigsplatz, including the immensely popular *Krokodil*, a boisterous hall with tiled walls, wooden ceiling and a well priced, eclectic menu. Around the corner, at Blumenstrasse 17, is *Trattoria Toscana*, a sophisticated and romantic Italian restaurant with updated versions of classic Italian fare.

Getting There & Away

Karlsruhe is a major train hub with service in all directions. Trains leave regularly to Baden-Baden (DM9.60, 15 minutes), Freiburg (DM35, one hour) and Cologne (DM83, three hours). Karlsruhe is on the A5 (Frankfurt-Basel) and the western terminus of the A8 to Munich. It is also crossed by the B3 and the B36. The Mitfahrzentrale (☎ 194 40) is at Rankestrasse 14.

Getting Around

Single rides on Karlsruhe's public bus and tram system cost DM3, four-block tickets are DM9. The best deal is the 24-hour Regio Card, which costs DM8 and entitles you to unlimited rides for two adults and two children in the city and surrounds.

BADEN-BADEN

- *pop 50,000*
- *area code* ☎ 07221

When Roman legionnaires came to Baden-Baden some 2000 years ago, they must have felt right at home. Just like Rome, this idyllic enclave at the foot of the Black Forest is built on numerous hills. The Romans discovered the curative powers of Baden-Baden's hot mineral waters that, since the 19th century, have made the town the playground of the privileged. From Queen Victoria to the Vanderbilts, from Bismarck to Brahms and Berlioz, they all came – the royal, the rich and the renowned – to take Baden-Baden's waters.

Today, Baden-Baden is the grande dame among German spas, ageing but still elegant. It offers a townscape of palatial villas, stately hotels, tree-lined avenues and groomed parks. Spared from WWII bombing (the French set up military headquarters here), Baden-Baden has been able to preserve its prewar grandeur and to maintain an Arcadian aura largely devoid of crime, poverty and other ailments of modern civilisation. As Germany's premier and ritziest health spa, it offers many salubrious activities in a sophisticated, yet relaxed, atmosphere that doesn't necessarily require super-deep pockets to enjoy.

Orientation

The train station is in the suburb of Oos, about 4km north-west of the town centre,

PLACES TO STAY

1 Hotel Schweizer Hof
9 Hotel Am Markt
12 Am Friedrichsbad
13 Hotel Römerhof

PLACES TO EAT

3 La Provence
11 Bratwurstglöckel
14 Leo's
20 Namaskaar
21 Zum Nest

OTHER

2 Post Office
4 Neues Schloss
5 Caracalla-Therme
6 Römische Badruinen
7 Friedrichsbad
8 Stiftskirche; Markt
10 Stadtmuseum; Weinstube Baldreit
15 Trinkhalle
16 Police
17 Sparkasse
18 Kurhaus; Casino
19 Theater
22 Tourist Office
23 Staatliche Kunsthalle

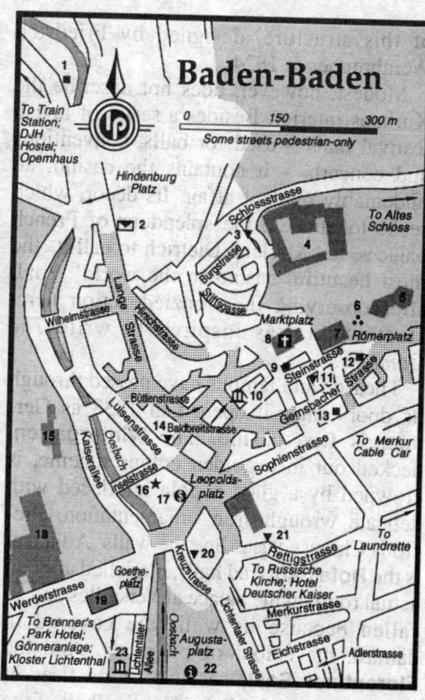

with the central bus station immediately in front. To get to the centre, take bus No 201, 205 or 216, all of which make frequent runs to Leopoldsplatz, the heart of Baden-Baden. Almost everything is within walking distance of this square.

Information

Tourist Office Baden-Baden's tourist office (☎ 275 20 0; fax 275 20 2) is at Augustaplatz 8 and is open daily from 9.30 am to 6 pm. If you're driving in from the autobahn, it's more convenient to stop at the office at Schwarzwaldstrasse 52, which you'll pass on your way into town. Hours here are 9 am to 8 pm between April and October and to 7 pm the rest of the year. If you're spending the night in Baden-Baden, you have to pay the resort tax of DM4 (DM1.50 in the suburbs) which entitles you to the *Gästekarte*, good for discounts on concerts, tours, lectures and more. Your hotel will obtain it for you and add the tax to your room rate. The tax does not apply to the hostel.

Money Most banks in Baden-Baden exchange money, including the Sparkasse on Leopoldsplatz and the Commerzbank at Augustaplatz 4. Both also have an ATM that accepts credit cards.

Post & Communications Baden-Baden's post office is inside the Kaufhaus Wagener, a department store at Lange Strasse 44.

Laundry The laundrette at Scheibenstrasse 14 is open Monday to Saturday from 7.30 am to 9 pm.

Kurhaus & Casino

In the heart of Baden-Baden, just west of the river Oos, looms the palatial Kurhaus, the town's cultural centre, set in an impeccably designed and groomed garden. Two colonnades of shops, flanked by chestnut trees, separate the complex from the Kaiserallee. Corinthian columns and a frieze of mythical griffins grace the relatively modest exterior of this structure, designed by Friedrich Weinbrenner in 1824.

Modest, however, does not describe the Kurhaus interior. Besides a series of lavish festival halls – used for balls, conventions and concerts – it contains the casino, an undeniably opulent affair. Its décor, which seeks to emulate the splendour of French palaces, led Marlene Dietrich to call it 'the most beautiful casino in the world'. And, after observing the frenzied action here, Dostoevski was inspired to write *The Gambler*.

The rich and famous have passed through its doors since it opened in 1838 as Germany's first casino. The **Wintergarten**, decked out in a golden colour scheme, is crowned by a glass cupola interlaced with delicate wrought-iron ornamentation. Precious Chinese vases line the walls. Adjacent is the **Rote Saal** (red hall), modelled after an actual room in the palace at Versailles and so called because its walls are covered in damask the colour of burgundy. And the **Florentiner Saal**, because of its fleet of chandeliers, is also known as the 'hall of the thousand candles'.

The casino is open daily from 2 pm to 2 am and to 3 am on Friday and Saturday; the baccarat tables are open to 6 am. You can also play French and American roulette, blackjack and poker. Admission is DM5 and you must bring your passport to enter. During the week, minimum bets are DM5, on weekends DM10. You do not have to gamble, but men must wear jacket and tie (these may be rented at DM15 each), and women a suit or dress (trousers and blazer are acceptable).

A more casual alternative is to take a guided tour (DM5) offered daily every 30 minutes from 9.30 am to noon. Between October and March, the first tour is at 10 am.

BADEN-WÜRTTEMBERG

Lichtentaler Allee

This elegant park promenade follows the flow of the sprightly Oos from Goetheplatz, adjacent to the Kurhaus, to Kloster Lichtenthal about 3km south. It's a gallery of trees and bushes brought here from around the world. Even today, it's not hard to imagine the movers and shakers of 19th-century Europe – royals, aristocrats, diplomats and artists – taking leisurely strolls along this fragrant avenue.

The gateway to Lichtentaler Allee is formed by the Baden-Baden **Theater**, a white and red sandstone neobaroque confection whose frilly interior looks like a miniature version of the Opéra-Garnier in Paris. Its inaugural performance in 1862 was the première of Hector Berlioz's opera *Béatrice et Bénédict*.

Nearby stands the **Staatliche Kunsthalle** (State Art Gallery; open from 11 am to 6 pm, Wednesday to 8 pm, closed Monday; DM8), a nearly windowless structure that features rotating international exhibits, mostly of contemporary art.

A bit farther on, notice on your left the **Brenner's Park Hotel**, one of the world's poshest. More of a mini-palace than a hotel, it oozes the kind of old world charm, glamour and perfection that has become largely extinct. It's the type of place where the concierge would remember your poodle's favourite food and where there are special waiting lounges just for chauffeurs.

About another km south of here is the **Gönneranlage**, an immaculate rose garden ablaze with more than 300 varieties. For a quick detour, check out the **Russische Kirche** (Russian church; 1882), just east of here on Maria-Victoria-Strasse. Built in the Byzantine style, it is topped with a shiny golden onion dome (open daily from 10 am to 6 pm; DM1).

Lichtentaler Allee concludes at the **Kloster Lichtenthal**, a Cistercian abbey founded in 1245. Generations of the margraves of Baden lie buried in its chapel, and there's also a **Museum of Religious Art** (closed mornings and all day Monday; DM3, discount DM1).

Altstadt

For a wonderful overview of the bucolic layout of Baden-Baden, it's worth climbing to the terrace of the Renaissance **Neues Schloss** in Schlossstrasse. Until recently, the palace was one of the residences of the margravial family of Baden-Baden, but acute cash flow problems forced them to auction off the rather substantial collection of furnishings and artworks. No one, however, bought the palace itself and so it stands empty until a buyer emerges. The nicest way to reach it is by climbing a series of stairs built into the hillside in the northern Altstadt.

On your way up, you're likely to pass the **Stiftskirche** on the Markt whose foundations incorporate the ruins of the former Roman baths and which is otherwise a hotchpotch of Romanesque, Gothic and baroque styles. Inside, look for the crucifix by Nicolaus Gerhaert; it is impressive for its heart-wrenchingly realistic depiction of the suffering Christ.

Nearby in Küferstrasse 3 is the **Stadtmuseum** (City Museum; open from 10 am to 12.30 pm and 2 to 5 pm, closed Monday; entry DM2) whose highlights include historic roulette wheels and other gambling paraphernalia, as well as furnishings, photos and paintings from Baden-Baden's *belle époque*.

Back in the city centre, swing by the **Trinkhalle** (pump room) at Kaiserallee 3 just north of the Kurhaus. Here you can amble beneath a 90m-long portico decorated with 19th-century frescos of local legends and myths. The building inside has unfortunately been taken over by a Black Forest kitsch store, but you can still get a glass of curative mineral water from Baden-Baden's own springs (open daily from 10 am to 5.30 pm, in winter to 4.30 pm; free with the Gästekarte).

Spas

The remains of the original **Roman baths** on Römerplatz are worth a quick look (open Easter to October daily from 10 am to noon and 1.30 pm to 4 pm; DM2.50, discount DM0.50). Vastly more fun, though, is taking the waters yourself at the two extraordinary spas that are among Baden-Baden's main attractions. Built on either side of Römerplatz are the Friedrichsbad and the Caracalla-Therme. Try to make a visit to one or both part of your stay.

The 19th-century **Friedrichsbad** looks more like an extravagant neo-Renaissance palace than a bathhouse. Most stunning is the circular pool ringed by columned arcades that blend into a graceful cupola adorned with ornamentation and sculptures. Two bathing options are offered: the Roman-Irish (DM36) and the Roman-Irish Plus (DM48) programmes. Your three or more hours of humid bliss consist of a timed series of hot and cold showers, saunas, steam rooms and baths that leave you feeling scrubbed, lubed and loose as a goose. The highlight of the Plus programme is the all-too-short soap-and-brush massage. At the end of the session, you're wrapped in a blanket for a half-hour's rest.

No clothing is allowed inside, and several of the bathing sections are mixed on most days, so check your modesty at the reception desk. The Friedrichsbad is open Monday to Saturday from 9 am to 10 pm, Sunday from 2 pm. Mixed bathing is all day on Wednesday and weekends, and from 4 pm on Tuesday and Friday.

The **Caracalla-Therme**, opened in 1985, has more than 900 sq metres of outdoor and indoor pools, a hot and cold-water grotto, various whirlpools, therapeutic water massages, a surge channel and a range of saunas. Admission gives you access to all areas and bathing suits must be worn everywhere, except in the upstairs sauna section. Suits are not available for hire and, oddly, neither are towels. Prices are DM19/25/33 for two/three/four hours. The baths are open daily from 8 am to 10 pm, but the last admission is two hours before closing time.

Hiking

The low mountains around Baden-Baden make for good hiking excursions. The tourist office has put together a collection of pamphlets (DM9.80) with suggested hikes from the short and easy variety to some more serious climbs. Popular destinations are the Geroldsauer waterfalls, the Yburg castle ruin in the surrounding wine country, the Altes Schloss above the town and Mount Merkur. The Merkur cable car, running daily every

15 minutes from 10 am to 6 pm (DM7 return) will take you up to the 660m-high summit of Mount Merkur, from where there are fine views and numerous 'terrain treatment' trails, each with a specific gradient designed to therapeutically exercise your muscles (take bus No 205 from Leopoldsplatz to the cable car station).

Places to Stay

The closest camping ground is *Campingplatz Adam* (☎ 07223-231 94), at Bühl-Oberbruch, about 12km south-west of town (no direct bus service). Baden-Baden's *DJH hostel* (☎ 522 23) is at Hardbergstrasse 34, 3km north-west of the centre, and costs DM22/27 for juniors/seniors (from the train station, take bus No 201 to Grosse Dollenstrasse, then walk for 10 minutes).

As one would expect from a swanky spa resort, hotel accommodation in Baden-Baden itself is not cheap, though there are ways to get around paying top Deutschmark. The tourist office has a free room-reservation service and can help you find a *private room* starting at DM30 per person. A good alternative to the hostel is the *Altes Schloss* (☎ 269 48), up on the hill at Alter Schlossweg 10, which has simple singles/doubles with shared shower and WC for DM40/80. Unfortunately the Schloss can only be reached by car or foot.

Many hotels still have rooms with shared bath that are more affordable. At the traditional *Deutscher Kaiser* (☎ 721 52; fax 721 54), Lichtentaler Hauptstrasse 35, you can get away with as little as DM50/75 for snug but quiet singles/doubles; if you want your own shower and toilet, you'll have to fork out DM95/130. Another good place is the *Schweizer Hof* (☎ 304 64 6; fax 304 64 6) at Lange Strasse 73, where basic rooms start at DM50/100 and those with private bath are DM85/150.

The *Hotel Am Markt* (☎ 227 47; fax 391 88 7), Markt 17, up by the Stiftskirche, charges DM54/100 for simple rooms and DM90/140 for those with private facilities. Classier is the *Hotel Römerhof* (☎ 234 15; fax 391 70 7), at Sophienstrasse 25, where bright clean rooms with private bath cost DM85/170; those without are DM10 less per person. Another nice place is *Am Friedrichsbad* (☎ 271 04 6; fax 383 10), at Gernsbacher Strasse 31, with singles from DM67 to DM99 and doubles from DM99 to DM190.

Places to Eat

A good place to sample local Baden cuisine is at *Bratwurstglöckel* (closed Tuesday) at Steinstrasse 7. It's rustic and small and has dishes priced at DM15 to DM20. Locals favour *Zum Nest*, Rettigstrasse 1, which serves up regional specialities from DM14. A hang-out for young people is *Leo's* in Louisenstrasse 10 near Leopoldsplatz, a trendy bistro with movie-themed décor that has large salads and creative pasta dishes. At *Weinstube Baldreit* (closed Monday), a bit hidden away in a courtyard beneath the Stadtmuseum at Küferstrasse 3, you can have filling snacks to go with deliciously crisp Baden wines or a full meal of regional fare in a cosy ambience.

Vaulted ceilings, Art Nouveau mirrors and hanging baskets of dried flowers are just some of the stylish touches that contribute to the elegant atmosphere of *La Provence* (☎ 255 50) at Schlossstrasse 20. Techno fiends to portly burghers dig into sizable portions of mouthwatering Franco-German food costing around DM15 to DM25. It's hugely popular so it's best to make reservations for dinner. For those with shallower pockets La Provence also has a dirt-cheap (DM7 and under) daytime menu, but it's limited to spaghetti, schnitzel and other simple dishes. If you fancy something exotic, head to *Namaskaar* (closed Tuesday), an Indian restaurant at Kreuzstrasse 1, with imaginative meat, fish and vegetarian meals from DM15 per main course.

Entertainment

The Baden-Baden cultural scene is due to reach another milestone in 1998, with the opening of the new *Opernhaus* on Lange Strasse at Robert-Schumann-Platz, incorporating the historic Alter Bahnhof (old train station). Only top-notch orchestras, soloists and ensembles are scheduled to perform, including London's Royal Opera, Seiji Ozawa, and the Vienna Philharmonic.

Baden-Baden's *Theater* at Goetheplatz offers a repertory of classical and modern drama and musical theatre. Tickets range from DM11 to DM38 (afternoon performances slightly cheaper).

The *Baden- Badener Philharmonie* performs in two concert halls in the Kurhaus and charges DM20 to DM36 per performance. Students get a 50% discount. Buy your tickets for either the theatre or a concert at the box office inside the Kurhaus (☎ 932 70 0).

Getting There & Away

Air In 1997, Baden-Baden inaugurated its own airport, about 15km west of town in the suburb of Söllingen. It's big enough to handle Boeing 747s, but will be mostly used for hops within Germany and Europe and charter flights.

Bus A number of buses to nearby Black Forest towns depart from Baden-Baden. Bus No 212 makes hourly trips to Rastatt, while bus No 218 goes to Iffezheim, the location of a prestigious annual horse race. Bus No 245 takes you to the Mummelsee on the Black Forest Highway twice daily (see the Schwarzwald-Hochstrasse section).

Train Baden-Baden is on the main north-south rail corridor. Trains leave every two hours for Basel (DM43, 1½ hours) and Frankfurt (DM46, 1¾ hours). There's a service several times hourly to Karlsruhe (DM9.60, 20 minutes) and Offenburg (DM11.80, 30 minutes).

Car & Motorcycle Baden-Baden is close to the A5 connecting Frankfurt and Basel (take the Baden-Baden exit). The town is on the B3 and also the northern terminus of the B500, the scenic Schwarzwald-Hochstrasse.

Getting Around

Bus The Stadtwerke Baden-Baden (☎ 277 1) operate a decent bus system. Single tickets cost DM3 and four-block tickets are DM9. By far the best deal, though, is the Day Pass (DM8), which entitles two adults and two children under 16 to unlimited travel in Baden-Baden and surrounds for 24 hours.

Car & Motorcycle To cut down on traffic through the centre, the main road goes underground near Verfassungsplatz in the north and emerges just south of the town centre. There are only a few exits from this tunnel, so if you want to go to the centre, try to stay above ground. Be warned, though, that much of the central area is either pedestrianised or blocked off from traffic. It's best to park your vehicle on the street or in a parking lot and walk.

Bicycle Baden-Baden is very hilly and a bicycle is not the easiest method of transport. If you want to try it anyway, you can rent from the Fahrradverleih at the train station or from the BBP bike shop at Geroldsauerstrasse 137a.

SCHWARZWALD-HOCHSTRASSE

The scenically beautiful Black Forest Highway, officially the rather mundanely named B500, wends its way from Baden-Baden to Freudenstadt, about 60km to the south. Large segments go right through the forest and along the ridge with expansive views of the Upper Rhine Valley and, further west, the Vosges Mountains in Alsace, which form the border between Alsace and Lorraine in France.

The road also skirts a number of lakes, of which the Mummelsee is the best known. It's at the foot of the Hornisgrinde, at 1164m the tallest mountain in the northern Black Forest. According to legend, the lake is inhabited by a gaggle of water nymphs who emerge from the lake at night to party till the stroke of 1 am, when the lake king orders them back. There are endless variations on this tale which, naturally, has provided much fodder for writers, including the poet Eduard Mörike. The Mummelsee is a popular destination and therefore bustles with tourists in season. If you want some quiet, rent a pedal boat (DM8 for 30 minutes).

The Schwarzwald-Hochstrasse is lined with hotels and you'll find a *DJH hostel* (☎ 07804-611) in Zuflucht, about 17km north of Freudenstadt, with its own bus stop. Bed & breakfast costs DM22/27 juniors/ seniors. For truly rock bottom-priced lodging, though, check out the *Naturfreundehaus* (☎ 07226-238), about 2km from the B500 (bus stop Bühl-Sand), which charges only DM8 per bed provided you have your own sheets.

If you're not driving, you can get to the Mummelsee from Baden-Baden's central bus station by taking bus No 245. From Freudenstadt's Stadtbahnhof, take bus No 12 during the week and either bus No 2 or No 11 on weekends. Service is more frequent on Saturday and Sunday.

FREUDENSTADT

- *pop 23,500*
- *area code* ☎ 07441

Freudenstadt is a spa town on the eastern border of the Black Forest, about 60km south of Baden-Baden. It was the brainchild of Duke Friedrich I of Württemberg who, in 1599, decided to build one of the first planned residences north of the Alps. Together with his own architect, Heinrich Schickardt, he scoured Bologna and Rome for inspiration and came back with the idea for a town laid out like a square spider web. At Freudenstadt's centre is a gigantic market square, Germany's largest in fact, with each side measuring 220m. It is framed on each side by streets set up in three concentric squares. Friedrich hoped to adorn the square with a palace, but this grandiose design never came to fruition. After his death in 1610, Freudenstadt fell into obscurity from which it did not raise itself until the mid-19th century when a rail connection brought in the first waves of tourists. In WWII it was wrecked by the French, but thanks to exemplary restoration, Freudenstadt retains some of its unique, quasi-urban charm.

Orientation & Information

Freudenstadt has two train stations, the Stadtbahnhof, centrally located about five minutes walk north of the Markt, and the Hauptbahnhof, about 2km south-east on Dietersweilerstrasse, on the corner of Bahnhofstrasse. Some trains link the two, as does the No B bus, but the latter only runs every two hours. The central bus station (ZOB) is right outside the Stadtbahnhof.

The tourist office (☎ 864 73 0; fax 851 76) is at Am Promenadeplatz 1 in the Kurhaus complex and is open weekdays from 10 am to 6 pm (in winter to 5 pm) and Saturday to 1 pm. If the office is closed, see if someone inside the Kurhaus can help. If you're spending the night, you have to pay the DM3 daily Kurtaxe.

Several banks on Markt exchange money, including Kreissparkasse, Dresdner Bank and Deutsche Bank. The main post office is also on Markt and has a late counter open on weekdays until 7 pm.

Things to See & Do

From the Stadtbahnhof and bus station take a short walk south along Martin-Luther-Strasse to the **Markt**. It's quite a sight to behold and almost too huge to truly feel like a square, especially since it's bisected by a major thoroughfare. It's entirely lined by Italianate arched arcades providing weather-proof access to dozens of shops.

On the south-western corner, the Markt is anchored by the **Stadtkirche** (1608), whose two naves are built at a right angle, another unusual design idea by the geometrically minded duke. It's a bit of a style mixture, with Gothic windows, Renaissance portals and baroque towers. Of note inside are a baptismal font from the early 12th century with intricate animal ornamentations, a crucifix from around 1500 and a wooden lectern from 1140 carried on the shoulders of the four Evangelists.

In its early days, the church also provided a safe place of worship for the many Protestants who settled in Freudenstadt after having been banished from their Austrian homeland.

For exercise, relaxation or indulgence visit the **Panorama-Bad**, a complex with various pools, a nearly 50m-long slide, whirlpool, massage jets, steam rooms and

BADEN-WÜRTTEMBERG

saunas. It's at Ludwig-Jahn-Strasse 60 and opens from 9 am to 10 pm (weekends to 8 pm). Entry costs DM10.50, discount DM8 without sauna and DM19/14.50 with sauna. Prices go up by DM1 on weekends and holidays.

Located at elevations of 750 to 1000m, Freudenstadt is a place for moderately good winter sports, especially cross-country skiing with eight groomed tracks between 4 and 12km long. There are also two ski lifts. For snow conditions, call ☎ 07442-692 2.

Places to Stay & Eat

If you want to camp, head to *Camping Langenwald* (☎ 286 2), about 3km west of town along the B28 (take bus No 12 in the direction of Kniebis). Freudenstadt's *DJH hostel* (☎ 772 0) is at Eugen-Nägele-Strasse 69, about 500m from the Stadtbahnhof and 2.5km from the Hauptbahnhof. Bed & breakfast here costs DM22/27 juniors/ seniors, and you can rent bicycles and cross-country ski equipment.

Go to the tourist office if you need help with finding a *private room* (no booking fee). These start at DM30 per person with private bath, but there's no shortage of central and reasonably priced hotels. Right on the southern end of Markt, at No 41, is *Gasthof Pension Traube* (☎ 288 0), which charges DM50/100 for singles/doubles. Nearby is *Gasthof Ochsen* (☎ 266 7) with identical room rates. Between Stadtbahnhof and Markt at Forststrasse 15-17 is *Hotel Adler* (☎ 915 20), which charges DM66/110. On the same street at No 6 is *Hotel Schwanen* (☎ 915 50), a family-run operation where contemporary rooms cost DM60/116. Right on the market square at No 12 is *Hotel Jägerstüble* (☎ 238 7), whose rooms cost DM60/114. All prices are for rooms with private shower and WC and include breakfast. All of them also have rather good, traditional restaurants serving the usual range of German and regional cuisine at prices around DM12 to DM25.

Getting There & Away

Bus No 7628 makes a few trips on weekdays to/from Tübingen. Bus No 7161 travels daily along the Kinzig Valley with stops in Alpirsbach, Schiltach, Wolfach and Hausach.

A better alternative on this route is the Kinzigtalbahn train, leaving at two-hour intervals from the Stadtbahnhof. If you're northward-bound, there's the hourly Murgtalbahn to/from Rastatt (DM14.20, 1½ hours), which stops at both the Stadtbahnhof and the Hauptbahnhof.

Freudenstadt marks the southern terminus of the Schwarzwald-Hochstrasse (B500) which meanders northward for 60km to Baden-Baden. It also lies on the B462, the Schwarzwald-Täler-Strasse (Black Forest Valley Road) from Rastatt to Alpirsbach.

Getting Around

Freudenstadt has a city bus network (☎ 895 0 for information) with four lines running at two-hour intervals. Each trip costs DM2.50. There's a bike-rental station in the Kurhaus.

Central Black Forest

KINZIG VALLEY

The horseshoe-shaped Kinzig Valley begins south of Freudenstadt and follows the little Kinzig River south to Schiltach, then west to Haslach and north to Offenburg. Near Strasbourg, after 95km, the Kinzig is eventually swallowed up by the mighty Rhine. A 2000-year-old trade route through the valley links Strasbourg with Rottweil. The valley's inhabitants survived on mining and shipping goods by raft for centuries, and to this day you'll see plenty of felled trees awaiting shipping.

Getting There & Away

Bus The Kinzig Valley has direct connections with Freiburg by bus No 1066 with four daily departures (two on weekends). Bus No 7160 traverses the valley on its route between Offenburg and Triberg. Bus No 7161 shuttles between Freudenstadt and Hausach.

Train From Freudenstadt Stadtbahnhof, the Kinzigtalbahn has departures every two hours with stops in Alpirsbach, Schiltach, Wolfach and Hausach. Here it hooks up with the Schwarzwaldbahn with hourly connections north to Haslach, Gengenbach and Offenburg and south to Triberg, Villingen, Donaueschingen and Konstanz.

Car & Motorcycle The B294 follows the Kinzig from Freudenstadt to Haslach, from where the B33 leads back north to Offenburg. If you're going south, you can pick up the B33 to Triberg and beyond in Hausach.

Alpirsbach

- *pop 7000*
- *area code* ☎ 07444

The main attraction of this village, 18km or so south of Freudenstadt, is the 11th-century **Klosterkirche St Benedict**, formerly a part of a monastery and now a Protestant parish church. An almost unadulterated Romanesque basilica, its austere red-sandstone façade matches the streamlined interior with its flat ceiling and row of columned arcades. The entire building is based on strictly symmetrical proportions: the central nave with its choir is exactly twice as long as the transept. The transept itself is just as wide as the central nave, but only half as wide as the aisles. Guided tours cost DM4 and take place at 10 and 11 am and at 2, 3 and 4 pm daily, except Sunday mornings.

The tourist office (☎ 951 62 81; fax 951 62 83) is at Hauptstrasse 20 inside the Haus des Gastes. The *DJH hostel* (☎ 247 7), at Reinerzauer Steige 80 above town, about 2km from the train station, charges DM22/27 juniors/seniors.

Schiltach

- *pop 4100*
- *area code* ☎ 07836

If you like half-timbered houses, then you should not miss this timeless jewel of a town about 18km south of Alpirsbach at the confluence of the Kinzig and the Schiltach rivers. The wealth acquired by Schiltach in former times translated into a picture-perfect village that is at its most scenic around the triangular **Markt** built against a steep hill. Take a closer look at the step-gabled **Rathaus**, whose murals provide a pictorial record of the town history.

At Hauptstrasse 5, you'll find Schiltach's tourist office (☎ 648; fax 585 8). *Campingplatz Schiltach* (☎ 728 9) is at Bahnhofstrasse 6 not far from the tourist office. There's no hostel here, but *private rooms* are available from DM25 per person, though some require a three-day minimum stay. At the traditional *Gasthaus Adler* (☎ 368), Hauptstrasse 20, singles/doubles go for DM60/90.

Wolfach

- *pop 6150*
- *area code* ☎ 07834

The main reason to stop at Wolfach, about 9km west of Schiltach, is to visit the **Dorotheenhütte**, a glass blowing workshop at Glasshüttenstrasse 4, where you can watch glasses and vases and other objects being blown by hand. The finished items can be admired in the adjacent **museum**. The complex is open daily from 9 am to 4.30 pm. Admission is DM5, discount DM3. To learn more about the importance of mining and logging in the area, you can visit the **Flösser- und Heimatmuseum** (Museum of Rafting & Local History), in the 17th-century palace of the former Württemberg landgraves. It's open Tuesday, Thursday and on weekends from 2 to 5 pm, Sunday also from 10 am to noon. In winter it's only open on Thursday from 2 to 5 pm. Admission is DM3. Wolfach's tourist office (☎ 835 35 1; fax 835 38 9) is at Hauptstrasse 41.

Gutach

- *pop 2200*
- *area code* ☎ 07685

Technically not in the Kinzig Valley, but only a 4km detour south along the B33, which parallels the Gutach river, is one of the Black Forest's biggest tourist draws, the **Schwarzwald Freilicht Museum** (Black Forest Open-Air Museum). It's worth braving the hordes of coach tourists for a first-hand look

STUTTGART-MARKETING GmbH

DAVID PEEVERS

DAVID PEEVERS

DAVID PEEVERS

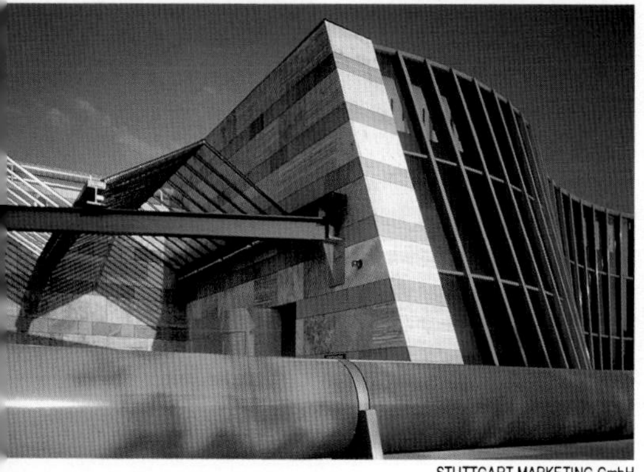

STUTTGART-MARKETING GmbH

DAVID PEEVERS

A	B
C	D
E	F

Baden-Württemberg

A: Rosensteinpark, Stuttgart
B: Schiller's birthplace, Marbach
C: Market square & castle, Heidelberg
D: Mercedes Museum, Stuttgart
E: Staatsgalerie, Stuttgart
F: Titisee, Black Forest

DAVID PEEVERS

DAVID PEEVERS

DAVID PEEVERS

DAVID PEEVERS

DAVID PEEVERS

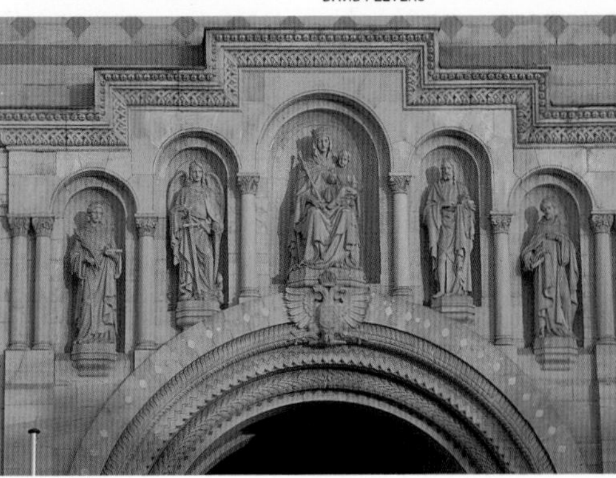
DAVID PEEVERS

A	B
C	D
E	F

Rhineland-Palatinate

A: Burg Eltz, Moselle Valley
B: Gobelin tapestry, Burg Eltz
C: Bend in the Moselle River
D: Kupferberg Memorial Barrel, Ma
E: Winemaker, Moselle Valley
F: Detail of Speyer Cathedral

at the full range of historical farmhouses from the entire region that have been assembled here.

The museum centres around the **Vogtbauernhof**, which has stood in the valley since 1570 and was saved from demolition in 1962 by Hermann Schilli, a former professor at the University of Freiburg and the museum's creator. The other farmhouses – along with a bakery, sawmill, chapel and granary – have been moved here from their original locations. It's not entirely kitsch-free, but the houses are authentically furnished and craftspeople at work inside seem to know what they're doing. The museum is open April to October daily from 8.30 am to 6 pm (last admission 5 pm) and costs DM7, discount DM5.

Haslach

- *pop 6600*
- *area code* ☎ 07832

Back in the Kinzig Valley, the next town worth a brief stop is Haslach. In the Middle Ages, it enjoyed a certain prosperity from the nearby silver mines, but when these were exhausted, it became a simple market town. Even today it still is something of a shopping hub for the immediate region, with 30 clothing stores alone. Haslach has a pretty Altstadt with some half-timbered houses, but the most interesting building is the former Capuchin monastery, which now contains the **Trachtenmuseum** (Museum of Folkloric Garments).

Most impressive in this exhibit are the women's headdresses of which there are two basic types, the *Bollenhut* and the *Schäppel*. The Bollenhut is a chalked straw bonnet festooned with woollen pompoms, red for unmarried, black for married women. Originally, it hails from the village of Gutach, but is now a symbol of the entire Black Forest. The Schäppel is a fragile-looking crown made from hundreds of beads that can weigh as much as 5kg. These headdresses, along with their appropriate costumes, are still worn on important holidays, during processions and, occasionally, at wedding ceremonies. It's astonishing that the outfits have stayed pretty much the same over the centuries, which just goes to show that change comes very slowly to this hilly forest area. The museum is open Tuesday to Saturday from 9 am to 5 pm and from 10 am on Sunday. From November to March, hours are reduced to Tuesday to Friday 1 to 5 pm. Admission is DM3.50.

While here, make sure to step into the tourist office (☎ 706 71; fax 590 9), housed in the same building as the museum. It has lots of information on Haslach and its surrounds and a friendly, English-speaking staff. What's more, they have great hours: from April to October it's open Monday to Saturday from 9 am to 5 pm and Sunday from 10 am. The rest of the year, hours are 9 am to noon and 1 to 5 pm on weekdays only. They can help with finding *private rooms* and hotel accommodation.

The nearest camping ground is *Campingplatz Kinzigtal* (☎ 812 2) in Steinach, about 3km north of Haslach. *Gasthaus Rebstock* (☎ 979 79 7), at Kirchgasse 6, charges from DM38/46 for singles/doubles.

Gengenbach

- *pop 10,500*
- *area code* ☎ 07803

Another symphony in half-timber is this romantic village, about 11km south of Offenburg. Gengenbach is often compared to Rothenburg ob der Tauber, but actually has remained relatively unspoiled by mass tourism. You can stroll through its narrow lanes, past imposing patrician town houses with crimson geraniums spilling out of flower boxes, and to the Stadtkirche with its lovely baroque tower.

On the market you'll find a fountain with a knight statue, a symbol of the village's medieval status as a 'free imperial city'. Masks and costumes worn during the local version of Carnival, called *Fasend* can be admired on the seven floors of the **Narrenmuseum** (open weekends from 2.30 to 5.30 pm, Sunday also 10 am to noon between April and October; DM2). The tourist office (☎ 930 14 3; fax 930 14 2) is at the Winzerhof building.

TRIBERG

- *pop 6000*
- *area code* ☎ 07722

Wedged into a narrow valley and framed by three mountains (hence the name) about 17km south of Hausach, Triberg is the undisputed capital of cuckoo-clock country. Countless shops, decorated with flags from around the world, simply crawl with international coach tourists thinking they're buying 'typical' German trinkets when the label on that cute doll more likely says 'Made in Taiwan'. This is not to say that you can't find some authentic, locally made items including clocks, though usually at a high price. Triberg also boasts not just one, but two of the 'world's largest cuckoo clocks' (see boxed text entitled An Entirely Cuckoo Affair). Fortunately, though, there are also some attractions unrelated to cuckoo clocks, including Germany's largest waterfall, some fine local museums and a historic Black Forest farmhouse where they still smoke their own hams.

Orientation & Information

Triberg's only thoroughfare is the B500, which bisects the valley and is called Hauptstrasse in town. The train station is at its northern end, where the B500 meets the B33. It's a little over a kilometre to walk from the station to the Markt and there's also bus service. The Markt is the hub for regional buses.

Triberg's tourist office (☎ 953 23 0; fax 953 23 6) is at Luisenstrasse 10 inside the Kurhaus, just east of the waterfalls. It's open 9 am to 5 pm weekdays and in summer also on Saturday from 10 am to noon. The daily resort tax is DM2. The Deutsche Bank at Markt 59 exchanges money and has an ATM that also accepts credit cards. There's also a Sparkasse at No 64. The main post office is at the train station, but there's another in town at Markt 55 next to the Rathaus.

Things to See

Niagara it ain't, but Germany's tallest **waterfalls** certainly exude their own wild romanticism. Fed by the Gutach river, they plunge 163m in seven cascades bordered by mossy rocks. The energy generated has been harvested since 1884 when it was first used to fuel the town's electric street lamps. The falls are a pretty neat sight to behold, though you have to drop DM2.50 to even access the wooded gorge. Its worth taking the 20 to 30-minute hike to the top of the falls.

For a thorough and quite imaginative overview of Triberg's history and social life in the region, head for the **Schwarzwaldmuseum** at Wallfahrtstrasse 4. It's open daily from 9 am to 6 pm (November to April 10 am to 5 pm, closed mid-November to mid-December) and costs DM5, discount DM2. Continuing on Wallfahrtstrasse will get you to the baroque pilgrimage church **Maria in der Tanne** (Our Lady of the Pines), a single-nave structure with a flat wooden ceiling whose simplicity contrasts with the extravagant high altar decked out in a veritable biblical who's who.

One of Triberg's two 'world's biggest cuckoo clocks' can be found another kilometre or so onward at Untertalstrasse 28. It's inside a snug little house which you can enter to see the large clockwork (open daily from 9 am to noon and 1 to 6 pm; DM1). Its rival is on the B33 in Triberg-Schonachbach and integrated into a large shop (open Monday to Saturday from 9 am to 6 pm and from Easter to October also on Sunday from 10 am; DM2).

Hiking

Triberg is premier hiking territory, and the tourist office has lots of maps and suggestions. One particularly enjoyable destination – reached after about a one-hour hike towards Schwarzenbach, south-west of Triberg – is the **Reinertonishof**, a historic Black Forest farmhouse from 1619. Inhabited until 1980, its chambers, stables and smokehouse can now be explored on a self-guided tour. The place is owned by Frau Duffner, who speaks excellent English, and who still smokes her own bacon while her husband makes schnapps so strong it will take the enamel off your teeth. The farm-

An Entirely Cuckoo Affair

Schwarzwälders know how to make capital with their cuckoo clocks, and like Texans and Alaskans, they have gone to absurd lengths in their claims of big, bigger, biggest.

The 'War of the Cuckoos' centres on Triberg and Schonach, which are pretty much the same village except perhaps to those who live there. As you enter Triberg on the B33 from the Gutach Valley, signs direct you to 'The World's Biggest Cuckoo Clock', a small house in which nests the Schwarzenegger of all cuckoos.

Problem is, as you exit Triberg in the direction of Schonach, you'll find the *other* 'World's Biggest Cuckoo Clock', also a legitimate contender.

The War of the Cuckoos hasn't yet come to an exchange of gunfire, but the acrimony over the issue is quite real. Civic pride is on the line.

Meanwhile, in elegant Wiesbaden, hundreds of kilometres away from the Black Forest, *another* 'World's Biggest Cuckoo' pops out of a storefront, chirping derisively at its deluded mountain cousins. ■

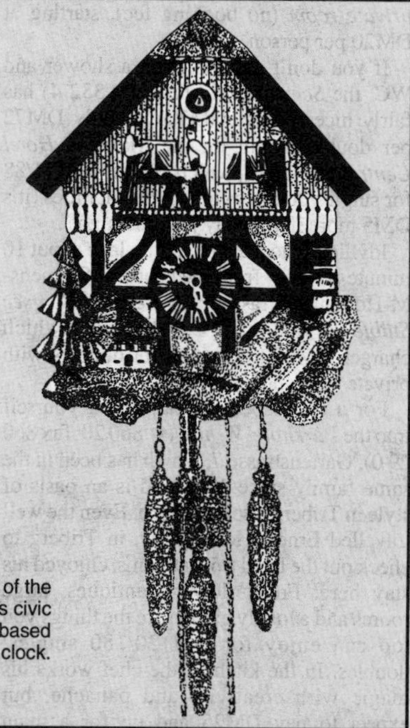

The Black Forest is the land of the cuckoo clock, where a town's civic pride has been known to be based on the size of its biggest clock.

house is open Tuesday to Sunday from 2 to 5 pm and admission is DM2.

Most traditional Black Forest farmhouses are built into a hillside, with an entrance to the living quarters at the bottom of the slope and an opening to the threshing floor on the uphill side to provide easy entry for hay wagons. Animals, humans and fodder are all housed under the same low-hanging, shingled roof. Smoke plays an important role in these chimney-less homes because it not only cures the bacon but also heats the rooms and keeps the wood worm-free. Larger farms, like the Reinertonishof, also have a separate granary, sawmill, bakehouse, distillery and chapel.

If you continue on the trail in the direction of Neustadt, after about another hour or so you'll get to the **Danube source**. Technically, of course, this modest little freshet springing from a stone is not yet the Danube but the Breg, the mighty Donau's main feeder, which merges with the Brigach in Donaueschingen (see that section) and then flows for another 2840km east to the Black Sea.

Places to Stay & Eat

Triberg's *DJH hostel* (☎ 411 0) is scenically, if a bit inconveniently, located on a ridge on the southern outskirts of town at Rohrbacher Strasse 3. It's a 45-minute walk from the train station, but you can cut this back by taking any bus to the Markt, from where it's a 1200m walk uphill. The charge is DM22/27 juniors/seniors for bed & breakfast.

The tourist office can help you find a *private room* (no booking fee), starting at DM20 per person.

If you don't mind sharing a shower and WC, the *Schwarzwaldstüble* (☎ 332 4) has fairly nice rooms and charges only DM72 per double. Right on the Markt is *Hotel Central* (☎ 436 0), which charges DM51/88 for singles/doubles with all the facilities (it's DM5 more if you stay just one night).

Idyllically located on a little lake about 10 minutes on foot from the centre at Clemens-M-Hofbauer-Strasse 19 is *Pension Bergsee Stüble* (☎ 603 6; fax 961 82 0), which charges DM80 to DM120 for doubles with private bath and balcony.

For a truly special treat, check yourself into the *Parkhotel Wehrle* (☎ 860 20; fax 860 29 0), Gartenstrasse 7, which has been in the same family since 1707 and is an oasis of style in Triberg's sea of kitsch. Even the well travelled Ernest Hemingway, in Triberg to check out the local trout streams, enjoyed his stay here. Fresh flowers, antiques, large rooms and a lovely garden are the things you too can enjoy for DM120/180 singles/doubles. In the kitchen, the chef works his magic with creativity and panache, but expect to pay DM25 and up for a main course.

All other hotels mentioned above have restaurants too, serving regional and German cuisine at average prices, from DM10 for a simple snack to DM20 for a plate laden with meat, potatoes and vegetables. Another good place to try is the *Bergcafé* at Hermann-Schwer-Strasse 6. It's a 15-minute trek uphill, but the views and reasonably priced good food are worth the effort. Back in town at Markt 63 is *Le Bistro* (closed Tuesday), a funky café popular with Triberg's young bloods and serving snacks mostly under DM10.

Getting There & Away

Triberg is well connected to other Black Forest towns. The three main bus lines are No 7160, which travels north through the Gutach and Kinzig valleys to Offenburg; No 7265, which heads south to Villingen via St Georgen (one hour); and No 7270, which makes the trip to Furtwangen in 35 minutes.

Triberg is a stop on the Schwarzwaldbahn train from Konstanz to Offenburg with service in either direction about once an hour. It's at the junction of the B500 and the B33.

Getting Around

There's local bus service between the train station and the Markt and on to the nearby town of Schonach. Trans-Alp (☎ 211 20), at Hauptstrasse 6, rents mountain bikes, though you'll need to be in fairly good shape to bicycle around Triberg.

FURTWANGEN

- *pop 10,000*
- *area code* ☎ 07723

Furtwangen, about 15km south of Triberg, is considered one of the birthplaces of clock making in Germany which, after 1700, became the dominant industry in large parts of the Black Forest. By 1870, more than 1.5 million clocks had been sold, and the sector continues to play a role here to this day. The earliest models were rather primitive, often had only an hour-hand, relied on a field stone as a weight and were about as accurate as an Italian train schedule. Gradually, they became more sophisticated and, by 1800, the cuckoo had set up house in the Black Forest clock. You can learn about this and more at the **Deutsches Uhrenmuseum** (German Clock Museum) with its absorbing and comprehensive exhibit on historical timepieces from around the world. The museum is at Gerwigstrasse 11 and is open daily from 9 am to 5 pm (from 10 am in winter); admission is DM4, discount DM2.

Besides the museum, there's little to see in Furtwangen. The tourist office (☎ 939 11 1; fax 939 19 9) is at Markt 4. The town is easily reached by bus No 7270 from Triberg, bus No 70 from Villingen-Schwenningen, bus No 71 from Donaueschingen and bus No 7272 from Freiburg.

VILLINGEN-SCHWENNINGEN

- *pop 80,000*
- *area code* ☎ 07221 *(Villingen)*
  ☎ 07720 *(Schwenningen)*

When Villingen and Schwenningen were joined in 1972, the union couldn't have been more incompatible. Villingen is a spa town that has largely preserved its medieval layout. Schwenningen, a clock-making centre, obtained town rights only earlier this century. What's worse, Villingen formerly belonged to the Grand Duchy of Baden, while Schwenningen was part of the duchy of Württemberg – historically separate allegiances that apparently cannot be reconciled. As one local was overheard to say, 'They decided to merge before they understood. Now they understand and can no longer decide.'

From the tourist's point of view, Villingen has more to offer, though Schwenningen has a couple of worthwhile museums.

Orientation & Information

Villingen's Altstadt is entirely contained within the ring road that follows the old fortifications. The train station is just east of the ring on Bahnhofstrasse; regional buses depart from here also. Most of the sights are in the northern half of the Altstadt. Bus No 20 connects Villingen with Schwenningen every 20 minutes in the daytime.

The Villingen tourist office (☎ 822 34 0; fax 821 20 7) is at Rietstrasse 8 and is open weekdays from 8.30 am to 7 pm, Saturday to 4 pm and Sunday 1 to 4 pm. There's also an information office inside the Schwenningen train station. The daily resort tax is DM1. The Sparkasse on the Markt in Villingen exchanges money, and the main post office is at Bahnhofstrasse 6. Schwenningen's post office is at Friedrich-Ebert-Strasse 22.

Things to See

Unless noted otherwise, museums mentioned here are closed on Monday and cost DM3, discount DM1.50.

Villingen Villingen has a few sights clustered in the Altstadt, which wraps around two main streets laid out in the shape of a cross. Sections of the town wall and three towers still stand. The focal point is the vast **Münster**, with its striking pair of disparate spires, one completely overlaid with coloured tiles. The Romanesque church had its origins in the 12th century, though the choir, added after a major fire in 1271, is in the high Gothic style.

Head west of here to Schulgasse, then south for a couple of blocks until you get to Rietgasse 2 and the **Franziskaner Museum** (open weekdays from 10 am to noon and also from 2 to 5 pm on Tuesday and Thursday to Saturday, from 2 to 8pm on Wednesday and from 1 to 5pm on Sunday and holidays). Housed in a former Franciscan monastery is a moderately interesting collection illuminating all aspects of the town's art and culture through the centuries; another department presents a wide range of folkloric and craft items.

At the eastern end of the Altstadt, just near the Bahnhof, is the 31m-high **Kaiserturm** (1372), once a town gate, whose five floors have exhibits on Villingen's medieval fortifications. It's open on Wednesday from 4.30 to 6.30 pm and Saturday 2 to 4 pm.

Schwenningen Housed in the former factory of the oldest clock company in Württemberg at Bürkstrasse 39 is the **Uhrenindustriemuseum** (DM5, discount DM3), which highlights the industrial-production aspects of clock making. The **Uhrenmuseum**, at Kronenstrasse 16, on the other hand, showcases the actual finished products, with a special section dedicated to typical Black Forest clocks and another tracing the evolution of the timepieces. Both are open from 10 am to noon and 2 to 6 pm.

Places to Stay & Eat

The Villingen *DJH hostel* (☎ 541 49) is at St Georgener Strasse 36 at the north-western town edge (bus No 3 or 4 to Triberger Strasse) and charges DM20/25 juniors/seniors. Hotels in Villingen-Schwenningen are surprisingly expensive, but the tourist office has a free booking service that includes *private rooms* from DM23 per person. The cheapest option is *Gasthof Schlachthof* (☎ 225 84), Schlachthausstrasse 11, which has a few shared-bath singles/doubles for DM42/75; rooms with private bath are DM65/110. If you can spend a little more, the central *Hotel Bären* (☎ 555 41), Bärengasse 2, has modern and spacious rooms that go for DM56/98 with private shower. Both hotels are in Villingen.

A good place for filling German fare is the *Ratskeller*, inside the Obere Tor at Obere Strasse 37, with daily specials from DM9. The *China-Haus*, inside the Hotel Bären, has three-course lunches for around DM10.

Entertainment

Villingen's strip at night is the Färberstrasse, lined with a collection of dimly lit and down-to-earth bars.

Getting There & Away

From Villingen, bus No 7265 makes regular trips north to Triberg via St Georgen. Bus No 7281 goes to Rottweil and No 7282 to Donaueschingen. To get to Furtwangen, take bus No 70. IR trains between Kassel and Konstanz stop at Villingen-Schwenningen every two hours. The town is on the Schwarzwaldbahn line from Konstanz to Offenburg, and there's also direct service to Donaueschingen and Rottweil. To get to Freiburg, you have to change in Donaueschingen.

Villingen-Schwenningen is just west of the A81 (Stuttgart-Singen) and is also crossed by the B33 to Triberg and the B27 to Rottweil.

Getting Around

There's a bike-rental office at the station in Schwenningen. The tourist office has a 1:30,000 bike map called *Rad- und Wanderwege in Villingen-Schwenningen* for sale (DM9.80).

DONAUESCHINGEN

- *pop 20,000*
- *area code* ☎ 0771

Donaueschingen lies on the Baar Plateau, about 50km east of Freiburg and nearly the same distance north-west of Konstanz on Lake Constance. The town marks the official beginning of one of the great European rivers, the Danube, formed by the confluence of the Brigach and the Breg. In the 15th century, the village was purchased by the princes of Fürstenberg, who made it their residence from 1723 to 1806, a legacy that survives in the impressively large palace and park.

Orientation & Information

Donaueschingen is small enough to explore on foot. The train station is on the southern periphery of the centre on Bahnhofstrasse. Walk north of here on Josefstrasse, then turn right into Fürstenbergstrasse where you'll find the Schloss. For the commercial town centre, turn left off Josefstrasse onto Karlstrasse.

At Karlstrasse 58 is the tourist office (☎ 857 22 1; fax 857 22 8), open weekdays from 8 am to noon and 2 to 5 pm, and in July and August also on Saturday 9 am to noon. Nearby, at No 47, is the Dresdner Bank with an ATM that takes credit cards. The post office is back on Bahnhofstrasse, opposite the train station.

Things to See

Donaueschingen's main sights are all clustered around the palace on the eastern end of the town centre. The **Schloss** itself is a grand structure. Many rooms, however, are rather lavishly furnished and can be seen on guided tours between 9 am and noon and 2 and 5 pm between Easter and September, closed Tuesday (DM5, discount DM3.50). The palace looks out over the sprawling **Schlosspark**, divided by the Brigach River with the half nearer to the palace laid out as a formal French garden, and the other side designed as a wildly romantic English park.

Next to the palace looms the **Stadtkirche St Johann** (1742), built in the Bohemian baroque style and topped with a pair of onion-domed towers. Inside you'll find lots of elements typical of the baroque such as a double row of windows, richly adorned pillars and the illusion of a balcony. On the left by the main entrance is the *Donaueschinger Madonna*, the only surviving piece from the Gothic church that preceded the current one.

About 100m north of the Schloss, in a former warehouse at Karlsplatz 7, are the **Fürstlich Fürstenbergische Sammlungen**. The collections amassed by genera- tions of members of the Fürstenberg family are displayed here. Their interests extended to such diverse fields as geology, mineralogy, prehistory and zoology and – to many, much more engaging than rocks and stuffed animals – art. The highlight of the **Gallery of Paintings** that occupies the 2nd floor is the *Grey Passion* by Hans Holbein the Elder, a cycle of 12 altar paintings from the late 15th century. Also look for vivid works by the so-called Zürcher Nelkenmeister, including the frightening *Temptation of St Anthony* from around 1510. The collections can be viewed from 9 am to noon and 1.30 to 5 pm, closed Monday and in November; admission is DM5, discount DM3.50.

Cycling

Donaueschingen is the gateway to the Donauradwanderweg (Danube Bike Trail), which ends 583km farther east in Passau on the Austrian border. The booklet *Donauradwanderführer* provides plenty of 1:50,000 maps and descriptions of the entire route and is available from bookshops or the tourist office for DM16.80. The tourist office also has a free brochure in English called *Tips, Info and Facts for Carefree Travels along the German Danube*, which gives useful information about all the towns on the river, along with listings of camping facilities, hostels and bike-rental and repair places.

Places to Stay & Eat

Riedsee Camping (☎ 555 1) is beautifully located on a natural swimming lake about 6km south-east of town at Am Riedsee 11. It charges from DM8 per tent space, plus DM8 per person; take bus No 7282 in the direction of Immendingen to Pfohren-Riedsee.

Donaueschingen does not have a hostel but it has a *Naturfreundehaus* (☎ 298 5) at Alte Wolterdinger Strasse 72 west of the centre and about a 15-minute walk from the train station (or bus No 90 to Kreiskrankenhaus). The charge is DM25 per bed in small dorms with shared facilities, breakfast included.

For help with finding accommodation, either turn to the tourist office (no charge) or, if it's closed, to the automated reservation terminal outside the office. A few *private rooms* are available from DM30 per person.

A fairly central hotel is *Gasthof zum Hirschen* (☎ 254 9), at Herdstrasse 5, with nice, comfortable singles/doubles with full bath from DM50/90. *Gasthof Adler* (☎ 240 1), at Bregstrasse 3, has a few doubles for DM100. The traditional *Schwarzwaldhotel Grüner Baum* (☎ 809 10; fax 809 12 50) is at Friedrich-Ebert-Strasse 59 and has cosy rooms with private facilities for DM85/140.

All hotels also have restaurants serving the usual assortment of German home-style cuisine. A good place for a snack is *Michael's Café Treff*, at Hagelrainstrasse 6, which is a younger crowd hang-out. *Zur Tränke*, at Karlsstrasse 12, is a beer pub that also has a small menu of simple yet filling German dishes. For somewhat more substantial fare, head to *Wirtshaus Trödler* at Dürrheimer Strasse 16.

Getting There & Around

Bus No 7259 goes to Titisee-Neustadt (50 minutes, no service on Sundays). Villingen-Schwenningen is reached by bus No 7282 (30 minutes). Bus No 7260 makes regular trips to the Wutachmühle (20 minutes), an excellent base for hiking explorations of the Wutach Gorge (see the Wutachschlucht section). Some buses also continue on to Bonndorf (45 minutes).

Donaueschingen is at a rail junction in the south-eastern Black Forest. IR trains between Kassel and Konstanz stop here every two hours. The town is also on the Schwarzwaldbahn from Konstanz to Offenburg, and the eastern terminus of the Höllentalbahn line to Freiburg.

Donaueschingen is at the junction of three highways: the B27 (Stuttgart-Schaffhausen);

the B31 (Freiburg-Lindau); and the B33 (Offenburg-Konstanz). It's about a one-hour drive to either Konstanz or Freiburg. If you want to rent a bicycle in Donaueschingen, go to Josef Rothweiler (☎ 131 48) at Max-Egon-Strasse 11.

Southern Black Forest

Getting Around

In order to get people out of their cars and onto the bus, SüdbadenBus offers special tickets that are very good value and valid on all routes in the South Baden area. The region encompasses locales like Freiburg, St Peter, Titisee, Feldberg, Donaueschingen, Bonndorf, Villingen-Schwenningen and Schiltach and reaches all the way east to Konstanz on Lake Constance.

The SBG-Freizeit-Ticket costs DM8 for one person or DM12 for a family of two adults accompanied by their own children under 13 and is valid for unlimited travel on one weekend day or holiday. Those spending more time in the Black Forest can get the 7-Tage-SüdbadenBus-Pass, which costs DM38 for one person, DM55 for two people and DM68 for a family. Tickets are available from bus drivers.

FREIBURG IM BREISGAU

- *pop 180,000*
- *area code* ☎ 0761

The gateway to the southern Black Forest, Freiburg (as it is usually abbreviated) has a relaxed atmosphere accentuated by the city's large and thriving university community. Founded in 1120 by Duke Bertold III and his brother Konrad of the Zähringer family, Freiburg came under the rule of the counts of Urach after the last Zähringer died childless in 1218. The Urachs proved to be immensely unpopular and so, just 150 years later, the people of Freiburg got rid of the family: they paid them the proud sum of 15,000 silvermarks, then voluntarily placed themselves under the protection of the House of Habsburg. Freiburg prospered until 1677, when France's Louis XIV took such a liking to the city that he felt the need to occupy it for 21 years. The Austrian court got the city back in 1698 and – only briefly interrupted by the French once again – the Habsburgs governed here until 1805 when Freiburg became part of the Grand Duchy of Baden.

Though badly destroyed in WWII, Freiburg recovered well and quickly. It is framed by the velvety hills of the Black Forest and endowed with a respectable list of historical attractions, led by the awe-inspiring Münster. Add to this a lively cultural scene and an excellent range of restaurants, bars and clubs, and it's easy to understand why Freiburg makes for a terrific city to visit and to base yourself for Black Forest exploration.

Orientation

The Hauptbahnhof and central bus station (ZOB) are on Bismarckallee, about 10 minutes west of the Altstadt. Follow either Eisenbahnstrasse or Bertoldstrasse east until you hit Kaiser-Joseph-Strasse, the centre's main artery. The cathedral is on Münsterplatz, another block east. All sights are within walking distance from here.

Information

Tourist Office From May to October, Freiburg's tourist office (☎ 38818 80; fax 370 03), at Rotteckring 14, is open weekdays from 9.30 am to 8 pm, Saturday to 5 pm and Sunday and holidays from 10 am to 2 pm. The rest of the year, it closes on weekdays at 6 pm, Saturday at 2 pm and Sunday and holidays at noon.

The official city guide booklet is available in English and is a worthwhile investment (DM6). Also ask about guided walking tours in English (DM10, children DM5) offered daily between April and October (less frequent the rest of the year).

Money There's an American Express office inside the tourist office where you can change money and travellers' cheques. Most banks in Freiburg, including the Volksbank opposite the Hauptbahnhof and the Deutsche Bank opposite the tourist office (open to 7

pm on Thursday) also change money; many have ATMs that accept credit cards.

Post & Communications The main post office is at Eisenbahnstrasse 58-62. The poste restante is here. Letters should be clearly marked *Hauptpostlagernd* and addressed to you at Hauptpost, 79001 Freiburg. There's a public fax phone here and also one inside the Hauptbahnhof.

Bookshops The Herder Verlag bookshop, at Kaiser-Joseph-Strasse 180, has a good assortment of foreign-language books, periodicals and maps. Rombach Verlag, at Bertoldstrasse 10, is another quality bookstore.

Laundry The central Café Fleck Waschsalon, at Predigerstrasse 3, is open daily until 1 am and has an adjoining café.

Medical Services & Emergency For an ambulance, contact ☎ 192 22 and for 24-hour emergency medical care ☎ 809 98 00. There's a police station on Rotteckring near the corner of Bertoldstrasse, diagonally opposite the tourist office.

Münster

Nothing dominates Freiburg's townscape more than its magnificent cathedral in the bustling market square. Begun as the burial church for the dukes of Zähringen, the financial burden for its construction was entirely shouldered by the local citizenry after the ruling family had died out in 1218. A mere parish church until 1827, it was granted cathedral status when Freiburg became the seat of the Upper Rhenish bishopric, previously located in Konstanz.

The cathedral has been called 'the most beautiful in Christendom'. Its oldest part is the singular **square tower** whose ground level is adorned with particularly rich sculptural ornamentation depicting scenes from the Old and New Testaments in a rather helter-skelter fashion. Look for allegorical figures such as Voluptuousness (the one with snakes on her back) and Satan himself on the west wall. The sturdy tower base gives way to an octagon, crowned by a filigreed 116m-high spire. An ascent of the tower (DM2) provides excellent perspectives on the architectural intricacies of this cathedral, with the added bonus of great views reaching as far as the Kaiserstuhl and, in France, the Vosges Mountains on a clear day.

Inside the cathedral, the kaleidoscopic **stained-glass windows** are truly dazzling. The **high altar** features a masterpiece triptych of the coronation of the Virgin Mary by Hans Baldung, which is best viewed on a guided tour (DM1) of the ambulatory with its ring of richly outfitted side chapels.

South of Münsterplatz

Unless noted, museums mentioned here are open daily, except Monday, from 10 am to 5 pm and charge an admission of DM4, discount DM2.

Immediately south of the cathedral on Münsterplatz stands the arcaded, reddish-brown **Historisches Kaufhaus** (1530), a merchants' hall used as the central trade administration in the Middle Ages. The coats of arms in the oriels, as well as the four figures above the balcony, represent members of the House of Habsburg and indicate Freiburg's allegiance to these rulers.

The sculptor Christian Wenzinger built himself the **baroque town house** east of the Kaufhaus in 1761. Inside is a wonderful staircase whose wrought-iron railing guides the eye to the elaborate ceiling fresco. Nowadays, the building is occupied by the **Museum für Stadtgeschichte** (Town History Museum), where you can learn all about Freiburg's past up to the 18th century.

Admission to this museum also covers entrance to the **Augustinermuseum** (and vice versa) in a former monastery at Salzstrasse 32 on Augustinerplatz. Its large collection of medieval art includes paintings by Baldung, Matthias Grünewald and Cranach, while its assembly of stained glass from the Middle Ages to the present ranks as one of the most important in Germany.

The **Museum für Neue Kunst** (free), a few steps farther south in a turn-of-the-century former school building at Marienstrasse 10, makes an artistic leap forward into the 20th century with its collection of expressionist and abstract art.

Also in this neighbourhood, on Oberlindenstrasse, is the muralled 13th-century **Schwabentor**. Following the little canal west through the **Fischerau**, the former fishing quarter, will soon get you to the **Martinstor**, the only other surviving town gate. It's right on Freiburg's main artery, Kaiser-Joseph-Strasse.

Western Altstadt

An eclectic mix of old and new buildings constitutes the **university quarter** extending just west of the Martinstor. The **Kollegiengebäude I** is an Art Nouveau concoction while the **Alte Universitätsbibliothek** (old university library) is baroque. Heading north from the Martinstor along Kaiser-Joseph-Strasse leads you to the **Bertoldsbrunnen**, a fountain marking the spot where the central roads have crossed since the city's founding.

North-west of here is the chestnut-tree-studded **Rathausplatz** with another fountain that's a popular gathering place. Several interesting buildings surround the square. To

BADEN-WÜRTTEMBERG

the west rises the **Neues Rathaus**, a symmetrical structure in which two Renaissance town houses flank a newer, central arcaded section. The petite tower contains a Glockenspiel (daily at noon). Nearby is the **Altes Rathaus** (1559), also the result of merging several smaller buildings and a good example of successful postwar reconstruction. Freiburg's oldest town hall, the so- called **Gerichtslaube** from the 13th century, is in Turmstrasse immediately west of the square.

The north-eastern side of Rathausplatz is taken up by the medieval **Martinskirche**, which formerly belonged to the Franciscan monastery. Though completely destroyed in WWII, it was rebuilt in the ascetic style typical of churches of this mendicant order. The antithesis to the Martinskirche is the extravagant, reddish-brown **Haus zum Walfisch** (House of the Whale), with its gilded late Gothic oriel garnished with gargoyles. Located behind the church in Franziskanergasse, the building was the temporary refuge of the philosopher Erasmus von Rotterdam after his expulsion from Basel in 1529.

Farther west, in a little park opposite the tourist office, is the neo-Gothic **Colombischlössle**, a villa housing the **Museum für Ur- und Frühgeschichte** (Museum of Pre- and Early History; free, donation requested). Via an unusual cast-iron staircase, you'll reach an eclectic bunch of archaeological exhibits spanning from prehistory to the Middle Ages.

Freiburg Beneath Your Feet

As you stroll the town, be sure to look down at the pavement for the cheerful **mosaics** usually found in front of shopfronts. A diamond, for instance, marks a jewellery shop, a cow is for a butcher, a pretzel for a baker and so on. Also be careful not to step into the **Bächle**, the permanently flowing, Lilliputian-like rivulets that parallel many pedestrian lanes. Unique to Freiburg, they were originally part of the sewage system and were also used to fight fires. Now they function literally as 'tourist traps' but can provide welcome relief for hot feet on sweltering summer days. Also, now that you've got your eyes to the ground, try to spot the unusually decorative **canalisation lids** bearing Freiburg's coat of arms.

Schauinsland

A ride on the cable car to the 1286m Schauinsland peak is a popular trip to the Black Forest highlands and a welcome escape from summer heat. Numerous easy and well marked trails make the Schauinsland area ideal for walks. From Freiburg take tram No 4 south to Günterstal and then bus No 21 to Talstation. Cable-car tickets cost DM13/20 one way/return (discount DM10/17). It operates daily year round, except during maintenance periods in early spring and late autumn. Ring ☎ 197 03 to check on the weather conditions atop the mountain.

Places to Stay

Camping *Camping Hirzberg* (☎ 350 54; open all year), at Kartäuserstrasse 99, is the most convenient camp site. Take tram No 1 from Stadtbahnbrücke near the Hauptbahnhof to Messplatz (direction: Littenweiler), then go under the road and across the stream. Charges are DM5 to DM7 per site, DM7 per person, DM3.50 per car. It's very busy in summer.

Hostel Freiburg's *DJH hostel* (☎ 676 56), farther east at Kartäuserstrasse 151, is often full with groups of German students, so phone ahead. Take the same tram No 1 as for the camping ground to Römerhof and follow the signs down Fritz-Geiges-Strasse (about a 10-minute walk). Bed & breakfast costs DM22/27 juniors/seniors.

Private Rooms & Long-Term Rentals The tourist office has a room-reservation service (DM5 per booking). Finding an affordable room anywhere near the town centre can be difficult. The tourist office may be able to find a private room for you, but don't count on it. For long-term rentals, there's the Mitwohnzentrale (☎ 194 45) at Konradstrasse 15a.

Hotels The least expensive place that's still fairly central is *Hotel Schemmer* (☎ 272 42 4), at No 63 on busy Eschholzstrasse behind the train station, where singles/doubles cost DM55/85 (DM90 for doubles with shower). Rooms with shared bath cost DM65/80 at the *Gasthaus Deutscher Kaiser* (☎ 749 10), south of the Altstadt in Günterstalstrasse 38, but it also has singles/doubles with private bath for DM95/125. *City-Hotel* (☎ 388 07 0; fax 388 07 65), at Weberstrasse 3 in the northern Altstadt, starts at DM80/120 for basic rooms, but charges up to DM120/195 for those with shower and WC.

The new *Hotel & Boardinghouse An den Kliniken* (☎ 896 80; fax 809 50 30), at Breisacher Strasse 84, charges DM93/120 for modern rooms with full facilities. The historic *Hotel zum Schützen* (☎ 720 21; fax 720 19), at Schützenallee 12 on the way to the hostel, is a reasonable compromise for location and good value, with rooms from DM75/110. Just north of the Altstadt, at Karlstrasse 7, is *Hotel-Restaurant Kolpinghaus* (☎ 319 30; fax 319 32 02), which has rooms for DM105/146.

If you can afford it, go for *Oberkirch's Hotel & Weinstuben* (☎ 310 11; fax 310 31) right at the Dom on Münsterplatz 22, which charges up to DM180/300 for singles/doubles. For a traditional atmosphere, try the classy *Hotel zum Roten Bären* (☎ 387 87 0; fax 387 87 17), near the Schwabentor gate, which claims to be the oldest guesthouse in Germany (since 1311). It charges from DM195/250.

BADEN-WÜRTTEMBERG

Places to Eat

As a university town, Freiburg virtually guarantees cheap eating. If you can produce student ID, the university-subsidised *Mensas*, at Rempartstrasse 18 and Hebelstrasse 9a, have salad buffets and lots of filling fodder. All in all, there are around 700 restaurants to choose from in Freiburg.

You'll find a good number of eating houses around the Martinstor, including the popular *Uni-Café*, on the corner of Universitätsstrasse and Niemenstrasse, which serves snacks and build-your-own breakfasts. Nearby at Löwenstrasse 1 is *Salatstuben*, with a wide choice of wholesome salads for DM2.29 per 100g (after 5 pm the price goes down to DM1.89) and filling daily specials for around DM7.50. It's open to 8 pm on weekdays and to 4 pm on Saturday.

Upstairs in the *Markthalle*, at Martinsgasse 235, you'll be hit with a wonderful confusion of smells from Mexican, Italian, Indian, French and other self-service counters offering fast, delicious and cheap lunches. Speaking of aromas, for a quick caffeine fix, head around the corner to the *Kolben-Kaffee-Akademie*, at Kaiser-Joseph-Strasse 233, an old-fashioned stand-up coffeehouse with large cups for DM2.50 (closed after 6.30 pm and on Sunday).

Pubs and restaurants also cluster along Konviktstrasse, where at No 12, you'll find *Engler's Weinkrügle*, which serves affordable Badener food and wine and has four-course meals from around DM20 (closed Monday). A haunt of the in-crowd is the *Hausbrauerei Feierling*, in a renovated old brewery at Gerberau 46, which has imaginative dishes like meatloaf with curry sauce and salad (DM10.50). It also operates the huge beer garden across the alley. Basically next door, at Insel 1, is *Sichelschmiede*, a snug wine bar decked out in wood and wrought iron.

Entertainment

The free cultural events listing *Freiburg Aktuell* is published monthly and available at hotels and at the tourist office.

Also look for *Freizeit & Kultur* and *Jazz Journal*, both a tad edgier and packed with up-to-date insider's tips.

Until the restoration of the municipal theatre is completed, most performances will take place in the *Theater am Park* (☎ 348 74) in the Technisches Rathaus in the Eschholzpark (tram Nos 1, 4 and 5 to Technisches Rathaus) and other venues around town. At Schnewlinstrasse 1 is the *Jazzhaus* (☎ 397 3), one of Germany's hottest music venues, with live jazz nearly every night (admission generally costs no more than DM20) and appearances by internationally acclaimed artists.

On the same street, at No 7, is *Cräsh*, a hard-core dance club open Friday and Saturday after 10 pm (free, except for concerts). Somewhat more tame is *Sound* at Nussmannstrasse 9, open Tuesday to Sunday from 9 pm where they play rock, pop and oldies (free for students on Wednesday).

Getting There & Away

Bus Freiburg is a major hub for buses to rural Black Forest communities. Bus No 1066 travels to Hausach in the Kinzig Valley with some departures continuing on to Wolfach and Schiltach. Bus No 7200 goes to the Europa Park Rust (see Around Freiburg), No 7205 and 7209 to St Peter, No 7211 to Breisach and No 7272 to Furtwangen.

Train Freiburg lies on the north-south train corridor, and is therefore highly accessible. There are frequent departures for Basel (DM15.60, 40 minutes) and Baden-Baden (DM27, 45 minutes). Freiburg is the western terminus of the Höllentalbahn to Donaueschingen via Titisee-Neustadt. There's a local connection to Breisach (DM7.80, 30 minutes).

Car & Motorcycle The A5, linking Frankfurt and Basel, also passes through Freiburg. The usually clogged but very scenic B31 leads east into the Höllental (Hell's Valley) and on to Lake Constance. The B294 leaves the town northward into the central Black Forest. Car-rental agencies include Europcar (☎ 515 10 0) at Zähringer Strasse 42 and Avis (☎ 197 19) at St-Georgener-Strasse 7.

Ride Services The Citynetz Mitfahr-Service (☎ 194 44) is at Belfortstrasse 55.

Getting Around

Freiburg has an efficient public transport system that is part of a regional network called Regio extending to all communities within a radius of approximately 30km. It is divided into three zones with tickets costing DM3.20/5.50/7.80 for one/two/three zones. The 24-hour ticket is available either for one zone (DM7.50 one person, DM10 two people) or all zones (DM15/20); up to four children under 15 travel for free on this ticket. Buy tickets from vending machines or the driver and be sure to validate upon boarding.

AROUND FREIBURG

Breisach

- *pop 12,000*
- *area code* ☎ 07667

About 25km west of Freiburg, separated from France by the Rhine, is Breisach, an ancient town that has often been caught in the crossfire of conflict. The Romans first built a fortress atop the volcanic Breisachberg. After becoming an imperial city under Rudolf von Habsburg in 1275, Breisach became involved in a power struggle between Staufian and Habsburg rulers, the French and the Austrians. In 1793, the French demolished the town, and in 1815 it fell to the Grand Duchy of Baden.

Not to be missed on any visit to Breisach is the huge **Münster of St Stephan**, a lordly presence above the town. It is reached after a short walk from the train station: cross Bahnhofstrasse to Poststrasse, then keep going straight to the Gutgesellentor and up the Münsterberg. The cathedral was built between the 12th and the 15th centuries and rebuilt after being badly damaged during WWII. Of note inside is the fairly faded **fresco cycle** (1491) of the *The Last Judgment* by Martin Schongauer in the west end and the sweeping **rood loft** from around the same period. There's also a nice Renaissance **pulpit** (1597) and a silver shrine containing the relics of the town's patron saints. Top billing, though, goes to the magnificent **high altar triptych** (1526), with figures carved entirely of linden wood by an artist simply known as Master HL. From the cathedral terrace, there's a great view across the Rhine into France and the Vosges Mountains.

The tourist office (☎ 940 15 5; fax 940 15 8) is on Markt and can help with accommodation if you want to spend the night here. You'll find *Camping Münsterblick* (☎ 939 30;

open April to October) in the suburb of Hochstetten, about 2km south of town. The *DJH hostel* (☎ 766 5), about a 15-minute walk south of the train station at Rheinuferstrasse 12, charges DM22/27 juniors/seniors.

Bus No 7211 shuttles between Freiburg and Breisach at least once an hour (40 minutes) and there's also direct train service (30 minutes) several times daily except Sunday.

Kaiserstuhl

North-west of Breisach is the Kaiserstuhl, a 560m-high mountain that is actually a long-extinct volcano. Its terraced slopes constitute one of Germany's finest wine-growing areas, noted especially for its late burgundies. The wines owe their quality to an ideal microclimate that is the result of plenty of sunshine and the fertile loess soil that retains the heat during the night. Another popular grape variety here is the Grauburgunder (pinot gris). On weekends between April and October, at least one wine estate opens for cellar tours and tastings on a rotating basis. For details, see the tourist office in Breisach.

The Kaiserstuhlbahn train from Breisach to Riegel is a good way to get to the area, though it's best explored by foot, for example by hiking the 15km Winzerweg (wine growers' trail) from Riegel to Achkarren. By bicycle, you could pedal along the Kaiserstuhl Radwanderweg, a 64km loop trail starting in Breisach. Bikes may be rented at the train station in Breisach or at Zweirad-Sütterlin, Im Gelbstein 19 (☎ 639 9).

St Peter

- *pop 2300*
- *area code* ☎ 07660

Little St Peter, on the southern slopes of Mt Kandel (1243m), is one of those supernaturally bucolic Black Forest villages that appears to be caught in a time warp. Framed by forests, meadows and fields, it has preserved its rural character and is seemingly immune from the ills of civilisation. The fresh-faced people of St Peter are deeply committed to their ancient traditions and customs. One third of them still live in neat farmhouses often owned by the same family for centuries. On important holidays or family events like weddings, you can see the villagers – from young boys and girls to grey-haired matriarchs and patriarchs – proudly sporting their colourful *Trachten* (folkloric costumes), hand-fashioned locally by skilled craftspeople.

The most outstanding feature of St Peter is the former **Benedictine Abbey** (1727), a baroque-rococo jewel designed by the masterful Peter Thumb of Vorarlberg. Its predecessor was founded in 1093 by Duke Berthold II of Zähringen as a private monastery and burial place for his family. Secularised in 1806, it has been the seminary of the archdiocese of Freiburg since 1842.

The baroque church, which is always open, is a festive and light-flooded single-nave construction with six side chapels. Many of the period's top artists collaborated on the sumptuous interior decoration, including Joseph Anton Feuchtmayer, who carved the statues of the various Zähringer dukes affixed to the pillars. The high altar shows the coronation of the Virgin Mary and was painted by Johannes Cristoph Storer. The wall and ceiling frescos, with scenes from the life of St Peter, are ascribed to Franz Joseph Spiegler. The church is occasionally used for concerts.

On a guided tour of the monastery complex (times vary so check first with the tourist office; DM5), you will also see Thumb's splendid **library**, an elegant oval hall that contains some 20,000 tomes. Life-sized sculptures of the Muses perch on the undulating gallery. The large ceiling fresco shows scenes from the Old and New Testaments.

The tourist office (☎ 910 22 4; fax 910 24 4) is next to the monastery at Klosterhof 11 and is open weekdays from 8 am to noon and 2 to 5 pm. From June to October, it's also open Saturday from 11 am to 1 pm.

From Freiburg's central bus station, you can take bus No 7205 (one hour). Bus Nos 7209 and 7216 take only about 40 minutes but operate less frequently.

If you're driving, take the B3 north, then turn east in the direction of Glottertal. This puts you right onto the **Schwarzwald Panorama Strasse** (Black Forest Panorama Road), a scenic route across a plateau with dreamy views of the Feldberg and other mountains. After passing through St Peter, St Märgen and Breitnau, it ends after about 50km in Hinterzarten where you can catch the equally scenic B31 through the Höllental (see that section) back to Freiburg.

Europa Park Rust

So you don't have time to go to Paris, London, Amsterdam and Venice during your trip to Europe? Don't despair. The people of the Europa Park have brought the continent's best sights together right here at their theme park in Rust, about 30km north of Freiburg. Sure, it's not the real thing, but where else can you meander effortlessly from a Swiss mountain village to a Spanish *avenida* and be back in time for lunch at the Rock-Café – without even taking your passport? And if you need to brush up on German architectural styles, just take a walk down 'Main Street Germany' where you'll find it all – Gothic red brick and cute half-timber to curvy baroque. Add to that a bunch of rides, restaurants and glitzy shows and the fun is complete – provided you're into that sort of thing. They even have a big mouse walking around... doesn't that remind you of that other theme park?

The park (☎ 07822-770) is open daily from 9 am to 6 pm (longer in peak season) from late March to early November. Admission is DM36.

From Freiburg's bus station, bus No 7200 makes daily trips directly to the park with several departures in the morning and return trips to Freiburg starting at 4 pm. By car, take the A5 north to the Herbolzheim exit.

Höllental

When in Freiburg, you shouldn't miss a ride through 'hell', the wildly romantic Höllental (Hell's Valley) to be precise, stretching east of the city en route to Titisee. It's easily seen by car along the B31 or by rail on the Höllentalbahn from Freiburg to Donaueschingen, although to truly experience its natural splendour, you should walk.

In a wonderful twist of names, the western gateway to 'hell' is the village of **Himmelsreich** (Kingdom of Heaven) after which you're plunged into the narrow, craggy stone canal that in parts is so steep that the sunlight doesn't reach the bottom until mid-morning. Near-vertical jagged rock faces, alternating with tree-covered hillsides, dwarf everything beneath them. A famous landmark is the **Stag's Leap**, the narrowest point of the valley between Himmelsreich and Posthalde, and allegedly the spot where a male deer being pursued by hunters rescued itself by leaping across the crevice.

The valley was virtually impassable until the construction of its railway at the turn of the last century. This was another amazing feat of engineering accomplished by Robert Gerwig, who also built the Schwarzwaldbahn. On its way, the train passes through nine tunnels and travels along the 222m-long viaduct over the Ravenna Gorge before coming out of the valley at Hinterzarten.

Hiking Located at the northern foot of the Feldberg, the entire Höllental is terrific hiking territory. A convenient and particularly scenic base for your explorations is the Hofgut Sternen in Höllsteig, an inn and restaurant at the mouth of the Ravenna Gorge. The Hofgut Sternen is a Höllental institution and was already here in 1770 when the ill-fated Marie-Antoinette, daughter of Habsburg Empress Maria Theresa (1717-80), spent the night on her way from Vienna to Paris to marry Louis XVI. And only a few years later, Johann Wolfgang von Goethe too stopped by for a visit.

Today, the Sternen is a sprawling, largely kitsch-free Black Forest inn run with aplomb by energetic outdoor enthusiasts who know the area extremely well and are full of tips, information and suggestions. If you want to stay at the Sternen (☎ 07652-901 0), expect to pay about DM93/146 for warmly furnished and very large singles/doubles with full facilities. Also ask here for the *Breitnau Wanderkarte* (1:25,000) hiking map.

Hike 1: Through the Höllental A particularly scenic, fairly steady and moderate hike (once you've worked your way out of the valley to an elevation of about 1000m) takes you above the Höllental towards Freiburg for a total of about 10km.

First you traverse the breathtaking, if claustrophobic, Ravenna Gorge that links up with the Querweg Freiburg-Bodensee. After about 5.5km on the Querweg you reach Nessellachen with great views of Freiburg. From there it's on to Himmelsreich, where you can catch the Höllentalbahn back to Hinterzarten. It's about a 30-minute walk from here to the Sternen.

Hike 2: To the Feldberg Peak You need to be in reasonably good shape for this quite strenuous hike to the top of the Feldberg (1493m). It starts off with a challenging 6.5km uphill climb through the forest to Rinken at an elevation of 1200m. From here it's only another 300m gain to the top of the Feldberg. Hike back down to Feldberg-Ort where you can catch a bus to Bärental, then the Dreiseenbahn to Titisee and from there the Höllentalbahn to Hinterzarten, followed by the same 30-minute walk back to the Sternen.

FELDBERG

- *pop 1800*
- *area code* ☎ 07655

At 1493m the Feldberg is the highest mountain in the Black Forest and the region's premier downhill skiing area, with a dense network of runs and ski lifts. On clear days, the view of the chain of Alps in the south is stunning indeed. The actual mountain top is treeless and not particularly attractive, looking very much like a monk's tonsured skull. This lack of trees is not because of an unusually low tree line, as some tourist brochures would have you believe, but the result of heavy logging by the area's early settlers.

Feldberg is also the name given to a cluster of five resort villages of which **Altglasshütten** is the administrative centre and site of the tourist office (☎ 801 9; fax 801 43) at Kirchgasse 1. It's open weekdays from 8 am to 6 pm, in winter to 5.30 pm. During peak seasons (June to October and December to March) it's also open Saturday from 9 am to noon and Sunday 10 am to noon. The daily resort tax is DM2.10. The post office is about 100m north of here on Bärentaler Strasse, with a bank immediately adjacent. Together with **Neuglasshütten**, Altglasshütten used to be a centre for glass blowing, a tradition kept alive by just a single workshop today.

Just north of these twin communities is **Bärental** where traditional Black Forest farmhouses snuggle against the hillsides. Germany's highest train station (967m) is here. East of Bärental is **Falkau** in the Haslach Valley, a family-friendly resort with a cute waterfall for a nearby attraction. Also not far is the idyllic **Windgfällweiher**, a good lake for swimming or rowing.

About 7km west of these four villages, there's **Feldberg-Ort** (area code ☎ 07676) right in the heart of the 42-sq-km nature preserve that covers much of the mountain. All the ski lifts are here, as is the popular chair lift to the Bismarck monument for wonderful panoramic views (DM10 return, DM8 up only, DM7 down only).

Skiing

The Liftverbund Feldberg comprises a network of 26 ski lifts, and you'll only need one ticket to use them all. There are 36 runs totalling 50km in length. Day lift tickets are DM36, morning tickets (to 1 pm) are DM22 and afternoon tickets (after 1 pm) are DM25. Discounts on multi-day tickets are available. If you prefer cross-country skiing, you can choose from among four groomed trails ranging from 2.5 to 20km in length.

The snow season usually lasts from November to the end of February. For the latest snow conditions, ring the Schneetelefon (☎ 07676-121 4). Four different ski schools offer a variety of packages. If you want to rent downhill or cross-country skis look for signs saying '*Skiverleih*' or try Skiverleih Schubnell (☎ 07655-560).

Schwarzwaldkaufhaus Faller (☎ 07676-223) rents snow- boards. There's free shuttle service from all Feldberg communities to the ski lifts if you have a lift ticket or your Gästekarte.

Hiking

In summer, the Feldberg area is a great place for hiking with some rather challenging trails. Since much of the region is part of a nature preserve, you're quite likely to encounter rare wildflowers or animal species such as mountain hens and chamois. The trail to the top of the Feldberg is gravel-covered. Show up early to avoid the throngs of coach tourists headed up here in ant-like processions. The Westweg trail (Pforzheim to Basel) also crosses the Feldberg. The tourist office has suggestions and an assortment of maps, including the *Wanderkarte Feldberg* (1:30,000), which costs DM5.80. (See the Höllental section for two recommended hikes around the Feldberg.)

Places to Stay

The DJH *Hebelhof* (☎ 07676-221), at Passhöhe 14, is perched at an elevation of 1234m right in Feldberg-Ort (take bus No 7300 from the Bärental train station to Hebelhof). The hostel charges DM22/27 juniors/seniors for bed & breakfast, plus resort tax, and offers paragliding courses year round and snowboard training in winter. If you're interested in the courses, call ahead for details.

In Altglasshütten, at Am Sommerberg 26, is the newly renovated *DJH Jugendgästehaus* (☎ 206), about a 15-minute walk south of that village's train station. Beds in modern four and two-bed rooms cost DM36 per person, including breakfast buffet. If you want a little more comfort, you can get a double for DM52 per person in the 'seminar wing'.

Still in the process of renovation at the time of writing was the *Naturfreundehaus* (☎ 07676-336) at Franz-Klameyer-Weg 28 in Feldberg-Ort. It may well have reopened by the time you're travelling, so just call ahead for prices and vacancies.

A more comfortable yet still affordable option is *Berggasthof Wasmer* (☎ 07676-230), at An der Wiesenquelle 1, which charges DM55/110 for rooms with full bath. It's right next to the ski-lift area.

If you need help finding a room that suits your budget, contact the tourist office (no service charge).

Getting There & Away

Bärental and Altglasshütten are stops on the Dreiseenbahn train from Titisee to Seebrugg on the Schluchsee. From the station in Bärental, bus No 7300 makes direct trips every 30 minutes to Feldberg-Ort.

If you're driving, take the B31 (Freiburg-Donaueschingen) to Titisee, then the B317 to Feldberg-Ort via Bärental. To get to Altglasshütten, catch the B500 in Bärental.

TITISEE-NEUSTADT

- *pop 12,000*
- *area code* ☎ 07651

Titisee, named for the glacial lake on which it is located, is an extraordinarily popular summer holiday resort with too much infrastructure for its own good. The village hugging the lake's north-eastern end is one giant beehive of activity filled with souvenir shops, kiosks, cafés and restaurants and swarming mostly with families and elderly tourists taking advantage of the healthy air of what is the Black Forest's oldest spa.

The lake itself – 2km long, 750m wide – is reasonably scenic and best appreciated from the relative isolation of a rowing or pedal boat. Until the Schluchsee, about 10km south, was dammed earlier this century, Titisee was the largest lake in the region. Surfing and sailing are popular activities here, and equipment for both sports may be rented. The scenic trails around the lake provide more escape routes from tourists.

Neustadt is Titisee's less commercial twin town, about 3km east in the Gutach Valley at the foot of Mt Hochfirst (1190m). Titisee's train station is at Parkstrasse, only a short walk from the lake shore. The Bahnhof in Neustadt is also centrally located at Bahnhofstrasse. Post offices and banks are in the immediate vicinity of both stations. The tourist office (☎ 980 40; fax 980 440) is at Strandbadstrasse 4 in Titisee. The resort tax is DM2.80 (DM1 if staying at the hostels).

Places to Stay

Titisee has a good selection of camping grounds, including *Terrassencamping Sandbank* (☎ 824 3; open April to mid-October) right on the lake shore and *Campingplatz Bühlhof* (☎ 160 6; open mid-December through October). The *DJH hostel* (☎ 238) in Titisee is at Bruderhalde 27 on the northern lake shore (bus No 7300 from the train station to Feuerwehrheim/Jugendherberge or 30 minutes on foot). There's a second *hostel* (☎ 736 0) in Neustadt, at Rudenberg 6 on the eastern town edge (20 minutes' walk from Neustadt train station). Both hostels cost DM22/27 juniors/seniors for bed & breakfast.

Private rooms start at DM18 per person, though there's often a small surcharge for stays of one or two nights. The tourist office has a free room-finding service. As for hotels and pensions, Titisee-Neustadt is flooded with options.

Getting There & Away

Bus Titisee-Neustadt is a transport hub for the southern Black Forest. Bus No 7257 makes hourly trips to Schluchsee. From Titisee train station, bus No 7300 goes to Feldberg before continuing on to Basel in Switzerland. From Neustadt's train station, there are hourly links to Bonndorf with bus No 7258 and to St Märgen with bus No 7261.

Train The Höllentalbahn from Freiburg to Donaueschingen stops at both Titisee and Neustadt train stations. The Dreiseenbahn to Feldberg and Schluchsee leaves from Titisee station. Neustadt is linked roughly every two hours with Donaueschingen and Ulm on the Donautalbahn.

Car & Motorcycle Titisee-Neustadt is at the junction of the B31 and the B500.

Getting Around

Bus No 7257 connects Titisee with Neustadt every hour. There's a free shuttle to the Feldberg ski area if you hold a lift ticket. Bikes may be rented from Ski-Hirt (☎ 749 4), at Wilhelm-Stahl-Strasse, and Harry's Mountain Bike Verleih (☎ 409 3), at Scheuerlenstrasse 15, both in Neustadt, as well as from Bootsvermietung Drubba (☎ 981 20 0) at Seestrasse 37 in Titisee.

SCHLUCHSEE

- *pop 2600*
- *area code* ☎ 07656

Schluchsee, the name of both a lake and town, is about 10km south of Titisee. Less commercial than its neighbour to the north, it's also a popular summer holiday-resort area and centre for outdoor activities of all kinds, especially water sports. Originally, the Schluchsee was a 2km-long natural glacial lake (*Schluch* is a variation of *Schlauch*, meaning 'tube'). In the 1930s, a 64m-high dam was built, which tripled the lake's length. An old farmhouse and other buildings fell victim to the raised water level and lie submerged. Because water from the Schluchsee is used to generate electricity, levels are not always constant. Water drained to power the turbines during the daytime is pumped back up from the Rhine – about 50km away and 600m lower in elevation – during the night.

Orientation & Information

The railway tracks and road run parallel to the Schluchsee's eastern shore. The community of Aha is at the north end of the lake, the town of Schluchsee is about two thirds down and Seebrugg forms the southern end. The western shore is accessible only by bike or on foot. The lake's circumference is 18.5km.

The tourist office (☎ 773 23 3; fax 775 9), inside the Haus des Gastes at Fischbacher Strasse 7, is open weekdays from 8 am to noon and 2 to 6 pm, in summer 8 am to 6 pm and also weekends 10 am to noon). The daily resort tax is DM2.10. The post office is on Lindenstrasse, a short walk north-west from the tourist office.

Water Sports

The most popular activity at the Schluchsee is swimming, which is free and permitted everywhere. Keep in mind that even in summer, water temperatures rarely climb above 20°C (the lake usually freezes over in winter). If that's too cold, you might prefer Aqua Fun, an outdoor pool complex with slides, playgrounds and a surge channel – though you better be fond of squealing children. It's open daily to 7 pm and costs DM5.50, discount DM3.50.

Those into windsurfing or sailing, can rent equipment at the Segel+Surfschule Schluchsee (☎ 366), at the landing docks in Aha. Surfboards are DM15/60 per hour/day. Sailing boats cost DM20/100.

It's not the Caribbean but scuba diving is another activity practised in the Schluchsee. Visibility is relatively high, though below 12m a diver's torch is needed. Besides oodles of fish, the buildings and streets that were submerged by the damming are of particular interest. Tauchschule Lang (☎ 1699) in Seebrugg rents equipment, but in order to dive on your own, you must present certification by a major international diving association (PADI, NAUI, BSAC etc). For the uninitiated, there are introductory courses (one hour of theory, one hour of practice, one dive) for DM100, including equipment.

Hiking

Thanks to its location at the foot of the Feldberg, the forests around Schluchsee offer some wonderful hiking on about 160km of trails. Even in winter, about 60km of paths are groomed for walking in the snow. To hike around the lake will take about four hours. Ask for the Schluchsee hiking map (1:25,000; DM3) at the tourist office.

Places to Stay & Eat

Campingplatz Wolfsgrund (☎ 573; open year round) is a modern facility on the eastern lake shore, just north of the Schluchsee town centre. The *DJH hostel* (☎ 329) is nicely located on the peninsula jutting into the lake, about a 10-minute walk north of the Schluchsee train station. There's a second *hostel* (☎ 494) in Haus Nr 9 in Seebrugg, about a five-minute walk from the Seebrugg train station. Bed & breakfast in either hostel is DM22/27 for juniors/seniors, plus resort tax.

As you'd expect, the whole gamut of accommodation from top resorts to simple *private rooms* (from DM22 per person) is available along the Schluchsee. The tourist office can help you wade through the bewildering number of choices at no charge. Among the less expensive places is *Pension am See* (☎ 513) at Im Wolfsgrund 1, which charges DM32/64 singles/doubles. *Haus Pfrommer* (☎ 867), Hinterer Giersbühlweg 4, whose rooms have nicely painted furniture, charges the same. A bit more up-market is *Pension Simone* (☎ 420), Dresselbacher Strasse 17, which charges DM57/114 for rooms with balcony. All prices are for rooms with full baths.

Good restaurants are at *Hotel Sternen*, Dresselbacher Strasse 1, and at *Hotel Haldenhof* on the same street at No 11, as well as at *Hotel Schiff*, Kirchplatz 7. If you're hiking or biking on the western lake shore, stop in at the *Vesperstube*, a rustic – and solar-powered – restaurant with hearty and filling food.

Getting There & Away

Bus No 7257 makes regular trips to/from Titisee-Neustadt, though it's probably more convenient to take the Dreiseenbahn train with hourly service between Titisee and Seebrugg. From the south, Seebrugg is also served by bus No 7319 to/from St Blasien. To get to the Wutach Gorge, take bus No 7343 to Bonndorf.

Schluchsee is on the B500 which hooks up with the B31 in Titisee.

Getting Around

Bicycles are available for rent at Haus Süsser Winkel (☎ 206) at Faulenfürster Strasse 4 in Schluchsee town. The tourist office has a map with bike trails available for DM3.

In season, G Isele (☎ 449) offers boat service around the Schluchsee, departing up to eight times daily with stops in Aha, at the dam (Staumauer), in Seebrugg and in Schluchsee town. You can get on and off as you please; the whole round trip takes one hour and costs DM9 (less for single stops).

ST BLASIEN

- *pop 4200*
- *area code* ☎ 07672

St Blasien is a health resort at the southern foot of the Feldberg, about 8km south of Schluchsee town. Despite its dwarfish size, St Blasien has been a political and cultural giant in this region throughout its 1000-year history. This is reflected in its almost urban appearance and flair that's hardly typical of the Black Forest.

St Blasien's power was anchored in the Benedictine monastery, founded in the 9th century, whose influence reached its zenith in the 18th century under the prince-abbot Martin Gerbert. He was the one responsible for St Blasien's outstanding landmark, the magnificent Dom. After secularisation in 1806, the monastery did time as an ammunition then weaving factory before being turned into a boarding school by the Jesuits in 1933. Today, it ranks as one of Germany's top private schools.

Thanks to its healthy, fogless climate, St Blasien has also been a popular spa resort since the late 19th century. In winter, it offers a small range of cross-country skiing tracks and ski lifts. The community of Menzenschwand (area code ☎ 07675), about 8km north-west, is now a part of St Blasien.

Orientation & Information

The Dom and former monastery complex dominate St Blasien's small centre. Bus No 7321 shuttles between here and Menzenschwand. The tourist office (☎ 414 30; fax 414 38) is at Am Kurgarten 1-3 and is open weekdays from 9 am to noon and 2 to 5 pm and Saturday 10 am to noon. The tourist office in Menzenschwand (☎ 07675-930 90; fax 170 9) is in the Rathaus at Hinterdorfstrasse 15 (same hours). The daily resort tax is DM2.60.

To exchange currency, there's a Sparkasse in St Blasien at Bernau-Menzenschwander Strasse 1, with the post office on the same road at No 5.

Dom St Blasien

The massive cathedral crowned by an enormous copper cupola seems oddly out of place in this remote town. It's an early masterpiece by French architect Pierre Michel d'Ixnard, who paved the way from the baroque period to neoclassicism. The former monastery complex surrounding the Dom is of equally generous proportions, measuring 105m x 195m. The cupola has a diameter of 33.5m, making it the third largest in Europe after the Pantheon in Rome and the Église du Dôme, containing Napoleon's tomb, in Paris.

Having entered the Dom through a columned portico, you find yourself in a light-flooded rotunda of overwhelming symmetry and harmony. Twenty Corinthian columns support the cupola whose massiveness is mitigated by 18 windows. The rectangular choir has the same length as the cupola's diameter. It's all bathed in white.

Throughout the summer, the Dom is used as a venue for a series of free classical concerts. It's open to 6.30 pm between May and September and to 5.30 pm during the rest of the year.

Skiing

Positioned at the foot of the Feldberg, St Blasien and Menzenschwand provide access to seven ski lifts at elevations of 900 to 1400m. There are downhill runs rated for beginners to the more advanced and about a dozen cross-country tracks. You can rent both types of ski at Sport Leber (☎ 504) in St Blasien, and at Skischule Gfrörer (☎ 733) at Albweg 11 and Wintersport Maier (☎ 498) at Vorderdorfstrasse 35, both in Menzenschwand. For up-to-date snow conditions, call ☎ 414 25.

Places to Stay & Eat

The *DJH hostel* (☎ 07675-326) is in Menzenschwand at Vorderdorfstrasse 10 in a gorgeous Black Forest farmhouse. It charges

DM20/25 juniors/seniors for bed & breakfast, plus resort tax.

The tourist office can help with finding a *private room* from DM23 per person.

Pension Glatt (☎ 266 8), at Klingnauer Strasse 2 in St Blasien, has rustic rooms for DM35 to DM55 per person.

Roomy singles/doubles at *Hotel Klostermeisterhaus* (☎ 848), Im Süssen Winkel 2 in St Blasien, cost DM55/90.

A typical Black Forest guesthouse, not far from the ski lifts in Menzenschwand, is *Gasthof Birkenhof* (☎ 107 9), at Hinterdorfstrasse 25, which charges DM30/60. All prices above are for rooms with shower and WC.

Except for Pension Glatt, all hotels have a restaurant. In St Blasien you might also try the *Gasthaus Alter Hirschen* (closed Friday) at Hauptstrasse 39 and in Menzenschwand the *Hotel Sonnenhof* at Vorderdorfstrasse 58. They serve regional and standard German food, well priced daily specials and an inexpensive *Vesper* (supper) menu.

Getting There & Away

Train tracks into the southern Black Forest terminate in Seebrugg at the southern end of the Schluchsee, about 6km north of St Blasien. Seebrugg is reached on the Dreiseenbahn from Titisee (25 minutes). The cross-country IR train from Norddeich in Friesland via Cologne, Mainz and Baden-Baden also terminates in Seebrugg. Bus No 7319 provides an almost hourly connection from Seebrugg to St Blasien (20 minutes). Bus No 7343 makes the trip from St Blasien to Bonndorf, the gateway to the Wutach Gorge (see the following Wutachschlucht section).

St Blasien is on the B500, which crosses the B31 (Freiburg-Donaueschingen) in Titisee.

Getting Around

Use your own two feet to get about town; should you need a taxi, ring ☎ 907 09 0 in St Blasien. Mountain bikes may be rented for DM20 to DM25 a day from MTB Zentrum Kalle (☎ 107 4) at Grosse Bachwiesen 4 in Menzenschwand.

WUTACHSCHLUCHT

In a country as developed and densely populated as Germany, there are very few nature paradises left. The Wutach Gorge near Bonndorf, often billed as the 'Grand Canyon of the Black Forest' by tourist brochures, is one of them. It's a lovely ravine whose craggy rock faces make a near vertical rise skyward. Below lies a fertile habitat that harbours about 1200 types of wildflowers including orchids, rare birds like grey egrets, and countless species of butterflies, beetles and lizards.

Lined by ancient trees, the valley follows the flow of the 90km-long Wutach (loosely translated as 'angry river'), which originates as the placid Gutach (meaning 'good river') on the Feldberg at 1450m before flowing into the Rhine near Waldshut.

To appreciate the Wutach Gorge in all its splendour and complexity, you should take the 13km hike from the Schattenmühle in an easterly direction to the Wutachmühle (or vice versa). This can be accomplished in about 4½ hours. If you have the energy, add the 2.5km-long wildly romantic Lotenbach-Klamm (Lotenbach Glen) to your tour. The Bonndorf tourist office (☎ 07703-760 7; fax 750 7), at Schlossstrasse 1, has maps and details about hiking in the Wutachschlucht.

To get to either trail head, take bus No 7344 from Bonndorf. The bus also stops in Boll, about 4km east of the Schattenmühle and 9km west of the Wutachmühle, which is a good place to end your hike if you don't want to walk the entire distance.

Bonndorf itself is served by buses from all directions. If you're coming from Neustadt, take bus No 7258 (40 minutes). From Donaueschingen, bus No 7260 travels to Bonndorf via the Wutachmühle (20 minutes). From St Blasien and the Schluchsee, bus No 7343 cuts west in about one hour.

If you're driving, take the B31 or B500 to Titisee, then the B315 in the direction of Bonndorf.

More Things to Do in the Black Forest

If you have more time and you want to explore the Black Forest by car or on foot, there is a huge range of routes.

Scenic Roads Brochures on each of these drives are available from local tourist offices or from the Schwarzwald Tourismusverband (☎ 0761-313 17; fax 360 21), Bertoldstrasse 45, 79098 Freiburg im Breisgau.

- Schwarzwald-Täler-Strasse (Black Forest Valley Road) runs 100km through the Murg Valley from Rastatt to Alpirsbach in the Kinzig Valley
- Schwarzwald-Bäder-Strasse (Black Forest Spa Road) is a loop connecting all of the region's spa towns
- Badische Weinstrasse (Baden Wine Road) goes from Baden-Baden 160km south to Lörrach
- Deutsche Uhrenstrasse (German Clock Road) is a 320km loop starting in Villingen-Schwenningen
- Schwarzwald-Panoramastrasse (Black Forest Panorama Road) leads from Waldkirch to Hinterzarten over a stretch of 50km
- Grüne Strasse (Green Road) travels for 160km from the Vosges Mountains in France across the border as far as Titisee
- Schwarzwald-Hochstrasse (Black Forest Highway) connects Baden-Baden with Freudenstadt 60km south

Long-Distance Hikes Information on these and other hikes can be obtained from the Schwarzwaldverein (☎ 0761-380 53 0; fax 380 532 0), Bismarckallee 2a, 79098 Freiburg im Breisgau.

- Westweg: Pforzheim to Basel via Mummelsee, Hausach, Titisee, Feldberg; 280km, 12 days
- Mittelweg: Pforzheim to Waldshut via Freudenstadt, Schiltach, Schluchsee; 233km, nine days
- Ostweg: Pforzheim to Schaffhausen via Freudenstadt, Villingen; 239km; 10 days
- Querweg Freiberg to Bodensee via Höllental, Wutachschlucht, Konstanz; 177km, eight days
- Querweg Gengenbach to Alpirsbach; 50km, three days
- Querweg Schwarzwald to Kaiserstuhl from Donaueschingen to Breisach; 110km, five days ■

BADEN-WÜRTTEMBERG

Lake Constance

Lake Constance (Bodensee) is a perfect cure for travellers stranded in landlocked southern Germany. Often jokingly called the 'Swabian Sea', this giant bulge in the sinewy course of the Rhine offers a choice of water sports, relaxation and cultural pursuits. It has a circumference of 273km, of which the southern 72km belong to Switzerland, the eastern 28km to Austria and the remaining northern and western 173km to Germany. It measures 14km at its widest point and 250m at its deepest level. The distance from Konstanz at its western end to Bregenz in the east is 46km. The snow-capped Swiss peaks provide a breathtaking backdrop when viewed from the German shore. During stormy weather, Lake Constance can get quite dangerous, with huge waves crashing onto the shores.

The Lake Constance region is popular with tourists and gets extremely crowded in July and August. It may be hard to find a room for the night, and drivers are bound to get very frustrated by the constantly choked roads. Be sure to call ahead to check on room availability and be prepared to head into the hinterland to find a place to stay. The public transport system is well coordinated and a good alternative to the car.

April and May are among the best times to visit Lake Constance because that's when the fruit trees are flowering. Summers are humid, but at least the lake is warm enough for swimming (around 20° to 23°C), though the autumn wine harvest is also a pleasant time to come. Winters are often foggy or misty at best.

Getting Around

Although most of the towns on Lake Constance have train stations (Meersburg is an exception), buses provide the easiest land connections. By car or motorbike, the B31 hugs the northern shore of Lake Constance, but it can get rather busy. By far the most enjoyable way to get around is on the ferries (☎ 07531-281 39 8) which, from March to early November, call several times a day at all the larger towns on the lake; there is a 50% discount for holders of most rail passes. The seven-day Bodensee-Pass costs DM57 and gives two free days of travel plus five days at half-price on all boats, buses, trains and mountain cableways on and around Lake Constance, including its Austrian and Swiss shores.

An international bike track circumnavigates Lake Constance, tracing the shoreline between vineyards and beaches. The route is well signposted, but Regio Cart's 1:50,000 *Rund um den Bodensee* cycling/hiking map (DM9.80) is useful and available at tourist offices.

KONSTANZ

- *pop 76,000*
- *area code* ☎ 07531

Konstanz (Constance in English) is the largest town on the lake and is its cultural and economic centre. Bordering on Switzerland, it has an attractive location on a spit of land separating the Obersee (the main section of Lake Constance) from the Untersee. Its picturesque Altstadt never suffered through fire or war damage. Konstanz was first settled by the Romans and played a leading role in the Middle Ages when it was the centre of the Duchy of Swabia – whose territory included

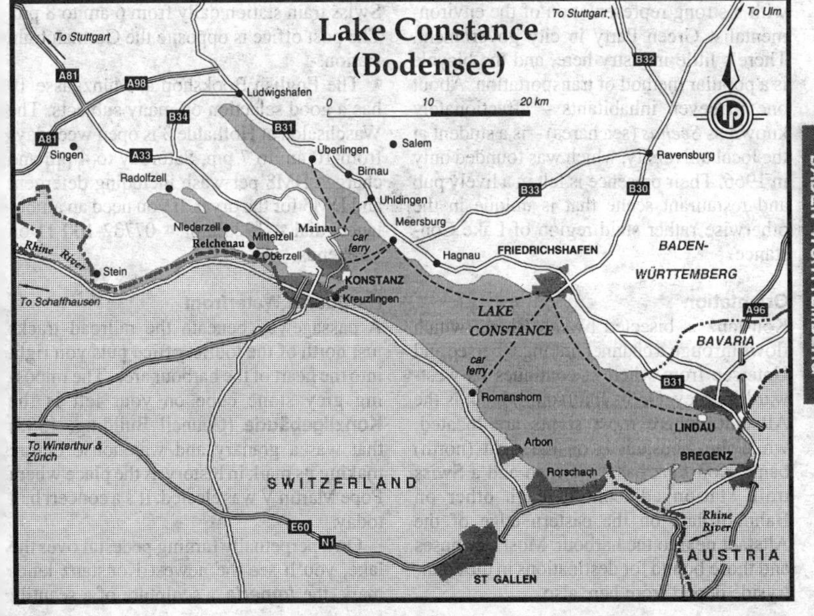

much of Central Europe – and was also the largest bishopric north of the Alps. The town reached its historical apex in the 15th century when the Council of Constance convened here from 1414 to 1418.

The primary mission of the council delegates was to heal the schism that had split the Catholic Church and resulted in three rival popes based in Rome, Avignon and Pisa. The negotiations concluded with the election of Otto Colonna as Pope Martin V, replacing the other three. This marked the first and last time a pope was chosen on German soil. While in session, the delegates also took care of the threat posed by the Bohemian reformer Jan Hus by declaring him a heretic and burning him at the stake in Konstanz in 1415. The council meeting was the last great moment on the world stage for Konstanz, which then plunged abruptly into relative obscurity. The final blow came in 1821 when the bishopric – in existence for 1000 years – was dissolved and moved to Freiburg.

Today, Konstanz is a rather liberal town with a strong representation of the environmentalist Green Party in city government. There's little industry here, and the bicycle is a popular method of transportation. About one in seven inhabitants – affectionately known as *Seehas* (sea hares) – is a student at the local university, which was founded only in 1966. Their presence is felt in a lively pub and restaurant scene that is unique in the otherwise rather staid region of Lake Constance.

Orientation

Konstanz is bisected by the Rhine, which flows through a channel linking Obersee and Untersee from where it continues its westward journey. On its left (south) bank is the Altstadt, where most sights are located, while the Neustadt is on the right (north) bank. Konstanz has a German and a Swiss train station adjacent to each other on Bahnhofplatz on the eastern edge of the Altstadt next to the harbour. Most city buses and those bound for destinations in the countryside depart from here also.

Information

The tourist office (☎ 133 03 0; fax 133 06 0) is at Bahnhofsplatz 13, about 150m to the right as you exit the train station. Between May and September, it's open weekdays from 9 am to 6.30 pm. The rest of the year, hours are 9 am to noon and 2 to 6 pm. From April to October, it's also open Saturday from 9 am to 1 pm. If you're staying more than one night, your hotel or pension will give you the Gästekarte, which entitles you to unlimited bus rides and various discounts, for instance at the island of Mainau. The daily resort tax is DM1.50 (April to October only).

In summer, the tourist office also sells the Konstanzer 2-Tages-Ticket (DM32) good for various boat rides, admission to Mainau, a guided city tour and an information package.

The Reisebank inside the train station is open weekdays from 8 am to 12.30 pm and 1.30 to 5.30 pm, Saturday 8 am to 2.30 pm and Sunday to 12.30 pm. You can also change money at the ticket counter of the Swiss train station daily from 6 am to 8 pm. The post office is opposite the German train station.

The English Bookshop at Münzgasse 10 has a good selection on many subjects. The Waschsalon at Hofhalde 3 is open weekdays from 10 am to 7 pm, Saturday to 4 pm and charges DM8 per wash including detergent and DM5 for the dryer. If you need an ambulance, dial ☎ 192 22 or ☎ 07732-100 11 on weekends.

Harbour & Waterfront

A passageway beneath the railroad tracks just north of the tourist office puts you right into the heart of the harbour area. The imposing grey stone cube on your left is the **Konzilgebäude** (Council Building, 1388) that was a granary and warehouse before making its mark in history as the place where Pope Martin V was elected. It's a concert hall today.

On a perpetually turning pedestal over the lake, you'll see the newest Konstanz landmark, the ***Imperia***, a sculpture of a scantily clad, voluptuous woman. Imperia was allegedly a prostitute who plied her trade in the days of the Council of Constance and was immortalised in a novel by Honoré de Balzac. Upon its unveiling in 1993 the sculpture aroused plenty of controversy – and even more publicity – for its unabashed mockery of authority. In the palms of her hands – so to speak – she triumphantly grips two puny and grotesque figures, one with an imperial crown and the other wearing a papal tiara. They symbolise the worldly and religious powers of the men at the council. Imperia's bemused smirk reveals her thoughts about where the *real* power lies.

A few steps from here is the **Zeppelin Monument**, in honour of the airship inventor Count Ferdinand von Zeppelin. He was born in 1838 in the building on the **Insel**, a mere blip of an island a short stroll north through a small park. This handsome structure has housed a hotel since 1875 but actually began life as a Dominican monastery in 1235. Just past the lobby is the former cloister with 19th-century murals depicting the history of Konstanz. Practically opposite the Insel is the **Theater**, whose façade sports a comical semi-relief showing the Fool's banishment from the theatre. The nearby **Rheinbrücke** links the Altstadt and Neustadt. Take a look across at Seestrasse on the opposite shore with its row of handsome Art Nouveau villas. The one at No 21 houses the city **Casino**.

Münster

The Münster, where the Council of Constance held its sessions, sits on a slightly raised square that marks the highest point in Konstanz's Altstadt. It's a showcase of architectural styles from nine centuries, starting with the original Carolingian church, built in 1000, which collapsed a mere 52 years later. Its reconstruction incorporated the original crypt beneath the choir that's decorated with large gilded copper medallions and – highly unusual for a crypt – bathed in muted daylight streaming in from a little window.

The new church in the Romanesque style still forms the core of today's structure. Between the 12th and the 15th centuries, the Gothic vaulted side aisles, with their chains of chapels, were added, as were the masterfully carved oak main portal and choir stalls. The Renaissance brought the organ which perches on a stone balcony, while the high altar dates to the baroque era. The 19th century gave the church its neo-Gothic spires.

The Münster contains a number of treasures. A highlight is the **Schnegg** (literally 'snail'; 1438) in the northern transept, a vividly decorated spiral staircase. Exit left into the cloister, then keep right to get to the **Mauritius Rotunda** with the 13th-century **Heilige Grab** (holy sepulchre), inspired by the one purportedly of Christ in Jerusalem. It's a crown-shaped, 12-sided, stone structure festooned with highly emotional and artistic sculptures, including the apostles perched between each of the gables. Time and the elements have taken a toll on the Münster, which has not been without scaffolding since 1961. Views from the 76m-high tower are superb, though it too may still be closed for renovation.

Niederburg

The Niederburg is the oldest quarter of Konstanz and stretches north of the Münster to the Rhine. The site of the original Roman settlement, it was later the quarter of the craftspeople and small merchants. An almost medieval atmosphere still permeates this maze of alleyways lined with centuries-old houses, some containing lovely antique stores, a snug wine bar or a lively restaurant.

In Brückengasse, at No 15, is the only surviving convent in Konstanz, **Kloster Zoffingen**, founded in 1257 and still in the hands of Dominican nuns who also run a girls school. On the Rheinsteig, running parallel with the river, stands the 15th-century **Rheintorturm**, a defensive tower whose upper section is covered by a mantle of wooden planks and topped by a steep tent roof. About 200m farther west is the **Pulverturm** (1321), with walls that are 2m thick. Nearby in Rheingasse is the **Domprobstei** (1609), a red baroque structure that used to be the residence of the cathedral provosts.

Museums

At Rosgartenstrasse 5 stands the former guildhall of the butchers, now occupied by the **Rosgartenmuseum**, founded in 1871 and dedicated to regional art and history. The museum is open Tuesday to Thursday from 10 am to 5 pm, Friday to Sunday to 4 pm; admission is DM3, discount DM1.50.

The **Archäologisches Landesmuseum** (Archeological State Museum) is inside a former monastery, at Benediktinerplatz 5, and has three floors filled with locally found objects, models and reconstructions. It's open from 10 am to 6 pm, closed Monday; admission is DM4, discount DM3.

Activities

Personenschiffahrt Wilfried Giess (☎ 811 01 75) offers one-hour cruises from the harbour landing docks daily in season between 10.30 am and 5.30 pm for DM8, discount DM7.

If you prefer to do your own pedalling, you can rent boats in the nearby Gondelhafen for DM8/14 per half-hour/hour.

Every Thursday at 7 pm between April and September wine tastings (DM13) take place at the Spitalkellerei at Brückengasse 16. It's best to call ahead for reservations on ☎ 288 34 2.

Organised Tours

Guided two-hour city tours in English (DM10) take place from May to September on Thursday at 10.30 am. Contact the tourist office for details.

Places to Stay

Camping Open late March to September, *Campingplatz Klausenhorn* (☎ 637 2) is on the shore of the Überlinger See in the northern suburb of Dingelsdorf (take bus No 4 to Klausenhorn).

Other options are *Campingplatz Bruderhofer* (☎ 313 88), at Fohrenbühlweg 50, and *Campingplatz Litzelstetten-Mainau* (☎ 943 03 0), at Grossherzog-Friedrich-Strasse 43 in Konstanz-Litzelstetten, about a 20-minute walk to Mainau Island.

Hostels Konstanz's *DJH hostel* (☎ 322 60) is pretty basic and located in a tower at Zur Allmannshöhe 18 in the northern suburb of Allmannsdorf (from the train station take bus No 4 to Jugendherberge or bus No 1 to Allmannsdorf-Post). The charge is DM20/25 juniors/seniors for beds in large dorms, breakfast included.

Private Rooms & Long-Term Rentals The tourist office has a room reservation service for which it charges DM5 per booking. Private rooms are available from DM30 per person. The Mitwohnzentrale (☎ 194 45) has an office at Zokerstrasse 12.

Pensions & Hotels In general, accommodation in Konstanz is frightfully expensive. Your cheapest option is *Pension Gretel* (☎ 232 83), Zollernstrasse 6, which charges DM50/95 singles/doubles for no-frills rooms with shared facilities. Next up is *Sonnenhof* (☎ 222 57), literally right on the Swiss border at Otto-Raggenbass-Strasse 3, which has a few shared-shower/WC rooms for DM70/100. Those with private bath will cost you from DM90/120. At the newly renovated *Hotel Gerda* (☎ 235 59, fax 226 03; for non-smokers only), centrally located at No 18 of the pedestrianised Bodanstrasse, the most simple rooms cost DM62/115 and go up to DM105/170 for those with full bath. Decent value, if you can get one of the cheaper rooms, is the traditional *Hotel Barbarossa* (☎ 220 21; fax 276 30), also in a central location at Obermarkt 8-12, which asks DM55/98 for rooms with shower, but at least DM70/155 for those with full bath. One of the best places in town is the classy *Hotel Halm* (☎ 121 0; fax 218 03), Bahnhofplatz 6, with fancy rooms from DM152/205.

Places to Eat

Konstanz has a great variety of interesting eating and drinking establishments, many of them low-priced.

At the *Seekuh*, a student-patronised bar with black, white and red décor and a beer garden in summer, they serve up salads, pasta and pizza for around DM11, and there's occasionally live music. *Heimat* at

Schreibergasse 2 in the Niederburg quarter is similar. An excellent bargain is the food at *Sedir*, a lively and down-to-earth Turkish restaurant at Hofhalde 11 where you can get Turkish pizza, super salads and wonderfully spiced noodle casseroles for under DM10.

On the corner of Salmannsweiler and Hohenhausgasse is *Pan*, a popular Greek restaurant that has preserved the beer hall look of its predecessor. *Zur Wendelgard* (closed Monday) at Inselgasse 5 has traditional German food, plus a surprising range of tofu-based dishes, all for DM20 and up. *Brauhaus Johann Albrecht*, Konradigasse 2, is a rambling beer hall with a rustic menu featuring daily specials and main courses under DM20.

Entertainment

The *Konstanz Stadttheater* (☎ 130 05 0), at Konzilstrasse 11, has a good regional reputation. It performs a repertoire of classical and contemporary drama and comedies. About 10% of the local Casino's profits are earmarked for financing the theatre.

There's no shortage of lively pubs and bars in Konstanz, though unfortunately most close by 1 am, weekends at 2 am. A good place for beer and talk is the bubbly *Blue Note* at Hofhalde 11, where you can also catch the occasional jazz concert. The *Salzbüchsle*, Salmannsweiler 26, one of the first student pubs in Konstanz, has a James Dean/Marilyn Monroe memorial gallery gracing the walls. *Weinstube zum Küfer Fritz*, opposite at No 11, is a hole-in-the-ground wine bar, where wines of the day are listed on a blackboard. It's smoky and rustic and attracts a more mature crowd. A wine bar for younger folks is the *Hintertürle* (closed Sunday) at Konradigasse 3 (it also has a snack menu).

Getting There & Away

Bus Bus No 7394 provides express service on weekdays to Meersburg (35 minutes) and Friedrichshafen (70 minutes). Bus No 7372 goes to the island of Reichenau (20 minutes) from outside the Swiss train station.

Train Konstanz is connected to Frankfurt (DM104, 4½ hours) by IR train every two hours. It is also the southern terminus of the scenic Schwarzwaldbahn, which travels hourly through the Black Forest to Offenburg.

To get to towns on the northern shore of Lake Constance – Salem, Friedrichshafen, Lindau – you must change in Singen, which is also where you catch the hourly Gäubahn to Stuttgart (DM54, 2½ hours).

Car & Motorcycle Konstanz is reached via the B33, which connects with the A81 to/from Stuttgart in Singen. (See also the following Boat section for details of the car ferry to Meersburg.)

Ride Services There's a Mitfahrzentrale (☎ 214 44) at Münzgasse 22.

Boat Between March and early November, Weisse Flotte (☎ 281 39 8) offers several departures daily between Konstanz and Bregenz (Austria) at the east end of Lake Constance. Boats stop at Meersburg (DM4.40, 30 minutes), Friedrichshafen (DM10.80, 1¾ hours), Lindau (DM18, 3¼ hours) and smaller towns in between. A second ferry headed for Überlingen (DM9.60, 1½ hours) travels also via Mainau and Meersburg. Prices quoted above are one way.

The Schweizerische Schiffahrtsgesellschaft Untersee und Rhein (☎ 004152-625 42 82) offers service to Schaffhausen, Switzerland, and its Rhine Falls (Europe's largest waterfalls; DM33 return, 3½ hours) via Reichenau Island and Stein am Rhein. Boats leave from the harbour.

The best way to get to the northern shore with your car or motorcycle is by taking the car ferry to Meersburg. It operates day and night with departures every 15 minutes between 5.30 am and 8.30 pm. Cars cost DM9.50 to DM14.50, plus DM2.20 per person. Bicycles are DM1.50 and motorcycles DM3. Boats leave from the landing docks in the north-eastern suburb of Staad.

Getting Around

The bus system is operated by Stadtwerke Konstanz. Single tickets around town cost DM2.20. Day passes are DM7 and good for two adults and up to four kids after 9 am. For a taxi, ring ☎ 222 22. Bicycles may be rented from Kultur-Rädle (☎ 273 10), at Blarerstrasse 19, for DM17 a day.

AROUND KONSTANZ

Mainau Island

Mainau is one of the finest attractions in the Lake Constance region and is something of a surprise. What was initially the island compound for the large Schloss of the Knights of the Teutonic Order has been transformed into a vast Mediterranean garden complex by the Bernadotte family, which is related to the royal house of Sweden. The current landowner, Count Lennart, has worked for more than 50 years to refurbish the island, which takes its name from the German *Maienaue*, meaning 'May meadow'.

More than two million visitors a year make their way over a narrow causeway to stroll around 45 hectares of splendid gardens and arboretums, visit the baroque church or attend special events and concerts. To avoid the crush of the crowds, it's a good idea to arrive early in the day or in late afternoon.

Each season offers different spectacular displays. In late April and May, you'll find millions of tulips, narcissi and hyacinths in bloom beneath the cherry trees. These displays segue into the rhododendron season of May/June, and then roses take over the stage for the duration of summer. By September, 20,000 dahlias usher in the onset of autumn foliage.

The **Tropical Garden** is a lush hothouse brimming with banana trees, bamboo, orchids and other exotic flowers. The **Italian Cascade** integrates bursting patterns of flowers with waterfalls and makes for a lovely photograph. The newly added **Butterfly House** is another highlight: you walk through a network of bridges and small canals while butterflies of the world flit and dart obliviously around your head.

Different restaurants serve food from snacks to romantic dinners, though it's prob ably more fun to bring your own picni Pathways are accessible to the disable there's a tactile and fragrant garden for th blind, and children have their own whimsic topiary garden areas to play in.

Between mid-March and early Novembe Mainau is open daily from 7 am to 8 pm (th just means you can get onto the island unt 8 pm; you can stay later if you want) an admission is DM16.50, discount DM9. I winter, opening hours are reduced to 9 am t 5 pm and so is admission, which is a fl DM8 for everybody, except children unde 15 who get in for free. In the summer seaso you can get a combined bus/admission ticke from the tourist office for DM17, childre DM6. See Information in the Konstan section for other discount options.

Reichenau Island

- *pop 3300*
- *area code* ☎ 07534

In 724, a hard-working missionary name Pirmin founded a Benedictine monastery o Reichenau, the largest island (4.5km b 1.5km) in Lake Constance, located in th Untersee section about 12km west of Kor stanz. Pirmin soon moved on to found othe monasteries in the Upper Rhine area, but th abbots and monks he left behind ensure that, by the end of the 8th century, Reichena had become a prominent cultural and artisti centre in south-west Germany. During it heyday from around 820 to 1050, it had mor than 100 monks and one of the largest librar ies anywhere. The so-called Reichenaue School of Painting produced stunnin illuminated manuscripts and vivid frescos.

Decline set in along with church reform in the high Middle Ages, and the monastery' prime was essentially over by 1200, thoug it wasn't dissolved until 1757. Of its man buildings scattered across the island, thre surviving churches provide silent testimon to the Golden Age of Reichenau. Toda about two thirds of the island is taken up b vegetable cultivation, the prime source income for the islanders. A 2km-long cause way connects the island with the mainland

Oberzell The main attraction of Reichenau's easternmost village is the late 9th-century **church of St Georg**, a supreme example of Carolingian architecture. The only section added later was the Romanesque vestibule (about 1100) through which you enter the church. Its most stunning features are the intense 10th-century **frescos** gracing the walls of the boxy central nave. Arcades carried by sturdy pillars lead the eye to the nine monumental panels depicting the miracles of Christ. The last one on the north side, for instance, shows the healing of the blind man, while the first one on the south side presents the re-awakening of the dead Lazarus.

Mittelzell The oldest of the monasteries is the **Münster** in the village of Mittelzell begun in the early 9th century, though with alterations from the 11th century. Its most unusual feature is the vaulted wooden ceiling above the central nave, whose appearance has been compared to an upturned ship's hull. A baroque wrought-iron gate separates the nave from the choir.

In the **Schatzkammer** (treasury) are five luxurious reliquaries shaped like houses. These are still carried during processions on important holy days. Also note the so-called Jug of Kanan, a 5th-century marble pitcher used to mix water and wine, and a small silver crucifix from the 11th century.

Niederzell The last in the trio of churches is **Saints Peter & Paul** in this village at the island's far north-western tip. Consecrated in 799, its significant age is concealed by a lavish rococo interior dating from 1757. The Romanesque frescos (around 1100) in the apsis, though, deserve closer attention. Rediscovered only in 1900, they show Christ flanked by the church patrons above one row of 10 figures representing New Testament apostles and another underneath depicting 10 prophets from the Old Testament. Originally, there were 24 figures in all, but the Gothic window, put in several centuries later, put paid to four of them.

Getting There & Away The best way to get to and around Reichenau from Konstanz is by taking bus No 7372. Buses leave from the Swiss train station. Reichenau is a stop on the Schwarzwaldbahn train, but the station is just off the island. The ferries from Konstanz to Schaffhausen and from Konstanz to Radolfzell also travel via Reichenau.

MEERSBURG

- *pop 5200*
- *area code* ☎ 07532

Meersburg is a picturebook romantic village, scenically perched on a rocky plateau overlooking Lake Constance and surrounded by vineyards and orchards. Small as it is, Meersburg is divided into two sections, the Oberstadt (upper town) and the Unterstadt (lower town). The historic Oberstadt has a labyrinth of narrow car-free lanes that are lined by gorgeous red-tiled, half-timbered houses and stately baroque buildings. There are two castles, the Altes and the Neues Schloss (old and new palace) which lord over the bustling Unterstadt along the lake shore. Much more commercial and catering for tourists, the Unterstadt has a pretty promenade with plane trees, cafés and souvenir shops.

Located 17km west of Friedrichshafen and reached by ferry from Konstanz, Meersburg makes for an extremely popular day excursion, and in July and August its tiny alleys are choked with visitors. If you're travelling in those months, try to show up early or late in the day to catch some of Meersburg's magic.

Orientation & Information

A steep vineyard separates the Oberstadt from the Unterstadt and there's a scenic set of steps connecting the two (enter between the Altes and Neues Schloss). The northern boundary of the old part of the Oberstadt is the B33, here called Stettener Strasse.

Meersburg's tourist office (☎ 431 11 0 or ☎ 194 33; fax 431 12 0) is at Kirchstrasse 4 in the Oberstadt and is open weekdays from 9 am to noon and 2 to 5.30 pm. Between April and September, it's also open on Saturday from 10 am to 2 pm. The daily resort tax is

DM1.50. The Volksbank on Marktplatz exchanges money and has an ATM that accepts credit cards. The post office is at Am Bleicheplatz, just north of Stettener Strasse. You'll find the police station (☎ 902 6) at Daisendorfer Strasse 26-28. Unless noted otherwise, museums in Meersburg are closed between November and March.

Altes Schloss

Meersburg's landmark is the Altes Schloss, overlooking Lake Constance from its lofty Oberstadt perch. Its origin supposedly goes back to the 7th-century Merovingian king Dagobert I, after whom the massive central keep, with its distinctive stepped gables, is named. Between 1268 and 1803, the bishops of Konstanz owned the castle, using it as a summer residence before moving in permanently in 1526 after the Reformation. As a result of secularisation, it fell to the Grand Duchy of Baden and was earmarked for demolition before being purchased in 1838 by Baron Joseph von Lassberg. He turned the castle into something of an artists' colony. His sister-in-law, the celebrated German female poet, Annette von Droste-Hülshoff (1797-1848), resided here for many years, and the Brothers Grimm and Ludwig Uhland were among those that also flocked to Meersburg.

The Altes Schloss is your quintessential medieval castle complete with defensive walkways, knights' hall, moats, dungeons and subterranean tunnels. On a self-guided tour (English pamphlet available) you'll see the usual collection of furniture and arms and armoury but also a frightful 9m-deep prison hole for which the condemned only got a one-way ticket. You'll also pass through Droste-Hülshoff's living quarters, primly furnished in Biedermeier style.

The castle is open daily year round from 9 am to 6.30 pm (in winter 10 am to 6 pm) and admission is a rather steep DM9/8/5.50 for adults/students/children.

Neues Schloss

In 1710, the prince-bishop Johann Franz Schenk von Stauffenberg determined that the Altes Schloss was no longer suitable to meet the representational needs of his exalted office and began building the Neues Schloss on the terrace just east of the old castle.

Construction continued under his successor, Damian Hugo von Schönborn, who added the impressive staircase, designed by Balthasar Neumann (1741), the chapel with stucco by Joseph Anton Feuchtmayer, and frescos by Gottfried Bernhard Göz (1743). The pink baroque palace was finally completed in the late 18th century, only a few years before the Grand Duchy of Baden gained its possession through secularisation. It then went through incarnations as a prison, a nautical school, an institution for the deaf and dumb, and a boys' high school. Now state-owned, it houses the **Municipal Gallery** with changing exhibits. On the 1st floor is the very interesting **Dornier Museum** dedicated to Claude Dornier, the inventor of the seaplane.

The museums are open daily from 10 am to 1 pm and 2 to 6 pm. Admission is DM5, discount DM4.

Other Museums

Tiny Meersburg has an astonishing wealth of museums outside the two castles, including the **Deutsches Zeitungsmuseum** (open daily from 11 am to 5 pm; DM3, discount DM2) at Schlossplatz 13, whose three floors trace the history of German newspapers.

To learn more about Annette von Droste-Hülshoff, visit the exhibit in the **Fürstenhäusle** (open daily from 10 am to 12.30 pm and 2 to 5 pm, closed Sunday am; DM5, students DM3.50) in Stettener Strasse 9. The poet bought this little garden house with the income from her first collection of poems. Though she never actually lived here, she frequently visited it for inspiration. By the way, you'll see Droste-Hülshoff's portrait on the DM20 note along with several Meersburg landmarks. In her honour Meersburg presents an award every three years to a female poet writing in the German language.

At Vorburgstrasse 11 is the diminutive but interesting **Weinmuseum** (open Tuesday,

Friday and Sunday from 2 to 5 pm; DM1), where you can see historical wine casks, including a giant one that holds more than 50,000 litres. There's also a wine press from 1607 that remained functional until the 1930s, plus lots of wine-making tools. Tastings take place here on Friday at 7 pm and cost DM15; ask at the tourist office for details.

Places to Stay

The nearest camping grounds are in Hagnau, 4km east of Meersburg: *Camping Schloss Kirchberg* (☎ 641 3), *Camping Seeblick* (☎ 562 0) and *Camping Alpenblick* (☎ 721 0). The area code for Hagnau is ☎ 07545. The nearest *DJH hostels* are in Konstanz and Friedrichshafen (see Places to Stay in those sections).

Meersburg is expensive turf thanks to its popularity, and even *private rooms* cost DM35 per person and up. The tourist office can help with reservations for free. The cheapest rooms are in small pensions outside the Altstadt like *Waldhaus Mainaublick* (☎ 940 8), at Unteruhldinger Strasse 88, which has singles/doubles for DM40/90. *Ferienhof Mohr* (☎ 657 2) is at Stettener Strasse 57 and charges DM50/95. At the *Gasthaus zum Letzten Heller* (☎ 614 9), Daisendorfer Strasse 41, which also has a popular restaurant, rooms are DM45/94. If you want to stay in a classic place, try the historical *Gasthof zum Bären* (☎ 432 20; fax 432 24 4), at Markt 11 in the Oberstadt, whose traditionally furnished, comfortable rooms go for DM85/150. All prices listed above include breakfast and are for rooms with private bath.

Places to Eat

Restaurants and cafés rub shoulders along the busy lakeside promenade in the Unterstadt. Almost all have a daily dish priced well under DM20. Fish caught in the lake, like Felchen (salmon trout) are specialities, and you'll find them on every menu. For coffee and cake or a snack, there's the *Burgcafé* inside the Altes Schloss, which also has a little terrace with fantastic views.

In the Oberstadt, the *Winzerstube zum Becher* in Höllgasse is a classy establishment whose chef infuses traditional Baden dishes with an international flavour. Also on the gourmet level is *Bistro 3 Stuben*, opposite the tourist office, which serves light bistro fare in a yuppie-inspired contemporary décor (DM15 to DM35). The *Restaurant 3 Stuben* in the same building (enter on Winzergasse) has extremely good food at outrageous prices (three-course menu DM120, wine extra).

Getting There & Away

Bus Lacking a train station, Meersburg relies on buses for connections with the outside world. On weekdays, express bus No 7394 makes the trip to Konstanz (45 minutes) and Friedrichshafen (30 minutes). The latter is also served more frequently (and on weekends) by bus No 7395. To get to Salem, take bus No 7397. Bus No 7373 connects Meersburg with Ravensburg and Konstanz four times daily except on Sunday.

Car & Motorcycle Meersburg is just south of the B31 and reached via Daisendorfer Strasse. In the Oberstadt, it merges with the B33, which begins in Meersburg and continues north-eastward to Ravensburg.

Boat From March to November, Meersburg is a stop on the Weisse Flotte boat service between Konstanz and Bregenz and Konstanz and Überlingen. Some boats travel via the island of Mainau. The car ferry to Konstanz operates day and night and is the most efficient way to cross the lake. All boats leave from the ferry harbour in the Unterstadt (see Getting There & Away under Konstanz for more details).

Getting Around

The best – actually the only – way to get around Meersburg is by foot. Those travelling by car or motorbike must drop their vehicle off in one of the pay car parks (signs will direct you), though even those can be full in high season. For excursions, you can rent a bicycle from Hermann Dreher (☎ 517 6) at Stadtgraben 5.

AROUND MEERSBURG

Birnau

The rococo pilgrimage church of Birnau is one of the artistic highlights of the Lake Constance region and is a sight worth braving the hordes for. Sitting majestically on a bluff overlooking the lake and surrounded by lush orchards, it looks more like a palace than a church. It was built by the prolific Peter Thumb of Vorarlberg, the master architect of the rococo, who also gave the world the abbey in St Peter (see that section) and many other churches in the region. He was joined by two other ubiquitous artists of the time, the stucco master Joseph Anton Feuchtmayer and the fresco painter Gottfried Bernhard Götz.

The impression upon entering the church is awe-inspiring, the décor being so intricate and profuse you don't know where to look first. Light streaming in from two rows of windows separated by an undulating gallery bathes the church in a festive and friendly glow. Your gaze is drawn to the ceiling, where Göz worked his usual magic, seemingly opening up the room to the heavens. The church is filled with whimsical details, such as the tiny **mirror** in the cupola fresco in which you can see yourself if standing in a certain spot in the choir. The church is a celebration of the life of Mary, the mother of Jesus. The high altar is dedicated to her and is flanked by **life-size sculptures**. The most famous church denizen, though, is the **Honigschlecker** (honey sucker), a cheeky cherub clutching a beehive and licking his finger; it stands adjacent to the right side altar.

Birnau is on the B31 about 10km north of Meersburg between Uhldingen and Überlingen. Bus No 7395 from Friedrichshafen and Meersburg stops right at the church.

Schloss Salem

The 7km-long Prälatenweg (Prelates' Path) connects the church at Birnau with its mother church, the former Cistercian abbey of Salem. Founded in 1137, it was the largest and richest monastery in southern Germany. The huge complex, now named Schloss Salem, became the property of the Grand Duchy of Baden after secularisation and is still the main residence of the family's descendants. The west wing is occupied by a private elite boarding school, founded in 1920 by Prince Max von Baden and Kurt Hahn, that was also briefly attended by the later Prince Philip, Duke of Edinburgh and husband of Queen Elizabeth II.

The focal point is the **Münster** (1414), whose Gothic purity has been diluted by the addition of a dominant high altar and 26 alabaster altars fashioned in an early neoclassical style by Johann Georg Dirr and his son-in-law, Johann Georg Wieland. The palace contains the lavishly decorated living, working and representational rooms of former abbots and monks. Of note are the study of Abbot Anselm II, with superb stucco ornamentation, and the **Kaisersaal**, which contains a bewilderingly detailed amount of sculpture and stucco.

The complex has been turned into something of a low-key amusement park, integrating museums, artisans' workshops, a golf driving range, gardens and various restaurants. Schloss Salem is open late March to October from 9 am to 6 pm (Sunday from 11 am). Admission is a steep DM19 (children under 16 are free), but that includes a lot: guided tours of palace and church, entry to all museums, access to the driving range, a welcome glass of wine, a bottle of wine to take away and more.

Bus No 7397 travels to Salem from Meersburg via Oberuhldingen. From Friedrichshafen, catch bus No 7396 or the Bodensee-Gürtelbahn train with departures roughly every 30 minutes.

FRIEDRICHSHAFEN

- *pop 53,000*
- *area code* ☎ 07541

Friedrichshafen is surely one of Germany's most beautifully located industrial towns, stretched out for 11km along a placid bay of Lake Constance. It's a modern town which

DAVID PEEVERS

DAVID PEEVERS

DAVID PEEVERS

DAVID PEEVERS

A	
B	C
D	

Hesse

A: Orangerie in Karlsaue park, Kassel

B: World's biggest cuckoo clock, Wiesbaden

C: Opera House, Frankfurt

D: Ebbelwei (apple wine) vendor, Frankfurt

DAVID PEEVERS

DAVID PEEVERS

DAVID PEEVERS

DAVID PEEVERS

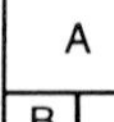

North Rhine-Westphalia
A: Rape seed field
B: Beethoven monument, Bonn
C: Moated Burg Vischering, the Münsterland
D: Palais Schaumburg, Bonn

despite its modest size, derives a big city flair from its trade show and convention activity. Historically, its name will forever be associated with the Zeppelin airships, first built here under the stewardship of Count Ferdinand von Zeppelin at the turn of the century. For decades, Friedrichshafen was the launching pad of these gentle giants. A new generation of Zeppelins is currently under construction and expected to be launched in 1998. Friedrichshafen is a relatively young town, formed only in 1811 when King Friedrich of Württemberg merged the former imperial city of Buchhorn with the priory of Hofen. In WWII it was blown to smithereens and therefore has little to offer in the way of historical sights. The extraordinary Zeppelin Museum, however, should not be missed.

Orientation

Friedrichshafen has two train stations, the Stadtbahnhof and the Hafenbahnhof, though you're most likely to arrive at the former. The central bus station is also at the Stadtbahnhof, as is the tourist office. A few metres south, across busy Friedrichstrasse, is the lakeside promenade along which you'll find most of the worthwhile sights. It's called Uferstrasse between the station and Gondelhafen, then turns into Seestrasse where it culminates in the Zeppelin Museum.

Information

Tourist Office The tourist office (☎ 300 10; fax 725 88) is right outside the Stadtbahnhof and open weekdays from 8 am to noon and 2 to 5 pm (Friday to 1 pm in winter). If they're closed, information may also be picked up at the Schulmuseum at Friedrichstrasse 14, about a five-minute walk west of the station.

Money The Sparkasse on Seestrasse opposite the Zeppelin Museum exchanges currency and also has an ATM that accepts credit cards.

Post & Communications The post office is immediately to the right as you exit the Stadtbahnhof.

Bookshops Buchhandlung Gessler, at Friedrichstrasse 53, has a small selection of foreign-language books. There are a few more bookstores along Wilhelmstrasse and Karlstrasse in the pedestrianised shopping district, a block inland from Seestrasse.

Laundry The self-service laundrette City Wash is at Schwabstrasse 16 and open daily from 8 am to 11 pm.

Emergency Police headquarters (☎ 701 0) are at Friedrichstrasse 85.

Zeppelin Museum

At the eastern end of Friedrichshafen's pleasant, café-lined promenade, you'll find the town's top tourist attraction. Inaugurated on 2 July 1996 in the reconstructed Hafenbahnhof, exactly 96 years to the day of the inaugural launch of the first Zeppelin airship, the museum is built around a full-scale, 33m-long, recreated section of the *Hindenburg*, at 245m the largest airship ever. You can walk through its reconstructed passenger rooms and also examine the filigree of the aluminium framework.

Legacy of the Zeppelins

Like many before him, Count Zeppelin (1838-1917) was obsessed with the idea of flying. With his vision and determination, he contributed significantly to the development of modern aircraft when the first Zeppelin made its inaugural flight over the Bodensee in 1900.

Unlike today's non-rigid airships (such as the Goodyear blimp), Zeppelins had an aluminium framework covered by a cotton-linen fairing. The cigar-shaped behemoths were soon used for passenger flights, outfitted as luxuriously and comfortably as ocean liners. The most famous of them all, the *Graf Zeppelin*, made 590 trips, including 114 across the Atlantic and, in 1929, travelled around the world in only 21 days.

The largest airship ever built was the 245m-long *Hindenburg*, which was destroyed in a terrible accident – or possible act of sabotage – while landing in Lakehurst, New Jersey, in 1937, killing 36 passengers and crew. ■

Exhibits, interactive information terminals (in German and English) and a series of short movies provide technical and historical insights. The top floor contains an eclectic collection of art. The museum is open from 10 am to 6 pm (to 5 pm in winter) and closed Monday; admission is DM10, discount DM5.

Schlosskirche

The western end of the promenade is anchored by the twin onion-domed, baroque Schlosskirche, built between 1695 and 1701 by Christian Thumb. It's the only accessible part of the Schloss, still inhabited by the ducal family of Württemberg. The church exudes a festiveness that results from the completely whitewashed walls and the heavily ornamented stuccoed ceiling. Unfortunately, the original stucco was destroyed in WWII but was recreated in 1950 by the appropriately named Joseph Schnitzer (*Schnitzer* means 'carver'). Of note too are the vividly carved choir stalls whose end pieces represent, clockwise from the front left, Moses, St Benedict, an abbot and King David. The church is open mid-April to the end of October from 9 am to 6 pm.

Activities

Like most towns on Lake Constance, Friedrichshafen is an ideal base for cycle tours of the lake area. The tourist office has put together a well designed and useful folder (DM9.80), outlining 20 day trips with detailed map and sightseeing information (though in German only).

For excursions on the lake, you can rent motorboats (DM45 an hour for up to four people) as well as pedal and rowing boats (DM14 for up to two people) from the rental office at the Gondelhafen.

Places to Stay

You'll find a *municipal camping ground* (☎ 420 59) – operating on a first-come, first-served basis – on Meersburger Strasse in the suburb of Fischbach. The private *Campingplatz Dimmler* (☎ 734 21) is at Lindauer Strasse 2, east of the centre.

Immediately opposite, at Lindauer Strasse 3, is Friedrichshafen's *DJH hostel* (☎ 724 04), which charges DM22.50/27.50 juniors/seniors (bus No 7587 from the Stadtbahnhof). It's often full, especially in summer, so be sure to call ahead.

The tourist office has a room reservation service (DM5 fee for walk-ins). To find out what's available, you can also call ☎ 194 12 any time of day. Additionally, there's a free automated booking terminal outside the office. Updated lists of available *private rooms* are posted in the window.

One of the cheapest places in town is *Gasthof Rebstock* (☎ 216 94), Werastrasse 35, which charges DM60/95 for singles/doubles with shared facilities and DM80/120 for rooms with private bath. *Hotel Schöllhorn* (☎ 218 16), Friedrichstrasse 65, has similar prices.

For good value, head to *Hotel-Restaurant Knoblauch* (☎ 607 0; fax 607 22 2) at Jettenhauser Strasse 30-32, where rooms with full bath range from DM90 to DM115 singles and DM135 to DM160 doubles. One of the top traditional places is *Buchhorner Hof* (☎ 205 0; fax 326 63), at Friedrichstrasse 33, which will set you back up to DM180/260 per night.

Places to Eat

Numerous cafés, snack bars and restaurants line the Seestrasse promenade.

A gathering place for the young and the hip – or both – is the *Pavillon am See* at the yacht harbour.

For Swabian specialities around DM15 and fish and meat dishes for DM20 and up, you could try *Old City*, on the 1st floor of the Hotel Zur Krone at Schanzstrasse 7. *Weber & Weiss* is an upscale bakery with delectable pastries that go down even better with a cappuccino (DM2.40) from its stand-up café. It's at Wilhelmstrasse 23 and also at Charlottenstrasse 11.

For good fast food, there's a *Kochlöffel* at Wilhelmstrasse 20. Gourmet international cuisine with prices to match is served at the restaurant of the *Hotel Buchhorner Hof*.

Entertainment

The tourist office publishes a free monthly events schedule and also has copies of the biweekly *Kultur-Blätter* covering the entire Lake Constance area. For performance art, live music and cultural events of all sorts, there's the *Kulturhaus Caserne* (☎ 371 66 1), at Fallenbrunnen 17, and the *Bahnhof Fischbach* (☎ 442 26), in an old train station at Eisenbahnstrasse 15.

Getting There & Away

Air Friedrichshafen has a small airport north-east of the city centre with domestic flights as well as some to Zurich, plus holiday charters.

Bus On weekdays, a fast way to get to Konstanz, via Meersburg, is on the express bus No 7394 (70 minutes). For local service to Meersburg and on to Birnau, take bus No 7395. Bus No 7395 makes the trip to Salem in 45 minutes.

Train Friedrichshafen is a stop on the Bodensee-Gürtelbahn between Singen and Lindau and the Südbahn, which goes to Ulm via Bad Schüssenried and Ravensburg and also to Lindau.

Car & Motorcycle Friedrichshafen is on the B31 along the northern lake shore and is also the starting point of the B30 to Ravensburg.

Boat Friedrichshafen is a regular stop on the Konstanz-Bregenz route of the Weisse Flotte. See Getting There & Away under Konstanz for details.

Friedrichshafen is also the springboard for the car ferry (☎ 201 38 9) to Romanshorn in Switzerland, the fastest way to get across the lake. Service is year round with departures about every hour between 5.30 am and 9.30 pm. The trip takes 45 minutes and costs DM8.80 per person, DM5.40 for students. Bicycles cost DM7, motorcycles DM20 (including driver) and cars DM28 to DM36 (including two people). All prices are one way.

Getting Around

The Airport The Lake Constance-Oberschwaben-Bahn train reaches Friedrichshafen's airport from the Stadtbahnhof in six minutes. A taxi ride takes about 20 minutes and costs DM21.

Bicycle Bikes may rented at the Fahrradladen (☎ 583 69 7), on König-Wilhelm-Platz, and at the Stadtbahnhof (☎ 201 38 5). Expect to pay from DM8 to DM12 a day.

LINDAU

- *pop 25, 000*
- *area code* ☎ 08382

If you arrive in Lindau by boat, you'll immediately know that you're in Bavaria when you see the statue of a lion, Bavaria's symbol. Other than this short segment in the north-eastern corner of Lake Constance, the lake's German stretch belongs entirely to Baden-Württemberg. More than one million people a year flock to see Lindau's picturesque Altstadt, scenically located on a little island reached via a bridge. They come to stroll along the pedestrianised **Maximilianstrasse**, lined by statuesque town houses. These reflect the prosperity Lindau enjoyed in the Middle Ages thanks to its location on a major north-south trading route. In the early 13th century, it was made a free imperial city and even hosted a session of the imperial diet in 1496.

The Markt, in the north-east of the island, is dominated by the **Haus zum Cavazzen** (1730), a beautiful baroque construction with murals that almost appear three-dimensional. It contains the attractive **Stadtmuseum** with a fine collection of furniture and mechanical instruments, among other exhibits. Even more impressive are the **frescos** of the Passion of Christ, painted by Hans Holbein the Elder, inside the former **Peterskirche** (around 1000) that is now a war memorial. Another visual highlight is the **Altes Rathaus** (1436), which has a stepped gable from the 16th century; the almost gaudy murals, however, were added only in 1975 and are based on 19th-century designs.

You'll find the train and bus stations, as well as a large pay car park, on the western side of the island. The tourist office (☎ 260 30; fax 260 02 6) is opposite the Bahnhof.

Getting There & Away

Train Lindau has train connections to/from Friedrichshafen several times each hour (DM7.20, 35 minutes). It is the eastern terminus of the Bodensee-Gürtelbahn line to Singen and the southern terminus of the Südbahn to Ulm via Ravensburg.

Car & Motorcycle Lindau is on the B31 and also connected to Munich by the A96. The scenic Deutsche Alpenstrasse (German Alpine Road), which winds eastward to Berchtesgaden, begins in Lindau.

Boat Weisse Flotte boats stop in Lindau several times daily between March and November on the route from Konstanz to Bregenz.

For details, see Getting There & Away in the Konstanz section.

Rhineland-Palatinate

When French occupational forces patched together the state of Rhineland-Palatinate (Rheinland-Pfalz) after WWII from parts of Bavaria, Hesse and Prussia, they joined together territories and people that had never been under the same government. But they have one thing in common: the Rhine.

Europe's third-largest river flows for 1320km from its source in the Swiss Alps to Rotterdam, but nowhere has it shaped the land and its people more than along the 290km stretch traversing the Rhineland-Palatinate. Here you'll find romanticism and industry intermingling to create the state's unique identity.

The headquarters of some of Europe's largest corporations, including the chemical giant BASF in Ludwigshafen, dominate the Rhine banks south of Mainz, the state capital. These firms have brought economic prosperity to the Rhineland-Palatinate, making it number one in the nation in terms of exports. To find the state's great natural beauty – interspersed with legend and lore – that has drawn artists and tourists here since the 19th century, you have to travel north of Mainz to the Rhine Valley. Here, steep, vine-clad slopes guide the river's northward journey past turreted hill-top castles, snug wine villages and dense forests.

As the Rhine River flows through the Rhineland-Palatinate, so do its rivers of wine. About two thirds of all wine produced in Germany comes from one of the six growing regions here: the Ahr Valley, the Moselle-Saar-Ruwer, the Middle Rhine, the Nahe, the Rheinhessen and the Rheinpfalz with the German Wine Road (the latter being the only region not on a river). The local people's *joie de vivre* finds expression in the many wine festivals organised by the villages, however small they may be.

The Romans first brought grapevines with them when they established a number of settlements in this region in the 1st centuries AD. They left their legacy everywhere, including in Bad Neuenahr-Ahrweiler on the Ahr River, Boppard and Bingen on the Rhine and, above all, in Trier. Nowhere north of the Alps will you find more and better preserved Roman monuments than in this town on the Moselle.

The Middle Ages are represented by some of Germany's finest ecclesiastical architecture, most notably the magnificent trio of Romanesque cathedrals at Mainz, Worms and Speyer. This period also saw the construction of the popular Rhine castles.

HIGHLIGHTS

- A boat trip on the Rhine between Koblenz and Bingen
- Burg Eltz, the quintessential medieval castle
- Porta Nigra and other Roman monuments in Trier, the best preserved Roman landmarks north of the Alps
- Exploring the network of tunnels at Burg Rheinfels in St Goar
- Wine tasting and an overnight stay at a wine estate
- Historical Museum of the Palatinate in Speyer

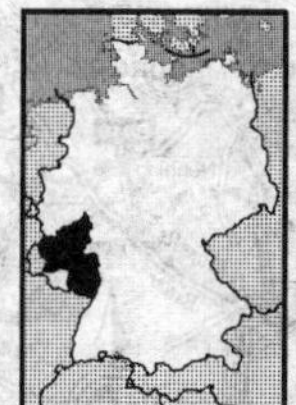

• **Population:** 4m • **Capital:** Mainz • **Area:** 19,850 sq km

Rhineland-Palatinate Luminaries: Hildegard von Bingen, Friedrich Engels, Johannes Gutenberg, Helmut Kohl, Karl Marx

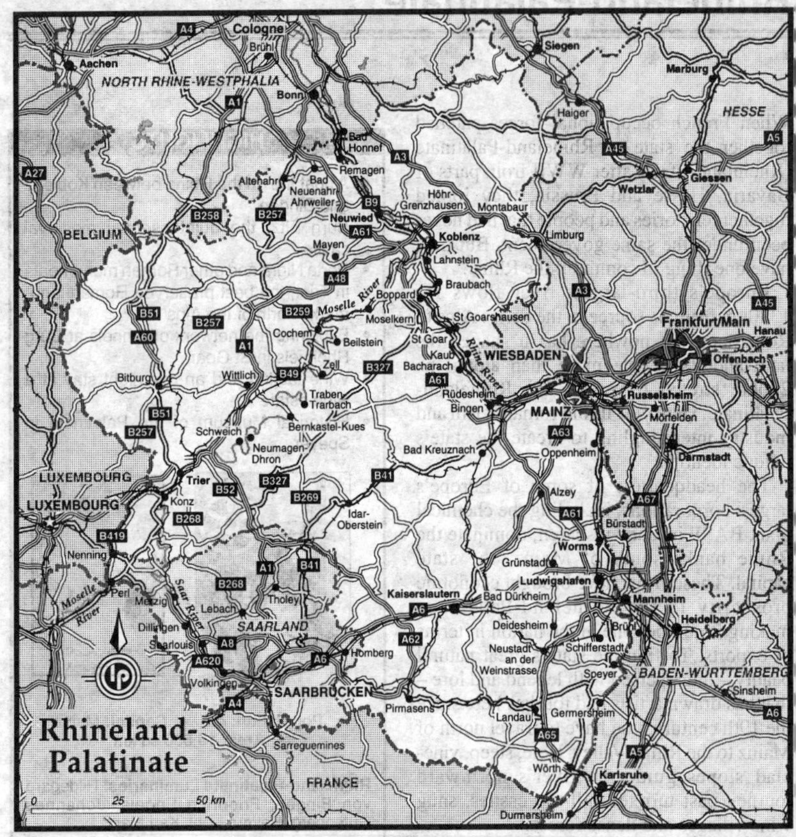

Idealised today, their original purpose was anything but romantic. In fact, most were erected by a medieval Mafia of robber barons who extorted huge tolls from merchant ships by blocking their passage along the river with iron chains. Most of the castles were ruined by the passage of time and by French troops under Louis XIV during the War of the Palatine Succession in 1689. Some were restored in the 19th century.

Its gorgeous landscapes and innumerable attractions have been both a blessing and a curse to the Rhineland-Palatinate. Mass tourism has tainted some of the towns. But getting away from the maddening crowds is easy. The low mountain areas of the Eifel, the Westerwald and the Hunsrück offer numerous escapes and plenty of outdoor recreation.

You'll also find ample accommodation choices. Inexpensive private rooms abound as do camping grounds, often located right on the river banks. Most of the Rhineland-Palatinate's hostels have recently been overhauled and now offer upgraded accommodation. Hotels run the gamut from simple guesthouses to full-service resorts. Or you could always take a room at one of the wine estates with grapes ripening just outside your window.

Thanks to its mix of autobahns and highways, exploring the Rhineland-Palatinate is never a problem. Those dependent on public transport will find a perfectly coordinated rail system. One of the greatest rail journeys in Europe is a trip through the Rhine Valley where tracks hug both sides of the river. Elsewhere in the state, buses pick up where the tracks leave off.

Rheinhessen Region

MAINZ

- *pop 175,000*
- *area code* ☎ 06131

Mainz, the state capital, wears its cathedral like a crown and drapes the Rhine like a royal robe. Indeed, Mainz's location at the confluence of the Main and Rhine rivers is one of its greatest assets and certainly among the reasons why the Romans founded a military camp here in 39 BC. Called Monuntiacum – possibly after the Celtic god Mogon – the settlement evolved into the capital of Germania Prima province by 300 AD.

After the Romans left in the 5th century, the town took a 250-year nap before being awoken by St Boniface, who established an archbishopric here in 746. Throughout the Middle Ages the archbishops of Mainz were immensely powerful, largely because they also held the position of prince-electors and thus managed to influence the politics of the Holy Roman Empire. In the 15th century movable type was invented by Johannes Gutenberg (around 1446) and the university was founded (1476).

It is still students who give Mainz its rather easy-going aspect, and overall its population seems to have retained a healthy dose of French savoir-vivre from that country's brief occupation (1798-1814). Mainz is a media city too, being the seat of the ZDF, one of Germany's earliest television stations.

During WWII, almost 80% of the Altstadt, including many medieval half-timbered buildings, were lost. It has since been restored and once again forms a bustling centre of activity cherished by locals and visitors alike.

Orientation

Much of the city centre consists of pedestrianised shopping areas, and it's possible to make the 20-minute walk from the Hauptbahnhof to the Dom without having to dodge a car. You'll find the train station at the southern end of one of the city's main arteries, Kaiserstrasse.

To get to the Dom from the station, head south-east on Bahnhofstrasse, then left onto Grosse Bleiche and right into Lotharstrasse, which turns into a series of outdoor shopping streets before spilling out onto Markt.

The most scenic part of the Altstadt is just south of the Dom around Augustinerstrasse.

Information

Tourist Office The tourist office (☎ 286 21 0; fax 286 21 55) is at Brückenturm am Rathaus and is open on weekdays from 9 am to 6 pm and to 1 pm on Saturday. Staff sell the MainzCard (DM10), which entitles you to museum admissions (though most are free anyway), unlimited public transport, plus hotel, theatre and other discounts. It is valid for one day during the week, or both weekend days.

Money There's an exchange counter inside the tourist office and a Reisebank in the Reisezentrum of the Hauptbahnhof (open to 7 pm, but only to 3 pm on Wednesday and Saturday). The post office also changes money.

Post & Communications The main post office is at Bahnhofstrasse 2 and is open to 6.30 pm weekdays, to 1 pm on Saturday and from 10 am to noon on Sunday. There's a public fax-phone here and another in the Reisezentrum inside the train station.

Bookshops The Gutenberg Buchhandlung at Grosse Bleiche 29 has a good assortment

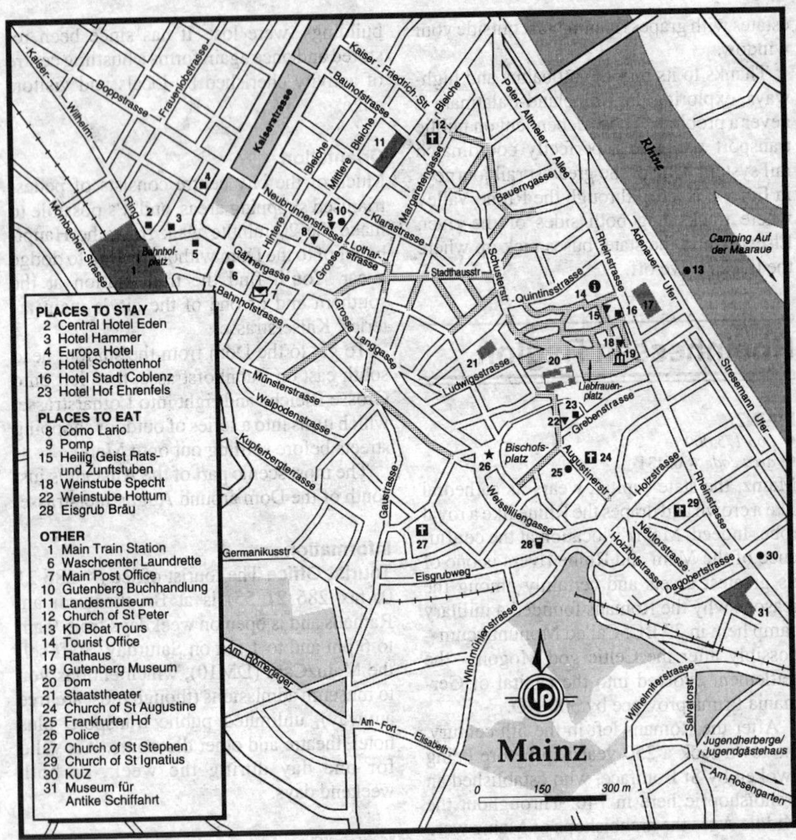

of books and periodicals in English and French.

Laundry For a centrally located laundrette, go to the Waschcenter on the corner of Gärtnergasse and Parcusstrasse. Opening hours are 6 am to 11 pm, and it charges DM6 per wash, DM1 to use the dryer.

Medical Services & Emergency For an ambulance, call ☎ 192 22. After-hours emergency medical help is available at ☎ 192 92. There's a police station (☎ 650) at Weissliliengasse 12 in the Altstadt.

Churches

Dom Mainz's cathedral is a mountain of reddish-brown sandstone whose fanciful architectural details reflect the changing styles during its long building period. It literally experienced a baptism by fire when the first structure, erected around the year 1000, burned down just one day before its consecration. Rebuilt by 1136, only the bronze portal facing the market square survives from that period. In fact, most of what you see today dates from the 12th and 13th centuries.

Important interior features are the 60

memorial tombstones of archbishops and other rulers from the 13th to 18th centuries. Some are fastened to the bulky pillars flanking the central nave, where they form a veritable portrait gallery. The murals above show scenes from the life of Christ but, despite their medieval appearance, they only date back to the last century.

The **Dom- und Diözesanmuseum** (open weekdays from 10 am to 4 pm, Thursday to 5 pm, Saturday to 2 pm; free entry) is reached via the cloister. Works spanning 2000 years are exhibited here in vaulted rooms. Note especially the expressive features of the *Turbaned Head* sculpture (1240), ascribed to the Master of Naumburg.

Church of St Stephen Located on a hill at Kleine Weissgasse 12, St Stephen would be just another Gothic church were it not for the nine brilliant stained-glass windows made by the Russian-born Jewish artist Marc Chagall in the last years of his life (he died in 1985 at the age of 97). Predominantly blue, they exude a cool, yet meditative, quality and show scenes from the Old Testament intended to symbolise Christian-Jewish reconciliation. The church is open on weekdays from 10 am to noon and 2 to 5 pm.

Baroque Churches Mainz also has a trio of stunning baroque churches, which together illustrate the evolution of this architectural style. The classically baroque **Church of St Augustine**, at Augustinerstrasse 34, dates back to 1768, has never been destroyed and features a delicate ceiling fresco of the saint by Johann Baptist Enderle. **Church of St Peter**, at Peterstrasse 3, shows off the sumptuous glory of the rococo style and is noted for its richly adorned pulpit and altars. **St Ignatius**, Kapuzinerstrasse 36, marks the transition from rococo to neoclassicism. Oddly, the architects, artists and stonemasons who worked on this church lie buried in the crypt alongside the priests. The large Crucifixion sculpture outside is a copy of the one made by Hans Backoffen (the original is in the Dom- und Diözesanmuseum).

Museums

Gutenberg Museum Since 1900, Mainz has had a museum dedicated to its most famous son, Johannes Gutenberg (1398-1468), the inventor of movable type. Enlarged and altered through the decades, the three-floor exhibit now displays not just his revolutionary accomplishments but also puts them in the context of the history of printing. In the basement, you'll find a recreation of Gutenberg's workshop, where occasional demonstrations take place, as well as a modern print shop for comparison. Another highlight awaits on the 1st floor, where an original 42-line Bible from the 1450s is displayed along with other early printed texts.

The museum is on Liebfrauenplatz 5 and is open from Tuesday to Saturday from 10 am to 6 pm, on Sunday to 1 pm, but is closed on Monday, holidays and all of January. Admission is DM5, discount DM2.50.

Landesmuseum The wonderfully eclectic collection of this state museum, housed in the former prince-elector's stables at Grosse Bleiche 49-51, provides a thorough history of the region from the Stone Age till today. A circuitous tour first leads to a light-flooded hall filled with Roman monuments, including the **Jupitersäule**, a 1st-century AD triumphal column with reliefs of 28 gods. In Room 6, you'll find the façade of the 14th-century **Kaufhaus am Brand**, a trading and storage house, with reliefs depicting church and civil officials. Upstairs is a small who's who of 19th and 20th-century art. Admission is free, and opening hours are Tuesday to Sunday from 10 am to 5 pm (Friday only to 4 pm).

Museum für Antike Schiffahrt Excavations for the Mainz Hilton Hotel in 1981 unearthed a spectacular collection of 4th-century Roman shipwrecks, now housed in the Museum of Roman Ships.

The remains of five war ships and two full-size replicas form the centrepieces of this new museum in the former market hall of the Südbahnhof on Holzhofstrasse, on the corner of Rheinstrasse. It is open Tuesday to

Sunday from 10 am to 6 pm; admission is free.

Cruises

Several operators offer boat tours up and down the Rhine. These include the Köln-Düsseldorfer (KD) line (☎ 224 51 1), whose fleet leaves from the quay near the Rathaus, and Mainz-Wiesbadener Personenschiffahrt (☎ 231 65 8), which departs from Fischtor and Stresemannufer. A return trip from Mainz to Rüdesheim with KD will cost you DM34.80, to Bacharach DM54.80.

Places to Stay

Camping Mainz's camping ground, *Auf der Maaraue* (☎ 06134-438 3), is nicely located at the confluence of the Rhine and Main in Mainz-Kostheim with a great view of the city. From the Hauptbahnhof, take bus No 17 or 19 to Castel Bahnhof, from where it's a five-minute walk.

Hostels Mainz has a nice combined *Jugendherberge/Jugendgästehaus* (☎ 853 32) in two buildings at Otto-Brunfels-Schneise 4 near a city park. Bed & breakfast in the Jugendherberge costs DM21.50; sheets are DM5. The two-bed (DM35.50 per person) and four-bed rooms (DM26.30 per person) in the Jugendgästehaus all have private bath; prices include sheets and breakfast. To get there from the train station, take bus No 1 to the Jugendherberge or bus No 22 to the Viktorstift stop.

Hotels The tourist office can make room reservations (DM5). During the summer months, special weekend rates may be available at some hotels. One of the cheapest options in town is *Hotel Stadt Coblenz* (☎ 227 60 2) at No 49 of busy Rheinstrasse, with singles costing between DM50 and DM80 and doubles between DM80 and DM120. In the heart of the Altstadt, at Grebenstrasse 5-7, is *Hotel Hof Ehrenfels* (☎ 224 33 4) whose modern rooms go for DM95/140.

Right outside the Hauptbahnhof, on Bahnhofplatz 6, is *Hotel Hammer* (☎ 611 06 1; fax 611 06 5) with pleasantly furnished singles/doubles costing from DM120/165. Next door at No 8, in a stately red-brick building, is *Central Hotel Eden* (☎ 276 0; fax 276 27 6), with rooms starting at DM135/ 180. Nearby at Schottstrasse 6 is the friendly *Hotel Schottenhof* (☎ 232 96 8; fax 221 97 0) which charges DM129 for singles and DM168 for doubles.

One of the top hotels in town – and worth the splurge – is the elegant *Europa Hotel* (☎ 975 0; fax 975 55 5) at Kaiserstrasse 7 whose generously sized rooms cost from DM140/190.

Places to Eat

Mainz is a wine town with many wine taverns concentrated in the Altstadt. Try *Weinstube Specht*, hidden away behind the Gutenberg Museum in Rotekopfgasse, and *Weinstube Hottum* at Grebenstrasse 3. Both are rustic and smoky, have a cluttered living room atmosphere, delectable wines and a small menu with inexpensive, simple hot and cold dishes.

If beer is your thing, head for *Eisgrub Bräu*, Weissliliengasse 1a. This brewery's network of vaulted chambers regularly buzzes with a mixed crowd that orders beer by the metre (12 glasses, DM28) and pub fare, including some vegetarian choices, for DM14 to DM25.

For a more sedate environment, there's the *Heilig Geist Rats- und Zunftstuben*, housed in a beautifully restored medieval hospital at Rentengasse 2. Those with somewhat larger budgets can dine here on refined regional cuisine in a large vaulted hall.

If you hunger for superb Italian food, jostle for a table at *Como Lario* in Neubrunnenstrasse 7, whose candlelit environment and Italian food packs a crowd most nights.

Thirty-somethings may feel comfortable at *Pomp*, a sparse but warmly lit bistro at Grosse Bleiche 29, where you can have breakfast till midnight, talk the day away over large cups of coffee or have a small meal.

Entertainment

Look in the tourist office, in cafés and in pubs for a copy of the free magazine *Fritz*, which lists events and other information for Mainz, Wiesbaden and Frankfurt.

The newly enlarged *Staatstheater* (☎ 285 12 22) on Gutenbergplatz 7 has its own ensemble and stages plays, opera and ballet. Students get a 50% discount. Mainz has two cultural centres worth checking out. The programme at the *Frankfurter Hof* (☎ 220 43 8) at Augustinerstrasse 55 runs the gamut from classical music to ethno jazz.

KUZ (☎ 286 86 0), in an old factory at Dagobertstrasse 20b, is a bit more edgy and has lots of big party events, usually with live music.

Getting There & Away

Air Frankfurt airport is 30km north-east of Mainz and easily reached by S-Bahn No 8, which departs several times hourly from the Hauptbahnhof.

Train Mainz is a major hub for IC trains in all directions. There are regional connections to Wiesbaden and Frankfurt several times an hour. Services to Koblenz (DM23.20, 50 minutes) and to Worms (DM11.80, 45 minutes) run almost as frequently. There are also regional trains to Saarbrücken (DM44, two hours) and Idar-Oberstein (DM23.20, 1¼ hours).

Car & Motorcycle Mainz is easily accessible by autobahn. It is encircled by a ring road with connections to the A60, the A63 and the A66 in all directions.

Ride Services The nearest Mitfahrzentrale is in Wiesbaden (☎ 0611-333 55 5).

Getting Around

Public Transport Mainz operates a joint bus and tram system with Wiesbaden for which single tickets cost DM3.20 and day passes DM8.50. Tickets are available from vending machines and must be validated before boarding.

Taxi There's a taxi rank at the Hauptbahnhof. To book a taxi call ☎ 910 91 0.

Bicycle There's a bike rental station (☎ 238 10 8) on the ground level of the CityPort-Parkhaus in Bingerstrasse near the Hauptbahnhof (open from 10 am to 3 pm). Maps and the booklet *Wandern und Radwandern in Mainz und Rheinhessen* are available at the tourist office and bookshops.

WORMS

- *pop 75,000*
- *area code* ☎ 06241

About 50km south of Mainz lies Worms. Today a sleepy provincial town, Worms has somehow managed to play a role in major moments in history. In 413 AD, it became the capital of the short-lived, but legendary, Burgundian kingdom whose rise and fall was later immortalised in the 12th-century Nibelungen epic, the basis of Richard Wagner's equally epic opera cycle *Der Ring des Nibelungen*.

After the Burgundians' downfall just about every other tribe had a go at ruling Worms, including the Huns, the Alemans and finally the Franks. Worms began to flourish under Charlemagne and rose to prominence under the succeeding Salian and Hohenstaufen emperors. From the early 11th century, a large Jewish community thrived in Worms. In 1517 the town hosted the Imperial Diet during which reformer Martin Luther refused to renounce his beliefs and was subsequently placed under imperial ban, effectively making him an outlaw. Not long afterwards, a succession of wars brought about Worms' demotion from imperial city to minor market town.

The most poignant reminder of Worms' heyday is its majestic late-Romanesque cathedral. Part of the Rheinhessen wine-growing region, Worms is also known as the birthplace of Liebfraumilch. Since that name could not be trademarked, the original still produced here has nothing in common with the plonk served in pubs all over the world (to try the original, you must ask for the wine made by the Liebfrauenstift Kirchenstück).

Orientation

Worms' train and bus stations are about 250m north-west of the ring road that encircles the Altstadt. To walk from here to the Dom, head east on pedestrianised Wilhelm-Leuschner-Strasse, one of the main shopping streets, to Kämmererstrasse. Turn right here and continue on for another 200m or so.

Information

The tourist office (☎ 250 45; fax 263 28) is just east of the Dom on Neumarkt 14 and is open on weekdays from May to October from 9 am to 6 pm (to noon on Saturday).

A number of banks exchange money, including the Volksbank at Markt 19, as does the main post office at the corner of Ludwigsplatz and Korngasse (both are open until 6 pm).

For after-hours medical help, call ☎ 192 92 or ☎ 594 50 4. The main police station (☎ 852 0) is at Hagenstrasse 5.

Kaiserdom

Worms' landmark St Peters cathedral, with its four towers and two domes, dominates the city skyline. Built in the 11th and 12th centuries in the late-Romanesque style, it ranks as one of the greatest accomplishments of medieval architecture.

The **Kaiserportal** on the north side was allegedly the scene of a fierce argument between the Burgundian queens Kriemhild and Brunhild – as commemorated in the Nibelungen epic – which triggered the downfall of their nation. Today you enter through the Gothic **Südportal** (1300), richly decorated with figures from the Old and New Testaments.

Inside, the cathedral's lofty dimensions impress as much as the lavish, canopied high altar (1738-42) in the east choir. Designed by the master of the baroque, Balthasar Neumann, it shows sculptures of Saints Peter and Paul flanking a figure of the Madonna. A claustrophobic crypt off the south aisle holds the stone sarcophagi of several ancestors of the later Salian emperors, themselves regional counts.

Also of interest is the wooden scale model of the huge original complex, which until 1689 also encompassed the imperial and bishop's palace north of the Dom. You'll find it upstairs at the end of the south aisle.

Jewish Quarter

From the early 11th century onward, a sizeable Jewish community – with a Talmudic school and synagogue – lived in the north-east corner of the Altstadt along Judengasse and its side streets.

The first synagogue from 1034 was burned down by the Nazis, but by 1961 the new **Alte Synagogue** (open daily to 4 pm in summer and to 5 pm in winter, closed at lunchtime; free entry), off Judengasse, had risen from its ashes. It's a serene, white-washed vaulted hall, divided by two central Corinthian columns. An adjacent room features an exhibit on the symbolism and decorations used on Jewish tombstones, as well as the oldest such stone (1036) from Worms' Jewish cemetery.

Behind the synagogue, in Hintere Judengasse, is the modern **Raschi Haus**, constructed on the 14th-century foundations of a former dance hall that also saw incarnations as a hospital and school. Named after Rabbi Salomon ben Issak of Troyes (aka Raschi), a celebrated 11th-century Talmudic commentator who studied in Worms, it now holds the **Judaica Museum** (open from 10 am to noon and 2 to 4 pm, closed Monday; DM3, discount DM1.50).

Across town, in the south-west corner of the Altstadt on Willy-Brandt-Ring, is the Jewish cemetery called **Heiliger Sand** (open daily to sundown, in summer to 8 pm). It is Europe's oldest Jewish cemetery and has more than 2000 graves. The distance of the cemetery from the Jewish quarter reflects the Jewish belief that contact with the dead causes impurity among the living. This also explains why the graves appear neglected and untended. A solemn jumble of tombstones protrudes from a lush meadow, their inscriptions worn away by time and the elements.

Among the graves is that of the marty Rabbi Meir of Rothenburg, who died in 129.

after being imprisoned by Habsburg King Rudolf for leading a group of would-be emigrants to Palestine.

Museums

Museum der Stadt Worms Worms' local history museum is housed in the former Andreasstift church, which has Romanesque origins and later Gothic additions and alterations. Exhibits chronicle Worms' turbulent history from prehistoric times onward. The museum is on Weckerlingplatz, behind the hostel. Its hours are from 10 am to noon and 2 to 4 pm (closed Monday). Entry is DM4, discount DM2.

Kunsthaus Heylshof In a little park north of the Dom, on the grounds of the former imperial and bishop's palace, stands a palace housing an important private art collection. Besides Italian, Dutch, French and German paintings from the 15th to 19th centuries – including works by heavyweights Tintoretto, Rubens and Lenbach – the assortment of Venetian, Bohemian and German glass is also impressive. Opening hours are 10 am to 5 pm in summer and 2 to 4 pm in winter, closed Monday. Admission is DM3, discount DM1.

Places to Stay

The nearest camping ground to Worms is in Bad Dürkheim, an inconvenient 30km south-west of Worms (see Places to Stay in the Bad Dürkheim section).

The location of Worms' *Jugendgästehaus* (☎ 257 80) at Dechaneistrasse 1, just south of the Dom, beats that of any five-star hotel. It has an unimpeded view of the entire cathedral and has just been renovated, with some rooms offering private bath. A night in a four-bed room costs DM26.30, in a two-bed room DM35.50; sheets and breakfast are included.

The tourist office provides a free hotel reservation service, and when it's closed an automated system indicates hotel vacancies and allows unlimited free calls to those of interest. The following prices are for rooms with private bath and breakfast.

One of the cheapest choices is *Hotel Lortze-Eck* (☎ 263 49) at Schlossergasse 10-14, which charges DM70 for singles and DM120 for doubles. *Hotel Kriemhilde* (☎ 627 8; fax 627 7) at Hofgasse 2-4 charges from DM85/120. Best of the bunch (and worth the extra DM10 or DM20) is *Hotel Central* (☎ 645 70; fax 274 39) at Kämmererstrasse 5, the beginning of the pedestrianised shopping strip. Its charming owner runs the place with great panache and a personal touch. Rooms are largish and cost DM95/145.

Places to Eat

Worms may not be a paradise for gourmets, but it offers a bunch of options for those on a budget. There's a plethora of Italian eateries with the usual pizza, pasta and salad selection starting at DM8. One of the more stylish establishments popular with locals is *Ristorante Kupferkeller* at Andreasstrasse 1. Good fast food (half a chicken for DM4.25) can be had at the *Kochlöffel*, on the corner of Kämmererstrasse and Stephansgasse.

The cluttered *Weinkeller* at Wollstrasse 7-9 has a distinctly young clientele and serves mouthwatering Flammekuche (an Alsatian style of pizza) on wooden boards (open Friday to Sunday only). Yuppies congregate behind the panorama windows of the multi-floor *Café Jux*, on the corner of Judengasse and Friedrichsstrasse. There's occasionally live music on weekends.

Getting There & Away

Worms has frequent train connections with Mannheim, a major hub for long-distance trains in all directions. The regional service to Frankfurt (DM15.60, 1¼ hours) and Mainz (DM11.80, 40 minutes) leaves several times hourly. Worms lies at the intersection of the B47 and B9 highways, the former being also the main access road to the A61 (Koblenz to Speyer), 5km west of Worms.

Getting Around

The Stadtwerke Worms operates a thorough bus system. Single tickets are DM2.60 (one zone) and DM3.20 (two zones). Day passes cost DM10 and allow travel for up to five people after 9 am. For a taxi, call ☎ 410 0 or ☎ 415 0.

Palatinate

SPEYER

- *pop 45,000*
- *area code* ☎ 06232

On the left bank of the Rhine about 50km south of Worms lies 2000-year-old Speyer, famed for its magnificent Romanesque cathedral.

First a Celtic settlement, then a Roman market town, the town catapulted to prominence in the early Middle Ages when a succession of emperors from the Salian dynasty made it one of the centres of the Holy Roman Empire. For more than seven centuries from 838, the town hosted 50 sessions of the imperial parliament. These sessions included the famous one in 1529 – at the height of the Reformation – when the term 'Protestant' was coined after the reformed regional rulers formally 'protested' against the Catholic majority's unilateral decision-making.

In 1076, the king and later Holy Roman Emperor Heinrich IV – having been excommunicated by Pope Gregor VII – launched his penitence walk to Canossa in Italy from Speyer. He crossed the Alps in the middle of winter, an action that even warmed the heart of the pope who granted him forgiveness and revoked his excommunication. He lies buried in the Kaiserdom.

Speyer's importance waned after being razed by the troops of France's King Louis XIV in 1689 during the War of the Palatine Succession. In the next century, the town was completed rebuilt and – having been spared from war destruction since – the city centre still retains its baroque appearance.

From 1792 to 1825, Speyer belonged to France, then became part of Bavaria until 1945 before being incorporated into the Rhineland-Palatinate after WWII. Today, this provincial town possesses a lively spirit which, together with some interesting sights, makes it well worth a stop of a day or two.

Orientation

The train station is on Bahnhofstrasse, about 1km north-west of the city centre. Most buses heading south will drop you off at the Altpörtel city gate, from which Speyer's lifeline, the broad Maximilianstrasse, leads you straight to the Dom in about 10 minutes.

Information

Tourist Office The tourist office (☎ 142 39 2; fax 142 33 2) is at Maximilianstrasse 11 and is open between May and October from 9 am to 5 pm on weekdays, 10 am to noon on Saturday (also 11 am to 3 pm on Sunday).

Money Several banks along Maximilianstrasse exchange money during normal business hours, with the Sparkasse opposite the tourist office open late (until 6 pm) on Thursday.

Post & Communications The main post office is on Postplatz 1 at the end of Maximilianstrasse behind the Altpörtel gate.

Medical Services If you need a doctor after hours call ☎ 192 22.

Kaiserdom

In 1030 Emperor Konrad II of the Salian dynasty laid the cornerstone to the majestic Dom, whose towers float above Speyer's rooftops like the smokestacks of a giant ocean liner. It's the grandest of the trio of imperial cathedrals (the others are in Mainz and Worms) and has been a UNESCO World Heritage Site since 1980. Eight Salian emperors and kings, along with some of their queens, lie buried here.

Most startling about the interior are the awesome dimensions and dignified symmetry. The height of the central nave, the clear lines of construction and unadorned walls create a solemn atmosphere. Make sure you walk up the staircase at the end of the right aisle to get an overview of its full size. Another set of steps leads down to the cathedral's oldest section – the large, darkly festive crypt whose candy-striped arches, with different coloured bands of sandstone, resemble Moorish architecture. From here, a few more steps lead back up to the tiny room beneath the altar area crammed with the austere granite sarcophagi of the Salian emperors. The cathedral is open weekdays from 9 am to 7 pm and to 6 pm on weekends (in winter to 5 pm).

Historisches Museum der Pfalz

Though it may be hard to get excited about regional history museums, this one is a clear exception and should be a part of any visit to Speyer. The permanent collection values quality over quantity, and each artwork is presented in a unique, intimately lit fashion.

One of the highlights is the **Goldener Hut von Schifferstadt**, downstairs in the first Prehistory Room. This is an incredibly ornate, perfectly preserved, gilded hat in the shape of a giant thimble that dates back to the Bronze Age (14th century BC). On the same floor are the rooms of the **Wine Museum** with ancient wine presses and a bottle of a jellied substance from the 4th century AD purported to be the world's oldest wine. Two more floors below is the **Cathedral Treasury** where the simple bronze crown of Emperor Konrad II is displayed, among other items.

The museum also hosts international exhibitions. It is immediately south of the Dom and is open from 10 am to 6 pm (Wednesday to 8 pm, closed Monday). Entry is DM8, discount DM5; admission is free on Tuesdays after 4 pm.

Along Maximilianstrasse

Roman troops and medieval emperors had already marched down broad Maximilianstrasse long before it became Speyer's main thoroughfare. Lined by a phalanx of baroque houses, this road and its side streets are the places to visit for shopping, sitting in cafés and checking out a few more sights.

Just south of the Dom, in Judenbadgasse, is the **Mikwe** (open April to October from 10 am to noon and 2 to 4 pm weekdays and 10 am to 5 pm weekends; entry DM1.50, discount DM0.50), an underground ritual Jewish bathhouse dating from 1128, the oldest such complex in Germany.

Just a few steps north of the Dom, in Johannesstrasse, is the **Dreifaltigkeitskirche** (Trinity Church), built in the early 18th century as a Lutheran baroque church. The lofty interior, with its two galleries, is made of carved and painted wood. Entry is only possible with a guided tour, but you can always catch a glimpse through the glass door in the entrance.

Among the baroque buildings on Maximilianstrasse, the **Rathaus** with its red façade and lavish rococo interior and the **Alte Münze** (Old Mint) deserve closer looks. The road finally culminates at the only part of the town wall still standing: the main city gate called the **Altpörtel**. It contains a viewing gallery and an exhibit about the city's fortification (opening hours same as for the Mikwe).

Technik Museum

A few minutes' walk south of the Dom, at Geibstrasse 2, is the Museum of Technology which, in an exhibition space of 8000 sq metres, sheds light on the evolution of engineering. Displays in this former aircraft manufacturing hall include classic cars, aeroplanes, fire engines, trains and ships. The complex also includes an IMAX cinema which has a five-storey screen and shows movies like *The Blue Planet*, about the earth seen from space, *The Grand Canyon* and *The Serengeti*.

The museum is open daily from 9 am to 6 pm; the last IMAX screening is at 7 pm Monday to Thursday and at 9 pm Friday to Sunday. Admission to either the museum or the cinema is DM12, children DM8; a combined ticket is DM22/15.

Places to Stay

The nearest camping ground to Speyer is in Bad Dürkheim on the German Wine Road (see that section for details) but, unless you have a car, it is very inconvenient. The town's *Jugendgästehaus* (☎ 753 80), recently renovated and enlarged, is at Geibstrasse 5 near the Rhine and offers state-of-the-art facilities and rooms with private bath. Bed, breakfast and sheets in four-bed rooms cost DM26.30, in two-bed rooms DM35.50.

The tourist office can help you find rooms in hotels and pensions. The closest to a budget option is the small *Pension Grüne Au* (☎ 721 96), fairly central at Grüner Winkel 28, whose singles/doubles with shower and WC on the floor go for DM50/70; doubles with private bath cost DM85. Rooms at the *Motel am Technik Museum* (☎ 671 00; fax 671 02 0) at Geibstrasse 2 are modern and functional and a good deal at DM75/105, including private bath. Just one block south of Maximilianstrasse, at Webergasse 5, is *Hotel und Weinstube Trutzpfaff* (☎ 601 20; fax 601 23 0), which charges DM90/130. Top of the list is the *Hotel Resort Binshof* (☎ 647 0; fax 647 19 9) in Binshof 1, which prides itself on being the only five-star accommodation in the state. It's located on a cluster of lakes a few minutes' drive north of Speyer and caters to those willing – and able – to part with DM220/380 and up per night.

Places to Eat

Most of Speyer's 200 restaurants are abuzz with locals and visitors alike most days of the week, and there's no shortage of culinary options around the Dom. One of the most popular places is *Domhof*, a sprawling brewery pub on Grosse Himmelsgasse 6, which specialises in traditional regional dishes. Similar but more refined fare characterises the menu of *Ratskeller* at Maximilianstrasse 12.

A good place to sample local wines is at *Zum Alten Engel* where you can also get small regional and Alsatian meals starting at DM10. For a younger crowd and a chatty atmosphere, head for *Café Wunderbar* in Salzgasse 2. Almost next door, at Johannesstrasse 1, is the yuppie hang-out *Zweierlei*, a postmodern bistro serving pricey German *nouvelle cuisine*.

Getting There & Away

Buses departs from the train station for Ludwigshafen (No 677) and Heidelberg (No 7007), but the train is more efficient. Speyer is on a minor rail line, and most trips require a change in Ludwigshafen or Schifferstadt. Regional trains to both destinations leave frequently, and there are good connections from Ludwigshafen on to Worms. There is also an hourly direct service to Heidelberg via Mannheim, the latter being a major hub for IC and other long-distance trains, including those to Frankfurt.

Getting Around

Most sights are within walking distance, but for the weary there's the City-Shuttle minibus (bus No 565). Running at 10-minute intervals, it loops between the train station and all major sights from 6 am to 8.45 pm at the incredible price of DM1 for unlimited trips all day. Other local buses connect the suburbs with the centre, but you're not likely to need them.

Speyer is a good base for exploring the surrounding wine country by bicycle. The booklet *Radspass im Süd-Westen* (DM7.50), available at the tourist office, has descriptions of 21 bike tours of various lengths. Rental bikes (DM20 a day) are available from Radsport Stiller (☎ 759 66) at Gilgenstrasse 24 but you must book ahead.

GERMAN WINE ROAD

The German Wine Road (Deutsche Weinstrasse) begins about 15km west of Worms in Bockenheim and runs south through Germany's second-largest wine-growing area. On its 80km route to the Deutsches Weintor (German Wine Gate) in Schweigen on the French border, it traverses countless wine communities – islands in a giant ocean of grapevines. To the west, the road is fringed by the velvety hills of the Palatinate Forest, with the Rhine plains unfolding to the east. It's a sun-drenched region (with an annual average of 1700 hours of sunshine) whose mild, almost Mediterranean climate supports the cultivation of kiwi fruit, lemons, almonds and figs alongside the grapes.

Crowds flock to the more than 200 wine festivals, but otherwise the German Wine

Road is not terribly commercialised. Especially south of Neustadt, the towns take on a decidedly French flair. Streets are lined by an endless string of wine estates, their façades festooned with vines that often form an arch over the road to the building on the opposite side. Ornate ironwork guild signs stick out over the pavement, announcing a wine tavern or other business. This is a great place to taste the crisp white Pfälzer wines: just look for the sign saying *Weinprobe*.

Information

The local tourist offices are the best sources of specific information on each town and can usually help with finding accommodation as well. Most will also have information about other towns on the German Wine Road. The central clearing house for information about all communities is the Deutsche Weinstrasse office (☎ 06321-912 33 3; fax 128 81) at Chemnitzer Strasse 3 in Neustadt.

Also in Neustadt, the Pfalz-Touristik office (☎ 06321-912 32 8; fax 128 81) at Landauer Strasse 66 is in charge of the entire Palatinate. Its web site is at www.diepfalz.de.

Getting There & Away

Neustadt is a central base from which to explore the German Wine Road and is served every half-hour by trains from Kaiserslautern (DM9.60, 30 minutes) and Saarbrücken (DM26, one hour), and hourly from Karlsruhe (DM14.20, 45 minutes). There's also a bus service from Speyer.

Getting Around

Having your own vehicle is a great advantage when exploring the German Wine Road (follow the signs marked with a bunch of grapes), though it's still possible to travel much of the route by public transport. Local trains connect Neustadt with Bad Dürkheim and Deidesheim to the north every 30 minutes.

For towns south of Neustadt, you first have to take a bus or a train to Landau, from where there are buses to Bad Bergzabern and on to Schweigen.

Bad Dürkheim

- *pop 16,500*
- *area code* ☎ 06322

Bad Dürkheim is the third-largest wine-growing community in Germany and one of four spa towns in the Rhineland-Palatinate. It has generous park areas and is fringed by the foothills of the Palatinate Forest.

One of the main attractions here is the **Dürkheimer Riesenfass**, a gigantic wine cask built in 1935 for the Dürkheimer Wurstmarkt (Sausage Fair). It has never contained any wine, though; instead, it's a restaurant seating 650 people. The festival, which attracts half a million visitors, has been held on the second and third weekend in September for the past 500 years. The goings-on during this major event are given hilarious expression in the **Wurstmarktbrunnen**, the fountain on the square outside the train station which shows several scenes of people making merry at the festival. The town's **thermal bath** is in Kurbrunnenstrasse (entrance DM13, sauna an extra DM14). There's also a hammam, or Turkish bath, at the nearby Kurmittelhaus (DM45 for two hours' use).

Bad Dürkheim's tourist office (☎ 935 15 6; fax 935 15 9) is at Mannheimer Strasse 24 and is open from 8 am to 5 pm (Thursday to 6 pm) on weekdays only. If it's closed, you can also get information at the Kurmittelhaus. The post office is opposite the train station.

Bad Dürkheim's *camping ground* (☎ 613 56), at Am Badesee, is open from February to October. The nearest hostel is in Neustadt an der Weinstrasse, some 15km south (see the Neustadt an der Weinstrasse section). One of the cheapest places to stay is *Pension Schillerstube* (☎ 632 69), Schillerstrasse 8, which charges DM35/60 for singles/doubles with shared bath. If you want to sleep at a wine estate, try *Weingut Karst* (☎ 611 61) at Im Salzbrunnen 11, where rooms with shower and WC cost DM44/79.

Deidesheim

- *pop 3650*
- *area code* ☎ 06326

Deidesheim has taken the stage as the town

where German Chancellor Helmut Kohl brings official state visitors to dinner. At the stuffily stylish Deidesheimer Hof, the elite are served a gourmet version of the Palatinate speciality called Saumagen: a sheep's stomach stuffed with meat, potatoes and spices, boiled, then cut in slices and briefly fried. It sounds more intimidating than it is.

Beyond that, Deidesheim is one of the area's most popular wine villages and has a fine historical town centre. The Markt is framed by half-timbered and proud houses, along with the church of **St Ulrich** and the **Rathaus** with its double-sided, canopied exterior staircase. Inside the Rathaus is a small **Wine Museum** (open from Wednesday to Sunday from 4 to 6 pm; DM2, children DM1).

On Bahnhofstrasse you'll find the **Goat Fountain** which represents an unusual local custom, the Goat Festival. According to an ancient contract between Deidesheim and the nearby town of Lambrecht, the latter has to make an annual 'payment' of one goat for using pastureland belonging to Deidesheim. The presentation of this goat, and its subsequent auctioning, gives rise to this raucous festival held yearly in historical costumes on the Tuesday after Whit Sunday.

The tourist office (☎ 502 1; fax 502 3) is in a low building complex adjacent to the Goat Fountain at Bahnhofstrasse 11 and is open weekdays from 9 am to noon and 2 to 5 pm (also on Saturday morning in summer). The post office is at Bahnhofstrasse 16.

There's no camping ground here and the nearest hostel is in Neustadt, 8km south (see the following section). The tourist office can help you find accommodation, including private rooms for DM25 per person. For DM80 per double you can sleep at the *Winzerhaus Funk* wine estate (☎ 525 2) at Bennstrasse 49. A central option is the comfortable *Gästehaus Ritter von Böhl* (☎ 972 20 1; fax 972 20 0), integrated into a 15th-century hospital complex at Weinstrasse 35. Its extremely spacious, modern rooms cost DM80/130 for singles/doubles.

For dinner, try the posh *Deidesheimer Hof* on Markt 1 or, if you prefer a more casual ambience, head for the *Turmstübl* in Turmstrasse 3, a contemporary, artsy wine café that also serves salads and simple dishes.

Neustadt an der Weinstrasse

- *pop 54,000*
- *area code* ☎ 06321

Neustadt, the heart of the German Wine Road and a gateway to the Palatinate Forest, is the largest wine-growing community in Germany. It's a busy, modern town whose high-rise skyline conceals a charming **Altstadt** with row upon row of half-timbered houses flanking pedestrianised streets. Neustadt owes its historical appearance to escaping the war destruction that befell just about every other town in the Rhineland-Palatinate. Other surviving buildings include the Gothic **Stiftskirche** in the centre, a red-sandstone concoction shared by a Protestant and a Catholic congregation since 1708 (open only during services).

The tourist office (☎ 926 89 2; fax 926 89 1) is at Exterstrasse 2 (by the Treff-Page Hotel near the train station) and is open from 9 am to 5 pm on weekdays, and also on Saturday morning from April to October. The post office is just east of the train station.

Neustadt's *DJH hostel* (☎ 228 9) was scheduled to close for renovation until mid-1998. Call to see if it's back in business. A low-budget alternative is the *Naturfreundehaus* (☎ 881 69), at Heidenbrunnerweg 100, which charges only DM24 per person for a double room. Rooms at the *Gästehaus Villa Deco* (☎ 210 5), in an old park at Haltweg 30, have pantry kitchenettes and cost DM75/105 singles/doubles.

Neustadt has a wonderful selection of restaurants, especially in the Altstadt. At Hintergasse 26 is *Novalis Cafe*, which serves such things as baked potatoes and grilled feta for less than DM10. At No 6 of the same street, the traditional *Gerberhaus* serves home-style German food. At *Backblech*, Hintergasse 18-20, the speciality is Flammekuche. *Wespennest* is an alternative-culture pub at Friedrichstrasse 36 which has vegetarian lunch specials and other fare, plus live music at night.

Around Neustadt

On a bluff a few kilometres south of Neustadt is the **Hambacher Schloss**. First built in the 11th century by the Salian emperors, this palace passed into the possession of the bishops of Speyer 100 years later who turned it into their summer residence.

The palace was badly destroyed by the French in 1689, and its ruins were the site of a massive demonstration for a free, democratic and united Germany on 27 May 1832, during which the German tricolour of black, red and gold was raised for the first time. An exhibit commemorates this event (DM5, discount DM2.50).

The palace got its current look only a quarter of a century ago. There's a splendid view over the vineyards and the Rhine plains. Daily opening hours are from 9 am to 6.30 pm (closed December to February). Admission to the grounds is free. From Neustadt, bus No 502 makes the trip up to 10 times daily.

Ahr Valley

The river Ahr has carved its scenic 90km valley from the High Eifel to the Rhine, which it joins near Remagen. It is one of Germany's few red-wine regions, with grapes growing on steeply terraced slopes along both banks.

The landscape is surprisingly diverse and at its most idyllic between October and May, when the crowds have disappeared. The most scenic stretch begins beyond Ahrweiler, where the valley narrows dramatically and the gentle hillsides give way to craggy cliffs.

The entire road is lined by inns and wine taverns and easily explored by car, train, bicycle or even on foot.

BAD NEUENAHR-AHRWEILER

- *pop 25,000*
- *area code* ☎ 02641

Formerly two separate communities, the twin towns of Bad Neuenahr and Ahrweiler have very different characters. The elegant spa town of Bad Neuenahr attracts a fairly sophisticated clientele and has drawn such luminaries as Karl Marx, Johannes Brahms and English royals. Ahrweiler, on the other hand, is a dreamy medieval village encircled by a town wall, with lots of half-timbered houses and narrow, pedestrian-only lanes. What the two have in common is wine, which can be enjoyed at wine estates and numerous taverns.

Orientation & Information

Bad Neuenahr forms the eastern half of the town, Ahrweiler the western half. The Bad Neuenahr train station is right in its city centre from where it's a five-minute walk west to the pedestrian-only Poststrasse, the main drag. To reach Ahrweiler's medieval core, just head west on Wilhelmstrasse from the Ahrweiler train station for a couple of hundred metres.

The main tourist office is in Bad Neuenahr (☎ 977 35 0; fax 297 58) at Hauptstrasse 60, next to the train station. There's a second branch at Markt 21 in Ahrweiler (☎ 977 36 2; fax 352 00). Both are open from 9 am to 6 pm on weekdays, 10 am to noon on Saturday and 10.30 am to 4 pm on Sunday. Between November and Easter, opening hours are from 8 am to 5 pm on weekdays and 10 am to noon on Saturday. There is a regional information office (☎ 02641-977 330; fax 977 37 3) at Markt 11 in Ahrweiler.

To change money, go to the Sparkasse at Telegrafenstrasse 20 or to the post office at the corner of Kölner Strasse and Hauptstrasse in Bad Neuenahr.

Things to See

The focal point of Bad Neuenahr is the grandiose **Kurhaus**, a turn-of-the-century neobaroque confection that also contains the posh **Casino**, the first to appear in post-WWII Germany. Here you can play roulette, slot machines and various card games (DM5 or DM10 minimum at most tables). Admission is DM5, and you must bring your passport. It's a fairly elegant affair and men must wear a jacket and tie. Opening hours are from 2 pm to 1 am.

The octagonal spire of the Gothic **Church of St Laurentius** characterises Ahrweiler's skyline. It is the oldest hall church in the Rhineland and contains 14th-century frescos and a hexagonal baptismal font from 1570.

Many lovely houses line Ahrweiler's narrow lanes. Look out for **Haus Wolff** in Niederhutstrasse, which was one of only 10 houses to survive the fire storm triggered by marauding French troops in 1689. Its most ornate feature is an octagonal oriel buttressed by generously sculpted and painted beams. All four **town gates** are still standing; the fortress-like Ahrtor is the most impressive.

In 1980, construction workers unearthed the remains of a large **Roman villa** on the north-western edge of town. It's extremely well preserved and sections – like the floor heating system – are still functional. The whole thing is now a museum (open between April and mid-November from Tuesday to Friday 10 am to 6 pm, weekends to 5 pm) at Silberberg 1, just north of the B267. Admission is DM7, discount DM3.50.

Activities

Hikers will enjoy trekking along the scenic Red Wine Hiking Trail which leads you right through grape country on its 35km route from Sinzig/Bad Bodendorf to Altenahr. Its most scenic stretch goes from Ahrweiler to Altenahr. The trail is marked by little signs with grape symbols, and you can walk as far as you like and return on the Ahrtalbahn train. The tourist office has a detailed trail description and maps.

If your muscles are sore from hiking, you could soothe them in the Ahr-Therme, Bad Neuenahr's state-of-the-art thermal mineral pools. Unfortunately the prices are anything but relaxed: two hours in the pools and sauna cost DM19 (DM27 for four hours; day pass DM36). It's at Felix-Rüttenstrasse 3 and is open daily from 9 am to 11 pm.

Places to Stay & Eat

The *camping ground* (☎ 356 84) is in Ahrweiler and open April to October. The snazzy, fairly new *Jugendgästehaus* (☎ 349 24) is in St-Pius-Strasse, about halfway between Ahrweiler and Bad Neuenahr (a 15-minute walk from the Ahrweiler train station). Rooms are cosy and have private bath. Bed & breakfast in double rooms costs DM35.50 per person, in quads DM26.50, sheets included.

The tourist office staff can help you find a room (no charge). There's plenty of accommodation, but budget options are scarce. Halfway reasonable is *Hotel Zum Ännchen* (☎ 977 70; fax 977 99) at Niederhutstrasse 11-13 in Ahrweiler, which has singles for DM80 and doubles for DM120. For something special, the elegant *Hotel Rodderhof* (☎ 399 0; fax 399 33 3) in an old monastery at Oberhutstrasse 48 in Ahrweiler has rooms starting at DM125/190.

Budget eating places are also hard to come by here. The rustic *Ahrweinstuben* at Markt 12 in Ahrweiler serves regional dishes for DM17.50 and up. In the spacious *Weingalerie* (closed Monday) at Adenbachhutstrasse 6, you can sample the local wines and main courses for around DM20.

Getting There & Away

There's bus service (No 841) from Remagen, but it's quite slow. To get here by train you must change to the local Ahrtalbahn in Remagen. It stops at both the Bad Neuenahr and Ahrweiler stations. If you're driving, take the A61 and exit at Bad Neuenahr-Ahrweiler to the B267, which connects all towns on the Ahr river.

Rhine Valley

KOBLENZ

- *pop 107,000*
- *area code* ☎ 0261

One of Germany's oldest cities, Koblenz traces its beginnings to a Roman military camp established around 10 BC. The Romans named it Confluentes for its location at the confluence of the Moselle and

Rhine rivers. Four low mountain ranges also converge here: the Hunsrück, the Eifel, the Westerwald and the Taunus. Koblenz itself was badly damaged in WWII and is now a modern city that blends sophistication with Rhine/Moselle romanticism.

Apart from offering a few worthwhile sights of its own, Koblenz is also an excellent base for exploration, especially along the rivers.

Orientation

Koblenz's core is on the left bank of the Rhine and the right (south) bank of the Moselle. The Altstadt is roughly bordered by the Moselring and the Friedrich-Ebert-Ring roads. The main train and central bus stations are a few hundred metres south-west of this ring on Löhrstrasse. From here, it's about a 10 to 15-minute walk north on Löhrstrasse to the heart of the Altstadt.

Information

Tourist Office The tourist office (☎ 313 04; fax 129 38 00) is in a pavilion right opposite the Hauptbahnhof and has opening hours that vary according to the season. In March, April and October, it is open daily from 9 am to 6 pm (from 10 am on weekends). Between May and September opening hours are from 9 am to 8 pm (again from 10 am on weekends). From November to February, it is open weekdays only from 9 am to 6 pm. Ask for the free bimonthly brochure *Koblenz: Was, Wann, Wo*, which provides comprehensive events listings and other useful information.

Money The Sparkasse near the Hauptbahnhof at Emil-Schüller-Strasse 22 exchanges money, and there's an ATM machine inside the train station.

Post & Communications The post office is to the right (south) of the train station.

Bookshops For a decent assortment of books in English and French, try Buch Reuffel's branches at Löhrstrasse 62 and Löhrstrasse 92.

Laundry The Waschcenter laundrette on the corner of Rizzastrasse and Löhrstrasse is open till midnight and charges DM6 per load, plus DM1 for the dryer.

Medical Services & Emergency If you require emergency medical assistance or an ambulance call ☎ 192 22.

There's a police station (☎ 103 2) at Moselring 10.

Walking Tour

The busy Löhrstrasse becomes a pedestrianised shopping street in the Altstadt. Look up above the rather dull shop-fronts for ornate details on the façades. At the intersection with Altergraben, the four 17th-century corner buildings, festooned with gorgeously restored carved and painted oriels each capped with a slender turret, clamour for attention.

Turn right onto Altergraben to get to **Am Plan**, a square that has seen incarnations as a butchers' market, a stage for religious plays, a place of execution and an arena for medieval tournaments.

Duck through the arched walkway on Am Plan's north-eastern end to get to the **Liebfrauenkirche**, built in a harmonious hotchpotch of styles. While the nave and western end still point to its Romanesque origins, the Gothic choir dates back to the early 15th century and the baroque onion-domed turrets were added in 1693.

Continue north through Mehlsgasse to Florinsmarkt, dominated by the **Florinskirche**.

Also here is the **Mittelrhein-Museum**, housed in a late-Gothic former department store. Highlights of its collection include a series of romantic Rhine landscapes, including a 1906 painting of the Marksburg by Emil Nolde.

The figure just beneath the clock on the building's façade shows the so-called **Augenroller** and commemorates a mistakenly executed medieval robber baron. You can watch it rolling its eyes and sticking its tongue out on the half and full hour.

The Moselle is just one block north. Strolling east along its banks will get you to the Deutsches Eck (see the Deutsches Eck section) and also to the **Basilika St Kastor**, an incredibly gloomy, almost spooky, church from the late 12th century. The contemporary art collection of the **Ludwig Museum** is in the adjacent Deutschherrenhaus, once owned by the Teutonic Knights. The **Rheinpromenade**, leading from the Deutsches Eck to Pfaffendorfer Brücke and beyond, is among the finest along the Rhine.

Ehrenbreitstein

This monumental fortress resting on a craggy hillside 118m above Koblenz is the world's second-largest after the one in Gibraltar and was named for its founder, the knight Ehrenbert. When Koblenz came under the jurisdiction of the archbishop of Trier in 1018, he recognised its strategic importance and had it enlarged. Destroyed by Napoleonic troops in 1801, it got a new lease of life from the Prussians who needed 15 years to turn it into Europe's strongest fortification. Indeed, walking beneath its massive bulwarks makes you feel like Gulliver among the giants of Brobdingnag. Needless to say, the view over the Rhine and Moselle rivers is fantastic. The fortress now houses the city's hostel, two restaurants and several public offices.

To get up there, you can take bus No 7, 8 or 9 from the central bus station to Bahnhof Ehrenbreitstein followed by a 20-minute walk uphill. Between Easter and October, a ferry across the Rhine operates daily until around 7 pm (DM2 each way, children DM1). In season between 10 am and 5 pm, there's also a chair lift up to the fortress (DM7, return DM10, discount DM4/6 for children, students and hostel guests). At the time of writing, admission to Ehrenbreitstein was still free, but a small fee was under consideration.

Deutsches Eck

The Deutsches Eck is a promontory built on a sandbank in the Moselle right at the confluence of the Moselle and Rhine rivers. It derives its name from the Deutscher Ritterorden (Order of Teutonic Knights) which had its headquarters in the building now occupied by the Landesmuseum from the 13th century. The spot is dominated by a statue of Kaiser Wilhelm I, put up in 1897 but blasted during WWII. In the 1980s, a wealthy local publisher donated DM3 million so that a replica could be mounted on the stone pedestal.

Schloss Stolzenfels

With its crenellated turrets, ornate gables and fortifications, this castle exudes the romanticism for which this stretch of the Rhine is famed. Only 5km south of Koblenz, Schloss Stolzenfels rests on a knoll, framed by woods. In 1823, the city donated the castle, which had been destroyed in 1689, to King Wilhelm IV of Prussia who had it restored and turned into a summer residence.

The guided tour takes you through the small and large Knights' Halls and past displays of furniture, ceramics, weapons and other objects. The castle is open from 9 am to 6 pm between Easter and September and to 5 pm the rest of the year (closed in December). Admission with guided tour is DM5, discount DM2. Bus No 6050 from the central bus station drops you off near the car park; it's a 15-minute walk to the castle.

Places to Stay

Of Koblenz's two camping grounds only *Campingplatz Rhein-Mosel* (☎ 802 48 9) accepts tents. It's on Schartwiesenweg right opposite the Deutsches Eck and is open from April to mid-October. There's a fairly frequent ferry service across the Moselle.

The *DJH hostel* (☎ 737 37) is dramatically, if a bit inconveniently, located inside the Ehrenbreitstein fortress and is often full with school groups. Beds cost DM22.50, including breakfast.

The tourist office has a free booking service for hotels, pensions and private rooms. *Hotel Jan van Werth* (☎ 365 00), at Von-Werth-Strasse 9, has imaginatively furnished singles/doubles for DM70/120. The family-run *Hotel Hamm* (☎ 303 21 0), at

St-Josef-Strasse 32-34 near the Hauptbahnhof, charges from DM75/120.

Hotel Am Schängel (☎ 338 13), at No 1 of lively Jesuitenplatz in the Altstadt, charges DM75/ 150.

Rooms at the old-fashioned but comfortable *Hotel Kleiner Riesen* (☎ 320 77; fax 160 72 5) on the Rhine at Kaiserin-Augusta-Anlagen 18 cost from DM100/150. If your taste veers towards the eccentric, you'll like *Hotel An der Mosel* (☎ 406 50; fax 406 51 88), at Pastor-Klein-Strasse 11 in the suburb of Rauental, which charges DM134.50 /159.50 singles/doubles. You can't miss it: it's the purple building with the whimsically painted façade.

Places to Eat

Most of Koblenz's restaurants and pubs are in the Altstadt and along the Rhine. Of the traditional restaurants framing Am Plan, the cosy *Alt Coblenz* has a good reputation but serves dinner only. Main courses here cost from DM20. Old-fashioned too is *Zum Deutschen Kaiser*, a wine tavern in a 16th-century building at Kastorstrasse 3, which serves simple fare but in generous portions, most under DM15. Note the fan vaulted ceiling on your left as you enter.

Young people congregate at *Pfefferminze* (closed Monday), a café at Mehlgasse 12, which has sandwiches and other snacks from DM4.50. *Faustus*, a smart brasserie at the corner of Am Alten Hospital and Eltzerhofstrasse, serves classic bistro fare – such as steak with chips (French fries) and Flammekuche – at surprisingly decent prices.

The restaurant row along the promenade south of the Deutsches Eck ends at the *Weindorf* near the Pfaffendorfer Brücke, a cluster of four wine restaurants in faux half-timbered buildings framing a pseudo village square. Of course, this place thrums with day-trippers in season, but if you want cheap, filling food and a good selection of local wines, you too might want to give it a try.

Getting There & Away

Bus Koblenz is the hub for buses to the nearby country towns. Bus No 6053 goes to Mayen in the Eifel, No 6050 to Boppard via Stolzenfels Castle. Other Rhine towns served include Braubach/Marksburg (bus No 6130) and St Goarshausen/Loreley (bus No 6129). To get to Höhr-Grenzhausen in the Westerwald, take bus No 6118.

Train Koblenz is served by hourly IC train connections to major cities both north and south. Regional trains headed for Cologne (DM23.20, one hour) and Bonn (DM14.20, 30 minutes) depart from Koblenz several times hourly, as do trains heading south through the Rhine Valley and on to Frankfurt Hauptbahnhof (DM34, 1¼ hours) via Frankfurt airport. There's also regular service up the Moselle to Trier (DM29, 1½ hours).

Car & Motorcycle Several highways converge in Koblenz, including the B9 from Cologne/Bonn and the B49 from the Westerwald. The nearest autobahns are the A61 (Cologne-Speyer) and the A48/A1 to Trier.

Boat The landing stages of several boat operators are along the Konrad-Adenauer-Ufer on the Rhine just south of the Deutsches Eck. Boats usually run from Easter to late October.

Rhein- und Mosellschiffahrt Hölzenbein (☎ 377 44) travels between Koblenz and Rüdesheim three times daily. Boats stop at all the little villages along the way, allowing you to make your trip as long or as short as you want. A trip to Rüdesheim costs DM32/ 38 one way/return, to Bacharach it's DM12/ 15.50.

KD line (☎ 310 30) makes similar trips up the Rhine and also goes into the Moselle Valley. The one-way trip to Cochem costs DM34.60, to Winningen DM9 (for details on discounts see The Rhine between Koblenz and Mainz section).

The newest vessel on the Rhine is the space-age RMF1 Enterprise (☎ 914 17 30). Daily trips from Koblenz to St Goar leave at 11 am and cost a stratospheric DM48 one way, DM59 return (DM36/44 for students).

Getting Around

Local buses operated by KEVAG (☎ 392 17 88) are easily recognised by their orange-yellow colour scheme. Their comprehensive system is separated into zones, with most trips within the city costing DM2. Two zones (eg to the hostel) cost DM3 and day passes are DM9.

To book a taxi call ☎ 330 55. Fahrradhaus Zangmeister (☎ 323 63), at Am Löhrrondell, rents bicycles for DM12 a day, while PRO JU (☎ 911 60 15) at Hohenzollernstrasse 127 charges from DM8.

Ask at the tourist office for the biking brochure *Radfahren in Koblenz*.

AROUND KOBLENZ

Höhr-Grenzhausen

- *pop 8200*
- *area code* ☎ 02624

This little town lies in the heart of the Westerwald, a sparsely populated rural region of gentle hills and laid-back villages.

Thanks to its huge deposits of clay, the area has been renowned for its pottery since the Middle Ages. It is today the largest ceramic-producing region in Europe.

Höhr-Grenzhausen is one of the main towns on the **Kannenbäckerstrasse** (literally 'pot bakers' road'), a themed route that connects 10 communities. At many of the 40 potteries along the way you can watch the artists at work.

Everywhere you go along this route, you'll find the grey-blue glazed ceramics typical of the area.

A friendly and instructive pottery place to visit in Höhr-Grenzhausen is **Töpferhof Mühlendyck** at Lindenstrasse 39, just 200m up the street from the **Keramik Museum Westerwald** (open from 10 am to 5 pm, closed Monday; DM4, discount DM3). This modern and spacious museum houses a comprehensive collection of both artistic and functional ceramics – from historical to contemporary – and also explains the production process.

To get to Höhr-Grenzhausen, you can take bus No 6118 from the central bus station in Koblenz.

THE RHINE FROM KOBLENZ TO MAINZ

The Rhine's best scenery lies between these two cities, as this mythical river carves deeply through the Rhenish slate mountains. Heading downstream (north) from Bingen, you'll encounter the most dramatic landscape, with fertile vineyards clinging to steep cliffs, dreamy wine villages of Roman origin and imposing castles framed by thick forests.

The Rhine Valley has been a favourite among travellers since the 19th century, and although visitor numbers have declined in recent years, the tiny towns are still regularly swamped by tourists, usually arriving by the bus load.

Unfortunately, these hordes have turned some otherwise lovely towns into tourist traps with tacky shops and overpriced cafés and restaurants. The countryside surrounding these kitsch centres is, however, brilliant at any time. The busiest season is from May to September so, if you can, visit in early spring or late autumn when the crowds have disappeared. The area all but shuts down in winter.

Hiking & Cycling

The Rhine Valley is great hiking and biking territory, and each tourist office has specific suggestions and maps for long and short trips. One hiking option is the long-distance *Rheinhöhenweg*, which parallels the left river bank between Bonn and Oppenheim, south of Mainz, over a distance of 240km. Another path travels along the right bank between the Bonn suburb of Bonn-Beuel and Wiesbaden, for a total of 272km. Trails are marked with an 'R'.

A detailed brochure outlining these routes is available from local tourist offices, as are detailed maps. Bicycle paths also run along both banks.

Wine Tasting

Much of the cheap stuff sold in shops around the world as 'Rhine wine' has nothing to do with the real thing, as you will soon discover when sampling some of Germany's finest at the many vineyards here. Just look for the signs saying *Weinprobe*. Some vintners will only do wine tastings for groups, but if you're really interested just go to the winery and ask. Most will happily comply if they can tell you are serious. Don't drink too much without buying at least a bottle or too, though. In many places, the tourist offices organise scheduled wine tastings for individuals as well.

Festivals

Every little river village holds at least one wine festival each year, with most of them crammed into the months of August and September, just before harvest time. The brochure *Veranstaltungskalendar Rheinland-Pfalz,* with a complete listing of all festivals, is available from the local tourist offices.

The region's greatest festival is called the **Rhine in Flames**. Water and fire combine in one spectacular show in splendid settings five times every year. Castles, boats, monuments and the river banks are swathed in brilliant light and form the backdrop to gargantuan fireworks displays. The following table shows where and when the festival is held.

Siebengebirge: Linz to Bonn
First Saturday in May
Bingen/Rüdesheim
First Saturday in July
Koblenz to Braubach/Spay
Second Saturday in August
Oberwesel
Second Saturday in September
Loreley: St Goar/St Goarshausen
Third Saturday in September

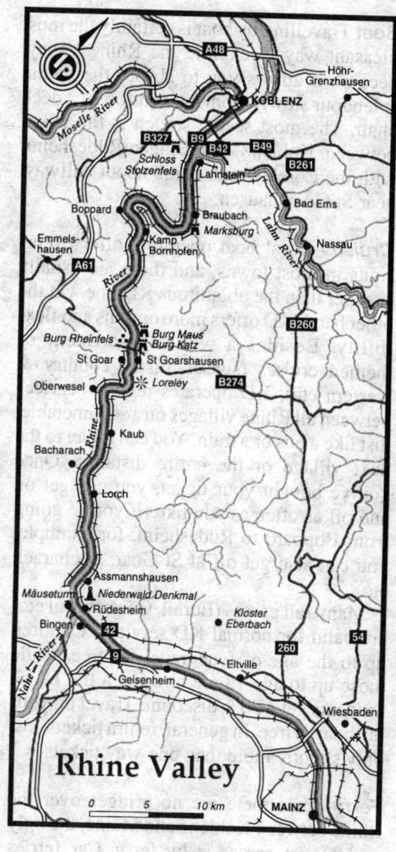

Getting There & Away

Koblenz and Mainz are the best starting points for touring the region. For details on how to get to these towns, see their Getting There & Away sections. If you're pressed for time, you can also explore the Rhine Valley on a long day trip from Frankfurt, though obviously that won't do justice to the region.

Getting Around

Train Train travel is an efficient and convenient way to go village-hopping along the Rhine. Local trains connect all Rhine villages on the left river bank between Koblenz and Mainz at least once an hour. The entire trip takes 1¾ hours. Some trains stop only at the bigger towns, and IC trains make the trip between the two cities in 50 minutes with no stops. Both cities are also gateways for trains to Rhine villages on the right bank, though services on this route are slightly less frequent.

Car & Motorcycle The B9 highway travels along the left bank of the Rhine from Koblenz to Bingen, from where the A60 leads on to Mainz. On the right bank, the B42 hugs the river.

RHINELAND–PALATINATE

Boat Travelling by boat is certainly the most pleasant way to explore the Rhine Valley, because it allows you to absorb the scenic splendour slowly from the comfort of a deck chair. The most scenic stretch is the 70km between Koblenz and Bingen/Rüdesheim, with the Loreley rock being about halfway, near St Goarshausen.

Cruises Local boat operators offer excursions in most towns, and these are usually cheaper than the ubiquitous KD line. On the other hand, KD offers more options and flexibility. Besides a whole assortment of themed cruises (sunset, disco, country & western etc), KD operates regular services between all Rhine villages on a set timetable, just like a bus or a train. You can travel to the next village or the entire distance. Once you've bought your ticket, you can get on and off as often as you like (if you're going from Boppard to Rüdesheim, for example, you can also get off at St Goar, Bacharach etc).

Many rail passes (Eurail, GermanRail etc) are valid for normal KD services. Children up to the age of four travel for free, while those up to age 13 are charged a flat DM3. Students get a 30% discount. Travel on your birthday is free. In general, return tickets cost only slightly more than one-way tickets.

Ferry Since there are no bridges over the Rhine between Koblenz and Mainz, the only way to get across is by ferry. Car ferries operate between Boppard and Filsen/Kamp Bornhofen, St Goar and St Goarshausen, Bacharach and Kaub, Trechtinghausen and Lorch, and Bingen and Rüdesheim. Car ferries also transport foot passengers, and additional passenger ferries also make the runs. Prices vary slightly but you can figure on around DM5 per car (including driver), DM1.50 per additional person and DM1 per bike.

Marksburg

Framed by vineyards and rose gardens, the snug 1300-year-old town of Braubach, about 8km south of Koblenz, unfolds against the dramatic backdrop of the Marksburg. This hill-top castle's main claim to fame is that it has never been destroyed, thanks to several layers of fortification added by a succession of counts and landgraves. It has withstood all attacks, including those by the French in 1689, who laid to waste most other Rhine castles.

A tour takes in the citadel, the Gothic hall and the large functioning kitchen, plus the grisly torture chamber in the cellar with its hair-raising assortment of pain-inflicting instruments. The castle is open from 10 am to 5 pm (to 4 pm in winter) and admission is DM7 (discount DM5). Take bus No 6130 from the Koblenz central bus station.

Boppard

- *pop 16,500*
- *area code* ☎ 06742

Boppard is about 20km south of Koblenz on a horseshoe-shaped bend of the Rhine and has been settled since Celtic times. Its attractions are bunched in the 200m-wide band between the Rhine and the train tracks. The town's main thoroughfare is the pedestrianised Oberstrasse.

Boppard's tourist office (☎ 388 8; fax 814 02) is on Markt and is open on weekdays in summer from 8 am to 5.30 pm (to 4 pm in winter) and on Saturday from 9 am to noon. Staff run English-language city tours every Tuesday at 3 pm in season.

To change money, there's a Sparkasse at Oberstrasse 141 which is open until 6.30 pm on Thursday. The post office is on Heerstrasse, just east of the train station.

Things to See A church has stood on the site of what once were Roman thermal baths at Markt since the 5th century. Today's twin-towered **Church of St Severus** dates to the 13th century and has a web vaulted ceiling. The triumphal cross above the main altar (1225) is considered the finest in the region.

A couple of blocks east of the church, on Burgstrasse, is the **Museum der Stadt Boppard** (open from 10 am to noon and 2 to 5 pm during the season, closed Monday; free entry) housed in a 14th-century palace. The highlight of the permanent exhibit is the furniture of Boppard's most famous son, Michael Thonet (1796-1871). He distinguished himself by developing a process that allowed the bending and shaping of wood strips which were then assembled into pieces of furniture, mostly chairs. You'll still find his characteristic swirling designs – which are often referred to as Viennese coffeehouse style – today. Thonet had in fact moved to Vienna in 1842 at the urging of none other than the Austrian chancellor, Klemens von Metternich, who was quite impressed by the talent of the man from Boppard.

Some remnants of Boppard's Roman past, including a 55m stretch of wall, survive in the **Archaeological Park** in Angertstrasse, east of the train station.

Activities It's a 20-minute ride via chair lift (DM7, return DM10) from the Mühltal station to the hill top above the Rhine bend, from where you have the illusion of looking at four lakes instead of a river. This is also a good starting point for hikes.

On its scenic 8km trip from Boppard to Buchholz in the Hunsrück mountain region, the Hunsrückbahn train travels through five tunnels and across two viaducts while ascending 330m. From Buchholz it continues on to Emmelshausen. Return tickets to Buchholz are DM6, to Emmelshausen DM9.20.

The local Hebel-Linie (☎ 242 0) runs boat trips to Rüdesheim (DM24), Bacharach (DM17) and other towns; staff offer discounts to children up to the age of 12. KD line (☎ 223 2) charges DM18 to St Goar, DM20 to Koblenz and DM29.80 to Rüdesheim. All prices are for return trips.

The tourist office organises wine tastings with different vintners at different estates on Thursday at 8 pm in the season (DM8 for five wines).

The area around Boppard is good for hiking and cycling. If you need to rent a bike, go to Fahrrad-Studio Lüdicke (☎ 473 6) in Oberstrasse 105 (DM10 per day; discounts for longer rentals). Maps are available from the tourist office.

Places to Stay & Eat The nearest camping ground is *Camping-Park Sonneck* (☎ 212 1), beautifully located on the Rhine about 5km north of Boppard and with modern facilities and a pool (bus No 6050, ask the driver to drop you off). The nearest *DJH hostel* is in St Goar (see the following St Goar section).

The tourist office has a free reservation service, with private rooms starting at DM32 for a single with shared facilities and doubles costing DM43 and up.

If you want to stay in a central hotel, try *Weinhaus Sonnenhof* (☎ 322 3), at Kirchgasse 8, which charges DM58/98 for singles/doubles. The American-owned *Günther Garni* (☎ 233 5) has a riverside location at Rheinallee 40 and rooms from DM54/84.

Wine taverns serving traditional German food include the *Felsenkeller*, Mühltal 21, and *Weinhaus Heilig Grab* in Zelkesgasse 12. For a more up-market meal, go to the snug *Schnuggel-Elsje*, Untere Marktstrasse 24, in a historical half-timbered house. Boppard also has its share of inexpensive pizzerias.

Getting There & Away The trip from Koblenz to Boppard by train costs DM5.60 and takes 15 minutes. From Mainz, the trip costs DM18.80 and takes 40 minutes.

St Goar

- *pop 3500*
- *area code* ☎ 06741

St Goar, 10km upstream from Boppard, is a routine stop on the tourist circuit, largely because of its proximity to the legendary Loreley rock. More impressive are the sprawling ruins of Burg Rheinfels above the town. St Goar's sister town, St Goarshausen, is across the river and accessible by ferry. St Goar's train station is a couple of blocks inland on Oberstrasse, but train tickets must be bought at Reisebüro Müller at Oberstrasse 93.

Most of the action takes place on Heerstrasse where, at No 86, you'll find the tourist office (☎ 383; fax 720 9). It's open on weekdays (plus Saturday morning in season) and closed at lunchtime. The Kreissparkasse across the street at No 81 is a convenient place to change money. The post office is next to the train station.

Things to See Don't miss **Burg Rheinfels**, built in 1245 by Count Dieter V of Katzenelnbogen as a base for his extortionate toll-collecting operation. Once the mightiest fortress on the Rhine, its size and labyrinthine layout is astonishing, as is the network of underground tunnels and mine galleries, most of which are accessible to the public. Daily opening hours are from 9 am to 6 pm in season, and fine weekends from November to March. Admission is DM5, children DM3.

From Rheinfels you have a good view of two castles on the Rhine's right bank. Downstream is **Burg Maus** (Mouse Castle), originally called Peterseck and built by the archbishop of Trier in an effort to counter Count Dieter's illegal toll practices. In a show of medieval muscle-flexing, the latter responded by building yet another, and much bigger, castle above St Goarshausen. He called it **Burg Katz** (Cat Castle) and so, to highlight the obvious imbalance of power between count and archbishop, Peterseck soon came to be known as Burg Maus.

One of the most anticipated sights of any trip down the Rhine Valley is the **Loreley** rock. Though nothing but a giant slab of slate, it owes its fame to the mystical maiden whose siren songs lured sailors to their death in the treacherous currents. You can make the one-hour trek to the top from St Goarshausen, but once there you'll most likely be joined by throngs of day-trippers who came up by coach.

Places to Stay & Eat *Camping Loreleyblick* (☎ 206 6) is right on the Rhine opposite the Loreley; it's open all year but tends to be full in season. *Camping Friedenau* (☎ 368) at Gründelbachstrasse 103 (a 20-minute walk west of the train station) is open from April to October. There's no public transport to either and both are rather old-fashioned. St Goar's *DJH hostel* (☎ 388) is right below Rheinfels Castle at Bismarckweg 17 and charges DM21.50 for bed & breakfast; sheets are DM5.

Private rooms and true budget hotels are scarce. One of the cheaper digs is *Hotel Keutmann* (☎ 169 1), at An der Loreley 24, where singles go for DM47.50, with doubles costing DM95. *Hotel Zur Loreley* (☎ 161 4; fax 255 0), at Heerstrasse 87, has rooms for DM70/120.

You'll find plenty of restaurants along Heerstrasse. Next to the train station is *Weinstube Zur Krone*, which serves good German food under DM20. Another option is the rustic *Vielharmonie* (closed Monday), the more casual of the two restaurants in Rheinfels Castle.

Getting There & Away The trip by train from Koblenz costs DM9.60 and takes 30 minutes. From Mainz to St Goar it costs DM14.20 and takes 1½ hours.

Bacharach

- *pop 2400*
- *area code* ☎ 06743

Unlike most other wine towns in the Rhine Valley, Bacharach hides its not inconsiderable charms behind a time-worn town wall and is therefore easily missed. Walk beneath one of its thick arched gateways, though, and you'll find yourself in a beautifully preserved medieval village with gorgeous half-timbered houses, including the **Altes Haus** on Oberstrasse, the town's main street. About a 15-minute walk above town looms **Burg Stahleck**, a 12th-century castle occupied by the hostel. Halfway up the hill you'll pass the fragile frame of the **Wernerkapelle**, a medieval chapel destroyed, like so much else around here, by the French in 1689.

Back on Oberstrasse stands the late Romanesque **Peterskirche**, which has a particularly graphic set of capstones. Look for the one of the naked woman with snakes sucking her breasts and another showing a man whose beard is being stroked by dragons (both are warnings about the consequences of adultery) at the end of the left aisle.

The diminutive tourist office (☎ 296 8; fax 315 5) is at Oberstrasse 1 and can help with finding accommodation. *Campingplatz Sonnenstrand* (☎ 175 2) is on the Rhine about 500m south of the town centre and open from April to mid-November.

The *DJH hostel* (☎ 126 6) in Burg Stahleck has recently been renovated and charges DM22.50 for bed & breakfast; sheets are DM5. One of many wine taverns to try is *Zum Grünen Baum*, at Oberstrasse 63, which has delicious wines and a friendly proprietor.

Bingen

- *pop 24,000*
- *area code* ☎ 06721

Strategically located at the confluence of the Nahe and Rhine, Bingen has seen its share of conflicts throughout the centuries, having been destroyed and rebuilt eight times since it was founded by the Romans in 11 BC. Far less touristy than Rüdesheim across the river, Bingen is a good alternative as a base from which to explore the southern section of the Rhine Valley and the Rheingau, the only section of the river that flows due west.

The Nahe cuts right through Bingen, with the city centre spreading out on its eastern bank. Of Bingen's two train stations, the smaller Hauptbahnhof is near the Rhine west of the Nahe. Most long-distance trains stop here. Local trains stop here as well and also at Bahnhof Bingen (Rhein) Stadt, only a couple kilometres further east.

Bingen's tourist office (☎ 184 20 5; fax 162 75) is at Rheinkai 21 and is open from 8.30 am to 6 pm on weekdays and on Saturday morning in summer. On Mainzer Strasse are both a Sparkasse branch at No 26 and the main post office at No 43.

Things to See & Do One of Bingen's landmarks is **Burg Klopp**, resting on a hill top right in the town centre and occupied by the city hall and a **Heimatmuseum** (open from Easter to October, closed Monday; entry DM1, discount DM0.50), whose prized exhibit is a complete set of Roman surgical instruments. Up on Rochus Hill east of town is the neo-Gothic **Rochuskapelle** (closed, but the interior is visible through a glass screen), a pilgrimage church with a splendid canopied altar showing scenes from the life of Hildegard von Bingen (see the Hildegard von Bingen aside) to the left of the main altar.

On an island in the Rhine is the bright ochre **Mäuseturm** where, according to legend, the sadistic Bishop Hatto was devoured

Hildegard von Bingen

She's hip and holistic, a composer, dramatist and a courageous campaigner for the rights of women. She heals with crystals and herbs, her music frequently hits the New Age charts ... and she's been dead for more than 800 years.

Hildegard von Bingen was born in 1098 at Bermersheim (near Alzey), the 10th child of a well-off and influential family. At the age of three she experienced the first of the visions that would occur over the course of her extraordinarily long life. As a young girl she entered the convent at Disibodenberg on the Nahe River and eventually became an abbess who founded abbeys of her own at Rupertsberg and Eibingen. During her preaching tours – an unprecedented female activity in medieval times – she lectured both the clergy and the common people, attacking social injustice and ungodliness.

Pope Eugen III publicly endorsed her, urging her to write down her theology and visionary experiences. This she did in a remarkable series of books that encompassed ideas as diverse as cosmology, natural history and female orgasm. Her overarching philosophy was that man is a distillation of all of God's greatness and should comport himself accordingly. Her accomplishments are even more remarkable considering her life-long struggle against feelings of worthlessness and the physical effects of her mysterious visions, which often left her near death.

Hildegard von Bingen was a force of nature who remains as much a cult figure today as she was during her life. She died in 1179. ■

by mice after setting fire to a barn in which he had locked a group of starving peasants who had asked him for grain after a bad harvest. In reality, though, the name is a mutation of *Mautturm*, or toll tower, which is what the building was during the Middle Ages.

Bingen-Rüdesheimer Fahrgastschiffahrt organises boat excursions into the Rhine Valley. Return trips to Bacharach are DM16, to St Goar DM23. Tickets are available from the tourist office.

Places to Stay & Eat The *camping ground* (☎ 171 60) is on the Rhine in the eastern suburb of Bingen-Kempten (open from May to October; bus No 1 or 3). The *DJH hostel* (☎ 321 63) is in the northern suburb of Bingerbrück at Herterstrasse 51 and has bed & breakfast for DM19.50 and sheets for an extra DM5. It's a 10-minute walk from the Hauptbahnhof.

The tourist office can make reservations for you, but charges DM3 per person per night. Private singles/doubles go for DM35/ 70.

The best hotel deal is offered by *Binger Weinstube/Haus Clara* (☎ 144 25), which has basic singles from DM50 and doubles from DM80; rooms with private bath are DM10 more. The top hotel is the business-style *Atlantis-Rheinhotel* (☎ 706 0; fax 796 50 0) where you'll pay from DM162/231 for small but fully equipped rooms.

For eats, try *Brunnenstübchen* behind the tourist office at Vorstadtstrasse 58, whose creative young cook does modern versions of regional favourites. Also popular with a younger crowd is *Life & Art*, a bistro-cum-gallery at Rathausstrasse 24.

Getting There & Away Bingen is served by several hourly trains from Mainz (DM9.60, 30 minutes).

Getting Around City-Linie minibuses shuttle between all major points of interest every 30 minutes and are a good deal at DM1, discount DM0.50, per trip. The car/passenger ferry to/from Rüdesheim operates continuously throughout the day till midnight.

Rüdesheim

- *pop 9200*
- *area code* ☎ 06722

Rüdesheim is the capital of the Rheingau, one of Germany's most famous wine-growing regions. It is on the right bank, about 25km west of Wiesbaden, at the only section of the Rhine where it flows due west. Rüdesheim is a quintessential wine town and a mecca for some three million yearly visitors – most of them middle-aged or older. Their 'shrines' are the wine bars and restaurants along the narrow Drosselgasse, the main drag. Every day between May and September, the ornate half-timbered houses here vibrate with polka music and the laughter of a rollicking crowd fond of a good time. As soon as you wander beyond these 100m of drunken madness, Rüdesheim is actually quite a pleasant place.

The area of interest to visitors is the thin strip bordered by Rheinstrasse along the Rhine and Oberstrasse about 100m away from the river. The train station and ferry landing dock are a few hundred metres to the west.

The tourist office (☎ 296 2; fax 348 5) is at Rheinstrasse 16 and is open from 8.30 am to 6.30 pm on weekdays, 1.30 to 5.30 pm Saturday and 2 to 6 pm Sunday. There's an American Express office here to change money. The post office is about 100m west on Rheinstrasse.

Things to See & Do Rüdesheim is too small for you to avoid the Drosselgasse razzmatazz completely but, once you've squeezed your way past the boisterous crowds, head for **Siegfrieds Mechanisches Musikkabinett** (open daily between mid-March and mid-November from 10 am to 10 pm) in the Brömserhof at Oberstrasse 29. This historical building contains a fun collection of mechanical musical instruments, such as pianolas, from the 18th and 19th centuries, many of which are demonstrated during the guided tour. Admission is a steep DM9, discount DM5, but it's actually worth it.

Also of interest is the **Weinmuseum** (open daily between mid-March and mid-November from 9 am to 6 pm; entry DM5, discount DM3), in the 1000-year-old Brömserburg castle at Rheinstrasse 3, with a large collection of rare drinking vessels from Roman times onward.

For a bird's-eye view over the Rhine Valley and the vineyards, either walk or take the gondola up to the bombastic **Niederwald Denkmal** (1883). This giant monument glorifies the establishment of the German Reich in 1871 with a heroic figure of Germania. The gondola leaves from Oberstrasse and gains 200m in elevation during its 1500m journey (DM6.50, return DM10; children DM3.50/5). There's also a chair lift from the neighbouring town of Assmannshausen (same prices), an island of red-wine production in a sea of white Riesling. If you go up on the gondola and down on the chair lift, the cost is DM10 (children DM5).

The only wine estate that does wine tastings for individuals is Weingut Georg Breuer at Grabenstrasse 8. Its wines are delicious, and the DM11 charge to try four or five wines is waived if you're buying.

Places to Stay & Eat The *Auf der Lach* camping ground (☎ 252 8), east of town on the Rhine, is open from May to October. The *DJH hostel* (☎ 271 1) is in the vineyards above Rüdesheim at Am Kreuzberg and costs DM21 for juniors, DM25 for seniors. It's about a 30-minute walk from the train station; there's no bus.

Hotel Zur Guten Quelle (☎ 275 7), at Katharinenstrasse 3, is one budget option, with singles/doubles for DM50/110. You'd never expect to find a modern, stylish and artsy hotel off the Drosselgasse, but that's just what the family-run *Rüdesheimer Schloss* (☎ 905 00; fax 479 60) at Steinstrasse 10 is. Spacious rooms with one-of-a-kind furniture cost from DM140/180 and are well worth the splurge.

Getting There & Away There are buses to/from Wiesbaden (No 5480) and Rüdesheim. The town is well connected by train to Mainz, Wiesbaden, Frankfurt and Koblenz.

Around Rüdesheim

Kloster Eberbach If you saw the 1986 film *The Name of the Rose*, starring Sean Connery, you've already 'visited' this one-time Cistercian monastery, where a number of scenes were shot. Dating back to the 12th century, the graceful structure went through periods as a lunatic asylum, jail and sheep pen after secularisation in the 19th century. In 1918, it was turned into a state-owned winery.

You can walk through the monks' refectory and dormitory, as well as to the austere Romanesque basilica, the site of a classical concert series from May to October. Wine tastings are held on weekends and holidays (April to October) in the musty cellars (DM7.50 for three wines). Hours are from 10 am to 6 pm daily (in winter to 4 pm) and admission is DM5, discount DM3. Eberbach is about 20km from Rüdesheim but, if you're not driving, the only way to get here is by taking the train or bus to Eltville, followed by a one-hour signposted walk.

Moselle Valley

TRIER

- *pop 95,000*
- *area code* ☎ 0651

Trier is not only one of Germany's oldest towns but also its first metropolis. Founded by the Romans as Augusta Treverorum in 15 BC, it became the capital of the Western Roman Empire in the 3rd century and also an imperial residence.

Along with Rome, Constantinople and Alexandria, Trier was one of the most important cities in the empire. You'll find more Roman ruins here than anywhere else north of the Alps and, despite a host of architectural gems from later ages, they are still Trier's prime asset.

Trier's second heyday began in the 13th century when its archbishops also acquired the rank and power of prince-electors. In the following centuries, the town seesawed between periods of prosperity and poverty.

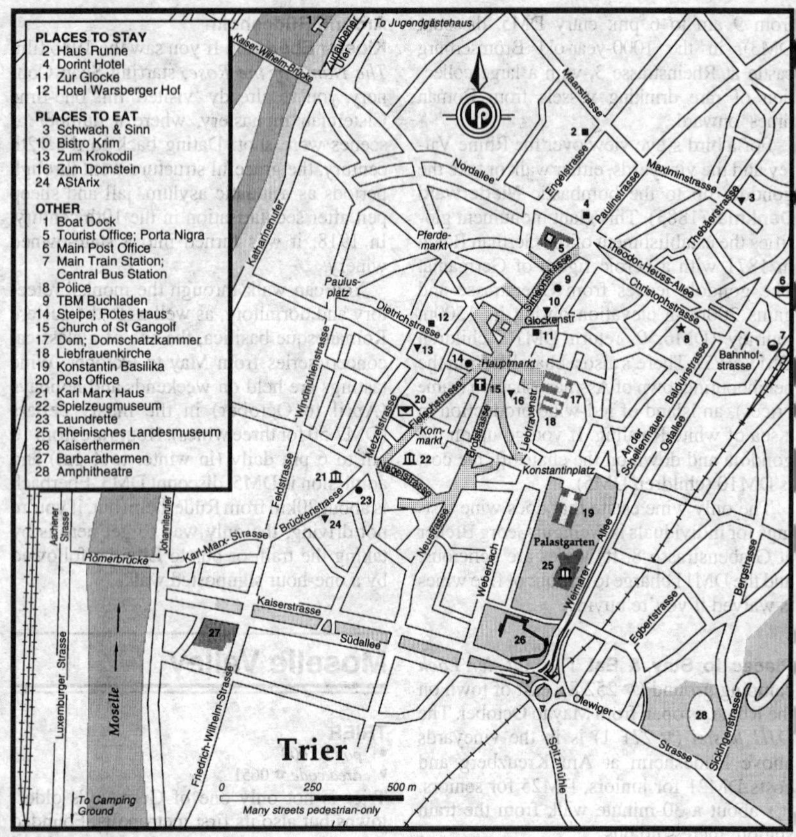

Trier was briefly French in the early 19th century before being swallowed up by Prussia in 1815.

The town is beautifully located on the Moselle, with its terraced vineyards, and framed by the Eifel and Hunsrück mountains. Its proximity to Luxembourg and France can be tasted in the local cuisine, and about 18,000 students do their part to infuse the town with a lively spirit.

Trier is an inspiring place that deserves at least a couple of days of exploration. It also makes an excellent base for trips down the Moselle River or into the nearby mountains.

Orientation

The city centre, where most of the major sights are located, occupies an area of approximately 1 sq km. It is bordered by a ring road on three sides and by the Moselle River to the west.

From the Hauptbahnhof, in the north-eastern corner, head west on Bahnhofstrasse and then Theodor-Heuss-Allee to the Porta Nigra, the Roman gate that is Trier's main landmark.

From here, walk south along the Simeonstrasse pedestrianised zone to Hauptmarkt, the pivotal centre of the old city.

Information

Tourist Office The tourist office (☎ 978 08 0; fax 447 59) is right at the Porta Nigra and has lots of maps and booklets in English and French and personnel fluent in both. Its hours are from 9 am to 6.30 pm from Monday to Saturday and to 3.30 pm on Sunday between April and mid-November. For the rest of the year it's open from Monday to Saturday from 9 am to 5 pm.

Ask here about daily guided walking tours in English held between April and October (DM9, children DM1) and rides aboard the Römerexpress, a motorised 'train' that ticks off the main sights in three languages and 30 minutes (DM10, DM5 for children up to the age of 14).

The TrierCard gives you free or reduced admission to the city's main attractions and museums and is good for three consecutive days. It costs DM17 for one person, DM32 for families.

TrierCardPlus includes public transport and costs DM25/ 44.

Money Most banks in Trier change money, including the Sparkasse at Simeonstrasse 55 near the tourist office and the Citibank in Grabenstrasse 12. Both also have ATM machines that accept credit cards.

Post & Communications Trier's main post office is at the Hauptbahnhof and has a counter open until 8 pm on weekdays. It's also open until 2 pm on Saturday and from 11 am to noon on Sunday. A second branch is at Am Kornmarkt.

Bookshop TBM Buchladen at Simeonstrasse 22 has a smattering of foreign-language novels and a good selection of maps.

Laundry There's a convenient laundrette, the Waschcenter, at Brückenstrasse 19-21, which charges DM6 per wash and DM1 to use the dryer.

Medical Services & Emergency To reach a doctor or pharmacist on night duty, call ☎ 115 0. There's a police station (☎ 977 00) at Christophstrasse 5 near the train station.

Walking Tour

Start your tour at Trier's chief landmark, the **Porta Nigra** (open daily; DM4, discount DM2), the imposing 2nd-century city gate that was once part of the 6.4km-long Roman wall.

Made from giant blocks of blackened sandstone held together by iron clamps, it has a central courtyard and two four-storey defensive towers jutting out from its northern façade, facing away from the city. In the 11th century, it was turned into the church of St Simeon, whose surviving apse can be seen when touring the interior.

A short walk south on Simeonstrasse leads to the **Hauptmarkt**, framed by a harmonious ensemble of restored buildings.

The Gothic **Steipe**, a former banqueting house at the corner of Dietrichstrasse, is the most noteworthy. Buttressed by an arched arcade, the three-storey building is topped by an unusual tent-shaped roof.

Next door is the Renaissance **Rotes Haus** with its early baroque gable. The flowery portal on the square's south side leads to the 14th-century **Church of St Gangolf**, with a muscular Gothic tower that was once used to watch for fires. The sculptures on the painted fountain in the square's centre represent St Peter and the four virtues.

Standing in the Hauptmarkt, the walls of the compact **Dom** (open daily to 6 pm, in winter to 5.30 pm), which is a veritable microcosm of town history, rise up to the east. The cathedral is mostly Romanesque, but incorporates an earlier Roman structure as well as Gothic and baroque elements.

Inside, it has a solemn simplicity, enlivened by a lavish stucco ceiling in the west apse, whose lower walls are clad in delicate inlaid panelling.

A curiosity is the organ which, seemingly suspended from the ceiling, looks a bit like the fuel tanks of the NASA space shuttle. The **Domschatzkammer** (treasure chamber; open daily; entry DM2, discount DM1) is accessible from within the cathedral.

Next door is the **Liebfrauenkirche** (open daily, but closed at lunchtime), one of the oldest Gothic churches in Germany and built on the southern wing of the earlier Roman church. The cross-shaped structure is supported by a dozen round pillars symbolising the 12 apostles and has a light, mystical quality despite its strict symmetry.

Heading south on Liebfrauenstrasse will get you to another architectural masterpiece, the **Konstantin Basilika** (open daily to 6 pm, restricted hours in winter), a 4th-century building that was first the throne room of Roman Emperor Constantine, later part of the residence of the prince-electors and is now a Protestant church. Its dimensions are mind-blowing: the rectangular brick edifice measures 67m long and 36m high. No pillars or galleries support the immense coffered ceiling.

In the 13th century, the prince-electors of Trier integrated it into their residence, and it wasn't freed of its medieval alterations until King Friedrich Wilhelm IV of Prussia had it restored as a Roman basilica in the 19th century.

The prince-electors' residence, a pink rococo confection, still leans against the south side of the basilica. Here begins the stylised **Palastgarten**, the green axis ending at the Kaiserthermen ruins. On your way there, you'll pass the **Rheinisches Landesmuseum** (Tuesday to Friday from 9.30 am to 5 pm, weekends from 10.30 am; entry DM5, children DM3) at Weimarer Allee 1, one of Germany's finest museums of prehistoric, Roman, early Christian and medieval art.

The ruins of the **Kaiserthermen** (Imperial Thermal Baths; open daily; DM4, discount DM2) from the early 4th century are a highlight of Trier. The arched remains of the eastern wall of these thermal baths rise 19m and preside over a labyrinthine system of heating ducts, hot and cold-water pools and a sauna-like hot air bath.

A few hundred metres east on Olewiger Strasse is the **Amphitheatre** (open daily; DM4, discount DM2), capable of holding 20,000 spectators during gladiator tournaments and animal fights. The visit includes the dank cellars once used to keep the imprisoned people, caged animals and corpses.

The final Roman structure is the **Barbarathermen** (open daily; DM4, discount DM2), reached by walking about 1.5km west on Kaiserstrasse. Only the foundation and the cellars remain of these baths, whose stones were used to build a school in the 17th century. It's still a good place to get a look at the 1800-year-old floor heating system.

From the baths, walk a few steps back east on Kaiserstrasse before turning north onto Lorenz-Kellner-Strasse and then take the second right into Brückenstrasse. At No 10, you'll find the **Karl Marx Haus** (open from 10 am to 6 pm, Monday from 1 pm, with curtailed hours in winter; DM3, discount DM2). The exhibit in this respectable town house, where the socialist philosopher was born, encompasses photographs, first edition books, documents and manuscripts. Marx left Trier at age 17 to study law, philosophy and history at the universities of Bonn, Berlin and Jena.

Children will especially enjoy the whimsical collection of the **Spielzeugmuseum** (open from 10 am to 5 pm, in winter noon to 4 pm, closed Monday; DM7.50, discount DM4), a block north-west at Nagelstrasse 4-5. Apart from the usual assortment of dolls and teddy bears, this toy museum contains some real rarities, including a miniature train environment on the 2nd floor. Turning right on Nagelstrasse and right again on Fleischstrasse will get you back to the Hauptmarkt.

A combined ticket to the four main Roman sights is DM9, discount DM4, and available at each (but *not* at the tourist office).

Cruises

Daily boat trips to Bernkastel-Kues and back are offered by the Gebrüder Kolb Line (☎ 263 17), in addition to various one-hour and evening excursions. Boats leave from the docks at Zurlaubener Ufer, near the hostel (also see the Getting There & Away section in the Moselle Wine Road section).

Places to Stay

The modern *Trier-City* municipal camping ground (☎ 869 21; open all year) is nicely positioned on the Moselle at Luxemburger Strasse 81. The newly renovated DJH *Jugendgästehaus* (☎ 146 62 0), at An der Jugendherberge 4 by the river, charges DM26.30 per person in four-bed dorms or DM35.50 in double rooms (all with shower and WC), sheets and breakfast included. Take bus No 3 or 40 from the train station, change at Porta Nigra to bus No 7 or 8, get off at the bridge, then walk for five minutes north along the river.

Trier's tourist office operates a free and efficient room-reservation service, and there's a surprisingly large number of good budget hotels. The central but simple *Hotel Warsberger Hof* (☎ 975 25 0) at Dietrichstrasse 42 charges DM37/74 for very basic singles/doubles, and also runs the independent *Jugendgästehaus* with beds for DM25. Better value still is *Zur Glocke* (☎ 731 09), Glockenstrasse 12, which has functional rooms for DM40/70 (DM80 with private bath).

Worth paying a little extra for are the rooms at *Haus Runne* (☎ 289 22) at Engelstrasse 35, where clean, sunny rooms with private facilities cost DM45/90. Its restaurant is known for its excellent Franco-German cooking. The view doesn't get any better than that from the rooms facing the Porta Nigra of the *Dorint Hotel* (☎ 270 10; fax 270 11 70) at Porta Nigra Platz 1, but you have to pay DM212/315 for the privilege.

Places to Eat

Trier is a great place to sample Franco-German cooking. One place to try it is at *Zum Krokodil*, a historical inn on Nikolaus Koch Platz, which has half a dozen daily set menus for between DM15 and DM27. *Bistro Krim*, an innovative bar and eatery at Glockenstrasse 7, serves three-course 'Mediterranean' set menus, including coffee, for DM28.50 and interesting à-la-carte dishes, many under DM20. Across the street, at No 12, is *Zur Glocke*, a miniature beer hall that also has good wines and hearty food. For something highly unusual, try the 'Roman' dishes served at *Zum Domstein* on Hauptmarkt 5. Such variations as veal cutlet in pine-nut sauce were inspired by a 3rd-century cookery book and cost DM25 and up.

A favourite student hang-out is *AStArix*, down an arcade at Karl-Marx-Strasse 11. Pasta, baked feta and casseroles all cost well under DM10 and are served until 11.30 pm, unless it's staging a performance or disco. *Schwach & Sinn*, at Maximinstrasse 17 north of the Porta Nigra, has similar prices.

Getting There & Away

Regional buses into the Eifel or Hunsrück mountains leave from the central bus station in front of the Hauptbahnhof. Trier has several hourly train connections to Saarbrücken (DM21.20, one hour) and Koblenz (DM29, 1½ hours). There are also trains to Luxembourg and, in France, Metz. The city is connected to the A1 and A48 via the short A602 and is also crisscrossed by several *Bundesstrassen* from all directions. There's a Mitfahrzentrale (☎ 474 47) at Kaiserstrasse 13.

Getting Around

Trier's comprehensive public bus system covers all corners of the city, though the city centre is largely pedestrianised. Tickets for the entire city area cost DM2.50 per ride or DM7 for a day pass; five-ticket blocks are DM10. Buy the tickets from the bus driver.

Rental bikes are available from Radstation Bahnhof (☎ 148 85 6) in the Hauptbahnhof and at the Warsberger Hof (☎ 975 25 24) at Dietrichstrasse 42.

MOSELLE WINE ROAD

The German section of the Moselle runs 195km north-east from Trier to Koblenz. The river follows a slow, winding course, revealing new scenery at every bend.

Exploring the vineyards and wineries of the Moselle Valley is an ideal way to get a taste for German culture, people and, of course, some wonderful wines. Slow down and do some sipping.

There is, however, more to the Moselle than wine. You'll encounter many historical sites and picturesque towns built along the river below steep, rocky cliff-side vineyards (they say locals are born with one leg shorter than the other so that they can work the vines more easily). This makes the Moselle one of the country's most romantically scenic regions. Though the entire route is packed with visitors from June to October, getting off the beaten path is always easy.

Wine Tasting

The main activities along the Moselle Valley are eating and drinking. Wine tasting and buying are why most people visit the area – just pick out a winery and head inside. Wine connoisseurs speak an international language, but a few tasting tips might help: indicate whether you like a *trocken* (dry), *halbtrocken* (semi-dry) or *lieblich* (sweet) wine; smell the wine as you swish it around in the glass; taste it by rolling it around in your mouth before swallowing; and don't drink too much at a tasting without buying a couple of bottles.

Hiking

The Moselle Valley is especially scenic walking country, but expect some steep climbs if you venture away from the river. The views are worth the sore muscles. The Moselle region is covered by a series of three 1:50,000-scale hiking maps; each sheet costs DM8.80.

A popular long-distance hike is the Moselhöhenweg, which runs on both sides of the Moselle for a total of 390km. The southern route through the Hunsrück Mountains stretches over 224km between Koblenz and Palzem on the border to the Saarland, while the northern route through the Eifel is only 166km long and goes from Wasserbillig on the border with Luxembourg to Koblenz. A detailed booklet is available, usually free, at local tourist offices.

Cycling

Cycling along the Moselle is a popular activity, and for much of the river's course there's a bike track separate from the road. The *Mosselland-Radwanderführer* (DM14.80) is an excellent guide, with detailed maps and information on bike rentals and repair shops, sights, accommodation and other useful hints and tips. It's available at local tourist offices and in bookshops.

An alternative is the ADFC map *Radtourenkarte Mosel-Saarland* (DM13.80), which is also useful for hiking.

Between May and October, you can take your bike on some of the Moselbahn buses travelling between Trier and Bullay.

Getting There & Away

Begin your Moselle Valley trip either in Trier or Koblenz. If you have private transport and are coming from the north, however, you might head up the Ahr Valley and cut through the scenic High Eifel mountain area. If you're coming from the Saarland, your route will lead you through the Hunsrück Mountains.

Getting Around

Bus There's scheduled bus service to all villages on the Moselle between Trier and Bullay, about three-fifths of the way towards Koblenz. The Moselbahn (☎ 0651-210 76) runs eight buses in each direction on weekdays, five on Saturday and three on Sunday (DM16.60, three hours each way). It's a highly scenic route following the river's winding course and passing through numerous quaint villages along the way. Buses leave from outside the train stations in Trier and Bullay.

Train Rail service between Trier and Koblenz (DM29, 1½ hours) is frequent but, except for the section between Bullay and Koblenz, trains travel several kilometres north of the river through the Eifel. If you want to enjoy the beautiful scenery along the Moselle, the Moselbahn buses (see the previous Bus section) are a better choice. One exception is the Moselweinbahn, which shuttles between Bullay and Traben-Trarbach. There's also regular service to

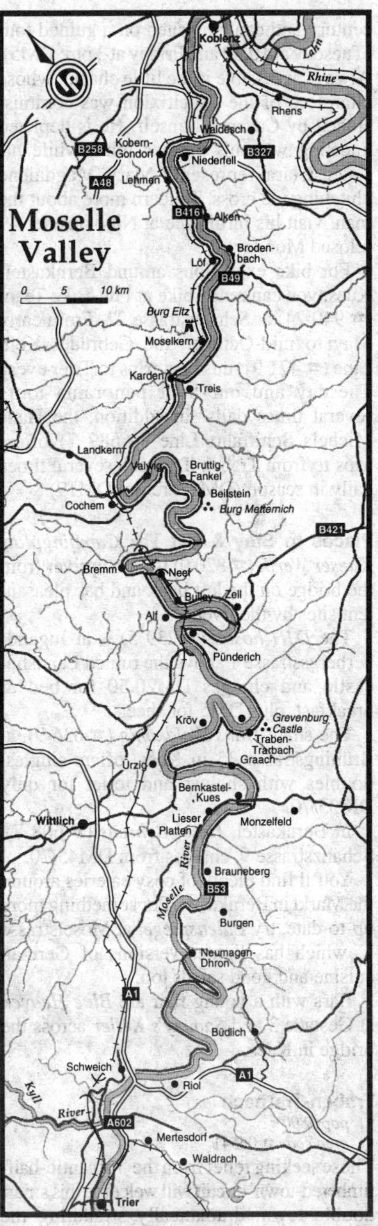

Koblenz from Saarbrücken (DM52, 2½ hours).

Car & Motorcycle The B53 from Trier, which continues as the B49 just north of Traben-Trarbach, follows the course of the Moselle all the way to Koblenz, crossing the river several times. Driving along the Moselle is ideal, though you may risk a cramped neck (not to mention nervous passengers) from looking up at the majestic slopes. Also keep in mind that, even though the distances are not great, driving along this constantly winding road actually takes quite a long time.

Boat A leisurely boat trip is a great way to experience the idyllic landscape of the Moselle. The most scenic stretch is between Trier and Bernkastel-Kues, where the river narrows and vineyards get steeper by the minute. While much of the river's charm comes from its constantly winding course, this does make water travel particularly slow. Add to that a fair number of locks – needed to compensate for the 70m difference in elevation between Koblenz and Trier – and it's easy to understand why the scheduled ferry service over the entire stretch takes two days.

Most boats operate between early May and mid-October. The fleet of the KD line sails several times daily from Koblenz to Cochem (DM38.20 one way). Many rail passes (Eurail, GermanRail etc) are valid for normal KD line services. Children up to the age of four travel for free, those up to age 13 are charged a flat DM3. Students get a 30% discount. Travel on your birthday is free. In general, return tickets cost only slightly more than one-way tickets.

Between Cochem and Trier, the Gebrüder Kolb Line (☎ 02673-151 5) is the dominant operation. Its scheduled boats run between April and October, and its repertory also includes day excursions and one-hour panorama tours from various towns. In most villages, local boat operators offer additional options.

Bernkastel-Kues

- *pop 7500*
- *area code* ☎ 06531

About 70km downriver from Trier, at a dramatic river bend, lies the 700-year-old double town of Bernkastel-Kues. It's the heart of the Middle Moselle region and a routine stop on many visitors' itineraries, making it pretty busy during the season. Bernkastel, on the right bank, is prettier and more commercial, though Kues, snuggled within the bend, is not without appeal. The bus station is next to the boat docks in Bernkastel.

The tourist office (☎ 402 3; fax 795 3) is at Am Gestade 5 and is open on weekdays from 8.30 am to 12.30 pm and 1 to 5 pm. In summer, it's also open from 10 am to 4 pm on Saturday. Staff can help find accommodation for a fee of between DM3 and DM5. The Volksbank right next to the tourist office changes money, as does the Sparkasse a few metres downriver. The post office is in Kues on Mozartstrasse.

Things to See & Do Bernkastel's main attraction is the **Markt**, a romantic ensemble of colourful and statuesque half-timbered houses with beautifully decorated gables. Note the medieval pillory to the left of the Rathaus. On Karlsstrasse, south-west of Markt, you'll find the **Spitzhäuschen**, a tiny building looking a bit like a giant bird's house with its narrow base topped by a much larger upper floor, which leans precariously. More such crooked gems line Römerstrasse and its side streets. Also take a look inside the 14th-century **St Michael's Church**, whose tower – ringed by a crown of eight smaller turrets – was originally part of the fortification wall.

Kues, across the bridge, is the birthplace of Nicolaus Cusanus (1401-64), a theologian (he died as general vicar of Rome) and one of the first German humanists to suggest that the earth was not at the centre of the universe. He built the town a hospice for exactly 33 men (one for every year of Christ's life) above the age of 50. The library has precious manuscripts from as far back as the 9th century and can be visited on a guided tour (Tuesday at 10.30 am, Friday at 3 pm; DM5). Always accessible is the little chapel, whose altarpiece of the Crucifixion was commissioned by Cusanus himself. He is depicted kneeling with his brother John, while his sister Clara represents Mary Magdalene clutching the cross. To learn more about the man, visit his birthplace at Nikolausufer 49 (closed Monday).

For bike excursions around Bernkastel-Kues, you can rent a bike at Fun-Bike Team (☎ 940 24) at Schanzstrasse 22. From early May to mid-October, the Gebrüder Kolb Line (☎ 471 9) runs boat trips to Trier every Tuesday and one-hour panorama tours several times daily. In addition, the Hans Michels Schiffahrt Line (☎ 689 7) offers trips to/from Traben-Trarbach several times daily in season (DM12, return DM19).

Places to Stay & Eat The *Campingplatz Kueser Werth* (☎ 820 0) is 1km upriver from the bridge on the left bank and has pleasant tent sites by the river.

The *DJH hostel* (☎ 239 5) is at Jugendherbergsstrasse 1 above the ruined Landshut castle and charges DM20.50 for bed & breakfast, plus DM5 for sheets.

The small *Haus Waldkönig* (☎ 636 9), at Brüningstrasse 35 in Kues, offers singles/doubles with shower and toilet for only DM35/70.

In Bernkastel, *Hotel Behrens* (☎ 608 8), Schanzstrasse 9, charges from DM45/70.

You'll find plenty of cosy eateries around the Markt in Bernkastel. For something more up-to-date, try *Eulenspiegel* at Moselstrasse 7, which has lighter versions of German cuisine and good salads too.

Bars with a young flair are *Blue Heaven* at Gestade 3 and *Sammy's Keller* across the bridge in Kues.

Traben-Trarbach

- *pop 5800*
- *area code* ☎ 06541

Those seeking relief from the 'romantic-half-timbered-town' circuit will welcome this smart double town, dramatically straddling the river in the middle of one its loops. Art Nouveau (known as Jugendstil in Germany) is the architectural style that characterises Traben-Trarbach, and several grand old villas contribute to its provincial sophistication. It was the trading – and not the production – of wine that brought wealth to this town. At one time, Traben-Trarbach was the second-largest trading centre in Europe after Bordeaux. Beneath the street surface lies a huge network of cellars where the wine was stored.

Traben, on the left bank, is the commercial centre and was joined to Trarbach in 1904. The train station (with service to Bullay via the Moselweinbahn) is in Traben as well. It's a five-minute walk south on Bahnstrasse to the centre and the tourist office (☎ 839 80; fax 839 83 9) at Bahnstrasse 22. It's open on weekdays from 8 am to 5 pm (closed at lunchtime in winter). From May to October, it's also open on Saturday from 1 to 4 pm. Most banks here change money, including the Deutsche Bank at Bahnstrasse 38 and the Kreissparkasse at No 41 in Traben. The post office is on Poststrasse in Traben.

Things to See Architecture fans will delight in touring Traben-Trarbach in search of its fanciful **Art Nouveau villas**, which it actually owes to two fires (1857 and 1879) that destroyed most of the older buildings. Several of the prosperous wine merchants chose to employ the Berlin architect Bruno Möhring, who was already in town to build a bridge across the Moselle. The bridge itself was destroyed in WWII and replaced by the current steel monstrosity, but the **Brückentor**, on the Trarbach side, survived. This sturdy gateway with its two towers and ornamentation is actually more representative of the style of Historicism, which flourished in the late 19th century, than it is of Art Nouveau.

One of the best preserved and purest Art Nouveau villas is the **Hotel Bellevue** (1903) on the Moselpromenade, whose distinctive exterior incorporates an oriel with a slate-covered turret shaped like a champagne bottle. The dark oak lobby is bathed in muted light from stained-glass windows. The stylish restaurant has a slightly vaulted ceiling and walls decorated with stencilled friezes.

Unfortunately, the Hotel Bellevue is the only Art Nouveau house accessible to the public, since all the other villas are privately owned. But they are still worth admiring from the outside, especially **Haus Adolph Huesgen** (1904) at Am Bahnhof 20 and **Haus Breucker** (1905) at An der Mosel 7.

Of the surviving pre-19th century buildings, the baroque **Haus Böcking** in Enkircher Strasse in Trarbach deserves special mention. Its former owners once hosted Goethe, whose journey down the Moselle was unfortunately interrupted when his boat capsized. It now houses the **Mittelmoselmuseum** (open from 9.30 am to noon and 1.30 to 5 pm, weekends to 11.30 am, but closed on Monday; entry DM3, discount DM1), a local history museum whose exhibits also shed light on Traben-Trarbach's two ruined castles, the Grevenburg and Mont Royal.

High above the craggy hillside of Trarbach is the medieval **Grevenburg**, reached from the Markt via a steep footpath. Because of its strategic importance, the castle was destroyed 13 times between 1620 and 1734 by various enemy troops before being razed by the French in 1735.

Under King Louis XIV the French were also the architects of the giant **Mont Royal** fortress, built in 1697 on a high plateau on the left bank as a base from which to secure and expand France's power over the Rhineland. Little remains of the giant structure today, but it offers good views over the river valley.

Activities Traben-Trarbach is also a spa town with hot mineral springs in the suburb of Bad Wildstein. You can experience these soothing waters at the Moseltherme, a state-of-the-art pool on Wildsteiner Weg, complete with sauna, indoor and outdoor pools and Jacuzzis. Day passes to both the pool and sauna are DM21, though you can spend as little as DM7 for one hour in the pool only.

Though Traben-Trarbach is not a major wine-growing area, the tourist office has tastings and cellar tours with different vintners every weekday at 7 pm (DM8). Pick up a schedule at their offices. Guided tours through the vineyards are held every Thursday and Saturday.

If you want to rent a bicycle, you can do so at Zweirad-Wagner (☎ 164 9) at Alte Marktstrasse 4 in Traben; staff can also help with repairs. For information on boat trips, see the Bernkastel-Kues section.

Places to Stay & Eat For campers, there's the *Campingplatz Rissbach* (☎ 311 1; open April to mid-October) at Rissbacher Strasse 170. Beds at the newly modernised *DJH hostel* (☎ 927 8) at Hirtenpfad in Traben cost DM25.10 in four-bed rooms and DM31.20 in doubles, sheets and breakfast included (to get there take bus No 6206 to Schulzentrum, or it's a 20-minute uphill walk from the train station).

The tourist office operates an efficient room-reservation service at no charge. If it's closed, you should find a list of vacancies posted on the door. For those on tighter budgets, there's the *Altstadt Café* (☎ 460 5), at Mittelstrasse 12 in Trarbach, which charges DM45/80 for singles/doubles with private bath. If you're going to splurge, spend the money on the Art Nouveau *Hotel Bellevue* (☎ 703 0; fax 703 40 0). Attention to detail and quiet and friendly service make a stay here a real treat; there's a small sauna and pool. Dining in the classy gourmet restaurant is a celebration of food. All this starts at a comparatively reasonable DM100/170 for large singles/doubles with full facilities.

For a more rustic eatery, try the whimsically decorated *Alte Zunftscheune* on Neue Rathausstrasse or the *Historische Weinschänke Storcke Stütz* at Brückenstrasse 4.

Cochem

- *pop 5300*
- *area code* ☎ 02671

Cochem, about 50km upriver from Koblenz, has all the trappings of a picture-postcard German village, replete with castle, narrow alleyways, half-timbered houses and town gates. But it's almost too cute for comfort. Attracting more than its fair share of day-trippers, Cochem is best to visit out of season or in the early morning.

Cochem's train station is at the northern end of town, from where it's only a short walk down Ravenéstrasse or Moselstrasse to the centre. On your way there, you'll pass the tourist office (☎ 397 1; fax 841 0) at Ravenéstrasse 61 next to Endertplatz.

The Volksbank on the Markt changes money, as do other banks around town. On Ravenéstrasse, towards the train station, are the post office and the police station.

Things to See & Do Cochem's *pièce de résistance* is the **Reichsburg** poised atop a bluff south of town. It matches everyone's imagined version of a medieval castle, but in fact this one only dates from the last century. Although a castle has stood here since the 11th century, the original fell victim to frenzied Frenchmen during their destructive crusade brought on by the War of the Palatine Succession in 1689. The walk up to the castle takes about 15 minutes. Guided tours (mid-March to November) last 45 minutes and cost DM6, children DM3; English translation sheets are available. The view of the valley, though, is free.

For an even better view, head up to the **Pinnerkreuz** on the chair lift leaving from Endertstrasse (Easter to mid-November from 10 am to 6 pm). The trip up costs DM6.90 (DM8.90 return), and it's a nice walk back down through the vineyards.

Activities If you want to explore the area by bicycle, you can rent one at Fahrradshop Kreutz, Ravenéstrasse 42, for DM14 a day; staff also do repairs.

Many wineries offer wine tastings only to groups but will often let you join one. Every Thursday at 8 pm, tastings for individuals are held in a different vineyard (DM10); ask at the tourist office for details.

The Cochem area is also good for hiking. Ask for the 1:25,000 *Ferienland Cochem* map at the tourist office. The Gebrüder Kolb

Line runs boat trips to Traben-Trarbach between May and mid-October and also goes to Beilstein several times daily.

Places to Stay For lovely riverside camping, go to the *Campingplatz Am Freizeitszentrum* (☎ 440 9; open 10 days before Easter to the end of October) in Stadionstrasse, about 1.5km downstream on the right bank.

Cochem's *DJH hostel* (☎ 863 3) is practically on the way, at Klottener Strasse 9, with bed & breakfast costing DM20.50; sheets are an extra DM5.

The tourist office staff can help you find a room, and if it's closed, you can call ☎ 194 12 to find out about room availability.

A good budget place is *Pension Dapper* (☎ 747 1), at Moselstrasse 24 near the train station, which has basic doubles from DM54 (or from DM62 with private shower and toilet).

The *Union Hotel* (☎ 244) at Moselpromenade 16 charges DM60/120 for singles/doubles. On summer weekends and during the wine harvest (mid-September to mid-October), you can forget about finding any bargain accommodation anywhere.

Places to Eat A good sit-down fast-food choice is *Kochlöffel* on Markt where a schnitzel with salad and chips (French fries) costs only DM7.50. A few paces uphill, at Schlaufstrasse 11, is *Zum Fröhlichen Weinberg*, which offers German home-style cooking for around DM14.

Getting There & Away Trains to Cochem leave Koblenz several times every hour (DM11.80, 30 minutes).

Around Cochem

Beilstein On the right bank, about 12km upriver from Cochem, is Beilstein (population 160), a pint-sized village right out of the world of fairy tales. It consists of little more than a cluster of houses squeezed into whatever space has not been taken up by steep vineyards.

Its romantic townscape is further enhanced by the ruined **Burg Metternich**, a hill-top castle reached via a set of steps. There's little to do here but to soak in the atmosphere during a stroll through the tiny lanes, taste some wine in one of the many cellars or walk up to the castle.

One of the finest buildings is the **Zehnthauskeller** where, in the Middle Ages, wine delivered as a tithing was stored. It now houses a romantically dark vaulted wine tavern.

To get to Beilstein from Cochem, take bus No 8060 or the boat (see Activities in the Cochem section).

Burg Eltz Victor Hugo thought this castle was 'tall, terrific, strange and dark', adding

Burg Eltz, the epitome of the medieval castle, has been in the same family for 1000 years.

that he'd never seen anything like it. Indeed, Burg Eltz, hidden away in the forest above the left bank of the Moselle, epitomises to many what medieval castles should look like.

The compact and impenetrable exterior is softened by scores of little turrets crowning it like candles on a birthday cake. Eight residential towers – looming up to 45m – stand gathered around an oval courtyard.

Burg Eltz has been owned by the same family for almost 1000 years and has never been destroyed. Highlights of the often crowded guided tour include the **Flag Room** with its fan vaulted ceiling and the festive **Knights' Hall**.

The **Treasury**, which extends four floors beneath the rock, features a rich collection of jewellery, porcelain and precious weapons.

The only direct access to Eltz, about 30km from either Koblenz or Cochem, is by private vehicle via the village of Münstermaifeld; it's a 10-minute walk from the parking lot. Alternatively, take a train to the village of Moselkern (DM9.60, 30 minutes from Koblenz) and take the scenic 40-minute walk along the Elzbach stream up to the castle.

The castle is open daily between April and October from 9.30 am to 5.30 pm. Admission is DM8, discount DM5.50; entry to the treasury is an extra DM4/2.

Hunsrück Mountains

IDAR-OBERSTEIN

- *pop 36,000*
- *area code* ☎ 06781

The twin town of Idar-Oberstein lies in the Nahe river valley at the southern tip of the Hunsrück Mountains, about 80km east of Trier and about 90km north-east of Saarbrücken. Since the Middle Ages, its history and development has been inextricably linked to the gemstone trade. Records of local agate mines go back to 1454, but the industry really took off after a bunch of adventurers left Idar-Oberstein for South America in the early 19th century. There they harvested raw stones as if they were potatoes, then sent them back home to be processed.

Idar-Oberstein soon evolved into Germany's gem-cutting and jewellery manufacturing centre – and remains so to this day. The world's first combined jewellery and gemstone exchange opened here in 1974.

About one million day-trippers swamp the town of 36,000 annually, drawn by mines, museums and the minerals sold in countless shops (open seven days a week in high season). All this attention is well deserved, however, for Idar-Oberstein offers a range of sights unique in Germany and, in some cases, even Europe.

Orientation & Information

Idar-Oberstein is a collection of communities spread out along the Nahe River for about 20km (you won't see much of the river, though, since it's been built over). The main centre is in Oberstein, where the train station is located. The Markt is about 500m east of here. Bus Nos 1, 2, 3 and 4 regularly shuttle between Oberstein and Idar.

The tourist office (☎ 644 21; fax 644 25) is at Georg-Maus-Strasse 2, about 300m north of the train station, and is open weekdays from 9 am to 5 pm, plus Saturdays from 9.30 am to 1 pm between May and October.

The Kreissparkasse on the Markt in Oberstein changes money and has a special counter open on weekends. The post office in Oberstein is at Hauptstrasse 34, about 200m north-west of the tourist office. The post office in Idar is inside the gemstone exchange building on Schleiferplatz.

Things to See

Not surprisingly, most of Idar-Oberstein's attractions involve gemstones. Though not all of them are right in the city centre, they are easily reached by car or bus.

West of Idar are the **Edelsteinminen Steinkaulenberg** (open daily from 9 am to 5 pm between mid-March and mid-November; guided tours DM7, discount DM4), the only gemstone mines in Europe open to visitors (take bus No 3 to Strassburgkaserne from the train station). Agates were still mined in this glittering underground world until 1870, but nowadays only hobby mineralogists dig for treasure in a designated 'miner's tunnel'.

For DM25 (discount DM10), you can keep whatever gemstones you unearth during three hours of digging. Finds are guaranteed.

For a close-up look at how gemstones were traditionally processed, visit the **Weiherschleife** (open daily from 9 am to 5 pm; admission DM5, discount DM2.50), a 17th-century cutting mill on Tiefensteiner Strasse (take bus No 1 from the train station to Weiherschleife). Lying belly-down atop tilting benches in front of water-driven wheels, the cutters demonstrate the stages of sawing, grinding, sanding and polishing. This is a tortuous process and in the old days, the lives of cutters were horrifyingly short.

The 9000 objects on display at the **Deutsches Edelsteinmuseum** (open daily from 9 am to 6 pm, in winter to 5 pm; DM8, discount DM6) should dazzle even the most, well, jaded of visitors. Housed in a lovely turn-of-the-century villa at Hauptstrasse 118 in Idar, the museum showcases a full catalogue of the world's gemstones, first in a raw state, then as a jewel. There's a 12.555 carat topaz from Brazil and copies of the famous Hope and Koh-i-Nor diamonds. Interesting too are the local agates that have been used as currency in parts of Africa since the 19th century. The top floor features jewellery and stunningly engraved stones. Take bus No 1, 2 or 3 to the Börse stop.

The **Museum Idar-Oberstein** (open daily from 9.30 am to 5.30 pm; DM5, discount DM1.50), on the Markt in Oberstein, is essentially a local history museum, which here means a focus on gemstones. It has an important collection of crystals and quartz, including the largest ever imported to Europe.

Right above the museum, and reached via 230 steps, is Idar-Oberstein's major non-gemstone-related attraction, the landmark 15th-century **Felsenkirche** (open from 10 am to 6 pm from April to October; DM3, discount DM1). Legend has it that this medieval chapel, wedged into a stark cliff, was built by a knight inhabiting the castle above the church to atone for killing his brother over a woman. Inside there's a steadily trickling well and an impressive altarpiece by a master from the School of Mainz. From the castle remains above, there's a great view over the valley.

Places to Stay & Eat

All places mentioned in this section are in Oberstein.

The smallish *Campingplatz Im Staden* (☎ 318 21; open April to October) is in the suburb of Tiefenstein and charges DM5 per person, DM2 per car and DM2 per tent.

Idar-Oberstein's modernised *DJH hostel* (☎ 243 66) is at Alte Treibe 23 in the hills above Oberstein and charges DM25.10 per person in four-bed rooms and DM31.20 in double rooms (including private bath, breakfast and sheets). From the train station, take bus No 5 to the Café Weber stop or walk for 15 minutes. An alternative is the *Naturfreundehaus* (☎ 224 50) next door, which charges DM28.80 per bed in doubles with shared bath, including breakfast.

The tourist office has a free hotel reservation service. One of the cheapest options is *Pension Trarbach* (☎ 256 77) at Wüstlautenbach 11, about a five-minute walk from the train station, where singles/doubles with shared facilities cost DM28/50 (DM31/70 with private bath). *Gasthaus Homericher Hof* (☎ 241 13), Homerich 38-40, charges a reasonable DM42/77 per night in rooms with shower and WC. More up-market is the *Edelstein Hotel* (☎ 230 58; fax 264 41), Hauptstrasse 302, where rooms are DM90/135.

Unless you're a vegetarian, you shouldn't leave Idar-Oberstein without trying the local speciality, the Spiessbraten. This is a giant hunk of beef or pork, marinated in raw onion, salt and pepper, then grilled over a beechwood fire, which gives it its characteristic spicy and smoky taste. A good place to try this dish is at *Restaurant Kammerhof* (closed Tuesday) on In der Kammer. For lighter, meatless fare, go to *Café Extrablatt* (closed Monday night) at Kirchweg 1.

Getting There & Away

Idar-Oberstein has direct train links to Saarbrücken (DM18.80, one hour) and to Mainz (DM23.20, 1¼ hours) at least once an hour. There are also direct trains to Frankfurt (DM34, two hours) every two hours.

Regional bus No 6440 leaves for Trier from the train station. The B41 and the B422 cross in Idar-Oberstein.

Saarland

Excluding the city-states of Berlin, Hamburg and Bremen, the Saarland is Germany's smallest state, covering a mere 2570 sq km. Yet this little piece of land has been hotly contested throughout its long history.

Already settled in Celtic and Roman times, the region was periodically governed by France throughout the Middle Ages. After Napoleon's defeat at Waterloo in 1815, it was divided by Prussia and Bavaria, both of whom coveted the area for its rich pockets of coal to fuel the burgeoning German economy. Under the Treaty of Versailles following WWI, Germany lost the Saarland, and it became an independent territory administered by the League of Nations under French guidance. In a referendum held in 1935, however, some 90% of all voters decided in favour of rejoining Germany. History repeated itself after WWII: the Saarland again became an autonomous region under French administration until another plebiscite in 1955 returned it to Germany. The Saarland has been a German *Land* since 1957.

With the steady decline of coal mining and steel production since the 1960s, the Saarland became one of the poorest and most depressed regions in western Germany. Restructuring began late – in the 1980s – and is still under way, with high-tech and service industries now making up for some of the jobs lost. The state's scenery and its historical sights are assets that have been largely untapped, and the tourism industry is still in its infancy. This means that you won't find the same kind of infrastructure that you will along the Moselle, for instance, or in the alpine regions. On the other hand, you will find lots of natural beauty and a people unspoiled by the commercial trappings of mass tourism.

HIGHLIGHTS

- A visit to the monstrous Völklinger Hütte ironworks
- A cruise along the Saarschleife river loop

- **Population:** 1.1m • **Capital:** Saarbrücken
- **Area:** 2570 sq km

Saarland Luminary: Erich Honecker

SAARBRÜCKEN

- *pop 200,000*
- *area code* ☎ 0681

Saarbrücken is the state capital of the Saarland and, though probably not tops on anybody's travel itinerary, it has a couple of museums and architectural sights worth exploring. It's also a good base from which to venture out to some of the other attractions in the Saarland. About 90% of the city was flattened in WWII and, in general, reconstruction has not been flattering. The proximity of smoking steel mills doesn't add much to its charm either.

But Saarbrücken can hardly be called an industrial wasteland, as the entire city has been, and still is, undergoing a major facelift. Vestiges of Saarbrücken's 18th-century heyday under Prince Wilhelm Heinrich (1718-1768) survive in the baroque buildings designed by his court architect, Friedrich Joachim Stengel. Foodies will also find a trip to Saarbrücken rewarding – there are many atmospheric and well priced places in the historical centre around St Johanner Markt.

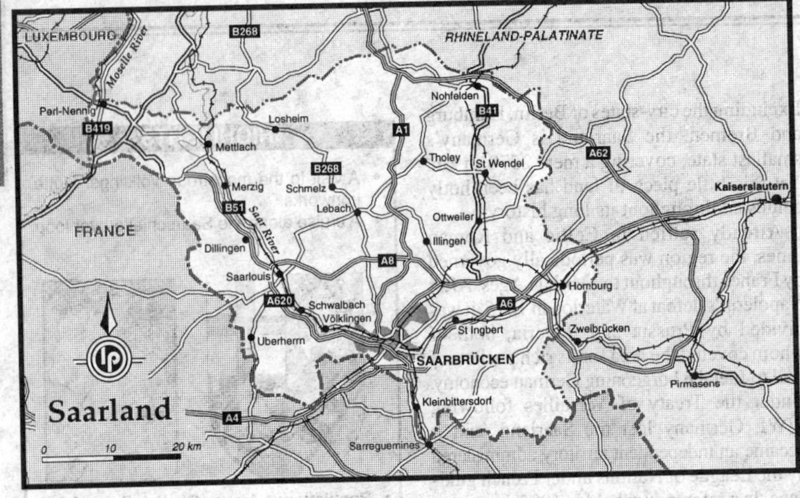

Orientation

Saarbrücken's centre is fairly compact. It's bisected by the Saar River, which runs north-west to south-east, parallel to the A620, the main artery through the Saarland. The train station is at the north-western end of the centre on St Johanner Strasse. From here it's about a 15-minute walk south-east to St Johanner Markt.

Information

Tourist Offices The main tourist office (☎ 369 01; fax 390 35 3) is at Grossherzog-Friedrich-Strasse 1 and is open weekdays from 7.45 am to 5 pm. More convenient is the branch office (☎ 365 15; fax 905 33 00) outside the Hauptbahnhof (turn left as you exit), open weekdays from 9 am to 6 pm and Saturday to 3 pm. Available here and in pubs and restaurants around town is *Kakadu*, the free monthly entertainment guide.

Money The Reisebank inside the Hauptbahnhof exchanges currency and travellers' cheques and is open weekdays from 7 am to 7.45 pm, Saturday from 8 am to 4 pm and Sunday from 9 am to 3 pm. In the foyer is an ATM that takes all major credit cards.

Post & Communications The main post office is at the Hauptbahnhof; there's another one in the city centre on the corner of Dudweilerstrasse and Kaiserstrasse.

Laundry The Waschcenter at Beethovenplatz 7 is open from 8 am to 10 pm daily and charges DM7 for a small load, DM15 for a large load and DM2 for the dryer.

Emergency There's a police station on the corner of Karcherstrasse and Beethovenstrasse.

Walking Tours

Northern Saar Bank Start your tour at the Hauptbahnhof. Just opposite is the **Saar-Galerie**, a huge, modern indoor shopping mall. Just east (left) of it begins Bahnhofstrasse, which was recently pedestrianised and is lined by department and chain stores. Continue for about 600m to Betzenstrasse where, on the left, you can make out the cathedral-like **Rathaus** (1900). It's an imposing neo-Gothic red-brick pile by the architect Georg Hauberisser, who also built the town halls in Munich and Wiesbaden.

Continuing on Bahnhofstrasse you will

soon reach **St Johanner Markt** which, along with its many alleyways and side lanes, forms Saarbrücken's historical core. In the centre of the square is the **Grosse Marktbrunnen**, a fountain designed by Stengel with a filigreed wrought-iron balustrade; from its centre rises an ornamented obelisk crowned by a vase. The oldest houses are those at Nos 8 and 49 with windows from the late Gothic and early Renaissance periods.

The row of houses at Nos 18-28 dates to the baroque era. No 24 houses the **Stadtgalerie** (open Tuesday to Sunday from 10 am to 7 pm; free entry), which showcases cutting-edge contemporary art, including video and performance art. Farther on you reach Türkenstrasse, from where you can make a short detour north for a look at **St Johannes Basilica**, another Stengel work.

Head back south on Türkenstrasse, then turn left (east) into Bismarckstrasse; at No 11-19 you'll find **The Saarland Museum** (open from 10 am to 6 pm, Wednesday from noon to 8 pm, closed Monday; DM3, discount DM1.50). The main building houses the **Moderne Galerie**, whose permanent collection includes some nice works by German impressionists such as Slevogt, Corinth and Liebermann. There's also French 19th and 20th-century art, and sculptures by artists like Richard Serra and Sigmar Polke.

In the building opposite at Karlstrasse 1 is the **Alte Sammlung** (same hours and prices) with almost a millennium's worth of paintings, porcelain, tapestries and sculptures from south-west Germany and the Alsace-Lorraine region of France. There are often special exhibits in either gallery (different prices apply).

Head west on Bismarckstrasse to the **Staatstheater** (☎ 322 04 for information and tickets), a grandiose yellow structure inspired by neoclassicism – a good example of the pompous architecture in vogue during the Third Reich. The theatre opened in 1938 with Richard Wagner's *The Flying Dutchman*.

Today's ensemble stages opera, ballet, musicals and drama (from classic to absurd). Just north of here is the **Alte Brücke**, a stone bridge that has connected the Saar's banks since 1546.

Southern Saar Bank Cross the Saar on Alte Brücke and head up to the **Saarbrücker Schloss**, which has risen from the ashes more times than a flock of phoenixes. The current incarnation dates back to 1810 and is a relatively plain, neoclassical U-shaped structure dominating the spacious Schlossplatz. The modern glass tower in the middle section was designed by Gottfried Böhm and put in place in 1989. Today, the palace houses administrative offices and sections of the **Historisches Saarmuseum** (open from 10 am to 6 pm, closed Monday; DM5, discount DM3) in the basement of the right wing; there's more in the adjacent modern building. The museum documents the history of the Saarland with themed sections on WWI, the Third Reich and post-WWII reconstruction.

Also on Schlossplatz, at No 16, is the **Museum für Vor- und Frühgeschichte** (Museum of Early History and Prehistory), open Tuesday and Thursday to Saturday from 9 am to 5 pm, Wednesday from noon to 8 pm and Sunday from 10 am to 6 pm; free entry.

Opposite the Schloss is the **Alte Rathaus**, originally built by Stengel in 1750 but simplified after WWII. Inside is the **Abenteuer Museum** (open Tuesday and Wednesday from 9 am to 1 pm, Thursday and Friday from 3 to 7 pm and Saturday from 10 am to 2 pm; DM3), with a peculiar assortment of ethnic masks, sculptures and the like collected by Heinz Rox-Schulz on his solitary expeditions to Asia, Africa, South America and New Guinea. There's a panoramic view of the river and town from atop the wall to the east of the palace.

From the Schloss, head west along Schlossstrasse to Eisenbahnstrasse and the impressive **Ludwigskirche** (1775), Stengel's crowning achievement. The festive sandstone structure dominates the generously sized Ludwigsplatz, lined with a collection of late-baroque town houses. Its main façade features a railing festooned with figures from the Old and New Testaments. As you enter, you may experience acute whiteout, for the entire interior is bathed in a pure, brilliant white – from the walls to the floor to the pews. A huge organ sits on a balcony above the main altar. The church has erratic opening hours but you can usually get at least a glimpse through the glass doorway.

Cruises

Saarbrücker Personenschiffahrt (☎ 340 84) runs three-hour boat trips from the landing near the Staatstheater, but don't expect too much in the way of scenery. It costs DM22 and includes a cup of coffee and a piece of cake. Every second Saturday, from May to early September, boats travel across the border to Sarreguemines in France (DM20, return DM26), sometimes also on market days.

Places to Stay

Camping The *Campingplatz Saarbrücken* (☎ 517 80), open April to September, is at Am Spicherer Berg near the Deutsch-Französischer Garten south of the city centre. The nearest bus stop is Goldene Bremm, reached on bus Nos 11 and 19. There's also *Campingplatz Kanuwanderer* (☎ 792 92 1; open year round) at Mett- lacher Strasse 13 (no bus service).

Hostel Saarbrücken's DJH *Jugendgästehaus* (☎ 330 40) is at Meerwiesertalweg 31 near the university in the north-east of town (take bus No 49 from the train station or bus No 19 from Beethovenplatz near the Rathaus to Prinzenweiher). A place in a two-bed room costs DM35.50, in a four-bed room DM26, including private shower and WC, breakfast and sheets.

Hotels The tourist office offers a free room-reservation service, but prices are relatively high because most hotels cater for business travellers.

One of the cheapest places is *Hotel Zur Klause* (☎ 582 22 5) which has singles/doubles with shower and WC for DM60/100 but is about 1.2km east of the centre at Deutschherrnstrasse 72. Near the train station, at Ursulinenstrasse 57, is *Hotel Drei Kronen* (☎ 360 32), which has rooms with shower but no toilet for DM65/95. Also in the heart of the city, at Cecilienstrasse 5, is *Hotel Madeleine* (☎ 322 28; fax 374 70 4), where rooms with private bath cost DM95/120.

The small and rustic *Hotel Im Fuchs* (☎ 936 55 0; fax 936 55 36), Kappenstrasse 12, charges DM98/138 for rooms with private facilities.

The *City-Hotel* (☎ 340 88; fax 320 35) at Richard-Wagner-Strasse 67 is funky and old-fashioned, with large rooms and friendly service. Singles/doubles with full bath cost DM115/150.

Places to Eat

Saarbrücken has an active and attractive restaurant and bar scene that centres on St Johanner Markt. Here you will find the immensely popular *Stiefelbräu* (enter from Froschgasse), where you can enjoy the house brew and regional specialities at pub prices. If you want more refined – and pricier – fare, go next door to the affiliated *Gasthaus Zum Stiefel*, the oldest restaurant in town.

At St Johanner Markt 17 is *Hauck, Das Weinhaus* where you can enjoy just a glass of fine wine or choose from a smallish selection of wonderfully imaginative salads, soups and seasonal dishes. It's often filled with theatregoers after the curtain has come down.

Inside the Stadtgalerie at St Johanner Markt 24 is the *Kulturcafé*, a stylish chrome-and-metal establishment with huge picture windows, large cups of coffee and an assortment of cakes.

North of the Rathaus at Johannisstrasse 17 is *Auflauf*, where you choose from the menu or create your own casserole from a selection of 20 ingredients. Small portions cost around DM14, large ones DM18.

La Carotte (closed Sunday), on the 1st floor of Karcherstrasse 15, specialises in vegetarian food, with snacks and salads from DM5. Daily specials are around DM12.50.

Getting There & Away

Bus The central bus station for local and regional buses is on Bahnhofsplatz outside the train station. Bus No 40 takes you right to the Völklinger Hütte (see the following section), though the train is faster and more frequent.

Train Saarbrücken has at least once-hourly connections with Trier (DM21.20, one hour), Idar-Oberstein (DM18.80, one hour), Mainz (DM44, two hours) and Karlsruhe (DM45, three hours). Regional services to Völklingen (DM4.60, 10 minutes) and Homburg (DM9.60, 30 minutes) leave about every half hour. IC trains to Frankfurt (DM58, two hours) and Dresden (DM183, eight hours) depart every two hours.

Car & Motorcycle Saarbrücken is bisected by the A620 leading north along the Saar to Merzig. It's also served by the A6 from Kaiserslautern and the A1 from the Moselle Valley. The B40 and B51 also cross the city.

Ride Services The Mitfahrzentrale (☎ 194 40) has an office at Grossherzog-Friedrich-Strasse 59.

Getting Around

Public Transport Saartal-Linien (☎ 500 33 44) operates the buses for the city and surrounding area, which is divided into three zones. Most likely you'll only need the DM1.50 ticket, which is good for any four consecutive stops, or the DM2.50 ticket, valid in the entire city area. Note that tickets cost DM0.50 more if you buy them from the driver instead of the machines at each stop. The four-block tickets for DM6/10 require validation. Good value is the 24-hour card which costs DM7 for the city or DM10 for the entire region. It's also available for families with children, under the name *City-Familien Karte* or *Regio-Familien-Karte* (same prices). If you validate this pass after 5 pm on Friday, you can use it for the entire weekend.

Car & Motorcycle Rent an Oldie (☎ 614 02) is an alternative car-rental agency where you can get away with DM49 a day for a small used car with 400km included free. Their weekend rate is DM99 and good from Friday at 1 pm to Monday at 9 am.

Taxi You can book a taxi on ☎ 330 33.

Bicycle Bicycles may be rented from Der Fahrradladen (☎ 370 98) at Nauwieserstrasse 19; they charge from DM10 a day for five-gear touring bikes and DM15 for 21-gear mountain bikes. There's a DM50 deposit.

VÖLKLINGER HÜTTE

About 10km down the Saar is the former Völklingen ironworks, one of Europe's great industrial monuments and a highlight of any visit to the Saarland. When it was founded in 1873, the Völklinger Hütte was among the last ironworks to be erected in Western Europe. Having survived the ravages of war, it fell into disuse as German manufacturing tapered off, was finally closed in 1986 and succumbed to rust and corrosion: an abandoned set from a version of *Metropolis* that was never filmed.

Today it exists as a testament to the Machine Age; its vast blast furnaces and the smelting houses that once spewed molten iron are now ice cold. Yet it has dignity, this industrial cathedral, and its sheer immensity will have some people exclaiming, 'My God – *people* built this?'. So that future generations might understand the world of its time, the Völklinger Hütte was placed on UNESCO's World Heritage List in 1994.

The only way to see the plant is to take its two-hour guided tour, offered daily except Monday from March to November at 10 am and 2 pm (DM6, discount DM4).

Völklingen is reached every 30 minutes by train from Saarbrücken. Völklinger Hütte is a short walk from the train station.

HOMBURG

- *pop 44,000*
- *area code* ☎ 06841

About 35km north-east of Saarbrücken, in the gentle forested valleys of the Saarland-Palatinate, is this placid country town with a small student population from The Saarland University's School of Medicine.

Looking out over the town is the Schlossberg where you'll find one of Homburg's main attractions, the **Schlossberghöhlen** caves, open from 9 am to noon and 1 to 5 pm but closed mid-December to early January (DM5, discount DM3). The interior of the mountain has been hollowed out over six centuries, resulting in an amazing network of coloured sandstone caverns and tunnels that is purported to be the largest in Europe. Their original purpose was to provide an escape route and emergency supply channel for Hohenburg Castle, a fortress built atop the Schlossberg in the 12th century. Later they were used as ammunition magazines, as military barracks and, in WWII, as an air-raid shelter. Three of the 12 levels are accessible.

To get to the caves by foot, take the trail marked 'Zu den Höhlen' from the Markt in Homburg. If you're driving, take the Schlossberghöhenstrasse to the top, from where it's a short walk back downhill to the entrance.

While you're in Homburg, it's also worth stopping by the **Römermuseum** (Roman Museum; open from 9 am to 6 pm, closed Monday, in winter open only on weekends from 10 am to 4.30 pm; DM5, discount DM4) in the suburb of Schwarzenacker. The Romans settled here between the 2nd and 3rd centuries AD. Some of their ruined houses and streets have been excavated and reconstructed, including a tavern and a house that supposedly belonged to an eye doctor. It still has a functioning under-floor heating system; the skeleton of a Roman dog, who died trapped inside the ducts, lies here too.

Homburg's tourist office (☎ 206 6) is in the Rathaus, Am Forum, and can help with finding accommodation. A pretty basic *DJH hostel* (☎ 367 9) at Sickinger Strasse 12 charges DM19.50 per bed & breakfast.

Homburg is easily reached in half an hour by trains leaving from Saarbrücken every 30 minutes (DM9.60). There are also frequent direct connections from Neustadt on the German Wine Road in Rhineland-Palatinate (DM15.60, one hour). If you're driving, take the Homburg exit off the A6 (Mannheim-Saarbrücken).

METTLACH

- *pop 11,500*
- *area code* ☎ 06864

Mettlach, about 30km downriver from Saarbrücken, was founded around 690 AD by the Merovingian Duke Luitwin, who served as bishop of Trier from 692 to 705. His bones lie buried in the octagonal **Alter Turm** (old tower), built around 990. Nearby is the former **Benediktiner Abtei** (Benedictine abbey), a baroque structure from the 18th century. The building was later sold to a paper manufacturer before being acquired by Johann Franz Boch-Buschmann, who turned it into a porcelain factory that is now known as Villeroy & Boch. The abbey houses the company headquarters and a fairly commercial, if interesting, multimedia exhibit on their products called *Keravision* (open weekdays from 9 am to noon and 2 to 5 pm, Saturday from 10 am to 1 pm; free entry). The historical porcelain collection is in Schloss Ziegelberg, also in Mettlach (open from 10 am to 1 pm and 2 to 5 pm, closed Monday, and in winter also on Sunday; DM3, discount DM1.50).

The most scenic spot along the Saar River is the **Saarschleife**, where the river makes a spectacular hairpin loop. It's in the community of Orschholz, located in a large nature park about 5km west of Mettlach (bus No 6300). The best viewing point is in Cloef, just a short walk through the forest from the village. Just look for signs saying Cloef or ask for directions. If you want to experience the loop from a boat, you can take a 1½ hour tour (DM11) offered by Saar-Personenschiffahrt (☎ 06581-991 88) on Tuesday and Wednesday at 11 am, 2 and 4 pm and on Thursday and Saturday at 11 am and 2 pm. Boats leave from the docks in Mettlach/ Schleusung.

Mettlach's tourist office (☎ 833 4; fax 832 9) is at Freiherr-vom-Stein-Strasse 64. A *DJH hostel* (☎ 270) in the community of Dreisbach charges DM19.50 per person for bed & breakfast.

Mettlach is on the Trier-Saarbrücken rail line, with services in either direction at least once an hour (DM11.80, 45 minutes in either direction).

By road, take the Merzig-Schwemlingen exit off the A8 (Saarbrücken-Luxembourg) and then follow the B51 north.

PERL-NENNIG

- *pop 6350*
- *area code* ☎ 06866

Right on the border with Luxembourg, about 15km west of Mettlach and 40km south of Trier, is Perl-Nennig. It is the Saarland's only wine-growing community and specialises in burgundies. On weekends between April and October, the wine growers open up their cellars for tastings on a rotating basis.

Perl-Nennig's real claim to fame, though, is the stunning, 160-sq-m **floor mosaic** in a 3rd-century reconstructed **Roman villa**. Composed of three million tiny chips of coloured stone, it is the largest and best preserved such mosaic north of the Alps and shows scenes from a performance at an amphitheatre. A farmer discovered it while digging in his garden in 1852. Between April and September, the villa is open from 8.30 am to noon and from 1 to 6 pm, closed Monday. The rest of the year (except December, when it's closed) afternoon closing hours are at 3.30 or 4.30 pm. Admission is DM1, discount DM0.50.

Perl-Nennig's tourist office (☎ 143 9) on Bübinger Strasse has information on the villa, wine tastings and accommodation. *Moselcamping Dreiländereck* (☎ 322; open mid-March to mid-October) is at Sinzer Strasse 1.

Perl-Nennig can be reached from Mettlach by bus No 6300. It also makes for an easy excursion from Trier, from where it is served by train at least every two hours (get off at Nennig; DM9.60, 50 minutes).

If you're coming from Saarbrücken, you also must change in Trier. Drivers can take the A8 from Saarbrücken or the B419 from Trier.

Hesse

HESSE

The Hessians, a Frankish tribe, were among the first people to convert to Lutheranism in the early 16th century. Apart from a brief period of unity in that century under Philip the Magnanimous, Hesse (Hessen) remained a motley collection of principalities and, later, of Prussian administrative districts until it was made a state in 1945. Its main cities are Frankfurt, the capital Wiesbaden and Kassel.

Frankfurt is Germany's most important transport hub but it can also be used as a base from which to explore some of the smaller towns in Hesse – those that remind you that you're still in Germany.

Wilhelm and Jakob Grimm were born in Hesse and while they lived in Kassel they began compiling fairy tales. *Grimm's Fairy Tales* is now available in almost 200 languages and is read to children all over the world.

HIGHLIGHTS

- Ebbelwei (apple wine) and Handkäse mit Musik ('hand-cheese with music') and, oh yes, Frankfurt's Museum Mile
- Steffi Graf's tennis shoes at the Shoe Museum in Offenbach
- Wilhelmshöhe Park in Kassel
- Elisabethkirche, Germany's first Gothic cathedral, in Marburg
- Wiesbaden's cable car up the Neroberg
- Hessian stops on the Fairy-Tale Road

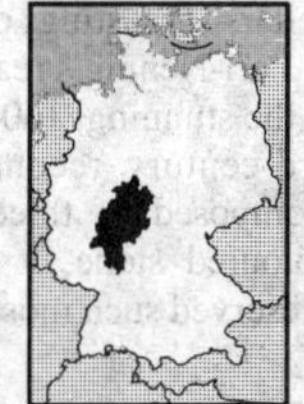

• **Population:** 6m • **Capital:** Wiesbaden
• **Area:** 21,114 sq km

Hesse Luminaries: Georg Büchner, Anne Frank, Johann Wolfgang von Goethe, Wilhelm & Jakob Grimm, HJC von Grimmelshausen, Paul Hindemith, Heinrich Hoffmann, the Rothschilds, August Weismann

FRANKFURT-AM-MAIN

- *pop 650,000*
- *area code* ☎ 069

They call it 'Bankfurt' and 'Krankfurt' and 'Mainhattan' and more. Skyscraper-packed Frankfurt-on-the-Main (pronounced 'mine') is the financial and geographical centre of western Germany and plays host to some important trade fairs, including the world's largest book, consumer-goods and musical-instrument markets.

If you're not here for a trade fair, you're probably here because of air, train and road connections. Everybody, but *everybody*, changes planes in Frankfurt at some time or another.

Frankfurt produces a disproportionately large part of Germany's wealth. It is home to the most important stock exchange in the country, the Bundesbank (Germany's central bank) and the European Monetary Institute, which will become the central bank for countries in the European Monetary Union. The Rothschilds – the wealthy side of the family anyway – hail from here.

A large part of the city's taxes are devoted to the arts though the percentage has been reduced since the highs of the 1980s; in Frankfurt you'll find some of the richest museums in the country.

Frankfurt isn't representative of Germany any more than New York is of the USA, so if you only have a few days you'll do better heading off to more traditional German destinations. If you have some time to explore, though, don't be surprised if you find this cosmopolitan melting pot more interesting – and a lot more fun – than you had expected.

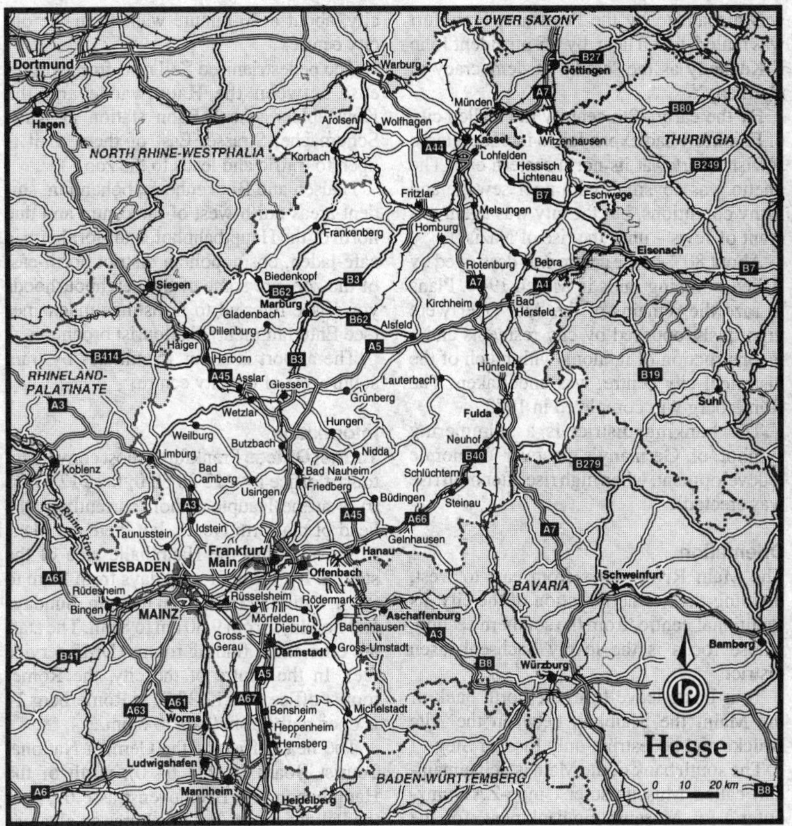

History

The first official mention of Frankfurt was in a document signed by Charlemagne in 794, which granted the town to the convent at St Emmeram – though by then it had been long established as a trading centre. Later, Frankfurt held a place of power in the Holy Roman Empire of Germany.

As its market flourished, so did its importance as a trade city; by the 12th century the 'Frankfurt Fair' attracted business from the Mediterranean to the Baltic.

From the election of Frederick I (Barbarossa) in 1152, Frankfurt became the site of the election and coronation of all German kings.

Throughout the history of the city and its market, Jews were invited to participate and then killed or driven out in pogroms. Frankfurt was among the first cities to convert to Protestantism.

The last German emperor was elected in 1792 and by the time the Holy Roman Empire collapsed in 1806 the region was under French control.

It was in Frankfurt in 1848 that Germany's first-ever parliamentary delegation met at St-Pauls-Kirche. Though that parliament was disbanded by the Prussians, Frankfurt was hailed, much later, by US president John F Kennedy as the 'cradle of democracy in Germany'.

By the early 20th century the walled city of Frankfurt had expanded to include a large Jewish quarter at its north-eastern end. The ghetto was abysmal, with poor sewage and filthy conditions, but the city was again tolerant of Jews – until the rise of Nazism.

About 80% of the centre was destroyed by Allied bombing raids in March 1944. Plans to raze the remains of the Alte Oper were vigorously opposed by city residents and a reconstruction of it, along with much of the historical city centre, was undertaken. The Römerberg was completed in 1983.

The banking district is a shimmering symbol of Germany's postwar economic redevelopment, when high rise after high rise was erected.

Orientation

The Main River flows from east to west, dividing the northern section of the city, its traditional centre, from the southern section, whose focus is the lovely Sachsenhausen district.

Tour boats leave from the north bank of the Main, the Mainkai, between the Alte Brücke and pedestrian-only Eisener Steg.

The south bank of the Main is Schaumainkai, called Museumsufer ('moo-ZAY-umz-oofer'), or Museum Embankment, for the high concentration of museums there.

Sachsenhausen's north-eastern corner, south of the DJH hostel, is known as Alt Sachsenhausen; it's full of quaint old houses and narrow alleys and plenty of places to sample the local apple wine.

From the Hauptbahnhof, walk east along Taunusstrasse to Goetheplatz and then on to a large square called An der Hauptwache. (The Hauptwache itself, a lovely baroque building, was once the local police station; now it's a restaurant.)

The area between the Hauptwache and the Römerberg, the tiny vestige of Frankfurt's original old town, is the city centre. The Hauptbahnhof is on the western side of the city, about a 10-minute walk from the old city centre.

The pedestrianised Zeil runs from west to east between the Hauptwache and the Konstablerwache S-Bahn station at Kurt-Schumacher-Strasse. East of there, Zeil is open to traffic and leads to the zoo.

Hausen and Bockenheim, bohemian, student areas north-west of the centre and due north of the Hauptbahnhof, and Bornheim, a café-laden, cosmopolitan district north-east of the zoo, are some of the neighbourhoods you'll see referred to in listings magazines (see Entertainment) and tourist brochures.

The airport is about 15 minutes by train south-west of the city centre.

Information

Tourist Offices Frankfurt's most convenient tourist office (☎ 212 38 80 0; fax 212 37 88 0) is at the Hauptbahnhof, currently at the head of platform No 23, but there are plans to move it into the Haupthalle area of the station. It's open on weekdays from 8 am to 9 pm, Saturday from 8 am to 8 pm, Sundays and holidays from 9.30 am to 8 pm. The staff are efficient at finding rooms (DM5 service fee). In the centre of the city, the Römer tourist office (☎ 212 38 7) at Römerberg 27 is open daily from 9 am to 6 pm.

The head office of the German National Tourist Board (☎ 974 64 0), north of the Hauptbahnhof at Beethovenstrasse 69, near the Palmengarten, has brochures on all areas of the country and very friendly staff.

Ask at any tourist office about the one/two-day FrankfurtCard, which costs DM10/15 and gives 50% reductions on admission to 15 museums and galleries, the zoo and the airport visitors' terraces, as well as unlimited travel on public transport.

The German auto association (ADAC) has an office (☎ 250 92 9) on Börseplatz, opposite the stock exchange.

Foreign Consulates Among the countries with consular representation in the city are:

Australia – Gutleutstrasse 85/IV (☎ 273 90 90)
Austria – Am Weingarten 25 (☎ 979 91 30)

Denmark – Am Leonhardsbrunn 20 (☎ 970 90 00)
France – Ludolfstrasse 13 (☎ 795 09 60)
Greece – Zeppelinallee 43 (☎ 979 91 20)
Italy – Beethovenstrasse 17 (☎ 753 10 19)
Netherlands – Beethovenstrasse 5 (☎ 752 02 1/2)
Norway – Bethmannstrasse 56 (☎ 131 08 15)
Spain – Nibelungenplatz 3 (☎ 596 10 41)
Sweden – Bethmannstrasse 50-54 (☎ 288 81 2)
UK – Bockenheimer Landstrasse 42 (☎ 170 00 20)
USA – Siesmayerstrasse 21 (☎ 753 50)

Money The Hauptbahnhof has a branch of Reisebank (☎ 264 82 01) near the southern exit at the head of platform No 1; it is open daily from 6.30 am to 10.30 pm. There's an exchange machine accepting foreign currency at the head of platform No 15. There are several banks at the airport, most of them open till about 10 pm, and exchange offices and ATMs are dotted around the various arrival and departure halls.

There are American Express (☎ 21050) and Thomas Cook (☎ 134 733) offices opposite each other on Kaiserstrasse at Nos 8 and 11 respectively.

Post & Communications The main post office is near Hauptwache at Zeil 108-110. It's open weekdays from 9 am to 6 pm, and to 1 pm Saturday; limited after-hours services are offered until 7 pm weekdays (to 8 pm on Thursday) and until 4 pm on Saturday.

Another post office, on the 1st floor of the Hauptbahnhof above McDonald's, is open from 6 am to 9 pm Monday to Friday, 8 am to 6 pm on Saturday and 11 am to 6 pm on Sunday and public holidays. The one at the airport (in the waiting lounge of departure hall B) is open daily from 7 am to 9 pm.

Online Services There are several cybercafés in town; the largest is Cybers – The Internet Zone (☎ 294 96 4), in stall 74 of the Zeilgalerie. The charge is DM8 for 30 minutes, or four hours for DM45. Others cafés include Cyberyder (☎ 913 96 75 4), Tönesgasse 31, and the smaller euroNET (☎ 242 93 70), on Willy-Brandt-Platz.

Travel Agencies Especially good deals on round-the-world tickets are available at outlets such as STA Travel (☎ 703 03 5), Bockenheimer Landstrasse 133; there is another branch in Bornheim (☎ 430 19 1) at Berger Strasse 118. Connections (☎ 705 06 0), Adalbertstrasse 8 in Bockenheim, is another agency to try. Last-minute tickets can be bought at the airport; the prices are usually lower than scheduled airfares.

There's a Lufthansa office (☎ 282 89 59 6) downstairs in the Hauptwache subway.

Bookshops The British Bookshop (☎ 280 49 2), Börsenstrasse 17, has the largest selection of English-language books in town. Hugendubel (☎ 289 82 1), Steinweg 12, also has English-language books, Lonely Planet titles and other travel resources and couches where you can sit and read before you buy.

Sussmann's Presse & Buch, on Hauptwache behind the Katharinenkirche, has a wonderful selection of English-language magazines.

Schmitt & Hahn has two branches in the Hauptbahnhof: one at the head of tracks 15/16, the other around the corner in the station's central hall area. Both have very good selections of fiction.

Bauer Press International, with a dozen branches throughout the airport, has a good selection of best-selling English-language books.

Libraries The library at Amerika Haus (☎ 971 44 82 0; see International Centres) is an excellent reference source on economic and business matters.

The city's central library (☎ 212 38 35 3), Zeil 17, and the Stadt- und Universitätsbibliothek (☎ 212 39 25 6), above the Bockenheimer Warte U-Bahn station, both have good English-language sections.

Campuses Johann Wolfgang von Goethe University (☎ 798 21), with 28,000 students, has its main campus at Bockenheimer Warte, near the Palmengarten. University buildings are scattered throughout the city, housing schools of economics, law and social sciences.

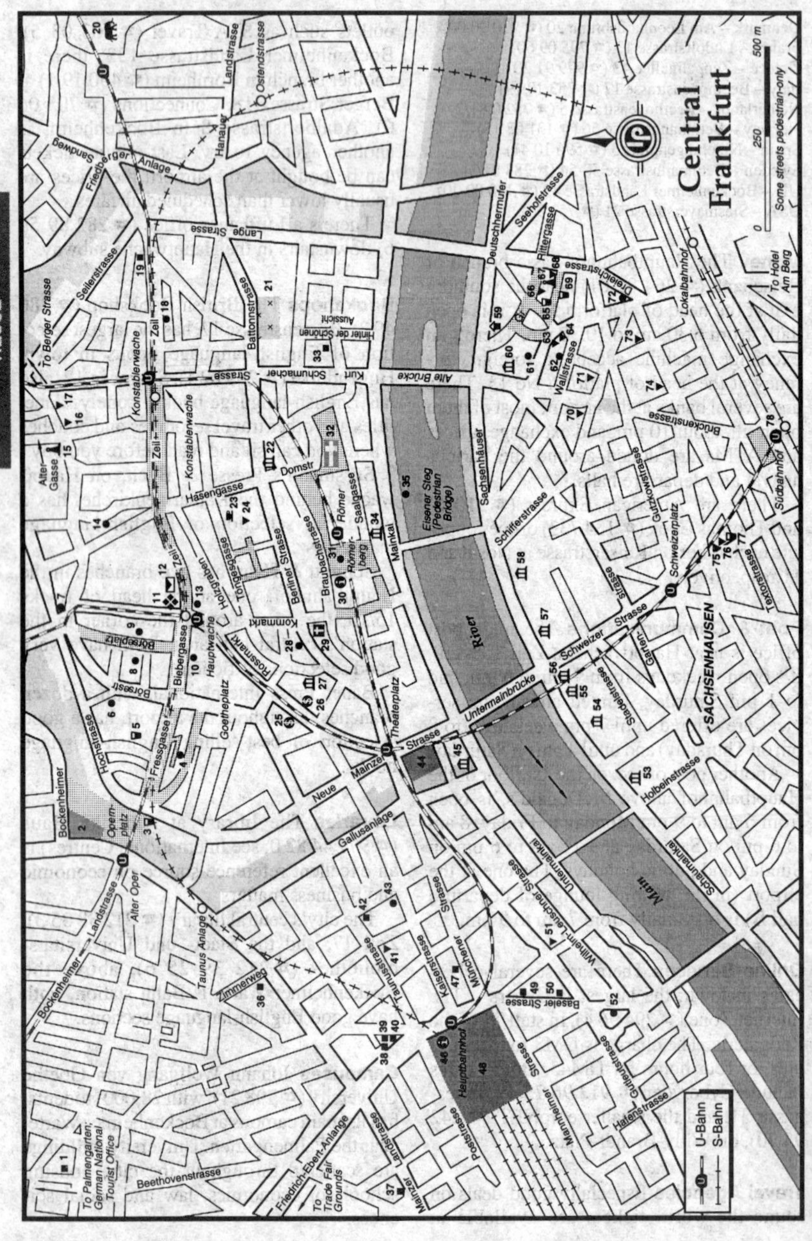
Central Frankfurt
0
250
500 m
Some streets pedestrian-only
U-Bahn
S-Bahn
Main
River
SACHSENHAUSEN
Hauptbahnhof
Eiserner Steg (Pedestrian Bridge)
Alte Brücke
Untermainbrücke
Römerberg
Römer
Zeil
Hauptwache
Konstablerwache
Opernplatz
Alter Oper
Goetheplatz
Theaterplatz
Taunus Anlage
Gallusanlage
Friedrich-Ebert-Anlage
Friedberger Anlage
Lange Strasse
Seilerstrasse
To Berger Strasse
Alter Gasse
Hasengasse
Domstr
Saalgasse
Mainkai
Braubachstrasse
Berliner Strasse
Töngesgasse
Holzgraben
Kornmarkt
Rossmarkt
Biebergasse
Börsenplatz
Börsenstr
Hochstrasse
Fressgasse
Bockenheimer Landstrasse
Beethovenstrasse
To Palmengarten; German National Tourist Office
To Trade Fair Grounds
Mainzer Landstrasse
Neue Mainzer Strasse
Taunusstrasse
Kaiserstrasse
Münchener Strasse
Poststrasse
Baseler Strasse
Wilhelm-Leuschner-Strasse
Untermainkai
Zimmerweg
Hanauer Landstrasse
Ostendstrasse
Sandweg
Battonnstrasse
Kurt-Schumacher-Strasse
Hinter der Schönen Aussicht
Deutschherrnufer
Seehofstrasse
Rittergasse
Dreieichstrasse
Wallstrasse
Sachsenhäuser
Schifferstrasse
Gutzkowstrasse
Brückenstrasse
Schweizer Strasse
Schweizerplatz
Stresemann Strasse
Gartenstrasse
Holbeinstrasse
Schaumainkai
Textorstrasse
Südbahnhof
Lokalbahnhof
To Hotel Am Berg
Hafenstrasse
Gutleutstrasse
Mannheimer Strasse

PLACES TO STAY

1 Hotel-Pension Gölz; Pension Sattler
19 Hotel Zeil
33 Hotel-Pension Station
36 Hotel Atlas
37 Hotel Glockshuber
38 Hotel Adler
39 Hotel Carlton
40 Concorde Hotel
42 Pension Schneider
47 Hotel Münchener Hof
49 Hotel Wiesbaden
50 Hotel Teheran
59 Haus der Jugend

PLACES TO EAT

16 Iwase
17 Lahore Palace
23 Café Mozart
24 Kleinmarkthalle
41 Royal Bombay Palace
51 Ginger Brasserie
63 Meshur Kebab Haus
64 L'Emir Sandwich
66 Lorsbacher Tal
68 Mexir
70 Cafe Satz
71 Tagtraum
73 Reformhaus
74 Zum Fauerrädchen
75 Zum Gemalten Haus
76 Wagner Adolf

OTHER

2 Alte Oper
3 Rob Roy
4 Jazzkeller
5 Blaubart Gewölbkeller
6 British Bookshop
7 Turm-Palast
8 Börse (Stock Exchange)
9 ADAC
10 Hugendubel Books
11 Zeilgalerie
12 Main Post Office
13 Sussman's Presse & Buch
14 Sinkkasten
15 Gay & Lesbian Memorial
18 City Library
20 Zoo
21 Jewish Cemetery
22 Museum of Modern Art
25 American Express
26 Thomas Cook
27 Goethe Haus
28 Jazz-Kneipe
29 St-Pauls-Kirche
30 Römer Tourist Office
31 Fountain
32 St Bartholomäus Dom
34 Historical Museum
35 Tour Boat Stand
43 English Theatre
44 Frankfurt Oper
45 Jewish Museum
46 Tourist Office
48 Main Train Station
52 ADM-Mitfahrzentrale
53 Städel Art Institute
54 Postal Museum
55 German Architecture Museum
56 German Film Museum
57 Museum of Ethnology
58 Museum of Arts & Crafts
60 Icon Museum
61 HL Markt
62 Wasch-Centre Laundrette
65 Far Out
67 Frau Rauscher Brunnen
69 O'Dwyers Pub
72 Harmonie Cinema
77 Hueck
78 Südbahnhof

International Centres Amerika Haus (☎ 971 44 82 0), Staufenstrasse 1, is hugely popular with Germans who want to learn more about life and study in the USA. The Goethe Institut (☎ 961 22 70), Hedderichstrasse 108-110, is *the* German cultural organisation, with concerts, openings, wine tastings and other events to introduce German culture to foreigners.

Laundry The Wasch-Centre chain has coin-operated laundrettes at Wallstrasse 8 in Sachsenhausen (very near the hostel) and at Sandweg 41, just north-east of the city centre.

They're open daily from 8 am to 10 pm and from 6 am to 11 pm respectively and charge DM6 per wash, DM1 for the spinner extractor and DM1 for 15 minutes use of the dryer. Münz Waschcenter has branches in Gallus at Mainzer Landstrasse 310 and in Bornheim at Sandweg 41.

Medical Services Lists of English-speaking doctors are available at the UK and US consulates.

The Uni-Clinic (☎ 630 11), at Theodor Stern Kai 7 in Sachsenhausen, is open 24 hours a day. Also in Sachsenhausen is the Krankenhaus Sachsenhausen (☎ 660 50), Schulstrasse 31. There's an emergency clinic (☎ 475 0) at Friedberger Landstrasse 430.

For routine medical queries, contact the 24-hour doctor service on ☎ 192 92. Pharmacies take turns staying open round the clock (*Notdienst*, emergency service); to find out which one's open, check the list placed in all pharmacy windows or call ☎ 115 00 for recorded listings.

Dangers & Annoyances The area around the Hauptbahnhof is a base for Frankfurt's trade in sex and illegal drugs. To contain the problem of junkies publicly shooting up, *Druckraumen* – shooting-up rooms – have

HESSE

been established in which drugs can be taken but not sold and where clean needles are distributed.

However, you *will* probably see junkies shooting up during your visit. Frequent police patrols of the station and the surrounding Bahnhofsviertel keep things under control. It is advisable to use 'big city' common sense, though.

The Frankfurter Rechtshilfekommitee für Ausländer (☎ 729 16 1) helps foreigners in legal trouble.

Zeilgalerie

The Zeilgalerie should be your first stop in Frankfurt because its rooftop observation deck is free of charge and provides a complete orientation of the city in one fell swoop. (The Zeilgalerie is also home to Frankfurt's Planet Hollywood restaurant, an IMAX – high-resolution, large format films shown on four-storey-high screens – cinema, a cyberbar and tonnes of other shops.)

From the roof you'll see, to the southwest, **Römerberg**, the original city centre and beyond it, across the river, **Sachsenhausen**. To the west is the **banking district**, with several noteworthy architectural features.

From west to north you'll see the **Commerzbank**, designed by British architect Sir Norman Foster. It has a 258m-high triangular tower and spiral winter gardens every eight floors.

The **Dresdener Bank** building was one of the earliest skyscrapers; water-filled plastic 'cushions' were used to stabilise the building on the city's sandy soil. When the structure was completed, the water was emptied and the cushions refilled with cement.

The **Kronenhochhaus** is the skyscraper with the crown pointing towards the Römerberg – an architectural nod to the city's origins. In front of this building, on the corner of Karlsstrasse and Mainzer Landstrasse, is the **sculpture** by Coosje van Bruggen and her husband Claes Oldenburg called *Inverted Collar and Tie*, a playful jab at the suits who work in the building.

Further left are the **Trianon** and **Twin Towers** buildings, now owned by Deutsche Bank.

Behind the **Citibank** building you can still see the reddish 256m-high peak of what locals dub **The Pen**, the Frankfurt Trade Fair building.

Römerberg

The Römerberg, west of the cathedral, is Frankfurt's old central square, where sympathetically restored 14th and 15th-century buildings, including **St-Pauls-Kirche**, provide a glimpse of the beautiful city this once was. It's especially lovely during December's *Christkindlmarkt*.

The old town hall, or **Römer**, in the northwestern corner of Römerberg, consists of three recreated stepped-gable 15th-century houses. The Römer was the site of celebrations of the election and coronation of emperors during the Holy Roman Empire. Today it's both the registry office and the office of Petra Roth, Frankfurt's mayor. Inside, you can view the **Kaisersaal** (open daily from 10 am to 1 pm and 2 to 5 pm; DM3/1.50), with portraits of 52 rulers. Flags flying outside the building indicate the Kaisersaal is being used for official functions, in which case you won't be able to get inside.

Right in the centre of Römerberg is the *Gerechtigkeitsbrunnen*, the 'Font of Justice'. In 1612, at the coronation of Matthias, the fountain ran with wine, not water.

St Bartholomäus Dom

The newly restored St Bartholomäus Dom, east of Römerberg, is behind the **Historical Garden**, a recreation of Roman and Carolingian foundation remains. Dominated by the elegant, 15th-century, 95m-high Gothic **tower** (completed in the 1860s), it is one of the few structures left standing after the 1944 raids.

You can climb to one of the two viewing platforms (at 40m/180 steps or 75m/328 steps) daily from 9 am to 1 pm and 2.30 to 6 pm; DM3, discount DM1.

The small **Wahlkapelle** (Voting Chapel) on the cathedral's southern side is where seven electors of the Holy Roman Empire chose the emperor from 1356 onwards; the adjoining **choir** has beautiful wooden stalls.

Museum of Modern Art

The triangular Museum für Moderne Kunst (☎ 212 30 44 7), Domstrasse 10, dubbed the 'slice of cake' by locals, has permanent and temporary exhibitions of modern art. The permanent collection contains works by Roy Lichtenstein, Andy Warhol, Claes Oldenburg and Joseph Beuys; temporary exhibits highlight local, national and international artists. It's open Tuesday to Sunday from 10 am to 5 pm (to 8 pm on Wednesday); admission is DM7/3.50.

Goethe House

Anyone with an interest in German literature should visit the Goethe Haus at Grosser Hirschgraben 23-25. Johann Wolfgang von Goethe was born in this house in 1749. This newly renovated museum and library is open Monday to Saturday from 9 am to 6 pm, Sunday and public holidays from 10 am to 1 pm (shorter hours in winter); entry costs DM4/3. Much of the furniture is reproduction, but some originals remain. There are guided tours in German daily at 10.30 am and 2 pm (mornings only on Sunday). At other times, the staff might point out the highlights but don't miss Goethe's original writing desk and the library on the top floor.

Alte Oper & Börse

Built in 1888, Frankfurt's lovely Renaissance Alte Oper (☎ 134 04 00), Opernplatz 8, bears a striking resemblance to Dresden's Semperoper. Destroyed in WWII, the Alter Oper – after a vote to save it from being razed to clear a path for 1960s-style cubes – underwent a DM220 million renovation. The outside is as original as possible but the inside is modern. There are statues of Goethe and Mozart on the building.

Between Opernplatz and Börsenplatz is pedestrianised **Fressgasse** (Munch Alley), a somewhat overrated mall scattered with snack bars and restaurants. If you're visiting in September stop at the very nice Rheingau wine festival held here.

The city's **Börse** (stock exchange , 1874) is open to visitors who can watch the traders' frantic hand-gesturing from an observation section Monday to Friday from 11 am to noon. Admission is free; enter from the small door under the glass awning on the east side of the front of the building.

Museums

Entry to most museums in Frankfurt is free on Wednesdays.

Museumsufer A string of museums lines the southern bank of the Main River. The pick of the crop is the **Städel Art Institute** (☎ 682 09 8), Schaumainkai 63, with a world-class collection of works by artists including Botticelli, Dürer, Van Eyck, Rembrandt, Renoir, Rubens, Vermeer and Cézanne plus artists native to Frankfurt, including Hans Holbein. Entry costs DM8/4 and is open Tuesday to Sunday, from 10 am to 5 pm and to 8 pm on Wednesday when admission is free.

The **German Architecture Museum** (☎ 212 38 84 4), Schaumainkai 43, is something of a disappointment – only rotating exhibitions and no permanent collection of the architecture of Frankfurt or even of Germany. Admission is DM8/4.

The **German Film Museum** (Deutsches Filmmuseum; ☎ 212 33 36 9) is, in contrast, a fascinating place. It has constantly changing exhibitions, extensive archives, plus premieres and special film events, all in their original languages, in the Kommunales Kino. Check with *MainCity* or the other listings magazines (see Entertainment). The museum is absolutely worth the admission of DM5/2.50.

The **Postal Museum** (☎ 606 00), Schaumainkai 53, in addition to the collection of the former Reichspostmuseum in Berlin, has displays on the history of communication; admission is free, so why not?

Other museums along this strip include the **Museum of Arts & Crafts** (DM6/3), Schaumainkai 17; the **Museum of Ethnology**, which will reopen in 1998; and the

Museum of Ancient Sculpture (DM5/2.50), Schaumainkai 71, with classical, medieval, baroque and Renaissance sculptures and an exhibition of Egyptian art.

The **Icon Museum** (☎ 212 36 26 2), Brückenstrasse 3-7, houses a collection of Russian religious paintings. It's open Tuesday to Sunday from 10 am to 5 pm; admission is DM2/1.

Historical Museum This museum (☎ 212 35 59 9), just south of Römerplatz at Saalgasse 19, is worth visiting even if you skip the permanent exhibition (DM5/2.50) on Frankfurt in the Middle Ages in favour of the spectacular **model** (DM1) of the city from the 1930s in the foyer. Built by the Treuner brothers, the detail of the city centre is nothing short of wonderful. It's especially nice to go on Wednesday when pensioners, taking advantage of the free admission, stand around the model and point out shops and streets remembered from their youth. In the same foyer is a model of the ruins of the city after the war.

Jewish Museums The city has two notable museums on Jewish life in Frankfurt which call attention to the fact that the Jewish community here, with 35,000 people, was once one of the largest in Europe. The main **Jüdisches Museum** (☎ 212 35 00 0), in the former Rothschildpalais at Untermainkai 14-15, is an enormous place with an exhibit of Jewish life in the city from the Middle Ages to present day, with good detail on well known Frankfurt Jews persecuted, murdered or exiled by the Nazis. Religious items are also on display. The museum is open Tuesday to Sunday from 10 am to 5 pm (Wednesday to 8 pm), closed Monday. Admission is DM5/2.50, free on Saturday.

The **Museum Judengasse** (same hours), along the north-eastern boundaries of the old city fortifications, is the annexe to the Jüdisches Museum. On display here are remains of ritual baths and houses from the Jewish ghetto which was destroyed by the Nazis. Admission is DM3/1.50, or DM6/3 when combined with the Jüdisches Museum.

Nearby, a **memorial** at Börneplatz off Battonnstrasse is a must-see: it's a long wall with metal cubes bearing the names of all Frankfurt-born Jews murdered during the Holocaust, some with the date of death, others with merely a notation of the camp in which they died. The cubes allow visitors to place stones or pebbles, a Jewish tradition that shows that a grave is tended and the person not forgotten.

Palm Garden

The botanical **Palmengarten** (entry DM7, students DM3, or DM5/2 with a valid RMV transport ticket) is an easy way to escape the city. It has rose gardens and formal gardens, a playground for kids, a little pond with rowing boats (DM4/3 adults/children plus DM1 per person per half-hour) and a mini-gauge train that puffs round the place (DM2/1). It's opposite the German National Tourist Board office and very near the university, one block from Bockenheimer Warte (U-Bahn No 6 or 7).

Monuments

On the corner of Alter Gasse, the city's main gay and lesbian drag, and Schaffergasse, north of Zeil, is a **memorial**, one of three in Europe, to homosexuals persecuted and killed by the Nazis during WWII. It is deliberate that the statue's head is nearly severed from the body.

In an altogether wacky departure from that sombre sight, the **Frau Rauscher Brunnen** on Klappergasse in Sachsenhausen is a treat. It's a bronze statue of a bulky, bitchy-looking *Hausfrau* who periodically spews a powerful stream of water about 10m onto the footpath. Stand around for a few moments east of the statue and you'll undoubtedly see pedestrians drenched. The idea is based on a popular Frankfurt song about drinking apple wine.

Frankfurt Zoo

The zoo (DM11/5, U6 to Zoo station), with its creative displays, signs and exhibits, is another relief from the cosmopolitan chaos. Just as creative, perhaps, and beloved by kids are the two visitors' terraces at Frankfurt airport (DM7, free with a FrankfurtCard) in Terminal 1, Level 3, and in Terminal 2, Level 4. It's only 11 minutes away by S-Bahn (see Getting Around).

Language Courses

Due to the high percentage of foreign residents here there are a number of language schools in the city. The most respected – and expensive – option is the Goethe Institut (☎ 961 22 70), Hedderichstrasse 108-110.

Inlingua (☎ 231 02 1), Kaiserstrasse 37, offers one, two and four-week intensive German courses for less money and we hear generally good things about the classes. One of the authors took a one-month course at Inlingua in Munich (DM500) and recommends it highly. Berlitz (☎ 280 87 5), Grosse Eschenheimerstrasse 1 and Kaiserstrasse 66, is the most commercially minded of the schools, with prices to match.

Organised Tours

During weekends and holidays the city's *Ebbelwei-Express* (☎ 213 22 32 5) tram circles Frankfurt, stopping at the zoo, Hauptbahnhof, Südbahnhof, Frankensteiner Platz (near the Haus der Jugend hostel) and back several times a day. The fare is DM4/2.

Kulturothek Frankfurt (☎ 281 01 0) runs 90-minute walking tours through the city, in English, on a variety of subjects. Show up at 2 pm at the meeting point (it changes weekly); the cost is DM15/10.

The tourist offices offer excellent 2½-hour city tours which include visits to the Historical Museum and Goethe House, leaving daily at 10 am and 2 pm from the Römer tourist office at Römerberg 27. There are shuttle services from the Hauptbahnhof to Römer for the tours as well. The cost is DM44/22. They also offer themed excursions, like Jewish Frankfurt, Frankfurt architecture and Goethe tours.

Elisabeth Lücke (☎ 06196-457 87) runs 2½-hour group tours (up to 30 people for DM150) in English, German and Spanish.

Half-hour rickshaw tours are available from Asien Am Main (☎ 212 38 70 8). The peddle-powered carriages make a 30-minute loop around the city for DM39. Pick one up near the Font of Justice in the centre of Römerplatz.

One to three-hour boat rides along the Main are available at varying prices from the docks on the northern embankment, just east of the Eisener Steg bridge.

Special Events

Frankfurt festivals include:

Dippemess
: March and September. Fun fair, apple wine and food.

Kunsthandwerk Heute
: Late May/early June. Paulsplatz; arts and handicrafts.

Sound of Frankfurt
: July. Along the Zeil, local and visiting groups play soul, blues, jazz and rock.

Frankfurt Book Fair
: Late September/early October

Christkindlmarkt
: December. Christmas fair in Römerberg with mulled wine, choirs and traditional foods.

Places to Stay

Camping The most recommended camping ground is *Heddernheim* (☎ 57 03 32; open all year) in the Heddernheim district northwest of the city centre at An der Sandelmühle 35. It charges DM10 for a site and DM9 per person and is a 15-minute ride on the U1, U2

The Frankfurt Book Fair

If you're in publishing, there's no avoiding the world's largest book fair, held in Frankfurt in late September/early October. Over 250,000 publishers, agents, authors, wannabes, yahoos, drunks, Lonely Planet staffers and other nefarious characters descend on Mainhattan with a vengeance.

It's a scene and a half, and hotels are booked out a year in advance. If you plan to visit Frankfurt during the fair, you should reserve accommodation well in advance.

General admission to the Frankfurt Messe (tram No 19), where the fair is held, is DM12 for one day, or DM36 for the duration of the fair. ■

or U3 from the Hauptwache U-Bahn station (one zone); get off at the Heddernheim stop.

Campingplatz Offenbach Bürgel (☎ 862 94 6), in a pretty spot on the Main River north-east of the centre at Gerhard-Becker-Strasse 104, charges DM7 per tent and DM7 per person. It can be reached via the No 101 bus from the centre.

Hostel The sparkling *Haus der Jugend* (☎ 61 90 58; fax 61 82 57), on the south side of the Main River at Deutschherrnufer 12 (which is what Schaumainkai becomes if you continue east past all the museums), is within easy walking distance of the city centre and Sachsenhausen, across the Alte Brücke. It's also perfectly located for the night life and cafés of the Alt-Sachsenhausen district and is big, bustling, spotless and fun. The only downside we've encountered on several visits is the sometimes rude manner of the hostel's desk staff.

Rates (including breakfast) for beds in large dorms are DM19.50/24.50 for juniors/seniors; in four-person rooms DM35/47. Evening meals cost DM8.70. From the Hauptbahnhof, take bus No 46 to the Jugendherberge stop; or S-Bahn line No 2, 3, 4, 5 or 6 to Lokalbahnhof. Check-in begins at 1 pm and it can get very crowded; the post code for bookings by mail is 60594 Frankfurt/Main. There's a lock-out from 9 am to 1 pm and curfew from midnight to 6.30 am.

Private Rooms The tourist office books private rooms during trade fairs only. At all other times, contact one of the three Mitwohnzentrale offices in town: City Mitwohnzentrale (☎ 296 11 1), An der Steinmauer 3; Mitwohnzentrale Mainhattan (☎ 597 55 61), Falkensteiner Strasse 68; and Frankfurter Mitwohnzentrale (☎ 447 70 6), Sandweg 106. All three can book rooms from about DM40 to DM100 per double.

Hotels – bottom end to middle In Frankfurt, 'cheap' can mean paying over DM100 for a spartan double room. During the many busy trade fairs, even that price may turn out to be unrealistic since most hotels and pensions jack up their prices – in some cases close to double the standard rate. But don't give up hope; one of the authors showed up in Frankfurt without a reservation on the opening day of the book fair and got a pleasant room for under DM100 through the booking service at the tourist office.

Bahnhofsviertel Most of Frankfurt's low-end accommodation is in the rather sleazy Bahnhofsviertel area surrounding the main train station. A typical, though not unpleasant, example is the *Hotel Teheran* (☎ 233 02 3) at Baseler Strasse 14, which has basic singles/doubles for DM60/80 and triples with shower and WC for DM150; the mark-up during fairs is only around 10%. The *Hotel Münchener Hof* (☎ 230 06 6) at Münchener Strasse 46 also has cheap singles/doubles from DM85/100 with shared shower. *Pension Schneider* (☎ 251 07 1), Taunusstrasse 43, has nicer rooms from DM70/115.

The *Hotel Adler* (☎ 233 45 5), on the 4th floor at Niddastrasse 65 just north of the Hauptbahnhof (access via an arcade from Düsseldorfer Strasse), has passable rooms for DM70/105 (DM105/195 during fairs). A bit more up-market is *Hotel Carlton* (☎ 232 09 3), just around the corner at Karlsstrasse 11, where rooms with TV, telephone, shower and WC cost DM69/100 (DM149/260 during trade fairs). Next door to that is the even nicer *Concorde Hotel* (☎ 233 23 0), Karlsstrasse 9, with very friendly service and rooms from DM120/180.

The most cheerful budget hotels in Bahnhofsviertel, however, are the *Wiesbaden* (☎ 232 34 7) at Baseler Strasse 52 (to the right of the station exit) and the *Glockshuber* (☎ 742 62 8), Mainzer Landstrasse 120, both of which offer clean and bright rooms from around DM75/120.

City Centre Away from the sleaze but still a convenient distance from the Hauptbahnhof is the modern *Hotel Atlas* (☎ 723 94 6), Zimmerweg 1, with simple singles/doubles from DM68/100 (DM85/142 during fairs). The *Hotel Byblos* (☎ 290 86 3), Vilbeler

Strasse 32 (entrance on Elefantengasse 1), has doubles for DM100.

A similar place closer to the centre is *Hotel-Pension Station* (☎ 287 87 7), at Hinter der Schönen Aussicht 16. Even more central is *Hotel Zeil* (☎ 283 63 8), at Zeil 12, where rooms with private toilet and shower cost DM80/120 (DM120/190 during fairs).

Sachsenhausen Apart from the hostel, Sachsenhausen has disappointingly few budget places to stay, but the *Hotel Am Berg* (☎ 611 20 21), in a lovely old sandstone building at Grethenweg 23 in the quiet back streets a few minutes' walk from Südbahnhof, charges DM60/115 (DM85/140 during fairs) for simple rooms without breakfast; it's clean, pleasant and friendly.

Other Areas Quite a number of budget pensions lie tucked away in Frankfurt's inner northern suburbs. Close to the quieter Palmengarten area, along Beethovenstrasse at No 44 and No 46 respectively, are *Hotel-Pension Gölz* (☎ 746 73 5) and *Pension Sattler* (☎ 746 09 1). Their rooms start at around DM65/135, but at those prices they're almost always full. The *Pension Backer* (☎ 747 99 2), at Mendelssohnstrasse 92 in Westend, offers rooms from DM50/80.

The friendly and clean *Pension Adria* (☎ 594 53 3), at Neuhausstrasse 21 in Nordend, has pleasant rooms overlooking garden lawns from DM65/110 (without breakfast). The *Hotel Uebe* (☎ 591 20 9), at Grünebrugweg 3 near the Botanical Gardens (Palmengarten) in Westend-Nord, offers simple singles for DM75 and doubles with private shower for DM105. In the interesting Bornheim district north-east of town is the *Pension Zur Rose* (☎ 451 76 2) at Berger Strasse 283. Basic rooms go for DM60/100 or DM120/140 with shower and toilet.

Hotels – top end

If you're in Frankfurt on an expense account, there are several ways of staying here without having your hotel bill sent directly to the Raised Eyebrow Department back at work. Note that all these prices rise during fairs.

The brand new *InterCity Hotel* (☎ 273 91 0; fax 273 91 99 9), attached to the Hauptbahnhof at Poststrasse 8, is a very nice place, with singles/doubles from DM120/ 160. It's newer than the *Bauer Hotel Domicil* (☎ 271 11 0; fax 253 26 66), Karlsstrasse 14, and the rooms are larger but the Bauer has a quiet location and much more personal service. Rooms are DM166/216.

There are two grand dames of the Frankfurt hotel scene. The stupendously grandiose *Steigenberger Frankfurter Hof* (☎ 215 02; fax 215 90 0), am Kaiserplatz, has similarly grand rooms and great service. For DM305/ 390 singles/doubles you even get a sweet on your pillow.

A friend who gets IBM to spend the DM375/445 singles/doubles to put him up for the night at the *Arabella Grand Hotel Frankfurt* (☎ 298 10; Konrad Adenauer Strasse 7) says he'd rather stay in a simple Holiday Inn, which is what the place is like: boxy rooms, not a whole lot of space but certainly friendly service.

Places to Eat

Bahnhofsviertel The area around Hauptbahnhof is filled with predominantly Southern European, Middle Eastern and Asian eating houses.

At the *Restaurant India House*, at Kaiserstrasse 54 (almost next door to the English Theatre), a serving of dhal and rice costs just DM8.90. For more convincing curry-and-coriander creations head for the nearby *Royal Bombay Palace* (☎ 233 93), Taunusstrasse 17, which offers set four-course menus (vegetarian or meat) for DM30 per person.

The *Ginger Brasserie* (☎ 231 77 1) at Windmühlestrasse 14 has everything Asian on the menu – from good Sichuan to bad sushi, great salads, tandoori and Thai – with most main courses between DM18 and DM23.

For snacks and fast food, the Hauptbahnhof has a McDonald's at the head of track 22 that's open for breakfast from 4 am, and a good *Kaffee Mit* nearby. There are dozens of stalls in the station and in the subway leading up to it selling doner kebabs, pizza, fish sandwiches, Chinese and wurst. Downstairs in the underpass running east from the Hauptbahnhof is a *Pizza Hut* and an overpriced *supermarket*, open daily.

Fressgasse & Northern Centre Known to locals as Fressgasse (Munch Alley), the Kalbächer Gasse and Grosse Bockenheimer Strasse area between Rathenauplatz and Opernplatz has many cheap restaurants and fast-food places with outdoor tables.

Moving east to Vilbeler Strasse, near Alte Gasse, are two excellent, if expensive, eateries. *Lahore Palace* (☎ 280 85 4), Vilbeler Strasse 27, is a pricey but mind-blowing Indian restaurant with excellent service and out-of-this-world food. The vindaloo is hot enough to make your nose run and the mixed starters (DM10 to DM12) are super. Main courses range from DM23 to DM30.

A few doors down is *Iwase* (☎ 283 99 2), a good Japanese restaurant that's cheaper at lunchtime (DM23 for seven pieces of sushi, one handroll salad, miso soup and fruit) than at dinner (DM38) but it always has a seven piece/one roll takeaway plate for DM20.

Zeil & Römerberg If you're here and hungry, the best place for snacks or picnic supplies is the *Kleinmarkthalle* off Hasengasse just south of Zeil. It's an active little city market (open Monday to Friday from 7.30 am to 6 pm, Saturday to 3 pm) selling fruit, vegetables, meats, fish and hot food. Stalls have Italian, Turkish, Chinese and German food and you can get salads and fresh fruit juices as well as wine and beer. At the western end of the hall there is a large mural of a bird's-eye view of Frankfurt. The nearby *Café Mozart* at Töngesgasse 23 is popular with tourists for its cakes and coffee. Across the street from the market, *Café Paragon* has a mostly gay clientele but is open to all and has a nice outdoor terrace.

The biggest news is the opening of a *Planet Hollywood* restaurant in the Zeilgalerie; owned by a group of American film stars, the place is packed with memorabilia, the food's good and the prices, if they follow the PHs in the rest of the world, aren't as shocking as you'd think.

Sachsenhausen Sachsenhausen's everyone-friendly (gays, lesbians, heteros) *Tagtraum* (☎ 618 75 7; open daily), at Affentorplatz 20, features inspired salads as well

Ebbelwoi & Handkäse mit Musik

Frankfurt eating and drinking traditions are best experienced in the city's apple-wine taverns which serve *Ebbelwoi* (Frankfurt dialect for Apfelwein), an alcoholic apple cider, along with local specialities like *Handkäse mit Musik* ('hand-cheese with music') and *Frankfurter Grüne Sosse* (Frankfurt green sauce).

The best Ebbelwoi taverns are in Alt Sachsenhausen – the area directly behind the DJH hostel – which is filled with eateries and pubs. In most of these you'll be served the stuff in *Bembel* jugs; it's something of a tradition to scrunch closer and closer to your neighbours and try to grab some from their pitcher too.

Classic Ebbelwoi joints include the Lorsbacher Tal, Grosse Rittergasse 49; the Wagner Adolf, tucked away at Schweizer Strasse 71; and Zum Gemalten Haus, a lively place full of paintings of old Frankfurt, nearby at Schweizer Strasse 67.

Handkäse mit Musik is a name you could only hear in German. It describes a round cheese marinated in oil and vinegar with onions, served with bread and butter and with a knife only – no fork. As you might imagine, cheese marinated in oil and onions would tend to give one a healthy dose of wind – the release of which, ladies and gentlemen, is the 'music' part.

Frankfurter Grüne Sosse is made from parsley, sorrel, dill, burnet, borage, chervil and chives mixed with yoghurt, mayonnaise or sour cream; it's served with potatoes and meat or eggs – Goethe's favourite food. ■

as daily specials that average DM15 per main course. A block away at Schifferstrasse 36 is the airy *Café Satz*, with vegetarian couscous (DM10.50) and chilli con carne (DM8.50) on offer.

Tucked away in a peaceful little courtyard with a garden and fountain, *Zum Feurrädchen* (☎ 621 31 3), Textorstrasse 24, has a wonderful enclosed stained-glass section; there's a beer garden/apple wine café in front. Main courses include goulash with Spätzle and salad (DM13) and pork schnitzel with fried potatoes and salad for DM15. It's closed on Monday.

Then there's *Mexir* (☎ 962 01 15 8), Klappergasse 8, Sachsenhausen's newest Mexican-Iranian – that's right – speciality spot. We can think of a whole lot of possible jokes for this one but the owners are so sweet and the place, next to the Frau Rauscher Brunnen, is very comfortable, so we don't have the heart.

For snacks and fast food, vegetarians will appreciate the *Reformhaus* (☎ 605 98), Textorstrasse 10, with vegie, tofu and soy burgers from DM2.50 to DM3, salads, awesome bread, vegie rolls, frozen foods and a wine bar, all reasonably priced.

There's spiffing felafel and meat dishes at *L'Emir Sandwich* (☎ 623 33 3), Paradiesgasse at Elisabethenstrasse; most sandwiches cost about DM6. A couple of doors down is the almost-as-good *Meshur Kebab Haus*, Paradiesgasse 38, a sit-down place with a doner window.

For self-caterers, there are excellent *markets* every Friday from 8 am to 6 pm in the square in front of the Südbahnhof, about 10 minutes south of the hostel. Beat the extortionate prices of the hostel's bottled water and soft drinks at the *HL Markt*, around the corner at Elisabethenstrasse 10-12.

Bornheim It is worth going well out of your way for the pizza and pasta at *Pizzeria Da Franco* (☎ 459 56 7), Saalburgstrasse 41, right near Bornheim-Mitte (U4) station in the cosmopolitan Bornheim area, north of the zoo. The smell will hit you when you're down the street and, while it's basic, its staff are charming. Pizzas range from DM6 to DM10, pastas from DM6.50 to DM12 – recommended is the tagliatelle al salmone (DM11).

Café Gegenwart (☎ 497 05 44), at Berger Strasse 6, is a stylish bar/restaurant serving traditional German dishes from DM13; if the weather cooperates you can sit outside. The zanier *Café Provisorisch* next door does particularly good breakfasts.

Bockenheim Over to the west in bohemian Bockenheim, past the university, Leipziger Strasse branches off from Bockenheimer Landstrasse and is a very pleasant shopping and cheap snack area. (Take the U6 or U7 to Bockenheimer Warte or Leipziger Strasse.) If you're at the Palmengarten or the university, you're close to *Fisch Bader*, Leipziger Strasse 55, where a huge plate of fried bass with vegetables is DM6 and fish soup is DM5.50. Across the street, the *Schwarzwälder Specialitäten* delicatessen sells Frankfurt's traditional smoked or air-dried bacon, onion bread and eat-in speciality soups for DM5.

A bit further down, at No 26, is *Bistro Hong Kong* (☎ 777 84 9), with good soups, all under DM4, and almost all of the 25 or so main courses under DM10. It's absolutely great.

Stattcafé at Grempstrasse 21 offers vegetarian and meat dishes from around DM13. Near the university, on the corner of Gräfstrasse and Bockenheimer Warte, is the *Depot Café*, a popular student hang-out serving great breakfasts. Another restaurant that offers decent servings at student prices is *Pielok* (☎ 776 46 8), Jordanstrasse 3.

The Nordend area, east of Bockenheim, also attracts students and trendoids. For fare with flair, try *Grössenwahn* (☎ 599 35 6), Lenaustrasse 97, a lively pub where you can eat for under DM20.

Entertainment

Frankfurt is truly a *Weltstadt* – an 'international city' – with an exhaustive amount of evening entertainment.

Listings The most indispensable source of information for travellers in Frankfurt is the excellent *MainCity* magazine (DM5), available at newsstands everywhere. It's edited by Irish tornado Angela 'Beer!' Cullen, who manages to crank out what amounts to a complete and practical guide to the city every month with restaurant reviews, entertainment listings and feature articles. If you're staying longer, the *MainCity Newcomer's Guide* has everything you'll ever need to know about the city – from driving licences to rubbish collection.

Fritz and *Strandgut* are free magazines with listings (in German) of concerts, clubs, restaurants etc available throughout the city in clubs and bars.

Gay & Lesbian *Fritz* has a gay listings page in every issue. Lesben-Informations und Beratunsstelle (☎ 282 88 3), Alte Gasse 38, provides information and assistance to lesbians; Rosa Telefon Mainz (☎ 06131-194 46) does the same for gay men.

The Oscar Wilde Bookshop on Alte Gasse sells gay and lesbian books and tapes and is a great source of local information. Pick up a copy of *Frankfurt von Hintern* (Frankfurt from Behind), a good gay guide to the city.

Cinemas Films in English are denoted in newspapers and programmes by the initials 'OF' or 'OmU'. Look for yellow Kino posters in U-Bahn stations; if the description's in English, so is the movie.

The *Turm-Palast* (☎ 281 78 7), at Am Eschenheimer Turm, is a multi-screen cinema that shows new films in original languages.

The *Kommunales Kino* (☎ 212 38 83 0) at the German Film Museum (see Museums) screens a range of old and new films, series and other special events. An IMAX cinema should be open in the Zeilgalerie by the time you read this.

Another venue is *Berger Kinos* (☎ 456 04 5), Berger Strasse 177 in Bornheim. *Harmonie* (☎ 213 55 0), Driechstrasse 54 in Sachsenhausen, shows art films in their original languages.

Discos & Clubs *Far Out*, Klappergasse, just west of the Frau Rauscher Brunnen, is a disco and café that is non-smoking on Wednesday night. It's open Thursday to Sunday too.

There's techno at *Dorian Gray* at the airport in Terminal 1, Hall C, and at *Omen*, Junghoferstrasse 14; acid jazz at *Cooky's*, Am Salzhaus 4; and funk, soul and groove at *Funkadelic*, on Brönnerstrasse.

Gay & Lesbian Frankfurt's premier gay street is Alte Gasse, just to the east of Konstablerwache and Brönnerstrasse; here you'll find gay and lesbian discos, cafés and baths. *Construction 5*, Alte Gasse 5, is mainly gay but with monthly gay and lesbian nights; *The Blue Angel*, Brönnerstrasse 17, is strictly gay. Lesbian clubs include *Papillon*, Bleicherstrasse 34, and *Tangerine*, Stiftstrasse 39.

Theatre The *English Theatre* (☎ 242 31 62 0), at Kaiserstrasse 52, performs English-language plays and musicals with performances from Tuesday to Sunday.

The *Chaincourt Theatre Company* (☎ 798 23 16 3), administered by Frankfurt University's English Department, performs at the theatre at Kettenhofweg 130.

Die Städtischen Bühnen (☎ 212 37 99 9) runs the *Kammerspiel*, *Oper* and the *Schauspielhaus*. It also runs *TAT* (☎ 212 37 66 6), Bockenheimer Warte, with experimental and alternative theatre, concerts and special events.

The *Freies Schauspiel* (☎ 596 94 90), Hebelstrasse 15-19, is another slightly offbeat venue.

Cabaret There's cabaret at the *Tiger Palast* (☎ 920 02 25 0), Heiligkreuzstrasse 16-20, with *variété* performances featuring acrobats, jugglers and other popular circus-like acts. A popular venue in Bornheim is *Mousonturm* (☎ 405 89 52 0), Waldschmidtstrasse 4, a converted soap factory that offers dance performances and politically oriented cabaret.

Classical Ballet, opera and theatre are strong points of Frankfurt's entertainment scene. For information and bookings, contact the Oper Frankfurt (☎ 212 36 06 1), Untermainanlage 11, or the Hertie concert and theatre-booking service (☎ 294 84 8), Zeil 90. There are three venues within the *Alte Oper* (☎ 134 04 00), Opernplatz 8: the *Mozart Saal, Hindemith Saal* and *Grosser Saal*, featuring an array of classical concerts, ballet and theatre.

Rock Catch leading reggae and rock bands at *Sinkkasten* (☎ 280 38 5), just north of the city centre at Brönnerstrasse 5.

There are concerts in the interesting space at the *Südbahnhof Musik Lokal*, inside the Südbahnhof, every Sunday night with rock, oldies, soul and sometimes Dixieland and jazz.

Jazz Top acts perform at the *Jazzkeller* (☎ 288 53 7), Kleine Bockenheimer Strasse 18a, and the *Jazz-Kneipe* (☎ 287 17 3) at Berliner Strasse 70. There's also a good crowd at *Mampf*, Sandweg 64 in Bornheim.

Folk Music There's Irish folk music every Sunday night at *O'Dwyers Pub*, Klappergasse 19 (another entrance on Affentorplatz).

Pubs & Bars The Irish influence on Frankfurt's drinking scene can't be ignored; there are currently six Irish pubs in town. We liked *O'Dwyers Pub* (see Folk Music); the *Shamrock*, Rittergasse 4; and the nearby *Irish Pub*, Rittergasse 11. *Planet Hollywood* promises to be an American-style meat market in the Zeilgalerie. *Down Under*, Klappergasse 13, is, well, guess what?

Friends both love and hate *Rob Roy* (also called *Billy's*), in the Möwenpick restaurant at Opernplatz, but it's definitely a cool gimmick: a 70s-style bar with a 60s-style bartender right out of *Dragnet* – invisible service, but the bartender remembers everyone's face and their drink. It's a banker, Brit and suit scene, but where else will you find the perfect Manhattan in Mainhattan?

Off Fressgasse is the admirable *Blaubart Gewölbkeller*, in the cellar at Kaiserhofstrasse 18, a vaulted chamber of a self-service watering hole that's fun and cheap with good beer.

If you're self-congratulatory you'll love *Hueck*, Schweizer Strasse 73, a very slick yuppie place with neon, medium-priced chichi food and interesting cocktails – no cell phones allowed.

Gay & Lesbian A popular gay bar is *Zum Schwejk* at Schäffergasse 20 (just off Zeil), while *Harvey's* (☎ 497 30 3), a restaurant on Friedberger Platz, is a favoured meeting place for Frankfurt's guppies and luppies.

Things to Buy

The shopping in Frankfurt is excellent and it's an ideal place to satisfy any souvenir requirements before boarding the plane or train home. If you live outside the USA, Frankfurt's enormous Duty Free shops offer some significant bargains on electronics, perfumes, cosmetics, cigarettes and booze. But if you're returning to the USA, prices are generally as good, or better, there.

Markets There's a great flea market along Museumsufer every Saturday between 8 am and 2 pm. Other city markets, which run from about 8 am to about 1 pm, include those at Bockenheimer Warte (Thursday) and Höchstrasse (Tuesday, Friday and Saturday).

Shopping Centres Frankfurt's main shopping street is Zeil, particularly between the Hauptwache and the Konstablerwache. It's reputed to do more business than any other shopping district in Europe – by some reports accounting for 1% of all money spent in Germany – but is generally expensive. More interesting areas for shopping are Schweizer Strasse in Sachsenhausen and Berger Strasse north-east of the city centre, where there are shops stocking all sorts of weird and wonderful stuff.

Getting There & Away

Air Flughafen Frankfurt/Main is Germany's largest airport, with the highest freight and passenger turnover in continental Europe (it's second to Heathrow in passenger turnover). This high-tech town has two terminals linked by an elevated railway called the Sky Line.

Departure and arrival halls A, B and C are in the old Terminal 1, the western half of which handles Lufthansa flights. Halls D and E are in the new Terminal 2.

Bus connections are currently on Level 1 of Terminal 1, train connections are on Level 0 (ground floor) and the S-Bahn is on Level 1. A new airport train station, expected to open in 1999, will accommodate faster InterCity trains.

The airport information number is ☎ 690 30 51 1.

If you arrive well before your departure, be sure to bring a snack: cafés and bars are unforgivably expensive. And take a book, or you'll probably end up in Dr Müller's – Germany's only airport sex shop/adult movie theatre.

If you're here in transit, especially after a long flight from Asia or Australasia, you should know that for a mere DM6 you can enjoy a hot shower in sparkling, lockable, private stalls and the soap, shampoo and towel are provided. The showers are in Hall B; ask at the information counter for directions.

Bus Long-distance buses leave from the southern side of the Hauptbahnhof where there's a Europabus office (☎ 230 73 5/6). It caters for most European destinations, but the most interesting possibility is the Romantic Road bus (see the Bavaria chapter). The Europabus head office is Deutsche Touring (☎ 790 30), Römerhof 17, 60486 Frankfurt.

Train The main train station handles more departures and arrivals than any other station in Germany, so finding a train to or from almost anywhere is not a problem. The information office for train connections, tickets etc is at the head of platform No 9. For train information call ☎ 194 19.

Car & Motorcycle Frankfurt features the Frankfurter Kreuz, Germany's biggest autobahn intersection – modelled, it would seem, after the worst in Los Angeles. All major (and some minor) car-rental companies have offices in the main hall of the Hauptbahnhof and at the airport.

Ride Services The ADM-Mitfahrzentrale (☎ 194 40) is on Baselerplatz, three minutes' walk south of the train station. It's open Monday to Friday from 8 am to 6.30 pm and Saturday till 2 pm. A sample of fares (including fees) is: Berlin DM54, Hamburg DM51 and Munich DM40. The Citynetz Mitfahr-Service (☎ 194 44), at Homburger Strasse 36, has slightly cheaper rates.

Getting Around

The Airport S-Bahn line No 8 runs at least every 15 minutes between the airport and Frankfurt Hauptbahnhof (11 minutes), then continues on to Ostbahnhof via Hauptwache and Konstablerwache; a standard fare of DM5.70 applies to/from all these stations. At the Hauptbahnhof you can also jump on any train that stops at the airport if you have a valid S-Bahn ticket; see the list posted on every track that says, in English, German and French, 'Trains to Frankfurt Airport'.

Bus No 61 runs to/from the Südbahnhof in Sachsenhausen. Taxis charge about DM40 for the trip into town but are slower than the train.

Public Transport Frankfurt's excellent transport network (RMV; ☎ 0130-235 14 51) integrates all bus, tram, S-Bahn and U-Bahn lines. The RMV has automatic ticket machines at every station and virtually every tram and bus stop (press the left-hand button for explanations in English).

A zonal system applies – the core zone (press the *Preisstufe 3* button) covers the large central area of Frankfurt, but to get to or from the airport you'll need a two-zone *(Preisstufe 4)* ticket. Short trips (up to 2km irrespective of zones) cost DM2.60, while a longer single trip costs DM3.30/5.70 for one/two zones. If you plan to do much city travelling, buy a 24-hour central-zone ticket for DM8.80 (DM5.30 for students) or a seven-day ticket for DM28.50 (students DM21.50). These are also valid for the airport.

Car & Motorcycle Traffic flows smoothly in central Frankfurt, but the one-way system makes it extremely frustrating to get to where you want to go. You're better off parking your vehicle in one of the many car parks (DM3 per hour, DM5 overnight) and proceeding on foot. Throughout the centre you'll see signs on lampposts for car parks, which give directions and the number of parking places left in each.

Taxi Taxis are quite expensive at DM3.80 flag fall plus a minimum of DM2.15 per kilometre. There are taxi ranks throughout the city, or you can ring for one on ☎ 230 00 33, ☎ 250 00 1 or ☎ 545 01 1.

The BahnTaxi stand (DM12 per couple) is at the eastern end of the Hauptbahnhof near the City exit.

Bicycle The city is good for cyclists, with designated bike lanes on most streets. Bikes are treated by the law as cars, so watch out for red lights. Bikes can be rented at the Hauptbahnhof's luggage counter for DM10 a day, or for slightly more at Per Pedale (☎ 707 23 63), Leipzigstrasse 4; Radschlag (☎ 452 06 4), Hallgartenstrasse 56; or Theo Intra (☎ 342 78 0), Westerbacherstrasse 273.

DARMSTADT

- *pop 141,000*
- *area code* ☎ 06151

Some 35km south of Frankfurt, Darmstadt is a city with a long history of artistic accomplishment – home to writers, composers and the Matildenhöhe, the art colony that truly brought the Art Nouveau (Jugendstil) style into vogue. It's a nice little side trip and if you decide to stay, there's a couple of very cool Irish pubs here too.

Orientation & Information

The Hauptbahnhof is at the eastern end of the city, connected to the Altstadt by a long walk (or quick ride on bus D or F) down Rheinstrasse, which runs directly into Luisenplatz, in the pedestrianised heart of the city. The Hessisches Landesmuseum and Schloss are right in the centre. The Matildenhöhe is about 1km from the centre.

The city tourist office (☎ 132 78 0) is right in front of the Hauptbahnhof and is open Monday to Friday from 9 am to 6 pm, Saturday 9 am to noon; a second office is in the Luisencentre at Luisenplatz (☎ 132 78 1; same weekday hours but open Saturday to 1 pm).

There's a post office at the Hauptbahnhof and another in Luisenplatz.

Books can be bought at the large international stand at the Hauptbahnhof; Lonely Planet titles and English-language books are available at Gutenberg Buchhandlung, Am Luisenplatz 4.

Things to See & Do

Established in 1899 at the behest of Grand Duke Ernst-Ludwig, the artists' colony at **Matildenhöhe** churned out some impressive works of Art Nouveau between 1901 and 1914. The **Artists' Colony Museum** (☎ 133 38 5; entry DM6, discount DM3) displays some of these works in its beautiful grounds. Take tram No 1 from the Hauptbahnhof. Also in the grounds is the **Braun Form Collection**, displaying 300 types of Braun products – from razors to radios – and a stunning **Russian Orthodox chapel**, built 1897-99 and designed by Louis Benois for the Russian Tsar Nicholas II after he married Princess Alix of Hesse in 1894.

One of the oldest art museums in Germany is the **Hessisches Landesmuseum** (☎ 125 43 4; closed Monday; DM5/1) at Friedensplatz 1. It houses Hessian artworks from 1550 to 1880, natural sciences and geology.

The **Schloss Museum** (open Monday to Thursday; DM2.50), in a former margrave's residence with an 18th-century castle, is packed with ornate furnishings, carriages and paintings, including *The Madonna of Jakob Meyer, Mayor of Basle* by Hans Holbein the Younger.

Organised Tours

There are 1½ to two-hour guided tours (DM15/8) of the city every Saturday and Sunday; they depart from the statue of Grand Duke Ernst-Ludwig in the centre of Luisenplatz. Get tickets at the tourist offices.

Places to Stay & Eat

The *Hostel* (☎ 452 93) is at Landgraf-Georg-Strasse 119 and has beds for juniors/seniors for DM23.50/28.50, including breakfast. South of the centre, the *Hotel Zum Weingarten* (☎ 522 61), Weingartenstrasse 36, has the cheapest singles/ doubles in town at DM35/45; prices for rooms with shower and WC begin at DM45/60. The nicely renovated *Hotel Atlanta* (☎ 178 90), north of the Herrngarten at Kasinostrasse 129, has rooms from DM90/130.

There's a *McDonald's* at the Hauptbahnhof, along with a good bakery. The Luisencentre is paradise for snackers and light eaters, with half a dozen options including *Le Gourmet* for sausages, meats and cheeses; *Obstgarten Schadt* for fruit and vegies; and *Bormith* bakery, along with fresh fruit juice and crêpe stands (DM2.40 to DM3).

Sidle up next to gangsters at *Bistro Da Gino*, which has cheap Italian specials all day. *Ann Sibin*, Landgraf-Georg-Strasse 125, is a killer Irish pub with good beer, as is *Die Krone*, which also has a cinema, piano room, pool table, live music and positively ghastly toilets.

Getting There & Away

There's frequent S-Bahn service (DM11.20/30 minutes) from Frankfurt's Hauptbahnhof.

OFFENBACH

- *pop 17,000*
- *area code* ☎ 069

Offenbach's ethnically diverse population gives it a rich range of eating options, and prices for everything, including food and lodging, are cheap by Frankfurt standards. Quiet and close to Frankfurt, it makes a good base for exploring the region.

Orientation & Information

S-Bahn trains arrive in a subway under Berliner Strasse, Offenbach's main drag, which neatly bisects the city. The Kaiserlei stop is close to the riverside beer gardens, the Ledermuseum is near many of the restaurants and hotels, and the Markt is in the centre. The train station is a 10-minute walk south of the centre. Frankfurt is a 30-minute walk west along the Main River.

The tourist office (☎ 806 56 52 9) is near the Marktplatz S-Bahn stop at Stadthof 17. It's open weekdays from 8 am to 12.30 pm and 1.45 to 6 pm. The post office is at Marienplatz 80.

Things to See & Do

Offenbach was, until WWII, a centre for leather manufacturing and mansions that belonged to the tanners line Main Strasse on the river and Frankfurter Strasse to the west.

The leather industry never returned, but the city is home to the national **Leather Museum** (☎ 81 30 21; open daily from 10 am to 5 pm; DM5), Frankfurter Strasse 86. Authentic down to the smell, anything and everything pertaining to tanned animal hides is celebrated in this large building. There is also a **Shoe Museum** here. Its highlight: Steffi Graf's trainers (in an airtight case).

The **riverfront** on Main Strasse has recently been spruced up and several boat clubs call this stretch home; each operates a café serving simple food and beer. In good weather, you can sit outside to watch the constant parade of commercial ships and barges on the Main.

Places to Stay

The non-HI *Jugendgästehaus-Offenbach* (☎ 832 45 1), Am Waldschwimmbad 30, is 20 minutes south of the centre and next to a good public pool. Doubles begin at DM34. Take bus No 104 from the train station or bus No 105 from the Marktplatz S-Bahn stop.

South of the city, *Hotel Matthäus* (☎ 894 46 6), Bieberer Strasse 64, charges DM72 for doubles without bath and *Hotel Traube* (☎ 891 18 0), Aschaffenburger Strasse 22, charges DM70/DM80 for doubles with/

without bath. Both are accessible by bus No 102 from the centre.

The quiet *Hansa Hotel* (☎ 82 98 50), Bernardstrasse 101, has doubles without bath from DM90. Near the Ledermuseum S-Bahn stop, *Hotel Ravel International* (☎ 800 45 24) and *Low'nhotel* (☎ 812 65 0) are on Ludwigstrasse at 91 and 95 respectively. Staff from both say their well-equipped doubles with baths start at DM150, but you can probably bargain them down.

Places to Eat

Iskender Kebab, across from the train station at Kaiserstrasse 4, has good doner for DM4.

The *Green Hill Vegetarian Restaurant*, Mainstrasse 11, has tofu-laden entrees from DM15 as well as main courses. Nearby, *Bistro Café Li*, Speyer Strasse 30, has large windows overlooking the river and is open for drinks and sandwiches all day and well into the night.

Pizzeria-Ristorante Da Bruno, Ludwigstrasse 117, is a tiny place with low prices. Excellent pizzas and pasta dishes average DM12.

Datscha, Kaiserstrasse 8a, has medium-priced Russian food and 20 types of vodka, but if you have a hankering for Hessian hootch, *Apfel-Wein Klein*, Bettina Strasse 16, has jugs of local apple wine to wash down pork-dominated main courses from DM15. You can sit outside in summer.

We loved *Wundertüte*, Goethestrasse 59, a friendly and relaxed bar serving cheap salads, sandwiches and pastas from 8 pm to midnight.

Getting There & Away

The S-Bahn train S8 makes the 25-minute journey between Offenbach and Frankfurt's Hauptbahnhof four times an hour from 4 am to midnight.

FULDA

- *pop 58,000*
- *area code* ☎ 0661

With a large baroque district and many fine and interesting churches, Fulda, 45 minutes from Frankfurt, is definitely worth a visit.

Orientation & Information

The train station is at the north-eastern end of Bahnhofstrasse, five minutes from the baroque Altstadt, which begins just west of Universitätsplatz. Turn right there and you'll get to the Stadtschloss, at the northern end of the Altstadt. The Dom and St-Michaels-Kirche are just west of the Stadtschloss. The bus station is at the southern end of the train station.

The tourist office, in the Stadtschloss (entrance DM2), is open Monday to Friday from 8.30 am to 4.30 pm (Thursday to 5.30 pm), Saturday from 9.30 am to 2 pm. It's closed on Sunday.

Change money at the Sparda bank, just to the left as you exit the train station. The main post office is a block north-west of the station at Heinrich-von-Bibra-Platz.

There are English-language books at the Buchexpress im Hauptbahnhof. The city library (☎ 974 90) is at Heinrich-von-Bibra. There's a Waschsalon in Vor dem Peterstor. Ärtzlicher Notdienst (☎ 192 92), Würtstrasse 1, on the corner of Leipziger Strasse, is an emergency medical service.

Things to See & Do

The **Stadtschloss**, completed in 1788, was the residence of prince abbots. It's now the city administration buildings. The **museum** (open Tuesday to Sunday from 10 am to 6 pm, Friday from 2 to 6 pm; DM6.50, discount DM4.50) has a residence, ballrooms and, from the **Green Room**, views over the **gardens** to the **Orangerie**. On the hill is the Frauenberg Franciscan Friary.

Built next to a monastic cemetery, **St-Michaels-Kirche** (1820-22) is fascinating; the rotunda dates to the original construction and in the cellar you can see original support pillars. The reconstructed **Dom** (1704-12) is across the street on the grounds of the Ratgar Basilica, which stood here from 819 to 1700. The cathedral has a richly decorated western portal.

Downstairs is the **tomb of St Boniface**, the English missionary who died a martyr in 754. Upstairs is an amazing painting of the **Assumption of Mary** and another of the

Holy Trinity and a Gothic relief of **Charlemagne** (15th century) at the east. There are organ recitals (DM3/2) here every Saturday at noon during May, June, September and October.

The **Cathedral Museum** (DM4/3), in the former Stiftskirche, is the highlight of a visit to Fulda.

In the cloakroom look through the glass floor at the foundations of the original basilica. The collection here includes Jewish gravestones (in the lovely front yard, packed with artefacts), the painting *Christus und die Ehebrechern* by Lucas Cranach the Elder (1512); a fashion show of bishop's vestments and a spooky thing that they say is the skull of St Boniface.

Places to Stay & Eat

There's camping at *Ferienplatz Eichenzell-Rothemann* (☎ 06659-228 5), Mulkuppenstrasse 15 in Rothemann, 12km south of Fulda. From the Hauptbahnhof take bus No 5043; the last one leaves Fulda at 6.30 pm. If you're driving, take the B27 (direction: Gersfeld).

The *hostel* (☎ 733 89), Schillmann Strasse 31, south-west of the city centre (bus Nos 1A and B), has dorm beds for DM24/30.50 for juniors/seniors.

Weinstube Dachsbau (☎ 741 12) is expensive but worth it, with good regional food and service. Don't mistake it for the Bistro Dachsbau across the street.

The *Zum Schwarzen Hahn* (☎ 240 31 2), right in the centre at Friedrichstrasse 18, also does Hessian specialities from DM15 to DM20.

The restaurant at the *Romantic Hotel Goldener Karpfen* is very, very expensive but has good service and international food, with a vegetarian menu and regional specialities.

Getting There & Away

S-Bahn trains make the journey from Frankfurt every half-hour for DM27, but IR trains do the journey about 15 minutes faster and ICE trains (DM41) take less than an hour.

WIESBADEN

- *pop 268,000*
- *area code* ☎ 0611

An hour west of Frankfurt, the Hessian capital of Wiesbaden is best known for a range of odd attractions: thermal baths, casinos, the state Parliament building and a Russian Orthodox church.

Visitors to Wiesbaden – an expensive and ugly capital – tend to be wealthy Germans passing through for relaxation in the spas, or Americans visiting family at the nearby Rhein-Mein air-force base, south-east of the city.

Orientation

From the Hauptbahnhof, bus Nos 1 and 8 take you north along Bahnhofstrasse to the city centre.

The cable car leading to the Russian Orthodox church at the top of Neroberg (Nero Hill) is at the northern end of the city. The Kurhaus is at the north-eastern end of the city. Bus No 1 goes to both of these.

Information

The tourist information office (☎ 172 90), Marktstrasse 6, is at the western end of the Markt. It's open Monday to Friday from 9 am to 6 pm, Saturday and Sunday from 10 am to 4 pm. Staff book rooms in hotels and pensions (but not private rooms) for DM6 and sell tickets to the spas and attractions.

Change money at the Reisebank at the Hauptbahnhof. The central post office is at Kaiser-Friedrich-Ring 81, next to the Hauptbahnhof.

The Bauer Buchhandlung bookshop has an English-language section at the Hauptbahnhof, along with foreign newspapers and magazines. Wash clothes at the SB Münzwascherei (☎ 488 82), Eltviller Strasse 8; there's another laundrette closer to the centre in Wellritzstrasse, on the corner of Wallramstrasse.

For a doctor, call ☎ 461 01 0 or ☎ 670 60.

Things to See & Do

Schlossplatz is the centre of the city and contains the stunning Gothic **Marktkirche**

(1852-62) and the **Neues Rathaus** (1884-87) surrounding the newly renovated **Marktbrunnen**, originally built in 1537.

Take bus No 1 to the **cable car** (DM2) for the trip up the Neroberg to the **Russian Orthodox Church**, often mistakenly called the 'Greek Chapel', built between 1847 and 1855 as the burial place of Elizabeth Mikhailovna, wife of Duke Adolf of Nassau and niece of a Tsar of Russia. Elizabeth died here during childbirth in 1845 and Adolf built this five-domed church, modelled on the Church of the Ascension in Moscow.

The **Museum Wiesbaden** (☎ 3680), south-east of the centre at Friedrich-Ebert Allee 2, houses many paintings by Russian expressionist Alexei Jawlensky, who lived and died here. It is open Tuesday to Sunday from 10 am to 4 pm.

The **Kurhaus Wiesbaden** (☎ 172 92 90), Kurhausplatz 1, at the eastern end of the centre, is a restored classical building (1907) that's been converted into the city's main theatre, convention centre and casino. You can view the obscenely lavish rooms with a guide (see Organised Tours) or just walk up to the desk staff and ask them to let you snoop around.

The grounds are lovely to stroll in and on Sunday there's a brunch buffet, accompanied by jazz, on the patio (DM45 per person). Admission to the grounds is free.

There are two main thermal baths in the city. **Kaiser-Friedrich-Bad**, where nude people cavort in hot, cold and steam baths and relax in cabins (containing the Irish-Roman Thermal baths) at the end of Landgasse just north of the centre; and the more conservative **Thermal Bad** with saltwater baths. Both have solarium and sauna. Bus No 18 takes you there from the centre. A day pass to the Kaiser-Friedrich-Bad costs DM20, to the Thermal Bad DM10.

Organised Tours

The tourist office runs bus tours on Wednesday at 2.30 pm, Saturday at 2 pm and Sunday at 9.45 am. Leaving from the Theatre Colonnade in front of the Hessische Staatstheater, the tours take in the Kurhaus, Neroberg and the castle at Biebrich. On Saturday and Sunday, the tour includes a glass of wine. The cost is DM20, DM10 for children up to age 14.

Places to Stay

Campingplatz Rettbergsau (☎ 312 27; bus No 4 or 14 to the riverbank), on the island in the middle of the Rhine, has camping sites for DM8.

The city's *hostel* (☎ 486 57), at Blücherstrasse 66, is a 10-minute walk west of the city centre. Despite the unattractive building, the staff are inordinately helpful and, though the place isn't sparkling, it's clean enough. A place in a six-bed dorm costs DM24/29 juniors/seniors. There's a cafeteria downstairs that serves beer and apple wine. From the train station, take bus No 14 (direction: Klarenthal) to Gnaisenastrasse.

Places to Eat

Schmitt, a drinks shop right near the hostel on the corner of Blücherstrasse and Nettelbeckstrasse, sells cheap mineral water, soft drinks and beer to bring over to your room. *Kaiser Vollkorn Bäckerei*, Blücherstrasse 8, has excellent organic bread, cakes and pastries and a stehcafé.

In the pedestrian zone west of Schlossplatz there are several fast-food options, especially along Friedrichstrasse where the popular *China Bistro* (☎ 373 52 9) at No 41 has cheap and good lunch specials (everything under DM10); fried rice and noodle dishes cost around DM7.50. There's a *Pizza Hut* next door.

Mauerstrasse, running off Schlossplatz, is another wonderful food street with lots of little bistros and restaurants. The cheery *Bistro Mauer Blümchen* (☎ 307 89 6), at Mauerstrasse 25, has nice lunch specials like a gyros platter with French fries and salads for DM13. At the corner of Marktstrasse and Mauerstrasse is *Fisch-Thiel am Markt*, with a wonderful atmosphere and fresh fish specials from DM15 every day.

The *Rhein Main Grill* (☎ 373 55 4), Rheinestrasse 27, has great service and good

German food at reasonable prices – figure on spending DM14 to DM16 on a main course.

Right in the centre is *Zum Dortmunder* (☎ 302 09 6), Langgasse 34, offering a full menu of international and German cuisine. A good vegetarian selection is available at the *Domäne Mechtildshausen* (☎ 737 46 0), which serves up only organically grown vegies. It's out by the US air-force base in Hofgut Mechtildshausen. From the centre, take bus No 28 out to the air base; ask the driver if the bus stops there (most do). Otherwise, take bus No 5 to Erbenheim and a taxi (about DM12) to the restaurant. Oh yeah, bring lots of cash or a credit card: a full meal will cost about DM100 per person.

Getting There & Around

S-Bahn trains leave every 20 minutes from Frankfurt's Hauptbahnhof (DM9.80, 45 minutes). There's an ADM Mitfahrzentrale office (☎ 333 55 5) just north of the train station at Bahnhofstrasse 51-53; look for the big banner.

City buses cost DM3.60 for a single ticket or DM8.50 for a 24-hour pass.

MARBURG

- *pop 76,400*
- *area code* ☎ 06421

Some 90km north of Frankfurt, Marburg is a university city known for its charming Altstadt and the splendid Elisabethkirche – Germany's first Gothic church. The Brothers Grimm studied here for a short time, and Phillips University (1527) was Europe's first Protestant university.

It's also a great place to get fit: much of the city is built on a hillside and staircases and ramps abound. There are lifts for the disabled to some of the sights.

Orientation

The Lahn River flows south and separates the Altstadt from the Hauptbahnhof area. The Altstadt takes up the hill on the west bank of the river and it's divided into the Unterstadt at the bottom and the Oberstadt at the top of the hill.

Bahnhofstrasse leads from the train station to Elisabethstrasse, which takes you south past Elisabethkirche to a fork in the road; bear right for the Oberstadt and left for the Unterstadt. See the Altstadt section for information about the lifts that run between the two.

Phillips University (☎ 202 16 2), Neue Kasseler Strasse 1, has 21 schools including law, medicine, physics, languages and history. The campus is spread throughout the city but the Old University building is in the centre of the Altstadt.

Information

The tourist office (☎ 991 20; fax 991 21 2) is in the Unterstadt at Pilgrimstein 26, opposite the Hotel Sorat and next to the lifts between the Unterstadt and Oberstadt. It's open Monday to Friday from 9 am to 6 pm, Saturday from 9 am to 1 pm.

There are ATMs in the train station and a Sparkasse opposite the train station. The main post office is at Bahnhofstrasse 6.

Universitäts Buchhandlung (☎ 170 90), Reitgasse 7-19, has lots of English books and Lonely Planet guidebooks. There are always cheap English-language paperbacks (about DM5) in the bins outside Wohlfeile Bücher (☎ 669 19), Neustadt 9.

Wash your clothes in style at the Bistro-Waschbrett (☎ 123 54), Gutenbergstrasse 16, a café-laundrette three minutes' walk from the hostel. Wednesdays are cheap days there; a wash costs DM5.

The main Uni-Klinikum (University Hospital; ☎ 283 69 7) is on the east side of the Lahn in Baldingerstrasse.

Elisabethkirche

The Elisabethkirche, Germany's first Gothic cathedral, was begun in 1235 and completed in 1283, though the twin spires weren't finished for another three decades. If you want to view the high choir and anything behind the screen they've erected (mean-spiritedly, we think), you'll have to pay DM3 (discount DM2) or join one of the tours (DM1) which run from Monday to Friday and on Sunday at 3 pm. You could just attend a Sunday service (at 8.30 am and 6 pm).

Altstadt
From Elisabethkirche, walk south, take the left jig and get on to Steinweg, which leads up the hill. Steinweg becomes Neustadt and Wettergasse, which finally leads into the **Markt**.

In the centre of the Markt is the **Rathaus** (1512). Its beautiful clock strikes hourly with lots of pomp and it has an odd half **gable** on the west side. A market is held here every Saturday morning.

Facing the Rathaus, turn round and you'll look straight up at the **Landgrafenschloss** (1248-1300), a massive stone structure that was the administrative seat of Hesse.

Follow the ramps up the amazingly steep **Land-Graf-Phillip-Strasse** to the top where there is a **Local History Museum** (DM3/2) and a great view.

Concerts are held in the **Schlosspark** throughout the year.

Walk back to the Markt and turn down Reitgasse and you'll reach the **Universitätskirche** (1300), a former Dominican monastery, and the **Alte Universität** (1891), still part of the campus and still bustling.

Finally, walk round the church and across the Weidenhäuser Brücke; on the south side of the bridge and the east side of the Lahn is a stand with rowing boats (DM10 per hour).

If you want to see the Markt but don't want to climb Steinweg, begin this tour by walking south from Elisabethkirche, bear left at the fork and follow the Pilgrimstein to **Rudolphsplatz**.

There's a monstrously steep **stone staircase** at Enge Gasse, which was once a sewage sluice.

Free **lifts** carry you from Rudolphsplatz up to Reitgasse from 7 am to 11.30 pm.

Other Sights
The **Universitätsmuseum für Bildende Kunst** (☎ 282 35 5), on the east bank of the river at Biegenstrasse 11, has artworks from the 19th and 20th centuries.

The former city **Botanical Gardens**, just to the north-west of the museum, are now open as a city park. Admission to both is free.

Organised Tours
The tourist office arranges two-hour walking tours of Elisabethkirche and Landgrafenschloss on Saturday, from April to October, for DM5; they leave from the Elisabethkirche at 3 pm. One-hour tours of the Markt and Altstadt leave Wednesday at 11 am from the Rathaus (DM3).

Places to Stay
Camping *Campingplatz Lahnaue* (☎ 213 31), Trojedamm 47, just south of the hostel (directions follow) is a fine option, right on the river, with tent sites for DM5 to DM6 plus DM6 per person and DM3 per car (DM1 per bicycle).

Hostel Marburg's spotless and welcoming *DJH hostel* (☎ 234 61) is at Jahnstrasse 1, about a 10-minute walk downstream along the Lahn from Rudolphsplatz in the Altstadt. Rates for juniors/seniors are DM28/33 for one night, DM24/29 for two nights. Staff can help plan outings, rent three-person canoes (DM35 a day) and arrange bicycle rental.

From the train station, take bus No 1 to Rudolphsplatz. From there, walk south, cross the Weidenhäuser Brücke, take the stairs to the right at the east end of the bridge, turn south (towards the waterfall) and it's five minutes ahead on the left.

Private Rooms Book private rooms at the tourist office; it's a free service.

Hotels & Pensions Hotels in town are uniformly expensive, but a good deal can be had if you get in at the tiny *Gästehaus Einsle* (☎ 234 10), tucked away at Frankfurter Strasse 2a, on the west side of the Lahn near the hostel. Tacky but clean singles/doubles go for DM50/60.

The boxy *Europäischer Hof* (☎ 696 0), Elisabethstrasse 12 near Bahnhofstrasse, is a good deal for what it looks like: it's slightly seedy and pretty unreasonable at DM85/150.

The *Hotel Sorat* (☎ 918 0; fax 918 44 4) was so new there wasn't any furniture in the lobby (and only a little in the rooms) when we last visited Marburg. But staff say it will be nice and their weekend deal sounds good for a top-end place: DM125/165 singles/doubles. During the week, rates shoot up to DM225/265.

Places to Eat

There's a delicious bakery at Fleckenbühler Backwaren, Steinweg 2-5. On the way to the train station, stop off at *Pizzeria da Pepe* (☎ 627 07), Bahnhofstrasse 18a, a very popular but tiny place with smiling staff and good pizzas from DM3.

The hostel's *restaurant* serves lunch every day for DM8.50. Over on that side of the river there's also very good Turkish food at *Kebab Asbendos* (☎ 152 29), Erlenring 2, near the Weidenhäuser Brücke. Doners cost from DM6, platters from DM12 and vegetarian sandwiches from DM4.

The *Brasserie* (☎ 219 92), opposite the Universitäts Buchhandlung on Reitgasse, has good breakfast and prices.

Across the street, *Bistro News Café* (☎ 212 05), Reitgasse 5, has the same stuff for the same prices, but it's much bigger. At the *Café Local*, Steinweg 1, you can fill up on food priced from DM8.

Two very nice places on Barfüsserstrasse include the romantic *Café 1900*, at No 27, with snacks and light meals for under DM10 and good bean soup for DM5.50; and *Café Barfuss* (☎ 253 49), at No 23, is a wacky place with toy aeroplanes and ads hanging from the ceiling, with pasta from DM9 to DM11, vegetarian dishes from DM10 to DM12.

Entertainment

Pick up a free copy of *Marburger Magazin Express* for listings and music dates.

The Kammer Filmkunstprogramm-Kino (☎ 672 65), Steinweg 4, shows films in their original language

There are two cool places downstairs from the Bistro News Café at Reitgasse 5: on the 1st level down is *Hemingways*, an American bar with happy hour daily from 6 to 7.30 pm, and *Dance Down Under*, a bar and disco.

Getting There & Around

Trains to Marburg run hourly from Frankfurt (DM23, one hour) and twice an hour from Kassel (DM26, one hour).

Velociped (☎ 245 11), Auf dem Wehr 3, hires bicycles for DM15 per day and also runs tours of nearby towns from DM15, and overnight bike trips from DM255. The hostel can also arrange an itinerary for you if you have your own bike.

Bus No 1 runs from the train station to Rudolphsplatz and costs DM2.

KASSEL

- *pop 63,000*
- *area code* ☎ 0561

The term 'architectural crimes' could well have been coined to describe the reconstruction of Kassel, a once lovely city on the Fulda River, 1½ hours north of Frankfurt.The label fits, but the sprawling town is doing its best to regain some of its former appeal.

Since reunification placed it once again in the geographical centre of the country, Kassel was chosen by the national train line to be a major ICE transfer point, which brought money and business to the area. Industry has moved out of the centre; the major factories have been converted to a liberal arts university that now boasts more than 18,000 students.

There are a couple of must-sees here, including the city's unusual Museum of Death and Wilhelmshöhe, a glorious nature park with waterfalls, a Roman aqueduct, two castles and the city's emblem – the massive Hercules monument.

Wilhelm and Jakob Grimm lived and worked in Kassel and there's a museum here celebrating their work.

Every five years Kassel is host to one of Weestern Europe's most important modern art shows, the *documenta*. Lasting 100 days, it attracts up to 700,000 visitors. The next documenta will be held in 2002.

Orientation

There are two main train stations. ICE, IC and IR trains pull into the new ICE-Bahnhof Wilhelmshöhe (everyone calls it the ICE-

Bahnhof), 3km west of the city centre. The Hauptbahnhof (in name only) is at the western end of the centre at Bahnhofsplatz and now serves as a train station for slower trains as well as a cultural centre.

Wilhelmshöhe and its attractions are all at the western end of Wilhelmshöher Allee, which runs straight as an arrow from the centre of the city to the castle.

The mostly pedestrianised centre of the city focuses on Königsplatz.

The Universität Gesamthochschule campus is on the grounds of the former Henschl factory complex, south of the centre, and at Holländischer Platz at the north-east of the city.

Information

There are two tourist offices: Kassel Service (☎ 707 70 7), Königsplatz 53, open Monday to Thursday from 9.15 am to 6 pm, Friday to 4.30 pm, closed Saturday and Sunday; and another at ICE-Bahnhof Wilhelmshöhe (☎ 340 54; fax 315 21 6), open Monday to Friday from 9 am to 1 pm and 2 to 6 pm, Saturday to 1 pm, closed Sunday.

Both offices sell the Kassel ServiceCard (DM12/19 for one/three days), which gives you unlimited access to public transport, guided coach or walking tours and free or reduced admission to the area's attractions.

Change money at either of the train stations or at the Deutsche Bank or Commerzbank at Königsplatz.

The main post office is at the north-east corner of the centre on Königsstrasse, just south of Holländischer Platz, but there's a post office in both train stations and another at Wilhelmshöher Allee.

Freyschmidts Buchhandlung (☎ 729 02 10), Königsstrasse 23, has English-language novels and Lonely Planet guidebooks.

There's a Schnell und Sauber Waschsalon at Friedrich-Ebert-Strasse 83, four blocks south of the hostel.

Wilhelmshöhe

Seven kilometres west of the centre, within the enchanting **Habichtswald** (Hawk Forest), stands the city's symbol – a massive statue of Hercules atop a huge stone pyramid atop an octagonal amphitheatre atop an impressive hill – which should be your first stop. You can spend an entire day here walking through the forest, down the hiking paths (all levels of difficulty) and, if you avoid the tour buses, it can be a very romantic spot to have a picnic.

The Hercules Herkules, at 600m above sea level, was built between 1707 and 1717 as a symbol of the area's power. The mythical hero himself (scantily clad as usual) looks down at the defeated Encelados, but the main attraction here, if you can climb the 449 steps (DM3, discount DM2) to the top, is the unbelievable view you have in all directions.

Facing the town, you'll see Wilhelmshöhe Allee running due west towards the town. Until reunification, the hills east of the town formed the border with the GDR. To the south and north-west is the Habichtswald, with over 300km of hiking trails. At the bottom of the hill you'll see Schloss Wilhelmshöhe and, to its south, Löwenburg.

To get to Herkules from the ICE-Bahnhof, take tram No 3 to the terminus and change for bus No 43, which goes right up to the top once or twice an hour from 8 am to 8 pm.

Schloss Wilhelmshöhe Home to Elector Wilhelm and later Kaiser Wilhelm II, this palace (1786-1798) houses the **Old Masters Gallery**, featuring works by Rembrandt, Rubens, Jordaens, Lucas Cranach the Elder, Dürer and many others.

During renovation (until 1999) Dutch paintings are stored in the Neue Galerie (see Museums), while Italian and German works are at the **Hessischen Landesmuseum**.

To reach Schloss Wilhelmshöhe from the ICE-Bahnhof, take tram No 1 to the last stop. From there you can take bus No 23, which makes a loop around the lower regions of the park including the aqueduct and Schloss Löwenburg, or walk, following the well marked hiking trails, straight to the top.

Schloss Löwenburg Modelled on a medieval Scottish castle, Löwenburg (1801) is only open to visitors on guided tours (DM3/1.50), which take in the castle's **Museum of Armaments** and **Museum of Chivalry**.

Fountains From April to October every Wednesday to Sunday the **Wasserspiel** takes place along the hillside. The fountain's water cascades from the Herkules down to about the halfway point, then follows underground passages until it emerges at the **Grosse Fontane** in a 52m-high jet of water. The waterworks begin at 2 pm – follow the crowds.

Museums
Billed as 'a meditative space for funerary art', Kassel's excellent and undervisited Museum für Serulkralkultur, or **Death Museum** (☎ 918 93 0), Weinbergstrasse 25-27, is certainly an interesting way to become familiar with German death rituals. Designed to end the taboo of discussing death, the museum's permanent collection consists of headstones, hearses, dancing skeleton bookends and sculptures depicting death. Upstairs are temporary exhibitions. It's open Tuesday to Sunday from 10 am to 5 pm and entry costs DM5/3.

The **Brothers Grimm Museum** (☎ 787 20 33), in the Bellevue Schlösschen at Schöne Aussicht 2, has displays on the brothers' lives, their work (before and after publishing the tales) and the tales themselves, with original manuscripts, portraits and sculptures. It's open daily from 10 am to 5 pm; admission DM3/2.

Across the street is the **Neue Galerie**, temporary home to the Dutch paintings from the Old Masters collection at Wilhelmshöhe. It is open Tuesday to Sunday from 10 am to 5 pm and admission is free.

Organised Tours
There are two-hour city bus tours which include Wilhelmshöhe on Saturday from May to mid-November at 2 pm; they leave from Königsplatz and cost DM18/12.

Walking tours also leave from Königsplatz throughout the year; call by when you're in town to join one.

Two shipping companies offer cruises along the Fulda River from the docks on the east side of town. Rehbein Linie Kassel (☎ 185 05) and Söllner-Kasel (☎ 774 67 0) run one to six-hour cruises into the hinterland from where you can walk or take a train back. Prices start at DM10/6 one way and DM16/8 return.

Places to Stay
Camping *Campingplatz Beier* (☎ 224 33), between Auestadion and the Messehallen on the Fulda River, is a very peaceful spot with tent sites for DM15 per person, including tent and parking. From the centre, take tram No 7 to Auestadion.

Hostel Kassel's clean *hostel* (☎ 776 45 5), Am Tannenwäldchen, Schenkendorfstrasse 18, is one of the best in the country. It is huge and airy with friendly staff, good food and activities. Beds are DM24/29 for juniors/seniors, sheets an extra DM5, towels DM2. The café on the main floor is open all day. It's 10 minutes from the Hauptbahnhof on foot; follow Kölnische Strasse west, past the Martini Pils brewery to Schenkendorfstrasse, turn right and the hostel is at the end of the street on the right-hand side. Or take tram No 4 or 6 from the Hauptbahnhof to Annastrasse and walk north four blocks.

Private Rooms Book private rooms and flats at either tourist office (DM5 for the service). Rooms average DM40 to DM60 per person; flats, they say, are too complicated to even quote a price on.

Hotels & Pensions The best deal on a room is at the *hostel*, where you can get a duplex (covering two floors) single/double for DM52.50/81.60. The bath is down the hall, but you have a WC and sink in the room.

Cheaper for a single, but somewhat stark, is the *Hotel Stock* (☎ 647 98), Harleshäuser Strasse 60, about 10 minutes' walk north of the Hauptbahnhof, with rooms from DM40/92. Things are coming apart at the seams, but the service is very friendly.

The well situated and friendly *Hotel Garni*

Kö 78 (☎ 716 14), Kölnische Strasse 78, has very fine singles/doubles from DM69/99. It is a bit closer to town than the hostel and is bright and comfortable.

Above that you're pretty much looking at health spas and business hotels, of which there are several. Right in the area of the ICE-Bahnhof are the *Ramada Hotel* (☎ 933 90; fax 933 91 00), a very nice place with good service and a sauna. Singles or doubles start at DM150.

A brand new *InterCity Hotel* (☎ 938 80; fax 938 89 99), attached to the east side of the station at Wilhelmshöher Allee 241, has rooms from DM190/230; and the luxury *Best Western Kurfürst Wilhelm I* (☎ 318 70; fax 318 77 7), opposite the station at Wilhelmshöher Allee 257, has rooms from DM180/240.

Places to Eat

Other than the *Burger King* at the Hauptbahnhof and the *Markt im Bahnhof* at the ICE-Bahnhof, the best place for a quick bite is along Königsstrasse's pedestrian zone. Try the excellent pastries, cookies, pizzas and breads at *Uden Hausener Brotstube*, just outside the Kaufhof, a couple of doors down from the bookshop. There are a few *Nordsee* restaurants along here, but the best is at No 45, with awesome Bratkartoffeln and good salads along with a wide selection of hot meals and sandwiches.

The hostel *restaurant* is of good quality and value, with full lunches available from noon to 1.30 pm and dinners from 6 to 7 pm for DM8.80. No dinner is served on Sunday night.

Marmara (☎ 713 37 5), Friedrich-Ebert-Strasse 66 on the corner of Annastrasse near the hostel, serves huge portions of Turkish food and service is so friendly it's almost embarrassing. Felafel costs DM6, doners are from DM6 and there are great salads from DM5.50.

Café Paulus (☎ 978 89 0), Königsstrasse 28 at Opernplatz, is a very popular place for lunch and pastries when it opens the footpath café. If you're a student, its daily breakfast buffet is a good deal at DM12.50; the rest of us pay DM18.50.

Right near the hostel, *Wok* (☎ 711 14 4), Kölnischestrasse 125 on the corner of Schenkenorfstrasse, has good Thai food with a menu catering to vegetarians as well as carnivores; noodle dishes are from DM12 to DM16, meat dishes DM16 to DM25 and vegie main courses from DM13 to DM17. There's a beer garden out the back.

Tucked away in the Hauptbahnhof, *Gleis 1* (☎ 780 16 0) has absolutely no right to be as hip as it is. Looking much more like New York than Hesse, this very cool place has an American-style bar, a restaurant and live music and disco at nights. You can get baguettes from DM7.50, starters or snacks like antipasti or chilli con carne from DM7 to DM8.50, pastas from DM9 to DM12.50 and full main courses from DM16 to DM25.

Entertainment

The Hauptbahnhof is now called the Kultur Bahnhof (or KüBa) and has cafés (Gleis 1), bars (*Caricatur*), art openings and original-language movies playing constantly. Stop in or check out the magazine *KüBa*, available throughout the city at bars and pubs.

There's a disco at Gleis 1 and live music at *More* (☎ 103 00 0), Friedrich-Ebert-Strasse 7 at Annastrasse, where different styles happen on different nights. Wednesdays are erotic nights for men and women – sometimes just for women, with male strippers.

At *Joe's Garage*, across the street at Friedrich-Ebert-Strasse 60, there's live music most nights and occasional piercing and tattoo nights too.

Getting There & Away

ICE connections to/from Frankfurt/Main leave/arrive at the ICE-Bahnhof two to three times an hour (DM73, 1¼ to 1½ hours). Most ICE trains between major northern and southern German cities stop here, including trains from Frankfurt to Hamburg (twice hourly, DM106, two hours), Berlin-Zoo (hourly, DM123, 3¼ hours) and Hanover (twice hourly, DM61, one hour).

To/from Fulda, trains leave from either the ICE-Bahnhof (twice hourly, DM41, 30 minutes), or the Hauptbahnhof (hourly, DM29, 1½ hours)

To/from Marburg, trains leave from ICE-Bahnhof and the Hauptbahnhof (DM26, 1½ hours).

Getting Around

The KVG-Transport Centre (☎ 194 49), Königsplatz 36b, sells bus tickets (DM8 for 24 hours, DM24 for a week), which you can also get at kiosks and at the train stations.

Rent bicycles from Fahrrad Hof (☎ 313 08 3), at the eastern end of the ICE-Bahnhof, for DM20 per day. For mountain bikes, head to Edelmann (☎ 177 69), Goethestrasse 37-39. The prices vary, and a DM500 deposit is required.

WARBURG

- *pop 3000*
- *area code* ☎ 05642

Some 40 minutes north-west of Kassel by train is the quaint village of Warburg. It makes a romantic day trip – an untouched German village filled with half-timbered houses, pleasant walking trails and nice churches.

If you have a bike, bring it along; trails through the woods are clearly marked here. Don't lose faith when you pull into the station and see the Südzucker sugar refinery!

Orientation & Information

The Altstadt is south of the Neustadt and the train station.

From the station, follow Bahnhofstrasse south to the T-junction; to the right is Hauptstrasse, leading to Neustadt's main drag, to the left is the post office and Kasseler Strasse. Follow Kasseler to Bernhardi-Strasse, the Altstadt's main street, which brings you to Altstadt Platz.

Things to See & Do

Along Bernhardi-Strasse you'll come across numerous half-timbered houses, including the **Glockengiesserhaus** (1538), a Renaissance burgher's house; the **Eisenhoithaus** (1526), with its half-painted, half-carved doorway; and the absolutely massive **Arnoldi Haus**.

On the main Altstadt square is the also huge **Alter Rathaus** (1336-7), now home to a pizzeria and beer garden.

For a bird's-eye view, walk through the narrow streets up the hill to the north of Bernhardi-Strasse. You'll first pass the **Altstadt Kirche** (1290-1297). From there, follow the ramps leading uphill, past the Gasthaus zur Alm, to the top of the hill, on which sits the late 12th-century **Pfarrkirche**, with its choir stalls from the early 14th century.

A very interesting cultural series runs here throughout the year, with art openings, music nights (from organ concerts to swing), barbecues and dinners.

Look south from the stone terrace for a wonderful view over the town: to the south is **Der Biermannsturm** (1443), to the east and west a view like a storybook illustration of medieval Germany.

Places to Stay & Eat

Most people don't make Warburg any more than an afternoon excursion, but if you want to stay, try the *Warburger Hof* (☎ 610 0), Bahnhofstrasse 19a, a clean, modern place which has a restaurant downstairs. Singles/doubles start at DM60/100.

Imbisstro in Altstadt Platz has cheap fast food plus vegetarian specials from DM5.

Halfway up the hill, the *Gasthaus zur Alm* has a lovely terrace overlooking the town, nice staff and lunch from DM8 to DM11.

Back in the Altstadt, try the pizza at *Auf'm Alter Rathaus* (DM6 to DM10), if only for the atmosphere. *Gaststätte Spiegel* nearby has a very nice beer garden.

Getting There & Away

Trains leave from Kassel's Hauptbahnhof every hour (DM15) for the 40-minute journey. In Warburg on weekdays only, you can take bus No 509 from the train station to the Altstadt (DM2.25).

Fairy-Tale Road

The 650km Fairy-Tale Road (Märchenstrasse) is one of Germany's most popular tourist routes. It's made up of cities, towns and hamlets in four states (Hesse, Lower Saxony, North Rhine-Westphalia and Bremen), some of them associated with the works of Wilhelm and Jakob Grimm.

The Brothers Grimm, grammarians heralded in academic circles for their work on *German Grammar* and *History of the German Language*, travelled extensively through central Germany in the early 19th century documenting folklore. First published in 1812 as *Kinder- und Hausmärchen*, their collection of tales (whose origins can be traced to Germany, Central Europe, Asia and India) gained international edition after the release in 1823 of *Grimm's Fairy Tales*, most famously including *Hansel & Gretel, Cinderella, The Pied Piper, Rapunzel* and scores of others.

Every town, village and hamlet along the Fairy-Tale Road has an information office of sorts. For advance information, contact the central Fairy-Tale Road Tourist Information office (☎ 0561-787 80 01), Postfach 102660, 34117 Kassel. Also most helpful is the office in Hamelin (☎ 05151-202 61 8), Deister Allee 3, just outside the old town (there is also a counter in the Hochzeitshaus from April to October).

For an organised tourist route, getting around the Fairy-Tale Road isn't very organised. There's no equivalent of the Romantic Road bus and, because the route covers several states, local bus and train services outside the major cities on the route aren't coordinated. The easiest way to follow the Fairy-Tale Road is by car. The ADAC map of the Weserbergland covers the area in detail. Several local trains a day travel between Hanover and Hamelin (40 minutes). From Hamelin's train station about a dozen buses a day (Nos 2612 to 2614, 40 minutes) travel to Bodenwerder. There are also buses between Bodenwerder and Höxter, and Höxter-Kassel buses pass through Bad Karlshafen.

There are over 60 stops on the Fairy-Tale Road. Major stops include:

Hanau This town east of Frankfurt on the Main River features a monument to its most famous sons: Jakob (1785-1863) and Wilhelm (1786-1859) Grimm, which is the obvious starting point of the Fairy-Tale Road. The puppet museum features some recognisable characters.

Steinau The Grimm brothers spent their youth here. The Renaissance Schloss contains exhibits on their work. The Amtshaus, Renaissance palace of the counts of Hanau, was their grand home. The puppet theatre stages some of their best-known tales.

Marburg This university town on the Lahn River was where the Brothers Grimm were educated and began their research into German folk tales and stories. You can visit the study of the brothers.

Kassel The Brothers Grimm collected a major part of their stories and legends in and around Kassel, where they lived from 1805 to 1830. The Brothers Grimm Museum has exhibits on their lives and works.

Göttingen The brothers were professors at the university (before being expelled in 1837 for their liberal views). In the summer months the Göttingen People's Theatre Company performs versions of the Grimms' fairy tales at the woodland stage in Bremke, south-east of Göttingen.

Bad Karlshafen This meticulously planned, baroque village is a major highlight of the Fairy-Tale Road. Originally the city was planned with an impressive harbour and a canal connecting the Weser River with the Rhine in the hope of diverting trade away from Hanover and Münden in the north. The plans were laid by a local earl with help from Huguenot refugees. The earl's death in 1730 prevented completion of the project, but even today his incomplete masterpiece and the influence of the Huguenots is too beautiful to miss.

Bodenwerder The Rathaus is said to be the house in which the legendary Baron von Münchhausen was born. The baron's fame was due to his telling of outrageous tales, the most famous of which was how he rode through the air on a cannonball. This very cannonball is in a room dedicated to the baron in the Rathaus. Also interesting is the statue of the baron riding half a horse, in the garden outside the Rathaus. This was, of course, another of his stories.

Hamelin The biggest stop on the Fairy-Tale Road is the quaint city of Hamelin (Hameln), associated forever with the legend of the Pied Piper. Hired by the city to rid the town of rats (he played his flute and the rats followed him out of town), the city later welched on paying the Piper, and legend has it that he then played his flute to rid the town of its children! The helpful city tourist office (☎ 05151-202 61 8), Deister Allee 3, just outside the old town (there is also a counter in the Hochzeitshaus from April to October), has maps and local information.

Among the most interesting sights is the Rattenfängerhaus (Rat Catcher's House) on Osterstrasse, the old town's main street, built at the beginning of the 17th century. On the Bungelosenstrasse side is an inscription that tells how, in 1284, 130 children of Hamelin were led past here by the piper, never to be seen again. Also have a look at the Rattenfänger Glockenspiel at the Weser Renaissance Hochzeitshaus (Marriage House) at the Markt end of Osterstrasse (plays daily at 1.05, 3.35 and 5.35 pm). More of the story is at the museum in the ornate Leisthaus (DM2; closed Monday). For the other beauties of Hamelin – the restored 16th to 18th-century half-timbered houses with inscribed dedications – stroll through the south-eastern quarter of the old town, around Alte Markstrasse and Grossehofstrasse or Kupferschmeidestrasse.

Bremen Last stop on the route is the old Hanseatic city-state of Bremen, home to the *Town Musicians of Bremen*. The route that began with a statue of the Brothers Grimm ends at the statue of the famous foursome, at the western end of the Rathaus not far from the giant Roland statue (see the Bremen chapter for other town highlights). On Sundays in the summer months, a troupe performs a re-enactment of the charming tale.

North Rhine-Westphalia

Few German states have to contend with as many negative perceptions as North Rhine-Westphalia (Nordrhein-Westfalen). Billowing chimneys and heavy industry; crowded, faceless cities; a barren landscape devoid of trees and flowers – those are the images that first come to the minds of many. Few, however, realise that forests, fields and lakes cover about 75% of the state, that the cities are pulsating cultural centres and that high-tech and speciality industries – not coal and steel – form the backbone of North Rhine-Westphalia's economy today. There's a greater density of theatres, orchestras and museums here – many of international stature – than anywhere else in Germany. Churches, palaces and castles bulge with art treasures. And unique discoveries like the Neanderthal skeleton unearthed in a valley near Düsseldorf point to a historic richness that reaches back to prehistory.

HIGHLIGHTS

- The soaring cathedrals of Cologne and Aachen
- Schloss Augustusburg in Brühl
- The carved altars in Kalkar's St Nikolai church
- An evening of drink and merriment in Düsseldorf's Altstadt
- House of the History of the Federal Republic of Germany in Bonn

- **Population:** 17.8m • **Capital:** Düsseldorf • **Area:** 34,070 sq km

North Rhine-Westphalia Luminaries: Konrad Adenauer, Pina Bausch, August Bebel, Joseph Beuys, Ludwig van Beethoven, Heinrich Böll, Annette von Droste-Hülshoff, Max Ernst, Herbert Grönemeyer, Heinrich Heine, Heino (Heinz Georg Kramm), Wilhelm Leibl, Udo Lindenberg, August Macke, Friedrich Wilhelm (FW) Murnau, Peter Paul Rubens, Claudia Schiffer, Michael Schumacher, Wim Wenders

History

As a modern political entity, North Rhine-Westphalia only came into existence in 1946. The British, who occupied the area after WWII, fused large portions of the former Prussian Rhine province with the province of Westphalia; the tiny state of Lippe-Detmold was incorporated a year later. It is Germany's most densely populated state: 17 million people (about one fifth of the total population) inhabit an area of 34,000 sq km, roughly the size of Belgium and Luxembourg combined. Most live in cities with over half a million inhabitants, and five of Germany's 10 largest metropolises are here: Cologne, Essen, Dortmund, Düsseldorf and Duisburg.

Many towns, including Cologne and Xanten, were founded by the Romans who settled here for about three centuries, having kicked out the Celts between 58 and 51 BC. Between the 3rd and the 5th centuries AD, Frankish tribes claimed the Lower Rhine area for themselves, while the Saxons took over today's Westphalia. This only lasted until the 8th century, when Frankish strongman Charlemagne subjugated Saxon Duke Widukind and incorporated the Saxon territory into the Holy Roman Empire.

Charlemagne's imperial headquarters were in Aachen, a city that belongs to any journey through North Rhine-Westphalia. Also a must is Cologne, which exhilarates with its breathtaking Gothic cathedral and

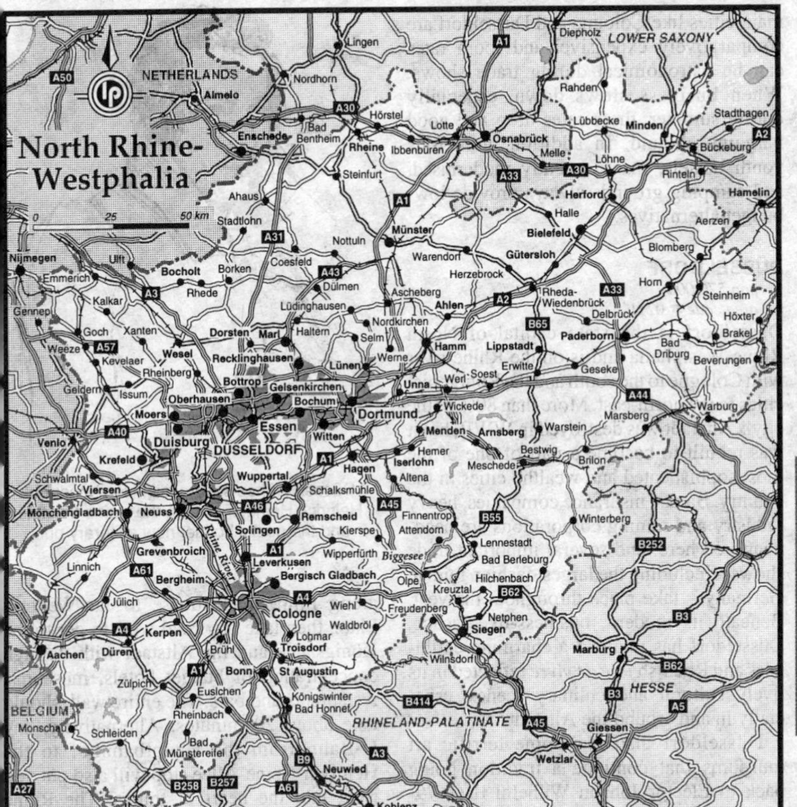

first-rate art museums. A fascinating range of world-class museums also adds to the appeal of Bonn, which served as West Germany's 'temporary capital' for a little over four decades.

The state capital Düsseldorf is an elegant and cosmopolitan city that also possesses an earthy conviviality best experienced in the brewery pubs of its Altstadt. The cities of the Ruhrgebiet – Essen, Dortmund and Bochum – surprise with their wide spectrum of top-notch cultural events and vast green spaces. To get completely off the main tourist path, head to the lush nature parks of the Sauerland and Siegerland, both popular getaways that Germans have kept largely to themselves. The skylines of the Westphalian towns of Soest and Paderborn are studded with the spires of medieval churches packed with a wealth of art treasures. And if there were still an independent Westphalia, Münster, with its great Dom, university and historic centre would surely be its capital.

Travelling in North Rhine-Westphalia is extremely easy, as the state is criss-crossed by a dense network of autobahns, country roads and major rail lines; even the smallest towns are served by trains and/or buses. The main cities like Cologne and Düsseldorf are comparatively expensive, and room rates can be astronomical during trade shows. When business slows down, especially during summer, these rates drop and good bargains abound. In addition, numerous youth hostels, many recently modernised, and camping grounds always provide low-budget alternatives.

DÜSSELDORF

- *pop 570,000*
- *area code* ☎ 0211

Düsseldorf is the state capital of North Rhine-Westphalia and is on the Rhine river with Cologne to the south and the Ruhrgebiet cities to the north-east. More than 80% of the city's Altstadt was destroyed in WWII, but it was rebuilt to become a part of one of the most sophisticated and wealthy cities in the country. Banks, insurance companies, heavy industry and mining corporations are headquartered here, and several important trade shows – including the largest fashion fairs in Germany – take place throughout the year. Beneath its modern, business-like façade, Düsseldorf has retained a charming earthiness and Rhenish *joie de vivre* reflected in its lively cultural and culinary scenes, especially in and around the Altstadt.

Düsseldorf also has some terrific art museums that continue a tradition going back to Elector Johann Wilhelm II (1679-1716) – popularly known as Jan Wellem – an avid collector of quality paintings. His collection was sent to Munich to protect it from Napoleon's troops, but it was never returned and in fact now forms the basis of that city's Pinakothek museum. The late-baroque period also saw the founding of the Düsseldorf School of Painting. It reached its zenith in the 19th century under Wilhelm von Schadow and still enjoys a fine reputation today as the Academy of Fine Arts. Düsseldorf is also the birthplace of the poet Heinrich Heine (1797-1856).

Orientation

The Hauptbahnhof is at the south-eastern periphery of the city centre. Walk north-west along Immermannstrasse to Jan-Wellem-Platz, then take any road west to get to the Königsallee and the Altstadt with its high concentration of budget hotels, museums, restaurants and bars. The entire walk should take about 20 minutes. Alternatively, any U-Bahn from the Hauptbahnhof to the Heinrich-Heine-Allee stop will also put you right into the heart of things. The Rhine forms the Altstadt's western border. The main shopping areas are along Königsallee and Schadowstrasse.

Düsseldorf has several sights in honour of Heinrich Heine, including the Heine Institute and the poet's house, now a literary pub.

Information

Tourist Office The tourist office (☎ 172 02 0; fax 161 07 1) is opposite the main exit of the Hauptbahnhof towards the northern end of Konrad-Adenauer-Platz. The information service is open from 8.30 am to 6 pm weekdays and 9 am to 12.30 pm on Saturday. The room reservation service stays open until 8 pm and even longer during trade shows.

Foreign Consulates Many countries have consulates in Düsseldorf, including the UK (☎ 944 80) at Yorckstrasse 19, France

(☎ 487 73 0) at Cecilienallee 10, Canada (☎ 172 17 0) at Prinz-Georg-Strasse 126, and the USA (☎ 470 61 23) at Kennedydamm 15-17.

Money There's no shortage of banks in the city centre, but if you need one after normal business hours, the Reisebank in the Hauptbahnhof's main hall is open daily to 9 pm. The American Express office is at Königsallee 98a.

Post & Communications The main post office is at Immermannstrasse 1, just north of the tourist office. It's open weekdays until 8 pm and Saturdays until 2 pm. The poste restante is here. Have letters clearly marked 'Hauptpostlagernd' (which means poste restante at the main post office) and addressed to you at 40029 Düsseldorf 1. There's a public fax-phone in the information and reservations office (Reisezentrum) in the Hauptbahnhof.

Medical Services & Emergency At night and on Sunday, call ☎ 192 92 for medical emergency assistance and ☎ 666 29 1 for dental help. If you need the police in an

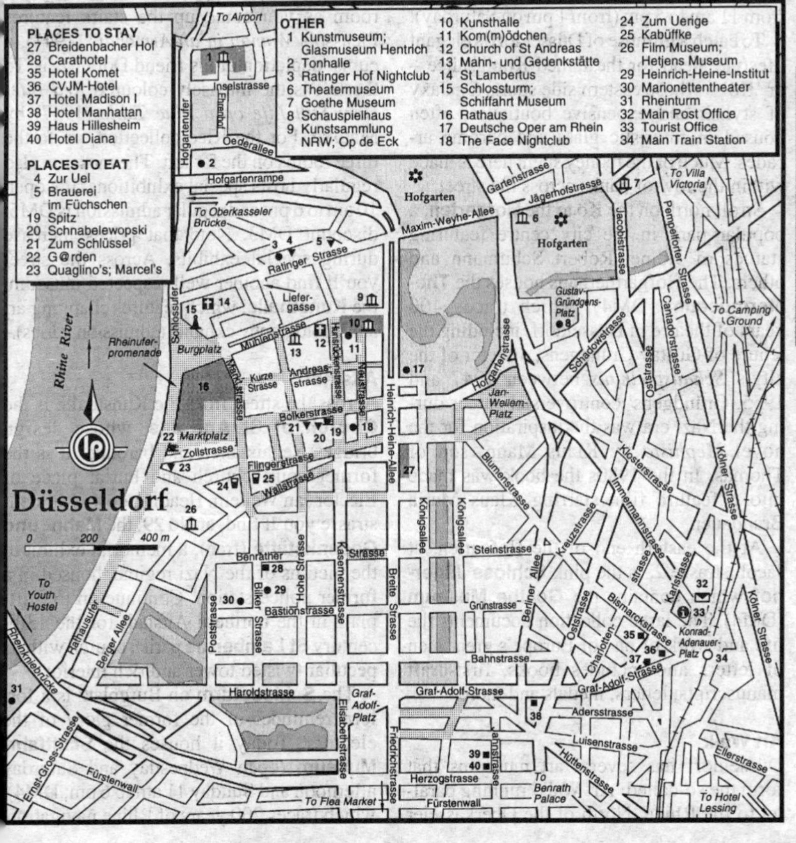

emergency call ☎ 110; their headquarters are at Jürgensplatz 5. The municipal lost and found office (Städtisches Fundbüro) is at ☎ 899 32 85.

Dangers & Annoyances As with most German cities, the area around the Hauptbahnhof attracts a murky element and should be avoided after dark. The same is true of the city parks, the preferred place for drug dealers and other unsavoury characters.

Königsallee & Hofgarten

Düsseldorf's museums are closed on Monday. Except where noted, a 50% discount is available to students, and opening hours are from 11 am to 5 pm (from 1 pm on Saturday).

To catch a glimpse of Düsseldorf's elegant lifestyle, head for the famed Königsallee – or 'Kö' – whose eastern side sports a galaxy of stylish and expensive boutiques, often housed in futuristic glass and chrome arcades. Much of the money spent here is made within the row of banks across the street.

Stroll north on the Kö to the **Hofgarten**, a popular park in the city centre featuring statues of Heine, Robert Schumann and others. The Hofgärtnerhaus houses the **Theatermuseum** (DM4), which traces 400 years of theatre in Düsseldorf, including the tenure of Gustav Gründgens, director of the city's *Schauspielhaus* between 1947 and 1955. Gründgens' controversial career during the Nazi era was the inspiration for the novel *Mephisto* by Klaus Mann, son of Thomas. In the 1980s the book was made into a feature film starring Klaus Maria Brandauer.

At the eastern end of the Hofgarten, at Jacobistrasse 2, is the pink **Schloss Jägerhof** which contains the **Goethe Museum** (DM4). The large collection documents the life and work of one of Europe's great men of letters and includes books, first-draft manuscripts, letters, medals and more.

Art Walk

Düsseldorf has several art museums that form the so-called 'Art Walk' running parallel to the Rhine. North of the Oberkasseler Brücke, at Ehrenhof, is the **Kunstmuseum** (open daily 10 am to 6 pm; DM5). This collection of European art spanning the Middle Ages to the present includes *Venus and Adonis* by Rubens and 19th-century landscape paintings by members of the Düsseldorf School. The museum also incorporates the **Glasmuseum Hentrich** with historic and contemporary glass exhibits.

Top billing goes to the **Kunstsammlung Nordrhein-Westfalen**, housed in a curved building with a black polished syenite façade at Grabbeplatz 5. Its exquisite permanent collection includes works by every leading light of the early 20th century, including Klee, Picasso, Braque and Kirchner. The first room as you come up the stairs features Picasso's *Woman in an Armchair* (1941), a cubist depiction of his friend Dora Maar. To the left is the intensely coloured *Red Interior: Still Life on a Blue Table* (1947) by Matisse. For the Klee collection, go to the three rooms on the far left. The museum also regularly hosts special exhibitions. It's open 10 am to 6 pm and regular admission is DM5, discount DM3. Note that prices increase during special exhibits. Across the street you'll find another well respected museum, the **Kunsthalle**, which features changing art and photography exhibits (admission varies).

Altstadt

Across the street from the Kunsthalle is the **Church of St Andreas**, whose design bridges Renaissance and baroque. It is the former court church and burial place of Elector Jan Wellem. Heading down Mühlenstrasse you'll find, at No 29, the **Mahn- und Gedenkstätte** (free), a memorial exhibit to the victims of the Nazi regime, housed in a former police station. Continue on to Stiftplatz in the northern Altstadt for the 13th-century **St Lambertus** parish church with its peculiar twisted tower and rich interior.

The **Schlossturm** on Burgplatz is a forlorn reminder of the former glory of the electors. Today it houses the **Schiffahrt Museum** (open Wednesday and Saturday afternoon and Sunday 11 am to 6 pm; DM4) which traces 200 years of Rhine navigation in summer, the town's youth congregate on the steps below the tower. From here you can stroll along the river on the **Rheinufer-promenade**. It spills into the Rheinpark, which contains the 234m **Rheinturm**. Its viewing platform offers terrific bird's-eye views of the city (DM5, no discount).

Back in the heart of the Altstadt, the Renaissance **Rathaus** (1573) looks out over the **Jan Wellem statue**, which dominates the Markt. German-literature buffs will also want to visit the **Heinrich Heine Institut** at Bilker Strasse 12-14, which documents this famed Düsseldorfer's career (DM4), or his house at Bolkerstrasse 53, now a literary pub called Schnabelewopski. The Palais Nesselrode at Schulstrasse 4 houses both the **Film Museum** and the **Hetjens Museum** with ceramics spanning a period of 8000 years (open 11 am to 5 pm, Wednesday to 9 pm; DM6).

Schloss Benrath

This pleasure palace and park 12km from the centre in the southern suburb of Benrath was built in 1755 by Elector Karl Theodor and makes for a lovely excursion. Its harmonious design – integrating architecture, garden landscaping, sculpture and decorative arts – is typical of the transition from late baroque to the neoclassical style. The rooms, which can be viewed on a one-hour guided tour, are decorated with inlaid parquet floors, wood-panelled walls and lots of stucco. The large mirrors in the **Audienzsaal** make the room appear much grander than it really is. Outside, the terraced park invites leisurely strolls.

The palace is at Benrather Schlossallee 104 (tram No 701 from Jan-Wellem-Platz or S-Bahn No 6 from the Hauptbahnhof) and is open from 10 am to 5 pm. Admission to the palace and the park is DM7, discount is DM3.50.

Places to Stay

Room rates in Düsseldorf fluctuate enormously and can be outright extortionate during major trade shows. On the other hand, when nothing's going on (usually in summer), you can often stay at top hotels for less than the cost of a private room. It's best to call the tourist office ahead of arrival to find out whether such bargains are offered during your stay. Prices quoted below should just be used as a guideline. If you're driving, keep in mind that parking your car in a hotel or public garage may add DM20 or more to your room rate.

The tourist office charges DM5 per person for a room reservation. If the office is closed, there's a list of hotels with addresses and phone numbers posted in the window so that you can call them directly. There's also a computerised room-reservation terminal in the train station (towards the main exit, next to the InterCity Hotel entrance). Via a touch screen, you can find out about room availability at each participating hotel and then dial the one of your choice for free. Naturally, most of the hotels listed belong to the middle to upper categories.

Places to Stay – bottom end

Camping There are two camping grounds fairly close to the city. *Campingplatz Nord Unterbacher See* (☎ 899 20 38; open April to September) is at Kleiner Torfbruch in Düsseldorf-Unterbach (S-Bahn No 7 to Düsseldorf-Eller, then bus No 735 to Kleiner Torfbruch). There's another camping ground on the southern lake shore, but it does not accept tourists, only long-term campers. *Camping Oberlörick* (☎ 591 40 1; open mid-April to mid-September) is at Lütticher Strasse beside the Rhine in Düsseldorf-Lörick (U-Bahn No 70, 74, 76 or 77 to Belsenplatz, then bus No 828 or 838).

Hostels The 280-bed *Jugendgästehaus* (☎ 557 31 0) is at Düsseldorfer Strasse 1 in posh Oberkassel across the Rhine from the Altstadt. Bed & breakfast in three to six-person rooms cost DM33.30/37 for juniors/seniors. Take U-Bahn No 70, 74, 76 or 77 from the Hauptbahnhof to Luegplatz. From there it's a 10-minute walk. If they're full, you could call the *DJH hostel* (☎ 229 97) at Götschenbeck 8 in nearby Ratingen to try your luck (take S-Bahn No 6 to Ratingen Ost, then bus No 750).

Hotels At the *Hotel Manhattan* (☎ 370 24 7), Graf-Adolf-Strasse 39, basic singles start at DM68 and doubles at DM100; rooms with private bath are DM95/150 and up. *Hotel Komet* (☎ 178 79 0) at Bismarckstrasse 93 has rooms with shower but no private WC ranging from DM60 to DM150 for singles and DM95 to DM225 for doubles. The *CVJM-Hotel* (☎ 172 85 0), as the YMCA is called in German, is at Graf-Adolf-Strasse 102; basic singles/doubles start at DM65/111. On Jahnstrasse, *Hotel Diana* (☎ 375 07 1) at No 31 and *Haus Hillesheim* (☎ 371 94 0) at No 19 have rooms with private bath from DM80/120, without from around DM55/80.

Places to Stay – middle & top end

Near the station and popular with artists is *Hotel Madison I* (☎ 168 50; fax 168 53 28) at Graf-Adolf-Strasse 94 whose singles cost DM170, doubles from DM210 to DM280. The *Carathotel* (☎ 130 50; fax 322 21 4), on the southern end of the Altstadt at Benrather Strasse 7a, is an elegant city hotel charging from DM155/200. Less central, but near a large park, is *Hotel Lessing* (☎ 977 00; fax 977 01 00) at Volksgartenstrasse 6, where you can pay as little as DM170/200 to as much as DM250/310.

If you like English country manor-style décor and happen to have from DM307 to DM334 to spend for a night in a hotel, then the all-suite *Villa Victoria* (☎ 469 00 0; fax 469 00 60 1), in a turn-of-the-century building at Blumenthalstrasse 12, may be your thing. Those with refined tastes might also enjoy the traditional *Breidenbacher Hof* (☎ 130 30; fax 130 38 30), Heinrich-Heine-Allee 36. Expect to shell out from DM330/440 for a plush room with full facilities in this classic hotel.

Long-Term Rentals

Düsseldorf has two Mitwohnzentralen: one at Hüttenstrasse 52 (☎ 383 48 0), the other at Charlottenstrasse 1 (☎ 363 02 5).

Places to Eat

The Altstadt has been nicknamed the 'world's longest bar' for good reason. But because men and woman do not live by beer alone, there are also plenty of eateries here. One of the typical rustic Rhenish beer halls where they dish out huge portions of hearty German food for DM10 to DM15 is *Brauerei im Füchschen* at Ratinger Strasse 28. It's a smoky, crowded Düsseldorf institution that attracts all ages. On the same street, at No 16, is *Zur Uel*, a popular hang-out for student types who munch on basic fare (the baked potato is a classic) listed on a blackboard.

Another happening street is Bolkerstrasse where, at No 45, you'll find *Zum Schlüssel*, Düsseldorf's oldest restaurant ('since 1628') whose menu features such regional favourites as Sauerbraten (marinated beef) and sauerkraut soup. At No 53, in Heinrich Heine's birthplace, is the literary pub *Schnabelewopski*, named after a Heine character. On the corner of Bolkerstrasse and Hunsrückenstrasse are the two floors of the trendy *Spitz*, which also has good breakfasts and a menu that changes daily.

For places with a touch more class, head to the pedestrianised Rheinuferpromenade along the Rhine. In warm weather, restaurant tables spill out onto the promenade, making it a perfect place for people-watching. At No 5 is *Quaglino's* which serves Italian fusion food to a self-important crowd at surprisingly decent prices (under DM20). Next door is *Marcel's*, an elegant bistro fit for those who know their carpaccio and cappuccino and pay DM20 and up for a plate of food. Then there's the futuristic *G@rden* where you can surf the net (DM5 for half an hour), sip creative cocktails, have high-energy breakfasts (around DM10) and, on Saturday, dance the night away in the disco. Culturally refined types might also like *Op de Eck*, inside the Kunstsammlung museum, which has a very nice terrace.

Entertainment

Listings Good sources for finding out what's on in and around Düsseldorf are the ıonthly magazines *Prinz* (DM5) and *Über-lick* (DM4.50), on sale at newsagents.

Discos & Clubs Düsseldorf's discos tend to e chic and trendy and fairly expensive. A rink minimum, in addition to a high admis-ion charge (DM15 to DM25), is common. n some places, dim doormen decide on who its in with the crowd and who doesn't. Most lubs are open only Wednesday, Friday and aturday and don't even get started until 11 m, though it's considered uncool to show p before midnight.

An Altstadt institution that has always idden the waves of the latest music trend currently it's techno) is *Ratinger Hof* at Ratinger Strasse 10. At Neustrasse 42 is *The ace*, a tiny cellar usually jammed with oungsters writhing to everything from acid azz to house.

heatre & Classical Music Düsseldorf's nain stage for theatre is the *Schauspielhaus* (☎ 369 91 1) on Gustaf-Gründgens-Platz. or opera and musicals, head to the *Deutsche Oper am Rhein* (☎ 890 82 11) at Heinrich-Ieine-Allee 16a. Classical concerts are erformed in the *Tonhalle* (☎ 899 61 23) at hrenhof 1, north of the Altstadt. A gem nside the baroque Palais Wittgenstein at Bilker Strasse 7 is the *Marionettentheater* (☎ 328 43 2), which performs beautifully rchestrated operas and fairy tales.

Between Kunsthalle and St Andreas is the *Com(m)ödchen* (☎ 325 42 8), the town's abaret known nationally for its unrelent-ngly satirical shows.

Beer Halls On evenings and weekends, specially in good weather, the atmosphere n the pedestrian-only streets of the Altstadt s electric and, occasionally, a bit rowdy. The everage of choice is Alt, a dark and semi-weet beer typical of Düsseldorf. The best lace to soak up the atmosphere along with e beer is *Zum Uerige* at Berger Strasse. veryone from company executives to street leaners gulp down huge amounts of Uerige ier, the house brew here. It flows so quickly om the giant copper vats inside that the waiters – called 'Köbes' here and in Cologne – just carry around trays and give you a glass when you're ready. Across from the Uerige, at Flingerstrasse 1, is the *Kabüffke* where, besides Alt, you can also taste Killepitsch, a herb liqueur sold only here. If you like it, you can buy a bottle at the little shop next door. Also see *Brauerei im Füchschen* and *Zum Schlüssel* in the Places to Eat section.

Things to Buy

Düsseldorf prides itself on being Germany's fashion capital and, indeed, for *haute couture* there are few places as exclusive as the boutiques along the Kö. Department stores and more reasonably priced shops are on Schadowstrasse and its side streets.

The Schadow Arcade offers stunning contemporary architecture and a nice mix of shops. If funky club wear is your thing, better head to the Altstadt. There's a flea market on Aachener Platz every Saturday from 9 am to 2 pm (tram No 712 from Jan-Wellem-Platz).

Getting There & Away

Air Düsseldorf's Lohausen airport (☎ 421 0) is busy with many national and international flights. Construction of a larger, state-of-the-art airport is currently under way, after the April 1996 fire that claimed 17 lives. Major airlines with offices at the airport include British Airways (☎ 421 66 86), American Airlines (☎ 421 60 42) and Air France (☎ 421 62 72). British Airways also has an office in the city centre at Am Wehrhahn 2a (☎ 162 161).

Train Düsseldorf is part of a dense S-Bahn network in the Rhine-Ruhr region, and regular services run to Cologne and Aachen as well; international rail passes are valid on these lines. ICE trains to Munich (DM194, six hours) leave hourly, while there's direct service every two hours to Hamburg-Altona (DM111, 3½ hours), Berlin-Zoo (DM162, five hours) and Frankfurt/Main (DM69, 2¾ hours). Direct links also exist to Amsterdam (two hours) and Moscow (13 hours). For information, phone ☎ 194 19. Plenty of lockers are available for DM2 and DM4.

Car & Motorcycle Autobahns from all directions lead to Düsseldorf; just follow the signs to the city centre. As to be expected, parking in the city centre is pretty much limited to parking garages charging DM2 to DM2.50 an hour.

Ride Services There's a Mitfahrzentrale at Konrad-Adenauer-Platz 13, on the corner of Graf-Adolf-Strasse (☎ 371 08 1 or ☎ 194 40) and a second one at Kruppstrasse 102 (☎ 771 94 4 or ☎ 194 44).

Getting Around

The S-Bahn Nos 7 and 21 shuttle between the airport and the Hauptbahnhof every 20 minutes. The 15-minute taxi ride to/from the station averages DM25.

Düsseldorf has an extensive network of U-Bahn trains, trams and buses operated by the Rheinische Bahngesellschaft (☎ 582 28). It is divided into zones, and prices vary according to how many zones you travel through. Single tickets are DM3.10 for one zone, DM5.80 for two, DM11.70 for three. Better value are the four-trip tickets that sell for DM9.20/15.70/34.50; day passes are DM10/14.50/27. If you want to take a bicycle on board, it's DM2.50. It is best to buy tickets from the orange vending machines at stops, though bus drivers sell them also. All tickets must be validated when boarding.

For a taxi call ☎ 333 33 or ☎ 194 10.

Rhineland

XANTEN

- *pop 16,500*
- *area code* ☎ 02801

It was Roman Emperor Traian who, around 100 AD, first put Xanten – about 60km north of Düsseldorf – on the map. He gave city status to a residential settlement adjacent to one of his military camps and named it Colonia Ulpia Traiana. Extending over some 73 hectares and inhabited by up to 15,000 people (almost the same population as today), it lasted until the 4th century when the Roman Empire began to crumble – an its buildings along with it. The stones wer later used in the construction of the Xante Dom, named for the Roman martyr St Victo The city's surviving foundations have bee excavated and form the basis of the Archaeological Park, Xanten's main attraction.

In the Middle Ages Xanten thrived be cause of its location at the crossroads o major trade routes. Prosperity declined in th 16th century when the town lost its direc waterway access after the Rhine change course. Xanten was badly damaged in WWI and, despite winning several conservatio awards, today is a shadow of its medieva self. A few buildings, though, most notabl the Dom, warrant a closer look. Xanten i also the legendary birthplace of Siegfrie one of the heroes of the Nibelungen epic wh figures prominently in Richard Wagner' opera cycle *Der Ring des Nibelungen*.

Orientation & Information

The Dom and city centre are about a 10 minute walk north-east of the train statio via Hagenbuschstrasse or Bahnhofstrasse The Archaeological Park is a further 1 minutes north of here.

The tourist office (☎ 772 0; fax 772 30 5 is in the Rathaus on the eastern end of th Markt and is open weekdays from 10 am t 5 pm April to September. On weekends there's an information booth on the squar open from 10 am to 4 pm. In winter, openin hours are from 10 am to 4.30 pm Monday t Thursday and to 2 pm on Friday. Betwee May and September, free walking tour depart from here on Saturdays at 11 am.

Xanten's post office is on the corner c Bahnhofstrasse and Poststrasse. There's police station a few metres north of th tourist office on the corner of Rheinstrass and Niederstrasse.

Altstadt

The crown jewel of Xanten's Altstadt is th **Dom St Viktor**, just west of the Mark Framed by a walled close called a 'immunity', it can only be entered throug the fortress-like gate from the Markt.

Immediately in front are the flying buttresses and flamboyant façade characteristic of a Gothic structure (13th century). However, the sturdy twin towers at the Dom's western end were built first in the late-Romanesque style (late 12th century).

The five-nave interior has a sombreness that is gratefully enlivened by a stunning collection of art treasures. Foremost among them is the **Marienaltar**, halfway down the right aisles, whose altar base (or predella) features an intricately carved version of the genealogical *Tree of Jesse* by Heinrich Douvermann (1535). Other masterpieces include the candelabrum in the central nave with its **Doppelmadonna** (1500), and the 28 stone statues of the apostles and other saints affixed to the pillars.

Just outside the Dom is the entrance to the **Regional Museum** (closed Monday; DM3, discount DM1.50) with Roman objects gleaned from the nearby excavation site on display, as well as presentations on the history of Xanten from the Ice Age to today. Turning right as you exit the Immunity, follow the signs to Klever Strasse; at the end of that street you'll come upon the **Klever Tor** (1393), the only surviving double town gate on the Lower Rhine. Used as a prison until 1906, it now contains holiday apartments (see Places to Stay). The windmill visible from here is the **Kriemhildmühle**, also once part of the fortifications. It forms the terminus of Brückstrasse, where you can still admire some fine Gothic houses, including the **Arme Mägde Haus** with its step-gabled facade at No 9.

Archäologischer Park

Colonia Ulpia Traiana is the only Roman settlement north of the Alps that has never been built upon, allowing archaeologists to unearth the foundations of the fortification wall, streets and many buildings. In the mid-1970s, some of these were reconstructed and opened to visitors. Critics have ridiculed the results and indeed the place sometimes feels like a Roman theme park – especially the restaurant, where toga-clad personnel serve such 'Roman' fare as chicken Mumidia; it's about as tacky as Caesar's Palace Hotel in Las Vegas. But overall, the reconstruction has been done faithfully and tastefully and helps amateurs to visualise what a Roman colony looked like.

The self-guided tour begins at the **Herberge**, the inn which, along with the restaurant, snack bar and furnished rooms, also contains an **Info-Center** with models and explanatory panels. Next door, the **Badehaus** points up the fairly high standard of hygiene enjoyed by the Romans 2000 years ago (note the communal toilet). Other highlights include the **Amphitheatre**, which seats about 12,000 people during Xanten's summer festival, and the only partly rebuilt **Hafentempel**. Be sure to walk around the back for a glimpse of the original foundation. At the **Spielehaus**, you can play a round of authentic antique board games, including backgammon (rules explained on the wall in German).

The Archäologischer Park is open daily from 9 am to 6 pm (10 am to 4 pm in winter) and admission is DM7, or DM8 in combination with the Regional Museum; various discounts are available.

Places to Stay & Eat

Xanten has two camping grounds but they are inconvenient unless you have a car. Both are on Urseler Strasse west of the centre with *Campingplatz Bremer* (☎ 473 0) at No 25 being about 3km away and *Wald-Camping Speetenkath* (☎ 176 9), at No 18, 5km away. The nearest *hostel* (☎ 02832-826 7) is 18km away in Kevelaer.

A low-budget alternative may be a night in the barn of the *Mörenhof* (☎ 02804-375), a farm at Mörmterer Strasse 7 in the north-western suburb of Marienbaum, which charges DM22, including a hearty breakfast. If you're staying three days or more, the small apartments inside the Klever Tor sleep up to four and can be let for DM75 per night (book at the tourist office). The tourist office also operates a free reservation service, with private rooms costing from DM25 to DM40 per person.

As far as hotels go, your best bet is the

central *Galerie an de Marspoort* (☎ 105 7; fax 614 2), at Marsstrasse 78, which has cosy singles for DM70 and doubles for DM110. The top address in town is the historic *Hotel van Bebber* (☎ 662 3; fax 591 4) at Klever Strasse 12, which charges DM99/190 for singles/doubles with all the facilities. Both hotels also operate decent restaurants.

Otherwise, Xanten has a huge number of ethnic eateries. On or around the Markt, you will find Greek, Yugoslav, Japanese-Korean, Chinese, Italian and Turkish restaurants. Young people gather for a beer and a chat at *Vips* at Bahnhofstrasse 18, *Mäx* at Klever Strasse 30 and *Zentrale* at Brückstrasse 2.

Getting There & Away

Buses to nearby Kalkar and Kleve leave daily except Sunday from outside the train station (bus No 44, hourly). The only train stopping at Xanten's tiny one-platform station is the hourly shuttle to and from Duisburg (DM11.80, 50 minutes). Xanten lies on route B57 (Kleve-Dinslaken). If travelling on the A57, take the Alpen exit, then route B58 east to B57 north. Bikes may be rented from the owner of the *Bummelzug* café (☎ 913 8) inside the train station. He charges DM12 on weekdays and DM15 at the weekend, and it's best to call ahead.

AROUND XANTEN

Kalkar

- *pop 11,500*
- *area code* ☎ 02824

About 15km north of Xanten lies the little town of Kalkar with a fairly intact medieval core anchored by the **Church of St Nikolai** and its seven carved altars. You'll find it on Jan-Joest-Strasse just west of the Markt. A rather bland Gothic brick building on the outside, St Nikolai's interior explodes with an extraordinary number of masterpieces. Many were created by artists from the Kalkar School of Woodcarving, founded in the late Middle Ages by Kalkar's wealthy burghers. Sadly, some of the treasures had to be sold off in the early 19th century to pay for the church's restoration, but enough is left to be admired.

Top billing goes to the **high altar**, a depiction of the Passion of Christ in dizzying detail. For a close look, walk through the choir at the end of the left aisle to a small walkway passing in front of the altar. The work was begun in 1490 by Master Arnt of Zwolle who died before finishing it, a task then undertaken by Jan Halderen and Master Loedewig. Turn around and lift the first seat of the upper choir chair on the right – once reserved for the duke of Cleves – to reveal the relief of a **monkey on a chamberpot**. Another eye-catcher is the **Altar of the Seven Sorrows** by Heinrich Douvermann in the right aisle. It perches on a predella containing another version of the *Tree of Jesse*, reminiscent of the one in Xanten's Dom. If you look closely you can make out Jesse, the father of David, framed by two prophets, and Solomon with the sceptre.

The church is currently undergoing another face-lift, which may require the moving of some of the altars. It's generally open from 2 to 5 pm, in summer also 10 am to noon. There's no admission as such, but you're requested to drop a minimum of DM2 in the collection box.

COLOGNE

- *pop 930,000*
- *area code* ☎ 0221

Cologne (Köln) is not just the largest city in North Rhine-Westphalia, it is also one of its most attractive and should be on everyone's must-see list. It spoils visitors with a cornucopia of sightseeing choices and activities: great architecture in its magnificent cathedral, churches and public buildings; internationally renowned museums with first-rate collections; funky boutiques and giant department stores; a unique local cuisine and beer; cutting-edge dance clubs; first-rate theatre and concerts.

History

Cologne has been a major player in European history for two millenia, not least for its location on the Rhine and at a major trade crossroads. It's one of Germany's oldest cities, founded by the Romans around 50 BC

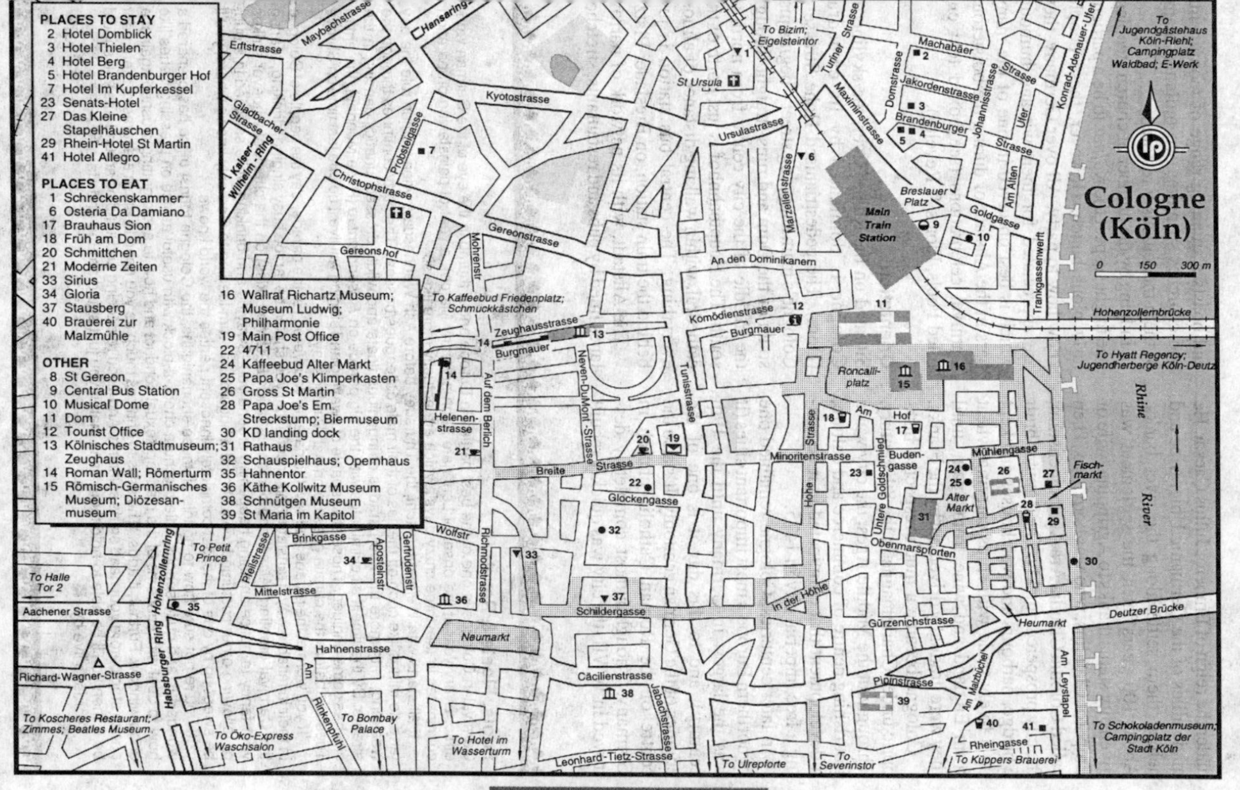

NORTH RHINE-WESTPHALIA

under the reign of Emperor Julius Caesar. He made allies of the Germanic Ubier tribe and helped them settle along the river banks. About 100 years later, the settlement was given city status thanks to Agrippina, wife of Emperor Claudius, who was born here. Then called Colonia Claudia Ara Agrippinensium, the city prospered quickly. The Romans built a bridge, harbours and warehouses and kept up a lively trade with ships carrying wheat from England and wine from Spain, until they were gradually driven out by the Franks.

Cologne became a much-respected bishopric under Charlemagne in the 8th century. Throughout the Middle Ages, the city was a flourishing centre of commerce and culture, a development that culminated in it becoming a free imperial city in 1475.

In later centuries, Cologne remained one of northern Europe's most important cities (it was the largest in Germany until the 19th century), and to this day it is one of the engines of the German economy. It's also the centre of the Roman Catholic church in Germany. Though almost completely destroyed in WWII, the city was quickly rebuilt and boasts a stunning range of monument and churches spanning two millenia, man of them meticulously restored.

Judging by the number of church steeples one might suspect the *Kölner* to be a particu larly pious bunch. However, these peopl know how to party. All over Germany, the are appreciated for their wit and humou which is best observed in one of the man bars in the Altstadt or during the boisterou Carnival celebrations (see boxed text en titled Fools, Floats & Revelry).

Orientation

Situated on the Rhine River, the skyline o Cologne is dominated by its cathedra (Dom). The pedestrianised Hohe Strasse - Cologne's main shopping street – begins jus south of the Dom and runs straight throug the middle of the city centre from north t south. The Hauptbahnhof is just north of th cathedral, within walking distance of almos everything. The central bus station is jus behind the train station, on Breslauer Platz.

The Altstadt, with its network of narrov lanes lined by pubs and restaurants, stretche

Fools, Floats & Revelry

Carnival in Cologne is one of the best parties in Europe and a thumb in the eye of the German work ethic. Every year at the onset of Lent (late February/early March), a year of painstaking preparation culminates in the 'three crazy days', which are actually more like six.

It all starts with *Weiberfastnacht*, the Thursday before Ash Wednesday, when women rule the day (and do things like chop off the ties of their male colleagues/bosses). The party continues through the weekend, with more than 50 parades of ingenious floats and wildly dressed lunatics dancing in the streets. By the time it all culminates with the big parade on *Rosenmontag* (Rose Monday), the entire city has come unglued. Those still capable of swaying and singing will live it up one last time on Shrove Tuesday before the curtain goes up on Ash Wednesday.

'If you were at the parade and saw the parade, you weren't at the parade,' say the people of Cologne in their inimitable way. Translated this means that you should be far too busy singing, drinking, roaring the Carnival greeting '*Alaaf*!' and planting a quick *Bützchen* (kiss) on the cheek of whoever strikes your fancy to notice anything happening around you. Swaying and drinking while sardined in a pub, or following other costumed fools behind a huge bass drum leading to God only knows where, you'll be swept up by one of the last completely innocent parties the world knows.

If you're not sure how to handle all these shenanigans, the Cologne tourist office has prepared a wonderful, and quite serious, little brochure chock-a-block with useful advice on pressing issues like how to deal with concerns of the bladder, sexual conduct and how to avoid getting crushed against a shop window. Further, it adds: 'The art is to drink as much as you need to attain a degree of merriment and to stop before your head starts spinning. And if you're dancing and jumping around – as you should be – then you'll be able to hold more drink than if you just stand around and stare.'

Words to live by. ■

out along the few blocks parallel to the western bank of the Rhine, between Hohenzollernbrücke and Deutzer Brücke.

A series of ring roads encircles Cologne's core, each chronicling the states of the city's growth like the rings of a tree. While the Roman city was roughly confined to today's Altstadt area, the road called the Ring marks the line of the medieval fortifications. The next circle is the Gürtel (beltway), built with Prussian efficiency in the 19th century. And around it all wraps the ambitious six-lane autobahn, the Kölner Ring, demanded by this century's technological advances and population growth.

Information

Tourist Office The tourist office (☎ 221 33 45; fax 221 33 20) is conveniently located opposite the cathedral's main entrance at Unter Fettenhennen 19. Opening hours are Monday to Saturday from 8 am to 10.30 pm and Sunday from 9 am. Winter hours are Monday to Saturday from 9.30 am to 9 pm and Sunday from 9.30 am to 7 pm. Apart from the usual array of brochures, maps and books, the office also has an ATM machine that accepts all major credit cards, as well as a public fax-phone. Here you can also buy the Cologne Bonbon (DM26), a booklet with vouchers for a free guided city bus tour and admission to nine municipal museums, plus various discounts for other attractions.

Money The bank inside the Hauptbahnhof is open daily from 7 am to 9 pm. Other banks abound, and most have ATM machines that accept credit cards. American Express has an office at Burgmauer 14, and Thomas Cook is at Burgmauer 4 near the tourist office.

Post & Communications The main post office is inside the WDR Arkaden shopping mall on the corner of Breite Strasse and Tunisstrasse and is open weekdays from 8 am to 8 pm and Saturday to 4 pm. The poste restante is here. Have mail clearly marked *Hauptpostlagernd* and addressed to you at 50441 Köln, Breite Strasse 6-26. There's also a public fax-phone and a photocopy machine.

Bookshops Ludwig im Bahnhof, inside the Hauptbahnhof, has international newspapers and magazines. For travel guides in English, try Kösel on Roncalliplatz south of the cathedral.

For a great selection of foreign-language novels, go to Gonski in Neumarktpassage on the north side of Neumarkt square.

Laundry Öko-Express Waschsalon (Monday to Saturday 6 am to 11 pm) is at Weyerstrasse near Barbarossaplatz. Washing costs DM6 per load, 10 minutes of drying is DM1.

Medical Services & Emergency For an emergency doctor call ☎ 192 92. Police headquarters (☎ 229 1) are on the corner of Nord-Süd-Fahrt and Blaubach.

Dom

The Kölner Dom with its soaring twin spires is the Mt Everest of cathedrals, Cologne's geographical and spiritual heart and main tourist draw. It's easy to spend at least half a day exploring it. Building began in 1248 in the French Gothic style but was suspended in 1560 for lack of money. For nearly 300 years, the structure lay half-finished and was even demoted to a horse stable and prison by Napoleon's troops. In the 1820s, the original architectural plans were found, and in 1880 the cathedral was finally completed, thanks to a generous cash infusion from Prussian King Friedrich Wilhelm IV. Strangely, it survived WWII's heavy night bombing almost intact.

For an overall impression of the Dom's dimensions, first head to the south side. Despite its overwhelming mass and height – it soars to 157m – its lacy spires and flying buttresses create a sensation of lightness and fragility.

The interior is just as overwhelming. A phalanx of pillars and arches supports the lofty central nave. An ethereal light shines through the radiant stained-glass windows, which rank as a highlight among the Dom's many art treasures. These also include the **Gero Crucifix** from 970, a monumental work that shows a larger-than-life-sized Christ figure with his eyes closed, and the largest **choir stalls** in Germany, which were carved in 1310. But the *pièce de résistance* is the **Shrine of the Three Magi** behind the altar, said to contain the bones of the kings who followed the star to the stable in Bethlehem where Jesus was born. The richly bejewelled and gilded sarcophagus was spirited out of Milan in 1164 as spoils of war by Emperor Barbarossa's chancellor, instantly turning Cologne into a major pilgrimage site. On the south side, in a chapel off the ambulatory, is the 15th-century **Adoration of the Magi altarpiece**.

The Dom is open daily from 7 am to 7 pm. Invest a mere DM1 in the informative, multi-language *Cologne Cathedral* booklet sold at the tourist office. Guided tours in English, including a slide show, are held Sunday to Friday at 2.30 pm, Saturday at 10.30 am and cost DM6, discount DM4. Meet at the Domforum information office opposite the main portal. Tours in German are more frequent and cost DM5, discount DM3.

Tower For an exercise fix, pay DM3 (students DM1.50) to climb the 509 steps up the Dom's south tower to the base of the stupendous steeple, which dwarfed all buildings in Europe until the Eiffel Tower was erected (open daily to 6 pm from May to October, to 4 or 5 pm during the rest of the year). Look at the 24-tonne **Peter Bell**, the largest working bell in the world, on your way up. At the end of your climb, the view from the vantage point at 98.25m is absolutely breathtaking (so to speak). With clear weather you can see all the way to the Siebengebirge beyond Bonn.

Domschatzkammer The cathedral treasury, just inside the north entrance, is pretty average. It is open April to October from 9 am to 5 pm Monday to Saturday (to 4 pm in winter), 1 to 4 pm Sunday; admission DM3. Cologne's archbishops are interred in the crypt.

Romanesque Churches

The wealth Cologne enjoyed during its medieval heyday is reflected in the abundance of Romanesque churches, built between 1150 and 1250. Many survived intact until they were hit by a barrage of bombs in WWII. A dozen have since been rebuilt; they are all scattered within the medieval city bordered by the Ring. The tourist office has a slim, multi-language guidebook with information on all of them for DM2.

Gross St Martin (open 10 am to 6 pm, Sunday 2 to 4 pm only), with its four slender turrets grouped around a central spire, towers above Fischmarkt and wins top honors for having the most handsome exterior. Inside, the impressive clover-leaf choir is modelled on that in **St Maria im Kapitol** (open daily 9.30 am to 6 pm) on Marienplatz. Among this church's treasures is a carved door that predates its consecration date of 1065 by a few years. The church with the most spectacular interior, though, has to be **St Gereon** (open from 9 am to 12.30 pm and 1.30 to 6 pm, closed Sunday morning) on Christophstrasse, whose four-storey decagonal dome was an astonishing architectural accomplishment in the early 13th century.

Museums

All museums are closed on Monday. Unless noted, a 50% discount on the admission prices listed here applies to children, students and seniors. A good deal is the Museumscard, valid for two days' admission to eight museums and free public transportation on the first day. It costs DM20 per person (DM36 for families) and is available at the tourist office and museums.

Römisch-Germanisches Museum Next to the cathedral at Roncalliplatz 4, this first-rate museum displays one of the most thorough collections of Roman artefacts found along the Rhine. Highlights are the giant **Poblicius grave monument** (30-40 AD) and the 3rd-century **Dionysus mosaic** around which the museum was built.

Keen insight into daily Roman life is gained from such items as toys, tweezers, lamps and jewellery, the designs of which have changed little over the centuries. The museum is open weekdays from 10 am to 5 pm (Thursday to 8 pm) and weekends from 11 am. Admission is DM5.

Wallraf Richartz Museum & Museum Ludwig Housed in a spectacular, modern building just south of the Dom at Bischofsgartenstrasse 1, this museum complex ranks as one of the country's finest art galleries. Its design makes brilliant use of natural light. The 1st floor is devoted to the Cologne Masters of the 14th to 16th centuries, known for their distinctive use of colour. Further along, look for familiar names like Rubens, Rembrandt and Dürer. The exhibit continues with 19th-century romanticists like Caspar David Friedrich and Lovis Corinth and 20th-century impressionists including Monet, Van Gogh and Renoir.

The Museum Ludwig picks up where its neighbour leaves off and enjoys stature as a European mecca of postmodern art, including works by Rauschenberg and Warhol. There's also a unique photography collection from the former Agfa Museum in Leverkusen. Opening hours are weekdays from 10 am to 6 pm (Tuesday to 8 pm) and weekends from 11 am. Admission is DM10.

Schnütgen Museum At Cäcilienstrasse 29, the former Church of St Cecilia houses an overwhelming display of medieval ecclesiastical treasures, including many religious items, manuscripts and early ivory carvings. It's open weekdays from 10 am to 5 pm (Wednesday to 8 pm) and weekends from 11 am; admission is DM5. At the **Diözesanmuseum** on Roncalliplatz, which also has religious treasures, admission is free (closed Thursday).

Other Museums In a bank branch at Neumarkt 18-24 is the **Käthe Kollwitz Museum** (open daily 10 am to 5 pm,Thursday to 8 pm; entry DM5, discount DM2). On display are sculptures and stunning black-and-white graphics of the acclaimed socialist artist. One of the highlights of the **Kölnisches Stadtmuseum**, at Zeughausstrasse 1-3, is a scale model showing old Cologne; there's also a fine weapons and armour collection. It's open daily from 10 am to 5 pm, to 8 pm on Tuesday; admission is DM5. Learn everything about the history of making chocolate in a 'hands-on' way in the **Schokoladenmuseum** (weekdays from 10 am to 6 pm, weekends from 11 am to 7 pm; DM10) on the river in the Rheinauhafen near the Altstadt; it's not just for those with a sweet tooth. Fans of the Fab Four may want to visit the **Beatles Museum** at Heinsbergstrasse 13 (open Monday to Friday from 10 am to 2 pm and 3 to 7 pm, Saturday to 3 pm; DM5), which documents their career.

Roman Cologne

Lots of remnants from the former Roman settlement lie scattered around town. Starting from the cathedral's main door, you will see the remains of the arch of a **Roman gate** from the ancient north wall. If you walk west along Komödienstrasse over Tunisstrasse, you reach the **Zeughaus** (containing the Kölnisches Stadtmuseum), the Burgmauer side of which was built along the line of the **Roman wall**. On the pavement at the west end is a plaque tracing the Roman wall's line on a modern street plan (other plaques appear around the city near Roman sites). Continue west until you find a complete section of the north wall, which leads to the Römerturm, a corner tower standing among buildings on the street corner at St-Apern-Strasse. Walk south one block and you come to another tower ruin near Helenenstrasse.

On the southern wall of the Römisch-Germanisches Museum are the remains of the **Roman harbour street**, which led to the banks of the Rhine, and two **Roman wells**. You can also take a lift down and walk through the **Roman sewer** and see the remains of the **Praetorian palace** under Cologne's medieval town hall (entry on Kleine Budengasse; closed Monday). The **Rathaus** itself, with its Gothic tower and Renaissance loggia, is open from 7.30 am to 4.45 pm weekdays (to 2 pm only on Friday).

Cruises

Between April and October KD River Cruises (☎ 208 83 18) runs at least four one-hour cruises daily (DM9.50) that let you enjoy the Cologne panorama from the Rhine. It also operates day excursions, for example to Königswinter in the Siebengebirge (DM39.80 return) and Linz (DM52.80 return) on the Rhine. Rail passes (Eurail, German Rail, etc) are valid for normal KD Line services. Children up to age 4 travel free, up to age 13 for a flat DM3. Students get a 30% discount. Travel on your birthday is free. In general, return tickets cost only slightly more than one-way tickets.

Organised Tours

The daily guided city bus tour in English departs from the tourist office at 10 and 11 am and at 3 pm (from November to March at 11 am and 2 pm only). It lasts two hours and costs DM25.

Places to Stay – bottom end

Cheap accommodation in Cologne is not plentiful and practically nonexistent during trade shows when hoteliers are not shy about ratcheting up their rates by 50% or more. On the other hand, if nothing is going on, you may be able to stay in an exclusive hotel at a cheap rate. Just contact the hotel directly and ask for the special rates. Prices quoted below should just be used as a guideline.

The tourist office operates a room-finding service for DM5 per person. If you're driving, keep in mind that parking your car in a hotel or public garage may add DM20 or more to your room rate.

Camping The most convenient (though not very) camp sites are the municipal *Campingplatz der Stadt Köln* (☎ 831 96 6; open from May to at least the end of September) on Weidenweg in Poll, 5km south-east of the city centre on the right bank of the Rhine (take U16 to Marienburg, then walk across the bridge); and *Campingplatz Waldbad* (☎ 603 31 5; open all year), on Peter-Baum-Weg in Dünnwald, about 10km north of the city centre (no public transport).

Hostels Cologne has two DJH hostels. The big, 374-bed *Jugendherberge Köln-Deutz* (☎ 814 71 1), at Siegesstrasse 5a in Deutz, is a 10-minute walk east from the Hauptbahnhof over the Hohenzollernbrücke or three minutes from Bahnhof Köln-Deutz. Juniors pay DM27 to DM30 per bunk; for seniors it's DM32 to DM37, including sheets and buffet breakfast. The *Jugendgästehaus Köln-Riehl* (☎ 767 08 1) is north of the city in the suburb of Riehl, by the river at An der Schanz 14 (U16 to Boltensternstrasse). Here, the cost is a flat DM37, including breakfast and sheets.

Hotels Rates listed below refer to basic rooms with toilet and shower in the corridor. Expect to pay about DM20 more for rooms with private bath.

The area north of the train and bus stations has a high concentration of low-budget, no-frills hotels and pensions. Options include *Hotel Berg* (☎ 912 91 62), Brandenburger Strasse 6, with singles/doubles from DM52/90. *Hotel Brandenburger Hof* (☎ 122 88 9), at Brandenburger Strasse 2, and *Hotel Thielen* (☎ 123 33 3) at No 1 of the same street, have rooms from DM50/75. At Probsteigasse 6, in the northern Altstadt, you'll find *Hotel Im Kupferkessel* (☎ 135 33 8), which starts at DM44/88.

Two more candidates are near Fischmarkt, south of the Dom. They are *Rhein-Hotel St Martin* (☎ 257 79 55) in Frankenwerft 31-33, with rooms from DM55/95, and *Das Kleine Stapelhäuschen* (☎ 257 78 62), which charges from DM48/120.

Places to Stay – middle

There are several mid-priced hotels centrally located in the Altstadt. The following room prices include private bath. *Hotel Allegro* (☎ 240 82 60; fax 240 70 40) is at Thurnmarkt 1-7 and has singles/doubles from DM90/140. At the business-like, yet pleasant, *Senats-Hotel* (☎ 206 20; fax 206 22 00) at Untere Goldschmied 9-17, you can get a good-sized room from DM95/110. Nice too is the *Domblick* (☎ 123 74 2; fax 125 73 6),

Domstrasse 28, where room rates start at DM115/135.

Places to Stay – top end
Being a major trade show centre, Cologne has the usual number of international chain hotels catering mainly to business travellers. The one with the nicest view over the entire Cologne panorama is the *Hyatt Regency* (☎ 828 12 34; fax 828 13 70), Kennedy-Ufer 2a, where a night in a full-facility room costs from DM305/345 for singles/doubles. An extremely classy and modern designer hotel is the *Hotel Im Wasserturm* (☎ 200 80; fax 200 88 88) in Kaygasse 2, which starts at DM419/548.

Long-Term Rentals
Cologne's Mitwohnzentrale (☎ 240 64 45) is at Lindenstrasse 77.

Places to Eat
Beer Halls Much like in Munich, beer reigns supreme in Cologne. There are more than 20 local breweries, all producing a variety called Kölsch, which is relatively light and slightly bitter. The breweries run their own beer halls and serve their brew in skinny glasses holding a mere 200 ml, but you'll soon agree it's a very satisfying way to drink the stuff. They also serve filling, if hearty, regional dishes that usually cost DM20 or less. The local colour around you, of course, is free.

Brauhaus Sion at Unter Taschenmacher 9 is a big beer hall, packed most nights and for good reason: you'll eat your fill for well under DM20, including a couple of beers. *Brauerei zur Malzmühle*, at Heumarkt 6 off Am Malzbüchel south of the Deutzer Brücke, is smaller but similar. *Päffgen* at Friesenstrasse 64-66 is another good bet, as is *Früh am Dom* at Am Hof 12-14. For a place that the locals have reserved for themselves – so far – try *Schreckenskammer* behind St Ursula at Ursulagartenstrasse 11.

Ethnic Restaurants Thanks to Cologne's large multicultural population, you can take a culinary journey around the world. The cheapest options include the numerous pizzerias where you can fill up for around DM10. For a more elegant Italian restaurant with prices to match, head to *Osteria Da Damiano* at Marzellenstrasse 66. For excellent Turkish food, there's no place like Weidenstrasse, where you'll find lots of snack bars serving Turkish pizza and doner kebabs, as well as sophisticated places like *Bizim* at No 47, where such delicacies as lamb medallions or quail will set you back DM50 and up.

Cologne has two kosher restaurants, both near Barbarossaplatz. One is the *Koscheres Restaurant der Jüdischen Gemeinde*, which means that it's affiliated with the Jewish congregation. It's at Roonstrasse 50. The other is *Zimmes* on nearby Rathenauplatz. For DM15 vegetarian dishes and Indian curries, seek out *Bombay Palace* at Am Weidenbach 21 (closed Monday).

Cafés Coffee-house culture is big in Cologne and traditional 'Kaffee und Kuchen' (literally 'coffee and cake') cafés can be found at just about every corner. Two favourites are on Breite Strasse. *Schmittchen* at No 38 has a bistro character and also serves small meals, from herring to steaks, for DM15 to DM25. *Moderne Zeiten*, on the corner of Breite Strasse and Auf dem Berlich, is popular with media types from the WDR radio/TV studios across the street. The menu here also extends to pizza, pasta and casseroles costing DM15 or less. Nearby, in a former cinema at Apostelnstrasse 11, is *Gloria*, a place popular with those keen on caffeine and a chat.

Fast Food *Kaffeebud* stand-up coffee bars, charge DM1.99 for all the coffee you can drink. There's one on the eastern end of Alter Markt and also on Friesenplatz. *Stausberg* at Schildergasse 92 is a bustling stand-up snack bar where you can get good, hot, fast food for under DM10. Vegetarians and health food freaks will enjoy the wholesome dishes served at *Sirius* on the 2nd floor of the Olivandenhof mall in Zeppelinstrasse 9. Salads, stews and casseroles are sold by weight, with 100g going for as little as DM1.49.

Entertainment

Listings For an overview of cultural events during your stay, pick up a copy of the bilingual what's-on monthly *Monatsvorschau* (DM2) or the magazines *Kölner Illustrierte* (DM4) and *Prinz* (DM4.50), available at newsagents and bookshops.

Discos & Clubs One of Cologne's main venues for rock concerts is *E-Werk* (☎ 962 79 0), a converted power station at Schanzenstrasse 28 across the Rhine in the suburb of Mülheim. It turns into a huge techno disco on Friday and Saturday night (event information at ☎ 962 79 0). *Halle Tor 2* (☎ 491 20 5), a former factory for oil drills at Girlitzweg 30 in the western suburb of Müngersdorf, has now evolved into a dance hot spot. More central are several clubs on Hohenzollernring between Friesenplatz and Gereonshof. These include *Petit Prince* (☎ 122 24 9) at No 90 where it's salsa one night, reggae the next and acid jazz on Tuesday.

Theatre & Classical Music Lovers of classical music should not miss a concert at the *Kölner Philharmonie* at Bischofsgartenstrasse 1, in the same building as the Wallraf Richartz Museum but below ground. The box office is at KölnTicket on Roncalliplatz (☎ 280 1). Repertory theatre is based at the *Schauspielhaus* on Offenbachplatz, where the *Opernhaus* is also located. The box office for both is in the opera house foyer (☎ 221 84 00).

Gaudí, a musical loosely inspired by the story of the Catalonian architect Antonio Gaudí (1852-1926), is being performed in the new blue caterpillar-like structure Musical Dome on the Rhine just north of the Hauptbahnhof (toll-free ☎ 0180-530 20 20). Fortunately, the painfully skimpy storyline is overshadowed by a well performed extravaganza of song, dance and special effects.

Jazz The standbys for jazz in Cologne are *Papa Joe's Klimperkasten* at Alter Markt 50 and *Papa Joe's Em Streckstrump* at Buttermarkt 37. The first is large and lively, with a wonderful old pianola, whereas the second is more intimate. For something different, try *Schmuckkästchen*, a newish but already well established jazz joint in Venloer Strasse 40.

Pubs & Bars Evenings and weekends in the Altstadt are like miniature carnivals, with bustling crowds and lots to do and see. The beverage of choice is, of course, beer, and there are plenty of places to enjoy it. If selection is what you want, head to the *Biermuseum* at Buttermarkt 39, which serves 39 varieties. For more pubs and bars in this quarter, see Local Cuisine under Places to Eat.

Another local favourite is south of the centre at Alteburger Strasse 157. *Küppers Brauerei* is a historic brewery (normal pub hours) which also functions as a 'beer museum' (Saturday from 11 am to 4 pm only). There's also a beer garden in summer. Take U16 to Bayenthalgürtel.

Spectator Sport

Cologne's soccer team, 1. FC Köln, was founded in 1948 and has been a mainstay in Germany's Bundesliga (First League) for a long time, though its last reign as German champion was in 1978. The team's home base is in the Müngersdorfer Stadion on Aachener Strasse west of the city centre (tram No 1 from Neumarkt). Prices range from DM14 for standing-room tickets to DM52 for top seats. Tickets are usually available at the stadium on game day, except when teams from Dortmund, Mönchengladbach and Munich come to town.

Things to Buy

Cologne is a fantastic place to shop, with its large variety of eccentric boutiques, cool designer stores and trendy second-hand shops, plus the usual selection of chain and department stores. The main shopping area is the pedestrianised Hohe Strasse, which meanders south from the Dom then forks off into In der Höhle and Schildergasse leading on to Neumarkt. Breite Strasse and adjoining side streets like Apostelnstrasse form another shopping haven with an eclectic mix of stores – some funky, some elegant.

If you want to bring something home to mother, consider a bottle of *eau de Cologne*, the not terribly sophisticated but refreshing perfume invented – and still being produced – in its namesake city. The most famous brand is called 4711, after the number of the house where it was invented. There's still a perfumery and gift shop by that name on the corner of Glockengasse and Schwertnergasse. (Try to catch the Glockenspiel, with characters from Prussian lore parading above the store hourly from 9 am to 9 pm.)

Getting There & Away

Air Cologne/Bonn airport has many connections within Europe and to the rest of the world. For flight information, ring ☎ 02203-404 00 1. The Lufthansa office (☎ 925 49 90), and a general travel agency, is at Am Hof 30.

Bus Deutsche Touring's Eurolines buses go to Paris and back six times weekly (some trips overnight) for DM75 (return DM133). Buses to/from London run daily and cost DM108/159. Trips to Prague are scheduled three times a week for DM105/180. The office is at the bus station outside the Breslauer Platz exit of the Hauptbahnhof.

Train Cologne is a major train hub. S-Bahn and main-line trains service Bonn (DM9.40, 20 minutes), Düsseldorf (DM11.80, 20 minutes) and Aachen (DM18.80, one hour) several times each hour. Hourly IC trains include those to Hamburg (DM118, four hours), Frankfurt and Frankfurt airport (DM59, 2¼ hours), Hanover (DM82, three hours) and Munich (DM166, 5¾ hours). Trains to Leipzig (DM150, six hours) and Berlin-Zoo (DM170, 5½ hours) leave every two hours. For information on tickets and schedules, call ☎ 194 19.

Car & Motorcycle Cologne is also a major autobahn hub and encircled by the immense Kölner Ring that has exits to the A1, A3, A4, A57, A555 and A559 leading in all directions. Note that the ring road tends to be jammed with traffic in the day time.

Ride Services The ADM Mitfahrzentrale (☎ 194 40) has two branches at Triererstrasse 47 and at Maximinstrasse near the Hauptbahnhof. Citynetz Mitfahr-Service (☎ 194 44) is at Saarstrasse 22 near Barbarossaplatz.

Boat An enjoyable way to travel to/from Cologne is by boat. KD River Cruises (☎ 208 83 18) Frankenwerft 15, has services all along the Rhine (also see Cruises).

Getting Around

The Airport Bus No 170 runs between Cologne/Bonn airport and the main bus station every 15 minutes (DM8.20, 20-minute trip). The taxi ride to/from the airport costs about DM45.

Public Transport Cologne's mix of buses, trams, U-Bahn and S-Bahn trains is operated by the Verkehrsverbund Rhein-Sieg (VRS; ☎ 208 08 0) and is integrated with the Bonn public transport system. Their fairly complicated tariff structure is explained in the English-language brochure *Bus and Train Travel Made Easy*, available at VRS offices, such as the one at the Hauptbahnhof.

Short trips within the city cost DM2, while tickets covering most of the city area are DM3.20. If you're travelling as a group, the best deal is the Minigruppenkarte, which costs DM11 and is valid for up to five people travelling together after 9 am on weekdays and all day on weekends. Buy your tickets from the orange ticket machines and be sure to validate them when boarding.

Car & Motorcycle Driving in Cologne, especially around the Dom area, can be confusing and frustrating. Unless you're careful, you could easily end up in a tunnel or on a bridge going across the Rhine. Street parking in the city is usually reserved for residents, so it's best to head for one of the many underground parking garages (DM2.50 an hour). Note that some close at night and charge an overnight fee.

Most major car-rental companies have branches in Cologne. Among them are Avis (☎ 234 33 3) at Clemensstrasse 29-31 and Hertz (☎ 515 08 47) at Bismarckstrasse 19-21.

Taxi Taxis cost DM3.20 at flag fall plus DM2.15 per kilometre (DM0.20 more at night); add another DM1 if you order by phone (☎ 288 2). There are taxi ranks on the city's larger squares. The BahnTaxi stand (DM17 per couple) is at the west end of the Hauptbahnhof near the B Tunnel exit.

Bicycle Exploring Cologne by bike is a healthy alternative to motorised vehicles but requires major attention and skills because of the traffic and the absence of bike lanes in the city, unlike elsewhere in Germany. Kölner Fahrradverleihservice (☎ 723 62 7) at Sedanstrasse 27 in the Altstadt next to the Deutzer Brücke rents bikes for DM4/10/20 per hour/three hours/day.

AROUND COLOGNE

Brühl

- *pop 40,000*
- *area code* ☎ 02232

About 15km south of Cologne, Brühl offers two major attractions that bring in the crowds. Aficionados of history, culture and architecture flock to **Schloss Augustusburg**, considered the most important baroque residential palace on the Rhine. Three well known architects of the period – Johann Conrad Schlaun, François Cuvilliés and Balthasar Neumann – worked on this elegant edifice that is surrounded by a rigidly formal French garden. Completed in 1745, the palace was commissioned by Clemens August (1723-1761), the flamboyant prince-elector and archbishop of Cologne. A member of the Wittelsbach family, the Bavarian ruling dynasty, he was a brilliant and immensely powerful man whose diplomatic finesse helped put his brother Karl onto the imperial throne in 1742.

Not a modest man, his palace interior is a visual extravaganza that seems to incorporate every architectural and decorative element the baroque style had to offer. But it also glorifies the Wittelsbachs – in particular Clemens August – with its liberal use of literal and allegorical references. The most impressive feature is the ceremonial staircase by Neumann. A symphony in stucco, sculpture and faux marble, it is bathed in muted light and crowned by a multicoloured ceiling fresco by Carlo Carlone that is a homage to the arts. The palace opens daily from 9 am to noon and 1.30 to 4 pm, except Monday. Admission is DM5, discount DM3 and includes a one-hour guided tour.

Brühl's other attraction is **Phantasialand** (☎ 362 00), one of Europe's earliest Disneyland-style amusement parks (it turned 30 in 1997) that is naturally a winner with children. Settings include a Chinatown, Petit Paris, Viking ships, a fairy-tale park and a wild water ride. The park is open April to October from 9 am to 6 pm (to 9 pm in the summer months) and is located at Berggeiststrasse 31-41. Day admission is DM33, children measuring up to 1.2m get in for free. Brühl is regularly served by regional trains from Cologne. If you're driving, exit Brühl-Süd from the A553.

BONN

- *pop 300,000*
- *area code* ☎ 0228

When this friendly, relaxed city on the Rhine became West Germany's 'temporary' capital in 1949 it surprised almost everyone, including its own citizens. Soon it was given the nickname 'Federal Village' for its supposed provincialism and lack of sophistication. While Bonn is no world capital, the charges are not entirely fair. A large foreign population (one in seven inhabitants, many of them diplomats) imbues it with a certain international feel, while the university's 37,000 students do their part to enliven the city. Then there's a host of first-rate museums, some packed with the biggest and the brightest names in art. Artists, in fact, also play a large role in the city's history. Bonn was the

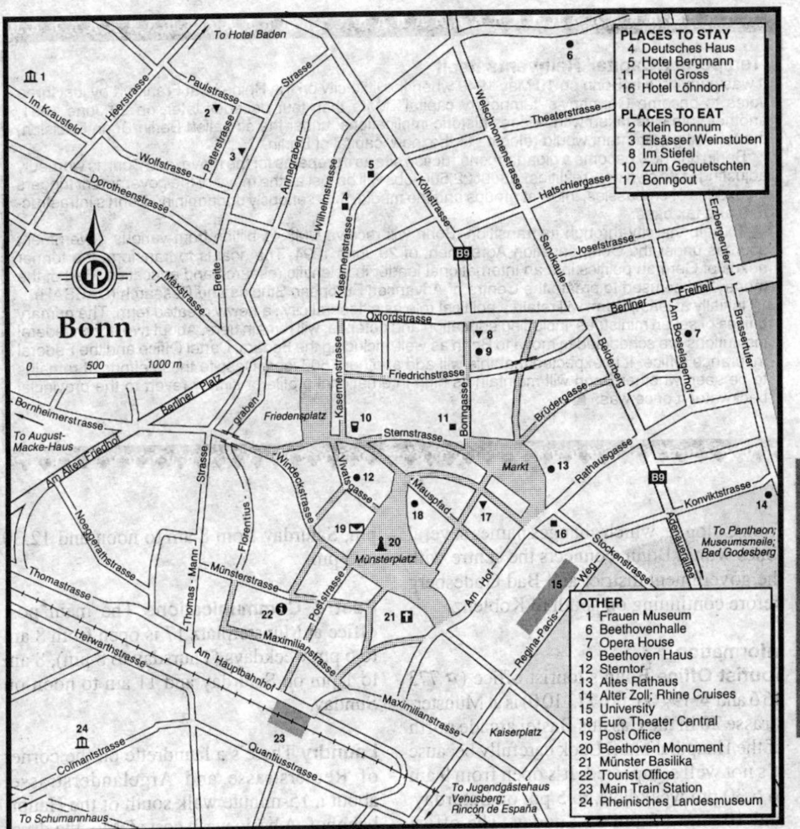

birthplace of Ludwig van Beethoven (1770-1827); the painter August Macke had his studio here; and Robert Schumann lived here for a time.

Settled in Roman times, Bonn celebrated its 2000th anniversary in 1989. From the late 16th to the 18th century, it was the permanent residence of the prince-electors and archbishops of Cologne, including the eccentric Clemens August (see the Brühl section). Some of the baroque architecture from this era survived the ravages of WWII and the postwar demand for modern government buildings. Faced with government relocation to Berlin by the year 2000, the city is now in the process of reinventing itself (see boxed text entitled 'Temporary Capital' Reinvents Itself).

Bonn is an easy day trip from Cologne and a good base for exploring the nearby spa town of Bad Godesberg and some of the sights along this section of the Rhine.

Orientation

Bonn is about 30km south of Cologne and just north of the Siebengebirge (Seven Mountains) nature preserve. The Hauptbahnhof is right in the city centre. The B9

'Temporary Capital' Reinvents Itself

It was party time in Bonn on 10 May 1949 when the little city on the Rhine beat Frankfurt by just three votes to become Germany's 'temporary capital'. More than four decades later, on 20 June 1991, another vote was taken with no less historic implications: under the so-called Berlin-Bonn Decision, the federal government would relocate to the 'new' capital of Berlin.

Berlin has now become a gigantic construction site as it prepares for the move, and Bonn is worriedly adjusting to its own new realities. About 22,500 jobs will be lost as the move of the government triggers an exodus of embassies, interest groups and the media, thus seriously undermining Bonn's infrastructure and tax base.

To help the city through its transition, Bonn will receive DM3.41 billion from various government sources under the Compensation Agreement of 29 June 1994. The goal is to transform the former nexus of German politics into an international leader in scientific research and education. Part of the money will be used to create the Centre of Advanced European Studies and Research (CAESAR).

Initially at least, Bonn will retain a political role as a 'federal city', a newly created term. The primary offices of seven ministries, including education and defence, will remain here. About two dozen federal institutions are scheduled to move to Bonn as well, including the Federal Cartel Office and the Federal Insurance Office. It is expected that this will add another 7500 jobs. Despite these efforts, it remains to be seen whether Bonn will maintain its high international profile or simply revert to the provincial backwater it once was. ■

from Cologne, which changes names several times within Bonn, connects the centre with the government district and Bad Godesberg before continuing on south to Koblenz.

Information

Tourist Office Bonn's tourist office (☎ 773 46 6 and ☎ 194 33; fax 773 10 0) is at Münsterstrasse 20 in the Cassius Bastei arcade north of the Hauptbahnhof. Look carefully because it's not well signposted. It's open from 9 am to 6.30 pm weekdays, to 5 pm on Saturday, and 10 am to 2 pm on Sunday. The office has good city maps and brochures (some in English) and also sells the BonnCard (DM12, families DM24), which is valid for 24 hours and provides unlimited use of public transportation within the city after 9 am and admission to most major museums.

Foreign Consulates & Embassies As long as the German Foreign Ministry remains in Bonn, most of the foreign embassies will stay too. See the Facts for the Visitor chapter for a complete list.

Money The bank in the train station changes cash and travellers' cheques and is open weekdays from 9 am to 1 pm and 1.30 to 6 pm, Saturday from 8 am to noon and 12.30 to 3 pm.

Post & Communications The main post office at Münsterplatz 17 is open from 8 am to 6 pm weekdays (Thursday to 8 pm), 8 am to 1 pm on Saturday and 11 am to noon on Sunday.

Laundry There's a laundrette on the corner of Reuterstrasse and Argelanderstrasse, about a 15-minute walk south of the Hauptbahnhof. A basic wash costs DM6, the dryer costs DM1.

Medical Services For medical emergencies ring ☎ 192 92. A recorded message listing dentists on call is available at ☎ 115 00.

Walking Tour

The tourist office runs a combined walking/bus tour of the city (between April and October from Monday to Saturday at 2 pm and on Sunday at 10.30 am; between November and March on Saturday at 2 pm; DM18) but you can easily cover the sights on your own. Cars are banned from much of the city centre, making it a pleasure to walk.

Start on Münsterplatz, dominated by the

five soaring spires of the **Münster Basilika**. Saints Cassius and Florentius, two martyred Roman officers who are the patron saints of Bonn, are honoured here in what is a good example of the Rhenish transitional style of architecture between Romanesque and Gothic. The Romanesque cloister ranks among the finest in northern Europe.

At the centre of the square stands the bronze **Beethoven monument**, unveiled in 1845 for the composer's 75th birthday. The yellow building on the north-western side of the square was once the Palais Fürstenberg and now houses the main post office.

Walk past it and turn left into Vivatsgasse to the **Sterntor**, a remnant of the old city wall. Turn right into Sternstrasse towards the Markt, a triangular square dominated by the pink, grey and gold rococo **Altes Rathaus**. Politicians from Charles de Gaulle to John F Kennedy have stood atop its stairway. Exiting the square onto Stockenstrasse and passing through the arches of the Stockentor leads you to the main building of the **Rheinische Friedrich-Wilhelm University** (1725), the one-time residence of the prince-electors. The university opened in 1818. It is flanked by the Hofgarten, a small park and popular gathering place for students.

Cross Adenauerallee towards the river to get to **Alter Zoll**, a small section of the stone ramparts that once encircled Bonn. The embarkation point for river cruises is nearby.

Government District

The federal government's move to Berlin looms, but for now politics are still the name of the game in Bonn. The government district lies about 1.5km south-east of the Hauptbahnhof between the B9 (here called Adenauerallee) and the banks of the Rhine. It's a potpourri of historic and modern buildings, of which the most statuesque are the **Villa Hammerschmidt** and the Palais Schaumburg, both off-limits to the public. The former is the second official residence of the federal president (the other one is Schloss Bellevue in Berlin) and was built in the last century on Roman foundations.

Visible only from Adenauerallee is the

Ludwig van Beethoven: Bonn's most famous product.

19th-century **Palais Schaumburg** which, in 1945, served as Allied headquarters in Bonn. From 1949 to 1976, it housed the chancellery and is now primarily used for representational functions. The chancellery moved next door to the cluster of low black buildings, said to reflect the austere tastes of then-Chancellor Helmut Schmidt. Also on Adenauerallee is the **Adenauer monument**, a gigantic bronze head with important events in the former chancellor's life engraved on the back.

Heading towards the Rhine, you'll come to the **Bundeshaus** complex at Görresstrasse. Its centrepiece is the modern circular steel, glass and wood **Plenary Hall** where the Bundestag, Germany's lower house, has convened since 1992. It stands right next to the Bauhaus structure where the country's first postwar parliament gathered in 1949. Free guided tours of the plenary hall (in German) provide insight into the German political system (daily on the hour, except during parliamentary sessions; departing from Entrance IIa).

Museums

Bonn has a fascinating variety of fine museums. It's worth getting the BonnCard (see the Information section above) if you plan to visit more than one or two. Unless noted otherwise, museums are closed on Monday and offer a 50% discount to students.

Beethoven House The modest appearance of the pink three-storey building at Bonngasse 20 belies its historic importance as the birthplace of Ludwig van Beethoven. Inside are letters, musical scores, paintings, the composer's last grand piano and public docments. Particularly memorable are the giant brass ear trumpets used by the composer to combat his growing deafness. There's also a haunting death mask, poignantly displayed next to the room where he was born. The Beethoven Haus is open Monday to Saturday from 10 am to 5 pm (4 pm in winter), Sunday from 11 am to 4 pm. Admission is DM8.

Frauen Museum Housed in a former department store at Im Krausfeld 10, this museum showcases contemporary paintings, installations, sculpture and other art forms by international women artists. It's all displayed in a friendly environment and complemented by readings, concerts, lectures and theatre performances. Men are welcome, of course. The museum is open Tuesday to Saturday from 2 to 5 pm, Sunday 11 am to 5 pm and admission is DM6 (tram No 61 to Rosenthal).

Rheinisches Landesmuseum The most prized exhibit in this museum at Colmantstrasse 14-16 is the top of a 50,000-year-old Neanderthal skull found in a valley near Düsseldorf. It is the starting-point for a journey through the ages that documents art and life in the Rhineland. Of note too are a golden cup from the Bronze Age; helmets, dishes, tombstones and other items from the days of Roman occupation, as well as the 14th-century *Pietà Roettgen*. Opening hours are weekdays from 9 am to 5 pm (Wednesday to 8 pm) and weekends from 10 am to 5 pm. Entry is DM4.

Museumsmeile The Museum Mile consists of four museums all located along the B9 in the heart of the government district. It begins with the **Museum Alexander Koenig** (open weekdays 9 am to 5 pm, Saturday to 12.30 pm, Sunday 9.30 am to 5.30 pm; DM4) at Adenauerallee 160. This is an old-fashioned museum of natural history with vast racks and cases displaying life forms from mosquitos to elephants.

If you visit only one museum in Bonn, make it the **Haus der Geschichte der Bundesrepublik Deutschland** at Adenauerallee 250 (open daily 9 am to 7 pm; free). Five levels of rampways present an entertaining multi-media chronology of the entire post-WWII history of Germany – from bombed-out obliteration to the industrialised and unified powerhouse of today. This fascinating exhibit is a must for anyone interested in recent German history.

The **Kunstmuseum Bonn** (open daily from 10 am to 6 pm; DM5, discount DM3), Friedrich-Ebert-Allee 2, is known for its 20th-century collection, especially an armload of works by August Macke and Joseph Beuys. It's all housed in a postmodern building with a generous and light-flooded interior. The hostile glares from overzealous security personnel can be a bit disturbing.

Immediately next door is the **Kunst- und Ausstellungshalle der Bundesrepublik Deutschland** (Tuesday and Wednesday 10 am to 9 pm, Thursday to Sunday to 7 pm; DM8), which features changing exhibitions of German, European and world culture, science and the arts. The creation of Viennese architect Gustav Peichl, the building features three distinctive cones jutting from its rooftop garden and a line of 16 columns representing the states of Germany.

Other Museums August Macke had his first and only studio at Bornheimer Strasse 96, now the **August Macke Haus** (weekdays 2.30 to 6 pm, Saturday 11 to 1 pm, Sunday to 5 pm; DM4). Macke lived here from 1910 until he was killed during WWI in 1914.

Fans of the composer Schumann can study pictures, letters and documents in the two memorial rooms devoted to him in a former sanatorium at Sebastianstrasse 182, now called the **Schumannhaus** (opening hours vary, call ☎ 773 65 6; free). The composer suffered severe depressions and checked himself into the asylum in 1854 after trying to take his own life. He and his wife, Clara, are buried in **Alter Friedhof** in Bornheimer Strasse.

Cruises

KD River Cruises (☎ 632 13 4) and Bonner Personen Schiffahrt (☎ 636 36 3) both run cruises along the Rhine from Brassertufer at Alter Zoll.

Places to Stay

The nearest *camping ground* (☎ 344 94 9; open all year) is right on the Rhine in Mehlem about 5km south of Bad Godesberg. Bonn's hostels are about as luxurious and modern as these places can get.

The *Jugendgästehaus Venusberg* (☎ 289 97 0), Haager Weg 42, is about 4km south of the Hauptbahnhof (take bus No 621) and has a bistro and a garden terrace. Such relative luxury has its price: DM37 per bunk, including breakfast. Not to be outdone, *Jugendgästehaus Bad Godesberg* (☎ 317 51 6), at Horionstrasse 60 in Bad Godesberg, offers much the same at the same price, plus buffet-style breakfast (bus No 615 from Bad Godesberg train station to Vrennerstrasse).

The tourist office operates a room-finding service (no phone reservations, fee of DM3 for rooms costing up to DM100, otherwise DM5).

True budget hotels are rare here, but you'll find two basic options on Kasernenstrasse. The better bet is the small *Hotel Bergmann* (☎ 633 89 1) at No 13 where singles/doubles with shared shower go for DM60/100. At No 19 is *Deutsches Haus* (☎ 633 77 7), where rates start at DM80/120. Another kilometre or so north gets you to *Hotel Baden* (☎ 633 60 0; fax 631 01 9), which charges DM95/160 for rooms with all facilities. South of the train station, at Mozart- strasse 1, is *Hotel Mozart* (☎ 659 07 1; fax 659 07 5), where basic rooms cost DM85/105.

Hotel Gross (☎ 654 08 0; fax 636 39 3) is right in the pedestrian zone in Bonngasse 17 near the Beethoven Haus and has singles for DM87 and doubles for DM140. At Stockenstrasse 6, you'll find *Hotel Löhndorf* (☎ 634 72 6; fax 695 71 2), which has basic singles/doubles for DM80/100, and several rooms with private bath for DM130/170.

Places to Eat

The city centre around the Markt is the place to find traditional Rhenish restaurant-pubs. One of them is *Zum Gequetschten* at Sternstrasse 78, which has generous main courses for under DM20. The historic *Im Stiefel* at Bonngasse 30 next to the Beethoven Haus is similar. At the trendy *Bonngout* at Remigiusplatz 4, you can simply linger over a *big* cup of coffee, munch on a salad or have a hot meal. Snack bars aren't hard to find in this area, and there's a colourful *produce market* in front of the Rathaus daily except Sunday. In summer, you can grab a sandwich and join the throngs of students lounging in the Hofgarten near the university.

Another quarter brimming with restaurants and bars is the Altstadt north-west of the pedestrian zone. *Klein Bonnum* at Paulstrasse 5 is popular for its creative menu, including several vegetarian dishes, all under DM20 (evenings only). At Breite Strasse 67 is *Elsässer Weinstuben*, which offers 11 varieties of Flammekuche, an Alsatian variation on the pizza, all around DM11.

South of the centre, at Karthäuserplatz 21, is *Rincón de España*, where reasonably priced paella, tapas and other Spanish dishes are so popular that the place bursts with people, night after night.

One of Bonn's finest restaurants is the stylishly cosy *Sankt Michael*, tucked away in a gorgeous Art Nouveau villa at Brunnenallee 26 in Bad Godesberg. A set four-course meal costs DM49 and à la carte is available.

Entertainment

To find out what's on in Bonn, pick up a copy of the monthly *Bonner Illustrierte* (DM3.80) at any newsagent. The tourist office also has a smaller schedule of events called *Bonn-Info* (DM1.50).

Classical concerts take place in the

Beethovenhalle at Wachsbleiche 17 by the Rhine and also in the small *chamber music hall* next to the Beethoven Haus in Bonngasse 24-26. The Beethoven Festival is held every two or three years (the last one was in 1997). Bonn's *Opera House* is at Am Boselagerhof 1 in the city centre. The diminutive *Euro Theater Central* at Mauspfad between the Markt and Münsterplatz stages plays in their original language. For biting satire, go to *Pantheon* on Bundeskanzlerplatz where there's also a disco every Friday and Saturday after 11 pm. The transvestite show at *Zarah L*, Maxstrasse 2, from Wednesday to Friday has been a long-time Bonn feature. On other days it's a pub.

Getting There & Away

Air Bonn shares an airport with Cologne that has connections within Germany, Europe and everywhere beyond.

Train Trains to Cologne (DM9.40, 20 minutes) leave several times an hour. IC trains to Hamburg (DM127, 4½ hours) and Frankfurt (DM50, two hours) depart hourly. There are also frequent trains to the Ruhrgebiet cities and Koblenz (DM14.20, 40 minutes).

Car & Motorcycle Bonn is at the crossroads of several autobahns, including the A565, the A555 and the A59. The B9 highway cuts north-south through the city.

Ride Services You'll find a Citynetz Mitfahrzentrale branch (☎ 693 03 0) at Herwarth Strasse 11.

Getting Around

Express bus No 670 shuttles between the Hauptbahnhof and Cologne/Bonn airport every 20 or 30 minutes (DM7.70). A taxi to the airport from Bonn costs about DM60.

Bonn's efficient public transportation system (☎ 711 48 13) is made up of buses, trams and the U-Bahn. It is divided into four zones. Single tickets are DM3.20/5.10/8.40/13.50, depending on the distance you travel. Day passes, valid for up to five people travelling together after 9 am, cost DM11/16/22.50/33. Tickets must be validated when boarding.

For a taxi, ring ☎ 555 55 5.

AROUND BONN

Siebengebirge

On the eastern side of the Rhine across from Bonn begins the Siebengebirge, a low mountain chain that is Germany's oldest nature preserve (1923). More than 200km of hiking trails lead through mostly deciduous forests, often allowing tremendous views of the Rhine, the Eifel and the Westerwald.

The Ölberg (461m) may be the highest of the seven mountains, but the **Drachenfels** (321m) is the most heavily visited. You can reach the summit on foot, by horse carriage, on the back of a mule, or by riding the historic cogwheel train that has made the 1.4km climb since 1883 (the station is in Drachenfelsstrasse just east of the B42).

About halfway up the steep slopes, you will pass the neo-Gothic **Drachenburg**, the Rhenish answer to King Ludwig's Neuschwanstein in Bavaria. Further uphill is the ruined **Drachenfels Castle** (1147), which was abandoned in 1634.

The base for explorations of the Siebengebirge is **Königswinter**, reached from the Bonn Hauptbahnhof via U66. The adjacent **Bad Honnef** was the home of the late federal chancellor Konrad Adenauer for many years. His house at No 8c in the street named after him has been turned into a museum (open 10 am to 4.30 pm, closed Monday; free).

AACHEN

- *pop 250,000*
- *area code* ☎ 0241

Aachen was known even in Roman times for its thermal springs. Charlemagne was so impressed by their revitalising qualities that he settled here and made it the capital of his kingdom in 794 AD. The famous cathedral begun in his reign is Aachen's main draw and one of the reasons why the town holds special significance among the icons of German nationhood.

Aachen is now a commercial and industrial city of 260,000, but its sulfurous springs

NORTH RHINE - WESTPHALIA

still attract spa visitors who come to take the waters recommended for rheumatism and other degenerative disorders. With the Netherlands and Belgium so close, Aachen has a distinctly international feel. It is also a university town with a lively cultural scene.

Orientation

Aachen's compact city centre is contained within two ring roads that roughly follow the old city walls, and is easily covered on foot. The inner ring road encloses the Altstadt proper and is called Grabenring because the segments it's composed of all end in 'graben' (meaning 'ditch'). The Hauptbahnhof is south-east of the town centre just beyond Alleenring, the outer ring road. Wend your way north from here to the Altstadt and the Dom, about a 10 to 15-minute walk. The central bus station is at the north-eastern edge of the Grabenring on the corner of Kurhausstrasse and Peterstrasse.

Information

Tourist Office Aachen's tourist office (☎ 180 29 60/1; fax 180 29 30) is at Elisenbrunnen on Friedrich-Wilhelm-Platz and is open weekdays from 9 am to 6 pm and to 2 pm on Saturday.

Money Nearly all banks exchange money and travellers' cheques, but the Sparkasse at Friedrich-Wilhelm-Platz 1-4, opposite the tourist office, has the longest hours: weekdays from 8.30 am to 6 pm and Saturday to 1 pm. The ATM machine inside the train station accepts all major credit cards.

Post & Communications The main post office is at Kapuzinergraben 19 and is open to 6 pm, Saturday to 1 pm. In addition to the usual array of services, there's a fax-phone and photocopy machine.

Medical Services & Emergency For after-hours emergency medical service call ☎ 192 92; for dental problems, call ☎ 709 61 6. The municipal Lost Property Office (☎ 432 32 43) is on Bahnhofsplatz.

Charlemagne's Court Chapel in Aachen cathedral: coronation site of 30 emperors.

Dom

Aachen's drawing card is its cathedral (open daily from 7 am to 7 pm), the coronation church of some 30 Holy Roman emperors, starting with Otto I in 936. The church was the brainchild of Charlemagne, who is buried here. It has been a major pilgrimage site since his death in 814, not least for its religious relics. In 1981, the Dom was included on UNESCO's World Heritage List.

Following the tradition of Constantine the Great, Charlemagne fancied himself as successor of the Roman emperors and also as God's representative on earth. Inspired by Byzantine architecture, the cathedral core was built as an octagon and was the largest vaulted structure north of the Alps when consecrated as Charlemagne's court chapel in 805.

A two-storey gallery, supported by antique pillars imported from Ravenna and Rome, rises towards a folded dome which was installed after the city fire of 1656 destroyed the original tent roof.

The rainbow-coloured **mosaics** covering walls and vaults replaced the rococo décor about 100 years ago. A colossal brass **chandelier**, added to the octagon by Emperor Friedrich Barbarossa in 1165, hangs pendulously overhead.

Also of note are the **high altar** with its 11th-century gold-plated pala d'oro (altar front) depicting scenes of the Passion and the gilded copper ambo – or **pulpit** – donated by Henry II.

Unless you join a German-language tour (DM3), you'll only catch a glimpse of Charlemagne's white marble **throne** in the first gallery of the octagon. Six steps lead up to it – the same number, supposedly, as those leading to the throne of King Solomon. To accommodate the flood of pilgrims flocking to the cathedral, it was enlarged with the addition of the Gothic **choir** in 1414.

Most came to see the gilded **Karlschrein**, Charlemagne's final resting place, which stands at its eastern end. Commissioned by

Barbarossa, it was completed under his grandson, Emperor Friedrich II, who allegedly insisted on personally placing Charlemagne's remains within this elaborate coffin on his coronation day in 1215.

The entrance to the **Domschatzkammer**, with one of the richest collections of religious art north of the Alps, is on nearby Klostergasse. It is open Monday from 10 am to 1 pm, Tuesday to Sunday to 6 pm (Thursday to 9 pm). Admission, which includes a pamphlet, is DM5, discount DM3.

Rathaus

North of the cathedral, the 14th-century Rathaus overlooks the Markt, a lively gathering place in summer, with its fountain statue of Charlemagne. The eastern tower of the Rathaus, the Granusturm, was once part of Charlemagne's palace. Some 50 statues of German rulers, including 31 kings crowned in Aachen, adorn the building's façade. The 1st floor has fancy stuccowork and wall panelling, but the highlight is the grand Empire Hall on the 2nd floor, where Holy Roman emperors enjoyed their coronation feasts. The Rathaus is open daily from 10 am to 1 pm and 2 to 5 pm. Admission is DM3, discount DM1.50.

Museums

Unless noted, admission to museums listed below is DM6, discount DM3. A combination ticket to all of Aachen's municipal museums is DM10 and is available at the tourist office. Museums are closed on Monday.

Ludwig Forum for International Art In a former umbrella factory at Jülicherstrasse 97-109, this museum has works by Warhol, Lichtenstein, Baselitz and other pop artists. Frequent performances complement the exhibits. It's open Tuesday and Thursday from 10 am to 5 pm, Wednesday and Friday to 8 pm, Saturday and Sunday from 11 am to 5 pm.

Zeitungsmuseum This international collection of newspapers at Pontstrasse 13 is comprised of some 150,000 titles spanning four centuries with many first, last and special editions. It's open Tuesday to Saturday from 9.30 am to 1 pm and 2.30 to 5 pm (in winter only to 1 pm on Saturday). Admission is free.

Suermondt Ludwig Museum This museum surveys art from the Middle Ages to modern times. Highlights include portraits by Lucas Cranach and Rubens and sculptures from the late Middle Ages. It's located at Wilhelmstrasse 18 and is open from 11 am to 7 pm on Tuesday, Thursday, Friday; to 9 pm on Wednesday and to 5 pm on weekends.

Kornelimünster

The romantic suburb of Kornelimünster is worth a short excursion. The main attraction here is the former Benedictine **Abbey Church of St Kornelius**. Upon its consecration in 817, Charlemagne's son, Ludwig the Pious, bestowed several important relics to the monastery. These are said to include Jesus' loin cloth and shroud, which are exhibited to the faithful every seven years. Take bus No 68/166 from the train station.

Places to Stay

Camping The nearest camping ground to Aachen is *Hoeve de Gastmolen* (☎ +31-43-306 57 55), across the Dutch border in Vaals, about 6km west of town at Lemierserberg 23. Take bus No 15 or 65 and get off at Heuvel.

Hostels The *DJH hostel* (☎ 711 01) is 4km south of the train station at Maria-Theresia-Allee 260 on a hill overlooking the city (take bus No 2 from Bushof to Ronheide or bus No 12 to Colynshof). A bunk and breakfast cost DM25/30 for juniors/seniors (a small discount applies to longer stays); sheets are DM6.

Hotels The tourist office's room-reservation service at ☎ 180 29 50/1 is for hotels, pensions and private rooms (from DM30/40 for singles/doubles). Unless noted, prices below include breakfast.

Rooms at the *Etap Hotel* (☎ 911 92 9),

outside the city centre at Strangenhäuschen 15 (take bus No 51), are plain but have private bath and cost only DM61/73 for singles/doubles (breakfast DM8.90 extra per person). Close to the train station, at No 33-35 of quiet Hubertusstrasse, is *Hotel Marx* (☎ 375 41; fax 267 05), with basic rooms from DM60/100 and those with facilities from DM85/130.

Central too is *Hotel Reichshof* (☎ 238 68; fax 238 69) at Seilgraben 2, which tops out at DM112/160 for rooms with all facilities. Small, comfortable and friendly is *Hotel Brülls am Dom* (☎ 317 04; fax 404 32 6), located within view of the cathedral at Hühnermarkt. They ask DM140/170 for rooms with private bath. *Hotel Benelux* (☎ 223 43; fax 223 45), Franzstrasse 21-23, is a well run, elegant place where you pay from DM145/165 for singles/doubles, although the cheap rooms are likely to be taken.

About 8km south-east of the centre, at Napoleonsberg 132 in the suburb of Kornelimünster, is the stylish 12-room *Hotel zur Abtei* (☎ 02408-21 48; fax 41 51), which charges from DM90/140 for individually designed rooms with private bath. The hotel's French restaurant is first-rate.

Places to Eat

Being a university town, Aachen is full of lively cafés, restaurants and pubs, especially along Pontstrasse. *Café Kittel*, at No 39 of that street, is the place to linger over huge cups of coffee or to have an inexpensive meal. There's also a lively beer garden out back. The café *Chico Mendes* in the Katakomben Studentenzentrum at No 74-76 is popular with vegetarians and for breakfast, while *Pizzeria la Finestra* at No 123 has developed a loyal following for its authentic large pizzas starting at DM8.50.

Gaststätte Labyrinth, at Pontstrasse 156-158, is a rambling beer-hall-type place that lives up to its name. Good, filling meals cost DM8 to DM15, and the menu offers a satisfying range of vegetarian dishes. The place for wine, cheese and French bistro fare is *Egmont* at Pontstrasse 1 which operates the popular 'Café Chantant' entertainment evenings in spring and autumn. Just off Pontstrasse, at Neupforte 25, you'll find *Efes*, a clean, contemporary café specialising in Turkish grilled meat and vegetarian dishes, many for around DM10.

Aachen has lots of nice coffee houses, but the classic one is *Leo van den Daele* in a historic house on the corner of Büchel and Körbergasse. Leather-covered walls, tiled stoves and antique furniture create an old-world atmosphere. The restaurant *Am Knipp* (closed Tuesday), Bergdriesch 3, has been around since 1698 and serves regional specialities for around DM20. *Goldene Rose*, housed in the former cathedral kitchen at Fischmarkt 1, is busy and boisterous with more than a touch of style, and slightly above-average prices. On Katschhof, the square between the cathedral and the Rathaus, there's a produce and flower *market* on Tuesday and Thursday from 8 am to 1 pm.

Entertainment

Classic theatre, concerts and opera are staged at *Theater Aachen* (☎ 478 42 44) on Theaterplatz most nights. If you like your productions experimental and, well, bizarre, there's *Theater K* (☎ 151 15 5) at Ludwigsallee 139.

Aachen has a lively dance club scene and the unpronounceable *Aoxomoxoa* at Reihstrasse 15 is one of the cutting-edge venues. At *B9* at Blondelstrasse 9, it's music across the board, from hip hop to jazz and techno. Both open at 10 pm and are closed Sunday. The more mature crowd heads for *Club Voltaire*, Friedrichstrasse 9, which doesn't start swinging to funk and other black music until after midnight.

The existentialist atmosphere of the *Domkeller*, around the side of the cathedral at Hof 1, has drawn students since the 1950s; there's live music on weekends.

Things to Buy

Aachen is known for its Printen, a crunchy spiced cookie reminiscent of gingerbread. Traditionally shaped like a log, Aachen bakeries now churn out this confection in a variety of shapes from the Easter Bunny to Santa Claus. One of the best places to buy them is Leo van den Daele (see Places to Eat). The main shopping area is along the pedestrianised Adalbertstrasse.

Getting There & Away

Air Airports serving Düsseldorf and Bonn/Cologne are nearly equidistant from Aachen (about 90km away).

Train There are several trains an hour to Cologne (DM18.80, one hour) with some carrying on to Dortmund and other cities in the Ruhrgebiet. If you're heading to cities south, you'll probably have to change in Cologne. Four trains a day go directly to Berlin-Zoo (DM169, seven hours).

Car & Motorcycle Aachen is easily reached via the A4 (east-west) from Cologne and the A44 (north-south) from Düsseldorf. The B57, B258 and B264 also meet here.

Ride Services The ADM Mitfahrzentrale (☎ 1 94 40) is at Roermonder Strasse 4, on the corner of Ludwigsallee.

Getting Around

Shuttles to/from Düsseldorf airport operate daily every 90 minutes; reservations are not required. To catch one of the four buses leaving for Cologne/Bonn airport (weekdays only), you must make a reservation by calling ☎ 1 82 00 23. Buses depart from Bushof, and rides cost DM32 each way.

Aachen's points of interest are clustered within the city centre which is best walked. Those arriving with private transport can dump their cars in one of the many parking garages or lots. Bus tickets for travel within the area encircled by Alleenring cost a flat DM1.60 (six-ticket block DM7.80). Otherwise, you can cover the entire city of Aachen – and the adjoining Dutch communities of Vaals and Kelmis – with the Zone 1 ticket for DM2.30 (six-ticket block DM12.60). The best deal, though, are day passes, which cost DM8 and are valid for up to five people travelling together. Tickets are available from the drivers.

For a taxi, call ☎ 511 11 1.

The Ruhrgebiet

About 7.4 million people live in this region stretching along the rivers Ruhr, Lippe and Emscher from the Dutch border to the eastern Westphalian flatlands. Yet, the Ruhrgebiet is neither a political, geographical or historic unit, but comprises the 53 cities and communities that belong to the Kommunalverband Ruhrgebiet (Association of Ruhrgebiet Communities). This organisation was founded in 1920 to coordinate the building of infrastructure to meet the demands of quickly expanding industry. The Ruhrgebiet became Europe's largest industrial region and was target No 1 for Allied bombers in WWII, whose thousands of raids produced the desired effect. During the rebuilding process, architectural aesthetics were unfortunately of secondary importance.

The days when the coal and steel industries provided employment to millions are long gone, and the Ruhrgebiet has undergone many changes over the past 30 years. Yet, the region and its people don't deny their history. In fact, they seem to embrace it, as is especially evident in the numerous former factories and mines now enjoying reincarnations as trendy restaurants, movie theatres, concert venues and nightclubs. Universities and academic institutes abound. Many cities support their own theatre ensembles and opera houses. And, thanks to the wave of musicals like *Les Miserables* and *Starlight Express* that have opened here in recent years, the Ruhrgebiet is now billing itself as 'Broadway on the Ruhr'.

Getting Around

All Ruhrgebiet cities are connected to each other by an efficient network of S-Bahn and regional trains, managed by the Verkehrsverbund Rhein-Ruhr (VRR; ☎ 0209- 194 49). In addition, each city has its own public transport system of buses, trams and, in some cases, U-Bahn trains. The same tariffs apply within the entire region. There are four categories depending on the distance you intend to travel. Look at the displays on the orange ticket vending machines to see which price applies in your case. Single tickets are DM2/3/5.80/11.70. Better value are the four-trip tickets at DM5.60/9.20/ 15.70/34.50. Day passes are DM10/14.50/27 (not available for *Kurzstrecken*, or short trips).

ESSEN

- *pop 630,000*
- *area code* ☎ 0201

Essen is the largest city in the Ruhrgebiet and sixth-largest in Germany. A settlement developed around a monastery founded here in 852 and obtained town rights in 1244. In the early 19th century, Essen plunged headlong into the Industrial Age, with the first 150 years dominated by steel and coal production. Essen is the home of the Krupp family of industrialists, and it was Friedrich Krupp who founded the first factory producing cast steel in 1811. All of Essen's mines and steel works have closed now, but it remains an industrial city as the headquarters of many important energy corporations. Nevertheless, Essen's fine collection of museums, generous green areas and lively cultural scene make it well worth a trip. It's also a popular town for shopping.

Orientation

Essen's sights are rather spread out, but all are easily reached by public transport. The Hauptbahnhof Nord (North) exit plunges you right onto the centre's main artery, the pedestrianised Kettwiger Strasse. The museum complex and the recreational areas are both south of the station.

Information

Tourist Office Essen's tourist office (☎ 194 33; fax 887 20 44) is on the ground floor of the Handelshof building opposite the north exit of the Hauptbahnhof and is open weekdays from 10 am to 5.30 pm and Saturday 10 am to 1 pm.

Money The Reisewelt bank inside the Hauptbahnhof is open daily but has odd hours that change frequently. If they're closed, the ATM machine outside the bank accepts all major credit cards. The American Express (☎ 245 13 0) office is at Gutenbergstrasse 68.

Post & Communications The main post office is just on the left opposite the northern exit of the Hauptbahnhof and is open from 8 am to 7 pm weekdays, 8.30 am to 2 pm Saturdays and 10 am to noon Sundays.

Bookshop At the Baedeker bookshop at Kettwiger Strasse 35 in the heart of the shopping zone, you'll find a wide selection of maps and guidebooks. They also have a fair number of English and French titles, mostly novels.

Medical Services In medical emergencies, contact ☎ 192 92; if it's a dentist you need, dial ☎ 202 20 2.

City Centre

Essen's reputation as a shopper's haven reaches far beyond the city limits. All along Kettwiger Strasse you'll find boutiques, speciality shops and department stores vying for your Deutschmarks. In the midst of all this are a couple of fine sights. Chief among them is the **Münster** at Burgplatz 1 off Kettwiger Strasse, the seat of the Ruhr diocese founded only in 1958. Of average architectural appeal, it is stocked with major Ottonian works of art from around 1000 AD, including a **seven-armed candelabrum** and the blue-eyed **Golden Madonna**.

The **Schatzkammer** (admission DM2) is one of Europe's richest cathedral treasuries and has various gemstone-studded processional crosses and a crown of Emperor Otto III.

East of the cathedral, at Steeler Strasse 29, you'll find the **Alte Synagogue** (closed Monday; free), an aesthetically challenged edifice built between 1911 and 1913. It's the largest synagogue north of the Alps and contains a memorial exhibit on the Holocaust.

NORTH RHINE - WESTPHALIA

Museum Complex
About 2km south of the Hauptbahnhof and flanked by Goethestrasse and Bismarckstrasse is Essen's museum complex (tram Nos 101, 107, 127 and U11 to Rüttenscheider Stern). The moderately interesting **Ruhrlandmuseum** focuses on the prehistory and geology of the Ruhrgebiet. The adjacent **Folkwang Museum**, on the other hand, enjoys an international reputation for its extensive collection of post-1800 art. However, because of extensive renovation, most of the collection cannot be seen until autumn 1998 months. Call ☎ 884 53 00 to see whether you can once again admire works by such major romanticists as Caspar David Friedrich and Lovis Corinth, plus a veritable who's who of impressionists, expressionists, cubists, Bauhaus artists and others. Both museums are open from 10 am to 6 pm, to 9 pm on Thursday, closed Monday. Admission is DM5, discount DM3.

Green Belt
The Ruhr flows right through Essen's southern suburbs and has been turned into the **Baldeney See**, a reservoir popular with water-sports enthusiasts. A series of parks and forests fringes its northern shore. One of them contains **Villa Hügel** (1869-73), the neoclassical mansion inhabited by the Krupp industrial dynasty until 1945. You can stroll through the same generous salons, halls and galleries where the Krupps once received royalty. On the upper floor of the adjacent building, the family history is chronicled, while an exhibit on the ground floor showcases the latest Krupp products. Occasionally, the space is also used for internationally acclaimed exhibits. The park and villa are open daily except Monday; admission is DM1.50 for both (take S-Bahn No 6 to Essen-Hügel).

Another recreational area north-west of here is the **Grugapark** (take U11 to Gruga), a huge city park incorporating the Botanical Garden and Bird Park, with the trade show complex on the eastern edge. The park is open daily. Admission is DM4, children DM2; in winter there's a 50% discount.

South of the lake, at Brückstrasse 54 in Essen-Werden, stands the superb **Basilica St Ludgerus** (1256). This late-Romanesque abbey succeeded the earlier monastic church (799) founded by the Frisian missionary Liudger who is buried here. The **Schatzkammer** (DM2) contains some important treasures.

Places to Stay
Essen has two camping grounds. *Stadtcamping Essen-Werden* (☎ 492 97 8) is at Im Löwental 67, near the Essen-Werden train station (take S-Bahn No 6 from Hauptbahnhof). Also in Werden, at Pastoratsberg 2, is the newly renovated *DJH hostel* (☎ 491 16 3), which costs DM22.50 to DM25 for juniors and DM27.50 to DM30 for seniors. From Werden station, take bus No 190 or walk for 10 minutes.

The tourist office operates a free hotel-booking service, but availability of budget options is slim, and private rooms are unfortunately nonexistent.

Among the cheaper places in the centre is *Hotel Zum Deutschen Haus* (☎ 232 98 9; fax 230 69 2) in Kastanienallee 16, which charges DM90/150 for simple singles/doubles with private bath. *Hotel Lindenhof* (☎ 233 03 1; fax 234 30 8), Logenstrasse 18, charges from DM120/150 while *Parkhaus Hügel* (☎ 471 09 1; fax 444 20 7) at Freiherr-vom-Stein-Strasse 209 in the green suburb of Bredeney costs DM110/175.

Artistic types will feel right at home in *Mintrops Burghotel* (☎ 571 71 0; fax 571 71 47), Schwarzensteinweg 81, where gorgeous rooms start at DM140/205.

Places to Eat
Essen's city centre is strangely devoid of pleasant eateries, and so it's best to head to the southern suburb of Rüttenscheid ('Rü' for short) with its clusters of pubs, bars and restaurants of all kinds, including *Schote* at Emmastrasse 25 and the Mexican *Sala Dolores* at Alfredstrasse 56. The restaurant in *Zeche Carl* (see Entertainment) also has inexpensive snacks and simple dishes. Essen's coal-mining tradition is celebrated in

the rustic *Brauhaus Graf Beust*, in a disused mine at Kastanienallee 95. Lots of local colour, though not that many locals.

A great option for vegetarians is *Zodiac*, Witteringstrasse 41, which offers 12 dishes from 12 countries every day.

Entertainment

As with most Ruhrgebiet cities, Essen has a very lively cultural scene. For a thorough listing of current hot spots and events schedules, pick up a copy of the magazine *Prinz* (DM5) or the free *Coolibri* (available in bars, restaurants, some shops and the tourist office).

A classic and contemporary repertoire is presented at the *Grillo-Theater* (☎ 812 22 00) on Theaterplatz off Kettwiger Strasse in the city centre. The students of the Folkwang School for Music, Theatre and Dance give regular performances in an old abbey in Essen-Werden (free for students). The *Aalto Theater*, Rolandstrasse 10, is the main venue for opera, ballet and musicals.

Gritty industrial chic is offered at the *Zeche Carl*, an old mine housing a trendy cultural centre with live concerts, disco nights, cabaret, theatre and art exhibits. It's at Wilhelm-Nieswandt-Allee 100 in the northern suburb of Altenessen (tram No 101 or 106 to Karlsplatz). Essen's current temple for techno and other sounds is the labyrinthine *Mudia Art*, in a former factory at Frohnhauser Strasse 75. Expect designer clothes, doormen who screen you and hefty entry fees.

NORTH RHINE - WESTPHALIA

Getting There & Away

Air Essen has its own small airport, but you're more likely to arrive or depart via Düsseldorf airport, approximately a 30-minute drive south-west on the A52.

Bus Eurolines offers regular bus service primarily to Eastern European cities – eg to Warsaw (daily, DM95/170 one way/return) and Prague (twice weekly, DM95/160). It also goes to Paris four times a week (DM92/163). For information and tickets, go to the Bahntouristik (☎ 182 41 88) office at the station's north exit. Buses leave from the stop outside the Hauptbahnhof South exit.

Train IC trains leave in all directions hourly or every other hour for such cities as Frankfurt (DM81, three hours), Munich (DM188, 6¾ hours) and Hamburg (DM100, three hours). Essen is also efficiently linked to other cities in the Ruhrgebiet, as well as to Düsseldorf and Cologne, via the VRR network. For ticket and schedule information call ☎ 194 19.

Car & Motorcycle Essen is well connected in all directions via autobahns A40 and A52, but because of heavy commuter traffic these roads often slow down to a crawl during rush hour.

Ride Services The ADM Mitfahrzentrale (☎ 194 40) is at Freiheit 4 outside the Hauptbahnhof South exit.

Getting Around

S-Bahn No 21 provides an hourly direct link to Düsseldorf airport, while S-Bahn No 1 operates more frequently but requires an easy change at Düsseldorf Unterrath.

Essen's public transportation system (☎ 826 12 34) is exemplary, composed as it is of buses, trams, U-Bahns and S-Bahns servicing every corner of the city. For prices, see Getting Around at the beginning of the Ruhrgebiet section.

You can order a taxi on ☎ 866 55.

BOCHUM

- *pop 385,000*
- *area code* ☎ 0234

Located in the heart of the Ruhrgebiet, halfway between Essen and Dortmund, Bochum's history contains a healthy dose of industrial pioneer spirit. By 1735, there were already 25 coal mines here. In 1799, Germany's first steam-powered drill ushered in the 19th century, and in 1841 the process of casting steel was invented here. Coal and steel were the economic engines that fuelled Bochum's huge population growth – by some 12 times – between 1875 and 1929.

After WWII, the two industries at first brought renewed prosperity, but by the 1960s the boom was over and by 1973 all mines had closed. Many of those made redundant found employment at the large Opel car factory which began production in 1961 and now ranks among the region's major employers. The construction of the Ruhrgebiet's first university – the Ruhr-Universität Bochum – in 1965 was another major component in the restructuring of the city's economy. Today, the university, which enjoys a fine reputation nationwide, has 35,000 students.

Of no great physical beauty, Bochum has much of cultural value. Two of Germany's best and most popular technical museums are here. The Schauspielhaus ranks as one of the leading theatres in the German-speaking world. The musical *Starlight Express*, staged in a custom-designed hall, has been packing them in here since 1988.

Alternative culture also thrives, and many former industrial sites have been converted into cutting-edge performance spaces. The south of Bochum is given over to a lush recreational area – complete with medieval castles and a lake – stretching out along both banks of the Ruhr meadows.

Orientation

Bochum's almost completely pedestrianised city centre lies within an irregular loop made up of segments all ending in 'ring'. The Hauptbahnhof and bus station are on its south-eastern edge. The Bermudadreieck (Bermuda Triangle) pub district concentrates within the area between Südring and Konrad-Adenauer-Platz, about 200m west of the station. Bochum's sightseeing attractions are scattered across town but easily reached by public transport.

Information

The tourist office (☎ 963 02 0; fax 963 02 55) is to the right of the Hauptbahnhof North exit and is open weekdays from 9 am to 5.30 pm and Saturday from 10 am to 1 pm. There are numerous banks in the city centre, including a Sparkasse at Dr-Ruer-Platz and a Deutsche Bank at Husemannplatz 5a. The main post office is behind the train station at Wittener Strasse 2.

The Brockmeyer bookshop, diagonally opposite the Rathaus on the corner of Victoriastrasse and Bongardstrasse, stocks English and French-language books. There's a coin-operated laundrette at Südring 34 that is open daily from 6 am to 11 pm. For after-hours medical assistance call ☎ 192 92, for dental emergencies ☎ 770 05 5.

Deutsches Bergbaumuseum

It may not seem a crowd-pleaser, but the exhibits at the German Museum of Mining are among the finest and most thorough on the subject you can find anywhere in the country.

The dominant external feature is a turquoise 68m mining tower, which can be ascended (DM2) for bird's-eye views of the city and surrounds. More unique and elucidating, though, is a trip beneath the earth's surface for a first-hand look at tunnels and mine shafts as well as the machinery miners used and the working conditions they had to endure. The exhibit itself is huge and imaginative and touches on every aspect of the industry. Of particular interest is the section on the role of women in mining.

The museum, located north of the city centre at Am Bergbaumuseum 28 (take U-Bahn No 35 from the train station), is open Tuesday to Friday from 8.30 am to 5 pm, weekends from 10 am to 4 pm. Admission is DM6, discount DM5.

Eisenbahnmuseum

In Bochum's southern suburb of Dahlhausen, this wonderfully nostalgic train museum faithfully documents the evolution of trains from steam-powered to electric. Based in a historic train station, its collection includes 160 vehicles, including 16 original steam locomotives. Between April and October, the museum organises rides through the Ruhr Valley aboard some of its oldest 'iron horses'. The museum is located at Dr-C-Otto-Strasse 191 and is open Wednesday and Friday from 10 am to 5 pm,

Sunday to 1 pm. Admission is DM6.50, discount DM3.50. Rides are DM10 one way, return DM17 (children under 12 pay DM6/10). Take tram No 318 or bus No 345 to Dahlhausen Bahnhof then walk for 1300m or take the historic Schweineschnäuzchen ('little pig snout'!) rail-bus shuttle to the museum grounds.

Other Sights

A couple of historic sights are located along the Ruhr on the boundary with the town of Hattingen. **Burg Blankenstein** (open daily; free), resting on a hillside above the river, is the place where Bochum was given its town rights in 1321. The view from its 30m tower gives you a good impression of how green parts of the Ruhrgebiet actually are. Right on the Ruhr banks along Kemnaderstrasse, **Haus Kemnade** (closed Monday; free) is a moated Renaissance castle built atop a structure from the 12th century. Inside, there's a Gothic chapel, a Knights' Hall and a collection of Gobelins. Bus No C31 will take you to both Haus Kemnade and Burg Blankenstein.

Back in the city centre, at Kortumstrasse 47, is the **Museum Bochum** (open 11 am to 5 pm, Wednesday to 8 pm, Sunday to 6 pm; admission varies), which specialises in art after 1945 with a particular focus on Eastern European works. There are also frequent changing exhibits.

Places to Stay

There's no camping ground in Bochum, and the nearest hostel is the one in Essen (see that section). If you don't mind basic accommodation, among the cheapest options in town are the rooms at the *Kolpinghaus* (☎ 601 90), where singles with shared shower cost DM48 and doubles are DM76.

The business-style *Ibis Hotel* (☎ 333 11; fax 333 18 67), right behind the Hauptbahnhof, charges DM108/138 for a functional room with private bath. If you can spend just a little more, your best bet is *Art Hotel Tucholsky* at Victoriastrasse 73, very close to the Bermudadreieck pub quarter whose modern and quite stylish rooms with shower and WC cost DM80/150.

Places to Eat

The restaurants in Bochum's centre seem to cater largely to a younger crowd. Traditional German restaurants are a rarity, though the genre is nicely represented with *Altes Brauhaus Rietkötter* at Grosse Beckstrasse 7, whose German and regional specialities (DM13 to DM35) include Westphalian pea soup. Otherwise, congenial cafés and bistros abound. One long-time favourite is *Café Ferdinand* behind the train station at Ferdinandstrasse 44. The décor is part Viennese coffee house, part modern and the food surprises with its French touches; it is especially popular for breakfast. Trendies put up with frosty service at the cool *Café Treibsand* at Castroper Strasse 79, which serves big breakfasts until the afternoon and small dishes too for under DM15.

Turkish fast-food places abound in the city centre, but for refined Turkish food try the *Kokille*, Südring 24, which serves such imaginative morsels as chicken fillet with walnut mousse (DM20 and up). The Art Deco ambience of *Tucholsky*, Viktoriastrasse 73, regularly draws a crowd of artists and actors (the Schauspielhaus is nearby) and is the kind of place where you can spend hours perusing the paper over a cup of coffee. They also have a small, reasonably priced menu and a good hot breakfast selection. The elegant *Zentral* at Luisenstrasse 15-17, with its large bar and wooden floors, is also a popular hang-out and has a creative Italian menu.

Entertainment

Listings The magazines *Prinz* (DM5, at newsagents) and *Coolibri* (free, at bars, pubs, restaurants etc) are good for finding out what's on in Bochum and the Ruhrgebiet.

Discos & Clubs Live music, wild dance parties and a decent restaurant are part of the repertory of the *Zeche*, a one-time coal mine at Prinz Regent Strasse 50-60. *Bahnhof Langendreer*, in a former train station at

Walbaumweg 108 in the eastern suburb of Langendreer, has a similarly eclectic programme. *Café du Congo*, downstairs at Kurt-Schumacher-Platz 1 near the train station, is a small but stylish 'club' disco (meaning doormen decide who gets in) popular with wearers of designer clothes. Another hot spot is *Planet* at Kortumstrasse 135.

Theatre The *Schauspielhaus* (☎ 333 31 42) looks back on a long tradition as one of the leading stages in Germany and has counted Peter Zadek (now of the Berliner Ensemble) and Claus Peymann (now at the Burgtheater in Vienna) among its directors. Currently, the young Leander Haussmann holds the reins, producing lots of updated Shakespeare and contemporary playwrights. Tickets cost from DM14 to DM39. Bochum's independent theatres include *Prinz Regent Theater* (☎ 771 11 7) in the Zeche complex (see Discos & Clubs) and *Theater Ecce Homo* (☎ 953 61 85) at Hiltroper Strasse 13.

The Andrew Lloyd Webber musical extravaganza *Starlight Express* plays in its custom-designed hall (☎ 0180-544 44) at Am Stadionring 24.

Pubs & Bars The people of Bochum are serious pub and bar crawlers, and people from neighbouring towns love to join them. As soon as the last winter storms have blown through, the Bermuda Triangle (so called because the area's three streets form a triangle where it's easy to get lost, so to speak) begins to look more like an Italian piazza with crowds gathered beneath umbrella-covered tables. Anyone can find a favourite bar here. In summer, the biggest crowds gather in the huge beer garden of the *Mandragora*. Inside, this is a warmly lit café where you can also get inexpensive soups, salads, crêpes and galettes. Two of the hippest joints are *Café Konkret* on the corner of Kortumstrasse and Kreuzstrasse and *Sachs* at Victoriastrasse 55.

Getting There & Away

There are frequent train links to other Ruhrgebiet cities from Bochum via the VRR network (see Getting Around at the start of the Ruhrgebiet section). Bochum is also an IC train stop with regular service in all directions. Regional trains to Cologne (DM26, one hour) and Münster (DM18.80, 45 minutes) leave frequently too. Bochum is served by a number of autobahns, including the A40 and the A43 (Wuppertal to Münster) as well as the B51. For hitchhikers, the Mitfahrzentrale (☎ 377 94) is at Ferdinandstrasse 20.

Getting Around

Bochum's network of U-Bahns, trams and buses reaches every corner of the city. See Getting Around at the beginning of the Ruhrgebiet section for tariffs. For a taxi, call ☎ 605 11 or ☎ 964 55 5. The Fahrradstation (☎ 684 34 0) inside the Hauptbahnhof rents (from DM4 per day) and repairs bicycles. A DM50 deposit is required for all rentals.

DORTMUND

- *pop 587,000*
- *area code* ☎ 0231

Dortmund is the second-largest city in the Ruhrgebiet and celebrated for its six huge breweries – Ritter, Union, Kronen, Actien, Thier and Stifts – which collectively make 600 million litres of the amber brew. (Only the US city of Milwaukee and the Warsteiner brewery in the Sauerland produce more.) Historically, Dortmund goes back to 880 when a settlement sprang up around a Saxon castle (today's Hohensyburg) conquered by Charlemagne. In 1220, Dortmund became a free imperial city and a member of the Hanseatic League shortly thereafter.

The location on the Hellweg, an important trade route, brought the town prosperity. The Thirty Years' War eventually plunged it into an economic slumber from which it awoke only with the onset of industrialisation in the early 19th century. Dortmund was a prime target in WWII, and aesthetics weren't a priority when the city was rebuilt. Nevertheless, it's an enjoyable down-to-earth place with a lively cultural and pub scene and several first-class sights and museums.

Orientation
Most attractions are located within an area with a ring road boundary made up of segments ending in 'wall'. The Hauptbahnhof and the central bus station are on Königswall on the north side of the ring. Cross Königswall from the southern exit of the train station, then take any road to the pedestrianised Westenhellweg (which turns into Ostenhellweg), the main artery that bisects Dortmund's circular centre.

Information
Tourist Office The tourist office (☎ 502 21 74; fax 163 59 3) is opposite the Hauptbahnhof Süd (South) exit at Königswall 20 and is open weekdays from 9 am to 6 pm and Saturday to 1 pm.

Money There's a Sparkasse in Freistuhl 2 and a Commerzbank at Hansaplatz 2 to change money and travellers' cheques.

Post & Communications The main post office is on Kurfürstenstrasse about 75m to the left outside the Hauptbahnhof Nord (North) exit and is open weekdays from 8 am to 6 pm and Saturday 9 am to 1 pm. There's a public fax-phone inside and an ATM machine that accepts all major credit cards by the entrance.

Bookshops C L Krüger at Westenhellweg 9 stocks foreign-language books, as does the Universitätsbuchhandlung at Vogelpothsweg 85.

Laundry Cleanator is a coin-operated laundrette at Kaiserstrasse 19 that is open daily from 6 am to 10 pm and charges DM6 per load and DM1 for the dryer.

Emergency Police headquarters (☎ 132 0) are at Markgrafenstrasse 102.

Walking Tour
Dortmund's main attractions are conveniently grouped within walking distance from the Hauptbahnhof. Turn left from the station and head to Hansastrasse 3 where the **Museum für Kunst und Kulturgeschichte** (Museum of Art & Cultural History; open from 10 am to 5 pm, closed Monday; DM4, discount DM2) displays an eclectic mixture of pre-1900 paintings, arts and crafts, graphics, photography, archaeology, municipal history and lots more in 23 departments on seven floors. Housed in an Art Deco building that was once a bank, its collection also includes a bevy of 4th and 5th century coins unearthed locally.

Head south to Westenhellweg to the Gothic **Petrikirche** on the corner of Kampstrasse. Its undeniable show stopper is the massive 7.4 by 5.6m altar carved in Antwerp around 1520 with 633 gilded figurines depicting the Passion of Christ and the Legend of the Cross in 30 scenes.

Stroll east to Ostenhellweg and you'll come to the **Reinoldikirche**, named after the city's patron saint and crowned by a 105m tower, a Dortmund landmark. According to legend, after Reinoldus was martyred by stone masons, the church bells began peeling and the carriage containing his dead body rolled – without explanation – to Dortmund to the spot now occupied by the church. Of note here are the late Gothic high altar and the life-sized statues of the saint and his uncle, Charlemagne, near the choir entrance.

The last in this trio of churches is the **Marienkirche** across the road, considered the oldest vaulted church in Westphalia. It has a 12th-century Romanesque nave and a late-14th century Gothic choir. The star exhibit here is the Marienaltar with a triptych painted by the indefatigable Conrad von Soest in 1420. The **Berswordt Altar** (1390) in the northern nave is noteworthy too.

Walk south from here along Kleppingstrasse, then east on Viktoriastrasse to Ostwall and the **Museum am Ostwall** (open from 10 am to 5 pm, closed Monday; DM4, discount DM1) at No 7. The museum frequently hosts changing exhibits, but the permanent collection focuses on 20th-century art with fine examples by Ernst Barlach, Max Beckmann, Paul Klee and many other big names, including avant-garde artists Christo and Beuys.

Industrial Museums

As a city of industry, it's only natural that Dortmund has its share of museums inspired by industrial themes. A visit to any of these makes a nice change from the usual 'church-castle-art museum' circuit and opens up different perspectives on German culture and history.

At the **Brauerei Museum** (open from 10 am to 5 pm, closed Monday; free entry) in Märkische Strasse, you can learn all about the fine art and history of brewing beer (take U41, U45 or U47 to Markgrafenstrasse).

A distinctly unusual museum is the **Deutsche Arbeitsschutz-Ausstellung** (open 9 am to 5 pm, Sunday from 10 am, closed Monday; free) at Friedrich-Henkel-Weg 1-25 in the suburb of Dorstfeld. This 13,000 sq metre, state-of-the-art exhibit focuses on workplace health and safety, machine protection, hazardous working materials and protective clothing and equipment (take S-Bahn No 1/21 to Dortmund-Dorstfeld-Süd).

The abandoned coal mine, Zeche Zollern II/IV at Grubenweg 5 in the suburb of Bövinghausen (S-Bahn to Dortmund-Marten Süd, then bus No 462), has been designated as the **Westfälisches Industriemuseum** (Westphalian Museum of Industry). It's noted for its beautiful neo-Gothic features and an impressive Art Nouveau machine hall. An exhibit (open weekends from 10 am to 6 pm only; free entry) documents working and living conditions in the region at the turn of the century. The grounds are accessible daily from 9 am to 6 pm.

Hohensyburg Casino

The glass-and-chrome complex of Dortmund's casino rises above the Ruhr Valley, framed by the parks and forest of the recreational area around the ruined Hohensyburg castle. Here you can play roulette, black jack, baccarat and slot machines. It requires 'proper attire' (jacket and tie for men), a passport and DM5 to get in. The casino is at Hohensyburgstrasse 200 and is open daily 3 pm to 2 am, to 3 am on weekends (bus No 444 from the train station).

Places to Stay

The nearest *camping ground* (☎ 774 37 4) is at Syburger Dorfstrasse 69 in the suburb of Syburg (take bus No 444). There's no *hostel* in Dortmund itself, and the closest one is about 26km away in Hagen (☎ 02331-502 54) at Eppenhauser Strasse 65a (DM21/26 for juniors/seniors). Take the regional train to the Hagen station, then bus No 522 or 523 to Emster Strasse.

Budget hotel accommodation in Dortmund's centre is scarce indeed, but the tourist office should be able to help. If you don't mind simple rooms with shared facilities, you might try *Pension Cläre Fritz* (☎ 571 52 3) at Reinoldistrasse 6, which charges DM50/83 for singles/doubles.

Down the same street at No 14 is *Stadthotel Dortmund* (☎ 571 00 0; fax 577 19 4) where you pay DM120/150 for rooms with private bath. Near the train station, on the corner of Burgwall and Bornstrasse, you'll find *Akzent-Hotel Esplanade* (☎ 585 30; fax 585 32 70), which charges DM140/160 for rooms with all facilities.

Places to Eat

Not-so-bitter Bitterbier and very rustic meat dishes are the draw of *Hövel's Hausbrauerei* at Hoher Wall 5. In summer, the beer garden brims with folks from all walks of life.

Antique furniture meets modern art at the hip *Chat Noir* at Alter Burgwall 2-6 with simple but affordable dishes under DM20. After a rainy day, the salsa rhythms at *La Cucaracha*, Humboldtstrasse 4, may be just what the doctor ordered – along with a dose of creative, Latin-inspired dishes that won't break the bank. The same cannot be said about the top-rated *Römischer Kaiser* at Kleppingstrasse 27 where a somewhat ostentatious clientele munches on French gourmet food. It's pricey, so bring your credit card.

Entertainment

Listings For comprehensive information on what's going on, get a copy of the magazine *Prinz* (DM5), a monthly guide to the entire Ruhrgebiet region. The free *Coolibri* is similar and can be picked up at bars, restaurants, some shops and the tourist office, often along with other freebie guides. Rosa Zone Verlag publishes a *Stadtplan für Schwule und Lesben* (City Map for Gays and Lesbians) with up-to-date information on the latest clubs and hot spots. Copies are free and available at the tourist office.

Discos & Clubs The following venues open on weekends only, after 10 pm. Right in the Hauptbahnhof, there's a Dortmund mainstay, the *Life Station*, open Friday to Sunday. Hit the dance floor to musical varieties including soul, funk and 1930s nostalgia, plus regular live concerts. *Le Fou* at Nordmarkt 26 in the Nordstadt quarter is a classy cocktail and dance bar for post-teenagers that plays everything but techno (or so they say). For good jazz, go to *Jazzclub Domicil*, also in Nordstadt at Leopoldstrasse 60, which runs the gamut from modern and new jazz to Afro and Latin rhythms.

Theatre & Classical Music Dortmund's municipal theatre stages drama and musicals at the *Schauspielhaus* at Hiltropwall 15. Regular tickets range from DM12 to DM30. For opera and classical-music concerts, there's the *Opernhaus* on Hansastrasse, which charges between DM15 to DM50 per ticket. Prices depend on the day of the performance and various discounts are available. Call the box office on ☎ 163 04 1.

Getting There & Away

Dortmund's train station is among Germany's biggest, with IC trains leaving every hour in all directions, and regional and local trains running even more frequently. For motorists, Dortmund is well connected with the surrounding area via the A1, A2 and A45. The B1 runs right through the city and is the link between the A40 to Essen and the A44 to Kassel. (The B1 is also known as the Ruhrschnellweg – literally 'Ruhr Fast Route' – a perfect misnomer for this notoriously clogged road.) The Mitfahrzentrale office (☎ 194 44) is at Grüne Strasse 3.

Getting Around

Dortmund has an extensive system of public transportation that includes U-Bahns, trams and buses. For details on the price structure, see Getting Around at the beginning of the Ruhrgebiet section. For a taxi call ☎ 144 44 4 or ☎ 194 10. There's a bike-rental service with ADFC (☎ 136 68 5) at Hausmannstrasse 22, on the corner of Saarlandstrasse. The staff there are full of ideas for bike excursions around Dortmund.

WARNER BROTHERS MOVIE WORLD

This sprawling amusement park – 'Hollywood in Germany', as the brochures modestly call it – is the Ruhrgebiet's answer to EuroDisney. Opened by the movie giant Warner Brothers in 1996, it's a collection of thrill rides, restaurants, shops and shows providing 'nonstop entertainment' for those who like this kind of thing. You'll meet many familiar characters like Batman in the Batman Adventure Ride, the Gremlins in the Gremlins Invasion and Bugs Bunny in the Looney Tunes Studio Tour. Things get a bit more serious in Agfa's Museum of German Film History but are definitely on the silly side in the Cartoon Theatre.

Day admission costs a whopping DM36 per adult, DM30 for children up to age 11. The park is open daily from late March to early November. Opening hours until 31 May are 10 am to 6 pm weekdays and 9 am to 7 pm weekends. In June, the park is open from 10 am to 7 pm weekdays and 9 am to 8 pm weekends. In July and August, hours are 9 am to 9 pm daily. From September to early November, it's open from 10 am to 6 pm on weekdays and to 7 pm on weekends.

Getting There & Away The park (☎ 02045-899 0) is located at Warner Allee 1 in Bottrop-Kirchhellen, about 15km north of Essen. If you arrive by train, you must get off at the Feldhausen stop. There are frequent direct connections from Essen and Oberhausen (both DM5.80, 30 minutes). If you're driving, take the Kirchhellen exit off the A31.

NORTH RHINE - WESTPHALIA

Westphalia

MÜNSTER

- *pop 267,000*
- *area code* ☎ 0251

Münster is an attractive university town and administrative centre in the flatlands of northern Westphalia, about an hour's drive north of the Ruhrgebiet cities. Patrician town houses and baroque city palaces characterise the Altstadt, but perhaps more than anything it is the bicycles – called *Leeze* by locals – that give the city its flair. On any given day, something in the region of 100,000 of them take over Münster's streets, making liberal use of special driving regulations and numerous designated bicycle parking lots. Germany's fourth-largest university and its 50,000 students are responsible for blowing the cobwebs out of this otherwise conservative and Catholic town.

Münster got its start as a monastery founded in 794 by the Frisian missionary Liudger to help Charlemagne teach the obstreperous Saxons a thing or two about Christianity. In 805, Münster was made a bishopric and, in 1170, it got its town rights. In 1648, the Thirty Years' War came to an end here with the signing of the Peace of Westphalia. During WWII, Münster received more than its share of bombs, but the city was rebuilt in accordance with the historic layout.

Orientation

Most of the main sights are within the confines of the easy-to-walk Altstadt. The Schloss, now the main building of the university, is just west of the city centre, while the Hauptbahnhof is to the east. Simply follow any of the streets ahead of you as you exit the train station and you'll be in the centre within minutes. The main recreational area is around the Aasee lake, south-west of the Altstadt.

Information

Tourist Office The tourist office (☎ 492 27 10; fax 492 77 43) is at Klemensstrasse 9 and is open from 9 am to 6 pm on weekdays and to 1 pm on Saturday. If you read German, the handy brochure *Münster Aktuell* (DM1) contains current information on events, hotels and useful addresses. English-language tours depart Saturdays at 11 am (May to October; DM6).

Money Most banks exchange money and cash travellers' cheques during regular hours, but the Commerzbank in the Karstadt department store on Salzstrasse is also open on Saturday to 4 pm.

Post & Communications There are post offices on Domplatz and at the Hauptbahnhof, both open to 7 pm weekdays and to 2 pm on Saturday.

Bookshop Poertgen Heinrich-Herdersche Buchhandlung in Salzgasse 56 has a huge assortment of books over four floors, including a fair amount of English and French volumes.

Dom

The Dom's two massive towers are in proportion to the rest of the 110m-long structure and the enormous square it overlooks (approach from the south for the maximum effect). The three-nave construction was built in the 13th century on the cusp of the transition from Romanesque to Gothic. Enter from the south through a portal, called the Paradies, festooned with magnificent sculptures. Once inside, you're greeted by a 5m **statue of St Christopher**, the patron saint of travellers (yes, that's a real tree branch in his left hand).

The cathedral's main attraction is the **astronomical clock** on the right side of the ambulatory. Look beneath the projecting pedestal in the gable of this 24-hour clock for a summary of its functions: it indicates the time, the position of the sun, the movement of the planets, and the calendar with the moveable feasts – ie Catholic holy days up to the year 2071.

Walk to the ambulatory encircling the altar area. The second chapel contains the **tomb**

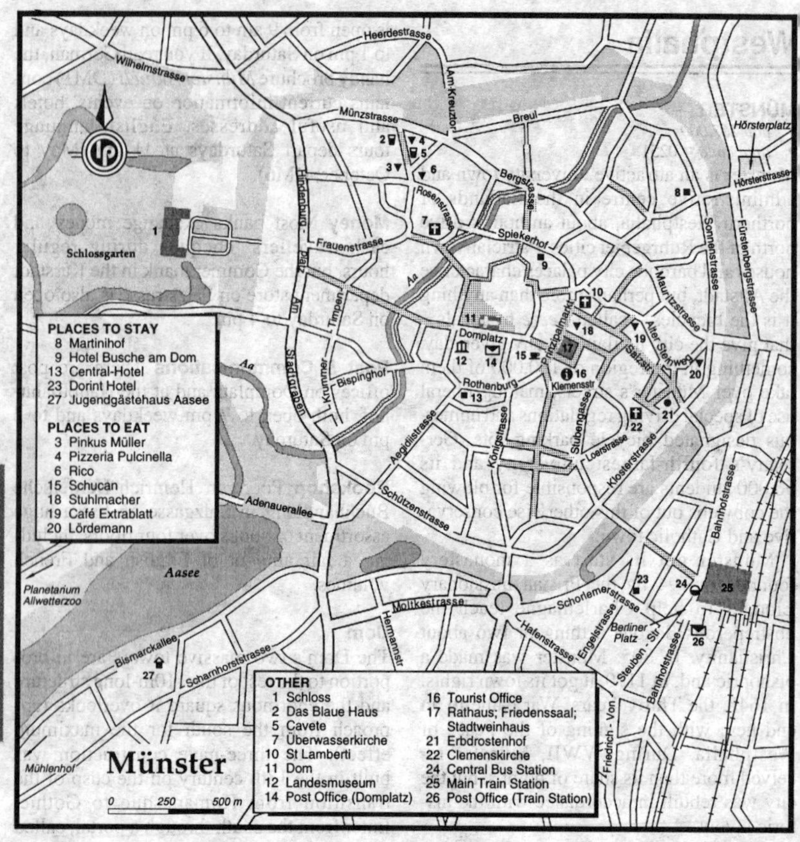

of Clemens August Cardinal von Galen, a vociferous opponent of the Nazi regime who – successfully – defended the right to display crucifixes in schools, which had been outlawed in 1936. The cathedral treasury in the **Domkammer** (DM1; closed Monday, Sunday morning and at lunchtime) can be reached via the cloister. Its highlight is the 11th-century gem-studded golden head reliquary of St Paul, the cathedral's patron.

Around Domplatz

A few steps north-west of the Dom is the **Überwasserkirche**, a 14th-century Gothic hall church with handsome stained-glass windows and an ornate square tower. It stands adjacent to Münster's tiny stream, the Aa, whose tree-lined promenade invites leisurely strolls. In the 16th century, the iconoclastic Anabaptists (see St Lamberti Church below) tore all sculptures out of this church, but fortunately many could be saved and are now on view on the ground floor of the **Landesmuseum** (closed Monday; DM5, discount DM2, prices increase during special exhibits) on the southern end of Domplatz. Head upstairs for an excellent cross section of the works of accomplished

Westphalian painters, including Conrad von Soest and Hermann and Ludger tom Ring and other members of this artistic family. Two rooms are dedicated to August Macke, a member of the Blue Rider group, an association of painters formed in Munich in the early 20th century that also included Franz Marc, Paul Klee and Wassily Kandinsky.

Prinzipalmarkt

Münster's main artery is the Prinzipalmarkt, which is not a market at all but a road a few metres to the east of the Dom. Among its most pleasant features are the gabled façades of the stately town houses, which look down on covered arcades of elegant boutiques and cafés.

The most majestic façade belongs to the **Rathaus**, begun in the late 12th century and enlarged and altered several times since. Inside is the **Friedenssaal** (open daily, DM1.50) where, in 1648, the Peace of Westphalia was signed, ending the calamitous Thirty Years' War. It is a spectacular hall with wood-panelled walls; note especially the elaborate carvings on the cabinet behind the mayor's table with their clever mix of secular and religious themes.

The open cabinet contains an incongruous display of the **Goldener Hahn** (golden rooster) statue, as well as a mummified hand and a slipper. As you exit, note the adjacent **Stadtweinhaus**, once used for wine storage and now part of the Rathaus.

Look north from here for a fine view of the Gothic **St Lamberti Church** and the three iron cages dangling from its slender openwork spire. These once held the dead bodies of the three leaders of the Anabaptists, a brutal Protestant movement that sought to do away with money and institute adult baptism and polygamy. In 1534, the group's crazed leader, Jan van Leyden, proclaimed Münster the capital of the utopian 'New Jerusalem' with himself as king. Troops of the prince-bishop soon stormed the town, arrested Leyden and his main cohorts, publicly tortured them to death with red-hot tongs (now on view at the Stadtmuseum at Salzstrasse 28), then stuck them in the cages to die.

Baroque Buildings

Münster boasts several beautiful baroque buildings, most of them the work of architect Johann Conrad Schlaun. At Salzstrasse 38 in the Altstadt, you'll find the **Erbdrostenhof** (1753-57), a town *palais* and former residence of the deputy prince-bishops. Nearby in Klemensstrasse is the small **Clemenskirche** (1744-53), whose domed ceiling is completely covered by a lavish fresco and supported by turquoise faux-marble pillars. The **Schloss** (1767-73), the former residence of the prince-bishops and now the main university building, is another example of Schlaun's understated northern baroque style.

Aasee

South-west of the Altstadt, the Aa flows into the Aasee, which, in good weather, is a popular place for picnics and activities like sailing and windsurfing. On or near the northern lake shore are three more of Münster's attractions. The **Mühlenhof** (open daily; DM5, discount DM3), at Theo-Breider-Weg 1, is an open-air museum with mills, a bakery and other buildings typical of Westphalia. The **Planetarium** is at Sentruper Strasse 285 and has several shows daily except Monday (prices vary). On the western lake end is the **Allwetterzoo** (open daily; DM13, discount DM6.50) with more than 2000 animals, including dolphins and Asian elephants.

Places to Stay

Campingplatz Münster (☎ 311 98 2) is open year round and located about 5km south-east of the city centre at Laerer Werseufer 7 next to a public outdoor pool (bus No 320 or 330 to Kinnebrock). Charges are DM4 to DM8 per tent and DM6 per person. Münster's modern hostel, the lakeside *Jugendgästehaus Aasee* (☎ 532 47 0), is at Bismarckallee 31 (bus No 10 or 34 to Hoppendamm). Beds cost DM37.50 (in four-bed rooms) and

DM46.50 (in two-bed rooms) inclusive of sheets, towel and buffet breakfast.

The tourist office's hotel-reservation service is free but budget hotels are practically nonexistent. If you want to rent a private room, try the agency Bed & Breakfast (☎ 142 68 6). Otherwise, the traditional *Martinihof* (☎ 418 62 0; fax 547 43) at Hörsterstrasse 25 has basic singles/doubles for DM71/114 and several with full facilities for DM105/156. The super-central but quite old-fashioned *Hotel Busche am Dom* (☎ 464 44), Bogenstrasse 10, charges DM90/160 for rooms with shower and WC.

The *Central-Hotel* (☎ 510 15 0; fax 510 15 50), Aegidiistrasse 1, has large rooms with modern furniture and private bath for DM150 for singles and from DM185 for doubles.

At the top end of the spectrum is the *Dorint Hotel* (☎ 417 10; fax 417 11 00) at Engelstrasse 39 near the train station with DM223/280 singles/doubles.

Places to Eat

The quarter to go for a bite, a beer or a full meal is the Kuhviertel just north of the Dom. The main drag is Kreuzstrasse, where you'll find the classic student pubs *Cavete* at No 38 and *Das Blaue Haus* at No 16. *Pizzeria Pulcinella*, with pasta and pizza from DM8, is at No 28 of the same street. A Münster institution and very popular with tourists is the brewery restaurant *Pinkus Müller*, which occupies half the western side of the street. It has rambling, wood-panelled rooms where tasty Westphalian and German dishes cost DM20 and up. The casual *Rico*, at Rosenplatz 7 nearby, serves wholesome and delicious vegetarian dishes for around DM8 (lunch only).

A Münster mainstay is *Stuhlmacher* next to the Rathaus; it specialises in updated Westphalian dishes and is quite expensive. *Schucan* across the street is an old-world coffee house with delectable pastries which you can also buy to take away. At Salzstrasse 7, on a pedestrianised shopping street, you'll find *Café Extrablatt*, a trendy bistro with good breakfasts and big portions for smallish budgets. At the rustic *Lördemann*, on the corner of Alter Steinweg and Sonnenstrasse, you order your sausage – served with potato salad – by the half metre (DM12.50) or the metre (DM20).

A colourful produce market takes place on the Domplatz every Wednesday and Saturday morning, with another selling only organic produce from 1 to 6 pm on Friday.

Getting There & Away

Train Fast IC trains link Münster with Munich (DM208, 7½ hours) and Stuttgart (DM145, five hours) every two hours. There are also IC trains every hour to Frankfurt (DM101, four hours), Hamburg (DM75, 2¼ hours) and the Ruhrgebiet cities (under one hour). Convenient touch-screen terminals in the main hall can give you exact train connections in German, English or French.

Car & Motorcycle Münster is on the A1 from Bremen to Cologne and is the starting point of the A43 in the direction of Wuppertal. It is also at the crossroads of the B51, B54 and B219. Parking in the centre is largely confined to parking lots and garages (DM2 per hour).

Ride Services There are several Mitfahrzentralen, including Citynetz (☎ 404 00) at Aegidiistrasse 20a and Flottweg Mitfahrzentrale (☎ 601 41) at Hamburger Strasse 8.

Getting Around

Bus Münster has a well organised bus system (☎ 694 16 80). Tickets, available from the driver, cost DM2.80 (valid throughout the city); four-trip tickets are DM9.70. There are also various group and family tickets.

Bicycle When in Münster, do as the locals do and ride a bike! One of the most convenient places to rent one is at the train station (☎ 691 32 0). Alternatives are ADFC (☎ 811 12) at Sentruper Strasse 169 and Hansen KG (☎ 449 98) at Hörsterstrasse 7. Expect to pay around DM10 per day. The tourist office has a wide selection of biking maps of the city and surrounding area, the so-called Münsterland, from DM8.80 to DM14.80.

MÜNSTERLAND CASTLES

Bounded by the Ruhrgebiet to the south, the Netherlands to the west, Lower Saxony to the north and the Teutoburg Forest to the east, the Münsterland has a dense concentration of well preserved moated castles and palaces. In these rural flatlands, water was often the only way to protect the residences of bishops, counts, dukes and landed gentry against rebels.

Some of these places are attractive destinations, either because of their unusual architecture, their idyllic country setting or both. Unfortunately, most are still in private hands and often can only be viewed from the outside. Unless you are driving, visiting these castles is not easy. Almost none are directly served by public transport and, if so, then only infrequently. As a rule, the bicycle is the best method of travelling through this region. Bikes may be rented in Münster (see Getting Around) and at nearly all local train stations. Maps are available from the Münster tourist office and bookshops.

Among the castles that make for a pleasant day trip from Münster are Burg Vischering and Schloss Nordkirchen, both located near each other about 30km south of town. More detailed information on these and other castles is available from *Münsterland Touristik* (☎ 02551-939 29 1) at Hohe Schule 13 in Steinfurt.

Burg Vischering

Burg Vischering is the quintessential medieval moated castle, the kind that conjures romantic images of knights and damsels in distress. It was built in 1271 by the bishop of Münster who gave it to a member of the Droste family so that they could rein in the independent-minded knights of Lüdinghausen. Though still owned by the same family today, Vischering is open to the public and is perhaps the castle with the greatest appeal to visitors.

Surrounded by a system of ramparts and ditches, the complex consists of an outer castle and the main castle, which are connected by a bridge. The main castle is circular, with a yard that measures only 38m in diameter. The **Münsterland Museum** (open daily to 5.30 pm, in winter to 4.30 pm; DM2) is housed here. Admission allows you to see the Knights' Hall, late-Gothic frescos and ornate oven plates (rectangular iron plates – often with elaborate reliefs – which formed the walls of heating stoves).

Schloss Nordkirchen

Very different in character from Burg Vischering, Schloss Nordkirchen is a grandiose baroque red-brick structure sitting on an island accessible via three bridges and surrounded by a lavish, manicured park. Nicknamed the 'Westphalian Versailles', this symmetrical palace was commissioned at the beginning of the 18th century by the prince-bishop of Münster, Christian Friedrich von Plettenberg. Gottfried Laurenz Pictorius began building it in 1703 and Johann Conrad Schlaun completed it in 1734. Now owned by the state government, it houses a college for economic studies.

The palace is well worth visiting just for the gardens and the exterior, though the interior with its stuccoed ceilings, the Jupiter Festival Hall, the dining room and other chambers can be viewed during guided tours (DM2). These are offered to individual travellers on weekends only, but on other days you may be able to join a pre-booked group tour.

Getting There & Away

Burg Vischering is in the north of Lüdinghausen. There are several trains daily between Münster and Lüdinghausen (DM11.60, 50 minutes), with a change in either Dülmen, Lünen or Coesfeld; connections tend to be quite good. Schloss Nordkirchen is another 8km south-east in the hamlet of Nordkirchen, which does not have a train station. Consult your bike map for the route between the two castles. On Saturday from April to October, the Münster tourist office also operates guided bus tours to these and other castles for around DM40.

SOEST

- *pop 43,000*
- *area code* ☎ 02921

Soest, a charming small town of neat, half-timbered houses and a web of idyllic lanes, has largely preserved its medieval appearance. It lies about 45km east of Dortmund and is the northern gateway to the Sauerland (see below). Soest is also a very green town, not just because of its parks and gardens but because of the unusual green sandstone used in constructing many of its buildings, notably churches. Brimming with outstanding works of art, these churches reflect the wealth Soest enjoyed in the Middle Ages when its products – mostly textiles, salt and corn – were in great demand around Europe. They are also what makes Soest a popular destination for day-trippers from the nearby Ruhrgebiet cities and the Sauerland.

Orientation & Information

Soest is small enough to explore on foot. To get a sense of its dimensions, take a walk atop or along the almost completely intact town wall (about 3.5km long). To get to the town centre from the train or bus stations, both located just north of the Altstadt, weave your way through the medieval lanes to the centre around St Patrokli. This should take around 15 minutes.

The tourist office (☎ 103 32 3; fax 330 39) is nearby at Am Seel 5 and is open weekdays from 8.30 am to 12.30 pm and 2 to 4.30 pm (Thursday to 5.30 pm); on Saturday from 9.30 am to noon. You'll find a Deutsche Bank at Markt 14 and a Volksbank at Marktstrasse 6. The post office is in Hospitalsgasse 3. For emergency medical assistance or an ambulance call ☎ 770 55.

Things to See

Soest's main attractions are its churches and their wealth of artworks. Closest to the train station is the exquisite 14th-century **St Maria zur Wiese** (open daily 10 am to 5 or 6 pm, in winter to 4 pm), known as Wiesenkirche and easily recognised by its filigreed Gothic twin spires. Of the series of luminescent stained-glass windows the one immediately in front of you as you enter is particularly dazzling. It depicts the **Westphalian Supper**, so called because the dinner depicted in this version of Christ's and the Apostles' Last Supper consists of the local staples of ham, rye bread and beer. There are four altars, including a 16th-century carved one from Brabant. Its lower panels depict the Christmas cycle while the upper show the Passion of Christ.

Just west of the Wiesenkirche is the smaller **St Maria zur Höhe** (open daily 9.30 am to 5.30 pm, in winter to 4 pm), better known as Hohnekirche, a squat and architecturally less accomplished hall church from the early 13th century. Its most surprising feature is the ceiling, which was painted white and then spruced up with ornamentation and naive depictions of birds and other animals. There's another fresco, in shimmering blue, above the altar. It's worth taking a closer look at the **altar** (1475) itself, ascribed to the Westphalian painter Master of Liesborn, and at the **Scheibenkreuz** in the right aisle, a large wooden cross usually found in Scandinavian countries and the only one in Germany. To help you see better, there's a light switch on your left as you enter.

While the Wiesenkirche and the Hohnekirche are both Protestant churches, **St Patrokli** (open daily) near the Markt in the city centre is Soest's main Catholic church. Locals refer to this Romanesque structure with three naves as the Dom. It dates back to 965 and sports a stout square tower known as the Tower of Westphalia. Turn left as you enter through the Paradies, the intricate portal, to find yourself faced with the delicate frescos of the 12th-century **Marienchor**. The bright colours of the painting above the **high choir**, on the other hand, seem gaudy and strangely out of place.

Of almost mystical simplicity is the tiny two-nave **Nikolaikapelle**, a few steps south-east in the Thomästrasse, also from the 12th century and containing a masterful **altar painting** by the 15th-century artist Conrad von Soest. It is open only on Tuesday, Wednesday, Friday and Sunday from 11 am to noon. **St Petri** (closed Monday), west of the Dom, is considered the oldest church in Westphalia, with origins in the 8th century.

Places to Stay & Eat

Soest's *DJH hostel* (☎ 162 83) is at Kaiser-Friedrich-Platz 2 just south of the Altstadt (take bus No 549 or 550 from the train station) and charges DM20 for juniors and DM25 for seniors.

The tourist office does not offer a room-reservation service, so you have to call the hotels directly. In town, you might try *Hotel Stadt Soest* (☎ 362 20; fax 362 22 7) in Brüderstrasse 50 near the train station, which has full-facility singles from DM85 and doubles from DM140. At Markt 11 is the *Hotel Im Wilden Mann* (☎ 150 71; fax 140 78) in a historic half-timbered building whose façade features the sculpture of a prehistoric man holding a club in one hand and the key to the city in the other. Rooms in this landmark cost DM95/160, and there's a restaurant on the ground floor. The *Pilgrim Haus* (☎ 182 8; fax 121 31) is on the south-western periphery of the Altstadt at Jakobistrasse 75 and is the oldest guesthouse in Westphalia, dating back to 1304. Singles/doubles are DM120/175.

Most restaurants serve artery-clogging Westphalian dishes, including the *Brauhaus Christ*, at Walburger Strasse 36. Young people gather at *Anno 1888*, a music pub at Thomästrasse 6 (evenings only). The Italian restaurant in the *Georgenkeller* on the Markt has lunch specials for DM10 but is pretty pricey otherwise.

Getting There & Away

There's regular bus service to the northern Sauerland, including the Möhnesee lake (bus No 549), Warstein (bus No 551) and Arnsberg (No 550). Depending on where you're coming from, getting to Soest by train often requires a change in Hamm or Dortmund. There are several trains an hour to/from both cities, as well as to Paderborn. Through trains to Münster (DM15.60, one hour) leave hourly. If you're driving, take the Soest exit from the A44. Soest is also at the crossroads of the B1, B229 and B475.

PADERBORN

- *pop 123,000*
- *area code* ☎ 05251

Paderborn is a bustling, modern city about 90km north-east of Dortmund that gets its name from the Pader, Germany's shortest river. More than 5000 litres a second spurt from about 200 springs in the city centre to form the little river that merges with the Lippe after only 4km. Charlemagne used the royal seat and bishopric he had established here to control the Christianisation of the Saxon tribes. In 799, he received a momentous visit from Pope Leo III here that ultimately resulted in Charlemagne's coronation in Rome and the foundation of the Holy Roman Empire, with Charlemagne at the helm.

Orientation & Information

Paderborn's centre is fairly small and easily explored on foot. The train station lies about 1km south-west of the Altstadt. Turn right into Bahnhofstrasse as you exit and continue straight through the pedestrianised shopping area to the Dom and the other sights.

At Marienplatz 2a you'll find the tourist office (☎ 882 98 0; fax 882 99 0), open weekdays from 9.30 am to 6 pm and Saturday 9 am to 1 pm, which can help you book a room in town. There's a Deutsche Bank at Bahnhofstrasse 1 and a Dresdner Bank at Rathausplatz 12. For the post office, go to Liliengasse 2. There's a police station (☎ 306 0) at Riemekestrasse 60-62.

Walking Tour

Except where noted, Paderborn's museums are open from 10 am to 6 pm and closed on Monday. A 50% discount applies to children and students.

Start your tour where Paderborn began, at Charlemagne's palace, the **Carolingian Kaiserpfalz** just north of the Dom. Its foundations were discovered beneath the rubble left by WWII bombs and were excavated in the 1960s.

Right behind looms the 11th-century **Ottonian Kaiserpfalz**, reconstructed in the 1970s and partly built atop portions of its

Carolingian predecessor. The low rectangular structure is about 50m long and exudes a dignified atmosphere because of its simple design and understated décor. It contains a museum (DM2) with items unearthed on display. Immediately adjacent is the tiny and austere **Bartholomäuskapelle** (1017), the oldest hall church north of the Alps, with other-worldly acoustics.

As you enter the Gothic **Dom** (1220-70), a three-nave hall church, through the north portal, note the base of Charlemagne's open-air throne kept here. Also look for the **Hasenfenster** in the cloister (follow the signs), a window depicting three rabbits with their ears intertwined. It originally represented the Holy Trinity and has become the city's symbol. The crypt contains the grave of St Liborius, whose remains were brought to Paderborn from Le Mans in France in 836.

To see the shrine containing the actual bones, though, exit through the sculpture-studded south portal – the Paradies – and head to the **Diözesanmuseum** (DM4), housed in a 1970s architectural eyesore right outside the Dom on the Markt. The interior is attractive but confusing and occasionally feels like an M C Escher drawing, with many open staircases connecting the different floors which sometimes seem to lead nowhere. There are lots of sculptures and paintings, but for the highlights from the Dom treasury – including Liborius' relics – you have to go to the basement.

From the Markt, walk west to Rathausplatz, dominated by the **Rathaus** (1620), a magnificent structure with ornate gables, oriels and other decorative touches typical of the Weser Renaissance architectural style. Just south of here is the **Jesuitenkirche**, whose curvilinear baroque exterior contrasts with the more subdued Gothic vaulted ceiling and rounded Romanesque arches inside. This mix of styles, however, is typical of Jesuit churches from the late 17th century.

Rathausplatz merges with Marienplatz, where the attractive **Helsingsche Haus** with its elaborate façade stands adjacent to the tourist office. A short walk north via Am Abdinghof will lead you to the **Paderquellgebiet**, a small park perfect for relaxing by the gurgling springs of the Pader source. This is the eastern starting point of a lovely walk along the little river that leads through other parks to **Schloss Neuhaus**, a moated water palace, about 5km west.

Just east of the Paderquellgebiet, the twin Romanesque towers of the **Abdinghofkirche** (1015) come into view. The austerity of this former Benedictine monastery with its whitewashed walls, flat wooden ceiling and completely unadorned interior is almost overwhelming. Right behind are the Dom and the Carolingian Pfalz and Ottonian Pfalz.

Heinz Nixdorf MuseumsForum

This interactive museum, established by the founder of one of Germany's big computer-technology companies, lets you take a journey through 5000 years of information technology – from the origins of the written language in Mesopotamia to the Internet. You can play computer games, get live news from around the world and learn about individual exhibits via touch-screen terminals. The museum is at Fürstenallee 7 (bus No 11 from Westerntor) and is open 9 am to 6 pm on weekdays and from 10 am on weekends. Admission is DM6.

Places to Stay

Paderborn has two camping grounds north of the city centre, of which only *Campingplatz Stauterrasse* (☎ 450 4) at Auf der Thune 14 is directly accessible by public transport (bus No 1, 8 or 11 to Schloss Neuhaus, then bus No 58 to Am Thunhof).

The other, *Campingplatz Am Waldsee* (☎ 737 2), Husarenstrasse 130, is a 2km walk from the Husaren- strasse stop (bus No 11).

Paderborn's *DJH hostel* (☎ 220 55) is conveniently located at Meinwerkstrasse 16 in the city centre, but needs an overhaul. Bed & breakfast is DM21/26 for juniors/ seniors.

The snug and central *Haus Irma* (☎ 233 42), scenically located at the Paderquellgebiet in Bachstrasse 9, is an excellent deal at DM55/80 for singles/doubles with shower and WC. More pricey and artsy is the *Galerie-Hotel Abdinghof* (☎ 122 40; fax 122 41 9) at No 1a of the same street, where singles/doubles with private facilities cost DM115/145. Also central at Mühlenstrasse 2 is the traditional *Hotel Zur Mühle* (☎ 107 50; fax 107 54 5), which charges from DM120/175 for rooms with shower & WC.

Places to Eat

The highest concentration of restaurants, student pubs and chic bars is in the Ükern quarter in the northern section of the Altstadt along Kisau, Mühlenstrasse, Hathumarstrasse and Ükern. Candle-lit and casual *Café Klatsch* at Kisau 11, serves up imaginative Turkish-bread pizzas (around DM8), plus the usual assortment of inexpensive German pub grub. Next door, the traditional *Deutsches Haus* serves huge portions of home-style German food at reasonable prices to a mixed crowd; daily specials cost around DM15. Also check out *Adam's* at Mühlenstrasse 2, where the chrome tables seat a fair share of trendy poseurs, but the food is actually quite decent (lunch only).

Getting There & Away

Paderborn has direct train links every two hours to Kassel-Wilhelmshöhe (DM28, 1½ hours), Erfurt (DM68, 2¾ hours), Düsseldorf (DM49, two hours) and the Ruhrgebiet cities (eg Dortmund; DM29, one hour). Trains to Soest (DM14.20, 40 minutes) leave several times hourly. Paderborn is located on the A33, which connects with the A2 in the north and the A44 in the south. The B1, B64, B68 and B480 also go through Paderborn. The Mitfahrzentrale (☎ 194 40) is at Bahnhofstrasse 10.

Sauerland

This gentle mountain range in the south-east of North Rhine-Westphalia is a playground for people from the densely populated Ruhrgebiet cities to the north-west. Five nature parks straddle the self-proclaimed 'land of the thousand mountains', which is at its most scenic around the Kahler Asten, at 841m the area's highest mountain. Outdoor enthusiasts will find lots of hiking and biking trails, lakes for water sports and rivers for fishing. For culture buffs, there are museums, tidy half-timbered towns and hilltop castles. Though perhaps not worth a special detour, the Sauerland is a fine destination for a brief respite.

Information

The Sauerland tourist office (☎ 02961-943 22 9) is at Heinrich-Jansen-Weg 14 in Brilon and offers information and a central room-reservation service (☎ 02961-943 22 7). For specific information about a particular town, it is best to go to a local tourist office. Most resorts charge a daily visitor's tax ranging from DM2.50 to DM5.

Skiing

Both downhill and cross-country skiing are available in the Sauerland. The season generally runs from December to March, but snow levels are not always reliable. The most dependable area is the High Sauerland, where elevations reach 700m. For daily updates (in German) on snow conditions, call the Snowphone (☎ 0291-115 30). Expect big crowds after major snow falls, especially on weekends.

The brochure *Loipen und Pisten* (Cross-Country Trails & Downhill Runs) contains route descriptions and can be picked up at tourist offices. The entire Sauerland has around 170 groomed cross-country tracks, 126 ski lifts and 44 ski schools. Equipment-rental shops abound; look for the sign saying 'Skiverleih' and figure on spending about DM20 for cross-country and DM25 for downhill skis and boots per day. Lift tickets cost around DM30 per day.

Hiking

More than 12,000km of hiking trails, mostly through dense beech and fir forest, crisscross the Sauerland. There's something for hikers of every level, from leisurely lakeside walks to long-distance treks. Maps and trail descriptions are available from the local tourist offices or in bookshops. A popular medium-level hike of 5km leads from Winterberg to the peak of the Kahler Asten. The new German Unity trail – cutting across the nation from Aachen to Görlitz at the Polish border – also traverses the Sauerland.

Water Sports

Sailing, surfing, diving, kayaking, swimming, fishing, rowing – the many artificial lakes in the Sauerland offer plenty of choices.

For a list of equipment-rental places, contact the local tourist offices. The Biggesee in the southern Sauerland and the Möhnesee in the north are prime destinations. The less active might enjoy a two-hour cruise on the Biggesee (April to October; DM12, children DM6).

Getting There & Away

The A45 cuts through the Sauerland, connecting the Ruhrgebiet with Frankfurt. The area is also easily reached via the A4 from Cologne. For regional buses into the northern Sauerland, see Getting There & Away in the Soest section earlier.

Regular train service – even to the smallest towns – exists though you may have to make a number of changes. Travelling from the north, you'll most likely have to change in Hagen. Coming from points south usually requires a change in Siegen.

Getting Around

It is most convenient to travel around the Sauerland by car, though with some planning, it can also be explored by train and bus. Once you are based in a town, there are special buses heading for the hiking areas and the surrounding towns. Each tourist office has specific information on the services available. If you're spending some time in the region, consider investing in the Sauerland Urlauberkarte (DM15), which buys unlimited public transportation for three days (DM30 for 10 days) for up to two adults and four children. It's available from bus drivers and the tourist offices, which also have route maps and timetables.

ATTENDORN

- *pop 21,700*
- *area code* ☎ 02722

This typical Sauerland town on the northern shore of the Biggesee offers a grab-bag of attractions that makes it well worth a stop. Foremost among them is the **Attahöhle**, one of Germany's largest and most impressive stalactite caves. The 45-minute tour (daily, DM8) covers a network of rooms with names like Candle Hall and Alhambra Grotto. Highlights include a 5m column and an underground lake.

In town, you'll find the **Church of St John the Baptist**, locally known as Sauerland Cathedral, whose main attraction is a 14th-century Pietà. The lower section of the square tower reveals the Romanesque origins of this church, which is otherwise Gothic. The **Kreisheimat Museum** is a well presented local history museum housed in the Gothic old town hall on Alter Markt (DM2, discount DM1; closed Mondays). Its whimsical tin figure collection warrants a close look.

Attendorn's tourist office (☎ 642 29; fax 477 5) is in the Rathauspassage in the new town hall and is open weekdays from 9 am to 6 pm.

The nearest *camping ground* (☎ 955 00) is beautifully situated on the Biggesee at Waldenburger Bucht 11. The nearest *DJH hostel* (☎ 02721-812 17) is east of Attendorn in a medieval castle at Von-Gevore-Weg 10 in Lennestadt-Bilstein (train to Lennestadt-Altenhundem, then bus to Bilstein). Beds are DM21.50/26.50 for juniors/seniors. Attendorn has few hotels and none of them are cheap. The six-bed private pension *Beate Wicker* (☎ 503 07) is at Bremger Weg 110 and charges DM50/100 for singles/doubles with shared bath. In town, *Hotel zur Post* (☎ 246 5; fax 489 1) in Niederste Strasse 7 has rooms with private bath for DM95/160 for singles/doubles. *Hotel Rauch* (☎ 924 20; fax 924 23 3), Wasserstrasse 6, has similar prices. If you're driving, the small *Surenhof*

(☎ 569 3) at Höhenstrasse 165 in nearby Weltringhausen offers seclusion and character at DM65/110 for rooms with full facilities.

Attendorn is on a minor railway line and is served by the Biggesee-Express, which shuttles between Finnentrop and Olpe. Finnentrop is a stop on the Hagen-Siegen route.

ALTENA

- *pop 24,000*
- *area code* ☎ 02352

The main attraction of this slightly industrialised town in the steep Lenne Valley is the 12th-century **Burg Altena**, romantically perched on a bluff. Originally the seat of the counts of Altena-Mark, this castle has spent time as an orphanage, a military command and a jail. In 1912, it became the world's first youth hostel whose spartan furnishings have been preserved as a museum. In the basement, you'll find the dormitory with 14 massive wooden bunks. Upstairs is the dank day room, which features a small open kitchen and long polished tables on a stone floor.

Two other museums are contained within the thick walls of the castle. The **Museum der Grafschaft Mark** is a regional history museum with a splendid assortment of weapons and armour, furniture, ceramics, glassware and minerals.

The **Smithy Museum** traces this ancient craft through the ages and attests to the importance of the region's metal-working acumen. The museums are open Tuesday to Friday from 10 am to 5 pm and on weekends from 9.30 am. Admission is DM5, discount DM2.50.

Altena's tourist office (☎ 209 21 2; fax 209 20 3) is at Lüdenscheider Strasse 22 and is open from 8 am to noon and 1.30 to 3.30 pm (Friday only to noon).

The *DJH hostel* (☎ 235 22) in Burg Altena is a 15-minute walk uphill from the train station. Its 38 beds fill up quickly and cost DM20/25 for juniors/seniors. There are few hotels, with the central *Hotel Würschmidt am Markt* (☎ 229 05) charging DM38/79 for singles/doubles with shared bath, and DM5 per person extra for rooms with shower. A step up is *Hotel Alte Linden* (☎ 712 10; fax 750 94), where singles/doubles with full facilities cost DM85/135.

There are hourly direct trains from Siegen (DM18.80, one hour). From Essen you must change in Hagen (DM18.80, 1½ hours).

WINTERBERG

- *pop 13,500*
- *area code* ☎ 02981

Appropriately named Winterberg in the High Sauerland is the region's winter-sport centre, in particular for downhill and cross-country skiing. Along with its many slopes, Winterberg also has a 1600m-long bobsled run where German and European championships are occasionally held. For a special treat, you too can feel like a champ by going down the ice canal with an experienced driver, reaching speeds of up to 150km/h. Alas, the whole trip only takes 60 seconds and costs DM50. There's also an ice-skating rink (DM6, discount DM4.50) in the Kurpark; it costs DM6 to rent skates.

In summer, the forests around Winterberg offer some excellent hiking opportunities. One popular destination is the Kahler Asten, at 842m the Sauerland's highest mountain. Views from the tower here (DM1) are great. Maps and route descriptions are available at the tourist office. If mountain biking is your thing, they're available for rent at Pro Biker (☎ 171 5) at Am Waltenberg 49 for DM30 a day.

The tourist office (☎ 925 00; fax 375 1) is at Hauptstrasse 1 and is open weekdays from 9 am to 5 pm and Saturdays 10 am to noon. The office has plenty of maps and information on outdoor activities, and the helpful staff provide sightseeing tips.

Winterberg has two camping grounds. *Campingplatz Hochsauerland* (☎ 324 9), at Remmeswiese 10, is a five to 10-minute walk from the town centre along the B480. If it's full, try *Campingplatz Winterberg* (☎ 177 6) at Kapperundweg 1 along the B236 in the direction of Bad Berleburg. The *DJH hostel* (☎ 228 9) is at Astenberg 1 and charges DM21.50/26.50 for juniors/seniors (take the bus to JH Neuastenberg from the train station). In town, the cosy family-run *Hotel Jägerhof* (☎ 170 6; fax 334 7), Am Langen Acker 1, has singles/doubles with private bath for DM48/96. *Haus Herrloh* (☎ 470; fax 811 14) at Herrlohweg 3 charges DM65/130. Both hotel restaurants serve good local cuisine. Keep in mind that accommodation can be tight on snowy winter weekends.

There are no direct rail links to Winterberg. Coming from Dortmund, you have to change in Schwerte and in Bestwig (DM31, 2½ hours). Coming from Cologne (DM49, three hours) means changing in Hagen and Bestwig.

Siegerland

The hills and mountains of the Sauerland continue southward into the Siegerland region, with the city of Siegen as its focal point. Frankfurt, the Ruhrgebiet and Cologne are all about 100km away.

SIEGEN

- *pop 106,000*
- *area code* ☎ 0271

Historically, Siegen has strong connections with the House of Nassau-Oranien (Nassau-Orange in English), which has held the Dutch throne since 1813. Around 1403, the counts of Nassau who ruled the area, obtained large possessions in the Netherlands to which they added, in 1530, the principality of Orange in southern France. When the Netherlands became a hereditary monarchy in 1813, the crown went to Wilhelm Friedrich of the House of Nassau-Oranien.

Two palaces and other buildings survive from those glory days. Though encircled by a lovely hilly landscape, modern Siegen has been scarred by steel production.

Siegen was the birthplace of Peter Paul Rubens (1577-1640) and the museum has a small collection of the Flemish painter's works.

Orientation & Information

Siegen's centre slopes up from the train station in the north-west to the Oberes Schloss in the east, where the Altstadt is at its most scenic. It's traversed by the river Sieg.

The tourist office (☎ 404 13 16; fax 226 87) is located in Room B219 of the Rathaus at Markt 2 and is open weekdays from 8.30 am to noon and 2 to 4.30 pm (closed Wednesday and Friday afternoons). There's also an Information Pavilion outside the train station open to 6 pm weekdays and to noon on Saturday. Another information source is the regional tourist office (☎ 333 10 20) at Koblenzer Strasse 73. You can change money at the Commerzbank at Bahnhofstrasse 2 or the Dresdner Bank next door. The main post office is at Hindenburgstrasse 9.

Things to See

In 1623, the ruling family of Nassau-Oranien was split into two branches feuding over the Reformation. This required the construction of a second palace, the baroque **Unteres Schloss**, by the Protestant side, while the Catholic counts continued to live in the 13th-century Oberes Schloss. The former is a short walk south-east from the train station. Today, it's primarily used as office space and only the family crypt has survived.

More interesting is the **Oberes Schloss**, reached via Burgstrasse. It houses the **Siegerland Museum** (open 10 am to 5 pm, closed Monday; DM4, discount DM2), a moderately interesting regional history museum. Its major drawing cards are eight original paintings by Rubens, including a self-portrait and *Roman Charity*.

The Oraniersaal, with portraits of members of the dynasty, is another highlight. On a clear day, the view of the town and wooded surroundings from the tower can be superb.

Below the Oberes Schloss is the late Romanesque **Nikolaikirche**, whose galleried, hexagonal main room is unique in Germany. Also note the baptismal plate, made by Peruvian silversmiths in the 16th century and brought back by the counts of Nassau who were involved in the colonisation of South America.

NORTH RHINE - WESTPHALIA

Places to Stay & Eat

The nearest DJH hostel is the *Freusburg* (☎ 02741-610 94) in a castle at Burgstrasse 46 in Kirchen-Freusburg, a village about 17km west of Siegen in the Sieg Valley. The hostel is not easily reached by public transport and is a 20-minute walk from the Freusburg-Siedlung train station. Beds are DM21.50/26.50 for juniors/seniors.

Both the local and the regional tourist offices can help with room reservations. Of Siegen's few hotels *Hotel Bürger* (☎ 625 51), Marienborner Strasse 132, has the lowest room rates with singles/doubles for DM68/80.

The family-run *Hotel Jakob* (☎ 232 72 0; fax 232 72 11), north of the train station at Tiergartenstrasse 61, charges DM63/126 for singles/doubles with shower & WC.

The poshest place is *Queens Hotel Siegen* (☎ 501 10; fax 501 11 50) at Kampenstrasse 83, where full-facility rooms cost DM130/260.

The very central *Stadtschänke* at Am Kornmarkt serves German food in a family atmosphere at reasonable prices. At Burgstrasse 28, there's *Am Hasengarten*, which is similar and has a beer garden. Somewhat more up-market Italian food is on the menu at *Efeu* (closed Monday) at Marienborner Strasse 7.

Getting There & Away

There's frequent and direct train service to Cologne (DM26, 1½ hours). Trips to Frankfurt require a change in Siegen-Weidenau (DM36, 1¾ hours). To get to the Ruhrgebiet cities, you have to change in Hagen. Siegen is off the A45 connecting the Ruhrgebiet with Frankfurt and is also easily reached from Cologne via the A4.

FREUDENBERG

- *pop 21,700*
- *area code* ☎ 02734

About a dozen kilometres north of Siegen, the little town of Freudenberg would be unremarkable were it not for its stunning **Altstadt**, whose immaculate half-timbered houses are set up in the 17th-century equivalent of a planned community. Built in rows, the houses all face the same way, are roughly the same height and sport the same white façades, the same pattern of wooden beams and the same black-slate roofs. Conceptualised by Duke Johann Moritz of Nassau-Oranien, the area is called Alter Flecken (literally 'old borough') and was given preservation status in 1966. There's also a **museum** at Mittelstrasse 4 (Wednesday and weekends 2 to 5 pm; DM1.50). To get to Freudenberg from Siegen, take bus No 45 from the train station.

Bremen

Only 404 sq km, the state of Bremen comprises just two cities: Bremen, the capital, and the port of Bremerhaven, about 65km to the north. Along with Bavaria, Bremen is one of the oldest political entities in Germany and the second-oldest city republic in the world after Italy's San Marino. Bremerhaven is Germany's most important port after Hamburg.

HIGHLIGHTS

- The architecture around the Markt
- Böttchergasse and the historic Schnoor quarter
- The pub and restaurant scene in Das Viertel and Auf den Höfen

• **Population:** 680,000 • **Capital:** Bremen • **Area:** 404 sq km

BREMEN

- *pop 550,000*
- *area code* ☎ 0421

This metropolis on the Weser River is celebrated for three things: beer (Beck's); liberal politics (the Green Party had its major breakthrough here); and a fairy tale *(The Town Musicians of Bremen)*. Of course, that charming quartet from the Brothers Grimm fable never actually made it through the town gates, but *you* should, for Bremen is an energetic city with much to offer. Besides a bevy of historical sights and museums, it has delightful parks, a vibrant nightlife and interesting restaurants. Bremen is also the end of the Fairy-Tale Road, which winds northward from Hanau, in Hesse, the Grimms' birthplace.

Like many German cities, Bremen has origins as an archbishopric. Founded in 787 by Charlemagne, it was the main base for Christianising Scandinavia, which earned the city its moniker as the 'Rome of the North'. Bremen grew by leaps and bounds and by 1358 was ready to join the Hanseatic League. In 1646 it became a free imperial city, a status it still enjoys today as a 'Free Hanseatic City'. The Roland statue on the Markt is a symbol of Bremen's independent spirit and the focal point of a congenial Altstadt that is wonderful to explore on foot.

Orientation

Bremen's city centre is fairly compact and easy to get around on foot. To the north, the Altstadt is bounded by a lovely park called Wallanlagen that follows the old city walls and moat. The Hauptbahnhof and central bus station are just north of here. The centre's southern periphery is the Weser River.

To get to the Markt from the stations, walk along Bahnhofstrasse to Herdentorsteinweg, then continue along the pedestrianised Sögestrasse for another few minutes to Obernstrasse. The Rathaus and Markt are just east of here. The main entertainment quarter is east of the Altstadt along Ostertorsteinweg.

Information

Tourist Offices The main tourist office (☎ 308 00 0 or ☎ 194 33; fax 308 00 30) is in a pavilion outside the Hauptbahnhof. Opening hours are Monday to Wednesday from 9.30 am to 6.30 pm, Thursday and Friday to 8 pm, weekends to 4 pm. There's also a smaller information kiosk at Liebfrauenkirchhof near the Rathaus that keeps the same hours.

Both offices hand out a free map of the city

and annual-events schedule. They sell the BremenCard, good for unlimited public transport, a 50% discount on museums and reductions of 10% to 20% on theatre tickets, sightseeing tours, guided walks etc. The two/three-day card for one adult and one child costs DM19.50/26. A group card good for up to five people costs DM35/46.

Foreign Consulates The UK consulate (☎ 590 90) is at Herrlichkeit 6. There's a French consulate (☎ 305 31 15) at Töferbohm 8.

Money Practically all banks in Bremen exchange money and travellers' cheques, but the Reisebank in the Hauptbahnhof has the best hours: weekdays from 7 am to 7 pm, Saturday from 8 am to 12.15 pm and 1 to 4 pm. If they're closed, the ATM outside accepts all major credit cards. The American Express office (☎ 174 60 0) is at Am Wall 138.

Post & Communications The main post office is on Domsheide, but one with better opening hours is right outside the Hauptbahnhof (weekdays from 8 am to 8 pm, Saturday from 9 am to 2 pm). There's a public fax-phone inside.

Bookshops Most major bookshops, including Storm Buchhandlung with branches at Langenstrasse 10 and Obernstrasse 18, stock a selection of foreign-language titles.

Laundry You'll find Schnell & Sauber laundrettes at Vor dem Steintor 105 and at Am Dobben 134. Expect to pay about DM6 per wash, plus DM1 for the dryer. They're open from 6 am to 11 pm.

Emergency There's a police station (☎ 362 1) at Am Wall 201.

Markt

Most of Bremen's main sights are concentrated around Market Square, anchored on the northern side by the imposing **Rathaus** (1410) with its intensely ornate façade. Above the arched arcades is a row of tall windows separated by a cycle of sandstone figures representing Charlemagne and seven prince-electors. The balcony in the middle, added between 1595 and 1618 and crowned by three gables, is a good example of the flowery Weser Renaissance style. Tours of the Rathaus (in German) take place weekdays at 10 and 11 am and noon (from May to the end of October only), Saturday at 11 am and noon (year round) and cost DM4, discount DM2. The highlight of the tour is the Upper Hall, with its wood-beamed ceiling and heavy brass chandeliers alternating with historic ship models.

In front of the Rathaus, the 13m-tall **Roland statue**, which has been a symbol of justice and freedom in Germany since the Middle Ages, stands guard over the Markt. It's the original statue dating from 1404, though it has had to be restored numerous times, most recently in 1983. While Roland is often thought to be the symbol of Bremen, another statue – banished to the western side of the Rathaus – shows the friendly foursome that people associate more with the city. These are the **Town Musicians of Bremen** – the donkey, dog, cat and rooster who star

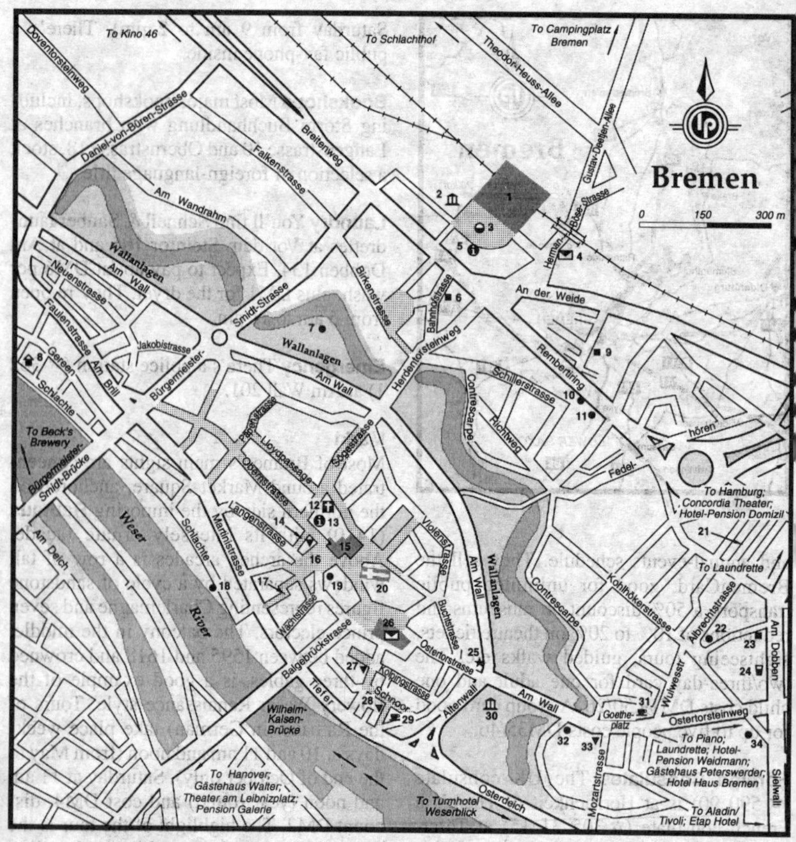

in the Brothers Grimm fairy tale. The bronze statue, by sculptor Gerhard Marcks, was erected in 1951. On Sunday at noon and again at 1.30 pm between May and October there's a charming reenactment here of the story by the Waldau Theater troupe (free).

Immediately beside the statue loom the spires of the **Kirche Unser Lieben Frauen**, Bremen's oldest parish church. Its earliest section is the 11th-century crypt from the Church of St Vitus, which once stood on the site. A Romanesque structure followed from which only the south tower, with its round arches and arcades, survives. The church acquired its early-Gothic appearance in the middle of the 13th century and has been altered several times since. Today it's a three-nave hall church with bare red-brick walls that were originally plastered over and painted. Most of the interior decoration fell victim to iconoclastic zealots during the Reformation. Note the baroque memorial on the wall of the north tower and the carved pulpit.

The western side of the Markt is taken up by a row of stately town houses containing several bars and restaurants. If it weren't for the modern building immediately opposite, you would find yourself in an almost per-

PLACES TO STAY

6 Hotel Schaper-Siedenburg
8 Jugendgästehaus Bremen
9 Hotel Bremer Haus
23 Hotel Weltevreden

PLACES TO EAT

14 Beck's Bistro
21 Auf den Höfen: Soufflé; Dos Mas; Zum Hofheurigen
27 Gasthof zum Kaiser Friedrich
28 Scusi
29 Schnoor Teestübchen
31 Café Engel
33 Casablanca

OTHER

1 Main Train Station
2 Übersee Museum
3 Central Bus Station
4 Post Office Bahnhof
5 Tourist Office Bahnhof
7 Windmill
10 Woody's Disco
11 Stubu Disco
12 Kirche Unser Lieben Frauen
13 Tourist Office Liebfrauenkirchhof
15 Rathaus; Ratskeller
16 Marktplatz
17 Böttcherstrasse
18 Martinianleger
19 Haus der Bürgerschaft
20 Dom St Petri; Dommuseum; Bleikeller
21 Auf den Höfen: Blue Bar; Carnevale Bar
22 Türke
24 Airport Bar
25 Police Station
26 Post Office Domsheide
30 Kunsthalle; KuKuk Café
32 Theater am Goetheplatz
34 Lagerhaus; Lagerhaus Kafé

fectly preserved medieval square. But with the **Haus der Bürgerschaft** (State Assembly; 1966), the 20th century asserts itself loudly and clearly. It houses the parliamentary hall for both the city and the state governments. Though not an architectural disaster as such, the angled steel and concrete structure does not harmonise well with the historic ensemble framing the Markt.

Dom St Petri

This magnificent cathedral, with its two landmark towers, stands to the east of the Rathaus. Its western portal is graced by two bronze doors with biblical scenes and flanked by sculptures of David and Moses (north door) and Peter and Paul, with a goofy-looking mustachioed Charlemagne in the middle. The Reformation got in the way of plans to turn this Romanesque basilica into a Gothic hall church, and therefore only the northern aisle sports a Gothic net vaulting while the southern aisle has retained its low ceiling. Have a look at the 17th-century pulpit with its neat carvings and the sandstone rood loft, which separates the central nave from the choir. The relief in its centre commemorates the founding of Bremen by Charlemagne and Bishop Willehad. Between Easter and October, you can climb the 265 steps to the top of the church tower (daily, DM1).

Also part of the cathedral complex is the **Dommuseum** at Sandstrasse 10-12, with sculptures, murals, liturgical books and items such as rings and vestments dug up recently from the graves of medieval archbishops. It's open weekdays from 9 am to 5 pm (November to April from 1 to 4.30 pm), Saturday to noon and Sunday from 2 to 5 pm; DM3, discount DM2.

A trip to the cathedral's **Bleikeller** (Lead Cellar) is a unique, if somewhat macabre, experience (open Easter to October on weekdays from 10 am to 5 pm, Saturday to noon and Sunday from 2 to 5 pm; DM2, discount DM1). Here you can admire eight mummified corpses in black coffins, including that of a soldier with his mouth opened in silent scream and another of a student who died in a duel in 1705. It's still not known why corpses placed beneath the cathedral do not decompose.

Böttcherstrasse

Off the south side of the Markt towards the Weser winds this narrow 110m-long lane, the creation of Ludwig Roselius, a merchant who made his fortune from the invention of decaffeinated coffee at the beginning of this century.

His dream became reality in 1931 in the form of a pleasing ensemble of red-brick gabled houses infused with expressionist,

Art Nouveau and Art Deco architectural elements. Soon after the lane's completion, the Nazis declared it a prime example of 'degenerate art' and ordered it destroyed. It survived only because Roselius cleverly convinced the authorities to keep the street as a 'warning' to future generations of the depravity of 'cultural Bolshevism'

A huge luminous golden relief greets you at the northern entrance to Böttcherstrasse. Called the ***Lichtbringer*** ('Bringer of Light', 1936), it shows a scene from the Apocalypse with the Archangel Michael fighting a dragon. It was created by Bernhard Hoetger (1874-1959), one of the main designers of Böttcherstrasse. He also designed the **Haus Atlantis**, a stunning composition of steel, concrete and glass with a show-stopping spiral staircase. The building's interior is intended to evoke the mythical lost city of Atlantis. In 1965 it was given a new façade by Ewald Mataré.

Museums Hoetger also designed the **Paula Becker-Modersohn Haus**, another prime example of expressionist architecture, with its rounded edges and wall reliefs. Inside is a museum showcasing the art of the painter also known as Paula Modersohn-Becker (1876-1907), a member of the Worpswede artists colony, who paved the way for the development of German expressionism. Inspired by Cézanne and Gauguin, she created a series of portraits, still lifes and landscapes in muted, earthy colours that evoke a certain melancholy. The artist died suddenly at age 31, just after the birth of her first daughter. Note that Roselius put the artist's maiden name first in his museum to acknowledge her greatness before she married the landscape painter Otto Modersohn.

The upper floors of the same building contain the **Sammlung Bernhard Hoetger**, the sculptor of whom Auguste Rodin said: '(He) found the way I was searching for ... the way to monumental art, which is the only proper way.' You'll find Hoetger's own portrayal of the Town Musicians of Bremen in the fountain of the **Handwerkerhof**, the courtyard where craftsmen used to have their workshops, in the same building complex.

The museums are connected via a walkway to the **Roselius Haus** (1588), the oldest house on the Böttcherstrasse. Integrated into this furnished town house is Roselius' private collection of medieval art. Highlights are paintings from Lucas Cranach the Elder and the Westphalian artist Conrad von Soest. There's also an emotional wooden sculpture by Tilmann Riemenschneider.

The museums are open from 11 am to 5 pm daily except Monday. The admission price (DM8, discount DM4) allows entry to all three.

Der Schnoor

The south-eastern section of the Altstadt is occupied by the Schnoor quarter, whose name stems from the word *Schnur*, or 'string', and refers to the straight way in which its snug cottages line up along the quarter's alleyways. Once inhabited by fisherfolk, traders and craftspeople, these homes from the 15th and 16th centuries survived the bombings of WWII but almost succumbed to the destructive building boom of the 1950s. In the end they were spared, put under protection order and revived as a picturesque neighbourhood filled with cafés, restaurants and shops. You'll often find swarms of tourists squeezing through the tiny lanes, but otherwise it's an idyllic and peaceful place that warrants a stroll.

Museums

Kunsthalle Located at Am Wall 207, the Kunsthalle ranks as Bremen's premier art museum and contains works spanning five centuries – from old masters like Rembrandt and Dürer to German expressionists, as well as paintings from the Worpswede artists' colony and sculptures by Rodin.

The museum was being renovated at the time of writing and was scheduled to reopen in spring 1998.

Übersee Museum The collection of the Overseas Museum, next to the train station at Bahnhofsplatz 13, had its origins in a colonial trade exhibit from 1890, where merchants displayed goods imported from abroad. Items, which include a Japanese teahouse and an Alaskan totem pole, are arranged by continent and grouped in rooms around two skylit courtyards. The museum is open from 10 am to 6 pm (closed Monday). Admission is DM6, discount DM3.

Beck's Brewery

Keen students of the amber brew can hone their knowledge with a look behind the scenes at **Beck's**, one of Germany's largest breweries. Tours of the facility cost DM15, last two hours and include a movie presentation and beer tasting. The brewery is located at Am Deich on the southern bank of the Weser, just west of Bürgermeister-Smidt-Brücke. Tours take place on weekdays between 10 am and 5 pm; on Saturday the last tour is at 3 pm. Some tours are in English; call ahead on ☎ 509 45 55 5 for details.

Organised Tours

Basic, two-hour bus sightseeing tours of Bremen with English commentary depart daily at 10.30 am from the central bus station and cost DM25 (children DM15). Buy your tickets at the tourist offices. A city walking tour leaves from the tourist office outside the Hauptbahnhof daily at 2 pm (DM9, free for children up to age 14). The guides will provide English commentary upon request.

Schreiber Reederei (☎ 321 22 9) operates a 75-minute Weser and harbour tour up to five times daily between March and October. Meeting point is the Martinianleger (Martini landing) in the city centre (DM13, students DM9.50, children DM7).

Places to Stay

The tourist office runs a room reservation service with a charge of DM3 per booking. You must leave a down payment of 10% with them, which counts towards your final bill.

Camping The closest camping ground is *Campingplatz Bremen* (☎ 212 00 2; open April to October) at Am Stadtwaldsee 1. It's reasonably close to the university – take tram No 5 from the Hauptbahnhof to Kuhlenkampfallee, then bus No 28 to the Campingplatz stop. Tent sites cost DM4.50 to DM9, plus DM7.50 per person and DM2.50 per car.

Hostel *Jugendgästehaus Bremen* (☎ 171 36 9; closed between Christmas and New Year) is at Kalkstrasse 6 across the Weser from the Beck's brewery. The cost for juniors/seniors is DM27/32. From the Hauptbahnhof it's about a 15-minute walk or a short ride on bus No 26 or tram No 6 to Am Brill.

Private Rooms If you'd like a private room, you should contact Bed & Breakfast Bremen (☎ 536 07 71), a private agency at Kornstrasse 147.

Hotels One of the cheapest options in town is *Hotel-Pension Weidmann* (☎ 498 44 55) at Am Schwarzen Meer 35, which charges DM40 to DM50 per single and DM80 to DM100 for a double.

Another place with decent prices is *Gästehaus Peterswerder* (☎ 447 10 1), Celler Strasse 4, which charges from DM55/90 for singles/doubles. *Hotel Garni Gästehaus Walter* (☎ 558 02 7), Buntentorsteinweg 86-88, charges from DM40 to DM70 per single and DM70 to DM110 per double.

Quite a bit south-east of the centre, at Borgwardstrasse 10, is the chain hotel *Etap* (☎ 837 35 0), whose basic but functional rooms cost DM66/87. Also south of the Weser River, at No 46 of busy Thedinghauser Strasse, is the family-run *Pension Galerie* (☎ 530 75 3), with singles for DM55 to DM70, doubles for DM80 to DM105 and free use of their bikes.

Rooms at the *Hotel-Pension Domizil* (☎ 347 81 47; fax 342 37 6) at Graf-Moltke-Strasse 42 start at DM78/120 for singles/doubles. *Hotel Weltevreden* (☎ 780 15; fax 704 09 1), Am Dobben 62, has rooms without bath for DM60/100; those with facilities cost up to DM90/120. Another option is *Hotel Haus Bremen* (☎ 432 72 0; fax 432 72 22) at Verdener Strasse 47, which offers nice, quiet rooms for up to DM110/150 (though a few cheaper ones are available).

A good hotel in the upper category is *Schaper-Siedenburg* (☎ 308 70; fax 308 78 8) at Bahnhofstrasse 8, only a few minutes' walk from the Hauptbahnhof. They serve a great breakfast and charge from DM130/160 for singles/doubles. *Hotel Bremer Haus* (☎ 3 29 40; fax 329 44 11) at Löningstrasse 16-20, only 300m from the Hauptbahnhof, charges from DM135/160. For a room with a view, go to *Turmhotel Weserblick* (☎ 791 97 9; fax 791 97 88) at Osterdeich 53 in one of Bremen's poshest neighbourhoods. Singles/ doubles here cost from DM160/190.

Long-Term Rentals The Home Company Mitwohnzentrale (☎ 194 45) is at Humboldtstrasse 28.

Places to Eat

Markt In good weather, the western half of the Markt takes on the feel of an Italian piazza as parcel-laden shoppers, bohemians and grey-haired ladies jostle for a place in the sun at dozens of café tables. One of the most popular is *Beck's Bistro*, Markt 9, whose regular menu is complemented by inexpensive daily specials (around DM10). From here you can spot the entrance to the *Ratskeller*, with its cosy network of vaulted cellar rooms decorated with large carved barrels. They serve regional and international cuisine and an astonishing 600 varieties of German wine. This is stored in huge rooms that, at any given time, hold 50,000 bottles and countless casks containing half a million litres of wine.

Schnoor Interesting cafés and restaurants clustered in this neat neighbourhood include the wonderfully old-fashioned teahouse *Schnoor Teestübchen*, Wüstestätte 1, which has a reasonably priced vegetarian menu. Down the same lane at No 11 is *Scusi*, a popular Italian cellar restaurant. Prices for creative pizza and pasta concoctions are only slightly higher than those at your average pizzeria. A popular gathering place of sea captains some 200 years ago, *Gasthof zum Kaiser Friedrich* at Lange Wieren 13 is now popular with office workers and tourists alike (closed Sunday). Its many rooms sport hundreds of black & white photographs of famous and not-so-famous guests. The food is hearty, plentiful and priced fairly.

Das Viertel The place to go for food and drink at night is Das Viertel (The Quarter), an area along Ostertorsteinweg, east of Goetheplatz. Here you'll find an eclectic mix of trendy restaurants, multicultural cafés, funky bars and bustling pubs, almost all of them offering good value. Many are open from breakfast till the wee hours.

Casablanca at Ostertorsteinweg 59 is a fashionable and noisy bistro. The menu includes 10 salads (DM10 to DM12), plus soups, baguettes and baked potatoes. The breakfast buffet is good, though service is often slow. In a former pharmacy at Ostertorsteinweg 31, you'll find *Café Engel*, a popular student hang-out that matches black & white tiled floors with dark wood furniture and offers two-course daily specials for around DM11.

At Am Wall 207, inside the Kunsthalle, you'll find *KuKuk*, a café-cum-restaurant with a nice view of the Wallanlagen park. The décor is sober and clean, the clientele artsy and the food reasonably priced Italian (mostly under DM20). A Bremen classic is *Piano* at Fehrfeld 64, where you dine in Art Deco rooms of subdued ambience on creative, Mediterranean-inspired dishes.

Auf den Höfen This narrow courtyard off Auf den Häfen offers a multicultural mix of restaurants, bars and cafés. On a balmy night, it's as jammed as a Rolling Stones concert with an atmosphere almost as electric. *Soufflé* offers creative casseroles for under DM16. *Dos Mas* has tapas, tortillas and nachos plus main courses for around DM15 to DM20. The Austrian *Zum Hofheurigen* seems almost incongruous with its southern German décor but the schnitzel is quite good (around DM15).

Entertainment

Listings For events information and tips on what's on and where in Bremen, buy a copy of *Prinz* (DM5) or *Bremer* (DM4.50) at any newsagent, or look for a free copy of *Mix* at the tourist office or in bars and restaurants. The monthly events guide *Bremer Umschau* is available for DM3.

Cinema Bremen has plenty of movie theatres but most films are dubbed into German. One of the biggest cinemas, whose repertory includes lots of movies in the original language (look for the acronym 'OmU') is *Kino 46* at Waller Heerstrasse 46 (tram No 2 or 10 to Gustavstrasse). Tickets cost DM9, discount DM8, which is a steal compared with most mainstream theatres.

Discos & Clubs You won't hear any techno sounds at *Chagall*, Rembertiring 4, which offers a varied mix of blues, hard rock and pop from the last three decades. It's open Wednesday to Saturday from 10 pm. *Aladin/Tivoli*, at Hannoversche Strasse 11 in the suburb of Hemelingen, has a disco (mostly hard rock) on Wednesday, Saturday and Sunday after 9.30 pm, and blues and rock concerts on other days. *Stubu*, at Rembertiring 21, is an old favourite which specialises in oldies and 1980s music. Next door is *Woody's*, which changes its musical emphasis nightly from Tuesday to Sunday.

Cultural Centres *Schlachthof*, a 19th-century slaughterhouse at Findorffstrasse 51, has ethnic and world-music concerts and also theatre, cabaret and variété, complemented by exhibits and a café. The *Lagerhaus*, at Schildstrasse 12-19, has a varied schedule of theatre, dance parties, movies, live concerts and more (see also Pubs & Bars).

Theatre Bremen has a total of nine stages, including *Theater am Goetheplatz* (☎ 365 33 04), which stages opera, operettas and musicals (take tram No 2 or 3 from the Domsheide stop near the Rathaus). The *Schauspielhaus* (☎ 365 33 33), next door at Ostertorsteinweg 57a, does the lot, from updated classic to avant-garde drama. Dance theatre dominates at the small *Concordia* (☎ 365 33 33) at Schwachhauser Heerstrasse 17 (tram No 1 or bus No 30, 31, 33 or 34 to Parkstrasse).

One of Bremen's private theatre troupes is the acclaimed Bremer Shakespeare Company, with 10 of the Bard's plays in repertory. It performs at the *Theater am Leibnizplatz* (☎ 503 37 2) about 500m south of the Weser off Friedrich-Ebert-Strasse (tram No 1 or 5).

Besides contacting the theatre box offices directly for tickets, you can also call the tourist office or the central Ticket Service Center at ☎ 353 63 7. All theatres offer discounts to students and children.

Pubs & Bars Bremen's best nightspots convene in Das Viertel (see Places to Eat). At Beim Steinernen Kreuz 13 is *Türke*, a mainstay of the quarter and so named because it once had a Turkish proprietor. For true night owls, there's the dimly lit *Airport* at Am Dobben 70, which doesn't even open until 11 pm and serves killer cocktails. Also popular is the large *Lagerhaus Kafé* inside the cultural centre by the same name at Schildstrasse 12-19. In the courtyard of Auf den Höfen, you'll find *Blue*, a trendy drinking place with minimalist blue and silver décor. Also here is the exotic Caribbean-themed *Carnevale*.

Things to Buy

Bremen's main shopping area is between Hauptbahnhof and Markt and centres around Sögestrasse and Obernstrasse. Along Ostertorsteinweg in Das Viertel are eccentric boutiques, ethnic food stores and funky second-hand shops. There are also two flea markets: one along the north bank of the Weser, roughly between Bürgermeister-Smidt-Brücke and the bridge at Balgebrückstrasse (Saturdays from 8 am to 4 pm year round) and the other on the Bürgerweide, north of the Hauptbahnhof (Sundays from 7 am to 2 pm, April to December).

Getting There & Away

Air Bremen's small international airport (☎ 559 50) is about 4km south of the centre and has more than 300 weekly flights to destinations in Germany and Europe. Airlines with offices here include British Airways (☎ 0180-340 34 0), Lufthansa (☎ 01803-803 80 3) and KLM (0180-521 42 01).

Bus Eurolines has a service to London every Monday, Thursday and Saturday. The journey takes 17 hours and costs DM124, return DM226. They also offer daily trips to Amsterdam (DM60/95, five hours). If you're under 26, you get a 10% discount.

Train Bremen has hourly IC train connections to Dortmund (DM59, 1¾ hours, every two hours) and Frankfurt (DM159, 3¼ hours). There are several trains each hour to Hamburg (DM31, one hour). Going to Berlin requires a change in Hanover. Lockers are plentiful in the station, located in the north aisle (DM4/2 big/small).

Car & Motorcycle The A1 (from Hamburg to Osnabrück) and the A27/A7 (Bremerhaven- Hanover) intersect in Bremen. The city is also on the B6 and B75. All major car-rental agencies have branches at the airport, including Avis (☎ 558 05 5), Hertz (☎ 555 35 0) and Alamo (☎ 552 02 6).

Ride Services The ADM Mitfahrbüro (☎ 194 40 or ☎ 720 11) is at Körnerwall 1.

Boat Schreiber Reederei (☎ 321 22 9) offers regular scheduled service up and down the Weser River. The boats leave from the Martinianleger landing in the city centre between early May and early October. Boats travelling the entire distance from Bremen to Bremerhaven (DM21/34 one way/return, 3½ hours), with numerous stops in between, depart at 8.30 am every Wednesday, Thursday and Saturday. Shorter tours ending at Brake (DM15/24, 2¼ hours) depart on Tuesday and Sunday at 2 pm. Additional boats on these days depart at 9.30 am for Vegesack (DM12/17, one hour). Students and children pay half price. Travel on your birthday is free, provided you can prove it with an ID.

Getting Around

Airport Tram No 5 from the Hauptbahnhof gets you to and from the airport in under 20 minutes (DM3.30). A taxi ride will cost about DM18.

Public Transport The Verkehrsverbund Bremen/Niedersachsen (☎ 536 32 88) operates a good system of buses and trams that extends to most corners of town. The main hubs are in front of the Hauptbahnhof and at Domsheide near the Rathaus. Short trips cost DM1.50 while a DM3.30 ticket covers most of the Bremen city area. Four-trip tickets are better value at DM10, but if you're doing a lot of travelling around, nothing beats the Day Pass (Tageskarte) for DM8.

Taxi You can book a taxi on ☎ 140 41.

Bicycle Bremen is a bicycle-friendly town, with lots of specially designated bike paths. In fact, if you're walking, you'd better watch out for cyclists since they also seem to claim the pedestrian areas (and just about any other ground) by proprietary right. It's safer just to join them. The Fahrradstation (☎ 302 11 4) just outside the Hauptbahnhof has bikes for DM15 for 24 hours and DM35 for three days, plus a DM50 deposit. You should also take your passport along.

AROUND BREMEN

Bremen-Nord

Technically still a part of Bremen proper and only 20km north of the city centre, the communities of Bremen-Nord – Vegesack, Burglesum and Blumenthal – have retained their own identity. The maritime tradition is still alive in these villages on the Weser River, which built Germany's first artificial harbour (1619-22), constructed merchant ships and sent hardy whalers on their journeys to the Arctic. Bremen-Nord is also the birthplace of the German Sea Rescue Service.

Sightseeing attractions include the ***White***

Swan of the Lower Weser, a recently restored, fully rigged windjammer used as a training ship for sailors and as a museum (open daily, closed at lunchtime on weekdays; DM3). It lies at anchor in the mouth of the Lesum River at Friedrich-Klippert-Strasse 1 in Vegesack.

Besides old villas, warehouses and captains' houses, you'll also find the 300-year-old moated **Schloss Schönebeck**, a stately red-brick building now occupied by a local history museum. The exhibit concentrates on shipbuilding, seafaring, whaling and other activities important to the region's past. Opening hours are Tuesday, Wednesday and weekends from 3 to 5 pm (Sunday also from 10 am to 12.30 pm); admission costs DM2. To get to the Schloss, take bus No 78 or 79 from Bahnhof Vegesack to Herbartstrasse.

To get to Bremen-Nord, take the Stadt-Express train from Bremen's Hauptbahnhof to Bahnhof Vegesack.

Worpswede

- *pop 9000*
- *area code* ☎ 04792

Worpswede is a pretty village with an artistic tradition about 30km north-east of Bremen, which actually places it within the borders of Lower Saxony. The town surrounds the 55m-tall **Weyerberg**, a sand dune at the centre of a large peat bog called **Teufelsmoor** (Devil's Moor). This barren, melancholic landscape – where big clouds form dramatic skyscapes and the light creates deep shadows – drew painters here in 1889.

The original artists' colony formed here included Fritz Mackensen, Otto Modersohn, Fritz Overbeck, Heinrich Vogeler and Hans am Ende. An exhibition of their works at the Glaspalast in Munich in 1895 catapulted the group to prominence overnight. Others, including writers, actors and composers, then began to flock to Worpswede as well. One of the colony's biggest names was Paula Modersohn-Becker, who joined the group in 1898 and is buried in the village cemetery. The future co-creator of Bremen's Böttcherstrasse, Bernard Hoetger (see the earlier Bremen section), arrived here in 1914. As the density of studios and galleries shows, Worpswede continues to cast its creative spell on artists from all fields.

To admire the works of the founding members, check out the **Grosse Kunstschau**, a museum at Lindenallee 3. Also here is the **Ludwig Roselius Museum**, which has a large collection of items from European prehistory. Both museums are open daily from 10 am to 6 pm and admission is DM5 (discount DM3).

At Ostendorfer Strasse 10 stands the **Barkenhof**, a half-timbered structure remodelled in the Art Nouveau style at the turn of the century by its then-owner Heinrich Vogeler. At one time, this house and studio formed the creative centre of the colony. Vogeler also designed the Art Nouveau **train station**. The rail line closed in 1978, and the structure is now a restaurant.

For detailed information visit the tourist office (☎ 950 12 1) at Bergstrasse 13, which is open weekdays from 9 am to 1 pm and 2 to 6 pm, weekends from 10 am to 3 pm (restricted hours in winter).

Getting There & Away To get to Worpswede from Bremen, take bus No 140 from the central bus station, which makes the 50-minute trip about every 1½ hours. Personenschiffahrt Ruth Haferkamp (☎ 04404-351 4) offers boat trips from Bremen-Vegesack (three hours; DM17/23 one way/return) via the Lesum and Hamme rivers every Wednesday and Sunday at 9.15 am from May to September. In August, there's an additional boat on Thursday. You can also always take the bus back to Bremen.

BREMERHAVEN

- *pop 130,000*
- *area code* ☎ 0471

Some 65km north of Bremen lies Bremerhaven, the state's only other city. It owes its existence to the silting up of the Weser in the early 19th century and the vision of the wily Bremen mayor at the time, Johann Smidt. For 73,000 thalers, he bought the land at the mouth of the river from King George of

Hanover and laid the foundations for a brand new harbour here in 1827. It was good timing, for the era of regular steamer traffic between Europe and North America was just picking up. Throughout the 19th and 20th centuries, Bremerhaven was the major exit ramp for about six million emigrants to the US and other countries.

Bremerhaven *is* its port. The biggest city on Germany's North Sea coast boasts one of the largest and most modern container terminals in the world, handling 1.3 million of these giant steel crates each year. At the separate Banana Terminal, some 450,000 tonnes of cargo are discharged annually, while the Automobile Terminal loads and unloads about 750,000 cars.

Things to See & Do

Bremerhaven isn't pretty, but there's a certain excitement from all the activity surrounding the gigantic port. You can stroll along the **waterfront promenade** or walk to the top of the **viewing platform** near the container terminal in the North Harbour to get an overview of its vastness (between March and October; free).

Bremerhaven's main draw, though, is the **Deutsche Schiffahrtsmuseum** (German Maritime Museum; open 10 am to 6 pm, closed Monday; DM6, children DM3) at Hans-Scharoun-Platz 1 near the radar tower in the city centre. (To get there take bus No 2, 3, 5, 6, 8 or 9 to Theodor-Heuss-Platz.) It's the kind of place that can be enjoyed even by those who can't tell the bow from the stern. The museum's several floors are meant to resemble the decks of a passenger liner. The prized exhibit is the wooden hull of a merchant boat from 1388, the so-called ***Hanse Kogge***. It was pieced together from thousands of fragments found during excavations in another harbour in 1962. Unfortunately, this gem from the briny deep cannot yet be viewed by the public. For preservation purposes, it's sitting in a giant steel tank, submerged in a chemical bath until at least the year 2000. A 1:10 scale model reveals what this early seafaring ship looked like.

But what you *can* see is a thorough exhibition documenting the evolution of shipbuilding. The collection of about 500 ship models includes whalers, brigantines, three-masters and steamers. The entire range of ship and boat types is represented here, from an 11,000-year-old dugout to the engine control room of the nuclear-powered *Otto Hahn*. Outside, the **Museum Harbour** has a parade of eight historical ships open for viewing between April and September. They include the wooden sailing vessel *Seute Deern* (1919), the polar research ship *Grönland* (1868) and the fire ship *Elbe 3* (1909).

To get a glimpse of life on a U-boat, climb aboard the WWII-vintage ***Wilhelm Bauer***, which is moored here as well (open April to October daily from 10 am to 6 pm; DM3, discount DM1.50). The only surviving boat of the XXI type, it was the first to go faster under water than above and was outfitted with a special snorkel that allowed it to stay submerged for extended periods.

Another museum worth investigating is the **Morgenstern Museum** (open from 10 am to 6 pm, closed Monday; DM3, children DM1.50) in a modern complex at An der Geeste. It brings to life the early history of the port town with such exhibits as an old harbour pub, a fish shop, an American jeep representing the occupation era after WWII, and older technology used to move cargo. Take bus No 5 or 6 to the Borriesstrasse stop.

Bremerhaven's tourist office (☎ 946 46 10; fax 460 65) at Van-Ronzelen-Strasse 2 is open weekdays from 8 am to 6 pm (in winter to 4 pm on Thursday and to 3.30 pm on Friday). There's also an information pavilion (☎ 430 00; fax 430 80) at Obere Bürger 17 in the Columbus-Center mall, open Monday to Wednesday from 9.30 am to 6 pm, Thursday and Friday to 8 pm and Saturday to 4 pm.

Getting There & Away

Train from Bremen to Bremerhaven are frequent and take about one hour (DM15.60). By car, Bremerhaven is quickly reached via the A27 from Bremen; get off at the Bremerhaven-Mitte exit. A slower alternative is a leisurely boat ride from Bremen (see Getting There & Away in the Bremen section).

Lower Saxony

Lower Saxony (Niedersachsen) is Germany's second-largest state after Bavaria. Part of its attraction lies in its amazingly varied natural landscape which spans the forested highlands of the western Harz Mountains, the northern German lowlands around Lüneburg, the low hills of the Weser region and the flat coastal area of Friesland with its offshore islands. Its natural resources are another major asset. Silver brought wealth to Goslar in the Middle Ages, and the salt mines in Lüneburg and the iron-ore deposits in Salzgitter contributed to those towns' riches. Fishing still provides a source of income to the coastal communities. And one of the largest car factories in Europe is the VW plant in Wolfsburg.

British occupational forces created the *Land* of Lower Saxony in 1946 when they amalgamated the states of Braunschweig (Brunswick), Schaumburg-Lippe and Oldenburg with the Prussian province of Hanover, formerly the Kingdom of Hanover. Between 1714 and 1837, Hanover and Britain were governed by the same series of rulers. Today, Hanover is the capital of the state and its largest city. Badly destroyed in WWII, its charms lie in its wonderful museums and parks rather than in harmonious historic appearance. Every year, it hosts the world's largest industrial fair at the Hannover Messe. The city will also be the site of Expo 2000.

North of Hanover is the Lüneburg Heath and the town of Lüneburg with its splendid townscape dominated by red-brick Gothic buildings. Celle, once a residence of the Lüneburg dukes, boasts a picturesque half-timbered Altstadt. South of the state capital is Hannoversch-Münden, where the Weser River begins its 440km-long journey through a rural area of valleys, meadows, ruined castles and palaces before emptying into the North Sea near Bremerhaven. Göttingen is a lively university town whose hallowed halls have produced at least 40 Nobel Prize winners. The student life here is particularly lively, as is the nightlife.

HIGHLIGHTS

- A visit to the Bergen-Belsen concentration camp
- The Herzog Anton Ulrich Museum in Braunschweig
- The half-timbered houses in Celle
- Hanover's Markthalle
- Volkswagen factory tours in Wolfsburg

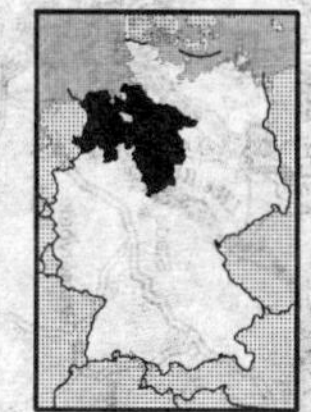

• **Population:** 7.8m • **Capital:** Hanover • **Area:** 47,338 sq km

Lower Saxony Luminaries: Wilhelm Bausch, Leo von Klenze, Robert Koch, Wilhelm Raabe, Erich Maria Remarque, Georg Friedrich Bernhard Riemann, Werner von Siemens

Braunschweig is Lower Saxony's second-largest town and most closely associated with Heinrich der Löwe (Henry the Lion) who governed Bavaria and Saxony from here after making the town his residence in 1166. He is buried in the Dom.

Unlike anything else in Germany are the coastal areas of Friesland. The land is flat as a pancake, and the people, who maintained republic-like governments until the late Middle Ages, are reserved and independent-minded. Friesland borders the Wattenmeer, a shallow sea which retreats twice daily with the tides, exposing the muddy ocean floor.

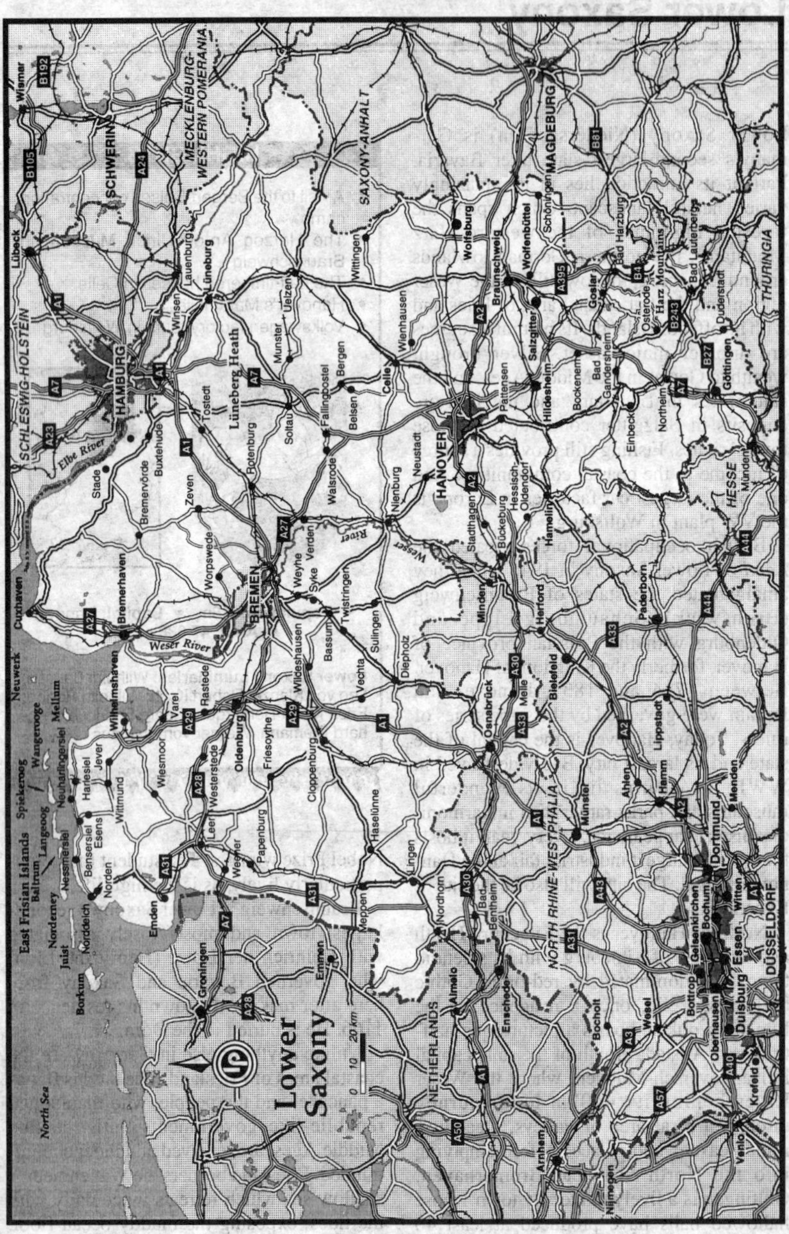

Lower Saxony

It's all part of a 565,000-hectare national park that teems with birds and wildlife. To the north, the Wattenmeer is separated from the North Sea by the seven East Frisian Islands, small windswept places popular with holiday-makers.

Like most other German regions, it's quite easy to travel around Lower Saxony, though you may find a car useful in Friesland and in the rural regions along the Weser. The Harz Mountains, the East Frisian Islands and the picturesque towns along the Fairy-Tale Road (see the Hesse chapter) are the most popular tourist destinations and offer plenty of tourist information, accommodation options and travel connections.

Accommodation

The big surprise in Lower Saxony are the *Heu Hotels*, literally 'hay hotels'. Usually set up in farmhouses and similar to bunk barns in the UK, the classic hay hotel is a barn in which visitors can sleep usually for a very low – and usually odd – fee, like DM14.14 per night. They're a great way to get into the countryside, and are usually much more comfortable (if odoriferous) than they sound. Some have horse riding, lakes for swimming, sledding in winter, and other activities. While some are bare-bones, all are heated in winter and many get downright luxurious. Check with tourist offices in the region for listings of local hay hotels.

Food & Drink

Regional specialities include *Braunkohl mit Bregenwurst*, meaning – hold on to your hats – marinated cabbage with brainmeat sausage. Yummy, we're sure.

The sandy soil of the Lüneburger Heide produces some exceptionally good vegetables – potatoes are fantastic. In spring, look for excellent locally produced asparagus.

The delicious *Steinhudemeer* – smoked eel, served cold and great at any time of year – is a great treat around Hanover and the lower Lüneburger Heide. Also very good is locally caught trout.

In summer a favourite is *Rote Grutze*, seasonal red fruits served under a vanilla cream sauce.

In Hanover, especially during Schutzenfest, people drop literally dozens of shots of Lutje Lage, a shot glass each of Korn schnapps and Weissbier, which you balance between first, second and third fingers (schnapps on top) and drink simultaneously (amateurs are given paper bibs).

Hildesheim's digestive hooch is Lutter-trunk, in a distinctive round bottle, available only in pharmacies.

HANOVER

- *pop 520,000*
- *area code* ☎ 0511

Hanover (Hannover), the capital of Lower Saxony, was savaged by heavy bombing in 1943 that destroyed much of the city's Altstadt. Reconstruction produced a city that may not be packed with architectural gems, but is certainly on a human scale. Much of the centre is pedestrianised, and the city is dotted with large parks, lakes and public artworks.

Best of all, so much of it is walkable. It's a 20-minute stroll from the Hauptbahnhof to the Spengler Museum and the northern end of the Maschsee – a nice change from cities in which you're lost without public transport or a car.

With an excellent range of cultural, artistic and entertainment offerings, Hanover is worth a couple of days.

History

Hanover was established around 1100 and became the residence of Heinrich der Löwe later that century. An early Hanseatic city, Hanover became a prosperous seat of royalty and a major power by the time of the Reformation.

Hanover has close links with Britain through a series of intricate marriages. In 1714, the eldest son of Electress Sophie of Hanover – a granddaughter of James I of England (James VI of Scotland) – ascended the English throne as George I while simultaneously ruling Hanover. This English/

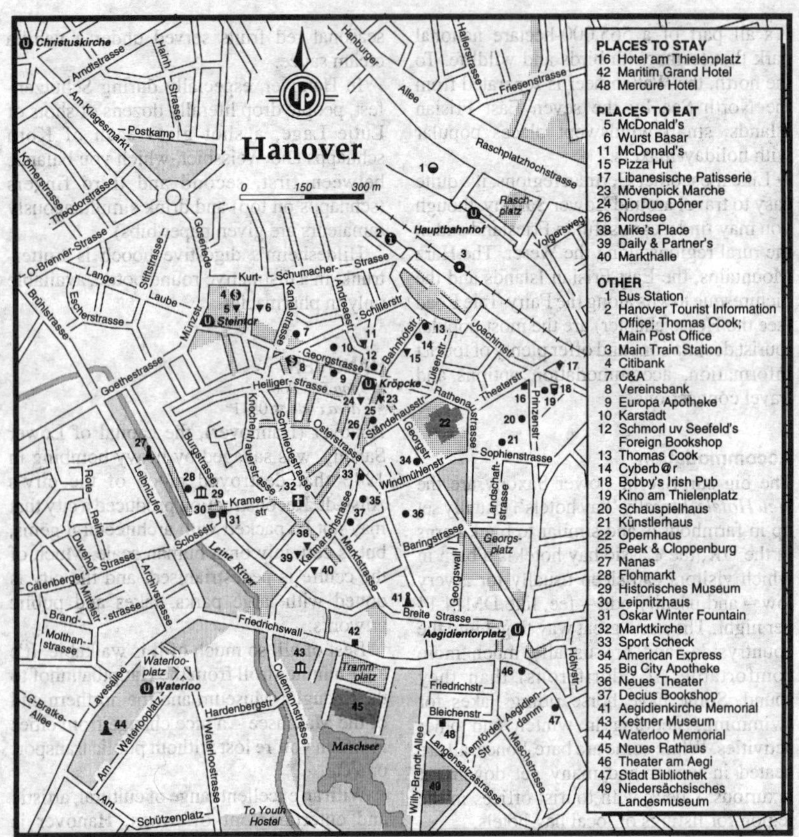

German union lasted through several generations until 1837.

In 1943 up to 80% of the centre and 50% of the entire city was destroyed by Allied bombing. The rebuilding plan, supervised by British forces, limited the height of new buildings, created sections of reconstructed half-timbered houses and painstakingly reconstructed the city's pre-war gems, such as the Opera House, Markt Kirche and Neues Rathaus.

Trade fairs have long played a role in Hanoverian economics, and after WWII the city was keen to get right back into them. It held its first postwar trade fair in August 1947 in the midst of all the rubble. As the majority of the city's hotels had been destroyed, the mayor made an appeal to the people of the city: make rooms in your flats available so we can bring in international money. The people did, the money came and it's become a tradition: today there are about a third more beds for rent in private flats than in hotels.

The granddaddy of all fairs is CeBit – the world's largest office information and telecommunications trade fair, attended by over 800,000 people annually. Look for CeBit's new home-electronics fair eventually to bring in even more than that. And Expo 2000, which will run here May to October, 2000, will attract an estimated 40 million visitors.

Orientation

The Hauptbahnhof is at the north-eastern end of the city centre. The centre contains the largest pedestrianised area in Germany, focusing on Georgstrasse and Bahnhofstrasse. Bahnhofstrasse runs south-west from the Hauptbahnhof, Georgstrasse west-east from Steintor to the square at Kröpke; the large indoor shopping mall called Galerie Luise is at the north-eastern end of Kröpke.

Beneath Bahnhofstrasse is the Passarelle, a major pedestrian subway-cum-shopping mall running from just south of the Hauptbahnhof to just south of Kröpke.

The city centre's limits are within the rough ring formed by Raschplatzhochstrasse north of the Hauptbahnhof, Berliner Allee at the east, Marienstrasse, Aegidientor Platz and Friedrichswall at the south and Leibnizufer at the west. Willy-Brandt-Allee runs south from Friedrichswall to the Landes and Stengel museums and on to Maschsee.

The city has painted a red line on pavements around the centre; follow it, with the help of the multilingual *Red Thread Guide* (DM3) available from the tourist information office, for a quick do-it-yourself tour of the city's main highlights.

The Herrenhäuser Garten is about 4km north-west of the city centre.

The Messegelände, the main trade fairgrounds and home to CeBit and other large fairs, are in the city's south-west, served by tram/U-Bahn No 8, IC and, soon, ICE trains. Expo 2000 will be held in a newly constructed area that expands on the present trade fairgrounds.

Information

Tourist Offices The excellent Hanover Tourist Information Office (HTIO; ☎ 301 42 0), Ernst-August-Platz 2 next to the main post office near the main train station, opens Monday to Friday from 8.30 am to 6 pm, Saturday from 9.30 to 2 pm. It provides a wide range of services, including hotel and private room booking (the latter only during trade fairs and festivals), concert and theatre ticket sales, tours and excursions and sale of the HannoverCard, which entitles you to unlimited public transport and discounted or free admission to museums and other attractions. It costs DM14 for a day, DM23 for three days.

There's a second HTIO information counter (no telephone) in the Rathaus.

During CeBit and other major trade fairs, there are special tourist information offices in the airport and an information pavilion at the trade fairgrounds. These are full-service offices that also book hotel and private rooms.

The German auto association (ADAC) has an office (☎ 850 00) in the extreme north-east of the city at Hindenburgstrasse 37.

Foreign Consulates There are several foreign consulates (H denotes honorary) in Hanover, including:

Belgium (H)
  Hans-Böckler-Allee 20 (☎ 857 25 54)
Finland (H)
  Mühlenfeld 18 (☎ 722 33 2)
Greece
  Podbielskistrasse 34 (☎ 628 35 6)
Italy
  Bischofsholer Damm 62 (☎ 283 79 0)
Netherlands (H)
  Büttnerstrasse 25 (☎ 938 22 85)
South Africa
  Heisterholzwinkel 10 (☎ 517 95 24)
UK (H)
  Berliner Allee 5 (☎ 388 38 08)

Money Change money at any of a dozen banks in and around the Hauptbahnhof and in the pedestrian zones, including Citibank (☎ 124 03 0), Kurt-Schumacher-Strasse 37, and Vereinsbank (☎ 327 29 6), Georgstrasse 8a. American Express (☎ 363 42 8) is at Georgstrasse 54 and Thomas Cook (☎ 327 07 6) is at Bahnhofstrasse 8.

Post & Communications The main post

office is north-west of the Hauptbahnhof in the same building as the HTIO.

Online Services Web surf at Cyberb@r (☎ 305 18 18), upstairs at Bahnhofstrasse 6.

Travel Agencies There's a Thomas Cook agency in the HTIO which also offers currency exchange. See the previous Money section for more Thomas Cook and American Express locations.

Explorer (☎ 326 82 1) is a discounter at Röselerstrasse 1 near Aegindietor Platz on the corner of Osterstrasse. Flügborse has an office (☎ 320 21 0) at Lavestrasse 61, and we've heard good things about the Last Minute Shop (☎ 342 20 0).

Bookshops & Libraries In the Passarelle on the corner of Georgstrasse is Schmorl uv Seefeld's Foreign Bookshop (☎ 367 50). Upstairs (separate entrance at Bahnhofstrasse 14) is a travel section with maps and Lonely Planet guides. A smaller selection is at Decius Buchhandlung (☎ 364 76 52), further south on the corner of Marktstrasse and Karmarschstrasse.

The Stadt Bibliothek (city library) is on Georgstrasse just south of Aegidientorplatz.

Campuses Hanover University has four campuses; the main one is west of the centre in and around the former Guelf Palace (1857-78); (tram/U-Bahn No 4 or 5 to Universität). The university's 34,000 students are split into faculties of medicine, veterinary medicine, music and art.

Laundry PANO is a laundrette at Hildesheimerstrasse 118 (take the U-Bahn or several trams to Alter Bekenerdamm).

Medical Services There are several hospitals, including Krankenhaus Heidehaus (☎ 790 60), in the centre at Am Leineufer 70. There's a clinic (☎ 304 31) at Marienstrasse 37. The biggest pharmacies are in the pedestrian zone, including Big City Apotheke (☎ 329 90 7), 33-35 Karmarschstrasse, and Europa Apotheke (☎ 326 18), Georgstrasse 16, just west of Grosse Packhofstrasse.

Dangers & Annoyances The Passarelle and the area around the Hauptbahnhof feel a bit dodgy after dark; there's a huge police presence, but use your common sense.

The red-light district hugs the western side of the pedestrian zone around Steintor. This area, along with legal brothels on and around Ludwigstrasse north of the railway tracks, attract nefarious characters galore. They're mainly beggars, but there are also pimps and prostitutes of both genders. Use extreme caution at night in these areas, where robbery rates are the highest in the city.

Herrenhäuser Garten

These gardens, especially the baroque **Grosser Garten** (Great Garden) and the **Berggarten** (open until 8 pm on summer evenings; DM4, discount DM2, free with HannoverCard), are some of the last of their kind in Europe, and justifiably a favourite Hanoverian haunt. Established on the estate of Duke Johann Friedrich in 1666, up to 200 gardeners can be seen toiling on the grounds daily in summer.

The **Great Fountain**, at the southern end of the park, once blasted a stream of water (in perfectly still weather) some 82m high. It operates in summer.

The gardens open daily. In summer, international fireworks contests, concerts and theatrical performances are held regularly; many events are free or have small admission charges (see Entertainment). And if you've never walked through a real **maze**, now's your chance – just don't see *The Shining* before you do it. It's at the north-west end of the Grosser Garten. There you'll also find the **Fürstenburg Museum** (entry DM5/3), with royal treasures and exhibits on the royal link between Britain and Hanover, and the **Wilhelm-Busch-Museum** of caricature and satirical art (closed Monday; DM4/2/free with HannoverCard), which contains the work of Busch and other such artists.

The Berggarten, north of the Grosser Garten, has a great range of flora from a boisterous rhododendron grove to desert and heath plants and a marshland pond.

Tram/U-Bahn Nos 4 and 5 stop right at the northern end of the gardens.

Altstadt

What remained of the Altstadt after WWII was razed and rebuilt, with several liberties taken. The focal point of the Altstadt is the 14th-century **Marktkirche** (1349-59); apart from its truncated tower, it's characteristic of the northern German red-brick Gothic style. Its original stained-glass windows are particularly beautiful. The city has created an entire row of reconstructed **half-timbered houses** that line Kramerstrasse and Burgstrasse between the church and the Historical Museum.

The **Altes Rathaus** (begun 1455) across the marketplace was built in various stages over a century. Another highlight of the Altstadt is the **Ballhof** (1649-64), originally built for 17th-century badminton-type games, but today staging plays.

Historical Museum

This museum (☎ 168 30 52), Pferdstrasse 6, is popular with children. The exhibits include videos (with great postwar footage), and original gilded stagecoaches of the royal family. Downstairs is a section of the city's original fortification, around which the museum was built. Upstairs, don't miss the section on old German cars, with 1924 and 1928 Hanomags, early production automobiles, and the itty-bitty BMW Jsetta 300. It's open Tuesday from 10 am to 8 pm, Wednesday to Friday from 10 am to 4 pm, Saturday and Sunday from 10 am to 6 pm.

Admission is DM5/3 (free with the Hannover Card).

Leibniz House & Fountain

Next to the Historical Museum, the home of mathematician and philosopher Gottfried Wilhelm Leibniz (1646-1716) is an impressive dwelling with a reconstructed Renaissance façade. Out front, walk up the little steps to the Oskar Winter fountain and, if you make a wish and turn the brass ring embedded in the ironwork three times, it'll come true – or so local lore tells us.

Flohmarkt

On Saturday from 7 am to 1 pm year round, there's a weekly flea market at Hohen Ufer, behind the Historical Museum, along the Leine River Canal. It's a favourite with kids and the whole affair is watched over by public art, the three playful **Nanas**, by Nicki de St Paulle.

Neues Rathaus

In the domed Neues Rathaus (1901-13), on Friedrichswall west of Willy-Brandt-Allee (tram/U-Bahn No 10), the star of the show is the dome **lift** (elevator). Open from April to November daily from 10 am to 12.45 pm and 1.30 to 4.45 pm; DM3/2), it carries passengers in a shaft along the exterior of the dome (that's right, the lift slants as you go up) to a viewing platform at 98m. Not to be attempted with a hangover.

Inside the main lobby are four detailed city models that show what has been lost and gained in the march of time (free entry). From the display you'll gain a new appreciation of how extensive the WWII bomb damage was.

Kestner Museum

Opened in 1889, the original building (containing the core collection) of the Kestner Museum (☎ 168 21 20) was rebuilt and restored after WWII, and is now enclosed within the modern one. On the ground floor are rotating exhibitions and a small, permanent coin and medal collection.

The 1st floor is dedicated to **decorative art** from the Middle Ages to the present, including amazing oak chests. On the 2nd floor, turn left at the top of the stairs to view the museum's excellent **Egyptian collection**, including a bust of the Pharaoh Akhenaten. To the right at the top of the stairs is the **ancient art** section.

The museum opens Tuesday, Thursday and Friday from 10 am to 4 pm, Wednesday from 10 am to 8 pm, Saturday and Sunday from 10 am to 6 pm. Admission is DM5/3, free on Wednesday and with a Hannover Card.

Aegidienkirche Memorial

On Breite Strasse near the corner of Osterstrasse, at the ruin of the Aegidienkirche Memorial (1350), bashed by artillery in 1943, is an eloquent steel-cross memorial simply to *Unsere Töten* (our dead); the peace bell inside is a gift from one of Hanover's sister cities – Hiroshima. Every 6 August at 8.15 am, the date and time of the atomic detonation at Hiroshima, a delegation from both cities meets here to ring the bell.

Niedersächsisches Landesmuseum

The Lower Saxony State Museum (☎ 883 05 1) was scheduled to reopen after renovation in 1998. It's home to an enormous display of natural history of the region. It also has paintings by Monet, Corinth and Cranach the Elder, along with 14th to 16th-century Dutch and 17th and 18th-century European works. It's at Am Maschpark 5, on Willy-Brandt-Allee at the east side of the Maschpark, 10 minutes' walk from the Neues Rathaus (tram/U-Bahn No 10 to Aegidentorplatz). It's usually open Tuesday to Sunday from 10 am to 5 pm (to 7 pm on Thursday).

Sprengel Museum

South of the Lower Saxony State Museum, the Sprengel Museum (☎ 168 38 75), Kurt-Schwitters-Platz, is a highly respected modern art museum with permanent and large rotating exhibitions and innovative programmes for children.

The highlights of the impressive permanent collection include works by Picasso and Max Beckmann, Edvard Munch, Francis Bacon, Marc Chagall and the Hanoverian Kurt Schwitters. There's at least one Duane Hansen here as well.

The KinderForum programme for children has thematic presentations that change monthly, as well as weekly painting, drawing and sculpting classes on Saturday from 2 to 6 pm and Sunday from 10 am to 1 pm and 2 to 6 pm. Admission is DM6/3, free with a HannoverCard.

Other Museums

There are several noteworthy museums that have rotating exhibits. The **Kestner Society** (☎ 327 08 1), Warmbüchenstrasse 16, has long been on the cutting edge of modern art shows (for which it was shut down by the Gestapo in 1936).

The **Kunstverein** (☎ 324 59 4), Sophienstrasse 2, Hanover's Art Association, has a great space in the Künstlerhaus (1853-56), highlighting the work of many local artists.

The **Theatermuseum** at the Schauspielhaus, Prinzenstrasse 9, has exhibitions related to ongoing performances.

Out at Laatzen, south-west of the Messegelände, the **Luftfahrtmuseum** (☎ 879 17 91), Ulmer Strasse 2, is a museum of the history of aviation, with 30 aircraft including biplanes and triplanes, and British, German and Russian aircraft. It's open Tuesday to Sunday from 10 am to 5 pm; admission is DM8/4.

Maschsee

The 2m-deep artificial Maschsee, a half-hour walk (or five-minute tram/U-Bahn ride) south of the Hauptbahnhof, was built by the unemployed in one of the earliest Nazi-led public works projects. Today, it's a favourite spot for swimming and boating (see Activities).

Motorboats aren't permitted, as the lake is a prime breeding ground for carp; carp are harvested in time for New Years' celebrations, a traditional dish at that time of year. A ferry plies around the lake from Easter to October in good weather; it costs DM5/2.50 to cross and DM10/5 for a tour.

The Strandbad, a swimming beach, is at the south-east side of the lake; the DJH hostel is on the west side.

Waterloo Memorial

West of Maschsee is another city park (tram/U-Bahn No 3, 7 or 9 to Waterloo) with a 42m-high column (1832) commemorating the German forces who fought here.

Activities

Cycling There are bike paths throughout the

city parks, and marked trails in the surrounding areas; get bike maps from the HTIO. Some hotels, including the Fora Hotel, allow guests the use of mountain bikes. For rental information, see Getting Around later.

Boating From Easter to October there are three boat rental stands around the Maschsee; you can rent sailing/rowing/pedal boats for DM20/12/16 per hour.

Swimming From May to August, you can swim free at the Strandbad at the south-east end of Maschsee. The city runs an enormous Stadtbad und Sauna (☎ 867 64 7) at Hildesheimerstrasse 118.

Special Events

The city's main festival is the annual Schutzenfest during the first two weeks of July, a marksmanship festival in which a 14km parade with horse-drawn carriages, brass bands and thousands of participants, winds its way from the Landesmuseum through the centre and finishes at Schutzenplatz. The following nights and days of drinking Lutje Lage (see the introductory Food & Drink section) are legendary.

The annual Maschsee festival, with drinking, performances and an enormous fireworks display, runs annually from 30 July to 17 August.

The international fireworks festival at Herrenhäuser Gärten is another biggie, taking place throughout the summer months, and Fäsching, the German version of pre-Lenten Carnival, is a fun time as well.

Places to Stay

Hanover's hotel scene becomes hectic during large trade shows: the city is positively awash with people and even the hotel industry approves of the HTIO booking private rooms as a pressure release valve. Come CeBit time, hotel prices quadruple, quintuple and are generally outrageous: singles/doubles for DM450/550 are booked solid a *year* in advance. Many businesspeople stay in Hamburg and take the 55-minute IC train ride to/from Hanover ride.

Hanover has dozens of hotels catering to expense-account holders. Check first – the more desirable mid to top-range places always sell out before the cheapies.

Camping There are three camping grounds in the area. *Campingplatz Blauer See* (☎ 05137-121 00 3), west of the city, has tent sites for DM3.90 plus DM9.50 per person. It also has dorm beds/singles/two-room cabins, all with kitchens, for DM39/49/79, but you need your own blankets. Take tram/U-Bahn No 4 to Garbesen EKZ then bus No 126 to Waldschänke Garbsen, from where it's a kilometre on foot; if you're driving take the A2 to Garbsen and follow the signs.

Campingplatz Arnauer See (☎ 05101-353 4), south of the city, has tent sites for DM7.50 plus DM6 per person. Take bus No 364 or 384 from the bus station to Arnum Mitte from where it's a five-minute walk: by car or motorcycle take the A7 south to Laatzen, or the B3 from Arnum and follow the signs.

Most expensive and inconvenient is *Campingplatz Birkensee* (☎ 529 96 2), south-east of the city in Laatzen, with tent sites for DM8 plus DM10 per person. There's no public transport; take the A7 to Laatzen and the B143 to Birkensee.

Hostels The *DJH Jugendherberg* (☎ 131 76 74), Ferdinand-Wilhelm-Fricke-Weg 1, is 3km from the centre. The price for juniors/seniors is DM21/25 with breakfast. Take U-Bahn No 3 or 7 from the Hauptbahnhof to Fischerhof, then cross the river on the Lodemannbrücke bridge and turn right.

The *Naturfreundehaus in der Eilenriede* (☎ 691 49 3), in the city park at Hermann-Bahlsen-Allee 8, has single rooms for DM41.80 (DM39.80 for stays of over three days) and dorm beds for DM33.80/30.80 per person.

The *Jügendgästehaus Hannover* (☎ 864 44 0), Wilkenburgerstrasse 40, has rooms for DM35 per person with shared bath, DM49 with private bath.

Private Rooms In a situation unique to western German cities, rooms in privately owned flats today play an enormous role in Hanover's accommodation scene (see the introductory History section). By agreement, the rooms are only available during trade fairs and shows. You can book rooms through the city's tourist information offices (☎ 811 35 00; fax 811 35 50; mailing address: Ernst-August-Platz 2, 30159 Hanover). Prices start at DM50 but average about DM80 and can go higher. The booking fee is DM10 to DM20 per stay.

Hotels – bottom end The city centre has some affordable hotel options, such as *Hospiz am Bahnhof* (☎ 32 42 97), in sight of the main station at Joachimstrasse 2, with basic singles/doubles from DM60/110 and access to a shower (DM3). It's sometimes closed, so reserve.

Similar but bigger is *Hotel am Thielenplatz* (☎ 327 69 1), Thielenplatz 2, with some rooms starting at DM85/140. *Hotel Flora-Garni* (☎ 342 33 4), Heinrichstrasse 36, has rooms with shared bathroom from DM60/100 (with private bathroom up to DM130/210).

Hotels – middle We've heard good things about the Best Western-run *Hotel Föhrenhof* (☎ 615 40), Kirschhorster Strasse 22, with singles/doubles from DM130/170, and the nicely located *Mercure Hotel* (☎ 800 80), Willy-Brandt-Allee 3, is worth checking out, with prices from DM135/155. Out at the airport there's a good *Holiday Inn Crowne Plaza* (☎ 770 70), Petzelstrasse 60, with rooms of the usual Holiday Inn standard for DM154/184.

Hotels – top end Some of the top-end places away from the centre and the convention area offer great amenities. Don't overlook the *Fora Hotel* (☎ 970 60; fax 670 61 11), Grosser Kolonnenweg 19, towards the airport. It's a modern, comfortable place with a great atmosphere, slick furnishings and one of the best breakfast buffets in Germany. Some rooms have kitchens, and the prices (from DM195/215 on weekdays, DM130/150 on weekends) include breakfast, a sauna, use of a mountain bike and a tram/U-Bahn ticket (tram/U-Bahn No 8 stops right outside).

The *Maritim Grand Hotel* (☎ 367 70; fax 325 19 5), Friedrichswall 11, has especially friendly staff and service, but the rooms – even its DM1700 per night presidential suite – are a little like those at your grandparents' house: dated furniture, aged appliances and, when you really look closely, all kind of coming apart at the seams. Still, its location is superb, facing the Neues Rathaus, and the service really makes up for a lot of the shortcomings. Singles/doubles start at DM255/308. For the same price, there's a newer *Airport Maritim* (☎ 973 70; fax 973 75 70) at Flughafenstrasse 5.

Places to Eat

Hanover is a nosh capital of Germany, with little eating places practically everywhere you turn.

Restaurants *Restaurant Gilde-Hof*, near the Hauptbahnhof at Joachimstrasse 6, has big servings of typical German food from DM10. If you've had your fill of this fare, try the slightly more expensive *Kreuzklappe*, a Turkish restaurant on the corner of Kreuzstrasse and Kreuzkirchhof.

The Mövenpick *Marché*, next to the Kröpke passage, is about as stylish as a Mövenpick chain restaurant can be, with main courses from about DM18 to DM25. There's an attached snack-food stand and café as well.

A Hanover tradition is the somewhat expensive *Brauhaus Ernst August* (☎ 306 03 0), Schmiedestrasse 13, serving traditional German food in a great atmosphere – with wooden tables and copper vats used to make its microbrew called Hannöversch.

Cafés A very cool place for breakfast or lunch is *Daily & Partners* (☎ 306 42 8), Karmarschstrasse 46 across from the Markthalle. Its huge breakfast buffet (daily from 7 to 10 am) is DM9.99; at lunch it does sandwiches (DM2.50 to DM5) in a chic setting. Aussies should head for *Mike's Place* next door; it has Vegemite (but it's DM10 for a small jar) and a good Aussie wine selection. Vegetarians will like the Markthalle (see the following Snacks & Fast Food section), or *Hiller*, at Blumenstrasse 3.

Snacks & Fast Food You're a fool if you don't spend at least one lunch hour or pre-picnic shopping spree at the *Markthalle*, on the corner of Karmarschstrasse and Leinstrasse south of the Marktkirche. It has dozens of stalls selling a huge array of food, and on weekdays it's a major networking spot for local yuppies. Try *Angelo Masala*, which does great hams, meats, cheeses and bottles of Italian wine from DM6 to DM7; *Vital Center* has freshly squeezed fruit and vegetable juices from DM2.50 to DM3; *Salad Erdal* has a dozen different salads (100g from DM1 to DM2.30), and full meals for DM8.50. There are places here selling sausage and meats, doner kebab, pizza, spices, teas, cakes, bread ... it's wonderful. The Markthalle opens Monday to Wednesday from 7 am to 6 pm, Thursday and Friday from 7 am to 8 pm, Saturday from 7 am to 2 pm.

There's a *Nordsee* at the southern end of the pedestrian zone on the corner of Karmarschstrasse, diagonally opposite the Sport Scheck. Great Greek food, doner kebabs, chicken doner and pizzas are available at *DioDue Döner*.

Across the street from the Kino Am Thielenplatz (the building with the superbly restored Renaissance façade, see Entertainment) is *Libanesische Patisserie* (☎ 134 82 30 0), Lavestrasse 82, a friendly, cheap place doing Lebanese sweets, breads, coffee and snacks.

The *WurstBasar* stand at the western end of Georgstrasse is fantastic: roast chickens (DM4.50/7.50 for a half/whole), cheap sandwiches (DM2 to DM4) and it's all good. In the back there's a good fruit, cheese and meat market as well.

Entertainment

The best place to get tickets, rather than the box offices, is through the HTIO's booking service.

Listings *Magascene* is an excellent and comprehensive free monthly publication packed with listings on music, concerts, gallery openings, museum exhibitions, theatre, film and football.

Cinema American and British films are shown in their original language every day at the *Kino Am Thielenplatz* (☎ 321 87 9), Am Thielenplatz 2, with starting times from 2 to 8 pm, 10 pm on Friday and Saturday. There are always at least three films showing in English; admission is DM8 to DM10, DM7 for students on weekday afternoons and for everyone on Wednesday. Films change every Thursday.

Kino im Künstlerhaus (☎ 168 47 32), in the Künstlerhaus at Sophienstrasse 2, screens a good range of foreign films in their original languages with German subtitles.

Discos & Clubs There's a great combination of film and disco in *The Capitol* (☎ 444 06 6), Schwarzer Bär 2, tram/U-Bahn No 3, 7 or 9 to Schwarzer Bär), a converted cinema that has disco while movies play on Friday and Saturday nights. On other nights it's a good live music venue. *Palo Palo* (☎ 331 07 3), behind the Hauptbahnhof at Raschplatz 8a, is a barn-like dance hall with pretty mainstream music and character that has been around forever.

Gay & Lesbian The HTIO hands out the excellent pamphlet *Hannover für Schwule und Lesben* with listings of clubs and bars for gays and lesbians, and a laudable pick-up section in German including key phrases for safe sex. *The Hole*, Franckestrasse 5, is about what it sounds like – the leather and rubber crowd. The *Schwule Sau* (☎ 700 05 25), Schaufelder Strasse 30a, is men only on Friday and women only on Saturday.

Theatre & Classical Music The *Schauspielhaus* (☎ 168 67 10), at Prinzenstrasse 9, and the *Neues Theater* (☎ 363 00 1), at

Georgstrasse 54, are the big players in town for straight drama. *Theater am Aegi* (☎ 989 33 33) on Aegidientorplatz is home to comedies and musicals. *TaK* (☎ 445 56 2), Stephanusstrasse 29, is the city's cabaret theatre venue.

The city's main classical music and opera venue is the mid-19th century *Opernhaus* (☎ 268 62 40), Opernplatz 1 (several trams/U-Bahn to Aegidientorplatz). Curtain time is usually at 7.30 pm.

Rock & Jazz *The Capitol* (see Discos & Clubs) and *Stadionsporthalle* behind the Niedersachsenstadion are the venues for big rock concerts.

Jazz, world music and the like are available at the *Kulturzentrum Pavilion* (☎ 344 55 8), Lister Meile 4, and at the *Jazz Club Hannover* (☎ 454 44 5), Am Lindener Berge 38. There's a great jazz brunch at the *Fora Hotel* every Sunday from 11 am to 2 pm for DM39. And there are jazz evenings on Sunday at *Marlene Bar & Bühne* (☎ 368 16 87), on Alexanderstrasse on the corner of Prinzenstrasse.

Pubs & Bars Some guy named Bobby has two cool places in Hanover. *Bobby's Irish Pub* (☎ 328 40 6), at Lavestrasse 3 around the corner from the Kino Am Thielenplatz, is a fun place with good specials but looking more American than Irish. There's also *Bobby's Altstadt Pub* (☎ 363 19 47), Am Markt 13.

Another Irish place is *McMurphy's Irish Pub* (☎ 131 60 64), Königsworther Strasse 13, and great beer is on tap at the *Brauhaus Ernst August* (see Places to Eat).

Getting There & Away

Air Flights land at Hanover's sparkling airport (☎ 977 12 23), from which there's great transport to the city and the fairgrounds. City airline offices include:

British Airways – ☎ 778 75 5
ČSA – ☎ 977 28 80
Iberia – ☎ 977 28 90
KLM – ☎ 0180-521 42 01
Lufthansa – ☎ 0180-380 38 03
Sabena – ☎ 728 18 14
SAS – ☎ 730 86 3
Swissair – ☎ 0180-525 83 73

Bus Short-hop regional buses depart from the bus station north of the Hauptbahnhof.

Train Hanover is a major hub for train lines. Trains to/from Hamburg (DM47, one to 1½ hours), Munich (DM192, 4½ hours), Frankfurt (DM125, 2¼ hours) and Berlin (DM68, 3½ to four hours) leave virtually every hour from 5 or 6 am.

Car & Motorcycle Hanover is well situated, with autobahns to the above four cities. There are also good autobahn connections to Bremen, Cologne, Amsterdam and Brussels.

Getting Around

The Airport Bus No 60 (DM9) shuttles between the Hauptbahnhof's city air terminal and the airport, 10km north-west of the city centre, from 5 am to 11 pm, and back from 5.25 am to 10.20 pm. During fairs bus No 69 shuttles between the airport and the fairgrounds (DM15/20 one way/return) every half-hour from 8 am to 9 pm.

The Fairgrounds From the Hauptbahnhof take tram/U-Bahn No 8 directly to Messegelände. It's a two-zone, 15-minute ride. Someone else paying? Grab the helicopter shuttle from the airport (arrivals level, gate Nos 1 to 6) to the helipad at the western end of the fairgrounds. They leave constantly during CeBit and some other fairs, and the eight-minute trip costs DM120.

Public Transport The excellent Hanover transit system of buses and a combination tram/U-Bahn line (the trams go underground in the centre of the city and pop up later) is run by üstra (☎ 01803-194 49). The tourist brochure *Travel Tips for Visitors* is packed with information on how to get around town and to most attractions. Pick up a copy at the üstra office in the Passarelle.

There are three zones: Hanover, Umland,

and Region. Single tickets/strips of six tickets for one zone cost DM3/16, two zones DM4/18, and single tickets/strips of four tickets for three zones DM5/18; 24-hour tickets for the zones respectively cost DM7.50/9.50/12. The HannoverCard (see Information earlier) includes free transport in all three zones.

There's late service on weekends leaving Kröpke at quarter to the hour from 12.45 to 3.45 am Friday and Saturday, and on Sunday to 4.45 am. Night travellers can ask transport personnel to order a taxi to meet their tram/U-Bahn or bus. The service is free but you pay for the taxi.

Taxi Flag fall is DM4, and it's DM2.20 per km. A taxi from the centre to the fairgrounds costs about DM30; from the airport about DM60. The BahnTaxi stand (DM15 per couple) is at the south-west end of the Hauptbahnhof near the Ernest-August-Platz exit.

Bicycle Tram/U-Bahn tickets allow one bicycle per person. Biking is pretty easy, though it's restricted or forbidden in pedestrian zones. Don't forget to lock it!

Pro-Rad (☎ 313 96 7), Friesenstrasse 48, rents bikes for DM15 per day; ADFC Hanover (☎ 348 23 22) does it for DM20 per day.

Lüneburger Heide

North of Hanover along the sprawling Lüneburg Heath lies a land of beautiful villages and opportunities to get out into nature. The region is packed with history. Lower Saxony was ruled from here before the court moved to Hamburg, and royal treasures and sagas, along with beautiful, exquisitely preserved buildings, await you in Celle. In Lüneburg, whose riches came from the salt trade in the Middle Ages, you can see fascinating museums and the largest Rathaus in Germany to have survived from the Middle Ages.

The area in between, along the Lüneburger Heath, can be covered on foot, by bike or in a boat, and there are plenty of hay hotels and camping grounds along the way. This is one of northern Germany's most rewarding areas; at the very least you should try to visit the two main cities, Celle and Lüneburg.

CELLE

- *pop 73,000*
- *area code* ☎ 05141

The hundreds of half-timbered buildings that line the tourist-thronged cobblestone streets are the main attraction in Celle. Many of the buildings, which date from the 16th century, were constructed by just the sort of strict, hardworking Germans who would take time to adorn the façades with inscriptions like 'Without the Lord's protection you need no guards' (that is, guards cannot save you) and 'Work harder'.

Celle has a lot to offer, with a great tourist office, an excellent museum, one of the few surviving synagogues in northern Germany and a fascinating ducal schloss. Carriage rides from here to the Lüneburger Heath are easy to arrange (see Organised Tours). It's a friendly town, and definitely worth an overnight stay – the spooky hostel notwithstanding.

Orientation

The centre is the mainly pedestrianised Altstadt, about 700m east of the train station. The Aller River flows around the northern section of the Altstadt with a tributary encircling it to the south. The Schloss is on the south-west corner.

The main street, running from the Schloss at the west to the Altstadt walls at the east, is Zöllnerstrasse. At the southern end of the Altstadt are the Französisch Gärten (French Gardens).

Bahnhofstrasse connects the train station with the Altstadt by way of Westcellertorstrasse. Note that the large yellow castle-like building on the north side of Bahnhofstrasse, behind the park, is not the city Schloss, but rather the city prison!

The Markt is the heart of the Altstadt.

Hehlentorstrasse runs north over the Allerbrücke to Torplatz; from there Bremer Weg leads north north-west and eventually to the hostel, west of the railway tracks 1.5km north of the station, at the intersection of Peterburgstrasse and Bremer Weg.

Information

Tourist Office Tourist Information Celle (TIC; ☎ 121 2), Markt 6, is an incredibly helpful place that offers walking and cycling tours and books rooms. It's open between May and mid-October from Monday to Friday from 9 am to 6 pm, Saturday from 9 am to 1 pm and 2 to 5 pm. In winter, it's open Monday to Friday from 9 am to 5 pm, Saturday from 10 am to noon.

The ADAC has an office (☎ 1060) at Nordwall 1a.

Money Change money at the Commerzbank, Westcellertorstrasse 8, or the Sparkasse, Schlossplatz 10.

Post & Communications The main post office is at Rundestrasse 7, diagonally opposite the Schloss.

Bookshops & Libraries Schulzesche Buchhandlung (☎ 224 24), Bergstrasse 49 has English-language books and maps. Brandt Buchhandlung (☎ 228 04), Zöllnerstrasse 8, has a similarly sized collection.

The city library (☎ 123 46), Arno-Schmidt-Platz 1, is on the south-west side of the Altstadt.

Medical Services The city hospital is Algemeines Krankenhaus (☎ 720), at Siemensplatz 4, just north-east of the centre. For routine matters, contact the Sankt-Josef-Stif clinic (☎ 751 0), Canonenstrasse 8, south-west of the city centre. The Löwenapotek, on the Stechbahn (see later in this section) is a pretty fabulous pharmacy.

Schloss

This magnificently restored ducal palace (☎ 123 73) is open to visitors on guided tours only but, unfortunately, there are no regular tours in English. If you do want an English-language tour, it'll cost you (see Organised Tours for details).

Built in 1292 by Otto Der Strenge (Otto the Strict) as a town fortification, the building was expanded and turned into a residence in 1378. The last duke to live here was Georg Wilhelm (1624-1705), the last royal was the

The Sad Tale of Queen Caroline

Queen Caroline-Mathilde (1751-75) of Denmark was the last royal to live in Celle palace after she was exiled there by her brother, England's George III. The story of how a queen of Denmark came to live in a German castle by order of an English king is a little convoluted, but bear with us – it's a good and gory one.

Caroline's husband, King Christian VII of Denmark (1749-1808), was a schizophrenic who needed constant looking after, so the German physician Dr Struensee (1737-72) was hired to come to Denmark and watch out for the king's welfare. Struensee did his job so well that he gradually managed to take over the day-to-day running of the country.

Struensee was something of a bleeding heart, freeing the serfs and the press; acts which didn't sit well with the Danish aristocracy, who wanted to flay the good man. But Struensee was smart enough not to push things too far – until he turned his attentions to the king's wife.

When Caroline gave birth to a daughter by Struensee, he was arrested. First they cut off his right hand and beheaded him, and then cut his body into four pieces, lengthwise and then crosswise at the waist. The body parts and his head were placed on stakes to warn the public not to do what he did.

Caroline was placed under house arrest at Kronborg, near Copenhagen, and was only released after appeals from George III, who then stuck her in the disused castle in Celle to keep her out of trouble.

For the next three years she wrote to her brother repeatedly, begging to return home to England. But she died of a fever here in 1775, a few weeks shy of her 24th birthday. ■

DAVID PEEVERS

DAVID PEEVERS

DAVID PEEVERS

DAVID PEEVERS

remen

op left: Town Musicians of Bremen

ottom left: Bremen Rathaus & Roland statue

Top right: Bremerhaven

Bottom right: Port scene, Bremerhaven

MARIE OAMEK

DAVID PEEVERS

MARIE OAMEK

DAVID PEEVERS

DAVID PEEVERS

A	B
C	D
E	F

Lower Saxony

A: Market in front of the Rathaus, Lüneburg

B: Detail of half-timbered house, Göttingen

C: The red roofs of Lüneburg

D: Siemens House, Goslar

E: Idyllic village, Fulda Valley

F: Hanover public park

exiled Queen Caroline-Mathilde of Denmark, who died here in 1775 (see the boxed text entitled The Sad Tale of Queen Caroline).

Court Chapel The intricate, Gothic chapel dates from the late 15th century. Many of the paintings are by the Flemish artist Martin de Voss. Inscriptions along the pews were installed after the Reformation, and are therefore in German, not Latin. The duke's pew was above; the shutters were added later so his highness could snooze during the three-hour services.

On the ground level, in the niche at the far left, is a painting of the Father marrying Adam and Eve and, above them in the triangle, God holding the earth in his hands.

At the westernmost end of the chapel, on the left side right near the glass, is the chapel's prize – *Temptation*, represented by a woman (the New Church) surrounded by devils in various forms trying to lead her astray, but an angel descending from Heaven protects her.

The painting on the south wall – De Vos' *Last Judgment* – is flanked by two others: on the left, *Faith*, and the right, *Love*. To the left of these is the sandstone pulpit (1565).

Bomann Museum

Across from the palace, the Bomann Museum (☎ 125 44), Schlossplatz 7, is the town's history and modern art museum. It's housed in an enchanting series of buildings, parts of which span every architectural period in Celle's history, including aspects of half-timbered, Gothic, Renaissance, baroque and modern 20th-century architecture. The historical museum is in the older building; the modern art collection and rotating exhibitions are in the new wing.

The museum is from Tuesday to Sunday from 10 am to 5 pm. Admission, including entry to the palace's east wing, is DM4/2.

Altstadt

The heart of the Altstadt is the Renaissance **Rathaus** (1561-79) in the Markt, with its trompe l'oeuil stone façade. At the northern end is a wonderful Weser Renaissance stepped gable, topped with a golden weather vane above the ducal coat of arms. On the south side are two whipping posts with shackles, used from 1786 to 1850. Prisoners guilty of minor offences were shackled by the neck to the posts for up to 12 hours; although prisoners weren't whipped, this time allowed their neighbours to insult them, throw eggs and apples, and spit at them.

On the western end of the Rathaus is the exceptional Gothic **City Church** (1292-1308), originally the Catholic Marienkirche, but Protestant since the Reformation. The church steeple dates from 1913. You can climb up the 234 steps to the top for a view of the city (DM1) or just watch as the city trumpeter climbs the 220 steps to the white tower below the steeple for a **trumpet fanfare** in all four directions. The ascent takes place at 8.15 am and 5.15 pm (9 am and 6 pm on Saturday and Sunday).

Inside the church is an incredible organ (now under restoration) once played by Johann Sebastian Bach. It is covered with gold and other decoration, and has carved faces on the pipes. The church opens from Tuesday to Saturday 9 am to 12.30 pm and 3 to 6 pm. The tower opens in summer, Tuesday to Saturday from 3 to 4 pm. Services are held year round on Sunday at 10 am.

Stechbahn

In front of the church, jousting tournaments were held on the Stechbahn. The little horseshoe at the corner on the north side of the street marks the spot where a duke was slain during a tournament; step on it and make a wish and local lore holds that it will come true.

Just north of the Stechbahn, one misspelled inscription on a building *(Von Gottes Gnaden Frierich Herzogz v Braunschweig)* purports to say piously 'By God's Grace, Friedrich, Duke of Braunschweig' but actually says 'By God's Grace I'm Freezing, Duke of Braunschweig'!

Synagogue

Celle's synagogue, the oldest in Lower

Saxony, was partially destroyed on Kristallnacht, but is still open today as a museum (there aren't enough Jews in the area to form a *minyan* to hold services). From outside it looks like just another half-timbered house.

The synagogue is open to the public Tuesday to Thursday from 3 to 5 pm, Friday 9 to 11 am and Sunday 11 am to 1 pm. At other times you can get the key (free) from the TIC, and let yourself in, or organise a guided tour, also through the TIC. The synagogue is at the south-eastern end of the Altstadt at Im Kreise 24, just off Wehlstrasse.

French Gardens

This lovely bit of green at the southern end of the Altstadt is densely planted with flowers and grass and makes a great place to walk in summer. It's also home to the Lower Saxon Beekeeping Institute (☎ 605 4). Guided tours weren't being held when we visited, but check when you're here – it could be interesting.

Other Sights

The **Hoppenerhaus** (1532), on the corner of Poststrasse and Rundestrasse, is one of the best of the Altstadt's Renaissance buildings, with a richly ornamented façade. This street contains buildings from the 16th to 20th centuries, culminating in the ugly Karstadt department store (1965).

Walk a block south to Bergstrasse, stand at the little blue **Trinkwasser** fountain and look south at the tiny alley between the pink and yellow Sparkasse buildings. One flight up you'll see a little box with a window – this was a **baroque toilet**. It's less glamorous than the name implies: waste would flush directly down into the alley.

Continuing east on Zöllnerstrasse you'll pass **No 37** (1570), with its heart-warming inscription, *'Work! No chatting, talking or gossiping!'*. Head one block north to Neue Strasse, whose highlights include the **green house** (1478) with the crooked beam at No 32, and at No 11, the **Fairy-Tale House**, the façade decorated with characters such as a jackass crapping gold pieces at the upper right.

Boating

Canoeing Hennings (☎ 287 91), near the Aller Brucke at the northern end of the Altstadt at Fritzenwiese 49, rents canoes for DM15 per hour. They can suggest several itineraries.

Organised Tours

The TIC runs city tours (DM3, free for children) in German on most days. From April to December, tours depart Monday, Wednesday and Saturday at 2.30 pm, Sunday at 11 am. From November to March tours operate on request.

From June to September bicycle tours leave from the bridge in front of the palace on Saturday at 10.30 am. The tours last 6½ hours and cost DM5 for adults, DM3 for students and children; you must book in advance at the TIC.

In summer there are half-hour, horse-drawn carriage rides through the old city from DM5 per person. For longer carriage tours, check with the TIC; it has a list of about 20 companies offering two to three-hour tours onto the Lüneburg Heath (about DM20 per person).

Places to Stay

Camping *Camping Silbersee* (☎ 312 23; fax 337 58) is the nicest and closest camping ground, about 4km from the centre; tent sites cost DM5 plus DM5 per person, DM3 for children. From Schlossplatz take city bus No 1, which stops 100m from the entrance at the Silbersee stop. There are laundry facilities.

Older and further (about 6.5km) away is *Camping Alvern* (☎ 600 0), Beedenboteler Weg 7 in the Lachendorf section of town, which charges DM5 for a tent plus DM4 per person, DM3 for kids. From the bus station take the KVC regional bus No 1 in the direction of Lachendorf (DM4.50, 15 minutes); the first bus into town in the morning is at 7.07 am, the last bus back is 6.30 pm. They run every two hours.

Hostel If Dracula himself popped out of the spooky DJH *Celle Hostel* (☎ 532 80), you wouldn't be surprised at all. Inside it's modern-ish and clean and comfortable; the cost is DM20 for juniors, DM25 for seniors, including breakfast buffet. There are no laundry facilities. To get to the hostel from the train station, walk under the tracks (west) to Kampstrasse and then north for about 15 minutes to Bremer Weg, turn left and walk the long block to Petersburg Strasse and the hostel's the apparition on the right. Or take bus No 3 to the Jugendherberge stop (DM2.20, every 20 minutes from 7 am to 7 pm).

Private Rooms The TIC books private rooms for no booking fee. Rooms average DM40 to DM45 per person in town, DM25 to DM30 per person in the countryside.

Hay Hotel Ingrid Knoop (☎ 930 40 0) runs a large hay hotel in her farm on Lachtehäuser Strasse 28, 3km north-east of the centre. A spot costs DM14.14 for adults, DM11.11 for kids, including breakfast. From Schlossplatz or the train station take city bus No 2 to Lachtehäuser at Am Silberberg and ask for directions. There are showers, a kitchen and a washing machine, but no dryer.

Hotels *Hotel Sattler Am Bahnhof* (☎ 107 5), Bahnhofstrasse 46, is a weird place with surprisingly pleasant rooms near the train station. Given the neighbourhood, you may try bargaining down the DM68 to DM85 for singles and DM110 to DM135 for doubles.

The rest of the town's hotels are outrageously expensive. Celler Residenz Hotels (☎ 201 14 1; fax 201 12 0) operates several nice places: the *Nordwall*, Nordwall 4, with singles DM85 to DM195, doubles DM125 to DM280; *Borchers*, Schuhstrasse 52, with singles DM98 to DM225, doubles DM145 to DM320; and the central *Celler Hof*, Stechbahn 11, opposite the Stadtkirche, with singles DM110 to DM225, doubles DM145 to DM320.

The new *Steigenburger Esprix* (☎ 200 0; fax 200 20 0), Nordwall 22, is a very pleasant place with singles/doubles from DM120/140, but probably the nicest in town is the *Hotel Caroline Mithilde* (☎ 320 23; fax 320 28), Bremer Weg 37/43, with spotless rooms at DM110/135, and a good pool and sauna.

Places to Eat

Local specialities include Roher Celle Roulade, rolled, thinly sliced raw beef in a mustard marinade, and smoked or fried trout from local rivers. The local hooch is the *très* powerful Ratzeputz, 58% alcohol, brewed from ginger and said to cure all that ails you; and Heidegeist, a 50%-alcohol brew made from 30 herbs that tastes predominantly of aniseed. You can buy both of these at the distillery's outlet at Zöllnerstrasse 20; a sampler of three little bottles costs DM7.50, larger flasks cost DM14.50 and DM23.

Restaurants A local favourite with good food and prices is the *Ratsstuben* (☎ 246 01), Neue Strasse 27, with good ol' German and Celle specialities. The atmosphere and food are good, with large salads from DM9.50 to DM15, mains DM13 to DM19, lunch specials DM10 to DM14.

Up the road, *Schweine Schulze* (☎ 229 44), Neue Strasse 39, is another long-time local favourite (it's been around since 1842) specialising in – what else? – pork dishes from DM15 to DM25.

Kartoffelhaus (☎ 781 5), Mauernstrasse 8, has good potato dishes from DM12 to DM18 and good service.

The town's *Ratskeller* (☎ 290 99) is the oldest restaurant in northern Germany, open since 1378. The food's fine – not spectacular – and it's overpriced (from DM18 to DM35 with main courses averaging DM25), but service is good and the atmosphere lovely.

Cafés The best place for cheap, great food is *H Kielhorn* (☎ 228 15), Brandplatz 2, a stand-up café with sumptuous, hearty soups (like split pea, bean, meat and cream of vegetable), for DM4 a huge bowl. Heaving plates of typical German fare – sausage, salad and potatoes and the like – cost DM7.50 at lunchtime. It's popular with locals, is packed at lunchtime and opens for breakfast as well.

Café Fricke, opposite Kielhorn at the

south-east corner of Brandplatz does crêpes from about DM7 to DM10.

Out on Bahnhofstrasse again, *Café Celler Loch* at No 24 is a smoky, laid-back place filled with hippies; it's open until 1 am Sunday to Thursday, 2 am on Friday and Saturday.

Snacks & Fast Food There are several pizzerias in town. *Pizzeria Molise*, on Pilzer Strasse, has huge slices for DM3 to DM3.50 and good service. On the corner of the Markt and Zöllnerstrasse is a *Nordsee*, selling cheap sandwiches for DM3 to DM5.

Along Bahnhofstrasse from the train station towards town are a number of fast-food options, including *Tandur* (☎ 234 29), with takeaway doner kebab for DM5, DM7 to eat in; it's at No 39, next to the tiny *Imbiss Fölsche*, which does bratwurst and other 'sausagey' things from DM3.

Entertainment

Listings *Celle Szene* is a monthly listings guide to bars, banks, the tourist office etc. Another goodie is *Im Spiegel des Monats*, with the same type of information plus a good street map.

Discos & Clubs In town 'action' on Friday nights can be found at *Flash* (☎ 250 29), at the side entrance of Anja's Lolipop, Bahnhofstrasse 14.

Other discos, also only on weekends, are out, or on the edge, of town. *Incognito*, in the Westercelle suburb in the city's south, has techno and house music on Tuesday, Friday and Saturday nights; admission is DM5, the crowd is aged about 16 to 30. You'll need a car – take the B3 south towards Hanover; it's about 6km from the centre on the right-hand side of the road.

In the north-eastern outskirts, *Club Freedom*, in Altenhagen, attracts a younger crowd (16 to 22 or 25 maximum), and plays more cutting-edge German music. Admission is also DM5. Take the B191 north towards Uelzen; it's about 4km from the centre on the right-hand side.

Theatre & Classical Music Concerts are held at the 360-seat Schlosstheater in the Schloss. Ticket prices and programmes are erratic, so check with the tourist office when you're in town. The Congress Union (☎ 919 3), Thaerplatz 1, also holds occasional concerts. In summer the City Church has free recitals every Wednesday at 6 pm.

Getting There & Away

Celle is practically a suburb of Hanover, with trains making the 17 to 37-minute trip three times an hour (DM11.50). There's also regular service to/from Lüneburg (DM21, 45 minutes) and Braunschweig (DM26, 1½ hours).

If you're driving, take the B3 straight into the centre.

Getting Around

Bus City buses run frequently from two main bus stations – one at the train station, the other at Schlossplatz, where all lines meet. Single tickets are DM2.10, six-ticket strips DM10.50. There are no family or day cards.

Regional buses serving Bergen-Belsen and Wienhausen operate from the bus station at the train station and are run by KVC (☎ 881 18 0) and Lembke & Koschick (☎ 418 59), respectively.

Taxi Taxis (☎ 444 44) cost DM4 at flag fall, DM2.20 per kilometre.

Bicycle Rent bikes from 2-Rahd Meyer (☎ 413 69), Neustadt 42a, 1.5km west of the centre, for DM15 a day. You can cycle from here to nearby Wienhausen; ask at the shop about the shortcut through farms that saves you 5km each way.

BERGEN-BELSEN

It's difficult to overstate the impact of a visit to Bergen-Belsen, some 12km north of Celle. It's the most infamous Nazi death camp on German soil (the largest Nazi concentration camp, Auschwitz-Birkenau, is in Poland). During WWII, 80,000 to 100,000 people were murdered here – 35,000 in 1945 alone.

Part of the emotional impact a visit to the camp has on people who were not directly affected by the Holocaust is that this is where Anne Frank died. The German-born Jewish girl was captured, along with her family, after two years of hiding in an Amsterdam attic. Anne and her sister, Margot, were brought to Bergen-Belsen from Auschwitz (near Kraków in Poland), and succumbed to typhoid only weeks before the camp was liberated.

The 13-year-old's diary was published by her father in 1947 as *The Diary of Anne Frank*. Her story brought people into the life of a bright, idealistic girl, on the cusp of adolescence, trying to come to terms with life in hiding, and it had the effect of humanising the statistics.

Established in 1940 as a POW camp, Bergen-Belsen officially became a concentration camp in December 1944, when SS captain, Josef Kramer, was put in command of the camp's 15,257 prisoners.

The prisoners – at first Russian and other Allied POWs, then later Jews, Poles, homosexuals and Romanian Gypsies – were subjected to some of the cruellest treatment ever perpetrated in human history. Beatings and torture were commonplace; many were starved to death or worked in the fields until they dropped. Prisoners, including children and the elderly, were used for 'medical experimentation'. As WWII progressed, prisoners were brought in from other camps, and as overcrowding became desperate, disease ran rampant. Death from dehydration was common.

British troops liberated the camp on 15 April 1945. The photographs and motion pictures taken by the liberating forces are so graphic and horrifying they literally defy description, and we won't attempt it here.

All told, approximately 50,000 concentration camp prisoners were murdered in Bergen-Belsen. Another 30,000 to 50,000 killed were POWs.

When the camp incinerators couldn't keep up with demand, mass graves were dug. These too were insufficient and thousands of corpses littered the compound. Days before liberation, the SS who hadn't fled the camp ordered a work force of 2000 Jews to begin dragging bodies to mass graves, but on 15 April several thousand bodies remained unburied.

In May 1945, British troops incinerated the camp's barracks to prevent the spread of typhus.

After WWII, the troop barracks were used by the Allied forces as a displaced-persons (DP) camp, the largest of a series of camps that housed refugees from the war, mainly Jews, waiting to emigrate to third countries. Those who didn't find their way to other countries ended up in Israel after its establishment in 1948. The DP camp at Bergen-Belsen closed in September 1950.

The Memorial

The camp is directly behind a large NATO training area, and you may hear artillery and small-arms fire during your visit.

Many photographs taken by liberating forces are on view in the main memorial, and a 25-minute documentary including the film shot on liberation day is shown daily, on the hour from 10 am to 5 pm. Free brochures sketch the layout and provide a historic outline; a fully illustrated guide to the exhibits is available in several languages, including English, Dutch, German, Hebrew and Polish, for DM5; the one in Russian is free. Another free booklet, *Guide for Visitors to the Belsen Memorial*, has an excellent overview of the camp, suggested further readings, a chronology of the camp and the memorial.

The **Documentation Centre** is the main visitors' centre and has two theatres screening the documentary. Pick up booklets and buy guides here as well, before walking through the exhibition area, mainly photographs taken by the liberating forces but also containing uniforms, shoes (the children's shoes are particularly chilling) and other camp paraphernalia.

The **Belsen Memorial** is a large cemetery with group and individual graves. At the southern end are symbolic tombstones and a **Jewish monument**. Enter through the gate to the right of the Documentation Centre.

The **Hörsten Soviet Prisoner of War Cemetery** is at the north-western end of the camp and consists entirely of mass graves. There's a **Soviet memorial** here.

Getting There & Away

It's easy to reach Bergen-Belsen by car but unforgivably difficult by public transport.

Bus There are only two direct buses per day to, and one from, the camp. From the train station in Celle, take the KVC Belsen bus (DM7.50/14.50 single/return, one hour) to the camp. These buses leave Celle at 11.55 am and 3.45 pm. The only direct bus back leaves the camp at 4.54 pm. There are buses to the town of Belsen, 4km away, but you'll have to walk to the camp.

Car & Motorcycle Take Hehlentorstrasse north over the Aller River, and follow Harburger Strasse straight north out of the city. This is the B3; continue north-west to the town of Bergen and follow signs to Belsen.

Taxi Taxis from Celle's Schlossplatz cost about DM30.

LÜNEBURG

- *pop 65,000*
- *area code* ☎ 04131

Lüneburg is a pleasant university town with a rich history, gorgeous buildings and a continuing vibrancy, even though it's not the boomtown it was when salt was king. Bombing of the city was negligible during WWII, leaving the city with most of its buildings intact.

Established in 956, many sources misinterpret the origin of the town's name to be from Luna, the Roman goddess of the moon. In fact, Lüneburg hails from the Lower Saxony word *hliuni*, or 'refuge', granted at the duke's castle to those fleeing other territories. The Luna connection came later, in a deliberate attempt to anchor the city name to something grandiose. Nonetheless, there's a lovely fountain with a statue of the goddess in the town's market square, in front of the wonderfully quirky Rathaus.

In 1371, the townsfolk realised that they could run the mines themselves, so they ran the feckless Duke Magnus out of town and destroyed his castle. But when salt production began winding down in the 17th century, the dukedom (apparently finding its feck) returned: the Ducal Palace from that period is on the north side of the Markt, and on the west side is the town's far more spectacular and wonderful Rathaus (1720).

The salt mines finally closed in 1980.

Orientation

The Hauptbahnhof is east, and the city centre west, of the Ilmenau River. The main sights are between the Markt and Am Sande and in the Altstadt, which is west and south of the Rathaus. Most of the city centre is pedestrianised. Stintmarkt, dubbed 'the Stint' by students, is a veritable 'restaurant row' on the west bank of the Ilmenau and also good for pubs and bars.

The German Salt Museum is in the southwest corner of the Altstadt, south-west of Lamberti Platz. Some 3km further southwest is Lüneburg University.

Information

Tourist Office Reluctant staff at the Lüneburg Tourist Information Office (LTIO; ☎ 309 59 3), Am Markt in the south-western corner of the Rathaus facing the square, mete out information Monday to Friday from 9 am to 6 pm, Saturday 9 am to 1 pm, Sunday (summer only) 9 am to 1 pm. It can also book private rooms (see Places to Stay).

The ADAC has an office (☎ 320 20) at Berlinerstrasse 2, just west of the Altstadt.

Money There's a Deutsche Bank branch (☎ 301 00) at Bardowicker Strasse 6 and a Sparkasse (☎ 288 0) at An Der Münze 4 on the Markt.

Post & Communications The main post office (☎ 727 0) is at Sülztor 21, and there's a large branch (☎ 840 92 7) at the train station, Bahnhofstrasse 14.

Bookshops & Libraries Perl Buchhandlung (☎ 440 28), Kleine Bäckerstrasse 6, has the best selection (though it is a poor one) of English-language books in town.

The city library is just across the street from the north-west corner of the Rathaus, and has a fairly good collection of English literature. The university's library (☎ 780) is behind building No 9 on the campus at Scharnhorststrasse 1.

Campuses Universität Lüneburg (☎ 780) was established in 1946 and has been expanding ever since. Today it includes colleges of education, business and cultural and environmental studies. From the train station or Am Sande take bus No 11 or 12 to Blücherstrasse.

Medical Services In emergencies contact the Stadt Krankenhaus (☎ 770), Bögelstrasse 1.

Rathaus & Markt

The focal point of the town is still the Markt, packed with shoppers and farmer's stalls during markets held every Wednesday and Saturday morning. The Rathaus (begun in the 12th century, rebuilt in the 14th and 15th centuries), has a spectacular baroque façade (1720), and the steeple, topped with 41 Meissen china bells, was installed on the city's 1000th birthday in 1956. The top row of **statues** on the façade is the most important, representing (from left to right): Strength, Trade, Peace (the one with the big sword); Justice and Moderation.

On the north side of the Rathaus is the former **Court of Justice**, the little gated-in grotto-like area with paintings depicting scenes of justice being carried out throughout the centuries.

At the northern end of the Markt, opposite the Rathaus is the former **Ducal Palace**, now a courthouse, and west of that, on the corner of Murmeisterstrasse and Am Ochsenmarkt, is the home of the parents of poet Heinrich Heine – note the sandstone dolphins along the top of the building's façade. Heine, who hated Lüneburg, wrote the *Laurelei* here.

The Rathaus occupies the block running west from the Markt, 111m down to Reitendedienerstrasse. Heading west on Am Ochsenmarkt you'll pass the entrance (tours leave Tuesday to Sunday at 10 and 11 am and 2 and 3 pm; DM5, discount DM3.50) which now houses city offices.

Diagonally opposite the mayor's offices, nine **16th-century row houses** line tiny Reitendedienerstrasse.

Damaged Buildings

Many of the city's buildings are leaning, some more than 2m off true. Over the centuries, as salt was removed from the mines, ground shifts and settling occurred. From 1994 to 1995, parts of the town sank an astounding nine cm into the ground.

The many buildings with bulging façades, though, are due to incompetence: artisans using gypsum plaster as mortar didn't maintain a uniform drying temperature, leaving the mortar susceptible to water absorption through rain or flooding, which caused the plaster to swell, resulting in the 'beer-bellied' buildings you see today.

Churches

At the eastern end of divided Am Sande is the clunky **St Johanniskirche** from the 14th century, whose 106m-high spire leans 2.2m off true.

Other churches include the partially reconstructed brick Gothic **St Nikolaikirche** (15th century; DM2), on the corner of Lüner Strasse and Koffmannstrasse. Behind it sits one of the best examples of the town's few half-timbered houses. At Johann-Sebastian-Bach-Platz is **St Michaelskirche** (1376-1418). The Catholic **St Marienkirche**, a modern, round building, is on Friedenstrasse, three blocks south of Am Sande.

Museums

The **Deutsche Salz Museum** (☎ 450 65), Sülfmeisterstrasse 1, has taken the examination of salt to the extreme. With hands-on and

The Killer Drink

Local legend has it that the architect of the Johanniskirche was so upset by its leaning steeple that upon its completion he was ready to do himself in. Up the hated steeple he climbed, and when he reached the top he stood high with his arms spread. Then he leapt, he thought, to certain death.

But as fate would have it, the architect merely bounced down the side of the steeple, slowing his descent, and finally landed quite safely in a full haycart.

To celebrate what seemed to be divine intervention, the architect made his way to the local pub where he told the story over and over, drinking until he fell off the bar and hit his head on the corner of a table, killing himself instantly. ■

interactive displays on the history of salt, salt production, salt tasting, salt boiling and even a salt tour of the city, salt fans will certainly feel they've had their money's worth – and it has a good section on the history of the city, too. It's open May to September, from Monday to Friday from 9 am to 5 pm, Saturday and Sunday from 10 am. From October to April it's open daily between 10 am and 5 pm. Admission costs DM6/4/5. There are one-hour guided tours daily which cost an extra DM1.50.

The city's **Brewery Museum** (☎ 410 21), Heiligengeiststrasse 39, shows the history of brewing in the city (once home to over 80 breweries) and the art of beer making. It's open daily 10 am to noon and 3 to 5 pm; entry is DM3/1. Beer is no longer produced here, but you can get a taste of Lüneburger Pilsner at the bar.

Organised Tours

The LTIO arranges tours in German daily at 11 am (DM5) and can also organise English-language tours on request.

Special Events

Lüneburg Bach weeks, usually held in September but recently held in June, are a series of Bach concerts in the area.

Places to Stay

Camping There's camping about 2km south of the centre at the friendly *Rote Schleuse Lüneburg* (☎ 791 50 0) open January to October. Tent sites are DM3, plus DM5.50 per person. From Am Sande, take bus No 605 or 1977 (direction: Deutschebern/Uelzen) directly there.

Hostel The city's *DJH hostel* (☎ 418 64) is at Soltauer Allee 133, just west of the university, but the entrance is on Wichernstrasse. Juniors/seniors pay DM20/24, including breakfast. From the Hauptbahnhof, take bus No 11 (direction: Rettmer) or No 12 (direction: Bockelberg) to Scharnhorststrasse.

Private Rooms Book private rooms at the LTIO; expect to pay DM28 to DM45 with breakfast.

Hotels Most hotels offer reduced-price weekend packages, including accommodation, some meals and a welcome drink through Aktion Aktive Lüneburger Hoteliers; contact the LTIO for more information. A bit out of town is the modern *Park-Hotel Lüneburg* (☎ 411 25), Uelzener Strasse 27, with clean and comfortable singles/doubles from DM 65/95.

Hotel Heidepark Lüneburg (☎ 650 91), Vor dem Neuen Tore 12, looks for all the world like a motel; clean, modern rooms start at DM75/119. Probably the loveliest place in town is the *Hotel Bremer Hof* (☎ 224 0; fax 224 22 4), Lüner Strasse 12-12 in the shadow of the Nikolaikirche, with charming, rustic rooms and great staff; rooms cost from DM79/133. There's a beautiful restaurant there as well.

Rooms at the flashy *Mövenpick Hotel Bergström* (☎ 308 0), Bei der Lüner Mühle, are clean and nice, some with great views of the Ilmenau River. They cost DM97 to DM165; its restaurant is in a wonderful location and does good food, but it's expensive.

Places to Eat

Restaurants & Cafés We had a tasty cream of tomato soup at the stylish *Casablanca*, above the Old Dubliner bar on the corner of An den Rosen and Stintmarkt. The service is great, it's gay-friendly and the atmosphere is very chic.

There are three good options on Schröderstrasse, east of the Rathaus: *Café Central* (☎ 405 09 9), at No 1, with huge, excellent breakfasts for DM5.50 and awesome café au lait and Bratkartoffeln; *Schröder's* (☎ 477 77), at No 5, specialises in casseroles (Aufläufe) and salads, and lends you board and electronic games to play while you are there; and the slightly more expensive *Brasserie Mäxx* (☎ 732 50 5) at No 6. At all three, main courses range from DM7 to DM16.

La Pampa Argentine, just south of the Markt on Schröder der Münze, is a very nice, if small, place, doing Argentine beef from DM22 to DM30, and fish from DM12 to DM15. They also have a good range of vegetarian dishes from DM8 to DM14. The staff are friendly.

Service is particularly friendly at *Hemmingways* (☎ 232 25 5), Bardowicker Strasse 27-28, which does Mexican and American specialities, appetisers from DM6 to DM9 and dinners DM12 to DM25. It may also be the only place in northern Germany to offer a bottomless cup of coffee. It also offers a good Sunday breakfast buffet (DM15.50) from 10 am to 3 pm. *Mövenpick Brasserie* (☎ 308 0), Bei der Lüner Mühle, where the dining room and the terrace both have good views of the Ilmenau, has main courses from DM18 to DM34. Its Sunday brunch is, while admittedly bigger and more varied than the one at Hemmingways, is outrageously priced at DM40 per adult, DM20 for kids up to 150cm tall.

The restaurant at *Hotel Bremer Hof* is excellent with very attentive staff, though main courses are a steep DM25 to DM40. It has great local specialities and chicken.

Snacks & Fast Food There are loads of doner kebab and gyros stands on Am Sande. We really liked *Istanbul* (☎ 359 29), on the corner of Lüner Strasse and Wendischen. *Camus* (☎ 428 20), Am Sande 30 next to the Johanniskirche, is a popular student hangout and has good pizzas, pasta and salads, from DM6 to DM16. Another student favourite is *Tolstefanz* (☎ 433 85), Am Berge 26 near Am Sande; with chi-chi sandwiches, lots of salads and full meals for under DM10.

Between Am Sande and Stintmarkt is the inconspicuous *Lanzelot* (☎ 404 81 3), Wantfärberstrasse 7, worth trying for a wide variety of German and international meals, in a neat old half-timbered house with a quiet beer garden.

Bäcker 8, Grosse Bäckerstrasse 8, has good takeaway pizza, ice cream and Asian fast food.

Entertainment

Listings *21Zwanzig* magazine, the biggest 'what's on' guide, is available at the LTIO, pubs and bars.

Cultural Centres *Theater Lüneburg* (☎ 421 00), An den Reeperbahnen 3, hosts drama, musicals, opera and classical-music concerts. There are also classical concerts and recitals in *St Johanniskirche*, *St Nikolaikirche* and *St Michaelskirche*.

The *Glockenhaus*, an arena seating 200-plus, holds art exhibits, classical and jazz concerts and occasional craft fairs. *Heinrich Heine Haus* hosts literature forums, lectures and small concerts as well.

For concert ticket information call or visit LZ Veranstaltungskasse (☎ 410 64) at Am Sande 16.

Pubs & Bars *Brauerei Museum* is a popular place to drink, but the most popular places are the bars along Stintmarkt. Lined with tables in summer, the Stint rocks. You can also have your beer on the river bank – pay a deposit for the glass. Try the arty *Café Caro*, the *Old Dubliner* and, with live music, *Ulous* and *Dialog*. *Hemmingways* (see Places to Eat) is a good place to start the evening; it has nachos, dip and a 1.5-litre pitcher of beer all for DM17.50.

Across the bridge from Stintmarkt is *Pons* (☎ 316 87), very popular for cheap drinks, and a tiny bit up the road is *Clax-American Billiards*, which does American billiards.

Getting There & Away

Bus Regional bus information is available at Reisezentrum Lüneburg (☎ 194 19) at the Hauptbahnhof.

Train There's frequent train service to Hanover (DM33, one hour), Celle (DM21, 30 minutes), Schwerin (DM24, 1½ hours), Rostock (DM45, 3¼ hours) and Hamburg (DM12, 45 minutes).

Car & Motorcycle From Hamburg, take the A7 south to the B250. From Schwerin take the B6 south to the A24 west and then exit No 7 (Talkau). From there, turn south on the B209, and you'll eventually get to town. From Hanover, take the A7 north to the B209.

Getting Around

Bus Buses leave from the bus centre near Am Sande, and most stop at the Hauptbahnhof as well. Most buses stop running at around 7 pm. Tickets are DM2.20.

Taxi There are several taxi companies in town, including Burchardt Horst Taxi (☎ 575 76), and Taxi Zentral-Ruf (☎ 194 10). For somewhat cheaper shared taxis, available after 8 pm, call AST (☎ 533 44).

Bicycle Rent bicycles at the Hauptbahnhof (☎ 557 7) for DM7 per day, DM15 per weekend. There's a local branch of the ADFC (☎ 478 23) at Katzzenstrasse 2. Bike broken? Fix it yourself at Fahrradselbsthilfewerkstatt KonRad (☎ 405 62 0), Scharnhorstrasse 1, building No 12, on the university campus.

South of Hanover

HILDESHEIM

- *pop 110,000*
- *area code* ☎ 05121

Established as a bishopric in the 9th century, Hildesheim grew as monasteries were established; by the 11th century it was a powerful market town. A new town (Neustadt) was formed, and the two merged in the 19th century.

The centre was completely destroyed by firebombs on 22 March 1945. Rebuilt in the 1950s in classic German Postwar Hideous, windowed concrete cubes took the place of the city's glorious half-timbered buildings. In the late 1970s a town movement was begun to rip them down and 'reconstruct' the town's historic heart. It was completed in 1989.

Today Hildesheim makes a pleasant day trip from Hanover. The Egypt collection at the Roemer - und Pelizaeus-Museum alone is worth the journey, but make sure it's there when you are – much is on loan.

The painstaking recreation of the town's architectural gems is spectacular, and the city is rightly proud of it. But the overall effect is that many of the town's recreated streets *feel* recreated. While it's undeniably very pretty, it's just not, well, real. So while you're 'oohing' and 'aahing' at the buildings in the Markt, remember that they are, quite literally, five years younger than *Miami Vice*.

Ironically, the town focuses its attention on these recreations more than on a section of town that actually survived the period: the old Jewish quarter at the southern end, and much of the Neuestadt, centred on Neuemarkt. Here are surviving 16th-century half-timbered houses and a reconstruction of the outline of the city synagogue, destroyed on Kristallnacht.

Orientation

The train station is 750m north of the Markt, the centre of the old town. Kennedydamm runs north-south at the eastern end of town and becomes the B494 heading north to Hanover.

Bahnhofs Allee leads from the train station south to Kaiserstrasse, which marks the northern limit of the Altstadt. Pedestrianised Almsstrasse runs south-west from there and becomes Hohner Weg; these, along with Shuhstrasse, marking the southern limit of the Altstadt, are the main shopping streets. Markt Platz is 100m east of Hohner Weg.

The old Jewish quarter and Neuestadt are south of Shuhstrasse. At Shuhstrasse's eastern end it becomes Goslarsche Strasse.

Information

Tourist Office The tourist office (☎ 179 80) is east of the Markt at Am Ratsbauhof 1c. Get a copy of *Hildesheimer Rosenroute* (DM3), a guide to the city's buildings and their history. The name comes from the tourist trail that is marked by roses painted on the streets of the town.

Money Around the train station are several banks, including Citibank (☎ 369 16), at Scheelenstrasse 13. The main post office is at Bahnhofsplatz, directly opposite the train station. There's a PANO laundrette (☎ 133 78 6) at Bahnhofsallee 10.

Medical Services The main city hospital is the Stadtisches Krankenhaus (☎ 890, emergency room/casualty department ☎ 894 33 1) at Weinberg 1.

Churches

The first thing you should do in Hildesheim (if you're physically up to it) is climb the 364 steps to the top of **St Andreas Church** (DM3, discount DM2). The viewing platforms at the top are on two levels. The bottom level has telescopes (DM0.50) and helpful directional indicators. The second offers the best view of the area.

The **Hildesheimer Dom** is an imposing reconstruction of the Gothic cathedral destroyed in 1945. The reconstructed interior is quite severe, but many of the church's treasures remain, including the almost 5m-high **Bernwardstüren** (Bernward bronze doors), the wheel-shaped **chandelier** 6m in diameter and the star of the show (commanding an extra DM0.50/0.30 admission), the **Tausendjähriger Rosenstock**, a 1000-year-old rosebush. Alleged to be the very one on which Emperor Ludwig the Pious hung his gear in 815 AD, the rosebush climbs the walls of the chapel's apse.

The Dom is open Tuesday to Saturday from 10 am to 5 pm, Sunday from noon to 5 pm. It's at Domhof, south-west of Markt. Next door, the **Diocesan Museum** (same hours; DM4/3) contains the cathedral treasury.

North-west of the Dom is the simple but enormous Romanesque **St Michael's Church** (1022), another reconstruction (1945-60). The choir stalls and Gothic Altar of St Mary are highlights.

Markt

The only thing that survived here was the **Marktbrunnen**, the fountain in front of the **Rathaus** on the east side of the square. The recreated highlights of the square are, on the west side, the **Knochenhauerhaus**, with entrance to the local history museum from the alley behind it and up a floor (DM2/1); and the **Bäckeramtshaus**. They are now both part of the Zum Knochenhauer restaurant. On the northern side of the plaza is the **Rococo Haus**, (now the Forte Hotel Hildesheim). At the east is the **Wool Weaver's House**, and, at the south, the **Wedekindhaus**.

Lappenberg

Lappenberg, the former **Jewish Quarter**, is the oldest section of town. On Kristallnacht, as they let the synagogue burn, fire brigades saved the other houses around the square, including the former **Jewish school** (now owned by St Godehard's Church) on the corner.

In 1988, on the 50th anniversary of Kristallnacht, a memorial was installed on its site: an archaeological dig unearthed the synagogue's foundation, which was built up to indicate the dimensions. They were extended onto the pavement to be a constant reminder – you have to notice it because you have to walk around it. The memorial itself is topped by a model of Jerusalem.

Roemer- und Pelizaeus Museum

The Roemer- und Pelizaeus Museum (☎ 936 90), Am Steine 1-2, has one of Europe's best collections of Egyptian art and artefacts, and runs special temporary shows as well. The museum sends chunks of its core collection around the world, so check to see what's on and what's here during your visit. It's open Tuesday to Sunday 9 am to 4.30 pm. Admission is DM12/7 during special exhibits, DM3/1 at other times.

Swimming

The biggest swimming pool is Wasser Paradies (☎ 150 70), Bischof-Janssen-Strasse two blocks west of the train station. It's a water theme park with multiple pools, some with kiddy slides and rides, saunas and solariums. Opening hours are Monday to Friday from 9 am to 2 pm and Saturday and Sunday from 9 am to 6 pm is DM8 for two hours without sauna, DM12 with; from 2 to 10 pm it's always DM12/18.50. Admission for children at the above times is DM4.50/8 and DM7/10.

Hallenbad Himmelstur (☎ 246 46), at Julianenaue 17, is an indoor swimming pool and sauna. Two lakes, Hohnsensee to the south and Müggelsee to the north, both have swimming areas.

Organised Tours

There are two-hour tours of the city (DM5) in German leaving from in front of the Rathaus daily at 2 pm, with an extra tour on Saturday at 10 am.

Places to Stay

Camping Müggelsee, north of the city near the autobahn, is a beautiful private area with a small unofficial *camping ground* (☎ 531 51), on the corner of Kennedydamm and Bavenstedterstrasse about 1km off the A7's Drispenstedt exit.

Campingplatz Derneburg (☎ 05062-565; fax 878 5) is 13km south-east of the city and open from April to mid-September. The cost is DM6 per person, DM6 per tent and DM3 per car.

From Hildesheim's bus station take bus No 2320 directly to the camping ground (the last bus is at 4.15 pm, though there's an indirect one at 6.15 pm to Derneburg Siedlung, a short walk from the place).

Hostel The modern DJH *Hildesheim Hostel* (☎ 427 17), in the pretty house at the top of the hill, has friendly staff and awesome views. From the centre, take bus No 1 or 4, ask for the Jugendherberge stop, then walk 750m up the hill; the entrance is on the right. Register from 8 to 9.30 am and 5 to 7 pm. There's a curfew at 10 pm. Beds cost DM20 for juniors, DM25 for seniors.

Hay Hotel *Hof-Café Wittenburg* (☎ 05068-376 5; fax 05068-438 0), about 3km west of the city, is a hay hotel with places for DM17.17 per night. Take a train to Elze, then city bus No 2524 to Wittenburg. By car, take the B1 towards Hamelin (Hameln).

Hotels Rooms are expensive in town. At *Burgermeisterkapelle Hotel* (☎ 140 21), Rathausstrasse 8 opposite the tourist office, they're small but clean, though the hotel is stingy with soap and towels; singles/doubles are DM100/150. The best place is the new *Forte Hotel Hildesheim* (☎ 300 0; fax 300 44 4), Markt 4 in the splendid Rococo Haus. Rooms vary as do prices, which run from DM100 to DM200 for singles, DM200 to DM400 for doubles.

Places to Eat

Restaurants *Leopold* (☎ 382 82), Kurzer Hagen 4, has enormous portions of everything, great service and a good atmosphere. Salads from DM11.80 to DM15.80, soup – especially their killer cream of tomato soup with shrimp – DM7.50) and grill plates getting a little pricey at DM18 to DM23 but with huge portions.

Oma Pütt (☎ 134 35 1), Osterstrasse 18 at the corner of Wallstrasse, is said to have good steaks, Bratkartoffeln, egg dishes and crêpes.

The restaurant in the *Burgermeisterkapelle Hotel* has good fish dishes, but it's expensive.

Cafés *Alex Brasserie*, between the post office and the Hotel Schweitzer Hof, is very chic with a good deal at lunchtime: a buffet including soup, salad, a choice from several main courses and pastas for DM9.50. It attracts a hip university crowd. Across the street, the *Café-Brasserie Hindenburg* is a good place with huge steaming bowls of cappuccino and French-style food for DM10 to DM13.

Friesenstrasse, parallel to and south of Schuhstrasse, has several places in which to be seen: it's *really* stylish at *Café Brazil* (☎ 386 05), No 15, with sandwiches from DM5 to DM8.50, chili con carne at DM6.50 and breakfast (DM4.80 to DM9). It's open 7 am to midnight every day and has Brazilian music.

Next door, *Maxim's* (see Entertainment) does Mexican specials like jalapeño poppers – so called because you pop them into your mouth (DM8) – and nachos (DM7).

Marmaris (☎ 133 86 5), at No 19, seems like a good late-night venue. It offers doner kebab (DM5) and good pizzas (DM3 to DM8), and opens to 2 am Sunday to Thursday, to 3 am Friday and Saturday.

Limerick (☎ 133 87 6), Kläperhagen 6, is a wonderful bar and café with a wood-fired oven and pizzas from DM6.70 to DM11.90. Great service, fun crowd. Look for the red phone booth just inside the front door.

Snacks & Fast Food Hildesheimer Pumpernickel, an almond-flavoured, very hard and dry cake is available in some local *Konditorei*; try *Borchhardt* (☎ 363 38), Scheelenstrasse 11, or *Café Engelke* (☎ 532 49), Bahnhofsplatz 5. There's a good snack bar called *Culinaria* in the train station serving up sausages for DM3, half chickens for DM4.50. It has a fruit stand as well. Great pizzas cost DM3.50 to DM5 at *Mario Pizza & Pasta* (☎ 349 87), Almsstrasse 4.

Entertainment

Listings *Hildesheim Aktuell* is a monthly entertainment guide put out by the city (free at the tourist information office) with excellent listings for cultural events. *Public* is another freebie that has information on discos, pop and rock concerts, parties and music reviews. Get tickets at the tourist office or at the venues themselves.

Cultural Centres There's no concert hall in Hildesheim, but the large churches and the town's Stadttheater chip in to host classical concerts and ballet every weekend during winter. *Vier Linden* (☎ 272 44), Alfelder Strasse 55B, has a disco in the cellar and, on the ground floor, a concert hall which hosts many types of concerts. There's a restaurant and a *Weinstube* as well.

Der Kultur Fabrik (☎ 553 76), in an old paper mill behind the train station at Langer Garten 1, has alternative attractions including performance art.

Rock, Jazz & Folk Music Rock, jazz and pop concerts are held at *Bishof's Mühle* (☎ 340 88), Dammstrsse 34. Out of town in Derneburg, opposite Schloss Derneburg (home of the German painter Georg Baselitz and not open to the public), is *Das Glashaus* (☎ 05062-440), Schlossstrasse 17, in the former castle gardening centre. It has a wide range of cultural offerings, including folk and other concerts and experimental theatre. Trains to Derneburg (DM5.50, 13 minutes) leave once an hour from Hildesheim's train station. From the station turn left, walk under the tracks and turn right – it's about a 1.5km walk to the Glashaus – follow the signs. The last train back to Hildesheim is at 9.30 pm.

Pubs & Bars *Maxim's* (☎ 132 21 5), Friesenstrasse 15a, has American beer, drinks and service and German prices. Happy hour is from 4 to 7 pm daily. Across the street at Friesenstrasse 6 is the *Two Pence Pub* (☎ 353 58), which is – surprise! – an English pub. *Limerick* (☎ 133 876), Kläperhagen 6, is an Irish pub with draught Guinness, Kilkenny and Fosters on tap.

Potters (☎ 146 98), Friesenstrasse 17-18, is much more up-market – marble, crystal, expensive. Stop at the beautiful, cosy *Zur Roten Nase* (☎ 341 07), Brühl 27, and get your nose red, too.

Getting There & Around

Train There's frequent service between Hildesheim and Hanover (DM9.50, 30 minutes), as well as to Braunschweig (DM11.50, 30 minutes) and Göttingen (DM22, 30 minutes to one hour).

Car & Motorcycle From Hanover, the A7 runs right into town.

Ride Services MFZ Reisen (☎ 390 51), Annenstrasse 15 on the corner of Goschenstrasse, runs a Mitfahrzentrale.

Bicycle Rent bikes for DM10 a day from Heyco (☎ 380 58), Bahnhofs Allee 12. You can book with them directly or through the tourist office.

The local ADFC (☎ 130 66 6) is at Wollenweberstrasse 30.

BRAUNSCHWEIG

- *pop 250,000*
- *area code* ☎ 0531

The busy, sprawling city of Braunschweig (Brunswick in English) saw 90% of its centre destroyed in WWII. It was rebuilt to look the part of the border town it was between East and West Germany until reunification.

The former home of Heinrich der Löwe, the city was created by absorbing, London-style, all the former suburbs and filling them with solid granite buildings and wide boulevards. You can still today see where the old towns were – each had its own market square and town hall.

Today Braunschweig's population is falling and its importance is waning, but the city does offer some fine museums and attractions and is worth some time. To escape the business-class prices of the area's hotels and the oppressive nature of the city in general, consider staying in the lovely city of Wolfenbüttel, 10 minutes to the south, where you'll have the benefit of Braunschweig's excellent museums without a lot of the hassles.

Orientation

The Hauptbahnhof is about 3km south-east of the centre, and is connected by Kurt-Schumacher-Strasse, which leads to John-F-Kennedy-Platz, and the south-eastern corner of the centre. The boundaries of the centre form a distorted rectangle, with Lange Strasse to the north, Bohlweg the east, Konrad Adenauer Strasse the south and Gülden Strasse the west. There's an annoying one-way system on the east (see Getting Around).

The pedestrianised shopping district, at the very core, centres on Kohl Markt.

Burg Platz is one block west of Bohlweg at the northern end of the pedestrian zone.

Information

Tourist Offices The tourist office (☎ 273 55 0; fax 273 55 19), in the Hauptbahnhof, opens Monday to Friday 8 am to 6 pm, Saturday 9 am to noon. There's a second office, Tourist-Büro Bohlweg-Pavillon (☎ 273 55 30/31), Bohlweg 70, open Monday to Friday from 9 am to 6 pm, Saturday from 9 am to 12.30 pm. Both have the usual excellent selection of brochures and lots of city tours are available (see Organised Tours).

The ADAC has an office (☎ 456 56), Lange Strasse 63, open Monday to Friday 9 am to 6 pm.

Money Thomas Cook has three offices in Braunschweig, including one at Kleine Burg 15 (☎ 406 98/9).

Post & Communications The main post office is next to the Hauptbahnhof.

Online Services Surf the net at Cyberb@r, on the top floor of the Karstadt building, on the corner of Bohlweg and Karrenführerstrasse.

Travel Agencies Flugbörse (☎ 448 54; fax 126 93 8) is at Hagenbrücke 15. Discount travel (☎ 242 72 0) has an office at Steinweg 44.

Bookshops & Libraries There's an excellent collection of English-language books lining the staircase, and Lonely Planet books upstairs, at Buchhandlung Karl Pfankuch (☎ 453 03), in the Burg Passage mall between Damm and Kleine Burg. The university's language library (☎ 391 35 06), Mülenpfordstrasse 22-23, is at the western end of the university campus.

Campuses Technische Universität Braunschweig is the oldest technical university in Europe. There are 12,000 students. The main campus is at the northern end of town, with smaller institutes throughout the city.

Laundry There is a laundrette at Arndt Waschsalon (☎ 577 623), Hinter der Masch 15.

Burgplatz

Landesmuseum The State Museum (☎ 484 26 02) covers Braunschweig and German history from the town's creation to the Trabant. There are great money exhibitions, with notes and coins from several periods, a coin press, and the best notes you could want: Weimar Republican *zweihundert milliarden* (200 million) and *zwanzig millionen* (20 million) mark notes, emergency Braunschweig notes and Reichmarks. There is also good Nazi propaganda and uniforms, and the 1950s and 60s section is a hoot – the Trabi doesn't look out of place there at all.

The museum's other displays – uniforms, excellent furniture and weapons – are all worth the trip and admission price (DM5/2.50).

The Dom In the crypt under St Blasius Cathedral (1173-95), the city's Romanesque and Gothic Dom, is the tomb of Heinrich der Löwe and Mathilde – an Englishwoman who was, depending on whom you believe, either his wife or (more probably) his 'consort'. Inside are some amazing murals from the 13th century, and large stone sculptures of Bishop Heinrich III of Hildesheim and Albert the Fat.

The Dom opens Monday to Friday from 10 am to 1 pm and 3 to 5 pm, with tours Monday to Friday at 5 pm. There are Protestant services on Sunday at 10 am. Entry to the crypt costs DM2, students and children free, but it's pretty much the honour system. Turn right at the bottom of the stairs for the tomb.

Burg Dankwarderode The main attraction at this former residence of Heinrich himself is his original **lion statue**, copies of which stand in the square outside the museum and all over town. Upstairs is the enormous, spectacularly adorned **Knights' Hall**. Admission is DM5/2.50.

Jewish Museum

In the former monastery of the **Aegidinkirche** (undergoing renovation), on Mönch Strasse at the south-eastern end of the centre, is Braunschweig's pathetically underfunded Jewish Museum (☎ 484 26 30). Inside are exhibits on Jewish life in northern Europe, the camp at Bergen-Belsen, remains from the synagogue in the village of Hornburg, including one of its Torah scrolls and photos of the synagogue before its destruction by Nazis in 1940. Other displays are more Torah scrolls, ceremonial artefacts from throughout Germany and Poland, Shofar horns and other exhibits. It's open Tuesday to Sunday from 10 am to 5 pm, Thursday to 8 pm. Admission is DM5/2.50.

Other Sights

The **Museum of Photography** (☎ 750 00), Helmstedter Strasse 1, has rotating exhibitions by local and international photographers. They're open Tuesday to Friday from 1 to 6 pm, Saturday and Sunday from 2 to 6 pm, and admission is DM5/3.

The Gothic **Altstadt Rathaus** at the northern end of Altstadt Markt may be imposing and spooky, but its arches are adorned with some interesting statues. Inside is the Dronse meeting hall. The neo-Gothic

Herzog Anton Ulrich Museum

Braunschweig's Herzog Anton Ulrich Museum is home to one of the best collections of Dutch, French and Italian paintings in northern Germany, with works from artists including Rubens, De Vos, Rembrandt and Vermeer, among many others.

The paintings are on the 1st floor. The 2nd floor houses sculpture, furniture, the most complete publicly owned collection of Fürstenburg porcelain, tapestries and other applied arts.

The staff are helpful but don't speak English. The museum is at Museumsstrasse 1, on the corner of Bohlweg and Ritterbrennen north-east of the centre, about a five-minute walk east of the Tourist-Büro Bohlweg-Pavillon.

The museum is open Tuesday to Sunday from 10 am to 5 pm (Wednesday to 8 pm). Admission is DM5, discount DM2.50. When special exhibitions are on, admission is an additional DM1/0.50.

Infuriatingly, instead of captions the paintings have numbers that correspond to a very pricey catalogue (DM20) you can buy at the cashier's desk. The text is in English, German, French and Italian. To save you money the museum's highlights follow.

1st Floor

The main painting galleries are in the large central halls, with separate halls in the wings to the right and left of the centre, along the building's exterior walls.

Central Galleries In front of the stairs is the *Gemäldegalerie*, home to Simon Vouet's *Bildnis Eines Junges Mannes*; Giovanni Lanfranco's *Die Auffindung des Moses*, Orazio Gentileschi's *Die Dornenkrönung Christi*, and Pierre Francesco Mola's *Bacchus and Ariadne*.

Continue to Alessandrovarotari Padovanino's *Venus and Adonis*, and further on, Cornelis van Haarlem's *Demokrit und Heraklit*, Cornelis de Cos' *Allegorie der Nichtigkeit des Reichturms* and Jan Victors' *Harmann Bittet Ester um Gnade*.

Nearby is De Vos' *Familienbild*; Jacob Jordaens' *Demokrit and Heraklit* and one of the stars of the show, Peter Paul Rubens' *Judith mit dem Haupt des Holofernes*.

Side Galleries From the west (stairway) side of the building, beginning on the right-hand side, highlights include: Vermeer's *Das Mädchen mit dem Weinglas*; Joachim Antonisz Uytewael's *Die Hochzeit von Paleus und Thetis*, Gert van der Neer's *Winterlandschaft*; two Rembrandts next to each other – *Familienbild*, perhaps the most famous painting in the museum, and *Christus and Magdalena*; Nickolaus Knüpfer's *Salomos Götzendienst*; David Teniers' (the Younger) *Der Alchymist*, De Voss' *Heilige Magdalene*; and the Braunschweig Monogramist's (probably Jan van Amstel) large *Last Supper*.

The centre side gallery has a stunning inlaid crossbow; continue around to the left-side galleries, passing an impressive carved oak chest, and you'll find: Van Haarlem's *Die Sintflut*; Johan Georg Platzer's *Merkur und Herse* and *Atalantes Weytlauf mit Hippomene*; Johann Kupezky's *Der Künstler und Sein Sohn* leaps right out at you, and lastly, Louis de Silvestre's *Nymphen und Satyrn*.

2nd Floor

The 2nd-floor exhibition rooms are on the left and right as you reach the top of the stairs, with no central galleries.

Starting on the left from the staircase, highlights include: Egyptian statuettes and pendants; the awesome sculpture *Michaels Sied über den Satan*; a pretty unbelievable lacquer *Kabinettschrank* (wardrobe closet) with clock and writing desk *mit dem Wappern der Herzög von Braunschweig-Lüneburg*.

Continue to a stunning amber *Kabinettschrank*; next to it is a gorgeous perpetual calendar. In the next case over is the table clock, a simple name for such a glorious piece.

The rooms at the end, opening to the right wing (but sometimes you have to retrace your steps and start from the stairs again on the right side), hold a spectacular 17th-century inlaid chess set, 17th-century combs, *palekh* boxes and candlesticks.

The right wing contains mainly porcelain, dolls, an incredible stone mosaic table, and in the last room, an intricate lacquer and inlaid trunk, cabinets and the biggest backgammon set in the world. ■

Neues Rathaus (1894-1900) has a pretty riotous façade of its own, but nothing in town is outdone by the step-gabled Renaissance **Gewandhaus** (1303, façade 1590) at the southern end of Altstadt Markt.

Don't miss the playful **Cats statue** on the corner of Damm and Kattreppeln, in front of the Nordsee, and the lovely **Till Eulenspiegel Fountain** at Bäckerklint with Till sitting above owls and monkeys.

Boating

From Easter to the end of October, weather permitting, a boat-rental stand is set up at the foot of the bridge over the Oker River, at the eastern end of Kurt-Schumacher-Strasse. Rentals cost DM8 to DM12 per hour.

Organised Tours

The tourist office organises several tours weekly, all in German. The two-hour Mumme-Bummel tour is a favourite, with a walk around the town followed by a beer and a shot of Mumme, a local concoction dating from the Middle Ages, when it was used as an antidote to scurvy. It's sweet, malty and syrupy, but the beer cuts through all that quite nicely. The tours leave from in front of the Rathaus at 6.30 pm every Friday from January to October and cost DM8.

City tours lasting 1½ hours leave from the Tourist-Büro Bohlweg-Pavillon every Sunday at 10.30 am year round, with additional tours Saturday at 2.30 pm. The cost is DM5.

Places to Stay

It's not easy finding cheap accommodation in Braunschweig, and because of the sprawling character of the city, it's not even possible to find stuff reasonably outside the centre, including camping grounds or hay hotels.

Hostel The non-DJH *Jugendgästehaus* (☎ 622 68), Salzdahlumer Strasse 170, near the hospital, has clean and comfortable rooms from DM18 to DM26 without breakfast and from DM25 to DM43 with. It's aging: their once-cool swimming pool is now closed. Take bus No 11 or 19 to Krankenhaus.

Hotels & Pensions Book hotels, pensions and guesthouses at the tourist information offices (free service).

Simoné (☎ 577 89 6), Celler Strasse 111, is the cheapest pension in the city, with singles/doubles from DM38/72 with breakfast – but the reception only opens at 3 pm. From here the scene gets depressing, with *Gästehaus Waldschlösschen* (☎ 621 61), Heidbleekangter 16, charging DM60/100.

City-Hotel Mertens (☎ 241 02 4), at Friedrich-Willhelm Strasse 27-29, has pretty standard singles/doubles from DM100/160. The new *Ramada Hotel* (☎ 481 40; fax 481 41 00), Auguststrasse 6-8, is clean and modern with good service, and on weekends the rate of DM139 for singles or doubles is worth a look.

The very traditional *Deutsches Haus* (☎ 120 00), Ruhfäutchenplatz 1, has rooms for less than you'd think: DM135/ 210, and suites DM240 to DM460. Around the same price is the *Hotel Mercure Atrium* (☎ 700 80), Berliner Platz 3 opposite the Hauptbahnhof and convenient to the post office, with rooms at DM138/158.

The renovated *Best Western Stadtpalais* (☎ 241 024; fax 241 025), Hinter Liebfrauen 1a, is an excellent place for a high price. Huge rooms, great service and lots of extras (they'll haul an exercise bike up to your room free for the asking). Drinks and snacks are available in your room 24 hours a day (no service charge), and they'll bring breakfast to your room at no extra charge (although there's a good breakfast buffet downstairs). If you're going to pay DM165 to DM185 for a single or DM225 for a double (DM250 for a suite), you should do it here. On weekend nights, it's a good deal at DM118/148.

Places to Eat

Restaurants The very nice *Vegetarisches Vollwert Restaurant Brodocz* (☎ 422 36), in the courtyard at Stephanstrasse 1, has excellent vegie and vegan offerings; lunch specials daily cost DM8.50, main courses at other times DM10 to DM16.

Java Indonesian (☎ 435 11), August-Strasse 12-13 gets quite pricey at night, but it too does good lunch specials from DM8 to DM14, including spring roll or soup; at night main courses are DM16 to DM19, satay DM18 to DM21.

Good German food and micro-brewed beer are available at *Zum Löwen* (☎ 124 51 1), Waisenhausdamm 13. Main courses are DM18 to DM20, and there are some lunch specials. It brews its own Pilsner and an Öbergälges Weizen in the huge copper vats in the middle of the restaurant. When they're brewing, the whole place smells, well, interesting.

Restaurant Dubrovnik (☎ 430 85), Kohlmarkt 11, serves up paprika-laced main courses for between DM9 and DM15, averaging DM12.

The inevitable *Ratskeller* serves up predictable Ratskeller fare with main courses from DM23 to DM26.

The flashiest place in town is *Gewandhaus Restaurant*, Altstadtmarkt 1, (☎ 242 77 7), a three-star place in a gorgeous setting. Main courses start at DM30 and average DM35.

Cafés *Emigré Café*, west of August Strasse on Hinter Liebfrauen, has a charming, intimate atmosphere with plenty of offerings for meat eaters and vegies alike. *Am Kohlmarkt*, at the Kohlmarkt, is a comfy neighbourhood kind of a bar-café; with a pleasant setting.

Stechinelli's Kartoffel Keller is probably more of a restaurant, but it's great to use it as a café for a quick lunchtime snack of huge baked potato (DM5) or an order of Bratkartoffeln. Its standard main courses – all with huge helpings of potatoes – average DM12. It's at the eastern end of the Gewandhaus, on the corner of Altstadtmarkt and Brabandstrasse.

Snacks & Fast Food There's a good *bakery* at the Hauptbahnhof and *Stehcafé* serve up breakfasts. We liked *Melek-Market* (☎ 135 85), Langedammstrasse 12, two minutes from the Herzog Anton Ulrich Museum and Stadtmuseum. It does small pizzas (DM3.50 to DM8), sandwiches, tzaziki and good vegie salads for DM1 to DM2 per 100g.

On the ground floor of the *Landesmuseum* there's a bistro with coffee and cake etc – try to get a seat on the glass floor over the foundation.

There are lots of Turkish food places in and around the pedestrian zones of the centre. *Dalyan Grill Restaurant*, Friedrich-Willhelm Strasse 25, does excellent vegie and meat dishes, good pizza and great apple tea, all with friendly service. Pick up organic fruits, vegies, nuts and dried goods, in addition to loads of natural products at *Ambrosia* (☎ 417 61), Friedrich-Willhelm Strasse 38.

There are two more great places for salads and the like. *Delicato* (☎ 400 71 6), Münzstrasse 9, near the corner of Kattreppeln, has awesome speciality salads, roast potatoes, heaps of vegie offerings and hot dishes like lasagne. Everything is under DM7.50. In the City Point Shopping Centre, *Gemüse Paradies* has much the same, but with more elaborate, exotic salads (with fish, weird vegies and odd combinations) from DM1.50 to DM5 per 100g.

Entertainment

Listings The city prints the free monthly *Braunschweig Bietet* with listings of concerts and plays. There are several privately published listings rags as well, including *Das Programm*; the more up-market *Subway*; *Extra Dry*, which dabbles in politics and has music reviews; and *Da Capo*, which seems to be the most well rounded. These are available at the tourist information offices and in bars and cafés.

Discos & Clubs *Panopticum* (☎ 181 28), Gieslerstrasse 3, is a popular disco and bar that plays independent music. *Jolly Joker* (☎ 894 28 5), Broitzemerstrasse 220, is a mainstream top-100 dance charts kind of place, but People in Black (PIBs) head for either *ChicSeal* (☎ 185 30), Bohlweg 55, or *Brain*, on Kalenwall, for techno.

Theatre & Classical Music The main *Staatstheater* (☎ 484 28 00), Am Theater, hosts theatrical performances, classical concerts and ballet performances. The smaller

Staatstheater Kleine Haus, Magnitorwall 18, hosts smaller events.

There's children's theatre and educational and fantasy, role-playing games at the *Kinder und Jugendzentrum Mühle* (☎ 470 25 71), An der Neustadtmühle 3. There's a *Frauen Café* here as well.

The *Stadthalle* (☎ 707 70), Leonhardplatz, is an all-round venue, host to rock concerts as well to performances by the *Philharmonic Stadtsorchestra*. Buy tickets at the Konzert Kasse (☎ 166 06), Schild 1a, or at the venues themselves.

Folk & Traditional Music *Brücke* (☎ 470 48 61), Steintorwall 3, is a cabaret and folk theatre. There are small live performances of modern music, classical and folk guitar and even flamenco (but not rock) at *Brunsviga* (☎ 238 04 0), Karlstrasse 35. There's live Irish folk music at *RP McMurphy's* pub (see Pubs & Bars).

Pubs & Bars This isn't exactly the most fun bar town in Germany, but the beer is pretty good at *Zum Löwen* (see Restaurants under Places to Eat), and at *RP McMurphy's* (☎ 336 09 0), Bültenweg, an Irish pub that also has live Irish folk music and music on most weekends. *Kottan* (☎ 40 53 2), Leopoldstrasse 7, is a heavy metal kind of place.

Getting There & Away

Train There are hourly connections to Hanover (DM15.50, 45 minutes), Leipzig (DM 49.50, 2¼ hours), Frankfurt (DM118, 2¾ hours) and Berlin (DM69, 2½ hours).

Car & Motorcycle The A2 runs east-west between Hanover and Magdeburg across the northern end of the city. This connects with the A39 about 25km east of the city, which heads north to Wolfsburg. The A39 heads south from the city.

Ride Services There's a Mitfahrzentrale (☎ 194 40) at Vollmarkt 3.

Getting Around

Bus & Tram Ticket prices are determined by time, not distance; 90 minute-tickets cost DM2.80, two 90-minute tickets cost DM4.80; 24 hour-tickets cost DM7, for families DM9. You can buy 90-minute tickets in blocks of 10 for DM23, or the much more sensible seven-day City-Kärtchen for DM22.

Car & Motorcycle Roads aren't in pristine condition, and parking enforcement is stringent in the centre. Watch the one-way system that kicks in just north of the corner of Bohlweg and Ritterbrennen. From there, Bohlweg splits off; the right fork heads north only up Ritterbrennen and the left fork is south only along Wendenstrasse and Bohlweg. To get to Lange Strasse from, say, the Hauptbahnhof, you have to go north on Ritterbrennen, west on Fallersleber Strasse and back south again on Bohlweg.

Bicycle Rent bicycles at Glockmann & Sohn (☎ 333 33 3), Hamburger Strasse 273, which opens Monday to Friday from 9 am to 6.30 pm, Saturday 9 am to 1 pm.

WOLFENBÜTTEL

- *pop 53,000*
- *area code* ☎ 05331

This charming little city, about 10 minutes by train south from Braunschweig's Hauptbahnhof, is definitely worth a day trip, if not an overnight stay – it's a lot nicer staying here than in Braunschweig. Wolfenbüttel was untouched by WWII, and it's almost a time capsule of half-timbered houses – there are over 600 of them, 300 of which have been beautifully restored.

You can see all the town's sites on foot.

Orientation & Information

The train station is a five-minute walk southwest of the centre of the mostly pedestrianised Altstadt; the Schloss is just west. Herzog Ernest Bibliothek is north of the Schloss. Kornmarkt, adjacent to Altstadtmarkt, is the main transfer point.

The tourist office (☎ 864 87), in the city

library building at Stadtmarkt 9, opens Monday to Friday 9 am to 12.30 pm and 2 to 4 pm (April to October it also opens Saturday 9 am to 1 pm).

The main post office is on Bahnhofstrasse, across the street from the train station.

Schloss Museum

From 1432 to 1754, the city's **ducal palace** was home to the dukes of Braunschweig-Lüneburg. The Schloss Museum (☎ 571 3) takes up 12 rooms. The dukes spent a lot of money on the mind-bogglingly intricate inlaid wood and ivory walls in the main dining room and on all the furniture. On the staircase at the entrance are trompe l'oeuil pillars. The museum opens Tuesday to Saturday from 10 am to 5 pm, Sunday 10 am to 1 pm. Admission is DM3, free for children and students.

August-Bibliothek

This is one of the best reference libraries in the world for books from 17th century. It consists of two main buildings, the Zeughaus (Armory) and the Bibliothek itself. A third building is a **museum** (DM6, discount DM4) in the home of writer Gotthold Lessing.

Established by Duke August the Younger, the collection in the **Bibliothek** exceeds 800,000 volumes, including what's billed as the 'World's Most Expensive Book', an evangelistery (gospel book) owned by Heinrich der Löwe.

To the right as you enter (DM6/4) is the research reading room. There's a huge collection of books in English, and you can request that books on any subject be pulled from the stacks for free.

To the right of the main hall is the **vault** where in September, you can see the original *Welfen Evangelia*, Heinrich der Löwe's evangelistery, valued at DM35 *million*. At other times facsimiles are on display.

Downstairs there are fascinating maps and globes, and displays on book illustrations, with lots by Picasso.

The **Zeughaus** is the main storage facility for the library's catalogue. It's in an enormous former armory with massive vaulted ceilings, and worth a glance.

Altstadt Platz

The city's Altstadt Platz, surrounded by half-timbered buildings, is dominated by the **Rathaus** (1602). Take the stairs to the right as you enter to the mezzanine floor for a look at where the original building was extended.

Across the square at No 15 is the weddings **Registry building** (1736) – outside the front door are two intertwined hearts in the stone sidewalk, and two more on the building's gable. Walk through to a lovely shared courtyard where choral performances are held in summer.

Kornplatz

Behind Altstadt Platz is Kornplatz, home to the Renaissance **Marienkirche** (1608). Its massive organ dominates the interior. The crypt houses the tombs of several dukes, but is closed to the public. Looking east from Kornplatz is the baroque **Trinity Church** on the site of the former Kaisertor.

Places to Stay

Camping Open from mid-September to August, the small *Campingplatz im Freibad* (☎ 298 72 8) charges DM3.50 per tent site and DM6.50 per person. Take bus No 97 or 98 from Kornmarkt.

Hostel The non-DJH *Jugend Gästehaus* (☎ 271 89) has clean, comfortable dorm beds for DM18 for kids under 14, DM22 for people 14 to 25 years old, and DM28 for everyone else (prices include breakfast). From Kornmarkt take bus No 95 to the Finanzamt stop, or bus No 91, 92 or 94 to Westring Adersheimer Strasse and walk back east, about 150m.

Private Rooms You can book private rooms at the tourist office. Rooms run from DM35 to DM50 including breakfast.

Hotels *Hotel Waldhaus* (☎ 432 65), Adersheimer Strasse 75, is an agreeable, traditional but renovated place with clean singles/

doubles from DM85/130. Nicer and just north-west of the city centre is *Landhaus Dürkop* (☎ 705 3/4), Alter Weg 47, with spotless rooms, a pleasant restaurant and a sauna/solarium. Rooms start at DM99/150.

The most expensive place in town is the *Park Hotel Altes Kaffeehaus* (☎ 888 0; fax 888 10 0), Harztorwall 18 on the south-eastern corner of the centre, with older rooms from DM130/170.

Places to Eat

Restaurants *Kartoffel Haus* (☎ 584 6), Kommisstrasse 10, behind the tourist office, has potato dishes from DM6 to DM13.50, salads DM8 to DM12 and full dinners DM20 to DM30. In the higher strata are two others: *Leibniz Restaurant* (☎ 140 4), Schloss Platz 5, which does up-market Italian food, and the *Ratskeller*, with dinners from DM25 to DM40.

Cafés *Vollkorn Bäckerei Brot & Wein* (☎ 297 76), Kleiner Zimmerhof 3, is a wonderful place for coffee and tea and excellent organic rolls and bread.*Vinum Italicum* (☎ 298 47 8), Krambuden 12, is a real Italian delicatessen with a little café in the back. It has great sandwiches from DM2 to DM5, and a really good salad/olive/vegie bar for DM8.

Snacks & Fast Food In front of the Karstadt department store on Grosse Ducal Weg, a van sets up every Thursday selling incredibly good roast chickens; DM4.50 for half, and the aroma fills the whole block.

Salat Fruchten, Krambuden 4, is great for sandwiches, both meat and vegetables, salads from DM1.25 to DM3 per 100g, and lots of olives; there's a fruit stall outside. Across the street at No 16 is *Pizzeria Capri*, doing slices and small pies from the window from DM3 to DM6, and inside in the restaurant from DM8 to DM12. Two doors down, offering among the best cookies (DM1.25) on earth is the *Altstadt Bäckerei*.

Getting There & Around

Trains connect Wolfenbüttel with Braunschweig's Hauptbahnhof (DM4.50) twice an hour. There's a good bus service in town; the main transfer point is Kornmarkt. Buses cost DM2.50 per ticket, or DM15 for a block of 10.

WOLFSBURG

- *pop 128,000*
- *area code* ☎ 05361

In Wolfsburg, 40km north-east of Braunschweig, you'll feel like a real bastard driving a Ford. Since its founding in 1938 under a Nazi plan to produce an economical car that every German could afford, Wolfsburg has been home to the Volkswagen (VW) factory.

The city was built to make that car, and to serve as a model factory town for propaganda purposes: *Mutter* and *Vater* with smiling *Kinder*, great salaries, perfect working and living conditions and the satisfaction of serving the people of the Reich.

During WWII, POWs and other forced labourers were put to work in the factory, which was producing jeeps, and plane and V2 parts.

The 1950s and 60s saw the Volkswagen (also known as the Beetle) grow in popularity throughout Germany, the UK and the USA. Pretty soon VW became a household name worldwide.

Today, though the town suffers from almost 20% unemployment, due to VW cutbacks and relocation of production, and most hotels are overpriced, expense-account traps, it's a lively place. There's plenty of culture and a lot of parks, hiking and biking trails, swimming and leisure opportunities.

You can tour the VW factory, which may well be the largest under one roof in the world: the roofed factory area is the approximate size of Monaco.

Orientation

Wolfsburg's centre is just south of the Hauptbahnhof. Its main shopping street is the pedestrianised Porschestrasse, which runs north-south. Major suburbs include Alt Wolfsburg north-east of the centre, with the Schloss and artificial Allersee; Fallersleben to the west, with the Hoffmann Museum and Altes Brauhaus; and Rabenberg and Detmerode, south of the centre, with access to Hattorfer Holz, the huge forested area packed with cycling, hiking and horse-riding trails.

The factory entrance is on the north side of the Hauptbahnhof. The hostel is at the south-east end of the city, off Berliner Ring.

Information

Tourist Offices Wolfburg's friendly, well stocked tourist office (☎ 282 82 8) is at the pavilion in the centre of Porschestrasse, where Pestalozziallee meets Goethestrasse.

EASI (☎ 291 89 0), on the 1st floor of the Südkopf Center, is dedicated to handing out information on non-commercial cultural and natural attractions in the area and has great staff.

The ADAC has an office (☎ 150 10) at Heinrich-Nordhoff-Strasse 125.

Money Along Porschestrasse there's a Citibank, at No 19, a Deutsche Bank, at No 36, and a Sparkasse, at No 70.

Post & Communications The central post office is at Porschestrasse 43c. Some suburbs have different telephone codes; unless otherwise indicated the main code in use is ☎ 05361.

Travel Agencies Flugbürse has an office (☎ 250 20; fax 151 57) at Rothenfelder Strasse 5. The TUI Centre (☎ 291 15 0) is at Porschestrasse 43e.

Bookshops & Libraries Salzmann Presse-Centrum in the Südkopf Center (☎ 125 39) has a good selection of English-language books. The main library is in the Kulturzentrum, Porschestrasse 51.

Laundry The only place in town that has coin-operated washing machines is the Campingplatz Allersee (☎ 633 95; see Places to Stay), which charges DM5 for washing and DM2 for the dryer. It's open to guests and nonguests alike.

Medical Services The city hospital (☎ 800, emergency room/casualty department (☎ 801 64 9) is at Sauerbruchstrasse 7.

Volkswagen Factory Tour

Free two-hour tours of the Volkswagen factory (☎ 924 270) leave Tuesday to Sunday at 1.15 pm. You'll see many aspects of car production – from the body press shop to the final product being loaded onto trains, and hear some of the mind-boggling facts about the enormous factory, its harbour, railway station, 75km of track, huge car parks etc.

Show up at the factory, just north of the Hauptbahnhof, at around 12.45 pm to get your free ticket.

Volkswagen Car Museum

Ferdinand Porsche (1875-1951) designed the air-cooled *Käfer mit dem Brezel Fenster* (Beetle with the pretzel rear window), a car that could run forever on tiny sips of fuel and practically no oil, could float, resist rust, and be fixed with spit and paper clips and which became a symbol of 1960s hippy lifestyle in the USA.

The VW Car Museum (☎ 520 71), Dieselstrasse 35, is a great trip back in time, with hundreds of cars from the original Käfer to concept cars, including a Beetle balloon gondola, amphibious vehicle and catamaran; the original 1938 Cabriolet presented to Adolf Hitler on his 50th birthday, and the 1988 Passat embossed with the names of 134,535 VW workers at the factory on its 50th anniversary.

The museum opens daily 10 am to 5 pm, closed 24 December to 1 January. Admission is DM7.50, discount DM4.50, DM18 per family.

Schloss Wolfsburg

The castle as it appears today was begun in 1600, but there's mention of a castle being here as early as 1302. From 1742 to 1942 the family of Graf von der Schulenburg lived here.

Today the castle has a museum of the city's history from 1938 to 1955, a small regional history museum, two art galleries that host rotating exhibitions, and some concerts in summer.

Its courtyard is the site of the Wolfsburg Summer Festival in June. Nearby, from May to September, there's also a **Museum of Agriculture** in the brewer's barn on the castle grounds.

Fallersleben

This lovely section of town is lined with original half-timbered houses from the mid-18th century. It was home to August Heinrich Hoffman (1798-1874), more commonly known as Hoffmann von Fallersleben, writer of the lyrics to Germany's national anthem in 1841 including the now infamous passage *Deutschland, Deutschland über Alles*.

Hoffmann was a liberal man, remembered far more for his charming children's songs. The 'über Alles' words themselves were a call for an end to petty fiefdoms – a far cry from the nationalistic fervour they were later used to incite. In fact, the words mean 'Germany, Germany above everything (else)' – not 'above all' or 'everyone (else)', which is what most non-Germans believe the translation to be. The words are etched in the rear beam of the **Hoffmann Haus**, the place of his birth, now a hotel.

Nearby in the **Fallersleben Schloss** is a **Hoffmann Museum** (☎ 05362-526 23), with exhibits on his life and great exhibits for kids on his children's songs – the tree puzzle in the kids' room plays recordings of them when you plug in the pieces. It's open Tuesday to Friday from 10 am to 5 pm, Saturday from 1 to 6 pm and Sunday from 10 am to 6 pm. Admission is DM2.50/1, Sunday DM2/0.50.

Allersee

The artificial Allersee, just north of the city centre, is a favourite spot for locals in summer, who gather on the lake's **beach** for swimming and baking.

Off the north-west side of the lake is **Badeland** (☎ 630 61), an enormous swimming complex with a wave pool, waterfalls, wildwater rapids and kiddie pools, plus sauna. Entry tickets to the pool and sauna cost DM14/7, DM26 for a family ticket Monday to Friday, and DM18/9/30 on Saturday, Sunday and holidays.

Across the street is the **Eispalast Wolfsburg** (☎ 630 91), a skating rink in winter and go-kart track in summer. In winter there are skating sessions on Wednesday and Saturday at 2 and 5 pm, Saturday at 2, 5, 6 and 9 pm and Sunday at 2 and 5 pm.

City Centre

In front of the **Stadttheater** on the hill just south-west of the southern end of Porschestrasse is **Planetarium Wolfsburg** (☎ 219 39), built in 1982 after VW bartered Golfs for Zeiss projectors with the GDR. It's got laser and rock shows, star shows and spoken-word performances set to the stars, like *The Little Prince*. Tickets are DM7, discount DM5.

Both are in front of the city's historic landmark, the **Esso Station**, built in 1951 and restored in 1995 to its original splendour.

Shopping centres include **Kaufhof Passage** at the northern end of Porschestrasse and **Südkopf Center** at the southern end.

Also at the southern end is the excellent **Kunst Museum** (☎ 266 90), Porschestrasse 53. It opened in 1993, and the building, designed by Hamburg architect Peter Schweger, is a delight in its own right, with an airy, modern but welcoming feel.

It's home to temporary exhibitions of modern art. Admission is DM7/4. It's open Tuesday 11 am to 8 pm, Wednesday to Sunday 11 am to 6 pm.

Places to Stay

It's expensive to stay in Wolfsburg unless you're camping or in a hostel. Hotels are geared entirely to business travellers.

Camping *Camping Allersee* (☎ 633 95), right on the Allersee, is a somewhat rundown spot, but it's open year round and has great access to the water. It costs DM8 per site plus DM7 per person and there's a washer/dryer, but there's a 10 pm curfew.

Hostel The *Jugendgästehaus* (☎ 133 37), Lessingstrasse 60 in the centre, has bare-bones dorm beds for DM22/27 juniors/seniors.

Hotels *Hotel Hoffmannhaus Fallersleben* (☎ 05362-300 2), Westerstrasse 4 in Fallersleben, is a charming country-inn sort of place with singles/doubles from DM135/175 including breakfast. In Wolfsburg proper, *Parkhotel* (☎ 505 0), Unter den Eichen 55, has clean rooms from DM110/160. In the *Holiday Inn* (☎ 207 0), Rathausstrasse 1, the rooms (which start at DM145/ 175) are dim and depressing. However, the hotel's location, near the southern end of Porschestrasse, makes it a favourite with business travellers.

Places to Eat

Restaurants *Zum Tannenhof* (☎ 152 33), Kleiststrasse 49, is somewhat hidden and not well known, but it does good German specialities (main courses DM9 to DM13) and has a terrific variety of German and imported beer. In summer it runs a beautiful beer garden out the back. There's live music on some weekends and an intimate atmosphere with good service.

There are lots of Italian places in town. We've heard great things about the food at *Come Prima* (☎ 142 86), Saarstrasse 5, with freshly made pasta and a good wine list. Prices range from DM10 to DM35 and average about DM14.

The restaurant at *Hoffman Haus Hotel* has a hushed atmosphere and high prices (main courses DM18 to DM26), but the food's about average. Better to head to the nearby and stunningly charming *Altes Brauhaus* (☎ 314 0), Schlossplatz in Fallersleben. It's a great place to eat and drink – long wooden tables, a beer hall atmosphere and boisterous crowds gathered round the copper brewing kettles. Killer soups cost DM5 to DM6.50, potato specialities DM11 to DM15 and main courses DM17 to DM23.

The *Alter Wolf*, out near the Schloss, does good, traditional northern German cooking, especially, in winter, the dreaded Bregenwurst (brain sausage). Main courses cost DM18 to DM28, full menus DM30 to DM60.

Cafés *Café Extreme* (☎ 322 44), Breslauerstrasse 198, is a student hang-out, with a big alternative scene; those who don't fit in elsewhere will be here. It's gay and lesbian-friendly, with sort of an art gallery décor. *Frauen Café Rotezora* (☎ 240 72), Porschestrasse 90, is for women and girls only. It's a great source of information for women in the city.

Café Schrill (☎ 715 25), Harttorfer Strasse 23 in Mürse, is similar to Café Extreme.

Snacks & Fast Food The *Glöckler*, on Porschestrasse next to the Imperial Cinema, does Currywurst (DM6.50) and other Wurst plus burgers, doner kebab, shashlik etc from DM3 to DM7.

The two main shopping malls in town are the best places for snacks and fast food. In Südkopf Center there's a little food court with some fine offerings while *Steinecke's Heidebrot Bäckstube* does really good sandwiches and pizza from DM2 to DM5

Entertainment

Listings *Wo und Was* is a free monthly magazine with listings of bars, restaurants and what's happening in town. *Indigo* has more of the same. They're both available at bars, restaurants and clubs around the city.

Discos & Clubs Disco cover charges are around DM5 – when there is one. The most popular disco is *Stardust* (☎ 542 55), in the industrial zone at the southern end of the Allersee (take bus No 1). It has typical, middle-of-the-road dance hits and a very young crowd.

Theatre & Classical Music The city's 777-seat *Stadtheater* hosts visiting performers from around the world: symphonies, theatrical performances and other events.

Rock & Jazz The main car park of the *Volkswagen Werk* and *Allersee Park* are the sites of large outdoor concerts, especially by bands sponsored by VW – past performances included Pink Floyd, Genesis, Bon Jovi and the Rolling Stones. Smaller concerts – with bands like the Toten Hosen – take place in the *Congress Park*.

Esplanade (☎ 129 40), Wielandstrasse 1, is an MTV kind of place with some nights set aside for local and independent music. It stays open very late. There's also live music at the *Altes Brauhaus* every Friday and Saturday night.

Pubs & Bars At the *Broker's Inn*, on Porschestrasse, the price of drinks depends on how much alcohol they're selling – prices are updated every 10 minutes or so. About 11 pm, you can get a glass of whisky for around DM0.50, but the more everyone buys the more expensive it gets. At around 2 am you'll be drinking piña coladas (they get cheaper!).

The *Altes Brauhaus* is a great place to knock back a few – it has a squared-off Cheers-style bar, and a sort of trough area in the back by the kettles. It brews and serves up Fallersleben Schlossbräu, a Pilsner, that's unfiltered and contains no additives.

Getting There & Away

Train Wolfsburg's train station should be accepting ICE traffic by the time you read this, which will increase service and reduce the required changes on trips to Berlin. At the time of writing, there was a frequent service from Wolfsburg to Braunschweig (DM14, 45 minutes), Hanover (DM18.50, 1¼ hours), Wernigerode (DM23, change required, 2¼ hours) and Berlin (DM54, change required, 3¼ hours).

Car & Motorcycle From Braunschweig, take the A2 east to the A39 north, which brings you right into town. Alternatively, take the B248 north to the A39.

Getting Around

Bus There's a comprehensive bus network in Wolfsburg. Tickets are sold in blocks of five for DM8.80, or 24-hour tickets for DM6.20. The major bus transfer point is at the northern end of Porschestrasse. To get to the Schloss, Badeland, Eispalast and Camping Allersee, take bus No 1. For Fallersleben, it's bus No 3.

The city has been experimenting with a free shuttle called City Mobil, which runs from the Hauptbahnhof down Porschestrasse with stops at the tourist office, Kaufhof, Südkopf Center and the Kunst Museum from Monday to Friday from 10 am to 8 pm, Saturday from 10 to 4 pm. Let's hope it continues.

Car & Motorcycle This is a city built for the ease of cars, but that's been a little frustrated by the pedestrianising of Porschestrasse. Nonetheless, driving's the best way to go. There are car parks throughout the centre. The one behind the Planetarium and Stadttheater is free.

Taxi There are taxi ranks at the Hauptbahnhof and at the northern end of Porschestrasse. Taxis cost DM2.40 at flag fall, DM1.90 per kilometre and DM3.50 for a telephone order. To order one call Alstadt Taxi (☎ 777 77).

Bicycle Rent bicycles from Fritz Schael (☎ 140 64), Kleiststrasse 5, for DM10 per day or DM8 a day for more than three days.

GÖTTINGEN

- *pop 134,000*
- *area code* ☎ 0551

Göttingen, on the Leine River about 100km south of Hanover, is a historic university town with a pleasant atmosphere, a lively student scene and plenty of open space. Its compactness and accessibility to the surrounding countryside make it a pleasant place in which to spend a few days between forays into Germany's larger cities. The university's 30,000 students set the tone of the place, making it a much more vibrant city than its size would suggest. This liveliness extends to a strong anarchist scene, which has attracted the attention of police. Nevertheless, the days are gone when plain-clothes police made up half the numbers in the more notorious student *Kneipen* (bars).

History

First mentioned in 953, Göttingen was the scene of some regional politicking until Henry the Lion destroyed its castle in 1180. Soon afterwards, it developed into a small merchant centre, gaining the status of a town in 1210. A network of walls and moats was constructed and improved upon up to the 18th century. From 1351 to 1572 Göttingen belonged to the Hanseatic League – the town owned half a ship – and enjoyed a period of relative prosperity.

The establishment of the Georg-August University in 1734 later revived flagging fortunes. The Brothers Grimm, founders of modern German philology, once taught here, and Otto von Bismarck was one of its more famous students. More than 40 Nobel Prize laureates have either studied, taught or lived in Göttingen at some time or other, and plaques on buildings around town show who lived where and when.

Orientation

The circular city centre is surrounded by the ruins of an 18th-century wall and is divided by the Leine Canal, an arm of the Leine River. The centre has a large pedestrian mall,

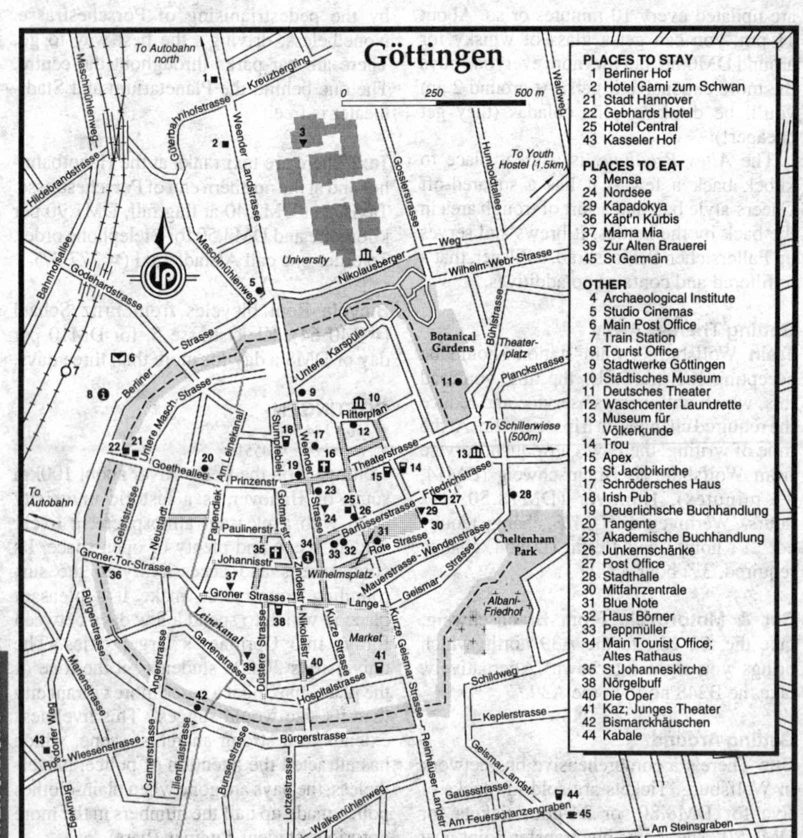

the hub of which is the Markt, a 10-minute walk east of the train station.

Information

Tourist Offices The tourist office (☎ 540 00; fax 400 29 98) is in the Altes Rathaus at Markt 9. April to October it's open weekdays from 9 am to 1 pm and 2 pm to 6 pm, weekends from 10 am to 4 pm. November to March it has the same weekday hours but closes on Saturday at 1 pm and is closed all day Sunday. There's a smaller tourist office (☎ 560 00), with the same hours, outside the main entrance to the train station.

Reasonable hiking and cycling maps are sold at the tourist office for DM12.80 and DM5 respectively.

Money There are plenty of banks in the centre where you can change cash or travellers' cheques, or get cash advances on credit cards. Most banks have ATMs that accept major credit cards.

Post & Communications The main post office is next to the train station at Heinrich von Stephanstrasse 1-5, and there's a large branch at Friedrichstrasse 3 near Wilhelmsplatz.

Bookshops Akademische Buchhandlung Calvör, in the mall at Weender Strasse 58, is excellent for ordering in English-language books quickly – many within 24 hours. Deuerlichsche Buchhandlung, across the street at No 33, also has good stocks. Peppmüller, Barfüsserstrasse 11, has a wide range of English-language books upstairs.

Laundry The central Waschcenter, Ritterplan 4, opens daily 7 am to 10 pm and costs DM5 per load.

Medical Services The main hospital is the Universitätsklinik (☎ 390) at Robert-Koch-Strasse 40.

Emergency There's a police station (☎ 491 41 5) at Markt 3.

Around the Markt

The **Altes Rathaus**, at Markt 9, dates back to 1270. It once housed the merchants' guild and was enlarged between 1369 and 1463. The rich decorations of the **Great Hall** were added during 19th-century restoration work. Frescos depict the coats of arms of the Hanse cities, as well as local bigwigs, grafted onto historic scenes. The **Gänseliesel**, the bronze statue in front of the Altes Rathaus, is both the symbol of Göttingen and its 'most kissed woman'. Traditionally, those who have just passed their doctoral exams make a beeline to Gänseliesel and plant a kiss on her cheek. Nearby is the **statue** of Georg-Christoph Lichtenbergan, aphorist and physicist, which was cast from old monuments to Lenin and Hoxha by an Albanian artist.

Half-Timbered Houses

The **Junkernschänke**, Barfüsserstrasse 5, is the prettiest of Göttingen's half-timbered buildings. Its colourful Renaissance façade dates from alterations made around 1548, and the building now houses a good restaurant. Further along at Barfüsserstrasse 12 is **Haus Börner**, built in 1536. Paulinerstrasse and Kurze Strasse are other historic streets worth a stroll for their fine buildings. **Schrödersches Haus**, Weender Strasse 62, was commissioned by a clothmaker and now houses a men's fashion store.

Churches

Göttingen counts six Gothic churches. The 72m tower of **St Jacobikirche** (1361) in Weender Strasse rises elegantly above the pedestrian mall. One of the twin towers of **St Johanniskirche** , behind the Altes Rathaus, can be climbed Saturday 2 to 4 pm (entry DM1). The tower was used by watchmen from the 15th century onwards – the last one died in 1921 – and it's now inhabited by students, who admit visitors on open days.

Museums

The **Städtisches Museum**, Ritterplan 7-8, has displays on local history, a good collection of porcelain and interesting models of the city ramparts. It's open Tuesday to Friday from 10 am to 5 pm, weekends until 1 pm. Entry is DM3/1 for adults/students.

In the **Archäologisches Institut**, at Nikolausberger Weg 15, you can view reproductions of over 1500 classical sculptures. Entry is free, but visits must be arranged in advance (Monday to Friday, 9 am to 4 pm). When the university is in session there are guided German-language tours on a particular theme on Sunday at 11.15 am.

The **Museum für Völkerkunde**, Theaterplatz 15, has a collection of ethnographic art, including objects brought back from the Pacific by Captain Cook. It's open on Sunday only from 10 am to 1 pm, or by prior arrangement. Admission costs DM3.

Parks & Gardens

Ideal for summer picnics, the small **Botanical Gardens** were Germany's first, and there's a pond and a section devoted to Alpine plants. The gardens are open year round, on weekdays from 8 am to 6 pm, weekends until 3 pm. The tropical greenhouses – highly recommended in winter – open daily from 9 am to noon, and 1.30 to 2.45 pm. The best entry point is from Untere Karspüle.

A 20-minute walk east of the Markt is the **Schillerwiese**, a large park that backs onto forest and has mini-golf. To reach it, follow Herzberger Landstrasse east, then turn right into Merkelstrasse.

Walks

Walking tours, in German and only available in summer, leave from the main tourist office daily at 2.30 pm and cost DM5; group tours in English cost DM75. A better idea is to get hold of the excellent brochure *A Walk through the City* (DM2) and do it yourself.

City Wall Highly recommended is a walk along the 18th-century city wall. It takes less than an hour, and the best starting point is the entrance near Cheltenham Park. This takes you past **Bismarckhäuschen** (Bismarck's Cottage) where, tradition holds, the town fathers banished 18-year-old Otto for rowdy behaviour in 1833. While this incident might be a case of rewriting history; the future Iron Chancellor was, however, later found guilty of the more serious offence of witnessing an illegal duel. The cottage opens Tuesday from 10 am to 1 pm and Thursday from 3 to 5 pm (admission free). Nearby are two old **water mills**, one of which operated until 1945. The walk ends near the **Deutsches Theater**.

Forest The Stadtwald is a 20-minute walk east from Wilhelmsplatz. One place to enter is from Borheckstrasse (near where Herzberger Landstrasse forms a hairpin bend). A bitumen track open to hikers and cyclists winds towards Hainholzhof-Kehr, a hotel and restaurant (see Places to Stay) another 45 minutes away. Another option is to take bus A to Hainholzhof-Kehr from Jüdenstrasse and walk north-west back through the forest into town. From the terminus a path leads to **Bismarckturm**. This stone tower has spectacular views over the Leine Valley and opens April to September on weekends and public holidays from 11 am to 6 pm. Admission costs DM2/0.50 adults/ children.

Places to Stay

Camping *Camping am Hohen Hagen* (☎ 05502-214 7), about 10km west of town in Dransfeld, is reached by bus No 120 from the train station. Open year round, it charges DM10.50 per tent site (including car parking) and DM8.50/4.20 per adult/child. The per person charges are 20% less in winter.

Hostel The *Jugendherberge Göttingen* (☎ 576 22), Habichtweg 2, has beds in single, double and dormitory rooms for DM22/27 juniors/seniors. It also has a laundry and rental bicycles (DM9 a day, book ahead). To reach the hostel, cross Berliner Strasse from the Hauptbahnhof, go south to Groner-Tor-Strasse and take bus No 6 from the stop across Groner-Tor-Strasse to the Jugendherberge stop.

Hotels All prices quoted here include breakfast unless otherwise stated. *Hotel Garni Zum Schwan* (☎ 448 63), Weender Landstrasse 23, has basic singles/doubles for

DM46/73 without shower and WC, DM56/87 with facilities. *Berliner Hof* (☎ 383 32 0), at No 43, has clean singles/doubles with shower from DM70/98. Some 10 minutes on foot south of the train station and in a quieter area at Rosdorfer Weg 26, *Kasseler Hof* (☎ 720 81) has homely, well priced rooms from DM53/95. Apartments with cooking facilities are available for a minimum of four days at DM65/95. Check-in, after 2 pm on Sunday, should be arranged in advance.

More expensive but still good value is *Hotel Central* (☎ 571 57; fax 571 05), Jüdenstrasse 12, which has singles/doubles with shared facilities for DM75/110, with shower for DM90/ 120, and with bath and WC for DM180/250.

Landgasthaus Lockemann (☎ 209 02 0), Im Beeke 1, 3km east of Göttingen in Herberhausen, has basic singles/doubles from DM45/70, doubles with shower and WC from DM100. Bus No 10 from Jüdenstrasse stops nearby. There's an excellent restaurant here (see Places to Eat).

Less convenient is *Hotel-Restaurant-Café Hainholzhof-Kehr* (☎ 750 08), in the forest at Borheckstrasse 66. Singles/doubles with shared facilities go for DM65/85, DM85/110 with shower and WC. Take bus A from Jüdenstrasse (on the corner of Barfüsserstrasse) to the terminus, or the more frequent bus No 11 from the Hauptbahnhof to the Vor dem Walde stop. Continue east along Schöneberger Strasse to Vor dem Walde itself, which leads to the hotel, a 15-minute walk away. Be warned that the Hainholzhof-Kehr is often booked out on weekends.

For a spot of luxury try *Gebhards Hotel* (☎ 496 80; fax 49 68 110), Goetheallee 22-23, with singles/ doubles from DM140/190; or the *Stadt Hannover* (☎ 459 57; fax 454 70), Goetheallee 21, where rooms start at DM98/145.

Places to Eat

The *Nordsee* chain of fish restaurants and snack bars offers good value at lunchtime, with herring rolls for around DM4.50, meals about DM12. You'll find one at Weender Strasse 50. Almost directly opposite at No 25 is *Cron & Lanz*, a quality café with delicious confectionery and cakes. The best value in town for students is the *Mensa*, the university cafeteria. There is one next to the Blue Note disco at Wilhelmsplatz 3, and a second on campus at Platz der Göttinger Sieben.

Kapadokya, on Wilhelmsplatz, serves excellent Turkish dishes (some vegetarian) for under DM20, amid kitsch plaster bas-reliefs. Similarly priced is the very Bavarian *Zur Alten Brauerei*, in a courtyard behind the half-timbered house at Düstere Strasse 20 (under the gallery walkover and to the right). The restaurant is at No 20a.

Käpt'n Kürbis, Groner-Tor-Strasse 16, is a lunchtime health-food restaurant with main dishes for around DM12.

Mama Mia, Groner Strasse 53, is one of the better Italian eateries in Göttingen. Expect to pay upwards of DM20 for main meat dishes. It's best to book for the French restaurant *St Germain* (☎ 464 64) at Geismar Landstrasse 21a. Open evenings only, it has fixed-price menus from DM23 to DM45. A popular place for quality German cuisine is *Junkernschünke*, Barfüsserstrasse 5, where many dishes cost around DM22. The restaurant at the *Landgasthaus Lockemann* (see Places to Stay) specialises in game. Expect to pay between DM20 and DM30 for main courses.

Entertainment

Listings The free magazine *Character* has limited listings in German of what's on in town. Brochures from the tourist office are good sources of information as is the *Göttinger Tageblatt*, the local newspaper.

Cinema The three *Studio* cinemas in the Iduna Zentrum, Weender Landstrasse 3, screen films in English.

Discos & Clubs Göttingen has no shortage of clubs. Live-music venues don't get going until about 10 pm, discos much later. *Blue Note*, Wilhelmsplatz 3, regularly has music and live bands. The *Irish Pub*, Mühlenstrasse 4, is an old favourite with cover bands and free admission. *Nörgelbuff*, Groner Strasse

23, is a small live venue with an emphasis on blues.

Tangente, Goetheallee 8a, is the top disco in town for a slightly older student crowd. *Die Oper*, upstairs at Nikolaistrasse 1b, is young, restless and very hip. There are a couple of lively bars downstairs.

Theatre & Classical Music The *Deutsches Theater*, Theaterplatz 11, and the innovative *Junges Theater*, Hospitalstrasse 6, are the two big venues for German-language plays. Classical-music concerts are held regularly in the *Stadthalle* at Albaniplatz and in the *Aula*, a beautifully appointed hall upstairs on Wilhelmsplatz. The Händel Festival, held over several days in late May and early June, is a must for those keen on music. Enquire about tickets at the tourist office.

Pubs & Bars *Apex*, Burgstrasse 46, opens at 5.30 pm and offers good food, drink and company in a warm atmosphere. It is also an art gallery and a performance area upstairs (mainly comedy, readings and music). *Trou*, 30m along Burgstrasse towards Wilhelmsplatz, is a small Gothic cellar where students meet to drink. *Kaz*, Hospitalstrasse 6, shares a 19th-century building with the Junges Theater. On summer evenings the square, which is also a fruit and vegetable market (year round on Tuesday, Thursday and Saturday from 7 am to 1 pm), turns into a lively beer garden. *Kabale*, Geismar Landstrasse 19, is another cosy place. Downstairs is the *Theaterkeller*, a nocturnal haunt for anarchists.

Getting There & Away

Bus Buses leave from the terminus alongside the Hauptbahnhof to surrounding towns and the Harz Mountains. Timetables and information can be obtained from the Regionalbus Braunschweig (RBB; ☎ 488 01 70), Bahnhofplatz 2.

Train Frequent EC, ICE and IR train services link Göttingen with many towns. There are frequent direct ICE services to Kassel (DM26; 18 minutes), Frankfurt (DM87, 1¾ hours), Munich (DM161; 3½ hours), Stuttgart (DM136; three hours), Hildesheim (DM35; 30 minutes), Hanover (DM46; 30 minutes), Hamburg (DM94; 1¾ hours), Magdeburg (DM65; 1¾ hours) and Berlin (DM106; three hours). Indirect regional services run to Halle via Eichenberg (DM47; three hours) and to Weimar via Bebra (DM52; three hours). Regional trains leave hourly for Goslar (DM20; one hour). All prices are one way.

Car & Motorcycle Göttingen is on the A7 running north-south. The closest entrance, often used by hitchhikers, is 3km south-west along Kasseler Landstrasse, an extension of Groner Landstrasse. The Fairy-Tale Road (B27) runs south-west to the Weser River and north-east to the Harz Mountains.

Ride Services The Mitfahrzentrale (☎ 194 44) is at Burgstrasse 7 (on Wilhelmsplatz). Sample prices include: Berlin DM32; Hamburg DM26; Frankfurt DM26.

Getting Around

Bus Single-journey tickets can be bought on board for DM2.60; six tickets cost DM11.80 when purchased from Stadtwerke Göttingen (☎ 301 39), the city works office which runs the buses, at Weender Strasse 80. You can change buses within one hour in any one direction.

Taxi There's a taxi rank alongside the Altes Rathaus at Markt 9. To book a taxi by phone ring ☎ 340 34. PUK Minicar (☎ 484 84 8) is good value, especially for women travelling either alone or with children after 8 pm (9 pm in summer): it gives a night discount of about DM3.50.

Bicycle Göttingen is a cyclist's dream, with plenty of bike lanes throughout the city. At the train station, Fahrrad Parkhaus am Bahnhof (☎ 599 94; open daily) rents bicycles for DM12 to DM15 per 24 hours. The Jugendherberge Göttingen (see Places to Stay) also rents bikes.

West of Hanover

OSNABRÜCK

- *pop 162,000*
- *area code* ☎ 0541

Osnabrück is a bustling modern university town that made its major mark on history in the 17th century. Together with Münster, about 60km to the south, it co-hosted the negotiations that brought about the Peace of Westphalia ending the devastating Thirty Years' War (1618-48).

Osnabrück has origins as a bishopric established by Charlemagne after he defeated the Saxon duke, Widukind, in 783. The battle, the last between Franks and Saxons, took place nearby. It wasn't just a military victory, but also a triumph of Christianity over paganism: two years after this encounter Widukind had himself baptised.

The Middle Ages brought relative wealth to Osnabrück as the town became an early and important member of the Hanseatic League. Most of the half-timbered and stone merchants' homes in the Altstadt date back to this era and are the few that survived the blazes that swept through Osnabrück during WWII. War and its devastation also played a major role in the works of native son, Erich Maria Remarque (1898-1970), who gained fame with his novel *All Quiet on the Western Front*.

Orientation

Osnabrück's egg-shaped city centre grew up within the boundaries of the old fortifications and is divided into the northern Altstadt and the southern Neustadt, with the Neumarkt at its centre. The Hauptbahnhof – an impressive two-level construction from the last century – is on the eastern edge of the city centre. It's about a 20-minute walk from here to the Altstadt, where most sights are clustered. The little Hase River traverses the centre in a north-south direction.

Information

Tourist Office The tourist office (☎ 323 22 02; fax 323 27 09), Krahnstrasse 58 near the Markt, opens weekdays from 9 am to 6 pm and Saturday from 9.30 am to 1 pm.

Money Most of Osnabrück's banks exchange money, including the Sparkasse, Krahnstrasse 9-10, near the tourist office. The main branch is at Wittekindstrasse 2-4.

Post & Communications Look for the post office as you exit the Hauptbahnhof; it's just south on Theodor-Heuss-Platz.

Laundry The large, central laundrette on the corner of Johannistorwall and Kommenderiestrasse is open daily from 6 am to 11 pm. A wash costs DM7, plus DM1 for the spin and another DM1 for the dryer.

Emergency Police headquarters (☎ 327 1) are at Kollegienwall 7.

Markt & Around

The two buildings that dominate the relatively small Markt are the Rathaus on its western side and the Marienkirche on its northern side. The façade of the **Rathaus** is festooned with neo-Gothic sandstone sculptures of Holy Roman emperors; the one above the portal is Charlemagne. It was from the town hall's double-sided open stairs that the Peace of Westphalia was proclaimed on 25 October 1648.

The peace negotiations took place in the **Friedenssaal** (peace hall), a stark rectangular room dominated by a flamboyant wrought-iron chandelier. Long wooden benches line the walls, which are decorated with portraits of the peace negotiators. The room is on the left as you enter the Rathaus. On the right is the small **Schatzkammer** (treasure chamber) with medieval manuscripts granting various town rights and several goblets including the impressive late-13th century *Kaiserpokal*. The figurine inside the goblet was originally the knob of the goblet lid, but it migrated when replaced by a bigger figure of Charlemagne.

The four richly ornamented cross gables of the **Marienkirche** loom above the square. The church was first mentioned in 1177, but the current design dates back to the early 14th century. It was completely burned down in WWII and has been painstakingly rebuilt. Of note inside are a baptismal font from the workshop of Johann Brabender whose reliefs show scenes from the life of Christ, and a triumphal cross from 1320.

Opposite the Marienkirche, a small exhibit on **Erich Maria Remarque** (closed Monday and at lunchtime; free) chronicles the writer's life and work with photos, documents and a copy of his death mask.

The streets south of the Markt have various historic houses that provide glimpses of what the Altstadt must have looked like before WWII. At Bierstrasse 24 is the baroque **Walhalla** (today a hotel), with a portal flanked by cheeky cherubs. At Krahnstrasse 4 you'll find a beautiful **half-timbered house** (1533) with Café Läer taking up the ground floor (see Places to Eat). Best of the bunch, though, is the Renaissance **Haus Willmann** (1586), at No 7, with its carved relief of Adam and Eve.

The western boundary of the Altstadt is the **Heger Tor**, a former town gate turned triumphal arch. Nearby at Heger-Tor-Wall 28 is the **Kulturgeschichtliche Museum** (Cultural History Museum; open Tuesday to Saturday from 9 am to 5 pm, Sunday from 10 am; DM1), which provides insights into local and regional history. A short walk north along Natruper-Tor-Wall gets you to the Bocksturm, also formerly part of the fortification, which contains a hair-raising collection of torture implements – Osnabrück was a centre of witch persecution – and a unique wooden crate used to imprison an unpopular count in the 15th century.

Dom St Peter

The bulky cathedral on Domplatz in the eastern Altstadt is distinctive for its two towers; the slender Romanesque tower dwarfed by the much bigger Gothic one. This incongruous assembly does not reflect the idiosyncracy of some medieval architect but, rather, the need for a sturdy tower to house the new and bigger church bells. The cathedral interior contains a number of interesting art treasures. In the chapel immediately on your left as you enter is the 13th-century bronze **baptismal font** in the shape of a pail perched on feet so that a little fire could be built underneath to heat the water.

In the central nave is the **triumphal cross** (1230), at 6.8m by 4.2m the largest in Lower Saxony. On the wall in the north transept is a little stone **sculpture** of Mary holding the Infant Jesus carved by the Master of Osnabrück in 1520. She's depicted, as usual, smiling angelically while stomping on a serpent, a symbol of evil from the Garden of Eden. Also, take a look at the **wrought-iron gates** with their unusual vanishing point perspective at the entrance to the square ambulatory, especially the one in the south transept. More treasures can be admired in the **Diözesan Museum** (open Tuesday to Friday from 10 am to 1 pm and 3 to 5 pm, weekends from 11 am to 2 pm; DM1) reached via the cloister.

Places to Stay

Camping Osnabrück's municipal *Campingplatz Niedersachsenhof* (☎ 772 26), Nordstrasse 109, is a modern, clean facility, about 5km north-east of the city centre (take bus No 73 to the Nordstrasse stop, then walk about 400m).

Hostel The nice 145-bed *Jugendgästehaus* (☎ 542 84; 567 83) is at Iburger Strasse 183a, about 2km south of the city centre next to a forest. Bed & breakfast costs DM26/31 for juniors/seniors. From the train station, take bus No 8, 13, 15, 62 or 83 to Neumarkt, then bus No 23 or 27 and get off at Kinderhospital.

Pensions & Hotels The tourist office has a free room-reservation service. Prices quoted below are for rooms with private bath.

One of the cheapest options is *Intour Hotel* (☎ 466 43), Maschstrasse 10, whose friendly owner charges DM75/98 for homely singles/doubles. Also affordable is the central *Dom Hotel* (☎ 215 54), Kleine Domsfreiheit 5, where rooms cost DM75/120. Somewhat more pricey and occasionally

DAVID PEEVERS

MARIE OAMEK

DAVID PEEVERS

DAVID PEEVERS

A	
B	C
D	

Hamburg

A: Overview of Hamburg

B: Jungfernstieg

C: Hamburg waterfront

D: Harry's Hamburg Harbour Bazaar

DAVID PEEVERS

DAVID PEEVERS

DAVID PEEVERS

Schleswig-Holstein
Top: Crowd on Town Hall Square during the Kieler Woche, Kiel
Left: View over the Altstadt, Lübeck
Right: Holstentor, Lübeck

quite noisy is *Hotel Westermann* (☎ 981 14 0; fax 981 14 11), Koksche Strasse 1 just south of the Altstadtring. It charges DM85/140. At the *Schlosspension* (☎ 338 33 0; fax 338 33 37), Schlossstrasse 15, in a lovely, tiny but cosy villa, rooms cost from DM75/180. Top of the line is the traditional *Hotel Walhalla* (☎ 349 10; fax 349 11 44), Bierstrasse 24, near the tourist office. Stylish rooms at this historic place cost DM135/195.

Places to Eat

Pubs Osnabrück has a wonderful range of pubs (most open in the evening only) that also serve inexpensive, simple food. Among them is the student-run *Unikeller* in the west-wing cellars of the Schloss (now part of the university) at Neuer Graben 29; the menu (DM4.50 to DM9) includes some vegetarian dishes. Right across at No 40 is the *Unicum*, which is similar and has good casseroles and stuffed pancakes from DM6. In the Altstadt, Heger Strasse 4-5, you'll find *Stiefel*, a dark and wooden pub. *Zwiebel*, at No 34, has low ceilings and a wine bar in the back. Carnivores should try *Grüne Gans*, Grosse Gildewart 15, which serves a beer, a Schnapps and a pepper steak for DM10. And yes, there's a 'green goose' sculpture in the window.

Cafés Open at lunchtime, the *Mensa* (university cafeteria) has won awards for its food and is open to non-students who pay a tad more. It's in the park south of the Schloss, the main university building.

For traditional Kaffee und Kuchen (coffee and cake), there's *Café Läer* in the ornate historic building at Krahnstrasse 4. Potato dishes prepared every way imaginable dominate at the *Kartoffelhaus*, Bierstrasse 38. Dishes 'as Grandma makes' is on the menu at *Spökenkieker*, Hakenstrasse 25.

Entertainment

Osnabrück's *municipal theatre* (☎ 323 33 14/40), Domhof 10/11, offers classical concerts, ballet and drama. The *Lagerhalle*, Rolandsmauer 26, is a large alternative cultural centre with a grab-bag of concerts, disco nights, movies, poetry readings and so on (evenings only, closed Monday; take bus No 2, 3 or 8 to Heger Tor).

Hyde Park, Fürstenauer Weg, is a disco with indie, metal and punk canned music and occasional live concerts. It's open weekends after 8 pm and costs only DM1 admission (take bus No 83 to Sportpark).

Getting There & Away

Train There are hourly IC trains to Hamburg (DM63, 1¾ hours), Cologne (DM55, 2¼ hours) and Dortmund (DM28, 55 minutes). Regional trains to Hanover also leave hourly (DM35, 1¾ hours).

Car & Motorcycle Osnabrück is well connected by road via the A1 (Bremen to Dortmund) and the B51, B65 and B68.

Ride Services There are two Mitfahrzentralen: one at Kleine Hamkenstrasse 4 (☎ 266 00; 194 40) and another at Martinistrasse 9 (☎ 429 47; 473 33).

Getting Around

Bus The Stadtwerke Osnabrück (☎ 344 72 4) operates the city bus network. The best deal is the 24-hour ticket for DM5. The Mini-Gruppen-Karte is valid for up to four adults or eight children and costs only DM10.

Taxi If you need a taxi, dial ☎ 277 81 or ☎ 830 83.

Bicycle To rent a bicycle, try Pedals Fahrradstation (☎ 259 13 1) at the Hauptbahnhof, which charges from DM5 a day.

OLDENBURG

- *pop 155,000*
- *area code* ☎ 0441

Oldenburg, about 50km west of Bremen and 100km north of Osnabrück, is the economic and cultural centre of the Weser-Ems region. The town has a reputation for its high quality of life and, unlike most provincial towns, has seen its population figures climb steadily in recent years. It has a young university, founded in 1970, with 12,000 students.

Oldenburg began life as Aldenburg in 1108. Around that time, it became the residence of the counts of Oldenburg, a family whose 'crowning' glory came in 1448 when Count Christian of Oldenburg became the king of Denmark. Though the Thirty Years' War bypassed the town, the 17th century nevertheless brought destruction in the form of a huge fire (1676) which spared only a few of the medieval buildings. After a century under Danish rule, Oldenburg was elevated to a duchy in 1773. The Schlosspark, the promenade and numerous neoclassical buildings date from that time.

Oldenburg escaped WWII almost unscathed, but swelled to a big city almost overnight when it had to absorb more than 40,000 German refugees from the east (Poland, the Sudetenland) after 1945. It's a pleasant town with a few sights worth exploring on a day trip from the Friesland coast or en route to Bremen or beyond.

Orientation

Oldenburg's centre is entirely pedestrianised and bounded by Heiligengeistwall to the north, Theaterwall to the west and Schlosswall to the south. The Hauptbahnhof is about a 10-minute walk north-east of the city centre.

Information

Tourist Office The tourist office (☎ 157 44; fax 248 92 02), Wallstrasse 14, opens weekdays from 9 am to 5 pm and Saturday from 10 am to 1 pm.

Money The Commerzbank, Heiligengeiststrasse 29, opens weekdays to 6.30 pm and exchanges cash and travellers' cheques. There's also an ATM here that accepts all major credit cards.

Post & Communications The main post office, just west of the Hauptbahnhof at Bahnhofsplatz 10, has a special counter open weekdays to 8 pm, Saturday to 2 pm and Sunday 10 to 11 am.

Bookshop For a decent bookshop with volumes in English, go to Bültmann & Gerriets, Lange Strasse 57.

Laundry There's a self-service laundrette at Bloherfelder Strasse 200.

Emergency Police headquarters (☎ 790 1) are at Raiffeisenstrasse 25. The number for medical emergencies after hours is ☎ 750 53.

Around the Markt

Most of Oldenburg's main sights are a few steps from each other in the southern Altstadt. The **Lambertikirche** (open weekdays from 11 am to 12.30 pm and 2.30 to 5 pm, and Saturday from 11 am to 12.30 pm) with its five sky-piercing spires dominates the Markt. It has a curious architectural history. When the original 13th-century Gothic hall church partly collapsed in 1791, Duke Peter Friedrich Ludwig used the stones to build a new church in the neoclassical style. Based on the Pantheon in Rome, the interior of this square building features a large galleried rotunda with ionic columns which support a giant cupola. By the late 19th century, however, tastes had changed again and the entire edifice was encased in a neo-Gothic, red-brick shell with landmark towers.

Also on Markt is the **Alte Rathaus** (open to 4 pm from Monday to Thursday, to 1 pm on Friday), an unusual flat-iron building trimmed with little turrets. It dates only from the last century and is a good example of the style of historicism in vogue at the time. Inside, the assembly hall and the staircase warrant a quick look. Opposite the main portal of the town hall is the **Haus Degode** (1502), one of the few medieval buildings to survive the 1676 fire.

Schlossplatz

The **Schloss**, the former residence of the counts and dukes of Oldenburg, makes a rather unexpected appearance at the southern end of the Altstadt shopping district. It's a large yellow structure built in 1607 in transitional style from the Renaissance to the baroque; its harmonious appearance conceals the many additions and alterations made in subsequent centuries. In the 18th century it was enlarged by a residential wing; a kitchen wing, library and carriage house followed. About 100 years ago, the neo-Renaissance wing was added.

Today, the Schloss contains the **Landesmuseum für Kunst und Kulturgeschichte** (State Museum for Art and Cultural History; open Tuesday to Friday from 9 am to 5 pm, Saturday from 10 am; DM4, discount DM2). The 1st floor features the representational rooms of the dukes of Oldenburg, preserved in their original neoclassical style. The Marble Room and the Idyllenzimmer with 44 paintings by court artist Heinrich Wilhelm Tischbein, a friend of Goethe, deserve special attention. Also noteworthy is the gallery of old masters focusing on Italian and Dutch art, including Rembrandt's *Angel in the House of Tobias*.

The 2nd floor provides insight into the lifestyle of the aristocracy between the 16th and 19th centuries, while the 3rd floor sheds light on the living conditions and customs of the working classes.

The museum's collection of 20th-century art has been farmed out to the **Augusteum** on Elisabethstrasse 1 (same hours). Showcased here are works by Heckel, Kirchner, Macke, the surrealist Franz Radziwill and others. Admission to the Landesmuseum includes entrance to the Augusteum.

Opposite the Schloss, the four simple columns of the **Neue Wache** (1839), also in the neoclassical style, come into view. A guard house until 1918, it is now part of the Sparkasse of Oldenburg, the oldest savings bank (1786) in the world. Unfortunately, the Bauhaus-style behemoth next to it, which houses most of the bank's administrative office, is not quite as classy a building.

Behind the Schloss is the sprawling English-style Schlosspark. Its pond, rose garden and masses of rhododendron bushes invite a leisurely stroll or a picnic.

Places to Stay

Camping The nearest camping ground is *Camping-Park Flötenteich* (☎ 328 28; open April to September) about 3km from the city centre at Am Flötenteich. A tent site with car parking cost DM9 plus DM6 per person.

Hostel At Oldenburg's *DJH hostel* (☎ 871 35), Alexanderstrasse 65, about 10 minutes north of the Hauptbahnhof, bed & breakfast costs DM22/26 for juniors/seniors.

Private Rooms The tourist office can help you find a room (DM4 per reservation), but budget options are basically nonexistent. Private rooms are your best bet, but even they still cost around DM60/80 singles/doubles, and that's without breakfast.

Hotels If you don't mind sharing shower and toilet, you can get away with DM50/100 at *Hotel Sprenz* (☎ 870 33), Heiligengeiststrasse 15. Rooms with private bath cost DM85/125. The family-run, somewhat rustic *Hotel zum Lindenhof* (☎ 951 91 0), Bloherfelder Strasse 210, won't break the bank either, with rooms including private bath going for DM75/110. At *Hotel Alexander* (☎ 980 20; fax 820 00), Alexanderstrasse 107, you can expect to pay from DM100/140 for full-facility rooms. Top of the line is *CCH City Club Hotel* (☎ 808 0; fax 808 10 0), Europaplatz 4-6 next to the Weser-Ems congress hall, which charges DM150/210 for its business-class singles/doubles.

Places to Eat

One of the main eating drags at night is Wallstrasse, near the Lappan Tower, an Oldenburg landmark. This car-free lane offers a strange but interesting hybrid of Parisian-style brasseries and American-style bars. In fine weather you can sit in wicker chairs under cheerful awnings. Otherwise, the décor in most places blends wood and brass into a fashionable ambience. Most serve a menu of tasty, filling snacks, such as baguettes, pizza, nachos and the like. One of the most popular haunts is *Alex Grand Café*, Wallstrasse 1, with a sweeping staircase. Most places are licensed to stay open until 5 am.

For inexpensive but superb Italian food in a wonderfully romantic atmosphere, go to *Chianti Classico*, Achternstrasse 40. It's in a crooked half-timbered house tucked away in an alley. Upstairs at No 63 is *Die Stube*, which bans smoking and serves vegetarian food for around DM11. For large portions of sit-down fast food, there's a Kochlöffel at No 8 on the same street. If you'd like to dine in smart Art Nouveau rooms, go to the *Bahnhofsgaststätten*, Bahnhofsplatz 12a.

Entertainment

Look for the free publications *Domino Kultur-Journal* and *Mox* in pubs or at the tourist office for up-to-date event information.

Performances at the *Oldenburgische Staatstheater* (☎ 222 51 11), Theaterwall 28, include musicals, operas, drama, ballet and classical concerts. A slightly more alternative repertoire is on at the *Kulturetage* (☎ 924 80 0), Bahnhofstrasse 11, and at the *Unikum* (☎ 798 0), within the university building at Ammerländer Heerstrasse 114. For live jazz, check out *Jazzclub Alluvium* (☎ 719 70), Zeughausstrasse 73.

Things to Buy

Oldenburg's pedestrian-only shopping area is one of the largest and earliest (1967) in Germany and covers practically the entire Altstadt. It stretches along Heiligengeiststrasse, Achternstrasse and Lange Strasse and has department stores, boutiques, chain stores and glass arcades. There's also a flea market every second Saturday of the month held in the Weser-Ems-Halle from December to March and on Schlossplatz from April to November.

Getting There & Away

Train Oldenburg is at the junction of rail lines to the north and to Bremen. There are trains at least once an hour to Bremen (DM11.80, 30 minutes) and Osnabrück (DM30, two hours) with further connections in all directions.

Car & Motorcycle Oldenburg is at the crossroads of the A29 to/from Wilhelmshaven and the A28 (Bremen-Dutch border).

Ride Services The Mitfahrzentrale (☎ 710 41) is at Ofener Strasse 45.

Getting Around

Bus Oldenburg's thorough bus system is fairly easy to use. Single tickets for the entire city area cost DM2.50; short trips only DM1.80. Day passes are DM8. Buy your tickets from the driver.

Taxi If you need a taxi, call ☎ 225 5.

Bicycle The preferred method of transportation is the bicycle. If you'd like to join the pedalling crowds, you can rent a bike at Fahrradstation. It's in a pavilion in Neue Strasse opposite the tourist office, and charges DM12/25 a day/three days.

EMDEN & AROUND

- *pop 50,000*
- *area code* ☎ 04921

The little town of Emden is located in the north-westernmost corner of Lower Saxony – and of Germany – about 80km west of Oldenburg, where the Ems River meets the North Sea. With a past spanning some 12 centuries, Emden is an old town, but with a modern flair. The driving force behind the economy is the huge Volkswagen factory, employing 9000 people. After being essentially flattened in WWII, Emden was rebuilt successfully and aesthetically. Its largely pedestrianised city centre features red-brick walkways that match the architecture. The harbour and little canals add some picturesque touches. What makes a visit to Emden truly worthwhile, though, are its museums. Art aficionados especially will be rewarded by the Kunsthalle whose collection of 20th-century art can compete with similar houses in much larger cities.

Orientation

Emden's train and bus stations are about a 10-minute walk west of the city centre. As you exit, take Larrelter Strasse east to Neutorstrasse past the Kunsthalle, then head south to the small medieval harbour called Ratsdelft.

Information

Tourist Office The tourist office (☎ 974 00; fax 974 09) is in a pavilion next to the car park at the harbour. Between May and October it's open weekdays from 9 am to 6 pm, Saturday from 10 am to 1 pm, and Sunday from 11 to 1 pm. From November to April, the hours are weekdays from 9 am to 1 pm and 3 to 5.30 pm, Saturday from 10 am to 1 pm. The information terminal outside is useful when the office is closed.

Money A number of banks around town exchange money and travellers' cheques, including the Commerzbank, adjacent to the tourist office, and the Citibank, on Neuer Markt, which also has an ATM that accepts all major credit cards. Most banks close at lunchtime.

Post & Communications The main post office is just north of the Hauptbahnhof.

Laundry You can wash your dirty laundry in the one-storey building next to the Hafentor in the harbour along Am Delft. Ask for the key and tokens at the kiosk across the street. A full load, including dryer, costs about DM4.

Emergency There's a police station on Larrelter Strasse near the Wasserturm.

Kunsthalle

Emden owes its place on the map of great art museums to local boy Henri Nannen who left his home town to become the founder, publisher and editor-in-chief of the magazine *Stern*, which is still one of Germany's most widely read publications. Upon retirement, he returned to Emden and donated the Kunsthalle to his home town to display his vast collection of paintings and sculpture. The red-brick building with blue wooden window frames blends harmoniously into its idyllic setting on a little canal.

Inside, its whitewashed, light-flooded rooms show off a stunning assembly of German Expressionism and New Realism. Emil Nolde alone is represented by about 30 paintings. There are works by the Russian Alex Jawlensky, Max Beckmann, Oskar Kokoschka, Erich Heckel, Max Pechstein and many more top names in 20th-century art. Not all works are permanently displayed and part of the space is used for travelling exhibits. Three times a year, the museum closes its doors for one week while exhibits are changed.

The Kunsthalle (☎ 975 00) is at Hinter dem Rahmen 13, about a five-minute walk east of the train station. It's open Tuesday from 10 am to 8 pm, Wednesday to Friday to 5 pm and weekends from 11 am to 5 pm. Admission is DM8, discount DM4.

Ostfriesisches Landesmuseum

Inside the historic Rathaus is this regional history museum with a vast collection spread over three floors. It's particularly famous for its fine assortment of swords, halberds, pikes, muskets and other antique weapons from the 16th to the 18th centuries.

Also on display are models, historic maps, costumes and other objects that document the history and lifestyle of East Friesland. There's also a gallery of old Dutch masters where you'll find such masterpieces as the evocative *Spaziergang nach Sandvoort* (Strolling to Sandvoort, 1642) by Isaack Luttichuijs and numerous works by the local 17th-century painter Ludolf Backhuyzen. From the Rathaus tower, you have a lovely view over the town.

From April to September the museum opens weekdays from 11 am to 1 pm and 2 to 5 pm, Saturday from 1 to 5 pm and Sunday from 11 am to 5 pm. The rest of the year, the museum closes at 4 pm and on Mondays.

Suurhusen

About 6km north of Emden, along the B70, stands the little church of Suurhusen (1262) which would be fairly unremarkable were it not for its unbelievably tilting tower. Currently leaning 2.43m off true, it allegedly outdoes even the famous tower in Pisa by 4.7cm. The overhang is apparently the result of the decreasing groundwater levels in the peat-rich soil.

Activities

The flatlands in Emden and around are premier bicycling territory, and the tourist office has at least half a dozen maps and even more suggestions on where to go (see Getting Around for bike rentals).

Another good way to travel is by water. The DJH hostel rents canoes and kayaks for paddling around the placid canals (DM15/25 a half-day/day).

Organised Tours

You can take a harbour cruise (DM8, discount DM4), which leaves several times daily between March and October from the Delfttreppe steps in the harbour. There are also canal tours leaving from the quay at the Kunsthalle between April and October on weekdays at 11 am and 3 pm and on Sunday at noon and 3 pm.

Places to Stay

Camping The nearest camping ground is *Campingplatz Knock* (☎ 567) at Am Mahlbusen about 10km west of town. There are no direct bus connections.

Hostel Emden's *DJH hostel* (☎ 321 61), An der Kesselschleuse 5, is about a 15-minute walk east of the city centre. From the train station, take bus No 3003 to Realschule/Am Herrentor. Bed & breakfast costs DM20/25 juniors/ seniors. It's closed in December and January and on the first and third weekends in November and February.

Private Rooms, Guesthouses & Hotels

The tourist office can help you find a room (no booking fee). Private rooms range from DM25 to DM50 per person. Small guesthouses that offer low-frills rooms at fairly low rates include *Gasthaus Rathausstübchen* (☎ 331 22), Brückstrasse 5, which charges DM70/100 for singles/doubles, and *Gasthof zur Quelle* (☎ 319 91), Bollwerkstrasse 51-52, whose doubles cost DM100. A step up is *Hotel Schmidt* (☎ 240 57 8), Friedrich-Ebert-Strasse 79, where rooms with private bath cost DM98/155, though it often has special weekend rates. The owner speaks good English.

Places to Eat

Emden may not be the place to come for gourmet food, but you can always get a decent bite at the many cafés and bistros lining Neuer Markt. These include *Take it Easy* (a US-style bar) and *Sam's* (which serves good breakfasts), both at No 20. The *Museumsstube* (closed at 6 pm) is the Kunsthalle's nicely located café-restaurant that serves regional dishes at civil prices (DM8 to DM15). For mainstream Italian food, try *Pizzeria Peppino* at Grosse Strasse 24, which charges from DM8 for pizza and pasta dishes. Some of the best fish in town can be had at *Nautilus*, a rustic restaurant aboard an old Dutch sailing boat (DM15 and up). They also have a good selection of pancakes. You can also satisfy your craving for seafood at a number of *Imbiss* stands around town.

Getting There & Away

Emden is connected by rail to Oldenburg (DM21.20, 1¼ hours), Bremen (DM33, 1¾ hours) and Hamburg (DM64, 2½ hours, change in Bremen). Despite its relative remoteness, it is also easily and quickly reached via the A31 which connects with the A28 from Oldenburg and Bremen. The B70/210 runs north from Emden to other towns in Friesland and to the coast.

Getting Around

Emden is small enough to be explored on foot but also has a bus system (DM1.50 per trip). The best transport method is the bicycle. Oltmanns (☎ 314 44), at Grosse Strasse 53-57, rents bikes at DM15 a day. Or else try MAC Zweiradverleih (☎ 275 00), Ringstrasse 17; it also rents motorcycles.

JEVER

- *pop 13,100*
- *area code* ☎ 04461

Jever is at the heart of Friesland, a region just north of Oldenburg. Though a visitor would never notice a difference, the Frieslanders insist on not being confused with the people of East Friesland (for instance, Emden, 50km to the west) and vice versa. In fact, both readily tell you about the so-called 'Golden Line', an imaginary border just a few km west of Jever. That this rivalry has profound historic reasons goes without saying.

Jever has been settled for many centuries, as Roman coins from the 1st and 2nd centuries found would suggest. In the Middle Ages the town rose to prominence, largely because of its harbour. This is hard to imagine, given that it's landlocked today, with the sea about 12km away. In those days, Jever was ruled by elected judges called *Häuptlinge* (chieftains). The last of these rulers was the most famous and a woman to boot – the legendary Fräulein Maria (see the boxed text 'Fräulein' Maria – the Last Chieftan later in this section), who is revered by the people of Jever to this day. However, it wasn't Maria who made Jever a household name in Germany, but the dry Pilsner beer produced here since 1848.

Orientation

Most of Jever's attractions are within a few hundred metres of each other in the eastern section of the Altstadt around the Schloss. The train station is at Anton-Günther-Strasse, the south-western segment of the ring road that encircles the historic core. From there, it's only a short walk to the Schloss and Jever's tourist office.

Information

Tourist Office The tourist office (☎ 710 10; fax 939 29 9), Alter Markt 18, opens from May to September, weekdays from 10 am to 6 pm and Saturday to 2 pm. The rest of the year, it's open Monday to Thursday from 9 am to 5 pm, Friday from 9 am to noon.

Ask for the *Radwanderkarte Friesland* (DM5.50) which has touring tips. There's an information terminal outside the office.

Money The Deutsche Bank, Alter Markt 17, and the Sparkasse, at No 4, exchange money.

Post & Communications At the time of writing, the post office was at Mühlenstrasse 14 east of the Schloss, though a move was under discussion.

Emergency There's a police station (☎ 921 10) at Ziegelhofstrasse 34.

Schloss

Jever's 14th-century castle was first built by chieftain Edo Wiemken the Elder to keep out his overly assertive neighbours, the counts of Oldenburg. The first structure proved too weak and was reconstructed and fortified in 1417 by Edo Wiemken the Younger, the father of Fräulein Maria. Today the palace houses the **Kulturhistorische Museum des Jeverlandes**, a cultural history museum with 60 rooms packed with objects chronicling the daily life of the Frieslanders and their accomplishments in crafts and art. Precious Gobelin tapestries, faïences, period rooms and a portrait gallery round off the exhibits.

The *pièce de résistance*, however, is the magnificent audience hall with a carved coffered oak ceiling of great intricacy. Fräulein Maria retained the Antwerp sculptor Cornelis Floris to create this 80-sq-metre Renaissance masterpiece. Look for the grotesque figurines amid the garlands. Also note the 18th-century leather wall coverings, gaudily decorated with gold leaf.

The Schloss is in the eastern section of the Altstadt and is open between March and mid-January from 10 am to 6 pm, closed Monday (except in July and August). Admission is DM4, discount DM2. From May to September you can also climb the Schloss tower which brings the entry fee up to DM5/3.

Friesisches Brauhaus zu Jever

This Frisian brewery (☎ 137 11), Elisabethufer 18, takes the mystique out of the beer-making process during tours of its production and bottling facilities. There's also a small museum. It's all capped off with a beer tasting. Tours take place weekdays from April to October at 9.30 am, 10.30 am, 11.30 am and 12.30 pm. The rest of the year,

'Fräulein' Maria – the Last Chieftain

German history has an unfortunate dearth of strong, celebrated women, but the city of Jever has a champ: Fräulein Maria. The locals are so proud of this woman – the last in a long line of *Häuptlinge* (chieftains) – that they like to refer to their town as 'Marienstadt'.

Maria's legacy is everywhere: in a school that bears her name; in the statue that stands near the Schloss where she lived; and in the nearby Glockenspiel. The people so love their Maria, in fact, that they are loath to let her depart this world even centuries after her death. Legend has it that she hasn't gone to meet her Maker, but is merely lost in the labyrinth beneath the palace. Every night at 10 pm (or 9 pm during winter), you'll hear the bells of the Stadtkirche pealing in an effort to guide Maria back to those who are waiting for her.

When Maria succeeded her chieftain father in 1517, she and her two sisters were immediately entrapped in a chauvinistic power play. Her political nemesis, Count Edzard of East Frisia, paternalistically occupied Maria's palace and declared himself 'protector' of the young women. He should have left well enough alone: his promise that his three sons would marry the three daughters was soon broken. And Maria – proving that a woman scorned is not without options – promptly grabbed the reins of power for herself.

Her rule was tough but fair, the locals say. She gave Jever its town rights and, as a staunch Protestant, nipped in the bud the local propensity for public drinking orgies. Having dealt with debauchery, she hurled her formidable energy into enlightening her people by founding a Latin school. When she died, the mantle of 'chieftain' was interred with her. But even in death she was to prove an agitator.

This century, feminists argued that the diminutive term 'Fräulein' – which originally referred to an unmarried, ie supposedly virginal, woman – was derogatory when applied to a mature woman such as Maria. But as she apparently died a virgin, this argument was soon dropped. 'Fräulein' Maria she will remain, and the bells of Jever will continue to ring in the hope that the last – and possibly greatest – chieftain will find her way home again. ■

they're given on Tuesday and Thursday at 10.30 am only. The cost is a fairly steep DM10, though that includes a pretzel and a commemorative glass mug. Reservations are necessary.

Other Sights

Most of Jever's sights are in some way connected to Fräulein Maria. She, her father and other historic figures are featured in the **Glockenspiel** on the façade of the Hof von Oldenburg opposite the Schloss (daily at 11 am, noon and 3, 4 and 5 pm). Nearby, on Fräulein-Marien-Strasse, stands a **statue** of Fräulein Maria as a dignified matron wearing a large hat and accompanied by her dog. Head north, then turn left into Kleine Rosmarinstrasse to get to the **Stadtkirche** (open daily 8 am to 6 pm) containing the lavish **memorial tomb** of Edo von Wiemken, Maria's father. It miraculously survived a series of fires (the last one in 1959), though the church itself succumbed to the flames and was rebuilt in a rather modern way. The fantastical tomb is another opus by Cornelis Floris whose imagination went into overdrive on this project. A huge octagonal two-level wooden canopy shelters the sarcophagus topped with the life-sized figure of the chieftain dressed as a knight. This arrangement is propped up by a flock of caryatids representing Justice, Wisdom, Hope, Love, War and Peace.

One attraction *not* related to Maria is the little shop of Georg Stark, a former teacher who recently revived the long-lost art and tradition of *Blaudruckerei*, a printing and dying process similar to batik. Using original wooden embossing stamps he finds in old barns, at flea markets, antique shops and secret places, he makes everything from table cloths to jeans in his workshop on Kattrepel (open weekdays from 10 am to noon and 2 to 4 pm, Saturday from 10 am to noon).

Places to Stay

Hostel You'll find the *DJH hostel* (☎ 359 0)

at Mooshütter Weg 12, about a five-minute walk from the train station, charges DM18/23 juniors/seniors for bed & breakfast. It's closed from November to the end of March.

Private Rooms, Pensions & Hotels Jever's tourist office doesn't make room reservations, though it can provide names and addresses. Private rooms start at DM22 per person.

There are only a few hotels in town, and they're quite inexpensive. *Hotel Weisses Haus* (☎ 683 9), Bahnhofstrasse 20, charges DM45/90 for singles/doubles. *Pension Am Elisabethufer* (☎ 949 60), Elisabethufer 9a, has one single for DM54 and seven doubles at DM90. Rooms at *Hotel Pension Stöber* (☎ 558 0), Hohnholzstrasse 10, cost DM60/100. All rooms have private shower and WC.

Places to Eat

One of the nicest restaurants is the historic *Haus der Getreuen*, Schlachtstrasse 1. It's famous for its regional fish specialities (DM15 to DM35) and has a menu changing daily. On Alter Markt, you'll find *Im Schmidt's*, a pub that also serves small meals, and *Pütt*, which is similar. Gourmets with deep pockets shouldn't miss *Alte Apotheke* (☎ 408 8), a stylish establishment at Apothekerstrasse 1 serving such delicacies as lamb with fetta crust.

Getting There & Away

If you're travelling to Jever by train, you must change in Oldenburg. By road, Jever is easily reached by taking the exit to the B210 from the A29 (direction Wilhelmshaven).

Getting Around

Jever is so small that all you need to explore it are your two feet. For explorations of the countryside, you can rent a bicycle at Rainer's Zweirad-Shop (☎ 735 98), Grosse Wasserpfortestrasse 14, or at Heinz Boeljes (☎ 139 4), Hauptstrasse 32.

East Frisian Islands

Trying to remember the sequence of the seven East Frisian Islands, Germans – with a wink of the eye – recite the following as a mnemonic device: '*Welcher Seemann liegt bei Nanni im Bett*?' (which translates rather saucily as 'Which seaman is lying in bed with Nanni?') Lined up in an archipelago off the coast of Lower Saxony, the islands are (east to west): Wangerooge, Spiekeroog, Langeoog, Baltrum, Norderney, Juist and Borkum. Like their North Frisian cousins Sylt, Amrum and Föhr (see the Schleswig-Holstein chapter), the islands are part of the Wattenmeer National Park. And here too, nature is the islands' prime attraction. Those who make the trek are rewarded with long sandy beaches fringed by dunes and the shallow waters of the Wattenmeer.

Friesland itself covers an area stretching from the northern Netherlands, along the German coast, up into Denmark. Many inhabitants speak a language that is the closest relative of English but virtually incomprehensible to other Germans. The islands are popular with holiday-makers, though the Germans have kept them largely to themselves. Visits here aren't cheap, but those that have fallen under the spell of these islands swear that the pure sea breeze and wide open spaces are as invigorating and mind-clearing as hours of therapy. The main season runs from mid-May to September.

Resort Tax

Each of the East Frisian Islands charges a so-called *Kurtaxe*, a slap in the face to most visitors. Paying the tax gets you a *Kurkarte* which entitles you to entry onto the beach and also gives you small discounts for museums, concerts and other events. The amount depends on the town and the season, though it rarely exceeds DM5 a day. If you're spending more than one night, your hotel will automatically obtain a pass for you for the length of your stay (the price will be added to the room rate).

Getting There & Away

Ferries to most of the islands don't operate on a fixed schedule because of the changing tides. It's best to call the ferry operator or Deutsche Bahn (DB), which also sells tickets, for details before you depart. Five of the seven islands don't allow cars, and you must leave your vehicle in a car park near the ferry pier, which can add up to an additional DM8.50 a day in expenses. If you're travelling by train, in most cases you'll have to change to a shuttle bus somewhere south of the harbour. For more details see the Getting There & Away sections under each island.

WANGEROOGE

Wangerooge looks back on a rather turbulent past that saw it governed by Russia, the Netherlands, France, the duchy of Oldenburg and, finally, Germany. These days it's regularly invaded by visitors, most of them families coming for the wonderful sandy beaches and the car-free environment. The island lies along the shipping canal to Hamburg, Bremen and Wilhelmshaven, and the big ships can often be seen from the shoreline. Attractions here include the historic 39m-tall **lighthouse**, which can be climbed, a couple of **bird sanctuaries** and the **Wattenmeer Information Centre** in the Rosenhaus. There's also a sea-water adventure pool and a large list of sports activities.

For information, go to the Kurverwaltung (spa administration; ☎ 04469-990; fax 991 14) on the Strandpromenade, which opens Monday to Thursday from 8 am to 1 pm and 2.30 to 5 pm. There's also the Verkehrsverein (☎ 04469-948 80) in the pavilion at the train station, which handles room reservations as well. A general warning: the tourist offices of the coastal spa towns change opening hours frequently and without notice. Call ahead if possible.

Getting There & Away

The ferry to Wangerooge leaves from Harlesiel two to four times daily (1¼ hours), depending on the tides. The one-way fare is DM24, same-day return tickets cost DM29. Large pieces of luggage are an extra DM5 each. If you want to take a bike along, it costs DM20. The price includes the tram shuttle to the village (4km). The ferry is operated by DB. If you're arriving by train, you must take the Bremen-Oldenburg-Wilhelmshaven line and get off in Sande, where you catch a shuttle bus to the ferry dock.

SPIEKEROOG

Rolling dunes dominate the landscape of minuscule Spiekeroog: about two thirds of its 17.4 sq km is taken up by these sandy hills. It's the tranquillity of this rustic island that draws people, although it gets fairly busy in July and August when most of the 50,000 annual visitors arrive. To prevent additional crowding, Spiekeroog is not only car-free but actually discourages bicycles too.

Spiekeroog's tourist office (☎ 04976-919 30; fax 919 34 7), Noorderpad 25 is open on weekdays from 9 am to 5 pm year round, to noon on Saturday (May to October only). For room reservations, telephone ☎ 04976-919 32 5.

An attraction is the pint-sized **Alte Inselkirche** (1696), a church with a surprising interior; its flat wooden ceiling painted with red stars and model wooden ships dangling down into the hall. There's also a Spanish Pietà that washed up ashore.

Getting There & Away

Neuharlingersiel to Spiekeroog takes 45 minutes and depends on the tides, which is why same-day returns aren't always possible. To get to the ferry by train, you must change to a shuttle bus in Esens or Norden. Prices are DM17.50 one way and DM28 for same-day return tickets. Each piece of luggage is an extra DM4, and bicycles are an extortionate DM36. Call either ☎ 04974-214 or any DB office for details and tickets.

LANGEOOG

Floods and pirates make up the story of Langeoog, whose population was reduced to a total of two following a horrendous storm in 1721. But by 1830 it had recovered sufficiently to become a resort town.

Langeoog's tourist office (☎ 04972-693 0; fax 658 8), in the Rathaus at Hauptstrasse 28, opens Monday to Thursday from 7.30 am to noon and 1.30 to 4.30 pm, Friday from 9 am to noon. In July and August, it's also open on Friday from 3 to 5 pm and Saturday from 10 am to noon. For room reservations ring ☎ 04972-693 20 1.

The island boasts the highest elevation in East Friesland (the 20m-high **Melkhörndüne**) and the **grave** of Lale Anderson, famous for her WWII song *Lili Marleen*. Nautical tradition is showcased in the **Schiffahrtsmuseum**, though the original **sea rescue ship** also on view is perhaps more interesting. In sunshine, the 14km-long beach is clearly the biggest attraction.

Getting There & Away

The ferry shuttles between Bensersiel and Langeoog up to nine times daily. The trip takes about one hour and costs DM18/28 one way/return. Luggage is DM5 a piece and bikes are DM30. For details, call ☎ 04971-250 1 or contact any DB office. To get to Bensersiel by train, you must change to a shuttle bus in Esens or Norden.

BALTRUM

Car-free Baltrum is tiny – only 1km wide and 5km long. It's so small that villagers don't even bother with street names. The houses, though, have numbers allocated on a chronological basis. Since houses 1 to 4 no longer exist, the oldest house is now No 5. Much of the available space is taken up by dunes and salty marshland. There's little to do except to go on walks or to the beach or visit the exhibit on the Wattenmeer National Park environment in house No 177.

Baltrum's tourist office (☎ 04939-800; fax 802 7), in house No 130, opens Monday to Thursday from 8.30 am to noon and 2 to 4 pm, Friday from 8.30 am to noon. For room reservations call ☎ 04939-137 7.

Getting There & Away

Ferries make the trip from Nessmersiel to Baltrum in 30 minutes. Departures depend on the tides which means day trips aren't always possible. Tickets are DM20/36 one way/return. Same-day return tickets cost DM24. Bikes are DM8 each way. Luggage is usually free. Details are available from ☎ 04939-913 00 or a DB office. To get to Nessmersiel by train, change to the shuttle bus in Norden.

NORDERNEY

Norderney is the 'Queen of the East Frisian Islands' and has been wooed by a long line of royal suitors, starting with Friedrich Wilhelm II of Prussia in 1797. He gave his blessing to the founding of Germany's first North Sea resort here. Georg V of Hanover liked Norderney so much that he made it his summer residence. Otto von Bismarck came here in 1844.

Norderney's tourist office (☎ 04932-918 50; fax 824 94), Bülowallee 5, opens weekdays from 9 am to 12.30 pm and 2 to 6 pm and Saturday from 10 am to 12.30 pm between May and September. In July and August, the office is also open on Saturday from 2 to 4 pm. The rest of the year, it's closed on weekends. It also handles room reservations.

The island's lavish **gardens**, **parks** and majestic architecture date back to this era of visits by the high and mighty. The red-brick post office and the **Kurhaus**, with its columns and arches and the many neoclassical homes give Norderney a glamorous flair. One particular attraction is **Die Welle**, an indoor ocean water wave and fun pool at Kurplatz. There's also an outdoor pool at Weststrand. Because it is comparatively large, Norderney also allows cars.

Getting There & Away

To get to Norderney, you have to catch the ferry in Norddeich with scheduled departures up to nine times daily (50 minutes). Prices are DM12/22.50 one way/return; same-day returns are DM25 (including resort tax). Bikes are DM9. Details are available at ☎ 04931-987 0 or any DB office. There's a train service to Norddeich Mole, the ferry landing stage.

JUIST

Juist, shaped like a snake, is 17km long and only 500m wide. The only ways to travel are by bike, horse-drawn carriage or on your own two feet. What makes Juist special is what is *not* here: no high rises, cars or shopping malls. Instead, you're often alone with the screeching sea gulls, the wild sea and the howling winds. Forest, brambles and elderberry bushes blanket large sections of the island.

Juist's tourist office (☎ 04935-809 0; fax 803 22 3), Friesenstrasse 18, opens Monday to Thursday from 8.30 am to noon and 3 to 5 pm and Friday from 8.30 am to noon. Between Easter and September, it's also open Friday from 3 to 5 pm and Saturday from 10 am to noon. Room reservations can be made on ☎ 04935-809 22 2.

One peculiarity of Juist is the idyllic **Hammersee** – the only fresh water lake on all the islands – which is also a bird sanctuary. There's also the Juister **Küstenmuseum** (Coastal Museum) on Loogster Pad.

Getting There & Away

Ferries to Juist also leave from Norddeich and take 1¼ hours. The cost is DM22/42 one way/return; same-day returns are DM30 and include the resort tax. Luggage costs DM5 a piece, bikes DM16. More information is available from ☎ 04931-987 0 or any DB office. The train goes straight to the landing dock in Norddeich Mole.

BORKUM

The largest of the East Frisian Islands is also one of the most popular. Until ripped apart by a flood in the 12th century, Borkum was even larger than today. For many centuries, the men of Borkum made a living as seafarers and whalers. Reminders of those brutal days are the whale bones that you'll occasionally find, stacked up side by side, as garden fences. It wasn't until 1830 that the locals realised that tourism was a safer way to earn a living.

Borkum's Kurverwaltung (☎ 04922-303 31 0; fax 383 3), Goethestrasse 1, opens weekdays from 9 am to 6 pm and Saturday from 10 am to noon from mid-May to the end of September. The rest of the year, hours are weekdays from 9 am to noon and 3 to 5.30 pm. There's another tourist office (☎ 04922-841), at the train station which also handles room reservations.

To learn about the whaling era and other stages in the life of Borkum, visit the **Heimatmuseum** (Local History Museum) at the foot of the old lighthouse. Also of interest is the museum fireship *Borkumriff* with its exhibit on the Wattenmeer National Park.

Getting There & Away

The embarkation point for ferries to Borkum is Emden. You can either take the car ferry, which takes two hours, or the catamaran, which makes the trip in half the time. Car-ferry tickets are DM25/47 one way/return. Same-day return tickets also cost DM25. Weekend return tickets are DM37 (valid from Friday after 5 pm to Sunday). Tickets for the catamaran are DM15 more each way. Transporting a bike costs DM18 return. For information call ☎ 04921-890 72 2.

Hamburg

- *pop 1.7 million*
- *area code* ☎ 040

A visit to Hamburg by Queen Elizabeth II of England presented city officials with a real dilemma. Local tradition dictated that the mayor receive all visiting dignitaries on the 1st floor of the Rathaus, requiring her to walk up the stairway alone. While a queen could hardly be expected to make the climb unescorted, there was a rigid tradition to uphold. In the end, a compromise was struck: the mayor would descend the stairs – halfway – to meet Her Majesty.

This anecdote illustrates why this northern German city is still called the 'Free and Hanseatic City' of Hamburg. At no time in history – with the exception of the Napoleonic occupation in the early 19th century – has Hamburg had to bow to any foreign ruler. Instead, it has always been ruled by commerce and business. In a letter from 1831, John Strang, then treasurer of Glasgow, called it 'the most mercantile city of the world' and, though in decline, Hamburg's bustling port is still the backbone of the city's wealth. And wealthy it is. Hamburg is home to more millionaires than any other German city, and in certain neighbourhoods – Blankenese, Harvestehude, Winterhude, to name just a few – their money is reflected in enormous mansions with matching cars.

But Hamburg is also a city of contrasts. Alongside a clubby elitism thrives a freewheeling liberalism, manifesting itself as much in the red-light district along the Reeperbahn as in the city's tolerance of left-wing radicals squatting on Hafenstrasse. And an eclectic mix of students, workers and foreigners coexists more or less harmoniously in such colourful neighbourhoods as the Schanzenviertel, Altona and St Pauli.

Rich or poor, Hamburgers are rightly proud of their city. Aesthetically it ranks highly among major German metropolises. It boasts a lively cultural scene, vast urban green spaces and gorgeous architecture, despite the destruction wreaked upon it by a major fire in the 19th century and two world wars in the 20th. Exploring Hamburg properly takes time and good shoes, for the best way to see this city properly is by trekking through its many neighbourhoods.

HIGHLIGHTS

- Shopping and rock 'n' roll at the Fischmarkt
- The collections of the Kunsthalle
- Hydraulic organ concerts in the Planten & Blomen park
- A boat trip through the Speicherstadt
- A Portuguese dinner near the St Pauli Landungsbrücken

- **Population:** 1.7m • **Capital:** Hamburg
- **Area:** 755 sq km

Hamburg Luminaries: Wolf Biermann, Johannes Brahms, Paul Dessau, Karl Lagerfeld, Felix Mendelssohn-Bartholdy, Helmut Schmidt, Michael Stich

History

Hamburg's recorded history begins in the 9th century when Charlemagne had the moated fortress of Hammaburg erected in what is today the city centre. His son, Ludwig der Fromme (Ludwig the Pious), immediately

recognised the strategic location of this new settlement and, by making it an archbishopric in 831, created a missionary stronghold in the northern territories.

Hamburg owes its development as a wealthy trading city largely to the ambitious Count Adolf III. One of his prime accomplishments was the building of the Neustadt, a new part of town immediately west of the bishop-controlled Altstadt.

More importantly, though, in 1189 the count managed to wrangle a royal charter from Emperor Friedrich I – better known as Barbarossa – which granted free trade rights and exemption from customs to residents of the Neustadt. This privilege was extended to the Altstadt after the two were united in the 13th century. Hamburg soon became an important port city and a leading member of the Hanseatic League, which it joined in 1321. In 1460 and again in 1510 Hamburg was raised to the status of 'free imperial city'.

Neutrality and religious tolerance were the hallmarks of the city's politics from the 15th to the 18th centuries. It joined the Reformation, but also became a haven for persecuted Catholics. At the same time, it strengthened its role as a centre for European trade. This period also saw the founding of Germany's first stock exchange (1558) and bank (1619).

The Napoleonic occupation from 1806-14, which engendered a trade blockade against England, caused a temporary economic decline. The Great Fire of 1842, which burned one third of the city, was another blow. With the founding of the German Reich in 1871, Hamburg joined the German Customs Federation – essentially revoking the rights granted it by Barbarossa in 1189 – but got its free port instead. By 1913, Hamburg's population exceeded one million, and it was again one of the premier ports in Europe.

After WWI, most of Hamburg's merchant shipping fleet (almost 1500 ships) was forfeited to the Allies as a reparations payment. WWII left more than half of all housing, 80% of the port and 40% of the industry in rubble. Fire bombs dropped by the Allies on 28 July 1943 created a conflagration so great that tens of thousands of civilians were killed, and entire streets were vaporised. Equal numbers of people perished at the hands of the Nazis in the concentration camps of Fuhlsbüttel and Neuengamme, including 8000 Jews.

After the war, Hamburg showed its usual resilience and recovered quickly. Today it is Germany's second-largest city after Berlin, with some 1.6 million people, about 15% of them immigrants. The University of Hamburg has 41,500 students, making it the fifth-largest after the universities at Munich, Berlin, Cologne and Münster.

Hamburg is Germany's media capital, with more than 3300 companies in the fields of publishing, advertising, film, radio, TV and music. It is one of three city-states (the others being Berlin and Bremen) and an autonomous *Land* within the Federal Republic of Germany.

Orientation

Like Venice and Amsterdam, Hamburg is a city shaped by water. Three rivers – the Elbe, the Alster and the Bille – run through it, as does an idyllic grid of narrow canals called

Fleete. The beautiful Inner and Outer Alster lakes in the city centre contribute further to the maritime feel. Hamburg boasts 2400 bridges – six times the number found in Venice.

Most of Hamburg's main attractions are concentrated in the half-moon-shaped city centre, which arches north of the Elbe and is bordered by large roads whose names all end with *wall* (literally 'rampart') that follow the former fortifications. The area is cut in half diagonally by the Alsterfleet, the canal that roughly separates the Altstadt from the Neustadt, though the two merge seamlessly today.

The Hauptbahnhof is on Glockengiesserwall on the city centre's north-eastern edge, with the central bus station (Zentraler Omnibus Bahnhof or ZOB) behind it to the south-east. Hamburg has three other train stations: Altona in the west; Harburg in the south; and Dammtor, just north of the city centre. The spiky top of the huge TV Tower and the bronze helmet-like spire of the Michaeliskirche provide handy visual orientation throughout the town.

Hamburg is a sprawling city made up of many distinct neighbourhoods. West of the city centre lies the red-light and entertainment district of St Pauli which, further west, merges with Altona. Just north of St Pauli (and technically still part of it) is the Schanzenviertel. The city's choicest neighbourhoods hug the 400-acre Outer Alster Lake north of the city centre, with Winterhude and Uhlenhorst on the eastern and Harvestehude and Rotherbaum on the western shores. The lively Universitätsviertel (University Quarter) takes up the western section of Rotherbaum.

The tourist offices hand out excellent free city maps.

Information

Tourist Offices The tourist office (☎ 300 51 20 0; fax 300 51 33 3) at the Kirchenallee exit in the Hauptbahnhof is open daily from 7 am to 11 pm and often gets very busy in summer. For shorter queues, head to the larger office (same ☎ & fax) at St Pauli harbour, between piers 4 and 5 (S/U-Bahn: St Pauli-Landungsbrücken). It's open daily from 10 am to 7 pm (in winter 9.30 am to 5.30 pm). Both offices provide brochures, a room-finding service (DM6 fee) and tickets to events around Hamburg. For information over the phone, room reservations or ticket sales, call the Hamburg Hotline (☎ 300 51 30 0) daily between 8 am and 8 pm (you can ask for an English-speaking operator).

All these places also sell the worthwhile Hamburg Card, which offers unlimited public transportation and free or discounted admission to many museums, attractions and boat cruises. The Day Card is valid after 6 pm on the day of purchase and the entire next day and costs DM12.50 (single) and DM24 (groups, ie up to four adults and three children under 12). The Multiple Day Card is valid on the day of purchase and the following two days (DM25.50/42). If you don't want public transportation included, you can get the Hamburg Light version, which is good for three days and costs DM8 for singles, DM16.50 for groups.

If you're under 27, the best deal around is the Jugend Pass (DM11.50 the first day; DM5 for each additional day), only available at DJH hostels (you don't need to stay there to buy one). Besides unlimited public transportation, it offers even greater discounts, plus a bunch of coupons good for savings on drinks, movie tickets and nightclubs.

Foreign Consulates Hamburg has about 100 foreign consulates. For a complete listing, check the phone book under Konsulate. The UK consulate (☎ 448 03 20) is at Harvestehuder Weg 8a. The USA has a small consulate at Alsterufer 27-28 (☎ 411 71 0; for after-hour emergencies ☎ 411 71 21 1). The French consulate (☎ 414 10 60) is at Pöseldorfer Weg 32.

Money Most major banks around town will exchange money, but it pays to compare rates and commissions. Normal opening hours are until 4 pm on weekdays only (to 6 pm on Thursday). Outside the city centre, many branches close at lunchtime. The Reisebank

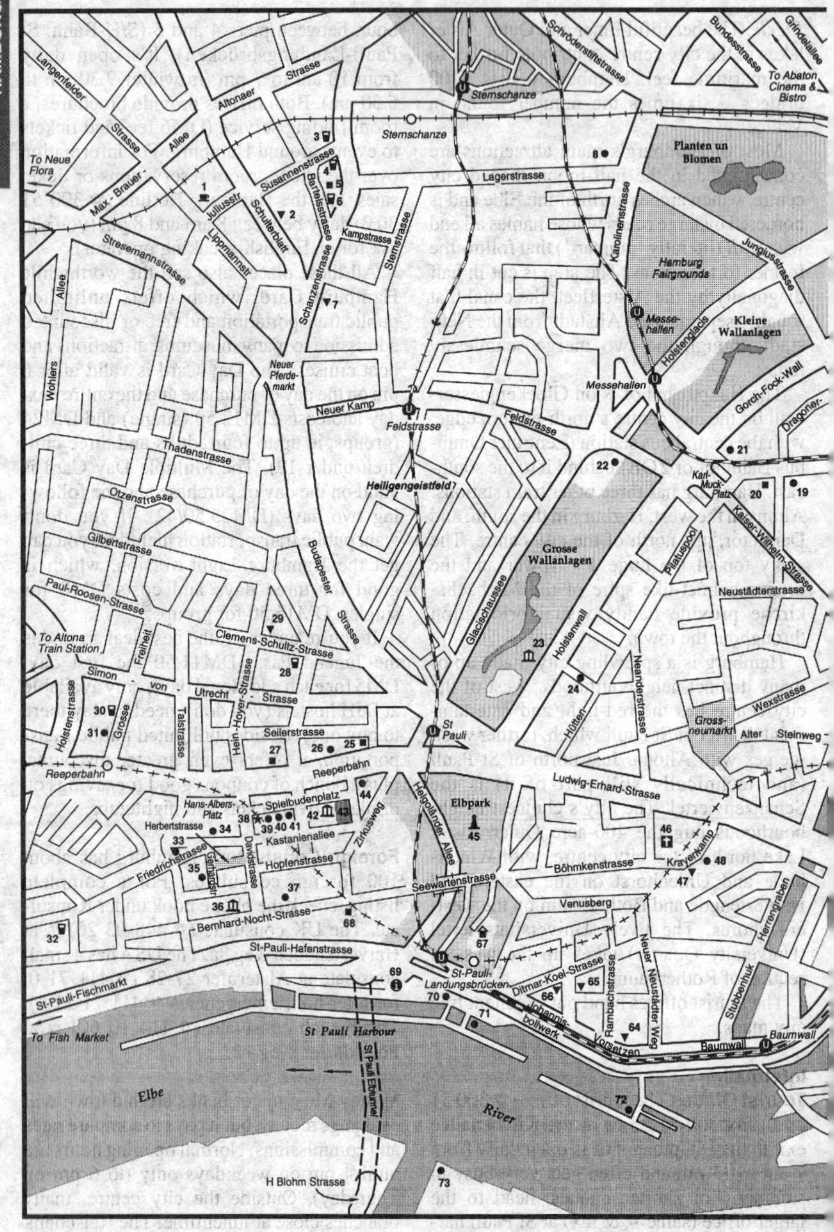

Langenfelder Strasse
Altonaer Strasse
Max-Brauer-Allee
To Neue Flora
Sternschanze
Schröderstiftstrasse
Bundesstrasse
Grindelallee
To Abaton Cinema & Bistro
Planten un Blomen
Lagerstrasse
Susannenstrasse
Bartelsstrasse
Juliusstr
Schulterblatt
Lippmannstr
Stresemannstrasse
Kampstrasse
Sternstrasse
Schanzenstrasse
Karolinenstrasse
Jungiusstrasse
Hamburg Fairgrounds
Messehallen
Kleine Wallanlagen
Holstenglacis
Gorch-Fock-Wall
Dragoner-
Allee
Wohlers
Neuer Pferdemarkt
Neuer Kamp
Feldstrasse
Thadenstrasse
Heiligengeistfeld
Karl-Muck-Platz
Otzenstrasse
Gilbertstrasse
Budapester Strasse
Grosse Wallanlagen
Glacischaussee
Pilatuspool
Kaiser-Wilhelm-Strasse
Neustädterstrasse
Paul-Roosen-Strasse
To Altona Train Station
Clemens-Schultz-Strasse
Simon von Utrecht Strasse
Grosse Freiheit
Holstenstrasse
Talstrasse
Hein-Hoyer-Strasse
Seilerstrasse
Holstenwall
Hütten
Neanderstrasse
Wexstrasse
Gross-neumarkt
Alter Steinweg
St Pauli
Reeperbahn
Ludwig-Erhard-Strasse
Hans-Albers-Platz
Spielbudenplatz
Herbertstrasse
Davidstrasse
Zirkusweg
Elbpark
Helgoländer Allee
Kastanienallee
Friedrichstrasse
Gerhardstr
Hopfenstrasse
Krayenkamp
Böhmkenstrasse
Seewartenstrasse
Venusberg
Bernhard-Nocht-Strasse
Herrengraben
St-Pauli-Hafenstrasse
St-Pauli-Landungsbrücken
Ditmar-Koel-Strasse
Rambachstrasse
Neuer Neustädter Weg
Stubbenhuk
St-Pauli-Fischmarkt
Johannisbollwerk
Vorsetzen
Baumwall
To Fish Market
St Pauli Harbour
St Pauli Elbtunnel
Elbe
River
H Blohm Strasse
1 2 3 4 5 6 7 8 19 20 21 22 23 24 25 26 27 28 29 30 31 32 33 34 35 36 37 38 39 40 41 42 43 44 45 46 47 48 64 65 66 67 68 69 70 71 72 73

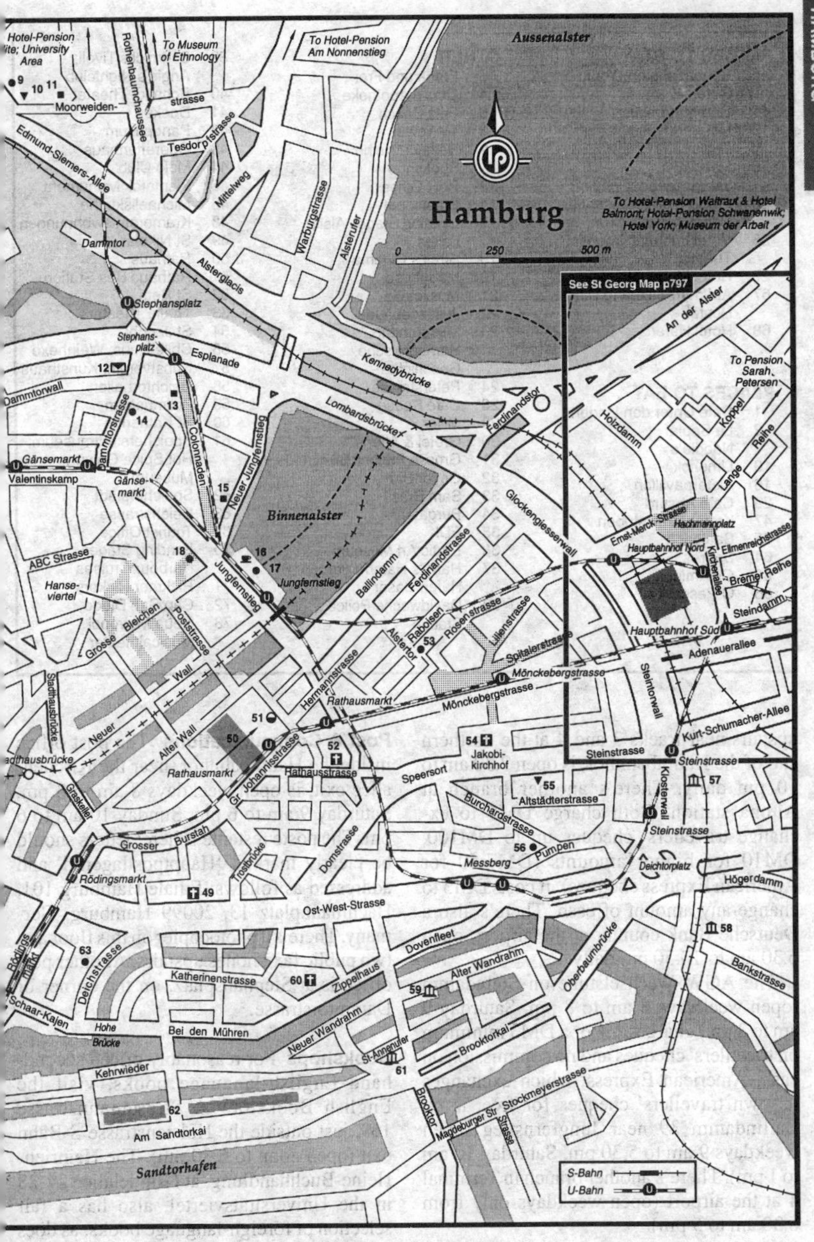
Hamburg
Aussenalster
Binnenalster
To Hotel-Pension Am Nonnenstieg
To Museum of Ethnology
To Hotel-Pension Waltraut & Hotel Balmont; Hotel-Pension Schwanenwik; Hotel York; Museum der Arbeit
See St Georg Map p797
To Pension Sarah Petersen
Dammtor
Stephansplatz
Gänsemarkt
Jungfernstieg
Rathausmarkt
Rödingsmarkt
Hauptbahnhof Nord
Hauptbahnhof Süd
Mönckebergstrasse
Steinstrasse
Messberg
Deichtorplatz
Sandtorhafen
S-Bahn
U-Bahn
0
250
500 m

PLACES TO STAY

5 Schanzenstern Youth Hotel
11 Dammtorpalais
13 Hotel-Pension Bei der Esplanade
15 Hotel Vier Jahreszeiten; Condi
20 Frauenhotel Hanseatin; Café Endlich
25 Hotel Imperial; Imperial Theatre
27 Hotel Monopol
67 Auf dem Stintfang DJH Hostel
68 Hotel Hafen

PLACES TO EAT

1 Café Unter den Linden
2 La Sepia
7 Noodle's
10 Limerick
16 Alsterpavillion
29 Café Absurd
47 Krameramtsstuben
55 Saalbach
64 Sagres
65 Os Amigos
66 O Pescador

OTHER

3 Frank und Frei
4 Oma's Apotheke
6 Fritz Bauch
8 TV Tower
9 Heinrich Heine Bookshop
12 Post Office
14 Staatsoper
17 Landing Stages Alster Lakes
18 Streit's Cinema
19 Madhouse
21 Musikhalle
22 Justizgebäude
23 Museum für Hamburgische Geschichte
24 Peterstrasse
26 Café Keese
28 Miller
30 Gretel & Alfons
31 Grosse Freiheit 36
32 Geyer Bar
33 Sam Brasil
34 Purgatory
35 EDK
36 Erotic Art Museum
37 Harry's Hamburger Hafen Basar
38 Davidwache Police Station
39 Schmidt's Tivoli; Angie's Nightclub
40 Schmidt Theater
41 Docks
42 Panoptikum
43 Operettenhaus
44 Mojo Club
45 Bismarck Monument
46 Michaeliskirche
48 Krameramtswohnungen
49 St Nikolai
50 Rathaus
51 Rathaus Bus Station
52 St Petri
53 Thalia Theater
54 St Jacobi
56 Chile Haus; Weinhexe
57 Kunstverein; Kunsthaus
58 Deichtorhallen
59 Zollmuseum
60 St Katherine
61 Speicherstadtmuseum; Hot Spice Gewürz Museum
62 Speicherstadt
63 Deichstrasse
69 Tourist Office
70 Landing Stages Harbour Cruises
71 Rickmer Rickers
72 Cap San Diego
73 Neue Metropol Musicaltheater

upstairs near tracks 3 and 4 at the northern end of the Hauptbahnhof, is open 7.30 am to 10 pm daily. There's another branch at Altona station. Both charge DM5 to exchange travellers' cheques up to DM100, DM10 for higher amounts (DM7.50 for American Express cheques). It costs DM3 to change any amount of cash. There's also a Deutsche Bank counter at the airport, open 6.30 am to 10.30 pm daily.

The AGW Wechselstube on Steindamm (open weekdays 8 am to 8 pm, Saturday 9 am to 3 pm) charges 1% or a DM3 minimum on travellers' cheques and no commission on cash. American Express, which exchanges its own travellers' cheques for free, is on Ballindamm 39 near Jungfernstieg (open weekdays 9 am to 5.30 pm, Saturday 10 am to 1 pm). There's another branch in Terminal 4 at the airport (open weekdays only from 6.30 am to 5 pm).

Post & Communications The post office inside the Hauptbahnhof, near the Kirchenallee exit, is open weekdays 8 am to 8 pm, Saturday 9 am to 6 pm, Sunday 10 am to 6 pm. The poste restante is here; letters should be clearly marked 'Hauptpostlagernd' and addressed as follows: Filiale Hamburg 101, Hachmannplatz 13, 20099 Hamburg, Germany. There's a photocopier on this floor and two public fax phones upstairs. Another post office is at Stephansplatz, on the corner of Dammtorstrasse.

Bookshops For reasonably priced secondhand English-language books, visit the English Bookstore at Stresemannstrasse 169, just outside the Holstenstrasse S-Bahn exit (open noon to 6.30 pm). The Heinrich-Heine-Buchhandlung, at Grindelallee 24-28 in the Universitätsviertel, also has a fair selection of foreign-language books, as does

Thalia Bücher, with branches at Grosse Bleichen 19 and Spitalerstrasse 8, both in the city centre. Just about every map under the sun is available at Dr Götze Land und Karte, Bleichenbrücke 9 in the Bleichenhof arcade (S-Bahn: Stadthausbrücke) with a smaller branch in the Wandelhalle shopping arcade in the Hauptbahnhof.

Laundry There's a laundrette at Nobistor 34 in St Pauli (S-Bahn: Reeperbahn) and another at Am Neuen Pferdemarkt 27 (U-Bahn: Feldstrasse). You might also try the one at Wandsbeker Chaussee 159, right outside the Ritterstrasse station U-Bahn exit.

Medical Services A medical emergency service is available at ☎ 228 02 2, as well as a 24-hour first-aid service (☎ 248 28 1) and dental emergency aid (☎ 115 00). There's also a private medical and dental emergency service at ☎ 331 15 5. An international pharmacy is located near the Kirchenallee exit of the Hauptbahnhof at Steindamm 2, corner of Adenauerallee.

Emergency There are police stations all over the city, including one on the corner of Kirchenallee and Bremer Reihe, east of the Hauptbahnhof. There's another at Spielbudenplatz 31, on the corner of Davidstrasse, in St Pauli.

The municipal lost and found office (☎ 351 85 1) is at Bäckerbreitgang 73.

Dangers & Annoyances Overall, Hamburg is a safe city with a low crime rate. Junkies and pushers congregate at several places around town, most notably at the Kirchenallee exit of the Hauptbahnhof, at Hansaplatz in the St Georg quarter and in Sternschanzenpark in the Schanzenviertel. These druggies are a nuisance but generally leave passers-by alone.

There are prostitutes all along St Pauli and also on Steindamm in St Georg. Locals claim that the area around the Reeperbahn is the safest place on earth because there are so many police around.

City Centre Walking Tours

Altstadt Starting at the Hauptbahnhof, head west down Mönckebergstrasse, one of the main shopping streets, to reach **St Petri**, the oldest of Hamburg's five main churches. Dating back to the 12th century, it was completely rebuilt in the neo-Gothic style after the Great Fire of 1842. Further on is the neo-Renaissance **Rathaus** built in 1897; tours lasting 40 minutes pass through the Parliamentary Meeting Hall, about the only austere room out of a total of 647 (allegedly more than Buckingham Palace). More typical is the opulent Emperor's Hall, where Emperor Wilhelm II gave a reception in 1895 to mark the opening of the Kiel Canal. The Great Hall, with its stunning coffered ceiling, is used for official banquets and concerts. English tours (DM2) run hourly Monday to Thursday from 10.15 am to 3.15 pm, Friday to Sunday to 1.15 pm.

Head south-west down Grosse Johannisstrasse and turn left at Börsenbrücke, which takes you to the historic **Trostbrücke**, the oldest bridge linking Altstadt and Neustadt. It features statues of Ansgar, Hamburg's first archbishop (801-65), and Adolf III, the founder of the Neustadt. Just beyond are the stark ruins of **St Nikolai**, now an anti-war memorial. While the medieval original succumbed to the Great Fire of 1842, the rebuilt St Nikolai was flattened by Allied bombers 100 years later.

The Great Fire broke out in **Deichstrasse**, which runs south from Ost-West-Strasse. The restored 1780 red-brick home at No 27 Deichstrasse is particularly fine. The best view of the street is from Hohe Brücke (turn left – east – at the southern end of Deichstrasse). Back on Ost-West-Strasse, the 115m-tall spire of **St Catherine Church**, capped by a figure of the saint, comes into view further east.

A little beyond the church begins the **Merchants' District**, characterised by mighty edifices – looking very much like red-brick ocean liners – designed by expressionist architect Fritz Höger. His crowning achievement was the magnificent **Chile Haus** – built for a merchant who derived his wealth from trading with Chile – located between Burchardstrasse and Messberg. To appreciate its eccentric shape fully, place yourself on the corner of Burchardstrasse and Pumpen.

North of the Chile Haus, on Steinstrasse, is **St Jacobi**, another of Hamburg's main churches. The main attraction here is a 17th-century organ built by Arp Schnitger.

Neustadt The distinctive tower of the **Michaeliskirche** is the star attraction of the Neustadt and Hamburg's most prominent landmark. Popularly known as 'Michel', it presides over northern Germany's largest, and arguably most beautiful, Protestant baroque church. The largely whitewashed interior of the church has a cheerful feel and is flooded by natural light and there's an elegantly curved upstairs gallery. It's often filled to its capacity of 2500 during concerts played on one or all of its three organs. For a splendid view of the city, take the lift up the tower (DM4, discount DM2; entrance door 2). The church and tower are open April to September from 9 am to 6 pm Monday to Saturday (10 am to 4.30 pm in winter), and 11.30 am to 5.30 pm on Sunday (to 4.30 pm in winter).

Just below the church, in an alley called Krayenkamp, are the **Krameramtswohnungen**, tiny half-timbered houses that are the last remaining original 17th-century buildings in Hamburg. For nearly 200 years up to 1863, they were residences for the widows of members of the Guild of Small Shopkeepers. When taken over by the city in 1863, they were used as apartments for seniors until 1969 and have since been a tourist attraction. Notice the twisted chimneys. One pint-sized home can be visited daily except Monday from 10 am to 5 pm (DM2, discount DM1).

Heading west on Ludwig-Erhard-Strasse and then north on Holstenwall leads you to cobbled **Peterstrasse** whose restored baroque houses provide another glimpse of old Hamburg. The house at No 39 has been set up as a memorial site to the composer Johannes Brahms, who was born here (DM1). For a thorough chronicle of Hamburg – from primal landscape to metropolis – visit the **Museum für Hamburgische Geschichte** (Hamburg History Museum) at Holstenwall 24. It's open Tuesday to Saturday 10 am to 5 pm, Sunday to 6 pm; entry costs DM8. Here you will learn that the Reeperbahn was once the quarter of the ropemakers (reep means rope) and how effective the firebombs dropped in 1943 were. Best of all, detailed legends in German and English accompany all exhibits. Further north on Holstenwall, you'll come to the **Justizgebäude** (Halls of Justice) and the neo-baroque **Musikhalle** (concert hall) on Karl-Muck-Platz. **Gänsemarkt**, to the east, is the gateway to Hamburg's elegant shopping district (see Things to Buy).

Hamburg's Unique Fish Market

The Fischmarkt around the old Fish Auction Hall on Grosse Elbstrasse has been drawing crowds ever since it opened in 1703, and it still defines the life and spirit of Hamburg. Early on Sunday morning you'll find Hamburgers from every segment of society here, either winding up a long Saturday night of partying, or simply shopping for produce and fish fresh off the boat. In the early light, along about 200m of the Elbe, the beer flows and you can buy everything from cheap sweatshirts and tulips to a hearty breakfast or a scorched Bratwurst.

The boisterous fishmongers, hawking their wares at the top of their lungs, provide the best free entertainment. With lascivious winks and leering innuendo, they boast of the quality and size of their eels. A surreal air pervades in the adjoining turn-of-the-century auction hall, where a band cranks out rock 'n' roll to crowds desperately in need of sleep.

Hamburg life thrives here – at the edge of the river – in the good stink of mud and oil and fish. If Bruegel were to paint a picture of Hamburg life, this is where he'd set up his easel. ■

Port of Hamburg

The port of Hamburg is still one of the largest in Europe. Each year about 12,000 ships deliver and take on some 70 million tonnes of goods. The area takes up 75 sq km, accounting for 12% of Hamburg's entire surface area. An excellent way to experience this vast port is by taking a harbour cruise (see Boating & Cruises). For a panoramic view of the frenetic shipping activity, walk up the steps above the St-Pauli-Landungsbrücken U/S-Bahn stop to the Stintfang stone balcony. Below, in the area of the harbour called City Sporthafen, lies the Rickmer Rickers, a three-masted, steel windjammer from 1896, now a museum ship (DM4, children DM2) and restaurant. Moored at the Überseebrücke (Overseas Pier) is the 160m-long behemoth, **Cap San Diego**, a 10,000-tonne freighter built in Hamburg and launched in 1962. It can also be visited (DM5, children DM1).

Just west of the St Pauli landing stages stands a sturdy grey structure topped by a giant copper cupola. It marks the entrance to the **St Pauli Elbtunnel** (1911), a 426m-long passageway beneath the Elbe River connecting St Pauli with the southern suburb of Steinwerder. It is still in use, although most cars now use the New Elbe Tunnel further west. Cars and pedestrians descend some 20m in a lift – evocative of Fritz Lang's silent film *Metropolis* – make their way through the tiled tube, then ride back up on the other end. After you've made the trip, be sure to look back across the Elbe at the port and the city skyline. For the best vantage point, turn left at the exit and walk towards the river bank.

Speicherstadt

Stretching from the Deichtorhallen in the east to Baumwall, where the Alsterfleet flows into the Elbe, is the Speicherstadt, the world's largest continuous warehouse complex, built between 1885 and 1927. The still waters of the narrow canals lacing this free port zone reflect the ornate gables and green copper rooftops of the solid storage buildings.

The building of a free port became necessary when Hamburg had to join the German Customs Union after becoming part of the German Reich in 1871. An entire neighbourhood had to be demolished, displacing around 24,000 people, to make room for its construction. Today, goods are still being stored customs-free in these beautiful brick buildings until the owner decides the time is right to sell. All this and more is explained at the **Speicherstadtmuseum** (DM4, children DM2), at St Annenufer 2. Other museums in the Speicherstadt are the **Deutsches Zollmuseum** (German Customs Museum; free) at Alter Wandrahm 15, and the **Hot Spice Gewürzmuseum** (DM3, discount DM1.50) at Am Sandtorkai 32. All three museums are open from 10 am to 5 pm daily except Monday.

The tourist office runs guided walking tours (in German) of the Speicherstadt every Tuesday at 2.30 pm between April and October (DM10, children DM5)

Kunstmeile

A string of museums extends from Glockengiesserwall to Deichtorstrasse between the Alster Lakes and the Elbe along a stretch known as the Art Mile. Their opening hours are Tuesday to Sunday from 10 am to 6 pm. On Thursday, the Kunsthalle and the Museum für Kunst und Gewerbe (Museum of Arts & Crafts) are open to 9 pm and admission to each is DM6, children DM1; entry to the others varies according to the exhibition.

Kunsthalle The green cupola and columns of the Kunsthalle dominate Glockengiesserwall just north of the Hauptbahnhof. It's considered Hamburg's most important art collection ranging from medieval to 20th-century minimalist. A bold new addition, called Galerie der Gegenwart (Gallery of Contemporary Art) opened in 1997, houses post-1960s artworks.

Top billing in the Gallery of Old Masters goes to the 36 panels from the main altar of St Petri (1379-83) by Master Bertram. An early work by Rembrandt called *Simeon in the Temple* heads the sampling of Dutch 17th-century work that also includes landscapes and seascapes by Averkamp and van Goyen.

The Kunsthalle's main strength is its collection of 19th-century German paintings. An entire room is dedicated to the romantic painter Caspar David Friedrich and his haunting landscapes, including the dramatic *Eismeer* (Polar Sea). Philipp Otto Runge, who signalled the trend towards subjectivity in painting, is strongly represented too, as is the impressionist Max Liebermann and the realist Wilhelm Leibl.

Among the early 20th-century expressionist paintings that survived the sweep by the Nazis in 1937 are works by Kokoschka, Beckmann, Nolde, Marc and Klee, who is represented with an evocatively simple work, *Der Goldfisch*. The Galerie der Gegenwart centres its collection around the 'new modernists', including Joseph Beuys, Richard Serra and Georg Baselitz. It's easy to spend several hours in the Kunsthalle, but if you're pressed for time, there's a handy pamphlet (DM1) with highlights available at the ticket office.

Museum für Kunst und Gewerbe In an ornate, yellow, 19th-century building at Steintorplatz 1, just south of the Hauptbahnhof, is the Museum of Arts & Crafts. Sculptures, furniture, jewellery, porcelain, musical instruments and even entire period rooms track the evolution of applied art and sculpture in Europe, from its roots in antiquity through to the 20th century. Highlights include an entire Art Nouveau room from the 1900 Paris World Fair and a Japanese tea house, where you can attend an actual tea ceremony. The museum café *Destille* is integrated into the exhibition space.

Other Kunstmeile Museums A few metres south, on Klosterwall 15 and 23, respectively, are the **Kunsthaus** (Art House) and the **Kunstverein** (Art Association). These are smallish spaces with changing exhibits. The Deichtorhallen, former markethalls on Deichtorstrasse 1-2, house important touring exhibitions featuring art, photography, design and architecture.

Other Museums

Museum der Arbeit One of the latest additions to Hamburg's museum scene is the Museum of Labour, located on the grounds of the former New York Rubber Company at Maurienstrasse 19, in the suburb of Barmbek (U/S-Bahn: Barmbek). As its name suggests, the museum chronicles the development of the workplace in the Hamburg area, with a particular focus on the changing rights and roles of working men and women. The museum is open Monday from 1 to 9 pm, Tuesday to Saturday 10 am to 5 pm and Sunday 10 am to 6 pm. Admission is DM6, discount DM3.

Museum für Völkerkunde The impressive Museum of Ethnology at Rothenbaumchaussee 64 (U-Bahn: Hallerstrasse) has exhibits such as ivory carvings from the kingdom of Benin and a complete, intricately carved Maori meeting hall. It's open Tuesday to Sunday 10 am to 6 pm (Thursday to 9 pm). Admission is DM6, discount DM3.

St Pauli

The Reeperbahn is St Pauli's main artery and getting off at the Reeperbahn S-Bahn station plunges you right into the heart of this legendary red-light district. Just north of the station is the Grosse Freiheit (literally 'Great Freedom') street with its bright lights, dark doorways and live sex nightclubs. Smarmy doormen try to lure the passing crowd into places like *Tabu* and *Safari*. If you're interested in one of these more traditional Reeperbahn haunts, be aware of the costs before entering; these clubs can be a lot more expensive than they appear. Admission tends to be fairly low (DM5 or DM10), but it's the mandatory drink minimum (usually around DM40) that drives up the cost. The Star Club was at Grosse Freiheit 39. At the live rock music venue Grosse Freiheit 36 the Beatles once played at the basement disco Kaiserkeller (or so the story goes).

Back on the Reeperbahn, head east past a

The Renaissance of St Pauli

The character of St Pauli and its main artery, the Reeperbahn, is unique. Where else will you find live sex shows, a wax museum filled with stiff Germans and a mediocre musical by an English knight – all on the same street?

On a good night there may be as many as 30,000 people cruising the rip-roaring collection of bars, sex clubs, variety acts, restaurants, pubs and cafés known collectively by locals as the 'Kiez'. It is, of course, ironic that Paul, for whom Hamburg's 'sin centre' is named, was in fact a saint who did not take kindly to lust.

St Pauli's popularity reached its zenith in the liberated 1960s when the Beatles cut their musical teeth at the legendary – and sadly defunct – Star Club. Prostitution boomed along the lurid, spidery streets spilling off the Reeperbahn. But then a wave of hard crime and drugs sent St Pauli on a downward spiral, and rip-offs were commonplace (eg serving cheap wine from expensive bottles). Germany's *Sündenmeil* (Sin Mile) had to reinvent itself to survive – which it did.

These days another layer of attractions has usurped the tired red-light activity as the number one draw for tourists. The musical *Cats* has been playing to sold-out houses since 1986. Stylish nightclubs keep a hip, moneyed clientele entertained until dawn, and there are surprisingly good restaurants, bars and clubs.

The sex industry is still in full swing but it has lost some of its rougher edges: pimps no longer loiter and leer. Rather, they've been seen to lower – via pulleys – a bracing flagon of whisky to their hard-working girls in the street. The place has a feeling of calamity infused with a weird gentility. ■

jumble of sex shops, peep shows and questionable hotels to Davidstrasse. The **Davidwache** (1913-14), is a dignified brick building, festooned with ornate ceramic tiles, designed by the celebrated architect Fritz Schumacher. It's the home base for 150 police. Thanks to their presence – and the mobs of people milling in the streets at all times of day – St Pauli has a reputation for being the safest area in Hamburg.

Herbertstrasse, a block-long bordello behind a metal wall about 50m south of the police station, is off limits to women and men under 18.

For tamer titillation follow Davidstrasse to Bernard-Nocht-Strasse where, at No 69, you'll find the **Erotic Art Museum** (open 10 am to midnight, closed Monday; admission DM15) in a restored warehouse. Erotic art from the 16th century to the present features, including Japanese wood prints, etchings, sculptures and paintings from artists such as Henry Miller, Jean Cocteau, Eugene Delacroix and Tomi Ungerer. The shop has an interesting collection of books and posters for sale.

A bit east, at No 89-91, you'll find **Harry's Hamburger Hafen Basar**, the life work of Harry Rosenberg, a bearded character known to seamen world-wide. For decades Harry has been buying trinkets and souvenirs from world travellers. The result is a shop crammed with oddities including Zulu drums, stuffed giraffes and even a shrunken head. The admission price of DM4 is refunded with a minimum purchase of DM10. Another unusual shop is the **Condomerie** back on Spielbudenplatz 18, a side street running parallel to the Reeperbahn (walk back on Davidstrasse, then right after the Davidwache). It has an amusing and extensive collection of sex toys and protection devices and offers DM100 to any gentleman who can properly wear the gargantuan condom hanging in the window. They say the prize money has been awarded twice, lucky devils.

Otherwise, Spielbudenplatz is the place to go for more 'respectable' entertainment. This is where *Cats* plays at the Operettenhaus and where a number of cafés and cabarets are located (see Entertainment). At No 3, you'll find the **Panoptikum**, a wax museum where models of prominent Germans from the arts, history and politics are on display. It's open weekdays from 11 am to 9 pm, Saturdays 11 am to midnight, and Sundays 10 am to 9 pm. Admission is DM7, discount DM4.

Schanzenviertel

The Schanzenviertel quarter, west of the TV Tower, has a village atmosphere – and grungy streets which graphically point out that not everyone in Hamburg lives in a palatial villa. Its main artery is Schulterblatt (literally 'shoulder blade'), which derives its name from a defunct 19th-century pub whose doorway was crowned by the shoulder bone of a whale. Immigrants, students, workers and left-wing radicals inhabit rows of tall apartment buildings with ornate façades which have certainly seen better days. Turkish grocers display their eggplants, oranges and other produce in artful pyramids right on the street, and there's no shortage of pubs and restaurants with character and decent prices.

On Schulterblatt, you cannot miss the graffiti-covered building that looks one step away from demolition. This is the **Rote Flora**, now an alternative culture centre, but once the famous Flora Theatre. Plans to make this historic venue into a musical theatre were thwarted by a neighbourhood alliance which feared that an influx of theatregoers and tourists would lead to an undesired beautification of the quarter, undermining its edgy character.

To tour the Schanzenviertel, walk south on Schanzenstrasse from the Sternschanze S-Bahn station. After about 0.5km, the road merges with Schulterblatt. Walk back north on Schulterblatt until you get to Susannenstrasse, then turn right again and head back to the S-Bahn.

TV Tower Properly known as Heinrich-Hertz-Turm, Hamburg's sleek TV Tower on Lagerstrasse looks out over the city from a height of just under 280m. The viewing platform, reached by a lift (DM6), and revolving restaurant, though, are 'only' at 128m. For a real scream – partially caused by having to part with DM250 to do so – you can leap from here in summer, attached to a bungee rope, of course.

Altona

Just west of St Pauli lies the neighbourhood of Altona, once a separate city that belonged to Denmark and Prussia before becoming part of Hamburg in 1937. Until then, the relationship between the two cities was based on a long-standing rivalry, which reached its peak around 1800 when Altona's merchant fleet was actually larger than Hamburg's. These days locals quip that the name Altona actually evolved from the Low German 'all to nah', meaning 'all too near'.

The **Stuhlmann fountain**, which you'll see when you turn south from the eastern exit of Altona train station, symbolises this age-old struggle for local supremacy. Just beyond lies the **Platz der Republik**, a rectangular park where locals congregate to play *boules* (bowls). Museumstrasse runs along its western side, and at No 23 you'll find the **Altona Museum** (open 10 am to 6 pm, closed Monday; admission DM8). Founded in 1863, its exhibits include exquisite models of sailing ships, harpoons, scrimshaw and other nautical memorabilia. An entire room is filled with an impressive display of ships' bowsprits. The museum restaurant is in an authentic 19th-century farmhouse.

At the southern end of the park looms the stately **Altona Rathaus** (1896-98), a white neoclassical affair whose southern wing was once the foyer of the city's first train station. Immediately in front is the equestrian **Kaiser Wilhelm I monument** (1896). South of the Rathaus is the **Palmaille**, a beautiful boulevard lined with linden trees and elegant, neoclassical, merchant houses built between 1790 and 1825; don't miss Nos 49 and 116. The name 'Palmaille' derives from the Italian *palla* for 'ball' and *maglio* for 'bat' and refers back to the street's intended (but never realised) use in the 17th century as a playing field.

Further west, it continues as Elbchaussee, one of Germany's grandest thoroughfares, lined by immense mansions with park-sized gardens.

Blankenese & Övelgönne

The people of Hamburg say that the better you're doing in life, the further west in the city you live. Those who reside in Övelgönne are making it; those who end up in Blankenese have arrived. **Övelgönne** was once home to captains who plied their trade on the Elbe River and North Sea. Its riverside walkway – past immaculate old homes and beneath a canopy of stately trees – is among the prettiest in Hamburg. At the **Museumshafen Övelgönne** on the Neumühlen ferry landing, some 20 old working and fishing vessels dating from the 1890s to 1930s bob lazily in the water. All found as wrecks, they've been restored to ship-shape condition (placards on the pier explain the ships). There are no official visiting hours but you can pretty much come anytime.

Heading west along the Elbe gets you to **Blankenese**, a former fishing village and haven for cutthroats that now boasts some of the most expensive property in Germany. The labyrinthine, narrow streets with clusters of fine houses are best explored on foot via the 58 stairways (ie 4846 steps) that wend their way through the neighbourhood. One of the most popular spots from which to view the Elbe (nearly 3km wide here), and the container ships putting out to sea, is from atop the 75m-high Süllberg hill.

Restaurants and cafés can be found at the Blankenese Landungsbrücke along Strandweg. The tiny bus No 48 – nicknamed the 'Mountain Goat' because of the steep, narrow alleys it has to navigate – shuttles between the hill-top town centre and the Elbe shores.

To get to Övelgönne by public transport, take bus No 112 from Hauptbahnhof. To get to Blankenese, take the S-Bahn No 1. From April to early September, there's also a scheduled boat service downriver from Pier 3 at St-Pauli-Landungsbrücken. The trip to Övelgönne takes 15 minutes and costs DM2.60 each way. To Blankenese it's 40 minutes and DM7 each way. Children up to age 16 pay half-price. On weekdays boats leave at 10.30 am and 2.30 pm; there are two additional sailings on weekends, at 11.30 am and 3.30 pm.

Parks & Gardens

Parks, forests, lakes and rivers cover about one quarter of Hamburg, and some 220,000 trees line its streets. The band of public gardens that stretches from the TV Tower to the banks of the Elbe begins with **Planten un Blomen**. This beautifully landscaped park encompasses a botanical garden with a tropical greenhouse, and an austerely handsome Japanese garden. The park lake features a hydraulic organ with light effects (nightly performances May to August at 10 pm, September at 9 pm).

South of here are the **Kleine Wallanlagen** und **Grosse Wallanlagen**. The latter has a roller-skating rink (ice-skating in winter) and a children's theatre. The stretch towards the Elbe is called the **Elbpark**. It contains the 15m-tall **Otto von Bismarck monument** (1906), homage to the nationalistic visionary and Germany's first chancellor. In a cruel irony, the 'Iron Chancellor' now looks down upon the lurid lights of the Reeperbahn.

Outside the city centre, in the northern suburb of Stellingen, is **Hagenbecks Tierpark**, Europe's largest privately owned zoo (open daily 9 am to 4.30 pm; U-Bahn: Hagenbecks Tierpark). It has more than 2100 animals representing 370 species housed in 54 enclosures. Admission is a hefty DM19 for adults and DM13 for kids (viewing the dolphins costs an extra DM6/4).

To the east, in the suburb of Winterhude, is the large **Stadtpark**, where many outdoor concerts are held in summer. The Planetarium, in a converted water tower, is also here. In Altona is the sprawling **Volkspark** with its vast stadium, the home of the Hamburger Sportverein (HSV) soccer club (see Spectator Sports).

Boating & Cruises

Boating on the Alster Lakes is a fine way to pass a sunny afternoon. Climb aboard one of the hourly ferries that call at 10 landing stages on the Outer Alster Lake and the river itself (DM1.50 per stop or DM12 for the entire trip). Or you can rent your own canoe, small sailing, rowing or pedal boat. You'll find boats for hire at Bodos Bootsteg at Harvestehuder Weg 1b in Harvestehude, or Dornheim at Isekai 1 in Eppendorf. Prices start at DM13 per hour, plus DM2 per person.

Alster Cruises The 50-minute Alster Lakes tour covers both the Inner and the Outer Alster (DM14). It departs twice an hour from 10 am to 6 pm between April and September and less frequently during the rest of the year. A scenic two-hour tour of the Fleet canals (DM23) takes you from the Alster to the Elbe and historic Speicherstadt, via a couple of locks. It leaves at 10.45 am, 1.45 pm and 4.45 pm between April and October. The idyllic two-hour Canal Tour (DM20) floats past stately villas and gorgeous gardens six times daily between May and September and four times daily in April and October. All boats leave from Jungfernstieg. There's a 50% discount for children under 16.

English-language pamphlets and cassettes with a description of the sights are available for the Alster Lakes and the Fleet cruises.

Port Cruises A one-hour steamer grand tour (DM15, children DM7.50), operated by the HADAG company (☎ 311 70 70), sails from Pier 2 half-hourly from 9.30 am to 6 pm between April and early October. The rest of the year, it leaves every 90 minutes between 10.30 am and 3 pm weekdays, and hourly between 10.30 am and 3.30 pm weekends. Tours with English commentary run daily at 11.15 am from March to November from Pier 1 only. Other HADAG tour options are outlined in the leaflet available at the pier or by calling ☎ 311 70 70.

Cycling

Hamburg is flat so cycling is an excellent way to explore the city and the surrounding countryside. The paved path around the Outer Alster is a popular route (also good for walking or inline-skating), while another takes you along the Elbe Banks from St Pauli to Blankenese and Wedel past gorgeous homes and forests (20km one way).

The excellent *Fahrradtourenkarte für Hamburg*, available at Dr Götze Land und Karte (see Bookshops), contains more ideas and itineraries. If you want to rent a bike, try Fahrradladen St Georg, Schmilinskystrasse 6 in St Georg, or Fahrrad Richter, Barmbeker Strasse 16 in Winterhude. Both charge DM15 a day and require a DM100 deposit.

Organised Tours

City sightseeing tours (Die Hamburgere Hummelbahn ☎ 792 89 79) in English on red double-decker buses run six times daily between 11 am and 4 pm in summer and twice at 11 am and 3 pm in winter (DM26, children DM13). They leave either from Kirchenallee next to the Hauptbahnhof or from St-Pauli-Landungsbrücken and last 1¾ hours; you can add on a harbour cruise for an extra DM12.

A more atmospheric way to go is on the double-decker Hummelbahn 'train' (actually more of a wagon ride through the streets) from the 1920s. Tours run hourly from 10 am to 5 pm between April and October and three times daily the rest of the year (DM20, children DM7).

The Cityhopper bus (Hamburg Vision ☎ 317 90 127) allows the greatest flexibility; you may get on and off as many times a day as you want at each of its 12 stops at or near the major sights. Buses leave hourly from the Hauptbahnhof between 10.20 am and 4.20 pm in summer and three times daily in winter. Tickets are available on the bus (DM20, children DM7).

Special Events

The **Hamburger Dom**, one of Europe's largest and oldest festivals, dates from 1329. Attracting 10 million visitors a year, it's held in late March, late July and late November on Heiligengeistfeld, a vast field west of the city centre.

The **Hafengeburtstag** (harbour birthday), a wild party ashore and in the water, commemorates the day in 1189 when Emperor Barbarossa granted Hamburg's Neustadt customs exemption in the lower Elbe area. It runs for five days, beginning 7 May, each year.

Places to Stay – bottom end

Accommodation in Hamburg is not cheap.

St Georg, east of the Hauptbahnhof, has most of the budget hotels, but be careful about walking into just any place. You may find yourself in a *Stundenhotel*, tawdry operations where rooms are rented by the hour. The places listed below, or in the hotel brochure available at the tourist offices, are safe choices. You can also book a room through the tourist offices or by calling the Hamburg Hotline (☎ 300 51 30 0). There's a DM6 booking fee for this service. Except where noted, all room rates listed below include breakfast.

Camping *Camping Buchholz* (☎ 540 45 32; open all year), at Kieler Strasse 374 in the suburb of Stellingen, is perhaps your best camping option. It's a 10-minute walk from the Hagenbecks Tierpark U-Bahn station. You can also take bus No 183 from Altona train station, which runs down Kieler Strasse. Tent sites cost from DM12.50 to DM18.50, plus DM7 per person. Warm showers are an extra DM1.50. You can also sleep in your car for DM10.50 plus DM7 per person.

On the same road at No 650 is the friendly *City Camp Tourist* (☎ 570 44 98; open all year) which charges DM10 to DM15 per tent site, DM7 per person and DM6 per car. To get there, it's best to take the U3 to Schlump, then change to bus No 182 and get off at the Reichsbahnstrasse stop; from here it's a 200m-walk.

The newish *Camping Schnelsen Nord* (☎ 559 42 25; open April to October) is at Wunderbrunnen 2 and costs DM11 to DM12 per tent site, DM7 per person and DM4.50 per car. From Hauptbahnhof take U2 to Niendorf Markt, then bus No 291 (direction Schnelsen Nord) to the Dornrösschenweg stop. From there it's 10 minutes on foot (follow the signs).

A bit outside of Hamburg, at Falkensteiner Ufer on the banks of the Elbe in Blankenese, is *Campingplatz Blankenese* (☎ 812 94 9; open March to October), which charges DM8 to DM12 per tent site plus DM6 per person. Take the S-Bahn No 1 to Blankenese, then bus No 189 (direction Wedel) to Tindtsthaler Weg; then it's a 10-minute walk down to the shore.

Hostels Hamburg's two DJH hostels are large but it's best to make a reservation, especially during the high season (June to September). *Auf dem Stintfang* (☎ 319 10 37) at Alfred-Wegener-Weg 5 has a great location atop a hill above the St-Pauli-Landungsbrücken. There are superb views of the Elbe and the harbour. There's room here for 350 people, but if all the beds are full, they let you flop on a mattress in the common area or refer you to an inexpensive hotel. After a recent renovation, the hostel now has self-catering kitchen facilities and laundry. Lockout is between 9.30 and 11.30 am for cleaning. Bed, breakfast and sheets are DM26 for juniors and DM32 for seniors. Hot and cold meals are available.

The other DJH hostel is *Horner Rennbahn* (☎ 651 16 71) and less convenient at Rennbahnstrasse 100 (U-Bahn: Horner Rennbahn, then 10 minutes on foot north past the racecourse and leisure centre). It's a modern 250-bed facility that serves buffet breakfast. Beds are DM32/37 for juniors/ seniors in six-bed dorms and DM5 more in three and four-bed rooms. There's a DM2.50 discount per day for stays of three nights and longer, but this only applies to bookings made in advance.

The *Schanzenstern* (☎ 439 84 41) at Bartelsstrasse 12 in the Schanzenviertel area is a privately run youth hotel in a building that was formerly the Mont Blanc pen factory. Beds in sparse but clean dorms are DM33. They also have singles/doubles/ triples for DM60/90/110. The breakfast buffet is DM10 per person and is served in an adjoining café where there is also a menu of healthy dishes at reasonable prices.

Private Rooms Private rooms are hard to come by in Hamburg and, at least for short-term stays, will not represent much of a saving over budget hotels. Rooms are usually in a flat shared by a group of people, often students.

Among the agencies worth trying are:

Agentur Zimmer Frei (☎ 412 07 0) at Baumkamp 58; *Bed & Breakfast* (☎ 491 56 66), Methfesselstrasse 49; *Hanseatische Zimmervermittlungs-Agentur* (☎ 655 56 00), Rhiemsweg 35; and *Mitwohnzentrale* (☎ 194 45) at Schulterblatt 112.

For short-term stays, expect to pay about DM50 for a single and DM85 to DM100 for a double per night. These rates usually include commission and tax (15%), but be sure to ask. Most agencies also rent rooms long term, which should cost from DM500 to DM800 per month. If you want a place of your own, simple one-bedroom flats start at DM800 per month, plus commission and tax. For one-month stays, the agencies usually charge 25-30% commission (more for longer stays).

Hotels – St Georg The *Hotel-Pension Kieler Hof* (☎ 243 02 4) at Bremer Reihe 15 has basic singles/doubles for DM60/100 and some with shower for DM70/110. Triples are DM165. At *Hotel-Pension Annenhof* (☎ 243 42 6), Lange Reihe 23, rooms with shower and WC go for DM56/98. Wedged between a sex shop and a pub at Steindamm 4, the *Hotel Village* (☎ 246 13 7), a former brothel, has retained ceiling mirrors, semi-lurid décor and sensual photographs in the hallways. Basic singles/doubles are DM92/ 102; those with shower and WC cost DM122/ 154.

The *Eden Hotel* (☎ 248 48 0), Ellmenreichstrasse 20, has modern rooms, all with TV and telephone. Expect to pay DM75/120 for a room with shared facilities and up to DM150/220 for those with private bath.

On the bustling Adenauerallee at No 7, you'll find the small, family-run *Polo Hotel* (☎ 241 04 3) which has a few no-frills singles/doubles from DM70/DM120. Rooms with private facilities cost up to DM130/240.

Hotels – Universitätsviertel There's a smattering of low-budget options in this colourful neighbourhood.

Hotel-Pension Preuss (☎ 445 71 6) is in the Dammtorpalais at Moorweidenstrasse 34, a huge brick building housing several hotels (also see Places to Stay – middle). Tasteful but basic singles/ doubles start at DM80/120 and reach DM110/150 for rooms with private facilities. Triples cost DM180. *Hotel-Pension Elite* (☎ 454 62 7), around the corner from the university at Binderstrasse 24, is decent value at DM90/110 for rooms with shower but shared toilet.

Places to Stay – middle

Hamburg has some medium-priced hotels and pensions that offer fairly good value. Many take up entire floors of a sprawling building or are upstairs from shops or restaurants. Often you must ring to enter. Expect to pay from DM85 to DM130 for rooms with shared facilities. Those with private bath cost around DM140/180.

St Georg *Hotel City-House* (☎ 280 38 50; fax 280 18 38), at Pulverteich 25, offers double rooms with shower and toilet from DM168 to DM198. *Hotel Mirage* (☎ 241 76 2; fax 246 66 5), Steindamm 49, has rooms with private baths that cost from DM110/ 140. *Hotel St Georg* (☎ 241 14 1; fax 280 33 70), at Kirchenallee 23 opposite the Hauptbahnhof, has basic singles/doubles from DM95/100 and rooms with showers (but no private toilet) for DM110/150. Next door is *Hotel Fürst Bismarck* (☎ 109 19 5; fax 280 10 96) where singles with private bath range from DM85 to DM120 and doubles from DM160 to DM180. Located in a pleasant and quiet part of St Georg on Holzdamm 43 is the tiny *Steen's Hotel* (☎ 244 64 2; fax 280 35 93), which has singles/doubles/triples with showers from DM90/130/180.

City Centre *Frauenhotel Hanseatin* (☎ 341 34 5; fax 345 82 5), at Dragonerstall 11, a busy street near the Musikhalle concert hall, accommodates women only. They charge DM100/140 for singles/doubles with shared bath and up to DM150/180 for those with private bath. *Hotel-Pension Bei der Esplanade* (☎ 342 96 1; fax 354 08 2) is located at No 45 in the historic Colonnaden pedestrianised street near the opera and the

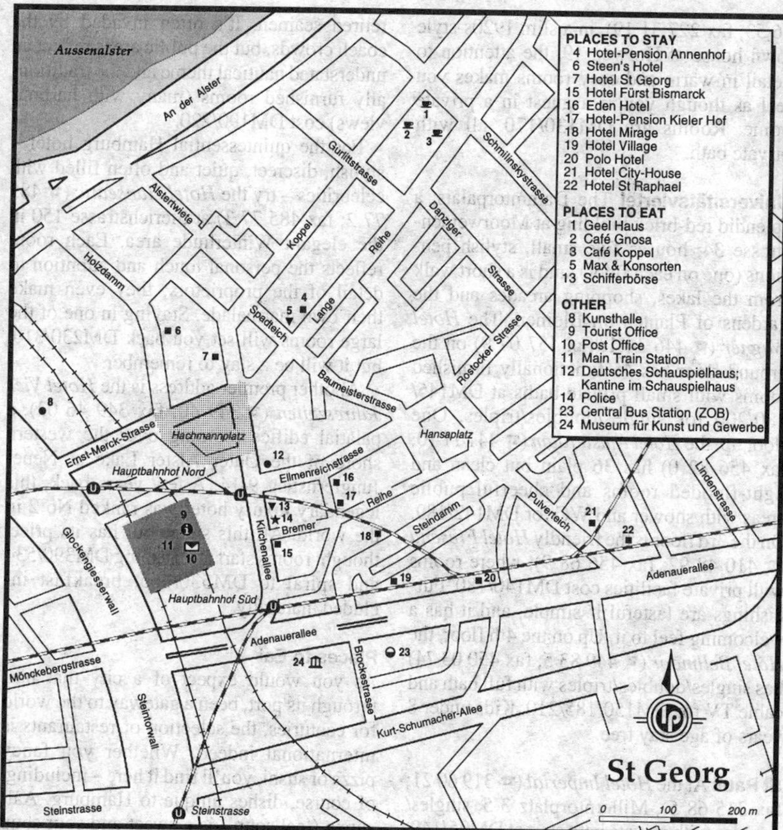

Jungfernstieg. Rooms, some quite large, are modern and have a shower. Singles/doubles/triples start at DM100/135/175.

Around the Alster Lakes *Hotel-Pension Am Nonnenstieg* (☎ 480 64 90; fax 480 64 94 9) is at Nonnenstieg 11, a quiet side street in up-market Harvestehude. Its entrance is jammed with knick-knacks, while the rooms are cheerfully decorated; some have kitchenettes. All rooms have private bath and range from DM85 to DM140 for singles and from DM130 to DM180 for doubles; optional breakfast is DM12 per person.

In a stately white building at Schwanenwik 30 you'll find two friendly hotels sharing a tasteful sense of décor and a lovely view of the Outer Alster Lake. *Hotel-Pension Waltraut* (☎ 221 00 7; fax 222 87 3) is on the ground floor, while the slightly swankier *Hotel Belmont* (☎ & fax 220 51 28) is upstairs. Fairly spacious singles/doubles with shower start at DM85/140 in both places. Next door, at No 29, is *Hotel-Pension Schwanenwik* (☎ 220 09 18; fax 229 04 46), whose very clean and modern rooms cost DM85/110 (shared bath) and DM135/160 (with all facilities). At the *Hotel York* (☎ 220

26 53; fax 227 31 19), in a slim 1920s-style town house at Hofweg 19, the attention to detail in warm and cosy rooms makes you feel as though you're a guest in a private home. Rooms are DM130/170, all with private bath.

Universitätsviertel The Dammtorpalais, a splendid red-brick building at Moorweidenstrasse 34, houses five small, stylish pensions (one on each floor), and is a short walk from the lakes, shopping arcades and the gardens of Planten un Blomen. The *Hotel Wagner* (☎ 446 34 1; fax 457 07 9) on the ground floor has 45 functionally furnished rooms with small private baths at DM145/180/200 for singles/doubles/triples. One floor up, the *Hotel Amsterdam* (☎ 441 11 10; fax 456 82 0) has 36 plain but clean and light-flooded rooms and cheerful public areas with shower and WC for DM142/189. On the 3rd floor is the friendly *Hotel Fresena* (☎ 410 48 92; fax 456 68 9), where rooms with private facilities cost DM140/180. Furnishings are tasteful if simple, and it has a welcoming feel to it. Up on the 4th floor, the *Hotel Bellmoor* (☎ 449 83 5; fax 450 03 74) has singles/doubles/triples with full bath and cable TV for DM150/185/210. Kids under 8 years of age stay free.

St Pauli At the *Hotel Imperial* (☎ 319 60 21; fax 315 68 5), Millerntorplatz 3-5, singles/doubles with private bath start at DM95/140. *Hotel Monopol* (☎ 311 77 0; fax 311 77 15 1), at Reeperbahn 48, has singles/doubles with full baths for DM150/200 and triples for DM195.

Places to Stay – top end

Near the Hauptbahnhof at Adenauerallee 41 is the business-style *Hotel St Raphael* (☎ 248 20 0; fax 248 20 33 3). The staff here are friendly and knowledgeable, and the modern rooms lack no creature comfort. Singles cost from DM190, doubles from DM240. In St Pauli, the urge to splurge is well directed towards the *Hotel Hafen* (☎ 311 13 0; fax 319 27 36), at Seewartenstrasse 9, a 19th-century former home for retired seamen. It's often invaded by the coach crowds, but the public areas reflect an understated nautical theme and the traditionally furnished rooms (many with harbour views) cost DM190/220.

For the quintessential Hamburg hotel – stylish, discreet, quiet and often filled with celebrities – try the *Hotel Hanseatic* (☎ 485 77 2; fax 485 77 3) at Sierichstrasse 150 in the elegant Winterhude area. Each room reflects the personal touch and attention to detail of the proprietors; they even make their own marmalade. Staying in one of the large rooms will set you back DM230/310, but it will be a stay to remember.

Another premier address is the *Hotel Vier Jahreszeiten* (☎ 349 40; fax 349 46 02), a palatial edifice looming over the western shore of the Outer Alster Lake at Neuer Jungfernstieg 9-14. A few years back, this legendary luxury hotel was ranked No 2 in the world. All this splendour has its price, though: rooms start at a gasping DM390/534 and spiral to DM530/665, breakfast included, naturally.

Places to Eat

As you would expect of a city that has, through its port, been a gateway to the world for centuries, the selection of restaurants is international indeed. Whether you fancy pizza or sushi, you'll find it here – including, of course, dishes unique to Hamburg. Aalsuppe ('eel soup') is a sweet and sour soup made with dried fruit, ham, vegetables, lots of herbs and, yes, even some eel. Labskaus consists of boiled marinated beef put through the grinder with red beets and mashed potatoes and served with a fried egg, herring and pickles. And then there's Birnen mit Bohnen und Speck, which is pears, beans and bacon, all cooked in one pot to allow the different flavours to mingle. (It all tastes better than it sounds.) Hamburg is one of the best spots in Germany for fresh fish.

City Centre For a splurge and a truly fishy Hamburg experience, head to *Schifferbörse* on Kirchenallee 46 opposite the Hauptbahnhof exit. Here, you sit amidst nautically themed décor beneath a giant wooden model ship dangling from the ceiling. Expect to pay about DM35 for a main dish and one drink. *Saalbach* at Steinstrasse 19 is a trendy self-service eatery (lunch only) with a salad bar and main dishes priced around DM10. You pay about the same to eat in the company of actors at the basement *Kantine* of the Deutsches Schauspielhaus theatre at Kirchenallee 39.

Popular with business and media types is the *Weinhexe* in the 'bow' of the Chile Haus at Burchardstrasse 13c. Stylish and cosy, it offers an opulent antipasti selection and daily specials starting at DM20. It's only open weekdays from 11 am to 8.30 pm. One of the best places for typical Hamburg fare is *Krameramtsstuben*, located in a charming half-timbered house at Krayenkamp 10 at the foot of the Michaeliskirche. The décor is old-fashioned, the cuisine solid but perhaps a bit pricey, with main courses around DM25.

For a chance to get a close-up look at Hamburg high society, treat yourself to an afternoon at the Biedermeier-style *Condi* in the Vier Jahreszeiten Hotel at Neuer Jungfernstieg 9. Expect to part with DM7 for a cappuccino, and if you're on a tight budget, don't even think about selecting one of the mouthwatering home-made cakes. The splendid view of the Inner Alster Lake, though, is free here, as it is at the *Alster-pavillion* across the street on Jungfernstieg. This is Hamburg's most established coffee house, frequented by Heinrich Heine in 1799 and now favoured by ladies with lap dogs. Things loosen up a little in spring when the terrace opens.

Home-made breads and cakes are just part of the menu at *Café Koppel* on Koppel 66 in St Georg. It's a quiet, non-smoking environment with lots of choices for vegetarians.

St Pauli & Port Area For fresh fish at reasonable prices, there's perhaps no better place than the small area just east of the St-Pauli-Landungsbrücken U/S-Bahn station, where about a dozen earthy Portuguese restaurants have set up shop. One of the best is *Sagres* at Vorsetzen 42, a snug establishment brimming with maritime décor and always packed to the gills. The menu includes every type of fish caught that day, many under DM20. If Sagres is full, try *Os Amigos* on the corner of Karpfanger Strasse and Reimarus Strasse or the more up-market *O Pescador* at the intersection of Reimarus and Dietmar-Koel-Strasse.

For European coffee specialities, go to *Café Absurd* on Clemens-Schultz-Strasse 86 in St Pauli. At night they also serve small dishes in a relaxed atmosphere, conducive to talking.

Schanzenviertel & Universitätsviertel In both areas there's a surprising selection of high-quality budget eateries. Grindelallee cuts right through the university area, and at No 18 you'll find *Limerick*, a casual student hang-out with daily lunch specials and good pizzas, cooked in a wood-fired oven, from DM6.50. Nearby, on Grindelhof 14a, inside the Abaton Cinema, is the *Abaton Bistro* where students increase their energy with biologically correct food and beverages. There are lots of options for vegetarians.

If you can tolerate the snotty service and arrogant stares of the alternative in-crowd at the *Café Unter den Linden* at Juliusstrasse 16 in the Schanzenviertel, you might enjoy the large coffees (DM6) served French-style in bowls. There's also a small bistro menu. More generous portions are served in the Mediterranean-style *La Sepia* at Schulterblatt 36. Feast on terrific fish dinners while seated at long, communal wooden tables. *Noodle's*, at Schanzenstrasse 2-4, specialises in, you guessed it, pasta. The salads are good too, and it's a friendly place.

Altona A feast for both eye and palate is lunch or dinner at *Eisenstein*, a postmodern symphony of stone, steel and wood wrapped around the brick chimney of an old ship propeller factory. It's all part of a shopping and entertainment complex called the Zeisehallen and located at Friedensallee 9. Eisenstein is known for its wood-fired pizza, but the salads and fish dishes are good, too.

A bit less pricey is the adjacent *Filmhauskneipe*, where barren wooden tables seat film executives and an intellectual crowd. For a very casual atmosphere, try *Auflauf* at Barnerstrasse 10a, which serves nothing but creative casseroles; some are vegetarian, and prices are below DM16. You can also put one together yourself.

Self-Catering You're likely to find several supermarkets in each district of Hamburg. Penny Markt outlets are, for example, on the corner of Lange Reihe and Schmilinskystrasse in St Georg; on Spritzenplatz in Altona; and at Schulterblatt 137 in the Schanzenviertel. Other stores are at Grindelhof 23 in the Universitätsviertel, on Bahrenfelderstrasse in Altona, and at Alter Steinweg 13 near Grossneumarkt in the city centre. An outlet of the Conti superstore is on Neuer Kamp, just to the left as you exit the Feldstrasse U-Bahn station.

Entertainment

Listings For cultural event and lifestyle information, look for the monthly magazines *Szene* (DM5), *Prinz* (DM5) and *Oxmox* (DM4.30). The *Hamburger* is a free English-language booklet with general and event information and is usually available at tourist offices and occasionally in bookshops, hotels and pubs. In the same places you might find the slightly more thorough *Hamburger Vorschau* (in German).

Cinemas Though practically every foreign film is dubbed into German, several Hamburg cinemas screen movies in the original language with subtitles. Look for the acronym 'OmU' in film listings and at cinemas. Venues include *Abaton* on the corner of Grindelhof and Allende Platz in the Universitätsviertel; *3001* in the Schanzenviertel at Schanzenstrasse 75; and *Streit's* on Jungfernstieg in the city centre. Movies tend to be quite expensive; tickets on Saturday night can set you back as much as DM17. Many cinemas charge less (as little as DM8) on Wednesday and sometimes for matinee shows. Some also give discounts to students with an ID.

Discos & Clubs Most nightclubs are located on the Reeperbahn and its side streets, but don't even bother showing up before 10 pm. *Mojo Club* at Reeperbahn 1 is open only on Friday and Saturday after 11 pm and attracts a trendy crowd with its dance-floor jazz. There's also a Jazz Café here (free), open at 9 pm.

If you enjoy dancing the tango, foxtrot and waltz, head across the street to 'Ball Paradox' at *Café Keese* at Reeperbahn 19, where it's always 'ladies choice'. Couples may go together, of course, and the atmosphere is highly respectable. It opens nightly after 8 pm and for Sunday tea from 4 pm. Dress smartly.

Upstairs from Schmidt's Tivoli (see Theatre) at Spielbudenplatz 27 is *Angie's Nightclub* (open nightly after 10 pm). Angie is a large black transsexual who knows how to throw a party. Occasionally there will be spontaneous concerts by accomplished (and sometimes even famous) guests.

Some may think they've died and gone to hell when they find themselves surrounded by lava lamps, velvet Jesuses and plastic flowers, but it's only *Purgatory* at Friedrichstrasse 8. The music is loud and the crowd occasionally pretty wild (open nightly after 10 pm). Nearby at *Sam Brasil* on Silbersackstrasse 27, you can go Latin after 9 pm while sipping exotic cocktails (closed Monday and Tuesday).

Outside St Pauli, *Madhouse* at Valentinskamp 46a near the Musikhalle has been a Hamburg mainstay for decades (open nightly after 10 pm). There's a small bar upstairs and a small dance floor downstairs, usually vibrating with rock, pop and hip-hop.

Opera & Musicals Hamburg's citizen-founded *Staatsoper* (1678), at Grosse Theaterstrasse 34 near Dammtorwall, is among the most respected opera houses in the world. Performances often sell out, but you can try calling either the Hamburg

Hotline (☎ 300 51 30 0) or the box office (☎ 351 72 1) at Grosse Theaterstrasse 35, about 50m from the opera house). Ticket prices vary by production and range from DM5 to DM260. *Cats*, which celebrated its 10th anniversary here in 1997, still plays at the Operettenhaus (☎ 270 75 27 0) on Spielbudenplatz 1 in St Pauli. Another St Pauli show is *Grease*, which packs them in at the Imperial Theatre (☎ 313 11 4), a former porno cinema at Reeperbahn 5. Since 1990, the *Phantom of the Opera* has haunted the halls of the Neue Flora (☎ 270 75 27 0) at Stresemannstrasse 159a in Altona. The yellow tent resembling a giant bee at Norderelbstrasse 6 in the free port area is the Neue Metropol Musicaltheater (☎ 300 51 30 0) which was purpose-built for the *Buddy Holly Story*. There's a shuttle service from Pier 1 of the St-Pauli-Landungsbrücken.

Theatre The *Deutsches Schauspielhaus* (☎ 248 71 3) at Kirchenallee 39 was voted Germany's Theatre of the Year in 1995. Its director, Frank Baumbauer, is well known for his solid productions of German classics as well as his experimental interpretations and original stage designs. With almost 1400 seats, the place is huge, so it's not usually a problem to obtain tickets. The *Thalia Theater* (☎ 322 66 6) at Alstertor 1 is another stage with a stellar reputation.

Hamburg also has a thriving private theatre scene. At the *English Theatre* (☎ 227 70 89), Lerchenfeld 14 in Winterhude, a cast of predominantly British actors performs fairly light fare, from mysteries to comedies. A former crane factory at Jarrestrasse 20-24, also in Winterhude, houses *Kampnagel* (☎ 270 94 94 9), one of the top venues for alternative and experimental theatre. For kids, there's *Theater für Kinder* at Max-Brauer-Allee 76 in Altona. Not at all suitable for the underaged are *Schmidt Theater* at Spielbudenplatz 24 and *Schmidt's Tivoli* (both ☎ 317 78 99) a few doors down at No 27. Both venues are much loved for their shrill variety shows, wild cabaret and very casual atmosphere.

Classical Music The premier address for classical concerts is the *Musikhalle* (☎ 346 92 0), housed in a splendid neobaroque edifice on Karl-Muck-Platz in the city centre (U-Bahn: Stephansplatz). It's the home of the Hamburg-based State Philharmonic Orchestra, the North German Broadcasting Network Symphony Orchestra and the Hamburg Symphonia.

Rock Wedged between live sex theatres and peep shows is *Grosse Freiheit 36*, named after its St Pauli address. It's one of the hippest places to go for live pop and rock concerts. The Beatles once played a gig in the *Kaiserkeller* disco in the basement. On weekends, one ticket gets you into both. *Docks*, another live venue, is nearby on Spielbudenplatz 19. The acoustics may not be perfect, but that hasn't stopped performers like Iggy Pop and Lou Reed from showing up. On Saturday nights, there's a dance club after 10 pm.

Fabrik, housed in a former foundry at Barnerstrasse 36 in Altona, is worth the trip. The crowds have been flocking to the pink building with a crane jutting from its roof since the 1970s. Blues and jazz greats, including Miles Davis, have performed here at the annual jazz festival. On most nights, the emphasis is on world music with international bands.

Pubs & Bars It seems as though you're never more than a five-minute walk from a bar or pub in Hamburg. In the Schanzenviertel, you'll find *Frank und Frei* at Schanzenstrasse 93, just opposite *Oma's Apotheke*, a converted pharmacy which uses the old counter as a bar. To soak up the area's politically radical atmosphere, head for *Fritz Bauch* at Bartelsstrasse 6, where punks, yuppies and environmentalists hunker over heavy wooden furniture in a room that's dark even in daylight.

Back in St Pauli on Grosse Freiheit is *Gretel & Alfons*, where you can have a drink in what purports to have been the Beatles' favourite watering hole. *Miller*, a bar on the corner of Clemens-Schultz-Strasse and

Detlev-Bremer-Strasse, has a warm ambience which invites conversation – possibly a problem if you try their tequila sampler (five shots) for DM9.90. Popular with Hamburg locals are the bars at Schmidt Theater and Schmidt's Tivoli (see Theatre). In summer the smallish *Geyer* sprawls out all over Hein-Köllisch-Platz and beyond.

St Georg also has its cluster of good bars, especially along Lange Reihe and parallel Koppel. *Geel Haus* at Koppel 76 is popular with actors from the nearby Deutsches Schauspielhaus while the smoky rooms of *Max & Konsorten* on Spadenteich 7 are somewhat of a Hamburg institution.

Gay & Lesbian Hamburg Hamburg has a thriving gay and lesbian scene. Look for the free magazine *hinnerk* which lists gay events around town. A favourite hang-out at Lange Reihe 93 is *Cafe Gnosa*, an old-fashioned coffee house with delectable cakes and bistro fare at night. The women-only *Café Endlich*, in the Frauenhotel Hanseatin at Dragonerstall 11, is a comfortable place not necessarily reserved for lesbians.

The bookshop Männerschwarm at Neuer Pferdemarkt 32 (U-Bahn: Feldstrasse) caters to men; the Frauenbuchladen at Bismarckstrasse 98 in Eimsbüttel to women. The nightclub *Camelot* at Hamburger Berg 12 in St Pauli features the 'Bad Boys Club' for gay men on Fridays and the 'Femme Fatal' for lesbians on Saturday. Popular with both gays and straights is the *EDK* club at Gerhardstrasse 3, also in St Pauli.

Spectator Sports

Hamburg's soccer fervour really heats up when both its teams play in the Bundesliga ('first league'). Most Hamburgers are fiercely loyal to one team or the other. The Hamburger Sportverein (HSV) (☎ 415 51 94 for tickets) plays in the Volkspark Stadium in Altona, which holds 60,000 people. The FC St Pauli (☎ 314 331) plays in the Millerntorstadium in St Pauli, which has a capacity of 25,000. At a game, you might want to avoid areas where the hard-core fans stand, since things can get rough if their team loses. Expect to pay about DM20 for standing tickets, from DM45 for seats. Students get significant discounts. The soccer season usually runs from February to July and then from September to December.

Hamburg also hosts the German Open men's tennis event at the stadium on Rothenbaumchaussee every year in early May. A major women's tournament is held in late April. For tickets, call ☎ 411 78 0.

Things to Buy

Hamburg has two main shopping districts, both in the city centre. East of the Hauptbahnhof, the Mönckebergstrasse (known as the 'Mö') cuts through the heart of the department store district, ending roughly at the Rathaus.

The more elegant shops are located within the triangle created by Jungfernstieg, Fuhlentwiete and Neuer Wall. Most of them are in a network of 11 shopping arcades, which are sophisticated, covered avenues of brick, chrome, steel, marble and tile. Some, like the Hanse Viertel, have domed glass roofs.

Shopping in Altona has a more relaxed feel. Along Ottenser Hauptstrasse west of the station, you'll find the Mercado mall with clothing stores and a Safeway supermarket. The quarter gets its Mediterranean feel from the many Turkish vendors who artfully display their fruit and vegies on the street. East of the station, department stores line the pedestrianised Grosse Bergstrasse. In the Schanzenviertel, you'll find a few funky stores along Schanzenstrasse.

Getting There & Away

Air Hamburg's international Fuhlsbüttel airport was among the first in Europe (opened 1911) and is located in Fuhlsbüttel, north of the city centre. It serves many cities within Germany and Europe, especially in Scandinavia. Lufthansa has an office here (☎ 359 26 66 0), but the main office of British Airways (☎ 309 66 36 3 or 01803-340 340 for reservations) is at Ballindamm 7 in the city centre. The Air France office (☎ 0180-536 03 70) is at Jungfernstieg 1.

Bus The central bus station is south-east of the Hauptbahnhof between Adenauerallee and Kurt-Schumacher-Allee. Look for the cylindrical bunker with the letters 'ZOB' (Zentraler Omnibus Bahnhof). You could shop around for the best deal in the string of travel agencies next to the bus boarding gates. Autokraft goes to Berlin several times daily for DM39 one way, DM52 return. Eurolines has buses to Paris for DM99/172; to London for DM133/235; to Amsterdam for DM70/105; and to Copenhagen for DM61/105. People under 26 get a 10% discount. Several agencies specialise in trips to Eastern European countries such as Poland, the Czech Republic and Hungary. Prices for these change constantly, so it's best to check when you get there. The station has lockers (DM2 and DM3) in the entrance hall and closes from 9 pm to 5 am.

Train Hamburg has no less than four train stations: Hauptbahnhof, Dammtor, Altona and Harburg. Many of the long-distance trains originate in Altona and stop at both Dammtor and Hauptbahnhof before heading out of the city. Be aware of this as you read the timetables, or you may end up at the wrong station at the wrong time.

There are several trains hourly to Lübeck (DM15.60, 45 minutes), Kiel (DM28, 1¼ hours), Hanover (DM48, 1½ hours) and Bremen (DM31, one hour). A direct service to Westerland on Sylt Island leaves every two hours (DM62, 2¾ hours).

There are good, direct connections to Berlin-Zoo and the airport in Berlin-Schönefeld (DM74, 2¾ hours), as well as to Frankfurt (DM172, 3½ hours), with some trains stopping at the airport there. Trains to Munich (DM243, six hours) and Cologne (DM118, four hours) leave hourly. There's a direct service to Copenhagen several times a day, but the only direct train to Paris is the night train. Going to Warsaw requires a change in Berlin. Hamburg-Harburg handles some regional services (for instance to Cuxhaven, the main port for Heligoland). Plenty of lockers are available at all four stations; large ones are DM4, small ones DM2.

Car & Motorcycle The autobahns of the A1 (Bremen-Lübeck) and A7 (Hanover-Kiel) cross south of the Elbe River. Three concentric ring roads manage traffic flow.

Ride Services The Citynetz Mitfahr-Zentrale (☎ 194 44) is at Gotenstrasse 19 (S-Bahn: Berliner Tor, then a five-minute walk). The office is open Monday to Saturday 8 am to 8 pm and Sunday from 10 am. Expect to pay about DM29 for a one-way trip to Berlin, DM50 to Frankfurt and DM71 to Munich.

Boat Scandinavian Seaways (☎ 389 03 71) operates the car ferry from Hamburg to the English port of Harwich. The journey takes 20 hours, and services operate year round at least twice a week in either direction (less frequently in January and February). The office is in the Edgar-Engelhard-Kai terminal (known as the England Ferry Terminal) at Van-der-Smissen-Strasse 4 off Grosse Elbstrasse, west of St Pauli harbour (S-Bahn: Königstrasse). It is open weekdays 10 am to 4.30 pm, weekends just before departures. The one-way passenger fare to Harwich ranges from DM93 to DM493, depending on the season, the day of the week and cabin amenities, size and location. A car costs an extra DM59 to DM121, a motorbike DM41 to DM81, and transporting a bicycle will cost DM26 in the high season and DM5 the rest of the year.

From May to August, there's also a ferry to Newcastle every four days. The trip takes 24 hours and costs from DM133 to DM513.

Getting Around

The Airport Airport buses (DM8/12 one way/return) make the 25-minute run to the airport from Hauptbahnhof every 20 minutes between 5.40 am and 9.20 pm. If you want to go more cheaply (DM4.10 each way), take the U1 or S-Bahn No 1 to Ohlsdorf, then change to bus No 10, which leaves every 10 minutes. The whole trip takes about 40 minutes. A taxi from the Hauptbahnhof to the airport should cost around DM25.

Public Transport Public transport in Hamburg consists of buses, the U-Bahn and the S-Bahn. The service area is set up by zones. The central area *(Nahbereich)* covers the city centre, roughly between St Pauli and Hauptbahnhof. The Greater Hamburg area *(Grossbereich)* covers the city centre plus the outlying communities like Blankenese. Hamburg State *(Gesamtbereich)* covers the entire Hamburg area.

Tickets for the S/U-Bahn must be purchased from the orange machines at station entrances; bus tickets are available from the driver. Single journeys cost DM2.60 for the central area, DM4.10 for Greater Hamburg and DM6.60 for Hamburg State. Children cost a basic DM1.50. The express Schnellbus or 1st-class S-Bahn supplement is DM1.90 per trip.

If you'll be using public transport a lot, day passes *(Tageskarte)* are a money-saving option. An individual day pass for travel after 9 am in Greater Hamburg is DM7.90 (DM12.60 for Hamburg State). Up to five people may travel together all day after 9 am for DM13.50/18.20. A three-day pass (available only for Greater Hamburg) is DM22.90. Weekly cards (valid Monday through Sunday) range from DM23.50 to DM48, depending on the distance you want to travel.

Outside rush hour, bicycles may be taken onto U-Bahn or S-Bahn trains. Most stations close from 1 to 4 am. The fine for riding without a valid ticket is DM60. Checks are sporadic but thorough: with up to five inspectors swooping into the U-Bahn or S-Bahn compartment, don't even think about trying to escape. From about midnight to dawn the night bus network takes over from the trains, converging on the main city bus station at Rathausmarkt. For transport options with the Hamburg Card, see the Information section at the beginning of this chapter.

Car & Motorcycle Driving around Hamburg is surprisingly easy. Major thoroughfares cut across town in all directions, and road signs are ubiquitous. Parking is expensive, though, especially in the city centre. Expect to pay about DM2 an hour at meters or in parking garages. Parking your car at a hotel usually adds between DM15 and DM25 to your room rate.

All major car-rental agencies have branches in Hamburg. Hertz and Budget have a counter in the Hauptbahnhof. A fully insured Opel Corsa will set you back DM119 per day at Budget, including tax. Hertz has a special weekend rate good from Friday noon to 9 am on Monday that will get you a Fiat Punto with unlimited kilometre, theft insurance and VAT (but no collision insurance) for DM99. Bigger models are available. Local agencies include Spar Car (☎ 474 06 3), where the options include a VW Polo for DM52 a day with 100 free km or for DM90 a day with 300 free km. The Spar Car office is at Ludolfstrasse 7 in the Eppendorf market square. Also in Eppendorf at Arnold-Heise-Strasse 16, is My Car (☎ 474 85 1), which offers VW Polos for DM65 a day (80 free km) and DM345 a week (500 free km).

Mot-In (☎ 550 03 33), at Heidlohstrasse 1 in Hamburg-Schnelsen, rents motorbikes from DM95 to DM205 a day (plus DM1200 deposit).

Taxi Book a taxi by ringing ☎ 211 21 1 or ☎ 221 12 2. The BahnTaxi stand (DM17 per couple) is at the north-east end of the Hauptbahnhof near the Post exit. At Bahnhof Altona it's at the south side of the station near the Museumstrasse exit.

Around Hamburg

STADE

- *pop 45,000*
- *area code* ☎ 04141

Stade, about 60km west of Hamburg, is one of the oldest Hanseatic towns in the north and was first mentioned in a public record about 1000 years ago. Most of Stade's medieval buildings were destroyed in the Great Fire of

1659; most of what you see today is post-17th century. Stade is an intensely neat little town with immaculately kept red-brick houses, manicured gardens and litter-free streets. Its Altstadt is very scenic, especially around the harbour, which is lined by restored town houses and historic warehouses. Add to that a couple of churches and museums and Stade is well worth a day trip.

Information

The tourist office (☎ 409 17 0; fax 409 11 0) is at Schiffertorstrasse 6 and is open weekdays from 9 am to 6 pm and Saturday to 2 pm.

Walking Tour

Stade's train station is south-west of the Altstadt, which is encircled by a moat and a ring road. Cross the moat via Bahnhofstrasse, then continue north-east on the pedestrianised Holzstrasse to Pferdemarkt, where you'll find the tourist office. Head east from here via Sattelmacherstrasse to Flurstrasse and the **St Wilhadi Kirche**, a 14th-century Gothic hall church with a badly leaning, squat tower. Of note here is the Baroque organ, built around 1730, by E Bielfeldt of Bremen and the ceiling frescoes which had been painted over and were only rediscovered during recent restoration. Heading back the same way, turn right onto Hökerstrasse, one of Stade's main shopping streets. On the right you'll see the **Rathaus** with its columned portal flanked by the figures of Truth (with the mirror) and Justice (with the scales).

Stade's oldest church, just north of here in a courtyard off to the right, is the **Church of Saints Cosmas and Damiani**. Its easily recognised for its octagonal tower crowned by a baroque helmet. Inside, the marble baptismal font is festooned with alabaster likenesses of three of the Evangelists. The organ was the first work of local son – and later master organ builder – Arp Schnitger. Hökerstrasse ends at Fischmarkt, which marks one end of the **Alter Hafen**, the canal-like harbour and the prettiest part of the Altstadt. Beautiful historic houses line it on both sides.

The houses on Wasser Ost were once owned by sea captains; the ones on the opposite side were merchants' homes. The **Kunsthaus** (DM2, discount DM1), at Wasser West 7, contains an exquisite collection of works by painters, including Paula Modernsohn-Becker, Fritz Mackensen and Fritz Overbeck, from the Worpswede artist colony (see Around Bremen in the Bremen chapter). The **Bürgermeister-Hintze-Haus**, a lacy stucco confection with tall gables and a fancy portal, is at No 23. The large building at the harbour's northern end is the **Schwedenspeicher**, used as a food warehouse by the Swedish garrison during their occupation of Stade after the Thirty Years' War. It is now a **regional history museum** (DM2, discount DM1).

Getting There & Away

There's a train service from Hamburg every 30 minutes (DM14.20, one hour). Coming from Bremen requires a change in Hamburg-Harburg (DM38, 1½. If you're driving from Hamburg, take the B73; from Bremen, Stade is reached via the B74.

From Hamburg, you can also hop on one of the super-fast Elbe-City-Jet catamarans which leave St-Pauli-Landungsbrücken, Pier 3, up to 17 times daily (fewer on weekends) and speed down the Elbe to the landing docks in Stadersand in 45 minutes. From there, free shuttle buses take you to Pferdemarkt in the town centre. The trip costs DM16 each way, children pay DM8 and bikes cost DM8.

BUXTEHUDE

- *pop 36,000*
- *area code* ☎ 04161

This bucolic town lies about 30km west of Hamburg on the Este River. The pedestrian-friendly Altstadt is at its dreamiest around the so-called **Fleth**, a Dutch-style (ie canal-like) harbour in the western Altstadt. The Fleth dates back to the town's founding in 1285 and until 1962 was used by lighters transporting cargo weighing up to 100 tonnes.

One of them, the **Ewer Margareta** (1897), is permanently moored here. Also here is the **Flethmühle**, a mill that was in operation until 1975 and has now been converted into apartments and shops.

Cafés and restaurants line both sides of the Fleth, and it's a nice place for a stroll. One block east of the Fleth, on the corner of Breite Strasse and the Markt, stands the ivy-clad **Rathaus**, a red brick edifice with a monumental sandstone portal and copper roof. Built in 1911, it replaced its 15th-century predecessor which was destroyed by fire. North of here, the spires of **St Petri** come into view. The light flooded, three-nave, vaulted Gothic basilica contains small but vividly carved choir stalls, circa 1400, and a sumptuous baroque pulpit supported by a statue of Atlas. The star attraction, though, is the late-Gothic **Halephagen Altar** below the organ, with scenes from the Passion of Christ, reminiscent of Lucas Cranach. If the church is closed, pick up the key from the **Buxtehude Museum** about 50m to the east at Am Stavenort 2. The museum (open Tuesday to Friday 1.30 to 5.30 pm, weekends from 10.30 am; DM2, discount DM1) focuses on regional history and also has special exhibits.

The Buxtehude tourist office (☎ 501 29 7; fax 526 93) is in the same building as the museum and is open Monday 9 am to noon and 1.30 to 4 pm, Tuesday to Friday to 5.30 pm and Saturday to 12.30 pm. If it's closed, though, general information and brochures are also available from the museum desk.

Getting There & Away

Buxtehude is easily reached by the same train connecting Hamburg Hauptbahnhof with Stade and Cuxhaven (DM9.60, 45 minutes). Drivers from Hamburg can catch the B73 west to Buxtehude. From Bremen, take the Rade exit off the A1, then travel via the B3 to the B73.

ALTES LAND

South of the Elbe, roughly bordered by Stade and Buxtehude is 'Hamburg's fruit basket', the Altes Land. All kinds of orchards blanket this fertile area that was reclaimed from marshy ground by Dutch experts in the Middle Ages. Thatched and panelled old houses and farms, romantic windmills and sweeping dykes characterise this stretch of land that's at its most brilliant in May when the trees are blossoming. The centre of the Altes Land is the little town of **Jork**, which can be reached from Hamburg by taking the S-Bahn No 3 to Neugraben and then bus No 257.

In fine weather, though, cycling is the most pleasant way to explore the region. The Obstmarschenweg is a particularly scenic bike path, following the Elbe. You can also travel here by boat. The HADAG cruise to Lühe from St-Pauli-Landungsbrücken, Pier 3, departs twice on weekdays and four times on weekends between April and October. The trip takes about 90 minutes and costs DM10 each way. The Elbe City Jet to Stadersand also stops at Lühe (DM12, 15 minutes).

Schleswig-Holstein

Schleswig-Holstein is a flat, windswept land of open skies, gentle hills and vast fields. Water has been the primary shaper in this northernmost of German states. From the beginning, Schleswig-Holstein's fate and prosperity have been inseparably linked to the savage North Sea in the west and the placid Baltic in the east. Its people have braved the seas as fisherfolk and whalers; its ports have been major launch sites for freighters, passenger ships and ferries. And, predictably enough, this predominantly agricultural land relies on its frequent rains.

Unlike some other states in Germany, Schleswig-Holstein doesn't owe its double-barrelled name to creative post-WWII mapping. The two territories were first united in 1460 under the Danish King Christian I. His oath that the two should 'remain forever undivided', however, was undermined only a generation later when his squabbling sons partitioned the land among themselves. For the next four centuries, both territories shuttled back and forth between independence and alliance with the Danish crown until, in 1864, a powerful Prussia ended the tug of war and both Schleswig and Holstein were incorporated into the German Reich. After WWI, the northern half of Schleswig was returned to Denmark following a referendum. The state – and national – border was moved southward to Flensburg, where it remains today.

With only 2.7 million people, Schleswig-Holstein is sparsely populated and almost devoid of cities. The largest is Kiel, the modern state capital internationally famous for its Kieler Woche – the world's largest sailing regatta – and as a gateway to Scandinavia. An absolute highlight for visitors is the old Hanseatic city of Lübeck, the birthplace of Thomas and Heinrich Mann; the picturesque Altstadt here has been included on UNESCO's World Heritage List. Also well worth a visit is Schleswig, whose heydays under the Vikings and then the dukes of Gottorf have left their legacies around the town. Flensburg's location on the Danish border is reflected in its architecture and street names, and there's even a sizeable Danish-speaking population here. On the west coast, Husum is a pretty little fishing town and a good jumping-off point for exploring the Halligen Islands. These are part of the archipelago of the North Frisian Islands, where you'll find some of Europe's finest beaches.

Since Schleswig-Holstein is as flat as a pancake, it's excellent for bike touring. Travelling by bus or train is also fairly easy though a car or motorbike is better because of the rural character of the state and the

HIGHLIGHTS

- The North Frisian Islands of Sylt, Amrum and Föhr
- The Landesmuseum in Schloss Gottorf in Schleswig
- The Holstentor in Lübeck
- Clambering through the WWII U-boat in Laboe

• **Population:** 2.7m • **Capital:** Kiel • **Area:** 15,730 sq km

Schleswig-Holstein Luminaries: Willy Brandt, Dietrich Buxtehude, Thomas & Heinrich Mann, Emil Nolde, Max Planck, Jil Sander, Theodor Storm, Carl Maria von Weber

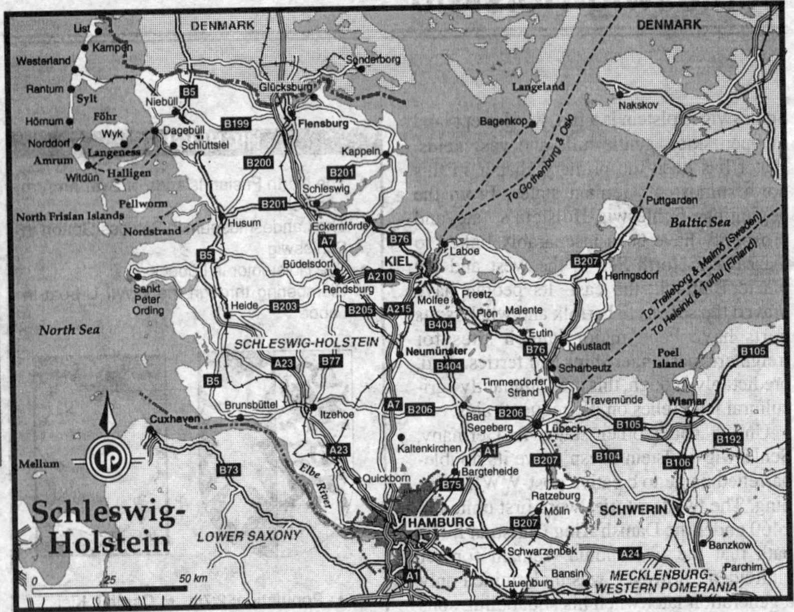

relatively long distances between towns. Accommodation is plentiful and cuts across the entire budget spectrum. But the coastal areas are very popular with Germans and, even though finding a place to stay should not be a problem, it's probably best to phone ahead during the peak summer months.

KIEL

- *pop 250,000*
- *area code* ☎ 0431

Kiel, about 75km north-west of Lübeck and 80km north of Hamburg, is the state capital of Schleswig-Holstein. It came into being more than 750 years ago but, sadly, little of historical importance survived the ravages of war. Located at the end of the 18km-long Kiel Firth, it has long been one of Germany's most important harbours on the Baltic Sea.

Under the Prussians, who annexed Schleswig-Holstein in 1864, it became the headquarters of the Imperial Navy. During WWII it was the base for enormous German U-boat activity, making it a prime target for Allied bombers, which left more than 80% of the city in ruin.

After the war, economic survival – not architectural aesthetics – was the issue on city-planners' minds and, as a result, you wouldn't use 'Kiel' and 'quaint' in the same sentence. Nevertheless, it's a vibrant city that's not without charm. Most of this comes from its rather scenic location on the water and the hubbub of its harbour. The city is the main gateway to Scandinavia, with about 2.3 million passengers annually boarding one of the colossal ferries headed for Oslo, Gothenburg and even St Petersburg in Russia. Kiel also has a long tradition as a venue for sailing regattas; it hosted the Olympic sailing events in both 1936 and 1972. The international Kieler Woche (Kiel Week) sailing spectacle has been taking place here since 1882.

Orientation

Kiel's main thoroughfare is the pedestrianised Holstenstrasse, about 100m inland from the firth. It starts at the Kieler Schloss and runs south for about 1.5km before culminating in the Sophienhof, a huge indoor shopping mall. This is where the tourist office is located. The Hauptbahnhof is just east of here, with the central bus station (ZOB) a few metres north of the station.

Information

Tourist Office The tourist office (☎ 679 10 0; fax 675 43 9) is on the ground floor of the eastern side of the Sophienhof mall, facing the Hauptbahnhof. It's signposted from within the station. Opening hours are Monday to Saturday from 9 am to 6.30 pm (closed Saturday after 1 pm in winter). In June and July, it is also open on Sunday from 9 am to 1 pm. Here you can buy the Kiel Card, which entitles you to unlimited public transport and discounts on museums, tours and cruises. It costs DM12/17/27 for one day/three days/seven days.

Money Banks closest to the Hauptbahnhof are the Sparkasse at Sophienblatt 21 and the Volksbank at the corner of Sophienblatt and Raiffeisenstrasse. Both are open to 6 pm on Monday and Thursday and closed Wednesday afternoon.

Post & Communications The main post office is at Stresemannplatz 5, about a five-minute walk north of the Hauptbahnhof. It has a public fax-phone and a copy machine.

Bookshops The Fabulus bookshop, inside the Holstentörn Passage connecting the Holstenstrasse outdoor mall with the Sophienhof, stocks a fair number of English-language books. Another bookshop called Eins zu Hundertausend, at Schülperbaum 15, has lots of maps and guidebooks.

Laundry The self-service Waschsalon at the corner of Knooper Weg and Ziegelteich charges DM6 per wash and DM1 for the dryer.

Emergency Police headquarters (☎ 598 1) are at Gartenstrasse 7.

Walking Tour

You can easily see the sights in central Kiel on a walk. From the train station, head through the nicely designed Sophienhof mall and then north onto Holstenstrasse. Turn left into Fleethörn to get to Rathausplatz and its impressive **town hall**, where baroque meets Art Nouveau. Completed in 1911, the Rathaus sports a 106m-tall **tower** that is a city landmark. Unfortunately, the interior of the Rathaus can only be visited on a guided city tour (May to October on weekends at 9.30 and 10.40 am, details at the tourist office).

Walk back to Holstenstrasse and continue north to Alter Markt and the **Nikolaikirche**, whose carved altar (1460), a triumphal cross (1490) and bronze baptismal font (1344) deserve a closer look. Outside stands the statue ***Der Geistkämpfer*** (The Ghost Fighter) by Ernst Barlach which was removed as 'degenerate art' during the Third Reich and was later found buried in the Lüneburg Heath.

Dänische Strasse north of here is one of the more successfully restored sections of old Kiel. The lovely red-brick building with a rococo portal at No 19 is the Warleberger Hof, which contains the **Stadtmuseum** (open daily from 10 am to 6 pm, closed Monday in winter; free) with changing exhibitions. The **Schloss** is only a few more metres north. The west wing is the only part of the original Renaissance palace to survive. It houses European art from the 17th to the 20th centuries, including works by Caspar David Friedrich and Philipp Otto Runge (open Tuesday to Friday from 10 am to 5 pm, weekends from 2 to 6 pm; DM2, discount DM1). North of here, at the other end of the little park, stands the **Kunsthalle** (open from 10.30 am to 6 pm, Wednesday to 8 pm, closed Monday; DM4, discount DM2, more for special exhibits) at Düsternbrooker Weg 1-3. It has a fine collection of paintings by Baltic artists and an entire section dedicated to Emil Nolde.

Finally, walk south along the waterfront to

the **Schiffahrtsmuseum** (Maritime Museum; open daily from 10 am to 6 pm, in winter to 5 pm; free) located in a former fish auction hall at Am Wall 65. It chronicles Kiel's maritime history with ship models, photographs and documents, and one section focuses on nautical inventions and innovations coming out of Kiel. The **Museum Harbour** has a number of historical ships on display (April to October).

Kiel Canal & Locks

Kiel is the point at which this 99km-long shipping canal (called Nord-Ostsee-Kanal in German) from the North Sea enters the Baltic. Inaugurated in 1895, the canal sees some 60,000 ships pass through it every year, and the *Schleusen* (locks) at Holtenau, 6km north of the city centre, are well worth a visit. Admission to the viewing platform on the southern side of the canal is DM2, discount DM1. Tours of the locks, offered daily at 9 and 11 am and 1 and 3 pm, depart from the northern side of the canal (DM3, discount DM2). To get to the locks, take bus No 4 to Wik, then walk north for about five minutes.

Special Events

Kiel's most famous attraction is the **Kieler Woche** (Kiel Week) in the last full week of June. It's a giant festival revolving around a series of yachting regattas and attended by more than 4000 of the world's sailing elite and half a million spectators. Even if you're not into boats, the atmosphere is electric – just make sure you book a room in advance if you want to be in on the fun.

Places to Stay

Camping Kiel's *Campingplatz Falckenstein* (☎ 392 07 8; open April to October) is at Palisadenweg 171, an inconvenient 15km north of the city centre (take bus No 40 to the Seekamp stop and then walk about 1.5km). Tent sites cost DM6 to DM12, plus DM7 per person.

Hostel Kiel's *DJH hostel* (☎ 731 48 8) is at Johannesstrasse 1 in the suburb of Gaarden, across the firth from the Hauptbahnhof; to get there, walk over the new drawbridge. Alternatively, take bus No 4 from the Hauptbahnhof to Kieler Strasse. The hostel charges juniors/seniors DM24/29 (including breakfast and sheets) in two and four-bed rooms.

Hotels If you need a room, you can make use of the free reservation service operated by the tourist office. Be warned, though, that even budget hotels are not exactly cheap and that hotels are booked solid during Kieler Woche. Private rooms are a good alternative and cost from DM30 per person.

One of the cheaper hotel options is *Hotel Zum Fritz Reuter* (☎ 579 75 0) at Langer Segen 5a, which has singles/doubles with shared shower & WC for DM60/92. The price goes up to DM95/135 for rooms with private bath. Then there's *Hotel Düvelsbek Garni* (☎ 810 21), Feldstrasse 111, which has well priced singles with shower & WC from DM69 to DM85 and doubles from DM105 to DM140. It's about 2km north of the city centre (bus No 1 to Esmarch-Strasse). *Muhl's Hotel* (☎ 997 90; fax 997 91 79), centrally located at Lange Reihe 5, charges up to DM130/190 for full-facility rooms.

If you can spend a bit more and want to unwind away from the bustle of the city, go for the classy *Hotel Birke* (☎ 533 10; fax 533 13 33), a snug country inn at Martenshofweg 2-8. It's excellent value for money, with rooms from DM125/160 and a sauna and fitness room on the premises. Three bus lines (Nos 2, 9 and 74) connect it regularly with the city centre.

Places to Eat

There are plenty of reasonably priced eateries. Students like *Oblomov*, a legendary pub with dirt-cheap pizza, salads and baguette sandwiches at Hansastrasse 82. Another favourite for a chat and cheap chow is the tiny *Viva* at Knooper Weg 169. Also near the university, at Olshausenstrasse 8, is *Frizz*, a small bistro serving inexpensive, simple fare.

For more sedate surrounds and regional specialities, try the traditional *Friesenhof* in the Rathaus, which has daily lunch specials priced around DM10 and tasty á la carte dishes starting at DM15. Best of all, between 3 and 5 pm you can order all dishes at half price plus DM2. The *Klosterbrauerei*, at Alter Markt 9, is a private brewery with a great atmosphere and lunch specials (including some vegetarian dishes) for under DM10.

A fun place to go on a warm day is the atmospheric *Forstbaumschule*, a big beer garden in a park about 3.5km north of the city centre. For a great view over the firth, head for *Kieler Ansichten* in a restored old building at Hasselfelde 20, which serves surprisingly affordable international cuisine.

Getting There & Away

Bus Kiel's ZOB is a major hub for buses into the nearby countryside and other towns in Schleswig-Holstein, although most are also served by trains that may be faster and more regular. Autokraft operates an express bus to Hamburg (2¼ hours) that runs up to a dozen times daily. There's also a special service direct to Hamburg airport. Bus No 1690 goes to Lübeck (2¾ hours) and bus No 1668 to Schleswig (1¾ hours) and Flensburg (2½ hours). To get to Husum (2¾ hours) take bus No 46 and change in Schleswig.

Train Numerous trains shuttle daily between Kiel and Hamburg-Altona and Hamburg Hauptbahnhof (DM28, one hour). Trains to Lübeck leave hourly (DM21.20, 1¼ hours). There are also regular local connections to Schleswig, Husum, Schwerin and Flensburg. The station has plenty of lockers costing DM2 and DM4.

Car & Motorcycle Kiel is connected with the rest of Germany via the A210 and the A215, which merge with the A7 to Hamburg and beyond. The B4, B76, B404, B502 and B503 also converge here.

Ride Services The ADM Mitfahrzentrale (☎ 675 00 1 or ☎ 1 94 40) is at Sophienblatt 54 near the Hauptbahnhof.

Boat Langeland-Kiel (☎ 974 15 0) runs two or three ferries a day to Bagenkop (2½ hours) on the Danish island of Langeland (though no boats sail from early January to mid-February). The trip costs DM7, return DM11 (DM9.50/18 in July and early August; DM9.90 return if you come back the same day). If you're taking a bicycle, you pay DM19/33. Cars cost DM22/42 (including up to four passengers) and DM39/73 in peak season, when the fare includes the driver only. The ferries leave from Oslokai in the northern city centre near the Schloss.

Stena Line (☎ 0180-533 36 00) operates the daily overnight Kiel-Gothenburg ferry (14 hours) leaving from Schwedenkai. From early November to April, the fare for pedestrians is DM66 (return DM104) on all but a few days. It rises to DM196/256 on peak days in July and August. If you're under 26, you can buy the super-cheap Tramper-Ticket for DM48 in low season and DM128 in peak season (available only for return trips). Sleeping berths in air-conditioned four-bed cabins with shower and WC are an additional DM30.

Color Line ferries (☎ 974 09 0) has services to Oslo (19½ hours) throughout the year. One-way fares start at DM136 in low season (around 30% extra in summer) per bed in very basic two-bed cabins. If you want a private shower and WC, expect to pay from DM236. Bikes are transported free; cars start at DM64. There's a 10% discount on return tickets, which are normally double the one-way fare. Ferries depart from the new Norwegenkai near the Hauptbahnhof. A 50% student discount (with ID) is available on selected dates.

Getting Around

Public Transport The main bus station is right outside the Hauptbahnhof on Auguste-Viktoria-Strasse. Single trips cost DM2.90, six-ticket blocks are DM13.20. For details on getting around with the Kiel Card, see Tourist Office in the earlier Information section.

Boat Ferry service along Kiel Firth operates daily until around 6 pm (5 pm on weekends) from the Bahnhofbrücke pier behind the Hauptbahnhof. Prices depend on how many zones you travel through and range from DM3.80 to DM5.50 (eg to Laboe). For information, ring ☎ 594 12 63.

AROUND KIEL

Laboe

At the mouth of the Kiel Firth and on its eastern bank lies the sleepy village of Laboe. It is home to the **U-boat** featured in Wolfgang Petersen's film *Das Boot* (1981). The sub, which served as a very real weapon of destruction during WWII, sits on struts in the sand and is now going through its third incarnation as a museum. The climb through its claustrophobic interior is well worth the DM3. You'll find it right below the **Marine Ehrenmal**, a naval memorial built in the shape of a ship's stern to commemorate sailors of all nations lost at sea. In fine weather, you can see all the way to Denmark from its 80m-tall tower. Inside is a **navigation museum** (DM4.50). Both the U-boat and memorial/museum are open daily from 9.30 am to 6 pm, in winter to 4 pm. From Kiel, take bus No 4 or the ferry (see Getting Around in the Kiel section for details).

Schleswig-Holsteinisches Freilichtmuseum

South of Kiel, at Alte Hamburger Landstrasse in Molfsee, the Schleswig-Holstein Open-Air Museum features some 70 traditional houses typical of the region and relocated from around the state. The houses, some of them furnished, provide a thorough introduction to the northern way of life. The museum is open from 9 am to 6 pm (closed Monday except in summer). In winter, it's only open on Sundays and holidays from 11 am to 4 pm. Admission is DM7, discount DM5. Take bus No 1680 from the Kiel bus station.

LÜBECK

- *pop 208,000*
- *area code* ☎ 0451

Lübeck, about 65km north-east of Hamburg, was actually founded twice, once in 1143 by Count Adolf II of Holstein and then again in 1159 – after a major fire had destroyed the modest settlement – by Saxon Duke Heinrich der Löwe (Henry the Lion). It was Heinrich who designed the orderly, grid-like street layout that still characterises the Altstadt today. He also laid the foundation stone for the grand Dom, having made Lübeck a bishopric in 1160.

Despite its many churches – by 1230 there were already five – Lübeckers proved to be incredibly adept at the rather secular art of trade and commerce. Within a century, Lübeck became the 'Queen of the Hanse', the flagship of the Hanseatic League, the powerful association of towns that ruled trade in much of Europe from the 13th to the 16th century. The legal, political and societal structures developed in Lübeck became a model for many other cities around the Baltic. Its power was further reflected in its status as a free imperial city, which it was given in 1226 and retained until the Nazis revoked it in 1937.

The Altstadt's proud merchants' homes and seven church spires still attest to Lübeck's medieval halcyon days. In 1987, UNESCO placed the entire area (including over 1000 historical buildings) on its World Heritage List. Yet the Altstadt is not just one giant museum but also an actual city centre, with lively shopping streets and a host of cosy pubs, elegant restaurants and interesting cultural venues. Along with its seaside resort and port of Travemünde, Lübeck is a must-see destination in Schleswig-Holstein that needs at least a couple of days to appreciate fully.

Orientation

Lübeck's Altstadt is set on an island ringed by the canalised Trave River. Lübeck's landmark, the Holstentor, forms the western gateway to the Altstadt, with the main train and bus stations a couple of hundred metres farther west of here. Car traffic is banned from the Altstadt between 11.30 am and 6 pm on weekdays (from 10 am on weekends) unless you're going to a hotel there.

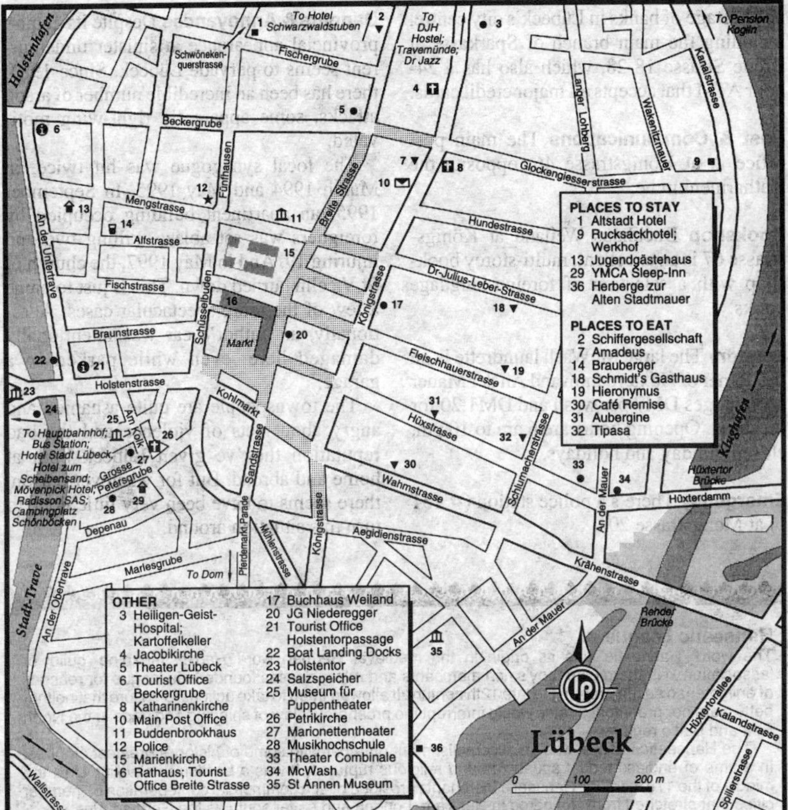

Information

Tourist Offices Lübeck's tourist office has four branches. The easiest to find is the one inside the train station (☎ 864 67 5; fax 863 024) which is open from 9 am to 1 pm and 3 to 6 pm Monday to Saturday.

The office in Holstentorpassage (☎ 723 39), on the corner of Holstenstrasse and An der Untertrave, is open weekdays from 10.30 am to 6.30 pm and Saturday from 10 am to 2 pm.

The office with the longest hours is at Breite Strasse 63 near the Rathaus (☎ 122 81 06), open weekdays from 9.30 am to 6 pm, and weekends from 10 am to 2 pm. Finally, there's the office at Beckergrube 95 (☎ 122 81 09; fax 122 81 90), open weekdays from 8 am to 4 pm.

At all four offices you can buy the Lübeck-Travemünde Card, good for unlimited public transport and discounts on cruises, cinemas, museums and other attractions. It costs DM9 for 24 hours and DM18 for three days.

Money The Wechselstube inside the Hauptbahnhof is a good place to exchange money and travellers' cheques and is open daily from 9.30 am to 6.30 pm. Otherwise, there's no shortage of banks in Lübeck's city centre, including the main branch of Sparkasse at Breite Strasse 18-28, which also has a 24-hour ATM that accepts all major credit cards.

Post & Communications The main post office is at Königstrasse 46, opposite the Katharinenkirche.

Bookshop Buchhaus Weiland at Königsstrasse 67 is an excellent, multi-storey bookshop with a selection of foreign-language books.

Laundry The large McWash laundrette is on the corner of Hüxterdamm and An der Mauer and charges DM7 per wash and DM1.20 for the dryer. Opening hours are 6 am to 10 pm, closed Sunday and holidays.

Emergency There's a police station (☎ 131 1) at Mengstrasse 20.

Dangers & Annoyances Despite its quaint, provincial appearance, a sinister undercurrent seems to pervade Lübeck. Since 1984, there has been an incredible number of arson attacks, some apparently right-wing motivated.

The local synagogue was hit twice, in March 1994 and May 1995. In September 1995, an apartment building occupied by foreigners was set ablaze, killing two and injuring 19. And in May 1997, the church of St Vicelin burned down. This is just to name a few of the more spectacular cases. Additionally, an author's car was intentionally damaged here, even while parked in a garage.

The townspeople are quite ashamed and angry about acts of violence and the bad reputation they've given Lübeck both at home and abroad. But for whatever reason, there seems to have been very little done to turn this situation around.

Hanseatic League

The word 'Hanseatic' has its origin in the medieval German word *Hanse*, meaning 'guild' or 'association'. Northern Germany's rich merchants and ruling classes founded the league for reasons of enlightened self-interest in the late 12th century. It allowed them to take actions to ensure that neither petty wars nor predatory pirates would interrupt the prosperous flow of shipping and trade in the North Sea and Baltic regions.

The Hanseatic League was an accomplishment on a par with some of history's greatest empires. In a time of endless feudal squabbles and religious ruptures, it was a bastion of stability. Until the middle of the 17th century, Hanseatic merchants presided over a commercial confederation of member cities that stretched from Novgorod in Russia to London and as far south as the German Alps.

By the time Lübeck became the centre of Hanseatic activity in the middle of the 13th century, the league was much more than a guarantor of privileges and rights for the wealthy. By virtue of its collective power – and virtual monopoly on many strategic trade routes – it actually became one of the dominant political forces in Europe. The league dictated policy by threatening to withhold trading privileges. It even went to war. When challenged by Danish King Valdemar IV over control of the south-western Baltic, the league's members raised an army to thwart Danish goals and ensure their mastery over the Baltic region. But normally, well placed bribes to foreign officials were more than adequate to ensure unfettered trade.

For more than 500 years – and with little more in the way of central authority than its periodic meetings in Lübeck – the Hanseatic League brokered, bludgeoned or bribed Europe into the shape desired by its merchant member cities. It certainly lined the pockets of the rich, but even Thomas Mann was forced to admire its power in creating what he called 'a humane, cosmopolitan society'. It may have monitored, or often fixed, the prices of such commodities as grain, fur and ore, but it also established outposts in nations as vastly different as Russia and England which served, additionally, as forums for political exchange.

In essence, the Hanseatic League formulated many of the ideas of pragmatism, mutual protection and assured stability that guide today's commercially driven democracies. It was the forerunner of such powerful associations as NATO, the EU and the UN. ■

Things to See

Unless noted otherwise, museums mentioned here are open from 10 am to 5 pm (to 4 pm October to March) and closed Monday. Admission is DM5, discount DM2.50. Except for the Holstentor, admission is free on the first Friday of the month.

Holstentor & Around Lübeck's landmark medieval town gate used to grace the old DM50 bill. Its distinctive round double towers, separated by a step gable, date back to 1464 and are the work of city architect Hinrich Helmstede. On closer inspection, the sturdy-looking gate is a rather crooked and off-kilter affair, the result of the swampy soil on which it was built. In the 19th century, only one vote in the city council tipped the scale in favour of restoration rather than demolition, though it took further strengthening earlier this century to anchor it successfully. The gate bears the inscription S.P.Q.L. which is Latin for the 'Senate and People of Lübeck' – a none-too-modest allusion to the signature S.P.Q.R. used by the Romans. Today it houses the **City History Museum**.

East of the Holstentor stands a quintet of pretty gabled brick buildings, the **Salzspeicher**, once used to store salt brought into town from Lüneburg. This 'white gold' contributed significantly to Lübeck's wealth in the Middle Ages. On the other side of the bridge (the Holstenbrücke), the towers of the **Petrikirche** come into view. Badly damaged in WWII, it is now used as a venue for concerts, lectures and even techno parties. You can take a lift to the top of the tower (May to October, open 9 am to shop closing time, which varies; DM3.50, discount DM2) for a superb view of the Altstadt.

Head to the church via Grosse Petersgrube, which is lined by merchants' houses from various periods. In the parallel Kleine Petersgrube, at No 4, is the **Museum für Puppentheater** (Puppet Theatre Museum), a beautiful assembly of some 1200 puppets, props, posters and more, from Europe, Asia and Africa (open daily from 10 am to 6 pm; DM6, students DM5, children DM3).

Markt & Around The majestic **Rathaus**, made of red and glazed-black bricks, flanks two sides of the Markt. Building began in 1230 and the complex grew over several centuries along with Lübeck's power and prosperity. The end result is a lavish, pan-shaped structure that's considered one of the most beautiful town halls in Germany. Most impressive is the southern façade of the north wing (1435), whose freestanding upper section sports three copper-clad spires and two large circular holes which lower the façade's resistance to wind, thus preventing it from being blown over. The cream-coloured Renaissance arcades are an embellishment from 1571. The comparatively plain, elongated middle section – part of the 'panhandle' – is an expansion from the turn of the 14th century.

South of here is the so-called **Kriegsstubenbau** (1444), which picks up the elements of the earlier sections – turrets, wind holes and arcades – with a row of coats of arms adding a splash of colour. The Breite Strasse side of this section boasts an elaborate Renaissance staircase. The inside of the Rathaus can only be seen on a guided tour (weekdays at 11 am, noon and 3 pm; DM4, discount DM2). A highlight is the **Audienzsaal** (audience hall), a light-flooded hall decked out in festive rococo with 10 allegorical paintings showing the virtues of a good town government – freedom, compassion, moderation, unity and so on.

Right behind the Rathaus rise the proud 125m-high spires of the **Marienkirche**, built between 1226 and 1350 by the town's secular leaders to demonstrate their power and independence from the church. The interior dimensions are overwhelming. The 80m-long centre nave rises 40m and is divided into two arcaded storeys. Floral ornamentation graces the vaulted ceilings and arches. Much of the interior decor- ation fell victim to WWII, whose destructiveness finds poignant expression in the chapel at the end of the south aisle: the shattered church bells – having crashed through the stone floor during a bombing raid – have been left where they fell as a memorial.

Another important chapel is the **Marientidenkapelle** (1518) behind the choir. Its stunning altar, a double triptych with predella, contains elaborate gilded carvings portraying scenes from the life of Mary. Back towards the entrance in the south aisle stands the exquisite wooden **statue of St John the Evangelist**, clutching a goblet with a snake emerging from it. (In quite a reversed role for a biblical reptile, a serpent once warned the apostle that he was about to quaff poisoned wine. Or so goes the legend…) Before you leave, look up at the **Buxtehudeorgel**, one of the church's two organs and supposedly the largest mechanical one in the world.

On the north side of the Marienkirche, at Mengstrasse 4, you'll find the **Buddenbrookhaus**, the house of the grandparents of literary giants Thomas and Heinrich Mann, which was immortalised in the former's 1929 novel *Die Buddenbrooks*. Today it houses an exhibit that documents, in chronological order, the literary accomplishments, family life, philosophical rivalry and years in exile of the brothers.

East of here, at Breite Strasse 89, is **JG Niederegger**, a mecca for lovers of marzipan, a delicacy for which Lübeck is famous. The store has museum-quality displays that are worth checking out even if you don't have a sweet tooth.

Dom & St Annen Heinrich der Löwe laid the foundation for the Dom – Lübeck's oldest church – in 1173. Today's structure, in the southern Altstadt, is 130m long and harmoniously blends Romanesque and Gothic styles. If you approach the Dom from the north-west, you have to go through Hölle (hell) and Fegefeuer (purgatory) – the actual names of the streets – to get to the **Paradies**, the lavish vestibule through which you enter the Dom. Inside, the flamboyant 17m-high **Triumphal Cross** (1477) by Bernt Notke dominates. Immediately behind is the equally ornate, arcaded rood-loft, topped with another set of amazing carvings by Notke. Take a closer look at the integrated clock face: the eyes of the sun at its centre move from left to right (or should: apparently this mechanism doesn't always work).

Ecclesiastical art is the focus of the **St Annen Museum**, close by at St-Annen-Strasse 15. Housed in a sprawling convent is a superb assortment of painted and gilded altars from the 15th and 16th centuries of which the **Passion Altar** (1491) by Hans Memling stands out in particular. Other exhibits illustrate the history of civilisation in Lübeck through to the end of the 18th century, with furniture, stoves, kitchen utensils, porcelain, and even doll houses.

Northern & Eastern Altstadt In the Middle Ages, this charming section of central Lübeck was the quarter of craftspeople and artisans. When demand for housing outgrew the available space, tiny single-storey homes were built perpendicular to the streets and made accessible via little walkways from the main roads. More than 100 such passageways still exist today, but you have to look carefully to find their arched entrances. There's one, for instance, at Aegidienstrasse 47.

Also typical of Lübeck – and the age – are the charitable housing estates built for the poor by civic-minded citizens. They too are accessible via walkways, the so-called **Stiftsgänge**. Examples are Bruskows Gang at Wahmstrasse 47-51 and Glandorps Gang at Glockengiesserstrasse 41-51.

Glockengiesserstrasse meets Königsstrasse, where you'll see the towerless **Katharinenkirche** built by the Franciscans. Part of the attractions here are the sculptures by Ernst Barlach and Gerhard Marcks set in niches in the façade and *The Resurrection of Lazarus* by Tintoretto, poorly displayed on the right as you enter. Continuing north on Königsstrasse will take you to the **Heiligen-Geist-Hospital**, the oldest hospital in Germany (1246). It functioned as a home for elderly people until 1972 and is now the site of Lübeck's Christmas market. Four slender octagonal spires alternating with gables dominate its distinctive exterior. Inside is an early-Gothic hall church with a rood-loft decorated with scenes from the life of St

Elisabeth. In the hospital hall you'll see the little chambers that were put in around 1820 to give the sick and old a certain degree of privacy. Admission to the complex is free.

Organised Tours

Guided two-hour city walking tours (DM8, discount DM6) depart daily from the tourist office at Breite Strasse 62 in May, June and October at 2 pm Monday to Saturday and at 11 am on Sunday. In the summer months, they're available at 11 am and 2 pm (Sunday at 11 am only). From November to April, they run at 2 pm on Saturday and 11 am on Sunday.

Between May and September, the open double-deck City-Tour bus operates hourly from 10 am to 5 pm. You can either take the entire one-hour tour for DM14 (children DM8) or buy a day ticket that lets you interrupt your journey as often as you like for DM25/15. The terminus is at the Musik- und Kongresshalle on Willy-Brandt-Allee.

A number of boat operators, like Quandt-Linie and Maak-Linie, run one-hour tours through the city canals encircling the Altstadt. Boats are scheduled to leave every half-hour, though many actually don't leave until they're at least half full. The landing docks are north of the Holstentorbrücke. Trips cost DM15/10 adults/children.

Places to Stay

The tourist offices at the Hauptbahnhof and the Holstentorpassage can help you find a room, but charge a DM5 booking fee. Unless noted, room rates listed below include breakfast.

Camping Lübeck's new camping ground, *Campingplatz Schönböcken* (☎ 893 09 0; open April through October), is located at Steinrader Damm 12 in the western suburb of Schönböcken, with a direct bus connection (No 7) to the city centre. Charges are DM8 per tent, plus DM6 per person.

Two more options are in Travemünde: *Strandcamping Priwall* (☎ 04502-717 92; open April through September), right on the beach and *Campingplatz Auf dem Priwall* (☎ 04502-223 4; open mid-March through September) at Mecklenburger Landstrasse 89a. Both are practically next to each other on the Priwall Peninsula on the southern side of the Untertrave River.

Hostels Lübeck has two DJH hostels. The excellent *Jugendgästehaus* (☎ 702 03 99), Mengstrasse 33, is well situated in the middle of the Altstadt, 15 minutes' walk from the Hauptbahnhof (or bus No 3 or 12 to Beckergrube). The cost for juniors/seniors is DM29/37.50 in three or four-bed rooms and DM31/40 in two-bed rooms. Rates include breakfast and sheets, and discounts on subsequent nights are available. *Folke-Bernadotte-Heim* (☎ 334 33) is at Am Gertrudenkirchhof 4, a little outside the Altstadt (bus No 1, 3, 11, 12 or 31 from the Hauptbahnhof to Gustav-Radbruch-Platz, then five minutes on foot). Bed & breakfast costs DM22/27 for juniors/seniors; sheets are DM7.

Another cheap option is the YMCA's *Sleep-Inn* (☎ 719 20) at Grosse Petersgrube 11, which charges DM15 per bed in dorms. A double room is DM40. They also have a two-bed apartment with private bath and kitchenette for DM30 per person and another that sleeps three to four people for DM40 per person. Breakfast and sheets are each an extra DM5. It's closed from mid-December to mid-January.

For budget accommodation, the small *Rucksackhotel* (☎ 706 89 2), Kanalstrasse 70, has beds in four to eight-bed rooms with shared facilities for DM21 to DM26. It also has a few doubles with private bath for DM75 and a four-bed room, also with shower and WC, for DM128. Prices do not include breakfast but there are cooking facilities. It only has 28 beds, so you'd be wise to book ahead.

In Travemünde, at Mecklenburger Landstrasse 69, is the *Jugendfreizeitstätte Priwall* (☎ 04502-257 6; open from April to mid-October), though it caters more for groups. Beds in rustic cabins cost DM13/19, plus a visitor's tax of DM5 in summer and DM2 in the off season.

Hotels Nonsmokers might like the no-smoking *Pension Koglin* (☎ 622 43 2), a bit north of the centre at Kottwitzstrasse 39, which charges from DM65/85 for singles/doubles with private shower and toilet. A place to flop is *Hotel zum Scheibenstand* (☎ 473 38 2) at Fackenburger Allee 76 south of the town centre. No-frills rooms here cost DM35/60 with shared shower and WC. Breakfast is extra.

For something central and a little more up-market, try *Hotel Stadt Lübeck* (☎ 838 83; fax 863 22 1), just outside the Hauptbahnhof at Am Bahnhof 21. Singles/doubles with private bath start at DM75/98. The family-friendly *Herberge zur Alten Stadtmauer* (☎ 737 02; fax 732 39), at An der Mauer 57, has simple singles/doubles for DM50/100 and ones with private shower & WC for DM70/120. Family rooms are available too. Another option is *Hotel Schwarzwaldstuben* (☎ 777 15; fax 705 41 4), where rooms with full facilities range from DM70 to DM100 for singles, DM135 to DM150 for doubles.

Several of the big chains have hotels in Lübeck, including the *Mövenpick Hotel* (☎ 150 40; fax 150 41 11) which has one of the best locations in town, right opposite the Holstentor, and standard rooms costing from DM140/170. A non-chain option in the heart of Lübeck is the *Altstadt Hotel* (☎ 720 83; fax 737 78) at Fischergrube 52. Its singles cost DM115 to DM155, doubles from DM185 to DM240. Top of the line is the *Radisson SAS* (☎ 142 0; fax 142 22 22) at Willy-Brandt-Allee 6 which charges from DM204/278 for state-of-the-art singles/doubles.

Places to Eat

Restaurants On Hüxstrasse at No 57 is the bistro-style *Aubergine*, decked out in cheerful yellowish décor and serving unusual dishes such as herring fried in garlic and tomatoes (DM12 to DM25). A lot more rustic is the *Kartoffelkeller* (closed Tuesday), downstairs at the Heiligen-Geist-Hospital at Koberg 8, where you can get potato-based dishes starting at DM5.30.

Hard to beat for style is the historical *Schiffergesellschaft* at Breite Strasse 2, the former guildhall of sailors. You sit beneath a painted and beamed wooden ceiling on long benches that resemble church pews. Above you are 17th-century models of ships while the walls are covered with large oil paintings. It's an atmosphere second to none, though you have to put up with tour groups and a menu starting at DM30.

Cafés & Pub-Restaurants One of the most popular student haunts is *Tipasa*, Schlumacherstrasse 14, which serves a variety of budget-priced meat, fish and vegetarian dishes as well as excellent pizzas. Another place that is always crowded is *Schmidt's Gasthaus*, Dr-Julius-Leber-Strasse 60-62. The menu is similar to Tipasa's.

For delicious freshly brewed beer, head to the cavernous *Brauberger* (closed Sunday) at Alfstrasse 36, which also serves pub fare and has a buffet with hot and cold dishes. Another winner is the rustic *Hieronymus* at Fleischhauerstrasse 81, a cosy restaurant spread over four floors of a narrow 17th-century building. Most dishes on the creative menu cost less than DM15 and are quite filling. If you want it really cheap, try lunch here (served until 5 pm) and choose from about a dozen specials priced around DM9.

Amadeus, Königstrasse 26, is a good place to linger over a cup of coffee or to have a small meal. It is also known for its generous breakfasts (open from 10 am). Hidden in a courtyard off Wahmstrasse 43-45 is the trendy *Café Remise* which has warm but sparse décor and a bistro menu of salads, moussaka, baguette sandwiches and the like.

A good place for a quick lunch is the basement of the Königspassage, where several self-service restaurants are clustered.

Entertainment

Listings For up-to-date event information, pick up a copy of *Lübeck Heute* from the tourist offices. Geared towards a younger audience is the magazine *Szene*, free in pubs, restaurants and also the tourist offices.

Ultimo and *Punktum* are similar, if a bit more subdued.

Theatre The place to go for drama, musicals, dance theatre and more are the two stages of the *Theater Lübeck* (☎ 745 52), an Art Nouveau building at Beckergrube 10-14. Avant-garde theatre by new authors is the focus of *Theater Combinale* (☎ 788 17) in the back at Hüxstrasse 115.

The *Marionettentheater* (Puppet Theatre), on the corner of Am Kolk and Kleine Petersgrube, is terrific entertainment – and not just for kids. Usually there is a children's show at 3 pm and one for adults at 7.30 pm, though times may vary. Afternoon seats cost DM7; evenings cost DM12 to DM16, depending on the play, discount DM9 to DM13. The theatre is closed on Mondays.

Classical Music The *Musikhochschule Lübeck* (Music Academy; ☎ 150 50), at Grosse Petersgrube 17-29, puts on a number of high-calibre concerts throughout the summer and winter semesters. Most concerts are free. The Brahms Festival takes place here at the end of April.

Lübeck is famous for its organ concerts played on the two organs of the *Marienkirche* at least once a week throughout the year. Tickets are available on the night of the performance only and cost DM5 to DM8, discount DM3 to DM5. There are also organ concerts in the Jacobikirche. Ask for the current schedule at the tourist offices or call ☎ 790 21 27.

Rock & Jazz One of Lübeck's premier concert venues – from rock and blues to flamenco – is the *Werkhof* (☎ 757 18) in Kanalstrasse 70. Nearby at Hüxterdamm 14 is the discotheque *Hüx* (☎ 766 33). The place for cool jazz is *Dr Jazz* (☎ 705 90 9) at An der Untertrave 1.

Getting There & Away

Bus Regional buses stop opposite the local buses on Hansestrasse, around the corner from the Hauptbahnhof. Kraftomnibusse services to/from Wismar terminate here, as well as Autokraft buses to/from Hamburg, Schwerin, Kiel, Rostock and Berlin.

Train Lübeck has connections to Hamburg at least once an hour (DM15.60, 45 minutes) and also to Kiel (DM21.20, 1¼ hours). A regional train goes to Rostock every two hours (DM34.60, two hours). A left-luggage office near the entrance of the Hauptbahnhof charges DM4 per day for large bags.

Car & Motorcycle If you're driving, Lübeck is easily reached via the A1 from Hamburg. The town also lies at the crossroads of the B75, the B104 to Schwerin, the B206 to Bad Segeberg and the B207 to Ratzeburg.

Getting Around

Public Transport Lübeck's city centre is easily walkable, but there's also an excellent bus system (☎ 888 28 28). A single journey on the Altstadt island, or to one stop beyond, costs DM2.80. A six-trip block costs DM14, though by far the best value is the 24-hour pass for DM4.

If you want to travel the entire Lübeck-Travemünde area, consider getting the Lübeck Karte, which is good for 24 hours and costs DM8 for individuals and DM15 for families (two adults, three children). This is different from the Lübeck-Travemünde Card (see Information at the start of the Lübeck section).

Bicycle Several companies rent bicycles at affordable rates, including Leihcycle (☎ 426 60) at Schwartauer Allee 39, with touring bikes for DM8 a day, and Laufrad (☎ 727 92), Beckergrube 13-17. You can also get bikes by the hour (DM1) at the rental station in the Bastion car park on Willy-Brandt-Allee near the Mövenpick Hotel. Bring your passport or ID.

TRAVEMÜNDE

- *pop 12,000*
- *area code* ☎ 04502

In 1329 when the rich city of Lübeck bought Travemünde, 20km to its north, for what must have been the pocket change sum of

1060 marks, the motivation wasn't beach but business. The goal was to control the spot where the Trave River flows into the Baltic Sea and therefore to secure access for ships to the harbour at Lübeck.

It wasn't until 1802 that Travemünde also became a resort town, the third on the German seaside after Norderney and Heiligendamm.

In 1894, Emperor Wilhelm II brought a spot of glamour to the town when he participated in the Travemünde Week, a sailing regatta and the town's answer to Kieler Woche. Henceforth, until WWI, it became an event *de rigueur* for the aristocracy and industrial elite.

Today, Travemünde is a much more down-to-earth coastal playground, often bursting with visitors during the summer months. They come to stroll on its promenade or catch the rays on its 4.5km of sandy beaches. Water sports – sailing, surfing, swimming, fishing – are popular here, and the casino offers glamorous entertainment at night. The AquaTop outdoor pool, with slides, jacuzzis and other fun installations, is a recent addition to the list of activities.

Next to Kiel, Travemünde is also a gateway to Scandinavia and ferries depart daily for Sweden and Finland (see Getting There & Away, below).

Getting There & Away

Bus From Lübeck's central bus station, bus Nos 30 and 31 provide direct service to Travemünde.

Train There are regular connections from Lübeck to Travemünde, which actually has three stations: Skandinavienkai, Hafenbahnhof and Strandbahnhof. Most trains stop at all three.

Car & Motorcycle From Lübeck, the B75 leads north-east to Travemünde. If you're travelling on the A1, catch the A226 connecting road to the B75.

Boat Ferry prices quoted below are for one-way trips. All boats leave from Skandinavienkai. In most cases, prices vary widely according to the season and the time of day.

TT-Line (☎ 040-360 14 42 in Hamburg) offers ferry service up to four times daily to Trelleborg, Sweden (7½ hours). Prices range from DM70 to DM100 (students DM42 to DM60). The tariff for a car plus driver is DM100 to DM250. Bikes are DM10.

Nördo Link (☎ 805 89) has one daytime and one overnight ferry to Malmö, Sweden, year round. Prices for daytime departures are DM77 per person plus DM50 for the cheapest two-bed cabin.

Overnight trips cost DM115 per person, plus another DM115 for the two-bed cabin. Bikes are a flat DM12. Various car packages are available.

The Finnjet-Silja Line (☎ 0451-589 92 22) runs ferry services several times weekly to Helsinki in Finland. The journey takes anything from 22 to 36 hours and costs from DM125 per person in a four-bed budget cabin. From June to August, the same cabin bed costs DM210. A normal car is DM160 (DM235 in high season). Bicycles are free. Discounts of about 20% are available to students.

An alternative is Poseidon Passagierdienst (☎ 0451-150 74 43 in Lübeck), which travels to the Finnish cities of Helsinki (37 hours) and Turku (34½ hours) year round at least once a week. The price per person in two-bed cabins is DM460, in three-bed cabins DM320.

In peak season, you pay DM570/450. Cars cost DM130 in low season, DM160 in high season.

Getting Around

Travemünde is small enough to be walked but, to get around quicker, you can rent a bicycle from Beitsch (☎ 662 2) at Kurgartenstrasse 67 (DM10 a day) and Bruders (☎ 534 0) at Mecklenburger Landstrasse 14 (DM8).

To get to Priwall, the southern shore of the Trave River, there's a car ferry from Vorderreihe and also a passenger ferry from the quay near Nordermole (summer only).

SCHLESWIG

- *pop 26,500*
- *area code ☎ 04621*

First mentioned in public records in 804, Schleswig is the oldest town in northern Europe and its long history has bestowed on it a plethora of first-rate sights and attractions. About 34km east of Husum and the same distance south of Flensburg, Schleswig is a placid town scenically wrapped around the lake-sized terminus of the Schlei – at 40km, the longest and narrowest Baltic Sea fjord. Schleswig muddled through the Middle Ages as a minor farming and artisans' town, not gaining much importance until 1544 when the dukes of Gottorf chose it as their residence. Thanks to their interest in art and science, Schleswig developed into a cultural centre in the late-Renaissance and baroque periods. The town's heyday lasted as long as the ducal power and, after 1721, Schleswig was once again relegated to provincial backwater.

After the German-Danish War of 1864, Schleswig went to Prussia and it has been part of the state of Schleswig-Holstein since the end of WWII. Despite its relatively small size, you'll need at least one full day to explore it entirely.

Orientation

Schleswig's train station is about 1km south of Schloss Gottorf and 3km from the city centre (take bus No 1, 2, 4 or 5). The central bus station is at the corner of Königsstrasse and Plessenstrasse, with the Altstadt and the Dom continuing to the south-east.

Information

The tourist office (☎ 248 78; fax 207 03) is at Plessenstrasse 7. Between May and September, it's open weekdays from 9 am to 12.30 pm and 1.30 to 5 pm, Saturday from 9 am to noon. In winter, it's closed on Friday afternoon and at weekends. Here you can get the SchleswigCard, which gives you unlimited access to public transport, admission to all museums and various reductions for three consecutive days (DM12, families DM28).

Banks exchanging money include the Sparkasse at Stadtweg 49, which also has an ATM machine that accepts all major credit cards. You'll find the post office practically next door at Stadtweg 53-55 (closed at lunchtime).

Bookshops with selections of English-language books are Liesegang at Stadtweg 8 and Die Eule at Mönchenbrückstrasse 10. There's a self-service Waschcenter next to Karstadt at Stadtweg 70, which is open 6 am to midnight and costs DM6 per wash plus DM1 for the dryer.

The police have a station (☎ 841) at Friedrich-Ebert-Strasse 8.

Dom St Petri

The centre of the Altstadt and a Schleswig landmark is the imposing Cathedral of St Petri, the oldest surviving building in town (around 1134), which is filled with wonderful art treasures. Upon entering, the first thing you will see is a wooden **statue of St Christopher** (1515), the patron saint of travellers. It was carved by Hans Brüggemann, who was also responsible for the **Bordesholmer Altar** (1521) in the east choir – and nothing will prepare you for this amazing display of complex, superb craftsmanship. The altar itself measures 12.6 by 7.14m, but it's the more than 400 figurines – carved with amazing emotional detail and perfectly composed– that impress most. In 24 scenes, they tell the story of the Passion of Christ. Bring your binoculars, if you have them, to truly appreciate this roped-off masterpiece and also the ceiling frescos above.

To reach the altar, you pass through the rood-loft, in this case an arcade with pointed arches held up by Corinthian columns and carrying a **Triumphal Cross**. South of the main altar you'll find the canopied **Dreikönigsaltar** (around 1300) which shows the three Magi with Mary and Jesus. In the niche north of the altar stands the monumental tomb of King Friedrich I of Denmark, formerly a Gottorf duke. Antwerp sculptor Cornelis Floris used black, green and red marble as well as alabaster for this work.

The Dom is open daily from 9 am to 5 pm between May and September and from 10 am to 4 pm the rest of the year. It's closed Friday afternoons and Sunday mornings. Concerts take place in the cathedral at 8 pm on Wednesday in summer.

Holm

Just east of the Altstadt is this traditional fishing village, which was an island until 1935. Even today, about 20 active fishermen haul in eel, perch, salmon and herring from the Schlei waters. Right in the centre of Holm is an almost toy-sized **chapel** ringed by a starkly symmetrical cemetery whose graves are curiously framed by low hedges. Only residents of Holm may be buried here. Continue along Süderholmstrasse to get to the **Johanniskloster**, a former Benedictine convent and a collegiate foundation for noble women since the Reformation. Its Romanesque church was redecorated in the baroque style. It can be seen during a guided tour with the prioress (call ahead on ☎ 262 63) or on an official walking tour of Holm (ask at the tourist office about upcoming walks).

Schloss Gottorf

The rather plain exterior of this palace does not hint at the marvellous design and wealth of art treasures – from the Middle Ages to the 20th century – awaiting within. The building itself has its origins in 1161, was the former residence of the dukes of Gottorf and later used as a military barracks. After WWII, it was chosen as the new home for the collections of the Schleswig-Holstein Landesmuseum, which lost its former domicile in Kiel to bombing raids.

It's easy to spend a day touring the palace's 132 exhibition rooms. Highlights include the medieval section on the ground floor (rooms 1-5) with altars, sculptures and paintings by such notables as Lucas Cranach the Elder. Upstairs you'll find an original wood-panelled 17th-century wine tavern from Lübeck with carvings by Hinrich Sextra II. The adjoining rooms shed light on the lifestyle of the Gottorf family, with fancy furniture, paintings, tapestries and books from the baroque period. Don't miss the circular Room 20, which boasts a fine collection of alabaster and marble sculpture. Also of note are the rooms (Nos 48-56) filled with Art Nouveau furniture, paintings and objects with works by Henry van de Velde, Peter Behrens and Wenzel Hablik.

Architecturally, one of the most interesting rooms is the **Königshalle** (Room 3), a Gothic hall in the south wing divided by a row of pillars supporting a cross-vaulted ceiling. Upstairs in the north wing is the **Schlosskapelle** (Room 26), a small church whose gallery is shouldered by a series of Ionic columns. Below is a small ebony altar with delicate silver decorations. The northern end of the gallery is taken up by the **Betstube**, a separate room reserved for the ducal family that is lavishly panelled with precious inlaid wood. It's the only room in the church that can be heated. Next door is the **Hirschsaal**, the former banquet hall, which derives its name from the deer frescos on the walls. These contrast with the monochrome scenes from Roman history painted on the vaulted ceiling.

Turn left as you exit the main building to get to the **Kreuzstall** whose three floors contain a striking collection of German 20th-century art, including paintings by Brücke members Kirchner, Heckel, Pechstein, Nolde, Schmidt-Rottluff and Otto Müller.

The museums are open daily between May and October from 9 am to 5 pm (some sections are closed on Mondays). In winter, hours are 9.30 am to 4 pm, closed Monday. Admission is DM7, discount DM3. If you read German, it pays to invest in the handy and thorough museum guide (DM8).

Wikinger Museum

The area of Haithabu, on the southern side of the Schlei Fjord, was the most important economic centre in northern Europe during the Viking era around the 9th century. The 24-hectare settlement is marked only by the remains of its semicircular wall. To make it all meaningful, visit the Viking Museum (open from 9 am to 5 pm, closed Monday; DM4, discount DM2), about 3km from the train station (bus No 1668), east of the B76.

A 30m-long Viking longboat has been artfully reconstructed inside, and objects displayed in glass cases provide insight into the everyday life of the Vikings. (For ferry service across the Schlei to Haithabu, see Getting Around.)

Places to Stay

The nearest camping ground is the well equipped *Campingplatz Haithabu* (☎ 324 50; open March through October), right on the southern shore of the Schlei in Haddeby with a great view of the Schleswig skyline (take bus No 1668). Schleswig's *DJH hostel* (☎ 238 93) is at Spielkoppel 1 and charges DM20/25 juniors/seniors for bed & breakfast. From the train station, take bus No 1, 2 or 4 to the Stadttheater stop, then walk.

The tourist office has a room-booking service (DM8). Lots of private rooms start at DM25 per person.

Some hotels charge less in the low season. One of the cheaper options is the small *Gaststätte zum Stadtfeld* (☎ 239 47), near the city centre at Stadtfeld 2a, which charges DM45/75 for rooms with shared facilities. Right on the harbour, at Hafenstrasse 40, is *Hotel Olschewski's* (☎ 255 77; fax 221 41), where rooms with private bath cost DM70 to DM80 per person; there's a good restaurant too. *Hotel Hohenzollern* (☎ 906 0; fax 906 16 9), Moltkestrasse 41, charges DM78/120 for singles/doubles with shower and WC.

Places to Eat

Schleswig's main street for restaurants and bars is Lollfuss, one of the roads connecting the Altstadt with Schloss Gottorf to the west, where, at No 3, you'll find *Patio*, a café-restaurant set in a lovely courtyard. Other places with a youthful ambience are *Classico* at No 76 on the same street and *Fanf* at No 79. All serve an assortment of dishes and snacks for smaller budgets. Another fun spot is the huge and rustic *Brauerei Schleswig* at Königstrasse 27. Wood-fire pizza can be had at *Panorama* at Plessenstrasse 15, which also has daily lunch specials for DM9.

For a proper fish restaurant, go to the nautical themed *Schleimöve* at Süderholmstrasse 8 where you get good-sized portions for under DM20. *Stadt Flensburg*, at Lollfuss 102, is small and cosy and serves a range of specialities from Schleswig-Holstein. One of the nicest – and priciest – places is *Senatorkroog*, in a historical building at Rathausmarkt 9-10.

Getting There & Away

There are several daily buses, with restricted service on weekends, to Kiel (No 1668), Flensburg (Nos 1668 and 1590) and Husum (No 1613). A direct train service to Hamburg (DM35, 1½ hours) is offered every two hours, while trains to Flensburg (DM9.60, 30 minutes) leave several times hourly. There's also an hourly link to Husum (DM9.60, 30 minutes) and Kiel (DM14.20, 50 minutes). If you're driving, take the A7 (Hamburg-Flensburg) to the Schuby exit, then continue east on the B201.

Boat From mid-June to early September, the Schleischiffahrt A Bischoff (☎ 233 19) operates scheduled boat service along the Schlei. Boats depart daily except Tuesday from the Schleihallenbrücke near Schloss Gottorf and travel as far as Ulsnis, about 15km to the north-east, which has a beautiful Romanesque church (about 1½ hours; DM8, return DM14). Trips from Schleswig all the way to the mouth of the Schlei into the Baltic Sea, just beyond Kappeln, are offered on Tuesday (3½ hours; DM13, return DM23). Children up to age 12 pay half price. The company also runs three-hour excursions on the Schlei every Sunday, Wednesday, Thursday and holidays from May to mid-June and through most of September (DM14).

Getting Around

Tickets for Schleswig's bus system cost DM1.70 per trip. Places that rent bicycles are Splettstösser (☎ 241 02) at Bismarckstrasse 13 and Peters (☎ 376 88) at Bahnhofstrasse 14. Ferries cross the Schlei channel, including to Haithabu, daily between May and September from 12.30 to 5.30 pm and cost DM3.50/6 one way/return; children pay DM2.50/4.

FLENSBURG

- *pop 90,000*
- *area code* ☎ 0461

Flensburg is the northernmost town on the German mainland – List on Sylt Island is still farther north – and located about 150km north of Hamburg on the Danish border. It's an attractive town, hugging the shores of the Flensburg Firth and ringed by low hills – a strange sight indeed on the plains of northern Germany. It's blessed with a handsome Altstadt, the work of visionary conservationists who, in the 1960s and 70s, silenced those in favour of razing and rebuilding. Flensburg is small enough to be explored in a day.

In 1284, Flensburg was awarded town rights but really only blossomed *after* the decline of the Hanseatic League in the 16th century. For centuries, squabbles between the dukes of Schleswig, the counts of Holstein and the Danish crown had kept Flensburg in the shadow of Lübeck and other Hanseatic cities. Only after King Christian 1 of Denmark was elected to also be duke of Schleswig and count of Holstein in 1460 did Flensburg evolve into one of the region's most important merchant towns.

In the 18th century, its ships sailed as far as the Caribbean and returned loaded with rum, and to this day the town is also known as the 'Rumstadt'. From this prosperous era date the many *Kaufmannshöfe* (merchants' courtyards) that are unique to Flensburg. These complexes usually consisted of a section facing the main street that contained the merchant's living quarters, often with an office or store on the ground floor. Directly behind was a series of low buildings, wrapped around a central courtyard, where workshops were located. A tall warehouse stood on the other end – the harbour side – which made it easier to load and unload goods quickly and cheaply. Today, these *Höfe* house restaurants, cafés, boutiques and galleries.

Flensburg escaped the bombing of WWII, and the local naval academy was in fact the seat of the last Third Reich government, under Admiral Karl Dönitz, who surrendered to the Allies here on 7 May 1945.

Orientation & Information

It's easy to orientate yourself in Flensburg, for most of its sights are strung along the pedestrian zone anchored by Südermarkt and Nordermarkt and its side streets. The harbour is just north-east of here, while the train station is about a 10-minute walk south of Südermarkt. The central bus station (ZOB) is at the end of Rathausstrasse on Süderhofenden near the harbour area.

The tourist office (☎ 230 90; fax 173 52) is inside the Amalien-Lamp-Speicher, a former warehouse, opposite the car park at Speicherlinie 40 and is open weekdays from 10 am to 6 pm (also on Saturday to 1 pm between June and September). The main branch of the Sparkasse bank is at Südergraben 8-14. The main post office is at Bahnhofstrasse 40 and there's a second branch on Nordermarkt. For a selection of English books, go to the Montanus bookshop at Holm 20. There are self-service laundrettes at Angelburger Strasse 45 and at Flurstrasse 27.

Walking Tour

From the train station, head north along Bahnhofstrasse to Neumarkt. Cross here, then continue on Rote Strasse, where you immediately come across some of Flensburg's typical **merchants' courtyards** – the Blumenhof at No 18-20 and the Krusehof at No 20-22.

Rote Strasse merges with Südermarkt, which is dominated by the **Nikolaikirche**, a Gothic red-brick hall church from 1390. The bronze baptismal font (1497) was the only piece of medieval decoration to survive the Reformation. An artful work by Peter Hansen, it is supported by statues of the four Evangelists and shows scenes from the life of Christ. The church's *pièce de résistance*, though, is the organ with its flashy Renaissance encasement by Heinrich Ringerink.

Continue north on Holm and look out for other courtyards, including the **Dethleffsen-Hof** at No 43-45, the **Borgerforeningen Hof** at No 17 with an enormous chestnut tree, and the oldest Hof, dating from the late 16th century, at No 19-21. Turning left (west) into

Rathausstrasse and heading uphill will get you to the **Städtisches Museum** (Municipal Museum; open Tuesday to Saturday from 10 am to 5 pm, to 1 pm on Sunday; DM5, discount DM2.50). The highlights are furnished farmhouse rooms from the 17th century and paintings by Emil Nolde. There's also a nice view from atop the Museumsberg.

Head back down Rathausstrasse and continue north on what is now Grosse Strasse where, after a short while, you'll pass the **Heiliggeistkirche** (1386), modestly integrated into a row of houses. It's the place of worship of the resident Danish minority and is decorated with late-medieval frescos and a baroque altar.

Just opposite, at Grosse Strasse 24, is the **Westindienspeicher** (West Indies warehouse) dating from 1706, a reminder of Flensburg's trade with the islands of the Caribbean. Parallel to Grosse Strasse (east) is the Speicherlinie with the tourist office.

Grosse Strasse spills into Nordermarkt above which rises the most magnificent of Flensburg's churches, the **Marienkirche**, begun in 1284. Of note are the frescos, the only decoration predating the Reformation. Most impressive, though, is the sumptuous **high altar** (1598) by Ringerink. It's topped by a superstructure of gables and giant portraits of the merchant couple who donated the altar. In fact, the great number of epitaphs in this church confirms that modesty was apparently not a trait of Flensburg's rich merchants. Check out the Niels Hacke epitaph at the end of the northern aisle, which integrates a painting by Heinrich Jansen, a student of Rembrandt.

If you continue beyond the Marienkirche on what is now Norderstrasse, you'll get to the **Nordertor** (1595), a Flensburg landmark and one of the few surviving town gates in Schleswig-Holstein. The town motto is inscribed on its north side: 'Friede ernährt, Unfriede verzehrt' (Peace nurtures, strife consumes).

To learn more about the history of shipping and the rum trade in Flensburg, visit the **Schiffahrtsmuseum** (Maritime Museum; open Tuesday to Saturday from 10 am to 5 pm, to 1 pm on Sunday; DM5, discount DM2.50), Schiffbrücke 39 at the harbour.

Activities

Between April and December, the Förde Reederei Seetouristik (☎ 864 0) makes daily cruises to Apenrade in Denmark. The return trip costs DM8, or DM5 if you come back by bus (DM12/8 in July and August). A limited number of bicycles may be taken on board for an extra DM5 each, and there's duty-free shopping as well. If you just want to take a short spin around Flensburg Firth, you can make the one-hour trip to Glücksburg (several times daily for DM6) with the Viking Reederei (☎ 276 86).

Places to Stay

The nearest camping ground is *Campingplatz Jarplund* (☎ 932 34; open April to October) on the B76 south of Flensburg. Flensburg's *DJH hostel* (☎ 377 42) is at Fichtestrasse 16 and charges DM20/25 for juniors/seniors. From the train station, take bus No 1 to ZOB, then No 3, 5 or 7 to the Stadion stop.

The tourist office reserves rooms for free. Private rooms start at DM15 per person without breakfast. As for hotels, *Pension Ziesemer* has two central 'branches': one at Wilhelmstrasse 2 (☎ 251 64) and another at Augustastrasse 8 (☎ 237 70). Singles/doubles with shared shower cost DM38/75. At Augustastrasse 2 is *Hotel Handwerkerhaus* (☎ 144 80 0), whose nicely furnished rooms cost DM45/80 with shared bath and DM85/135 with private bath. Top of the line is the state-of-the-art *Ramada Hotel Garni* (☎ 841 10; fax 841 12 99), with a great location on the harbour at Norderhofenden 6-9 and full-facility rooms for DM135/160.

Places to Eat

A cosy place to go for a glass of wine, accompanied by anything from a small DM5 snack to a succulent plate of shrimp for DM25, is the *Weinstube* at Rote Strasse 18-20 (dinner only). If beer is more to your liking, go to *Hansens Brauerei* at Grosse

Strasse 83 near Nordermarkt. Here you can watch beer being made, order the house brew by the gallon while sitting in a historic tram, and down big burgers, steaks and fish dishes at very reasonable prices.

At the smart *Brasserie Napoleon*, in a half-timbered building at the end of the courtyard at Grosse Strasse 42-44, you'll dine on well priced regional fare in wood-panelled rooms surrounded by gold-leaf mirrors and oil paintings.

For a quick snack, there's *Kochlöffel* at Grosse Strasse 42.

Getting There & Away

There's a regular bus service (No 1668) to Schleswig (one hour) and on to Kiel (2½ hours). Bus No 44 goes daily to Husum (1¼ hour).

Flensburg has rail connections with Kiel (DM21.20, 1¼ hours), Hamburg (DM46, 1¾ hours) and Schleswig (DM9.60, 30 minutes). Trips to Husum (DM14.20, 1½ hours) require a change at Jübeck.

Flensburg is at the beginning of the A7, which leads south to Hamburg, Hanover and beyond. The town can also be reached via the B76, B199 and B200. The ADM Mitfahrzentrale (☎ 194 40) is at St-Jürgen-Platz 1.

Getting Around

You can easily cover all of Flensburg on foot, though city buses do exist. To rent a bicycle, go to Fahrrad Petersen (☎ 254 55) at Hafermarkt 19.

GLÜCKSBURG

- *pop 6400*
- *area code* ☎ 04631

The little spa town of Glücksburg is a mere 10km north-east of Flensburg. The main reason to visit is for the dreamy, horseshoe-shaped **Wasserschloss** (moated palace), which virtually floats in the middle of a large lake. It's one of the state's most important Renaissance palaces and is partly furnished as a museum

Built between 1582 and 1622, it was the seat of the dukes of Glücksburg until 1779 and then temporarily fell under the rule of the Danes. It's a gleaming white structure, anchored by four octagonal corner towers, and can be explored either on a guided tour or by walking around independently.

On the ground floor, the lavish baroque palace chapel is a popular place for weddings. The raised room, connected with the chapel through a window, was reserved for the ducal family and allowed them to participate in the service without having to mingle with the servants. The altar and baptismal font are the work of Claus Gabriel of Flensburg.

Two sweeping staircases lead to the upper floors and the family's private quarters. Much of the furnishings you see here now were brought from Schloss Gottorf in Schleswig.

The **Kaiserin Salon** and **Kaiserin Schlafzimmer** (empress's salon and bedroom) were richly furnished in the rococo, Empire and Biedermeier styles for the German Empress Auguste Victoria in 1896.

Among the highlights on the 2nd floor is the series of **Gobelin tapestries** (1740) in the **Weisser Saal** (white hall). Also note the precious goat-skin wall coverings, vividly painted with hunting scenes. In the **Schatzkammer** (treasure chamber) look for the Vogelservice porcelain from the royal manufacturer in Berlin.

If it's a nice day, you might want to check out the **Rosengarten** north of the palace with more than 400 varieties of roses (DM3). Prime blooming season is usually around the end of June.

From May to September, the Schloss is open daily from 10 am to 5 pm. In April and October, hours are 10 am to 4 pm (closed Monday). From November to March it's open only on weekends, but daily from 17 to 30 December. Admission is DM7.50, discount DM5.

Getting There & Away

Bus No 21 makes regular trips between Flensburg and Glücksburg, though it's nicer to travel by boat along the Flensburg Firth (see Activities in the previous Flensburg section).

HUSUM

- *pop 21,000*
- *area code* ☎ 04841

About 80km north-west of Kiel and 42km south-west of Flensburg lies this peaceful, pleasant coastal town which has largely preserved its historical attributes. Husum was the birthplace of the famed 19th-century German novelist, Theodor Storm, who caustically referred to his hometown as 'the grey town by the sea', a description rather undeserved, especially when the crocuses are in bloom in late March or early April.

Husum was first mentioned in 1252 in connection with the killing of King Abel of Denmark in Husumbro castle. Both disaster and serendipity struck in 1362 when a major storm rearranged the coast and carved out Husum's inland harbour. This direct access to the North Sea proved very profitable in the following centuries, as trade with the Netherlands picked up.

Despite this commercial success, Husum didn't get its town rights until 1603. A quarter century earlier, it had become a royal residence when the dukes of Gottorf built themselves a palace here. Husum continued to thrive as a merchant town and was largely spared from destruction during WWII. Today it's a relaxing place that is a good base for bike touring and exploring the Halligen Islands.

Orientation & Information

Husum's train station lies on the southern periphery of the city centre. To get to the central bus station, walk about 300m north from the train station along Herzog-Adolf-Strasse; it's just east of the Nordfriesisches Museum. The Markt and the town centre are another 300m north. The harbour is about half a km west of the Markt, with the beach another 1.5km farther west.

The tourist office (☎ 898 70; fax 472 8) is in the historical town hall at No 27 of Grossstrasse (which merges with the Markt to the east) and is open weekdays from 9 am to noon and 2 to 4.30 pm (Friday to 3 pm). If you're interested in seeing all of Husum's five main museums, consider buying the Museumsverbundkarte for DM10, available here or at each museum.

Banks around the Markt, where you can exchange cash and travellers' cheques, include the Commerzbank and a Sparkasse branch. The main post office is behind the train station, but the more central one is at Markt. The self-service Waschcenter at Norderstrasse 12 charges DM6 per wash, plus DM1 for the dryer. There's a police station (☎ 668 0) at Poggenburgstrasse 9, near the train station.

Markt

The size of the Markt, and the merchants' houses that line it, attest to Husum's prosperity in the 16th and 17th centuries. The tower of the **Marienkirche**, which is supposed to symbolise a lighthouse, looms above the square. Built in the neoclassical style, the church replaced an earlier Gothic one, torn down in 1807. The interior is plain and streamlined with a flat ceiling and a phalanx of Doric columns holding up the gallery. The altar is framed by a construction that looks like the entrance to a Greek temple. The bronze baptismal font (1643) is one of the few pieces left over from the original church.

The **fountain** outside the church shows Tine, a young Frisian woman who figures in one of Storm's novellas. On the north side of the Markt is the old **Rathaus** (1601) where you'll find the tourist office. Adjacent is the **Herrenhaus**, whose gables sport a series of sandstone heads supposedly representing executed 15th-century rebels. The house at No 11 is the birthplace of Theodor Storm. He lies buried in Klosterkirchhof, reached via Norderstrasse, which runs east from the northern side of the Markt.

Schloss vor Husum

The Schloss is north of the Markt and easily reached via the narrow Schlossgang. The secondary residence of the dukes of Gottorf, it was built on a site formerly occupied by a Franciscan monastery. It was the Franciscans who, sometime in the Middle Ages, first planted oodles of crocuses in what is now the **Schlosspark**. If you happen to be in Husum in late March or early April, you will witness the stunning spectacle of the entire park bathed in a sea of purple blossoms. The palace was repeatedly altered through the centuries but finally got back its characteristic onion-shaped tower in 1980. Only the **Torhaus** (gateway), with its curvaceous gables, remained largely unchanged. Inside the Schloss is a moderately interesting collection of paintings and furniture, though the richly decorated fireplaces do warrant a closer look. The Schloss is open April to October from 11 am to 5 pm, closed Monday. Admission is DM5, discount DM2.50.

Schiffbrücke & Around

A short walk west from Markt will lead you to Schiffbrücke, the area around Husum's inland harbour. It is webbed by cobbled lanes of which **Wasserreihe** is the most picturesque. At No 31 stands the **Theodor Storm Haus** (open April to October daily from 2 to 5 pm, Tuesday to Friday also from 10 am to noon, and the rest of the year on Tuesday, Thursday and Saturday from 2 to 5 pm; DM3, discount DM2.50). The writer lived and worked in this town house from 1866 to 1880. On view are Biedermeier furniture, paintings and documents.

Across the street at No 52 is the curious **Tabak- und Kindermuseum** (Museum of Tobacco and Children), which seems like an unusual fusion until one meets Herbert 'Floi' Schwermer, its eccentric bearded owner. He has amassed a lifetime's worth of prams, teddy bears, toys and, of course, pipes and other smoking paraphernalia that are displayed in a charming, if somewhat chaotic, fashion. It's open daily from 10 am to 6 pm; DM3, discount DM2.50.

Wasserreihe parallels Hafenstrasse and the inland harbour on whose southern side stands the new modern Rathaus. A short way east of here, at Am Zingel 15, is the **Schiffahrtsmuseum Nordfriesland** (Maritime Museum of North Friesland; open daily 10 am to 5 pm from April to October; DM2, discount DM1) with a small but nicely displayed collection on Frisian shipping history. Exhibits include a historic ship's hull, scrimshaw and a good selection of ships in bottles. For an even wider look at local and regional history, go to the **Nordfriesisches Museum Nissenhaus** (open daily except Saturday from 10 am to 5 pm, in winter to 4 pm; DM5, discount DM2) in Herzog-Adolf-Strasse 25 near the train station.

Hiking & Biking

The tourist office publishes a useful booklet with decent maps (DM4) that outlines seven hiking tours of varying lengths throughout the Husum Bay area. Another volume details nine different biking tours (DM5). For bike-rental places see the Getting Around section below.

Places to Stay

Camping There are three camping grounds in the vicinity of Husum. The nearest one is *Campingplatz Doekkoog* (☎ 619 11; open late March through October), about 2km west of the town centre near the beach at Doekkoog 17. To reach it, take bus No 47, 51 or 53 from the train station to Hafen, then walk.

Another site is *Nordseecamping Zum Seehund* (☎ 399 9; open year round) in Simonsberg about 7km south-west of Husum (bus No 73 or 77). They also rent rooms for DM35 per person.

The third camping ground is the nicely located *Camping Seeblick* (☎ 332 1; open April to mid-October) at Nordseestrasse 32 north of Husum in Schobüll (bus No 51).

Hostel Husum's *DJH hostel* (☎ 271 4), at Schobüller Strasse 34 north-west of the city centre, charges DM22/27 for juniors/seniors. From the bus station, take bus No 51 to Westerkampweg.

Hotels The tourist office offers a free room-reservation service. Private rooms start from around DM25 per person. Some hotels drop their rates in the low season.

One of the least expensive places in town is *Hotel-Restaurant Rödekrog* (☎ 377 1) at Wilhelmstrasse 10, about five minutes walk south from the train station, which charges

DM35/70 for simple singles/doubles with private shower. In the same category is *Gaststätte Kielsburg* (☎ 739 25) at Kielsburger Strasse 1, which has three doubles with full facilities for DM80 to DM110.

If you can spend a little more, you should stay at the *Hotel am Schlosspark* (☎ 202 22 4; fax 620 62) at Hinter der Neustadt 76-86, a modern and quiet hotel with large rooms and a killer breakfast. Rooms with shower and WC cost DM99/150. The only five-star hotel in all of Schleswig-Holstein is the atmospheric *Hotel Altes Gymnasium* (☎ 833 0; fax 833 12), in a former school at Süderstrasse 6, where classy rooms start at DM187/234.

Places to Eat

One of Husum's main streets is Neustadt where, at No 66, you'll find the *Brauhaus*, a favourite gathering spot inside the Theodor Storm Hotel. You can sit among brewing vats or outside in the beer garden when the weather allows. Simple dinners like spare ribs cost around DM16. The intimate restaurant *Anna* is a neat little find in the basement of the Stadtpassage shopping arcade off Grossstrasse opposite the Karstadt store. The eclectic menu ranges from chilli con carne to fresh fish dishes from DM13.

In the harbour, at Kleikuhle 6, is the *Friesenkrog*, a rustic establishment with daily specials from DM12. If you want something even cheaper, grab a fish sandwich at one of several snack shops in the harbour area. Be sure to try the Husumer Krabben, the tiny brown shrimp for which Husum is famous. Sometimes, you can also buy the freshest catch right off the boat or from the *Fischereigenossenschaft* (fishers cooperative) at Am Aussenhafen 2. Sale hours depend on the tides, so it's best to call ahead in the morning at ☎ 503 3.

Getting There & Away

Husum has many bus connections with other towns in North Friesland, but the service is irregular. If you're planning to return the same day, be sure to check schedules in advance so as not to be stranded. For detailed information, call ☎ 0130-845 30 0. Bus No 44 travels daily to Flensburg (1¼ hours). Bus No 46 goes to Schleswig (one hour), though train service is more frequent and faster. Bus No 71 goes to the resort town of St Peter-Ording (40 minutes). Some buses will transport your bicycle for an extra DM2.

There are direct hourly train connections to Kiel (DM23.20, 1½ hours), Hamburg-Altona (DM41, 1¾ hours) and Schleswig (DM9.60, 30 minutes) and several links daily to Westerland on Sylt (DM18.80, one hour). Husum is at the crossroads of the B5, the B200 and the B201.

Getting Around

Husum is eminently walkable, though it's nice to have a bike to get around. You have a few rental companies to choose from. Zweirad Clausen (☎ 729 75), at Osterende 94, charges DM7.50 a day. The bikes of the Service Center (☎ 446 5), at Schulstrasse 4, cost DM10. And Eilrich (☎ 147 9), at Ostenfelder Strasse 12, charges DM7.

AROUND HUSUM

Halligen

Husum is a good springboard for exploring the Halligen, a handful of tiny wafer-flat islands scattered across the Nationalpark Wattenmeer. In the Middle Ages, some 50 of the North Sea islets supposedly existed, but the sea swallowed all but 10. Life here is rough and in constant conflict with the tides. Up to 60 times a year, floods drown the beaches and meadows, leaving the few reed-thatched farms stranded on the artificial knolls – or 'wharves' – they're built on. Electricity, water and even a few cars have reached these remote places, but essentially they're unique locales for walks in the sea breeze with your thoughts uninterrupted.

The largest island is **Hallig Langeness**, which measures about 10km in length and 1km in width and has 120 inhabitants. It can be reached by boat or by causeway via Oland. The prettiest islet is **Hallig Hooge**, which once sheltered a Danish king from a storm in the handsome **Königshaus** with its blue and white tiles and baroque ceiling fresco. Only 25 people on a single wharf eke out a living on **Hallig Oland** (2km by 500m), connected with the mainland by a 5km-long causeway. It's possible to rent rooms, though capacity is obviously limited and most people just experience the islands on day excursions.

From Husum, Wilhelm Schmid GmbH (☎ 04841-201 4) offers boat tours to the Halligen during the season. If you're prone to sea sickness, pick a day when the sea is fairly quiet. Boats leave from the Aussenhafen (outer harbour) in Husum and trips cost between DM18 and DM25. Some boats pass sandbanks with seal colonies.

The main jumping-off point for Halligen explorations, though, is Schlüttsiel, about 35km north of Husum. The Husum tourist office has information on the various operators and tours. Prices range from DM20 to DM40. If you're driving to Schlüttsiel, take the B5; if not, bus No 41 makes several runs daily from Husum right to the landing docks.

North Frisian Islands

SYLT

- *pop 21,000*
- *area code* ☎ 04651

Nature is the major draw of the North Frisian Islands, which lie west of the German mainland in the North Sea, and Sylt is no exception. On the west coast of the island, shaped not unlike an anchor attached to the mainland, the fierce surf of the North Sea gnaws mercilessly at the fragile shoreline. The wind can be so strong that the world's best windsurfers meet here for one of their World Cup events each year. By contrast, the mood on Sylt's eastern Wattenmeer (Watt means mud-flats) shore is tranquil and serene. It's a rather unusual sight to witness the shallow ocean retreat twice daily with the tides, exposing the muddy sea bottom. In Sylt's north, you'll find wide expanses of shifting dunes with candy-striped lighthouses above fields of gleaming yellow rape flower. Everywhere you go there are typical Frisian homes, thatched with reeds and surrounded by heath the colour of burnt sienna.

Landscapes like these have long inspired writers like Thomas Mann and Theodor Storm and painters like Emil Nolde and Lovis Corinth. For the past 40 years, Sylt has also been the preferred playground of the German jet set and has provided much of the smut for Germany's gossip press. These days, the couplings – or triplings or what have you – have quietened down to the point where *Playboy* writer Benno Kroll remarked that Sylt was experiencing a 'sort of post-coital hangover'. But judging by the glut of fancy restaurants, designer boutiques, mega-Deutschmark homes and luxury cars, the monied set has not disappeared yet.

It's easy enough, though, to leave the glamour and crowds behind and to get comfortably lost on the beach, in the dunes or on a bike trail.

Orientation

Sylt is 38.5km long and measures only 700m at its narrowest point. The largest town and commercial centre is Westerland in the centre of the island. At the northern end is List, Germany's northernmost town, while Hörnum is at the southern tip. Sylt is connected to the mainland by a trains-only causeway though you can take your car on board (see Getting There & Away for details). The train station is in Westerland.

Information

For information on the entire island, the best place to go is the Bädergemeinschaft Sylt (☎ 820 20; fax 820 22 2), near the Westerland Rathaus at Stephanstrasse 6. It is open weekdays from 9 am to noon and 1.30 to 4.30 pm (Friday to 3.30 pm). The office of Sylt Tourismus Zentrale (☎ 602 6) is at Keitumer Landstrasse 10b just outside of town in Tinnum and is open Monday to Saturday from 10 am to 6 pm. Local tourist offices are listed under each village.

If you need to exchange money, you can do so in Westerland at the Commerzbank at Strandstrasse 18 or the Volksbank at Friedrichstrasse 18. Other banks on the island also offer an exchange service and there are various ATM machines accepting all major credit cards. There's a post office in Westerland at Kjeirstrasse 17 and a police station (☎ 851 12) at Kirchenweg 21.

Resort Tax All the communities on Sylt charge visitors a *Kurtaxe* of DM2.50 to DM5.50 a day, depending on the town and the season. Paying the tax gets you a *Kurkarte*, which you need even to get onto the beach but which also entitles you to small discounts to museums or concerts and other events. If you're spending more than one night your hotel will automatically obtain a pass for you for the length of your stay (the price will be added to the room rate). If you're just there for the day you will need to obtain a *Tageskarte* (day pass) from a kiosk at the entrances to the beach. It's DM6 in all communities except Kampen, where it costs DM12.

Westerland

Westerland, the largest town on the island, is the Miami Beach of Sylt. In the centre, the view of the sea is sadly blocked by chunky high rises but there's a nice promenade along the beach. Another place to stroll along is the pedestrianised **Friedrichstrasse**, the main drag, where swanky nightclubs rub shoulders with tourist shops and restaurants.

Westerland became Sylt's first resort back in the mid-19th century, its people having moved much earlier from a little village to the east called Eidum. Don't look for it on the map though; in 1436 it was swallowed up by the sea during a horrendous storm. Miraculously, the wily villagers managed to save their little church's altar, which can today be admired in the **Alte Dorfkirche** on Kirchenweg to the east of the train station.

Nowadays, the only rising tide of real danger to Westerland is tourism. More than 2.5 million overnight stays were registered in 1995 and – thanks to cheap weekend tickets on Deutsche Bahn – a veritable deluge of day-trippers descends on Saturday and Sunday.

Westerland's tourist office (☎ 998 0) is at Strandstrasse 33.

Kampen

If Westerland is the Miami Beach of Sylt, Kampen is its St Tropez. This is the island's ritziest village and the one that attracts all sorts of major and minor celebrities and aristocrats. The main artery is **Stroenwai**, better known as Whiskey Alley, which is lined with restaurants, cars and boutiques – all expensive, naturally. Grab a table at one of the outdoor cafés, plonk down DM8 or so for a cappuccino and watch the action.

Kampen has its landmarks too, among them the island's oldest **lighthouse** (1855), which rises 60m above sea level. Locals have baptised it 'Christian' in honour of all the Danish kings by that name who ruled the island until it became German territory in 1866. There's also the **Uwe Dune**, at 52.5m Sylt's highest natural elevation and named for a local 19th-century freedom fighter, Uwe Jens Lornsen. You can climb to the top via 115 wooden steps for a 360° view over Sylt and, on a good day, to the neighbouring islands of Amrum and Föhr.

Kampen's tourist office (☎ 469 80) is at Hauptstrasse 12.

Keitum

About 3km east of Westerland is Keitum, the island's prettiest village. Here you'll find quiet streets flanked by old chestnut trees and lush gardens erupting in symphonies of colour. Historic reed-thatched houses, some of them the former homes of retired sea captains, abound.

In the old days, Keitum was Sylt's most important harbour and evidence of this nautical tradition abounds. **St Severin** is a late-Romanesque sailors' church known for its Gothic altar and pulpit, as well as for its romantic candlelight concerts. For excursions into the island's salty past, there's the Sylt **Heimatmuseum** (DM4) at Am Kliff 19 and the historic **Altfriesisches Haus** (DM3) at Am Kliff 13. Both are open daily from 10 am to 5 pm (in winter, Thursday to Saturday from 1 to 4 pm only).

Keitum's tourist office (☎ 337 0) is at Am Tipkenhoog 5.

List

List's tourist brochures are filled with superlatives, for everything here is 'Germany's northernmost' – harbour, beach, restaurant etc ... just fill in the blank. It's a windswept, tranquil land's end, but things usually liven up in the harbour when the ferry from Rømø dumps its load of day-tripping Danes in search of cheap drink. List has played important roles in both world wars. In WWI, Zeppelins headed towards England from its custom-built airport. In the 1930s, List became an army post and its airport again a launchpad, this time for fighter planes. Remnants of List's wartime past can still be found around the village.

North of List is the privately owned Ellenbogen (literally 'elbow'). Two families own this banana-shaped peninsula which has 35m-high moving dunes and beaches that are unfortunately off-limits because of dangerous currents. It's under a nature-preservation order and you must pay a toll at the entrance (DM8 per car).

List's tourist office (☎ 952 00) is at Listlandstrasse 11.

Activities

One of the most unusual ways to see the island is by taking a barefoot walk through the sludge of the Wattenmeer which stretches between Sylt's eastern shore and the mainland. It's a fragile environment that's part of the Nationalpark Wattenmeer, founded in 1985. Because of the danger from swiftly returning tides and treacherous channels, you should only venture out with a guide. The tourist offices have lists of tours on offer.

Horse riding is a popular activity on Sylt and offered both for beginners and the experienced. Usually you will need to go out as a member of a group, and in high season you should book at least a few days ahead. Rates start at DM20 per hour and the rides usually last for two hours. In Westerland, try Heikos Reiterwiese (☎ 560 0); in Keitum there's Reitstall Hoffmann (☎ 315 63).

Another activity unique to Sylt is a trip to the beach-side sauna. After you've heated up, the idea is to run naked into the chilly North Sea – brrrrr! To get to the sauna, take the road to Ellenbogen which branches off the main island road about 4km south-west of List. You will see a sign for the sauna on the left. The facilities are open from 11 am to 6 pm from Easter through October and admission is DM22.

In Westerland, a fun thing to do is visit the Sylter Welle indoor water park and health spa, especially when it's too cold for the beach. There are saunas, solariums, a wave pool and a slide. The complex is open daily from 10 am to either 9 or 10 pm (DM17 for two hours and DM22 for four).

Places to Stay

Private rooms tend to be the least expensive accommodation option on Sylt. They cost from DM30 per person and the tourist offices can help you find one. If you're planning a longer stay, renting a holiday flat is another possibility. This can cost as little as DM60 a day in low season and DM85 in high season (May to September). Unless it's a particularly slow time, though, proprietors may be reluctant to rent for fewer than three days. In general, keep in mind that prices fluctuate between low and high season and that the Kurtaxe is extra (see Resort Tax in the earlier Information section).

Camping Sylt has about half a dozen camping grounds, the nicest being *Campingplatz Kampen* (☎ 420 86; open April to mid-October), located among dunes on Möwenweg at the southern entrance to Kampen. It's about a five-minute walk to the beach. The largest camping facility is *Campingplatz Westerland* (☎ 994 49 9; open April to October), in the dunes off Rantumer Strasse.

Hostels The *DJH hostel* in Hörnum (☎ 880 29 4), at Friesenplatz 2, charges DM22/27 for juniors/seniors. From the bus station in Westerland take the bus to the Hörnum-Nord stop from where it's about a 1km walk. The other *DJH hostel* is about 2km north-east of

List (☎ 871 03 9), surrounded by dunes and just 800m from the North Sea. Buses run from Westerland to List-Schule and between April and September there's a shuttle to the hostel. Otherwise it's a 2.5km trek.

Hotels Prices quoted here are for the low season; rates increase by 10% to 20% in high season.

Among the cheaper options in Westerland is the lovely *Landhaus Nielsen* (☎ 986 90), Bastianstrasse 5, where singles/ doubles cost DM60/100. *Hotel Garni Diana* (☎ 988 60), Elisabethstrasse 19, is good value at DM85/ 150. An even better deal is *Haus Wagenknecht* (☎ 230 91), Wenningstedter Weg 59, where rooms are DM60/150. Top of the line is *Hotel Stadt Hamburg* (☎ 858 0; fax 858 22 0) at Strandstrasse 2, which offers traditional service and décor from DM150/240.

Places to Eat

Dining on Sylt can get pretty pricey though there are numerous shops and stands selling fresh fish meals for DM10 and under. Picnics on the beach are another fine option.

The traditional place for dinner in Westerland is the *Alte Friesenstube*, in a 17th-century building at Gaadt 4. It specialises in northern German and Frisian cooking, with main courses starting at DM25. For good, inexpensive fare, try *Toni's Restaurant* at Norderstrasse 3. It has a variety of main courses from around DM11 and a pleasant garden. *Blum's* on Neue Strasse 4 has some of the freshest fish for a sit-down meal or takeaway at very reasonable prices, but it has a bit of a cafeteria feel to it.

In Kampen, at Stapelhooger Wai, is *Kupferkanne*, where you can sit either inside a cosy Frisian house or outside in your private 'room', walled in by hedges, brambles and trees. Their giant cups of coffee and equally large slices of pie are not cheap, but the view of the Wattenmeer is complimentary. For a closer look at the German jet set, head to *Gogärtchen* on Stroenwai in Kampen where you can sit in the beer garden, on the terrace, or inside in the restaurant and munch on main courses from DM25.

List's harbour sports a number of colourful kiosks. One of them, *Gosch*, which – guess what? – prides itself on being 'Germany's northernmost fish kiosk', is an institution known far beyond Sylt. The food is delicious and, with prices starting at DM2.50 for fish sandwiches, nobody has to leave hungry.

A Keitum classic is the *Fisch-Fiete* at Weidemannweg 3, which also has a nice garden. Another treat is *Sansibar* on the beach between Rantum and Hörnum, south of Westerland. It looks like a shack but having a drink or dinner on its terrace at sunset, with a view of the crashing waves, ranks as a Sylt highlight. Of course prices are lower at lunchtime.

Getting There & Away

Getting to Sylt is a bit of an adventure and a pricey one to boot if you're driving. The island is connected to the mainland by the Hindenburgdamm, a causeway for trains only, which is no wider than a basketball court. Between 13 and 18 passenger trains a day make the direct three-hour trek from Hamburg-Altona to Westerland (DM62).

If you are travelling by car, you must load it onto a train in the town of Niebüll. There are constant crossings (usually at least once an hour) in both directions every day and no reservations can be made. The cost per car is a shocking DM135 return, but at least that includes all passengers. A cheaper alternative is to drive across the Danish border to the seaport of Rømø, connected to the mainland by causeway, and catch the ferry to List on Sylt's northern tip (one hour). There are up to 12 daily ferries year round in either direction. Return tickets are DM8 per person, DM13 if you're taking a bicycle. Cars cost DM88 return, which includes all passengers.

There are daily flights between Westerland airport and Hamburg, Munich and Berlin, and several weekly flights from other German cities.

If you want to visit the neighbouring islands of Amrum and Föhr, hop on one of the boats leaving from the harbour in

Hörnum. Day return cruises through the shallow banks that attract seals and sea birds are offered by WDR (☎ 04681-80 147 in Wyk) and Adler-Schiffe (☎ 04651-98 700 in Westerland) for DM32, children DM16. Bicycles are an extra DM7 or DM8.

Getting Around

Sylt is well covered by a bus system (☎ 702 7) with five lines serving every corner of the island. The main north-south connections run at 20-minute intervals during the day. There are seven price zones, costing from DM2 to DM10.50. Some buses have bicycle hangers.

The best mode of transport on the island is the bicycle and rental places abound. Look for the sign saying *Fahrradverleih* and expect to pay about DM10 a day.

In Westerland, the easiest place to find is Fahrrad am Bahnhof (☎ 580 3) at platform No 1 of the train station. In List, there's Esser (☎ 954 90) at Am Buttgraben 6a.

AMRUM

- *pop 2100*
- *area code* ☎ 04682

Amrum is the smallest of the North Frisian Islands – small enough in fact to walk around in a day. Yet it is also arguably the prettiest, blessed with the glorious Kniepsand – 12km of fine white sand, sometimes up to 1km wide – that takes up half the island. Amrum is much different in character from Sylt; not at all glamorous but tranquil, relaxing and far less touristed. Its landscape is a harmonious patchwork of dunes, woods, heath and marsh. Its villages have traditional Frisian architecture, with houses that are reed-thatched, gabled and with small doors. Besides the central village of Wittdün, there are Nebel, Norddorf, Steenodde and Süddorf.

Wittdün has northern Germany's tallest lighthouse (63m) which affords a spectacular view of the island and across to Sylt and Föhr (open April to October daily to 12.30 pm; admission DM2). In Nebel, you can visit the *Öömrang-Hüs* at Waaswai 1 (open year round from 10 am to 1 pm; also from 4 to 6 pm in summer), which is a historical sea captain's house with changing exhibits on North Frisian culture.

The friendly tourist office (☎ 891; fax 297 6) is right at the ferry landing in Wittdün.

Places to Stay & Eat

Campingplatz Schade (☎ 225 4; open mid-March to mid-October) has modern facilities and is about a 15-minute walk from the beach at the northern edge of Wittdün. Reservations are mandatory in summer. The *DJH hostel* (☎ 201 0) is practically on the beach at Mittelstrasse 1 in Wittdün, about 300m from the ferry landing. Bed & breakfast costs DM22/27 for juniors/seniors. Private rooms cost from DM30 per person.

As for hotels, *Haus Südstrand* (☎ 270 8), at Mittelstrasse 30 in Wittdün, has a few singles/doubles priced at around DM58/120. *Hüttmann* (☎ 922 0; fax 922 11 3), at Ual Saarepswai 2-6 in Norddorf, was the first hotel on the island – it opened more than 100 years ago – and is still owned by the same family. There's a sauna, steam room and other amenities. Rates are from DM90 for singles and DM140 for doubles.

Amrum has only a few restaurants and many of them close in winter. For local fare, try the nautical themed *Ual Öömrang* at Bräätlun 4 in Norddorf. This is Amrum's oldest restaurant and has main courses from DM24. For a relaxing teahouse atmosphere, try *Burg Haus*, built on an old Viking hill fort above the eastern beach at Norddorf. Note that restaurants can be closed by 7 pm in the low season.

FÖHR

- *pop 10,000*
- *area code* ☎ *04681*

Föhr is even more remote and tranquil. Its main village is Wyk, which has been a resort since 1819. The island's best sandy beach is in the south. In the north you'll find 16 tiny Frisian hamlets tucked behind dykes that stand up to 7m tall. In the old days, Föhr's men went out to sea to hunt whales, an epoch you can learn more about at the **Friesenmuseum** (open Tuesday to Sunday from 10 am to 5 pm; DM7.50, discount DM3.50) at Rebbelstieg 34 in Wyk. Many of these men are buried in the **cemetery of St Laurenti** in Süderende. Also worth visiting is the **church of St Johannis** in Nieblum. It dates from the 12th century and is sometimes called the 'Frisian Cathedral' because it seats up to 1000 people (ask about guided tours at the tourist office).

The information service on Föhr (☎ 304 0; fax 306 8) is at the harbour of Wyk. The spa administrations *(Kurverwaltungen)* in the various villages are also useful sources of information.

Places to Stay & Eat

Föhr does not have a camping ground. The *DJH hostel* (☎ 552 7) is in Wyk at Fehrstieg 41 on Südstrand beach, about 3.5km from the ferry landing. Bed & breakfast costs DM22/27 juniors/seniors, and you should call ahead to check availability. Private rooms cost from DM25 per person. Right on the beach in Wyk is the *Strandhotel* (☎ 587 00), which charges DM70/130 for singles/doubles. In Nieblum, on Strandstrasse, is *Timpe Te* (☎ 163 1; fax 507 57), a relaxing and elegant hotel whose rooms cost from DM90/150.

Wyk boasts a surprising number of restaurants. For local cuisine, head to the *Friesenkeller* in Mühlenstrasse or the *Friesenstube* in Süderstrasse. For fishy fast food, head to *Wyk End* on Mittelstrasse.

Getting There & Away

To get to Amrum and Föhr from the mainland, you must board a ferry operated by WDR (☎ 04681-801 40) in Dagebüll Hafen. To get there, take the Sylt-bound train from Hamburg-Altona and change in Niebüll. In summer, there are also some through trains. Up to 10 boats make the trip in season and, with prior reservation, it's possible to take your car aboard. The trip to Amrum takes 1½ hours, to Föhr about 45 minutes. The one-way trip to Wittdün costs DM15.80, day return DM23. Bikes are an extra DM7. One-way trips to Wyk cost DM9.80, day-return tickets are DM15.

For getting to Amrum and Föhr from Sylt, see Getting There & Away in the Sylt section.

Getting Around

On Amrum, buses travel at 30-minute intervals (hourly in winter) along the island spine from the ferry terminal in Wittdün to Norddorf. On Föhr, there's an hourly bus service to all villages (less frequent in winter). There are bike-rental places in every village on both islands. They charge between DM5 and DM10 a day.

HELGOLAND

Technically not part of the North Frisian Islands, Helgoland lies 45km from the mainland and is a popular day trip and duty-free port. Because of the North Sea's strong currents and unpredictable weather, however, the passage will be enjoyed only by those with iron stomachs. Helgoland was first ruled by the Danes, then by the British before it became German in 1891 in exchange for the African island of Zanzibar. It's a tiny place whose landmark is an 80m-tall red rock called 'Lange Anna' (Long Anna) sticking out from the sea in the south-west of the island.

In 1841, Heinrich Hoffmann von Fallersleben wrote the words to the German anthem in Helgoland. In WWII it was used as a submarine base and it's still possible to tour the remaining bunkers and underground tunnels. The island was heavily bombed and all of the houses are new.

Take a walk along Lung Wai (literally 'long way'), filled with duty-free shops, and then up the stairway (180 steps) to Oberland for the view. There's also a scenic trail around the island.

There are no decent beaches on Helgoland but to swim you can go to neighbouring **Düne**, a mere blip in the ocean that is popular with nudists. Little boats make regular trips to the pint-sized island from the landing stage in Helgoland.

There's a tourist office (☎ 04725-808 62; fax 426) on Lung Wai, open weekdays from 9 am to 4 pm, Saturday from 11 am to 4 pm

SCHLESWIG - HOLSTEIN

and Sunday from 11 am to 3 pm. The office can help with finding a room.

Places to Stay

There's a *camping ground* (☎ 04725-08 40) and a bungalow village on Düne Island.

Helgoland has a *DJH hostel* (☎ 04725-341), about 15 minutes on foot north-east of the landing stages, where bed & breakfast costs DM22/27 juniors/seniors. It's only open from April to October and you must call ahead. Private rooms are available too.

Getting There & Away

The WDR boat service (☎ 04681-801 40) makes the excursion from Hörnum on Sylt twice weekly (DM42). Ferries also travel to Helgoland from Dagebüll, Husum, Büsum, Cuxhaven, Bremerhaven, Wilhelmshaven and Borkum.

Glossary

(pl) indicates plural

Abfahrt – departure (trains)
Abtei – abbey
ADAC – Allgemeiner Deutscher Automobil Club (German Automobile Association)
Allee – avenue
Altstadt – old town
Ankunft – arrival (trains)
Antiquariat – antiquarian bookshop
Apotheke – pharmacy
Arbeitsamt – employment office
Arbeitserlaubnis – work permit
Ärztlicher Notdienst – emergency medical service
Aufenthaltserlaubnis – residency permit
Auflauf, Aufläufe (pl) – casserole
Ausgang, Ausfahrt – exit
Aussiedler – person of German descent who has returned to Germany (usually refers to post-WWII expulsions)
Autobahn – motorway
Autonom – left-wing anarchist
AvD – Automobilclub von Deutschland (Automobile Club of Germany)

Bad – spa, bath
Bahnhof – train station
Bahnsteig – train station platform
Bau – building
Bedienung – service
Berg – mountain
Bergbaumuseum – mining museum
Besenwirtschaft – seasonal wine restaurant indicated by a broom above the doorway
Bezirk – district
Bibliothek – library
Bierkeller – cellar pub
Bierstube – traditional beer pub
Bildungsroman – literally 'novel of education'; literary work in which the personal development of a single individual is central
Bratkartoffeln – fried or roasted potatoes
BRD – Bundesrepublik Deutschland or, in English, FRG (Federal Republic of Germany). The name for Germany today; orginally applied to the former West Germany.
Brücke – bridge
Brunnen – fountain or well
Bundesland – federal state
Bundesrat – upper house of German Parliament
Bundestag – lower house of German Parliament
Bundesverftssungsgericht – Federal Constitutional Court
Burg – fortress or castle
Busbahnhof – bus station

Christkindlmarkt – Christmas market; *see also* Weihnachtsmarkt

DB – Deutsche Bahn (German national railway)
DDR – Deutsche Demokratische Republik or, in English, GDR (German Democratic Republic). The name for the former East Germany. *See also* BRD.
Denkmal – memorial
Deutsche Reich – German Empire. Refers to the period 1871-1918.
DJH – Deutsches Jugendherbergswerk (German youth hostels association)
Dirndl – traditional women's skirt
Dom – cathedral
Dorf – village
DZT – Deutsche Zentrale für Tourismus (German National Tourist Office)

Eingang – entrance
Eintritt – admission
Eiscafé – ice-cream parlour

Fahrplan – timetable
Fahrrad – bicycle
Fasching – pre-Lenten carnival
Ferienwohnung, Ferienwohnungen (pl) – holiday flat or apartment
Fest – festival
Flammekuche – Franco-German dish consisting of a thin layer of pastry topped with

cream, onion, bacon and, sometimes, cheese or mushrooms, and cooked in a wood-fired oven. Found on menus in the Palatinate and the Black Forest.

Fleets – canals in Hamburg
Flohmarkt – flea market
Flughafen – airport
Föhn – an intense autumn wind in the Agerman Alps and Alpine Foothills
Forstweg – forestry track
Franks – Germanic peoples influential in Europe between the 3rd and 8th centuries
Freikorps – WWI volunteers
Fremdenverkehrsamt – tourist office
Fremdenzimmer – tourist room
FRG – Federal Republic of Germany; *see also* BRD
Frühstück – breakfast

Garten – garden
Gasse – lane or alley
Gastarbeiter – literally 'guest worker'; labourer imported from Turkey, Yugoslavia, Italy or Greece after WWII to help rebuild Germany
Gästehaus, Gasthaus – guesthouse
Gaststätte – informal restaurant
GDR – German Democratic Republic (the former East Germany); *see also* BRD, DDR
Gedenkstätte – memorial site
Gepäckaufbewahrung – left-luggage office
Gestapo – Nazi secret police
Glockenspiel – literally 'bell play'; medieval carillon, usually on a cathedral, sounded by mechanised figures often in the form of religious or historical characters
Gründerzeit – literally 'foundation time'; the period of industrial expansion in Germany following the founding of the German Empire in 1871

Hafen – harbour, port
halbtrocken – semi-dry (wine)
Hauptbahnhof – main train station
Hauptpostlagernd – poste restante
Heide – heath
Heilige römische Reich – the Holy Roman Empire, which lasted from the 8th century to 1806. The German lands compromised the bulk of the Empire's territory.
Herzog – duke
Heu Hotels – literally 'hay hotels'; cheap forms of accommodation usually set in farmhouses and similar to bunk barns in the UK
Hitlerjugend – Hitler Youth organisation
Hochdeutsch – literally 'High German'; standard spoken and written German developed from a regional Saxon dialect
Hochkultur – literally 'high culture'; meaning 'advanced civilisation'
Hof, Höfe (pl) – courtyard
Höhle – cave
Hotel Garni – a hotel without a restaurant where you are only served breakfast

Imbiss – stand-up food stall; *see* Schnellimbiss
Insel – island

Jugendgästehaus – youth guesthouse, usually of a higher standard than a youth hostel
Jugendherberge – youth hostel
Jugendstil – Art Nouveau
Junker – originally a young, noble landowner of the Middle Ages; later used to refer to reactionary Prussian landowners

Kabarett – cabaret
Kaffee und Kuchen – literally 'coffee and cake'; traditional afternoon coffee break in Germany
Kaiser – emperor; derived from 'Caesar'
Kanal – canal
Kantine – cafeteria, canteen
Kapelle – chapel
Karte – ticket
Kartenvorverkauf – ticket booking office
Kino – cinema
Kirche – church
Kloster – monastery, convent
Kneipe – bar
Kommunales Kino – alternative or studio cinema
Konditorei – cake shop
König – king
Konsulat – consulate

Konzentrationslager (KZ) – concentration camp
Kristallnacht – literally 'night of broken glass'; attack on Jewish synagogues, cemetaries and businesses by Nazis and their supporters on the night of 9 November 1938 that marked the beginning of full-scale persecution of Jews in Germany. Also known as Reichspogromnacht.
Kunst – art
Kunstlieder – early German 'artistic songs'
Kurfürst – prince elector
Kurhaus – literally 'spa house', but usually a spa town's central building, used for social gatherings and events and often housing the town's casino
Kurort – spa resort
Kurtaxe – resort tax
Kurverwaltung – spa administration
Kurzentrum – spa centre

Land, Länder (pl) – state
Landtag – state parliament
Lederhose – traditional leather trousers with attached braces
Lesbe, Lesben (pl) – lesbian
lesbisch – lesbian (adj)
lieblich – sweet (wine)
Lied – song

Maare – crater lakes in the Eifel Upland area west of the Rhine
Markgraf – margrave; German nobleman ranking above a count
Markgrafschaft – the holding of a Markgraf
Markt – market
Marktplatz (often abbreviated to Markt) – marketplace or square
Mass – one-litre tankard or stein of beer
Meer – sea
Mehrwertsteuer (MWST) – value-added tax
Meistersinger – literally 'master singer'; highest level in the medieval troubadour guilds
Mensa – university cafeteria
Milchcafé – milk coffee, *café au lait*
Mitfahrzentrale – ride-sharing service
Mitwohnzentrale – an accommodation-finding service (usually long-term)

Münster – minster or large church, cathedral
Münzwäscherei – coin-operated laundrette

Norden – north
Notdienst – emergency service

Ossis – literally 'Easties'; nickname for East Germans
Osten – east
Ostler – old term for an Ossi
Ostpolitik – former West German chancellor Willy Brandt's foreign policy of 'peaceful coexistence' with the GDR

Palast – residential quarters of a castle
Pannenhilfe – roadside breakdown assistance
Paradies – architectural term for a church vestibule or ante-room
Parkhaus – car park
Parkschein – parking voucher
Parksheinautomat – vending machine selling parking vouchers
Passage – shopping arcade
Pfand – deposit for bottles and sometimes glasses (in beer gardens)
Pfarrkirche – parish church
Plattdeutsch – literally 'Low German'; German dialect spoken in northern Germany
Platz – square
Postamt – post office
Priele – tideways on the Wattenmeer on the North Sea coast

Radwandern – bicycle touring
Rathaus – town hall
Ratskeller – town hall restaurant
Reich – empire
Reichspogromnacht – *see* Kristallnacht
Reisezentrum – travel centre in train or bus stations
Reiterhof – riding stable or centre
Ruhetag – literally 'rest day'; closing day at a shop or restaurant
Rundgang – tour, route

Saal, Säle (pl) – hall, room
Sammlung – collection
Säule – column, pillar
Schatzkammer – treasury

Schiff – ship
Schiffahrt – literally 'boat way'; shipping, navigation
Schloss – palace, castle
Schnaps – schnapps
Schnellimbiss – stand-up food stall
Schwul, Schwule (pl) – gay
See – lake
Sekt – sparkling wine
Selbstbedienung (SB) – self-service (restaurants, laundrettes etc)
Skonto – discount
Sozialmarktwirtschaft – literally 'social market economy'; German form of mixed economy with built-in social protection for employees
Spätaussiedler – literally 'late repatriate'; people of German extraction resettled in Germany; usually refers to period after post-WWII expulsions in Eastern Europe
Speisekarte – menu
Sportverein – sport association
SS – Schutzstaffel; organisation within the Nazi party that supplied Hitler's bodyguards, as well as concentration-camp guards and the Waffen-SS troops in WWII
Stadt – city or town
Stadtbad, Stadtbäder (pl) – public bath
Stadtwald – city or town forest
Stasi – GDR secret police (from Ministerium für Staatssicherheit, or Ministry of State Security)
Stau – traffic jam
Staudamm, Staumauer – dam
Stausee – reservoir
Stehcafé – stand-up café
Strasse (often abbreviated to Str) – street
Strausswirtschaft – seasonal wine pub indicated by wreath above the doorway, also known as a Besenwirtschaft
Süden – south
Szene – scene (ie where the action is)

Tageskarte – daily menu or day ticket on public transport
Tal – valley
Teich – pond
Thirty Years' War – pivotal war in Central Europe (1618-48) that began as a German conflict between Catholics and Protestants
Tor – gate
Trampen – hitchhiking
Treuhandanstalt – trust established to sell off GDR assets after the Wende
trocken – dry (wine)
Trödel – junk
Turm – tower

Übergang – transit point
Ufer – bank

verboten – forbidden
Verkehr – traffic
Viertel – quarter, district
Volkslieder – folk song

Wald – forest
Waldfrüchte – wild berries
Wäscherei – laundry
Wattenmeer – tidal flats on North Sea coast
Wechselstube – currency exchange office
Weg – way, path
Weihnachtsmarkt – Christmas market; see also Christkindlmarkt
Weingut – wine-growing estate
Weinkeller – wine cellar
Weinprobe – wine tasting
Weinstube – traditional wine bar
Wende – 'change' of 1989, ie the fall of communism that led to the collapse of the GDR and ultimately German reunification
Weser Renaissance – an ornamental architectural style found around the Weser River
Wessis – literally 'Westies'; nickname for West Germans
Westen – west
Westler – old term for a Wessi
Wies – meadow
Wirtschaftswunder – Germany's post-WWII 'economic miracle'
Wurst – sausage

Zahnradbahn – cog-wheel railway
Zeitung – newspaper
Zimmer Frei – room available (accommodation)
Zimmervermittlung – room-finding service; *see also* Mitwohnzentrale
ZOB – Zentraler Omnibusbahnhof (central bus station)

Alternative Place Names

English place names are followed by their German equivalent.

Allgäu-Bavarian Swabia –
Allgäu-Bayerische-Schwäbisch

Baltic Sea – Ostsee
Bavaria – Bayern
Black Forest – Schwarzwald
Brunswick – Braunschweig

Cologne – Köln
Constance – Konstanz

Danube – Donau

East Bavaria – Ostbayern

Franconia – Franken

Hamelin – Hameln
Hanover – Hannover
Hesse – Hessen

Lake Constance – Bodensee

Lake Plains – Mecklenburger Seenplatte
Lower Saxony – Niedersachsen

Mecklenburg-Western Pomerania –
Mecklenburg-Vorpommern
Moselle – Mosel
Munich – München

North Rhine-Westphalia –
Nordrhein-Westfalen
Nuremberg – Nürnberg

Rhine – Rhein
Rhineland-Palatinate – Rheinland-Pfalz
Romantic Road – Romantische Strasse

Saxony – Sachsen
Saxony-Anhalt – Sachsen-Anhalt

Thuringia – Thüringen

Upper Bavaria – Oberbayern

Index

MAPS

TEXT

Map references are in **bold** type.

U

Ibis Hotel | Munich - 89 360830
Dachauer. 89 551930

DM.130 / Frühstuck

DM. 21 /

Ibis 55

LONELY PLANET PHRASEBOOKS

Building bridges,
Breaking barriers,
Beyond babble-on

- handy pocket-sized books
- easy to understand Pronunciation chapter
- clear and comprehensive Grammar chapter
- romanisation alongside script to allow ease of pronunciation
- script throughout so users can point to phrases
- extensive vocabulary sections, words and phrases for every situation
- full of cultural information and tips for the traveller

'...vital for a real DIY spirit and attitude in language learning' **– Backpacker**

'the phrasebooks have good cultural backgrounders and offer solid advice for challenging situations in remote locations' **– San Francisco Examiner**

'...they are unbeatable for their coverage of the world's more obscure languages' **– *The Geographical Magazine***

Arabic (Egyptian)
Arabic (Moroccan)
Australia
Australian English, Aboriginal and Torres Strait languages
Baltic States
Estonian, Latvian, Lithuanian
Bengali
Brazilian
Burmese
Cantonese
Central Asia
Central Europe
Czech, French, German, Hungarian, Italian and Slovak
Eastern Europe
Bulgarian, Czech, Hungarian, Polish, Romanian and Slovak
Ethiopian (Amharic)
Fijian
French
German
Greek
Hindi/Urdu
Indonesian
Italian
Japanese
Korean
Lao
Latin American Spanish
Malay
Mandarin
Mediterranean Europe
Albanian, Croatian, Greek, Italian, Macedonian, Maltese, Serbian and Slovene
Mongolian
Moroccan Arabic
Nepali
Papua New Guinea
Pilipino (Tagalog)
Quechua
Russian
Scandinavian Europe
Danish, Finnish, Icelandic, Norwegian and Swedish
South-East Asia
Burmese, Indonesian, Khmer, Lao, Malay, Tagalog (Pilipino), Thai and Vietnamese
Spanish (Castilian)
Basque, Catalan and Galician
Sri Lanka
Swahili
Thai
Thai Hill Tribes
Tibetan
Turkish
Ukrainian
USA
US English, Vernacular, Native American languages and Hawaiian
Vietnamese
Western Europe
Basque, Catalan, Dutch, French, German, Irish, Italian, Portuguese, Scottish Gaelic, Spanish (Castilian) and Welsh

---

LONELY PLANET JOURNEYS

JOURNEYS is a unique collection of travel writing – published by the company that understands travel better than anyone else. It is a series for anyone who has ever experienced – or dreamed of – the magical moment when they encountered a strange culture or saw a place for the first time. They are tales to read while you're planning a trip, while you're on the road or while you're in an armchair, in front of a fire.

JOURNEYS books catch the spirit of a place, illuminate a culture, recount a crazy adventure, or introduce a fascinating way of life. They always entertain, and always enrich the experience of travel.

THE GATES OF DAMASCUS

Lieve Joris

Translated by Sam Garrett

This best-selling book is a beautifully drawn portrait of day-to-day life in modern Syria. Through her intimate contact with local people, Lieve Joris draws us into the fascinating world that lies behind the gates of Damascus. Hala's husband is a political prisoner, jailed for his opposition to the Assad regime; through the author's friendship with Hala we see how Syrian politics impacts on the lives of ordinary people.

Lieve Joris, who was born in Belgium, is one of Europe's leading travel writers. In addition to an award-winning book on Hungary, she has published widely acclaimed accounts of her journeys to the Middle East and Africa. *The Gates of Damascus* is her fifth book.

'Expands the boundaries of travel writing' **– Times Literary Supplement**

KINGDOM OF THE FILM STARS

Journey into Jordan

Annie Caulfield

Kingdom of the Film Stars is a travel book and a love story. With honesty and humour, Annie Caulfield writes of travelling in Jordan and falling in love with a Bedouin. Her book offers fascinating insights into the country – from the traditional tent life of nomadic tribes to the first woman MP's battle with fundamentalist colleagues. *Kingdom of the Film Stars* unpicks some of the tight-woven Western myths about the Arab world, presenting cultural and political issues within the intimate framework of a compelling love story.

Annie Caulfield, who was born in Ireland and currently lives in London, is an award-winning playwright and journalist. She has travelled widely in the Middle East.

'Annie Caulfield is a remarkable traveller. Her story is fresh, courageous, moving, witty and sexy!' **– Dawn French**

PLANET TALK

Lonely Planet's FREE quarterly newsletter

We love hearing from you and think you'd like to hear from us.

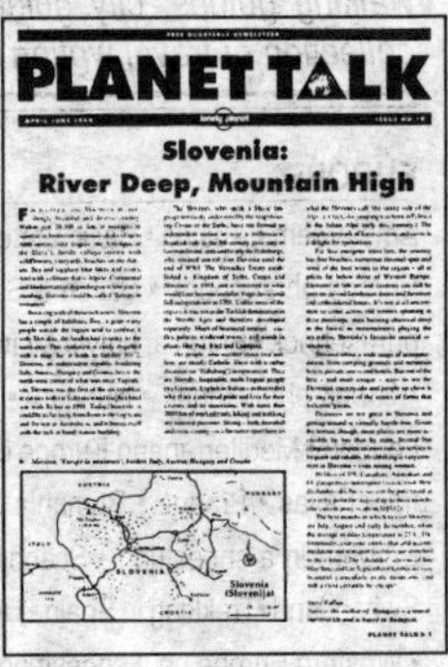

When... is the right time to see reindeer in Finland?
Where... can you hear the best palm-wine music in Ghana?
How... do you get from Asunción to Areguá by steam train?
What... is the best way to see India?

For the answer to these and many other questions read PLANET TALK.

Every issue is packed with up-to-date travel news and advice including:

- a letter from Lonely Planet co-founders Tony and Maureen Wheeler
- go behind the scenes on the road with a Lonely Planet author
- feature article on an important and topical travel issue
- a selection of recent letters from travellers
- details on forthcoming Lonely Planet promotions
- complete list of Lonely Planet products

To join our mailing list contact any Lonely Planet office.

Also available: Lonely Planet T-shirts. 100% heavyweight cotton.

LONELY PLANET ONLINE

Get the latest travel information before you leave or while you're on the road

Whether you've just begun planning your next trip, or you're chasing down specific info on currency regulations or visa requirements, check out Lonely Planet Online for up-to-the minute travel information.

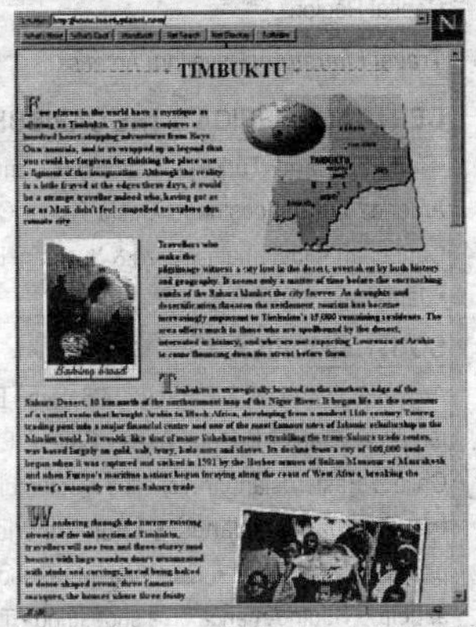

As well as travel profiles of your favourite destinations (including maps and photos), you'll find current reports from our researchers and other travellers, updates on health and visas, travel advisories, and discussion of the ecological and political issues you need to be aware of as you travel.

There's also an online travellers' forum where you can share your experience of life on the road, meet travel companions and ask other travellers for their recommendations and advice. We also have plenty of links to other online sites useful to independent travellers.

And of course we have a complete and up-to-date list of all Lonely Planet travel products including guides, phrasebooks, atlases, Journeys and videos and a simple online ordering facility if you can't find the book you want elsewhere.

www.lonelyplanet.com
or
AOL keyword: lp

LONELY PLANET PRODUCTS

Lonely Planet is known worldwide for publishing practical, reliable and no-nonsense travel information in our guides and on our web site. The Lonely Planet list covers just about every accessible part of the world. Currently there are nine series: *travel guides, shoestring guides, walking guides, city guides, phrasebooks, audio packs, travel atlases, Journeys – a unique collection of travel writing and Pisces Books - diving and snorkeling guides.*

EUROPE

Amsterdam • Austria • Baltic States phrasebook • Berlin • Britain • Canary Islands• Central Europe on a shoestring • Central Europe phrasebook • Czech & Slovak Republics • Denmark • Dublin • Eastern Europe on a shoestring • Eastern Europe phrasebook • Estonia, Latvia & Lithuania • Finland • France • French phrasebook • Germany • German phrasebook • Greece • Greek phrasebook • Hungary • Iceland, Greenland & the Faroe Islands • Ireland • Italian phrasebook • Italy • Lisbon • London • Mediterranean Europe on a shoestring • Mediterranean Europe phrasebook • Paris • Poland • Portugal • Portugal travel atlas • Prague • Romania & Moldova • Russia, Ukraine & Belarus • Russian phrasebook • Scandinavian & Baltic Europe on a shoestring • Scandinavian Europe phrasebook • Slovenia • Spain • Spanish phrasebook • St Petersburg • Switzerland •Trekking in Spain • Ukrainian phrasebook • Vienna • Walking in Britain • Walking in Italy • Walking in Switzerland • Western Europe on a shoestring • Western Europe phrasebook

Travel Literature: The Olive Grove: Travels in Greece

NORTH AMERICA

Alaska • Backpacking in Alaska • Baja California • California & Nevada • Canada • Chicago • Deep South• Florida • Hawaii • Honolulu • Los Angeles • Mexico • Mexico City • Miami • New England • New Orleans • New York City • New York, New Jersey & Pennsylvania • Pacific Northwest USA • Rocky Mountain States • San Francisco • Southwest USA • USA phrasebook • Washington, DC & the Capital Region

Travel Literature: Drive thru America

CENTRAL AMERICA & THE CARIBBEAN

•Bahamas and Turks & Caicos •Bermuda •Central America on a shoestring • Costa Rica • Cuba •Eastern Caribbean •Guatemala, Belize & Yucatán: La Ruta Maya • Jamaica

SOUTH AMERICA

Argentina, Uruguay & Paraguay • Bolivia • Brazil • Brazilian phrasebook • Buenos Aires • Chile & Easter Island • Chile & Easter Island travel atlas • Colombia Ecuador & the Galápagos Islands • Latin American Spanish phrasebook • Peru • Quechua phrasebook • Rio de Janeiro • South America on a shoestring • Trekking in the Patagonian Andes • Venezuela

Travel Literature: Full Circle: A South American Journey

ISLANDS OF THE INDIAN OCEAN

Madagascar & Comoros • Maldives• Mauritius, Réunion & Seychelles

AFRICA

Africa - the South • Africa on a shoestring • Arabic (Moroccan) phrasebook • Cairo • Cape Town • Central Africa • East Africa • Egypt • Egypt travel atlas• Ethiopian (Amharic) phrasebook • Kenya • Kenya travel atlas • Malawi, Mozambique & Zambia • Morocco • North Africa • South Africa, Lesotho & Swaziland • South Africa, Lesotho & Swaziland travel atlas • Swahili phrasebook • Tunisia • Trekking in East Africa • West Africa • Zimbabwe, Botswana & Namibia • Zimbabwe, Botswana & Namibia travel atlas

Travel Literature: The Rainbird: A Central African Journey • Songs to an African Sunset: A Zimbabwean Story

MAIL ORDER

Lonely Planet products are distributed worldwide. They are also available by mail order from Lonely Planet, so if you have difficulty finding a title please write to us. North American and South American residents should write to 150 Linden St, Oakland CA 94607, USA; European and African residents should write to 10a Spring Place, London NW5 3BH; and residents of other countries to PO Box 617, Hawthorn, Victoria 3122, Australia.

NORTH-EAST ASIA

Beijing • Cantonese phrasebook • China • Hong Kong • Hong Kong, Macau & Guangzhou • Japan • Japanese phrasebook • Japanese audio pack • Korea • Korean phrasebook • Mandarin phrasebook • Mongolia • Mongolian phrasebook • North-East Asia on a shoestring • Seoul • Taiwan • Tibet • Tibet phrasebook • Tokyo

Travel Literature: Lost Japan

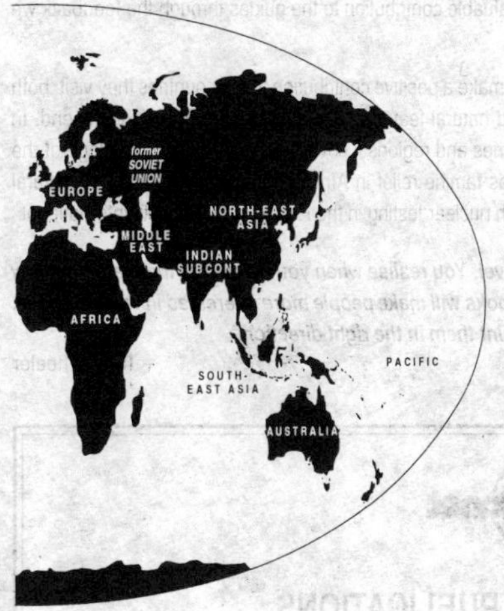

MIDDLE EAST & CENTRAL ASIA

Arab Gulf States • Arabic (Egyptian) phrasebook • Central Asia • Central Asia phrasebook • Iran • Israel & the Palestinian Territories • Israel & the Palestinian Territories travel atlas • Istanbul • Jerusalem • Jordan & Syria • Jordan, Syria & Lebanon travel atlas • Lebanon • Middle East • Turkey • Turkish phrasebook • Turkey travel atlas • Yemen

Travel Literature: The Gates of Damascus • Kingdom of the Film Stars: Journey into Jordan

ALSO AVAILABLE:

Brief Encounters • Travel with Children • Traveller's Tales

INDIAN SUBCONTINENT

Bangladesh • Bengali phrasebook • Delhi • Goa • Hindi/Urdu phrasebook • India • India & Bangladesh travel atlas • Indian Himalaya • Karakoram Highway • Nepal • Nepali phrasebook • Pakistan • Rajasthan • Sri Lanka • Sri Lanka phrasebook • Trekking in the Indian Himalaya • Trekking in the Karakoram & Hindukush • Trekking in the Nepal Himalaya

Travel Literature: In Rajasthan • Shopping for Buddhas

SOUTH-EAST ASIA

Bali & Lombok • Bangkok • Burmese phrasebook • Cambodia • Ho Chi Minh City • Indonesia • Indonesian phrasebook • Indonesian audio pack • Jakarta • Java • Laos • Lao phrasebook • Laos travel atlas • Malay phrasebook • Malaysia, Singapore & Brunei • Myanmar (Burma) • Philippines • Pilipino phrasebook • Singapore • South-East Asia on a shoestring • South-East Asia phrasebook • Thailand • Thailand's Islands & Beaches • Thailand travel atlas • Thai phrasebook • Thai audio pack • Thai Hill Tribes phrasebook • Vietnam • Vietnamese phrasebook • Vietnam travel atlas

AUSTRALIA & THE PACIFIC

Australia • Australian phrasebook • Bushwalking in Australia • Bushwalking in Papua New Guinea • Fiji • Fijian phrasebook • Islands of Australia's Great Barrier Reef • Melbourne • Micronesia • New Caledonia • New South Wales • New Zealand • Northern Territory • Outback Australia • Papua New Guinea • Papua New Guinea phrasebook • Queensland • Rarotonga & the Cook Islands • Samoa • Solomon Islands • South Australia • Sydney • Tahiti & French Polynesia • Tasmania • Tonga • Tramping in New Zealand • Vanuatu • Victoria • Western Australia

Travel Literature: Islands in the Clouds • Sean & David's Long Drive

ANTARCTICA

Antarctica

THE LONELY PLANET STORY

Lonely Planet published its first book in 1973 in response to the numerous 'How did you do it?' questions Maureen and Tony Wheeler were asked after driving, bussing, hitching, sailing and railing their way from England to Australia.

Written at a kitchen table and hand collated, trimmed and stapled, *Across Asia on the Cheap* became an instant local bestseller, inspiring thoughts of another book.

Eighteen months in South-East Asia resulted in their second guide, *South-East Asia on a shoestring*, which they put together in a backstreet Chinese hotel in Singapore in 1975. The 'yellow bible', as it quickly became known to backpackers around the world, soon became *the* guide to the region. It has sold well over half a million copies and is now in its 9th edition, still retaining its familiar yellow cover.

Today there are over 350 titles, including travel guides, walking guides, language kits & phrasebooks, travel atlases and travel literature. The company is the largest independent travel publisher in the world. Although Lonely Planet initially specialised in guides to Asia, today there are few corners of the globe that have not been covered.

The emphasis continues to be on travel for independent travellers. Tony and Maureen still travel for several months of each year and play an active part in the writing, updating and quality control of Lonely Planet's guides.

They have been joined by over 80 authors and 200 staff at our offices in Melbourne (Australia), Oakland (USA), London (UK) and Paris (France). Travellers themselves also make a valuable contribution to the guides through the feedback we receive in thousands of letters each year and on our web site.

The people at Lonely Planet strongly believe that travellers can make a positive contribution to the countries they visit, both through their appreciation of the countries' culture, wildlife and natural features, and through the money they spend. In addition, the company makes a direct contribution to the countries and regions it covers. Since 1986 a percentage of the income from each book has been donated to ventures such as famine relief in Africa; aid projects in India; agricultural projects in Central America; Greenpeace's efforts to halt French nuclear testing in the Pacific; and Amnesty International.

'I hope we send people out with the right attitude about travel. You realise when you travel that there are so many different perspectives about the world, so we hope these books will make people more interested in what they see. Guidebooks can't really guide people. All you can do is point them in the right direction.'

– Tony Wheeler

LONELY PLANET PUBLICATIONS

Australia
PO Box 617, Hawthorn 3122, Victoria
tel: (03) 9819 1877 fax: (03) 9819 6459
e-mail: talk2us@lonelyplanet.com.au

USA
150 Linden St
Oakland, CA 94607
tel: (510) 893 8555 TOLL FREE: 800 275-8555
fax: (510) 893 8572
e-mail: info@lonelyplanet.com

UK
10a Spring Place,
London NW5 3BH
tel: (0171) 428 4800 fax: (0171) 428 4828
e-mail: go@lonelyplanet.co.uk

France:
71 bis rue du Cardinal Lemoine, 75005 Paris
tel: 01 44 32 06 20 fax: 01 46 34 72 55
e-mail: bip@lonelyplanet.fr

World Wide Web: http://www.lonelyplanet.com
or *AOL keyword: lp*